The 2019 Edition of California Family Law Handbook For Paralegals

By: LW Greenberg, Esq.
© LW Greenberg 2019
lwgreenberg@californialegalbooks.com

Copyright © 2019 LW Greenberg

All rights reserved.

This book is the original work of LW Greenberg. All text, charts and lists were drafted and designed exclusively by LW Greenberg, and accordingly, LW Greenberg is the sole owner and retains ALL rights regarding this book.

No part of this book may be reproduced in any form, including the charts and the lists, the cover, by any mechanical or electronic method, and this includes but is not limited to photography, recording or using any information storage or retrieval system without the written permission of LW Greenberg.

ISBN- 9781793449993

DEDICATION

This book is dedicated to my wonderful husband of almost 40 years. Without his love and support I could not and would be writing these books.

PREFACE

Approximately 90 laws relating to family law were modified, deleted, repealed and rewritten effective January 1, 2019. Assembly Bill No 2684 was responsible for more than one-half of the code changes. This bill rewrote many codes that de-genderized the family codes such as "The Uniform Paternity Act" was changed to "The Uniform Parentage Act" and the word "paternity" was changed to "parentage" in many codes. Appendix Two is a list of the laws that changed and Appendix Three sets forth many of the new laws that will become effective/operative January 1, 2020.

This book updates most of the codes that became effective January 1, 2019. Also included are some new cases that were filed in 2018 and even 2019. And many of the "Educational Exercises" were re-worked toward helping the paralegal understand and even remember important cases and facts. NOTE: All CURRENT codes in this book have bolded.

If you are a paralegal teacher of family law, this book is the most updated California paralegal family law book on the market today. It is easy to read and understand. It is easy to teach from because each chapter starts with a summary (*In Brief*). And there are tests and syllabi available to teachers to help make the transition to this book easier. Email me at lwgreenberg@californialegalbooks.com to request this material.

Finally, please visit my website, www.californialegalbooks.com for additional information about the California paralegal books I have written and how you can get advance notice of updates of my books, both current and future.

TABLE OF CONTENTS *In Brief*

CHAPTER 1: Introduction to California Family Law 1
CHAPTER 2: The California Paralegal 9
CHAPTER 3: Jurisdiction & Venue 29
CHAPTER 4: Validity of Marriage 39
CHAPTER 5: Annulments, Dissolutions & Legal Separations 57
CHAPTER 6: Date of Separation 81
CHAPTER 7: Attorney Fees & Limited Scope Representation 91
CHAPTER 8: Initial Forms, Initial Filing & Checkboxes 121
CHAPTER 9: Timing, Electronic Filing & Service 141
CHAPTER 10: Service of Process & Proof of Service 151
CHAPTER 11: Discovery 159
CHAPTER 12: Mediation 177
CHAPTER 13: Child Custody 201
CHAPTER 14: Child Visitation 237
CHAPTER 15: Moveaways or Relocations 255
CHAPTER 16: Child Support 291
CHAPTER 17: Spousal & Family Support 323
CHAPTER 18: Disclosure & Fiduciary Duty 369
CHAPTER 19: Bifurcation 385
CHAPTER 20: Title, Kinds of Property & Valuation 395
CHAPTER 21: Community & Separate Debts/Liabilities 415
CHAPTER 22: Division, Tracing & Reimbursement 425
CHAPTER 23: Retirement & Disability 447
CHAPTER 24: Apportionment 457
CHAPTER 25: Degrees of Proof & Presumptions 471
CHAPTER 26: The Hearing 483
CHAPTER 27: *Ex Parte* 493
CHAPTER 28: Defaults 501
CHAPTER 29: Drafting Court Orders 513
CHAPTER 30: Marital Agreements 523

CHAPTER 31: Settlements, Trial & the Final Paperwork 563
CHAPTER 32: Enforcement 577
CHAPTER 33: Postjudgment 599
CHAPTER 34: Parentage 607
CHAPTER 35: Minors 653
CHAPTER 36: Domestic Violence 675
CHAPTER 37: Living Together/*Marvin* Actions 703
Appendix One: Johns' Intake Sheets & Timeline 727
Appendix Two: 2019 Family Code Changes & Bill Nos. 737
Appendix Three: Family Codes Effective 1/1/2020 745
GLOSSARY 757
INDEX (Terms & Cases) 781

Table of Contents

CHAPTER 1: Introduction to California Family Law ... 1
- Introduction ... 2
    1. The California Family Code ... 3
    2. The Judicial Council ... 4
    3. California Rules of Court (CRC) ... 5
    4. Family Law Rules, Local Rules & Websites ... 5
    5. Holdings of the Court ... 6
- EDUCATIONAL EXERCISES ... 7

CHAPTER 2: The California Paralegal ... 9
- Introduction ... 10
- California Paralegal Laws ... 10
    1. Business & Professions (B&P) Code § 6450 et seq. ... 10
    2. B&P Code §§ 6451 and 6452 ... 11
    3. B&P Code § 6453 ... 12
    4. B&P Code § 6454 ... 12
    5. B&P Code § 6455 ... 12
- The Unauthorized Practice of Law ... 13
- Attorney Liability for Paralegal Error & Misconduct ... 15
- Appropriate and Inappropriate Conduct ... 18
    1. A Paralegal Shall Not… ... 18
    2. A Paralegal Shall… ... 19
- A Paralegal Conflict ... 20
    - Paralegal Form: Conflict of Interest Record ... 23
- A Paralegal is a Professional ... 24
- Paralegal Duties and Initial Client Interaction ... 24
    1. Paralegal Duties ... 24
    2. Initial Client Interaction ... 26
- EDUCATIONAL EXERCISES ... 28

CHAPTER 3: Jurisdiction & Venue ... 29
- Introduction ... 30
- Jurisdiction: The Two Types ... 30

    1. Subject Matter Jurisdiction 30
    2. Personal Jurisdiction 31
  Jurisdiction: The Two Kinds 31
    1. *In Personam* Jurisdiction 31
    2. *In Rem* Jurisdiction 32
  Venue is Where the Action is Entertained 35
  EDUCATIONAL EXERCISES 37

CHAPTER 4: Validity of Marriage 39
  Introduction 39
  Solemnization 39
  The Marriage License 41
  Common Law Marriage 47
  Requirements of a Valid of Marriage 48
  Persons Authorized to Solemnize a Marriage 50
  The Confidential Marriage 51
  EDUCATIONAL EXERCISES 54

CHAPTER 5: Annulments, Dissolutions & Legal Separations 57
  Introduction 58
  Annulment 58
    1. Void Marriage Annulments 59
    2. Voidable Marriage Annulments 61
  CHART 1: Fraud Alleged - Annulment Granted 64
  CHART 2: Fraud Alleged- Annulment Not Granted 65
    3. The Putative Spouse 66
  Domicile and/or Residence 68
  Dissolution/Divorce 69
    1. Divorce History: Fault & Cooling Off Period 69
    2. The Grounds for Divorce 71
    3. The Residency Requirement 72
  Legal Separation 72
  CHART 3: Annulment vs. Dissolution vs. Legal Separation 74
  Summary Dissolution 75
  EDUCATIONAL EXERCISES 78

CHAPTER 6: Date of Separation 81

Introduction 82
Conduct Not Demonstrating a Final Break in the Marriage 83
    Spouses Living Separate for Economic Reasons 83
    Spouses Continuing Sexual Relationship, Attempting Reconciliation 85
    Spouses Seeing Meeting Regularly; Joint Title to Real Property 87
Conduct Demonstrating a Final Break in the Marriage 88
EDUCATIONAL EXERCISES 89

CHAPTER 7: Attorney Fees & Limited Scope Representation 91

Introduction 92
Authority to Award Attorney Fees Pursuant to the Family Code 93
    1.   FC §§ 270, 271, 274 93
    2.   FC § 2010 97
    3.   FC §§ 2030-2032 97
    4.   FC § 2107 103
    5.   FC § 2255 103
    6.   FC §§ 3027.1, 3120, 3121, 3150 104
    7.   FC § 3452 106
    8.   FC §§ 3557 and 3652 107
    9.   FC § 4324.5 107
    10.   FC §§ 6344 and 6386 108
    11.   FC §§ 7605 and 7640 110
Attorney Fees in Bankruptcy Actions 111
Limited Scope Representation 113
    1.   Definition and Explanation of "Limited Scope Representation" 113
    2.   Procedures and Forms 113
    3.   Requesting Attorney Fees 114
    4.   Responding to a Request for Attorney Fees 115
CHART 4: Family Code Attorney Fee Award Authority 118
EDUCATIONAL EXERCISES 119

CHAPTER 8: Initial Forms, Initial Filing & Checkboxes 121

Introduction 122
Definitions in the Rules of Court 122
Initial Forms 124
    1.   The *Petition* (Form *FL-100*) 124
    2.   The *Response* (Form *FL-120*) 125

	3. The *Summons (Family Law)* (Form *FL-110*) 125
	4. *Uniform Child Custody Jurisdiction and Enforcement Act* (Form *FL-105*) 127
	5. The *Income and Expense Declaration* (Form *FL-150*) 127

    Filing Paperwork with the Court 128
        1. Filing Rules 128
        2. Filing Fee/Fee Waivers 129
    Checkboxes 131
    CHART 5: Initial Forms for Dissolution, Legal Separation & Nullity 135
    CHART 6: Rules of Court and Codes RE: INITIAL FORMS 136
    EDUCATIONAL EXERCISES 139

CHAPTER 9: Timing, Electronic Filing & Service 141

    Introduction 142
    Computation of "Time" 142
    Codes and Rules 143
    The Timing for Discovery 144
    Electronic Service and Filing 145
    EDUCATIONAL EXERCISES 148

CHAPTER 10: Service of Process & Proof of Service 151

    Introduction 152
    Service of Process 152
    Proof of Service 155
    CHART 7: Judicial Council Forms RE: PROOF OF SERVICE 157
    EDUCATIONAL EXERCISES 158

CHAPTER 11: Discovery 159

    Introduction 160
    Family Law Discovery 161
    Methods of Discovery 164
        1. Interrogatories 164
        2. Document Inspection Demands 165
        2. Requests for Admissions 165
        3. Depositions 166
    Discovery Misuse and Sanctions 168
    Postjudgment Discovery 171
    EDUCATIONAL EXERCISES 176

CHAPTER 12: Mediation 177
Introduction 178
Conciliation Court 178
Superior Court Mediation 181
    1. The Mediation 181
    2. The Superior Court Mediator/Counselor 184
    3. Private Mediation 186
Child Custody Evaluators 189
EDUCATIONAL EXERCISES 198

CHAPTER 13: Child Custody 201
Introduction 202
Classifications of Custody 202
Custody Orders 207
Custody Acts (Statutes) 211
    1. Uniform Child Custody Jurisdiction and Enforcement Act (UCCJEA) 211
    2. Federal Parental Kidnapping Prevention Act 28 U.S.C. § 1738A 220
    3. The Missing Children Act 224
    4. The Hague Convention 225
    5. Indian Child Welfare Act ICWA 25 USCS § 1901 et seq. 229
    6. Juvenile Dependency Court 231
Pet Custody 233
EDUCATIONAL EXERCISES 234

CHAPTER 14: Child Visitation 237
Introduction 238
Court Orders for Visitation 238
Visitation Plans 239
Grandparent Visitation 240
Stepparent Visitation 247
Supervised Visitation 249
Adoption Severs All Parental Rights 250
EDUCATIONAL EXERCISES 254

CHAPTER 15: Moveaways or Relocations 255
Introduction 256
Factors Courts Must Consider When Allowing a Moveaway 257

Detriment to the Children Must Be Considered 262
Best Interests Must Be Considered-No Final Custody Order 264
Substantial Change of Circumstances - Custody Order 267
Custodial Parent Has a Presumptive Right to Move 269
Evidentiary Hearing Not Always Required 272
Superior Economic Position May not be Used in determining Custody 274
Other Moveaway Holding(s) 275
    1.   No Denial of Custody because of a Handicap 275
    2.   Siblings Cannot Be Separated Unless There Is a Compelling Reason 276
    3.   Mediation Is Necessary 277
    4.   Need Sufficient Protective Measures to Insure Compliance 277
    5.   Preferences of the Children Must be Considered 278
    6.   There are Different Moveaway Rules when the Parties have Joint Custody 279
CHART 8: Moveaway Cases by Holding(s) 280
EDUCATIONAL EXERCISES 287

CHAPTER 16: Child Support 291

Introduction 292
Parental Duties/Responsibilities 293
    1.   Duties 293
    2.   Health Insurance 293
    3.   Other Rules 295
Determining the Amount of Child Support 296
    1.   Calculating the Parents' Income and Timeshare 296
    2.   The State Guideline Child Support Formula 296
    3.   Presumptions RE: The Child Support Guideline Formula 300
    4.   Additional Child Support (Add-ons) 300
    5.   The Hardship Deduction 301
    6.   Computer Software to Calculate Amount of Child Support 301
Child Support Orders 302
    1.   Rules RE: Child Support Court Orders 302
    2.   Garnishment: Income Withholding for Support 305
    3.   Retroactivity of Child Support Orders 305
    4.   Arrearages 306
Modifications or Terminations of Child Support Orders 308
Child Support Agreements 309

	1.	Required Provisions in all Child Support Agreements	309
	2.	Stipulations for Child Support Less Than Guideline Amount	310
	3.	No Duty to Pay College Expenses	310

A Deferred Sale of the Home Order or *Duke Order* 313

Expedited Child Support 317

EDUCATIONAL EXERCISES 319

CHAPTER 17: Spousal & Family Support 323

Introduction 324

Awarding Spousal Support is a Discretionary Decision 326

The Spousal Support Order 329

	1.	FC § 4320	329
	2.	The Marital Standard of Living	330
	3.	Self-Supporting Goal FC § 4320(l)	332
	4.	Duration of the Marriage	334
	5.	Disparity of Income, Retraining or Education & Reconciliation	335
	6.	Retroactivity	335
	7.	Security for Spousal Support Orders	336
	8.	Spousal Support Enforceability	336
	9.	Documented Evidence of Domestic Violence	336
	10.	A Criminal Conviction Bars Spousal Support	338
	11.	Retirement	339
	12.	A Professional License That is Obtained During the Marriage	344

Temporary and Permanent Spousal Support 347

	1.	Temporary Support	347
	2.	Permanent Spousal Support	348

Modifiable and Nonmodifiable Spousal Support 349

	1.	Modification/Change of Circumstances	349
	2.	Nonmodifiable Spousal Support	355

Specific Reduction Spousal Support Orders 357

	1.	The Richmond Order	357
	2.	Substantive Stepdown	358
	3.	Jurisdictional Stepdown	359

Cohabitation 359

EDUCATIONAL EXERCISES 364

CHAPTER 18: Disclosure & Fiduciary Duty 369

Introduction 370
Family Code Disclosure Provisions FC § 2100 et seq. 370
    1.   FC § 2100 370
    2.   FC § 2101 371
    3.   FC § 2102 371
    4.   FC § 2103 372
    5.   FC § 2104 373
    6.   FC § 2105 373
    7.   FC § 2106 373
    8.   FC § 2107 374
    9.   FC § 2108 374
    10.   FC § 2109 374
    11.   FC § 2110 374
    12.   FC § 2111 375
    13.   FC § 2112 375
    14.   FC § 2113 375
Fiduciary Duty 379
Breach of Fiduciary Duty FC § 1101 382
    EDUCATIONAL EXERCISES 383

CHAPTER 19: Bifurcation 385
Introduction 386
Codes, Rules and Forms RE: Requesting a Bifurcation 386
    EDUCATIONAL EXERCISES 394

CHAPTER 20: Title, Kinds of Property & Valuation 395
Kinds of Property 396
    1.   Personal Property 396
    2.   Real Property 397
    3.   Separate Property 398
    4.   Quasi-Marital Property 401
    5.   Quasi-Community Property 402
    6.   Community Property 403
Transmuting or Changing the Character of Property 405
Valuation of Community Assets 410
    EDUCATIONAL EXERCISES 411

CHAPTER 21: Community & Separate Debts/Liabilities ... 415

Debts/Liabilities ... 416
1. Community Estate Debts/Liabilities ... 416
2. Separate Debts/Liabilities ... 419
3. The Court has the Discretion to Assign Assets and Debts Party ... 423

EDUCATIONAL EXERCISES ... 424

CHAPTER 22: Division, Tracing & Reimbursement ... 425

Introduction ... 426
Division of Community Property ... 426
Tracing Claims ... 428
1. The *Pereira* Method ... 429
2. The *Van Camp* Method ... 430

Reimbursement ... 432
1. The Right to Claim Reimbursement ... 432
2. *Epstein* Credits ... 432
3. *Watts* Charges ... 434
4. Community Contributions to Education ... 435
5. Other Reimbursements ... 436

Personal Injury ... 437
Community Estate Debts/Liabilities ... 438
1. Separate Debts/Liabilities ... 441
2. The Court has the Discretion to Assign Assets and Debts Party ... 445

EDUCATIONAL EXERCISES ... 446

CHAPTER 23: Retirement & Disability ... 447

Introduction ... 448
Pensions, Retirement and the Like ... 448
1. Definitions ... 448
2. Matured, Unmatured Vested and Nonvested Retirement Plans ... 449
3. The Time Rule ... 450
4. Court Orders ... 450
5. Joinder and Joinder Forms ... 452
6. Early Retirement ... 452

Disability Benefits ... 453
EDUCATIONAL EXERCISES ... 455

CHAPTER 24: Apportionment **457**

Introduction 458
Principal and Interest in a Mortgage Loan 458
Home Purchased Before Marriage, Title Changed During Marriage 460
Home Purchased Before Marriage, Title Not Changed 461
    1.   The *Moore* Case 462
    2.   The *Moore* formula: 464
    3.   The *Marsden* Case 465
    4.   The *Marsden* formula: 467
    5.   The Moore/Marsden Formula 468
EDUCATIONAL EXERCISES 469

CHAPTER 25: Degrees of Proof & Presumptions **471**

Introduction 472
Degrees of Proof 472
    1.   Preponderance of the Evidence 472
    2.   Clear and Convincing Proof 473
    3.   Beyond a Reasonable Doubt 473
Presumptions 473
    1.   Rebuttable Presumptions 473
    2.   Conclusive Presumptions 478
EDUCATIONAL EXERCISES 481

CHAPTER 26: The Hearing **483**

Introduction 484
Prior to Filing a Request for a Hearing 484
    1.   *Request for Order* and Responding to a *Request for Order* 484
    2.   Declarations: Supporting and Responding to the *Request for Order* 486
    3.   Other Rules 487
The Hearing 487
EDUCATIONAL EXERCISES 491

CHAPTER 27: *Ex Parte* **493**

Introduction 494
The Process 495
Temporary Ex Parte Orders 497
EDUCATIONAL EXERCISES 499

CHAPTER 28: Defaults 501
Introduction 502
The Two Kinds of Judgment Defaults 503
1. Default without an Agreement 503
2. Default with an Agreement 504

Default Procedures, Rules and Forms 504
1. To Prove Up or Not 506
2. Default Rules and Codes 507

Setting Aside a Default 508
Additional Forms 509
EDUCATIONAL EXERCISES 511

CHAPTER 29: Drafting Court Orders 513
Introduction 514
Court Orders 514
1. Stipulations 514
2. *Pendente Lite* Hearings and Court Orders 515
3. Postjudgment Modifications or Terminations 515
4. The *Findings and Order After Hearing* form 517

Forms for Stipulations, Court Orders and Attachments 519
1. Stipulations 519
2. Court Orders 519
3. Attachments to Stipulations and Orders 520

EDUCATIONAL EXERCISES 522

CHAPTER 30: Marital Agreements 523
Introduction 524
1. Premarital Agreements 524

CHART 9: Check List for a Premarital Agreement 549
2. Postmarital Agreements 553

CHART 10: Check List for a Post Marital Agreement 555
3. Marital Settlement Agreements 558

CHART 12: Marital Settlement Agreement - Check List 559
EDUCATIONAL EXERCISES 562

CHAPTER 31: Settlements, Trial & the Final Paperwork 563
Introduction 564

    Dissolutions 564
        1.   Uncontested Dissolutions 564
        2.   Contested Dissolutions 565
    The Final Paperwork 566
        1.   The Declaration of Disclosure 566
        2.   The Notice of Entry of Judgment FL-190 570
        3.   Judgments 571
    Filing the Final Paperwork 574
    The Six-Month Waiting Period 574
    EDUCATIONAL EXERCISES 576

CHAPTER 32: Enforcement 577

    Introduction 578
    The Writ of Execution 578
    The Abstract of Judgment 579
    The Elisor 580
    Contempt of Court 581
        1.   The Contempt Process 581
        2.   Proving a Contempt 581
        3.   Court Orders 583
        4.   The Statute of Limitations 588
    Judgments 588
    Income Withholding Orders for Support /Wage Assignment 590
        1.   Definitions 590
        2.   Arrearages 591
        3.   Court Orders 591
        4.   Obligor's Employer 592
        5.   Failure of an Employer to Withhold Employee Wages 594
        6.   Staying and Terminating Assignment Orders 594
        7.   Judicial Council Forms for Wage Assignment Orders 596
    Sanctions for Violations under the Family Code 596
    EDUCATIONAL EXERCISES 598

CHAPTER 33: Postjudgment 599

    Introduction 600
    The Appeal Process 600

Postjudgment Motions 601
Setting Aside the Judgment 603
    EDUCATIONAL EXERCISES 605

CHAPTER 34: Parentage 607

Introduction 608
Establishment of Parentage by Voluntary Declaration FC § 7570 608
    1. The Declaration of Parentage FC § 7571 609
    2. The Form for the Declaration of Parentage FC § 7574 610
    3. Declarations Signed on or Before December 31, 1996 611
    4. A Declaration Signed by a Parent Who is a Minor 612
    5. Custody, Visitation and Child Support 612
    6. Rescission of a Declaration of Parentage FC § 7575 614
The Uniform Parentage Act (UPA) FC § 7600 et seq. 615
    1. The Parent-Child Relationship 615
    2. The Presumption of Parentage FC § 7611 615
    3. The Parentage Action 621
    4. The Parentage Judgment 625
    5. Setting Aside or Vacating the Judgment of Paternity 626
    6. Assisted Reproduction 628
    7. Adoption and Termination of Parental Rights in Paternity Cases 632
Attorney Fees 639
CHART 13: Parentage Codes & Titles (Code No. Order) 642
CHART 14: Parentage Family Codes (Alphabetical by Subject) 645
    EDUCATIONAL EXERCISES 650

CHAPTER 35: Minors 653

Introduction 654
Minors and Contracts 654
The Coogan Trust Account/Coogan's Law 658
Medical Treatment 663
Parents' Rights 666
Emancipation of Minors 667
Termination of Parental Rights 672
    EDUCATIONAL EXERCISES 674

CHAPTER 36: Domestic Violence 675

Introduction 676
The Crimes 681
    1. Assault 682
    2. Assault with deadly weapon or by force likely to produce great bodily injury .. 682
    3. Battery 682
    4. Sexual Battery 682
    5. Traumatic Injury 682
    6. Murder in the First Degree 683
    7. Murder in the Second Degree 683
    8. Attempted Murder 683
Protective Orders 684
    1. The Emergency Protective Order (EPO) 684
    2. Restraining Orders (ROs) 686
    3. Emergency Orders 695
    4. The Restraining Order (RO) Paperwork 695
The Tort Action 696
Real-time GPS Monitoring 700
    EDUCATIONAL EXERCISES 701

CHAPTER 37: Living Together/*Marvin* Actions 703

Introduction 704
The Marvin Cases 705
Marvin Property Claims 710
    1. The Meretricious Agreement 710
    2. Parties Can Agree to Pool Assets Acquired During their Cohabitation 711
    3. Contributions and Sharing Can be Proportional 713
    4. When the Property is Held in Joint Title 714
    5. When the Real Property is only in the Name of One of the Parties 714
Marvin Support Claims (Palimony) 715
Remedies in Marvin Actions 718
Marvin Contract Breaches & the Statute of Limitations 719
CHART 15: (*Marvin*)/Living Together Rules from Case Law 722
EDUCATIONAL EXERCISES 725

Appendix One: Johns' Intake Sheets & Timeline 727

Appendix Two: 2019 Family Code Changes & Bill Nos. 737

Appendix Three: Family Codes Effective 1/1/2020 745
GLOSSARY 757
INDEX (Terms & Cases) 781

CHAPTER 1: Introduction to California Family Law

In Brief...

FAMILY LAW:
- Is never boring or routine because no two families are the same;
- Is like no other field of law because it includes many other areas of the law; and
- There are no jury trials in family courts because they are courts of equity.

CALIFORNIA FAMILY CODE, (FC):
- Consolidated most family laws into one book, **FC § 1**;
- Not all new law but restatements and continuation of other laws, **FC § 2**;
- Additionally, contained many Uniform Acts, **FC § 3**;
- Is gender neutral, **FC § 11**; and
- Became operative on January 1, 1994.

JUDICIAL COUNCIL:
- Adopts forms and procedures that are used in CA courts; and
- Authority from **FC § 211** and **California Constitution, Article VI § 6**.
- Create Judicial council forms that:
    - Are **prescribed** or **adapted** by the council, use is **mandatory**;
    - Are **approved** or **adopted** by the council, use is **optional**;
    - Date of revision/implementation lower left corner of the 1st page; &
    - Only latest version of forms will be accepted by the court for filing.

CALIFORNIA RULES OF COURT, (CRC):
- Apply to every action and proceeding to which the Family Code applies;
- Contain procedures and court forms for use in CA Courts;
- Can be found at *www.courts.ca.gov/rules.htm*; and
- Title Five-Family & Juvenile Rules used most often in family law offices.

Each county has their own local family law rules, forms & websites:
- Pursuant to **CRC Rule 5.4**;
- Contain local court procedures & special court forms are set forth;
- The website at *www.courts.ca.gov/forms.htm* provides a list of all counties and websites; &
- All counties are represented on the *www.courts.ca.gov/forms.htm* website.

All rules and codes:
- Should be reviewed at least every 6 months:
- Because most changes become effective January 1 and July 1 of each year.

COURT HOLDINGS vs. DICTA:
- Court holdings are statements of law in appellate/supreme court cases that are part of the decision;
- Court holdings are binding precedents; and

> - Trial courts do not hold anything because they do not create binding precedents.
> - Dicta is the plural form
> - Dictum is the singular form;
> - Dicta include arguments and general observations that are unnecessary to the decision;
> - Do not create binding precedents; and
> - Are not holdings of the court.

Introduction

What area of the law is never boring? What field of law includes many other areas of law? Since this is a family law book, the answer has to be family law. But isn't family law only about divorce, support and child custody? No, there is so much more to family law.

Family law is never boring or routine. Each case is different in some way because no two families are exactly alike. Family law encompasses many other areas of the law, such as probate, tax law, civil litigation and issues related to real property. These differences make family law unique and more interesting than any other field of law.

Family law is about the constantly changing rules and laws that affect home life and families. For example, think about how families have changed over the last one hundred years. Extended families living together were the norm one hundred years ago; that is not the norm today. Many modern families include other people, such as nannies, half siblings, stepsiblings, stepparents and maybe even an extra set of grandparents.[1]

And, yes, family law does include divorce, support and custody issues. Many people believe that a nasty divorce, where winner takes all, is what the practice of family law is about; this is a misconception. Unless the parties choose to make the divorce a contest of power, which only escalates the bitterness between the parties, most divorces are, at worst, unpleasant.

Certainly, there is no doubt that working in a family law office requires hearing depressing tales of unhappy family situations. And there is no question that these tales of woe can weigh heavily upon a person. But the feeling that accompanies witnessing parents with such love for their children that no sacrifice is too great can bring an unparalleled high; an unparalleled high that only happens in family law. It used to be that marriage and forever were synonymous. Perhaps that was because society as a whole was not willing to recognize that people sometimes change and grow apart. Today, more people are able to see divorce as a way to become more

---

[1] According to the Pew Research Center Report in 2011, forty-two percent (42%) of Americans have a step-relationship (stepparent, step or half sibling, step child).

content with life.[2] In any case, divorce no longer carries the same stigma that it did 50 years ago and, fortunately, neither does working in a family law office.

One final aspect of family law that sets it apart from other areas of the law is that there are no jury trials in family law courts. When California became a state in 1850, English common law was used as the basis for many of the laws that were enacted. When the California legislature met for the first time, they decided that California would adopt the English common law system where private rights and torts cases were tried in **courts of law** for monetary damages and **courts of equity** tried cases seeking non-monetary remedies.

> If the action has to deal with ordinary common-law rights cognizable in courts of law, it is to that extent an action at law. In determining whether the action was one triable by a jury at common law, the court is not bound by the form of the action but rather by the nature of the rights involved and the facts of the particular case – the *gist* of the action. A jury trial must be granted where the *gist* of the action is legal, where the action is in reality cognizable at law. On the other hand, if the action is essentially one in equity and the relief sought "depends upon the application of equitable doctrines," the parties are not entitled to a jury trial. (*C & K ENGINEERING CONTRACTORS v. AMBER STEEL COMPANY, INC.* (1978) 23 Cal.3d 1 at p. 9.)

Divorce and similar family law matters are considered cases of equity. *CASSIDY v. SAN FRANCISCO* (1883) 64 Cal. 266 at p. 267; *In re Marriage of GAGNE* (1990) 225 Cal.App.3d 277 at p. 289. Since California family law matters are cases of equity, there is no right to a jury trial and no jury is provided. This English common law system of trying family law matters in courts of equity where there is no jury became the law in 1850 and remains the law today.

1. The California Family Code

Prior to the establishment of the Family Code, the family law codes were included in the Civil Code, the Code of Civil Procedure, the Evidence Code and the Probate Code. The California Family Code became operative on January 1, 1994.[3] It consolidated most laws concerned with family law into one area, one book, one specific code, the California Family Code (**FC**). **FC § 1**. Many of the laws were "a restatement and continuation of" other laws relating to the same subject matter and not new law. **FC § 2**. The Family Code contains the set of rules that are most frequently employed in a family law office.

---

[2] Forty percent (40%) of all new marriages are remarriages for one or both of the parties. Pew Research Center Report 2014. In 1960 only thirteen percent (13%) present were married for the second time. In 2014, that number had risen to twenty-five percent (25%), Livingston 2014. According to the United States Bureau of Statistics (2007), thirty-six (36) million Americans are divorced or widowed.

[3] Forty percent (40%) of all new marriages are remarriages for one or both of the parties. Pew Research Center Report 2014. In 1960 only thirteen percent (13%) present were married for the second time. In 2014, that number had risen to twenty-five percent (25%), Livingston 2014. According to the United States Bureau of Statistics (2007), thirty-six (36) million Americans are divorced or widowed.

Following each specific law in the Family Code is the history of that law (when enacted), notes, historical derivation (former law from which it was drawn), comments and references. These comments explain how the current law compares with the prior law. The Law Revision Commission Comments that follow **FC § 2** contain a list and definitions of important terms.

Some Family Code provisions are drawn from Uniform Acts such as the Uniform Premarital Agreement Act (§§ 1600-1617), the Uniform Divorce Recognition Act (§§ 2090-2093), the Uniform Child Custody Jurisdiction Act (§§ 3400-3425), the Uniform Reciprocal Enforcement of Support Act (§§ 4800-4854), the Uniform Act on Genetic testing Tests to Determine Parentage (§§ 7550-7557) and the Uniform Parentage Act (§§ 7600-7730). **FC § 3** provides that "a provision of a uniform act, shall be construed to effectuate the general purpose to make uniform the law in those states which enact that provision." **FC § 4** governs the application of the laws enacted under the Family Code and the laws that change or modify sections in the Family Code.

When reviewing laws from the Family Code, note that the headings are not meant to affect the meaning or intent, and the tenses include past, present and future tenses. **FC §§ 5, 9**. Singular numbers include the plural and vice versa. **FC § 10**. References made to spouses or married persons include both persons who are lawfully married to one another and persons who were previously lawfully married to one another. **FC § 11**.

Finally, there is a great difference between the terms **shall** and **may**. **Shall is mandatory** and **may is permissive**. **Shall not** and **may not** are **prohibitory** (restricted). **FC § 12**.

2. The Judicial Council

In 1926 an amendment to the California Constitution created the Judicial Council to make policy decisions for the California Courts. The main focus of the Judicial Council was and is to enact uniform rules of court practice and procedure. The Judicial Council is chaired by the Chief Justice.

Most of its members are appointed by the Chief Justice or by the State Bar Board of Trustees. All council members are volunteers and receive no compensation. Most Judicial Council members serve three-year terms. Each year, about one-third of the membership rotates out, and a new group is sworn in.

The Judicial Council is responsible for adopting legal forms for use in the California Courts. The forms and rules have been enacted, adapted or adopted by the Judicial Council under the authority of **FC§ 211, article VI, section 6** of the **California Constitution** and other applicable law.

There are many judicial council family law forms that have been promulgated by the Judicial Council. Some of these forms are prescribed by the council and are mandatory; others are approved for optional use. The printed language in the lower left corner of the first page of each form specifies: **(1)** whether the form is adapted (mandatory) or approved (optional) and **(2)** the date of revision or implementation. Only the latest version of the form may be filed with the court.

3. California Rules of Court (CRC)

The California Rules of Court (**CRC**) provide information about procedures and court forms that are used in California courtrooms. The CRCs can be found on the Internet at ***www.courts.ca.gov/rules.htm***. These rules cover trial court rules, civil court rules, criminal rules, family and juvenile rules, probate rules, appellate rules, law practice rules for attorneys and judges, judicial administration rules and more. Title Five is entitled **Family and Juvenile Rules** and is the set of rules and forms most commonly used in family law offices.

The family law rules commence at **CRC Rule 5.2** et seq. and apply to every action and proceeding to which the Family Code applies and, unless these rules elsewhere explicitly make them applicable, do not apply to any other action or proceeding that is not found in the Family Code. **CRC Rule 5.2(c).**

Unless provided otherwise, all provisions of law applicable to civil actions generally apply to a proceeding under the Family Code if they would otherwise apply to such a proceeding without reference to this rule. To the extent that these rules conflict with provisions in other statutes or rules, these rules prevail in family law matters. **CRC Rule 5.2(d).**

All provisions of law applicable to civil actions generally apply in any action under the Family Code. **CRC Rule 5.2(e).**

Pursuant to **CRC Rule 5.4**, each county can adopt local rules and forms regarding family law actions and proceedings that are not in conflict with or inconsistent with California law, the Family Code or the California Rules of Court.

4. Family Law Rules, Local Rules & Websites

The local rules of each county provide the procedures and special forms that are employed in that county. For information about each county, visit ***www.courts.ca.gov/find-my-court.htm***. This website provides information about the superior courts in California, by county. All of the counties in California are represented in this list.

Most changes that are made to the family law forms become effective January 1st or July 1st of each year. Accordingly, the rules and forms should be reviewed at least every six months at both the local and the state superior court website (***www.courts.ca.gov/forms.htm***).

5. Holdings of the Court

Finally, understanding what the word **holding** encompasses is a vital part of understanding case law. In *In re Marriage of BOSWEL* (2014) 225 Cal.App.4th 1172, the appellate court stated:

> We use the word "holding" in its traditional and strict legal sense. Witkin uses the Latin phrase "*ratio decidendi*" to describe the word "holding." The *ratio decidendi* is the principle or rule that constitutes the ground of the decision, and it is this principle or rule that has the effect of a precedent.
>
> It is therefore necessary to read the language of an opinion in the light of its facts and the issues raised, to determine (a) which statements of law were necessary to the decision, and therefore binding precedents, and (b) which were arguments and general observations, unnecessary to the decision, i.e., dicta, with no force as precedents.
> We comment on the strict use of the word "hold" because there are cases where the appellate court casually characterizes a trial court's ruling as a "holding" or that the trial court "held" something. Since a trial court cannot create "binding precedent," it cannot "hold" anything. There are also cases where the appellate courts casually use the word "hold" when it actually means "conclude." (*Id.* at pp. 1176-1177.)

EDUCATIONAL EXERCISES

Read the quote above, then decide for each of the quotes that follow whether the quote is dicta or holding.

1. The following quote is from: *In re Marriage of CANTARELLA* (2011) 191 Cal.App.4th 916

> In the rare instance where a party failed to register public evidence of the marriage, such failure might be inadvertent or involuntary (as in the case of a rejected certificate) or might instead indicate a lack of consent at that time. We do not believe the Legislature intended a marriage to be thereby rendered invalid. True, the keeping of accurate and complete marriage records benefits the public. But this goal pales compared to the societal importance of recognizing the validity of marriages to which parties have consented. To hold that a failure by a party to register a certificate voids a marriage would invalidate "marriages already solemnized in this state and would, among other results, affect the marital status of the parties, their property rights and rights of inheritance." In wife's words, it would "negate the manifold mutual fiduciary and legal obligations the parties understood they were incurring," due to "a technical misstep along the way."

Dicta or holding? If there is dicta and holding, circle the holding.

2. The following quote is from: *Loeffler v. Medina* (2009) 174 Cal.App.4th 1495

> Further, in determining that the trial court did not abuse its discretion, we find it significant that that the trial court reduced Loeffler's request of $ 45,842.50 in fees and $ 2,934.85 in costs almost in half by awarding only $ 25,000 in fees and $ 1,504.85 in costs. The award granted was significantly reduced from the original request. Thus, it clearly appears that the trial court exercised its discretion. In these circumstances, we cannot conclude that the award of attorney's fees shocks the conscience or suggests that passion and prejudice had a part in it.

Dicta or holding? If there is dicta and holding, circle the holding.

3. The following quote is from: *FREDERICK v. SUPERIOR COURT* (2014) 223 Cal.App.4th 988

> The court concluded that the husband's death deprived it of jurisdiction to decide the remaining issues and on its own motion issued two minute orders abating the action and vacating its prior orders. (Id. at pp. 810–811.) The appellate court, treating the wife's appeal as a petition for writ of mandate, directed the trial court to substitute the estate of the husband as a party in the action and "determine the issues over which it [had] reserved jurisdiction at the time it entered its judgments of dissolution of marriage." (Id. at p. 812.) According to the appellate court, "the death of a party to a dissolution proceeding does not abate an action in which a decision has been rendered. ... When the trial court at bench entered judgment dissolving the status of the marriage it properly reserved jurisdiction to decide the collateral property issues. [The husband's] subsequent death neither abated the remainder of the dissolution action nor deprived the court of its retained jurisdiction to dispose of the remaining issues." (Ibid.)

Dicta or holding? If there is dicta and holding, circle the holding.

4. The following quote is from: *Jason P. v. Danielle S.* (2014) 226 Cal.App.4th 167

> By interpreting FC § 7613(b) only to preclude a sperm donor from establishing paternity based upon his biological connection to the child, while allowing him to establish that he is a presumed parent under FC § 7611 based upon a demonstrated familial relationship, we allow both statutes to retain effectiveness and promote the purpose of each.
>
> Our holding that a sperm donor is not precluded from establishing presumed parentage does not mean that a mother who conceives through assisted reproduction and allows the sperm donor to have some kind of relationship with the child necessarily loses her right to be the sole parent.

(Dicta) or holding? If there is dicta and holding, circle the holding.

5. The following quote is from: *MARVIN v. MARVIN* (1976) 18 Cal.3d 660

> We conclude that the judicial barriers that may stand in the way of a policy based upon the fulfillment of the reasonable expectations of the parties to a nonmarital relationship should be removed. As we have explained, the courts now hold that express agreements will be enforced unless they rest on an unlawful meretricious consideration.
> We add that in the absence of an express agreement, the courts may look to a variety of other remedies in order to protect the parties' lawful expectations.
>
> The courts may inquire into the conduct of the parties to determine whether that conduct demonstrates an implied contract or implied agreement of partnership or joint venture or some other tacit understanding between the parties.
>
> The courts may, when appropriate, employ principles of constructive trust or resulting trust. Finally, a nonmarital partner may recover in quantum meruit for the reasonable value of household services rendered less the reasonable value of support received if he can show that he rendered services with the expectation of monetary reward.
>
> Since we have determined that Michelle's complaint states a cause of action for breach of an express contract, and, as we have explained, can be amended to state a cause of action independent of allegations of express contract, we must conclude that the trial court erred in granting Marvin a judgment on the pleadings.
>
> The judgment is reversed and the cause is remanded for further proceedings consistent with the views expressed herein.

(Dicta) or holding? If there is dicta and holding, circle the holding.

CHAPTER 2: The California Paralegal

In Brief...

PARALEGAL RULES AND CODES:
Business & Professions (B&P) Code § 6450 et seq. provide the paralegals laws.
  B&P Code § 6450 provides:
  - A paralegal is qualified by education, training, or work experience.
  - The requirements for a CA paralegal certificate.
  - That only a certified paralegal can use the title **paralegal**.
  - A paralegal must always disclose paralegal.

  A PARALEGAL SHALL NOT:
  - Provide legal advice;
  - Represent a client in court;
  - Select, explain, draft, or recommend documents for client use without supervision;
  - Act as a runner or capper, as defined in Sections 6151 and 6152;
  - Engage in conduct that constitutes the unlawful practice of law;[1]
  - Contract with anyone other than the supervisor to perform paralegal services;
  - Induce a person to make an investment, purchase a financial product or service, or enter a transaction from which income or profit, or both, purportedly may be derived; or
  - Establish the fees to charge a client for the services the paralegal performs.

  B&P Code § 6451 provides:
  - A paralegal must always be supervised of an attorney.
  - Legal ethics for paralegals are the same as those for lawyers.
  - Paralegals should review the Rules of Professional Conduct.

  B&P Code § 6452(b) provides:
  - Attorneys are liable for the work & conduct of the paralegals that they supervise.

  B&P Code § 6453 provides that a paralegal:
  - Has the same confidentiality requirement as an attorney; &
  - Must always preserve the attorney-client privilege.

  B&P Code § 6454 provides:
  - **Paralegal**, **legal assistant**, **attorney assistant** can be used interchangeably.

PARALEGAL FORM: CONFLICT OF INTEREST RECORD
  Paralegals MUST keep records of the work that they perform.
A Paralegal is a Professional and should always act like a professional.
PARALEGAL DUTIES AND INITIAL CLIENT INTERACTION
Some tasks that are performed by paralegals pursuant to **FC § 6450** include:
  - Case planning, development and management;
  - Research;
  - Interviewing clients;

---

[1] See *In re ANDERSON, Debtor* (1987) 79 B.R. 482 set forth above.

Chapter 2: The California Paralegal

> - Fact gathering and retrieving information;
> - Drafting and analyzing legal documents;
> - Collecting, compiling and utilizing technical information to make an independent decision and recommendation to the supervising attorney.
>
> **There is no standardized Client Intake Form.**
> **Client Intake forms vary from law firm to law firm.**

Introduction

The focus of this chapter is California family law paralegals. While this is a family law book, the information in this chapter applies to most, if not all, California paralegals.

Being a certified paralegal is important to many attorney employers. Two reasons that attorneys should be concerned about a certified. How the paralegal acts and conducts his or herself will be a reflection on not only the paralegal, but the law firm and supervising attorney, as well. Many attorneys rely on their reputation to obtain new clients and attorneys rely on the reputation of the paralegal when they are in the market for a paralegal.

Paralegal laws, rules and ethical issues are discussed in this chapter both written and not written.

California has passed laws that are specific to paralegals. Those laws follow.

California Paralegal Laws

1. Business & Professions (B&P) Code § 6450 et seq.

California has enacted specific laws for paralegals and they are set forth at **Business & Professions Code § 6450** et seq. (**B&P Code § 6450**). These codes first became effective on January 1, 2000. The codes were thereafter amended in 2001, 2002 and 2006.

B&P Code § 6450 provides in part:

> (a) "Paralegal" means a person who holds himself or herself out to be a paralegal, who is qualified by education, training, or work experience, who either contracts with or is employed by an attorney, law firm, corporation, governmental agency, or other entity, and who performs substantial legal work under the direction and supervision of an active member of the State Bar of California, as defined in Section 6060, or an attorney practicing law in the federal courts of this state, that has been specifically delegated by the attorney to him or her. Tasks performed by a paralegal include, but are not limited to, case planning, development, and management; legal research; interviewing clients; fact gathering and retrieving information; drafting and analyzing legal documents; collecting, compiling, and utilizing technical information to make an independent decision and

Chapter 2: The California Paralegal

> recommendation to the supervising attorney; and representing clients before a state or federal administrative agency if that representation is permitted by statute, court rule, or administrative rule or regulation.

B&P Code § 6450 also provides that a paralegal must possess one of the following:

> **(1)** A certificate of completion of a paralegal program approved by the American Bar Association.
> **(2)** A certificate of completion of a paralegal program at, or a degree from, a postsecondary institution that requires the successful completion of a minimum of 24 semester, or equivalent, units in law-related courses and that has been accredited by a national or regional accrediting organization or approved by the Bureau for Private Postsecondary and Vocational Education.
> **(3)** A baccalaureate degree or an advanced degree in any subject, a minimum of one year of law-related experience under the supervision of an attorney who has been an active member of the State Bar of California for at least the preceding three years or who has practiced in the federal courts of this state for at least the preceding three years, and a written declaration from this attorney stating that the person is qualified to perform paralegal tasks.
> **(4)** A high school diploma or general equivalency diploma, a minimum of three years of law-related experience under the supervision of an attorney who has been an active member of the State Bar of California for at least the preceding three years or who has practiced in the federal courts of this state for at least the preceding three years, and a written declaration from this attorney stating that the person is qualified to perform paralegal tasks. This experience and training shall be completed no later than December 31, 2003.

The continuing education of a paralegal is set forth in **B&P Code § 6450(d)** which provides that a paralegal is to complete four (4) hours of mandatory continuing legal education in legal ethics and four (4) hours of mandatory continuing legal education in either general law or in an area of specialized law every two years.

Identifying oneself as a **paralegal** requires that a paralegal has met the requirements set forth in **B&P Code § 6450(c)** and performs his/her paralegal duties under the supervision of an attorney who is an active member of the California State Bar. Also, the business card of a paralegal must include the name of the supervising attorney/law firm. **B&P Code § 6452**.

The rules for a paralegal are set forth in **B&P Code § 6450(d)**, which provides that a paralegal is to complete four (4) hours of mandatory continuing legal education in legal ethics and four (4) hours of mandatory continuing legal education in either general law or in an area of specialized law every two years.

2. B&P Code §§ 6451 and 6452

> It is unlawful for a paralegal to perform any services for a consumer except as performed under the direction and supervision of the attorney, law firm, corporation, government agency, or other entity that employs or contracts with the paralegal. Nothing in this chapter shall prohibit a paralegal who is employed by an attorney, law firm, governmental

Chapter 2: The California Paralegal

> agency, or other entity from providing services to a consumer served by one of these entities if those services are specifically allowed by statute, case law, court rule, or federal or state administrative rule or regulation. "Consumer" means a natural person, firm, association, organization, partnership, business trust, corporation, or public entity. B&P Code § 6451.

Paralegals MST be supervised by California licensed attorneys. If a paralegal performs work that is not appropriately supervised, and a consumer suffers an injury due to the work of the paralegal. That paralegal could be fined AND jailed.

A paralegal must always disclose his or her position as a paralegal. Identifying oneself as a **paralegal** requires that a paralegal has met the requirements set forth in **B&P Code § 6450(c)** and performs his/her paralegal duties under the supervision of an attorney who is an active member of the California State Bar. Also, the business card of a paralegal must include the name of the supervising attorney/law firm. **B&P Code § 6452**.

3. B&P Code § 6453.

A paralegal is subject to the same confidentiality duty as an attorney as set forth in **B&P Code § 6068(e)**[2], which is "to maintain inviolate the confidentiality, and at every peril to himself or herself to preserve the attorney-client privilege, of a consumer for whom the paralegal has provided any of the services described in subdivision (a) of Section 6450."

4. B&P Code § 6454

The terms paralegal, legal assistant, attorney assistant, freelance paralegal, independent paralegal, and contract paralegal are synonymous and can be used interchangeably, if one is entitled to use these labels pursuant to **B&P Code § 6451** set forth above. **B&P Code § 6454**.

5. B&P Code § 6455

A violation of **B&P Code § 6451** or **§ 6452**[3] is punishable upon conviction by a fine of up to two thousand five hundred dollars ($2,500) for the first violation and a fine

---

[2] "It is the duty of an attorney to do all of the following: ...
(e)
  (1) To maintain inviolate the confidence, and at every peril to himself or herself to preserve the secrets, of his or her client.
  (2) Notwithstanding paragraph (1), an attorney may, but is not required to, reveal confidential information relating to the representation of a client to the extent that the attorney reasonably believes the disclosure is necessary to prevent a criminal act that the attorney reasonably believes is likely to result in death of, or substantial bodily harm to, an individual."

[3] B&P Code § 6452 provides:
"(a) It is unlawful for a person to identify himself or herself as a paralegal on any advertisement, letterhead, business card or sign, or elsewhere unless he or she has met the qualifications of subdivision (c) of Section 6450 and performs all services under the direction and supervision of an

of two thousand five hundred dollars ($2,500) as to each consumer with respect to whom a violation occurs, or imprisonment in a county jail for not more than one year or by both fine and imprisonment for subsequent violations. **B&P Code § 6455.**

The Unauthorized Practice of Law

A paralegal cannot practice law. Additionally, paralegals cannot make court appearances, sign pleadings, give legal advice or take depositions. Paralegals must always disclose their position as a paralegal.

There is an abundance of cases involving paralegals engaging in the unauthorized practice of law. Since paralegals help lawyers with research, interviewing and document preparation, sometimes the precise boundaries of the scope of the duties of the paralegal can be blurred.

In the case that follows a paralegal was held to have been practicing law without a license.

> *In re: Katheryn Irene ANDERSON, Debtor*
> **UNITED STATES BANKRUPTCY COURT FOR THE SOUTHERN DISTRICT OF CALIFORNIA**
> **79 B.R. 482**
> **November 5, 1987**
> **(Anderson v. Bankruptcy Court)**
>
> When Ms. Anderson was having financial difficulties, she responded to an ad in a local newspaper by San Diego Paralegal Services, a sole proprietorship run by Tom Kavanaugh. She was attracted by the ad because it said that San Diego Paralegal would come to your home, and she was without transportation.
>
> She telephoned San Diego Paralegal and spoke with Kavanaugh. Kavanaugh explained he was a paralegal and that San Diego Paralegal was a typing service. She indicated she was thinking about filing bankruptcy and asked him to come to her home because her car was inoperative.
>
> Kavanaugh went to her house and questioned her about her assets, liabilities and financial affairs from a questionnaire which roughly parallels those questions asked by Official Form Nos. 6 and 7 prescribed by the Judicial Conference of the United States. Kavanaugh admits the answers to the questions were written down by him.
>
> During the interview, Anderson asked Kavanaugh a number of questions concerning the consequences of filing bankruptcy. She asked him whether she would lose her car if she

---

attorney who is an active member of the State Bar of California or an attorney practicing law in the federal courts of this state who is responsible for all of the services performed by the paralegal. The business card of a paralegal shall include the name of the law firm where he or she is employed or a statement that he or she is employed by or contracting with a licensed attorney.
(b) An attorney who uses the services of a paralegal is liable for any harm caused as the result of the paralegal's negligence, misconduct, or violation of this chapter."

Chapter 2: The California Paralegal

> filed Chapter 7; he said, "yes". She asked him if she would be able to keep her income tax refund. He indicated probably. He told her that the income taxes which she owed would have to be paid after bankruptcy. She mentioned that she had a pending civil lawsuit which would bring in extra money and inquired whether she needed to report it. He advised her not to worry about it and that it did not need to be reported.
>
> When she inquired about a Chapter 13 [bankruptcy], he indicated that it would cost her more money for a Chapter 13; that she would have three years to pay it off and that the payments would be $ 150 per month. Based on his statements, she decided not file Chapter 13.
>
> After the Chapter 7 was filed, Ms. Anderson received an income tax refund of $ 1,050, rather than the $ 500 refund she was expecting. She called Mr. Kavanaugh when she got the larger refund and asked if she should amend her bankruptcy schedules. He told her not to worry about it. Consequently, no amendment was ever filed.
>
> The term "practice law" or its equivalent, "the practice of law," has been repeatedly defined by our reviewing courts. They have uniformly said that "as the term is generally understood, the practice of law . . . . includes legal advice and counsel and the preparation of legal instruments and contracts by which legal rights are secured although such matter may or may not be depending in a court."
>
> If defendant had only been called upon to perform and had only undertaken to perform the clerical service of filling in the blanks on a particular form in accordance with information furnished him by the parties, or had merely acted as a scrivener to record the stated agreement of the parties to the transaction, he would not have been guilty of practicing law without a license. But the record supports the conclusion that he went further -- that he determined for the parties the kind of legal document they should execute in order to effectuate their purpose. This constituted the practice of law.
>
> After considering the testimony of Kavanaugh and debtor in light of the cases and opinions, the conclusion that Kavanaugh is engaged in the unauthorized practice of law is inescapable. Kavanaugh held himself out to be qualified to give advice concerning bankruptcies. He interviewed debtor and solicited information from her, from which he selected and prepared bankruptcy schedules. He advised Anderson of her legal rights vis-a-vis secured collateral and of the differences between a Chapter 13 filing and one under Chapter 7. He further (incorrectly) advised her regarding the necessity to file amendments to her schedules to accurately reflect an increased tax refund. It also appears that he selected her exemptions. All of these acts require the exercise of legal judgment beyond the knowledge and capacity of the lay person.
>
> Accordingly, an injunction will issue barring Kavanaugh, doing business as San Diego Paralegal Services, from engaging in any of the following activities for a fee: Advising debtors regarding exemptions, discharge ability or the automatic stay; providing advice concerning the differences and/or relative advantages of filing a Chapter 13 or Chapter 7 case; and, from interviewing debtors with an eye towards preparing statements or schedules. Kavanaugh will also be barred from soliciting any such employment in accordance with the prohibition contained in Cal. B&P Code § 6126.

In the case above, Mr. Kavanaugh was found to be practicing law without a license: **(1)** when he chose and filled in the forms for Ms. Anderson, **(2)** when he responded to Ms. Anderson's legal questions, and **(3)** when he advised Ms. Anderson about bankruptcy law.

Attorney Liability for Paralegal Error & Misconduct

The paralegal needs to be aware that his or her supervising attorney can be subjected to malpractice claims if the work product of the paralegal is subpar. The paralegal should also be aware that his or her conduct may also give rise to liability.

B&P Code § 6452(b) provides:

> An attorney who uses the services of a paralegal is liable for any harm caused as the result of the **paralegal's negligence, misconduct**, or violation of this chapter. (Emphasis added.)

The supervising attorney is always liable for the paralegal's conduct. A paralegal's illegal or unethical behavior can subject his or her supervising attorney to sanctions, disbarment and give rise to malpractice claims.

The two cases that follow demonstrate that the supervising attorney is, indeed, responsible for the work, lack of work and misconduct of his or her paralegal.

As the following case demonstrates, if a default is taken an attorney may set aside the default obtained because the paralegal miscalendared the dates that the attorney was to appear in court. Thus, relief may be obtained if a court can be persuaded that the **CCP § 473** applies.

> ***SYLVIA WEI-TING HU, Plaintiff and Respondent, v. AMY FANG, Defendant and Appellant.***
> COURT OF APPEAL OF CALIFORNIA, SECOND APPELLATE DISTRICT, DIVISION EIGHT
> 104 Cal.App.4th 61
> December 5, 2002, Decided
> (*Sylvia Wei-Ting Hu, Plaintiff and Respondent, v. Amy Fang*)
>
> Sylvia Wei-Ting Hu sued Amy Fang for breach of contract and common counts. Fang, represented by J. Flores Valdez, answered the complaint. On February 16, 2001, Valdez, failed to appear at a status conference. The trial court issued an order to show cause (OSC)[4] for failure to appear and for striking Fang's answer. Valdez was mailed a copy of the trial court's minute order.
>
> The hearing on the OSC was set for March 15, 2001, but Valdez again failed to appear. At the March 15, 2001 hearing, the case was transferred from West Covina to Pomona and the hearing on the OSC was continued to April 5, 2001. Valdez was given notice, but again failed to appear. The trial court ordered Fang's answer stricken and ordered counsel

---

[4] OSC–Order to Show Cause, (a request for a hearing) changed to *RFO–Request for Order* effective 1/1/2012.

Chapter 2: The California Paralegal

> for Hu to file a request for entry of default.
>
> On April 25, 2001, Valdez filed a motion, under CCP § 473, to set aside the order of default (Motion). The Motion was based, inter alia, on the declaration of Valdez and the declaration of his paralegal, Ben Lui. Valdez stated that "[t]here was a mistake on the part of my paralegal in the calendaring of my appearances" and consequently Valdez understood that the appearance was on April 6th before the Citrus Court instead of April 5th in Pomona. Lui stated "I am the paralegal/ calendar clerk for J. Flores Valdez" and "I made a mistake in calendaring the matter in that I set it for April 6th in Citrus Court instead of the noticed time and date of April 5th at the Pomona Court."
>
> At the hearing on the Motion, Valdez argued that his employee's mistake should be imputed to him. The trial court denied the Motion, finding "473 only grants relief for mistake, inadvertence, surprise, or excusable neglect of an attorney, not a paralegal." The court further concluded: "It's a tough call, but if you choose to use paralegals and have them do your work, then I don't think it's your mistake that they make a mistake." Subsequently, the trial court entered a default judgment. Fang timely appealed.
>
> We conclude the trial court abused its discretion in finding that Valdez was not the cause of the default judgment because the mistake was made by his paralegal. The attorney is the professional responsible for supervising the work of his or her legal assistants. "[E]ven though an attorney cannot be held responsible for every detail of office procedure, he must accept responsibility to supervise the work of his staff." Thus, Valdez was responsible for supervising Lui's work and is responsible for Lui's work product, including his mistake in calendaring the OSC hearing.
>
> Valdez, as required, acknowledged that Liu's error was attributable to the attorney and requested relief from default. The trial court should have granted the Motion and considered whether sanctions were appropriate. Granting relief from default does not condone Valdez's failure to appear, but serves the purpose of relieving "the innocent client of the burden of the attorney's fault . . . ."
> The judgment of default is reversed.

Not every **CCP § 473** motion will be granted. These cases are decided on a case-by-case analysis based upon the facts of a specific case. Excusable neglect is a somewhat subjective call by a judge, as the case that follows demonstrates.

> ***SUSAN HENDERSON, Plaintiff and Appellant, v. PACIFIC GAS AND ELECTRIC CO., Defendant and Respondent.***
> **COURT OF APPEAL OF CALIFORNIA, FIFTH APPELLATE DISTRICT**
> **187 Cal.App.4th 215**
> **August 5, 2010, Filed**
> **(Henderson v. Pacific Gas and Electric)**
>
> In March 2007, Henderson filed a complaint against her former employer, PG&E, asserting causes of action for employment discrimination in violation of the California Fair Employment and Housing Act and breach of contract.
>
> On May 8, 2008, PG&E moved for summary judgment. On June 20, 2008, the court granted Henderson's Ex Parte application to continue the summary judgment motion to September 22, 2008. At the September 22, 2008 hearing, the trial court denied

Henderson's application to [once again] continue the summary judgment motion [and] a written order granting summary judgment in PG&E's favor was filed on October 30, 2008. The court entered judgment against Henderson on November 14, 2008. On December 2, 2008, Henderson filed a motion for a new trial. By order filed January 29, 2009, the trial court denied the motion.

On March 20, 2009, Henderson filed a motion to set aside the summary judgment in accordance with § 473(b), based on [her attorney's] inadvertence, surprise or excusable neglect resulting from the action of a "former rogue employee". She argued [that her attorney] McClelland committed excusable neglect when he relied on the paralegal to prepare the opposition in its entirety.

On May 8, 2009, the court issued a written ruling denying the motion to set aside the October 30, 2008 order and November 18, 2008 judgment. This appeal followed. Henderson asserts [on appeal that] the trial court erred in failing to set aside the order granting summary judgment [because] the error was not attributable to her. In support of her motion, McClelland submitted a declaration in which he stated that he had entrusted preparation of the summary judgment opposition to his paralegal, who had just taken the California bar exam, because he was handling other matters related to his law practice.

McClelland claimed that throughout the month before the opposition was due, his paralegal, who was leaving for an Alaskan cruise on Friday, September 5, 2008, assured him the preparation was going well and the opposition would be filed timely. On Thursday, September 4, she left his office early to work on completing the opposition at home, taking the majority of Henderson's file with her without his consent. Later that day, she called him and said the opposition would be in his office on Friday morning, September 5, for his review and filing the following Monday. On his way to work on September 5, he received a voice mail message the paralegal left on his cell phone at 7:00 a.m., stating that her computer crashed the night before, so she took the entire file with her on the cruise and made arrangements to have the documents e-mailed to an employee of an attorney service in Fresno, who would then file and serve the documents on September 8. McClelland could not contact the paralegal [to confirm that the documents were filed] because she was without cell phone access.

McClelland was responsible for supervising his paralegal's work and is responsible for her work product, including the failure to have the opposition filed on time. Given this, the trial court reasonably could conclude that his paralegal's inability to complete the assignment within the deadline he gave her, thereby resulting in the late filing of the opposition, did not constitute either surprise or excusable neglect, and instead was inexcusable, as he failed to supervise his employee closely and trusted in her scheme to file and serve the documents from a remote, out-of-state location, without ensuring his ability to review and sign them.

Certainly McClelland knew by Friday morning that he did not have the documents to review and his paralegal was planning to attempt to transmit them from Seattle or the cruise ship. Instead of immediately informing opposing counsel or the court of this problem and requesting either a continuance of the hearing or an extension of time to file the opposition, he gambled that the paralegal's plan would work and the documents would be filed on time. He gambled and lost.

Since it was McClelland's negligence in failing to supervise his employee and to request relief sooner that led to the late-filed opposition, the trial court reasonably could conclude

Chapter 2: The California Paralegal

> that his conduct was inexcusable. While counsel might not have expected the paralegal's computer to crash, that she would take the client file with her on vacation, or that she would not have the documents filed while on her trip, ordinary prudence certainly could have guarded against these events. A reasonably prudent person would not have expected a paralegal, even a trusted one, to prepare an opposition to a summary judgment on her own and then, upon learning that the opposition would not be available for review before filing, simply wait to see if in fact the opposition is filed.
>
> For these reasons, the trial court's May 8, 2009 order is affirmed.

Appropriate and Inappropriate Conduct

California Codes and the cannons from many of the paralegal organizations provide some light into what conduct is appropriate and inappropriate. And, of course, California codes discuss paralegal conduct.

B&P Code § 6451 provides that a paralegal may not perform any services for a consumer unless he or she is under the direct supervision of an attorney licensed to practice law in the State of California.

B&P Code § 6452 provides that a paralegal must disclose his or her position as a paralegal and not mislead the public into believing that the paralegal is an attorney at any time.

The California codes and cannons set forth in many of the paralegal organizations provide the paralegal with knowledge of proper and improper behavior. The State Bar provides that paralegals are held to the same ethical conduct code as attorneys, The California Rules of Professional Conduct[5]. But there are unwritten rules that a paralegal should be aware of, as well. As a guide, a list of shall not and shall behavior for paralegals follows.

1. A Paralegal Shall Not...

B&P Code § 6450 provides that a paralegal shall not do the following:

> (1) Provide legal advice.
> (2) Represent a client in court.
> (3) Select, explain, draft, or recommend the use of any legal document to or for any person other than the attorney who directs and supervises the paralegal. (See the case that follows these rules for an understanding of what constitutes the practice of law.)
> (4) Act as a runner or capper, as defined in Sections 6151 and 6152.
> (5) Engage in conduct that constitutes the unlawful practice of law.[6]
> (6) Contract with, or be employed by, a natural person other than an attorney to perform paralegal services.

---

[5] The entire text of these rules can be found on the California State Bar site at: *http://rules.calbar.ca.gov/Rules/RulesofProfessionalConduct.aspx*.
[6] See *In re ANDERSON, Debtor* (1987) 79 B.R. 482 set forth above.

> **(7)** In connection with providing paralegal services, induce a person to make an investment, purchase a financial product or service, or enter a transaction from which income or profit, or both, purportedly may be derived.
> **(8)** Establish the fees to charge a client for the services the paralegal performs, which shall be established by the attorney who supervises the paralegal's work.

2. A Paralegal Shall...

a. Always act ethically and with integrity.
b. Prevent and assist whenever possible the unauthorized practice of law.
c. Always protect the confidences and secrets of clients.
d. Always be supervised by a member of the California State Bar Association.
e. Always avoid, if possible, any conflict of interest, including but not limited to, working for a law firm that accepts a client that the paralegal previously worked for at another law firm. (A conflict of interest occurs when a person has divided loyalties such as represented a husband and a wife in a divorce.)
f. Disclose to supervising attorney all possible conflicts of interest.
g. Always make it clear that he or she is a paralegal, not an attorney;
h. Always treat co-workers and office employees with courtesy and respect;
i. Address all people both clients and supervising attorney formally[7];
j. Dress professionally[8];
k. Conduct him or herself properly and ethically[9]
l. Be timely whenever possible[10];
m. Never make judgment calls[11];
n. Never tell personal stories[12]
o. Never flirt with a client
p. Never tell attorney jokes
q. Give anyone the impression that he or she practices law;
r. Not accept a case on behalf of a client without attorney supervision and consent;
s. Never accept a gift from a client; or
t. Never advertise or contract members of the public for the performance of paralegal functions.

---

[7] Whenever the paralegal references an attorney or attorneys, he or she should always refer to him or her formally (e.g. Mr. Jones). A client should also always be addressed formally.
[8] If the paralegal is dressed as a professional the first time a client sees him or her, he or she will be given more credence as a professional. Dressing appropriately means that the paralegal should always be well groomed and attired in clean respectable non-beach/playwear; short skirts or tank tops or any kind of revealing clothing should be avoided.
[9] The paralegal should always conduct himself or herself as a professional. A professional acts in a business-like manner in any work situation. Proper conduct also includes body language.
[10] The paralegal should never keep a client waiting if it can be prevented. This may require planning ahead so as not to be tardy.
[11] DO NOT JUDGE clients. The paralegal should never make comments to the client regarding the beliefs or conduct of the client. Also, the paralegal should be careful with facial expressions and body language. This includes rolling the eyes or making any kind of noise or movement that may show disapproval.
[12] A paralegal should never relay his or her personal life stories to the client. By sharing personal stories, the client may view the paralegal as a friend and ally.

Chapter 2: The California Paralegal

Finally, a paralegal must always be a professional and act like a professional.

A Paralegal Conflict

One conflict of interest for paralegals is pointed out by the case below.

> ***In re COMPLEX ASBESTOS LITIGATION et al., Plaintiffs and Appellants, v.***
> ***OWENS-CORNING FIBERGLAS CORPORATION et al., Defendants and Appellants***
> Court of Appeal of California, First Appellate District, Division Three
> 232 Cal.App.3d 572
> July 19, 1991
> (*Complex Asbestos Litigation v. Owens-Corning*)
>
> Attorney Jeffrey B. Harrison, his law firm, and their affected clients appeal from an order disqualifying the Harrison firm in nine asbestos related personal injury actions. The appeal presents the difficult issue of whether a law firm should be disqualified because an employee of the firm possessed attorney-client confidences from previous employment by opposing counsel in pending litigation. We hold that disqualification is appropriate unless there is written consent or the law firm has effectively screened the employee from involvement with the litigation to which the information relates.
>
> Michael Vogel worked as a paralegal for the law firm of Brobeck, Phleger & Harrison (Brobeck) from October 28, 1985, to November 30, 1988. At Brobeck, Vogel worked exclusively on asbestos litigation. During most of the period Brobeck employed Vogel, he worked on settlement evaluations. He extracted information from medical reports, discovery responses, and plaintiffs' depositions for entry on "Settlement Evaluation and Authority Request" (SEAR) forms. The SEAR forms were brief summaries of the information and issues used by the defense attorneys and their clients to evaluate each plaintiff's case. The SEAR forms were sent to the clients.
>
> Vogel attended many defense attorney meetings where the attorneys discussed the strengths and weaknesses of cases to reach consensus settlement recommendations for each case. The SEAR forms were the primary informational materials the attorneys used at the meetings. Vogel's responsibility at these meetings was to record the amounts agreed on for settlement recommendations to the clients. Vogel sent the settlement authority requests and SEAR forms to the clients. He also attended meetings and telephone conferences where attorneys discussed the recommendations with clients and settlement authority was granted. Vogel recorded on the SEAR forms the amount of settlement authority granted and distributed the information to the defense attorneys.
>
> The SEAR form information was included in Brobeck's computer record on each asbestos case. The SEAR forms contained the plaintiff's name and family information, capsule summaries of medical reports, the plaintiff's work history, and asbestos products identified at the plaintiff's work sites, and any special considerations that might affect the jury's response to the plaintiff's case. The SEAR forms also contained information about any prior settlements and settlement authorizations. Information was added to the forms as it was developed during the course of a case. Vogel, like other Brobeck staff working on asbestos cases, had a computer password that allowed access to the information on any asbestos case in Brobeck's computer system.
>
> Vogel also monitored trial events, received daily reports from the attorneys in trial, and

relayed trial reports to the clients. Vogel reviewed plaintiffs' interrogatory answers to get SEAR form data and to assess whether the answers were adequate or further responses were needed.

[Late 1988] Brobeck gave Vogel two weeks' notice of his termination, though his termination date was later extended to the end of November.

Vogel contacted a number of firms about employment, and learned that the Harrison firm was looking for paralegals. The Harrison firm recently had opened a Northern California office and filed a number of asbestos cases against Respondents. Sometime in the second half of November 1988, Vogel called Harrison to ask him for a job with his firm. Harrison offered Vogel a job starting after the holidays. During their conversations, Harrison told Vogel the job involved work on complex, nonasbestos civil matters, and later would involve processing release documents and checks for asbestos litigation settlements. Harrison did not contact Brobeck to confirm Vogel's claim that he made a full disclosure and obtained Brobeck's consent.

In March 1989, Snyder learned from a Brobeck trial attorney that Vogel was involved in asbestos litigation. In a March 31 letter, Snyder asked Harrison if Vogel's duties included asbestos litigation. Harrison responded to Snyder by letter on April 6. In the letter, Harrison stated Vogel told Snyder his work for the Harrison firm would include periodic work on asbestos cases, and that Harrison assumed there was no conflict of interest. Harrison also asked Snyder to provide details of the basis for any claimed conflict. There were no other communications between Brobeck and the Harrison firm concerning Vogel before the disqualification motion was filed.

On July 31, counsel for three Respondents demanded that the Harrison firm disqualify itself from cases against those Respondents. Three days later, the motion to disqualify the Harrison firm was filed; it was subsequently joined by all Respondents.

The trial court held a total of 21 hearing sessions on the motion, including 16 sessions of testimony. During the hearing, several witnesses testified that Vogel liked to talk, and the record indicates that he would volunteer information in an effort to be helpful.

A critical incident involving Vogel's activities at Brobeck first came to light during the hearing. Brobeck's computer system access log showed that on November 17, 1988, Vogel accessed the computer records for 20 cases filed by the Harrison firm. On the witness stand, Vogel at first flatly denied having looked at these case records, but when confronted with the access log, he admitted reviewing the records "to see what kind of cases [the Harrison firm] had filed."

The case information on the computer included the SEAR form data. Many of the 20 cases had been entered on the computer just over a week earlier, though others had been on the computer for weeks or months. The initial computer entries for a case consisted of information taken from the complaint by paralegals trained as part of Brobeck's case intake team. Vogel denied recalling what information for the Harrison firm's cases he saw on the computer, and Brobeck's witness could not tell what specific information was on the computer that day. During the course of the hearing, the Harrison firm terminated Vogel on August 25, 1989.

The trial court found that Vogel obtained confidential information when he accessed Brobeck's computer records on the Harrison firm's cases, and that there was a reasonable

> probability Vogel used that information or disclosed it to other members of the Harrison firm's staff.
>
> Harrison never told Vogel not to discuss the information Vogel learned at Brobeck and did not consider screening Vogel even after Brobeck first inquired about Vogel's work on asbestos cases.
>
> The evidence also amply supports the trial court's observation that Vogel was "a very talkative person, a person who loves to share information." Further, Vogel's willingness to use information acquired at Brobeck, and the Harrison firm's insensitivity to ethical considerations, were demonstrated when Vogel was told to call Respondent Fibreboard Corporation and Vogel knew the person to contact there.
>
> Beyond that, though, substantial evidence established a reasonable probability that Vogel used or disclosed to the Harrison firm the confidential attorney-client information obtained from Brobeck's computer records. Accordingly, the trial court was well within a sound exercise of discretion in ordering the Harrison firm's disqualification.
>
> The order of the trial court is affirmed.

The conflict in the case above happens when a paralegal changes jobs (employer #1) and gets hired at another law firm (employer #2) and both employers are involved in the same lawsuit but on different sides. If the paralegal worked on the case when employed by employer #1 and then worked on the case for employer #2, that paralegal presents a real problem for employer #2. Employer #2 could be removed from the case. And as shown from the case above, disqualifying a law firm can cost the law firm millions of dollars. So how can this be avoided?

This conflict can be avoided simply by keeping records of the cases that the paralegal work on. Attorneys must keep accurate records about their clients to make sure that they do not take conflicting cases. Paralegal need to also keep records. A form for conflict record keeping follows.

Paralegal Form: Conflict of Interest Record

	Month & Year	Name of Case	Plaintiff (P) Defendant (D)	Name of Client	Employer	Summary of Work Performed
1.						
2.						
3.						
4.						
5.						

© 2017 LW Greenberg, Esq.

Chapter 2: The California Paralegal

A Paralegal is a Professional

A professional is someone who:

1. Has special knowledge obtained through education or experience;
2. Acts and dresses in a business-like manner;
3. Never brings personal issues to his or her lace of business;
4. Cares about his or her reputation and how he or she is perceived; and
5. Exercises good judgment and common sense in the workplace.

Being a professional requires a blend of many qualities, such as integrity, accountability, self-confidence and responsibility. The professional paralegal additionally must interact with clients in a professional manner. Interacting with clients requires communicating effectively and appropriately and speaking courteously and politely. Family law issues usually involve intimate details of a client's personal life, and a client can become uncomfortable and embarrassed when responding to personal questions. Putting the client at ease and moving past any unease and/or embarrassment requires more guidance for the family law paralegal than for paralegals in other areas of the law. When the client perceives the paralegal as a professional just performing his or her duties, the client is usually less uncomfortable. This makes eliciting important and, perhaps, intimate information from a client somewhat easier

Professional ethics and attitude require the professional paralegal to keep a distance from the client. A paralegal must sensitive to the client's intimate facts, but should never become emotionally involved.

Paralegal Duties and Initial Client Interaction

1. Paralegal Duties

The family law paralegal will have many duties and should be prepared for some significant responsibilities. However, the actual tasks and responsibilities of the family law paralegal depend upon the supervising attorney. Most paralegals will work directly with the client to obtain information, schedule appointments and update the client with regard to the status of the case. Some tasks that are performed by paralegals are set forth in **FC § 6450**. They include:

- Case planning, development and management;
- research;
- interviewing clients;
- fact gathering and retrieving information;
- drafting and analyzing legal documents;
- collecting, compiling and utilizing technical information to make an independent decision and recommendation to the supervising attorney; and

- representing clients before a state or federal administrative agency if that representation is permitted by statute, court rule, or administrative rule or regulation.

Additional paralegal tasks may include:

- Screening prospective clients via telephone or email;
- Attending the Initial Client Interview to obtain client information;
- Taking notes at the Initial Client Interview;
- Preparing initial pleadings;
- Drafting Fee Letters/Agreements;
- Drafting correspondence to clients, courts and attorneys;
- Arranging for service of process;
- Preparing the client for the Family Court Services Meeting;
- Drafting any temporary orders, including injunctions;
- Noticing and setting hearings (including *Ex Parte*);
- Preparing initial disclosure forms;
- Preparing summaries/notes for conferences and settlement negotiations;
- Drafting stipulations for temporary orders after negotiations;
- Drafting subpoenas and arranging for service of process;
- Attending hearings and trials;
- Compiling checklists;
- Preparing child support worksheets and arrearage calculations;
- Preparing support orders;
- Drafting discovery requests;
- Assisting clients in gathering documents to respond to requests;
- Preparing the responses to discovery requests;
- Drafting settlement Briefs;
- Drafting proposed parenting plans for the supervising attorney's review;
- Drafting proposed property divisions;
- Researching legal questions;
- Drafting memorandums, judgments and other legal documents;
- Drafting Marital Settlement Agreements;
- Preparing trial exhibits and trial notebooks;
- Drafting trial briefs;
- Preparing final paperwork;
- Filing documents at the courthouse or arranging for filing;
- Preparing motions;
- Drafting attorney withdrawals from cases;
- Developing forms for gathering information from clients; and,
- Maintaining client office files.

Chapter 2: The California Paralegal

2. Initial Client Interaction

a. The Initial Client Interview

In most family law firms, prospective clients are screened by a paralegal before the initial client interview with the attorney. The screening can be conducted via email or telephone. Preliminary screening usually entails determining whether the client has a family law issue that is possibly within the purview of that family law firm. At this first interaction, the paralegal usually obtains basic information, such as the client's name, contact information and the reason for the call or email. Then the paralegal schedules an appointment for the initial client interview.

The purpose of the initial client interview is to obtain as much information as possible so that the case can be accurately evaluated to determine the legal action necessary to achieve the client's goals. The initial interview is also used to determine if an effective relationship can be established between the attorney, his or her paralegal and the prospective client.

At the first meeting, two things should be ascertained: **(1)** what the client seeks to achieve by hiring counsel and **(2)** the client's current state of affairs. With this information, the attorney can determine what action or actions to file and whether there is any urgency that will require emergency relief, such as restraining orders.

Preparations for the first interview are necessary. Most often, these preparations will be the responsibility of the paralegal and may include preparing a client intake sheet and fee agreement.

Most family law attorneys will include his or her paralegal in the initial client interview. At the beginning of the initial interview, the supervising attorney should introduce the paralegal to the client. The attorney should then explain that the paralegal's time is less expensive, and therefore, the client can interact with the paralegal at a lower rate.

At the first interview, it is the paralegal's job to take meticulous notes for the attorney/file, to listen very carefully to the client's story, keep track of the time, have a fee agreement ready to sign and to gather as much information about the client for the file as possible.

After the client leaves, the paralegal's job is to summarize the initial meeting. Also, the paralegal should arrange a telephone conference for additional information that may be needed to complete the necessary forms that will be filed with the court, as well as a follow-up, in-person appointment to procure the client's signatures on any documents require the client's signature.

Additionally, it is the paralegal's responsibility to prepare the client's office file such that the attorney can find all of the information that he or she seeks very quickly. This will require sections/tabs for:

Chapter 2: The California Paralegal

- Client intake sheet;
- Client contact information;
- Fee agreement;
- Forms received from opposing counsel or the opposing side;
- Notes;
- List of documents needed from the client;
- Correspondence to the client;
- Correspondence received from the opposing side and to opposing counsel;
- Information to give to and already given to the client;
- Specific client requests;
- List of documents needed from others; and
- Complete list of tabs on the first page to ensure quick access to all information/forms/correspondence in the file.

b. The Client Intake Form

There is no particular form for the client information sheet, and every law firm customarily has its own. An intake sheet at a minimum usually contains:

- Name of client;
- Address and contact information;
- Employment;
- Children of the marriage;
- Property: both real and personal;
- Bank Accounts and investments;
- Retirement; and
- Monthly expenses.

Chapter 2: The California Paralegal

EDUCATIONAL EXERCISES

I. **Match the B&P Code section with the appropriate sentence.**

   A. B&P Code § 6450
   B. B&P Code § 6451
   C. B&P Code § 6453
   D. B&P Code § 6454
   E. B&P Code § 6455

   1. __A__ A paralegal gathers information for the attorney supervisor.
   2. __C__ A paralegal should not share any information about a client.
   3. __B__ Attorney Wilson employs a paralegal.
   4. __D__ Maria properly calls herself a paralegal.
   5. __E__ Paralegal Paul was turned in to the authorities because without supervision he prepared divorce documents for Mary and now Mary is liable for the tax debt that her should-have-been-ex-husband caused.

II. **Perform the following:**

   a. List the education that a paralegal needs to obtain California certification. What is the code section that provides this information?
   b. Find the Rules of Professional Conduct on the State Bar website. Then write all of the headings of those rules.
   c. List the names of 3 paralegal associations. Do any of these associations provide legal education seminars for paralegals

CHAPTER 3: Jurisdiction & Venue

In Brief...

JURISDICTION is the right to exercise authority over persons and their property and apply the law of the land.

There are two types:

1. Subject matter jurisdiction:
- Is the power to hear and determine the cause and to describe the range of power to apply remedies in various fields of substantive law;
- Provides superior court authority to hear family law cases; **FC § 200**;
- Allows a court to render a judgment/make appropriate orders concerning:
    - The status of the marriage;
    - Custody issues;
    - Support issues;
    - Property issues; &
    - Attorney fees. **FC § 2010**.

2. Personal jurisdiction:
- Provides the court with the authority to make court orders that personally affect a person and his or her property;
- Provides that for a court to make orders that affect a person or his or her property, the person must have been served with a copy of the lawsuit;
- Gives a party notice of the lawsuit and an opportunity to be heard;
- Is necessary for both *in personam* and *in rem* jurisdiction; &
- May be obtained when a nonresident is served while he or she is present in the State of California in family law matters.

There are two kinds:

1. *In personam* jurisdiction:
- Gives the court the authority to make orders that personally affect a person and/or a person's rights;
- Is jurisdiction over the person; and
- Allows the court to make orders that personally affect a person and/or a person's rights, such as a court order requiring child support or specifying when a party can visit with his or her children.

2. *In rem* jurisdiction:
- Is jurisdiction over property or things;
- Is the kind of jurisdiction in a divorce action;
- Gives the Court the authority to decide matters involving a person's *real/personal* property;
- Only allows a court to change the nature of real property interests that are located within CA, **FC § 2660(a)**.

VENUE is where the action is filed or entertained, **CCP § 395(a)**:

Chapter 3: Jurisdiction & Venue

> - A court may relocate a case to a different venue if the ends of justice would be promoted by the change of venue, **CCP § 397**.
> - The court may change venue when both petitioner and respondent have moved, **CCP § 397.5**.
> - The court can order the proceedings transferred to the county of residence of either party, **CCP § 397.5**.
> - A superior court may specify by local rule the venue where certain types of actions or proceedings are to be filed and heard.
> - **If a case is filed in the wrong venue, the superior court cannot dismiss the case but has the jurisdiction to transfer the case or action to another location or venue, FC § 402.**

Introduction

California superior courts have exclusive authority to decide all issues arising from a family law matter. This authority is called jurisdiction. Jurisdiction gives the court the right to exercise authority over persons and their property and to apply the law of the territory. There are four (4) kinds of jurisdiction: subject matter, personal, *in personam* and *in rem* jurisdiction. Generally, jurisdiction to adjudicate matters in a marital case involve three requirements: **(1)** that the court have authority to adjudicate the specific matter raised by the pleadings (subject matter jurisdiction); **(2)** that the court have jurisdiction to terminate the marital status, divide property and make orders regarding property (*in rem* jurisdiction); and (3) that the court have jurisdiction over the parties to adjudicate personal rights and obligations (*in personam* jurisdiction). *MUCKLE v. SAN DIEGO COUNTY* (2002) 102 Cal.App.4th 218 at p. 225.

Jurisdiction: The Two Types

1. Subject Matter Jurisdiction

In *HAHN v. DIAZ-BARBA* (2011) 194 Cal.App.4th 1177 at p. 1188, the court defined subject matter jurisdiction as "the power to hear and determine the cause" and to "describe the range of power to apply remedies in various fields of substantive law."

In the State of California, the superior court has subject matter jurisdiction to hear family law cases. **FC § 200.** Specifically, pursuant to **FC § 2010,** the California Superior Court:

> In a proceeding for dissolution of marriage, for nullity of marriage, or for legal separation of the parties, the court has jurisdiction to inquire into and render any judgment and make orders that are appropriate concerning the following:
> **(a)** The status of the marriage, including any marriage under subdivision (c) of Section 308.
> **(b)** The custody of minor children of the marriage.

> **(c)** The support of children for whom support may be ordered, including children born after the filing of the initial petition or the final decree of dissolution.
> **(d)** The support of either party.
> **(e)** The settlement of the property rights of the parties.
> **(f)** The award of attorney's fees and costs.

2. Personal Jurisdiction

Acquiring personal jurisdiction provides the court with the authority to make court orders that personally affect a person and his or her property. Personal jurisdiction gives a party notice of the lawsuit and an opportunity to be heard. Personal jurisdiction is necessary for both *in personam* and *in rem* jurisdiction.

Jurisdiction: The Two Kinds

1. *In Personam* Jurisdiction

In personam jurisdiction is jurisdiction over the person. Obtaining *in personam* jurisdiction over a person allows the court to make orders that personally affect a person and/or a person's rights, such as a court order requiring child support or specifying when a party can visit with his or her children.

In order for a court to obtain personal jurisdiction over a person or his or her property, the person must have been served with a copy of the lawsuit. (Certain procedures must be followed that are discussed later in this chapter.) If both parties reside or are domiciled[1] in the State of California, acquiring personal jurisdiction is usually easily obtained by personal service. Personal jurisdiction becomes a problem when the nonmoving party or responding party is not a resident of the State of California. The United States Supreme Court held in *INTERNATIONAL SHOE CO. v. WASHINGTON* (1945) 326 U.S. 310 at p. 316 that in order for a court to obtain personal jurisdiction, "if he be not present within the territory of the forum, he must have certain minimum contacts with it such that the maintenance of the suit does not offend 'traditional notions of fair play and substantial justice.'"

However, personal jurisdiction in family law matters may be obtained when a nonresident is served while he or she is present in the State of California, even if that person does not have **minimum contacts** with California. *BURNHAM v. COUNTY OF MARIN* (2002) 495 U.S. 604. In *Burnham,*

Mr. Burnham, a resident of the State of New Jersey, was served with dissolution papers while he was in the State of California. Mr. Burnham made a special appearance in the California Superior Court, moving to quash the service of process on the ground that the court lacked personal jurisdiction over him because his only

---

[1] In California the term "residence" is synonymous with "domicile" when determining if the residency requirement has been met for a dissolution. *In re Marriage of Thornton* (1982) 135 Cal.App.3d 500 at p. 507.

contacts with California were a few short visits to the state for the purposes of conducting business and visiting his children. The Superior Court denied the motion to quash. Mr. Burnham appealed, contending that the Due Process Clause prohibited California courts from asserting jurisdiction over him because he lacked **minimum contacts** with the State.

The Court of Appeal affirmed, holding that since the defendant was served while in the forum state, that service was "a valid jurisdictional predicate for *in personam* jurisdiction." *Id.* at p. 607. Mr. Burnham then petitioned the Supreme Court of the United States for a *Writ of Certiorari*; it was granted. The United States Supreme Court held that California obtained personal jurisdiction over Mr. Burnham because he was personally served in the State of California, affirming the Appellate Court decision. Justice Scalia wrote in the opinion that "because the Due Process Clause does not prohibit the California courts from exercising jurisdiction over Petitioner based on the fact of in-state service of process" California acquired jurisdiction over Mr. Burnham when he was served within the state. *Id.* at p. 628.

2. *In Rem* Jurisdiction

In rem jurisdiction is jurisdiction over property or things. It gives the superior court of California jurisdiction to decide matters involving a person's property, both real and personal. However, a court only has jurisdiction over real property that is situated within its borders. (See *SCHLUTER v. SCHLUTER* (1933) 130 Cal.App. 780, where the court stated that "jurisdiction to affect the title to real estate by a judgment *in rem,* or directly against the thing itself, exists only in the courts of the state wherein the land is situated." *Id.* at p. 784.)

If the property is real property located in another state, the court must, if possible, divide the community property and quasi-community property as provided for in this division in such a manner that it is not necessary to change the nature of the interests held in the real property situated in the other state. **FC § 2660(a)**.

If it is not possible to divide the property in another state and not change the nature of the assets then the court may: **(1)** require the parties to execute conveyances or take other actions with respect to the real property situated in the other state as are necessary or **(2)** award to the party who would have been benefited by the conveyances or other actions the money value of the interest in the property that the party would have received if the conveyances had been executed or other actions taken. **FC § 2660(b).**

SARA FREDERICK, as Personal Representative, etc., Petitioner, v. THE SUPERIOR COURT OF LOS ANGELES COUNTY, Respondent; THELMA MARTIN, Real Party in Interest.
COURT OF APPEAL OF CALIFORNIA, SECOND APPELLATE DISTRICT, DIVISION ONE
223 Cal.App.4th 988; 167 Cal.Rptr.3d 773
February 6, 2014, Opinion Filed
(Frederick v. Superior Court of Los Angeles)

If a party dies between the time the court orally grants a judgment of dissolution and the time the court enters a written judgment of dissolution does the court lose jurisdiction to enter such judgment nunc pro tunc? For the reasons explained below, we hold the court does not lose jurisdiction to enter a nunc pro tunc judgment.

Alejandro and Thelma Martin were married on March 3, 2008, and separated on July 27, 2011. Alejandro petitioned for dissolution of the marriage on October 18, 2011. Thelma responded to the petition on December 12, 2011. Several months later, on April 3, 2012, Alejandro petitioned for bifurcation of the marital status, requesting that the trial court enter a judgment dissolving the marriage and reserve jurisdiction over all other issues. At a hearing on May 7, 2012, the court granted Alejandro's bifurcation petition. It granted a judgment of dissolution of marriage and reserved jurisdiction over all other issues. Alejandro's counsel submitted a written judgment to the court at the hearing. On May 22, 2012, Alejandro passed away. On May 25, 2012, the court entered the written judgment of dissolution.

On June 8, 2012, Alejandro's counsel appeared ex parte requesting that the trial court amend the May 25, 2012 written judgment nunc pro tunc[2] as of a date prior to Alejandro's death, as the judgment of dissolution had been granted and the written judgment had been submitted to the court on May 7, 2012. The court denied the motion without prejudice on the ground that no personal representative had been substituted in the action for Alejandro.

On September 24, 2012, Alejandro's daughter, Sara Frederick, was appointed as her father's personal representative. On November 7, 2012, she requested an order joining her in the action as Alejandro's personal representative and amending the May 25, 2012 written judgment nunc pro tunc to terminate the marital status effective May 7, 2012. The court granted her request on December 11, 2012. It entered an amended judgment and served notice of its entry on December 20, 2012. No appeal was taken from the amended judgment.

At a status and trial setting conference on July 3, 2013, the trial court announced on its own motion that it was vacating its nunc pro tunc order and amended judgment on the ground that it had lacked jurisdiction when it entered them. According to the court, it lost jurisdiction over the matter on May 22, 2012, upon Alejandro's death, and the matter was to be resolved in probate court.

On August 2, 2013, Frederick petitioned this court for a writ of mandate asking us to

---

[2] If due to a mistake, such as a party not signing or dating his or her agreement that is attached to the judgment and the judgment does not get processed at that time, when the mistake is corrected, a judgment can be back-dated to the day that the judgment would have been entered if there was no mistake. That back-dated judgment is a *nunc pro tunc judgment*.

Chapter 3: Jurisdiction & Venue

vacate the July 3, 2013 order. On September 3, 2013, at our direction, Thelma filed opposition to the petition. On October 3, 2013, we issued an order to show cause, scheduling the matter for oral argument and setting a due date of October 28, 2013, for Thelma to file a written return to the petition. She did not file a written return. Because we conclude that the trial court had jurisdiction when it entered the nunc pro tunc order and amended judgment, we grant the petition for writ of mandate and direct the court to vacate its order of July 3, 2013, which vacated the *nunc pro tunc* order and amended judgment.

DISCUSSION

The trial court vacated its nunc pro tunc order and amended judgment on the ground that it had lost jurisdiction over the matter upon the death of Alejandro. We disagree.

Code of Civil Procedure section 669 provides, "If a party dies after trial and submission of the case to a judge sitting without a jury for decision or after a verdict upon any issue of fact, and before judgment, the court may nevertheless render judgment thereon." This provision "applies to marital dissolution actions." (*In re Marriage of Mallory* (1997) 55 Cal.App.4th 1165, 1170 [64 Cal.Rptr.2d 667].) FC § 2346(a), provides that, "[i]f the court determines that a judgment of dissolution of the marriage should be granted, but by mistake, negligence, or inadvertence, the judgment has not been signed, filed, and entered, the court may cause the judgment to be signed, dated, filed, and entered in the proceeding as of the date when the judgment could have been signed, dated, filed, and entered originally, if it appears to the satisfaction of the court that no appeal is to be taken in the proceeding or motion made for a new trial, to annul or set aside the judgment, or for relief …" on certain grounds. The court may enter such judgment nunc pro tunc. (FC § 2346(c).)

These provisions demonstrate that the trial court had authority to enter the nunc pro tunc order and amended judgment as of the date it orally granted the judgment of dissolution of marriage and reserved jurisdiction over all other issues—a date prior to Alejandro's death.

In this case, on May 7, 2012, the trial court on the record announced judgment dissolving the marital status and reserved jurisdiction over all other matters. Alejandro's counsel submitted a written judgment to the court at the hearing. Alejandro passed away on May 22, 2012. The court entered the written judgment on May 25, 2012. Because the court had decided to dissolve the marriage and reserve jurisdiction over all other matters before Alejandro's death, the court maintained the authority to enter the December 11, 2012 nunc pro tunc order and the December 20, 2012 amended judgment recognizing the date of dissolution as May 7, 2012. The court, therefore, was incorrect on July 3, 2013, when it vacated the nunc pro tunc order and amended judgment on the ground that it lacked jurisdiction over the matter when it had entered them. Accordingly, the July 3, 2013 order must be vacated, and the nunc pro tunc order and amended judgment govern the action.

With the nunc pro tunc order and amended judgment in place, such that the dissolution of marriage is prior to Alejandro's death, the trial court may decide the remaining issues over which it reserved jurisdiction. "The death of one of the spouses abates a cause of action for dissolution, but does not deprive the court of its retained jurisdiction to determine collateral property rights if the court has previously rendered judgment dissolving the marriage." (*In re Marriage of Hilke* (1992) 4 Cal.4th 215, 220.) For example, in *Kinsler v. Superior Court* (1981) 121 Cal.App.3d 808, the trial court, "[o]n November 2, 1979, and January 22, 1980, respectively, … entered interlocutory and final judgments

> dissolving the status of the marriage only, and reserving jurisdiction to confirm the parties' separate property and divide their community property at a later date." (Id. at p. 810.) The husband died on January 28, 1980. (Ibid.) The court concluded that the husband's death deprived it of jurisdiction to decide the remaining issues and on its own motion issued two minute orders abating the action and vacating its prior orders. (Id. at pp. 810–811.)
>
> The appellate court, treating the wife's appeal as a petition for writ of mandate, directed the trial court to substitute the estate of the husband as a party in the action and "determine the issues over which it [had] reserved jurisdiction at the time it entered its judgments of dissolution of marriage." (Id. at p. 812.) According to the appellate court, "the death of a party to a dissolution proceeding does not abate an action in which a decision has been rendered. … When the trial court at bench entered judgment dissolving the status of the marriage it properly reserved jurisdiction to decide the collateral property issues. [The husband's] subsequent death neither abated the remainder of the dissolution action nor deprived the court of its retained jurisdiction to dispose of the remaining issues." (Ibid.)
>
> The petition for writ of mandate is granted. The trial court is directed to vacate its July 3, 2013 order and proceed in the matter with the December 11, 2012 nunc pro tunc order and December 20, 2012 amended judgment in place.

Venue is Where the Action is Entertained

The venue is where the action is filed or entertained pursuant to **CCP § 395(a)**, which provides in pertinent part:

> In a proceeding for dissolution of marriage, the superior court in the county where either Petitioner or Respondent has been a resident for three months next preceding the commencement of the proceeding is the proper court for the trial of the proceeding. In a proceeding for nullity of marriage or legal separation of the parties, the superior court in the county where either Petitioner or Respondent resides at the commencement of the proceeding is the proper court for the trial of the proceeding. In a proceeding to enforce an obligation of support under Section 3900 of the Family Code, the superior court in the county where the child resides is the proper court for the trial of the action. In a proceeding to establish and enforce a foreign judgment or court order for the support of a minor child, the superior court in the county where the child resides is the proper court for the trial of the action…

For good cause, the court may relocate a case to a different venue if the appropriate motion is made and **the ends of justice would be promoted by the change** of venue. Prior to determining whether a change of venue should or will be ordered, the court may consider motions for allowance of temporary spousal support, support of children, temporary restraining orders, attorneys' fees and costs and any other necessary orders. **CCP § 397**.

The court may order a change of venue when both the petitioner and the respondent have moved from the county and the convenience of the parties would be promoted by this change. **CCP § 397.5**. When ordering a change of venue pursuant to **CCP §**

397.5, the court can order that the proceedings be transferred to the county of residence of either party.

A superior court may specify by local rule the locations where certain types of actions or proceedings are to be filed. If a case is filed in the wrong venue according to those counties' local rules, the superior court cannot dismiss the case, but has the jurisdiction to transfer a case or action to another location or venue. **FC § 402**.

Chapter 3: Jurisdiction & Venue

EDUCATIONAL EXERCISES

I. Match the letter to the number

a. Real property
b. Property or things
c. Involving a person's property
d. Of venue
e. With authority
f. Jurisdiction over the person
g. Make orders that personally affect a person or a person's rights
h. Is served while present in the State
i. Family law cases
j. Filed or entertained
k. Been served with a copy of the lawsuit
l. Notice of the lawsuit

1. Personal jurisdiction gives the superior court of California jurisdiction to decide matters _____, both real and personal.
2. In order for a court to obtain personal jurisdiction over a person or his or her property, the person must have _____.
3. A court only has jurisdiction over _____ that is situated within its borders.
4. The court may order a change _____ when both the petitioner and the respondent have moved from county, and the convenience of the parties would be supported by the change.
5. In the State of California, the superior court has subject matter jurisdiction to hear _____.
6. Acquiring personal jurisdiction provides the court with the authority to make court orders that _____ a person and his or her property.
7. Personal jurisdiction gives a party _____.
8. Obtaining *in personam* jurisdiction over a person allows the court to _____, such as a court order requiring child support or specifying when a party can visit with his or her children.
9. Personal jurisdiction in family law matters may be obtained when a nonresident is _____.
10. *In rem* jurisdiction is jurisdiction over _____.
11. The venue is where the action is _____.
12. *In personam* jurisdiction is _____.

II. Briefly summarize the case *Frederick v. Superior Court* (2014) 223 Cal.App.4th 988 and explain why that case is included in this chapter.

III. Answer the following questions:

1. What is the Family Code section that gives the California the superior court subject matter jurisdiction family law cases?
2. List the different kinds and types of jurisdiction and give an example of each one.
3. What is venue? Give one example.

Chapter 3: Jurisdiction & Venue

CHAPTER 4: Validity of Marriage

In Brief...

SOLEMNIZATION, FC § 400 et seq.:
- Is the marriage ceremony where parties declare to be each other's spouse, **FC § 420**;
- Is required for a valid marriage; and
- Requires no particular form for the ceremony, **FC § 420**.

COMMON LAW MARRIAGE:
- Is uncodified law, as opposed to civil law that is codified; and
- There is no common law marriage in CA.

A VALID MARRIAGE REQUIRES:
- Consent of the parties, **FC § 300-305**;
- A marriage license, **FC § 350**; and
- Solemnization, **FC § 400**.

THE MARRIAGE LICENSE:
- Requires both parties to appear to request a marriage license from the county clerk, **FC § 354**;
- Allows parties to be married in any county in state of CA, **FC § 423**;
- Must be returned to county where it was obtained after completion by the authorized official who performed the ceremony, **FC §§ 359, 423**;
- Requires only one witness to sign the license, but there may be 2 witnesses, **FC § 422(b)**;
- Is the document issued by the county clerk until it is registered with the county recorder; and
- **Marriage certificate** issued to parties upon payment, **FC § 500.5**.

CONFIDENTIAL MARRIAGE, FC § 501 et seq.:
- The parties must be living together prior to requesting a confidential marriage license;
- Both parties must appear and request a confidential marriage license;
- Only a search confirming the existence of a marriage is allowed; and

Introduction

It is important to know the statutes and the case law that set forth the requirements for a valid marriage, so that it can be determined when the requirements have and have not been met. While there are many different actions in family law, the laws regarding a valid marriage provide a foundation for many of these actions. This chapter provides information, statutes and case law regarding valid marriages.

Solemnization

A valid marriage requires solemnization. Solemnization is the marriage ceremony where the parties declare in front of the official performing the ceremony that they

Chapter 4: Validity of Marriage

take each other as spouses. This law dates back to 1872 when the Nineteenth Session of the California Legislature enacted Civil Code § 71 which provided that "no particular form for the ceremony is required but the parties must declare, in the presence of the person solemnizing the marriage that they take each other as husband and wife."[1]

The solemnization law has changed very little since 1872. The current corresponding code is **FC § 420(a)**[2], which provides "No particular form for the ceremony of marriage is required for solemnization of the marriage, but the parties shall declare, in the physical presence of the person solemnizing the marriage and necessary witnesses, that they take each other as spouses."

In the case that follows, the Supreme Court of California considered the issue of whether keeping the solemnization a secret invalidated the marriage.

SARAH ALTHEA SHARON, Respondent, v. F. W. SHARON, Executor, etc., of William Sharon, Deceased, Appellant
Supreme Court of California
75 Cal. 1
January 31, 1888
(*Sharon v. Sharon*)

[The parties signed a declaration of marriage that contained an agreement that they would keep their declaration of marriage secret for a period of two years. Husband separated from Wife about 15 months later. Wife filed for a divorce from Husband and Husband died before the divorce was settled. The Executor of husband's estate claimed that the marriage between Wife and Husband was not valid. The trial court held that the marriage was valid. Husband's estate appealed. The Supreme Court agreed to review the trial court's decision regarding the validity of the marriage.]

The validity of the alleged marriage we are considering must depend upon the fact that it was not made known by the parties. By section 78 of the Civil Code, the solemnization of a marriage is mentioned as a thing distinct from the license to marry, from the authentication of the marriage, and from the record of the marriage certificate. A marriage is solemnized when, in the presence of a judicial officer, priest, or minister, the parties declare that they take each other as husband and wife (Civ. Code §§ 70, 71), and the officer or minister who witnesses this ceremony is said to "solemnize" the marriage. But, if between competent persons, the solemnization makes the marriage complete; although not preceded by license or succeeded by record. Such a marriage is valid, although retained within the knowledge of those present at its solemnization, without any communication of its existence to the community at large, which, in a certain sense, is said to have an interest in all marriages, or rather an interest that the institution of matrimony be maintained in its sacred purity. By the language of section 55 of the Civil Code, the solemnization completes the marriage, although not followed by a mutual

---

[1] Civil Code, Division I, Part III, Title I, Chapter I, Article II, § 71.
[2] Effective 2017, FC § 420 was amended as follows: (1) Amended the second sentence of subd (b) by (a) substituting "shall personally" for "must personally"; (b) deleting the comma after "not stationed overseas"; and (c) substituting "before a notary" for "by a notary"; (2) added the last sentence of subd (b); and (3) amended subd (c) by (a) substituting "A" for "No" at the beginning; and (b) adding "not".

Chapter 4: Validity of Marriage

> assumption of marital rights and duties; since such assumption is required only where there is no solemnization.
>
> It may be said, however, it is giving to the word "solemnization," in section 55, too narrow a meaning to confine it to the mere ceremony before the officer or minister; that it should be held to include the issuing of the license and the record of the certificate, with the publicity incidental to the license and record; that the purpose of the section must be to facilitate the proof of marriages by requiring their existence to be made public.
>
> It may be added, that when the propriety of requiring a public declaration to accompany unsolemnized marriages was directly called to the attention of the legislature of California, the legislature refused to act upon the suggestion, but permitted § 55 to remain as it now is. Among the amendments reported by the revisory commissioners, appointed in 1873, was one to make § 55 of the Civil Code read: "Marriage is a personal relation arising out of a civil contract, to which the consent of the parties is necessary. To render marriage hereafter contracted in this state valid, the contract must be accompanied by a solemnization, or by a public declaration, as provided in this chapter." While adopting many of the amendments proposed by the commissioners, the legislature rejected this one.
>
> The promise of the plaintiff not to make it known for a period of two years, except with the consent of the defendant, was a collateral agreement, and not a condition to the marriage contract taking effect. If the promise had been utterly disregarded, it could not be successfully contended that they were not married. The agreement to become husband and wife was complete.
>
> The judgment appealed from (entered on the nineteenth day of February, A. D. 1885) is affirmed.

The Marriage License

Parties seeking to be married must first obtain a marriage license from the county clerk. **FC § 350**. A marriage license contains:

- The identity of the parties to the marriage;
- The parties' full given names at birth, or by court order;
- The parties' mailing addresses; and
- The parties' dates of birth. **FC § 351**.

Each applicant for a marriage license is required to present authentic photo identification acceptable to the county clerk as to name and date of birth. Credible witness affidavit(s) are acceptable instead of photo identification. **FC § 354(a)**.

A marriage license includes an affidavit, which the applicants sign, affirming that they have received the brochure provided for in **FC § 358**[3]. The forms for the

---

[3] The brochure pursuant to FC § 358 contains information concerning the possibilities of genetic defects and diseases and a listing of centers available for the testing and treatment of genetic defects

marriage license must contain spaces for either or both parties to indicate a change in name. **FC § 355.**

A license to marry is obtained at the office of the county clerk. Both parties must personally appear to request the license. The purchased license must be presented to the official performing the ceremony who must fill out the following on the marriage license:

- The date of the marriage;
- The city and county where the ceremony took place;
- The printed names, signatures and mailing addresses of at least one, and no more than two, witnesses to the ceremony; and
- His or her name and mailing address and his or her official position or of the denomination of which that person is a priest, minister, rabbi or other authorized person of any religious denomination. **FC § 422**.

The license contains a place for two witnesses. However, only one witness is required. And there is no law that sets forth legal requirements for a witness.

After filling out the marriage license pursuant to **FC § 422**, the official must send the license to the county where the license was issued within ten (10) days of the solemnization. **FC § 359.** Only one officiant may sign the marriage license as the person who solemnized the marriage.

The solemnization or marriage ceremony must take place within 90 days after the license is issued; it expires after 90 days if no marriage and solemnization occurred. **FC § 356.**

If the clerk determines that either of the applicants appearing to obtain a marriage license lacks the capacity to enter into a valid marriage or is under the influence of an intoxicating liquor or narcotic drug, the clerk has the authority to refuse to issue the marriage license. **FC § 352.**

While the parties are free to marry in any county, the license must be returned to the county where it was obtained within 10 days after the ceremony. If one of the parties is a minor, the marriage license and a copy of the court order granting permission for the minor to marry must be sent to the registrar in the county where the license was obtained. **FC § 423**[4]. When the marriage license is received at the County Recorder's Office, it is registered and becomes public record. The document issued by the county clerk to the couple getting married is a marriage license until it

---

and diseases, information concerning acquired immunodeficiency syndrome (AIDS) and the availability of testing for antibodies to the probable causative agent of AIDS.

[4] Effective 1/1/2019, the person solemnizing the marriage must include the court order(s) granting permission with the signed license that is sent back to the county, if one or both of the parties are minors.

Chapter 4: Validity of Marriage

is registered with the county recorder, at which time the license becomes a marriage certificate. **FC § 300**.

The parties will not receive a copy of their marriage certificate unless they so request and pay for a certified copy from the County Clerk or County Recorder.

All of the information on the marriage license must be legible, clear and reproducible. No changes to the information added can be made to the marriage license. Crossed-out information or any use of correction fluid will require the payment for and issuance of a duplicate marriage license.

In the case that follows, the marriage was held to be valid, even though no marriage certificate was issued.

> *In re Marriage of JOSEPH S. and TANYA M. CANTARELLA. JOSEPH S. CANTARELLA, Appellant, v. TANYA M. CANTARELLA, Respondent.*
> COURT OF APPEAL OF CALIFORNIA, FOURTH APPELLATE DISTRICT, DIVISION THREE
> 191 Cal.App.4th 916; 119 Cal.Rptr.3d 829
> January 11, 2011, Filed
> *(Marriage of Cantarella)*
>
> In this case, we consider whether registration of a marriage certificate was vital to the validity of a marriage under the Family Law Act.
>
> In 1991, a judge conducted a marriage ceremony for Joseph S. Cantarella (husband) and Tanya M. Cantarella (wife). The marriage certificate, however, was twice rejected for registration due to a technical error on the document. After the second rejection, the parties decided not to resubmit the certificate for registration, possibly to avoid the tax consequences of marriage. As a result, the 1991 marriage was never registered. Nine to 11 years later (between 2000 and 2002), the parties were married in a new ceremony.
>
> In 2008, the parties dissolved the marriage. As part of the dissolution judgment, the family court ordered husband to pay wife spousal support for several years in accordance with an agreement between the parties.
>
> Husband subsequently sought modification of the spousal support order. At the hearing on his order to show cause, the parties disagreed about how long they had been married. Husband argued the parties were married in 2000. The court found the marriage was of long duration and therefore awarded wife permanent spousal support.
>
> Husband appeals from the spousal support order.
> [At the order to show cause hearing on August 2009], the court asked the parties' attorneys how long the parties had been married. Wife's counsel replied that the marriage took place in 1991. Husband disagreed and claimed the year of marriage was 2001. Wife's counsel then informed the court that the parties had a marriage license and ceremony in 1991, the license was submitted for registration but returned due to an error in the judge's address, and wife tried to have the error corrected. Husband countered the parties were "legally married" in 2002. Wife's counsel acknowledged that the parties "went through a second ceremony."

Chapter 4: Validity of Marriage

> The court asked husband whether, at the time of the 1991 ceremony, he believed the marriage was legal. Husband replied, "I want to say no." The court stated, "I don't believe you." The court's written findings and order after the hearing included a finding that the parties were married for 17 years, i.e., from 1991.
>
> In the rare instance where a party failed to register public evidence of the marriage, such failure might be inadvertent or involuntary (as in the case of a rejected certificate) or might instead indicate a lack of consent at that time. We do not believe the Legislature intended a marriage to be thereby rendered invalid. True, the keeping of accurate and complete marriage records benefits the public. But this goal pales compared to the societal importance of recognizing the validity of marriages to which parties have consented. To hold that a failure by a party to register a certificate voids a marriage would invalidate "marriages already solemnized in this state and would, among other results, affect the marital status of the parties, their property rights and rights of inheritance." In wife's words, it would "negate the manifold mutual fiduciary and legal obligations the parties understood they were incurring," due to "a technical misstep along the way."
>
> We affirm the family court's ruling that the parties were married for 17 years, holding the 1991 marriage is valid even though the marriage certificate was never registered.

In the above case, the license contained an error that was not the fault of the parties to the marriage. An error in the license that is not the fault of the parties does not invalidate the marriage. **FC § 306.**

In the case that follows, the official failed to return the license.

> ***Chaney v. Netterstrom,***
> 21 Cal. App. 5th 61
> Second Appellate District, Division Six
> March 8, 2018, Opinion Filed
> (*Chaney*)
>
> The parties began dating in 2008 and cohabiting in 2011. In the fall of 2011, Netterstrom agreed to what was, in her mind, a "commitment ceremony." She had reasons to avoid marriage: she had been married twice before; "I never wanted to get married again"; she did not want to lose her Social Security widow's benefits by remarrying; and Chaney gambled and was financially unstable. In Chaney's view, he proposed marriage to Netterstrom and she accepted.
>
> The parties obtained a confidential marriage license from the county clerk. Netterstrom claimed at trial that this was a ruse: The parties only wanted to appease relatives who disapproved of unwedded cohabitation. The trial court discredited Netterstrom's testimony, noting that the parties could have held a ceremony without a license, and her relatives would have been none the wiser.
>
> It is undisputed that the parties participated in a solemnization ceremony in Cambria on November 11, 2011. The officiant signed the marriage license and gave it to the parties with the understanding that they would file it. The trial court found that in doing so, the officiant did not perform his duty to return the license. It concluded, however, that this dereliction did not invalidate the marriage.

Chaney admittedly allowed the time for returning the license to lapse. Netterstrom asked him not to file it because she did not want to lose her Social Security benefits. Chaney told Netterstrom "it was her decision as to whether or not the marriage license would be returned to the county recorder's office"; she advised him that "she decided she didn't want to mail the certificate in." It is undisputed that neither of the parties returned the signed marriage license to the county. Instead, it remained in Chaney's desk, where Netterstrom found it in July 2015.

After exchanging vows, Netterstrom occasionally called herself Leanne Chaney, and the couple openly referred to each other as husband and wife. Despite telling friends and family that they were married, the parties pretended to be unmarried when it suited their financial interests. They filed tax returns as "single" people. They refinanced Chaney's home in 2013, stating on the loan application that they were unmarried. The deed of trust securing repayment of the loan is in the names of Chaney and Netterstrom as "unmarried" individuals.

In 2015, Chaney petitioned for dissolution of marriage. In response to the petition, Netterstrom declared that she and Chaney are not married. She asked the trial court to quash the summons and petition on the ground that there is no marriage, and to dismiss the action.

The trial court ruled that the parties are married. The statement of decision recites that the parties participated in a ceremony, then wittingly kept the completed marriage license instead of returning it to the county. Family members toasted the marriage at a party after the ceremony. Netterstrom announced the marriage on Facebook and thereafter referred to Chaney as her "husband." When the relationship ended, Netterstrom lamented the end of the "marriage."

The trial court acknowledged that the parties filed as "single" taxpayers throughout their marriage, to suit their financial interests. Nonetheless, it found that the parties consented to marriage by not calling off the ceremony before the exchange of vows. Though the parties agreed to retain the marriage license, the court deemed this "unconvincing" evidence that consent was lacking. The court wrote that the wedding officiant failed to perform his duty to return the license, but this did not invalidate the marriage.

DISCUSSION

"Marriage is a personal relation arising out of a civil contract between two persons, to which the consent of the parties capable of making that contract is necessary. Consent alone does not constitute marriage. Consent must be followed by the issuance of a license and solemnization … ." (§ 300, subd. (a).) To solemnize the marriage, "the parties shall declare, in the physical presence of the person solemnizing the marriage and necessary witnesses, that they take each other as spouses." (§ 420, subd. (a).)

Following solemnization, the marriage license "shall be returned" to the county. (§ 306.) "[R]eturned" means presented in person or postmarked before the statutory deadline. (§ 359, subd. (f).) A confidential marriage document "is a marriage license until it is registered with the county clerk, at which time the license becomes a marriage certificate." (§ 500.5.)

The statutory scheme does not contemplate what happens if the wedded couple retains the signed license. The Legislature did not address this eventuality because it has placed the

Chapter 4: Validity of Marriage

> burden of returning the license to the county for registration squarely upon the wedding officiant.
>
> The law on this point is clear. It states that a confidential marriage license "*shall be* returned by the person solemnizing the marriage to the office of the county clerk in the county in which the license was issued within 10 days after the ceremony." (FC § 506(c), italics added; see FC § 423 ["The person solemnizing the marriage *shall return* the marriage license … to the county recorder … within 10 days after the ceremony." (italics added)]; Health & Saf. Code, § 103150 [A marriage "*shall be* registered by the person performing the ceremony." (italics added)].) The word "[s]hall" means that the act is mandatory. (§ 12.)
>
> Applying the statutes addressing the creation of marriage, we conclude that the parties in this case are married. They applied in person for a confidential marriage license at the office of the county clerk. They exchanged vows declaring each other spouses at a solemnization ceremony. After the ceremony, the officiant authenticated the marriage license; he was not told that the wedding was a ruse. At that point, the parties were married. The officiant had a legal duty to return the license to the county. His failure to perform that duty "does not invalidate the marriage." (§ 306.)
>
> The registration of the certificate does not bear on the issue of consent and serves only a recordkeeping function "*after* the parties had solemnly consented to marriage in a ceremony and *after* the county clerk and the officiant had satisfied themselves the parties' consent was knowing, voluntary, and valid. Additionally, registration was the duty of an officiant … , i.e., of a *nonparty* whose noncompliance with statutory requirements did not void a marriage … ." (*Cantarella, supra*, 191 Cal.App.4th at p. 924)
>
> Nodding to the societal importance of recognizing the validity of marriages—given the significant property and inheritance rights marriage confers, with concurrent fiduciary and legal duties—the court concluded that the Legislature did not intend that a marriage be invalidated by the parties' failure to register the license. (*Cantarella, supra*, 191 Cal.App.4th at pp. 924–925.) The court recognized that its holding "could allow a party to conceal a marriage for tax reasons, but later claim it for purposes of spousal support" but determined that "[t]he tax consequences of our decision, if any, are not before us." (*Id.* at p. 926, fn. 12.)
>
> **CONCLUSION**
> Here we conclude that the parties' retention of the license does not invalidate the marriage after the solemnization ceremony has taken place. The "necessary step of solemnizing" the marriage makes the union valid. The exchange of vows to take each other as spouses "symbolize[s] the irrevocable decision to go through with the union. In the case of solemnization, once the parties say 'I do,' they cannot take the statement back. … [I]t is the point in the process at which the parties can no longer change their minds about their decision to form a union." (*Id.* at p. 1585.)
>
> The judgment is affirmed. Respondent is entitled to recover his costs on appeal.

However, if the parties knew about the license requirement but did not obtain a license prior to solemnization of the marriage, the marriage is invalid. (See *ESTATE of PASSE* (2002) 97 Cal.App.4th 92, where the parties went forward with the ceremony because one of the parties was dying and there was no time to get a license to marry. The marriage was held to be invalid. *Id.* at p. 108.)

Chapter 4: Validity of Marriage

Common Law Marriage

Common law is uncodified law, as opposed to civil law, which is codified. It is law that is unwritten and instead is the custom of the land. Common law marriage is a marriage that does not require legal formalities such as solemnization or recordation; it becomes a legal marriage after the couple meets the requirements that usually include residing together for some specified period of time. Many of the laws regarding common law marriages in the United States today were modeled after the Common Laws in England except that common law marriages in England required notice and recordation since 1753.[5] Today, there are states that do recognize common law marriage as a legal marriage. However, California has not been one of them since 1895.

California became the thirty-first state of the United States on September 9, 1850. At the First Session, on April 22, 1850, the California Legislature enacted laws regarding marriages.[6] Pursuant to these laws, the requirements for a valid marriage in 1850 were:

(1)	Consent of the two persons wanting to be married.
(2)	Consent from parents, unless the male was at least twenty-one of age and female was at least eighteen.
(3)	The marriage is performed by a person having the authority to perform marriage ceremonies.
(4)	Solemnization of the marriage.
(5)	Certificate of marriage made with Christian names and surnames.
(6)	Certificate of marriage sent to county recorder within 3 months of solemnization.

In 1872, the Nineteenth Legislative Session established the Civil Code. In that session, the marriage statutes were renumbered and amended to Division I, Part III, Title I, Chapter I, Articles I and II, sections 55-79.

The most significant change was CC § 75, which provided:

Persons married without the solemnization provided for in § 70[7] must jointly make a declaration of marriage, substantially showing: (1) The names, ages, and residences of the parties; (2) The fact of marriage; (3) The time of marriage; (4) That the marriage has not been solemnized.

Pursuant to this law, two people who were living together and who had followed none of the rules to be married could be married by making a declaration. In other

---

[5] Such as "An Act for the Better Preventing of Clandestine Marriages" that was enacted in England in 1753.
[6] Chapter 140 "An Act regulating Marriage."
[7] CC §70 provided: "Marriage may be solemnized by either a justice of the supreme court, judge of the superior court, justice of the peace, priest, or minister of the gospel of any denomination."

Chapter 4: Validity of Marriage

words, common law marriage was valid in California when this law was enacted in 1872. CC § 75 remained the law until it was repealed in 1895, ending common law marriage in California.

Requirements of a Valid of Marriage

The definition of marriage in California and the requirements for a valid marriage commence at **FC § 300** et seq. **FC § 300** provides:

> **(1)** Marriage is a personal relation arising out of a civil contract between two persons, to which the consent of the parties capable of making that contract is necessary. Consent alone does not constitute marriage. Consent must be followed by the issuance of a license and solemnization as authorized by this division, except as provided by Section 425 and Part 4 (commencing with Section 500).
> **(2)** For purposes of this part, the document issued by the county clerk is a marriage license until it is registered with the county recorder, at which time the license becomes a marriage certificate.

Therefore, in order to have a valid marriage in California there must be:

- Consent of the parties;
- A marriage license; and
- Solemnization.

Additionally, **FC § 301** adds to the above requirements the law with regard to the age of consent. **FC § 301**. **FC § 301** provides "two unmarried persons 18 years of age or older, who are not otherwise disqualified, are capable of consenting to and consummating marriage."

If a minor (a person under the age of 18 years) wishes to marry, permission must be obtained by a court order granting permission in accordance with requirements described in. **FC § 304**. **FC § 302**. The court and at least one parent must consent. **FC § 302**. If a minor has no parent or guardian who can provide consent, then a court order is necessary for the consent to marry. **FC § 303**. However, before a court grants permission for a minor to marry, the court must determine if pre-marital counselling is necessary. **FC § 304**[8].

Consent and solemnization of a marriage may be proved under the same general rules of evidence as facts are proved in other cases. **FC § 305**.

FC § 306.5[9] provides that parties to a marriage do not have to have the same name; that either of or both parties can change their middle or last names, or both, by

---

[8] FC § 304 was amended effective 1/1/2019 proving that "the parties shall not be required, without their consent, to confer with counselors provided by religious organizations…"
[9] 2017 change: (1) Deleted "hyphenated" before "combination" in subds (b)(2)(D), (b)(3)(C), and (b)(3)(D); (2) substituted "shall" for "may" wherever it appears in the second and fourth sentences of

entering the new name in the spaces provided on the marriage license application as long as there is no intent to defraud.

Since 1850 it has been the law that any marriage that is valid by the laws of the jurisdiction where the marriage took place is valid in the State of California. **FC § 308**.[10]

The age of majority, or the age that a couple was legally able to get married without permission from a parent or guardian in the 1930s, was the same for Nevada and California, 21 years of age for a male and 18 years of years of age for a female. At that time, Nevada law differed from California law in that California declared void a marriage with underage persons who did not obtain consent, while Nevada law did not provide that the marriage involving a minor without consent was invalid. Since a marriage with underage persons was valid in the State of Nevada, the marriage was valid in the State of California, as evidenced by the case below. **FC § 308**.

ALECIA McDONALD, Respondent, v. JAMES McDONALD III, Appellant
Supreme Court of California
6 Cal.2d 457
May 27, 1936
(*McDonald v. McDonald*)

In an action by the wife for separate maintenance, the husband filed a cross-complaint for an annulment of the marriage upon the ground that at the time of the marriage the defendant and cross-complainant was a minor, eighteen years of age, and, therefore, under the legal age of consent. The trial court sustained the wife's demurrer to the cross-complaint, without leave to amend. From the judgment entered in favor of the plaintiff wife, the defendant husband appeals.

The parties married in the state of Nevada, the husband being at that time but eighteen years of age and the wife but sixteen years old. Neither had the consent of parent or guardian. If the marriage had taken place in this state, it would have been subject to annulment for failure of the parties to procure such consent. But the marriage was valid in Nevada. The statute of that state relating to marriage and divorce (Compiled Laws of Nevada, 1861-1900, sec. 2, p. 112) provides, in so far as is material here, "that male persons under the age of twenty-one years and female persons under the age of eighteen years", in order to marry, shall first obtain the consent of parents or guardians. The Supreme Court of Nevada, construing the statute, held that, notwithstanding the proviso, as the statute did not expressly, nor by implication, render a marriage in disregard of its prescribed formalities void, a marriage entered into in that state while the parties were under the prescribed ages and without the required consent is, nevertheless, a valid binding contract.

---

subd (b)(5); and (3) deleted former subd (d) which read: "(d) This section shall become operative on January 1, 2009."

[10] In 1850 Chapter 140, "An Act regulating Marriage" § 5, provided: "All marriages contracted without the State, which would be valid by the laws of the country in which the same were contracted, shall be valid in all courts and places within this State." The current law (2017) is FC § 308 which provides: "A marriage contracted outside this state that would be valid by laws of the jurisdiction in which the marriage was contracted is valid in California."

Chapter 4: Validity of Marriage

> If we were to hold, in accordance with appellant's present contention, that, even though this marriage was valid in all respects in Nevada and, therefore, under section 63 of the Civil Code, valid in all respects here, but could be annulled for causes provided by our law, but not permitted by Nevada law, we would be holding that, although this marriage was valid in all respects, nevertheless, it was a marriage which never existed. Such a doctrine would repudiate not only the entire concept of annulment, but would also indirectly repudiate the doctrine of conflict of laws, universally recognized and embodied in section 63 of the Civil Code.
>
> § 63 of the Civil Code of California provides: "All marriages contracted without the state, which would be valid by the laws of the country in which the same were contracted, are valid in this state." Consequently, the marriage of these parties, being a valid marriage in the state of Nevada, is a binding and valid marriage in this state.
>
> The judgment is affirmed.

In 1850, permission from a parent or guardian was necessary for a male under the age of 21 and a female under the age of 18 to marry. In 1872, this law was amended, and the newly amended law provided that "[a]ny unmarried male of the age of eighteen or upwards, and any unmarried female of the age of fifteen or upwards, and not otherwise disqualified, are capable of consenting to and consummating marriage." CC § 56.

Note that consent to marry is not the same as permission to marry. A minor may consent to be married, but the marriage requires permission by his or her parents or a court order.

In 1921, the age that a person could consent to be married was revised to 21 years or older for a male and 18 years or older for a female. In January of 1970 when the Family Law Act became effective, CC § 56 was renumbered to CC § 4101, keeping the age of consent the same. In 1971, the age of consent was lowered to 18 years for both male and female. CC § 4101. In 1994, CC § 4101 was renumbered to **FC § 301** without substantial change. Thus, the current age requirements are at least eighteen (18) years old for both parties.

Persons Authorized to Solemnize a Marriage

The persons authorized to solemnize a marriage are set forth in **FC § 400**[11], which provides:

> **(a)** Although marriage is a personal relation arising out of a civil, and not a religious, contract, a marriage may be solemnized by a priest, minister, rabbi, or authorized person of any religious denomination who is 18 years of age or older. A person authorized by this subdivision shall not be required to solemnize a marriage that is contrary to the tenets of his or her faith. Any refusal to solemnize a marriage under this subdivision, either by an individual or by a religious denomination, shall not affect the tax-exempt status of any

---

[11] This is the current law; FC § 400 was amended effective 2017.

Chapter 4: Validity of Marriage

> entity.
> **(b)** Except as provided in subdivision (c), a marriage may also be solemnized by any of the following persons who are 18 years of age or older:
> **(1)** A judge or retired judge, commissioner of civil marriages or retired commissioner of civil marriages, commissioner or retired commissioner, or assistant commissioner of a court of record in this state.
> **(2)** A judge or magistrate who has resigned from office.
> **(3)** Any of the following judges or magistrates of the United States:
> **(A)** A justice or retired justice of the United States Supreme Court.
> **(B)** A judge or retired judge of a court of appeals, a district court, or a court created by an act of the United States Congress the judges of which are entitled to hold office during good behavior.
> **(C)** A judge or retired judge of a bankruptcy court or a tax court.
> **(D)** A United States magistrate or retired magistrate.
> **(4)** A Member of the Legislature or constitutional officer of this state or a Member of Congress of the United States who represents a district within this state, or a former Member of the Legislature or constitutional officer of this state or a former Member of Congress of the United States who represented a district within this state.
> **(5)** A person that holds or formerly held an elected office of a city, county, or city and county.
> **(6)** A city clerk of a charter city or serving in accordance with subdivision (b) of <u>Section 36501 of the Government Code</u>, while that person holds office.
> **(c)**
> **(1)** A person listed in subdivision (b) shall not accept compensation for solemnizing a marriage while holding office.
> **(2)** A person listed in subdivision (b) shall not solemnize a marriage pursuant to this section if they have been removed from office due to committing an offense or have been convicted of an offense that involves moral turpitude, dishonesty, or fraud.

The clerk can appoint a deputy commissioner of civil marriages, who may also solemnize a marriage. **FC § 401**. The license must be presented to the person solemnizing the marriage prior to the solemnization. **FC § 421**.

The Confidential Marriage

A confidential marriage is a marriage whereby the record of the marriage is not open to public inspection. The county clerk may conduct a search for a confidential marriage certificate for the purpose of confirming the existence of a marriage, but the date of the marriage and any other information contained on the certificate may not be disclosed. **FC § 511(c)**. California records indicate that secret marriages date back to the time when the first cases were decided.

The case *PEARSON v. PEARSON* (1873) 46 Cal. 609 was one of the earliest secret marriages recorded. In *Pearson* one of the issues was what evidence could be used to determine whether the secret marriage actually took place. The Supreme Court held that "the recitals in the will were competent evidence that established that there was a marriage." *Id.* at p. 634.

Chapter 4: Validity of Marriage

In *SHARON v. SHARON* (1888) 75 Cal. 1, there was a written declaration that the parties agreed to marry and keep the marriage confidential for two years. After approximately 14 months of marriage, Wife filed for a divorce. During the divorce, Husband died. Husband's estate sought to have the marriage declared invalid, which would deny Wife her community property share in Husband's estate. The trial court held that the marriage was valid. The Supreme Court affirmed stating that the:

> validity of the alleged marriage we are considering must depend upon the fact that it was not made known by the parties. The promise of the plaintiff not to make it known for a period of two years, except with the consent of the defendant, was a collateral agreement, and not a condition to the marriage contract taking effect. The agreement to become husband and wife was complete. (*Id.* at p.15.)

This 1888 case was the first case to address the issue of a secret or confidential marriage.

Today there are specific laws regarding confidential marriages. **FC § 500**[12] provides:

> When two unmarried people, not minors, have been living together as spouses, they may be married pursuant to this chapter by a person authorized to solemnize a marriage under Chapter 1 (commencing with Section 400) of Part 3.

The two parties to the marriage must be at least 18 years old to apply for a confidential marriage license. Minors may NOT purchase a confidential marriage license.

FC § 501 provides:

> Except as provided in FC § 502, a confidential marriage license shall be issued by the county clerk upon the personal appearance together of the parties to be married and their payment of the fees required by code sections 26840.1 and 26840.8 of the Government Code and any fee imposed pursuant to the authorization of § 26840.3 of the Government Code.

Thus, a confidential marriage: (1) requires that the parties be living together prior to the time that the license is obtained, and (2) the marriage must be solemnized by a person who is authorized to solemnize a marriage.[13]

The marriage license may be obtained from any county in California. The solemnization does not have to be performed in the county where the license was purchased; however, the ceremony must be performed in California.

---

[12] This is the 2017 version of FC § 500, which deleted "without the necessity of first obtaining health certificates" from the previous version.
[13] The persons who are authorized to solemnize a marriage are set forth in FC § 400 et seq. (amended 2017).

Chapter 4: Validity of Marriage

No witnesses are required to be at the ceremony, AND no witnesses sign the confidential marriage license.

The marriage license is a confidential record and is registered at the County Clerk's Office in the county where it was purchased. Only the married couple may purchase copies of the marriage certificate and must present valid picture identification together with the required fee to the County Clerk in order to do so.

Persons other than the parties to the marriage requesting copies of a confidential marriage certificate may only do so by presenting a court order to the County Clerk in the county where the license is registered.

A confidential marriage license is only valid for a period of ninety (90) days after issued, so the solemnization must occur within that period of time. **FC § 504**. "The document issued by the county clerk is a marriage license until it is registered with the county clerk, at which time the license becomes a marriage certificate."[14] **FC § 500.5**.

One of the forms necessary to obtain a license for a confidential marriage license includes an affidavit, which the parties must sign: **(1)** affirming that they meet the requirements for a confidential marriage and **(2)** that they have received a copy of the brochure provided for in **FC § 358**. This brochure contains: **(1)** information concerning the possibilities of genetic defects and diseases, **(2)** a listing of centers available for the testing and treatment of genetic defects and diseases, **(3)** information concerning acquired immunodeficiency syndrome (AIDS) and **(4)** the availability of testing for antibodies to the probable causative agent of AIDS. **FC § 505**.

The confidential marriage license is to be presented to the person solemnizing the marriage.

After the solemnization, the special solemnization section of the confidential license is completed by the person solemnizing the marriage. Then, the confidential marriage license must be returned by the person solemnizing the marriage to the office of the county clerk in the county where the license was issued within ten (10) days after the ceremony. **FC § 506**.

When parties are issued a confidential marriage license, they are provided with an application to obtain a certified copy of the confidential marriage certificate from the county clerk. **FC § 508**. The parties can obtain a confidential marriage certificate after the clerk receives the completed license and the parties have paid the fee. **FC § 509**.

---

[14] FC § 500.5 is the same law as FC § 300(b) above, except FC § 500.5 law applies to confidential marriages.

Chapter 4: Validity of Marriage

EDUCATIONAL EXERCISES

I. FILL IN THE BLANKS

1. A valid marriage requires _____, which is the marriage ceremony where the parties declare in front of the official performing the ceremony that they take each other as spouses. This law dates back to 1872 when the Nineteenth Session of the California Legislature enacted Civil Code § 71.
2. _____ is uncodified law.
3. _____ is civil law that is unwritten and is the custom of the land.
4. _____ is a marriage that does not require legal formalities such as solemnization or recordation; it becomes a legal marriage after the couple meets the requirements that usually include residing together for some specified period of time.
5. In 1872, the Nineteenth Legislative Session established the _____.
6. In 1872 CC § 75 was enacted and pursuant to this code, a common law marriage was valid in California because parties could make a declaration of marriage and without _____.
7. Pursuant to this law, two people who were living together and who had followed none of the rules to be married could be married by making a _____.
8. _____ was legal in California after the enacting of this law 1872.
9. CC § 75 remained the law until it was repealed in 1895, ending _____.
10. Since _____ it has been the law that any marriage that is valid by the laws of the jurisdiction where the marriage took place is valid in California. FC § 308.
11. Parties seeking to be married must first obtain a marriage license from _____. FC § 350.
12. Each applicant for a marriage license is required to present _____ acceptable to the county clerk as to name and date of birth.
13. Credible witness affidavit(s) are acceptable instead of _____. FC § 354(a).
List the four items that every marriage license contains.
14. A _____ is obtained at the office of the _____. Both parties must personally appear to request it.
15. The _____ contains a place for witnesses.
16. Only one _____ is required. And there is no law that sets forth legal requirements.
17. After filling out the _____ pursuant to FC § 422, the official must send the completed form to the county where the license was issued within ten (10) days of the solemnization. FC § 359.
18. The _____ or marriage ceremony must take place within _____ after the license is issued; it expires after 90 days if no marriage/solemnization occurred. FC § 356.
19. If the clerk determines that either of the applicants appearing to obtain a marriage _____ to enter into a valid marriage or is under the influence of an intoxicating liquor or narcotic drug, the clerk has the authority to _____. FC § 352.
20. While the parties are free to marry in any county, the license must be returned to the _____. FC § 423.
21. When the marriage license is received at the _____, it is registered and becomes public record. The document issued by the county clerk to the couple getting

Chapter 4: Validity of Marriage

married is a marriage license until it is registered with the county recorder, at which time the _____ becomes a _____. FC § 300.

22. The parties will not receive a copy of their _____ unless they so request and pay for a certified copy from the County Clerk or County Recorder.
23. An error in the license that is not the fault of the parties does no_____. FC § 306.
24. If parties know about the _____ but do not obtain a license prior to solemnization of the marriage, the marriage is _____.
25. The county clerk can appoint a deputy commissioner of civil marriages, who may also _____ a marriage. FC § 401. The license must be presented to the person solemnizing the marriage prior to the solemnization. FC § 421.
26. _____ is a marriage whereby the record of the marriage is not open to public inspection. It requires that (1) the parties _____ to the time that the license is obtained, and (2) the marriage must be _____ by a person who so authorized.
27. The marriage license may be obtained from any county in California. The solemnization does not have to be performed _____; however, the ceremony must be performed in California.
28. _____ are required to be at the ceremony, AND _____ sign the confidential marriage license.
29. The marriage license is _____ and is registered at the _____ in the county where it was purchased.
30. Only the _____ may purchase copies of the marriage certificate and must present valid picture identification together with the required fee to the County Clerk in order to do so.
31. Persons other than the parties to the marriage requesting copies of a confidential marriage certificate may only do so by presenting _____ in the county where the license is registered.
32. A confidential marriage license is only valid for a period of_____ days after issued, so the solemnization must occur within that period of time. FC § 504.
33. One of the forms necessary to obtain a license for a confidential marriage license includes_____.
34. After the solemnization, the special solemnization section of the _____ is completed by the person solemnizing the marriage. Then, the _____ must be returned by the person solemnizing the marriage to the office of the county clerk in the county where the license was issued within ten (10) days after the ceremony. FC § 506.
35. The parties can obtain a _____ after the clerk receives the completed license and the parties have paid the fee. FC § 509.

II. Answer the following

1. List the elements of a marriage.
2. What is common law and how does it differ from codified law?
3. What are the requirements to obtain a marriage license?
4. Explain solemnization and give an example.
5. What is a confidential marriage and how does it differ from a conventional marriage?

CHAPTER 5: Annulments, Dissolutions & Legal Separations

In Brief...

ANNULMENTS:
- If granted, provide the marriage never existed.
- **2 kinds of annulments, both based upon validity of the marriage:**
  - **Void marriage** never valid, requires adjudication, **FC §§2201, 2201**.
  - **Voidable marriage** has defect at onset of marriage but becomes voidable at request of one party, requires adjudication, **FC § 2210**.
- **Attorney fees** may be granted under certain conditions, **FC § 2255**.
- **Putative spouse** has reasonable good faith belief that the marriage is valid, when it is not, **FC § 2251**.

CHART 1: Fraud Alleged- Annulment Granted
CHART 2: Fraud Alleged- Annulment Not Granted
Domicile is a person's **legal address; residence** is **where a person resides**.

DISSOLUTION/DIVORCE
- Have the same meaning; &
- It is the procedure used to terminate a marriage, **FC § 2300-2333**.

LEGAL SEPARATION:
- Resolves all divorce issues,
- But the marital status of the couple remains intact, **FC §§ 2345, 2347**.

ANNULMENT vs. DISSOLUTION vs. LEGAL SEPARATION:
- **The same form** is used for all three kinds of actions, *FL-100*.
- **Residency** is only required for a dissolution, **FC § 2320**.
- **Legal grounds:**
  - **Dissolution/legal separation** - grounds: (1) irreconcilable differences & (2) permanent legal incapacity to make decisions, **FC § 2310**.
  - **Annulments** – grounds: void marriages are incest and bigamy; voidable marriages have different requirements, **FC §§ 2200, 2201, 2210-2212, 2250**.
- **Waiting/cooling off period** dissolutions: 6 months begins at *summons* service; Legal separations/annulments: no waiting period, **FC § 2339**.
- **Marital status** remains intact for legal separation; if annulment is granted, marriage never existed; and a judgment of dissolution changes the marital status from married person to unmarried person, **FC § 2339**.
- **Both parties must consent** & continue to consent to legal separation; ; no consent is needed for a dissolution or an annulment, **FC § 2345**.
- **Name restoration** is only available in a dissolution, **FC § 2080**.
- **Attorney fees** in a legal separation and dissolution may be granted to provide equal ability to retain representation, **FC § 2255**.
- **Only legal separation can be converted** into dissolution, **FC § 2321**.

Divorce History: Fault & Cooling Off Period
CHART 3: Annulment vs. Dissolution vs. Legal Separation
SUMMARY DISSOLUTION, **FC § 2400-2406:**

Chapter 5: Annulments, Dissolutions & Legal Separations

> - Requires that both parties consent to the procedure, **FC § 2400**;
> - Requires the parties file a *Joint Petition* form *FL-800;*
> - Requires the parties to meet the requirements set forth in **FC 2401**; &
> - Allows either party to revoke joint *Petition* and terminate summary dissolution proceeding any time prior to filing summary dissolution judgment, **FC § 2402**.

Introduction

This chapter examines the laws, rules and cases regarding terminating or erasing a marriage. After determining that there has been a valid marriage and that the couple wants to erase or terminate that marriage, the next step is to decide which of the three types of actions is appropriate for a particular client.

An annulment or nullity judgment[1] invalidates the marriage and declares that a marriage never existed. Dissolution or divorce[2] terminates the marriage and is an action that resolves all issues of the marriage, such as marital status, property, custody, child support, spousal support and division of property. Legal separation is an action that is identical to dissolution, except the marital status of the couple remains intact. Thus, a marriage is only erased by a judgment of nullity or terminated by a judgment of dissolution or by death. **FC § 310.**

Finally, there is no common law marriage in California regardless of how long the couple cohabitates. However, if a couple is married pursuant to the law in a state that allows common law marriage and the couple have met the requirements for a common law marriage while residing in that state and then the couple thereafter reside in California, the marriage is legal in California.

Annulment

An annulment is an action filed by a married person to change his or her marital status from a married person to an unmarried person. If an annulment is granted, the marriage never existed. **FC § 2212** provides that when a nullity is granted the parties are restored to the status of unmarried persons.

There are many myths regarding annulments such as: a very short marriage may be annulled; a marriage of long duration cannot be annulled; or a marriage that has been consummated cannot be annulled. These are all myths. In order to be granted an annulment, a party MUST meet the requirements that are set forth in **FC § 2200** or **FC § 2210**. The length of the marriage and act of consummation are NOT requirements for an annulment.

To obtain a judgment of nullity, the marriage must be void or voidable. A void marriage is a marriage that has never been valid and is void from the beginning. A

---

[1] An annulment and a judgment of nullity have the same meaning.
[2] *Black's Law Dictionary* defines divorce as "the legal dissolution of a marriage by a court." Page 549. Accordingly, divorce and dissolution have the same meaning.

Chapter 5: Annulments, Dissolutions & Legal Separations

voidable marriage is a marriage that had a defect at the onset of the marriage but becomes voidable at the request of one of the parties. Void and voidable marriages have different requirements that must be met in order to obtain a judgment of nullity. (See Chart 3: Annulment vs. Dissolution vs. Legal Separation, infra.)

1. Void Marriage Annulments

Void marriages are marriages that were never valid under any circumstances at any time. There are only two grounds for a void marriage: incest and bigamy/polygamy. **FC § 2200.** FC § 2200 provides that **the following marriages are incestuous**, and void from the beginning, whether the relationship is legitimate or illegitimate:

1. Between parents and children,
2. Between ancestors and descendants of every degree,
3. Between brothers and sisters of the half as well as the whole blood, and/or
4. Between uncles and nieces or aunts and nephews.

FC § 2253 provides that custody of the children in a void or voidable marriage is determined in the same way that custody is determined in a valid marriage.

Bigamy/polygamy is the only other ground for an annulment in a void marriage. FC § 2201 addresses the issue of annulment on the ground of bigamy. **FC § 2201** can be traced back to Civil Code § 61 enacted in 1872. In 1994, when the FC became effective, it became **FC § 2201**. In the 140 years from 1872 to the present, the language has remained virtually the same. **FC § 2201** provides that:

> (a) A subsequent marriage contracted by a person during the life of his or her former spouse, with a person other than the former spouse, is illegal and void, unless:
> (1) The former marriage has been dissolved or adjudged a nullity before the date of the subsequent marriage.
> (2) The former spouse (A) is absent, and not known to the person to be living for the period of five successive years immediately preceding the subsequent marriage, or (B) is generally reputed or believed by the person to be dead at the time the subsequent marriage was contracted.
> (b) In either of the cases described in paragraph (2) of subdivision (a), the subsequent marriage is valid until its nullity is adjudged pursuant to **FC § 2210(b)**.

If a party is seeking an annulment because the former husband or wife has been absent for five years or is believed to be dead, a judgment of nullity can restore the living party to a marriage-never-existed status. As the following case demonstrates, bigamous marriages are void from the onset.

> *In re Marriage of JEFFREY D. and PATRICIA L. SEATON. JEFFREY D. SEATON, Respondent, v. PATRICIA L. SEATON, Appellant*
> COURT OF APPEAL OF CALIFORNIA, THIRD APPELLATE DISTRICT
> 200 Cal.App.4th 800
> November 8, 2011, Filed
> *(Marriage of Seaton)*
>
> Patricia married Richard in November 1973. After separating from Richard in January 1987, she dated Henry for several months. Patricia met Jeffrey in January 1988 and broke

Chapter 5: Annulments, Dissolutions & Legal Separations

> up with Henry in February 1988. Patricia was a legal secretary and Jeffrey was a law student intern.
>
> [In an effort to stop Henry from constantly pursing her,] Patricia agreed to meet with Henry. When [Patricia] arrived, Henry asked to take Patricia to dinner in Reno to talk about their relationship. Patricia agreed. They arrived in Reno in the early afternoon, ate at a buffet, and began drinking. Several shots of tequila later, they ended up at a wedding chapel where Patricia and Henry were married. After spending the night in a hotel, they drove back to Sacramento early the next morning.
>
> Patricia's marriage to Richard was dissolved in December 1988. Her marriage to Henry was never dissolved or annulled. Patricia and Jeffrey were married in June 1991.
>
> In November 2008, Jeffrey filed a Petition for legal separation. Patricia responded with a request for dissolution. Over Patricia's opposition, Jeffrey was allowed to amend the Petition to request a judgment of nullity based on Patricia's former marriage to Henry.
>
> The trial court nullified the marriage on the ground that Patricia was married to Henry when she attempted to marry Jeffrey. [On appeal] Patricia contends her marriage to Henry was void even in the absence of an annulment decree, and thus her marriage to Jeffrey was valid. We agree.
>
> Patricia does not dispute that she married Henry in Nevada prior to marrying Jeffrey in California. And there is no dispute that the marriage to Henry was neither dissolved nor adjudged a nullity. Thus, the question of whether Patricia's marriage to Jeffrey was void turns on whether she was married to Henry when she married Jeffrey.
>
> The relevant Nevada statute provides that a marriage is "void without any decree of divorce or annulment or other legal proceedings" when either party has a "former husband or wife then living." [3] In Nevada, as in California, a bigamous marriage is void, not merely voidable at the option of one of the parties to the marriage. [4] There being no dispute that Patricia was still married to Richard when she married Henry, her marriage to Henry was "void without any decree of divorce or annulment or other legal proceedings."
>
> The judgment [nullifying Patricia's marriage with Jeffrey] is reversed.

Patricia married Richard in November 1973. Then Patricia married Henry in April 1988, while she was still married to Richard. Patricia's marriage to Henry was void because she was still married to Richard. Patricia then divorced Richard in December 1988. Patricia married Jeffrey in June 1991.

Patricia's marriage to Jeffrey was valid because her marriage to Henry was void and she had divorced Richard. Pursuant to the statutes in Nevada and California, when a married person marries another person, that marriage is void. However, in

---

[3] Nev. Rev. Stat. Ann. §125.290 provides that: "All marriages which are prohibited by law because of: 1. Consanguinity between the parties; or 2. Either of the parties having a former husband or wife then living, if solemnized within this state, are void without any decree of divorce or annulment or other legal proceedings. A marriage void under this section shall not bar prosecution for the crime of bigamy pursuant to NRS 201.160."

[4] FC §2201(b) provides that both a void and a voidable marriage require adjudication.

Chapter 5: Annulments, Dissolutions & Legal Separations

California pursuant to **FC § 2201**, an adjudication is required, but no such adjudication is required in Nevada.

2. Voidable Marriage Annulments

A voidable marriage is a marriage that may be declared invalid by an annulment judgment at some time after the marriage takes place because a defect existed at the time of the marriage.

FC § 2210 provides that a marriage is voidable and may be adjudged a nullity if certain conditions existed at the time of the marriage. The conditions are:

> **(a)** The party who commences the proceeding or on whose behalf the proceeding is commenced was under 18 years of age, unless the party entered into the marriage pursuant to Section 302 or 303.
> **(b) The spouse of either party was living** and the marriage with that spouse was then in force and that spouse (1) was absent and not known to the party commencing the proceeding to be living for a period of five successive years immediately preceding the subsequent marriage for which the judgment of nullity is sought or (2) was generally reputed or believed by the party commencing the proceeding to be dead at the time the subsequent marriage was contracted. (Emphasis added.)
> **(c) Either party was of unsound mind**, unless the party of unsound mind, after coming to reason, freely cohabited with the other as his or her spouse.
> **(d)** The **consent of either party was obtained by fraud**, unless the party whose consent was obtained by fraud afterwards, with full knowledge of the facts constituting the fraud, freely cohabited with the other as his or her spouse.
> **(e)** The **consent of either party was obtained by force**, unless the party whose consent was obtained by force afterwards freely cohabited with the other as his or her spouse.
> **(f) Either party was**, at the time of marriage, **physically incapable** of entering into the marriage state, and that incapacity continues, and appears to be incurable. (Emphasis added.)

Not only are there requirements that must be met in order to obtain a judgment of nullity, but there are time limitations as well. **FC § 2211** sets forth the time limitations to annul a marriage. These limitations vary with the annulment grounds alleged. If a party is under the age of consent, that party has four years after reaching the age of consent to file an annulment action. If a parent, guardian or legal representative of the underage party wishes to file for an annulment, that action must be filed before the underage party reaches the age of consent.

The allegation of fraud as a ground for annulment must be pleaded within four (4) years from the time that the fraud was discovered. However, if, after the fraud is discovered, the party freely cohabited with the other party as husband and wife, the issue of fraud is deemed waived; and a judgment of annulment will not be granted. Fraud appears to be one of the most pleaded allegations in requesting an annulment.

In the two cases that follow, fraud was the ground used to request a judgment of nullity. The court stated in both cases that the fraud must go to the very essence of the marriage.

Chapter 5: Annulments, Dissolutions & Legal Separations

> **AMIEL R. SCHAUB v. ELLEN SCHAUB [and her boyfriend Scott]**
> COURT OF APPEAL OF CALIFORNIA, SECOND APPELLATE DISTRICT,
> DIVISION THREE
> 71 Cal.App.2d 467
> October 31, 1945
> (*Schaub v. Schaub*)
>
> Plaintiff [Amiel Schaub] and defendant [Ellen Schaub] were married on July 8, 1941, and at that time he was 60 years of age and she was 34 years of age. Plaintiff [seeks a judgment of annulment alleging that] defendant falsely represent[ed] to plaintiff that she would be a good and faithful wife and would fulfill all the obligations of a wife.
>
> [Being suspicious that his wife was having an affair with Scott, Plaintiff Amiel hired detectives to follow her. On May 1, 1943, plaintiff and his detectives] entered the living room of Scott's house [finding his wife] was in bed, and Scott was "just getting out of bed" and was undressed that plaintiff went to the bed, pulled the blanket off defendant and [he saw that] she did not have any clothes on.
>
> The only fraud which will support a proceeding for annulment of marriage is one which goes to the essence of the marriage relation.
>
> The court found that defendant had an agreement with Scott that she would marry plaintiff, procure an interest in his property, and that she and Scott would continue their intimacies and sexual relations which had existed between them for some time prior to the inauguration of their plan. Whether they had such an agreement is immaterial; the question is whether defendant intended to break off or to continue her relations with Scott upon her marriage to plaintiff. Defendant's intentions, as established by the findings, were that she planned to marry a self-respecting old gentleman, acquire an interest in his property, and at the same time continue with her love affair. Defendant's association with Scott was open, flagrant and continuous.
>
> The judgment is affirmed.

In the *Schaub* case, the court stated that the fraud went to the very essence of the marriage and granted the annulment. However, in the case below the court found that the fraud did not go to the essence of the marriage and, accordingly, reversed the trial court's decision granting an annulment.

> ***In re Marriage of BRENDA and DONALD R. JOHNSTON. BRENDA JOHNSTON, Respondent, v. DONALD R. JOHNSTON, Appellant.***
> COURT OF APPEAL OF CALIFORNIA, FOURTH APPELLATE DISTRICT,
> DIVISION THREE
> 18 Cal.App.4th 499
> August 30, 1993, Decided
> (*Marriage of Johnston*)
>
> After a 20-month marriage, Brenda sought to have her marriage to Donald annulled. At the trial, Brenda testified she was unaware of Donald's severe drinking problem until after the marriage and she was upset to discover this and disappointed in his refusal to seek help. She knew before the nuptials that he was unemployed but did not realize he would refuse to work thereafter. She stated that he was dirty and unattractive. **In short,**

Chapter 5: Annulments, Dissolutions & Legal Separations

> **he turned from a prince into a frog.**[5]
>
> The court found Brenda's consent had been fraudulently obtained and annulled the marriage. Donald appeals.
>
> [On appeal]Donald complains the evidence is insufficient to support a finding of fraud. He is correct.
>
> Brenda testified Donald told her "he wanted to get a job and with my help in his life, maybe I could help him get himself back together and get his feet on the ground and go out and get a job. And he wanted to get married to me, to have a nice life with me." She also explained that prior to the marriage she saw him regularly and "he was just very polite. Very nice. Very respectful to me. Clean-shaven. Bathed. Just very nice." But after they were wed he "never treated me with respect after the marriage that is correct. And on many occasions [,] unshaven."
>
> Even if Brenda's testimony was believed by the trial court, she presented insufficient grounds for an annulment. In California, fraud must go to the very essence of the marital relation before it is sufficient for an annulment. Thus, the trial court erred in granting the annulment.
>
> The granting of a nullity of the marriage is reversed and a judgment of dissolution shall be entered.

Brenda knew that Donald was unemployed before the marriage. Maybe Brenda did not know about Donald's lack of desire to bathe. In any case, when one of the parties to a marriage turns out to be not exactly what is expected, this is not fraud that provides grounds for an annulment. Not bathing and/or shaving do not go to the very essence of a marriage. Also note, as set forth in the case above, when a nullity is denied, the only other method of marital termination available is dissolution.

---

[5] This is the actual language in the opinion. Emphasis added.

Chapter 5: Annulments, Dissolutions & Legal Separations

CHART 1: Fraud Alleged - Annulment Granted
Fraud that goes to the essence of the marriage

	Case Name & Cite	**YEAR**	**Fraud alleged**
1	*Marriage of Ramirez* 165 Cal.App.4th 751	2008	Wife entitled to annulment because her husband intended to continue simultaneous sexual relationships with her & her sister when wife & husband entered into a 2nd marriage.
2	*Marriage of Liu* 197 Cal.App.3d 143	1987	Where the parties' marriage was unconsummated and where the wife entered into the marriage to obtain a green card, the husband's consent to the marriage was obtained by fraud.
3	*Ruiz v. Ruiz* 6 Cal.App.3d 58	1970	Where minor knowingly misrepresented his age in procuring a marriage license, his misrepresentation was not a bar to procuring an annulment of the minor's marriage.
4	*Lamberti v. Lamberti* 272 Cal.App.2d 482	1969	Annulment of wife's marriage to her husband, who was an Italian citizen, was proper where the evidence revealed that the husband had no intention of fulfilling his promise to marry her in a religious ceremony after their civil ceremony.
5	*Handley v. Handley* 179 Cal.App.2d 742	1960	A wife's refusal to adopt the husband's name and to cohabit with the husband sufficiently proved that the wife committed fraud at the time of the marriage; the wife did not intend to perform duties vital to the marriage relationship.
6	*Douglass v. Douglass* 148 Cal.App.2d 867	1957	Wife entitled to annulment because husband committed fraud in misrepresenting that he did not have a criminal history; fraud so egregious that it placed her in an intolerable position.
7	*Rathburn v. Rathburn* 138 Cal.App.2d 568	1956	Annulment granted in favor of the husband was affirmed because the trial court found sufficient evidence that the wife went through the ceremony with an intention not to consummate the marriage by marital intercourse.
8	*Schaub v. Schaub* 71 Cal.App.2d 467	1945	A husband was granted an annulment because his wife committed fraud when she married him to gain his property. Further, she carried on an illicit affair with her lover and conspired with him to commit the fraud.
9	*Vileta v. Vileta* 53 Cal.App.2d 794	1942	A woman's concealment of her sterility was a fraud that vitiated a marriage contract and justified annulment, when her husband acted promptly upon his discovery of the fraud.
10	*Aufort v. Aufort* 9 Cal.App.2d 310	1935	The husband was entitled to an annulment on the ground of fraud because his wife was incapable of conceiving and bearing children by reason of an operation and did not disclose this fact to the husband prior to their marriage.

© 2019 LW Greenberg

CHART 2: Fraud Alleged- Annulment Not Granted
Fraud that does not go to the essence of the marriage

	Case Name & Cite	**YEAR**	**Fraud alleged**
1	*Marriage of Meagher & Maleki* 131 Cal.App.4th 1	2005	Although husband, prior to the marriage, misrepresented his financial status and fraudulently induced wife to invest in a business venture with him, was not fraud that went to the very essence of the marriage relation. lg
2	*Marriage of Johnston* 18 Cal.App.4th 499	1993	There was insufficient evidence to support a finding of fraud that would justify the annulment of the marriage when the wife discovered after the marriage that her husband refused to work, did not bathe frequently, and had a drinking problem.
3	*Bruce v. Bruce* 71 Cal.App.2d 641	1945	A husband was properly denied an annulment of his marriage where he failed to show that at the time of the marriage his wife had the present intention never to live with him.
4	*Foy v. Foy* 57 Cal.App.2d 334	1943	A judgment granting husband an annulment on the grounds that his wife had falsely represented, before marriage, that her daughter was legitimate was reversed because fraud regarding her chastity before marriage was not vital to the marriage relation.
5	*Sutton v. Sutton* 12 Cal.App.2d 355	1936	The husband was not entitled to an annulment. His testimony regarding the wife's behavior was largely based on matters occurring after the marriage. There was no evidence to support his claim that the wife had illicit relations or was of bad character.
6	*Marshall v. Marshall* 212 Cal. 736	1931	Denial of the wife's action for an annulment of marriage following consummation on the ground of fraud was proper because the husband's alleged representation that he was a man of means did not go to the very essence of the marriage.
7	*Mayer v. Mayer* 207 Cal. 685	1929	A wife was not entitled to an annulment on the basis of the husband's fraud when the husband's false representations to his wife as to his social and financial position were insufficient grounds to rescind the marriage contract.

© 2019 LW Greenberg

Chapter 5: Annulments, Dissolutions & Legal Separations

3. The Putative Spouse

A **putative spouse** is a spouse who reasonably and in good faith believes that his or her marriage is legally valid when it is not. This marriage can be void (a marriage that was never valid) or voidable (a marriage that had a defect at the beginning of the marriage but remains in effect until challenged) depending on the circumstances. The court determines whether one or both of the spouses are putative spouses. If the court so determines, then the marriage is called a putative marriage.

In a putative marriage, the innocent party is entitled to all of the benefits of a valid marriage. One such benefit is that all of the property acquired during the marriage is divided equally as though it was community property. (The property acquired during a putative marriage is called quasi-marital property. See Chapter 20 RE: Title, Kinds of Property & Valuation, *infra*.)

In certain rare situations, spousal support can be awarded to the putative spouse. Thus, the title of putative spouse can be advantageous.

California codified the concept of putative spouse commencing in 1969 with Civil Code § 4452, which was renumbered to Civil Code § 4800. In 1994, when the California Family Code came into effect, Civil Code § 4800 was changed to **FC § 2251**. The actual language has changed very little since its inception. **FC § 2251** provides that if a court finds that a marriage is void or voidable and the court finds that either party or both parties believed in good faith that the marriage was valid, the court must declare the party or parties to have the status of a putative spouse.

The following case is an amusing example in which the couple went through the marriage ceremony twice, and the court found that both marriages were void and that the wife was a putative spouse in the second marriage.

> *In re Marriage of JORGE L. RAMIREZ and LILIA LLAMAS. JORGE L. RAMIREZ, Appellant, v. LILIA LLAMAS, Respondent.*
> COURT OF APPEAL OF CALIFORNIA, FOURTH APPELLATE DISTRICT, DIVISION TWO
> 165 Cal.App.4th 751
> July 30, 2008, Filed
> (*Marriage of Ramirez*)
>
> [In 1999] Jorge, an immigrant from the State of Michoacán, Mexico [married] Lilia in a religious ceremony in Moreno Valley, California. The ceremony was performed by a priest or other official from the State of Jalisco, Mexico, and an "Acta de Matrimonio" [Mexican marriage license] was issued. No marriage license was issued by the State of California. In 2001, Jorge and Lilia became aware that the 1999 marriage was invalid. The parties were remarried in 2001 and obtained a confidential marriage license. [I]n May 2004, [Jorge] took Lilia out to dinner and asked for a divorce because he was in love with someone else and always had been. In June 2004, Jorge moved out.
>
> That same month, Lilia found out who the other woman was when she overheard a conversation between Jorge and Lilia's sister Blanca. Jorge had begun an affair with

Chapter 5: Annulments, Dissolutions & Legal Separations

> Blanca prior to the 2001 marriage, and it lasted until 2005. The intercepted conversation occurred in 2005. Lilia asked her teenaged son Victor to call Blanca, who babysat for Jorge and Lilia's daughter, on her cell phone to inquire if she would be joining them for lunch with the child. Blanca, at a restaurant with Jorge, had the cell phone in her purse. Instead of pressing the stop key, she pressed the button to answer the call, so the conversation she was having with Jorge was overheard on Victor's cell phone, which Lilia and Victor listened to by activating the loudspeaker. In this conversation, Jorge professed his love for Blanca, assured her that they would be together once he got his share of money and property from Lilia.
>
> The trial court concluded the 1999 marriage was void under the laws of Mexico and neither spouse was a putative spouse since neither acted in good faith.
> The court found the second marriage was also void because Jorge perpetrated a fraud on Lilia by carrying on an extramarital affair with Blanca. [This] fraud related to Jorge's marrying Lilia while carrying on a sexual relationship with Blanca which he intended to maintain. The court concluded Jorge wanted to "have his cake and eat it too" by carrying on sexual relationships with both women at the same time.
>
> The trial court held that this kind of fraud goes to the heart of the marital relationship and declared the 2001 marriage void on the ground of fraud. The court also found Lilia was a putative spouse.
>
> [R]egardless of whether Jorge subjectively believed the 1999 marriage was valid, a reasonable person would not have. Thus, we hold that Jorge was not a putative spouse as to the 1999 marriage.
>
> [H]istorically, annulments based on fraud have only been granted in cases where the fraud relates in some way to the sexual, procreative or child-rearing aspects of marriage. Jorge's actions here, in marrying Lilia while continuing to carry on a sexual relationship with her sister Blanca, directly relates to a sexual aspect of marriage—sexual fidelity. At the time of the 2001 marriage, Jorge purposely deceived Lilia into thinking that he would perform one of the central obligations of the marriage contract—the obligation of fidelity. Jorge committed fraud and Lilia is entitled to a judgment of annulment.
>
> The judgment is affirmed.

The court in the *Ramirez* case above defined a putative spouse as **an innocent party to an invalid marriage**.

The court in *Ramirez* further stated that:

> The determination of the party's good faith [that the marriage is valid] is tested by an objective standard. A subjective good faith belief alone, even by a party that is found credible and sympathetic, is insufficient. Instead, under an objective standard, a claim of putative spouse status must be based on facts that would cause a reasonable person to believe in good faith that he or she was married and that the marriage was valid under California law. *Id.* at p. 756.

The Appellate Court found that Jorge should have known that the first marriage performed in 1999 was invalid, as a reasonable person would not have believed that this marriage was valid. *Id.* at p. 757. Since the court held that no reasonable person would have believed such a marriage was valid, Jorge was not entitled to putative spouse status from that marriage. With regard to the 2001 marriage, the court found that Lilia was entitled to putative spouse status because she believed that this marriage was valid and had no knowledge of Jorge and Blanca's perfidy at the time of the second marriage.

Finally, it should be noted that a court can order a party to pay support to the other party during the nullity proceeding and upon judgment of nullity "in the same manner as if the marriage had not been void or voidable if the party for whose benefit the order is made is found to be a putative spouse." **FC § 2254.**

Domicile and/or Residence

The court in *SMITH v. SMITH* (1955) 45 Cal.2d 235 at p. 239 defines the term **domicile** as:

> ... the one location with which for legal purposes a person is considered to have the most settled and permanent connection, the place where he intends to remain and to which, whenever he is absent, he has the intention of returning, but which the law may also assign to him constructively... 'Domicile' normally is the more comprehensive term, in that it includes both the *act* of residence and an *intention* to remain; a person may have only one domicile at a given time, but he or she may have more than one physical residence separate from his domicile, and at the same time.

Thus, domicile is a person's legal address. It is where a person **intends** to make his or her permanent home. It is the address used when determining state income tax or eligibility to vote. A person can have only one domicile.
A domicile can also be a residence, provided that a person has only one dwelling or house. A person can have many residences. Summer, winter or vacation homes are examples of residences.

California law provides that there is a **residency** requirement that must be met before a judgment of dissolution can be entered. **FC § 2320(a)** provides:

> a judgment of dissolution of marriage may not be entered unless one of the parties to the marriage has been a resident of this state for six months and of the county in which the proceeding is filed for three months next preceding the filing of the *Petition*.

California law requires that a person live in the State of California for six (6) months and in the county where the dissolution *Petition* will be filed for three (3) months prior to the filing of the *Petition*. It is important to note that this residency code does not require a person to live at the same address for the six (6) or three (3) months prior to filing.

Dissolution/Divorce

A *Petition* for dissolution can be filed by a married person to terminate a marital relationship. "The effect of a judgment of dissolution of marriage when it becomes final is to restore the parties to the state of unmarried persons." **FC § 2300**.

1. Divorce History: Fault & Cooling Off Period

The first divorces in California were based upon fault. In fact, California fault divorces can be traced back to the Second Session of the California Legislature. In 1849 California sought statehood after the United States acquired a large area of the Southwest, including California, pursuant to a treaty signed by Mexico and the United States at the end of the Mexican War. Just six months after achieving statehood, California adopted its first divorce law in its Second Session of the Legislature on March 25, 1851. This first divorce law of California provided:

> **§ 1.** The several District Courts of this State, within their respective Districts, shall have exclusive jurisdiction to grant a divorce from bed and board, and from the bonds of matrimony.
> **§ 2.** Divorces may be granted from bed and board, or from the bonds of matrimony.
> **§ 3.** No person shall be allowed to apply for a divorce under the provisions of this Act, who has not been a resident of this State for a period of six months, immediately preceding such application.
> **§ 4.** Divorce from bed and board, or from the bonds of matrimony may be granted.

As set forth above, the divorce statutes enacted by the Second Session of the California Legislature distinguished between **two kinds of divorces: a divorce from bed and board** and **a divorce from the bonds of matrimony**. In order for a person to obtain a divorce from the bonds of matrimony, one party, the filing party, had to be completely blameless in fault. The divorce from the bonds of matrimony (*divorce a vincula matrimonii*) was a complete divorce, a dissolution, and the parties were free to remarry after the judgment was obtained. A divorce from bed and board (*divorce a mensa et thoro*) was granted when the person seeking the divorce wronged the other party in some way and thus, was not blameless. (This is called the doctrine of recrimination.[6]) A divorce from bed and board is roughly analogous to California's current legal separation, where neither party can remarry after the judgment.

In 1872, the California Legislature amended § 92 of the Civil Code to include that divorces may be granted for one of the following causes:

1. Adultery;
2. Extreme cruelty;

---

[6] Recrimination is a countercharge in a divorce action in which the filing party is shown to be guilty of an offense constituting a ground for divorce. It is often referred to as the "Doctrine of Recrimination". When both parties to the marriage have committed marital misconduct that would be grounds for divorce, neither may obtain a complete divorce, a divorce from the bonds of matrimony.

Chapter 5: Annulments, Dissolutions & Legal Separations

3. Willful desertion;
4. Willful neglect;
5. Habitual intemperance; and
6. Conviction of a felony.

Section 61 of the Civil Code provided:

> A subsequent marriage contracted by any person during the life of a former husband or wife of such person, with any person other than such former husband or wife is illegal and void from the beginning unless:
> 1. The former marriage had been annulled or dissolved; or
> 2. Unless such former husband or wife was absent, and not known to such person to be living for the space of 5 successive years immediately preceding such subsequent marriage; in which case the subsequent marriage is void only from the time its nullity is adjudged by a competent tribunal."

This section was enacted not only to make bigamy and polygamy illegal, but also to impose a one year waiting period.

In 1897, Civil Code § 61 was amended to add after "the former marriage had been annulled or dissolved", "provided that in the case it be dissolved, the decree of divorce must have been rendered and made at least one year prior to such subsequent marriage."

At that time parties were avoiding the one year waiting period by simply going to another state to get married. These marriages were valid in California even though they were entered into less than one year after a divorce had been granted to one of the parties in California.

In 1903 the statute was again amended making "the right to a divorce ineffective for the period of one year"; thus, making it impossible for the parties to remarry "anywhere until at least a year after the trial of the action of divorce had taken place."

In *Pereira v. Pereira* (1909) 153 Cal. 1, the court explains why the one year waiting period was necessary.

> While the law deems it necessary to provide that a divorce may be granted when conditions are such as to make the marriage relation intolerable, it is nevertheless true that the policy of the law does not favor the dissolution of marriages. It has been generally believed that many divorces were sought, not in good faith, but because a roving fancy had found another affinity more attractive, and that a dissolution was often desired solely for the purpose of forming a new marital connection. With the design of providing conditions under which it would be understood that ardent passions of this character must perforce have time to cool before a new marriage relation could be actually formed, the legislature, in 1897, enacted a law in effect providing that no marriage should be entered into by any divorced person, until at least one year had elapsed after the decree of divorce was rendered. *Pereira v. Pereira* (1909) 156 Cal. 1, 8).

Chapter 5: Annulments, Dissolutions & Legal Separations

In 1952, the Supreme Court of California, in *DeBURGH v. DeBURGH* (1952) 39 Cal.2d 858, held that cases supporting the doctrine of recrimination were disapproved. *Id.* at p. 871. Thus, from 1952 until the Family Law Act of 1970 became law, the court no longer distinguished divorces of **bed and board** and **bonds of matrimony**. If it was proven that one of the parties wronged the other party by committing adultery, extreme cruelty, willful desertion or neglect, habitual intemperance or had been convicted of a felony, then a complete divorce could be granted.

In 1966 California Governor Edmund G. Brown established the Commission on the Family "to begin what he termed a 'concerted assault on the high incidence of divorce.'" This commission was to **study and suggest revision**[7] of the current divorce laws. After a careful analysis of the current divorce situation, one recommendation of the commission in the **Report of the Governor's Commission on the Family** was to eliminate the fault grounds and allow a

> marital dissolution be permitted only upon a finding that the marriage has irreparably failed, after penetrating scrutiny and after the parties have been given by the judicial process every resource in aid of conciliation.[8]

A divorce would not require showing fault, if this suggestion became law, which it did approximately three years later. Governor Ronald Reagan signed the Family Law Act (Senate Bill 252 and Assembly Bill 530) and made California the first no-fault state in the United States. The Family Law Act became effective on January 1, 1970.

The Family Law Act changed the cooling off period from one year to six months. And the cooling off period changed from commencing at the end of the divorce to commencing at the time the soon-to-be-ex-spouse was served with the divorce paperwork.

2. The Grounds for Divorce

As of 1970, a failure of the marriage instead of the fault of the parties became the grounds for divorce. From 1970 until 2014, the only grounds for a dissolution or legal separation were irreconcilable differences, which caused the irremediable breakdown of the marriage or incurable insanity. **FC § 2310.**

The legislature has defined irreconcilable differences as grounds that are determined by the court to be substantial reasons for not continuing the marriage and which make it appear that the marriage should be dissolved. **FC § 2311.**

On January 1, 2015, **FC § 2312** became operative changing the **incurable insanity** grounds to **permanent legal incapacity to make decisions**. **FC § 2312** provides:

---

[7] "Report of the Governor's Commission on the Family," dated December 1966, p 28.
[8] See "Report of the Governor's Commission on the Family" dated December 1966.

Chapter 5: Annulments, Dissolutions & Legal Separations

> A marriage may be dissolved on the grounds of permanent legal incapacity to make decisions only upon proof, including competent medical or psychiatric testimony, that the spouse was at the time the petition was filed, and remains, permanently lacking the legal incapacity to make decisions.

Also, on January 1, 2015, **FC § 2332** became operative providing that if a *Petition* for dissolution of marriage is filed on the ground of legal incapacity to make decisions and the spouse who lacks legal capacity to make decisions has a guardian or conservator, the *Petition* and *Summons* must be served upon the spouse and the guardian or conservator. The guardian or conservator must defend and protect the interests of the spouse who lacks legal capacity to make decisions. **FC § 2332(a)**.

If, however, the spouse who lacks legal capacity to make decisions has no guardian or conservator, the court must appoint guardian ad litem,[9] who may be the district attorney or the county counsel to defend and protect the interests of the spouse who lacks legal capacity to make decisions. **FC § 2332(b)**.

3. The Residency Requirement

In order to obtain a judgment of dissolution today, just as in 1851,[10] it is required that one of the parties to the marriage must have been a resident of this state for six (6) months and of the county in which the proceeding is filed for three (3) months prior to the filing of the *Petition*. **FC § 2320**.

This residency requirement does not mean that the parties must have the same residence or that both have to meet the requirement. Only one of the parties must meet the residency requirement.

If, at the hearing for dissolution, at least one party meets the residency requirement and the court finds that there are irreconcilable differences that have caused the irremediable breakdown of the marriage, the court must order a judgment of dissolution of marriage or a legal separation of the parties. **FC § 2333**.

Sometimes after a dissolution *Petition* has been filed, the parties reconcile. When a reconciliation occurs after a dissolution action has commenced, the court can continue the proceeding up to thirty (30) days to allow the parties to decide if there is a chance that the marriage can be saved. **FC § 2334**. After thirty (30) days, either party may move for a dissolution or legal separation, or the court may enter a judgment of dissolution of the marriage or legal separation of the parties.

Legal Separation

A legal separation action can be filed by a married person who wishes to maintain his or her marital status but resolve all other issues of the marriage. A legal

---

[9] Guardian ad litem is a court-appointed adult that represents a minor child or legally incompetent person.
[10] California Civil Code § 3 was enacted by the Second Session of the Legislature, March 25, 1851.

separation procedure is virtually identical to a dissolution, except that the parties in the legal separation retain their marital status; they remain married and are not free to remarry. Just as in a dissolution, issues regarding child custody and child support, spousal support and the division of property are all resolved in a legal separation. Also, the grounds for a legal separation are the same as required in a dissolution: irreconcilable differences and permanent legal incapacity to make decisions.

Sometimes parties choose to file a legal separation because there is no residency requirement necessary.

Both parties must agree to the legal separation pursuant to **FC § 2345** unless there is a default[11] situation. If the responding party to a legal separation requests a dissolution instead of a legal separation, the court will not grant a judgment of legal separation. **FC § 2345**.[12]

In *In re Marriage of WALTON* (1972) 28 Cal.App.3d 108, the husband filed an action for a dissolution and the wife responded with a request for a legal separation, both listing the same ground, "irreconcilable differences which have caused the irremediable breakdown of the marriage." *Id.* at p. 475. Since the husband did not agree to the legal separation, the trial court could not grant the wife's request. Instead a judgment of dissolution was granted.

If, after the legal separation action is commenced, one or both parties desire to obtain a judgment of dissolution, the legal separation action can be converted into a dissolution action. **FC § 2321**.

A legal separation does not bar a subsequent judgment of dissolution. **FC § 2347**.

However, in order to convert the legal separation action into a dissolution action, the residency requirements set forth in **FC § 2320** must be met.

For some clients a legal separation may be preferable to a dissolution for the following reasons:

1. To maintain health insurance. When a judgment of dissolution or a termination of status becomes final, the nonemployee spouse's health insurance is terminated.
2. To file income taxes jointly. When the parties retain their marital status, they may file their income taxes jointly or separate. This may be an effective way for the couple to pay less tax.
3. The residency requirements have not been met. Unlike a dissolution, the filing of a legal separation action has no residency requirements.
4. For religious or moral reasons. Some religions do not allow divorce.

---

[11] A "default" is explained in Chapter 28 RE: Defaults & Default Judgments, *infra*.
[12] In the Kardashian/Humphries divorce, Kim Kardashian requested a divorce, but Chris Humphries requested a legal separation. Because the two were not in agreement, divorce was the only possible marriage termination method that could be used.

CHART 3: Annulment vs. Dissolution vs. Legal Separation

		ANNULMENT FC § 2200 et seq.	DISSOLUTION FC § 2300 et seq.	LEGAL SEPARATION FC § 2300 et seq.
1	**Judicial Council Form**	*Petition FL-100* FC §§ 297, 299, 2030, 3409	*Petition FL-100* FC §§ 297, 299, 2030, 3409	*Petition FL-100* FC §§ 297, 299, 2030, 3409
2	**Residency Requirement**	None	6 months in CA, 3 months in County prior to filing FC § 2320	None
3	**Grounds**	**Void Marriage** (1) Incest FC § 2200 (2) Bigamy FC §2201 **Voidable Marriage** (1) **Fraud** (most common) (2) No capability to consent (3) Spouse dead 5 years (4) Unsound mind (5) Consent by force (6) Physical incapacity FC §§ 2210, 2211	(1) Irreconcilable differences and (2) Permanent legal incapacity to make decisions FC §§ 2310, 2311, 2312	(1) Irreconcilable differences and (2) Permanent legal incapacity to make decisions FC §§ 2310, 2311, 2312
4	**Waiting or Cooling-off Period**	None	6 months FC §2339	None
5	**Marital Status Postjudgment**	Single/never married	Unmarried persons	Married
6	**Consent**	None	None; appropriate notice only FC § 2250	H & W must continue to consent
7	**Name Restoration**	None	Option to restore name	None
8	**Other**			Can convert to a dissolution FC § 2321 if the residency requirement is met

Chapter 5: Annulments, Dissolutions & Legal Separations

Summary Dissolution

A summary dissolution is a less expensive process for parties to dissolve their marriage and it is usually done without the participation of attorneys. It is less expensive because there is only one fee for filing a *Joint Petition for Summary Dissolution of Marriage* (form *FL-800*). A *Response* is not filed, thus saving the fee for filing a *Response*. The filing fee for the *Joint Petition* is the same as that charged for filing a *Petition-Marriage* (form *FL-100*). And no additional fee may be charged for the filing of any form prescribed for use in a summary dissolution proceeding. **CRC Rule 5.77**.

A summary dissolution requires that both parties consent to the procedure. Either party can revoke the *Joint Petition* and terminate the summary dissolution proceeding at any time prior to the filing of the judgment of summary dissolution, if they so desire. **FC § 2402**.

For a summary dissolution, the parties file a *Joint Petition for Summary Dissolution* (form *FL-800*, found at ***www.courts.ca.gov/documents/fl800.pdf***). It is signed under oath and provides that all of the conditions set forth in **FC § 2400** have been met prior to the filing of the *Joint Petition for Summary Dissolution*.

FC § 2400 provides that a marriage may be dissolved by the summary dissolution procedure if all of the following conditions exist at the time the proceeding is commenced:

> **(1) Either party has met the jurisdictional requirements** of Chapter 3 (commencing with FC § 2320) with regard to dissolution of marriage.
> **(2) Irreconcilable differences have caused the irremediable breakdown of the marriage** and the marriage should be dissolved.
> **(3)** There are **no children of the relationship** of the parties born before or during the marriage or adopted by the parties during the marriage, and the wife, to her knowledge, is not pregnant.
> **(4)** The **marriage is not more than five years in duration** as of the date of separation of the parties.
> **(5) Neither party has any interest in real property** wherever situated, with the exception of the lease of a residence occupied by either party which satisfies the following requirements:
>   **(A)** The lease does not include an option to purchase.
>   **(B)** The lease terminates within one year from the date of the filing of the *Petition*.
> **(6) There are no unpaid obligations in excess of four thousand dollars ($4,000)** incurred by either or both of the parties after the date of their marriage, excluding the amount of any unpaid obligation with respect to an automobile.
> **(7)** The **total fair market value of community property** assets, excluding all encumbrances and automobiles, including any deferred compensation or retirement plan, **is less than twenty-five thousand dollars ($25,000),** and neither party has separate property assets, excluding all encumbrances and automobiles, in excess of twenty-five thousand dollars ($25,000).
> **(8) The parties have executed an agreement** setting forth the division of assets and the assumption of liabilities of the community, and have executed any documents, title

> certificates, bills of sale, or other evidence of transfer necessary to effectuate the agreement.
> **(9) The parties waive any rights to spousal support.**
> **(10) The parties**, upon entry of the judgment of dissolution of marriage pursuant to § 2403, irrevocably **waive their respective rights to appeal and their rights to move for a new trial.**
> **(11) The parties** have read and **understand the summary dissolution brochure** provided for in § 2406.
> **(12) The parties desire that the court dissolve the marriage.** (Emphasis added.)

FC § 2406 provides that the brochure discussed above must state that:

(1) It is in the best interests of the parties to consult an attorney,
(2) The parties should not rely exclusively on the summary dissolution brochure,
(3) A summary of **FC §§ 2320-2322** and **FC §§ 2339-2344**,
(4) The services will be provided by conciliation court,
(5) No spousal support will be paid to either party,
(6) The rights and obligations of both parties upon judgment,
(7) Neither party can remarry until the judgment is entered, and
(8) Other matters that the Judicial Council considers appropriate.

The State of California maintains a website where a copy of the summary dissolution brochure is provided: ***www.courts.ca.gov/documents/fl810.pdf***. Further, pursuant to statute, all counties in California must have a website where a copy of the brochure can be found.

All of the requirements set forth in **FC § 2400** above must be met at the time of the filing of the *Joint Petition* in order for the court to grant a summary dissolution judgment. The residency requirements for a summary dissolution are identical to those needed for a dissolution. **FC § 2320.**

If the parties are granted a summary dissolution, at the entry of their judgment, the judgment is a final adjudication of their rights and obligations with respect to marital status and property rights.

Further, the judgment of summary dissolution provides that the parties have waived any rights that they may have with regard to spousal support, rights to appeal and the right to request a new trial. **FC § 2404.**

CCP § 473 is available as a remedy to set aside a summary dissolution judgment if there was fraud, duress, accident or mistake in procuring the judgment and the set-aside request is made within six (6) months from the date that the judgment was rendered. Also, if the court finds upon acceptable proof that the parties did not meet the requirements set forth in **FC § 2400** above, the court can set aside the judgment of summary dissolution. **FC § 2405.**

Chapter 5: Annulments, Dissolutions & Legal Separations

To comply with the preliminary disclosure requirements for a summary dissolution, each joint petitioner must complete and give each other copies of the following documents before signing a property settlement agreement or completing a divorce:

> **(1)** An Income and Expense Declaration (form FL-150).
> **(2)** Either of the following documents listing separate and community property assets and obligations:
> **(A)** Declaration of Disclosure (form FL-140) and either a Schedule of Assets and Debts *or a* Property Declaration (form FL-160) with all attachments; or
> **(B)** The completed worksheet pages indicated in Summary Dissolution Information (form FL-810).
> **(3)** A written statement of all investment, business, or other income-producing opportunities that came up after the date of separation based on investments made or work done during the marriage or domestic partnership and before the date of separation.
> **(4)** All tax returns filed by the spouse or domestic partner in the two year period before exchanging the worksheets or forms described in (2).
> **(b)** Fee for filing. CRC Rule 5.77.

Chapter 5: Annulments, Dissolutions & Legal Separations

EDUCATIONAL EXERCISES

I. FILL IN THE BLANKS

1. An _____ is an action filed by a married person to change his or her marital status from a married person to an unmarried person. If _____ is granted, the marriage never existed.
2. There are many _____ regarding annulments such as: a very short marriage may be annulled; a marriage of long duration cannot be annulled; or a marriage that has been consummated cannot be annulled.
3. These are all _____.
4. In order to be granted an annulment, a party MUST meet the requirements that are set forth in FC § 2200 or FC § 2210. The length of the marriage and act of consummation _____ for an annulment.
5. To obtain a _____, the marriage must be void or voidable.
6. _____ are marriages that were never valid under any circumstances at any time.
7. A _____ may be declared invalid by an _____ at some time after the marriage takes place because a _____ at the time of the marriage.
8. FC § 2210 provides that a marriage is _____ and may be _____ if certain conditions existed at the time of the marriage.
9. As of 1970, a _____ instead of the fault of the parties became the grounds for divorce. From 1970 until 2014, the only grounds for a dissolution or legal separation were irreconcilable differences, which caused the irremediable breakdown of the marriage or incurable insanity. FC § 2310.
10. In a _____, the innocent party is entitled to all of the benefits of a valid marriage. One such benefit is that all of the property acquired during the marriage is divided equally as though it was community property.
11. A _____ is a spouse who reasonably and in good faith believes that his or her marriage is legally valid when it is not. This marriage can be void (a marriage that was never valid) or voidable (a marriage that had a defect at the beginning of the marriage but remains in effect until challenged) depending on the circumstances. The court determines whether one or both of the spouses are putative spouses. If the court so determines, then the marriage is called a _____.
12. _____ is a person's legal address. It is where a person intends to make his or her permanent home. It is the address used when determining state income tax or eligibility to vote.
13. A person can have only one _____.
14. A domicile can also be a _____, provided that a person has only one dwelling or house. A person can have many _____.
15. Summer, winter or vacation homes are examples of _____.
16. California law requires that a person live in the State of California for _____ and in the county where the dissolution Petition will be filed for _____ prior to the filing of the Petition.

Chapter 5: Annulments, Dissolutions & Legal Separations

17. A _____ for dissolution can be filed by a married person to terminate a marital relationship. "The effect of a _____ when it becomes final is to restore the parties to the state of unmarried persons." FC § 2300.
18. The first divorces in California were based upon _____.
19. A _____ action can be filed by a married person who wishes to maintain his or her marital status but resolve all other issues of the marriage.
20. The legislature has defined _____ as grounds that are determined by the court to be substantial reasons for not continuing the marriage and which make it appear that the marriage should be dissolved. FC § 2311.
21. If, at the hearing for dissolution, at least one party meets the _____ and the court finds that there are _____, the court must order a judgment of dissolution of marriage or a legal separation of the parties. FC § 2333.
22. A _____ action can be filed by a married person who wishes to maintain his or her marital status but resolve all other issues of the marriage.
23. A _____ is virtually identical to a _____, except that the parties in the legal separation retain their marital status; they remain married and are not free to remarry.
24. Just as in a dissolution, issues regarding _____ are all resolved in a legal separation. Also, the grounds for a legal separation are the same as required in a dissolution: irreconcilable differences and permanent legal incapacity to make decisions.
25. In a dissolution action, if only one party requests a dissolution on the ground of irreconcilable differences and the court so determines, either by testimony or affidavit/declaration, a dissolution will be granted and _____ from the other party is unnecessary.
26. Both parties must _____ to the legal separation pursuant to FC § 2345 unless there is a default situation.
27. If the responding party to a legal separation requests a dissolution instead of a legal separation, the court will not grant a judgment of _____ FC § 2345.
28. If, after the legal separation action is commenced, one or both parties desire to obtain a judgment of dissolution, the legal separation action can be converted into a _____ action. FC § 2321.
29. A _____ does not bar a subsequent judgment of dissolution. FC § 2347.
30. In order to convert the _____ action into a dissolution action, the residency requirements set forth in FC § 2320 must be met.
31. The same _____ (form FL-100) is used to commence proceedings for an annulment, dissolution or legal separation. This form fulfills the requirements set forth in FC § 2330.
32. No _____ is necessary to obtain a judgment of nullity or legal separation. There is, however, one required for a dissolution. FC § 2320.
33. The grounds for a _____ are the same. FC § 2310 provides that the grounds for dissolution or legal separation are: (1) irreconcilable differences, which have caused the irremediable breakdown of the marriage, and (2) _____.

Chapter 5: Annulments, Dissolutions & Legal Separations

34. In the case of a _____, once the judgment of nullity has been granted, it is as if the marriage never occurred, so the parties are free to remarry.
35. In a _____, after the judgment becomes final, both parties are free to remarry. FC § 2339.
36. In a _____, there is no marriage, so no consent is necessary. In a voidable marriage, only one of the parties needs to prove that the requirements for a judgment of nullity have been met, making consent of the other party unnecessary.
37. Either party can have the action converted to a _____ at any time while the legal separation action is pending, provided the residency requirements are met.
38. With regard to a _____ at any time after an action has been commenced, the _____ can be converted into a _____, provided that the residency requirements set forth in FC § 2320 have been met.
39. A _____ is a less expensive process for parties to dissolve their marriage and it is usually done without the participation of attorneys. It is less expensive because *there is only one fee* for filing a *Joint Petition for Summary Dissolution of Marriage* (form FL-800).

II.   Answer the following questions:

1. List the two types of annulments and give an example of each.
2. What is a putative spouse and who makes the decision whether a marriage is putative or not?
3. Explain the difference between a domicile and a residence.
4. When Governor Reagan signed the Family Law Act in 1970, California became the first no fault state in the United States. Explain "no fault" and give an example of a no fault dissolution.
5. What is bigamy and how does one become a bigamist?
6. List one requirement that makes legal separation different from a dissolution.
7. What is a summary dissolution? List the factors that a couple must comply with to use this process.

CHAPTER 6: Date of Separation

In Brief...

FAMILY CODE § 70 RE: DATE OF SEPARATION BECAME EFFECTIVE JANUARY 1, 2017

FC § 70. Determination of date of separation
(a) "Date of separation" means the date that a complete and final break in the marital relationship has occurred, as evidenced by both of the following:
 (1) The spouse has expressed to the other spouse his or her intent to end the marriage.
 (2) The conduct of the spouse is consistent with his or her intent to end the marriage.
(b) In determining the date of separation, the court shall take into consideration all relevant evidence.
(c) It is the intent of the Legislature in enacting this section to abrogate the decisions in *In re Marriage of Davis* (2015) 61 Cal.4th 846 and *In re Marriage of Norviel* (2002) 102 Cal.App.4th 1152.

CONDUCT COURTS HAVE CONSIDERED TO DETERMINE THE DATE OF SEPARATION
1. Continuous and frequent contacts at the marital home
2. Eating dinner with spouse and family
3. Maintaining mailing address at the marital home
4. Sleeping at the marital home
5. Going to events with family (including wife).
6. Vacationing together without the children
7. Attending social occasions together
8. Sending Christmas, birthday, and anniversary cards to the other spouse
9. Filling in the children's enrollment cards at school listing both parents as living at the marital home
10. Filing joint income tax returns.
11. Maintaining voting registration at the marital home address
12. Paying all the household bills and supporting family
13. Bringing laundry home for wife to wash and iron
14. Moving out of the marital home
15. Filing a Petition for dissolution.
16. Continuing sexual relationship
17. Trying to resolve differences/reconcile with aid of marriage counselor.
18. Spending holidays together
19. Traveling together
20. Sending a note to the other spouse about ending the relationship.
21. After moving out, keeping belongings at the marital home.
22. Telling spouse to come and get belongings
23. Instructing attorney to draft a settlement agreement

Chapter 6: Date of Separation

> 24. A final agreement executed by the parties
> 25. Maintaining joint bank accounts and credit cards
> 26. Taking title to vehicle in joint names
> 27. Never moving back into the marital home.
> 28. The parties dating other people.
> 29. Acquiring real property in joint names
> 30. Spouses seeing each other regularly.
>
> **When the "date of separation" is disputed, the burden to so prove is "preponderance of the evidence".** *MARRIAGE of PETERS.*

Introduction

The following Family Code Section became effective January 1, 2017

> **FC § 70. Determination of date of separation**
> (a) "Date of separation" means the date that a complete and final break in the marital relationship has occurred, as evidenced by both of the following:
> (1) The spouse has expressed to the other spouse his or her intent to end the marriage.
> (2) The conduct of the spouse is consistent with his or her intent to end the marriage.
> (b) In determining the date of separation, the court shall take into consideration all relevant evidence.
> (c) It is the intent of the Legislature in enacting this section to abrogate the decisions in *In re Marriage of Davis*[1] (2015) 61 Cal.4th 846 and *In re Marriage of Norviel*[2] (2002) 102 Cal.App.4th 1152.

By enacting this code, the legislature decided that it was not a requirement that the parties live in separate residences in order to be separated. Moving or not moving from the marital home is but one factor that the court can consider in making a "date of separation" and in most cases, not all, the spouses are living in separate residences. However, as of January 1, 2017, it is no longer a threshold finding necessary to begin the analysis. The court must now determine if there was a final break in the marriage by finding whether one spouse told the other spouse that he or she wanted to end the marriage or by looking to the conduct of the parties.

But there must be enough facts for the court decide if there has been a final break in the marriage.

Case Remanded: Not Enough Facts Presented on Issue of Date of Separation

In *In re Marriage of UMPHREY* (1990) 218 Cal.App.3d 647, Husband and Wife were married on June 24, 1950, and had four children. On November 1, 1978, Wife

---

[1] The rule in *Davis* that is no longer the law was living in separate residences is an indispensable threshold requirement for a finding that spouses are living separate and apart.
[2] The rule in *Norviel* that is no longer law was living separate and apart requires the contemporaneous conjunction of intent to separate and conduct evidencing that intent. The statute requires the spouses to establish separate residences as a predicate to separation.

wrote Husband a note telling him she had decided to end their relationship. At her request, Husband moved out of the family home. On November 17, 1978, Wife filed a petition to dissolve their marriage, although she dismissed it shortly thereafter at Husband's behest. Wife claimed that after she dismissed the dissolution action, she considered their marriage to have resumed. When Husband was away from home for extended periods due to business commitments, he maintained "temporary living quarters from time to time and place to place." *Id.* at p. 653. However, his belongings remained at the family residence. Husband maintained that he never resided with or reconciled with Wife after November 1978.

In late 1983 or early 1984, when Wife requested that Husband make a payment on a property, Husband expressed a desire to enter into an overall marital settlement. Husband thereafter instructed his attorney to draft a settlement agreement, and the parties executed a final agreement in March of 1986. The agreement recited that all community and quasi-community property had been disposed of by prior agreement and recited a separation date of September 1979.

Wife stated that she never discussed a separation date with Husband. She accepted the date in the written agreement because she thought Husband had the legal right to choose the date. The court stated that the separation date chosen by Husband in the agreement was not conclusive as to whether the parties' conduct evidenced a complete and final break in the marital relationship and remanded the case to the trial court to determine a date of separation.

Conduct that the court considered:
1. Wife wrote Husband a note telling him she had decided to end their relationship.
2. At her request, Husband moved out of the marital home.
3. Wife filed a petition to dissolve their marriage, although she dismissed it shortly thereafter at Husband's behest.
4. Husband's belongings remained at the marital home.
5. Wife moved with their son to a townhouse in Foster City.
6. Wife wrote a note to Husband indicating that he should come and get his belongings.
7. After separation, each sold the condominiums in his or her name and kept the sale proceeds.
8. Husband expressed a desire to enter into an overall marital settlement.
9. Husband instructed his attorney to draft a settlement agreement.
10. A final agreement was executed by the parties.

REMANDED for the trial court to decide the date of separation

Conduct Not Demonstrating a Final Break in the Marriage

Spouses Living Separate for Economic Reasons

In *MAKEIG v. UNITED SECURITY BK. & T. CO.* (1931) 112 Cal.App. 138, Husband and Wife were married for 14 ½ years before Wife's death. However, they

Chapter 6: Date of Separation

lived together only for a period of about six weeks immediately following the marriage. Then, by agreement, Wife returned to San Francisco to her work as a saleswoman in a department store there. Three years later, Wife visited Husband for a week in El Paso, but because Husband did not have a steady job and had been moving from place to place working as a barber for three to four weeks in a place, Wife again returned to San Francisco. Wife continued to live in San Francisco working as a saleswoman in a department store from March 1914 to December 31, 1926. The parties visited back and forth, with Husband sometimes meeting Wife in San Francisco, while several times Wife visited Husband over weekends, occupying the same room. Whenever Wife and Husband were together, Wife was always introduced as his wife. They never settled down together.

Husband's explanation of their status was that his wife liked San Francisco and they were trying to save money together for a home. As he testified: "It was always said, 'Well, just as soon as you can get some money together we will come together.' She was always talking every time I was with her about saving money up -- was making a home." *Id.* at p. 141. Husband also testified that his wife said, "it won't be long now before we will be able to go to housekeeping and get a home," and that their only understanding in regard to money was that as soon as they got money enough together they would make a home. *Ibid.* Wife died June 8, 1928. Wife had some money in bank accounts when she died. The court found this money to be community property because there had been no final rupture of the marital relationship such that the parties were living separate and apart. The court held that because the parties were living separate and apart due to economic or social reasons, they were not separated.

Wife Continuing to Furnish Normal Wifely Contributions

In *In re Marriage of BARAGRY* (1977) 73 Cal.App.3d 444, Husband moved out of the family home after a quarrel with Wife on August 4, 1971. Husband lived for a time on his boat. Thereafter, he rented an apartment for himself and his 28-year-old girlfriend. Husband maintained continuous and frequent contact with his family. He ate dinner at home with Wife almost every night; he maintained his mailing address at the home; he took his family to basketball games; and took his Wife to Sun Valley for a week without the children.

Husband frequently took Wife to social occasions. He sent Wife numerous Christmas, birthday and anniversary cards after he had moved out of the family residence. The parties continued to file joint income tax returns, and Husband maintained his voting registration at the home address. He paid all the household bills and supported his family. He regularly brought his laundry home to Wife, who washed and ironed it twice a month.

Husband filed a *Petition* to dissolve the marriage claiming that the date of separation was the date he moved out of the family home. Wife contended that the date of separation was the date that Husband filed the *Petition* for dissolution.

In reversing the trial court's decision that the date of separation was the date that Husband moved out of the family residence, the court stated "Husband was presumably enjoying a captain's paradise, savoring the best of two worlds, and capturing the benefits of both. Husband was reaping the advantages of those services and may be presumed to owe part of his professional success during that four-year period to Wife's social and domestic efforts on his behalf. One who enjoys the benefit of a polygamous lifestyle must be prepared to accept its accompanying financial burdens. During the period that spouses preserve the appearance of marriage, they both reap its benefits, and their earnings remain community property." *Id.* at p. 449. The date of separation was, thus, held to be the date that Husband filed his *Petition* for dissolution.

Conduct that the court considered:
1. Wife's continuing to furnish wifely duties
2. Continuous and frequent contacts at the marital home.
3. Eating dinner with wife and family.
4. Maintaining mailing address at the marital home.
5. On occasion (Christmas) sleeping at the marital home.
6. Going to events with family (including wife).
7. Vacationing with wife (and not children).
8. Attending social occasions -- parties at friends' homes, dinners for professional and academic groups, outings with other doctors and their wives.
9. Sending Christmas, birthday, and anniversary cards to wife.
10. Filling in daughter's enrollment card at school listing both parents as living at the marital home.
11. Filing joint income tax returns.
12. Maintaining voting registration at the marital home address.
13. Paying all the household bills and supporting family.
14. Bringing laundry home for wife to wash and iron.

Court held: NOT SEPARATED

Spouses Continuing Sexual Relationship, Attempting Reconciliation

In *In re Marriage of MARSDEN* (1982) 130 Cal.App.3d 426 the parties were married on February 11, 1971. On April 12, 1975, Wife moved out of the house in which she had lived with Husband and moved into an apartment. On April 25, 1975, Wife filed a petition for dissolution of marriage. Wife testified although she filed the petition for dissolution in April of 1975, she did not want a divorce. Wife stated she simply wanted to work out the parties' differences. Wife rented the apartment because it was close to the house and she wanted to remain near her husband. The parties' sexual relationship continued after Wife moved out of the house. The parties also saw a marriage counselor during this period.

The appellate court affirmed the trial court's decision that the parties were not **living separate and apart**. Even though Wife had moved out of the marital home,

Chapter 6: Date of Separation

the parties continued their sexual relationship, sought marriage counseling and made multiple efforts at reconciliation.

Conduct that the court considered:
1. Wife moved out of the marital home.
2. Wife filed a Petition for dissolution.
3. Wife did nothing for more than 3 years after filing the *Petition*.
4. The parties continued their sexual relationship.
5. The parties attempted to resolve their marital differences with aid of marriage counselor.
6. The parties made multiple efforts at reconciliation.
7. Husband joined wife in Mexico and traveled with her to the Middle East.
8. The parties spent Christmas together in 1975 in Mexico.
9. The parties again traveled together.

Court Held: Not separated

Spouses Maintaining Joint Checking Accounts, Credit Cards

In *In re Marriage OF VON DER NUELL* (1994) 23 Cal.App.4th 730, the parties were married almost 28 years. The trial court found the parties separated on November 1, 1987 because they had parted on that date with no present intention of resuming marital relations. The appellate court reversed, stating that the final break in the marital relationship did not occur at that time because after that date: **(1)** the parties maintained joint checking accounts, credit cards and tax returns; **(2)** they took title to an automobile jointly; **(3)** Husband maintained close contact with Wife, including frequent visits to the home; **(4)** Husband took Wife on vacations; **(5)** they continued having sexual relations with one another; **(6)** Husband continued to contribute financially to the community; and **(7)** they attempted to reconcile. The court stated that "given these ongoing economic, emotional, sexual and social ties between the parties and their attempts at reconciliation, regardless of the parties' present intention on November 1, 1987, a complete and final break in the marriage did not occur at that time." *Id.* at p. 737.

Conduct that the court considered:
1. The parties maintained joint checking accounts, credit cards and tax returns.
2. The parties took title to an automobile jointly.
3. Husband maintained close contact with Wife, including frequent visits to the marital home.
4. Husband took Wife on vacations.
5. The parties continued having sexual relations with one another.
6. Husband continued to contribute financially to the community.
7. The parties attempted to reconcile.

Court held: NOT SEPARATED

Chapter 6: Date of Separation

Spouses Seeing Meeting Regularly; Joint Title to Real Property

In *In re Marriage of HARDIN* (1995) 38 Cal.App.4th 448, Doris and Victor Hardin married in 1961. On June 28, 1969, Victor walked out of their apartment, but he and Doris continued their economic relationship, saw each other often and communicated regularly. Fourteen years transpired between Victor's exiting the family residence and dissolution of the marriage. Even then, the matter was not entirely concluded. Although the parties dissolved their marriage in 1983, they neither divided their property nor established support obligations.

At the hearing, Doris contended that they separated in 1983 when Victor, wishing to remarry, went forward with the dissolution. The trial court held that the date of separation occurred on June 28, 1969, when Victor moved out of their residence.

The appellate court stated, in reversing the trial court's decision, that the **date of separation** is determined by more than when a party leaves the family residence or files a dissolution petition.

"The ultimate question to be decided in determining the date of separation is whether either or both of the parties perceived the rift in their relationship as final. The best evidence of this is their words and actions. The husband's and the wife's subjective intents are to be objectively determined from all of the evidence reflecting the parties' words and actions during the disputed time in order to ascertain when during that period the rift in the parties' relationship was final." *Id.* at p. 451.

Conduct that the court considered:
1. Husband moved out of the marital home after a heated argument.
2. Husband never moved back into the marital home.
3. Husband never again slept at the marital home.
4. The parties dated other people.
5. The parties did not attend business, social or family events together.
6. Wife filed 3 different petitions for dissolution specifying the same date of separation.
7. The parties saw each other regularly.
8. The parties' economic relationship remained unchanged.
9. The parties acquired real property together.
10. Husband continued to receive mail at the marital home.
11. Wife remained a corporate officer in the family business and signed, at Husband's request, all documents presented to her in connection with this business.
12. There remained bank documents indicating that they were married and all of their property was community.

The court held: NOT SEPARATED

Chapter 6: Date of Separation

Conduct Demonstrating a Final Break in the Marriage

In *In re Marriage of MANFER* (2006) 144 Cal.App.4th 925, Maureen and Samuel Manfer married on June 16, 1973. One week after their 31st wedding anniversary, the couple quarreled, and Samuel moved out of the family residence into an apartment he had previously leased. To keep up appearances, the couple continued to have sporadic social contact and take an occasional trip together, but they did not engage in sexual relations with one another, commingle their funds or support one another. The trial court found there was "a preponderance of the evidence that the Manfers' private conduct evidenced a final and complete break in their marital relationship in June of 2004." Nonetheless, it determined the date of separation was March 15, 2005, by expressly utilizing an "objective test" standard, i.e., "[W]ould society at large consider the couple separated?" *Id.* at p. 928.

The appellate court found that "the trial court's focus on the couple's 'public persona' was misdirected... The court found by a preponderance of the evidence that the marriage relationship was irretrievably over in June 2004, as shown by Maureen's subjective intent *and* specific instances of the parties' objective conduct demonstrating that intent (i.e., they physically separated, they did not have sexual relations, they did not commingle funds or support one another, they sought no counseling and they agreed to hide their separation). In the absence of any factual findings of equivocation, ambivalence or uncertainty, as a matter of law, the court could not defer the date of separation to coincide with the couple's public revelation of their split." *Id.* at p. 935.

Facts that the court considered:
1. Husband moved out of the marital home and into an apartment after a quarrel.
2. Husband leased an apartment before moving out of the marital home.
3. Wife made up her mind the stormy marriage was finally over.
4. Both parties agreed to hide their circumstances from family and friends.
5. The couple continued to have sporadic social contacts and take an occasional trip together.
6. The parties did not engage in sexual relations with one another.
7. The parties did not seek any counseling.
8. The parties did not commingle their funds, or support one another.
9. Husband and Wife told their daughters and friends they were not living together.

Court held: SEPARATED

Chapter 6: Date of Separation

EDUCATIONAL EXERCISES

I. Read the following scenario and answer the questions that follow it.

A client, Mark Wood, comes to the Family Law office where you work. He wants to divorce his wife Kathy Wood. Mark told Kathy that he wanted a divorce on March 3, 2016 and he moved out of the family residence 3 days later taking all of his clothes and personal possessions. He, thereafter, retained the services of a lawyer and signed the court documents requesting a divorce and the documents were filed April 1, 2016. After moving out, he started dating other people. On May 4, 2016 Mark asked if Kathy would meet him for dinner on May 7, 2016 at one of their favorite restaurants. Kathy agreed. At dinner, he told her that he really did not want a divorce and asked if she would agree to see a marriage professional. She agreed.

The couple went to see a marriage professional and they continued to see her until October 16, 2016. Mark won $25 million in the California lottery on October 18, 2016. He wants date of separation that will allow him to keep all of the money.

1. From Mark's perspective, what is the date of separation?
2. Make an argument for Mark to keep all of the lottery money.
3. List the conduct that a court would consider to determine their date of separation.
4. What should the court order with regard to the date of separation? Why?

II. The following is a class exercise.

Indicate whether the conduct is evidence of a final break in the marriage (Y), is not conduct conducive to a final break in the marriage (N) or possible either way (P). If possible either way, discuss what additional conduct would make it a final break.

1. _____ Continuous and frequent contacts at the marital home but only to see the children
2. _____ Eating dinner with spouse and family one night every two weeks to be with the children
3. _____ Maintaining mailing address at the marital home, waiting to get a more permanent address before changing

Chapter 6: Date of Separation

4. __P__ Sleeping at the marital home in the spare bedroom
5. __N__ Going to events with family with the spouse and the children
6. __N__ Vacationing together without the children but each having his or her own hotel room
7. __P__ Attending social occasions together, but meeting at the event, never driving together
8. __P__ Filling in the children's enrollment cards at school listing both parents as living at the marital home only for a short time and to avoid embarrassing until they get used to the divorce.
9. __P__ Filing joint income tax returns, only until the divorce is finalized because that is the most advantageous for both parties.
10. __P/__ Maintaining voting registration at the marital home address, waiting to get a more permanent address before changing.
11. __N__ Paying all the household bills and supporting family until a support plan is in place
12. __N/__ Moving out of the marital home into a friend's house until tempers cool
13. __P__ Filing a Petition for dissolution, but requesting that the attorney not go forward with it yet
14. __N__ Continuing sexual relationship but not being monogamous
15. __P__ Spending holidays together
16. __N__ Traveling together with the spouse and the children
17. __P__ Sending a note to the other spouse about ending the relationship.
18. __N__ After moving out, keeping belongings at the marital home.
19. __P__ Maintaining joint bank accounts and credit cards until can separate equally
20. __P__ Taking title to vehicle in joint names a vehicle that will only be driven by one of the children

CHAPTER 7: Attorney Fees & Limited Scope Representation

In Brief...

ATTORNEY FEES AWARDS ARE COMMON IN FAMILY LAW ACTIONS:
- For disparity in incomes between parties;
- When there is a prevailing party; and
- As sanctions.

FAMILY CODE ATTORNEY FEE AWARD AUTHORITY CODES INCLUDE:
- **FC § 270** awards fees if it is determined that the other party has the ability to pay.
- **FC § 271** is awarded as a sanction.
- **FC § 274** awards to an injured spouse as a sanction against the other spouse.
- **FC § 2010** awards fees in dissolutions, annulments and legal separations.
- **FC § 2030** awards fees for equal access in dissolution, annulment or legal separation.
- **FC § 2030(a)** is an award to retain an attorney in a timely manner before the proceedings.
- **FC § 2030(b)** awards fees for legal services incurred before or after the proceeding.
- **FC § 2030(c)** gives the court the authority to augment prior awards so that both parties continue to have the ability to hire counsel.
- **FC § 2030(d)** requires a party, not the spouse of another party, to pay attorney fees that are limited to an amount that is reasonably necessary to maintain or defend the action.
- **FC § 2031** awards fees and no notice to the opposing side is required.
- **FC § 2032(a), (b)** and **(c)** the court should consider the circumstances in each case and financial resources is only one factor. Pay of attorney fees can come from any type of property.
- **FC § 2032(d)** in cases designated as "complex" the court may award additional fees.
- **FC § 2107** awards fees as a money sanction for a breach of fiduciary duty.
- **FC § 2255** awards fees in annulment actions.
- **FC §§ 3027.1, 3120, 3121, 3150** awards fees in cases regarding the custody of children.
- **FC § 3120** awards fees to ensure both parties have equal access to legal representation.
- **FC § 3121(a)** provides an award of fees in an amount that is necessary based on an income and needs assessment for the cost of maintaining or defending the proceeding.

Chapter 7: Attorney Fees & Limited Scope Representation

> - **FC § 3121(b)** provides that when a request for fees is made, the court must make findings as to whether an award of fees is appropriate
> - **FC § 3452** awards fees under the (UCCJEA) to the prevailing party.
> - **FC §§ 3557** and **3652** awards to enforce existing order for child or spousal support.
> - **FC § 3652** awards fees to the prevailing party in an order that modifies, terminates or sets aside a support order.
> - **FC § 4324.5** awards fees where there is a criminal conviction for a violent sexual felony.
> - **FC §§ 6344** and **6386** the court may award fees to the prevailing party in domestic violence cases.
> - **FC §§ 7605** and **7640** awards fees under the UPA for equal access to legal counsel.
> - **11 U.S.C.S. § 523(a)(5)**, provides that any debt to a spouse, former spouse or child of the debtor for alimony to, maintenance for or support of such spouse or child, in connection with a separation agreement, divorce decree or other order of a court is nondischargeable in bankruptcy.
>
> **CHART 4: Family Code Attorney Fee Award Authority**
>
> *LIMITED SCOPE REPRESENTATION* is a relationship between an attorney and a person seeking legal services in which they have agreed that the scope of the legal services will be limited to specific tasks that the attorney will perform for the person.

Introduction

In other areas of law, a family or both spouses retain one attorney. In a divorce situation, each spouse may desire to retain an attorney; so, there are two attorneys to be paid. Since one spouse usually earns more than the other spouse in a family, the higher-earning spouse may be able to retain an attorney because he or she makes more money and supports less people; meanwhile, the lower-earning spouse, who has less money to support the same household that both parties were paying for, often cannot afford to retain an attorney.

In order to make representation available to both spouses, California legislature has passed laws that provide the court with the authority to level the playing field by examining the earnings of both spouses and ordering that the payment for both attorneys be shared by the spouses on a percentage of income basis. Thus, the spouse with more money to spend on attorney fees would be ordered to contribute or pay to the attorney fees and litigation costs of the other spouse.[1]

There are many code sections that provide a court with authority to make attorney fees orders, such as where there is a disparity in incomes between parties, as

---

[1] See FC § 2030 and *In re Marriage of Tharp* (2010) 188 Cal.App.4th 1295 at p. 1316 that is set forth in Chapter 27 RE: Attorney Fees & Limited Scope Representation, *infra*.

Chapter 7: Attorney Fees & Limited Scope Representation

explained above. Prevailing party fees are attorney fees that are awarded mainly to ensure that the action filed is likely to obtain its objective because the losing party is responsible for his or her own attorney fees, as well as the other party's attorney fees. Attorney fees paid as a sanction are to "promote settlement and encourage cooperation that will reduce litigation."[2] They monetarily penalize a party who files a meritless, frivolous action that is an "entirely needless expenditure of a huge amount of money and time."[3]

Of the many family codes that authorize a court to make attorney fees orders, some are completely discretionary, and some provide that a court must make an attorney fee order if certain conditions are met. Listed below in numeric order are the most common family codes that provide the court with the authority to make attorney fees orders.

Authority to Award Attorney Fees Pursuant to the Family Code

1. FC §§ 270, 271, 274

FC § 270 is the first section in the Family Code that considers the issue of attorney fees. It is in the Family Code under **General Provisions, Attorney's Fees and Costs**. **FC § 270** provides that if a court orders a party to pay attorney fees or costs pursuant to this code, the court must first determine that the party so ordered has or is reasonably likely to have the ability to pay.

In the following case, the attorney fee award ordered by the trial court pursuant to **FC § 270** was affirmed on appeal.

> *ALICIA R et al., Plaintiffs, Cross-defendants and Respondents, v. TIMOTHY M., Defendant, Cross-complainant and Appellant.*
> COURT OF APPEAL OF CALIFORNIA, SECOND APPELLATE DISTRICT, DIVISION SEVEN.
> 29 Cal.App.4th 1232
> October 27, 1994, Decided
> (*Alicia R. v. Timothy M.*)
>
> On November 26, 1988, knowing that Alicia R. (R.) was still legally married to another, Peter S. (S.) and R. entered into a marriage ceremony. When they married, R. moved from her residence in Malibu, California, to S.'s residence next door also in Malibu.
>
> The child was conceived in approximately December 1989 and was born on September 22, 1990. S. was present at the hospital when the child was born and was named as the father on all hospital records. R. signed the child's birth certificate, stating that S. was the father.

---

[2] *Parker v. Harbert* (2012) 212 Cal.App.4th 1172 at pp. 645-646.
[3] *Parker v. Harbert, supra* at p. 648.

Chapter 7: Attorney Fees & Limited Scope Representation

In May 1992, the child was baptized; R. was identified as the mother and S. as the father. Their friends and family attended the baptism.

On January 27, 1993, S. filed a proceeding for dissolution of his marriage to R. In his verified petition he identified the child as a child of the marriage.

In early February 1993, or October 1992, R. told S. that he was not biologically related to the minor child. Prior thereto R. had by statements and conduct induced S. to believe he was the child's father and the child knew S. as her father. After this announcement, R. and the child moved back into R.'s residence. S. continued to see the child but not as a parent.

S. agreed to have a blood test to determine whether he was the child's father and when it was established that he was not, he decided not to resist R.'s action to declare the marriage void and to an adjudication that there were no children of the marriage. [Accordingly,] a judgment of nullity was filed May 25, 1993, to the effect that the marriage between R. and S. was void ab initio.

R. had known M. since 1983 and they began having an affair in 1989. On August 12, 1993, she filed a complaint against M. to establish he was the biological father of the child and for child support. She also filed an order to show cause for child support, attorney fees and costs.

M. filed an answer to the complaint denying he was parent of the child and asserted that pursuant to Evidence Code § 621, a man other than M. was the father of the child.

At the hearing on the order to show cause, the court determined that it would be a travesty to employ the conclusive presumption of parentage as provided in Evidence Code § 621 and ordered the parties to take part in DNA tests.

These tests established that M. was the biological father of the child and M., based on these results, admitted he was the child's biological father. The superior court so found and ordered M. to pay a contributive share of attorney fees of $ 2,500 to S.'s attorney and $ 9,500 to R.'s attorney.

In support of [her request for] an award of attorney fees, R. declared in pertinent part that she is a flight attendant and earns approximately $ 1,900 gross per month, that she lives on a piece of property she owns in Malibu, that she receives some additional rent money from her mother who lives in a guest house on the property and from the rental of a trailer. R. declared that M. has a luxurious lifestyle on approximately 2 acres in Bel Air in a 3,500-square-foot house and that she is informed and believes that he earns more than $ 200,000 per year; he is a board-certified plastic surgeon and is on staff at both University of California, Los Angeles and the Veterans' Administration Hospital, that he lectures frequently on behalf of University of California, Los Angeles and she is informed that he receives research grants. R. filed an income and expense declaration setting forth her gross income and net monthly disposable income and her estimate of M.'s gross yearly income.

M. contends the trial court abused its discretion in awarding attorney fees because it made the award in the absence of any substantial evidence concerning the parties' respective abilities and needs.

FC § 270 provides that if a court orders a party to pay attorney fees or costs under this code, it shall first determine that the party has or is reasonably likely to have the ability to

Chapter 7: Attorney Fees & Limited Scope Representation

> pay. The income and expense declaration and the declaration of R. reflect that M. was a plastic surgeon whose income exceeded $ 200,000. M. did not counter that evidence and did not argue otherwise at the hearing. The evidence before the court made it reasonably likely that M. would have the ability to pay the attorney fees awarded and there was no abuse of discretion in making the award of attorney fees.
>
> **DISPOSITION**
> The order is affirmed.

An award of attorney fees and costs pursuant to **FC § 271** is in the nature of a sanction. A court may base an award of attorney fees and costs on the extent to which the conduct of each party or attorney furthers or frustrates the case. The court must take the parties' incomes, assets and liabilities into consideration when setting an amount. The court may not impose a sanction that imposes an unreasonable financial burden on the party against whom the sanction is imposed. Financial need is not a requirement to receive an award.

Notice and an opportunity to be heard are required. An award of attorney fees and costs pursuant to this section is payable only from the property, income or community property of the party against whom the sanction is imposed. This sanction code section can only be assessed against a party to the litigation. *KOEHLER v. SUPERIOR COURT OF SAN MATEO COUNTY* (2010) 181 Cal.App.4th 1153 at p. 1164.

FC § 271 sanctions are often requested for attorney fees spent in actions that are frivolous or filed to delay family law proceedings.

The case below is an example of a trial court properly sanctioning a father for conduct that "frustrated the policy behind **FC § 271**."

> ***CYNTHIA M. PARKER, Plaintiff and Respondent, v. LEE D. HARBERT, Defendant and Appellant.***
> COURT OF APPEAL OF CALIFORNIA, FIRST APPELLATE DISTRICT, DIVISION FIVE
> 212 Cal.App.4th 1172
> December 19, 2012, Opinion Filed
> (*Parker v. Harbert*)
>
> In September 2009, Harbert initiated contempt proceedings against Parker. He claimed Parker willfully violated both court orders by, among other things (1) refusing to bring his minor son to visit him while he was in prison; (2) refusing to give him access to their son's medical records; and (3) failing to help their son take "the full course of medication for his poison oak medical problem."
>
> Following a 13-day trial, the court issued a tentative decision finding "the evidence was insufficient to prove Ms. Parker guilty beyond a reason[able] doubt as to any of the charged offenses" and sanctioning Harbert in the amount of $87,000. The court advised Harbert: "[t]he proposed award with respect to the attorney's fees in favor of [Parker] will serve as notice ... of the court's intent to impose fees as a sanction pursuant to [FC § 271].

Chapter 7: Attorney Fees & Limited Scope Representation

Both parties objected to the tentative statement of decision. In October 2011, the court issued a detailed 30-page statement of decision examining the evidence offered in support of the contempt allegations and concluding it did not establish Parker was guilty beyond a reasonable doubt. The court also imposed $92,000 in attorney's fees and costs as sanctions pursuant to FC § 271.

The court initially imposed $87,000 but increased the amount to $92,000. Parker sought attorney's fees and costs of $121,113.90.) The court explained, "the evidence shows that none of the conduct alleged against Ms. Parker constituted the sort of egregious behavior that any objective party would have seen as warranting the pursuit of contempt allegations that could result in the imposition of a jail sentence." The court continued, "[w]hile the court cannot say that each allegation in the contempt petition is wholly frivolous, it is the court's view that many of the allegations were frivolous."

The court determined Harbert's conduct frustrated the policy behind FC § 271 because he "launched a host of contempt allegations against Ms. Parker as a means to force [her to] acquiescence to his child custody demands. Mr. Harbert initiated this proceeding even though any reasonable person could see that the evidence was insufficient to prove guilt beyond a reasonable doubt. As a consequence of this strategy, Mr. Harbert has caused the entirely needless expenditure of a huge amount of money and time in a vain attempt to punish Ms. Parker for violations of the previous court orders which at the very most were trivial."

DISCUSSION
The purpose of FC § 271 is to promote settlement and to encourage cooperation which will reduce the cost of litigation. "Family law litigants who flout that policy by engaging in conduct that increases litigation costs are subject to the imposition of attorneys' fees and costs as a sanction." (Citation omitted.)

Harbert's first claim is the court's finding that the contempt proceedings "were objectively unreasonable" somehow constitutes "prejudicial error." Harbert has not demonstrated why this conclusion was erroneous. He has not cited any authority precluding a court from imposing sanctions pursuant to FC § 271 when a court has previously issued an order to show cause or partially denied a motion for judgment of acquittal.

Second, and perhaps most importantly, the court was authorized to impose sanctions even in the absence of a finding of frivolity. FC § 271 vests family law courts with an additional means with which to enforce this state's public policy of promoting settlement of family law litigation, while reducing its costs through mutual cooperation of clients and their counsel. Thus, a party who individually, or by counsel, engages in conduct frustrating or obstructing the public policy is thereby exposed to liability for the adverse party's costs and attorney's fees such conduct generates. Sanctions under FC § 271 are justified when a party has unreasonably increased the cost of litigation.

Here, there can be no dispute Harbert's conduct delayed the resolution of various issues relating to child custody and increased litigation costs. Harbert's conduct also wasted the court and the parties' time. The court did not abuse its discretion by imposing sanctions pursuant to FC § 271.

As we have already stated, FC § 271 does not require the conduct be frivolous or taken solely for the purpose of delay.

Chapter 7: Attorney Fees & Limited Scope Representation

> **DISPOSITION**
> The judgment is affirmed.

FC § 271 can also be used to appropriately request sanction-based attorney fees. (See *In re Marriage of Perow* (2019) Court of Appeal, Second Appellate District, Division Two, where the court held that the request for sanctions-based attorney fees is not affirmative relief. As such, it does not require a separate motion or companion Request for Hearing (RFO). It is a sanction that can be responsive to a party's conduct in litigating his/her motion, allowing the court to consider the "party's conduct at the same time as his motion without the need for a separately filed motion for fees"; thus, avoiding possible duplicative, repetitious pleadings.

If a spouse is convicted of attempted murder or solicitation for murder of the other spouse, **FC § 274** provides that the injured spouse is entitled to an award of reasonable attorney fees and costs as a sanction. Notice and an opportunity to be heard are required. An award of attorney fees and costs is payable only from the property, income or community property of the party against whom the sanction is imposed. Financial need is not a requirement to receive an award.

2. FC § 2010

FC § 2010 gives the court authority to make attorney fees orders in a proceedings involving dissolutions, annulments and legal separations. (See *In re Marriage of GUASCH* (2011) 201 Cal.App.4th 942 at p. 947 where the court stated that **FC § 2010** confers broad authority on the court to make appropriate orders concerning "[t]he settlement of the property rights of the parties.")

3. FC §§ 2030-2032

FC §§ 2030-2032 provide the court with the authority to make attorney fee awards in dissolutions, annulments and legal separations and are the most utilized attorney fees and costs sections in the Family Code. **FC § 2030** ensures that each party has access to legal representation in a dissolution of marriage, nullity of marriage or legal separation action or subsequent to a related judgment. An order made under this section is based on the income and needs assessments of both parties.

Whatever amount is reasonably necessary for attorney fees and for the cost of maintaining or defending the proceeding may be ordered. The court must make findings on whether an award of attorney fees and costs under this section is appropriate, whether there is a disparity in access to funds to retain counsel and whether one party is able to pay for legal representation of both parties.

If the findings demonstrate disparity in access and the ability to pay, the court must make an order awarding attorney fees and costs. This code section also provides authority for the court to make an attorney fee order for an unrepresented litigant who lacks the financial ability to hire an attorney. If the other party has the financial

Chapter 7: Attorney Fees & Limited Scope Representation

ability to pay a reasonable amount, the court may make an order that allows the unrepresented party to retain an attorney in a timely manner before proceedings in the matter go forward. **FC § 2030(a).**

Attorney fees and costs may be awarded pursuant to **FC § 2030(b)** for legal services rendered or costs incurred before or after the commencement of the proceeding. **FC § 2030(c)** provides that the court must augment or modify the original award for attorney fees and costs as may be reasonably necessary for the prosecution or defense of the proceeding, or any proceeding related thereto, including after any appeal has been concluded.

FC § 2030(d) is an unusual section because it gives a court authority to make an attorney fee order to "a party who is not the spouse of another party to the proceeding." However, the amount of the order is "limited to an amount reasonably necessary to maintain or defend the action on the issues relating to that party."

During a proceeding for dissolution of marriage, nullity of marriage, legal separation of the parties or any proceeding subsequent to entry of a related judgment, an application for a temporary order for a retainer to hire an attorney, or that augments or modifies a previous order, may be made by filing a *Request for Order (RFO)*. The court has fifteen (15) days to rule on this request. This code section does not require notice and, accordingly, a request can be made by either party or the judge by an oral motion in open court at the time of the hearing of the cause on the merits or at any time before entry of judgment against a party whose default has been entered. **FC § 2031.**

The court may make an award of attorney fees that is just and reasonable under the relative circumstances of the respective parties. Reasonableness will be determined by taking into consideration the party's circumstances and need for each party to have sufficient financial resources to present the party's case adequately. Even if a party has sufficient resources to pay his or her own attorney fees, he or she can still make a request and be awarded attorney fees. A party's financial resources are only one factor for the court to consider in making an award. The payment of attorney fees may come from any type of property, whether community or separate, principal or income. **FC § 2032(a), (b) and (c).**

Either party can request that the court make a finding that the case involves complex or substantial issues of fact or law related to property rights, visitation, custody or support. Upon that finding, the court may in its discretion determine the appropriate, equitable allocation of attorney fees, costs, expert fees and consultant fees between the parties. The court order may provide for the allocation of separate or community assets, security against these assets and for payments from income or anticipated income of either party. Payments may be made by an agreement of the parties or order of the court. **FC § 2032(d).**

Although a trial court has a lot of latitude in making an attorney fees order, the court MUST follow the law. In the following case, the Appellate Court held that the trial court did not follow the law and, therefore, abused its discretion in not awarding attorney fees pursuant to **FC §§ 270, 271, 2030** and **2032.**

> *In re Marriage of CASEY O. and MARY BETH THARP. CASEY O. THARP, Respondent, v. MARY BETH THARP, Appellant.*
> COURT OF APPEAL OF CALIFORNIA, FIFTH APPELLATE DISTRICT
> 188 Cal.App.4th 1295
> October 1, 2010, Filed
> (*Marriage of Tharp*)
>
> Mary Beth and Casey were married on October 11, 1992. On August 27, 2007, Casey filed for dissolution of his marriage to Mary Beth. Casey was represented by Attorney Robert Koligian, Jr. Casey stated in the petition that there was an antenuptial agreement signed by both parties and counsel, which confirmed that all property owned by Casey was his separate property and all income of Casey's before, during, and after the marriage was his separate property. No schedule of assets and debts was included.
>
> On November 6, 2007, Mary Beth filed an order to show cause. She sought spousal and child support, an advance of $ 50,000 for attorney's fees. Mary Beth was represented by Attorney Dale R. Bruder.
>
> In her declaration in support of the order to show cause, Mary Beth provided information regarding Casey's income, the family expenses, and the expenses paid by E.M. Tharp, Inc. (hereafter the corporation). Mary Beth reported Casey's income in 2005 to be $ 132,534, which did not include the family expenses paid by the corporation. The corporation paid for the family cars, all expenses for those vehicles, property taxes and insurance for the family home, housekeepers and ranch hands employed at the family home, all utilities, cellular telephones, health insurance, country club dues, and credit card bills for personal credit cards used by the family.
>
> On December 18, 2007, the family court made [a] temporary order of family support in the amount of $ 5,000 payable by Casey to Mary Beth. Casey was ordered to pay $ 2,500 to Mary Beth's attorney based on disparity of income and to pay $ 2,500 for an "accounting evaluation."
>
> On January 25, 2008, Mary Beth asked the family court to designate the dissolution proceedings as "complex," pursuant to FC § 2032(d). Mary Beth again requested that Casey be ordered to advance $ 50,000 for her attorney fees and $ 20,000 for a forensic accountant. Mary Beth stated that she was unemployed, had no independent financial means to pay for an attorney or accountant, and that the services of these professionals were necessary in order to prepare and represent her adequately in the case.
>
> [At the hearing, the] family court denied the request to designate the proceedings as complex under FC § 2032(d), instead finding the case to be complex and ordering a case management plan be developed and implemented pursuant to FC § 2451. The family court ordered Casey to pay the sum of $ 20,000 to Mary Beth's attorney, reserving for the future a determination of whether that amount should be deducted from Mary Beth's share of the community property.
>
> In April 2008, Mary Beth moved to compel Casey to respond to discovery, specifically, form interrogatories, special interrogatories, and document production.

Chapter 7: Attorney Fees & Limited Scope Representation

At the May 8, 2008, hearing, the family court found that Casey had failed to answer the special interrogatories adequately and granted the motion to compel further responses to the special interrogatories, directing Casey to pay $ 1,500 in attorney's fees to Mary Beth's counsel as a sanction.

The issue of the premarital agreement and its validity was bifurcated at the request of Casey's counsel and set for trial on July 28, 2008. Casey and his counsel were ordered to produce a signed copy of the alleged agreement, and, if they could not produce a signed copy, to notify the family court and opposing counsel and remove the matter from the calendar.

On July 22, 2008, Mary Beth filed an order to show cause seeking to have Casey held in contempt for failing to comply with the May 8 order of the family court. Casey had not produced the documents and had not answered the special interrogatories as ordered.

On July 28, the date set for trial on the validity of the alleged premarital agreement, Casey and Harbottle did not appear. Instead, Harbottle sent a letter via facsimile to the family court stating that there was no executed premarital agreement. Bruder and Mary Beth were present for the trial.

On September 17, 2008, the family court considered the order to show cause filed [by Mary Beth on July 24 and] denied the request for attorney's fees and sanctions.

On November 26, 2008, Mary Beth filed a motion for attorney's fees, forensic accounting fees, and sanctions. A hearing was set for January 7, 2009. In her declaration in support of the motion, Mary Beth declared that she had no separate or community source of income with which to pay attorney's fees and costs, her only asset was a small 401k account, and her income was the temporary spousal support of $ 5,000 that had been awarded. As of July 18, 2008, Mary Beth had paid $ 12,770 in attorney's fees from her income, separate and apart from the $ 22,500 the family court had ordered Casey to pay. [Mary Beth had incurred $160,154.54 to date in attorney's fees and requested an additional $150,000 to prepare for trial.] [Also,] Mary Beth requested that Casey be sanctioned under FC § 271 and FC § 2100 et seq. for his bad faith conduct and his failure to disclose assets and debts.

Mary Beth's motion for attorney's fees was [denied at the hearing] on February 6, 2009 and the family court declined to award any sanctions against Casey. In its written order on the motion filed March 11, 2009, the family court stated that it was denying Mary Beth's request for attorney's fees and costs based on disparity of income under FC § 2032, finding no basis for a further award of needs-based fees.

Prior to the written order being signed, Mary Beth filed a motion for reconsideration. In [denying the motion for reconsideration, the family court issued a written ruling making] 32 findings that placed much of the blame for the protracted litigation on Mary Beth, including that she had made excessive discovery requests. The ruling stated that Mary Beth had means with which to pay the attorney's fees, specifically, from her $ 5,000 monthly support or by executing a lien against her share of the community property. Mary Beth had given Bruder such a lien. The family court, however, ordered it expunged.

On March 26, 2009, Mary Beth filed a third and final motion seeking to secure an award of attorney's fees. Mary Beth's third motion again pointed out that (1) she had been a homemaker for over eight years prior to separation; (2) she had no income other than the temporary support; (3) her only asset was a 401k in the amount of about $ 30,000; and (4) her monthly expenses for herself and her children exceeded $ 5,900.

Casey filed an opposition to the third motion for attorney's fees, attacking the reasonableness of the requested fees. In its ruling on this third motion, the family court [found] that Mary Beth engaged in "pro-longed [sic] and protracted discovery efforts regarding issues which are far removed from the facts before the court." The family court denied the request for an award of attorney's fees and costs previously incurred, again stating the fees and costs "are grossly excessive and unreasonable."[H]owever, the family court did make an award of future attorney's fees to cover the costs through trial, including pending custody matters. The award was for $ 20,000, but was payable upon the conclusion of trial and was subject to a request by Casey to charge the amount toward Mary Beth's distributive share of community property.

On May 5, 2009, Mary Beth filed a notice of appeal of the three attorney's fees orders. On that same day, she filed an order to show cause regarding a stay of the proceedings in light of the filing of the notice of appeal. Casey opposed a stay.

After the May 21 hearing, the family court issued a written ruling denying the request for a stay, finding that none of the pending hearings or the trial was affected by the orders being appealed.

Mary Beth filed a petition for writ of supersedeas[4] in this court, seeking a stay of all matters pending before the family court. On July 31, 2009, this court granted the petition and issued a writ of supersedeas.

DISCUSSION
This appeal involves three orders. The written orders are dated (1) March 11, 2009, denying the initial request for attorney's fees and sanctions, (2) April 22, 2009, denying the request for reconsideration, and (3) April 13, 2009, denying the third motion, but awarding $ 20,000 for the balance of the case to be paid at the conclusion of trial.
Mary Beth contends the family court abused its discretion by (1) repeatedly refusing to examine the time records and declarations submitted by Bruder, (2) failing to make a needs analysis and considering the relative ability of the parties to pay, and (3) failing to consider the trial tactics of Casey and his counsel. In this portion of the opinion, we address the first two points.

The family court previously determined this was a complex case and there was a disparity of income between the parties. It had ordered Casey to pay attorney's fees and costs in the sum of $ 2,500 on Mary Beth's behalf on December 18, 2007. The April 14, 2008, order provided that Casey pay $ 20,000 to Bruder. Both orders specified that Casey was being ordered to pay attorney's fees on behalf of Mary Beth because of the disparity in income between the parties.

While the family court has considerable latitude in fashioning or denying an attorney's fees award, its decision must reflect an exercise of discretion and a consideration of the appropriate factors as set forth in FC §§ 2030 and 2032. In assessing one party's relative need and the other party's ability to pay, the family court may consider all evidence concerning the parties' current incomes, assets, and abilities. Further, in determining whether to award attorney's fees to one party, the family court may consider the other

---

[4] A writ commanding that the legal proceedings in the trial court be stayed or stopped.

party's trial tactics.

Here, the record discloses that the family court abused its discretion by affirmatively refusing and failing to exercise that discretion. The statement by the family court that it was not going to review the billing records submitted by Bruder before summarily denying the attorney's fees requested is sufficient grounds, by itself, to reverse the family court's decision. The family court's abuse of discretion also is apparent when one considers the family court's failure to make a needs-based analysis. This was a nearly 15-year marriage. Mary Beth had not been employed outside of the home for the last eight years of the marriage. She filed declarations pointing out that her sole source of income was the $ 5,000 in support she received. She did not have any investment income or assets. Casey had a higher income and an ownership interest in numerous businesses. The family court had an obligation to make a needs-based analysis before ruling; an obligation it failed to fulfill.

The record evidence before the family court at the time of the hearings on the attorney's fees requests established that there was a considerable disparity of income and assets between Mary Beth and Casey, a strong indication Mary Beth was entitled to a needs-based award of additional attorney's fees.

The public policy purpose behind FC §§ 2030 and 2032 is "'leveling the playing field' and permitting the lower-earning spouse to pay counsel and experts to litigate the issues in the same manner as the spouse with higher earnings." Attorney's fees, financial experts, other experts, witness fees, and other costs are all awardable. A spouse should not have to utilize support payments designed to pay living expenses to fund litigation in the dissolution proceeding.

In order to level the playing field, funds must be available to Mary Beth to pay for attorneys, other experts, and costs of litigation, and those funds must be available and accessible prior to the conclusion of the case. The matter will be remanded so that a judicial officer can undertake an analysis of the billings supporting the attorney's fees request and make a needs-based analysis.

In October 2007, Casey had been asked to disclose and characterize fully the assets and debts of the marriage by completing the schedule of income and assets and answering form interrogatories. Instead of making an accurate and full disclosure, Casey asserted there was a signed premarital agreement and claimed everything owned by the couple or earned by him during the marriage was his separate property. After Mary Beth incurred additional legal fees to address this allegation, the family court finally determined at a hearing, at which Casey and Harbottle did not appear, that no such agreement existed.

Casey engaged in bad faith conduct as it pertains to discovery and breached his fiduciary duty [by failing to disclose his] income and assets throughout the case.

The plain language of FC § 2107(c) required the family court to award Mary Beth attorney's fees by way of sanctions "in an amount sufficient to deter repetition of the conduct or comparable conduct." This, the family court failed to do.

On remand, the family court will be directed to award sanctions against Casey, payable to Mary Beth, pursuant to FC §§ 271 and 2107. When making the award, the family court shall consider Casey's dilatory tactics and lack of full fiduciary disclosure and the policy of imposing sanctions in an amount sufficient to deter future similar conduct.

> Mary Beth has asked that this case be assigned to a different judicial officer on remand. Casey contends such a claim by Mary Beth is "outrageous." We agree that an assignment to a different judicial officer is warranted.
>
> The March 11, April 13, and April 22, 2009, orders denying an award of attorney's fees and costs to Mary Beth are reversed. This case is remanded to the family court for further proceedings. On remand, this case shall be assigned to a different judicial officer. The new judicial officer shall analyze the attorney's fees requests and award Mary Beth attorney's fees and costs pursuant to FC §§ 271, 2107, 2030 and 2032 in an amount commensurate with the complexities of the case.

4. FC § 2107

As shown in *In re Marriage of Thorpe, supra*, the court must impose money sanctions if a party breaches his or her fiduciary duty by failing to comply with any of the disclosure of assets and liability provisions set forth in **FC § 2107**. Additionally, the court must impose any other remedy provided by law against the noncomplying party. The sanctions imposed under this code section must be in an amount sufficient to deter repetition of the conduct or comparable conduct, and must include reasonable attorney fees, costs incurred or both, unless the court finds that the noncomplying party acted with substantial justification or that other circumstances make the imposition of the sanction unjust. (See *In re Marriage of FELDMAN* (2007) 153 Cal.App.4th 1470 at p. 1479 where the court stated that **FC § 2107(c)** provides "that sanctions are to be imposed to effectuate compliance with the laws that require spouses to make disclosure to each other [and that] the statute is not aimed at redressing an actual injury.")

5. FC § 2255

FC § 2255 gives the court authority to make an attorney fee order in an annulment action for either a void or voidable marriage. (See Chapter 5 RE: Annulment, Dissolution & Legal Separation, *supra*.) However, the party requesting the attorney fees and costs must be innocent of fraud or wrongdoing in inducing or entering into the marriage and free from knowledge of the then existence of any prior marriage or other impediment to the contracting of the marriage for which a judgment of nullity is sought. (See *In re Marriage of TEJEDA* (2009) 179 Cal.App.4th 973, where the court stated that "the Legislature intended to treat 'guilty' and 'innocent' parties to a putative marriage differently.

In the words of one commentator, 'the fact that the Legislature limited support and attorney fee rights to the 'good faith' (innocent) spouse ... may be some indication it also intended only the putative spouse to be entitled to quasi-marital property rights.' (Hogoboom & King, Cal. Practice Guide: Family Law (The Rutter Group 2009) ¶ 19:62, p. 19-20 (rev. # 1, 2007).' Here, the Legislature singled out the 'innocent' party in providing for fees." *Id.* at p. 984.)

6. FC §§ 3027.1, 3120, 3121, 3150

FC § 3027.1 provides that if a false accusation of child abuse or neglect is made against another person in a child custody proceeding, the court may impose money sanctions, including reasonable attorney fees and costs, to the party against whom the false accusation was made. The false accusation must be made during a child custody proceeding, and the party making the accusation must have known that the accusation was false at the time that the accusation was made. When the false accusation is made, a court may order an investigation or order sanctions based upon other evidence presented to it. The money sanctions ordered must be reasonable and not exceed all costs incurred by the party accused as a direct result of defending the accusation. (See *In re MARRIAGE of DEPRE* (2005) 127 Cal.App.4th 1517 at p. 1527 where the court held that the statute requires that the false statement be made during the child custody proceeding, but the falsity of the statement does not have to be established during the child custody proceeding.)

In any proceeding pursuant to **FC § 3120**[5], and in any proceeding subsequent to the entry of a related judgment, the court must ensure that both parties have access to legal representation, including access early in the proceedings, to preserve each party's rights by ordering, if necessary, based on the income and needs assessments, one party to pay to the other party, or to the other party's attorney, whatever amount is reasonably necessary for attorney fees and for the cost of maintaining or defending the proceeding during the pendency of the proceeding. **FC § 3121(a)**.

FC § 3121(b) provides that when a request for attorney fees and costs is made, the court must make findings on whether an award of attorney fees and costs under this section is appropriate, whether there is a disparity in access to funds to retain counsel, and whether one party is able to pay for legal representation of both parties. If the findings demonstrate disparity in access and ability to pay, the court must make an order awarding attorney fees and costs. A party who lacks the financial ability to employ an attorney may request, as an unrepresented litigant, that the court order the other party, if that other party has the financial ability, to pay a reasonable amount to allow the unrepresented party to retain an attorney in a timely manner before proceedings in the matter go forward.

Attorney fees and costs pursuant to **FC § 3121(b)** may be awarded for legal services rendered and costs incurred before or after the commencement of the proceeding. The court must augment or modify the original award for attorney fees and costs as may be reasonably necessary for the prosecution or defense of a proceeding described in **FC § 3120**, or any proceeding related thereto, including after any

---

[5] FC § 3120 provides: "[w]ithout filing a petition for dissolution of marriage or legal separation of the parties, a spouse may bring an action for the exclusive custody of the children of the marriage. The court may, during the pendency of the action, or at the final hearing thereof or afterwards, make such order regarding the support, care, custody, education and control of the children of the marriage as may be just and in accordance with the natural rights of the parents and the best interests of the children. The order may be modified or terminated at any time thereafter as the natural rights of the parties and the best interest of the children may require."

Chapter 7: Attorney Fees & Limited Scope Representation

appeal has been concluded. **FC § 3121(b), (c)** and **(d)**.

An application for a temporary order making, augmenting or modifying an award of attorney fees, including a reasonable retainer to hire an attorney or costs or both, must be made by filing a *Request for Order (RFO)*. The court has fifteen (15) days to rule on the motion. **FC § 3121(e)**.

Additionally, an order made pursuant to this section may be made by an oral motion without notice in open court at the time of the hearing of the cause on the merits or at any time before entry of judgment against a party whose default has been entered. **FC § 3121(f)**.

If the court determines that it would be in the best interests of the minor child, the court may appoint private counsel to represent the interests of the child in a custody or visitation proceeding. **FC § 3150**.[6] When an attorney is appointed pursuant to this section, the appointed attorney is entitled to "receive a reasonable sum for compensation and expenses." **FC § 3153**.

In the case that follows, a divorce was begun, and an attorney was appointed to represent the two children. Thereafter, counsel was relieved without prejudice and without being paid pursuant to a stipulation. After one of the spouses was killed, the other spouse argued that the court no longer had jurisdiction to pay the appointed counsel.

> *In re Marriage of KENNETH and PAMELA B. LISI. PAMELA B. LISI, Appellant, v. PEARL FRANKLIN VOGEL et al., Respondents.*
> COURT OF APPEAL OF CALIFORNIA, SECOND APPELLATE DISTRICT, DIVISION FIVE
> 39 Cal.App.4th 1573
> October 26, 1995, Decided
> (*Marriage of Lisi*)
>
> On November 4, 1992, Kenneth Lisi filed a petition to dissolve his marriage to Pamela Lisi. A bitter battle developed over the custody of the parties' two minor children. Pursuant to FC § 3150, which authorizes the court to appoint private counsel to represent the interests of children in a custody proceeding, the court appointed respondent Pearl Franklin Vogel to represent the two children. Ms. Vogel retained Honey Kessler Amado to assist in the representation of the children.
>
> On October 22, 1993, the court relieved Ms. Vogel as counsel for the children pursuant to stipulation and without prejudice, subject to reappointment on motion of one of the parties prior to time of trial. The court further ordered that "reasonable attorney's fees for Ms. Vogel will be determined at time of trial. Such fees will be paid out of the proceeds of the sale of the family residence subject to allocation of her attorney's fees as to each parties' [sic] share."
>
> On October 31, 1993, Mrs. Lisi's mother shot Kenneth to death. A judgment of

---

[6] FC § 3151 discusses the rights and duties of appointed counsel.

dissolution had not been entered. Thereafter, on March 29, 1994, Ms. Vogel sought an order fixing the amount of her fees and apportioning the obligation between the community or the parties. Mrs. Lisi opposed the motion, contending that Mr. Lisi's death abated the action and deprived the court of jurisdiction to make the requested order. She also contested reasonableness of the fees requested. On July 22, 1994, the court awarded attorney's fees in the amount of $27,205 to Ms. Vogel and $3,500 to Ms. Amado. The order required the fees to be equally shared by Mrs. Lisi and the estate of Kenneth Lisi. Mrs. Lisi appeals the order, stating in her opening brief that the appeal presents a single issue "Did the court in the dissolution action err in exercising jurisdiction to award fees subsequent to the death of Mr. Lisi?"

Counsel for children appointed pursuant to FC § 3150 "shall receive a reasonable sum for compensation and expenses, the amount of which shall be determined by the court. . . . [T]his amount shall be paid by the parties in the proportions the court deems just." FC § 3153(a). If the parties together are financially unable to pay all or a portion of the cost of appointed counsel, the portion the parties are unable to pay shall be paid by the county. FC § 3150(b). This clear legislative directive that counsel's fees are to be paid, either by the parties or by the county, imposes a mandatory duty upon the court to award attorney's fees to such counsel and vests in the attorney the right to receive a "reasonable sum for compensation and expenses" at the time the order is made.

The order determining the right to attorney's fees was made prior to the death of Mr. Lisi, but the court postponed the determination of the amount of reasonable fees to the date of trial. Since the right to fees had been adjudicated before Mr. Lisi's death, the court retained jurisdiction after his death to determine the amount of fees and allocate payment between the parties

Here, Ms. Vogel's and Ms. Amado's rights to attorney's fees for representing the children vested prior to Mr. Lisi's death and became a property right. Even though the fee had not yet been fixed, the right to the fee had been established and the calculation of the amount of the fee by the court after Mr. Lisi's death was the enforcement of a vested property right, an act within the court's jurisdiction.

DISPOSITION
The judgment is affirmed.

7. FC § 3452

FC § 3452 pertains to actions under the Uniform Child Custody Jurisdiction and Enforcement Act (UCCJEA). Pursuant to this section, the court must award to the prevailing party, including a state, necessary and reasonable expenses incurred by or on behalf of the party, including costs, communication expenses, attorney fees, investigative fees, expenses for witnesses, travel expenses and child care during the course of the proceedings, unless the party from whom fees or expenses are sought establishes that the award would be clearly inappropriate. **FC § 3452.** (See *In re NADA R. v. ABDULAZIZ R.* (2001) 89 Cal.App.4th 1166 at pp. 1181-1182 where the court held that this section does not apply to juvenile dependency cases.)

Chapter 7: Attorney Fees & Limited Scope Representation

8. FC §§ 3557 and 3652

FC §§ 3557 and 3652 are listed under the heading of support. When there is a disparity in access to funds to retain counsel in an action to enforce an existing order for child or spousal support and one party is able to pay for legal representation for both parties, upon determining that an award of attorney fees and costs under this section is appropriate, the court must award reasonable attorney fees to a custodial parent or other person to whom payments should be made. **FC § 3557.**

When an order is made that modifies, terminates or sets aside a support order, the prevailing party may be awarded attorney fees and costs. This section does not apply as against a governmental agency. **FC § 3652.**

9. FC § 4324.5[7]

FC § 4324.5 pertains specifically to spousal support. In any proceeding for dissolution of marriage where there is a criminal conviction for a violent sexual felony perpetrated by one spouse against the other spouse and the *Petition* for dissolution is filed before five (5) years following the conviction and any time served in custody, on probation or on parole, an award of spousal support to the

---

[7] FC § 4324.5 was amended effective January 1, 2019. The added language is bolded. (a) In any proceeding for dissolution of marriage where there is a criminal conviction for a violent sexual **felony or a domestic violence felony** perpetrated by one spouse against the other spouse and the petition for dissolution is filed before five years following the conviction and any time served in custody, on probation, or on parole, the following shall apply:
(1) An award of spousal support to the convicted spouse from the injured spouse is prohibited.
(2) If economic circumstances warrant, the court shall order the attorney's fees and costs incurred by the parties to be paid from the community assets. The injured spouse shall not be required to pay any attorney's fees of the convicted spouse out of the injured spouse's separate property.
(3) At the request of the injured spouse, the date of separation, **as defined in Section 70,** shall be the date of the incident giving rise to the conviction, or earlier, if the court finds circumstances that justify an earlier date.
(4) The injured spouse shall be entitled to 100 percent of the community property interest in the retirement and pension benefits of the injured spouse.
(b) As used in this section, the following definitions apply:
(1) "Domestic violence felony" means a felony offense for an act of abuse, as described in Section 6203, perpetrated by one spouse against the other spouse.
(2) "Injured spouse" means the spouse who has been the subject of the violent sexual felony or domestic violence felony for which the other spouse was convicted.
(3) "Violent sexual felony" means those offenses described in paragraphs (3), (4), (5), (11), and (18) of subdivision (c) of Section 667.5 of the Penal Code.
(c) If a convicted spouse presents documented evidence of the convicted spouse's history as a victim of a violent sexual offense, as described in paragraphs (3), (4), (5), (11), and (18) of subdivision (c) of Section 667.5 of the Penal Code, or domestic violence, as defined in Section 6211, perpetrated by the other spouse, the court may determine, based on the facts of the particular case, that one or more of paragraphs (1) to (4), inclusive, of subdivision (a) do not apply .
(d) The changes made to this section by the bill that added this subdivision shall only apply to convictions that occur on or after January 1, 2019.

convicted spouse from the injured spouse is prohibited. The injured spouse shall not be required to pay any attorney fees of the convicted spouse out of the injured spouse's separate property where economic circumstances warrant, the court shall order the attorney fees and costs incurred by the parties to be paid from the community assets. FC § 4324.5.[8]

10. FC §§ 6344 and 6386

FC §§ 6344 and **6386** are codes under the **Prevention of Domestic Violence** sections. In the first of these two codes, **FC § 6344** provides that after notice and a hearing, the court may issue an order for the payment of attorney fees and costs of the prevailing party. In any action in which the petitioner is the prevailing party and cannot afford to pay for the attorney fees and costs, the court shall, if appropriate, based on the parties' respective abilities to pay, order that the respondent pay the petitioner's attorney fees and costs for commencing and maintaining the proceeding.

If the respondent is ordered to pay attorney fees and costs for the prevailing petitioner, the amount ordered must be determined based upon: **(1)** the respective incomes and needs of the parties, and **(2)** any factors affecting the parties' respective abilities to pay.

In the case that follows, the trial court awarded attorney fees and costs to the prevailing party in a domestic violence action, and the Appellate Court affirmed.

> ***HOLLY LOEFFLER, Plaintiff and Respondent, v. WILLIAM M. MEDINA,***
> ***Defendant and Appellant.***
> COURT OF APPEAL OF CALIFORNIA, FOURTH APPELLATE DISTRICT,
> DIVISION ONE
> 174 Cal.App.4th 1495
> June 18, 2009, Filed
> (*Loeffler v. Medina*)
>
> Holly Loeffler (Loeffler) and William Medina (Medina) began living together in 1995 in a home they purchased together in Jamul, California. Their relationship ended in 2001, and Loeffler remained in the house. In April 2001, based on Loeffler's allegations about Medina's behavior toward her, the trial court issued a restraining order pursuant to FC § 6344 restraining Medina from, among other things, contacting, harassing, threatening, or coming within 200 yards of Loeffler and her teenaged daughter. The domestic violence restraining order was to expire in April 2004.

---

[8] FC § 4324.5 was primarily enacted through the efforts of a San Diego woman, Crystal Harris. At her divorce trial, Ms. Harris was ordered to pay spousal support in the amount of one thousand dollars ($1,000.00) to her soon-to-be ex-husband, Sean Harris, and twenty-five thousand dollars ($25,000.00) in attorney fees to Mr. Harris's attorney. At the time this order was made, Mr. Harris was out on bail awaiting trial for the rape of Ms. Harris. Mr. Harris was later convicted and sentenced to six years in prison for his sexual assault on Ms. Harris. Ms. Harris went public with her story in an effort to change the law. Ms. Harris told her story to the judiciary committee of the California State Assembly and, with the help of Assemblywoman Toni Atkins, FC § 4324.5 was enacted and went into effect on January 1, 2013.

Chapter 7: Attorney Fees & Limited Scope Representation

[I]n April 2004, Loeffler applied for an extension of the restraining order. In support of her application, Loeffler submitted a declaration detailing the reasons she was concerned that Medina might harass or harm her if the restraining order was not renewed. [O]n June 23, 2004, the trial court ruled that the "restraining order is extended indefinitely. No expiration."

Three months later, on August 23, 2004, Medina filed an application for an order terminating the permanent restraining order. The trial court denied Medina's application to terminate the permanent restraining order. There is no indication that Medina appealed this order.

Almost two years later, on June 7, 2006, Medina filed another application to terminate the permanent restraining order. In support of the application, Medina declared that he [now]resided in Arizona, had recently married, had minimal contact with the San Diego area, and wanted the restraining order lifted because it was impacting his employment on government contracts and his possible future activity as a reserve law enforcement officer.

In the statement of decision, the trial court [denied Medina's request and] awarded Loeffler $ 25,000 in attorney's fees and $ 1,504.85 in costs. [Loeffler had sought an award of $ 45,842.50 in fees, costs of $ 2,934.85 and sanctions pursuant to FC § 271.] The trial court appears to have implicitly denied that request by not making any express finding that sanctions were warranted.

Medina filed a timely appeal from the order denying his application to terminate the restraining order and challenges the trial court's award of attorney's fees and costs to Loeffler. As a predicate for his argument, Medina assumes that the trial court made the award under FC § 271(a), which authorizes the court in a family law matter to award attorney's fees and costs "in the nature of a sanction" when the conduct of a party or attorney "frustrates the policy of the law to promote settlement of litigation."

However, as we interpret the trial court's statement of decision, it did not award fees and costs to Loeffler as a sanction under FC § 271. Instead, it awarded fees and costs to Loeffler pursuant to FC § 6344(a), which states that in connection with a proceeding concerning a domestic violence restraining order, "[a]fter notice and a hearing, the court may issue an order for the payment of attorney's fees and costs of the prevailing party."

Because FC § 6344(a) provides authority for the trial court to award attorney's fees and costs to a party who prevails in defeating an application to terminate a domestic violence restraining order—and Loeffler prevailed in defeating Medina's application—we reject Medina's argument that there was no evidentiary basis for the attorney fee and costs award. [In a footnote, the Appellate Court added, we note that the availability of a fee award under FC § 6344(a) serves to dissuade a restrained party from continuing his or her harassing behavior by filing unwarranted applications to terminate the restraining order.]

Medina also argues that the award of fees and costs to Loeffler "shocks the conscience" because of its amount. In support of his argument, Medina claims that he purportedly spent only $ 5,000 to litigate the case, while Loeffler spent approximately $ 50,000.

Loeffler submitted detailed billing records from her attorney showing how each of the items of fees and costs related to this litigation. Medina [did not prove that] any specific

> item of fees or costs was not reasonably incurred by Loeffler. Accordingly, Medina has not met his burden to establish that the trial court abused its discretion in that the award was manifestly excessive in the circumstances.
>
> Further, in determining that the trial court did not abuse its discretion, we find it significant that that the trial court reduced Loeffler's request of $ 45,842.50 in fees and $ 2,934.85 in costs almost in half by awarding only $ 25,000 in fees and $ 1,504.85 in costs. The award granted was significantly reduced from the original request. Thus, it clearly appears that the trial court exercised its discretion. In these circumstances, we cannot conclude that the award of attorney's fees shocks the conscience or suggests that passion and prejudice had a part in it.
>
> The trial court's order is affirmed.

FC § 6386, provides that the court may order the respondent to pay reasonable attorney fees and costs incurred by the petitioner to enforce the terms of a protective order.

11. FC §§ 7605 and 7640

FC §§ 7605 and 7640, fall under the Uniform Parentage Act. **FC § 7605(a)** provides that in any proceeding to establish physical or legal custody of a child or a visitation and in any proceeding subsequent to entry of a related judgment, the court shall ensure that each party has access to legal representation to preserve each party's rights by ordering, if necessary, based on the income and needs assessments, one party, except a government entity, to pay to the other party or the other party's attorney, whatever amount is reasonably necessary for attorney fees and for the cost of maintaining or defending the proceeding during the pendency of the proceeding.

FC § 7605(b) provides that when a request for attorney fees and costs is made the court shall make findings on whether an award of attorney fees and costs is appropriate, whether there is a disparity in access to funds to retain counsel and whether one party is able to pay for legal representation of both parties. If the findings demonstrate disparity in access and ability to pay, the court shall make an order awarding attorney fees and costs. A party who lacks the financial ability to hire an attorney may request, as an in pro per litigant, that the court order the other party, if that other party has the financial ability, to pay a reasonable amount to allow the unrepresented party to retain an attorney in a timely manner before proceedings in the matter go forward.

Attorney fees and costs within this section may be awarded for legal services rendered or costs incurred before or after the commencement of the proceeding. **FC § 7605(c).**

The court must augment or modify the original award for attorney fees and costs as may be reasonably necessary for the prosecution or defense of a proceeding described in subdivision (a), or any proceeding related thereto, including after any

Chapter 7: Attorney Fees & Limited Scope Representation

appeal has been concluded. **FC § 7605(d)**.

Except where an oral motion is made in open court, an application for a temporary order making, augmenting or modifying an award of attorney fees, including a reasonable retainer to hire an attorney or costs or both, shall be made by motion with notice to the opposing party. The court must rule on an application for fees under this section within fifteen (15) days of the hearing on the motion or order to show cause. **FC § 7605(e)**.

An order made pursuant to an oral motion made in open court without notice must be made at the time of the hearing of the cause on the merits or any time before entry of judgment against a party whose default has been entered. **FC § 7605(f)**.

The second of the two sections under the Uniform Parentage Act, **FC § 7640**, provides that the court may order reasonable fees of counsel, experts, the child's guardian ad litem and other costs of the action and pretrial proceedings, including blood tests, to be paid by the parties, excluding any governmental entity, in proportions and at times determined by the court.

The most commonly used Family Codes for attorney fees are discussed above. Of the twenty-four (24) code sections[9] that were not discussed, some are addressed in other chapters.

Attorney Fees in Bankruptcy Actions

11 U.S.C.S. § 523(a)(5), provides that any debt to a spouse, former spouse or child of the debtor for alimony to, maintenance for or support of such spouse or child, in connection with a separation agreement, divorce decree or other order of a court is nondischargeable in bankruptcy.

Additionally, if an attorney fees award was ordered and that award was essential to a spouse's ability to sue or defend a matrimonial action, it was a necessary payment, which constitutes alimony or support. As such, the attorney fees award is not dischargeable in bankruptcy. *In re AUER* (1982) 22 B.R. 274 at p. 275. (See also *In re HORNER* (1991) 125 B.R. 458, where the court found that Ms. Overton's attorney fees were nondischargeable in bankruptcy because "without such an award Ms. Overton would have been unable to obtain or pay for legal representation in the pursuit of her support claims through the judicial labyrinth. Her attorney obtained an order awarding her spousal maintenance and support. The legal fees Ms. Overton incurred were necessary to her support and the court's order imposing payment upon Debtor was actually in the nature of support and maintenance within the meaning of 11 U.S.C. § 523(a)(5)(B)." *Id.* at p. 462-463.)

---

[9] They are: FC §§ 272, 273, 916, 1101, 1102, 2033, 2034, 2040, 2330.5, 2334, 3111, 3427, 3428, 3448, 4002, 4303, 4901, 4919, 5615, 6602, 8638, 8800, 8812 and 17803.

In *In re ROSEN* (1999) 232 B.R. 284 Mr. and Mrs. Rosen divorced in 1988. When the divorce judgment was entered, Mr. Rosen was ordered to pay Mrs. Rosen's attorney fees in the amount of $109, 216.27. In 1991, Mr. Rosen filed for a Chapter 7 bankruptcy seeking to have the attorney fees debt discharged. The court held that Mrs. Rosen:

> was not able to support herself sufficiently to pay her own attorneys' fees and therefore the state court's orders provided for the payment of the fees. Without the payment of such fees, she would not have been able to continue to have adequate representation in the divorce proceedings. The court found that the awards of legal fees were clearly necessary for Mrs. Rosen to defend and maintain her matrimonial action. Since the fee awards were in the nature of support and maintenance, they were nondischargeable pursuant to 11 U.S.C.S. § 523(a)(5). *Id.* at 293.

Thus, to make an attorney fee award that is not dischargeable in bankruptcy, the award must appear as part of an order for support. Additionally, it is more likely to be nondischargeable if it is labeled **for support** or **as additional support**.

Finally, pursuant to **FC § 2030(d)**, it is within a court's discretion to award attorney fees pendente lite where a ex-husband fraudulently transferred community property to his second wife, who was joined into the dissolution action. A court has the authority to award attorney fees "without regard to whether the moving party demonstrated a likelihood of success on the merits or whether there was a prima facie case linking the second wife to issues in the proceeding." *In re Marriage of BENDETTI* (2013) 214 Cal.App.4th 863 at p. 871.

Limited Scope Representation

1. Definition and Explanation of "Limited Scope Representation"

Limited scope representation is a relationship between an attorney and a person seeking legal services in which they have agreed that the scope of the legal services will be limited to specific tasks that the attorney will perform for the person. **CRC Rule 3.35.** Limited scope representation is sometimes called **unbundling**.

There are two types of limited scope representation. They are:
(1) Noticed representation, Rule 3.36, provides procedures for cases in which an attorney and a party notify the court and other parties of the limited scope representation.
(2) Undisclosed representation, Rule 3.37, applies to cases in which the limited scope representation is not disclosed. **CRC Rule 3.36.**

2. Procedures and Forms

Pursuant to **CRC Rule 3.36**, a party and an attorney may provide notice of their agreement to limited scope representation by serving and filing a *Notice of Limited Scope Representation* (form *MC-950*).

After the notice is received and until either a substitution of attorney or an order to be relieved as attorney is filed and served, papers in the case must be served on both the attorney providing the limited scope representation and the client.

An attorney who has completed the tasks specified in the *Notice of Limited Scope Representation* (form *MC-950*) may use the procedures in this rule to request that he or she be relieved as attorney in cases in which the attorney has appeared before the court as an attorney of record and the client has not signed a *Substitution of Attorney—Civil* (form *MC-050*). **CRC Rule 5.425.**

In a civil proceeding, an attorney who contracts with a client to draft or assist in drafting legal documents, but not to make an appearance in the case, is not required to disclose within the text of the documents that he or she was involved in preparing the documents. This rule does not apply to an attorney who has made a general appearance in a case. If a litigant seeks a court order for attorney fees incurred as a result of document preparation, the litigant must disclose to the court information required for a proper determination of the attorney fees, including:

(1) The name of the attorney who assisted in the preparation of the documents;
(2) The time involved or other basis for billing;
(3) The tasks performed; and
(4) The amount billed. **CFC Rule 3.37.**

An application to be relieved as attorney on completion of limited scope representation under **CCP § 284(2)** must be directed to the client and made on the *Application to Be Relieved as Counsel Upon Completion of Limited Scope Representation* (form *FL-955*).

The application to be relieved as attorney must be filed with the court and served on the client and on all other parties or attorneys for parties in the case. The client must also be served with a blank *Objection to Application to Be Relieved as Counsel on Completion of Limited Scope Representation* (form *FL-956*).

If no objection is served and filed with the court within fifteen (15) days from the date that the *Application to Be Relieved as Counsel on Completion of Limited Scope Representation* (form *FL-955*) is served on the client, the attorney making the application must file an updated form *FL-955* indicating the lack of objection, along with a proposed *Order on Application to Be Relieved as Counsel on Completion of Limited Scope Representation* (form *FL-958*). The clerk must then forward the order for judicial signature.

If an objection to the application is served and filed within fifteen (15) days, the clerk must set a hearing date on the *Objection to Application to Be Relieved as Counsel on Completion of Limited Scope Representation* (form *FL-956*). The hearing must be scheduled no later than twenty-five (25) days from the date the objection is filed. The clerk must send the notice of the hearing to the parties and the attorney.

If no objection is served and filed, and the proposed order is signed, the attorney who filed the *Application to Be Relieved as Counsel on Completion of Limited Scope Representation* (form *FL-955*) must serve a copy of the signed order on the client and on all parties or the attorneys for all parties who have appeared in the case. The court may delay the effective date of the order relieving the attorney until proof of service of a copy of the signed order on the client has been filed with the court.

In a family law proceeding, an attorney who contracts with a client to draft or assist in drafting legal documents, but does not make an appearance in the case, is not required to disclose within the text of the document that he or she was involved in preparing the documents.

3. Requesting Attorney Fees

If a litigant seeks a court order for attorney fees incurred as a result of document preparation, the litigant must disclose to the court information required for a proper determination of attorney fees, including the name of the attorney who assisted in the preparation of the documents, the time involved or other basis for billing, the tasks performed and the amount billed.

Chapter 7: Attorney Fees & Limited Scope Representation

CRC Rule 5.427 applies to attorney fees and costs based on financial need, as described in **FC §§ 2030, 2032, 3121, 3557, 7605**. **CRC Rule 5.427** provides that to request attorney fees and costs, a party must complete, file and serve the following documents:

(1) *Request for Order* (form *FL-300)*;
(2) Request for *Attorney's Fees and Costs Attachment* (form *FL-319*) or a comparable declaration that addresses the factors covered in form *FL-319*;
(3) A current *Income and Expense Declaration* (form *FL-150*);
(4) A personal declaration in support of the request for attorney fees and costs, either using *Supporting Declaration for Attorney's Fees and Costs Attachment* (form *FL-158*) or a comparable declaration that addresses the factors covered in form *FL-158*; and
(5) Any other papers relevant to the relief requested.

The party requesting attorney fees and costs must provide the court with sufficient information about the attorney hourly billing rate; the nature of the litigation; the attorney experience in the particular type of work demanded; the fees and costs incurred or anticipated; and why the requested fees and costs are just, necessary and reasonable.

4. Responding to a Request for Attorney Fees

To respond to the request for attorney fees and costs, a party must complete, file and serve the following documents:

(1) *Responsive Declaration to Request for Order* (form *FL-320*);
(2) A current *Income and Expense Declaration* (form *FL-150*);
(3) A personal declaration responding to the request for attorney fees and costs, either using *Supporting Declaration for Attorney's Fees and Costs Attachment* (form *FL-158*) or a comparable declaration that addresses the factors covered in form *FL-158*; and
(4) Any other papers relevant to the relief requested.

Pursuant to **CRC Rule 5.427**, in making a request for attorney fees and costs, a party must include an *Attorney's Fees and Costs Attachment* (form *FL-319*) or a comparable declaration that addresses the factors covered in form *FL-319*. Accordingly, the *FL-319* is not a mandatory form, as the case below demonstrates.

In re Marriage of LINDA and NORMAN SHARPLES. LINDA SHARPLES, Appellant, v. NORMAN SHARPLES, Respondent.
COURT OF APPEAL OF CALIFORNIA, FOURTH APPELLATE DISTRICT, DIVISION TWO
223 Cal.App.4th 160; 166 Cal.Rptr.3d 818
January 22, 2014, Opinion Filed
(*Marriage of Sharples*)

Wife filed an order to show cause (OSC) seeking modification of spousal support and an order to pay $20,000 for attorney fees and $10,000 for expert accounting fees. The OSC was supported by a memorandum of points and authorities, Wife's declaration, a declaration by Wife's counsel, and an income and expense declaration. According to Wife, Husband was the chief executive officer of Copan Diagnostics, Inc. (Copan), and had income in 2010 of $855,850. Wife was employed at Copan and made $700 per month. However, she believed Husband was trying to force her out of the company and she would soon have no income. She had $42,000 in assets and average monthly expenses of approximately $9,700. In his declaration, Wife's counsel set forth his qualifications as a certified family law specialist, his billing rates, and the need to retain the services of an accountant.

Husband opposed the OSC. He stated he had been giving Wife $3,000 per month and she would receive a portion of his bonus income. He also stated he had provided Wife's attorney with $10,000 for Wife's attorney fees. Wife's request that he pay more, he asserted, was unreasonable and there was no need for an accounting expert in this case. He argued that each side should pay for its own attorneys and experts. Husband did not assert there was any procedural defect in Wife's OSC.

Prior to the hearing on the OSC, Wife's attorney filed an amended declaration and an updated income and expense declaration. Counsel stated that this case had become more complicated because Husband failed to respond to discovery and his business was objecting to a subpoena, necessitating a motion to compel. The amounts sought for attorney fees and expert fees were increased to $30,000 and $20,000, respectively. The new income and expense declaration indicated that Wife had no income and that Husband's income was estimated to be $55,429 per month. Wife's assets had been reduced to $25,000 and her monthly expenses had increased to $9,950.

At the hearing on the OSC, the court stated it had read the documents that had been filed regarding the matter. [The court then stated that the family law form FL-319 was not filed], which is mandatory for you to be able to recover attorney's fees, so your request for attorney's fees is denied. The court made no other findings. The court's minute order regarding the hearing stated: "Motion for attorney fees (form 319 not filed) is denied." No other reasons were given.

DISCUSSION
Wife argues the trial court erred by failing to exercise its discretion with respect to the OSC and denying her request solely because of the erroneous conclusion that form FL-319 was mandatory. We agree.

Cal. Rules of Court, former rule 5.93(a) (hereafter former rule 5.93) was in effect at the time Wife filed her OSC and when the matter was heard. The rule provided that to request attorney's fees and costs, a party must complete and file a "Request for Attorney's Fees and Costs Attachment (form FL-319) or a comparable declaration that addresses the factors covered in form FL-319.

Under the plain language of former rule 5.93, a party seeking attorney fees and costs under section 2030 must file and serve either form FL-319 or a comparable declaration. Although filing form FL-319 or a comparable declaration is mandatory, neither is mandatory if the other is filed. Stated differently, the moving party has the option of filing form FL-319 or a comparable declaration.
A list of Judicial Council forms is included in an appendix to the California Rules of Court. The forms designated in the appendix with an asterisk (*) are "mandatory" forms; those without the asterisk are "optional." (Rules 1.31(b), 1.35(b).) Form FL-319 bears the

Chapter 7: Attorney Fees & Limited Scope Representation

words, "Form Approved for Optional Use" and is listed in the appendix to the rules without an asterisk. (Cal. Rules of Court, appen. A.)

The court rules and form FL-319 are unambiguous: The form is optional in the sense that it need not be filed if the moving party files a "comparable declaration." Here, there is no dispute that the declarations provided by Wife and her counsel provided the substance of what is called for in form FL-319; i.e., they are comparable to form FL-319. Therefore, the court erred in concluding that form FL-319 was mandatory.

It is also clear from our record that the denial of the OSC was based on the court's mistaken understanding that form FL-319 was mandatory and that the court did not consider the OSC on its merits. The only finding the court made was that Wife failed to file form FL-319, and the only explanation of its ruling is that it did "not see anywhere a family law form 319, which is mandatory for you to be able to recover attorney's fees."

Because the court based its denial of the OSC on an incorrect determination that form FL-319 was mandatory and did not exercise its discretion in considering the merits of the OSC, the order issued on May 29, 2012, denying to wife attorney fees and costs is reversed.

CHART 4: Family Code Attorney Fee Award Authority

Division/Part	Family Code	Case Example	RE:
General Provisions Attorney Fees	§ 270	ALICIA R. v. TIMOTHY M. (1994) 29 Cal.App.4th 1232	Ability to Pay
General Provisions Attorney Fees	§§ 271, 274	PARKER v. HARBERT (2012) 212 Cal.App.4th 1172 MARRIAGE of THARP (2010) 188 Cal.App.4th 1295	Sanctions for Frustration of Litigation/Delay
Nullity, Dissolution, Legal Separation Jurisdiction	§ 2010	MARRIAGE of GUACSH (2011) 201 Cal.App.4th 942	Authority to Award Atty Fees
Nullity, Dissolution, Legal Separation General Provisions	§§ 2030, 2031, 2032	MARRIAGE of THARP (2010) 188 Cal.App.4th 1295	Equal Access to Representation
Nullity, Dissolution, Legal Separation Disclosure	§ 2107	MARRIAGE of FELDMAN (2007) 153 Cal.App.4th 1470	Mandatory Money Sanction for Noncompliance
Nullity, Dissolution, Legal Separation	§ 2255	MARRIAGE of TEJEDA (2009) 179 Cal.App.4th 973	Innocent Party Atty Fees Award
Nullity, Dissolution, Legal Separation	§ 3027.1	ROBERT J. v. CATHERINE D. (2009) 171 Cal.App.4th 1500	Child Abuse Allegations Atty Fees/Sanctions
Custody of Children "Best Interests"	§ 3150	MARRIAGE of LISI (1995) 39 Cal.App.4th 1573	Appt. of Counsel to Represent Child
Custody of Children UCCJEA	§ 3452	IN RE NADA R. (2001) 89 Cal.App.4th 1166	Prevailing Party Reasonable Atty Fees
Support/Definitions General Provisions	§ 3557	MARRIAGE of CORONA (2009) 172 Cal.App.4th 1205	Atty Fee Awards for Disparity of Income
Support Modifications	§ 3652	MARRIAGE of LURIE (1995) 33 Cal.App.4th 658	Prevailing Party Modifications to Support
Support Spousal Support	§ 4324.5	MARRIAGE of PRIEM (2013) 214 Cal.App.4th 505	No Spousal Support, No Atty fees
Domestic Violence Issuance of Orders	§ 6344	LOEFFLER v. MEDINA (2009) 174 Cal.App.4th 1495	Atty Fees/Costs Prevailing Party
Domestic Violence Protection Orders	§ 6386	Restates former CCP § 553 no change; case with CCP § 553: HENDERSON v. DRAKE (1955) 134 Cal.App.2d 145	Atty Fees for Enforcement of Order
Parent and Child Uniform Parentage Act	§ 7605	KEVIN Q. v. LAUREN W. (2011) 195 Cal.App.4th 633	Equal Access to Representation
Parent and Child Uniform Parentage Act	§ 7640	BANNING v. NEWDOW (2004) 119 Cal.App.4th 438 KEVIN Q. v. LAUREN W (2001) 195 Cal.App.4th 633	Reasonable Atty Fees Determination of Parent © 2019 LW Greenberg

Chapter 7: Attorney Fees & Limited Scope Representation

EDUCATIONAL EXERCISES

I. DISCUSSION QUESTIONS

1. If both parties in a dissolution matter are employed, can a court order one party to pay attorney fees to the other party's attorney? Explain.
2. List four Family Code sections that give the court authority to award attorney fees in dissolution matters.
3. Can a judge award attorney fees to the other party in a family law matter without a request being made by either party?
4. What should a court consider before making an attorney's fee order?
5. What is limited scope representation?

II. NAME THAT CASE

For each of the summaries below, name the case.

1. A child was conceived and born to R. S. was present at the hospital when the child was born and was named as the father on all hospital records. R. signed the child's birth certificate, stating that S. was the father. R. told S. that he was not biologically related to the minor child. Prior thereto R. had by statements and conduct induced S. to believe he was the child's father and the child knew S. as her father. S. agreed to have a blood test to determine whether he was the child's father. He was not. R. had known M. since 1983 and they began having an affair in 1989. On August 12, 1993, she filed a complaint against M. to establish he was the biological father of the child and for child support. She also filed an order to show cause for child support, attorney fees and costs. **Name that case**

2. M. filed an answer to the complaint denying he was parent of the child and asserted that pursuant to Evidence Code § 621, a man other than M. was the father of the child. At the hearing on the order to show cause, the court determined that it would be a travesty to employ the conclusive presumption of parentage as provided in Evidence Code § 621 and ordered the parties to take part in DNA tests. These tests established that M. was the biological father of the child and M., based on these results, admitted he was the child's biological father. The superior court so found and ordered M. to pay a contributive share of attorney fees of $ 2,500 to S.'s attorney and $ 9,500 to R.'s attorney. **Name that case**

3. F initiated contempt proceedings against M. F claimed M willfully violated both court orders by, among other things (1) refusing to bring his minor son to visit him while he was in prison; (2) refusing to give him access to their son's medical records; and (3) failing to help their son take "the full course of medication for his poison oak medical problem." The court issued a detailed 30-page statement of decision examining the evidence offered in support of the contempt allegations and concluding it did not establish M was guilty beyond a reasonable doubt. The court also imposed $92,000 in attorney's fees and costs as sanctions pursuant to FC § 271.

Here, there can be no dispute F's conduct delayed the resolution of various issues relating to child custody and increased litigation costs. F's conduct also wasted the court and the parties' time. The court did not abuse its discretion by imposing sanctions pursuant to FC § 271. As we have already stated, FC § 271 does not require the conduct be frivolous or taken solely for the purpose of delay. **Name that case**

Chapter 7: Attorney Fees & Limited Scope Representation

3. H filed for dissolution. H stated in the petition that there was an antenuptial agreement signed by both parties and counsel, which confirmed that all property owned by H was his separate property and all income of H's before, during, and after the marriage was his separate property. No schedule of assets and debts was included. W requested a contribution toward her attorney fees. The family court made a temporary order of family support in the amount of $ 5,000 payable by H to W. H was ordered to pay $ 2,500 to W's attorney based on disparity of income and to pay $ 2,500 for an "accounting evaluation."

H failed to respond to discovery and pursuant to a motion to compel, directed H to pay $ 1,500 in attorney's fees to W's counsel as a sanction. W filed an order to show cause because H still failed to comply with the discovery order. At the bifurcated trial on the premarital agreement, H and his attorney did not show up. Instead a letter via facsimile to the family court stating that there was no executed premarital agreement. Thereafter, the family court considered denied W's request for attorney's fees and sanctions. W again requested attorney's fees, forensic accounting fees, and for H's bad faith conduct and his failure to disclose assets and debts. W's motion was denied. W filed a third and final motion seeking to secure an award of attorney's fees. H opposed. The family court awarded $20,000, but was payable upon the conclusion of trial.

On appeal the court stated that H engaged in bad faith conduct as it pertains to discovery and breached his fiduciary duty by failing to disclose his income and assets throughout the case. And that the family court failed to order attorney's fees by way of sanctions in an amount sufficient to deter repetition of the conduct or comparable conduct. The case was remanded, and it ordered that a different judicial officer preside. **Name that case**

4. W's mother killed H. Counsel appointed by the court sought an order fixing the amount of her fees and apportioning the obligation between the community or the parties. W opposed the motion, contending that H's death abated the action and deprived the court of jurisdiction to make the requested order. The order determining the right to attorney's fees was made prior to the death of H, but the court postponed the determination of the amount of reasonable fees to the date of trial. Since the right to fees had been adjudicated before H's death, the court retained jurisdiction after his death to determine the amount of fees and allocate payment between the parties. The court said that even though the fee had not yet been fixed, the right to the fee had been established and the calculation of the amount of the fee by the court after H's death was the enforcement of a vested property right, an act within the court's jurisdiction. **Name that case**

5. The victim of domestic violence applied for an extension of the restraining order. In support of her application, the victim submitted a declaration detailing the reasons she was concerned that the abuser might harass or harm her if the restraining order was not renewed. The restraining order was renewed. The victim requested attorney fees. The trial court awarded $ 25,000 in attorney's fees and $ 1,504.85 in costs. [the request was for $45,842.50 in fees, costs of $ 2,934.85]. The abuser appealed arguing that the award of fees and costs "shocks the conscience" because of its amount. The appellate court affirmed stating that they did not agree that the award of attorney's fees shocks the conscience. **Name that case**

CHAPTER 8: Initial Forms, Initial Filing & Checkboxes

In Brief...

INITIAL FORMS INCLUDE:

The *Petition* (*FL-100*).
- A *FL-100* must be used to request a dissolution, legal separation, annulment or domestic partnership. **CRC Rule 5.60.**
- The party filing the initial paperwork is the petitioner, and the other party or responding party is the respondent. **CRC Rule 5.16.**
- The *Petition* provides the petitioner's facts and story.
- Judicial Council form *FL-100* is a mandatory use form.

The *Response* (*FL-120*).
- The responding party must use the *FL-120* to respond to the *Petition*.
- The *Response* provides respondent's facts and respondent's side of the story.
- The paralegal must not copy the *Petition* but set forth respondent's information/facts.
- The *Response* must be filed and served on the petitioner within 30 days of the date that the respondent was served with the *Petition* and *Summons* in order to avoid a default. **FC § 2020.**

The *Summons* (*Family Law*) (*FL-110*).
- The *Summons* alerts the respondent that an action has been filed there are 30 days to answer.
- In a dissolution, legal separation or nullity, the clerk must issue a *Summons* that includes the **Standard Family Law Restraining Orders**. **FC § 233.**
- The **Standard Family Law Restraining Orders** on the back of the *Summons* are to maintain the status quo during the divorce proceedings.
- The **Standard Family Law Restraining Orders** are enforceable within CA by any law enforcement agency that has received notice of this paperwork. **FC § 232.**
- The **Standard Family Law Restraining Orders** take affect for the petitioner when the petitioner signs the *Petition,* for the respondent when the respondent is served with *Petition* and *Summons*.

The *Uniform Child Custody Jurisdiction and Enforcement Act* UCCJEA(*FL-105*) form:
- If children of the marriage, must be completed & served with *FL-100*, *FL-110*. **CRC Rule 5.52.**
- The respondent must also complete, file and serve upon the petitioner (usually with FL-120).

***Income and Expense Declaration* (*FL-150*):**
- If financial relief is requested, the *Income and Expense Declaration* must be completed and filed.

Chapter 8: Initial Forms, Initial Filing & Checkboxes

> - The *FL-150* provides income information upon which the court relies to make court orders.
> - Income tax returns are not attached but must be brought to court to provide income information.
>
> **FILING PAPERWORK WITH THE COURT**
> - All moving/supporting papers must be filed pursuant to **CCP § 1005.**
> - No paper may be rejected for filing because it was untimely submitted, **CRC Rule 3.1300.**
> - Filing fees must be paid at the time the papers are filed with the court.
> - The amount of the filing fee is established by **Government Code § 70670.**
> - If a party cannot afford to file an action, a fee waiver may be requested, **CRC Rule 5.41.**
> - A party is not required to file a new fee waiver application for an appeal, **CRC Rule 8.818.**
> - At judgment, the court may order either party to pay the waived fees, **CRC Rule 5.45.**
>
> **CHECKBOXES:**
> - Not checking a box may mean a client will not receive the relief that he or she needs or desires.
> - When an **Other Relief** checkbox is checked, an explanation of the relief sought by checking the box must be clear enough for a responding party to adequately respond to the claim.
> - Attorney fees box does not always have to be checked providing all parties have been noticed of request for attorney fees.
>
> **CHART 5: Initial Judicial Council Forms**

Introduction

There are forms for almost every action and court order in family law. This chapter discusses the initial forms that must be completed and filed to begin a family law case. It further discusses the importance of correctly completing these forms and ensuring that the right checkboxes are marked.

Definitions in the Rules of Court

CRC Rule 5.2 provides that in any action under the Family Code, the following definitions apply:

> (1) "Family Code" means that code enacted by chapter 162 of the Statutes of 1992 and any subsequent amendments to that code.
> (2) "Action" is also known as a lawsuit, a case, or a demand brought in a court of law to defend or enforce a right, prevent or remedy a harm, or punish a crime. It includes all the proceedings in which a party requests orders that are available in the lawsuit.
> (3) "Proceeding" is a court hearing in an action under the Family Code, including a

Chapter 8: Initial Forms, Initial Filing & Checkboxes

> hearing that relates to the dissolution or nullity of a marriage or domestic partnership, legal separation, custody and support of minor children, a parent and child relationship, adoptions, local child support agency actions under the Family Code, contempt proceedings relating to family law or local child support agency matters, and any action filed under the Domestic Violence Prevention Act, Uniform Parentage Act, Uniform Child Custody Jurisdiction and Enforcement Act, Indian Child Welfare Act, or Uniform Interstate Family Support Act.
> (4) "Dissolution" is the legal term used for "divorce." "Divorce" commonly refers to a marriage that is legally ended.
> (5) "Attorney" means a member of the State Bar of California. "Counsel" means an attorney.
> (6) "Party" is a person appearing in an action. Parties include both self-represented persons and persons represented by an attorney of record. Any designation of a party encompasses the party's attorney of record, including "party," "petitioner," "plaintiff," "People of the State of California," "applicant," "defendant," "respondent," "other parent," "other parent/party," "protected person," and "restrained person."
> (7) "Best interest of the child" is described in FC § 3011.
> (8) "Parenting time," "visitation," and "visitation (parenting time)" refer to how parents share time with their children.
> (9) "Property" includes assets and obligations.
> (10) "Local rule" means every rule, regulation, order, policy, form, or standard of general application adopted by a court to govern practice and procedure in that court.
> (c) The rules in this division apply to every action and proceeding to which the Family Code applies and, unless these rules elsewhere explicitly make them applicable, do not apply to any other action or proceeding that is not found in the Family Code.
> (d) Except as otherwise provided in these rules, all provisions of law applicable to civil actions generally apply to a proceeding under the Family Code if they would otherwise apply to such proceeding without reference to this rule. To the extent that these rules conflict with provisions in other statutes or rules, these rules prevail.
> (e) In any action under the Family Code that is not considered a "proceeding" as defined in (b), all provisions of law applicable to civil actions generally apply. Such an action must be commenced by filing an appropriate petition, and the respondent must file an appropriate response within 30 days after service of the summons and a copy of the petition.
> (f) The time within which any act is permitted or required to be done by a party under these rules may be extended by the court upon such terms as may be just.
> (g) In the exercise of the court's jurisdiction under the Family Code, if the course of proceeding is not specifically indicated by statute or these rules, any suitable process or mode of proceeding may be adopted by the court that is consistent with the spirit of the Family Code and these rules.

CRC Rule 1.5 provides:

> (a) The rules and standards of the California Rules of Court must be liberally construed to ensure the just and speedy determination of the proceedings that they govern.
> (b) As used in the rules and standards:
> (1) "Must" is mandatory;
> (2) "May" is permissive;
> (3) "May not" means not permitted to;
> (4) "Will" expresses a future contingency or predicts action by a court or person in the ordinary course of events, but does not signify a mandatory duty; and

> **(5)** "Should" expresses a preference or a nonbinding recommendation.
> **(c)** Standards are guidelines or goals recommended by the Judicial Council. The nonbinding nature of standards is indicated by the use of "should" in the standards instead of the mandatory "must" used in the rules.
> **(d)** In the rules:
> **(1)** Each tense (past, present, or future) includes the others;
> **(2)** Each gender (masculine, feminine, or neuter) includes the others; and
> **(3)** Each number (singular or plural) includes the other.

All forms adopted or approved by the Judicial Council for use in any proceeding under the Family Code are adopted as rules of court under the authority of **FC § 211, article VI, section 6** of the **California Constitution**.

Mandatory forms are Judicial Council forms prescribed under **Government Code § 68511**. Each mandatory Judicial Council form is identified as mandatory by an asterisk (*) on the list of Judicial Council forms in Appendix A to the California Rules of Court. The list is available on the California Courts website at *www.courts.ca.gov/forms*. Courts may not require that any mandatory Judicial Council form be submitted on any color of paper other than white.

Finally, it should be noted that an otherwise legally sufficient **court order** for which there is a mandatory Judicial Council form is not invalid or unenforceable because the order is not prepared on a Judicial Council form or the correct Judicial Council form. **CRC Rule 1.31**.

Initial Forms

1. The *Petition* (Form *FL-100*)

Before starting any family law case, the residency requirements for that particular action should be considered. If a party desires a dissolution, legal separation or annulment of a marriage or domestic partnership, he or she must file a *Petition* using a form approved or adapted[1] by the Judicial Council. **CRC Rule 5.60**. In civil litigation, the initial form that is required to file a claim is called a *Complaint*. It is prepared and filed by or on behalf of a plaintiff. The responding party is called the defendant. **CRC Rule 5.16** provides that in cases filed under the Family Code, the party starting the case is referred to as the petitioner, and the other party or responding party is called the respondent. The petitioner is similar to the plaintiff in civil litigation, and the respondent is similar to the defendant.

The initial paperwork filed by the petitioner is the *Petition*. The respondent answers the petitioner's paperwork by filing a *Response*.

---

[1] The printed language in the lower left corner of the first page of each Judicial Council form provides whether or not the form is approved. An "approved" form is optional, and an "adapted" form is mandatory.

Chapter 8: Initial Forms, Initial Filing & Checkboxes

FC § 2330 sets forth the information that is to be included in a *Petition*. Judicial Council form *FL-100* is the mandatory form that incorporates that information.

2. The *Response* (Form *FL-120*)

If a responding party desires to respond to a *Petition* (form *FL-100*), a *Response* (form *FL-120*) is mandatorily required. The *Response* must be filed and a copy served on the petitioner within thirty (30) days of the date that the *Petition* and *Summons* was served on the respondent in order to avoid a default. **FC § 2020.**

The *Response* is very similar to the *Petition*, except it is the respondent's rendition of his or her facts and requests. All of the information requests and checkboxes on the *Response* correspond to the information on the *Petition*. While many of the respondent's answers may be the same as those answered by the petitioner on the *Petition*, some of the respondent's answers will differ from the petitioner's answers on the *Petition*, and special care should be taken to ensure that the answers on the *Petition* are not automatically assumed to be the correct answers.

The information requested on the *Response* must be the respondent's information, and the relief sought must be pursuant to the needs and/or desires of the respondent.

3. The *Summons (Family Law)* (Form *FL-110*)

If a *Summons* is required to commence a family law case, the clerk of the court must issue the summons using the same procedure for issuing a summons as is used in civil actions. **CRC Rule 5.50.** The Family Law Judicial Council forms to be issued by the clerk of the court are: **(1)** a *Summons (Family Law*, form *FL-110*) for divorces, legal separations or annulment cases involving married persons or domestic partnerships; **(2)** a *Summons (Uniform Parentage—Petition for Custody and Support*, form *FL-210*) for parentage or custody and support cases; **(3)** a *Summons (UIFSA*, form *FL-510*) when a party seeks to establish or enforce child support orders from other states; and **(4)** a *Summons and Complaint or Supplemental Complaint Regarding Parental Obligations* (form *FL-600*), as specified in **CRC Rule 5.325. CRC Rule 5.50.**

The clerk of the court must not give the original *Summons* to the petitioner, but must maintain it in the court file, except for support cases initiated by a local child support agency. **CRC Rule 5.50, CCP § 412.10.**

CCP § 412.20 sets forth the information that is to be included on a *Summons* (form *FL-110*). The *Summons*, adapted by the Judicial Council to comply with this section, provides the responding party with notice that legal proceedings have been instituted against him or her and advises him or her that he or she has thirty (30) days to answer and there is a right to retain counsel.

The *Summons* (form *FL-110*) contains: **(1)** the petitioner's name, **(2)** his or her attorney's name, address and telephone number, **(3)** the case number, **(4)** the

Chapter 8: Initial Forms, Initial Filing & Checkboxes

address of the court where the case was filed, **(5)** how long the responding party has to answer the *Petition* without consequences and **(6)** the Standard Family Law Restraining Orders that personally affect the petitioner's and the respondent's conduct.

In a dissolution, legal separation or nullity of a marriage the clerk of the court must issue a *Summons* that includes the Standard Family Law Restraining Orders. **CRC Rule 5.50**.

The Standard Family Law Restraining Orders on the Summons are:

(1) Neither party may remove their child(ren) from the State of California without the prior written consent of the other party or an order of the court;
(2) Neither party can transfer, encumber, hypothecate, conceal or dispose of any property without the written consent of the other party or an order of the court, except in the usual course of business or for the necessities of life;
(3) Neither party can cash, borrow against, cancel, transfer or change the beneficiaries of any insurance or other coverage; and
(4) Both parties are restrained from creating a nonprobate transfer or modifying a nonprobate transfer in a manner that affects the disposition of property subject to the transfer, without the written consent of the other party or an order of the court.[2] **FC § 2040**.

The Standard Family Law Restraining Orders on the *Summons* are to maintain the status quo during the divorce proceedings. They are enforceable within the entire State of California by any law enforcement agency that has received notice of this paperwork. **FC § 232**. Also, they remain in effect until the final judgment is entered, the *Petition* is dismissed or until further order of the court. **FC § 233**.

The Standard Family Law Restraining Orders on the *Summons* (form *FL-110*) take affect for the petitioner when the petitioner signs the *Petition*. **They take effect for the respondent when the respondent is served with the *Petition* and the *Summons*.**

A *Summons* MUST accompany a *Petition* when the *Petition* is being filed and served. Also, note that whenever a *Petition* in a family law case is amended, a new *Summons* must be prepared to accompany the amended *Petition* when filing and serving.

---

[2] FC § 2040 (1) defines a "'Nonprobate transfer' as an instrument, other than a will, that makes a transfer of property on death, including a revocable trust, pay on death account in a financial institution, Totten trust, transfer on death registration of personal property, or other instrument of a type described in Section 5000 of the Probate Code. The nonprobate transfer does not include a provision for the transfer of property on death in an insurance policy or other coverage held for the benefit of the parties and their child or children for whom support may be ordered."

Chapter 8: Initial Forms, Initial Filing & Checkboxes

4. *Uniform Child Custody Jurisdiction and Enforcement Act* (Form *FL-105*)

The *Uniform Child Custody Jurisdiction and Enforcement Act* (form *FL-105*) is commonly referred to as the *UCCJEA*. If the petitioner and the respondent have children under the age of eighteen (18) from the marriage, and the petitioner filed a *Petition* and respondent filed a *Response*, then each must complete, serve and file the *FL-105*. **CRC Rule 5.52**. The *FL-105* form was adapted by the Judicial Council to comply with the *UCCJEA* and its use is mandatory. It is a required attachment to the *Petition* and *Response* in actions for divorce, to establish parentage, or actions for custody and support of minor children; it is filed and served with the *Petition* and *Summons*. The *UCCJEA* (form *FL-105*) provides vital information to the court, such as the number of children of the relationship, where the children of the relationship currently reside and with whom and where the children of the relationship have resided in the last five (5) years and with whom.

Additionally, the *FL-105* specifies if there are additional parties that may need to be joined in the action and if there are other parties that have had physical custody of the children.

Judicial Council form *FL-105* was adapted as part of the Uniform Child Custody Jurisdiction and Enforcement Act, (the Act). The Act was enacted to give uniformity to custody rules throughout the United States. A form of the Act has been enacted in every state in the United States in an effort to encourage cooperation between the states and minimize jurisdictional competition. The Act applies in all child custody proceedings. In any action or proceeding involving custody of a minor child, a party has a continuing duty to inform the court if he or she obtains further information about a custody proceeding in a California court or any other court concerning a child who is named in the *Petition*, *Complaint* or *Response*. In family law proceedings concerning children, each party must file an updated *UCCJEA* form (*FL-105*) with the court and have it served on the other party.

FC § 3402 defines words and phrases that are set forth on the *FL-105* and clarifies the information requested on this form.[3]

5. The *Income and Expense Declaration* (Form *FL-150*[4])

Whenever financial relief is requested by either party, such as child support, spousal support or attorney fees, the *Income and Expense Declaration* must be completed and filed with the court. The *Income and Expense Declaration* (form *FL-150*) is a

---

[3] The following words and/or phrases are defined in FC § 3402: abandoned, child, child custody determination, child custody proceeding, commencement, court, home state, initial determination, issuing court, issuing state, modification, person, person acting as a parent, physical custody, state, tribe and warrant.
[4] The Judicial Council has amended this form effective January 1, 2019.

Chapter 8: Initial Forms, Initial Filing & Checkboxes

four-page document that requests financial information of the party filing the *FL-150*, such as employment, education, tax filing status, average monthly income, assets, average monthly expenses and child support information.

The *FL-150* is used in both family law cases and probate cases, as set forth in **Probate Code § 1510.**

When there is a proceeding involving child, family or spousal support, the petitioner and the respondent, if the respondent has filed a *Response*, MUST each complete and submit copies of his or her state and federal income tax returns to the court, whether they are individual or joint returns.
The tax returns can be lodged with the court for the hearing and returned to the parties at the end of the hearing. If the income tax returns become part of a court file, they must be sealed as confidential and not be a part of the public file or all of the personal information on the tax returns should be redacted. **FC § 2024.5**. These income tax returns may be examined and are discoverable by the other party. **FC § 3552.**

The *FL-150* provides income information upon which the court relies to make court orders, such as child support orders, spousal support orders and attorney fees' orders.

Special care should be taken to fill in, if possible, an estimate of the other party's gross monthly income on the *FL-150*. This question is especially important because if a responding party defaults and does not file an *Income and Expense Declaration,* the court can make orders for child support, spousal support and/or attorney fees using this estimate.

The last page of the *FL-150* is not mandatory, if there are no children of the marriage.

Filing Paperwork with the Court

1. Filing Rules

CRC Rule 3.1300 provides that all moving and supporting papers must be filed in accordance with **CCP § 1005**, which provides in pertinent part:

> **(b)** Unless otherwise ordered or specifically provided by law, all moving and supporting papers shall be served and filed at least 16 court days before the hearing. The moving and supporting papers served shall be a copy of the papers filed or to be filed with the court.
>
> All papers opposing a motion so noticed shall be filed with the court and a copy served on each party at least nine court days, and all reply papers at least five court days before the hearing.
>
> The court, or a judge thereof, may prescribe a shorter time.

> **(c)** Notwithstanding any other provision of this section, all papers opposing a motion and all reply papers shall be served by personal delivery, facsimile transmission, express mail, or other means consistent with Sections 1010, 1011, 1012, and 1013, and reasonably calculated to ensure delivery to the other party or parties not later than the close of the next business day after the time the opposing papers or reply papers, as applicable, are filed.
>
> The court, or a judge thereof, may prescribe a shorter time.

CRC Rule 3.1300 provides further, "No paper may be rejected for filing on the ground that it was untimely submitted for filing. If the court, in its discretion, refuses to consider a late filed paper, the minutes or order must so indicate."

2. Filing Fee/Fee Waivers

Parties must pay filing fees to the clerk of the court at the time the papers are filed with the court. The amount of the filing fee in family court is established by the Uniform Civil Fees and Standard Fee Schedule Act of 2005 under **Government Code § 70670**, et seq. and is subject to change. The act covers fees the court may charge parties to file the initial papers in a family law proceeding, motions or other papers requiring a hearing. It also covers filing fees that courts may charge in proceedings relating to child custody or visitation (parenting time) to cover the costs of maintaining mediation services under **FC§ 3160**, et seq. **CRC Rule 5.40**. The current amount charged can be found on the Court of California website at: *www.courts.ca.gov/documents/filingfees.pdf*.

If a party cannot afford to file an action in family court, a party may request that the court waive fees and costs. **CRC Rule 5.41**. The procedure and forms needed to request an initial fee waiver in a family law action are the same as for all civil actions: *The Request to Waive Court Fees* (form *FW-001*). It is a mandatory use form. **CRC Rules 3.50-3.56** govern fee waivers in family law cases. **CRC Rule 5.41**.

Whether a party is eligible for a fee waiver is addressed in **CRC Rule 3.52**. Fee waiver applications and orders thereon are confidential documents. Only the court and authorized court personnel, any persons authorized by the applicant and any persons authorized by order of the court may view these documents. **CRC Rule 8.26**.

A party is not required to file a new application for waiver of court fees and costs for an appeal if the fee waiver issued by the trial court is still in effect. **CRC Rule 8.818**.

When a judgment or support order is entered in a family law case, the court may order either party to pay all or part of the fees and costs that the court waived and must consider and determine the repayment of waived fees. **CRC Rule 5.45**.

Chapter 8: Initial Forms, Initial Filing & Checkboxes

If the full amount of the filing fee is not paid or a check without sufficient funds is used to pay the filing fee, the clerk of the court will void the proceeding. **CCP §§ 411.20** and **411.21.**

CRC Rule 3.51 provides:

> An application for initial fee waiver under CRC Rule 3.55 must be made on a *Request to Waive Court Fees* (form *FW-001*). An application for initial fee waiver under CRC Rule 3.56 must be made on *Request to Waive Additional Court Fees (Superior Court)* (form *FW-002*). The clerk must provide the forms and the *Information Sheet on Waiver of Superior Court Fees and Costs* (form *FW-001-INFO*) without charge to any person who requests any fee waiver application or indicates that he or she is unable to pay any court fee or cost.

Unless otherwise ordered or specifically provided by law, all moving and supporting papers must be served and filed in accordance with **CCP § 1005. CRC Rule 3.1300(a)**.

The court, on its own motion or on application for an order shortening time supported by a declaration showing good cause, may prescribe shorter times for the filing and service of papers other than the times specified in **CCP § 1005. CRC Rule 3.1300(b)**.

The parties must serve the trial brief (if a trial brief is required) on all parties and file the brief with the court a minimum of five (5) court days before the trial or long-cause hearing. **CRC Rule 5.393(b).**

Papers submitted before the close of the clerk's office on the day the papers are due are deemed timely filed. **CRC Rule 3.1300(e)**.

A document is deemed filed on the date the clerk receives it. A filing is not timely unless the clerk receives the document before the time to file it expires. **CRC Rule 8.25(b)**.

The clerk may not reject moving or responding papers relating to a *RFO* for filing on the ground that it was untimely submitted for filing. The court, in its discretion, may refuse to consider a late filed paper. However, the minutes of the court or the court order must so indicate this refusal. **CRC Rule 5.94(d).**

The following list of documents, whether they are filed separately or attached to other documents, may not be filed unless they are offered as relevant to the determination of an issue in a law and motion proceeding:

- Subpoena;
- Subpoena duces tecum;
- Deposition notice and response;
- Notice to consumer or employee and objection;
- Notice of intention to record testimony by audio or video tape;

Chapter 8: Initial Forms, Initial Filing & Checkboxes

- Notice of intention to take an oral deposition by telephone, videoconference or other remote electronic means;
- Agreement to set or extend time for deposition, agreement to extend time for response to discovery requests and notice of these agreements;
- Interrogatories and responses or objections to interrogatories;
- Demand for production or inspection of documents, things and places, and responses or objections to demand;
- Request for admissions and responses or objections to request;
- Agreement for physical and mental examinations;
- Demand for delivery of medical reports and response;
- Demand for exchange of expert witnesses;
- Demand for production of discoverable reports and writings of expert witnesses;
- List of expert witnesses whose opinion a party intends to offer in evidence at trial and declaration;
- Statement that a party does not presently intend to offer the testimony of any expert witness;
- Declaration for additional discovery;
- A stipulation to enlarge the scope of number of discovery requests from that specified by statute and notice of the stipulation; and
- Offer to compromise, unless accompanied by an original proof of acceptance and a written judgment for the court's signature and entry of judgment. **CRC Rule 3.250.**

Checkboxes

There are many family law forms, and most of these forms are mandatory and must be used. Filling out family law forms must be carefully and thoughtfully executed. Although checking boxes seems relatively simple, not checking a box may mean that your client will not receive the relief that he or she needs or desires.

In the case set forth below, a necessary checkbox for child support was NOT checked. Because that checkbox was not checked, the City and County of San Francisco could not recover funds paid to the petitioner for the support of her child.

> *In re Marriage of ANGELA and RONALD LIPPEL. RONALD LIPPEL, Appellant, v. CITY AND COUNTY OF SAN FRANCISCO, Respondent*
> Supreme Court of California
> 51 Cal.3d 1160
> December 17, 1990
> (*Marriage of Lippel*)
>
> In March 1971 Ronald Lippel's wife, Angela Lippel (Angela), filed a Petition for dissolution of their marriage of 11 1/2 months, requesting custody of their infant daughter, Kristin. Angela initiated the action by filing a standard printed form Petition, which was statutorily authorized, that provided blank spaces for the entry of certain

statistical information and contained boxes to be checked to indicate what relief was being requested by the Petitioner.

Angela checked the boxes that indicated there was no property to be divided and that she was not requesting spousal support. She also checked the box that indicated she was requesting child custody. The form Petition also provided a box relating to the issue of child support, which stated: "Petitioner requests that: . . . (c) Support of children be awarded if need is found." This box was left blank. Both Angela and her attorney signed the Petition.

Ronald Lippel (Ronald) was served with a Summons and copy of the Petition and did not file a Response. Accordingly, in April 1971 his default was duly entered. At a default hearing in May 1971, an interlocutory judgment of dissolution of marriage was entered, awarding Angela custody of Kristin and reasonable visitation rights to Ronald. Despite the fact that Angela had not requested such relief in her Petition, the court made an order that Ronald was to pay $ 100 per month in child support. A notice of entry of that judgment, which merely indicated the book and page where the judgment was entered, was served on Ronald, by mail, on May 27, 1971. A similar notice of entry of the final judgment was served upon him on October 12, 1971. Ronald was never served with a copy of the judgment itself, nor did he ever receive a copy of the judgment.

During the next 16 years Ronald maintained a close relationship with his daughter through regular visits during holidays and summer vacations. Ronald bought her clothes, school supplies, and miscellaneous personal items, including a bedroom set and a stereo. He also paid for her dance classes and other extracurricular activities. Furthermore, for various periods during these 16 years, Ronald assumed, at Angela's request, custody of and total responsibility for Kristin. According to Ronald, moreover, Angela, with Kristin, participated in some holiday and other family gatherings of Ronald's family.

Angela never mentioned the support order to Ronald, and Ronald was unaware of the order's existence until the City and County of San Francisco (CCSF), which had been paying Aid to Families with Dependent Children (AFDC) to Kristin, commenced proceedings for assignment of his wages.

After more than 16 1/2 years from the date of the interlocutory judgment, in December 1987, CCSF filed a declaration requesting an assignment of Ronald's wages, alleging that he owed unpaid child support. The trial court found that Ronald owed $ 18,200 to the county for reimbursement of AFDC funds paid to support Kristin. The court ordered a deduction from Ronald's wages in the amount of $300 per month until the total amount was paid. CCSF then recorded an abstract of support judgment with the county recorder and served it upon Ronald by mail. As a result of this action by CCSF, Ronald moved to vacate the child support provision of the interlocutory judgment and to vacate the order assigning his wages. He argued that the underlying support order was void because it gave Angela relief she had not requested, and of which he had no notice before he allowed his default to be entered. He argued that the judgment denied him due process, in that, since he had never received notice of a request for child support, he was denied an opportunity to oppose the child support order itself and/or the amount of support ordered.

In July 1988 the trial court entered its order denying Ronald's motion to vacate the child support order and the order assigning his wages. The Court of Appeal, in a published opinion, reluctantly affirmed, stating: "We affirm the order under compulsion of existing California Supreme Court authority."

Chapter 8: Initial Forms, Initial Filing & Checkboxes

> The issue we address is whether due process permits a court to order child support in a default case where, as here, the plaintiff has not requested support in the Petition for dissolution of marriage, and consequently, the defendant has not received notice that it may be awarded.
>
> [I]t is clear that Angela and her lawyer carefully completed the form Petition. Angela requested child custody by checking the box so designated. She specifically denied seeking spousal support by checking the box so designated. She did not check the box requesting child support. Ronald was, therefore, never put on notice that child support would be placed in issue in the dissolution proceeding, since a copy of the Petition served on him did not raise child support as an issue.
>
> **DISPOSITION**
> The decision of the Court of Appeal is reversed, and the cause remanded with instructions to order the superior court to vacate its order of child support and its order assigning wages to the City and County of San Francisco.

While most of the checkboxes that must be checked on a form are self-explanatory, when an **Other Relief** checkbox or a checkbox that is not specific is checked, an explanation of the relief that is being requested must be clear enough for a responding party to adequately respond to the claim.

In the case below, a non-specific checkbox was checked. Next to the checkbox was typed "Relief for [Robert's] breach of fiduciary duty pursuant to Family Code sections 1100 et seq." No other explanation was offered in the pleadings.

> ***In re Marriage of JESSIE A. and ROBERT S. KAHN. JESSIE A. KAHN, Respondent, v. ROBERT S. KAHN, Appellant.***
> COURT OF APPEAL OF CALIFORNIA, FOURTH APPELLATE DISTRICT
> 215 Cal.App.4th 1113
> April 26, 2013
> (*Marriage of Kahn*)
>
> In this dissolution of marriage proceeding, husband Robert S. Kahn failed to respond to discovery propounded by wife Jessie A. Kahn. After a prove-up hearing, it entered a default judgment, which, among other things, awarded Jessie $275,000 against Robert for breach of fiduciary duty.
>
> [Robert's argument is that the] award of $275,000 exceeded the scope of the Petition.
>
> In this opinion, we agree that the award of $275,000 rendered the judgment void, because Jessie's Petition had not indicated that she was seeking any particular amount of damages for breach of fiduciary duty. Hence, we will remand to the trial court with directions to determine whether to modify the judgment by striking the award of $275,000 or to vacate the judgment in its entirety so that Jessie can file an amended Petition and seek damages for breach of fiduciary duty.
>
> Jessie filed her Petition using a Judicial Council form (No. FL-100), as required. The form provided checkboxes for the relief sought. Jessie checked the box for "Other," then typed in, "Relief for [Robert's] breach of fiduciary duty pursuant to Family Code sections

Chapter 8: Initial Forms, Initial Filing & Checkboxes

> 1100 et seq." However, she did not specify any factual grounds, nor did she specify an amount sought.
>
> CCP§ 580(a) provides: "The relief granted to the plaintiff, if there is no answer, cannot exceed that demanded in the complaint … ."
>
> " '[T]he primary purpose of the section is to guarantee defaulting parties adequate notice of the maximum judgment that may be assessed against them.'" "[D]ue process requires notice to defendants … of the potential consequences of a refusal to pursue their defense. Such notice enables a defendant to exercise his right to choose … between (1) giving up his right to defend in exchange for the certainty that he cannot be held liable for more than a known amount, and (2) exercising his right to defend at the cost of exposing himself to greater liability.
>
> "[A] default judgment greater than the amount specifically demanded is void as beyond the trial court's jurisdiction." CCP § 580 applies in a marital dissolution action.
>
> Jessie argues that her Petition gave Robert sufficient notice. Admittedly, we are dealing with a form complaint in a marital dissolution action; the checkbox for "other" relief is distinguishable from the checkboxes for a division of community property. It is a catchall category; it could encompass practically any kind of relief, including relief that is not statutorily required in a marital dissolution action. The Respondent is therefore entitled to notice of the specific nature and amount of any "other" relief sought before defaulting.
>
> Accordingly, we will remand with directions to determine whether to vacate or to modify the default judgment. The judgment is void to the extent that it awards Jessie $275,000 against Robert. The matter is remanded to the trial court with directions to determine whether the judgment should be modified by striking the award of $275,000 or wholly vacated.

Finally, even though an attorney fees request box is not checked on the initial form, attorney fees may still be awarded provided the other side has been sufficiently and properly noticed that the request is being made. (See *FATON v. AHMEDO* (2015) 236 Cal.App.4th 1160, where the court awarded attorney fees after the action had been completed because the requestor was the prevailing party and the other side had been properly noticed.)

Pursuant to **CRC Rule 5.170**, notice to the other parties in the matter may not be necessary with regard to the following actions/forms:

> **(1)** Applications to restore a former name after judgment;
> **(2)** Stipulations by the parties;
> **(3)** An order or judgment after a default court hearing;
> **(4)** An earnings assignment order based on an existing support order;
> **(5)** An order for service of summons by publication or posting;
> **(6)** An order or judgment that the other party or opposing counsel approved or agreed not to oppose; and
> **(7)** Application for an order waiving filing fees.

CHART 5: Initial Forms for Dissolution, Legal Separation & Nullity

FL-FORM	FORM NAME
FL-100	*Petition for Dissolution, Legal Separation, Nullity and Domestic Partnership*
FL-105	*Declaration under Uniform Child Custody Jurisdiction and Enforcement Act (UCCJEA)*
FL-107-INFO	*Legal Steps for a Divorce or Legal Separation*
FL-110	*Summons (Family Law)*
FL-117	*Notice and Acknowledgment of Receipt (Family Law)*
FL-120	*Response for Dissolution, Legal Separation, Nullity and Domestic Partnership*
FL-130	*Appearance, Stipulations, and Waivers (Family Law-Uniform Parentage-Custody and Support)*
FL-140	*Declaration of Disclosure (Family Law)*
FL-141	*Declaration Regarding Service of Declaration of Disclosure and Income and Expense Declaration*
FL-142	*Schedule of Assets and Debts (Family Law)*
Fl-150	*Income and Expense Declaration (Family Law)*
FL-160	*Petitioner's/Respondent's Community/Quasi-community/Separate Property Declaration*
FL-161	*Continuation of Property Declaration (Family Law)*

© 2019 LW Greenberg

CHART 6: Rules of Court and Codes RE: INITIAL FORMS

CRC/CODE	RULE *In Brief*
CRC Rule 1.21	Whenever a document is required to be served on a party, the service must be made on the party's attorney, if the party is represented.
CRC Rule 1.31	A legally sufficient court order not on Judicial Council form is not invalid.
CRC Rule 1.5	**Must** is mandatory; **may** is permissive.
CRC Rule 3.1300	All moving and supporting papers must be filed and served in accordance with CCP § 1005 and the proof of service of the moving papers must be filed no later than 5 court days before the time appointed for the hearing.
CRC Rule 3.51	An application for initial fee waiver under CRC Rule 3.55 must be made on a *Request to Waive Court Fees* (form *FW-001*). An application for initial fee waiver under CRC Rule 3.56 must be made on *Request to Waive Additional Court Fees (Superior Court)* (form *FW-002*). The clerk must provide the forms and the *Information Sheet on Waiver of Superior Court Fees and Costs* (form *FW-001-INFO*) without charge to any person who requests any fee waiver application or indicates that he or she is unable to pay any court fee or cost.
CRC Rule 3.52	Eligibility for a fee waiver
CRC Rule 5.16	Party starting case is the petitioner, and the other party is the respondent
CRC Rule 5.170	Notice to the other parties may not be necessary with: **(1)** Applications to restore a former name after judgment; **(2)** Stipulations by the parties; **(3)** An order or judgment after a default court hearing; **(4)** An earnings assignment order based on an existing support order; **(5)** An order for service of summons by publication or posting; **(6)** An order or judgment that the other party or opposing counsel approved or agreed not to oppose; **(7)** Application for order waiving filing fees.
CRC Rule 5.2	Definitions: Family Code, Action, Proceeding, Dissolution, Attorney, Party, Best interests of the child, Parenting time, Property and Local rule.
CRC Rule 5.40	The parties must pay filing fees to the clerk of the court at the time of filing. The amount of money required to pay filing fees in family court is established by the Uniform Civil Fees and Standard Fee Schedule Act of 2005 under Government Code section 70670 et seq. and is subject to change.
CRC Rule 5.41	If a party cannot afford the filing fee, that party can request that the court waive the fees and costs. The procedure and forms needed to request an initial fee waiver in a family law action are the same as for all other civil actions.
CRC Rule 5.45	When a judgment or support order is entered in a family law case, the court must consider and determine if either party should pay all or part of the fees and costs that the court waived.
CRC Rule 5.50	If a *Summons* is required to commence a family law case, the clerk of the court must issue a *Summons* using the same procedure for issuing a *Summons* in civil actions. The clerk of the court must not give the original *Summons* to the petitioner, but must maintain it in court file, except for support cases by local child support agency.
CRC Rule 5.52	If the petitioner and the respondent have children from the marriage, and the petitioner filed a *Petition* and respondent filed a *Response*, then each must complete, serve, and file the *FL-105* if there are children of their relationship under the age of eighteen (18) years.

Chapter 8: Initial Forms, Initial Filing & Checkboxes

CRC Rule 5.60	If a party meets the necessary residency requirements and that party desires a dissolution, legal separation or annulment of a marriage or domestic partnership, he or she must file an appropriate *Petition* or *Complaint* using a form approved or adapted[1] by the Judicial Council.
CRC Rule 5.62	A respondent is deemed to have appeared in a proceeding when he or she files a *Response*, motion to strike, motion to transfer the proceeding or a written notice of his or her appearance.
CRC Rule 5.68	A general appearance of the respondent is equivalent to personal service within this state of the *Summons* and the *Petition*. The petitioner must arrange to serve the other party with a *Summons, Petition*, and any other papers regarding the case filed with the court. Service may be effected by: **(1)** personal service, **(2)** substituted service (leaving a copy of the paperwork at a person's residence), **(3)** service by mail with a notice and acknowledgment of receipt, **(4)** service by publication (i.e. publishing in a newspaper) or **(5)** service by posting (announcing by affixing a notice in a public place). A *Response* to a family law *Petition* may be served personally or by mail providing the respondent agrees to it and signs a *Notice and Acknowledgment of Receipt*, (form *FL-117*).
CRC Rule 5.72	*Proof of service by Posting* (form *FL-985*) (or a pleading containing the same information as form *FL-985*) must be completed by the person who posted the documents and then filed with the court once posting is completed.
CRC Rule 5.83	Family Centered Case Resolution
CRC Rule 8.26	Only the court and authorized court personnel, any persons authorized by the applicant, and any persons authorized by order of the court may view the documents in a sealed file.
FC § 211	Provides authority for the Judicial Council to adopt or approve forms.
FC § 232	The Standard Family Law Restraining Orders on the *Summons* are enforceable within the entire State of California by any law enforcement agency that has received notice of this paperwork.
FC § 233	A *Summons* MUST accompany a *Petition* when a *Petition* is being filed and served. The *Summons* containing the Standard Family Law Restraining Orders must be issued and filed in the same manner as a *Summons* in a civil action. Only where the *Petition* and *Summons* have been personally served on the respondent or upon waiver and acceptance of service by the respondent, are the Standard Family Law Restraining Orders in effect.
FC § 2020	A responsive pleading must be filed and a copy served on the petitioner within 30 days of the date of the service of the *Petition* and *Summons* on the respondent in order to avoid a default.
FC § 2040	The Standard Family Law Restraining Orders on the *Summons*
FC § 2330	Information that is to be included in a *Petition* (form-*FL-100*).
FC § 2331	A copy of a *Petition,* together with a copy of a *Summons* must be served upon the other party to the marriage in the same manner as service of civil action papers.
FC § 3402	Defines words and phrases that are set forth on the *FL-105* form and help to clarify the information requested on this form.
FC § 3552	When there is a proceeding involving child, family, or spousal support, the petitioner and the respondent, if the respondent has filed a *Response*, MUST complete and submit copies of his or her state and federal income

---

[1] The printed language in lower left corner of the first page of each Judicial Council form provides whether the form is or approved. An "approved" form is optional and an "adapted" form is mandatory.
lg

Chapter 8: Initial Forms, Initial Filing & Checkboxes

	tax returns to the court, whether they are individual or joint returns. These income tax returns may be examined and are discoverable by the other party.
CCP §§ 411.20 and 411.21	If the full amount of the filing fee is not paid or a check without sufficient funds is used to pay the filing fee, the clerk of the court will void the proceeding.
CCP § 412.10	The clerk of the court must not give the original *Summons* to the petitioner, but must maintain it in the court file, except for support cases initiated by a local child support agency.
CCP § 412.20	The information that is to be included on a *Summons* (form *FL-110*) has been adapted by the Judicial Council.
CCP § 413.30	If the respondent cannot be found to be served a *Summons* and *Petition*, the petitioner may request an order for service of the *Summons* by publication or posting.
CCP § 414.10	Court paperwork may be served by any person who is at least 18 years of age and not a party to the action.
CCP § 415.10	Personal delivery of *Summons* is deemed complete at time of delivery.
CCP § 415.20	Substituted service
CCP § 415.30	Service by mail with a notice and acknowledgment of receipt
CCP § 415.40	Service on a person outside of the state.
CCP § 415.50	If respondent cannot be found to be served a *Summons* & *Petition*, petitioner may request order for service of *Summons* by publication or posting.
CCP § 417.10	If service is made by mail pursuant to CCP § 415.30, proof of service must include acknowledgment of receipt of *Summons* in the form provided by that section or other written acknowledgment of receipt of *Summons* satisfactory to the court. All proofs of personal service must be made on a form adapted by the Judicial Council.
CCP § 1013(a)	When service is effected by mail, the responding party has an additional 5 days to respond if the documents were mailed to a party who is within the State of California, 10 additional days if mailed to a party within the United States and 20 additional days if mailed internationally.
Government Code § 70670	The amount of the filing fee in family court is established by the Uniform Civil Fees and Standard Fee Schedule Act of 2005 under Government Code § 70670 et seq. and is subject to change. The act covers fees the court may charge parties to file the first papers in a family law proceeding, motions, or other papers requiring a hearing. It also covers filing fees that courts may charge in proceedings relating to child custody or visitation (parenting time) to cover the costs of maintaining mediation services under FC § 3160 et seq. CRC Rule 5.40.

© 2019 LW Greenberg

EDUCATIONAL EXERCISES

Using the information in the intake sheets of the Johns in Appendix One to complete the following list of forms:

For Petitioner

1. A Summons (FL-110)
2. A Petition (FL-100)
3. A UCCJEA (FL-105)
4. An Income and Expense Declaration

For Respondent

1. Response (FL-120)
2. A UCCJEA (FL0105)
3. An Income and Expense Declaration

CHAPTER 9: Timing, Electronic Filing & Service

In Brief...

WHEN COUNTING DAYS FOR SERVICE AND RESPONSE:
- **Calendar days** include weekends and holidays;
- **Court days** are days that the CA courts are open for official business, **CRC Guideline 1**;
- Mondays through Fridays are counted as court days, except for judicial holidays;
- The first day is excluded and the last day is included, **CCP § 12**;
- If the last day is a holiday, and then it is also excluded, **CCP § 12**; and
- If it is not specified whether it is court days or calendar days, it is calendar days.

TIME FOR FILING:
- And service for *RFO*s and motions is 16 court days before the hearing;
- And service for opposing papers is at least 9 court days before the hearing; and
- And service for reply papers is at least 5 court days before the hearing, **CCP § 1005(b)**; and
- May be shorter if a court so orders, **CCP § 1005, CRC Rule 3.1300(b)**.
- A document is deemed filed on the date the clerk receives it, **CRC Rule 8.25(b)**.
- Moving/supporting papers must be served and filed pursuant to **CCP § 1005. CRC Rule 3.1300(a)**.
- **The response time is extended if papers are served by mail,** 5 calendar days if service is within CA, 10 calendar days if service is affected outside of CA, but in the US; and 20 calendar days if outside of the US. **CCP § 1013(a)**.

A DROPBOX:
- Must be provided for depositing documents to be filed whenever a clerk's office filing counter is closed at any time between 8:30 a.m. and 4:00 p.m. on a court day. A court may provide a dropbox during other times. **CRC Rule 2.210(a)**.
- Documents deposited in a court's dropbox up to and including 4:00 p.m. on a court day are deemed to have been deposited for filing on that day. A court may provide for same-day filing of documents deposited in its dropbox after 4:00 p.m. on a court day. **CRC Rule 2.210(b)**.
- Documents deposited in a court's dropbox are deemed deposited for filing on the next court day if they are deposited on a court day after 4:00pm. or on judicial holiday. **CRC Rule .210(c)**.

TIMELY DISCOVERY REQUESTS REQUIRE:
- That the petitioner may not serve until 10 days after service of the *Summons* or appearance;
- That the respondent may serve at any time;

- That d**eposition notices** provide 10 days' notice, **CCP § 2025.270(a)**; and
- That **subpoenas for the production of business records** provide that production be 20 days after issuance of the subpoena or 15 days after service of the subpoena, whichever date is later, **CCP § 2020.410(c)**.
- **Motions to compel further responses to discovery requests** are due within 45 days after the responses were served.

ELECTRONIC SERVING AND FILING:
- Requires that consent be obtained for electronic service, **CRC Rule 2.251(a)(b)**;
- Is complete at the time of the transmission, **CRC Rule 2.521(h)**;
- Allows 2 extra court days to respond, **CCP § 1010.6(a)(4)**; and
- Proof of electronic service may be in electronic form. **CRC Rule 2.251(i)**.

Introduction

Court papers must be filed and served in accordance with the laws set forth in the Code of Civil Procedure, the Family Code and the California Rules of Court. However, pursuant to **CRC Rule 1.10(c)**[1] and **CRC Rule 5.2(f)**[2], a court can shorten or extend the time to file and/or serve court papers. The focus of this chapter is the codes and rules regarding the timely filing, responding and serving of papers filed with the court, including the rules for electronic filing and serving.

Computation of "Time"

Pursuant to **CCP § 583.240**, in computing the time within which service must be made, the time during which any of the following conditions existed must be excluded:

> **(a)** The defendant was not amenable to the process of the court.
> **(b)** The prosecution of the action or proceedings in the action was stayed and the stay affected service.
> **(c)** The validity of service was the subject of litigation by the parties.
> **(d)** Service, for any other reason, was impossible, impracticable, or futile due to causes beyond the plaintiff's control. Failure to discover relevant facts or evidence is not a cause beyond the plaintiff's control for the purpose of this subdivision. CCP § 583.240.

The time is computed by excluding the first day and including the last, unless the last day is a holiday, and then it is also excluded. **CCP § 12**.

---

[1] CRC Rule 1.10(c) provides: "Unless otherwise provided by law, the court may extend or shorten the time within which a party must perform any act under the rules."
[2] CRC Rule 5.2(f) provides: "The time within which any act is permitted or required to be done by a party under these rules may be extended by the court upon such terms as may be just."

Chapter 9: Timing, Electronic Filing & Service

> **(a)** The time in which any act provided by these rules is to be performed is computed by excluding the first day and including the last, unless the last day is a Saturday, Sunday, or other legal holiday, and then it is also excluded.
> **(b)** Unless otherwise provided by law, if the last day for the performance of any act that is required by these rules to be performed within a specific period of time falls on a Saturday, Sunday, or other legal holiday, the period is extended to and includes the next day that is not a holiday.
> **(c)** Unless otherwise provided by law, the court may extend or shorten the time within which a party must perform any act under the rules. CRC Rule 1.10.

Court days are days that the California courts are open for official business. Normally, Mondays through Fridays are counted as court days, except for judicial holidays. **California Rules of Court, Guideline 1**.

When the days in the code or rules are not specified, then **five (5) days** means five (5) calendar days. *IVERSON v. SUPERIOR COURT OF ORANGE COUNTY* (1985) 167 Cal.App.3d 544 at p. 548.

Close of business means 5 p.m., or the time that the court would not accept filing at the court's filing counter, whichever is earlier. **CCP § 1010.6(b)(3)**.

A dropbox must be provided for depositing documents to be filed with the clerk whenever a clerk's office filing counter is closed at any time between 8:30 a.m. and 4:00 p.m. on a court day. A court may provide a dropbox during other times. **CRC Rule 2.210(a)**.

Documents deposited in a court's dropbox up to and including 4:00 p.m. on a court day are deemed to have been deposited for filing on that day. A court may provide for same-day filing of documents deposited in its dropbox after 4:00 p.m. on a court day. If so, the court must give notice of the deadline for same-day filing of a document deposited in its dropbox. **CRC Rule 2.210(b)**.

Documents deposited in a court's dropbox are deemed to have been deposited for filing on the next court day if they are deposited on a court day after 4:00 p.m. or on a judicial holiday. **CRC Rule 2.210(c)**.

Codes and Rules

A *Request for Order* (*RFO*), and any moving and/or supporting papers must all be served and filed at least **sixteen (16) court days before the hearing**. The moving and supporting papers served must be a copy of all of the papers filed or to be filed with the court. **CCP § 1005(b)**.

All papers **opposing** a motion must be filed with the court and a copy served on each party at least **nine (9) court days before the hearing**. All **reply papers** must be filed with the court and a copy served on each party at least **five (5) court days** before the hearing. **CCP § 1005(b)**.

Chapter 9: Timing, Electronic Filing & Service

The *Proof of Service* of the *RFO* (form *FL-300*) and supporting papers must be filed at least five (5) court days before the hearing date. **CRC Rule 5.94(b)**.

The Timing for Discovery

Petitioners may serve discovery requests a minimum of ten (10) days after: **(1)** service of *Summons* on the party to be served discovery or **(2)** the appearance of the party to be served the discovery requests, whichever occurs earlier.

Respondents may serve discovery requests at any time.

Almost all responses to discovery requests are due 30 days after the requests were served, taking into consideration that if they are served by mail, additional time will be allowed to respond pursuant to **CCC § 1013(a)**.

Motions to compel further responses to discovery requests are due within 45 days after the responses were served.

When *Interrogatories*, *Demands for Inspections* and *Requests for Admission* have been prepared and served, the responding party and any other party may promptly move for a protective order. (See Chapter 11 RE: Discovery, *infra*.) This motion must be accompanied by a meet and confer declaration pursuant to **CCP § 2016.040**[3].

Deposition notices require ten (10) days' notice. **CCP § 2025.270(a)**. Additionally, deposition notices cannot be served on behalf of a plaintiff until at least 20 days after service of the *Summons* and the *Petition/Complaint* on the respondent/defendant. **CCP 2025.210(b)**.

Subpoenas only for the production of business records may demand production twenty (20) days after issuance of the subpoena or fifteen (15) days after service of the subpoena, whichever date is later. **CCP § 2020.410(c)**.

Subject to **CCP § 2020.410(c)**[4], a deposition subpoena must be served a sufficient time in advance of the deposition to provide the deponent a reasonable opportunity to locate and produce any designated business records, documents, electronically stored information, and tangible things and, where personal attendance is commanded, a reasonable time to travel to the place of deposition. **CCP § 2020.220(a)**.

---

[3] Pursuant to § 2016.040 "A meet and confer declaration in support of a motion shall state facts showing a reasonable and good faith attempt at an informal resolution of each issue presented by the motion."

[4] CCP § 2020.410(c) provides: "A deposition subpoena that commands only the production of business records for copying need not be accompanied by an affidavit or declaration showing good cause for the production of the business records designated in it. It shall be directed to the custodian of those records or another person qualified to certify the records. It shall command compliance in accordance with Section 2020.430 on a date that is no earlier than 20 days after the issuance or 15 days after the service of the deposition subpoena, whichever date is later."

A demand for an exchange of information concerning expert witnesses may be made by any party without leave of court. However, this demand may be made no later than the 10th day after the initial trial date has been set or seventy (70) days before that trial date, whichever is closer to the trial date. **CCP § 2034.220.**

The demand must specify the date for the exchange of lists of expert trial witnesses, expert witness declarations and any demanded production of writings, and that date must be fifty (50) days before the initial trial date or twenty (20) days after service of the demand, whichever is closer to the trial date, unless the court, on motion and a showing of good cause, orders an earlier or later date of exchange. **CCP § 2034.230(b).**

Electronic Service and Filing

The following definitions are set forth in **CCP § 1010.6(a):**

1. **Electronic service** is service of a document on a party or other person by either electronic transmission or electronic notification. Electronic service may be performed directly by a party, by an agent of a party—including the party's attorney—or through an electronic filing service provider.
2. **Electronic transmission** is the transmission of a document by electronic means to the electronic service address at or through which a party or other person has authorized electronic service.
3. **Electronic notification** is the notification of the party or other person that a document is served by sending an electronic message to the electronic address at or through which the party or other person has authorized electronic service, specifying the exact name of the document served and providing a hyperlink at which the served document may be viewed and downloaded.

When a document may be served by mail, express mail, overnight delivery or fax transmission, the document may be served electronically under **CCP § 1010.6**. However, the consent of the parties must be obtained for electronic service. **CRC Rule 2.251(a)(b).**

A party indicates that he or she agrees to accept electronic service by: **(1)** serving a notice on all parties that accept electronic service, **(2)** manifesting affirmative consent through electronic means by (a) filing "*Consent to Electronic Service and Notice of Electronic Service Address*" with the court and (b) agreeing to the terms of service agreement with an electronic service provider. **CRC Rule 2.251(b).**

A court may require parties to serve documents electronically in specified actions by local rule or court order, as provided in Code of Civil Procedure section 1010.6 and the rules in this chapter. **CRC Rule 2.251(c).**

A court that permits or requires electronic filing in a case must maintain and make available electronically to the parties and other persons in the case an electronic service list that contains the parties' or other persons' current electronic service addresses, as provided by the parties or other persons that have filed electronically in the case. **CRC Rule 2.521(e)**.

"Electronic service of a document is complete as provided in Code of Civil Procedure section 1010.6 and the rules in this chapter. If an electronic filing service provider is used for service, the service is complete at the time that the electronic filing service provider electronically transmits the document or sends electronic notification of service." **CRC Rule 2.521(h)**.

The time period or date to respond must be extended after service by electronic means by two court days, except the extension does not apply to a notice of intention to move for new trial, a notice of intention to move to vacate judgment under **CCP § 663a** or a notice of appeal. **CCP § 1010.6(a)(4)**.

This extension applies in the absence of a specific exception provided by any other statute or rule of court. **CCP § 1010.6(a)(4)**.

A document that is filed electronically has the same legal effect as an original paper document filed with the court. **CCP § 1010.6(b)(1)**.

Any document that is electronically filed with the court after the close of business on any day is deemed to have been filed on the next court day. **CCP § 1010.6(b)(3)**.

When the court receives a document filed electronically, it must issue a confirmation that the document has been received and filed. The confirmation will serve as proof that the document was filed. **CCP § 1010.6(b)(4)**.

The party filing the proof of electronic service must maintain the printed form of the document bearing the declarant's original signature and must make the document available for inspection and copying on the request of the court or any party to the action or proceeding in which it is filed, in the manner provided in **CRC Rule 2.257(a)**. **CRC Rule 2.251**.

Proof of electronic service may be by any of the methods provided in **CCP § 1013(a)**, except that the proof of service must state:

> (1) Proof of electronic service shall be made as provided in Code of Civil Procedure section 1013b.
> (2) Under rule 3.1300(c), proof of electronic service of the moving papers must be filed at least five court days before the hearing.
> (3) If a person signs a printed form of a proof of electronic service, the party or other person filing the proof of electronic service must comply with the provisions of rule 2.257(a). CRC Rule 2.251(i).

Chapter 9: Timing, Electronic Filing & Service

As of January 1, 2017, electronic filing documents with Courts of Appeal and the California Supreme Court must comply with **CRC 8.71**, which provides in pertinent part:

> **(a)** Except as otherwise provided by these rules, the local rules of the reviewing court, or court order, all parties are required to file all documents electronically in the reviewing court.
> **(b) Self-represented parties**
> **(1)** Self-represented parties are exempt from the requirement to file documents electronically.
> **(2)** A self-represented party may agree to file documents electronically. By electronically filing any document with the court, a self-represented party agrees to file documents electronically.
> **(3)** In cases involving both represented and self-represented parties, represented parties are required to file documents electronically; however, in these cases, each self-represented party may file documents in paper form.
> **(c) Trial courts** Trial courts are exempt from the requirement to file documents electronically, but are permitted to file documents electronically.

Chapter 9: Timing, Electronic Filing & Service

EDUCATIONAL EXERCISES

I. Answer the following:

1. An *RFO* is filed on September 14 and on the same day is served by mail to the opposing party. If the hearing is set for October 11 is the service valid?
2. Is it valid service if the hearing is on October 12?
3. Is it valid service if the hearing is on October 13?
4. If a RFO is filed on March 15 and served by mail on the same day for a hearing set on April 26 the response to the RFO must be served by mail on _____ or personally _____ served by to be valid.
5. If a response to a RFO is mailed to the opposing party on June 18 for a hearing set for July 20 when does the reply have to be served to be valid service?
6. Discovery was served by mail on May 26 and it is now July 29 and no responses have been received. What is the first day that the Motion to Compel can be filed?
7. A subpoena for business records was served on March 22. When is the first day that the business records can be due?
8. Documents were dropped in the court dropbox on May 27 at 4:10 p.m. What is the file date that the clerk will stamp on the documents?
9. If a deposition notice is mailed on August 17 for a deposition scheduled for September 6, is that valid service such that the deposition will go forward?
10. If the code does not specify court or calendar days, which is used?
11. When counting the days that a response is due, is the first, last or both days counted?

II. Match the letter with the appropriate number

      a. CRC Guideline 1
      b. CCP § 2020.410(c)
      c. CCP § 1013(a)
      d. CCP § 12
      e. CCP § 2025.270(a)
      f. CRC Rule 2.210
      g. CCP § 1005(b)
      h. CRC Rule 3.1300
      i. CCP § 1010.6(a)(4)
      j. CRC Rule 8.25(b)

1. _____ Unless otherwise ordered or specifically provided by law, all moving and supporting papers shall be served and filed at least 16 court days before the hearing. The moving and supporting papers served shall be a copy of the papers filed or to be filed with the court. However, if the notice is served by mail, the required 16-day period of notice before the hearing shall be increased by five calendar days if the place of mailing and the place of address are within the State of California, 10 calendar days if either the place of mailing or the place of address is outside the State of California but within the United States, and 20 calendar days if either the place of mailing or the place of address is outside the United States, and if the notice is served by facsimile transmission, express mail, or another method of

Chapter 9: Timing, Electronic Filing & Service

delivery providing for overnight delivery, the required 16-day period of notice before the hearing shall be increased by two calendar days.

2. _____ The time in which any act provided by law is to be done is computed by excluding the first day, and including the last, unless the last day is a holiday, and then it is also excluded.

3. _____ Court days refer to days on which the California courts are open for official business. Normally, Mondays through Fridays are counted as court days, except for judicial holidays.

4. _____ In case of service by mail, the notice or other paper shall be deposited in a post office, mailbox, subpost office, substation, or mail chute, or other like facility regularly maintained by the United States Postal Service, in a sealed envelope, with postage paid, addressed to the person on whom it is to be served, at the office address as last given by that person on any document filed in the cause and served on the party making service by mail; otherwise at that party's place of residence. Service is complete at the time of the deposit, but any period of notice and any right or duty to do any act or make any response within any period or on a date certain after service of the document, which time period or date is prescribed by statute or rule of court, shall be extended five calendar days, upon service by mail, if the place of address and the place of mailing is within the State of California, 10 calendar days if either the place of mailing or the place of address is outside the State of California but within the United States, and 20 calendar days if either the place of mailing or the place of address is outside the United States, but the extension shall not apply to extend the time for filing notice of intention to move for new trial, notice of intention to move to vacate judgment pursuant to Section 663a, or notice of appeal. This extension applies in the absence of a specific exception provided for by this section or other statute or rule of court.

5. _____ An oral deposition shall be scheduled for a date at least 10 days after service of the deposition notice. An oral deposition shall be scheduled for a date at least five days after service of the deposition notice, but not later than five days before trial. The party giving notice of the deposition is a subpoenaing party, and the deponent is a witness commanded by a deposition subpoena to produce personal records of a consumer or employment records of an employee, the deposition shall be scheduled for a date at least 20 days after issuance of that subpoena.

6. _____ A deposition subpoena that commands only the production of business records for copying need not be accompanied by an affidavit or declaration showing good cause for the production of the business records designated in it. It shall be directed to the custodian of those records or another person qualified to certify the records. It shall command compliance in accordance with Section 2020.430 on a date that is no earlier than 20 days after the issuance, or 15 days after the service, of the deposition subpoena, whichever date is later.

7. _____ The court receiving a document filed electronically shall issue a confirmation that the document has been received and filed. The confirmation shall serve as proof that the document has been filed.

8. _____ All moving and supporting papers must be served and filed in accordance with **CCP §1005** and, when applicable, the statutes and rules providing for electronic filing and service.
The court, on its own motion or on application for an order shortening time supported by a declaration showing good cause, may prescribe shorter times for the filing and service of papers than the times specified **CCP §1005**. Proof of service of the moving papers must be filed no later than five court days before the time appointed for the hearing.

Chapter 9: Timing, Electronic Filing & Service

9. _____ A document is deemed filed on the date the clerk receives it.
A filing is not timely unless the clerk receives the document before the time to file it expires.

A brief, an application to file an amicus curiae brief, an answer to an amicus curiae brief, a petition for rehearing, an answer to a petition for rehearing, a petition for transfer of an appellate division case to the Court of Appeal, an answer to such a petition for transfer, a petition for review, an answer to a petition for review, or a reply to an answer to a petition for review is timely if the time to file it has not expired on the date of:

Its mailing by priority or express mail as shown on the postmark or the postal receipt; or

Its delivery to a common carrier promising overnight delivery as shown on the carrier's receipt.

The provisions of (3) do not apply to original proceedings.

_____ Whenever a clerk's office filing counter is closed at any time between 8:30 a.m. and 4:00 p.m. on a court day, the court must provide a drop box for depositing documents to be filed with the clerk. A court may provide a drop box during other times.

Any document deposited in a court's drop box up to and including 4:00 p.m. on a court day is deemed to have been deposited for filing on that day. A court may provide for same-day filing of a document deposited in its drop box after 4:00 p.m. on a court day. If so, the court must give notice of the deadline for same-day filing of a document deposited in its drop box.

Any document deposited in a court's drop box is deemed to have been deposited for filing on the next court day if:

It is deposited on a court day after 4:00 p.m. or after the deadline for same-day filing if a court provides for a later time; or

It is deposited on a judicial holiday.

CHAPTER 10: Service of Process & Proof of Service

In Brief...

SERVICE OF PROCESS:
- Is delivering a copy of all of the paperwork filed with the court to the responding party;
- Is affected in the same manner as service of civil action papers, **FC § 2331**; and
- Any person 18 years old or older and not a party to the action may provide service, **CCP § 414.10**.
- Jurisdiction over a party begins when the *Summons/Petition* are served, **CCP § 410.50**.
- If the respondent cannot be found to be served, the petitioner may request an order for service by publication or posting under **CCP §§ 415.50** and **413.30**, respectively. By fax requires written confirmation of an agreement to so accept; and
- One copy of any document filed must be served on all parties and attorneys. A copy of the *Proof of Service* must be attached, **CRC Rule 8.25(a)**.
- The *Proof of Service* must be filed no later than 5 court days before the hearing. **CRC Rule 3.1300(c)**.
- When service is effected by mail, the responding party has an additional 5 days to respond if mailed within CA, 10 additional days if mailed within the US and 20 additional days if mailed internationally. **CCP § 1013(a)**.

KINDS OF SERVICE OF PROCESS:
- Personal service, (leaving a copy of the paperwork at a person's residence), **(CCP § 415.10)**;
- Substituted service **(CCP § 415.20)**;
- Service by mail with a notice and acknowledgment of receipt **(CCP § 415.30)**;
- Service on person outside of the state **(CCP § 415.40)**;
- Service by posting, (announcing by affixing a notice in a public place), **CCP § 415.50, CRC Rule 5.68**.
- Service by publication, (e.g. publishing in a newspaper) **(CCP § 413.30)**.
- A response to a family law petition may be served by the methods described in (a) but may also be served by mail without notice and acknowledgment of receipt. **CRC Rule 5.68**.

PROOF OF SERVICE:
- A proof of service form is used to provide a declaration stating that service has been made on the party/party's attorney and filed with court, **CRC Rule 1.21**.
- In family law the *FL-115* form is used for service of the *Summons*.
- The three most commonly used proof of service forms in family law are:

Chapter 10: Service of Process & Proof of Service

> - *Proof of Service of the Summons* (*Family Law*)(form *FL-115*),
> - *Proof of Service by Mail* (form *FL-335*), directions for completing this form and information regarding this form are provided on Judicial Council form *FL-335-INFO*;
> - *Proof of Personal Service* (form *FL-330*), Directions for completing this form and information regarding this form are provided on Judicial Council form *FL-330-INFO*.
> - By fax requires written confirmation of an agreement to so accept; and
> - One copy of any document filed must be served on all parties and attorneys. A copy of the *Proof of Service* must be attached, **CRC Rule 8.25(a)**.
> - The *Proof of Service* must be filed no later than 5 court days before the hearing. **CRC Rule 3.1300(c)**.
>
> **CHART 7: Judicial Council Forms RE: PROOF OF SERVICE**

Introduction

After all of the initial forms have been completed, carefully examined for errors and signed by the party and his or her attorney, if an attorney has been retained, the paperwork must be **filed** with the clerk of the appropriate department of the superior court. Usually an original document and two copies of each document must be submitted to the clerk for filing. All original documents are kept by the filing clerk and placed in a court file. The two copies are conformed[1] and returned to the person or service that is filing the paperwork or placed in a dropbox[2] to be picked up by an attorney, attorney's office or attorney's service.

Service of Process

When service is made by mail, service is complete at the time of the deposit (the mailbox rule).

When service has been effected by mail, the responding party has an additional five (5) calendar days to respond, upon service by mail, if the place of address and the place of mailing is within the State of California, ten (10) calendar days if either the place of mailing or the place of address is outside the State of California but within the United States, and twenty (20) calendar days if either the place of mailing or the place of address is outside of the United States. **CCP § 1013(a)**.

In the case of service by overnight delivery, service is complete at the time of the deposit, but after service of the document served by express mail or other method of delivery providing for overnight delivery, the response time is extended by two

---

[1] Conformed copies are exact and true copies of an original that are stamped and dated with an official court stamp. Conformed copies usually have stamped, printed signatures.
[2] Most courts have both a dropbox to drop off paperwork for the court to file and a dropbox to pick up paperwork that has been processed.

court days. **CCP § 1013(c)**.

If service is affected by facsimile, service is complete at the time of transmission, but after service by facsimile transmission, the response time is extended by two court days. **CCP § 1013(e)**.

If a *RFO* (form *FL-300*) is not timely served on the opposing party, the moving party must notify the court as soon as possible before the date assigned for the court hearing and request a new hearing date to allow additional time to serve the *RFO* (form *FL-300*) and supporting documents. **CRC Rule 5.94(c)**. The moving party must also request that the court reissue the *RFO* (form *FL-300*) and any temporary orders. To do so, the moving party must complete and submit to the court an *Application and Order for Reissuance of Request for Order* (form *FL-306*). **CRC Rule 5.94(c)**.

When a *Petition* is filed, the respondent must receive a copy of all of the paperwork that the petitioner filed with the court pertaining to the case so that he or she has notice of all of the claims in the lawsuit and an opportunity to respond to those claims. A copy of the *Petition,* together with a copy of a *Summons* must be served upon the other party to the marriage in the same manner as service of civil action papers. **FC § 2331**.

Serving a copy of all of the paperwork filed with the court is called **service of process**. It is the method used to bring the responding party into the proceeding, action or lawsuit and gives the court the authority to make orders in the case. Service of process is affected by delivering a copy of all of the paperwork filed with the court to the responding party. Improper service can result in a *void* judgment.

Service may be effected by: **(1)** personal service, **(2)** substituted service (leaving a copy of the paperwork at a person's residence), **(3)** service by mail with a notice and acknowledgment of receipt, **(4)** service by publication (e.g. publishing in a newspaper), or **(5)** service by posting (announcing by affixing a notice in a public place). **CRC Rule 5.68**.

The petitioner, or his or her attorney if represented, must arrange personal service on the respondent with a *Summons, Petition* and any other papers regarding the case filed with the court. **CRC Rule 5.68**. This paperwork may be served by any person who is at least 18 years of age and not a party to the action. **CCP § 414.10**. Personal delivery of a *Summons* is deemed complete at the time of such delivery. **CCP § 415.10**.

Whenever a document is required to be served on a party, the service must additionally be made on the party's attorney, if the party is represented. **CRC Rule 1.21**.

A responsive pleading must be filed, and a copy served on the petitioner within thirty (30) days of the date that the respondent was served with the *Petition* and *Summons*. **FC § 2020**.

After service is affected or the respondent has made an appearance, the respondent/his or her attorney is entitled to notice of all subsequent proceedings pursuant to the Family Code or in civil actions generally. If a party does not appear at a hearing after being appropriately and timely served, no notice of subsequent proceedings needs to be given to the respondent or responding party.

A *Response* to a family law *Petition* may be served by mail, providing the respondent agrees to it and signs a *Notice and Acknowledgment of Receipt* (form *FL-117*). **CRC Rule 5.68**.

A respondent is deemed to have appeared in a proceeding when he or she files a *Response*, motion to strike, motion to transfer the proceeding or a written notice of his or her appearance. **CRC Rule 5.62**. And a general appearance of the respondent is equivalent to personal service within this state of the *Summons* and the *Petition*. **CRC Rule 5.68. The Standard Family Law Restraining orders are only in effect when** the *Petition* and *Summons* have been personally served on the respondent or upon waiver and acceptance of service by the respondent. **FC § 233**.

After service, the court has jurisdiction over a party when the *Summons* is served on him or her. Jurisdiction of the court over the parties and the subject matter of an action continues throughout subsequent proceedings in the action. **CCP § 410.50**.

If the respondent cannot be found to be served a *Summons* and *Petition*, the petitioner may request an order for service of the *Summons* by publication or posting under **CCP §§ 415.50** and **413.30**, respectively.

To request service of a *Summons* by publication or posting, the petitioner must complete and submit to the court an *Application for Order for Publication or Posting* (form *FL-980*) and *Order for Publication or Posting* (form *FL-982*). *NOTE*: The *FL-982* has a second page that contains information and instructions upon completion.

Alternatively, the petitioner may complete and submit to the court pleadings containing the same information as forms *FL-980* and *FL-982*. The petitioner must list all the reasonable diligent efforts that have been made to find and serve the respondent.

Service of a *Summons* by posting may be ordered only if the petitioner has obtained an order waiving court fees and costs. If the petitioner's financial situation has improved since obtaining the approved order on court fee waiver, the petitioner must file a *Notice to Court of Improved Financial Situation or Settlement* (form FW-010). If the court finds that the petitioner no longer qualifies for a fee waiver, the court may order service by publication of the documents. A *Proof of service by*

Posting (form *FL-985*), or a pleading containing the same information as form *FL-985*, must be completed by the person who posted the documents and then filed with the court once posting is completed. **CRC Rule 5.72**.

Service by facsimile transmission is permitted only where the parties agree and a written confirmation of that agreement is made. In the case of service by facsimile transmission, the notice or other paper must be transmitted to a facsimile machine maintained by the person on whom it is served at the facsimile machine telephone number as last given by that person on any document which he or she has filed in the case and served on the party making the service.

Other than the *Petition*, which must be served personally, all documents that the rules require be served on the parties must be served personally or electronically. All parties represented by counsel are deemed to have agreed to accept electronic service. All self-represented parties may agree to such service. **CRC Rule 3.2222(b)**.

Unless the court-filed paper served is a *Response*, the party who serves a court-filed paper must retain the original with the original proof of service affixed. The original of a *Response* must be served, and it must be retained by the person upon whom it is served. All original papers must be retained until six (6) months after final disposition of the case, unless the court, on motion of any party and for good cause shown, orders the original papers preserved for a longer period. **CRC Rule 3.250**.

No judgment of dissolution is final such that either of the parties can remarry until six (6) months after the date of service of the *Summons* and *Petition* or the date of appearance of the respondent, whichever occurs first. **FC § 2339(a)**. The court may extend the six-month waiting period that commences after the judgment is rendered for a good cause. **FC § 2339(b)**.

Proof of Service

A copy of any document that is to be filed must be served on the attorney for each party separately represented, on each unrepresented party and on any other person in the action before the filing of that document. A *Proof of Service* must be attached to the document to be filed showing that the service was performed as required. **CRC Rule 8.25(a)**.

Parties must file a completed *Proof of Service* form to prove that the other party received the *Petition* or *Response to Petition* or other pleading. The proof of service of the summons may be a form approved by the Judicial Council or a document or pleading containing the same information required in *Proof of Service of Summons* (form *FL-115*). The proof of service of the *Response* to a *Petition* or *Complaint* may be a form approved by the Judicial Council or a document or pleading containing the same information required in *Proof of Service by Mail* (form *FL-335*) or *Proof of Personal Service* (form *FL-330*).

Chapter 10: Service of Process & Proof of Service

The *Proof of Service* of the moving papers must be filed no later than five (5) court days before the time appointed for the hearing. **CRC Rule 3.1300(c)**.

CRC Rule 1.21 provides:

> **(a)** Whenever a document is required to be served on a party, the service must be made on the party's attorney if the party is represented.
> **(b)** As used in these rules, unless a statute or rule provides for a different method for filing or service, a requirement to **"serve and file"** a document means that a copy of the document must be served on the attorney for each party separately represented, on each self-represented party, and on any other person or entity when required by statute, rule, or court order, and that the document and a proof of service of the document must be filed with the court.
> **(c)** As used in these rules, **"proof of service"** means a declaration stating that service has been made as provided in (a) and (b). If the proof of service names attorneys for separately represented parties, it must also state which party or parties each of the attorneys served is representing. (Emphasis added.)

If the service is of the *Summons* and *Petition*, then the petitioner must arrange to serve the other party with a *Summons*, *Petition* and other papers as required by one of the following codes:

> **(1)** Personal service (CCP § 415.10);
> **(2)** Substituted service (CCP § 415.20);
> **(3)** Service by mail with a notice and acknowledgment of receipt (CCP § 415.30);
> **(4)** Service on person outside of the state (CCP § 415.40);
> **(5)** Service on a person residing outside of the United States which must be done in compliance with service rules of the following:
>   **(A)** Hague Convention on the Service Abroad of Judicial and Extrajudicial Documents in Civil or Commercial Matters; or
>   **(B)** Inter-American Convention on Letters Rogatory and the Additional Protocol to the Inter-American Convention on Letters Rogatory.
> **(6)** Service by posting or publication (CCP §§ 415.50 and 413.30).
> **(b)** A response to a family law petition may be served by the methods described in (a) but may also be served by mail without notice and acknowledgment of receipt. CRC Rule 5.68.

The court has jurisdiction over the parties and control of all subsequent proceedings commencing when the *Petition* and *Summons* are served upon the responding party.

Parties must file with the court a completed *Proof of Service* form to prove that the other party received the *Petition* or *Response* or any other paperwork filed with the court and served upon the responding party. In family law there is a specific proof of service form used for service of the *Summons* (form *FL-115*). This form contains checkboxes that require that all documents accompanying the *Summons* are to include both a completed form and a blank form.

The three most commonly used proof of service forms in family law are: **(1)** *Proof of Personal Service* (form *FL-330*), **(2)** *Proof of Service by Mail* (form *FL-335*) and

(3) *Proof of Service of the Summons (Family Law)* (form *FL-115*), mentioned above.

When personal service has been affected of documents other than the *Summons*, the *Proof of Personal Service* (form *FL-330*) is used. Directions for completing this form and information regarding this form are provided on Judicial Council form *FL-330-INFO*.

When service is affected by mail, the *Proof of Service by Mail* (form *FL-335*) is used. Directions for completing this form and information regarding this form are provided on Judicial Council form *FL-335-INFO*.

It is important to note that when service is affected by mail, the responding party has an additional five (5) days to respond if the documents were mailed to a party who is within the State of California, ten (10) additional days if mailed to a party within the United States and twenty (20) additional days if mailed internationally. **CCP § 1013(a)**.

If service is made by mail pursuant to **CCP § 415.30**, the proof of service must include an acknowledgment of receipt of the *Summons* that is satisfactory to the court.[3] All proofs of personal service must be made on a form adapted by the Judicial Council. **CCP § 417.10**.

CHART 7: Judicial Council Forms RE: PROOF OF SERVICE

FL-FORM	FORM NAME
FL-115	*Proof of Service of Summons (Family Law)*
FL-117	*Notice and Acknowledgment of Receipt (Family Law)*
FL-141	*Declaration Regarding Service of Declaration of Disclosure and Income and Expense Declaration*
FL-330	*Proof of Personal Service*
FL-330-INFO	*Information Sheet for Proof of Personal Service*
FL-335	*Proof of Service by Mail*
FL-335-INFO	*Information Sheet for Proof of Service by Mail*
FL-980	*Application for Order for Publication or Posting*
FL-982	*Order for Publication or Posting*
FL-985	*Proof of service by Posting*

© 2019 LW Greenberg

---

[3] There is a special Family Law Judicial Council form entitled *Notice and Acknowledgement of Receipt* (form *FL-117*) that may be used. This is an optional form approved by the Judicial Council.

Chapter 10: Service of Process & Proof of Service

EDUCATIONAL EXERCISES

Using the information set forth in Appendix One, and specifically noting the dates on the Timeline prepare a Proof of Service form for the discovery sent on 3/2/2018 and the RFO sent on 4/6/2018.

CHAPTER 11: Discovery

In Brief...

***CIVIL DISCOVERY ACT APPLIES TO ALL FAMILY LAW DISCOVERY,* CRC Rule 5.12**.
- **There are restrictions on disseminating information** obtained by any method of discovery.
- **Time to respond is extended if discovery request is mailed, CCP § 1013(a):**
  - The response time extended by 5 days if mailed within CA;
  - The response time extended by 10 days if mailed outside CA, but within US; and
  - The response time extended by 20 days if mailed outside the US.

SOME OF THE COMMONALITIES IN THE DISCOVERY LAWS ARE:
- Discovery requests are not filed with the court.
- A copy of all discovery requests must be served upon all partied that have appeared in the action.
- The propounding party must retain both the original discovery and the original proof of service.
- If interrogatories, document inspection demands and/or requests for admissions are mailed to a party within CA, **CCP § 1013(a)** applies.
- The parties requesting and responding may agree to extend the time, but it must be confirmed in writing.
- If a party objects to discovery based on a claim of privilege, the response must provide sufficient factual information for other parties to evaluate the merits of that claim.
- Each answer must have the same identifying number and be in the same sequence as the request.
- If a party fails to obey an order-compelling discovery, the court may issue sanctions.
- The court must impose a monetary sanction against any party, person or attorney who unsuccessfully makes or opposes a motion for a protective order there is a substantial justification.

THE 4 METHODS OF DISCOVERY COMMONLY USED IN FAMILY LAW ARE:
- **Interrogatories a**re written questions served on an opposing party, **CCP § 2030.010** et seq.
- **Document inspection demands** are demands for inspection/copying of documents, **CCP §2031.01**.
- **Requests for Admission** are to admit genuineness of documents, truth of statements, **CCP §2033.010**.
- **Depositions** are proceedings to examine a parties or witness under oath, **CCP 2020.010** et seq.

***MISUSE OF THE DISCOVERY PROCESS INCLUDES,* CCP § 2023.010:**
- Persisting without justification to obtain information outside permissible scope;

Chapter 11: Discovery

> - Using in a manner that does not comply with the specified procedures;
> - Using discovery to annoy, embarrass, unduly burden or make the case costlier;
> - Failing to respond or to submit to an authorized method of discovery;
> - Making an unmeritorious objection to discovery;
> - Making an evasive response to a discovery request;
> - Unsuccessfully opposing any discovery motion; and
> - Failing to meet and confer.
>
> **SANCTIONS FOR DISCOVERY MISUSE:**
> - In the CCP also apply to family law discovery, **CRC Rule 5.2(d)**;
> - May be ordered for any misuse of the discovery process, **CCP § 2023.010**; and
> - Are usually a discretionary decision for the judge, **CRC Rule 5.2(d)**.
>
> **SPECIAL DISCOVERY RULES FOR POSTJUDGMENT MODIFICATIONS:**
> - After a judgment, parties may request a completed current *FL-150* from other party, **FC § 3664**.
> - A party may request a completed *FL-150* only once every 12 months, **FC § 3663**.
> - Discovery methods may only be used if motion for modification/termination is pending, **FC § 3662**.
> - The *Response* must include a completed *FL-150* and prior year's tax returns, **FC § 3665**.
>
> *FL-150* must be complete, accurate and include prior year's tax returns or can be sanctioned. **FC §3667**.

Introduction

Discovery consists of several procedures that are used to request necessary information and documents from an opposing party to prepare a client's case.

Family law discovery rules include all of the laws set forth in the Civil Discovery Act that is within the Code of Civil Procedure[1] and **FC §§ 2100** through **2113** regarding disclosure of assets and liabilities. **CRC Rule 5.12**. (Disclosure is covered in Chapter 30, *infra*.) Additionally, other laws in the Code of Civil Procedure apply to family law discovery, such as the laws pertaining to obtaining evidence, issuing subpoenas and discovery sanctions. **CRC Rule 5.2(d)**. Other rules in the Rules of Court may apply to family law actions in proceedings under the Civil Discovery Act. **FC § 210**.

There are special rules when discovery is requested postjudgment for modifications and termination of court orders.

---

[1] The Civil Discovery Act laws are set forth in CCP § 2016.010 through CCP §2036.050.

Family Law Discovery

In the Civil Discovery Act there are several laws that have provisions that in common: some of those laws are:

(1) Discovery requests are not filed with the court.
(2) A copy of all discovery requests must be served upon the party to whom the request is directed and to every other party that has appeared in the action.
(3) The propounding party[2] must retain both the original discovery request with the original proof of service affixed and the original of the sworn response until six months after final disposition of the action.
(4) If interrogatories, document inspection demands and/or requests for admissions are mailed to a party within the State of California, the responding party has an additional five (5) days to respond. If the interrogatories are mailed to a party who is not in California but is within the United States, the responding party has an additional ten (10) days to respond; if the interrogatories are mailed to an party internationally, there is an additional twenty (20) days to respond. **CCP § 1013(a)**.
(5) The party requesting the discovery and the responding party may agree to extend the time for service of a response, but it must be confirmed in a writing that specifies the extended date for the service of a response.
(6) When any discovery request has been made, the responding party may promptly move for a protective order.
(7) If a party objects to discovery based on a claim of privilege or a claim that the information sought is protected work product, the response must provide sufficient factual information for other parties to evaluate the merits of that claim.
(8) Absent exceptional circumstances, the court may not impose sanctions on a party or any attorney of a party for failure to provide electronically stored information that has been lost, damaged, altered or overwritten as the result of the routine, good-faith operation of an electronic information system.
(9) Each answer or objection in the responses to interrogatories, demands for documents and requests for admission must have the same identifying number or letter and be in the same sequence as the corresponding request, but the text of the particular request need not be repeated.
(10) If a party fails to obey an order-compelling discovery, the court may make those orders that are just, including the imposition of an issue sanction, an evidence sanction, a terminating sanction and/or a monetary sanction.
(11) The court must impose a monetary sanction against any party, person or attorney who unsuccessfully makes or opposes a motion for a protective order under this section, unless it finds that the one subject to the sanction acted with substantial justification or that other circumstances make the imposition of the sanction unjust.
(12) There are restrictions on disseminating information obtained by any method of discovery, as the court held in the following case.

---

[2] The term "propounded" means prepared or drafted.

Chapter 11: Discovery

> ***In re Marriage of DEBRA and THOMAS C. CANDIOTTI. DEBRA CANDIOTTI,
> Appellant, v. THOMAS C. CANDIOTTI et al., Respondents.***
> COURT OF APPEAL OF CALIFORNIA, FIRST APPELLATE DISTRICT, DIVISION THREE
> 34 Cal.App.4th 718
> April 27, 1995, Decided
> (*Marriage of Candiotti*)

Debra and Thomas dissolved their marriage after having two children together. Following the dissolution, the court retained jurisdiction over custody and visitation issues. Thomas subsequently married his present wife, Donna, who was joined as a party so that certain restraining orders would be applicable to her, as well as to Debra and Thomas.

The following year, the parties stipulated in lieu of a hearing to the children's Christmas vacation schedule and to certain practices to be followed when driving with the children.

Prior to the stipulation, Debra had noticed Donna's deposition and requested a number of documents, including personal information, driving records, and any criminal history. Donna's counsel had sought a protective order regarding the discovery demand, and the court discussed the issue with counsel in chambers. After reviewing the material and hearing argument, the court issued a temporary protective order directing Debra not to disseminate information regarding Donna's past driving record and other defined personal history to anyone besides certain specified individuals.

Debra opposed the order, arguing it violated her First Amendment free speech rights. She claimed the order hampered her ability to protect her children, because she was restricted from communicating the subject information to other appropriate parties.

Debra also argued that because some of the information was acquired through outside sources, rather than through the discovery process, the court could not restrict its dissemination. Specifically, Debra alleged she had received an anonymous telephone call from an individual who claimed to have information related to Donna. Debra thereafter investigated these allegations and obtained information about Donna's driving and personal history.

In support of the order, Thomas asserted Debra had no legitimate reason to disseminate the information and that her sole motivation was vindictive. He argued the court's concern for protecting the best interests of the children overrode Debra's free speech rights and that the First Amendment was not designed to protect this type of speech.
Donna argued in support of the temporary protective order, urging it promoted the best interests of the children. In addition, she claimed dissemination of the information violated her privacy rights.

In determining whether the temporary protective order should become permanent, the trial court weighed Debra's right of speech against the state's interest in protecting the minor children and Donna's right to privacy. As for Donna's privacy rights, the court noted that part of the information was public record, in which Donna had little or no privacy interest. The court also found that the other records, provided by Donna's counsel at the in camera hearing, legitimately raised privacy concerns.

The court explained, however, that its concern for the welfare of the children justified restrictions on Debra's conduct. In particular, the court stated it would be harmful for the children to hear from the "rumor mill" disparaging comments about their stepmother or to be taunted by peers at school. The court was concerned that Debra's purpose in making the information public was to embarrass and ridicule Donna, with that effect also falling upon the children. In this regard, the court chastised the parties for their continued fighting, particularly the animosity between Debra and Donna, and noted it had previously admonished the parties to "behave like adults" for the benefit of the children.

The court then directed the temporary protective order to remain in full force and effect for a period not to exceed three years.

DISCUSSION
This case arises from circumstances tragically common in our family law courts. Daily, judges are called upon to intervene when parents pursue their animosity toward each other to the detriment of their children. Such cases involve the most profound and compelling of interests. Matters of familial, parental, and personal autonomy must be balanced against traditional statutory and constitutional concepts. Trial judges are challenged to navigate between the Scylla of harm to innocent children and the Charybdis of undue governmental intervention. In this case, an experienced and insightful judge tried to shield two youngsters from the harmful effects of adult conflict swirling about them. We feel constrained to find, however, that the order, in part, ran afoul of constitutional principles. The order covers two separate kinds of information: that acquired during formal discovery and that independently obtained.

In terms of disclosure, courts have treated information obtained through discovery differently from that secured by other means. Restrictions on dissemination of discovery material have withstood First Amendment challenges. (Seattle Times Co. v. Rhinehart (1984) 467 U.S. 20, 31-37.)

[The United States Supreme Court stated in Settle Times, supra, that "the discovery process is a matter of legislative grace. A litigant has no First Amendment right of access to information made available only for purposes of trying his suit… [D]iscovered information does not raise the same specter of government censorship that such control might suggest in other situations." A rule upholding restrictions on dissemination of information obtained through discovery allows "parties to obtain relevant information pertinent to their case, while preventing potential abuse, such as use of the information to damage a person's reputation or invade their privacy rights. Such a rule properly furthers an important governmental interest." The court held that "when a protective order is properly issued on a showing of good cause and limits only the dissemination of information obtained through discovery and not other sources, it does not offend the First Amendment." Id. at 723.]

Here, the trial judge found a sufficient showing of good cause. Clearly the court was concerned with Debra's motivation for disseminating the information and the derivative harm that might befall the children. And, although Debra maintains that all of the material about Donna was obtained outside the discovery process, such an assertion runs counter to the record. The trial court specifically found that Debra obtained material both from private and court-compelled sources.

We conclude that the part of the protective order restricting the dissemination of information obtained through Debra's discovery request is a proper restriction. But, the scope of restrictions on material independently acquired violates Debra's rights under the California Constitution.

> That part of the order banning dissemination of information obtained through discovery is affirmed. That part of the order banning dissemination of independently acquired materials is reversed.

Methods of Discovery

There are six methods that can be used to obtain discovery. **CCP § 2019.010**.[3] However, in family law, only four of the six methods are commonly employed—interrogatories, document inspection demands, requests for admission and depositions.

1. Interrogatories

Interrogatories are a set of written questions that are served upon an opposing party. The interrogatory rules are set forth at **CCP §§ 2030.010** through and including **2030.410**. There are form interrogatories for family law (form *FL-145*). This form is downloadable at *www.courts.ca.gov/forms.htm*. At the top of the form are the instructions for filling it out. Because this form is approved and not adapted, its use is optional.

However, it is always a good place to begin discovery with the family law form interrogatories.

Both form and special interrogatories may be propounded. However, the number of special interrogatories that may be propounded to another party may not exceed thirty-five (35). If the number of additional special interrogatories exceeds thirty-five (35), an objection can be made on the ground that the limit has been exceeded. **CCP § 2030.030.**

Each special interrogatory must be prepared full and complete in and of itself. No interrogatory may contain subparts or compound, conjunctive or disjunctive questions. **CCP § 2030.060**.

Written interrogatories, including form interrogatories, are to be answered under penalty of perjury. **CCP § 2030.010.** Responses must be complete or an objection may be made. If an objection is made to only part of an interrogatory, the remainder must be answered. **CCP § 2030.240.** Responses to interrogatories constitute admissions that can be used as evidence at trial. **CCP § 2030.410.**

---

[3] Pursuant to CCP § 2019.010, the six discovery methods are: (1) oral and written depositions; (2) interrogatories to a party; (3) inspections of documents, things and places; (4) physical and mental examinations; (5) requests for admissions; and (6) simultaneous exchanges of expert trial witness information.

2. Document Inspection Demands

Document inspection demands are propounded and served on an opposing party, demanding to allow inspecting, copying, testing or sampling: **(1)** documents, **(2)** tangible things, **(3)** land or other property; and **(4)** electronically stored information in the possession, custody or control of any other party to the action. Any party to the action may use this method of discovery. **CCP § 2031.010(a)**.

A party may demand that any other party produce and permit the party making the demand, or someone acting on that party's behalf, to inspect and copy documents, photographs and/or electronically stored information that are in the possession, custody or control of the party on whom the demand is made. **CCP § 2031.010**.

A response must be verified and signed under penalty of perjury. Additionally, the response must identify the documents in the responding party's possession and indicate whether the documents will be made available for inspection and copying. **CCP §§ 2031.010** et. seq.

Many times, in family law cases, if both the propounding party and the responding party agree, the documents demanded may be copied and served upon the propounding party within the time permitted to respond. This is a much less costly method. If the parties so agree to this copying method, the agreement should be in writing and the propounding party should retain the right to inspect the originals.

In family law discovery, documents that are commonly demanded to be inspected are financial records, such as paystubs, income tax returns (both federal and state), bank records, credit card statements, IRAs, deferred compensation, pension and retirement plan information. Deeds, Deeds of Trust, registrations and certificates of title for vehicles, leases and rental agreements are often demanded, as well.

2. Requests for Admissions

Requests for Admissions are requests to an opposing party to admit the genuineness of specific documents and/or the truth of specific statements that are relevant to the action. This method of discovery is not used as often as the other three. However, requests for admissions can be a very effective way to reduce conference and court time by quickly eliminating undisputed facts/issues.

The Judicial Council has promulgated an official form for Requests for Admissions, DISC-020. It is not a family law form, but it may be used in family law discovery. It is downloadable at: ***www.courts.ca.gov/forms.htm?filter=DSC***.

At the top of the form are instructions for completing it. Because this form is approved and not adapted, its use is optional. The procedure for serving requests for admissions is the same as for interrogatories.

No party may request that any other party admit more than thirty-five (35) matters that do not relate to the genuineness of documents. If the initial set of admission requests does not exhaust this limit, the balance may be requested in subsequent sets. A party need only respond to the first thirty-five (35) admission requests served that do not relate to the genuineness of documents if an objection is made on the ground that the limit was exceeded. **CCP § 2033.030**.

The party to whom requests for admission have been directed must respond in writing under oath separately to each request. Each response must answer the substance of the requested admission or set forth an objection to the particular request. **CCP § 2033.210**.

3. Depositions

A deposition is a proceeding whereby one party is allowed to examine the other party or witness under oath in front of a court reporter. The deposition rules in the Civil Discovery Act are set forth at **CCP § 2020.010** et seq. The person whose deposition is being taken is called the deponent. The deponent is placed under oath by the court reporter and then asked questions by counsel. The oath taken is the same as the oath taken before testifying in court of law and has the same effect.

Any party may obtain discovery by taking the oral deposition of any person, including any party to the action. The person deposed may be a natural person, an organization, such as a public or private corporation, a partnership, an association or a governmental agency. **CCP § 2025.010**.

A party desiring to take the oral deposition of any person must give notice in writing. The deposition notice must include all of the information set forth in **CCP § 2025.220**. The information in the notice includes:

(1) The address where the deposition will be taken.
(2) The date of the deposition and the time it will commence.
(3) The name, the address and the telephone number of each deponent.
(4) The materials or category of materials to be produced by the deponent.
(5) Whether the deposition testimony will be by audio or video technology.
(6) Any intention to reserve the right to use at trial.
(7) The form in which any electronically stored information is to be produced.
(8) A statement disclosing the existence of a contract, if any is known to the noticing party, between the noticing party or a third party who is financing all or part of the action; and
(9) A statement disclosing that the party noticing the deposition, or a third party financing all or part of the action, directed his or her attorney to use a particular officer or entity to provide services for the deposition, if applicable.

The party who prepares a notice of deposition must give the notice to every other party who has appeared in the action. The deposition notice, or the accompanying proof of service, must list all the parties or attorneys for parties on whom it is served. **CCP § 2025.240**.

The deposition of a natural person, whether or not a party to the action, must be taken at a place that is, at the option of the party giving notice of the deposition, either within 75 miles of the deponent's residence or within the county where the action is pending and within 150 miles of the deponent's residence. **CCP § 2025.250**.

An oral deposition must be scheduled for a date at least ten (10) days after service of the deposition notice. If the party giving notice of the deposition is a subpoenaing party, and the deponent is a witness commanded by a deposition subpoena to produce personal records of a consumer or employment records of an employee, the deposition must be scheduled for a date at least twenty (20) days after issuance of that subpoena. **CCP § 2025.270**.

A deposition notice under **CCP § 2025.240** is effective to require any deponent who is a party to the action or an officer, director, managing agent or employee of a party to attend and to testify, as well as to produce any document, electronically stored information or tangible thing for inspection and copying. **CCP § 2025.270(a)**.

If the deponent is not a party to the action, the deponent must be served a deposition subpoena.[4] The deposition subpoena may require the attendance and testimony of a non-party, as well as the production by the deponent of any document, electronically stored information or tangible thing for inspection and copying. **CCP § 2025.270(b)**.

CCP § 2034.280 provides:

> **(a)** The service of a deposition notice under Section 2025.240 is effective to require any deponent who is a party to the action or an officer, director, managing agent, or employee of a party to attend and to testify, as well as to produce any document, electronically stored information, or tangible thing for inspection and copying.
> **(b)** The attendance and testimony of any other deponent, as well as the production by the deponent of any document, electronically stored information, or tangible thing for inspection and copying, requires the service on the deponent of a deposition subpoena under Chapter 6 (commencing with Section 2020.010).
> **(c)** A deponent required by notice or subpoena to produce electronically stored information shall provide a means of gaining direct access to, or a translation into a reasonably usable form of, any electronically stored information that is password protected or otherwise inaccessible.[5]

A deposition examination of the witness by all counsel, other than the witness' counsel of record, is limited to seven hours of total testimony. The court may allow additional time, beyond any limits imposed by this section, if needed to fairly

---

[4] The deposition subpoena is pursuant to CCP § 2020.010 et seq.
[5] Section (C) became effective January 1, 2017.

Chapter 11: Discovery

examine the deponent or if the deponent, another person or any other circumstance impedes or delays the examination. **CCP § 2025.290**.

Unless the parties agree otherwise, the testimony at a deposition is recorded and transcribed by the court reporter. The party noticing the deposition bears the cost of the transcription, unless the court, on motion and for good cause shown, orders that the cost be borne or shared by another party. Any other party or the deponent, at the expense of that party or deponent, may obtain a copy of the transcript. **CCP § 2025.510**.

For thirty (30) days after the testimony is transcribed, unless a shorter or longer period is stipulated to on the record, and after the testimony has been transcribed into a booklet, the deponent may change the form or the substance of the answer to any question and may either approve the transcript of the deposition by signing it or refuse to approve the transcription booklet by not signing it. **CCP § 2025.520(b)**.

The attorney that requested and noticed the deposition must retain custody of it until six (6) months after final disposition of the action. At that time, the transcript may be destroyed, unless the court, on motion of any party and for good cause shown, orders that the transcript be preserved for a longer period. **CCP § 2025.550**.

At the trial or any other hearing in the action, any part or all of a deposition may be used against any party who was present or represented at the taking of the deposition, or who had due notice of the deposition and did not serve a valid objection under **CCP § 2025.410**. However, admissibility pursuant to the Rules of Evidence applies as though the deponent were then present and testifying as a witness. **CCP § 2025.620**.

Discovery Misuse and Sanctions

Discovery sanctions in the Code of Civil Procedure also apply to family law discovery. **CRC Rule 5.2(d)**. A court may order sanctions against a party if the court finds that party has misused the discovery process. Sanctions are usually a discretionary decision for the judge. Pursuant to **CCP § 2023.010**, misuses of the discovery process include, but are not limited to, the following:

> **(a)** Persisting, over objection and without substantial justification, in an attempt to obtain information or materials that are outside the scope of permissible discovery.
> **(b)** Using a discovery method in a manner that does not comply with its specified procedures.
> **(c)** Employing a discovery method in a manner or to an extent that causes unwarranted annoyance, embarrassment, or oppression, or undue burden and expense.
> **(d)** Failing to respond or to submit to an authorized method of discovery.
> **(e)** Making, without substantial justification, an unmeritorious objection to discovery.
> **(f)** Making an evasive response to discovery.
> **(g)** Disobeying a court order to provide discovery.
> **(h)** Making or opposing, unsuccessfully and without substantial justification, a motion to compel or to limit discovery.
> **(i)** Failing to confer in person, by telephone, or by letter with an opposing party or

> attorney in a reasonable and good faith attempt to resolve informally any dispute concerning discovery, if the section governing a particular discovery motion requires the filing of a declaration stating facts showing an attempt at informal resolution has been made.

After notice to any affected party, person or attorney, and after opportunity for a hearing, the court may impose a monetary sanction ordering that the party engaging in the misuse of the discovery process, or any attorney advising that conduct, or both pay the reasonable expenses, including attorney fees, incurred by anyone as a result of that conduct. The court may also impose this sanction on one who unsuccessfully asserts that another has engaged in the misuse of the discovery process, or on any attorney who advised that assertion, or on both. **CCP § 2023.030(a)**.

When making a request for sanctions, a *Request for Order* (*RFO*) must be filed and properly served that specifies the type of sanction and identifies every person, party and attorney against whom the sanction is sought. Also, a memorandum of points and authorities and a declaration setting forth facts supporting the amount of any monetary sanction sought must accompany the *RFO*. **CCP § 2023.040**.

In the case that follows, the trial court applies **CCP § 1987.2**[6] in a dissolution action to award attorney fees as a sanction. The dates have been bolded so that the sequence of events is easier to discern.

> ***KERI EVILSIZOR, Plaintiff, v. JOSEPH SWEENEY, Defendant and Respondent; JOHN EVILSIZOR, Objector and Appellant.***
> COURT OF APPEAL OF CALIFORNIA, FIRST APPELLATE DISTRICT, DIVISION ONE
> 230 Cal.App.4th 1304
> October 28, 2014, Opinion Filed
> (*Evilsizor v. Sweeney*)
>
> The proceedings to dissolve Sweeney and Keri's marriage began in April 2013. During discovery, Keri produced documents showing she had a bank account with, and a credit card issued by Chase Bank.
>
> On **August 9**, Sweeney issued a subpoena to Chase seeking records of those two accounts. Unbeknownst to Sweeney, [Keri's father] John, had an interest in the accounts, and some of his financial information was contained in the records.
> According to Sweeney, John made no attempt to meet and confer to explore limiting the scope of the subpoena. Instead, John filed a motion to quash on **September 5** arguing he had been given insufficient notice of the subpoena. A hearing date of October 2 was set.
>
> Sweeney's attorney [received the motion to quash **September 9** and the next day] wrote to John's counsel stating the subpoena would be amended to exclude John's private

---

[6] CCP § 1987.2(a) provides that "the court may, in its discretion, award the amount of the reasonable expenses incurred in making or opposing the motion, including reasonable attorney's fees, if the court finds the motion was made or opposed in bad faith or without substantial justification or that one or more of the requirements of the subpoena was oppressive."

Chapter 11: Discovery

information. The letter demanded John drop his motion "immediately" and warned that if the motion was not withdrawn by September 16, Sweeney would seek "attorney fees and sanctions ... for the unnecessary time spent in resolving this dispute without court intervention."

An amended subpoena was issued to Chase on **September 12**. It sought records related to the same accounts as the first subpoena, except it requested Chase to "exclude any deposits for sums payable or disbursements to/by John Evilsizor" on the bank account and to "exclude any charges made by John Evilsizor" on the credit card account.

John's attorney was served by mail with the amended subpoena on **September 12**.

Sweeney's attorney [wrote to John on] **September 16** [stating that] Sweeney would seek sanctions for unnecessarily having to respond to the motion if John's motion to quash was not dropped "forthwith." It also state[d]: "Please be advised that the original subpoena has been withdrawn. Enclosed is our Amended Subpoena Deuces Tecum."

John's attorney wrote to Sweeney's attorney on **September 17** [acknowledging receipt of the Amended Subpoena but refusing] to drop John's motion unless the Amended Subpoena was withdrawn."

Sweeney's attorney wrote to John's attorney on **September 18** [warning] that if John did not "articulate a legal basis to proceed with a Motion to Quash after I have withdrawn the original subpoena and [he is] proceeding under the Amended Subpoena, [he would] will file a Response and seek attorney fees and sanctions per the Code." Sweeney's attorney asked for a response "before the end of business since my Response is due tomorrow."

On **September 19**, Sweeney filed a response to the motion to quash. In doing so, he focused solely on his demand for attorney fees incurred in responding to John's motion, without citing a statutory basis for such an award. He sought $4,450 for 10 hours of legal work, and his attorney submitted a declaration setting forth his hourly rate and listing the tasks he performed responding to the motion to quash. Sweeney also filed a declaration describing the communication between the parties.

The law office representing John contacted the trial court on Friday, **September 27**, stating John withdrew his motion to quash. Sweeney's counsel wrote to the trial court that same day requesting that the scheduled hearing set for the following Wednesday, October 2, go forward to decide whether John should pay attorney fees under CCP § 1987.2. John's attorney then wrote another letter that same day asking the trial court to take the motion off calendar because the original subpoena had been withdrawn.

The **October 2** hearing [remained on calendar and at] the hearing, the parties focused solely on whether Sweeney was entitled to attorney fees. His attorney argued that Sweeney was entitled to fees as the prevailing party "as required by the code." John's attorney argued that although CCP § 1987.2 permits an award of attorney fees in responding to a motion to quash where such a motion is made in bad faith or without justification, that was not the case here because John sought in good faith to protect the disclosure of his private financial records. The attorney also explained that it "took awhile" to confirm with Chase that the bank would not produce the requested records because counsel was unfamiliar with the process, but he pointed out that John withdrew the motion to quash as soon as he confirmed the bank would not produce records.

> The court reiterated its belief that John's original motion to quash was not filed in bad faith. The court focused on the timing, noting that John did not withdraw his motion until September 27 and ordered John to pay Sweeney $2,225 in attorney fees, half of what had been requested.
>
> **DISCUSSION**
> John argues that the award was unauthorized under CCP § 1987.2(a) because Sweeney did not prevail on the underlying motion to quash. We are not persuaded.
>
> The statute provides that in making an order on a motion to quash, "the court may in its discretion award the amount of the reasonable expenses incurred in ... opposing the motion, including reasonable attorney's fees, if the court finds the motion was made ... in bad faith or without substantial justification . ..." (CCP § 1987.2(a).) The trial court agreed with John that the motion did not appear to have been filed in bad faith.
>
> We first conclude that the record does not support a finding of bad faith. An award for sanctions based on bad faith generally requires a subjective element of bad faith. John's attorney explained he had wanted to confirm with Chase that it would not produce his financial records before he withdrew his motion. Even if, as Sweeney contends on appeal, this was objectively unreasonable, there is insufficient evidence in the record to support a finding of subjective bad faith.
>
> The trial court makes clear the court found that John's delay in withdrawing the motion lacked substantial justification under CCP § 1987.2. We recognize that some courts might have been more sympathetic than the trial court was to John's contention that he was justified in waiting to withdraw his motion until he confirmed with Chase that his financial information would not be disclosed. But we are not free to substitute our discretion for that of the trial court so long as its ruling "was a reasonable exercise of its discretion." (Citations omitted.)
>
> The trial court did not abuse its discretion in awarding Sweeney attorney fees because it was not outside the bounds of reason to conclude that John was not justified in waiting to withdraw his motion to quash.
>
> [We affirm] the October 2, 2013 sanctions order and hold that a trial court may impose sanctions under CCP § 1987.2 against a litigant for pursuing a motion to quash that, even though legitimately filed, was rendered unnecessary by a subsequent amendment or withdrawal of the subpoena.

When responding to a request for a completed *Income and Expense Declaration*, a copy of the prior year's federal and state personal income tax returns must be attached. **FC § 3665(a)**.

Postjudgment Discovery

There are special discovery rules to be used when filing for a modification or termination of a court order. These rules are "to permit inexpensive discovery of facts before the commencement of a proceeding for modification or termination of an order for child, family or spousal support." **FC § 3660**.

Chapter 11: Discovery

At any time following a judgment of dissolution of marriage or legal separation of the parties or a determination of paternity that provides for payment of support, either the party ordered to pay support or the party to whom support was ordered to be paid or that party's assignee, without leave of court, may serve a request on the other party for the production of a completed current *Income and Expense Declaration* (form *FL-150*). **FC § 3664(a)**.

If there is no response within thirty-five (35) days of service of the request, or if the responsive income and expense declaration is incomplete, the requesting party may serve a request on the employer of the other party for information limited to the income and benefits. The employer may require the requesting party to pay the reasonable costs of copying this information. The request must be served so that the employer has at least fifteen (15) days to respond. **FC § 3664(b).**

The information that is requested from the employer must also be served on the employee and the attorney of the employee, if represented. The requesting party shall serve, or cause to be served, on the employee described in this section or on his or her attorney a copy of the request served on the employer prior to the date specified in the request served on the employer for the production of income and benefit information. A notice must accompany the request to the employer with a notice that includes the conditions set forth in **FC § 3664(c)**, **FC § 3664(d), (e) and (f)**.

The discovery received may not be disclosed to anyone other than the court, the party's attorney, the party's accountant or other financial consultant assisting with matters relating to the proceeding or any other person permitted by the court. **FC § 3665(b).**

The methods of discovery other than those described in this article may only be used if a motion for modification or termination of the support order is pending. **FC § 3662**.

If there is no pending motion for modification or termination of a support order, a request for discovery pursuant to this article may be undertaken not more frequently than once every twelve (12) months. **FC § 3663**.

These special discovery requests may be enforced in the manner specified in **CCP §§ 1991**, **1991.1**, **1991.2**, **1992** and **1993** and any other statutes applicable to the enforcement of procedures for discovery. **FC § 3666**.

A court may sanction for all costs of the motion on the responding party if the *Income and Expense Declaration* was incomplete, inaccurate, missing the prior year's federal and state personal income tax returns or was not submitted in good faith. **FC § 3667**.

In the following case, the wife seeks to reopen discovery postjudgment.

> ### *In re Marriage of LINDA A. and STEVEN B. BOBLITT.* LINDA A. BOBLITT, Appellant, v. STEVEN B. BOBLITT, Respondent.
> COURT OF APPEAL OF CALIFORNIA, THIRD APPELLATE DISTRICT
> 223 Cal.App.4th 1004; 167 Cal.Rptr.3d 777
> February 7, 2014, Opinion Filed
> (*Marriage of Boblitt*)
>
> "Wife and respondent Steven Boblitt (husband) were married in December 1989 and separated in January 2004. Wife filed the petition for dissolution of the marriage in January 2004. "The marriage was dissolved by a status only judgment of dissolution in October 2006.
>
> "In April 2007, [the trial began and continued for] 19 days."
> [On] April 14, 2008, the court filed the statement of decision and a judgment on reserved issues that incorporated the statement of decision. The judgment and statement of decision did not conclusively and finally resolve all of the property issues, however.
>
> [In] March 2012—four years after the entry of judgment, husband filed a motion to compel the sale of [property that the parties owned as tenants in common.] The court then set the hearing on husband's motion for May 18. Ultimately, the court set trial for August 16 and 17.
>
> In mid-June, wife's attorney served husband's attorney with a request for production of documents, with the date of production set for July 13. On June 21, wife's attorney noticed husband's deposition for July 6.
>
> On June 26, the parties' attorneys exchanged letters. For her part, wife's attorney refused to limit husband's deposition "other than to limit the inquiry into the current postjudgment issues before the court" and refused to withdraw the request for production of documents. Wife's attorney threatened to file a motion to compel husband's deposition with no restrictions.
> For his part, husband's attorney asked wife's attorney to provide him with "authority that another deposition is allowed."
>
> [Wife then] filed a motion to compel husband's deposition (even though the scheduled deposition date had not yet arrived) [and] for evidentiary sanctions. Wife's motion was set for hearing on July 24, the same day as the settlement conference.
>
> Husband's deposition went forward on July 6 as scheduled, and he produced documents in response to wife's request for production on July 13 as scheduled.
>
> Adverting to the deposition of husband, the court asked wife's counsel if she got "an order allowing [her] to take that second deposition as required by the Code of Civil Procedure." She replied, "I don't know that that's required because this is postjudgment. It's a separate case." She later stated that she "didn't come for leave of Court because he said he would appear."
>
> The evidentiary hearing regarding division of the funds from the sale of the property began on August 16. After hearing argument on September 20, the court issued its

Chapter 11: Discovery

tentative ruling. Following written input from the parties, the court issued its statement of decision and order on October 12.

Wife timely appealed the court's order. Husband did not file a respondent's brief.

DISCUSSION

On appeal, wife first contends the trial court deprived her of due process when the court "grant[ed husband's] motion to add Ranchita Way reimbursements as an issue just three (3) weeks and (2) days before trial." According to wife, by doing this the court "terminated her discovery rights before they ever began, as discovery cut-off is 30 days before trial by statute." Without the right to conduct discovery and without "any factual pleading in support of [husband's] Ranchita Way reimbursement claims," wife contends she was "obliged to defend against [his] claims based on whatever occurred at trial." She concludes the "[f]undamental requirement of due process is [the] opportunity to be heard and the opportunity must be granted at a meaningful time and in a meaningful manner. A meaningful time for notice would include an opportunity to obtain evidence under the discovery statutes, an opportunity [wife was] denied."

Wife's due process argument is based on the assumption that she had the "right" to conduct discovery prior to the evidentiary hearing on husband's postjudgment motion to divide the proceeds from sale of the Hedge Avenue property. That assumption, in turn, appears to be based on the belief of wife's attorney that "in family law, [but] not in civil law, … postjudgment motions act as a separate and individual case …" for purposes of discovery. That belief is incorrect.

FC § 210 provides that "[e]xcept to the extent that any other statute or rules adopted by the Judicial Council provide applicable rules, the rules of practice and procedure applicable to civil actions generally … apply to, and constitute the rules of practice and procedure in, proceedings under this code." No statute or rule of court exempts a marital dissolution proceeding from the application of the Civil Discovery Act (CCP § 2016.010 et seq.).

Accordingly, the provisions of the Civil Discovery Act—including those provisions that govern the time for completion of discovery (CCP § 2024.010 et seq.)—apply to such proceedings. Under those provisions, discovery generally must be completed "on or before the 30th day … before the date initially set for the trial of the action" (id., § 2024.020(a), italics added) and, absent court order (or an agreement of the parties), "continuance or postponement of the trial date does not operate to reopen discovery proceedings" (id., § 2024.020(b)).

Wife does not point to, nor are we otherwise aware of, any provision that reopens discovery in a marital dissolution proceeding just because one of the parties has filed a postjudgment motion. The assertion of her attorney that "postjudgment motions act as a separate and individual case …" for purposes of discovery finds no support in the law.

The Family Code does contain an article that allows for limited postjudgment discovery relating to the "modification or termination of an order for child, family, or spousal support." (FC § 3660 et seq.) Under the provisions of that article, a party may request that the other party produce a current income and expense declaration even if no motion for modification or termination of the support order is pending. (Id., § 3664, subd. (a).) Under certain circumstances, the requesting party may also request information on the other party's income and employment benefits from the other party's employer. (FC §

Chapter 11: Discovery

> 3664(b).) "Methods of discovery other than that described in this article may only be used if a motion for modification or termination of the support order is pending." (Id., § 3662.)
>
> We do not understand the foregoing provision to imply that once a postjudgment motion for modification or termination of a support order is pending, discovery in the action automatically reopens and all of the other methods of discovery available under the Civil Discovery Act are available to the parties without agreement or court order. Rather, we understand the provision to mean simply that when there is no motion pending, the only discovery that may be conducted is a request for an income and expense declaration and, in some instances, a request for pay and benefit information from the other party's employer. In other words, if after judgment a party simply wants to explore the possibility of moving to modify support, the only discovery that is available is that provided for in Family Code section 3660 et seq.
>
> In any event, these provisions have no direct application here because husband's postjudgment motion did not seek to modify or terminate a support order.
>
> Once the discovery cutoff date has run and discovery has closed, the only means provided in the Civil Discovery Act for reopening discovery is a motion for leave of court. (CCP § 2024.050(a).) It is true that the statute specifically speaks only of the court granting "leave … to reopen discovery after a new trial date has been set" (italics added), and that is not exactly the situation in a marital dissolution case where a postjudgment motion has been filed.
>
> Nevertheless, we construe the statute as allowing a motion to reopen discovery after judgment in a marital dissolution proceeding because otherwise, in light of the fact that there is no basis for concluding that discovery automatically reopens for each and every postjudgment motion, not construing the statute in this manner would leave the parties without any access to discovery on postjudgment matters where it may be needed.
>
> Thus, we conclude there is no automatic right to conduct discovery under the Civil Discovery Act in connection with a postjudgment motion in a marital dissolution proceeding. To secure the right to conduct such discovery, a party must secure the agreement of the other party or must obtain a court order for leave to conduct discovery.

Thus, in a marital dissolution case, there is no automatic right to conduct postjudgment discovery unless the issue of the discovery request pertains to modification or termination of support.

EDUCATIONAL EXERCISES

Using the information in Appendix One, draft:

1. Two interrogatories for the petitioner to answer Trevor's allegation that he has seen a truck in the driveway at the family residence almost every day so that has been appears that Marilyn is living with a new "friend"; and

2. Two interrogatories for the respondent to answer Marilyn's allegation that several of her friends told her about seeing Trevor often at the casinos winning money.

CHAPTER 12: Mediation

In Brief...

CONCILIATION COURT, FC § 1830 et seq.:
- Is a service that fosters and protects the rights of children, family life and the institution of matrimony, **FC § 1801**;
- Provides reconciliation procedures to reconcile spouses, **FC § 1801**; and
- Requires a petition to invoke its services, **FC § 1831**.

SUPERIOR COURT MEDIATION:
- Is commonly called Family Court Services (FCS).
- Is defined as a process in which a neutral person or persons facilitate communication between the disputants to assist them in reaching a mutually acceptable parenting plan, **Evid. Code § 1115(a)**;
- Is a process where a neutral person assists parents to reach an agreeable parenting plan;
- Is required when an action is filed with disputed issues of custody and/or visitation, **FC § 3170(a)**, including disputed custody and/or visitation issues in paternity matters, **FC § 3172**;
- Is required to be set concurrently with the setting of the hearing. **FC § 3175**;
- Proceedings must be held in private and are to be confidential, **FC § 3177**;
- Does not allow *ex parte* communications between attorney(s) and mediator, **FC § 216**;
- Provides that any agreement reached will be reduced to a writing, **FC §§ 3178(a), 3186(a)**;
- Provides that any remaining disputed issues will be set for a hearing, **FC § 3185(a)**;
- Allows parties to agree to **private mediation**; the procedures for opting out of superior court mediation are usually set forth in the local rules of the county; and
- Agreements made in private mediation will be upheld.

THE SUPERIOR COURT MEDIATOR/COUNSELOR:
- Is a neutral person who assists to resolve custody/visitation disputes, **Evid. Code § 1115(b)**;
- Must be impartial, competent and uphold the standards contained in **CRC Rule 5.210(h)**;
- Must try to help parents develop an agreement in best interests of the children, **FC § 3161**;
- Has authority to exclude attorneys from the mediation proceedings, **FC § 3182**;
- Can make the discretionary decision to interview the children;
- May recommend an investigation before a hearing on the issues, **FC § 3183(b)**; and
- Must use best efforts to affect a settlement in the best interests of the child, **FC § 3180**.

Chapter 12: Mediation

> - A county's local rules provide procedures for problems related to mediation. **FC § 3163**.
>
> ***CHILD CUSTODY EVALUATORS:***
> - Must maintain objectivity, gathering balanced information from both parties;
> - Must protect the confidentiality of the parties and the children;
> - Must consider the health, safety, welfare and best interests of each child;
> - Must not pressure children to state a custodial preference;
> - May be appointed by the court if it is in the child's best interests to do so;
> - Must prepare a written report re: findings, **CRC Rule 5.220**; and
> - Must be sensitive to gender, race, ethnicity, culture, religion issues, **CRC Rule 5.220(h)**.
>
> ***THE EVALUATIONS:***
> - The scope of the evaluations is set forth in **CRC Rule 5.220(e)**;
> - The court may appoint an expert in a child custody case, **Evid. Code § 730**; and
> - A court can remove the expert for bias in violation of **CRC Rule 5.220(h)(1)**.

Introduction

Conciliation court is a mediation service provided by the superior court where court-appointed, experienced mediators try to assist couples to reconcile by resolving their differences in an effort to save their marriage. A *Petition* is required to invoke conciliation court services. Only some counties have conciliation courts because it is not a requirement that all superior courts provide this service. **FC § 3160**.

Mediation, called Family Court Services (FCS) in many counties, is completely different from conciliation court; it is a required service that must be provided by the superior court for divorcing or separating parties with children of their marriage. Only custody and visitation issues are discussed in the mediation. The mediators at FCS try to help parents reach a parenting plan with regard to custody and visitation of their children. Every divorcing or separating couple MUST attend FCS prior to setting any hearing, if there are any custody/visitation issues that are disputed.

Conciliation Court

The purpose of conciliation court is to "protect the rights of children and to promote the public welfare by preserving, promoting and protecting family life and the institution of matrimony." Additionally, conciliation court provides the means for the reconciliation of spouses and the amicable settlement of domestic and family controversies. **FC § 1801**.

Family conciliation court has jurisdiction to provide mediation services when a controversy exists between spouses or when a controversy relating to child custody or visitation exists between parents, regardless of their marital status. If the dispute could result in dissolution, nullity or legal separation of the parties or in the disruption of the household, and there is a minor child or children of the parents whose welfare might be affected thereby, the services of the conciliation court may be invoked. **FC § 1830(a)**.

However, the family conciliation court also has jurisdiction, whether or not there is a minor child of the parties or either of them, when the controversy involves domestic violence. **FC § 1830(b)**.

In the counties that have a conciliation court, the parties may, "at any time, pursuant to local rules of court, consult with the conciliation court for the purpose of assisting the parties to formulate a plan for implementation of the custody order or to resolve a controversy which has arisen in the implementation of a plan for custody." **FC § 3089**.

Parties must file a petition to invoke the services provided by the conciliation court. The petition must request an amicable settlement of their controversy in order to avoid litigation. **FC § 1831**.

At or after the hearing, the court may make orders if they are necessary to preserve the marriage or to implement the reconciliation of the spouses. The court orders can be with respect to the conduct of the spouses or the subject matter of the controversy. These orders are only effective for thirty (30) days after the hearing, unless the parties mutually consent to extend the time the order will remain in effect. **FC § 1839(a)**.

A reconciliation agreement is encouraged between the parties; if the parties do make such an agreement, it must be reduced to writing and, with the consent of the parties, made into a court order. **FC § 1839(b)**.

The conciliation court may make support orders to pay an amount necessary for the support and maintenance of the other spouse and for the support, maintenance and education of the minor children. Any support order made may be modified or terminated at any time, except as to an amount that accrued while the support order was in effect. **FC § 1839(c)**[1].

---

[1] FC § 1839 in its entirety provides:
"(a) At or after the hearing, the court may make orders in respect to the conduct of the spouses or parents and the subject matter of the controversy that the court deems necessary to preserve the marriage or to implement the reconciliation of the spouses. No such order shall be effective for more than thirty (30) days from the hearing of the petition unless the parties mutually consent to a continuation of the time the order remains effective.
(b) A reconciliation agreement between the parties may be reduced to writing and, with the consent of the parties, a court order may be made requiring the parties to comply fully with the agreement.
(c) During the pendency of a proceeding under this part, the superior court may order a spouse or parent, as the case may be, to pay an amount necessary for the support and maintenance of the other

Chapter 12: Mediation

Neither party may file a petition for dissolution, nullity or legal separation for thirty (30) days, commencing at the time of the filing of the petition in conciliation court. **FC § 1840**.

If a petition for dissolution, nullity or legal separation of the parties is filed in family court, the case may be transferred at any time during the proceeding to the conciliation court "for proceedings for reconciliation of the spouses or amicable settlement of issues in controversy" if a minor child whose welfare may be adversely affected is involved or if there is a possibility of a reconciliation between the parties. **FC § 1841**.

If there is no minor child whose welfare will be adversely affected, the matter can still be transferred to conciliation court, provided there is a reasonable chance for reconciliation and "the work of the court in cases involving children will not be seriously impeded by acceptance of the case." **FC § 1842**.

Pursuant to **FC § 1819**, a conciliation court judge can order that any record, paper or document filed or kept in the office of the supervising counselor of conciliation which is more than two (2) years old be destroyed. The judge can also order that any case be microfilmed.

A person employed as a supervising counselor of conciliation or as an associate counselor of conciliation must have all of the following minimum qualifications:

(1) A master's degree in psychology; social work; marriage, family and child counseling; or other behavioral science substantially related to marriage and family interpersonal relationships;
(2) At least two years of experience in counseling or psychotherapy, or both, preferably in a setting related to the areas of responsibility of the family conciliation court and with the ethnic population to be served;
(3) Knowledge of the court system of California and the procedures used in family law cases;
(4) Knowledge of other resources in the community that clients can be referred to for assistance;
(5) Knowledge of adult psychopathology and the psychology of families;
(6) Knowledge of child development, child abuse, clinical issues relating to children, the effects of divorce on children, the effects of domestic violence on children, and child custody research sufficient to enable a counselor to assess the mental health needs of children; and

---

spouse and for the support, maintenance and education of the minor children, as the case may be. In determining the amount, the superior court may take into consideration the recommendations of a financial referee if one is available to the court. An order made pursuant to this subdivision shall not prejudice the rights of the parties or children with respect to any subsequent order that may be made. An order made pursuant to this subdivision may be modified or terminated at any time, except as to an amount that accrued before the date of filing of the notice of motion or order to show cause to modify or terminate."

Chapter 12: Mediation

(7) Training in domestic violence issues as described in **FC § 1816**. **FC § 1819**.

FC § 1816 provides that an evaluator must:

> participate in a program of continuing instruction in domestic violence, including child abuse, as may be arranged and provided to that evaluator. This training may utilize domestic violence training programs conducted by nonprofit community organizations with an expertise in domestic violence issues … [And] … complete 16 hours of advanced training within a 12-month period. Four hours of that advanced training shall include community resource networking intended to acquaint the evaluator with domestic violence resources in the geographical communities where the family being evaluated may reside.

After an evaluator has completed the sixteen (16) hours of advanced training, that evaluator MUST also complete 4 hours of updated training annually.

Superior Court Mediation

1. The Mediation

Evid. Code § 1115(a) defines **mediation** as a process in which a neutral person or persons facilitate communication between the disputants to assist them in reaching a mutually acceptable parenting plan. **Evid. Code § 1115(c)** provides that a mediation consultation is a communication between a person and a mediator for the purpose of initiating, considering or reconvening a mediation or retaining the mediator.

Whenever any *Petition, Response, Request for Order* or other pleading is filed requesting a new order or to modify a current order for custody and/or visitation, the court MUST set the contested issues for mediation, prior to hearing the matter. **FC § 3170(a)**. Since many separating and divorcing family law clients that have children often find it difficult to decide custody and visitation issues, mediation is almost an everyday occurrence in family law.

Because a mediation date must be set in every contested custody and/or visitation matter set for a hearing, the legislature has enacted laws that require that mediation be available at every superior court.[2] Some of the smallest counties in California just have one mediator to aid family law litigants in deciding these issues.

Larger counties have more mediators. These mediation services are called by different names in the different counties. Some are called Family Court Services (FCS), Family Court Mediation Services and Child Custody Recommendation Counseling Services (CCRC). FCS is by far the most commonly used name for this service because at least half of the 58 counties in California currently call their

---
[2] "It is the policy of California to protect the rights of children and to promote the public welfare by preserving, promoting and protecting family life and the institution of matrimony, and to provide means for the reconciliation of spouses and the amicable settlement of domestic and family controversies." FC § 1801.

Chapter 12: Mediation

mediation services FCS. The State Court website at ***www.courts.ca.gov/selfhelp-familycourtservices.htm*** has a list of all of the counties with a link to the mediation that will be provided in that county.

Pursuant to **CRC Rule 5.210(e)**, all mediation processes must include:

> **(1)** Review of the intake form and court file, if available, before the start of mediation;
> **(2)** Oral or written orientation or parent education that facilitates the parties' informed and self-determined decision making about:
> **(A)** The types of disputed issues generally discussed in mediation and the range of possible outcomes from the mediation process;
> **(B)** The mediation process, including the mediator's role; the circumstances that may lead the mediator to make a particular recommendation to the court; limitations on the confidentiality of the process; and access to information communicated by the parties or included in the mediation file;
> **(C)** How to make best use of information drawn from current research and professional experience to facilitate the mediation process, parties' communication, and co-parenting relationship; and
> **(D)** How to address each child's current and future developmental needs…

The standards of practice for mediation cases involving custody and/or visitation must include: **(1)** considering the best interests of the children and **(2)** safeguarding the rights of children. The standards also include conducting the negotiations in such a way as to equalize power relationships between the parties, detailing factors to be considered in decisions concerning the child's future and making sure that the children have frequent and continuing contact with both parents. **FC § 3162(b)**.

Whenever a matter is set for mediation, the mediation must be set before or concurrent with the setting of the matter for hearing.[3] **FC § 3175**.

Notice of mediation must be given to each party and to each party's counsel of record when mediation is required to settle a contested issue of custody or visitation. When a stepparent or grandparent seeks visitation rights, notice must be given to the stepparent or grandparent seeking visitation rights, to each parent of the child, and to each parent's counsel of record. Notice must be given by personal service or certified mail, return receipt requested, postage prepaid, to the last known address. The notice of mediation pursuant to **FC § 3188** must state that all communications involving the mediator will be kept confidential between the mediator and the disputing parties. **FC § 3176**.

When there has been a history of domestic violence between the parties or where there is a protective order, at the request of the party alleging domestic violence in a written declaration under penalty of perjury or protected by the order, the mediator must meet with the parties separately and at separate times. **FC § 3181**. (See Chapter 36 RE: Domestic Violence, *infra*.)

---

[3] A hearing is set by filing a *Request for Order* (*RFO*) *FL-300*.

Chapter 12: Mediation

Mediation proceedings must be held in private and are to be confidential. All communications, verbal or written, from the parties to the mediator and vice versa made in the proceeding are official information within the meaning of **Evid. Code §1040**.[4] **FC § 3177**.

Unless the parties agree otherwise, there must not be any *ex parte* communications between the attorneys and the mediator. This rule extends to counsel appointed by the court. **FC § 216**.

An agreement reached by the parties as a result of mediation is limited to the resolution of issues relating to parenting plans, custody, visitation or a combination of these issues. The agreement will be reduced to a writing that will be mailed to the counsel of both parties and thereafter filed in the court file. **FC § 3178(a)** and **FC § 3186(a)**.

> An agreement may not be confirmed or otherwise incorporated in an order unless each party, in person or by counsel of record, has affirmed and assented to the agreement in open court or by written stipulation. FC § 3186(b).

If there are issues that remain unresolved after the parties have participated in mediation, the mediator must inform the court in writing,[5] and the court must set the matter for a hearing on the unresolved issues. **FC § 3185(a)**.

If the parties do not reach an agreement as a result of the mediation proceedings, the mediator may recommend to the court that an investigation be conducted or that other services be offered to assist the parties to affect a resolution of the controversy before a hearing on the issues. **FC § 3183(b)**. In these cases, after the mediator has first provided the parties and their attorneys, including counsel for any minor children, with the recommendations in writing in advance of the hearing, the mediator will submit his or her recommendation to the court. The mediation and recommendation process is referred to as **child custody recommending counseling. FC § 3183(a)**.

---

[4] Evidence Code §1040(b) provides: "A public entity has a privilege to refuse to disclose official information, and to prevent another from disclosing official information, if the privilege is claimed by a person authorized by the public entity to do so and:
(1) Disclosure is forbidden by an act of the Congress of the United States or a statute of this state; or
(2) Disclosure of the information is against the public interest because there is a necessity for preserving the confidentiality of the information that outweighs the necessity for disclosure in the interest of justice; but no privilege may be claimed under this paragraph if any person authorized to do so has consented that the information be disclosed in the proceeding. In determining whether disclosure of the information is against the public interest, the interest of the public entity as a party in the outcome of the proceeding may not be considered."
As used in this section, 'official information' means information acquired in confidence by a public employee in the course of his or her duty and not open, or officially disclosed, to the public prior to the time the claim of privilege is made." Evidence Code §1040(a).

[5] This writing to the court is called a "Recommendation".

Chapter 12: Mediation

If a stepparent or grandparent has petitioned for a visitation order, the court must set the matter for mediation so that the stepparent or grandparent has an opportunity to appear in court and be heard on the issue of visitation. **FC § 3171(a)** and **FC § 3185**. An agreement reached by a stepparent or grandparent seeking visitation rights must be limited to the resolution of issues relating to visitation. **FC § 3178)(b)**.

A natural or adoptive parent who is not a party to the proceeding is not required to participate in the mediation proceeding, but failure to participate is a waiver of that parent's right to object to a settlement reached by the other parties during mediation or to require a hearing on the matter. **FC § 3171(b)**.

A custody or visitation agreement reached as a result of mediation may be modified at any time at the discretion of the court, subject to Chapter 1 (commencing with **FC § 3020**[6]), Chapter 2 (commencing with **FC § 3040**[7]), Chapter 4 (commencing with **FC § 3080**) and Chapter 5 (commencing with **FC § 3100**[8]). **FC § 3179**.

Finally, mediation is also required and provided when there are disputed custody and visitation issues in paternity actions. **FC § 3172**.

2. The Superior Court Mediator/Counselor

Evid. Code § 1115(b) provides that a mediator is "a neutral person who conducts a mediation." The neutral person is usually called a counselor. The counselor assists the parties in resolving custody and visitation disputes.

In order for a couple to work effectively with a counselor, mediation must be conducted in an atmosphere that encourages trust in the process and a perception of fairness pursuant to the Code of Ethics for the Court Employees of California. **CRC Rule 5.210(h)**.

The counselor must be impartial, competent and uphold the standards of practice contained in **CRC Rule 5.210(h)**.

Counselors must use reasonable efforts and consider safety issues to:

> **(i)** Facilitate the family's transition and reduce acrimony by helping the parties improve their communication skills, focus on the child's needs and areas of stability, identify the family's strengths, and locate counseling or other services;
> **(ii)** Develop a comprehensive parenting agreement that addresses each child's current and

---

[6] FC § 3020 provides in pertinent part that any court order regarding physical or legal custody or visitation must be "made in a manner that ensures the health, safety and welfare of the child and the safety of all family members." This code was added to effective January 1, 2019.
[7] FC § 3040 sets forth the order preference of granting custody.
[8] FC § 3100(a) provides: "In making an order pursuant to Chapter 4 (commencing with Section 3080), the court shall grant reasonable visitation rights to a parent unless it is shown that the visitation would be detrimental to the best interest of the child. In the discretion of the court, reasonable visitation rights may be granted to any other person having an interest in the welfare of the child."

> future developmental needs; and
> **(iii)** Control for potential power imbalances between the parties during mediation. CRC Rule 5.210(d).

The counselors must strive to reduce acrimony that may exist between the parties and to help parents develop an agreement (parenting plan[9]) that ensures that the children will have continuing contact with both parents that is in the best interests of the children. **FC § 3161**.

The counselors have the authority to exclude attorneys from participation in the mediation proceedings pursuant to this chapter if, in the counselor's discretion, exclusion of counsel is appropriate or necessary. **FC § 3182**.

The counselors have the duty to assess the needs and interests of the child(ren) involved in the controversy and may interview the child(ren) if the mediator considers such interview is appropriate or necessary. **FC § 3180(a)**. Interviews with children are a completely discretionary decision to be made by the counselor.

Further, the counselor must "use his or her best efforts to affect a settlement of the custody or visitation dispute that is in the best interests of the child, as provided in **FC § 3011**."[10] **FC § 3180**.

The counselor may interview the child alone or together with other interested parties, including stepparents, siblings, new or stepsiblings or other family members significant to the child. When interviewing a child, the counselor must: **(1)** inform the child in an age-appropriate way of the mediator's obligation to disclose suspected child abuse and neglect; and, **(2)** with parental consent, coordinate interview and information exchange among agency or private professionals to reduce the number of interviews a child might experience. **CRC Rule 5.210(e)(3)**.

A counselor may be a member of the professional staff of a family conciliation court, probation department, or mental health services agency, or may be any other

---

[9] A "parenting plan" describes how parents or other appropriate parties will share and divide their decision-making and caretaking responsibilities to protect the health, safety, welfare, and best interest of each child who is a subject of the proceedings. CRC Rule 5.210(c).

[10] Effective 1/1/2019, FC § 3011 provides, in determining the best interests of the child, the court must consider:
"(a) The health, safety and welfare of the child;
(b)
(1) Any history of abuse by one parent or any other person seeking custody against any of the following:
(A) A child to whom he or she is related by blood or affinity or with whom he or she has had a caretaking relationship, no matter how temporary.
(B) The other parent.
(C) A parent, current spouse, or cohabitant, of the parent or person seeking custody, or a person with whom the parent or person seeking custody has a dating or engagement relationship."

person or agency designated by the court and must meet the minimum qualifications required of a counselor of conciliation as provided in **FC § 1815**. **FC § 3164**.

Pursuant to **CRC Rule 5.210(f)**, the requirement for training, continuing education and experience to be a counselor are:

> [1] Complete a minimum of 40 hours of custody and visitation mediation training within the first six months of initial employment as a court-connected mediator;
> [2] Annually complete 8 hours of related continuing education programs, conferences, and workshops. This requirement is in addition to the annual 4-hour domestic violence update training described in rule 5.215; and
> [3] Participate in performance supervision and peer review.
> [4] Each mediation supervisor and family court services director must complete at least 24 hours of additional training each calendar year...

A county's local rules provide procedures to respond to requests for a change of counselors or for general problems or complaints related to mediation. **FC § 3163**.

3. Private Mediation

As set forth above, whenever an action is filed and there are contested visitation and custody issues, mediation is required prior to a hearing on these issues. However, the parties can agree to private mediation. The procedures for opting out of the mediation provided by the superior court and agreeing to private mediation are set forth in the local rules of the counties where the actions are filed.

Agreements made in private mediation will be upheld, as case that follows demonstrates.

> *In re Marriage of ANNA and CLARK WOOLSEY. ANNA WOOLSEY, Respondent, v. CLARK WOOLSEY, Appellant.*
> COURT OF APPEAL OF CALIFORNIA, THIRD APPELLATE DISTRICT
> 220 Cal.App.4th 881
> October 22, 2013, Opinion Filed
> (*Marriage of Woolsey*)
>
> The parties married in September 2001. They had two children, who were born in California: Grant, who was born in July 2002, and Claire, who was born in February 2004. The parties lived in California until they moved to Missouri in December 2007. Clark and Anna separated on April 30 or May 1, 2009. Anna and the children moved back to California, where Anna had lived her entire life except for the 18 months she resided in Missouri.
>
> In July 2009, Anna filed a petition for legal separation.
>
> In August 2009, Clark hoped to achieve reconciliation with Anna and urged her to participate in mediation provided by Live at Peace Ministries. Anna was skeptical but agreed to participate.

Mediation began on August 20, 2009, but no agreement to reconcile was reached during the first two days. Thus, the focus of the mediation for the next two days was on division of community property, custody, and other issues related to dissolution of marriage. The mediation was successful, and the parties personally signed a marital settlement agreement on August 23, 2009. The agreement resolved issues of custody, division of community property, and set up a plan for communication between Clark and Anna.

On the same day the parties signed the marital settlement agreement, Clark was served with Anna's petition for legal separation.

[In October 2009] the parties entered a stipulation regarding custody and visitation in which they agreed Anna would have custody of the children "at all times" except for the period from October 30 to November 1, 2009, and the Thanksgiving holiday period of November 21 to 29, 2009. Anna was entitled to keep the children during the entire Christmas holiday.

In January 2010, Anna filed an amended petition to seek dissolution of marriage.

In February 2010, Anna moved to enter judgment to enforce the marital settlement agreement under CCP § 664.6. Clark opposed entry of judgment on the agreement, and a one-day trial occurred on August 16, 2010. During trial Clark represented himself while Anna had legal counsel. The trial court granted Anna's motion to enter judgment on the marital settlement agreement under CCP § 664.6. The court also awarded joint legal and physical custody, with a parenting schedule that confirmed Anna as the primary caregiver for the children.

Clark timely appealed from the judgment.

DISCUSSION
Private mediation, like nonjudicial arbitration, offers a speedy and less expensive approach to resolution of issues arising from marital dissolution. As recognized by the California Supreme Court, "mediation [is] a form of alternative dispute resolution encouraged and, in some cases required by, the Legislature." (Citations omitted.) Implementing alternatives to judicial dispute resolution has been a strong legislative policy since at least 1986.

Private mediation, like nonjudicial arbitration, offers an alternate approach to resolve disputed issues arising from a marital dissolution.

Clark argues the trial court erred in entering judgment on the marital settlement agreement because it did not comply with the requirements of rule 30.7 that such agreements be notarized. We conclude rule 30.7 is invalid insofar as the rule imposes requirements on a marital settlement agreement in addition to those required by Evidence Code § 1123, FC § 2550 and CCP § 664.6.

The Legislature has enacted statutes to further the strong public policy of encouraging out-of-court resolution of disputes. The Legislature has imposed specific requirements for settlement agreements and provided an expedient method of enforcing them. There is nothing in the Evidence Code or Family Code or in the Code of Civil Procedure that requires a marital settlement agreement to be notarized or contain talismanic language to inform unrepresented parties about the right to legal counsel. Thus, the addition of requirements to those imposed by the California codes for mediated marital agreements is inconsistent with the Legislature's specifications of the requirements for enforceability. It has long been settled that "[a] court may not by rule change or add to procedural requirements established by statutory provision. An order attempting to add requirements to those prescribed by a statute is to such an extent a nullity and void.

Thus, we conclude rule 30.7 is invalid insofar as it imposes additional requirements on entry of judgment on a mediated agreement that resolves marital dissolution issues.

We note that even the trial court in this case did not enforce rule 30.7, excusing performance because the marital settlement agreement comported with the intent underlying the rule. It would be incongruous to ignore the statutes governing mediated agreements in order to give trial courts discretion to ignore local rules of court.

We affirm the trial court's entry of judgment on the marital settlement agreement, but do so because rule 30.7 cannot impose requirements for enforcement of mediated settlement agreements in addition to those specified by statute.

In the trial court, Clark argued the marital settlement agreement is unenforceable because the mediator engaged in undue influence during the mediation. On appeal, he changes his argument to assert Anna exerted undue influence on him during the mediation. Clark acknowledges the confidentiality extended to mediation proceedings undermines his argument. Elsewhere, Clark even notes he objected to admission of evidence regarding the intent of the parties in entering into the marital settlement agreement "on the basis of mediation confidentiality." We conclude Clark's assertion of undue influence is precluded by the mediation confidentiality imposed by the Evidence Code. In addition, there is no presumption of undue influence in marital settlement agreements reached as a result of mediation.

Evidence Code § 1119(a) provides: "No evidence of anything said or any admission made for the purpose of, in the course of, or pursuant to, a mediation or a mediation consultation is admissible or subject to discovery, and disclosure of the evidence shall not be compelled, in any arbitration, administrative adjudication, civil action, or other noncriminal proceeding in which, pursuant to law, testimony can be compelled to be given." Construing Evidence Code § 1119, the California Supreme Court "conclude[d] that there are no exceptions to the confidentiality of mediation communications or to the statutory limits on the content of mediator's reports. Neither a mediator nor a party may reveal communications made during mediation." Accordingly, Clark cannot establish undue influence by Anna or any other participant in the mediation under the mediation confidentiality provisions of Evidence Code § 1119.

Accordingly, we reject Clark's undue influence argument. As Clark acknowledges, the mediation confidentiality provisions of Evidence Code § 1119 protect the mediation process and preclude any claim of undue influence. Further, there is no presumption of undue influence in marital settlement agreements reached as a result of mediation.

We conclude the trial court properly entered judgment on the marital settlement agreement and the custody and visitation terms in the judgment do not establish an abuse of discretion by the trial court; the trial court's statement of decision is adequate in addressing the issues presented for trial. Accordingly, we affirm the judgment.

Chapter 12: Mediation

Child Custody Evaluators

Evaluator means a supervising or associate counselor, as described in **FC §1815**; a mediator, as described in **FC § 3164**; a court-connected or private child custody evaluator, as described in **FC § 3110.5**[11]; or a court-appointed investigator or evaluator, as described in **FC § 3110** or **Evid. Code § 730**. **FC § 1816**.

It is important for the child custody evaluator to: **(1)** maintain objectivity, provide and gather balanced information for both parties, and control for bias; **(2)** protect the confidentiality of the parties and children; **(3)** consider the health, safety, welfare and best interests of the child in all phases of the process; **(4)** not pressure children to state a custodial preference; and **(5)** be sensitive to the socioeconomic status, gender, race, ethnicity, cultural values, religion, family structures and developmental characteristics of the parties. **CRC Rule 5.220(h)**.

In the case that follows, the evaluator lost his objectivity.

> *In re Marriage of CHRISTINA ADAMS and JACK A. CHRISTINA ADAMS,*
> *Respondent, v. JACK A., Appellant.*
> COURT OF APPEAL OF CALIFORNIA, FOURTH APPELLATE DISTRICT, DIVISION THREE
> 209 Cal.App.4th 1543
> October 16, 2012, Opinion Filed
> (*Marriage of Adams*)
>
> [The parents have a son, J., who was diagnosed at a young age with Asperger's syndrome, a form of high functioning autism. Mother has written a published book on autism, gives lectures on the subject, helps other families obtain services for their children with autism. Father is a special education attorney and has a master's degree in psychology.
>
> **1. 2008** –parents divorced; agreed in stipulated judgment to submit future disputes about J. to a special master.
> **2. 2010** - a dispute arose between the parents as to which middle school J. should attend.
> **3. March 16, 2010** e-mail father to mother –need to get a special master in time for the special master to gather information to make a school recommendation.
> **4. May 27, 2010**, mother filed OSC (*order to show cause*) (OSC)[12] requesting sole legal custody of J, an evaluation under Evidence Code § 730[13] and to modify the judgment's

---

[11] This code section was amended effective 1/1/2019. The following language was added:
"(5) He or she is licensed as a professional clinical counselor under Chapter 16 (commencing with Section 4999.10) of Division 2 of the Business and Professions Code and is qualified to assess couples and families pursuant to paragraph (3) of subdivision (a) of Section 4999.20 of the Business and Professions Code."
[12] OSC–Order to Show Cause (a request for a hearing). Changed to *RFO–Request for Order* 1/1/2012.
[13] Evid. Code § 730 provides in pertinent part: "When it appears to the court, at any time before or during the trial of an action, that expert evidence is or may be required by the court or by any party to the action, the court on its own motion or on motion of any party may appoint one or more experts to investigate, to render a report as may be ordered by the court and to testify as an expert at the trial of the action relative to the fact or matter as to which the expert evidence is or may be required." Evid. Code § 730 will be referred to as § 730.

Chapter 12: Mediation

special master requirement. Father responded with his own OSC, requesting the appointment of a special master.

5. July 21, 2010 stipulated order regarding an Evidence Code § 730 evaluation. Parties agreed that: (1) they would submit to a full psychological examination by David J. Jimenez for the purpose of making a recommendation as to child custody.

6. August 2, 2010 stipulated order - parties agreed that Jimenez would recommend a school for J. before addressing other issues and prior to completing his § 730 report.

7. August 2010, Jimenez wrote father's attorney; he had received a voice mail message from mother expressing concern about father's taking J. to Catalina on his boat. Jimenez contacted the and spoke to the harbormaster at the Marina del Rey harbor. Jimenez wrote a letter to father's attorney 'strongly discouraging both parties to refrain from this type of activity, or any other type of activity with J. which could be accidentally interpreted by others as child endangerment as defined by Penal Code § 273a(a)[14]. Father complied with Jimenez's discouragement and did not take a boat trip to Catalina with J.

8. September 2, 2010, Jimenez recommended J. be enrolled at mother choice for middle school.

9. October 2010, J. and father began making a "life mask"—"intended to be a remembrance of J. becoming a teenager." Jimenez phoned father to say mother had asked Jimenez to instruct father to stop creating a life mask of J. Father and J. stopped making the life mask.

10. November 29, 2010, Jimenez phoned father and said he (Jimenez) was parked in front of father's house and wanted to "look at the browsing histories on computers used by J., inspect [father's] knife collection and talk with" father without J. present. Father drove home as requested and let Jimenez examine the browsing histories of computers that might have been used by J. Jimenez also inspected each knife in father's collection. Father offered to "get rid of the collection" if Jimenez thought the knives were a problem. Jimenez said the knives were not a problem, but father should lock them up.

11. December 3 Jimenez wrote father's attorney that father's "failure to put the knife collection under lock and key" had caused Jimenez "'dismay and disappointment.' Dr. Jimenez referred to J.'s behavior in his letter as being 'unpredictable' with 'poor judgment, and poor impulse control.'"

12. December 12 father e-mailed mother informing her that J. had taken a pocket knife to her house and asking her "to please make sure that the pocket knife not be inadvertently left in [J.]'s sweatshirt pocket where it might accidentally end up at school with him." Jimenez phoned father later that day and instructed him to appear at Jimenez's office "the next day to explain the circumstances surrounding J. taking a pocket knife to his mother's house the previous day." Jimenez stated the requirement was "'non-negotiable.'" The next day, father traveled to Jimenez's office, which was located 50 miles from father's home and office. Jimenez showed father "an enlarged picture" of J.'s pocket knife. Jimenez read father the definition of criminal child endangerment from Penal Code § 273a, subdivision (a). Jimenez stated he was considering reporting father to child protective services for suspected child endangerment.

13. December 13 (the next day) Jimenez e-mailed father directing him to carefully walk through his house today and identify potential safety hazards for J. and prepare a 'safety plan' and fax it to him by the end of the business day.

---

[14] Penal Code § 273a(a) provides: "Any person who, under circumstances or conditions likely to produce great bodily harm or death, willfully causes or permits any child to suffer, or inflicts thereon unjustifiable physical pain or mental suffering, or having the care or custody of any child, willfully causes or permits the person or health of that child to be injured, or willfully causes or permits that child to be placed in a situation where his or her person or health is endangered, shall be punished by imprisonment in a county jail not exceeding one year, or in the state prison for two, four, or six years."

14. December 14 father faxed Jimenez a letter informing him that, on the advice of counsel, that he should contact father's attorney with any questions.

15. December 20, 2010, father filed an ex parte application to stay the § 730 evaluation and remove Jimenez as the evaluator, (father's removal motion). Jimenez had acted outside the scope of a § 730 evaluation and demonstrated a bias in favor of mother.

16. December 29, 2010, father's counsel asked Jimenez to voluntarily recuse himself.

17. December 30, 2011, the next day, Jimenez wrote father's counsel stating: (1) father and his attorney were not to communicate with Jimenez and (2) Jimenez would interpret any communications from them as "intrusive and an attempt to delay or otherwise interfere with [Jimenez's] completion of" the § 730 report.

18. January 2011, Jimenez wrote father's counsel a letter, taking "issue with a complaint that [father] filed with the Board of Psychology regarding [Jimenez's] conduct."

19. April 14, 2011, about an hour before father was to pick up J. at mother's house, J. contacted father to say he wanted to stay with mother instead of father over the weekend. Father said he would talk with J. about it when father came to mother's house at 5:00 p.m. J. said he would not be at mother's house at 5:00 p.m. Mother had taken J. away from her home so he could not be picked up.

19. April 22, 2011, the trial judge interviewed J. alone in chambers. Prior to the interview, mother's counsel advised the court, inter alia, that J. no longer wished to spend time with father and had "expressed the fact that he is afraid of his father … ." Two weeks had passed since mother last allowed J. to see father. Father's counsel argued "that [J.] has been primed and prepared to say what he says … ." In the interview, J. said he wished to see father only on some holidays or when mother was on vacation. When the court asked if anyone had coached J., the boy replied, "Well, not a whole lot." The court stated to the parents: Sometimes it seemed as though J. was trying to recall what he was supposed to say, but that was just an impression. And he told me that he hadn't been coached or told what to say.

20. May 4, 2011, mother filed an OSC seeking full legal and physical custody of J., with limited visitation for father. She declared that during "the § 730 evaluation, Dr. Jimenez's objective, psychological testing found that [father] is afflicted with depressive symptoms, has poor judgment and presents a mild risk of suicide.

Father pointed out that Jimenez omitted from his report significant results of the Millon Clinical Multiaxial Inventory-III psychological tests he administered to the parties, thereby revealing the evaluator's bias and lack of objectivity. The omitted results showed mother was "exhibiting psychological dysfunction of mild to moderate severity," while father was "experiencing no disorder or a minimally severe disorder."

22. May 13, 2011 the hearing re: father's removal motion. The court stated Jimenez, in an "ex parte communication" to the court that morning, had submitted his § 730 report to the court, but did not "want to give it to [the parties] until he had been paid." The court had no "idea what [Jimenez's] recommendations are, because [it had] not opened his report."

Father's counsel declared Jimenez had violated, inter alia, CRC Rule 5.220(h)(1)[15] by exhibiting bias and aligning himself with mother. "Additionally, Dr. Jimenez has violated his own stated protocols by examining documents not provided to [father's] counsel after stating in writing he would refuse to consider any document not copied to the other [party's] counsel first." Jimenez had interviewed J. in mother's home, but not in father's home. Jimenez conducted psychological testing of father, but not of mother. Jimenez's

---

[15] CRC Rule 5.220(h)(1) provides: "In performing an evaluation, the child custody evaluator must: (1) Maintain objectivity, provide and gather balanced information for both parties, and control for bias."

Chapter 12: Mediation

> billing revealed that he had spent [a total 14.0 hours in individual sessions with mother, compared with 9.0 hours with father.]
>
> Counsel declared that Jimenez's demands on father violated CRC Rules 5.220(h)(1), (5) and (9)[16], and CRC Rule 5.225(d)(14), (16) and (20)[17].
>
> The court stated father believes "that Dr. Jimenez has gone well outside the perimeter of a § 730 evaluation and has become essentially sort of a special master here, making decisions, directing the parties to take certain actions and conduct, without their consent for him to engage in that role." The court continued: "Quite frankly, [father] is right. ... I was surprised to see the things that Dr. Jimenez had done while being tasked to perform a completely neutral and objective child custody evaluation. If nothing else, he has lost his objectivity and he is no longer evaluating. [T]o the extent that Dr. Jimenez has lost his objectivity. I think that bears on the validity of his recommendation. I believe it is an appropriate area for cross-examination. I think it is an appropriate area for [father] to argue that [Jimenez's] recommendations are slanted, that they shouldn't be accepted."
>
> Father's counsel argued, inter alia, that "Dr. Jimenez was not using the balanced information gathering that he was required to do under the Rules of Court." As to the time and costs spent on the report, father's counsel argued that Jimenez began writing his report only after father filed his removal motion, and that Jimenez also did most of his work and billed much of his nearly $42,000 fee after father's removal motion was filed.
>
> The court denied father's removal motion, stating: "I don't believe the conduct as set forth in the declarations is so egregious as to justify the removal of Dr. Jimenez as the § 730 evaluator at this point." The court continued the hearing on mother's OSC seeking modification of custody.
>
> After a hearing on mother's request for sole legal custody and father's request for the appointment of a special master, the court granted mother's request and denied father's. The court granted mother sole legal custody based on its finding father "is unable to effectively coparent ..."

---

[16] CRC Rule 5.220 provides in pertinent part:
"(h) In performing an evaluation, the child custody evaluator must:
 (1) Maintain objectivity, provide and gather balanced information for both parties, and control for bias;
 (5) Strive to maintain the confidential relationship between the child who is the subject of an evaluation and his or her treating psychotherapist;
 (9) Not disclose any recommendations to the parties, their attorneys, or the attorney for the child before having gathered the information necessary to support the conclusion." (Only the pertinent sections are included here.)

[17] CRC Rule 5.225 provides: "(d) Education and training requirements Before appointment, a child custody evaluator must complete 40 hours of education and training, which must include all the following topics:
 (14) Ethical requirements associated with the child custody evaluator's professional license and rule 5.220;
 (16) The importance of understanding relevant distinctions among the roles of evaluator, mediator, and therapist;
 (20) How to maintain professional neutrality and objectivity when conducting child custody evaluations."

The court found it was in J.'s best interest for mother to have sole legal custody.

At the custody hearing, Dr. Jeffrey Arden, a psychologist who conducts § 730 child custody evaluations, testified he had a phone conversation with Jimenez around six months earlier. Jimenez said he was excited about being recently admitted to the Orange County child custody panel and that he had "caught his first case and it had, quote, 'deep pockets,' and that he was assigned simultaneously as child custody evaluator and special master ... ." Arden was surprised because those "are conflicting dual roles," and psychologists are required "to inform the court [of this] if the court does appoint us in simultaneous roles."

Finally, the court stated it had no authority to delete the special master provisions from the judgment, because the parties had agreed to the requirement. But the court declined to appoint a new special master because, so long as mother has sole legal custody, there is no need for a special master.

DISCUSSION

Because "the results of an independent evaluation generally are given great weight by the judge in deciding contested custody ... issues, the Judicial Council has adopted rules of court establishing uniform standards of practice for court-ordered custody evaluations." CRC Rule 5.220 governs child custody evaluators appointed under § 730 and requires them to "[m]aintain objectivity, provide and gather balanced information for both parties, and control for bias." (CRC Rule 5.220(h)(1)) Additionally, a court-appointed evaluator in a child custody proceeding under the Family Code is prohibited from engaging in ex parte communication with a party's counsel or with the court, except in limited circumstances. CRC Rule 2.235(c)[18].

[W]e must first evaluate whether the court properly denied father's motion to remove the evaluator before we can consider whether the court appropriately awarded mother sole legal custody. In reviewing the court's ruling on father's removal motion, our threshold inquiry is whether Jimenez exhibited bias against father (in violation of CRC Rule 5.225(h)(1) prior to father's filing of the removal motion. The facts (set forth in father's removal motion) are essentially undisputed. Although mother sought to explain and justify Jimenez's actions, she did not dispute they occurred. Thus, whether Jimenez was biased against father is a question of law we may review de novo. We need not do so, however, because the court made a factual finding that Jimenez lost his objectivity, a finding clearly supported by substantial evidence. Jimenez established a pattern of acting upon mother's complaints against father, resulting in the evaluator making escalating demands on father accompanied by unreasonable deadlines and threats. The trial court properly found Jimenez acted with bias against father.

Yet, despite that finding, the court denied father's motion to remove the evaluator. The court concluded the psychologist's behavior was not sufficiently "egregious" to justify the "draconian" step of removing him as evaluator. Jimenez's misconduct had two aspects: (1) he exceeded the scope of the § 730 evaluation, and (2) he exhibited bias against father. Thus, the court impliedly found that neither Jimenez's overstepping of his § 730 role, nor the degree of bias he exhibited, nor even the combined effect of both, was

---

[18] CRC Rule 5.235(c) provides: "In any child custody proceeding under the Family Code, ex parte communication is prohibited between court-connected or court-appointed mediators or evaluators and the attorney for any party, a court-appointed counsel for a child, or the court, except as provided by this rule."

> egregious enough to warrant his removal.
>
> It is unclear what standard of review applies to a court's ruling on a motion for removal of the evaluator. But, even if we apply the most deferential standard of review, we conclude, under the totality of the circumstances here, that the court abused its discretion by denying father's application to stay the evaluation and remove Jimenez as the evaluator.
>
> Jimenez made ex parte communications to mother's counsel and the court, and imposed an escalating series of accusatory demands on father. Most or all of these demands were made at mother's request. Father, quite reasonably, finally concluded he could no longer talk openly with Jimenez for fear Jimenez would try to present him in a negative light. Father then moved for Jimenez's removal and his counsel asked Jimenez to recuse himself. Jimenez refused to recuse himself, forbade father and his counsel from contacting him, and proceeded to write a biased report (described below). Under these circumstances, the court abused its discretion by denying father's motion for the removal of Jimenez as the evaluator.
>
> Here, the court saw no need for an evidentiary hearing on father's removal motion. It ultimately denied his removal motion and laid the onus on father to discredit, if necessary, the report. Subsequently, the court expressly relied on Jimenez's report in awarding mother sole legal custody and stated for the record that it found the report to be "detailed and useful."
>
> Jimenez's report, however, casts father in such an unfavorable light that we cannot discount the possibility that the evaluator's preexisting bias against father tainted the report's contents. The report omits the psychological test results described in father's declaration, which indicated that father has no psychological disorder or a minimal one, while mother exhibits psychological dysfunction of mild to moderate severity. Instead, the report's psychological sections portray mother more favorably than father; we do not divulge the details. The report states father has no homicidal or suicidal ideation.
>
> Unfortunately, Jimenez's bias may have tainted J.'s opinion of father. The evaluator's views probably carried great weight in the 13-year-old's mind. Because the court awarded mother sole legal custody based at least in part on Jimenez's biased report and on J.'s statements which may have been influenced by Jimenez's bias, the order must be reversed. At the hearing on father's removal motion, the court found Jimenez acted "outside the scope of a § 730 evaluation."
>
> We reverse the March 7, 2011 order denying father's removal motion and the June 9, 2011 legal custody modification order. (All bolding and numbering was added.)

(See also *LESLIE O. v. SUPERIOR COURT OF LOS ANGELES COUNTY* (2014) 231 Cal.App.4th 1191 at p. 1212 where the appellate court reversed the trial court's decision not to remove the evaluator for bias. The appellate court stated that *Leslie O.* was not distinguishable from *Adams* because the facts were "more egregious in *Adams*. *Adams* does not establish a low watermark which dictates that only evaluators who fall below it should be disqualified and all others should be immunized from removal." *Id.* at p. 1212.)

Chapter 12: Mediation

While **FC § 3118** primarily addresses the issue of child abuse, the duties of the mediator are the same, whether or not child abuse is present in a particular case. Pursuant to **FC § 3118(b)**, the evaluator or investigator must, at a minimum, do all of the following:

> **(1)** Consult with the agency providing child welfare services and law enforcement regarding the allegations of child sexual abuse, and obtain recommendations from these professionals regarding the child's safety and the child's need for protection.
>
> **(2)** Review and summarize the child welfare services agency file. No document contained in the child welfare services agency file may be photocopied, but a summary of the information in the file, including statements made by the children and the parents, and the recommendations made or anticipated to be made by the child welfare services agency to the juvenile court, may be recorded by the evaluator or investigator, except for the identity of the reporting party. The evaluator's or investigator's notes summarizing the child welfare services agency information shall be stored in a file separate from the evaluator's or investigator's file and may only be released to either party under order of the court.
>
> **(3)** Obtain from a law enforcement investigator all available information obtained from criminal background checks of the parents and any suspected perpetrator that is not a parent, including information regarding child abuse, domestic violence, or substance abuse.
>
> **(4)** Review the results of a multidisciplinary child interview team (hereafter MDIT) interview if available, or if not, or if the evaluator or investigator believes the MDIT interview is inadequate for purposes of the evaluation, investigation, or assessment, interview the child or request an MDIT interview, and shall wherever possible avoid repeated interviews of the child.
>
> **(5)** Request a forensic medical examination of the child from the appropriate agency, or include in the report required by paragraph (6) a written statement explaining why the examination is not needed.
>
> **(6)** File a confidential written report with the clerk of the court in which the custody hearing will be conducted and which shall be served on the parties or their attorneys at least 10 days prior to the hearing.

The scope of the evaluations is set forth in **CRC Rule 5.220(e)**. This rule provides that all evaluations include a written explanation of the process that clearly describes the purpose of the evaluation, the procedures used, the time required to gather and assess information and, if psychological tests will be used, the role of the results in confirming or questioning other information or previous conclusions.

Further, the scope and distribution of the evaluation report, the limitations on the confidentiality of the process and the cost and payment responsibility for the evaluation must also be included.

Custody evaluators are required to file a completed *Declaration of Court-Connected Child Custody Evaluator Regarding Qualifications* (form *FL-325*) when appointed by the court, certifying that he or she is qualified. There is a specific form that is used for a court order appointing a child custody evaluator. It is the *Order Appointing Child Custody Evaluator* (form *FL-327*).

A child custody evaluator must also prepare a written report regarding his or her findings. This report must: **(1)** summarize the data-gathering procedures, information sources and time spent and present all relevant information, including information that does not support the conclusions reached; **(2)** describe any limitations in the evaluation that result from unobtainable information, failure of a party to cooperate or the circumstances of particular interviews; and **(3)** provide clear, detailed recommendations that are consistent with the health, safety, welfare and best interests of the child if making any recommendations to the court regarding a parenting plan. **CRC Rule 5.220**.

A superior court may order child custody evaluations, investigations and assessments to assist them in determining the health, safety, welfare and best interests of children with regard to disputed custody and visitation issues. Many of the rules for mediation apply to custody evaluations, investigations and assessments as well. All child custody evaluators must meet the qualifications, training and continuing education requirements specified in **FC §§ 1815, 1816** and **3111**, and in **CRC Rules 5.225** and **5.230. CRC Rule 5.220(g)**.

The court, on its own motion or a motion of any party, may appoint an expert to investigate, render a report and testify as an expert in any child custody case.[19] **Evid. Code § 730**. Further, a court can remove the expert for bias in violation of **CRC Rule 5.220(h)(1)**. *In re Marriage of ADAMS* (2012) 209 Cal.App.4th 1543 at p. 1563.

FC § 3111 provides that a court may appoint a child custody evaluator when it determines that it would be in the child's best interests to do so.

> [1] A child custody evaluation shall be conducted in accordance with the standards adopted by the Judicial Council pursuant to Section 3117, and all other standards adopted by the Judicial Council regarding child custody evaluations. If directed by the court, the court-appointed child custody evaluator shall file a written confidential report on his or her evaluation. At least 10 days before any hearing regarding custody of the child, the report shall be filed with the clerk of the court in which the custody hearing will be conducted and served on the parties or their attorneys, and any other counsel appointed for the child pursuant to Section 3150. A child custody evaluation, investigation, or assessment, and any resulting report, may be considered by the court only if it is conducted in accordance with the requirements set forth in the standards adopted by the Judicial Council pursuant to Section 3117; however, this does not preclude the

---

[19] Evidence Code § 730 provides that the expert appointed for any kind of action where expert evidence is or may be required. The full text of Evidence Code § 730 is:
"When it appears to the court, at any time before or during the trial of an action, that expert evidence is or may be required by the court or by any party to the action, the court on its own motion or on motion of any party may appoint one or more experts to investigate, to render a report as may be ordered by the court, and to testify as an expert at the trial of the action relative to the fact or matter as to which the expert evidence is or may be required. The court may fix the compensation for these services, if any, rendered by any person appointed under this section, in addition to any service as a witness, at the amount as seems reasonable to the court."

> consideration of a child custody evaluation report that contains nonsubstantive or inconsequential errors or both.
> **[2]** The report may be received in evidence on stipulation of all interested parties and is competent evidence as to all matters contained in the report.
> **[3]** If the court determines that an unwarranted disclosure of a written confidential report has been made, the court may impose a monetary sanction against the disclosing party. The sanction shall be in an amount sufficient to deter repetition of the conduct, and may include reasonable attorney's fees, costs incurred, or both, unless the court finds that the disclosing party acted with substantial justification or that other circumstances make the imposition of the sanction unjust. The court shall not impose a sanction pursuant to this subdivision that imposes an unreasonable financial burden on the party against whom the sanction is imposed. This subdivision shall become operative on January 1, 2010.

And finally, **CRC Rule 5.225** provides the licensing, education and training and experience requirements for child custody evaluators who are appointed to conduct full or partial child custody evaluations under **FC §§ 3111** and **3118, Evid. Code § 730** or Chapter 15 (commencing with **CCP § 2032.010**). This rule is adopted as mandated by **FC § 3110.5**.

Chapter 12: Mediation

EDUCATIONAL EXERCISES

I.   Fill in the blanks using the Word List that follows.

1. The purpose of _____ _____ (2 words together) is to protect the rights of children and to promote the public welfare by preserving, promoting and protecting family life and the institution of matrimony.
2. The services of conciliation court are provided after the filing of a _____.
3. A _____ is encouraged between the parties; if the parties do make such an agreement, it must be reduced to writing and, with the consent of the parties, made into a court order.
4. A person employed as a _____ counselor of conciliation or as an associate counselor of conciliation must have the minimum qualifications set forth in **FC § 1819.**
5. **FC § 1816** provides that an evaluator must participate in a program of continuing instruction in _____ _____ (2 words together).
6. Whenever any *Petition*, *Response*, *Request for Order* or other pleading is filed requesting a new order or to modify a current order for _____ and/or _____, the court MUST set the contested issues for mediation, prior to hearing the matter. **FC § 3170(a)**.
7. Because a mediation date must be set in every contested custody and/or visitation matter set for a hearing, the legislature has _____ _____ (2 words together) that require that mediation be available at every superior court.
8. _____ _____ _____ (3 words together) is by far the most commonly used name for the mediation service because at least half of the 58 counties in California use this name for their mediation.
9. The standards of practice for mediation cases involving custody and/or visitation must include: **(1)** considering the _____ (2 words together) of the children and **(2)** _____ the rights of children.
10. Whenever a matter is set for mediation, the mediation must be set before or _____ with the setting of the matter for hearing. **FC § 3175**.
11. The notice that must be given to all parties and their attorneys of record must state that all _____ involving the mediator will be kept _____ between the mediator and the disputing parties. **FC § 3176**.
12. Unless the parties agree otherwise, there must not be any _____ _____ (2 words together) communications between the attorneys and the mediator. This rule extends to counsel appointed by the court. **FC § 216**.
13. A custody or visitation agreement reached as a result of mediation may be _____ at any time at the discretion of the court.
14. If the parties do not reach an agreement as a result of the mediation proceedings, the mediator may recommend to the court that can _____ be conducted or that other services be offered to assist the parties to affect a resolution of the controversy before a hearing on the issues. **FC § 3183(b)**.
15. **Evid. Code § 1115(b)** provides that a mediator is a _____ _____ (2 words together) who conducts a mediation. The neutral person is usually called a

Chapter 12: Mediation

counselor. The counselor assists the parties in resolving custody and visitation disputes.

16. The counselors must strive to reduce _____ that may exist between the parties.
17. A _____ _____ (2 words together) describes how parents or other appropriate parties will share and divide their decision-making and caretaking responsibilities to protect the health, safety, welfare, and best interest of each child who is a subject of the proceedings. CRC Rule 5.210(c).
18. The counselor may _____ the child alone or together with other interested parties, including stepparents, siblings, new or stepsiblings or other family members significant to the child.
19. A county's _____ _____ (2 words together) provide procedures to respond to requests for a change of counselors or for general problems or complaints related to mediation. **FC § 3163**.
20. Agreements made in _____ _____ will be upheld.
21. A _____ _____ (2 words together) is required to file a completed *Declaration of Court-Connected Child Custody Evaluator Regarding Qualifications* (form *FL-325*) when appointed by the court, certifying that he or she is qualified.

Word List

Reconciliation	Parenting plan
Interview	Enacted laws
Domestic violence	Supervising
Custody evaluator	Local rules
Conciliation court	Modified
Communications	Best interests
Investigation	Acrimony
Safeguarding	Visitation
Private mediation	Neutral person
Petition	*Ex parte*
Concurrent	Family Court Services
Custody	Confidential

II. **Find in the local rules in your jurisdiction, the information relating to how to handle a problem with a Family Court Services mediator.**

Chapter 12: Mediation

III.   Answer the following questions:

What is a conciliation court? How does one obtain the services of a conciliations court?

What continuing education programs must an evaluator participate in pursuant to **FC § 1816?**

When is medication required when filing for a hearing?

What happens when the parties do not reach an agreement during a mediation session?

Are attorneys allowed to participate in the mediation process? Why or Why not? What are the code sections that are relevant to this question?

CHAPTER 13: Child Custody

In Brief...

THE CLASSIFICATIONS OF CUSTODY, FC §§ 3000-3089:
- **Legal custody** is the right to make decisions regarding the health, education and welfare of the children. **FC § 3006**.
- **Sole legal custody** is where one parent has the right to make the decisions relating to the health, education and welfare of the children.
- **Joint legal custody** means both parents share the right/responsibility to make decisions.
- **Sole physical custody** is where the children reside with and are under the supervision of one parent, subject to the power of the court to order visitation. **FC § 3007**.
- **Joint physical custody** means that the both parents have significant periods of physical custody, such that there is frequent and continuing contact with both parents.

CUSTODY DECISIONS/ORDERS:

A change of custody requires:
- The best interests test be the test when there is no final custody order; and
- When there is a final custody order, the **change-in-circumstance rule (or changed-circumstance rule)** applies to modify that final order.

BEST INTEREST OF THE CHILD:
- There is a strong presumption against domestic abusers being awarded custody pursuant to **FC § 3020**, effective January 1, 2019.
- Prior to January 1, 2019:
- FC § 3010(a) provided that parents are equally entitled to have custody of their child.
- Reasonable visitation was granted unless the visitation would be detrimental to the best interest of the child.
- Since **FC § 3044** became effective, the court is required to grant reasonable visitation and/or custody **WHEN** the visitation/custody is in the best interest of the child to do so.

CUSTODY ACTS, (STATUTES):
1. **Uniform Child Custody Jurisdiction and Enforcement Act (UCCJEA):**
   - The UCCJEA takes a strict **first-in-time** approach to jurisdiction.
   - California may have jurisdiction and render a custody order if:
     1. This state is the home state of the child;
     2. The home state of the child has declined to exercise jurisdiction;
     3. All courts having jurisdiction have declined to exercise jurisdiction;
     4. No court of any other state has jurisdiction. **FC § 3421**
     5. Temporary emergency jurisdiction in emergency cases. **FC § 3424(a)**.

Chapter 13: Child Custody

> 2. **Federal Parental Kidnapping Prevention Act 28 U.S.C. § 1738A** addresses parental kidnapping and interstate/international child custody/visitation disputes.
> 3. **Missing Children Act or National Child Search Assistance Act** requires Federal, State, and law enforcement to report missing children under the age of 21. **42 USCS § 5779(a)**.
> 4. **The Hague Convention**
>   - Is a multilateral, international treaty that provides an expeditious procedure to return children who have been abducted and taken across international boundaries; and
>   - Applies to any child who was habitually resident in a Contracting State immediately before any breach of custody or access rights and ceases to apply when the child attains the age of 16 years.
> 5. **Indian Child Welfare Act** protects American Indian children. 25 USCS § 1901 et seq.
>
> ***JUVENILE DEPENDENCY COURT:***
> - Decisions take precedence over matters heard in the family court; and
> - Maintains jurisdiction until it decides that it no longer needs to intervene.
>
> ***PET CUSTODY:*** Pursuant to **FC § 2605** the court now has guidance with regard to pet custody. **FC § 2605** is set forth in its entirety at the end of this chapter.

Introduction

Child custody cases are quite possibly the most litigated cases in all of family law. Certainly, there is no other area of the law that carries with it such emotion and hostility. "Custody disputes are often fraught with emotionally charged issues and competing charges of impropriety.[1] Family law cases have a unique propensity for bitterness.[2] Controversies over custody are oftentimes long drawn out and bitter..."[3]

Custody issues are present in almost all family law cases, including paternity cases, because a valid marriage is not a requirement for a custody determination.

Classifications of Custody

The custody rules in the Family Code are set forth in **FC §§ 3000-3089**.

Joint custody: Joint custody means joint physical custody and joint legal custody. **FC § 3002**.

---

[1] *Steve H. v. Wendy S.* (1997) 57 Cal.App.4th 379 at p. 387.
[2] *Bidna v. Rosen* (1993) 19 Cal.App.4th 27 at p. 35.
[3] *Lucachevitch v. Lucachevitch* (1945) 69 Cal.App.2d 478 at p. 485.

Legal custody: The right to make decisions regarding the health, education and welfare of the children.

Sole legal custody: One parent has the right and the responsibility to make the decisions relating to the health, education and welfare of a child. **FC § 3006**.

Joint legal custody: Both parents share the right and the responsibility to make the decisions relating to the health, education and welfare of a child.

Sole physical custody: A child resides with and is under the supervision of one parent, subject to the power of the court to order visitation. **FC § 3007**. If a parent has sole physical custody, then the children live primarily with that parent and the other parent has visitation rights.

Joint physical custody: Each parent has significant periods of physical custody. Joint physical custody must be shared by the parents in such a way so as to assure a child of frequent and continuing contact with both parents, subject to **FC §§ 3011** and **3020**. **FC § 3004**.

In California, most courts grant parents joint legal custody, unless there is a very good reason why a court should not make this order.

If a court grants or denies a parent's request for legal custody, then that parent is entitled to request that the court state the reasons for the denial or the grant. The judge cannot simply state that his or her decision is in the best interests of the children. The judge must explain WHY his or her decision IS in the best interests of the children. **FC § 3082**. If a judge grants joint legal custody to the parents, the judge must explain what is required of parents who have legal custody and what the consequences are if those requirements are not followed. **FC § 3083**.

When the parents have agreed to joint custody, there is a presumption, affecting the burden of proof that joint custody is in the best interests of the minor child(ren). **FC § 3080**. Before making a decision regarding custody, the court may direct an investigation to be conducted. **FC § 3081**.

In making an order for joint physical custody, the court must specify the rights of each parent to physically control the children in sufficient detail to enable a parent deprived of that control to the implement laws for relief of child snatching and kidnapping. **FC § 3084**.

In making an order for joint physical custody or joint legal custody, the court may specify one parent as the primary caretaker of the children and one home as the primary home of the child(ren) for the purposes of determining eligibility for public assistance. **FC § 3086**.

If a court grants joint legal custody to the parents, the judge is under no obligation to grant the parents joint physical custody. **FC § 3085**.

Chapter 13: Child Custody

Effective January 1, 2019, the California Legislature declared that it is the public policy of this state to ensure that the health, safety, and welfare of children shall be the court's primary concern in determining the best interests of children when making any orders regarding the physical or legal custody or visitation of children.

"The Legislature further finds and declares that **children have the right to be safe** and free from abuse, and that the perpetration of child abuse or domestic violence in a household where a child resides is detrimental to the health, safety, and welfare of the child." **FC § 3020.**

(b) The Legislature finds and declares that it is the public policy of this state to ensure that children have frequent and continuing contact with both parents after the parents have separated or dissolved their marriage, or ended their relationship, and to encourage parents to share the rights and responsibilities of child rearing in order to effect this policy, except when the contact would not be in the best interests of the child, as provided in subdivisions (a) and (c) of this section and Section 3011. **(c)** When the policies set forth in subdivisions (a) and (b) of this section are in conflict, a court's order regarding physical or legal custody or visitation shall be made in a manner that ensures the health, safety, and welfare of the child and the safety of all family members.

Before **FC § 3044** became effective, (January 1, 2019), the court was required to grant reasonable visitation rights to a parent unless it is shown that the visitation would be detrimental to the best interest of the child. Now, after **FC § 3044** became effective, the court is required to grant reasonable visitation and/or custody **WHEN** the visitation/custody is in the best interest of the child to do so. In determining the best interests of the children, a court must take into consideration that children have a right to be safe and free from abuse. **FC § 3044.**

When making custody decisions, the best interests of the children are considered. It is the public policy of California to ensure that the health, safety and welfare of children are the court's primary concern in determining the best interests of children when making any orders regarding physical or legal custody or visitation of children. Also, it is the public policy of this state to ensure that children have frequent and continuing contact with both parents after the parents have separated or dissolved their marriage or ended their relationship, and to encourage parents to share the rights and responsibilities of child rearing in order to effect this policy, except where the contact would not be in the best interests of the child. **FC § 3020.**

A **best interests** determination in a family law proceeding[4] requires that the court consider:

---

[4] FC § 3021 provides that a family law proceeding includes:
" (a) A proceeding for dissolution of marriage.
(b) A proceeding for nullity of marriage.
(c) A proceeding for legal separation of the parties.
(d) An action for exclusive custody pursuant to Section 3120.
(e) A proceeding to determine physical or legal custody or for visitation in a proceeding pursuant to the Domestic Violence Prevention Act (Division 10 (commencing with Section 6200)).

> (a) The health, safety, and welfare of the child.
> (b)(1) Any history of abuse by one parent or any other person seeking custody against any of the following:
>   (A) A child to whom he or she is related by blood or affinity or with whom he or she has had a caretaking relationship, no matter how temporary.
>   (B) The other parent.
>   (C) A parent, current spouse, or cohabitant, of the parent or person seeking custody, or a person with whom the parent or person seeking custody has a dating or engagement relationship.
> (2) As a prerequisite to considering allegations of abuse, the court may require independent corroboration, including, but not limited to, written reports by law enforcement agencies, child protective services or other social welfare agencies, courts, medical facilities, or other public agencies or private nonprofit organizations providing services to victims of sexual assault or domestic violence. As used in this subdivision, "abuse against a child" means "child abuse" as defined in Section 11165.6 of the Penal Code and abuse against any of the other persons described in paragraph (2) or (3) means "abuse" as defined in Section 6203.
> (c) The nature and amount of contact with both parents, except as provided in Section 3046.
> (d) The habitual or continual illegal use of controlled substances, the habitual or continual abuse of alcohol, or the habitual or continual abuse of prescribed controlled substances by either parent. Before considering these allegations, the court may first require independent corroboration, including, but not limited to, written reports from law enforcement agencies, courts, probation departments, social welfare agencies, medical facilities, rehabilitation facilities, or other public agencies or nonprofit organizations providing drug and alcohol abuse services. As used in this subdivision, "controlled substances" has the same meaning as defined in the California Uniform Controlled Substances Act, Division 10 (commencing with Section 11000) of the Health and Safety Code.
> (e)
> (1) When allegations about a parent pursuant to subdivision (b) or (d) have been brought to the attention of the court in the current proceeding, and the court makes an order for sole or joint custody to that parent, the court shall state its reasons in writing or on the record. In these circumstances, the court shall ensure that any order regarding custody or visitation is specific as to time, day, place, and manner of transfer of the child as set forth in subdivision (c) of Section 6323.

If the children of the marriage are of sufficient age and capacity to reason so as to form an intelligent preference as to which one or both of the parents should have legal custody, the court must consider, and give due weight to, those wishes when making an order granting or modifying custody. **FC § 3042(a)**.

In an action under Section 6323, nothing in this subdivision shall be construed to authorize physical or legal custody, or visitation rights, to be granted to any party to a Domestic Violence Prevention Act proceeding who has not established a parent and child relationship pursuant to paragraph (2) of subdivision (a) of Section 6323.
(f) A proceeding to determine physical or legal custody or visitation in an action pursuant to the Uniform Parentage Act (Part 3 (commencing with Section 7600) of Division 12).
(g) A proceeding to determine physical or legal custody or visitation in an action brought by the district attorney pursuant to Section 17404.
 (e) A proceeding to determine physical or legal custody or for visitation in a proceeding pursuant to the Domestic Violence Prevention Act (Division 10 (commencing with Section 6200))."

Chapter 13: Child Custody

It is generally thought that by age 12 a child can make a decision about which parent he or she wishes to reside with and that because the child has reached this age, the court must follow the child's wishes. However, there is NO magical age such that a child can absolutely make this choice, and have it granted by the court.

However, when a child obtains the age of 14 years or older and wishes to address the court regarding custody or visitation, the child MUST be permitted to do so, unless the court determines that doing so is not in the child's best interests. In that case, the court must state its reasons for that finding on the record. **FC § 3042(c)**. Also, a child under the age of 14 years MAY address the court regarding visitation issues if the court determines that is in the child's best interests to do so. **FC § 3042(d)**.

When making a custody determination, the court may not deny a disabled parent custody because of his or her disability. *In re Marriage of CARNEY* (1979) 24 Cal.3d 725 codified at **FC § 3049**.

Nor can a court disqualify a parent, legal guardian or relative for a grant of custody because of his or her immigration status. **FC § 3040(b)**.

The court must not exhibit a preference or a presumption for or against joint legal custody, joint physical custody or sole custody, but must be allowed the widest discretion to choose a parenting plan that is in the best interests of the child. **FC § 3040(c)**.

Parents are equally entitled to the custody of their child(ren). **FC § 3010(a)**. If one parent dies, or is unable or refuses to take custody, or has abandoned the child, the other parent is entitled to custody of the child. **FC § 3010(b)**.

When granting custody, the following order of preference has been determined to be in the best interests of the child:

> **(1)** To both parents jointly pursuant to Chapter 4 (commencing with Section 3080) or to either parent. In making an order granting custody to either parent, the court shall consider, among other factors, which parent is more likely to allow the child frequent and continuing contact with the noncustodial parent, consistent with Sections 3011 and 3020, and shall not prefer a parent as custodian because of that parent's sex. The court, in its discretion, may require the parents to submit to the court a plan for the implementation of the custody order.
> **(2)** If to neither parent, to the person or persons in whose home the child has been living in a wholesome and stable environment.
> **(3)** To any other person or persons deemed by the court to be suitable and able to provide adequate and proper care and guidance for the child. FC § 3040(a).

In cases where a child has more than two parents, the court must make an order for custody and visitation that is in the best interests of the child, considering the child's need for continuity and stability by preserving established patterns of care and emotional bonds. The court may order that not all parents share legal or physical

Chapter 13: Child Custody

custody of the child, if the court finds that it would not be in the best interests of the child. **FC § 3040(d)**.

In counties that have a conciliation court, the court or the parties may, at any time, pursuant to the local rules of court, consult with the conciliation court for the purpose of assisting the parties to formulate a plan for implementation of the custody order or to resolve a controversy that has arisen in the implementation of a plan for custody. **FC § 3089**.

Custody Orders

FC § 3048 provides that the contents of a custody order must contain all of the following:

> (1) The basis for the court's exercise of jurisdiction.
> (2) The manner in which notice and opportunity to be heard were given.
> (3) A clear description of the custody and visitation rights of each party.
> (4) A provision stating that a violation of the order may subject the party in violation to civil or criminal penalties, or both.
> (5) Identification of the country of habitual residence of the child or children.

As set forth above, the California legislature and courts consider the best interests of the children when making custody orders. However, as the following case demonstrates when a final custody order in place, there is an adjunct to the best interests' custody rule.

> ***ALEX MONTENEGRO, Plaintiff and Respondent, v. DEBORAH DIAZ, Defendant and Appellant.***
> SUPREME COURT OF CALIFORNIA
> 26 Cal.4th 249; 27 P.3d 289; 109 Cal.Rptr.2d 575
> July 30, 2001, Decided
> (*Montenegro v. Diaz*)
>
> Montenegro and Diaz were unmarried when their son Gregory was born in November 1994. For the first 18 months after the birth, Montenegro had short visits with Gregory, usually in the home Diaz shared with her mother.
>
> In March 1996, Montenegro visited Gregory while Diaz was at work and Gregory was in the care of his grandmother. Although Montenegro had made no previous arrangements with Diaz, he took Gregory for an overnight visit. After that incident, Diaz refused to allow visitation without a court order. Montenegro then filed a complaint and order to show cause to establish paternity and requested joint legal and physical custody. Diaz conceded paternity but sought sole physical custody of Gregory. She also sought child support and a restraining order preventing Montenegro from harassing her at home or work. The trial court referred them to family court services, including mediation counseling.
>
> Montenegro and Diaz were both represented by counsel and initially stipulated to a temporary custody order after mediation. Under the order, Diaz retained physical custody

Chapter 13: Child Custody

and Montenegro had visitation rights that would increase by stages to one weekday a week and alternate weekends.

On September 30, 1996, the superior court entered another order, signed by the parents and their attorneys, captioned "Stipulation and Order to Show Cause for Judgment." The order stated that Montenegro was Gregory's biological father and that Diaz had "primary responsibility for the care, custody and control of the minor." The order included a detailed visitation schedule for Montenegro. The order further provided that "[t]his stipulation covers all matters in dispute in this Order to Show Cause. This Order when signed is the formal Order. No further documents are necessary." The minute order, however, was virtually identical in form to the previous temporary minute orders, and the end of the order contained a "Notice to Parties Without Attorneys" stating that "[t]his order, although temporary, shall remain in effect until further order of court."

On June 24, 1997, the trial court entered another stipulated order signed by the parents and their attorneys after both parents filed orders to show cause seeking to modify the custody arrangement. Prior to this stipulation, neither Montenegro nor Diaz claimed that the September 30, 1996 order was a final judgment as to custody. In the new stipulation, the parents agreed to joint legal custody. Diaz had "primary physical custody," and Montenegro had "secondary physical custody." The order also included [a] detailed visitation schedule. Although the June 24, 1997 order did not provide for further review, it never stated that it was a permanent custody order.

Not surprisingly, this order did not end the feuding as Montenegro and Diaz had a disagreement over Gregory's future school. As a result, Montenegro filed an order to show cause requesting that the June 24, 1997 order be modified to provide for joint physical custody, with Gregory living with each parent on alternating weeks. Diaz filed a responsive declaration indicating that a joint custody arrangement would not be feasible once Gregory began to attend regular school, and that it would be in his best interest to be with her.

Although she argued that Montenegro had not made "the requisite showing of a 'change in circumstances' or that a change in custody would be 'in the best interests' of" their child, she did not contend that the June 24, 1997 order was a final judicial custody determination.

Trial commenced on August 4, 1999. At the outset, both parents agreed that the triggering event for the hearing was Gregory's impending enrollment in kindergarten and the need to choose his school. They also agreed that the current custody arrangement would no longer be appropriate once Gregory began kindergarten, because his new daily schedule would necessitate that he spend the majority of his time with one parent.

On September 10, 1999, the trial court issued a statement of intended decision. In the decision, the court acknowledged that the parents had previously entered into stipulated orders concerning custody. It, however, concluded that "[t]his is an initial trial on custody" and held that a showing of changed circumstances was not required for a change in custody. Because Montenegro was more willing to share Gregory, the court ruled that it was in "the best interests of Gregory . . . that he be in the primary physical custody of the father . . . ." Consistent with these rulings, the trial court entered an order awarding physical custody to Montenegro and visitation to Diaz on alternate weekends, alternate holidays, and, during the summer, alternate weeks.

The Court of Appeal reversed. After reviewing the evidence presented at trial, the Court of Appeal determined that there was no evidence of a significant change of circumstances. We granted review.

DISCUSSION
In this case, the Court of Appeal held that the trial court abused its discretion by applying the best interest standard instead of the changed circumstance rule. We now reverse the Court of Appeal on the ground that the trial court properly applied the best interest standard. Because the trial court did not abuse its discretion by refusing to apply the changed circumstance rule, we do not consider whether the Court of Appeal erred in its application of this rule to the facts of this case.

Under California's statutory scheme governing child custody and visitation determinations, the overarching concern is the best interest of the child. The court and the family have "the widest discretion to choose a parenting plan that is in the best interest of the child." (FC § 3040 (c).) When determining the best interest of the child, relevant factors include the health, safety and welfare of the child, any history of abuse by one parent against the child or the other parent, and the nature and amount of contact with the parents. (FC § 3011.)

Although the statutory scheme only requires courts to ascertain the "best interest of the child," this court has articulated a variation on the best interest standard once a final judicial custody determination is in place. Under the so-called changed circumstance rule, a party seeking to modify a permanent custody order can do so only if he or she demonstrates a significant change of circumstances justifying a modification. (*Burgess, supra,* 13 Cal.4th at p. 37, 51.) According to our earlier decisions, "[t]he changed-circumstance rule is not a different test, devised to supplant the statutory test, but an adjunct to the best-interest test. It provides, in essence, that once it has been established that a particular custodial arrangement is in the best interests of the child, the court need not reexamine that question. Instead, it should preserve the established mode of custody unless some significant change in circumstances indicates that a different arrangement would be in the child's best interest. The rule thus fosters the dual goals of judicial economy and protecting stable custody arrangements." (*Burchard*, supra, 42 Cal.3d at p. 535.)

We hold that a stipulated custody order is a final judicial custody determination for purposes of the changed circumstance rule only if there is a clear, affirmative indication the parties intended such a result. In adopting this holding, we recognize the reality that many family court litigants do not have attorneys and may not be fully aware of the legal ramifications of their stipulations.

We conclude that neither the June 24, 1997 order nor the September 30, 1996 order constitutes a final judicial custody determination. Although these orders included detailed visitation schedules and did not provide for further hearings, they did not clearly state that they were final judgments as to custody. For example, the September 30, 1996 order, which did contain the words "for judgment" written by hand, also contained a notice stating that "[t]his order, although temporary, shall remain in effect until further order of Court."

Although the notice ostensibly applied to parties without attorneys, its inexplicable inclusion casts the finality of the judgment into doubt. Meanwhile, the June 24, 1997 order never mentioned the words "final," "permanent" or "judgment." Finally, the minute

Chapter 13: Child Custody

> orders confirming these stipulations resembled the minute orders confirming the parties' temporary stipulations. Thus, neither order contained a clear, affirmative indication that the parties intended it to be a final judicial custody determination.
>
> In reaching this conclusion, we do not dismiss the arguments of various amici curiae who contend this court should reevaluate the changed circumstance rule in light of new developments in social science and child psychology and development. Although we agree that the changed circumstance rule should be flexible and should reflect the changing needs of children as they grow up, we need not reach this issue today because we conclude that the changed circumstance rule does not apply. Accordingly, we leave any review of the changed circumstance rule for another day.
>
> We reverse the judgment of the Court of Appeal and hold that the trial court properly applied the best interest standard, rather than the changed circumstance rule. [This case is remanded] for further proceedings consistent with this opinion.

The best interests test is applied in determining custody when there is no final custody order; when there is a final custody order, there must be a substantial change in circumstances to modify that order. Under this **change-in-circumstance rule**, the court will not reexamine what is in the child's best interests. Instead, it:

> preserves the established mode of custody unless some significant change in circumstances indicates that a different arrangement would be in the child's best interest. The rule thus fosters the dual goals of judicial economy and protecting stable custody arrangements. *BURCHARD v. GARAY* (1986) 42 Cal.3d 531 at p. 535.

On January 1, 2019 **FC § 3020** was amended providing that children have a right to be free from abuse and safe. FC § 3020 provides:

> (a) The Legislature finds and declares that it is the public policy of this state to ensure that the health, safety, and welfare of children shall be the court's primary concern in determining the best interests of children when making any orders regarding the physical or legal custody or visitation of children. The Legislature further finds and declares that children have the right to be safe and free from abuse, and that the perpetration of child abuse or domestic violence in a household where a child resides is detrimental to the health, safety, and welfare of the child.
> (b) The Legislature finds and declares that it is the public policy of this state to ensure that children have frequent and continuing contact with both parents after the parents have separated or dissolved their marriage, or ended their relationship, and to encourage parents to share the rights and responsibilities of child rearing in order to effect this policy, except when the contact would not be in the best interests of the child, as provided in subdivisions (a) and (c) of this section and Section 3011.
> (c) When the policies set forth in subdivisions (a) and (b) of this section are in conflict, a court's order regarding physical or legal custody or visitation shall be made in a manner that ensures the health, safety, and welfare of the child and the safety of all family members.

Custody Acts (Statutes)

1. Uniform Child Custody Jurisdiction and Enforcement Act (UCCJEA)

In 1968, the Uniform Law Commissioners promulgated the Uniform Child Custody Jurisdiction Action (UCCJA). The UCCJA was designed to discourage interstate kidnapping of children by their non-custodial parents. In 1980, Congress adopted the Parental Kidnapping Prevention Act (PKPA) to address the interstate custody jurisdictional problems that continued to exist after the adoption of the UCCJA. Despite the UCCJA, some states continued to modify out-of-state custody orders, refusing to give the orders deference under the Full Faith and Credit Clause of the Constitution of the United States.

Part of the problem was that the UCCJA had no provisions regarding continuing exclusive jurisdiction, which produced conflicting custody decrees and different interpretations of how long continuing jurisdiction lasts. Additionally, in the UCCJA there was an ambiguity regarding whether a court has declined jurisdiction. *In re Marriage of NURIE* (2009) 176 Cal.App.4th 478 at p. 502.

In 1997, a revised version of the UCCJA was promulgated as the UCCJEA. It was enacted to harmonize inconsistent case law under the UCCJA and bring a uniform procedure to the law of interstate enforcement by providing a remedial process to enforce interstate child custody and visitation determinations. *In re Marriage of PAILLIER* (2006) 144 Cal.App.4th 461 at p. 469.

The purpose of the UCCJEA is to promote uniformity among the states, minimize competition among the jurisdictions and encourage states to cooperate with one another with regard to child custody matters. **FC § 3461**.

The UCCJEA takes a strict **first-in-time** approach to jurisdiction. Once the court of an appropriate state has made a **child custody determination**, that court obtains **exclusive, continuing jurisdiction**. All of the states have adopted the UCCJEA.

If no other state has taken jurisdiction or rendered a custody determination, then **FC § 3421** provides that if any of the following are true, California has the jurisdictional basis for making a child custody determination:

(1) **This state is the home state of the child** on the date of the commencement of the proceeding or was the home state of the child within six (6) months prior to the proceeding and the child is absent from this state but a parent or person acting as a parent continues to live in this state.

Chapter 13: Child Custody

(2) **The home state of the child has declined to exercise jurisdiction** on the grounds that this state is the more appropriate forum.[5]
(3) **All courts having jurisdiction have declined to exercise jurisdiction** on the ground that a court of this state is the more appropriate forum.
(4) **No court of any other state has jurisdiction**.
(5) **Temporary emergency jurisdiction** if the child is present in this state and has been abandoned or it is necessary in an emergency to protect the child because the child, or a sibling or parent of the child, is subjected to, or threatened with, mistreatment or abuse. **FC § 3424(a)**.

A child is defined as an individual who is under eighteen (18) years of age. A child custody proceeding is any proceeding in which legal custody, physical custody or visitation with respect to a child is an issue, including a proceeding for dissolution of marriage, legal separation of the parties, neglect, abuse, dependency, guardianship, paternity, termination of parental rights and protection from domestic violence. **FC § 3402(d)**.

The **home state** is the state in which a child lived with a parent or a person acting as a parent for at least six consecutive months immediately before the commencement of a child custody proceeding. In the case of a child less than six (6) months of age, the term means the state in which the child lived from birth with any of the persons mentioned. (See *SCHNEER v. LLAURADO* (2015) 242 Cal.App.4th 1276 at p. 1289 where the court held that the six months is measured backward.) A period of temporary absence of any of the mentioned persons is part of the period. **FC § 3402(g)**.

Physical presence of, or personal jurisdiction over, a party or a child is not necessary or sufficient to make a child custody determination. **FC § 3421(c)**.

If there is no previous child custody determination made pursuant to the rules set forth in the UCCJEA, then a child custody determination made under this section remains in effect until an order is obtained from a court of a state having jurisdiction. **FC § 3424(b)**.

If there is a previous child custody determination, then the order issued in this state remains in effect until an order is obtained from the other state within the period specified or the period expires. **FC § 3424(c)**.

A California court may communicate with a court in another state concerning a proceeding in which legal custody, physical custody or visitation is an issue. **FC § 3410(a)**. The court may allow the parties to participate in this communication. However, if the parties are not able to participate in the communication, they must be given the opportunity to present facts and legal arguments before a decision on

---

[5] Additionally, the child and the child's parents must have a significant connection with this state other than mere physical presence, and substantial evidence must be available in this state concerning the child's care, protection, training and personal relationships.

jurisdiction is made. **FC § 3410(b)**. A record must be made unless it concerns only schedules, calendars, court records and similar matters. **FC § 3410(c)**.[6]

A California court that has jurisdiction to make a child custody determination may decline to exercise its jurisdiction at any time if it determines that it is an inconvenient forum under the circumstances and that a court of another state is a more appropriate forum. The issue of inconvenient forum may be raised upon motion of a party, the court's own motion or at the request of another court. **FC § 3427(a)**.

Pursuant to **FC § 3453**, a California Court must accord full faith and credit to an order issued by another state and, consistent with this part, enforce a child custody determination by a court of another state unless the order has been vacated, stayed or modified by a court having jurisdiction to do so.

A California court must treat a foreign country as if it were a state of the United States for the purpose of applying the UCCJEA. **FC § 3405(a)**.

A child custody determination made in a foreign country under factual circumstances in substantial conformity with the jurisdictional standards of this part must be recognized and enforced. **FC § 3405(b)**.

Although the term **best interests** is a primary part of California custody determinations, it was eliminated when the UCCJEA was enacted because the term was being misused to attempt to override jurisdictional determinations, arguing that the best interests of the child should control such decisions.

The following UCCJEA case graphically confirms that the established mode of custody should be preserved unless there is some significant change in circumstances that would indicate that a different arrangement would be in the child's best interests.

In re Marriage of GHULAM and FIZZA RIZVI NURIE. GHULAM NURIE, Respondent, v. FIZZA RIZVI, Appellant. GHULAM NURIE, Plaintiff and Respondent, v. FIZZA RIZVI, Defendant and Appellant.
COURT OF APPEAL OF CALIFORNIA, FIRST APPELLATE DISTRICT, DIVISION TWO
176 Cal.App.4th 478; 98 Cal.Rptr.3d 200
August 7, 2009, Filed
(*Marriage of Nurie*)

Fizza Rizvi (Wife) and Ghulam Nurie (Husband) were both born in Pakistan, but Husband had lived in the United States for his entire adult life and is a naturalized United States citizen. They were married in a religious ceremony in Karachi on October 30, 2001. Shortly after the wedding, Wife came to live with Husband in his home of 16 years in Fremont, California. The couple were again married in a civil ceremony in Reno, Nevada, on January 31, 2002, and resided together in Fremont for the duration of their

---

[6] FC § 3410(e) provides that a "record" consists of information that is inscribed on a tangible medium or that is stored in an electronic or other medium and is retrievable in perceivable form.

Chapter 13: Child Custody

brief marriage. On September 16, 2002, their son (Son) was born in San Ramon, California.

On or about February 19, 2003, Wife took five-month-old Son to Pakistan, ostensibly on a four-week visit with the extended families. Husband bought round trip airfare for them on that understanding. At the end of that time, Wife said she wanted to extend her visit for a few more weeks, and Husband agreed. Husband later learned through a third party that Wife did not plan to return. Wife did not directly communicate to Husband that she did not intend to return to California until the end of May 2003.

On June 20, 2003, Husband filed for dissolution of the marriage in Alameda County Superior Court. He sought custody of Son under the UCCJEA. On July 29, 2003, he obtained an ex parte order to show cause granting him temporary custody. Wife was served in Pakistan on September 16, 2003.

On September 30, 2003, Margaret Gannon, an Oakland attorney, made a special appearance on Wife's behalf to contest subject matter jurisdiction under the UCCJEA and to quash service of summons. At that hearing, a briefing schedule was established and a hearing on the merits set for November 4, 2003.

Wife substituted in as her own attorney on October 16, 2003, before any briefs had been filed. Wife filed no briefs, did not appear at the November 4 hearing, and took no further action to challenge the court's jurisdiction. The court found that Wife had been served and had notice of the hearing. After hearing testimony from Husband about Son's birth and first months of life, as well as the circumstances under which Son was taken to Pakistan, the court found it had home state jurisdiction and awarded sole legal and physical custody to Husband. The court issued a written order on November 5, 2003 (2003 Custody Order.

Meanwhile, on October 1, 2003, Wife filed an action seeking custody of Son in the Court of the Civil Judge and Guardian Judge (Guardian Court) in Pakistan. She neglected to disclose the pendency of the California Dissolution Action. On October 3, the Pakistani court issued an order forbidding Husband to remove Son from Pakistan. In the custody application, Wife alleged she had been physically abused by Husband during their marriage.

Husband filed responsive papers, informing the Guardian Court of California's 2003 Custody Order. On December 1, 2003, the Pakistani court dismissed Wife's custody application, deferring to the California court's jurisdiction.

[Thereafter], the parties agreed to reconcile as a couple in the United States and share custody of Son. Under their agreement, Wife was to return to California with Son on or about December 31, 2003. She failed to do so, however, claiming that Husband had verbally abused her after the agreement was signed. Husband returned to the United States alone in late December 2003 or early January 2004.

On March 1, 2004, the district attorney's office issued an arrest warrant for Wife, alleging two felonies for child abduction and unlawful deprivation of custody. Also on this date, Wife, represented by new California counsel, Hannah Sims, sought an ex parte order to show cause in California, requesting that the court modify the 2003 Custody Order or, in the alternative, "abdicate" jurisdiction to Pakistan. Wife's request included a declaration by her alleging physical and psychological abuse at Husband's hands during their marriage, and detailing events in Pakistan leading up to and following the December

Chapter 13: Child Custody

2003 Order.

On March 5, 2004, the court denied Wife's ex parte application and set a hearing for May 5, 2004. Wife's attorney subsequently took her motion off calendar, as Wife would not risk arrest and prosecution to appear at the hearing.

Wife's default was entered and subsequently a judgment of dissolution was granted, with legal and physical custody awarded to Husband, again with notice to Wife's counsel. On February 1, 2005, Hannah Sims formally withdrew as Wife's counsel. Wife claims, however, that she had no knowledge of the default judgment until December 18, 2007.

Wife alleges that on October 26, 2007, Husband and three armed accomplices kidnapped Son from outside her lawyer's office in Karachi, as she brought him for the scheduled visitation. An order prohibiting Son's removal from Pakistan was issued by the Sindh High Court (SHC) on October 29, 2007, which was followed by a warrant for Husband's arrest and placement of Son's and Husband's names on an "Exit Control List" to prevent them from leaving Pakistan. Husband somehow escaped the country and returned to California with Son. On April 18, 2008, the SHC authorized issuance of an INTERPOL "red notice" for Husband's arrest.

Husband, for his part, claims the seizure of Son was perfectly legal and was conducted by the Pakistani Federal Investigation Agency (FIA), which was enforcing an INTERPOL "yellow notice" issued as a result of the abduction charges against Wife in California. Husband declares that he and Son left Pakistan with the cooperation of the United States government and arrived back in the United States on November 21, 2007.

Either way, Son was brought back to California and kept at an undisclosed location. He now lives with Husband in California and attends school here.

On January 8, 2008, Wife registered the July 2006 Order from Pakistan in Alameda County Superior Court and shortly thereafter filed an order to show cause to modify the earlier California custody order and to enforce the foreign order under section 3405. (See also §§ 3443, 3446.) The trial court consolidated the Registration Action with the Dissolution Action.

On February 21, 2008, the court denied registration and enforcement of the July 2006 Order. In that order the court found that (1) its jurisdiction under the UCCJEA and the issue of service were litigated and resolved in Husband's favor in the Dissolution Action; (2) the 2003 Custody Order entered in that action, and subsequently incorporated into the January 21, 2005 default judgment, was valid and enforceable; (3) Wife's then counsel was served with notice of entry of judgment; and (4) the time limitations for seeking relief from entry of a default judgment had passed.

The court issued a written order on May 12, 2008, reaffirming its findings in the February 21 order and concluding that California's jurisdiction under the UCCJEA was exclusive and continuing, that it did not lose jurisdiction by reason of Husband's prolonged presence in Pakistan or the loss of "significant connections" with Son, that the alleged kidnapping of Son by Husband did not require California to relinquish jurisdiction, and that California would not voluntarily decline jurisdiction as an inconvenient forum.

DISCUSSION

Thankfully, it is not our task to decide all of the hotly contested factual issues between

Chapter 13: Child Custody

these warring parties. We are, however, asked to decide between two core concepts in child custody jurisdiction that appear to compete in this case, namely "home state" jurisdiction and "exclusive, continuing" jurisdiction. (FC §§ 3421, 3422.) We conclude the method for resolving any conflict between these legal principles is dictated by the UCCJEA, and decide the case accordingly.

The exclusive method of determining subject matter jurisdiction in custody cases is the UCCJEA. Under the UCCJEA, a California court must "treat a foreign country as if it were a state of the United States for the purpose of" determining jurisdiction. (FC § 3405(a).) Moreover, with limited exception, "a child custody determination made in a foreign country under factual circumstances in substantial conformity with the jurisdictional standards of this part must be recognized and enforced" in California. (FC § 3405(b)).

There is no provision in the UCCJEA for jurisdiction by reason of the presence of the parties or by stipulation, consent, waiver, or estoppel.

Under the UCCJEA, the state with absolute priority to render an initial child custody determination is the child's home state on the date of commencement of the first custody proceeding or, alternatively, the state which had been his home state within six months before commencement if the child is absent from the home state but a parent continues to live there.[7]

A court that properly acquires initial jurisdiction has exclusive, continuing jurisdiction unless one of two subsequent events occurs: (1) a court of the issuing state itself determines that "neither the child, nor the child and one parent, nor the child and a person acting as a parent have a significant connection with this state and that substantial evidence is no longer available in this state concerning the child's care, protection, training, and personal relationships," or (2) there is a judicial determination by either the issuing state or any other state that "the child, the child's parents, and any person acting as a parent do not presently reside in" the issuing state. (FC § 3422(a)(1), (2).)

"The UCCJEA takes a strict 'first in time' approach to jurisdiction. Once the court of an appropriate state has made a child custody determination, that court obtains 'exclusive, continuing jurisdiction ….' The court of another state: (a) Cannot modify the child custody determination; [and] (b) Must enforce the child custody determination.[8]

The trial court found that California properly assumed initial UCCJEA jurisdiction over the child custody matter as Son's home state when the Dissolution Action was

---

[7] FC § 3421(a) provides that a court of this state has jurisdiction to make an initial child custody determination only if any of the following are true:
"(1) This state is the home state of the child on the date of the commencement of the proceeding, or was the home state of the child within six months before the commencement of the proceeding and the child is absent from this state but a parent or person acting as a parent continues to live in this state. (g) 'Home state' means the state in which a child lived with a parent or a person acting as a parent for at least six consecutive months immediately before the commencement of a child custody proceeding. In the case of a child less than six months of age, the term means the state in which the child lived from birth with any of the persons mentioned. A period of temporary absence of any of the mentioned persons is part of the period." (Only pertinent sections are included.)
[8] FC §§ 3421, 3422, 3423, 3443, 3445, 3446, 3448, 3453; *In re Marriage of Pailler* (2006) 144 Cal.App.4th 461 at p. 469.

commenced. That initial assertion of jurisdiction gave California exclusive, continuing jurisdiction under section 3422.

Nevertheless, Wife argues that the California dissolution judgment is void or should be set aside on three grounds: (1) she was deprived of due process and notice by the procedures employed; (2) Husband failed to notify the California court of the proceedings in Pakistan, as required by section 3429, subdivision (d); and (3) Husband made misrepresentations in the Dissolution Action that acted as a fraud upon the court.

The trial court found the due process and notice issues had been litigated in the Dissolution Action and that the time had expired for Wife to contest those matters.

Wife argues vigorously that the motivating force behind the UCCJEA is to prevent parental kidnapping, and that our decision in this appeal must be guided by that principle. While that is certainly one of the UCCJEA's underlying objectives, it is not the only one. We have previously identified the primary purposes of its predecessor, the Uniform Child Custody Jurisdiction Act (UCCJA), as (1) preventing the harm done to children by shifting them from state to state to relitigate custody, and (2) preventing jurisdictional conflict between the states after a custody decree has been rendered. Thus, among the primary purposes of the uniform acts is to encourage states to respect and enforce the prior custody determinations of other states, as well as to avoid competing jurisdiction and conflicting decisions.

Wife argued in the trial court that on October 1, 2003, when she filed her action for custody in Pakistan, California and Pakistan had "concurrent jurisdiction." Such claim ignores the fact that a major aim of the UCCJEA is to avoid "concurrent jurisdiction."

Wife argues that California lost jurisdiction as soon as Husband acquired a residence in Pakistan, essentially advocating the view that jurisdiction is self-terminating when the specified parties move out of the decree state. Accordingly, Wife goes to some length to prove that Husband "resided" for a substantial period in Pakistan from sometime in 2004 until October 2007, pointing out that he bought a house there and enjoyed regular visitation with Son. And, she argues, husband is estopped to deny residency in Karachi because he used a Karachi address on his pleadings in Pakistan.

Husband acknowledges that he visited Pakistan frequently, but insists he was there only to try to regain custody of Son and to keep in contact with him. Husband claims he stayed with his parents or friends while he was there. He claims the house in Karachi was purchased by his mother and is held in her name (Qamar Nurie). He never was employed in Pakistan, and never bought property or owned a car there. He always intended to return to California, not to move to Pakistan.

The crucial question under the statute is not whether Husband "resided" in Pakistan, but whether he stopped residing in California. On that point, Husband claims he never stopped residing in California because he continuously owned a house here, which he kept for his own use and never rented out, even paying a gardener to maintain the grounds in his absence. He always maintained a car, telephones and a fax machine here, paid taxes and utilities here, and had built his career as an electrical engineer and marketing manager in the Silicon Valley. He has lived in California since 1983 and considers it his permanent home. We may infer from his declaration that he maintained furnishings and other personal possessions in his home in Fremont. We infer from the record that he physically

Chapter 13: Child Custody

resided in California at least from October 2005 to April 2006, and his residence here during other periods has not been precluded.

Wife emphasizes the importance of "home state" jurisdiction, and insists that Pakistan became Son's home state, even as California lost connections entitling it to continuing jurisdiction. She claims that home state jurisdiction is "paramount" under the UCCJEA because it is ultimately in the child's best interests for that state to make the custody determination.

It is true that in initial custody determinations the child's home state is given absolute priority. (See FC § 3421(a)(1).) That is, in fact, the basis upon which California asserted initial jurisdiction in this case. However, it is not true that a change in the child's home state will automatically allow the new home state to acquire modification jurisdiction.

Wife argues that the December 2003 Order in Pakistan was a "valid modification of the earlier California order." FC§ 3402(k). She also contends that even if Pakistan was not Son's home state in 2003, as the trial court found, it had become his home state at least by July 12, 2006, when the SHC (Sindh High Court) issued the order Wife seeks to enforce.

Under FC §§ 3422 and 3423, however, it is not enough that a jurisdiction qualify factually as the child's home state for the courts to exercise modification jurisdiction. Rather, the UCCJEA makes clear that a change in the child's home state after a court has initially assumed jurisdiction does not result in the shifting of jurisdiction to the new home state.

The principles of the UCCJEA require a state at least to deferentially assess the status of any preexisting order before acting. For Pakistan to assume modification jurisdiction, either California would have had to voluntarily cede jurisdiction (which it did not), or else the Pakistani court would have had to find that "the child, the child's parents, and any person acting as a parent do not presently reside" in California. FC § 3423(a), (b).

Wife asserts that Pakistan gained jurisdiction because she and Husband entered into the 2003 Compromise. As the trial court noted, "it is unclear how a compromise regulating visitation pending the parents' return to California changed [the Guardian Court's] analysis."

As the trial court found, Pakistan appears to have asserted jurisdiction based on the parties' consent. This view is confirmed by subsequent observations in the Pakistani court filings that Husband had "surrendered" or "submitted" to Pakistan's jurisdiction. However, as noted, subject matter jurisdiction cannot be created by consent.

We conclude that the July 2006 Order did not substantially comply with UCCJEA principles and need not be enforced by a California court. (FC §§ 3405, 3443, 3446). In so holding, we conclude that the concepts of exclusive, continuing jurisdiction, restraint in exercising modification jurisdiction, and deference to prior-in-time decrees (except in limited circumstances) are among the key jurisdictional standards that must be adhered to by a foreign jurisdiction before its custody orders are entitled to enforcement in California. In other words, a party seeking to enforce a foreign custody order must show not only "factual circumstances in substantial conformity" (FC § 3405(b)) with the initial jurisdictional requirements of section 3421, but also that the foreign order substantially conforms to the policies of enforcing prior decrees and avoiding conflicting jurisdiction embodied in sections 3422, 3423 and 3426.

Chapter 13: Child Custody

Wife claims California has also lost jurisdiction based on FC § 3422(a)(1), which provides that a court may lose exclusive, continuing jurisdiction if "A court of this state determines that neither the child, nor the child and one parent, nor the child and a person acting as a parent have a significant connection with this state and that substantial evidence is no longer available in this state concerning the child's care, protection, training, and personal relationships."

California never lost jurisdiction. Wife contends that California nevertheless was required to relinquish jurisdiction under section 3428, which provides, in part: "if a court of this state has jurisdiction under this part because a person seeking to invoke its jurisdiction has engaged in unjustifiable conduct, the court shall decline to exercise its jurisdiction …."

The trial court rejected this argument without determining the merits of the kidnapping claim because the statute does not require it to relinquish jurisdiction properly acquired, but only to decline to accept jurisdiction if it is invoked as a result of wrongful conduct.

We are, of course, deeply troubled by Wife's allegation that Husband kidnapped Son from her in Pakistan with the help of three armed gunmen. Husband has declared under oath, however, that he retrieved Son lawfully through the Pakistan FIA and with the assistance of the United States government.

Finally, Wife argues that even if California technically could retain jurisdiction, it should nevertheless cede jurisdiction to Pakistan because it is a more convenient forum. Whether a trial court stays its proceedings on that basis is purely discretionary, and the ruling will not be disturbed on appeal unless there was a clear abuse of discretion.

The trial court examined each of eight factors pertinent to the inconvenient forum decision under section 3427.[9] In light of this thoughtful analysis, we cannot say that the trial court abused its discretion in refusing to declare Pakistan a more convenient forum.

A court should decline jurisdiction as an inconvenient forum only when there is concurrent jurisdiction elsewhere. Here, as discussed, California had exclusive, continuing jurisdiction, and Pakistan had no modification jurisdiction under UCCJEA principles.

DISPOSITION
The judgment is affirmed.

---

[9] The eight factors are:
(1) Whether domestic violence has occurred and is likely to continue in the future, and which state could best protect the parties and the child.
(2) The length of time the child has resided outside this state.
(3) The distance between the court in this state and the court in the state that would assume jurisdiction.
(4) The degree of financial hardship to the parties in litigating in one forum over the other.
(5) Any agreement of the parties as to which state should assume jurisdiction.
(6) The nature and location of the evidence required to resolve the pending litigation, including testimony of the child.
(7) The ability of the court of each state to decide the issue expeditiously and the procedures necessary to present the evidence.
(8) The familiarity of the court of each state with the facts and issues in the pending litigation.

Finally, parties must have notice and an opportunity to be heard before a court can make a child custody determination. (See *W.M. v. V.A.* (2018) 30 Cal.App.5th 64 where the court held that since father did not have notice of mother's action, mother's custody action was not first in time and did not give her custody pursuant to the UCCJEA. *Id.* at p. 79-80.)

2. Federal Parental Kidnapping Prevention Act 28 U.S.C. § 1738A

The Parental Kidnapping Prevention Act (PKPA) became law in 1980 to address parental kidnapping and interstate/international child custody and visitation disputes.[10] Its intent was to prevent forum shopping by preventing other states that were not the home state of the child from taking jurisdiction to decide custody disputes. Pursuant to the PKPA, a child's home state must be the state in which the child has lived with a parent for at least six (6) months prior to the commencement of the proceeding that resulted in that determination—not the state to which the child might have been taken. *In re Marriage of MICHALIK* (1991) 164 Wis.2d 544 at p. 557.

The PKPA was an effort to put the weight of full faith and credit behind the principles of the UCCJA.

The PKPA provided that once a state had exercised jurisdiction, it maintained continuing, exclusive jurisdiction until every party to the dispute has exited that state, so long as the requirements of the PKPA were met. The UCCJA provided only that a legitimate exercise of jurisdiction must be honored by any other state until the basis for that exercise of jurisdiction no longer exists. The PKPA was enacted to work in conjunction with the UCCJEA.

Despite its name, the PKPA:

> is not a criminal kidnapping law but rather a federal law regarding custody disputes.[11] Nevertheless, it was enacted to eliminate the incentive for one parent unhappy with a state's custody decree to "kidnap" his or her child and flee to another state in order to "relitigate the issue." *Louden v. THOMPSON* (1988) 484 U.S. 174 at p. 180.

Once a state exercises jurisdiction consistently with the provisions of the PKPA, no other state may exercise concurrent jurisdiction over the custody dispute, even if it would have been empowered to take jurisdiction in the first instance, and all states must accord full faith and credit to the first state's ensuing custody decree. **28 U.S.C. § 1738A(g).**

---

[10] Sen. Bill No. 668 (1999–2000 Reg. Sess.) Stats. 1999, ch. 867.
[11] Shapiro, Uniform Child Custody Jurisdiction Act (UCCJA) and the Parental Kidnapping Prevention Act (PKPA): A Comparative Study, 11 Wis. J. Fam. Law 1 (1991).

Chapter 13: Child Custody

Pursuant to **28 U.S.C. § 1738A**, every state must enforce the PKPA according to its terms and may not modify any custody determination or visitation determination made consistently with the provisions of this section by a court of another state.

The exclusive jurisdiction of a court of a state that has made a child custody or visitation determination consistently with the provisions of the PKPA continues as long as the requirement of subsection **28 U.S.C. § 1738A (c)(1)**[12] of this section continues to be met and such state remains the residence of the child or of any contestant.

A court of a state may modify a determination of custody of the same child made by a court of another state if:

(1) It has jurisdiction to make such a child custody determination; and
(2) The court of the other state no longer has jurisdiction, or it has declined to exercise such jurisdiction to modify such determination. **28 U.S.C. § 1738A (f)**.

A court of a state may not modify a visitation determination made by a court of another state unless the court of the other state no longer has jurisdiction to modify such determination or has declined to exercise jurisdiction to modify such determination. **28 U.S.C. § 1738A(g).**

Although the following case is a Wisconsin Court of Appeals case, it demonstrates how the PKPA gives the first state to exercise jurisdiction over a custody matter **home state** status and exclusive jurisdiction, thus discouraging interstate controversies over child custody actions.

> ***In re Marriage of Rita M. MICHALIK, Petitioner-Appellant, v. Kenneth E. MICHALIK, Respondent-Respondent***
> Court of Appeals of Wisconsin
> 164 Wis.2d 544; 476 N.W.2d 586
> September 10, 1991, Decided
> (*Marriage of Michalik*)
>
> Three minor children were born to Rita M. and Kenneth E. Michalik during the course of their marriage. The children are now eleven, nine, and seven. The Michaliks were granted a divorce by the Superior Court of Porter County, Indiana, by a Dissolution Decree entered by that court on October 1, 1987, nunc pro tunc to March 3, 1987.[13] The decree granted to Rita Michalik custody of the children subject to Kenneth Michalik's visitation rights, the nature of which were specified in the decree.

---

[12] 28 U.S.C. § 1738A (c)(1) provides that a child custody or visitation determination made by a court of a State is consistent with the provisions of this section only if such court has jurisdiction under the law of such State.
[13] Due to a mistake, such as a party not signing or dating the agreement that is attached to the judgment, the judgment does not get processed at that time. When the mistake is corrected, a judgment can be back-dated to the day that the judgment would have been entered if there were no mistake. That back-dated judgment is a *nunc pro tunc* judgment.

On May 1, 1989, Rita Michalik and the children moved to Milwaukee. As a result, the Michaliks agreed to a modification of the visitation schedule. On June 7, 1989, the Michaliks' written stipulation encompassing their agreement was approved by the Indiana court. [The parties also stipulated that] the Porter Superior Court, sitting in Valparaiso, Indiana shall retain in personam jurisdiction over the parties with reference to said dissolution action and all subsequent post-decree modifications therein.

On December 1, 1989, Rita Michalik brought this action against Kenneth Michalik in Milwaukee circuit court seeking, inter alia, a divorce, custody of the Michaliks' children, and a division of the parties' property.

On December 4, 1989, Kenneth Michalik complained to the Indiana court that Rita Michalik was interfering with his visitation rights, and sought temporary custody of the children. On December 28, 1989, the Indiana court found Rita Michalik in contempt of court and gave temporary custody of the children to Kenneth Michalik.

On January 22, 1990, the circuit court in Milwaukee County stayed proceedings in Rita Michalik's Wisconsin "divorce" action "until such time as this Court is notified that Indiana chooses not to exercise its jurisdiction and elects to allow Wisconsin to hear the matter, or an appellate court directs Wisconsin to hear the matter." Rita Michalik requested that the circuit court in Milwaukee County modify "the summer (school recess) visitation schedule of the parties." Kenneth Michalik objected, contending that the Wisconsin court should not hear the matter.

On October 16, 1990, the Wisconsin trial court entered an order finding that the children "have the closest and most significant connections with the State of Wisconsin," and that Wisconsin was the children's "home state" under the Uniform Child Custody Jurisdiction Act. Although concluding that it thus had "concurrent subject matter jurisdiction" with Indiana, the trial court decided to defer to the Indiana court "regarding determinations or modification of visitation issues arising under the Dissolution Decree, and Modified Stipulation." Rita Michalik appeals, and argues that because Wisconsin has "home state" jurisdiction over the children Indiana could not act in custody matters and any orders it may have entered were unenforceable because they were in violation of the [PKPA].

DISCUSSION
A. Article IV, section 1, of the United States Constitution requires that each state give "Full Faith and Credit" to the "public Acts, Records, and judicial Proceedings of every other State," and authorizes Congress to "prescribe the Manner in which such Acts, Records and Proceedings shall be proved, and the Effect thereof." Pursuant to this authority, Congress enacted the [PKPA of 1980]. Additionally, pursuant to Article VI, clause 2, of the United States Constitution, [t]he [PKPA[is thus conclusive on the issues to which it is applicable.

As pertinent to this appeal, the [PKPA] provides that:
The appropriate authorities of every State shall enforce according to its terms, and shall not modify except as provided in subsection (f) of this section, any child custody determination made consistently with the provisions of this section by a court of another State. A state's "child custody determination" is consistent with the provisions of 28 U.S.C. § 1738A, a precondition to Act's direction that the determination not be modified by any other state, if the state court making the "child custody determination" [has jurisdiction and is the home state.]

The jurisdiction of a court of a State which has made a child custody determination consistently with the provisions of this section continues as long as the requirement of subsection (c)(1) of this section [that the state has jurisdiction under its own law] continues to be met and such State remains the residence of the child or of any contestant. Furthermore, the Act bars the courts of any state from interfering with child custody disputes over which another state court is currently exercising jurisdiction in accordance with 28 U.S.C. § 1738A.

The [PKPA] thus preserves to the state that initially enters a child custody determination that is valid under its own law and is consistent with the Act, the sole prerogative to modify that determination, as long as any modification would also be valid under its own law and either the child or a contestant continues to live in the state.

The effect of §§ 1738A(d) and 1738A(f) is to limit custody jurisdiction to the first state to properly enter a custody order, so long as two sets of requirements are met. First, the [PKPA] defines a federal standard for continuing exclusive custody jurisdiction: the first state must have had proper initial custody jurisdiction when it entered its first order (according to criteria in the Act) and it must remain "the residence of the child or any contestant" when it later modifies that order. Second, the Act incorporates a state law inquiry: in order to retain exclusive responsibility for modifying its prior order the first state must still have custody jurisdiction as a matter of its own custody law. Even if the federal and state criteria for continuing jurisdiction are met, the first state's courts can, if they choose, voluntarily relinquish their jurisdiction in favor of a court better situated to assess the child's needs. These principles govern our analysis.

[T]he issue [is] whether Wisconsin may exercise child-custody-determination jurisdiction concurrent with Indiana [and this] depends on (1) whether the Indiana court's initial child custody determination was consistent with the provisions of 28 U.S.C. § 1738A, and, whether the Indiana court's on-going exercise of child-custody-determination jurisdiction is consistent with the provisions of 28 U.S.C. § 1738A.

The Indiana court's child custody determination and its ongoing exercise of child-custody-determination jurisdiction is consistent with the [PKPA] if Indiana was the "home State of the child[ren] on the date of the commencement of the proceeding;" that is, if the children lived with their parents in Indiana "for at least six consecutive months" prior to the commencement of the "proceeding,"

The [PKPA] was enacted to correct what Congress perceived was the failure of state courts hearing custody disputes that involved custody determinations by other jurisdictions "to give full faith and credit to the judicial proceedings of the other jurisdictions."[14] Thus, Congress believed that national full-faith-and-credit standards were needed in order to advance the following goals:

(1) promote cooperation between State courts to the end that a determination of custody and visitation is rendered in the State which can best decide the case in the interest of the child;
(2) promote and expand the exchange of information and other forms of mutual assistance between States which are concerned with the same child;
(3) facilitate the enforcement of custody and visitation decrees of sister States;

---

[14] Pub. L. No. 96-611, § 7(a)(4), 94 Stat. 3566, 3569.

Chapter 13: Child Custody

> (4) discourage continuing interstate controversies over child custody in the interest of greater stability of home environment and of secure family relationships for the child;
> (5) avoid jurisdictional competition and conflict between State courts in matters of child custody and visitation which have in the past resulted in the shifting of children from State to State with harmful effects on their well-being; and
> (6) deter interstate abductions and other unilateral removals of children undertaken to obtain custody and visitation awards.
>
> Pursuant to its authority under article IV, section 1, of the United States Constitution, Congress provided that a state's child custody determination is entitled to full faith and credit only if that state is the child's "home State." [A] child's "home State" for the purposes of determining whether an initial child custody determination was consistent with the [PKPA] must be the state in which the child has lived with a parent for at least six months prior to the commencement of the proceeding that resulted in that determination -- not the state to which the child might have been taken.
>
> Since the Michalik children lived in Indiana for at least six months prior to the commencement of their parents' divorce proceeding, and Indiana had jurisdiction under its own law to grant the decree and render the child custody determination, Indiana was the children's "home State."
>
> Thus, the October 1, 1987, Dissolution Decree was consistent with the provisions of the Parental Kidnapping Prevention Act. Additionally, since Kenneth Michalik continues to live in Indiana, and there is no claim that Indiana does not have on-going jurisdiction over the decree under its own law, Indiana has continuing child-custody-determination jurisdiction over the Michalik children. Under these circumstances, the [PKPA] precludes courts in Wisconsin from modifying the child custody determinations of the Indiana court and from interfering with that court's on-going exercise of its child-custody-determination jurisdiction.
>
> **DISPOSITION**
> Accordingly, the order of the trial court is affirmed.

3. The Missing Children Act

The Missing Children Act was enacted in 1990. Its actual name is the National Child Search Assistance Act (NCSA). The NCSA requires that "each Federal, State, and local law enforcement agency shall report each case of a missing child under the age of 21 reported to such agency to the National Crime Information Center of the Department of Justice." **42 USCS § 5779(a)**.

The NCSA provides that each state must:

> ensure that no law enforcement agency within the State establishes or maintains any policy that requires the observance of any waiting period before accepting a missing child or unidentified person report. [Each State must also] ensure that no law enforcement agency within the State establishes or maintains any policy that requires the removal of a missing person entry from its State law enforcement system or the National Crime Information Center computer database based solely on the age of the person. 42 USCS § 5780(1) and (2).

4. The Hague Convention

The Hague Convention (Convention) is a multilateral, international treaty that provides an expeditious procedure to return children who have been abducted and taken across international boundaries. It provides a legal method for countries to work together toward a resolution. The primary intention of the Convention is to preserve the status quo of the child custody order that exists when a child is wrongfully taken. Many countries, including the United States have joined.

The Convention provides:

> The interests of children are of paramount importance in matters relating to their custody. Desiring to protect children internationally from the harmful effects of their wrongful removal or retention and to establish procedures to ensure their prompt return to the State of their habitual residence, as well as to secure protection for rights of access. The parties to the Hague have agreed that the objects of the present Convention are to secure the prompt return of children wrongfully removed to or retained in any Contracting State; and to ensure that rights of custody and of access under the law of one Contracting State are effectively respected in the other Contracting States.
>
> The removal or the retention of a child is to be considered wrongful where
> [1] it is in breach of rights of custody attributed to a person, an institution or any other body, either jointly or alone, under the law of the State in which the child was habitually resident immediately before the removal or retention; and
> [2] at the time of removal or retention those rights were actually exercised, either jointly or alone, or would have been so exercised but for the removal or retention.
> The Convention applies to any child who was habitually resident in a Contracting State immediately before any breach of custody or access rights and ceases to apply when the child attains the age of 16 years.

The court where the Convention action is filed should not consider the merits of any underlying child custody dispute. The court should determine the country where the issues should be heard, and that is where the child will be returned, not to the parent who is left behind. Substantive rights are not altered by the Convention.

The Central Authority[15] of the state where the child is must take, or cause to be taken, all appropriate measures in order to obtain the voluntary return of the child.

The judicial or administrative authority may refuse to order the return of the child if it finds that the child objects to being returned and has attained an age and degree of maturity at which it is appropriate to take account of his of or her views. (Note that this does not mean that the child has to have reached the age of sixteen (16) years old to refuse.)

---

[15] The Office of Children's Issues is the Central Authority and is the primary contact for cases of children abducted both to and from the United States. Additionally, this office has the responsibility for implementation of the Abduction Convention in the United States. U.S. Department of State, Office of Children's Issues (CA/OCS/CI), SA-17, 9th Floor, WASHINGTON, DC 20522 – 1709, United States of America. Website: *www.travel.state.gov/childabduction*. Email: askci@state.gov.)

Chapter 13: Child Custody

No security, bond or deposit, however described, is required to guarantee the payment of costs and expenses in the judicial or administrative proceedings falling within the scope of this Convention.

To invoke the Convention, the aggrieved parent or interested party files an application for assistance with the **central authority** of the member country that establishes compliance with the Convention's procedures and an appropriate basis for invocation of its provisions.

The action must be brought within one year of the child's removal, unless the facts show the child's whereabouts had been deliberately concealed during that year.

In the case that follows, the trial court ruled pursuant to the UCCJEA that California was an inconvenient forum for adjudicating the custody of the Witherspoon children. Danny Witherspoon appealed the trial court's order pursuant to the Hague Convention.

> *In re Marriage of DANNY and JULIE WITHERSPOON. DANNY WITHERSPOON, Appellant, v. JULIE WITHERSPOON, Respondent.*
> COURT OF APPEAL OF CALIFORNIA, FOURTH APPELLATE DISTRICT, DIVISION THREE
> 155 Cal.App.4th 963; 66 Cal.Rptr.3d 586
> September 27, 2007, Filed
> (*Marriage of Witherspoon*)
>
> Danny was a high school band teacher in California when he began a sexual relationship with 16-year-old Julie, one of his students. In February 1994, the pair traveled to Las Vegas where Julie, then 17, married Danny, at the time 52 years old. The couple's daughter was born in September 1994, and a son was born in June 1996.
>
> In 1995, the couple moved to Garden Grove, California, where Danny again worked as a band teacher. In 1997, Julie joined the Army Reserve and later requested and received active duty orders. In August 1998, Julie left Danny and moved to Fort Hood, Texas, with her children. In December 2002, Julie was deployed to Germany, and her children followed one month later. The children attended school in Germany from January 2003 until the end of July 2006. In June 2003, Julie was transferred to Iraq, and returned to Germany in August 2004. During her Iraq deployment, Julie left the children in the care of a childcare provider, assertedly because Danny refused to take them.
>
> In July 2006, the children were hospitalized due to gastric problems. When Julie arrived to take the children home, the attending physician refused to release them because Julie was extremely intoxicated, hostile, and behaving in a bizarre fashion. According to social workers investigating the matter in Germany, Julie threatened to harm both the children and herself. As a result, the Army Community Service offices and the Jugendamt (Youth Welfare Office)[16] took custody of the children, and Julie was involuntarily committed to a mental institution for a brief period.
>
> Julie's commanding officer then contacted Danny and informed him the children had been placed in a foster home because the Jugendamt would not release them to Julie. The

---

[16] Each municipality in Germany has a Jugendamt. This is a local agency very similar to child protective services (CPS).

officer informed Danny the Jugendamt would release the children to him if he went to Germany.

According to Danny, Julie also called him and told him to come to Germany to pick up the children because they were in foster care and she was restricted to barracks. Danny traveled to Germany and, after speaking with those involved, returned to the United States. The children were sent to Danny shortly thereafter and, commencing in early August 2006, resided with him in Orange County.

On August 8, 2006, Danny filed for divorce in Orange County Superior Court, seeking sole legal and physical custody of the children, and requested an order denying Julie visitation absent treatment for alleged alcoholism and mental health problems. Danny included with his petition documents he received from the Army's Social Work Services Department and the Jugendamt detailing both the present and past abuse and neglect allegations relating to the children.

On October 20, 2006, Julie filed an order to show cause (OSC) seeking under the Convention the return of her children to Germany, and requesting the court place the children in protective custody pending the hearing on the OSC. In her accompanying declaration, Julie accused Danny of violence toward the children and repeatedly beating her.

She also accused Danny of having sex with other underage high school students, and sexually abusing a daughter from a previous marriage. Julie declared that Danny had met his three previous wives while they were his high school students. Julie also alleged that she had spoken with Beth, Danny's daughter from a previous marriage, who claimed Danny had molested her and beaten her mother, Diane, and that she witnessed Danny having sex with high school students.

Danny filed a responsive declaration denying his previous wives were ever his students that he ever beat any of his wives, including Julie, or that he was a sexual predator. Danny filed supporting declarations from Beth, who denied ever speaking with Julie or being sexually molested, and Diane, who denied she had been Danny's student or that she had been beaten by him.

At the OSC hearing, the trial court granted Julie's Convention petition and ordered the children returned to Germany. The court also ruled that under the Uniform Child Custody Jurisdiction and Enforcement Act, Family Code section 3400 et seq., California was an inconvenient forum for adjudicating child custody. The court also assumed temporary emergency jurisdiction under Family Code section 3424, and removed the children from Danny's custody. The court determined the children were threatened with mistreatment or abuse in Danny's care due to the parents' extreme difference in age.

[Danny Witherspoon appeals the trial court's order (1) requiring the return to Germany of his two children under the Hague Convention, (2) declaring California an inconvenient forum for adjudicating their custody dispute, and (3) awarding Julie temporary custody of the children pending their return to Germany.]

DISCUSSION
The trial court based its order in part on the Convention [which seeks] protect children internationally from the harmful effects of their wrongful removal or retention and to establish procedures to ensure their prompt return to the State of their habitual residence,

as well as to secure protection for rights of access. [Citation omitted.] Under Article 3 of the Convention, the removal or retention of a child is wrongful if: (a) it is in breach of rights of custody attributed to a person, an institution or any other body, either jointly or alone, under the law of the State in which the child was habitually resident immediately before the removal or retention; and (b) at the time of removal or retention those rights were actually exercised, either jointly or alone, or would have been so exercised but for the removal or retention. The parent filing a Convention petition bears the burden of proving wrongful removal by a preponderance of the evidence. If the petitioner demonstrates that the child was wrongfully removed, the court must order the child's return to the country of habitual residence unless the respondent demonstrates that one of four narrow exceptions applies. (Citations omitted.)

The parties do not dispute the children's habitual residence is Germany, where they had lived continuously for over three and one-half years. Danny, however, contends his removal or retention of the children did not breach Julie's custodial rights under German law. In support, Danny notes that German law gives both parents equal de jure custody over a child. Danny reasons that because he had equal custodial rights under German law, including the right to determine the children's residence, his removal or retention could not have been wrongful. Although Danny correctly cites German law, he misconstrues its effect under the Convention.

The Convention is not concerned with establishing the person to whom custody of the child will belong at some point in the future, nor with the situations in which it may prove necessary to modify a decision awarding joint custody on the basis of facts which have subsequently changed. It seeks, more simply, to prevent a later decision on the matter being influenced by a change of circumstances brought about through unilateral action by one of the parties. (Citations omitted.) Thus, Danny's removal or retention of the children is considered wrongful under the Convention even if Danny's actions did not violate German law.

Danny contends that Julie was not actually exercising her rights of custody at the time of removal or retention because the Jugendamt had intervened to take physical custody of the children. Article 5a of the Convention states that the term "rights of custody, shall include rights relating to the care of the person of the child and, in particular, the right to determine the child's place of residence …." (Citations omitted.) To determine whether Julie was exercising her rights of custody despite the Jugendamt's intervention, we consider the effect of that agency's actions upon Julie's rights under German law. [We determine that] under German law Julie continued to exercise "rights of custody" under the required "flexible interpretation" of that term. Julie has thus established a prima facie case for return under the Convention.

Once a petitioner under the Convention has demonstrated by a preponderance of the evidence that removal of a child was wrongful, the other parent may assert exceptions that, if proven, will prevent the return of the child. One exception to return exists when "there is a grave risk that his or her return would expose the child to physical or psychological harm or otherwise place the child in an intolerable situation." (Convention, art. 13b.) This exception must be proved by clear and convincing evidence.

Here, Danny contends Julie will place the children in an "intolerable situation" if she takes them back to Germany because the Jugendamt again will place the children in protective custody. Whether this would create an intolerable situation, however, is only part of the equation. Danny also provided evidence from Army and Jugendamt social

Chapter 13: Child Custody

> workers detailing Julie's drunken, hostile, and suicidal acts shortly before and after Julie's children were taken from her, resulting in her involuntary commitment to a mental institution. This evidence, if accepted, would suffice to demonstrate a risk of harm to the children by clear and convincing evidence, even construing the exception narrowly.
>
> Ironically, the trial court exercised emergency jurisdiction under FC § 3424 to remove the children from Danny, but refused to make any findings on the evidence demonstrating Julie posed a risk of potential harm to the children before awarding her custody. Contrary to its order, the trial court had jurisdiction to determine all of the issues raised by Julie's petition under the Convention, and erred by failing to fully consider the exceptions to return asserted by Danny and supported by the evidence.
>
> We recognize courts should expeditiously determine Convention petitions. But this case does not present the typical Convention situation. Danny did not simply abduct the children, but took them at the request of the Jugendamt, who removed them from Julie out of concern for their safety.
>
> We conclude the court abused its discretion by granting Julie emergency custody over the children without considering the evidence presented or making any finding whether doing so might potentially harm the children. [Further] the trial court erred in failing to make factual findings regarding certain enumerated exceptions to the children's return under the Convention, and in awarding temporary custody of the children to Julie without considering whether doing so would pose a substantial risk of harm to them.
>
> **DISPOSITION**
> We therefore reverse the order and remand for further proceedings.

5. Indian Child Welfare Act ICWA 25 USCS § 1901 et seq.

The Indian Child Welfare Act (ICWA) is an act that protects the interests of American Indian children and promotes the stability and security of Indian tribes and families. ICWA sets forth minimum federal standards, both substantive and procedural, effectuating these policies.

ICWA was enacted as a "response to the failure of States to recognize the essential tribal relations of Indian people and the cultural and social standards prevailing in Indian communities and families." **25 USCS § 1901(5)**.

ICWA is set forth **at 25 USCS § 1901** et seq. This act reflects a congressional determination that "it is in the best interests of the child to retain tribal ties and cultural heritage and in the interest of the tribe to preserve its future generations, a most important resource. Congress has concluded the state courts have not protected these interests and drafted a statutory scheme intended to afford needed protection. The courts of this state must yield to governing federal law."[17]

Pursuant to **U.S.C. § 1911(a)** an Indian tribe must have exclusive jurisdiction over any child custody proceeding involving an Indian child who resides or is domiciled

---
[17] *In re H.G. v. B.G.* (2015) 234 Cal.App.4th 906 at pp. 908-909.

Chapter 13: Child Custody

within the reservation of such tribe, except where such jurisdiction is otherwise vested in the State by existing federal law.

Further, proceedings regarding the foster care placement of, or termination of parental rights to, an Indian child not domiciled or residing within the reservation of the Indian child's tribe, must transferred upon petition and absent objection to the court to the jurisdiction of the tribe. **U.S.C. § 1911(b)**.

Pursuant to **U.S.C. § 1911(c)**, the Indian custodian of the child and the Indian child's tribe have a right to intervene at any point in a proceeding for the foster care placement of, or termination of parental rights to, an Indian child.

CRC Rule 5.480 provides:

> This chapter addressing the Indian Child Welfare Act (25 United States Code § 1901 et seq.) as codified in various sections of the California Family, Probate, and Welfare and Institutions Codes, applies to most proceedings involving Indian children that may result in an involuntary foster care placement; guardianship or conservatorship placement; custody placement under FC § 3041; declaration freeing a child from the custody and control of one or both parents; termination of parental rights; or adoptive placement. This chapter applies to:
> **(1)** Proceedings under Welfare and Institutions Code § 300 et seq.;
> **(2)** Proceedings under Welfare and Institutions Code §§ 601 and 602 et seq., whenever the child is either in foster care or at risk of entering foster care. In these proceedings, inquiry is required in accordance with rule 5.481(a). The other requirements of this chapter contained in rules 5.481 through 5.487 apply only if:
>   **(A)** The court's jurisdiction is based on conduct that would not be criminal if the child were 18 years of age or over;
>   **(B)** The court has found that placement outside the home of the parent or legal guardian is based entirely on harmful conditions within the child's home. Without a specific finding, it is presumed that placement outside the home is based at least in part on the child's criminal conduct, and this chapter shall not apply; or
>   **(C)** The court is setting a hearing to terminate parental rights of the child's parents.
> **(3)** Proceedings under FC § 3041;
> **(4)** Proceedings under the Family Code resulting in adoption or termination of parental rights; and
> **(5)** Proceedings listed in PC § 1459.5 and CRC Rule 7.1015.

If it is known or there is reason to know that a child is an Indian child, the court hearing must not proceed until at least ten (10) days after the parent, Indian custodian, tribe or the Bureau of Indian Affairs have received notice, except as stated in sections A2 and A3. **CRC Rule 5.482**.

> **(A)(2)** The detention hearing in dependency cases and in delinquency cases in which the probation officer has assessed that the child is in foster care or it is probable the child will be entering foster care described by rule 5.480(2)(A)-(C) may proceed without delay, provided that:
>   **[1]** Notice of the detention hearing must be given as soon as possible after the filing of the petition initiating the proceeding; and

> **[2]** Proof of notice must be filed with the court within 10 days after the filing of the petition.
> **(A)(3)** The parent, Indian custodian, or tribe must be granted a continuance, if requested, of up to 20 days to prepare for the proceeding, except for specified hearings in the following circumstances:
> **[1]** The detention hearing in dependency cases and in delinquency cases described by rule 5.480(2)(A)-(C);
> **[2]** The jurisdiction hearing in a delinquency case described by rule 5.480(2)(A)-(C) in which the court finds the continuance would not conform to speedy trial considerations under Welfare and Institutions Code § 657; and
> **[3]** The disposition hearing in a delinquency case described by rule 5.480(2)(A)-(C) in which the court finds good cause to deny the continuance under Welfare and Institutions Code § 682. A good cause reason includes when probation is recommending the release of a detained child to his or her parent or to a less restrictive placement. The court must follow the placement preferences under rule 5.484 when holding the disposition hearing.

The court must order transfer of a case to the tribal court of the child's tribe if:

> **(1)** The Indian child is a ward of the tribal court; or
> **(2)** The Indian child is domiciled or resides within a reservation of an Indian tribe that has exclusive jurisdiction over Indian child custody proceedings under section 1911 or 1918 of title 25 of the United States Code. CRC 5.483.

Finally, the:

> United States, every State, every territory or possession of the United States, and every Indian tribe shall give full faith and credit to the public acts, records, and judicial proceedings of any Indian tribe applicable to Indian child custody proceedings to the same extent that such entities give full faith and credit to the public acts, records, and judicial proceedings of any other entity. U.S.C. § 1911(c).

6. Juvenile Dependency Court

The Juvenile Dependency Court[18] has jurisdiction to hear many kinds of cases involving minors, including criminal acts that have been committed by minors. Even though the superior court and the juvenile court are equal branches of the court system, juvenile court decisions take precedence over matters heard in the family court. The Juvenile Court maintains jurisdiction over these matters until it decides that it no longer needs to intervene. Accordingly, when there is an action that is still current within the juvenile court, the family court does not have jurisdiction to hear the matter.

Additionally, the Juvenile Court has the power to terminate parental rights and preside over adoption proceedings.

---

[18] The "Juvenile Dependency Court", the "Juvenile Court and the "Dependency Court" are all names for the same court.

Chapter 13: Child Custody

Welfare & Institutions Code § 300 provides that any child who comes within any of the following descriptions is within the jurisdiction of the juvenile court which may adjudge that person to be a dependent child of the court:

> [1] The child has suffered, or there is a substantial risk that the child will suffer, serious physical harm inflicted nonaccidentally upon the child by the child's parent or guardian.
> [2] The child has suffered, or there is a substantial risk that the child will suffer, serious physical harm or illness, as a result of the failure or inability of his or her parent or guardian to adequately supervise or protect the child…
> [3] The Legislature finds and declares that a child who is sexually trafficked, as described in PC § 236.1, or who receives food or shelter in exchange for, or who is paid to perform, sexual acts described in PC § 236.1 or PC § 11165, and whose parent or guardian failed to, or was unable to, protect the child…
> [4] The child is suffering serious emotional damage, or is at substantial risk of suffering serious emotional damage, evidenced by severe anxiety, depression, withdrawal, or untoward aggressive behavior toward self or others, as a result of the conduct of the parent or guardian or who has no parent or guardian capable of providing appropriate care…
> [5] The child has been sexually abused, or there is a substantial risk that the child will be sexually abused, as defined in PC § 11165.1, by his or her parent or guardian or a member of his or her household, or the parent or guardian has failed to adequately protect the child from sexual abuse when the parent or guardian knew or reasonably should have known that the child was in danger of sexual abuse.
> [6] The child is under the age of five years and has suffered severe physical abuse by a parent, or by any person known by the parent, if the parent knew or reasonably should have known that the person was physically abusing the child.
> [7] The child's parent/guardian caused the death of another child through abuse or neglect.
> [8] The child has been left without any provision for support; physical custody of the child has been voluntarily surrendered pursuant to Health and Safety Code § 1255.7 and the child has not been reclaimed within the 14-day period.
> [9] The child has been freed for adoption by one or both parents for 12 months by either relinquishment or termination of parental rights or an adoption petition has not been granted.
> [10] The child has been subjected to an act or acts of cruelty by the parent or guardian or a member of his or her household, or the parent or guardian has failed to adequately protect the child from an act or acts of cruelty when the parent or guardian knew or reasonably should have known that the child was in danger of being subjected to an act or acts of cruelty.
> [11] The child's sibling has been abused or neglected and there is a substantial risk that the child will be abused or neglected.

FC § 3666.26 sets forth the procedures for terminating parental rights.

The Juvenile Dependency Court has jurisdiction to hear dependency matters. Dependency matters typically originate when Child Protective Services (CPS) or the County Department of Public Social Services (DPSS) remove a child from his or her home. This removal can be prompted by a report from the child's teacher, a doctor or any child abuse mandated person that there is a situation in which a minor may be in danger. In these matters, the juvenile dependency court has jurisdiction to decide the course of action that will be followed.

Pet Custody

As of January 1, 2019, the courts can now order a party to care for a family pet. **FC § 2605** provides:

> **(a)** The court, at the request of a party to proceedings for dissolution of marriage or for legal separation of the parties, may enter an order, prior to the final determination of ownership of a pet animal, to require a party to care for the pet animal. The existence of an order providing for the care of a pet animal during the course of proceedings for dissolution of marriage or for legal separation of the parties shall not have any impact on the court's final determination of ownership of the pet animal.
> **(b)** Notwithstanding any other law, including, but not limited to, Section 2550, the court, at the request of a party to proceedings for dissolution of marriage or for legal separation of the parties, may assign sole or joint ownership of a pet animal taking into consideration the care of the pet animal.
> **(c)** For purposes of this section, the following definitions shall apply:
> **(1)** "Care" includes, but is not limited to, the prevention of acts of harm or cruelty, as described in Section 597 of the Penal Code, and the provision of food, water, veterinary care, and safe and protected shelter.
> **(2)** "Pet animal" means any animal that is community property and kept as a household pet.

This new code provides some guidance for the court when family pets are the subject of a dispute. A request must be made for the court to assume jurisdiction pursuant to this code section. Once a request has been made, a court can order that a party care for a family pet.

EDUCATIONAL EXERCISES

I. Fill in the blanks using the Word List that follows.

1. _____ custody: One parent has the right and the responsibility to make the decisions relating to the health, education and welfare of a child.
2. _____ _____ custody (2 words together): Both parents share the right & responsibility to make decisions relating to health, education & welfare of a child.
3. _____ _____ custody (2 words together): A child resides with and is under the supervision of one parent, subject to the power of the court to order visitation
4. _____ _____ custody (2 words together): Each parent has significant periods of physical custody.
5. Joint physical custody must be shared by the parents in such a way so as to assure a child of frequent and continuing contact with both parents.
6. When the parents have agreed to joint custody, there is a _____, affecting the burden of proof that joint custody is in the best interests of the minor children.
7. In making an order for joint physical custody or joint legal custody, the court may specify one parent as the primary _____ of the children and one home as the primary home of the children for the purposes of determining eligibility for public assistance.
8. When making custody decisions, the _____ _____ (2 words together) of the children are considered.
9. When making a Custody _____, the court may not deny a disabled parent custody because of his or her disability.
10. A court cannot disqualify a parent, legal guardian or relative for a grant of custody because of his or her _____ Status.
11. The _____ was designed to discourage interstate kidnapping of children by their non-custodial parents.
12. The Uniform Child Custody Enforcement takes a strict _____ _____ _____ approach to jurisdiction.
13. Once the court of an appropriate state has made a child custody determination, that court obtains _____, continuing jurisdiction.
14. The _____ _____ (2 words together) is the state in which a child lived with a parent or a person acting as a parent for at least six consecutive months immediately before the commencement of a child custody proceeding.
15. In the case of a child less than _____, the term means the state in which the child lived from birth with any of the persons mentioned.
16. _____ _____ of (2 words together), or personal jurisdiction over, a party or a child is not necessary or sufficient to make a child custody determination.
17. A California Court must accord _____ _____ (2 words together) and _____ to an order issued by another state and, consistent with this part, enforce a child custody determination by a court of another state unless the order has been vacated, stayed or modified by a court having jurisdiction to do so.

Chapter 13: Child Custody

18. The Parental _____ Prevention Act (PKPA) became law in 1980 to address parental kidnapping & interstate/international child custody and visitation disputes.
19. The _____ _____ Act (2 words together) actual name is the National Child Search Assistance Act (NCSA). The NCSA requires that "each Federal, State, and local law enforcement agency shall report each case of a missing child under the age of 21 reported to such agency to the National Crime Information Center of the Department of Justice."
20. The _____ _____ (2 words together) is a multilateral, international treaty that provides an expeditious procedure to return children who have been abducted and taken across international boundaries. It provides a legal method for countries to work together toward a resolution.
21. An _____ _____ (2 words together) must have exclusive jurisdiction over any child custody proceeding involving an Indian child who resides or is domiciled within the reservation of such tribe, except where such jurisdiction is otherwise vested in the State by existing federal law.
22. The Juvenile _____ Court has jurisdiction to hear many kinds of cases involving minors, including criminal acts that have been committed by minors.

Word List

Best interests
Caretaker
Credit
Dependency
Determination
Exclusive
Exclusive
First in Time
Full Faith
Hague Convention
Home State Test

Immigration
Indian Tribe
Joint Legal
Joint Physical
Kidnapping
Legal
Missing Children
Physical Presence
Presumption
Sole Physical
UCCJEA

II. Perform/Answer the following:

1. List the different types of custody. Define and give an example of each one.
2. What is the full name of the UCCJEA? Why was this law enacted? Describe a situation where the UCCJEA would be relevant.
3. What is the Hague Convention? Why is it called the "Hague Convention"?

CHAPTER 14: Child Visitation

In Brief...

CHILD VISITATION COURT ORDERS:
- Must be made with the understanding that parents have a fundamental right to make decisions concerning the care, custody and control of their children;
- Should provide the maximum possible visitation time available to the noncustodial parent, with the proviso that such visitation be in the best interests of the child and not interfere with the custodial parent's time with the child because this is the policy of CA, **FC § 3020**;
- Must grant parents a reasonable amount of time to visit with their children unless it is shown that the visitation would be detrimental to the best interests of the child;
- Cannot give a disabled parent less visitation time because of his or her disability; and
- Cannot enforce an order for a parent to visit with his or her child.
- **Must contain all of the following, FC § 3048:**
  - The basis for the court's exercise of jurisdiction;
  - The manner in which notice and opportunity to be heard were given;
  - A clear description of the custody and visitation rights of each party;
  - A provision that a violation may subject the party to civil/criminal penalties; and
  - Identification of the country of habitual residence of the children.

VISITATION PLANS:
- Must be fashioned such that they are in the best interests of the child and the court has broad powers toward making these orders;
- That reflect a 20/80 percent timeshare have been called **Freeman orders**; and
- Where both parents have as much quality time as possible is the best visitation plan of all.

GRANDPARENT VISITATION:
- Will only be ordered if there is a preexisting relationship between the grandparents and the grandchildren that has engendered a bond such that visitation is in the best interests of the child, **FC § 3103(a)**;
- May be granted when one of the parents is deceased upon a finding that the visitation would be in the best interests of the minor child, **FC § 3102**; and
- Will only be ordered if the rebuttable presumption that grandparent visitation is not in the best interests if the child is rebutted when the parent does not agree that the grandparent have visitation rights. **FC § 3103.**

STEPPARENT VISITATION, FC § 3101:

- May be granted, if visitation by the stepparent is determined to be in the best interests of the minor child.
- Cannot be requested via a modification if there is a prior court order that denied visitation under **FC § 3101(a)**.

SUPERVISED VISITATION, **FC § 3200.5:**
- May be conducted by a professional provider who will be paid for the service; and
- Requires special training for professional providers of supervised visitation.

ADOPTION severs all parental ties between the child and biological parent, **Probate Code § 6451**.

A POSTADOPTION CONTRACT:
Is an agreement between the adoptive parents and the biological parent(s) whereby the parties can agree to allow contact after the adoption is completed. **FC § 8616.5**.

Introduction

It has been said that visitation of children is for the parents, not the children. This could be true, because many separated parents try to be with their children as much as possible. However, since a higher amount of time spent with their children equates to less money paid in child support, parents may not always have the best motives in trying to obtain as much visitation as they can.

Court Orders for Visitation

Since it is the policy of this state to grant the maximum possible visitation time available to the noncustodial parent, with the proviso that such visitation must be in the best interests of the child and must not interfere with the custodial parent's time with that child, the court must take this policy into consideration when making orders regarding visitation. **FC § 3020**. All parents must be granted a reasonable amount of time to visit with their children unless it is shown that the visitation would be detrimental to the best interests of the child. Further, the court has the discretion to grant visitation not only to the parents, but also to any other person having an interest in the welfare of the children. **FC § 3100**.

Pursuant to **FC § 3048**, every visitation order must contain all of the following:

(1) The basis for the court's exercise of jurisdiction.
(2) The manner in which notice and opportunity to be heard were given.
(3) A clear description of the custody and visitation rights of each party.
(4) A provision stating that a violation of the order may subject the party in violation to civil or criminal penalties, or both.
(5) Identification of the country of habitual residence of the child or children.

Chapter 14: Child Visitation

Even though many parents fight for as much visitation as they can, not every parent wants visitation time with his or her children. And if a parent refuses to exercise visitation, there is no authority to force that parent to visit with the child.

> The court cannot compel a noncustodial parent on dissolution of a marriage to care for and love and visit with the child… The court can only compel the parent to provide monetary support…California law gives a parent a right and privilege to visit his or her child. This right is not, however, reciprocal. *LOUDEN v. OLPIN* (1981) 118 Cal.App.3d 565 at pp. 567-568.

Finally, a court may not grant custody or less visitation time to one parent based upon the fact that the other parent has a disability. In *In re Marriage of CARNEY* (1979) 24 Cal.3d 725 the Supreme Court of California reversed the trial court's decision, holding that the trial court abused its discretion by relying on a physical handicap as prima facie evidence of a parent's unfitness to have custody. *Id.* at p. 736.) The Supreme Court of California stated that:

> The stereotype indulged in by the court mistakenly assumes that the parent's handicap inevitably handicaps the child. But children are more adaptable than the court gives them credit for; if one path to their enjoyment of physical activities is closed, they will soon find another. Indeed, having a handicapped parent often stimulates the growth of a child's imagination, independence, and self-reliance. Such stereotypes have no place in our law. *Id.* at p. 738.

The California legislature codified this decision at **FC § 3049** in 2010.

Visitation Plans

Trial courts have broad powers to fashion visitation plans that are in the best interests of the child, and the weight to be accorded to the applicable factors are left to the superior court's sound discretion. *In re Marriage of LaMUSGA* (2004) 32 Cal.4th 1072 at p. 1087-1088.

One common visitation plan is a 20/80 percent timeshare. With this plan the noncustodial parent has visitation alternating weekends from Friday at 6:00 p.m. to Sunday at 6:00 p.m., one mid-week dinner (or sometimes overnight) visit, equal division of holidays (odd/even)[1], two (2) uninterrupted weeks during summer for each parent and equal division of school vacations (winter/spring). The 20/80 percent timeshare has been called a **Freeman order**, after a judge who made such an order.

Some parents feel that sharing children equally is the best plan. However, unless the parents reside in the same school district, the children will be forced to spend many hours each week traveling between the two households. Of course, the best plan of

---

[1] Many visitation orders provide that in even-numbered years, one parent has specific holidays with the children, while the other parent has the children for those holidays in odd-numbered years.

Chapter 14: Child Visitation

all is one where both parents have as much quality time with their children as possible. (Perhaps traveling time is not the best quality time.) In any case, just as each family is different, a visitation plan should be developed for each family.

Grandparent Visitation

Often, grandparents wish to have their own special time with their grandchildren. However, unless there is a preexisting relationship between the grandparents and the grandchildren that has engendered a bond such that visitation is in the best interests of the child, a court most likely will not award the grandparents reasonable visitation rights. **FC § 3103(a)**. If the parent of a minor child dies, the grandparents of the deceased parent may be granted reasonable visitation with the child upon a finding that the visitation would be in the best interests of the minor child. **FC § 3102.**

FC § 3103 provides in pertinent part:

> [1] There is a rebuttable presumption affecting the burden of proof that the visitation of a grandparent is not in the best interest of a minor child if the child's parents agree that the grandparent should not be granted visitation rights.
> [2] Visitation rights may not be ordered under this section if that would conflict with a right of custody or visitation of a birth parent who is not a party to the proceeding.
> [3] Visitation ordered pursuant to this section shall not create a basis for or against a change of residence of the child, but shall be one of the factors for the court to consider in ordering a change of residence.

In 2000, the **United States Supreme Court** decided the following case regarding the constitutionality of a Washington State law granting visitation rights to grandparents.

> ***JENIFER TROXEL, ET VIR v. TOMMIE GRANVILLE***
> SUPREME COURT OF THE UNITED STATES
> 530 U.S. 57
> June 5, 2000, Decided
> (*Troxel v. Granville*)
>
> Tommie Granville and Brad Troxel shared a relationship that ended in June 1991. The two never married, but they had two daughters, Isabelle and Natalie. Jenifer and Gary Troxel are Brad's parents, and thus the paternal grandparents of Isabelle and Natalie. After Tommie and Brad separated in 1991, Brad lived with his parents and regularly brought his daughters to his parents' home for weekend visitation. Brad committed suicide in May 1993. Although the Troxels at first continued to see Isabelle and Natalie on a regular basis after their son's death, Tommie Granville informed the Troxels in October 1993 that she wished to limit their visitation with her daughters to one short visit per month.
>
> In December 1993, the Troxels commenced the present action by filing, in the Washington Superior Court for Skagit County, a petition to obtain visitation rights with Isabelle and Natalie. The Troxels filed their petition under Washington statute, Wash.

Rev. Code § 26.10.160(3) (1994) [which] provides: "Any person may petition the court for visitation rights at any time including, but not limited to, custody proceedings. The court may order visitation rights for any person when visitation may serve the best interest of the child whether or not there has been any change of circumstances." At trial, the Troxels requested two weekends of overnight visitation per month and two weeks of visitation each summer. Granville did not oppose visitation altogether, but instead asked the court to order one day of visitation per month with no overnight stay. In 1995, the Superior Court issued an oral ruling and entered a visitation decree ordering visitation one weekend per month, one week during the summer, and four hours on both of the petitioning grandparents' birthdays.

Granville appealed, during which time she married Kelly Wynn. Before addressing the merits of Granville's appeal, the Washington Court of Appeals remanded the case to the Superior Court for entry of written findings of fact and conclusions of law. On remand, the Superior Court found that visitation was in Isabelle and Natalie's best interests.

The Washington Court of Appeals reversed the lower court's visitation order and dismissed the Troxels' petition for visitation, holding that nonparents lack standing to seek visitation under § 26.10.160(3) unless a custody action is pending. In the Court of Appeals' view, that limitation on nonparental visitation actions was "consistent with the constitutional restrictions on state interference with parents' fundamental liberty interest in the care, custody, and management of their children." Having resolved the case on the statutory ground, however, the Court of Appeals did not expressly pass on Granville's constitutional challenge to the visitation statute.

The Washington Supreme Court granted the Troxels' petition for review and, after consolidating their case with two other visitation cases, affirmed. The court disagreed with the Court of Appeals' decision on the statutory issue and found that the plain language of § 26.10.160(3) gave the Troxels standing to seek visitation, irrespective of whether a custody action was pending. The Washington Supreme Court nevertheless agreed with the Court of Appeals' ultimate conclusion that the Troxels could not obtain visitation of Isabelle and Natalie pursuant to § 26.10.160(3). The court rested its decision on the Federal Constitution, holding that § 26.10.160(3) unconstitutionally infringes on the fundamental right of parents to rear their children.

We granted certiorari, and now affirm the judgment.

The Fourteenth Amendment provides that no State shall "deprive any person of life, liberty, or property, without due process of law." We have long recognized that the Amendment's Due Process Clause, like its Fifth Amendment counterpart, "guarantees more than fair process." The Clause also includes a substantive component that "provides heightened protection against government interference with certain fundamental rights and liberty interests."

[There is a] fundamental right of parents to make decisions concerning the care, custody, and control of their children [and] the Due Process Clause of the Fourteenth Amendment protects the fundamental right of parents to make decisions concerning the care, custody, and control of their children.

Section 26.10.160(3), as applied to Granville and her family in this case, unconstitutionally infringes on that fundamental parental right. The Washington nonparental visitation statute is breathtakingly broad. According to the statute's text, "any

Chapter 14: Child Visitation

> person may petition the court for visitation rights at any time," and the court may grant such visitation rights whenever "visitation may serve the best interest of the child." § 26.10.160(3) (emphases added). That language effectively permits any third party seeking visitation to subject any decision by a parent concerning visitation of the parent's children to state-court review. Once the visitation petition has been filed in court and the matter is placed before a judge, a parent's decision that visitation would not be in the child's best interest is accorded no deference.
>
> Section 26.10.160(3) contains no requirement that a court accord the parent's decision any presumption of validity or any weight whatsoever. Instead, the Washington statute places the best-interest determination solely in the hands of the judge. Should the judge disagree with the parent's estimation of the child's best interests, the judge's view necessarily prevails.
>
> First, the Troxels did not allege, and no court has found, that Granville was an unfit parent. That aspect of the case is important, for there is a presumption that fit parents act in the best interests of their children. Accordingly, so long as a parent adequately cares for his or her children (i.e., is fit), there will normally be no reason for the State to inject itself into the private realm of the family to further question the ability of that parent to make the best decisions concerning the rearing of that parent's children.
>
> The problem here is not that the Washington Superior Court intervened, but that when it did so, it gave no special weight at all to Granville's determination of her daughters' best interests. More importantly, it appears that the Superior Court applied exactly the opposite presumption.
>
> Because we rest our decision on the sweeping breadth of § 26.10.160(3) and the application of that broad, unlimited power in this case, we do not consider the primary constitutional question passed on by the Washington Supreme Court -- whether the Due Process Clause requires all nonparental visitation statutes to include a showing of harm or potential harm to the child as a condition precedent to granting visitation. We do not, and need not, define today the precise scope of the parental due process right in the visitation context. [T]the constitutionality of any standard for awarding visitation turns on the specific manner in which that standard is applied and that the constitutional protections in this area are best "elaborated with care."
>
> We therefore hold that the application of § 26.10.160(3) to Granville and her family violated her due process right to make decisions concerning the care, custody, and control of her daughters. Accordingly, the judgment of the Washington Supreme Court is affirmed.

As set forth in *Troxel* above, parents have a fundamental right to make decisions concerning the care, custody and control of their children. Because the Washington State law gave no consideration to the parent's wishes, it infringed upon this right. Although there was a marked division in the *Troxel* decision with Justices Stevens, Kennedy and Scalia dissenting, this decision remains the law with regard to constitutionality of statutes providing for grandparent visitation.

The following case was decided after *Troxel* and finds that **FC § 3104** is constitutional.

Chapter 14: Child Visitation

> ***In re Marriage of KAREN and CHARLES ERIK HARRIS. KAREN BUTLER,
> Appellant, v. CHARLES ERIK HARRIS et al., Respondents.***
> SUPREME COURT OF CALIFORNIA
> 34 Cal.4th 210
> August 23, 2004, Filed
> (*Marriage of Harris*)

The mother and father met in San Diego in October 1993, when the mother was a helicopter pilot in the Navy. They began living together two weeks after they met, later moving to a boat in the Chula Vista Marina. They married January 12, 1994, three months after they met. They separated on October 16, 1994, 10 days before the birth of their daughter, Emily. The mother filed for dissolution of marriage three months later.

The mother left the father shortly before Emily was born and stayed in hotels and with a friend. She lived with the paternal grandparents, respondents Leanne and Charles Harris, for more than a week after Emily was born and then moved into a shelter for battered women. She took Emily to visit the father regularly.

On July 21, 1995, the superior court, pursuant to stipulation of the parties, entered judgment dissolving the marriage and granting the mother sole legal and physical custody of Emily. The judgment also provided that the mother could move to Maryland with Emily on or after August 5, 1995. Also by stipulation, the paternal grandparents were joined as parties to the action.

On August 2, 1995, the paternal grandparents filed a motion for visitation, alleging that the mother would not permit visitation absent a court order. The paternal grandparents asked that Emily spend 10 days at their home every other month. The mother's response noted that Emily was 11 months old and was still nursing. She asked that all visitations take place in Maryland where she was living with her parents. Family court services counselor Sandra Boyles conducted a mediation session in which the mother participated by telephone.

On April 29, 1996, the mother filed a motion to terminate the paternal grandparents' visitation rights, alleging that their visits in January and April of 1996 "were extremely hostile and filled with conflict" and thus had been detrimental to Emily. Following a hearing, the court on October 30, 1996, denied the mother's motion to terminate the paternal grandparents' visitation rights and modified visitation.

[The mother moved to Utah and married Mark Butler, who had six children. When the paternal grandparents asked the mother if they could bring Emily, then four years old, to California on their next visit, the mother] declined, saying she was "not comfortable sending Emily to California." In January of 1999, the paternal grandparents again visited Emily in Utah for seven days. The mother did not permit overnight visits.

On February 9, 1999, the paternal grandparents filed a motion to modify the visitation order to permit them to bring Emily to California for visitation and to permit overnight visits in Utah.

On March 17, 1999, pursuant to court order, the mother, the father, and the paternal grandparents met with family court services counselor Sandra Boyles. The father became so agitated and hostile during the conference that Boyles asked him to leave. Boyles recommended that the paternal grandparents continue to have weeklong visits with Emily four times per year until she started school. Subsequent visits were to be at the grandparents' home in California.

On March 31, 1999, the mother filed a declaration objecting to the recommendation that Emily visit the paternal grandparents in California. At a hearing on May 5, 1999, the court adopted Boyles's recommendations permitting the paternal grandparents to have weeklong visits with Emily four times per year until she started school, with the next visit to take place in Utah and subsequent visits to take place in California.

On May 26, 2000, the paternal grandparents filed an order to show cause for visitation beginning when Emily started kindergarten in August 2000. The grandparents alleged they had had their fourth weeklong visit with Emily in California in April and were planning another before Emily started school.

In a responsive declaration filed on June 12, 2000, the mother objected to court-ordered visitation, noting that she never would prevent Emily from being with her paternal grandparents, but believed it was wrong to force Emily to leave her family against her will. In her supporting points and authorities, the mother asked that the paternal grandparents' request for visitation be denied.

At a hearing on July 10, 2000, the court stated that it would apply "a best interest standard" that focused on the "health, safety and welfare" of the child. The court concluded: "I think presently, at least, that it is in the best interest of this child to continue to have a significant relationship with the grandparents." The court noted that its conclusions were "tough calls because I do have to acknowledge that the grandparents are interfering to some degree with the mother's rights as a parent to the extent they exist to raise children ... ."

The court ordered that Emily fly unaccompanied to California on a nonstop flight beginning with the December visit if permitted by the airlines to do so, and required the mother to take Emily to the airport in Utah and pick her up. The paternal grandparents further were permitted to take Emily to visit other relatives in or out of California.

The mother appealed and the Court of Appeal reversed, holding that the visitation order denied the mother due process of law under both the federal and California Constitutions, explaining that the paternal grandparents should have been required "to show by clear and convincing evidence that the parents' decision [to deny or limit visitation] would be detrimental to the child." [The grandparents appealed to the California Supreme Court.]

DISCUSSION
Grandparents' rights to court-ordered visitation with their grandchildren are purely statutory. Three California statutes expressly address grandparent visitation: FC § 3102, which permits visitation by a deceased parent's children, siblings, parents, and grandparents if such visitation would be in the best interests of the child; FC § 3103, which permits a court in specified proceedings involving the custody of a child to grant grandparent visitation; and FC § 3104, which permits grandparents to petition for visitation if the grandchild's parents are not married or if certain other conditions are met.

The present case is governed by FC § 3104. The mother contends that FC § 3104 is unconstitutional both on its face and as applied in this case, because it unduly burdens her parental liberty interest in the custody, care, and control of her child. We first address the

Chapter 14: Child Visitation

mother's claim under the federal Constitution.

A sharply divided United States Supreme Court addressed the thorny issue of grandparent visitation in *Troxel v. Granville*, supra, 530 U.S. 57, 60, considering a Washington statute that permitted " '[a]ny person?' " to petition the superior court for visitation rights " 'at any time' " and authorized the court to grant such visitation if it would " 'serve the best interest of the child.' " The paternal grandparents petitioned for visitation with their two granddaughters after their son committed suicide and the children's mother notified them she wished to limit their visitation with her daughters to one short visit a month. The parents had never married and had separated two years before the father died. Before his death, the father had lived with the paternal grandparents and had regularly brought his daughters to his parents' home for weekend visits.

The decision in Troxel does not support the mother's argument here that FC § 3104 is unconstitutional on its face. FC § 3104 is significantly different from the Washington statute at issue in Troxel. The Washington statute was, in the words of the plurality in Troxel, "breathtakingly broad," permitting " '[a]ny person' " to petition the superior court for visitation rights " 'at any time.' " (*Troxel v. Granville, supra*, 530 U.S. 57, 67 (plur. opn. of O'Connor, J.)) FC § 3104 is more narrow, permitting grandparents of a minor child to petition the court for visitation rights only if the child's parents are not married or are separated or if other similar conditions apply. FC § 3104 requires that there be "a preexisting relationship between the grandparent and the grandchild that has engendered a bond such that visitation is in the best interest of the child" and directs the court to balance "the interest of the child in having visitation with the grandparent against the right of the parents to exercise their parental authority" before ordering grandparent visitation. (FC § 3104(a)(1),(2).)

[T]he Legislature limited FC § 3104 by creating rebuttable presumptions against grandparent visitation "if the [child's] parents agree that the grandparent should not be granted visitation rights" (FC § 3104(e)), or if the parent awarded sole custody objects to grandparent visitation (FC § 3104(f). These provisions prevent the situation that arose in Troxel in which the court ordered visitation over the objection of the child's sole surviving fit parent based upon a finding that such visitation was in the child's best interest. Unlike the Washington statute at issue in Troxel, FC § 3104 gives "special weight" to the parents' decision, if the parents agree that visitation is not in their child's best interest, or to the decision of a parent who has been awarded sole custody of the child. The high court recognized as much by citing with approval FC § 3104(e).

Accordingly, FC § 3104 does not suffer from the constitutional infirmities that plagued the Washington statute considered in Troxel. FC § 3104 does not violate the federal Constitution on its face, as Justice Souter concluded the Washington statute did, because it does not permit "judicially compelled visitation by 'any party' at 'any time' a judge believed he 'could make a better decision' than the objecting parent had done." FC § 3104 permits only grandparents to seek visitation and only if the parents are not married or are separated or if other specified circumstances exist. It requires that there be "a preexisting relationship between the grandparent and the grandchild that has engendered a bond such that visitation is in the best interest of the child," directs the court to balance "the interest of the child in having visitation with the grandparent against the right of the parents to exercise their parental authority" and creates rebuttable presumptions against visitation if the parents agree that grandparent visitation is not in their child's best interest or a parent with sole custody of the child objects to grandparent visitation. (FC §

Chapter 14: Child Visitation

> 3104(a)(1),(2).)
>
> Neither does the decision in Troxel support the mother's argument here that FC § 3104 violates the federal Constitution as applied in this case. Troxel involved an order for grandparent visitation that was opposed by the child's sole surviving fit parent. That was not the situation before the superior court in this case when it issued the visitation order under review. Rather, the parents of the child in the present case disagreed concerning grandparent visitation, and the father had not been declared unfit and his parental rights had not yet been terminated. Nothing in the decision in Troxel suggests that an order for grandparent visitation that is supported by one parent infringes upon the parental rights of the other parent.
>
> Although we conclude that the superior court erred in failing to utilize the rebuttable presumption in FC § 3104(f), it remains the case that the superior court did apply the statute and, thus, it is proper for this court to determine whether FC § 3104 is constitutional as applied in this case. We conclude, therefore, that FC § 3104 does not violate the federal or California Constitutions, either on its face or as applied.
>
> As noted above, FC § 3104(f) creates "a rebuttable presumption affecting the burden of proof that the visitation of a grandparent is not in the best interest of a minor child if the parent who has been awarded sole legal and physical custody of the child ... objects to visitation by the grandparent." In the present case, the mother was awarded sole custody of Emily and objected to grandparent visitation. Accordingly, the grandparents were required to overcome a rebuttable presumption that visitation is not in Emily's best interest. The record before us reflects that the superior court did not consider this presumption, but rather expressly utilized a "best interest of the child" standard.
>
> Accordingly, we will remand this case to the superior court to reconsider the visitation order in light of the presumption that grandparent visitation is not in Emily's best interest.

While deciding which of California's visitation statutes for grandparents apply to the facts in the *Harris* case, the court summarized **FC § 3103 and FC § 3104** as follows:

> **FC § 3103** provides that in specified proceedings involving the custody of a child, including proceedings for dissolution of marriage, the court may grant reasonable visitation to a grandparent of a minor child of a party to the proceeding if the court determines that visitation by the grandparent is in the best interest of the child.
> **FC § 3104** permits a grandparent to petition a court for visitation if the child's parents are not married or are living separately or if certain other conditions apply. The court may grant reasonable visitation if the court finds that there is a preexisting relationship between the grandparent and the grandchild that has engendered a bond such that visitation is in the best interest of the child and balances the interest of the child in having visitation with the grandparent against the right of the parents to exercise their parental authority.
> Both **FC § 3103 and FC § 3104** provide a rebuttable presumption that grandparent visitation is not in the child's best interest, if the parents agree that the grandparents should not be granted visitation.
> **FC § 3104** further applies the same rebuttable presumption against visitation if the parent who has been awarded sole legal and physical custody of the child in another proceeding ... objects to visitation by the grandparent. *Harris, supra* at p. 220.

FC §§ 3102, 3103 and **3104** have all been declared constitutional, provided certain conditions are met.

Finally, while grandparents' rights to visitation with their grandchildren are governed by the Family Code provisions, nothing in **FC § 3104** indicates it similarly governs visitation in a dependency context. *In re J.T v. JASMINE* (2014) 228 Cal.App.4th 953 at p. 961.

Stepparent Visitation

The court may grant reasonable visitation to a stepparent, if visitation by the stepparent is determined to be in the best interests of the minor child. Unless there is a substantial connection between the stepparent and the child, visitation will be denied if the parent or parents object to this visitation.

In **FC § 3101(d)(2)** a **stepparent** is defined as a person who is a party to the marriage that is the subject of the proceeding, with respect to a minor child of the other party to the marriage.

Adoption severs the ties of an existing parent to a child who is thereafter adopted from the time of the adoption forward; he is relieved of all parental duties towards, and all responsibility for, the adopted child and has no right over the child, as the case below demonstrates.

MARC WILFRIED MARCKWARDT, Petitioner, v. THE SUPERIOR COURT OF LOS ANGELES COUNTY, Respondent; ROBERT MICHAEL SOTO, Real Party in Interest
Court of Appeal of California, Second Appellate District, Division Seven
150 Cal.App.3d 471
January 4, 1984
(*Marchwardt v. Superior Court*)

Real party in interest Robert Soto (Soto) is the natural father of Kimberly Marckwardt and Melodie Marckwardt, ages seven and eight respectively. Their mother, Linda Marckwardt, obtained a decree of marital dissolution from Soto in 1981. The interlocutory decree awarded custody of the minor children to Linda Marckwardt. She thereafter married Marc Wilfried Marckwardt (Marckwardt), petitioner here.

Marckwardt then commenced proceedings for stepparent adoption of the children. In May of 1982, Soto executed two consents to this adoption, one for each child. Each consent recited that Soto was giving consent to adoption of his child by Marckwardt, "it being fully understood by me that with the signing of this document my consent may not be withdrawn except with court approval, and that with the signing of the order of adoption by the court, I shall give up all my rights of custody, services, and earnings of said child, and that said child cannot be reclaimed by me." Upon the filing of these consents and other attendant proceedings, Marckwardt's adoption petition was granted.

Soto thereafter filed a "petition to withdraw consent," seeking to set aside the adoption decree. The superior court denied this petition without prejudice to proceedings. Soto did not so proceed. Instead, on March 28, 1983, he obtained an "order to show cause re

Chapter 14: Child Visitation

> stepparent visitation" in the dissolution action. Asserting that although no longer the legal father of the minor children he must be deemed their stepparent, Soto sought to invoke visitation jurisdiction under Civil Code section 4351.5.
>
> Linda Marckwardt responded to the order to show cause by moving to dismiss the proceeding for lack of subject matter jurisdiction. Marckwardt then petitioned us for a writ of prohibition, alleging that upon entry of the adoption decree the dissolution court had lost jurisdiction to deal with the minor children and that the ongoing visitation proceedings involve an impermissible intrusion by Soto and the court into the Marckwardts' family affairs. We issued an alternative writ, staying the proceedings below.
>
> The question at issue in this proceeding is whether the superior court has jurisdiction, in the dissolution proceeding between Linda Marckwardt and Soto, to grant Soto visitation of the children whose adoption has finally transpired with his consent.
>
> Soto discounts the effect of Civil Code section 229[2] (adoption cuts off rights of natural parent or parents over child). [Further] Soto cannot be a stepparent. A "stepfather" is defined by a leading modern dictionary as "a man who succeeds one's father as the husband of one's mother." Black's Law Dictionary defines "stepparent" as "[the] mother or father of a child born during a previous marriage of the other parent and hence, not the natural parent of such child."[3] Under any definition, Soto is not the stepparent of his natural children, for he is not and never has been simultaneously the husband of their mother while not their legal father.
>
> Let a peremptory writ of prohibition issue, restraining respondent court from taking any further proceedings pursuant to the order to show cause re stepparent visitation filed March 28, 1983 other than to dismiss those proceedings for lack of subject matter jurisdiction.

If a minor child's parent is deceased, the children, siblings, parents and grandparents of the deceased parent may request and be granted reasonable visitation with the child during the child's minority if the court finds that it would be in the best interests of the minor child. **FC § 3102(a)**. In making this decision, the court must consider the amount of personal contact in making such a visitation order. **FC § 3102(b)**.

Finally, with regard to stepparent visitation, a stepparent cannot request a modification of a prior court order that denied visitation under **FC § 3101(a)**. Once the trial court denies on the merits a stepparent's request for visitation under **FC § 3101(a)**, no legal authority permits the court to reconsider a modification of this final order. *CHALMERS v. HIRSCHKOP* (2013) 213 Cal.App.4th 289 at p. 294-295.

---

[2] Currently,
[2] Black's Law Dict. (5th ed. 1979), p. 1268.FC § 8617, which provides "the existing parent or parents of an adopted child are, from the time of the adoption, relieved of all parental duties towards, and all responsibility for, the adopted child, and have no right over the child."
[3] Black's Law Dict. (5th ed. 1979), p. 1268.

Chapter 14: Child Visitation

Supervised Visitation

FC § 3200.5 provides that any standards for supervised visitation providers adopted by the Judicial Council pursuant to **FC § 3200** must conform to this section. A provider, as described in **FC § 3200**, must be a professional provider or nonprofessional provider.

A **nonprofessional provider** is a provider that is not paid for providing supervised visitation services. A **professional provider** is a provider that is paid. **FC § 3200.5(c)(1)** and **(2)**.

Professional providers of supervised visitation must have received twenty-four (24) hours of training that includes training in the following subjects:

(A) The role of a professional provider. **(B)** Child abuse reporting laws. **(C)** Recordkeeping procedures. **(D)** Screening, monitoring, and termination of visitation. **(E)** Developmental needs of children. **(F)** Legal responsibilities and obligations of a provider. **(G)** Cultural sensitivity. **(H)** Conflicts of interest. **(I)** Confidentiality. **(J)** Issues relating to substance abuse, child abuse, sexual abuse, and domestic violence. **(K)** Basic knowledge of family and juvenile law. FC § 3200.5(d)(1).

A court can order supervised visitation or limit a parent's custody or visitation if the court finds that:

(1) There is substantial evidence that the parent intended to interfere with the other parent's lawful contact with the child, and/or
(2) The other parent made a report of child sexual abuse, during a child custody proceeding or at any other time, that he or she knew was false at the time it was made. **FC § 3027.5(b)**.

Registered sex offenders may not be granted custody or unsupervised visitation with a child. **FC § 3030(a)**. Persons who were convicted of murder in the first degree will not be granted custody or unsupervised visitation of a child unless the court finds that there is no risk to the child's health, safety and welfare and states the reasons for its findings in writing or on the record. **FC § 3027.5(d)**.

A court may refuse to disclose a custodial parent's place of residence, place of employment or the child's school if the court finds that it is in the child's best interests to do so. **FC § 3027.5(e)**.

No parent shall be placed on supervised visitation, or be denied custody of or visitation with his or her child, and no custody or visitation rights shall be limited, solely because the parent (1) lawfully reported suspected sexual abuse of the child, (2) otherwise acted

Chapter 14: Child Visitation

> lawfully, based on a reasonable belief, to determine if his or her child was the victim of sexual abuse, or (3) sought treatment for the child from a licensed mental health professional for suspected sexual abuse. FC § 3027.5(a).

Finally, pursuant to **FC § 3020** effective January 1, 2019, the Legislature "finds and declares that children have the right to be safe…" Children now have this right whether the visitation is supervised or not.

Adoption Severs All Parental Rights

Any visitation rights granted before the adoption of the child automatically terminate if the child is adopted by a person other than a stepparent or grandparent of the child. **FC § 3102(c)**.

> *LARRY P. HUFFMAN et al., Plaintiffs and Appellants, v. PATRICIA GROB,
> Defendant and Respondent*
> Court of Appeal of California, Second Appellate District, Division One
> 172 Cal.App.3d 1153
> October 4, 1985
> *(Huffman v. Grob)*
>
> Appellants Larry P. Huffman, Kathleen Huffman, and Bernice Huffman (the Huffmans) appeal from an order of the superior court denying their petition for visitation rights with minor child Joseph Lee Grob in the matter of the adoption petition of Patricia Grob. We affirm.
>
> Joseph Grob (Joseph) was born Fermin Konkright Huffman in Laredo, Texas on May 25, 1972. Janice Huffman Konkright and her husband Ronald Konkright adopted Joseph shortly after birth. The child's name was changed to Joseph Lee Konkright by order of December 23, 1975.
>
> In December of 1978, Janice Konkright died of an illness arising out of her diabetic condition. Joseph continued to reside with Ronald Konkright in Texas for another five years. In 1983 Ronald Konkright contacted his deceased wife's longtime friend and Joseph's godmother, Patricia Grob (Grob), a resident of Southern California, and requested that Grob adopt Joseph. Grob agreed.
>
> Joseph moved to Grob's California home in 1983. A decree of adoption was signed by the court on October 27, 1983, and the child's name was changed to Joseph Lee Grob. Janice Konkright's mother, Bernice Huffman, brother, Larry Huffman, and sister, Kathleen Huffman, reside in Southern California and visited Joseph at Grob's home pending the adoption proceeding. After the proceedings were completed, Grob refused to permit the Huffmans to visit Joseph.
>
> On May 8, 1984, the Huffmans filed a petition for visitation with Joseph. The court requested that the Huffmans submit a memorandum of points and authorities in support of their petition, as the court was not aware of any legal authority in support of the Huffman's position. The Huffmans did so, and the court denied their petition. This appeal followed.

DISCUSSION

The sole issue presented by the Huffmans in this appeal is whether the court erred in refusing to permit the Huffmans to have an evidentiary hearing on the issue of visitation rights. The court below ruled properly on this issue.

When a child is adopted, the law creates a parent-child relationship between the adopting parent(s) and the child and severs the child's relationship with his or her natural family. "In an adoption proceeding the child receives a 'substitute' parent, and although he loses his right to look to the natural parent for support, he can now look to the adoptive parent." (Cite omitted.)

The initial adoption by the Konkrights created a familial relationship between Joseph, the Konkrights' adopted son, and the Huffmans, Janice Konkright's mother, brother, and sister. The subsequent adoption by Grob substituted Grob as Joseph's new mother and operated to sever Joseph's family ties with the Huffmans and the Konkrights.

Bernice Huffman, Janice Konkright's mother, cites Civil Code § 197.5 as authority for her claim of visitation rights. That section provides that the parents, grandparents, and children of a decedent may obtain court-ordered visitation rights with a minor child of the decedent under certain circumstances.

Under the terms of Civil Code § 197.5(c), Bernice Huffman is not entitled to court-ordered visitation rights in this case. Grob, who was neither a grandparent nor a stepparent, has adopted Joseph. Moreover, the terms of that statute do not bestow any right to visit Joseph upon Kathleen or Larry Huffman, sister and brother, respectively, of Janice Huffman Konkright.

The Huffmans are unable to cite one single opinion in which an appellate court of this state has granted former relatives of an adopted child visitation rights under the authority of Civil Code §§4600[4] and 4601 where Civil Code § 197.5[5] would bar such rights. Civil Code § 197.5, which specifically applies in this context, places strict limitations upon the court's authority to award visitation rights after an adoption has taken place. The effectiveness of Civil Code § 197.5 would be vitiated were we to adopt the Huffmans' position and hold that the operation of Civil Code §§ 4600 and 4601 nullifies the restrictions upon continuing contacts with former relatives after adoption imposed by Civil Code § 197.5.

Grob is Joseph's adoptive mother. She is statutorily entitled to full parental rights and subject to full parental obligations. The purpose of the laws severing old family ties after adoption is to permit the new, adoptive family ties to solidify and to confer upon the new parent(s) discretion to provide for the best interests of the adopted child without interference from the former relatives.

---

[4] Civil Code § 4600 was renumbered to FC § 3041 which provides in pertinent part that before "making an order granting custody to a person or persons other than a parent, over the objection of a parent, the court shall make a finding that granting custody to a parent would be detrimental to the child and that granting custody to the nonparent is required to serve the best interest of the child. Allegations that parental custody would be detrimental to the child, other than a statement of that ultimate fact, shall not appear in the pleadings. The court may, in its discretion, exclude the public from the hearing on this issue."

[5] FC § 3102 replaced Civil Code § 197.5 when the Family Code became effective in 1994.

Chapter 14: Child Visitation

> Were we to accept the Huffmans' broad interpretation of Civil Code § 4601, then any stranger, with or without some preexisting relationship to an adopted child, would have standing to apply at any time after the adoption decree to obtain visitation with an adopted child. Such a result is contrary to the policy of providing adopted children with stable homes free of protracted or repeated litigation concerning custody or visitation.
>
> **DISPOSITION**
> The order is affirmed.

Adoption severs all ties with the adopted child. As the court in *Huffman* above points out, the reason for severing the former family ties is to "solidify and to confer upon the new parent(s) discretion to provide for the best interests of the adopted child without interference from the former relatives." *Supra* at p. 1158.

However, there is a procedure where the adoptive and biological parents can make an agreement for continuing contact after the adoption. It is called a "kinship adoption agreement" or "postadoption agreement". FC § 8616.5 sets forth the rules that must be followed. FC § 8616.5 was amended effective 2017.

The postadoption contract is not generally known and it is not the duty of the court, the County Social Services or the attorneys involved to so advise the parents. *Kimberly S. v. Leanne W.* (1999) 71 Cal. App. 4th 405 at p. 409, 415-416.

The court in *Kimberly S. v. Leanne W.*, supra, at p. 412 stated the following regarding the intent behind FC § 8714.7, which was renumbered to **FC § 8616.6** in 2003:

> In practical terms, a kinship adoption agreement may be initiated by either the birth parent(s), other birth relatives, or by the prospective adoptive parents. When a birth parent is contemplating relinquishing a child for adoption by a relative, the birth parent may decide to condition such relinquishment on the adoptive parent's agreement to allow the birth parent to maintain some form of open relationship with the child, such relationship to be embodied in a kinship adoption agreement as provided by the statute.
>
> From the perspective of a prospective adoptive parent, that person may want the birth parent's continued involvement with the child, at some level, especially when the adoptive parent is a relative of the birth parent. The adoptive parent may view such involvement as beneficial for the child, may view such involvement as lessening tensions in the circumstance of an involuntary, dependency-related transfer of custody, [3] or may view such involvement as appropriate for a myriad of other reasons. In 1997, legislation was passed altering the long-standing rule mandating extinguishment of birth parents' rights after an adoption of their child. The Legislature determined that in limited circumstances the goal of providing stable homes to children may be fostered by allowing relatives of the child who are the prospective adoptive parent or parents, the birth relatives (including the birth parent or parents), and the child to enter into agreements providing for visitation, future contact, and/or sharing of information. Such an agreement is known as a kinship adoption agreement.
>
> "This bill was introduced through the collaborative efforts of the counties, State Department of Social Services, children's advocates and relative caregivers over the past

Chapter 14: Child Visitation

> year to identify barriers to adoption for children living with relatives and to create an adoption plan for relatives which recognizes the unique circumstances of children placed with relatives.
> "Currently, 40 percent to 46 percent of the approximately 100,000 children in foster care in California live with relatives, primarily because of the state's requirement to consider relatives as the first choice for placement. The majority of relative placements are grandparents, and the current foster care system has legal interventions and social worker involvement designed for foster parents that some maintain are not necessarily appropriate for relative placements or suitable for assuring the safety and long-term well being of children in these placements." (Sen. Rules Com. Rep., 3d reading analysis of Assem. Bill No. 1544 (1997-1998 Reg. Sess.) as amended Sept. 11, 1997.)
>
> Thus, a kinship adoption agreement may assuage the trepidations of a reluctant prospective adoptive relative parent because it allows the relative to adopt the child without appearing to advocate a role permanently severing all family ties with the birth parents. It is the intent of the Legislature that a kinship adoption agreement will encourage a qualified relative to move forward with an adoption, causing children to move out of foster care and into permanent homes, thereby expediting legal permanency. Given these reasons for kinship adoption agreements, it does not appear that the Legislature in any way intended to alter current dependency procedures to require that birth parents be advised of the availability of these agreements.

EDUCATIONAL EXERCISES

Answer/perform the following:

1. What is a "Freeman" order?
2. In what US Supreme Court case in 2000 was grandparent visitation an important issue? Give the case name and cite.
3. Describe a situation where a step parent may be granted visitation.
4. What are the 5 agreements that must be in every stipulated visitation/custody agreement pursuant to FC § 4065?
5. What section(s) of the Family Code are the issues of grandparent visitation addressed?
6. Discuss supervised visitation and when it should be ordered.
7. With regard to visitation and pursuant to FC § 3048, what must every court order contain?
8. List three different visitation plans and give an example of each.
9. Briefly summarize the grandparent visitation case.
10. What is the law that set forth the rules with regard to grandparent visitation?
11. Describe a situation where supervised visitation would be appropriate.

CHAPTER 15: Moveaways or Relocations

In Brief...

FACTORS COURTS MUST CONSIDER WHEN ALLOWING A MOVEAWAY: *Marriage of LaMusga*
- The children's interest in stability and continuity in the custodial arrangement;
- The distance of the move;
- The age of the children;
- The children's relationship with both parents;
- The relationship between the parents including their ability to communicate and cooperate effectively and their willingness to put the interests of the children above their individual interests;
- The wishes of the children if they are mature enough for such an inquiry to be appropriate;
- The reasons for the proposed move; and
- The extent to which the parents currently are sharing custody.

HOLDINGS IN MONTENEGRO v. DIAZ (2001) 26 Cal.4th 249
- Best interests must be considered if no final custody order:
- Modifying a permanent custody order requires a significant change of circumstances justifying a modification.
- A stipulated custody order is a final judicial custody determination for purposes of the changed circumstance rule only if there is a clear, affirmative indication the parties intended such a result.

HOLDINGS IN IN RE MARRIAGE of BURGESS (1996) 13 Cal.4th 25
- The court should consider the effects of relocation on the "best interest" of the children, including health, safety, welfare and amount of contact with both parents. **(FC § 3011(a) &(c).)**
- A court may consider the extent to which the minor children's contact with the noncustodial parent will be impaired by relocating.
- The custodial parent seeking to relocate, like the noncustodial parent doing the same, bears no burden of demonstrating that the move is "necessary."
- A parent entitled to the custody of a child has a right to change the residence of the child, subject to the power of the court to restrain a removal that would prejudice the rights or welfare of the child.
It is the intent of the Legislature to affirm the decision in *In re Marriage of Burgess* (1996) 13 Cal.4th 25 and to declare that ruling to be the public policy and law of this state.
- **A custodial parent is entitled to change the residence of his or her minor children, unless such removal would result in "prejudice" to their "rights or welfare." (FC § 7501.)**

OTHER MOVEAWAY HOLDINGS:

Chapter 15: Moveaways or Relocations

> - Court must assume that the move will occur and take the request seriously. *Jacob A. v. C.H.*
> - Courts must fashion a custody and visitation order that is in the best interests of the child based upon the move. *Mark T. v. Jamie Z.*
> - Evidentiary hearing not always required in a moveaway case. *Marriage of Brown and Yana*
> - Superior economic position is not a basis for a custody award. *Burchard v. Garay*
> - Handicap is no reason to deny custody. *Marriage of Carney*
> - Unless there is a compelling reason, siblings will not be separated. *Marriage of Williams*
> - Mediation is necessary in a moveaway case. *Marriage of MCGinnis*
> - Protective measures may be required to enforce custody order. *J.M. v. G.H., Marriage of Condon*
> - Preferences of child must be considered. *Marriage of Rosson*
> - There are separate rules for joint custody. *Niko v. Foreman*
> - Substantial change of circumstances not required when there is frustration of visitation. *Marriage of Ciganovich*
> - If detriment to the child is shown, moveaway will not be allowed. *Marriage of Melville*
>
> **CHART 8: Moveaway Cases by Holding(s)**

Introduction

When parties with children divorce, court orders and/or agreements are usually made that provide that a custodial parent or a parent who shares custody cannot move with the children to another county, state or country unless the other parent agrees to the move in writing or a court so orders.

Often parents will not agree, so a parent must obtain permission to relocate with the children by court order.[1] These cases are commonly called **moveaway** or **relocation** cases. Over the years, the legislature and the courts have carved out many rules that provide procedures and guidance for the trial court when determining whether or not to allow the moveaway. "Such a decision is one of the most serious decisions a family law court is required to make." *In re Marriage of McGINNIS* (1992) 7 Cal.App.4th 473 at p. 477. Just as all families are different in some way, each moveaway case presents different problems to be resolved.

---

[1] "When the parents are unable to agree on a custody arrangement, the court must determine the best interest of the child by setting the matter for an adversarial hearing and considering all relevant factors, including the child's health, safety, and welfare, any history of abuse by one parent against any child or the other parent, and the nature and amount of the child's contact with the parents." *In re Marriage of Seagondollar* (2006) 139 Cal.App.4th 1116 at p. 1126.

Chapter 15: Moveaways or Relocations

We live in a mobile society where "approximately one American in five changes residences each year and economic necessity and/or remarriage account for the bulk" of the moves. *In re Marriage of BURGESS* (1996) 13 Cal.4th 25 at p. 35-36.

This issue of relocation is thus occurring more and more often in family law making moveaway issues more and more common.

The following abbreviations are used in the text and charts of this chapter:

TC: Trial Court
M: Mother
F: Father
CP: Custodial Parent
NCP: Noncustodial Parent
DV: Domestic Violence
CtA: Court of Appeals
D: District of Court of Appeal
(#): Division of District of Court of Appeal
SupCt: Supreme Court of CA

Factors Courts Must Consider When Allowing a Moveaway

In re Marriage of LaMUSGA (2004) 32 Cal.4th 1072

In *LaMusga*, M and F were married on October 22, 1988, and had two children, born in 1992 and 1994. M filed a petition for dissolution on May 10, 1996, requesting sole physical custody of the children, who were living with her in the family residence. F objected and requested joint legal and physical custody. At a hearing on November 14, 1996, the TC awarded the parties joint legal custody of the children, with M having primary physical custody.

Because the parties could not agree on custody, the court ordered that Philip Stahl, Ph.D., a licensed psychologist, would conduct a child custody evaluation. In Dr. Stahl's report he stated that the parties verbally abused each other, were hostile toward each other and could not communicate with each other.
On February 13, 2001, M filed an order to show cause to modify the visitation order to permit her to relocate with the children to Cleveland, Ohio. She alleged that she had family in the Cleveland area and her husband had received an offer for a more lucrative job there.

F objected to M's plan to relocate with the children to Ohio and asked that primary custody of the children be transferred to him if M moved to Ohio. The TC court held that if M wished to relocate to the state of Ohio, she certainly could but if so, the court would implement the recommendations contained in Dr. Stahl's supplemental report, which provided that F would be awarded custody, at least during the school year. However, if M decided not to relocate, then the existing custodial arrangement would remain in effect.

M appealed, and the Court of Appeal reversed the judgment. The Court of Appeal concluded that the TC did not take into consideration that M had a presumptive right to relocate with the children and that there was a paramount need for stability and continuity. The Court of Appeal stated that the TC "placed undue emphasis on the detriment that would be caused to the children's relationship with F if they moved." *Id.* at p. 1093.

The Supreme Court granted a review, but right after that M filed a notice of abandonment of her appeal, supported by a declaration stating that she no longer intended to move to Ohio, but intended to move to Arizona instead. F objected, and the Supreme Court denied M's motion to dismiss the appeal.

In reversing the Court of Appeal's decision and remanding with directions to affirm the judgment of the trial court, the Supreme Court wrote:

> The Court of Appeal in the present case held that the superior court abused its discretion in ordering that primary physical custody of the children would be transferred to the father if the mother moved to Ohio. The Court of Appeal placed undue emphasis on the detriment that would be caused to the children's relationship with Father if they moved. The Court of Appeal erred in substituting its judgment for that of the superior court.
>
> W]e must permit our superior court judges—guided by statute and the principles we announced in Burgess and affirm in the present case—to exercise their discretion to fashion orders that best serve the interests of the children in the cases before them.
>
> Among the factors that the court ordinarily should consider when deciding whether to modify a custody order in light of the custodial parent's proposal to change the residence of the child are the following:
> [1] the children's interest in stability and continuity in the custodial arrangement;
> [2] the distance of the move;
> [3] the age of the children;
> [4] the children's relationship with both parents;
> [5] the relationship between the parents including their ability to communicate and cooperate effectively and their willingness to put the interests of the children above their individual interests;
> [6] the wishes of the children if they are mature enough for such an inquiry to be appropriate; the reasons for the proposed move; and
> [7] the extent to which the parents currently are sharing custody.
>
> [The decision of the Court of Appeal is reversed and the trial court's decision is affirmed.]

JANE J. v. SUPERIOR COURT (2015) 237 Cal.App.4th 894

Petitioner Jane J. (M) and Christopher J. (F) are the parents of two boys, an older son, born in the fall of 2002, and a younger boy, born in January 2006. The couple separated in 2006 and divorced in October 2009. At the time of the divorce, M lived

Chapter 15: Moveaways or Relocations

in Wisconsin with the two children. F was an active duty pilot in the military, stationed in Hawaii.

M and F agreed to a marital settlement, which was approved by a Wisconsin family court commissioner. The parents agreed to joint legal custody, but because of the family's "unique" situation, M was given 92% primary physical custody, with F having 8% physical custody.

The marital settlement agreement was signed by the Wisconsin family court commissioner and filed with the La Crosse County Circuit Court on October 22, 2009.

In 2012, M and the children moved from Wisconsin to Orange County, where M was living with her fiancé. The Wisconsin court held a hearing and approved M's moveaway.

F was transferred to various places from 2009 to 2013. In December 2013 F returned to the United States and received transfer orders to Fort Rucker in Alabama, where he relocated with his new wife.

In January 2014, F registered the October 2009 Wisconsin custody order in California. In April 2014, he filed a request for order (*RFO*) to modify the 2009 Wisconsin custody order, either to increase visitation, or to give him primary physical custody over the boys. He also sought to modify the support amounts.

M opposed F's *RFO* providing that she and F had serious disagreements with him concerning the children's future medical treatment and exact custody schedule.

On October 28, 2014, respondent court held an afternoon session on Father's *RFO*. Although the parties agreed to share the costs for an **Evid. Code § 730** evaluator to make recommendations regarding the children's best interests, respondent court did not appoint one.

On February 11, 2015, respondent court held the continued hearing on Father's *RFO*. The hearing lasted for 15 minutes in the morning and several hours in the afternoon.

At the conclusion of the hearing, respondent court determined that the 2009 Wisconsin custody order "wasn't a final order in any event" and that F did not have to establish changed-circumstances.

Respondent court stated that it was time [F] had an opportunity to parent the children and changed custody to F. The court declined M's counsel's request to defer the timing of any order until the end of the school year, and directed that its order take effect in four days, by February 16, 2015.

M filed a notice of the mandatory 30-day stay for out-of-state moveaway orders

Chapter 15: Moveaways or Relocations

in **CCP § 917.7**. In recognition of the code provision and over F's objection, respondent court stayed immediate removal of the children from California to Alabama.

In reversing the trial court's order, the Appellate Court stated:

> This is not an initial custody determination, where the family court has the "'widest discretion'" to make a de novo determination of the parenting plan that is in the best interest of the children. Neither is this a situation where the parents, pursuant to a final custody order, have shared physical and legal custody of the minor children.
>
> [A]s the noncustodial parent seeking a change of the existing custody order, F has the initial burden to make a substantial showing of changed circumstances affecting the children to change the final custody determination of the Wisconsin court.
>
> Because F is not the custodial parent, he does not have a presumptive right to relocate the children to another region of the country simply because he acts in good faith and for a legitimate reason. Instead, as the noncustodial parent who seeks a change in custody involving an out-of-state moveaway, F bears additional burdens of persuasion as part of the changed-circumstances standard.
>
> At a minimum, this requires a balancing of the children's current situation in California and their proposed new situation in Alabama, with the substantial burden of showing a change of circumstance imposed upon F, as the noncustodial parent, to establish that the children will not sustain detriment by the proposed move, and that the out-of-state moveaway will serve their best interests.
>
> Here are some of the factors a family law judge should consider in evaluating a noncustodial parent's moveaway request:
> (1) the children's ages (and, if age appropriate, the children's wishes);
> (2) community ties;
> (3) health and educational needs;
> (4) the attachment and past, present and potential future relationship of the children with each parent;
> (5) the anticipated impact of the move upon the children's existing social, educational and familial relationships; and
> (6) each parent's willingness to facilitate frequent, meaningful and continuing contact to the other parent.
>
> Respondent court abused its discretion in ordering a change in the existing custody arrangement, with its attendant out-of-state moveaway, without considering the relevant *LaMusga* factors. Respondent court acted precipitously in issuing its February 11, 2015 moveaway order and failing to weigh, in the context of F's substantial burden to show changed circumstances and best interests, the disruption to the children from losing their existing home, school and support structure against the potential benefits from an out-of-state relocation.
>
> Let a peremptory writ of mandate in the first instance directing respondent court to vacate its order granting Father physical custody of the minor children and requiring that they move away from their California residence with Mother to the state of Alabama, where

> Father resides. Respondent court shall conduct further proceedings regarding appropriate visitation and custody orders in accordance with this opinion.

In re Marriage of WINTERNITZ (2015) 235 Cal.App.4th 644

The parents married in 1985. F is an orthopedic surgeon. The couple had three children: Jill, Jana and Jamison. The couple separated in August 2001, shortly after Jamison's birth. Their marriage was dissolved in 2004. The TC thereafter allowed M to relocate with the children to San Diego. The order provided that custody would be modifiable on the children's best interests without showing a change in circumstance. After M moved to San Diego with the children, F relocated to San Diego and established an orthopedic surgery practice there.

Subsequent to her move to San Diego, M filed a moveaway request seeking an order to move Jamison with her to Chico in northern California, where she had purchased a home. In turn, F moved to modify custody and visitation, seeking physical custody of Jamison. The parties met at Family Court Services (FCS), and the FCS mediator recommended that M remain Jamison's primary caregiver. F did not agree with the FCS recommendation and, accordingly, requested a custody evaluation and evidentiary hearing. The TC granted F's request and appointed Robert Simon, Ph.D., to conduct a custody evaluation.

Dr. Simon submitted his custody evaluation report in March 2013, recommending that the move-away request be denied and Jamison be placed with F. M moved to strike Dr. Simon's report because it presented some serious issues concerning the technical preparation, including Dr. Simon's violation of his own rules concerning what was required of the parties and their lawyers, as well as his failure to conform to requests for discovery and to provide all of his records. The TC noted that many of M's objections to the report were valid, but found they went "to the weight of the contents of the report and were not sufficient to justify having the report stricken." It found Dr. Simon was not biased in favor of either party; accordingly, it considered the report and Dr. Simon's testimony in entering its decision.

After considering Dr. Simon's report, hearing testimony and argument from counsel, the TC denied M's move-away request and changed primary custody of Jamison to F. The TC found that F met his burden of showing that the planned move would cause substantial detriment to Jamison. It then addressed the *LaMusga* factors and found that changing custody to F was in Jamison's best interests. M appealed from the denial of the move-away order.

M appealed the denial of her move-away request, claiming that the TC court did not apply the correct legal standard in assessing her relocation request, including: **(1)** failing to consider her presumptive right to move under **FC § 7501, (2)** not weighing all of the factors set forth in *In re MARRIAGE of LAMUSGA* (2004) 32 Cal.4th 1072 and **(3)** not giving meaningful consideration to Jamison's custodial preference to remain in her care, as required by **FC § 3042**.

Court of Appeal rejected M's claims that the TC court did not apply the correct legal standard in assessing her relocation request, noting that the TC acknowledged in its Statement of Decision that **M had been the primary caretaker**, and denying M's request to move Jamison to Chico would result in a change of custody and a disruption in the current custody arrangement. Despite these concerns, the TC found **denying the move-away request was "clearly in the child's best interests."** That the TC found "**the factor concerning the ability and willingness of one parent to provide the other parent with the opportunity to spend as much time with the child as possible** and to be flexible with scheduling requests as a controlling factor" does not show that the family court failed to consider all other factors. With regard to M's claim that the TC did not give meaningful consideration to Jamison's preference to remain in M's care, the TC acknowledged that it was aware of Jamison's wishes. That the family court did not follow Jamison's wishes does not establish an abuse of discretion. *Id.* at p. 656.

Detriment to the Children Must Be Considered

F.T. v. L.J. (2011) 194 Cal.App.4th 1

In January 2006, Child was born to M and F, who had dated for five or six months. Child resided with M from his birth through February 17, 2007. On February 17, M burned Child's arm with a hot curling iron, apparently to teach him a lesson by showing him how hot it was. F filed a petition to establish paternity of Child and for an order granting him sole legal and physical custody of Child.
On March 2, F filed an order to show cause requesting orders granting him sole legal and physical custody of Child and granting M only supervised visits with Child. F then first sought to move to the State of Texas and then to the State of Washington. The TC denied F's request and F appealed.

The Court of Appeal held that the TC made several errors that required reversal. Three of those errors were: **(1)** It misunderstood the proper legal standards to be applied in determining whether that motion should be granted by failing to properly treat F's plan to move to Washington as a serious one; **(2)** by considering whether F's reasons for his proposed move to Washington were "sufficient" or "necessary"; and **(3)** by placing an undue, if not sole, emphasis on the probability that F's proposed move with Child to Washington could be detrimental to Child's relationship with M.

OSGOOD v. LANDON (2005) 127 Cal.App.4th 425

F and M were never married. Their son Daniel was born on July 30, 1998. On July 31, 2001, M filed a petition to establish paternity and named F as the father, which F later admitted. M filed a request to enter a default on September 12, 2001, and a default judgment was entered on October 3, 2001. The judgment granted M sole legal and physical custody of Daniel, with reasonable visitation to F.

On February 6, 2002, F filed a motion to modify visitation and to change custody to him based on M's plans to move to Tennessee to accept a job offer. The TC determined that F had a burden to establish detriment and that F failed to demonstrate that M's relocation caused any detriment. On appeal, the court affirmed. F argued that the TC court incorrectly applied the "changed circumstances" (rather than the "best interests of the child") standard to the proposed move, and that the error led to denial of his motion. However, this was not correct. The Court of Appeal, in affirming the TC's decision, stated that **the TC properly required that F establish that M's move would cause detriment to Daniel; F failed to establish such detriment; and substantial evidence supported the TC's order**.

In re Marriage of MELVILLE (2004) 122 Cal.App.4th 601

M and F were married in 1981. They had two sons, one of whom had Down's syndrome and a heart condition (Patrick). They separated in 1994, with M having primary physical custody of both children. In December of 2002, M was laid off from her job at America Online. The next day M told F that she planned to relocate and take Patrick to Klamath Falls, Oregon, where M had bought a house in 2000. F obtained an order barring any change of Patrick's residence pending a court hearing for a modification of Patrick's custody, due to this change of circumstance. M violated that order by taking Patrick to Oregon. Ultimately, the TC determined that M and F would share legal custody, and that F would have the majority of physical custody; M would have custody during the summer, with regular visitation during the rest of the year. M filed a notice of appeal from the order. The Court of Appeal affirmed the TC's order, finding no abuse of discretion and stating that the TC's findings demonstrate a substantial basis for the order that F have primary custody. **The relocation would have caused detriment to Patrick.** The court stated that this finding alone, supported by substantial evidence, requires affirmance of the TC's order. *Id.* at p. 692.

In re Marriage of CARLSON (1991) 229 Cal.App.3d 1330

The parties met and married in 1979 while they were in the United States Navy. They had two children, one born in the State of Pennsylvania and one born in California. In 1985 the family established a residence in Madera, California. When F filed the petition for marital dissolution, M stated that she wanted to move to Pennsylvania with the children. M grew up there and her family' resided there. M aspired to obtain a degree in counseling—a goal which would take six (6) years to achieve—and she wanted the emotional support of her parents, who could also help her care for the children while she attended college in Pennsylvania. The parents agreed to share joint legal custody of the children, with M to have physical custody and F to have reasonable visitation. In 1989, the court entered an order prohibiting each parent from moving with the children out of California without the prior consent of the other or court approval. In addition, it ordered joint legal custody and awarded M primary physical custody with specific visitation rights to F. The appellate court affirmed the trial court decision holding that: **(1)** the trial court did not err when it considered the effect M's contemplated move would have on F's exercise of visitation; and **(2)** F, as a NCP, did not have an affirmative burden to prove the move would be detrimental to the children in order to obtain the

Chapter 15: Moveaways or Relocations

restraining order preventing M from moving with the children.

Best Interests Must Be Considered-No Final Custody Order

MONTENEGRO v. DIAZ (2001) 26 Cal.4th 249

In *Montenegro* F and M never married. They had a son, Gregory, who was born in November 1994. M lived with her mother, and F had short visitations for the first 18 months.

One day in March of 1996, F visited Gregory while M was at work and Gregory was in the care of his grandmother. Although F had made no previous arrangements with M, he took Gregory for an overnight visit. After that incident, M refused to allow visitation without a court order. F then filed a complaint and order to show cause to establish paternity and requested joint legal and physical custody. M conceded paternity but sought sole physical custody of Gregory. The TC court's order was that M had primary responsibility for the care, custody and control of the minor.

There were several disputes concerning custody. Many OSCs[2] were filed and the parties continued to file them when there was a dispute; then, before the hearing, they would resolve the disputes with a stipulation.

However, because they could not agree on Gregory's impending enrollment in kindergarten and the choice of his school, there was a trial on the choice of school issue and what custody arrangement would be appropriate once Gregory started school.

The order of the TC was that because F was more willing to share Gregory, he was awarded physical custody with M having visitation on alternate weekends.

The Court of Appeal reversed. The court held that the TC should have applied the changed circumstance rule, rather than the best interests standard, because the stipulations that the parties had made were final agreements. The Court of Appeal found that there was no evidence of a significant change of circumstances and that application of the changed circumstance rule likely would have yielded a different result. The Supreme Court then granted review.

In reversing the order of the Court of Appeal, the Supreme Court stated:

> At the adversarial hearing, the court has " 'the widest discretion to choose a parenting plan that is in the best interest of the child' " (Citations omitted.)

---

[2] OSC–Order to Show Cause (a request for a hearing) was renamed to *RFO–Request for Order* effective 1/1/2012.

264

> Although the statutory scheme only requires courts to ascertain the "best interest of the child" (e.g., §§ 3011, 3020, 3040, 3087), this court has articulated a variation on the best interest standard once a final judicial custody determination is in place. Under the so-called changed circumstance rule, a party seeking to modify a permanent custody order can do so only if he or she demonstrates a significant change of circumstances justifying a modification. (*In re Marriage of Burgess* (1996) 13 Cal.4th at p. 37, 51 Cal.Rptr.2d 444, 913 P.2d 473.)
>
> [W]e hold that a stipulated custody order is a final judicial custody determination for purposes of the changed circumstance rule only if there is a clear, affirmative indication the parties intended such a result.
>
> Applying this holding to the facts presented here, we conclude that [none of the stipulated orders constituted a] final judicial custody determination. Although these orders included detailed visitation schedules and did not provide for further hearings, they did not clearly state that they were final judgments as to custody. Finally, the minute orders confirming these stipulations resembled the minute orders confirming the parties' temporary stipulations. Thus, neither order contained a clear, affirmative indication that the parties intended it to be a final judicial custody determination.
>
> Because the record amply supports the trial court's determination that Montenegro should have custody of Gregory, we affirm it under the deferential abuse of discretion standard.

JACOB A. v. C.H. (2011) 196 Cal.App.4th 1591

M challenged a postjudgment order that denied her request to relocate to the State of Washington with the minor child and to modify the parenting schedule accordingly. The trial court's order assumed that M would not move if a change of custody was ordered. In reversing the TC, the Court of Appeal held that the TC misapplied the relevant legal standard in deciding M's moveaway request. The issue that should have been addressed was what should the parenting plan be when M moved. **The TC was required to decide de novo what physical custody arrangement would be in the child's best interests**, assuming M would move and be living in Washington, not assuming she would not move if the right court order was prohibitive enough to prevent her from moving.

MARK T. v. JAMIE Z. (2011) 194 Cal.App.4th 1115

A dating relationship between M and F produced a child. F filed a petition to establish his paternity. The court entered an order establishing F's paternity, and entered a temporary custody order based on the time-sharing agreement that the parties had reached. Before the court entered a permanent custody order, M filed an order to show cause (OSC) requesting that the court permit her to relocate with the child to Minnesota. The TC denied M's moveaway request and issued an order establishing a legal and physical custody sharing arrangement. M appealed. In reversing the trial's court decision, the appellate court stated that the trial court misunderstood that it was required to proceed on the assumption that the parent will in fact be moving and **fashion a custody and visitation order that is in the best**

interests of the child based upon the move. Since the trial court failed to assume that M would be moving, it abused its discretion. *Id.* at p. 1132.

RAGGHANTI v. REYES (2004) 123 Cal.App.4th 989

The parties were never married and stopped seeing each other a few weeks after their child, Karyn, was born. The parties stipulated to paternity and a paternity judgment was entered in December 1997, when Karyn was eight months old. The temporary custody order attached to that judgment provided that Karyn was to live primarily with M and that F had visitation rights. In 1998 M threatened to move to Georgia. F obtained a restraining order, and the TC found that M's motive for moving was to deny F access to Karyn. The court ordered custody to F if M chose to move. M did not move and Karyn remained in her custody. In September 2000, M told F that she was going to move away with Karyn. This time she planned to relocate to Sacramento. M, thereafter, filed a motion seeking permission to move to Sacramento. The parties stipulated that there was no existing final custody order and, accordingly, the TC applied the best interests' analysis, considering all of the circumstances in making a custody determination. The TC found that it was in Karyn's best interests to live primarily with F. M appealed, contending that the TC erred because it did not find M's care deficient.

The Court of Appeal affirmed the TC's decision, holding that the TC correctly applied the best interests standard and considered all of the correct circumstances. Because the parties stipulated that there was no final custody determination, the TC's custody determination was an initial custody order, so applying the best interests analysis was correct. A best interests analysis does not require a finding of deficiency or detriment.

In re Marriage of BRYANT (2001) 91 Cal.App.4th 789

In a marital dissolution proceeding, the TC awarded primary physical custody of the two minor children to M. In making the award, the court found that the mother, who intended to move to New Mexico—where she had been raised—to be with her family was not acting in bad faith and that the custody award was in the best interests of the children. An evaluation conducted by a court-appointed expert showed that the mother was the "primary parent" and "had a greater level of involvement in the children's lives" than did the father. *Id.* at p. 792. The TC noted "it would be detrimental to the children to make a 'radical shift' to F as the primary parent." *Ibid.* The TC found that M was not motivated to move by bad faith and had not unreasonably interfered with F's visitation with the children.

The Court of Appeal affirmed. It held that, in light of the TC's findings: **(1)** M was not acting in bad faith, **(2)** that it was in the best interests of the children for custody to be with M and **(3)** that the TC did not abuse its discretion in awarding primary physical custody to M. The court held that a parent proposing a moveaway is not required to establish a need or even a justification for relocating to another

Chapter 15: Moveaways or Relocations

geographic area; the only exception is when the reason for the move is to frustrate the noncustodial parent's relationship with the child.

In re Marriage of EDLUND & HALES (1998) 66 Cal.App.4th 1454

In dissolution of marriage proceedings, TC granted the application of M, who was the primary caretaker and CP of the parties' three-year-old daughter, to move with the child to Indiana, where her fiancé had accepted a job and was already living. The move would allow M to stay at home with her child rather than working full-time outside the home. The TC relied upon the evaluator's opinion that M had not attempted to limit F's visitation in the past and acknowledged the importance of F's role as their child's father. The Court of Appeal affirmed, concluding that the superior court had not abused its discretion because the **TC carefully considered all the factors bearing on the child's best interests**, and that its decision was supported by substantial evidence of the strength and primacy of the bond between the child and her mother, M's ability to provide and care for the child on a full-time basis and the overwhelming, undisputed proof that F was not prepared to assume primary physical custody of his daughter.

CASSADY v. SIGNORELLI (1996) 49 Cal.App.4th 55

M and F were not married and their relationship ended when their child was born. F and M could not agree on support or visitation, and this led to a great deal of litigation. The initial TC order awarded joint custody, with M as the primary caretaker and F having visitation rights. The TC also ordered that M could not remove the child from the Bay Area. When M sought to move to Florida, the court entered an order that reiterated its previous ruling that M was prevented from removing the child from the Bay Area, F was to have overnight visitation with the child.

M appealed and the Court of Appeal affirmed. The court held that the TC did not err in concluding that it was in the child's best interests to continue the parties' joint custody arrangement in California and regular visitation with F, rather than follow M to move to Florida, where, although she intended to support herself as an academic parapsychologist, she did not have a job awaiting her.

Substantial Change of Circumstances - Custody Order

"Under the so-called changed circumstance rule, a party seeking to modify a permanent custody order can do so only if he or she demonstrates a significant change of circumstances justifying a modification." *In re Marriage of BURGESS* (1996) 13 Cal.4th 25 at p. 37.

"The changed-circumstance rule is not a different test, devised to supplant the statutory test, but an adjunct to the best-interest test. It provides, in essence, that once it has been established that a particular custodial arrangement is in the best interests of the child, the court need not reexamine that question. Instead, it should preserve the established mode of custody unless some significant change in circumstances indicates that a different arrangement would be in the child's best interest. The rule thus fosters the dual goals of judicial economy and protecting stable custody arrangements." *In re Marriage of BURCHARD* (1986) 42 Cal.3d at p. 535.

KEITH R. v. SUPERIOR COURT (2009) 174 Cal.App.4th 1047

After F filed for divorce, M claimed domestic violence against F and requested sole custody of their daughter. Following an investigation and a hearing, the TC denied M's requests. Subsequently, the TC entered an order granting both parents joint legal and physical custody and appointed a child custody evaluator, who recommended maintaining the current custody arrangements based on their daughter's parental attachments.

In early 2008, M sought a temporary restraining order against F, citing new allegations that he had stalked and was spying on her and was seen by a police officer parked outside M's apartment complex late at night. F sought mandate relief from an order of the TC of Orange County, which issued a moveaway order that allowed M to leave the state with the child. Thereafter, the TC issued a domestic violence order against F, and awarded M with sole legal and physical custody. Additionally, the TC required F to participate in a batterer's intervention program for a year. The order allowing M to relocate with the children was issued less than a year later. The TC found that F had not rebutted the presumption against custody to a domestic violence perpetrator. The TC applied the changed-circumstances standard and made no determinations as to the child's best interests.

The Court of Appeal held that the TC erred in applying the changed-circumstances standard because there had been no final judicial custody determination. The Court of Appeal issued a peremptory writ of mandate directing the Superior Court of Orange County to vacate its order. The case was remanded back to the Superior Court of Orange County to conduct a new trial on custody in accordance with this opinion before issuing a final or permanent judicial custody determination.

ENRIQUE M. v. ANGELINA V. (2004) 121 Cal.App.4th 1371

F and M dated from 1995 to 1997. In September 1997, after their relationship had ended, M gave birth to their son, X. In March 1998, F filed a complaint to establish a parental relationship and child custody and visitation. In the complaint, F alleged that M had refused to allow him to have any involvement with X. The court's order stated that the parents would share joint legal custody of the child, that X's primary residence would be initially with M and that F's custody rights would be gradually increased over time until the parents shared joint physical custody.

The parties could not agree on many points regarding X and sought help from the court and Family Court Services (FCS). In one such mediation with FCS, the counselor made a recommendation that F opposed. The parties subsequently entered into a handwritten stipulation and order signed by them and by the family court judge. The parties agreed that they would continue to share joint legal and physical custody, and that X's primary residence would be with M.

In August 2002, F filed a motion requesting that the parenting schedule be modified. On January 7, 2003, the court denied F's request. The court concluded that a modification of the parenting schedule required a substantial change in circumstances. F appealed from the TC's order of January 7, 2003, claiming that his request was **to modify the parenting schedule and not custody, so the changed circumstance rule did not apply.** The Court of Appeal reversed the TC's decision, holding that the TC erred in applying the changed circumstance rule.

Custodial Parent Has a Presumptive Right to Move

In re Marriage of BURGESS (1996) 13 Cal.4th 25

In *Burgess*, F and M married and had two children. Both parents were employed by the State Department of Corrections at the state prison in Tehachapi. They separated in May 1992, when the children were three and four years old. M petitioned for dissolution shortly thereafter.

In July 1992, the TC entered a **Stipulation and Order** dissolving the marriage and providing for temporary custody and visitation in accordance with a mediation agreement reached between the parties. The parents agreed that they would share joint legal custody of the children with M having sole physical custody of the children.

Thereafter, M requested permission to move to Lancaster, where she had accepted a job transfer. Living in Lancaster would permit greater access for the children to medical care, extracurricular activities, private schools and daycare facilities. The travel time between Lancaster and her home in Tehachapi was approximately 40 minutes.

The TC issued a ruling granting M's request, providing that F and M would share joint legal custody, with M having sole physical custody. F moved for reconsideration and for a change in custody; M opposed the change. The TC denied the motion.

F appealed from both the order denying reconsideration and the order denying change in custody; the appeals were consolidated, and the Court of Appeal reversed. It formulated the following test for relocation cases. The TC initially must determine whether the move will significantly impact the existing pattern of care and adversely affect the nature and quality of the noncustodial parent's contact with the child. The burden is on the NCP non-moving parent to show this adverse impact.

If the impact is shown, the TC must determine whether the move is **reasonably necessary,** and the **moving parent has the burden of showing such necessity.** If it

Chapter 15: Moveaways or Relocations

concludes that the move is necessary, either because not moving would impose an unreasonable hardship on the custodial parent's career or other interests or because moving will result in a discernible benefit that would be unreasonable to expect the parent to forgo, the TC must resolve whether or not the benefit to the child in going with the moving parent outweighs the loss or diminution of contact with the nonmoving parent.

The Court of Appeal concluded that **no showing of necessity was made**. It reversed the orders of the TC and remanded for further proceedings consistent with the opinion. The Supreme Court granted review.

The Supreme Court stated:

> The trial court's order was supported by substantial evidence concerning the "best interest" of the minor children. First, and most important, the minor children had been in the sole physical custody of the mother [as their primary caretaker] for over a year at the time the trial court issued its order concerning permanent custody. As we have repeatedly emphasized, the paramount need for continuity and stability in custody arrangements--and the harm that may result from disruption of established patterns of care and emotional bonds with the primary caretaker--weigh heavily in favor of maintaining ongoing custody arrangements.
>
> The record reflects that the trial court, as required by FC § 3011, considered the "health, safety, and welfare" of the children as well as the "nature and amount of contact with both parents." (FC § 3011(a) & (c).)
>
> In an initial custody determination, a parent seeking to relocate with the minor children bears no burden of establishing that the move is "necessary." The trial court must--and here did--consider, among other factors, the effects of relocation on the "best interest" of the minor children, including the health, safety, and welfare of the children and the nature and amount of contact with both parents. (FC § 3011(a) &(c).)
>
> A trial court may consider the extent to which the minor children's contact with their noncustodial parent will be impaired by relocating. In so doing, however, it is not restricted to any particular formula for contact or visitation; nor is it required to make a custody determination that preserves the predissolution status quo.
>
> Although this matter involved an initial order of custody and visitation, the same conclusion applies when a parent who has sole physical custody under an existing judicial custody order seeks to relocate: the custodial parent seeking to relocate, like the noncustodial parent doing the same, bears no burden of demonstrating that the move is "necessary."
>
> In a "moveaway" case, a change of custody is not justified simply because the custodial parent has chosen, for any sound good faith reason, to reside in a different location, but only if, as a result of relocation with that parent, the child will suffer detriment rendering it " 'essential or expedient for the welfare of the child that there be a change.'" (*Ibid.*)
>
> This construction is consistent with the presumptive "right" of a parent entitled to

Chapter 15: Moveaways or Relocations

> custody to change the residence of his or her minor children, unless such removal would result in "prejudice" to their "rights or welfare." (FC § 7501.) The dispositive issue is, accordingly, not whether relocating is itself "essential or expedient" either for the welfare of the custodial parent or the child, but whether a change in custody is "'essential or expedient for the welfare of the child.'" (*In re Marriage of Carney, supra*, 24 Cal.3d at p. 730.
>
> Where appropriate, it must also take into account the preferences of the child. (FC § 3042(a).) ["If a child is of sufficient age and capacity to reason so as to form an intelligent preference as to custody, the court shall consider and give due weight to the wishes of the child in making an order granting or modifying custody."].)
>
> For the reasons discussed, we reverse the judgment of the Court of Appeal.

The holding in *In re Marriage of BURGESS* was codified and added as **FC § 7501(b)** which provides:

> **(a)** A parent entitled to the custody of a child has a right to change the residence of the child, subject to the power of the court to restrain a removal that would prejudice the rights or welfare of the child.
> **(b)** It is the intent of the Legislature to affirm the decision in *In re Marriage of Burgess* (1996) 13 Cal.4th 25 and to declare that ruling to be the public policy and law of this state.

In re Marriage of ABARGIL (2003) 106 Cal.App.4th 1294

M and F were both Israeli citizens who came to the United States on tourist visas and overstayed. They married and had a son. When they separated, the child lived primarily with M and visited F. M returned to Israel to nurse her dying mother, taking their son with her. While she was in Israel, F filed for divorce. When M attempted to return to California, she was barred from entering the United States for 10 years as a sanction for having overstayed her visa. This sanction was stayed, however, to permit her to return to California to litigate the custody of the child. F asserted that he would be unable to visit his son if he moved to Israel, because F was applying for permanent residency in the United States and could not leave the country for an extended time.

Following a five-day trial, the court permitted the child to move to Israel with M, noting that she had been the child's primary caregiver and finding that she was more likely to facilitate visitation with the father than if the parental roles were reversed.

The Court of Appeal affirmed, holding that a CP has the presumptive right to move and take the child with her and that F did not meet his burden of proving that CP's decision to move was not in the child's best interests. The fact that M's visa violation meant she could not bring the child to the United States for 10 years was counterbalanced by the fact that F could not leave the United States for any extended time during the pendency of his application for permanent residency without jeopardizing his right to continue living in the United States. Also, the court took adequate steps to ensure its judgment would be enforceable in Israel, including the requirement that it be registered there, and compelled M's adherence by requiring her to post a bond or other surety.

Evidentiary Hearing Not Always Required

In re Marriage of BROWN and YANA (2006) 37 Cal.4th 947

In Brown and Yana, M and F dissolved their marriage in 1994, and in 1999, after a psychological evaluation, M was awarded sole legal custody and sole physical custody of their son, Cameron.

In June of 2003, M informed F that she was moving with Cameron to Las Vegas, Nevada, at the end of the summer. On June 27, 2003, F filed an order to show cause to restrain any change of residence for Cameron and to request a psychological evaluation and a contested evidentiary hearing on the moveaway issue.

At the hearing, TC denied F's requests for relief, stating that an evidentiary hearing and psychological examinations had occurred in 1999, which resulted in an award of sole legal and physical custody of Cameron to M. And that given that judicial custody order, F was required to assert some detriment to warrant an evidentiary hearing.

F appealed. The Court of Appeal reversed in a split decision, holding that, in a moveaway case, a parent with no legal or physical custody rights is entitled to an evidentiary hearing. The Supreme Court granted M's petition for review.

In affirming the TC's order, the Supreme Court stated that:

> The question presented is this: In a case where sole legal and sole physical custody of a child has been awarded to one parent after a contested custody dispute, and the custodial parent's subsequent decision to relocate with the child is opposed by the noncustodial parent, is the noncustodial parent entitled to an evidentiary hearing on the matter?
>
> [W]e hold an evidentiary hearing in a moveaway situation should be held only if necessary. Where, as here, one parent has been awarded sole legal and sole physical custody of a child, and the noncustodial parent opposes the custodial parent's decision to relocate with the child, a trial court may deny the noncustodial parent's requests to modify custody based on the relocation without holding an evidentiary hearing to take oral evidence if the noncustodial parent's allegation or showing of detriment to the child is insubstantial in light of all the circumstances presented in the case, or is otherwise legally insufficient to warrant relief.

ANDREW V. v. SUPERIOR COURT (2015) 234 Cal.App.4th 103

M and F married in 2003. They had two children, a girl born in 2002 and a boy born in 2005. F and M permanently separated in 2006 and the judgment of dissolution was granted in June of 2008, granting them joint legal and physical custody. In

2014, M filed a moveaway request that would allow her to relocate with the two children to the State of Washington, due to a job transfer and promotion. The parties stipulated for a full custody investigation. The investigation report was finished on December 22, 2014, and the court set a hearing for January 14, 2015. The child custody investigator was not available at the January 14th hearing. F's counsel was present but ill and not able to represent F. As a result, the hearing was continued until March 4, 2015 and the TC issued a temporary order allowing M to relocate with the children to Washington. On January 20, 2015, F filed a petition for writ of mandate and a request for an immediate stay. M filed a timely *Response*. M disenrolled the children from their school and two days later moved to the State of Washington with the two children. Respondent court failed to recognize the 30-day stay pursuant to **CCP § 917.7**.

Without any meaningful hearing, the TC modified the final custody order based upon the written report of the child custody investigator. The Court of Appeal granted F's request for a stay of Respondent court's temporary order and M was ordered to bring the children back to California forthwith. The Court of Appeal issued a writ of mandate directing respondent court to vacate its temporary order of January 14, 2015. **A meaningful hearing is a critical requirement of California law before any judicial determination regarding an out-of-state, moveaway request for a parent who shares joint legal and physical custody.** Here, a trial court issued a "temporary" moveaway order allowing M to relocate out-of-state with her minor children, thus depriving F of an opportunity to be meaningfully heard before granting the mother's moveaway request.

In re Marriage of SEAGONDOLLAR **(2006) 139 Cal.App.4th 1116**

The marriage of F and M was dissolved on May 20, 2003, awarding F and M shared legal and physical custody of their four children. Subsequently, the TC appointed counsel to represent the children in a custody dispute. At the request of the children's counsel, the court appointed Dr. Adam to conduct "a limited evaluation." Dr. Adam conducted his evaluation, and one of his recommendations was that "the court considers allowing all of the children to relocate to Virginia to live with M and her husband."

At the hearing, the TC denied F's request for a continuance and his request to schedule a day of the hearing to present his rebuttal witness to Dr. Adam, Dr. Philip Stahl. The TC granted M primary custody of the children and permitted her to relocate with the children to Virginia, conditioned on various orders regarding F's custody. The TC concluded that it was in the children's best interests to award M primary physical custody and to authorize her to relocate to Virginia with the children. The Court of Appeal reversed the TC's decision, stating that F was denied a fair hearing because he was not permitted to present his witness.

In re Marriage of CAMPOS **(2003) 108 Cal.App.4th 839**

F sought modification of a child custody and visitation order relating to his sons, aged 15 and 12, after M announced she would move with the children from Santa

Barbara to Moorpark, about two (2) hours away by car. The TC summarily denied F's request, finding that M did not have a bad faith reason for the move.

In reversing the trial court's order, the Court of Appeal held that, although the TC properly considered whether M had a bad faith reason for the move, the TC erred in failing to hold an evidentiary hearing on whether the move would cause detriment to the children. Although a change in custody is not mandated simply because a move will require more travel or changed visitation for a NCP, a NCP opposing such a move has a right to present evidence on both relevant issues, bad faith on the part of the custodial parent and detriment to the children. *Id.* at p. 843-44.

Superior Economic Position May not be Used in determining Custody

BURCHARD v. GARAY (1986) 42 Cal.3d 531

In *Burchard*, M became pregnant as a result of a brief liaison. When M told F that she was pregnant with his child, he refused to believe that he was the father. William, Jr., was born on September 18, 1979.

After the birth, M cared for her child, with the help of her father and others, while working two jobs and continuing her training to become a registered nurse. F continued to deny paternity and did not visit the child or provide any support. In the spring of 1980, M brought a paternity and support action. Court-ordered blood tests established that F was the father, and he stipulated to paternity and to support. A judgment of paternity was entered on November 24, 1980. Thereafter, M and F tried to live together as a family, but this only lasted six weeks.

After M and F separated, F requested visitation rights; M refused and filed a petition for exclusive custody. F responded with his own action, seeking exclusive custody. The parties then stipulated that, pending the hearing, M would retain custody, with F having a right to two full days of visitation each week.

The TC after hearing the evidence issued a statement of decision in which it impliedly ruled that the changed circumstances rule did not apply because there was no prior custody determination. The TC applied the **best interests** test and awarded custody to F. Its decision was based upon three considerations: **(1)** F was financially better off, had greater job stability, owned his own home and was better equipped economically to give constant care to the minor child and cope with his continuing needs; **(2)** F had married, and he and his new wife could provide constant care for the minor child and keep him on a regular schedule without resorting to other caretakers, whereas M had to rely upon babysitters and daycare centers while she worked and studied to become a nurse; and **(3)** the TC believed that F would be the most willing parent to allow visitation.

Thereafter, F took custody of the minor child. M appealed from the order and sought a writ of supersedeas. The Court of Appeal, however, denied supersedas and subsequently affirmed the TC's order. The Supreme Court granted a hearing in August 1984. M did not seek supersedeas from the Supreme Court, so the child remained in his father's custody, pending the appeal.

In reversing the TC's order, the Supreme Court concluded that although the TC had applied the correct standard, the best interests test, it had erred in applying that standard. The Supreme Court stated that the TC's

> reliance upon the relative economic position of the parties was impermissible. Its reliance upon the asserted superiority of [F]'s child care arrangement suggests an insensitivity to the role of working parents. And all of the factors cited by the TC together weigh less to our mind than a matter it did not discuss -- the importance of continuity and stability in custody arrangements. (*Id.* at p. 535.)

In re Marriage of FINGERT (1990) 221 Cal.App.3d 1575

M and F were married in 1980 and lived in Ventura County. They separated before their son Joshua was born. The parties agreed in their Marital Settlement Agreement that they would have joint legal custody, with M having actual physical custody. F was to have reasonable visitation rights. M decided to relocate to Chicago, Illinois, when Joshua was one year old; then she changed her plans and relocated to San Diego. The custody order was modified to provide for this change. M then moved to San Mateo County for a better job. M and F, through their attorneys, agreed to an informal modification of the visitation schedule.

Thereafter, M petitioned the court for permission to move to Chicago because her father was ailing. Her request was denied. In April 1988, M filed a motion to modify the custody order to provide for visitation to F, consistent with Joshua's school schedule. The judge ordered that Joshua's residence be in Ventura (where F resided) and could not be changed. The TC apparently based its decision on F's better economic position and the fact that F owned a home in Ventura. The appellate court vacated the trial court's order, stating that it is impermissible to make a custody award on the basis of a parent's superior economic position.

Other Moveaway Holding(s)

1. No Denial of Custody because of a Handicap

In re Marriage of CARNEY (1979) 24 Cal.3d 725

In *Carney*, William (F) and Ellen (M) were married in New York in December 1968. Two sons were born of the union, the first in November 1969 and the second in January 1971. The parties separated not long after the second son was born. Upon separating, M and F entered into a written agreement whereby M relinquished custody of the boys to F. For reasons of employment F eventually moved to the West Coast with the boys. Four years after relocating, F was injured in a jeep accident. The accident left him a quadriplegic, with paralyzed legs, and impaired use of his arms and hands. He spent the next year recuperating in a veterans' hospital; his children visited him several times each week, and he came home nearly every weekend. He also bought a van, and it was fitted with a wheelchair lift and hand controls to permit him to drive.

In May 1977, F filed action for dissolution of his marriage with M. M, thereafter, moved for an order awarding her immediate custody of both boys even though from the date of separation until a few days before the hearing (a five-year period), M did not once visit her young sons or make any contribution to their support. Nevertheless, the court ordered that the boys be taken from the custody of F and given into the custody of M. M requested and was granted permission to move with the children to New York state. F appealed from that portion of the decree, transferring custody of the boys to M.

In reversing the TC's decision that awarded the custody of the children to M as an abuse of discretion, the Supreme Court stated:

- There is a requirement that a custody award serve the best interests of the child, and the moral and legal obligation of society to respect the civil rights of its physically handicapped members, including their right not to be deprived of their children because of their disability.
- To justify ordering a change in custody there must be a persuasive showing of changed circumstances affecting the child.
- A request for a change of custody is addressed to the sound discretion of the trial judge.
- The burden of showing a sufficient change in circumstances is on the party seeking the change of custody.
- If a person has a physical handicap, it is impermissible for the court simply to rely on that condition as prima facie evidence of the person's unfitness as a parent or of probable detriment to the child.
- It is erroneous to presume that a parent in a wheelchair cannot share, to a meaningful degree, in the physical activities of his child, should both desire it.

2. Siblings Cannot Be Separated Unless There Is a Compelling Reason

In re Marriage of WILLIAMS **(2001) 88 Cal.App.4th 808**

F and M dissolved their marriage that produced four children. They shared custody. M remarried and moved to Utah with her new spouse. TC ordered two of the children to move with M and two to stay with F. Both parents appealed, asserting that the TC abused its discretion. The Court of Appeal reversed, holding that the separation of siblings requires "compelling circumstances warranting the separation of the siblings." *Id.* at p. 810.

3. Mediation Is Necessary

In re Marriage of MCGINNIS **(1992) 7 Cal.App.4th 473**

F and M were married in January 1983 and separated in 1988. There were three children of the marriage. F and M entered into a stipulated judgment of dissolution providing for joint legal custody of the children. The judgment was silent as to physical custody. F, who was a California Highway Patrol officer, became engaged and subsequently married a fellow officer. M married a football coach for the University of California at Santa Barbara. When the university disbanded its football program, M's new spouse obtained employment as a football coach in the Arcadia area. M sent F a letter providing that she was moving to Arcadia with the children. In response to M's letter, F filed a motion to prevent M from changing the children's residence to Arcadia. F requested an order maintaining the status quo until an independent evaluation could be done. The TC denied F's request and entered an order that provided that the parties would share legal custody but M would have physical custody so that so that she may move with the children and her present husband to Arcadia. F appealed, and the Court of Appeal reversed stating that **mediation is mandatory in a moveaway case**.

4. Need Sufficient Protective Measures to Insure Compliance

J.M. v. G.H. **(2014) 228 Cal.App.4th 925**

J.M. (F) and G.H. (M), an Israeli citizen, met in 1996 and soon were living together. They never married. When M gave birth to Joey in September 2005, F signed a voluntary declaration of paternity and the birth certificate. The couple separated in late 2007 when Joey was two, and F moved into another house in the summer of 2008, while M and Joey were in Israel visiting M's family. In July 2009, when Joey was nearly four, F filed a petition to establish his paternity of Joey, requesting joint legal and physical custody and reasonable visitation. In October 2009, he filed an order to show cause, requesting sole legal custody and shared physical custody (with primary custody to him), after M and Joey returned from a summer 2009 trip to Israel three weeks after the agreed-upon date of September 3, 2009. In response, M requested sole legal and physical custody of Joey, with the right to move to Israel with Joey, and reasonable visitation for F in the United States and Israel. The TC found that there was no risk of abduction by M and that no measures to prevent abduction were necessary. The fact that the TC did not require a bond was not an abuse of discretion, because M did not have the resources to post a bond and the **TC's order had made sufficient protective measures**. The TC found that there was sufficient evidence that the child had a closer relationship with M, such that it was in the child's best interests to reside primarily with M. The TC's decision was affirmed.

Chapter 15: Moveaways or Relocations

In re Marriage of CONDON (1998) 62 Cal.App.4th 533

In a dissolution of marriage proceeding, the TC entered an order awarding M and F joint legal and physical custody of their two minor sons and ruled that it was in the children's best interests that they be permitted to move with M to Australia—8,000 miles away from their current home in California, where the couple had been married and the children were born. The court permitted to move the children to Australia. Among the factors considered by the TC were the mother's ability to financially support herself in Australia, rather than be wholly dependent on F for support; the impact of the parties' stressful relationship on the children; M's extensive family in Australia; the children's primary emotional attachment to M; and the "children's lack of a firm long-time base in California." *Id.* at p. 540.

The Court of Appeal affirmed in part and reversed in part, remanding the case with instructions to amend its order to incorporate M's concession of continuing jurisdiction in the California courts and **appropriate sanctions to enforce that concession**. In other respects, the judgment was affirmed. The court held that the TC did not abuse its discretion in ruling that it was in the children's best interests that they be permitted to move with M to Australia. The court carefully balanced all of the competing factors unique to foreign relocations and took extraordinary pains to craft measures calculated to minimize the adverse effects of the move on the father-child relationship. However, the TC's order lacked guaranteed enforceability in the Australian courts, especially after the children had resided in Australia for more than one year. Thus, remand was necessary for the trial court to obtain from M an enforceable concession of the continuing jurisdiction of the California court, a concession that she volunteered to make, and to create sanctions calculated to enforce that concession.

5. Preferences of the Children Must be Considered

In re Marriage of ROSSON (1986) 178 Cal.App.3d 1094

M and F stipulated a judgment of dissolution, providing that the primary residence of their two children was to be with M. Seven years later, M started making arrangements to move for legitimate job reasons out of Napa, where both parents lived for a substantial period of time. F filed a motion for modification, requesting that he have custody of both children if M moved to San Francisco.

The TC granted F's motion to modify custody, holding that M's move constituted a change of circumstances affecting the children and justifying modification of the custody order. The TC heard testimony from the parents, the court mediator and the two children in a closed proceeding in chambers. The oldest child strongly preferred to remain in Napa, but the youngest really did not have a preference. The Court of Appeal affirmed the decision of the TC.

6. There are Different Moveaway Rules when the Parties have Joint Custody

***NIKO v. FOREMAN* (2006) 144 Cal.App.4th 344**
Niko (F) and Foreman (M), who were unmarried, had a romantic relationship which produced their son, Taylor, in 1991. At the same time F was dating M, he was also dating another woman, Elizabeth. Shortly after Taylor's birth, F married Elizabeth, and they remain married to the present time.
Despite F's marriage, however, F and M continued their romantic relationship on and off over the next several years. In September 1996, during a period of discord, F filed a Paternity Petition to formally establish his parental relationship with then five-year-old Taylor and requested a 50/50 time-sharing physical custody order.

While M readily admitted F's paternity, they continued to argue over what the appropriate custody arrangement would be for their son. Finally, in February of 2001, they reached an agreement and the court entered a stipulated judgment. It decreed F was both the natural and legal father of Taylor, and M was Taylor's biological and natural mother. This judgment also provided that F and M would have joint legal and joint physical custody and that neither party could change Taylor's residence to a location outside the State of California without the express written permission of the other party or, alternatively, by order of the court.

Thereafter, the TC granted M's relocation request and that significantly reduced F's physical custody time. F appealed the modification order, asserting that the TC applied the wrong standard in deciding M's modification petition. The Court of Appeal affirmed the TC's decision, finding no abuse of discretion.

When parents have joint physical custody:

[1] modification of coparenting arrangements does not require change of circumstances;
[2] **the joint custody moving parent does not have the presumptive right to change the child's residence** and bears no burden of proving the move is essential or imperative;
[3] the opposing, nonmoving parent bears no burden of showing substantial changed circumstances requiring a change in custody or that the move will be detrimental to the child.

CHART 8: Moveaway Cases by Holding(s)

Subject	Case & Cite	Trial Ct Permit Move?	Affirmed or Reversed	Holding(s) of the Court
Factors courts must consider before granting a moveaway request	*IRMO LaMusga* (2004) 32 Cal.4th 1072		Reversed Affirmed	NCP has the burden of showing that the planned move will cause detriment to the child in order for the court to reevaluate an existing custody order. If the NCP makes an initial showing of detriment, the court must perform the delicate and difficult task of determining whether a change in custody is in the best interests of the children considering the following: (1) children's interest in stability and continuity in the custodial arrangement; (2) distance of the move; (3) age of the children; (4) children's relationship with both parents; (5) relationship between the parents including, but not limited to, their ability to communicate and cooperate effectively and their willingness to put the interests of the children above their individual interests; (6) wishes of the children if they are mature enough for such an inquiry to be appropriate; the reasons for the proposed move; & (7) extent to which the parents currently are sharing custody.lw
	Jane J. v. Superior Ct. (2015) 237 Cal.App.4th 894; CtAD4(3)	YES	Reversed	When granting moveaway, court MUST consider *LaMusga* AND (1) community ties; (2) health and educational needs; (3) anticipated impact of the move upon the children's

				existing social, educational and familial relationships; and (4) Each parent's willingness to facilitate frequent, meaningful and continuing contact to the other parent.
	IRMO Winternitz (2015) 235 Cal.App.4th 644; CtAD4(1)	NO	Affirmed	TC did not err by: (1) focusing on child's relationship with NCP; (2) by emphasizing the respective attitude of each parent regarding visitation with the other parent; & (3) by not expressly referring to *LaMusga* factors and CP's presumptive right to move.
Detriment to the children must be considered	*Osgood V. Landon* (2005) 127 Cal.App.4th 425; CtAD3	YES	Affirmed	TC properly required F to establish that M's move would cause detriment to Daniel; F failed to establish such detriment; & substantial evidence supports TC..
	IRMO Melville (2004) 122 Cal.App.4th 601; CtAD1(4)		Affirmed	The TC determination that relocating to another state would cause detriment to the child was supported by substantial evidence.
	IRMO Carlson (1991) 229 Cal.App.3d 1330; CtA D5	NO	Affirmed	No abuse of discretion because NCP does not have affirmative burden to prove move would be detrimental to children to obtain restraining order preventing move.
Best interests test is used when there is no final order	*Montenegro v. Diaz* (2001) 26 Cal.4th 249		TC Reversed by CtA CtA Reversed	Finding that there was no final custody order, the TC correctly determined custody by using the best interests test. When there is a final custody order, a party seeking to modify that custody order can do so only if he or she demonstrates a substantial change of circumstances justifying a modification.
	Jacob A. v. C. (2011) 196 Cal.App.4th 1591	NO	Reversed	TC erred when it ordered joint legal and physical custody to the parents denying M's request to relocate to Washington with the parties' minor child and to modify the parenting schedule accordingly.

Chapter 15: Moveaways or Relocations

Best interests test is used when there is no final order con't				The TC's order in effect prevented M from relocating. TC was required to decide de novo what physical custody arrangement would be in the child's best interests, assuming the mother would be living in Washington, not assuming that mother would not move if the right court order was prohibitive enough to prevent the move.
	Mark T. v. Jamie Z. (2011) 194 Cal.App.4th 1115; CtAD4(1)	NO	Reversed	TC erred in applying wrong legal standard when it denied M's request to move to another state. TC must decide de novo custody arrangement that is in child's best interests, assuming mother would move, not assuming no move if TC ordered change in custody. TC must consider, among other factors, effects of relocation on best interests of minor children and effects of relocation on best interests of the minor children.
	F.T. v. L.J. (2011) 194 Cal.App.4th 1	NO	Reversed	TC applied incorrect legal standards: (1) in failing to determine custody arrangement that would be in child's best interests if F moved; (2) in making an order that coerced F to abandon his plan to move; (3) in considering whether F's reasons for proposed move were "sufficient" or "necessary"; & (4) in placing an undue focus on detriment to the child's relationship with the mother.
	Ragghanti v. Reyes (2004) 123 Cal.App.4th 989; CtAD6		Affirmed	TC was correct in applying best interests standard & in considering all pertinent circumstances because there was no existing final custody order. A finding of detriment was not necessary.

Chapter 15: Moveaways or Relocations

	IRMO Bryant (2001) 91 Cal.App.4th 789; CtAD2(6)		Affirmed	TC did not abuse its discretion because there was no bad faith and the best interests of the children were considered. A parent proposing moveaway is not required to establish need or justification for relocating to another geographic area; the only exception is where the reason for move is to frustrate NCP's relationship with child.
	IRMO Edlund & Hales (1998) 66 Cal.App.4th 1454; CtAD1(3)		Affirmed	TC did not abuse its discretion because it carefully considered all the factors bearing on the child's best interests.
	Cassady v. Signorelli (1996) 49 Cal.App.4th 55; CtAD1(5)		Affirmed	TC properly exercised its discretion by its consideration of the best interests of the child in not allowing M to move to Florida.
A substantial change of circumstances are required if there is a final order	*Montenegro v. Diaz* (2001) 26 Cal.4th 249			If there is a final order RE: custody, a modification of a custody order requires a substantial change in circumstances.
	Keith R. v. Superior Ct. (2009) 174 Cal.App.4th 1047; CtAD4(3)	NO	Reversed	TC erred in applying the changed-circumstances standard because there had been no final judicial custody determination. A DV order is not a final judicial custody determination.
	Enrique M. V. Angelina V. (2004) 121 Cal.App.4th 1371; CtAD4(1)		Reversed	TC erred in applying the changed-circumstances standard instead of the best interests test when F was requesting change in parenting time not in custody.
	IRMO Ciganovich (1976) 61 Cal.App.3d 289; CtAD3		Reversed	When there is frustration of visitation, no change of circumstances is necessary for a modification of custody.
Presumptive right to move is a right of the custodial parent	*IRMO Burgess* (1996) 13 Cal.4th 25	YES / CtA NO	TC Reversed By CtA / CtA Reversed by SupCt	M did not prove move was necessary. CP seeking to relocate does not have to prove the relocation is a necessity in initial custody determination. Parent entitled to custody has a presumptive right to change residence of child, subject to power of court

Chapter 15: Moveaways or Relocations

				to restrain move if would prejudice rights or welfare of the child, FC § 7501.
	IRMO Abargil (2003) 106 Cal.App.4th 1294; CtAD2(8)		**Affirmed**	CP has presumptive right to move and take child with him or her. NCP has burden of proving CP's decision to move was not in child's best interests.
Evidentiary hearing is not always necessary before a moveaway	*IRMO Brown & Yana* (2006) 37 Cal.4th 947		**Affirmed**	If TC in a moveaway case diligently considers the NCP's claims, evidence, & offers of proof but properly finds them insufficient to establish the detriment required for custody modification, then it is not abuse of discretion to deny a custody modification without holding an evidentiary hearing with live testimony. TC has wide discretion to deny evidentiary hearing in a moveaway case.
	Andrew V. v. Superior Ct. (2015) 234 Cal.App.4th 103; CtAD4(3)		**Reversed TC Order vacated**	TC order vacated; Writ issued. F was entitled to meaningful hearing before any judicial determination regarding an out-of-state moveaway request for parents who share legal and physical custody.
	IRMO Seagondollar (2006) 139 Cal.App.4th 1116; CtAD4(3)	**YES**	**Reversed**	TC denied F fair hearing when it modified a shared custody arrangement giving M permission to move when M did not request affirmative relief before custody evaluation & the purpose of the evaluation was not set forth. TC should have granted a continuance.
	IRMO Campos (2003) 108 Cal.App.4th 839; CtAD2(6)		**Reversed**	Although TC properly considered whether M had bad faith reason for move, TC erred in failing to hold an evidentiary hearing on whether move would cause detriment to children. TC has duty to consider all relevant issues in a moveaway case.
Superior economic position	*Burchard v. Garay* (1986) 42 Cal.3d 531	N/A	**Reversed**	TC's "reliance upon the relative economic position of the parties" was impermissible.

Chapter 15: Moveaways or Relocations

cannot be used to determine custody issues				The changed circumstance rule applies whenever final custody has been established by judicial decree.
	IRMO Fingert (1990) 221 Cal.App.3d 1575; CtA D2(6)	N/A	Reversed	TC based its custody decision on F's superior economic position. It is impermissible the make a custody award on this basis.
No denial of custody because of a handicap	*IRMO Carney* (1979) 24 Cal.3d 725	YES	Reversed	TC improperly ruled that F could not be awarded custody because his physical handicap was prima facie evidence that he was unfit and a detriment to the children.
Cannot separate siblings unless compelling reason	*IRMO Williams* (2001) 88 Cal.App.4th 808; CtAD2(6)		Reversed	TC abused its discretion in separating siblings. The separation of siblings is disfavored and should be done only under the most compelling circumstances.
Mediation is necessary before allowing a moveaway	*IRMO McGinnis* (1992) 7 Cal.App.4th 473; CtA D2(6)	YES	Reversed	Mediation is mandatory in a **moveaway** case.
Sufficient enforcement measures may be needed to enforce court orders	*J.M. v. G.H.* (2014) 228 Cal.App.4th 925; CtAD2(1)	YES	Affirmed	TC's determination that it was in the child's best interests to reside primarily with M abroad because the child had a closer bond with M was based on sufficient evidence. TC order contained adequate protective measures that guaranteed the enforceability of the CA custody order.
	IRMO Condon (1998) 62 Cal.App.4th 533; CtAD2(7)		Affirmed And Reversed	TC did not abuse its discretion in ruling that it was in the children's best interests that they be permitted to move with M to Australia. Reversed and remanded to incorporate M's concession of continuing jurisdiction in the California courts and appropriate sanctions to enforce the custody and visitation order.
Preferences of the	*IRMO Rosson* (1986)	NO	Affirmed	TC properly considered the preferences of the children and

Chapter 15: Moveaways or Relocations

children must be considered	178 Cal.App.3d 1094; CtA D1(5)			the fact that the parents shared physical custody of the children when changing a custody order.
Joint custody rules	*Niko V. Foreman* (2006) 144 Cal.App.4th 344; CtAD4(3)		Affirmed	When parents have joint physical custody, modification of coparenting arrangements does not require a change of circumstances; there is no presumptive right to change the child's residence and no burden of proving the move is essential or imperative. The nonmoving parent bears no burden to show substantial changed circumstances requiring a change in custody or that the move will be detrimental to the child. TC court has wide discretion in determining whether a child can testify as a witness regarding his or her preference as to custody. TC can require NCP to show detriment and can issue a conditional order so that custody/visitation order can be enforced.

© LW Greenberg 2019

EDUCATIONAL EXERCISES

I.   Using the following summaries about the some of the cases in this chapter, name the case that it described.

1. TC awarded the parties joint legal custody of the children, with M having primary physical custody.
M filed an order to show cause to modify the visitation order to permit her to relocate with the children to Cleveland, Ohio. She alleged that she had family in the Cleveland area and her husband had received an offer for a more lucrative job there. F objected to M's plan to relocate with the children to Ohio. The TC court held that if M moved F would be awarded custody, at least during the school year. M appealed, and the Court of Appeal reversed the judgment. The Supreme Court granted a review reversing the Court of Appeal's decision and remanding with directions to affirm the judgment of the trial court. **Name that case**

2. M and F are the parents of two boys. The couple separated and divorced. M and F agreed to a marital settlement, which was approved by a Wisconsin family court commissioner. The parents agreed to joint legal custody, but because of the family's "unique" situation, M was given 92% primary physical custody, with F having 8% physical custody. Then M and the children moved from Wisconsin to Orange County, where M was living with her fiancé with the Wisconsin court's approval. In December 2013 F returned to the United States where he relocated with his new wife in Alabama. F filed a request for order (*RFO*) to modify the Wisconsin custody order, either to increase visitation, or to give him primary physical custody over the boys. He also sought to modify the support amounts. M opposed F's *RFO*. Respondent court stated that it was time [F] had an opportunity to parent the children and changed custody to F. The Appellate Court reversed the trial Court's decision. **Name that case**

3. The parents married in 1985. F is an orthopedic surgeon. The couple had three children. Their marriage was dissolved in 2004. The TC thereafter allowed M to relocate with the children to San Diego. The order provided that custody would be modifiable on the children's best interests without showing a change in circumstance. After M moved to San Diego with the children, F relocated to San Diego and established an orthopedic surgery practice there. Subsequent to her move to San Diego, M filed a moveaway request seeking an order to move with one son (S) with her to Chico in northern California, where she had purchased a home. In turn, F moved to modify custody and visitation, seeking physical custody of (S). The TC denied M's move-away request and changed primary custody of (S) to F. M appealed the denial of her move-away request, claiming that the TC court did not apply the correct legal standard in assessing her relocation request. Court of Appeal rejected M's claims. **Name that case**

4. F and M never married. They had a son (S) M lived with her mother, and F had short visitations for the first 18 months. F filed a complaint and order to show cause

Chapter 15: Moveaways or Relocations

to establish paternity and requested joint legal and physical custody. M conceded paternity but sought sole physical custody of S. The TC court's order was that M had primary responsibility for the care, custody and control of the minor. There were several disputes concerning custody. Many OSCs were filed. The parties could not agree on S's impending enrollment in kindergarten and the choice of his school. The order of the TC was that because F was more willing to share S, he was awarded physical custody with M having visitation on alternate weekends. The Court of Appeal reversed. The court held that the TC should have applied the changed circumstance rule, rather than the best interests standard, because the stipulations that the parties had made were final agreements. The Court of Appeal found that there was no evidence of a significant change of circumstances and that application of the changed circumstance rule likely would have yielded a different result. The Supreme Court then granted review and reversed the Court of Appeal's decision. **Name that case**

5. A dating relationship between M and F produced a child. F filed a petition to establish his paternity. The court entered an order establishing F's paternity and entered a temporary custody order based on the time-sharing agreement that the parties had reached. Before the court entered a permanent custody order, M filed an order to show cause (OSC) requesting that the court permit her to relocate with the child to Minnesota. The TC denied M's moveaway request and issued an order establishing a legal and physical custody sharing arrangement. M appealed. In reversing the trial's court decision, the appellate court stated that the trial court misunderstood that it was required to proceed on the assumption that the parent will in fact be moving and fashion a custody and visitation order that is in the best interests of the child based upon the move. Since the trial court failed to assume that M would be moving, it abused its discretion. **Name that case**

6. F and M married and had two children. Both parents were employed by the State Department of Corrections at the state prison in Tehachapi. They separated when the children were three and four years old. M petitioned for dissolution shortly thereafter. The TC entered a Stipulation and Order dissolving the marriage and providing for temporary custody and visitation in accordance with a mediation agreement reached between the parties. The parents agreed that they would share joint legal custody of the children with M having sole physical custody of the children. Thereafter, M requested permission to move to Lancaster, where she had accepted a job transfer. Living in Lancaster would permit greater access for the children to medical care, extracurricular activities, private schools and daycare facilities. The travel time between Lancaster and her home in Tehachapi was approximately 40 minutes. The TC issued a ruling granting M's request, providing that F and M would share joint legal custody, with M having sole physical custody. F moved for reconsideration and for a change in custody; M opposed the change. The TC denied the motion.

F appealed from both the order denying reconsideration and the order denying change in custody; the appeals were consolidated, and the Court of Appeal reversed. The Court of Appeal concluded that **no showing of necessity was made**. It reversed

Chapter 15: Moveaways or Relocations

the orders of the TC and remanded for further proceedings consistent with the opinion. The Supreme Court granted review and reversed the judgment of the Court of Appeal. **Name that case**

7. M and F dissolved their marriage in 1994, and in 1999, after a psychological evaluation, M was awarded sole legal custody and sole physical custody of their son, (S). In June of 2003, M informed F that she was moving with S to Las Vegas, Nevada, at the end of the summer. On June 27, 2003, F filed an order to show cause to restrain any change of residence for Cameron and to request a psychological evaluation and a contested evidentiary hearing on the moveaway issue. At the hearing, TC denied F's requests for relief, stating that an evidentiary hearing and psychological examinations had occurred in 1999, which resulted in an award of sole legal and physical custody of Cameron to M. And that given that judicial custody order, F was required to assert some detriment to warrant an evidentiary hearing. F appealed. The Court of Appeal reversed in a split decision, holding that, in a moveaway case, a parent with no legal or physical custody rights is entitled to an evidentiary hearing. The Supreme Court granted M's petition for review and affirmed the TC's holding that an evidentiary hearing may not be absolutely necessary before a moveaway. **Name that case**

8. M and F married in 2003. They had two children. M filed a moveaway request that would allow her to relocate with the two children to the State of Washington, due to a job transfer and promotion. The parties stipulated for a full custody investigation. The investigation report was finished on December 22, 2014, and the court set a hearing for January 14, 2015. The child custody investigator was not available at the January 14th hearing. F's counsel was present but ill and not able to represent F. As a result, the hearing was continued until March 4, 2015 and the TC issued a temporary order allowing M to relocate with the children to Washington. On January 20, 2015, F filed a petition for writ of mandate and a request for an immediate stay. M filed a timely *Response*. M disenrolled the children from their school and two days later moved to the State of Washington with the two children. The Court of Appeal granted F's request for a stay of Respondent court's temporary order and M was ordered to bring the children back to California forthwith. The Court of Appeal issued a writ of mandate directing respondent court to vacate its temporary order of January 14, 2015. A meaningful hearing is a critical requirement of California law before any judicial determination regarding an out-of-state, moveaway request for a parent who shares joint legal and physical custody.
Name that case

9. M became pregnant as a result of a brief liaison. When M told F that she was pregnant with his child, he refused to believe that he was the father. After the birth of (S), M cared for her child, with the help of her father and others, while working two jobs and continuing her training to become a registered nurse. F continued to deny paternity and did not visit the child or provide any support. In the spring of 1980, M brought a paternity and support action. Court-ordered blood tests established that F was the father, and he stipulated to paternity and to support. A judgment of paternity was entered on November 24, 1980. Thereafter, M and F tried

to live together as a family, but this only lasted six weeks. After M and F separated, F requested visitation rights; M refused and filed a petition for exclusive custody. F responded with his own action, seeking exclusive custody. The TC after hearing the evidence issued a statement of decision in which it impliedly ruled that the changed circumstances rule did not apply and since F was financially better off, had greater job stability, owned his own home and was better equipped economically to give constant care to the minor child and cope with his continuing needs. TC granted F custody. F took custody and M appealed from the order and sought a writ of supersedeas. The Court of Appeal, however, denied supersedeas and subsequently affirmed the TC's order. The Supreme Court granted a hearing in August 1984. In reversing the TC's order, the Supreme Court concluded that although the TC had applied the correct standard, the best interests test, it had erred in applying that standard. **Name that case**

10. F and M dissolved their marriage that produced four children. They shared custody. M remarried and moved to Utah with her new spouse. TC ordered two of the children to move with M and two to stay with F. Both parents appealed, asserting that the TC abused its discretion. The Court of Appeal reversed, holding that the separation of siblings requires compelling circumstances warranting the separation of the siblings. **NAME THAT CASE**

II. **Answer/perform the following:**

1. What is a moveaway action? Describe a situation where a moveaway action would be filed.
2. What are the elements set forth in the LaMusga case with regard to moveaways?
3. Briefly summarize the Burgess case and the LaMusga case.

CHAPTER 16: Child Support

In Brief...

PARENTAL DUTIES/RESPONSIBILITIES INCLUDE:
- An equal responsibility to support their child, **FC § 3900**;
- Providing **health insurance** for their children, **FC § 3760(b)**; and
- Paying child support continues as to an unmarried child who has attained 18 years of age, is a full-time high school student unless the child has a medical condition documented by a physician, and who is not self-supporting until the child completes the 12th grade or attains 19 years of age, whichever occurs first. **FC § 3901(a)(1)**.

THE AMOUNT OF CHILD SUPPORT:
- Is determined by the parents' income and time-share (the time that the parent spends with the child);
- Is determined by the state guideline formula, **FC § 4055**;
- Established by the formula is presumed to be the correct amount, **FC § 4057(a)**;
- Is determined by using the income and timeshare of the parents;
- Is calculated by using computer software, **FC § 3830(a)**;
- May include a hardship deduction; this is a discretionary decision, **FC § 4071(a)**; and
- Must include the following add-ons:
- The reasonable uninsured health care costs for the children, **FC § 4063**, and
- Child care costs related to employment or education for employment, **FC § 4062(a)**;

CHILD SUPPORT ORDERS:
- MUST adhere to the statewide uniform guideline and can deviate from the guideline only for good cause, **FC § 4052, CRC Rule 5.260(b)**;
- Require that the payment of child support ordered by the court be made before the payment of any debts the paying parent owes to creditors, **FC § 4011**;
- Must include an *Income Withholding for Support* (form *FL-195*), (also called a **wage assignment**);
- May be made retroactive to the date of filing of the *Petition* if the request is made during the dissolution or legal separation action, **FC § 4009**;
- May be made retroactive back to the date of filing of the request, if the request is made postjudgment; **FC § 3653(a)**:
- May include **arrearages** (the amount of support ordered but not paid), **FC § 4503**; and
- May include **a deferred sale of the home order** (DUKE ORDER) that delays the sale of the home until the youngest child reaches the 18 years old, **FC §§ 3800-3809**.

MODIFICATION/TERMINATION OF CHILD SUPPORT ORDERS, **FC § 3651(a)**:
- May be made any time the court determines; and

Chapter 16: Child Support

> - Continues until terminated by court or by operation of law.
>
> ***CHILD SUPPORT AGREEMENTS:***
> - That are stipulated to must include:
>   - They are fully informed of their rights concerning child support;
>   - The order is being agreed to without coercion or duress;
>   - The agreement is in the best interests of the children involved;
>   - The needs of the children will be adequately met by the stipulated amount; and
>   - The right to support has not been assigned to the county pursuant to **Welfare and Institutions Code § 11477** and no public assistance application is pending. **FC § 4065(a)**.
> - May include an enforceable obligation to pay college expenses in an *MSA*, which is considered support for an adult. *Marriage of Rosenfeld & Gross* (2014) 255 Cal.App.4th 478.
>
> ***EXPEDITED CHILD SUPPORT*** may be necessary in some cases. **FC § 3623**.

Introduction

In almost all cases where there are children, the court orders that child support be paid to the custodial parent (CP). Parents have a duty to support their children, and this duty is a serious legal obligation. **FC § 4250**. There is a statutory guideline for the determination of the amount of child support, and there are several important principles relating to child support determinations, such as:

> **(1)** the interests of the child are the state's top priority;
> **(2)** a parent's principal obligation is to support his or her children according to the parent's circumstances and station in life;
> **(3)** both parents are mutually responsible for the support of their children;
> **(4)** each parent should pay for the support of the children according to his or her ability;
> **(5)** children should share in both parents' standard of living; and
> **(6)** in cases where both parents have high levels of responsibility for the children, child support orders should reflect the increased costs of raising the children in two homes and should minimize significant disparities in the children's living standards in the two homes. *In re Marriage of SCHLAFLY* (2007) 149 Cal.App.4th 747 at p. 754.

The state guide formula must be used to determine the amount of child support to be paid, unless the "application of the formula would be unjust or inappropriate." **FC § 4055(b)(7)**. The data necessary to utilize the formula is: **(1)** the income of the parents and **(2)** the amount of time that each parent spends with the children, which is called **timeshare**.

Calculating the amount of child support can be challenging in certain cases, such as where one or both of the parents is self-employed. When a parent is self-employed, that parent must submit a **Profit and Loss** statement.[1] On a profit and loss

---

[1] A Profit and Loss statement is required whenever there is self-employment income. It is a requested document that must be attached to and filed with the *Income and Expense Declaration*. In all hearings

statement, the business expenses actually expended, and the proposed expenses should be set forth. However, business expenses can include expenses that may be valid for the business, but not valid to reduce the amount of income that is available to pay child support. Further, some parents may not be as honest as they should be when declaring their income and preparing a profit and loss statement. Accordingly, calculating the amount of parents' income may require considerable time and effort.

Calculating the amount of child support also requires the timeshare of the parents. The parents may, and often do, disagree as to the timeshare. If the parents disagree, the timeshare amount must be calculated.

Parental Duties/Responsibilities

In almost all cases, the noncustodial parent (NCP) will pay the child support for the minor children to the CP. The NCP is then the payor or obligor; the CP, or the person that receives the support for the minor child is called the payee or obligee. **FC § 3550**.

1. Duties

Parents are legally obligated to contribute to the support and care of their child until that child reaches his or her majority. The parents of a minor child have an equal responsibility to support their child in the manner suitable to the child's circumstances. **FC § 3900**. This equal responsibility does not mean that the parents are obligated to pay the same amount of child support. It is the responsibility that is equal, not the amount of the child support.

The parents' duty of support imposed by **FC § 3900** continues for an unmarried child who has attained 18 years of age, is a full-time high school student unless excused due to a documented medical condition, and who is not self-supporting until the time the child completes the 12th grade or reaches 19 years of age, whichever occurs first. **FC § 3901(a)(1)**.

If a parent has the duty to provide for the support of his or her child and willfully fails to so provide, the other parent, or the child by guardian ad litem[2], may bring an action against the parent to enforce the duty. **FC § 4000**.

2. Health Insurance

Parents have a duty to provide health insurance for their children. Health insurance, health insurance plan, health insurance coverage, health care services, or health insurance coverage assignment includes vision and dental care coverage, whether

---

involving child support, both parties must complete, file, and serve a current *Income and Expense Declaration* (form *FL-150*) on all parties. CRC 5.260(a).
[2] A guardian ad litem is a court-appointed adult that represents a minor child or legally incompetent person.

Chapter 16: Child Support

the vision care or dental care coverage is part of existing health insurance coverage or is issued as a separate policy or plan. **FC § 3760(b)**.

In any case in which an amount is set for current child support, the court must require that health insurance coverage for a supported child be maintained by either or both parents if that insurance is available at no cost or at a reasonable cost to the parent. **FC § 3751(b)**.

All child support orders must include a provision requiring the child support obligor to keep the obligee informed of whether the obligor has health insurance made available through his or her employer or has other group health insurance and, if so, the health insurance policy information.

The support obligee under a child support order must inform the support obligor of whether the obligee has health insurance made available through his or her employer or other group health insurance and, if so, the health insurance policy information. **FC § 3752.5(a)**.

Whenever a parent accrues or pays costs on behalf of the minor child, if that parent wants to be reimbursed for his or share, that parent MUST provide the other parent with an itemized statement of the costs within thirty (30) days after accruing the costs. The parent incurring these costs must then be paid as follows:

> **(1)** If a parent has already paid all of these costs, that parent shall provide proof of payment and a request for reimbursement of his or her court-ordered share to the other parent.
> **(2)** If a parent has paid his or her court-ordered share of the costs only, that parent shall provide proof of payment to the other parent, request the other parent to pay the remainder of the costs directly to the provider, and provide the reimbursing parent with any necessary information about how to make the payment to the provider.
> **(3)** The other parent shall make the reimbursement or pay the remaining costs within the time period specified by the court, or, if no period is specified, within a reasonable time not to exceed 30 days from notification of the amount due, or according to any payment schedule set by the health care provider for either parent unless the parties agree in writing to another payment schedule or the court finds good cause for setting another payment schedule.
> **(4)** If the reimbursing parent disputes a request for payment, that parent shall pay the requested amount and thereafter may seek judicial relief under this section and Section 290. If the reimbursing parent fails to pay the other parent as required by this subdivision, the other parent may seek judicial relief under this section and Section 290.

A parent MUST utilize the health care insurance coverage, including, but not limited to, coverage for emergency treatment for the child(ren), provided by a parent pursuant to a court order at all times, consistent with the requirements of that coverage, unless the other parent can show that the health care insurance coverage is inadequate to meet the child's needs. **FC § 4063(e)(1)**.

If either parent uses a health care provider other than the preferred provider, the parent obtaining that care must bear the sole responsibility for any non-reimbursable health care costs in excess of the costs that would have been incurred under the court-ordered health care insurance coverage had the preferred provider been used. **FC § 4063(f)(2)**.

The cost of health insurance is in addition to the child support amount ordered, with allowance for the costs of health insurance actually obtained given due consideration under **FC § 4059(d)**. **FC § 3753**.

There is a rebuttable presumption that the costs actually paid for the uninsured health care needs of the children are reasonable. **FC § 4063(d)**.

An employer or insurer cannot deny enrollment of a child under the health insurance coverage of a child's parent because the child was born out of wedlock, is not claimed as a dependent on the parent's federal income tax return or does not reside with the parent or within the insurer's service area. **FC § 3751.5(a)**.

An employer or other person providing health insurance who willfully fails to comply with a valid health insurance coverage assignment order entered and served is liable to the applicant for the amount incurred in health care services that would otherwise have been covered under the insurance policy. **FC § 3768(a)**.

Additionally, the willful failure of an employer or other person providing health insurance to comply with a health insurance coverage assignment order is punishable by contempt of court. **FC § 3768(b)**.

3. Other Rules

If the custodial parent (CP) or other person having physical custody of the child, to whom payments are to be made, fails to notify the person ordered to make the payments, or the attorney of record of the person ordered to make the payments, of the happening of the contingency and continues to accept support payments, the CP or other custodial person must refund all moneys received that accrued after the happening of the contingency, except that the overpayments shall first be applied to any support payments that are then in default. **FC § 4007(b)**.

If a party who has been kept in ignorance or in some other manner, other than his or her own lack of care or attention, was fraudulently prevented from fully participating in the child support proceeding, an action or motion based on fraud must be brought within six (6) months after the date that the complaining party discovered, or reasonably should have discovered, the fraud. **FC § 3691(a)**.

Finally, a parent does not have the duty to support a child of the parent's child (grandchild). **FC § 3930**.

Chapter 16: Child Support

Determining the Amount of Child Support

1. Calculating the Parents' Income and Timeshare

If a parent has an employer, calculating his or her monthly income is not difficult; the amount that the parent earns each pay period is clearly set forth on that parent's paystub. The problems arise when the parent is self-employed and/or has decided to earn less income in an effort to pay less support. *In re Marriage of MCHUGH* (2014) 231 Cal.App.4th 1238, (*McHugh*), is such a case.

In *McHugh*, Charles McHugh (F) was fired from his job as a commissioned salesman because he was diverting business from his employer to his father's competing company to reduce his support obligations. The vice president of the company where F worked as a salesman testified that F had come to him and asked him to help him reduce his income because he faced a bitter divorce and wanted to minimize his earnings. The vice president offered to rehire F if he would fully disclose his misconduct and pay restitution for the lost business. F refused. The TC imputed income to F pursuant to **FC § 4058** based upon the money that he was earning before the divorce. The court of appeal affirmed, finding substantial evidence that supported the findings of the TC. *Id.* at 1256.

Timeshare is the time that is spent with the minor child(ren) and is usually calculated by determining the number of days in a year that the parent spends with the minor child(ren). The number of days is then divided by the number of days in the year, 365, in order to get a percentage of time. Parents can, and often do, dispute this figure. Sometimes the timeshare calculation can be determined by the number of hours that a parent spends with the child(ren) with that number divided by the number of hours in a year, which is 8,760.

The timeshare information can be ascertained if the parent kept a record of the number of days or hours that the child(ren) were with him or her.

The income of a parent's subsequent spouse may only be considered in the "extraordinary case" where excluding that income would lead to extreme and severe hardship to any child subject to the child support award. **FC § 4057.5**.

2. The State Guideline Child Support Formula

"In adopting the statewide uniform guideline provided in this article, it is the intention of the Legislature to ensure that this state remains in compliance with federal regulations for child support guidelines." **FC § 4050**.

FC § 4055 sets forth the formula to determine the amount of child support that the noncustodial parent (NCP) must pay to the custodial parent (CP) for the support of their children.

Chapter 16: Child Support

The formula is: CS = K[HN - (H%)(TN)].
CS = child support amount.
K = amount of both parents' income to be allocated for child support as set forth in paragraph (3).
HN = high earner's net monthly disposable income.
H% = approximate percentage of time that the high earner has or will have primary physical responsibility for the children compared to the other parent. In cases in which parents have different time-sharing arrangements for different children, H% equals the average of the approximate percentages of time the high-earner parent spends with each child.
TN = total net monthly disposable income of both parties.

In determining **K**, the amount of both parents' income to be allocated for child support:
K = 1 + H% (if H% is less than or equal to 50%) or 2 - H% (if H% is greater than 50%) times the following fraction:

1.6 if there are 2 children
2 if there are 3 children
2.3 if there are 4 children
2.5 if there are 5 children
2.625 if there are 6 children
2.75 if there are 7 children
2.813 if there are 8 children
2.844 if there are 9 children
2.86 if there are 10 children

If the amount calculated under the formula results in a positive number, the higher earner pays that amount to the lower earner. If the amount calculated under the formula results in a negative number, the lower earner pays the absolute value[3] of that amount to the higher earner. **FC § 4055(b)(5).**

Note that in any default proceeding where the proof is presented by declaration pursuant to **FC § 2336** or in any child support proceeding where a party failed to appear after being appropriately and timely noticed:

> H% shall be set at zero in the formula if the noncustodial parent is the higher earner or at 100 if the custodial parent is the higher earner, where there is no evidence presented demonstrating the percentage of time that the noncustodial parent has primary physical responsibility for the children. H% shall not be set as described above if the moving party in a default proceeding is the noncustodial parent or if the party who fails to appear after being duly noticed is the custodial parent. A statement by the party who is not in default as to the percentage of time that the noncustodial parent has primary physical responsibility for the children shall be deemed sufficient evidence. FC § 4055(b)(6).

---

[3] The absolute value of a number is the distance that the number is from zero on the number line. So if a number is
|-6|, then it is 6 away from 0, so the absolute value of -6 is 6.

Chapter 16: Child Support

In cases where the net disposable income per month of the obligor is less than one thousand five hundred dollars ($1,500), adjusted annually for cost-of-living increases, there is a rebuttable presumption that the obligor is entitled to a low-income adjustment. **FC § 4055(b)(7)**. This amount will be amended to one thousand dollars ($1,000) effective January 1, 2018. (See footnote 5 below.)

In calculating the amount of child support to be paid, the annual gross income of each parent means income from whatever source derived. The word **income** encompasses:

1. commissions,
2. salaries,
3. royalties,
4. wages,
5. bonuses,
6. rents,
7. dividends,
8. pensions,
9. interest,
10. trust income,
11. annuities,
12. workers' compensation benefits,
13. unemployment insurance benefits,
14. disability insurance benefits,
15. social security benefits, and
16. spousal support received from a person who is not a party to the proceeding. **FC § 4058(a)**.

The annual gross income does not include any income from child support payments that were actually received or income from any public assistance program where the eligibility is based on a determination of need. Child support received by a party for children from another relationship will not be included as part of that party's gross or net income. **FC § 4058**.[4]

Only income and timeshare are used to calculate the amount of child support to be paid except in an extraordinary case where excluding that income would lead to extreme and severe hardship to any child that is the subject of a child support award. In the extraordinary case, the court must also consider whether including that income would lead to an extreme and severe hardship to any child supported by the obligor or by the obligor's subsequent spouse or nonmarital partner. **FC § 4057.5**.

An **extraordinary case** could be where a parent voluntarily or intentionally quits working or reduces his or her income, or who intentionally becomes or remains

---

[4] FC § 4058 was amended effective January 1, 2019. The following language was added to 4058(b): "taking into consideration the overall welfare and developmental needs of the children, and the time that parent spends with the children."

unemployed or underemployed and relies on a subsequent spouse's income. **FC § 4057.5**.

If a parent is unemployed or underemployed, the court can consider the earning capacity[5] of a parent in lieu of the parent's income, consistent with the best interests of the children. **FC § 4058(c)**.

The California State Legislature enacted **FC § 4055** (the guideline child support formula) in 1993 to become operative in 1994, when the Family Code became effective. After its enactment, **FC § 4055** was amended in 1994, 1998, 2003, 2012 and again in 2013. In 2013, the legislature enacted another version of this code section to become effective January 1, 2018, repealing the current code section as of that date. The differences between the currently effective code section and the one that will become operative on January 1, 2018 affects only one section, **FC § 4055(b)(7)**, in both the current and future code sections.[6]

---

[5] Earning capacity is composed of: (1) the ability to work, including such factors as age, occupation, skills, education, health, background, work experience and qualifications; (2) the willingness to work exemplified through good faith efforts, due diligence and meaningful attempts to secure employment; and (3) an opportunity to work, which means an employer who is willing to hire. *In re Marriage of Regnery* (1989) 214 Cal.App.3d 1367 at p. 1372. The opportunity to work exists when there is substantial evidence of a reasonable likelihood that a party could, with reasonable effort, apply his or her education, skills and training to produce income. The statewide uniform guideline for determining child support permits the court, in lieu of using actual income, to impute income to a parent based on his/her earning capacity. *In re Marriage of Smith* (2001) 90 Cal.App.4th 74 at p. 77.

[6] **This section is repealed effective January 1, 2018.**
(7) In all cases in which the net disposable income per month of the obligor is less than one thousand five hundred dollars ($1,500), adjusted annually for cost-of-living increases, there shall be a rebuttable presumption that the obligor is entitled to a low-income adjustment. On March 1, 2013, and annually thereafter, the Judicial Council shall determine the amount of the net disposable income adjustment based on the change in the annual California Consumer Price Index for All Urban Consumers, published by the California Department of Industrial Relations, Division of Labor Statistics and Research. The presumption may be rebutted by evidence showing that the application of the low-income adjustment would be unjust and inappropriate in the particular case. In determining whether the presumption is rebutted, the court shall consider the principles provided in Section 4053, and the impact of the contemplated adjustment on the respective net incomes of the obligor and the obligee. The low-income adjustment shall reduce the child support amount otherwise determined under this section by an amount that is no greater than the amount calculated by multiplying the child support amount otherwise determined under this section by a fraction, the numerator of which is 1,500 minus the obligor's net disposable income per month, and the denominator of which is 1,500.
This section is operative as of January 1, 2018.
(7) In all cases in which the net disposable income per month of the obligor is less than one thousand dollars ($1,000), there shall be a rebuttable presumption that the obligor is entitled to a low-income adjustment. The presumption may be rebutted by evidence showing that the application of the low-income adjustment would be unjust and inappropriate in the particular case. In determining whether the presumption is rebutted, the court shall consider the principles provided in Section 4053, and the impact of the contemplated adjustment on the respective net incomes of the obligor and the obligee. The low-income adjustment shall reduce the child support amount otherwise determined under this section by an amount that is no greater than the amount calculated by multiplying the child support amount otherwise determined under this section by a fraction, the numerator of which is 1,000 minus the obligor's net disposable income per month, and the denominator of which is 1,000.

Chapter 16: Child Support

3. Presumptions RE: The Child Support Guideline Formula

The amount of child support established by the formula provided in **FC § 4055(a)** is presumed to be the correct amount of child support to be ordered. **FC § 4057(a)**. However, this presumption is a rebuttable presumption that affects the burden of proof; it

> may be rebutted by admissible evidence showing that application of the formula would be unjust or inappropriate in the particular case, consistent with the principles set forth in Section 4053, because one or more of the following factors is found to be applicable by a preponderance of the evidence, and the court states in writing or on the record the information required in subdivision (a) of Section 4056:
> **(1)** The parties have stipulated to a different amount of child support under subdivision (a) of Section 4065.
> **(2)** The sale of the family residence is deferred pursuant to Chapter 8 (commencing with Section 3800) of Part 1 and the rental value of the family residence where the children reside exceeds the mortgage payments, homeowner's insurance, and property taxes. The amount of any adjustment pursuant to this paragraph shall not be greater than the excess amount.
> **(3)** The parent being ordered to pay child support has an extraordinarily high income and the amount determined under the formula would exceed the needs of the children.
> **(4)** A party is not contributing to the needs of the children at a level commensurate with that party's custodial time.
> **(5)** Application of the formula would be unjust or inappropriate due to special circumstances in the particular case. These special circumstances include, but are not limited to, the following:
>   **(A)** Cases in which the parents have different time-sharing arrangements for different children.
>   **(B)** Cases in which both parents have substantially equal time-sharing of the children and one parent has a much lower or higher percentage of income used for housing than the other parent.
>   **(C)** Cases in which the children have special medical or other needs that could require child support that would be greater than the formula amount.
>   **(D)** Cases in which a child is found to have more than two parents.

4. Additional Child Support (Add-ons)

   a. Add-ons the Court MUST order are:
      i. Child care costs that are related to employment or to reasonably necessary education or training for employment skills and reasonable uninsured health care costs for the children. **FC § 4062(a);** and
      ii. The reasonable uninsured health care costs for the children as provided in **FC § 4063**.

   b. Add-ons the Court MAY order are:
      i. Costs related to the educational or other special needs of the children; or
      ii. Travel expenses for visitation. **FC § 4062(b)(2)**.

5. The Hardship Deduction

Hardships are: **(1)** extraordinary health expenses for which the parent is financially responsible, **(2)** uninsured catastrophic losses and **(3)** the minimum basic living expenses of natural or adopted children for whom the parent has the obligation to support from other relationships who reside with the parent. **FC § 4071(a)**.

A parent can request, and a court MAY allow, the income deductions pursuant to **FC § 4059** if that parent is experiencing an extreme financial hardship due to justifiable expenses resulting from the circumstances enumerated in **FC § 4071** above. **FC § 4070**.

If a hardship deduction is awarded to a parent, basic expenses for each child who resides with the parent will be deducted from that parent's income up to the amount of support allocated for each child subject to the order. **FC § 4071(c)**.

If a deduction for hardship expenses is allowed, the court must: **(1)** state the reasons supporting the deduction in writing or on the record and **(2)** document the amount of the deduction and the underlying facts and circumstances. **FC § 4072(a)**.

Hardship deductions are completely within the discretion of the court. The hardship deduction request is made on page 4, number 19 of the *Income and Expense Declaration, FL-150*. The court will not grant a hardship deduction if a completed *FL-150* has not been filed with the request.

6. Computer Software to Calculate Amount of Child Support

The child support guideline formula set forth in **FC § 4055** is extremely complicated. Accordingly, in almost all cases, computer software is used.

Computer software used to assist in determining the appropriate amount of child support must conform to rules of court adopted by the Judicial Council prescribing standards for the software, ensuring that it performs in a manner consistent with the applicable statutes and rules of court for determination of child support or spousal support. **FC § 3830(a)**.

CRC Rule 5.275 sets forth the standards for the software that are used to assist in determining the amount of guideline support. **CRC Rule 5.275** provides that the software must accurately compute the net disposable income of each parent as follows:

> **(A)** Permit entry of the "gross income" of each parent as defined by FC § 4058;
> **(B)** Either accurately compute the state and federal income tax liability under FC § 4059(a) or permit the entry of a figure for this amount; this figure, in the default state of the program, must not include the tax consequences of any spousal support to be ordered;
> **(C)** Ensure that any deduction for contributions to the Federal Insurance Contributions Act or as otherwise permitted by FC § 4059(b) does not exceed the allowable amount;

Chapter 16: Child Support

> **(D)** Permit the entry of deductions authorized by FC § 4049(c) through (f); and
> **(E)** Permit the entry of deductions authorized by FC § 4059(g) (hardship) while ensuring that any deduction subject to the limitation in FC § 4071(b) does not exceed that limitation.

Child Support Orders

1. Rules RE: Child Support Court Orders

A **support order** is a child, family or spousal support order. **FC § 3650**.

Pursuant to **FC § 4053**, the courts must adhere to the following principles when implementing the child support statewide uniform guideline:

> **(a)** A parent's first and principal obligation is to support his or her minor children according to the parent's circumstances and station in life.
> **(b)** Both parents are mutually responsible for the support of their children.
> **(c)** The guideline takes into account each parent's actual income and level of responsibility for the children.
> **(d)** Each parent should pay for the support of the children according to his or her ability.
> **(e)** The guideline seeks to place the interests of children as the state's top priority.
> **(f)** Children should share in the standard of living of both parents. Child support may therefore appropriately improve the standard of living of the custodial household to improve the lives of the children.
> **(g)** Child support orders in cases in which both parents have high levels of responsibility for the children should reflect the increased costs of raising the children in two homes and should minimize significant disparities in the children's living standards in the two homes.
> **(h)** The financial needs of the children should be met through private financial resources as much as possible.
> **(i)** It is presumed that a parent having primary physical responsibility for the children contributes a significant portion of available resources for the support of the children.
> **(j)** The guideline seeks to encourage fair and efficient settlements of conflicts between parents and seeks to minimize the need for litigation.
> **(k)** The guideline is intended to be presumptively correct in all cases, and only under special circumstances should child support orders fall below the child support mandated by the guideline formula.
> **(l)** Child support orders must ensure that children actually receive fair, timely, and sufficient support reflecting the state's high standard of living and high costs of raising children compared to other states.

The child support guideline formula is to be used except where the **application of the formula would be unjust or inappropriate**. A court MUST adhere to the statewide uniform guideline and can deviate from the guideline only in the special circumstances where the court finds a good cause to deviate. **FC § 4052. CRC Rule 5.260(b).**

If a court order for child support differs from the guideline amount set forth at **FC § 4055,** the court must state, in writing or on the record, the following information:

Chapter 16: Child Support

> **(a)(1)** The amount of support that would have been ordered under the guideline formula.
> (2) The reasons the amount of support ordered differs from the guideline formula amount.
> (3) The reasons the amount of support ordered is consistent with the best interests of the children.
> **(b)** At the request of any party, the court shall state in writing or on the record the following information used in determining the guideline amount under this article:
> (1) The net monthly disposable income of each parent.
> (2) The actual federal income tax filing status of each parent (for example, single, married, married filing separately, or head of household and number of exemptions).
> (3) Deductions from gross income for each parent.
> (4) The approximate percentage of time pursuant to paragraph (1) of subdivision (b) of Section 4055 that each parent has primary physical responsibility for the children compared to the other parent. FC § 4056.

During the pendency of any proceeding for a dissolution of marriage or for a legal separation, or any proceeding where there is at issue the support of a minor children for whom support is authorized, the court may order either spouse to pay any amount that is necessary for the support of the child. **FC § 3600**.

This order may, without a hearing, require a parent(s) to pay the amount required by **FC § 4055** for the support of their minor children during the pendency of that action. If the income of the obligated parent(s) is unknown, then the minimum amount of support is as provided in the **Welfare and Institutions Code § 11452**.[7]

In any proceeding where there is at issue the support of a minor child or a child for whom support is authorized under **FC § 3901** or **3910**, the court may order either or both parents to pay an amount necessary for the support of the child. **FC § 4001**.

Effective January 1, 2019, the obligation to pay child support is suspended if the child support payor is incarcerated for longer than 90 consecutive days. **FC § 4007.5**[8], which provides in pertinent part:

> (a) Every money judgment or order for support of a child shall be suspended, by operation of law, for any period exceeding 90 consecutive days in which the person

---

[7] Welfare and Institutions Code § 11452 provides in pertinent part: "(a)(1) Minimum basic standards of adequate care shall be distributed to the counties and shall be binding upon them. The standards are determined on the basis of the schedule set forth in this section, as adjusted for cost-of-living increases or decreases pursuant to Section 11453, which schedule is designed to ensure:
  (A) Safe, healthful housing.
  (B) Minimum clothing for health and decency.
  (C) Low-cost adequate food budget meeting recommended dietary allowances of the National Research Council.
  (D) Utilities.
  (E) Other items including household operation, education and incidentals, recreation, personal needs, and insurance.
  (F) Allowance for essential medical, dental, or other remedial care to the extent not otherwise provided at public expense."

[8] A similar section was effective 1/1/2011 to 7/1/2015, when it was repealed.

Chapter 16: Child Support

> ordered to pay support is incarcerated or involuntarily institutionalized, unless either of the following conditions exist:
> (1) The person owing support has the means to pay support while incarcerated or involuntarily institutionalized.
> (2) The person owing support was incarcerated or involuntarily institutionalized for an offense constituting domestic violence, as defined in Section 6211, against the supported party or supported child, or for an offense that could be enjoined by a protective order pursuant to Section 6320, or as a result of his or her failure to comply with a court order to pay child support.
> (b) The child support obligation shall resume on the first day of the first full month after the release of the person owing support in the amount previously ordered, and that amount is presumed to be appropriate under federal and state law. This section does not preclude a person owing support from seeking a modification of the child support order pursuant to Section 3651, based on a change in circumstances or other appropriate reason.

When making a child support order, the court must advise each parent, in writing or on the record, of his or her rights and liabilities, including financial responsibilities, and include in the order the time period for a parent to reimburse the other parent for the reimbursing parent's share of the reasonable additional child support costs. **FC § 4063(a)**.

In a proceeding for child support the court must consider the health insurance coverage, if any, of the parties to the proceeding. **FC § 4006**.

Upon a showing of good cause, the court may order a parent that has been required to make a payment of child support to give reasonable security for the payment. **FC § 4012**.

At the request of either party, the court must make appropriate findings with respect to the circumstances on which the order for support of a child is based. **FC § 4005**.

> In any case in which the support of a child is at issue, the court may, upon a showing of good cause, order a separate trial on that issue. The separate trial shall be given preference over other civil cases, except matters to which special precedence may be given by law, for assigning a trial date. If the court has also ordered a separate trial on the issue of custody pursuant to Section 3023, the two issues shall be tried together. FC § 4003.

The court may adjust the child support order to accommodate seasonal or fluctuating income of either parent, as it deems appropriate. **FC § 4064**.

The payment of child support ordered by the court must be made before the payment of any debts the paying parent owes to creditors. **FC § 4011**.

Either parent may file a noticed motion to enforce an order issued to reimburse costs accrued on behalf of the minor child. The court has the discretion to award filing costs and reasonable attorney fees if it finds that either party acted without reasonable cause regarding his or her obligations. **FC § 4063(c)**.

Chapter 16: Child Support

The statewide uniform guideline, as required by federal regulations, also applies in any case in which a child has more than two parents. The court must apply the guideline by dividing child support obligations among the parents based on income and amount of time spent with the child by each parent, pursuant to **FC § 4053**. **FC § 4052.5(a)**.

It is important to note that even if the CP refuses to allow the court ordered visitation, the NCP still MUST pay the support ordered. FC § 3556.

If the parents have reconciled and are living together, the support order is not enforceable during the time that they are living together, unless the order specifies otherwise. **FC § 3602**.

Finally, when the court orders a party to pay an amount for support or orders a modification of the amount of support to be paid, the court must include in its order an *INCOME WITHHOLDING FOR SUPPORT*, form *FL-195*. (See Chapter 32 RE: Enforcement, *infra*.)

2. Garnishment: Income Withholding for Support

When the court orders a party to pay child support, the court MUST include in its order an earnings assignment order, known as an ***Income Withholding for Support*** (IWO) or **wage assignment**.

An **IWO** IS A COURT ORDER for the payment of child support that orders the employer[9] of the obligor[10] to pay to the obligee[11] (the person to whom the support was ordered to be paid) that portion of the obligor's earnings due or to become due in the future, as will be sufficient to pay an amount to cover the monthly amount ordered by the court for support or arrearages.[12] **FC § 5230**.
(See Chapter 32 RE: Enforcement, *infra*.)

3. Retroactivity of Child Support Orders

> An original order for child support may be made retroactive to the date of filing the petition, complaint, or other initial pleading. If the parent ordered to pay support was not served with the petition, complaint, or other initial pleading within 90 days after filing and the court finds that the parent was not intentionally evading service, the child support order shall be effective no earlier than the date of service. FC § 4009.

---

[9] Pursuant to FC § 5210 an "Employer" includes all of the following:
"(a) A person for whom an individual performs services as an employee, as defined in CCP § 706.011.;
(b) The United States government and any public entity as defined in Government Code § 811.2.;
(c) Any person or entity paying earnings as defined under FC § 5206."
[10] "Obligor" is the person or employee who owes the support. FC § 5216.
[11] "Obligee" or "assigned obligee" means the person to whom support has been ordered to be paid, the local child support agency or another person designated by the court to receive the payment. FC § 5214.
[12] Arrearages are discussed in the next section. lg

Chapter 16: Child Support

If the request for child support is not the initial request, any order modifying or terminating a support order may be made retroactive to the date of the filing of the *Request for Order* (*RFO*) to modify or terminate, or to any subsequent date. **FC § 3653(a)**.

4. Arrearages

When a person who has been court-ordered to pay child support gets behind in his or her payments, the amount of money owed but not paid on time is called **arrearages**. **FC § 5201** defines **arrearages** as the amount necessary to satisfy a support judgment or order pursuant to **CCP § 695.210**.[13] Pursuant to **FC § 4503**[14] there is no statute of limitations on child support arrearages.

However, this does not mean that the court will always order that arrearages be paid. The request must be a reasonable one, as shown by the case below.

> *In re Marriage of VLADIXA and JOHN M. BOSWELL. VLADIXA BOSWELL, Appellant, v. JOHN M. BOSWELL, Respondent.*
> COURT OF APPEAL OF CALIFORNIA, SECOND APPELLATE DISTRICT, DIVISION SIX
> 225 Cal.App.4th 1172
> April 28, 2014, Opinion Filed
> (*Marriage of Boswell*)
>
> This is another frivolous family law appeal. As we shall explain, given well-known appellate rules, it was "dead on arrival" at the appellate courthouse. The family law court is a court of equity and fairness. Here the trial court, exercising its broad equitable discretion, refused to enforce a 25-year-old judgment for child support arrearages because appellant (mother) concealed the children for 15 years. It specifically ruled that doing so would be "inequitable," that the request was "untimely," "unjust" and "[t]his is just a terribly egregious situation." The trial court did not credit mother's factual explanation. It did credit respondent's (father's) factual explanation, i.e., he did not visit the children or pay child support because mother did conceal the children.
>
> Mother and father dissolved their marriage in October of 1985. The trial court awarded physical custody of the two children, Denise (born Feb. 1980) and John Jr. (born Mar. 1982) to mother. Father was ordered to pay $70 per month child support per child. He did so for two months and then mother "disappeared" with the children. She moved from

---

[13] CCP § 695.210 provides:
"The amount required to satisfy a money judgment is the total amount of the judgment as entered or renewed with the following additions and subtractions:
(a) The addition of costs added to the judgment pursuant to Section 685.090.
(b) The addition of interest added to the judgment as it accrues pursuant to Sections 685.010 to 685.030, inclusive.
(c) The subtraction of the amount of any partial satisfactions of the judgment.
(d) The subtraction of the amount of any portion of the judgment that is no longer enforceable."
[14] FC § 4503 provides: "If a parent has been ordered to make payments for the support of a minor child, an action to recover an arrearage in those payments may be maintained at any time within the period otherwise specified for the enforcement of such a judgment, notwithstanding the fact that the child has attained the age of 18 years."

California, changed the children's names, and did not notify father of their new addresses. Father did not see the children for approximately 15 years, almost their entire minority. After Denise reached the age of majority, mother "gave" custody of John Jr. to father in 1998 when he was 16 years old. He lived with father until he reached majority.

Fifteen years after that, i.e., in 2013, the children were over 30 years old. Then, mother sought to enforce the child support order and sought a judgment of $92,734.94.

DISCUSSION
Family law court is a court of equity. (Citations omitted.) Those who seek equity, must do equity and have "clean hands". (Citations omitted.)Family law cases are equitable proceedings in which the court must have the ability to exercise discretion to achieve fairness and equity.

Mother contends that the trial court abused its discretion and applied a faulty legal analysis in making its ruling. In addition, she claims that the trial court should have credited her declaration that she did not conceal the children.
We need not dwell upon or explicate in detail underlying principles of "active concealment," "estoppel," or "retroactive modification of child support." The only issue here is whether the trial court should have used judicial power to achieve an "inequitable result." It is sufficient to observe that mother did actively conceal the children. This equitably estops her from enforcing a child support judgment.

The trial court found that mother had been "unjust" in her unilateral decision to remove father from the children's lives. This is tantamount to a finding of "unclean hands." We reiterate our statement in Keith G. v. Suzanne H. (1998) 62 Cal.App.4th 853 at p. 853, "These are some of the dirtiest hands we have seen."

As expressly indicated by the trial court, this was terribly egregious. 'The "clean hands" rule is of ancient origin and given broad application. It is the most important rule affecting the administration of justice. Equity denies affirmative relief for such conduct even though it thereby leaves undisturbed and in ostensible full legal effect acts or proceedings which would affirmatively be set aside but for such consideration. (Citations omitted.) We hold that a family law court, in the exercise of its broad equitable discretion, and upon a finding of "unclean hands," may decline to enforce a child support arrearage judgment.

Mother contends that the trial court erroneously did not credit her factual showing of why father did not see his children for 15 years. This is folly. The trial court was not required to believe her and, sitting as trier of fact, had the power and the right to not do so, just as it had the power and right to believe father. We do not judge credibility on appeal. An adverse factual finding is a poor platform upon which to predicate reversible error. (Id. at p. 1097.) "We sit as a court [of law] to review errors of law and not [claimed] errors of fact."

Mother has no appreciation for the rules on appeal, i.e., the substantial evidence rule and the rules relating to the exercise of discretion by the trial court and the review thereof by the Court of Appeal. These rules are well known. They need not be repeated. We hold that where, as here, the family law court makes a fair and equitable ruling on contested issues of fact, its express or implied factual determinations are binding on appeal. The appellate court may not substitute its discretion for that of the trial court unless the appellant can demonstrate, as a matter of law, that the trial court's judgment is arbitrary,

Chapter 16: Child Support

> capricious, whimsical, or exceeds the bounds of reason. (Ibid.)
>
> As a separate basis for denial of the motion to enforce a child support arrearage judgment, the trial court ruled that there was a laches bar, i.e., she waited too long to enforce the order. This theory is erroneous as a matter of law and father so concedes. FC § 291(d) provides that the defense of laches only applies to child support owed to the state.
>
> Although the appeal is frivolous, we elect not to impose sanctions because mother believed, and apparently prosecuted this appeal because of the trial court's ruling on laches. This is the only thing that saves her and her attorney from a sanction order.
>
> The judgment is affirmed. Costs are awarded to respondent.

Modifications or Terminations of Child Support Orders

It is the intent of the Legislature to: **(1)** provide for commissioners to hear child support cases being enforced by the local child support agency; **(2)** adopt uniform and simplified procedures for all child support cases; and **(3)** create an Office of the Family Law Facilitator in the courts to provide education, information and assistance to parents with child support issues. **FC § 4250**.

A support order may be modified or terminated at any time as the court determines to be necessary. **FC § 3651(a)**. A support order may not be modified or terminated as to an amount that accrued before the date of the filing of the *RFO* to modify or terminate.

The court must require that a *Child Support Case Registry Form* (form *FL-191*) be completed by one of the parties and filed each time an initial court order for child or family support or a modification of a court order for child or family support is filed with the court. A party attempting to file an initial judgment or order for child or family support or a modification of an order for child or family support without a completed *Child Support Case Registry Form* (form FL-191) must be given a blank form to complete. The form must be accepted if legibly handwritten in ink or typed. No filing fees may be charged for filing the form. **CRC Rule 5.330(c)**.

Copies of the *Child Support Case Registry Form* (form *FL-191*) must be made available by the clerk's office and the family law facilitator's office to the parties without cost. A blank copy of the *Child Support Case Registry Form* (form FL-191) must be sent with the notice of entry of judgment to the party who did not submit the judgment or order. **CRC Rule 5.330(d)**.

At the request of either party, an order modifying, terminating or setting aside a support order must include a statement of decision. **FC § 3654**.

Except as against a governmental agency, an order modifying, terminating or setting aside a support order may include an award of attorney fees and court costs to the prevailing party. **FC § 3652**. (See Chapter 7 RE: Attorney Fees & Limited Scope Representation, *supra*.)

> Upon the filing of a supplemental complaint pursuant to Section 2330.1, a child support order in the original proceeding may be modified in conformity with the statewide uniform guideline for child support to provide for the support of all of the children of the same parents who were named in the initial and supplemental pleadings, to consolidate arrearages and wage assignments for children of the parties, and to consolidate orders for support. FC § 3651(b).

The court may, on any terms that may be just, relieve a party from a support order, or any part or parts thereof, after the six-month time limit of **CCP § 473** has run, based on the grounds, and within the time limits, provided in this section of the Family Code. **FC § 3690(a)**. **FC § 3690(b)** provides that before granting relief, the court must find that the facts alleged as the grounds for relief materially affected the original order and that the moving party would materially benefit from the granting of the relief.

An order for child support terminates by operation of law pursuant to **FC §§ 3900**[15], **3901**[16], **4007**[17] and **4013**[18]. **FC § 3601(a)**.

Child Support Agreements

1. Required Provisions in all Child Support Agreements

Parties may stipulate to an amount of child support, but this stipulation is subject to the approval of the court. The stipulation will not be approved unless the parties declare all of the following in the stipulation:

(1) They are fully informed of their rights concerning child support;
(2) The order is being agreed to without coercion or duress;
(3) The agreement is in the best interests of the children involved;
(4) The needs of the children will be adequately met by the stipulated amount; and
(5) The right to support has not been assigned to the county pursuant to **Welfare and Institutions Code § 11477** and no public assistance application is pending. **FC § 4065(a)**.

Additionally, parties can agree that the child support will be paid by an electronic funds transfer pursuant to **FC § 17309.5**.

---

[15] FC § 3900 provides that parents have equal responsibilities to support their child in the manner suitable to the child's circumstances.

[16] FC § 3901(a)(1) provides that a parent's duty of support "continues as to an unmarried child who has attained 18 years of age, is a full-time high school student, unless excused pursuant to paragraph (2), and who is not self-supporting, until the time the child completes the 12th grade or attains 19 years of age, whichever occurs first."

[17] FC § 4007(a) provides: "If a court orders a person to make specified payments for support of a child during the child's minority, or until the child is married or otherwise emancipated, or until the death of, or the occurrence of a specified event as to, a child for whom support is authorized under FC § 3901 or 3910, the obligation of the person ordered to pay support terminates on the happening of the contingency."

[18] FC § 4013 provides that "if obligations for support of a child are discharged in bankruptcy, the court may make all proper orders for the support of the child that the court determines are just."

Chapter 16: Child Support

2. Stipulations for Child Support Less Than Guideline Amount

If the parties stipulate to a child support order whereby the amount is lower than the amount established by **FC § 4055**, a change in circumstances is NOT necessary to obtain a modification of the child support order to the applicable guideline level or above. **FC § 4065(a)** and **CRC Rule 5.260(c)**.

> The provisions of an agreement between the parents for child support shall be deemed to be separate and severable from all other provisions of the agreement relating to property and support of either spouse. An order for child support based on the agreement shall be imposed by law and shall be made under the power of the court to order child support. FC § 3585.

One final word with regard to child support agreements: Agreements to pay less than the guideline amount will only be upheld if the court finds that it is in the children's best interests to do so, which is highly unlikely. (See *In re Marriage of FACTOR* (2013) 212 Cal.App.4th 967 where the court severed the child support agreement paragraph from the marital settlement agreement.)

3. No Duty to Pay College Expenses

Pursuant to **FC § 3901(a)(1)** the parents' duty of support continues until the time the child completes the 12th grade or attains 19 years of age, whichever occurs first.[19] Further, **FC § 3901(b)** provides that the parents are free to agree to provide additional support after their obligation ceases.

Accordingly, there is no parental duty to pay for college expenses. However, if the parties agree to pay college expenses, the court has jurisdiction to modify the amount of the payment as additional child support, if there is no provision providing otherwise, as the case below demonstrates.

> *In re Marriage of KIM LENORE ROSENFELD and MARK P. GROSS. LENORE DRESCHER, Appellant, v. MARK P. GROSS, Respondent.*
> COURT OF APPEAL OF CALIFORNIA, SECOND APPELLATE DISTRICT, DIVISION THREE
> 225 Cal.App.4th 478
> April 11, 2014, Opinion Filed
> (*Marriage of Rosenfeld & Gross*)
>
> Drescher and Gross were married in 1987 and separated in 2001. There are three children from the marriage: Joshua, born in 1992; Lila, born in 1994; and Noah, born in 1997.
>
> In June 2001, the parties executed a marital settlement agreement (MSA). At the time, the parties were both employed as attorneys earning six-figure incomes. [In the parties'

---

[19] The following language was added to §3901 effective 1/1/2019: "(2) A child is excused from the requirement to become a full-time high school student for the purposes of paragraph (1) if the child has a medical condition documented by a physician that prevents full-time school attendance."

Chapter 16: Child Support

MSA was the following provision.] "**D. Each party shall be responsible for payment of one-half (½) of all costs incurred on behalf of each minor child, for undergraduate California state college or university expenses, trade or other school or schools' costs incurred by such minor child, or other schools approved by the parties, so long as such minor child is continuing to reasonably matriculate at such school.**"

In October 2002, the final judgment of dissolution was entered. The judgment incorporates the MSA and orders child custody, spousal support and child support as set forth therein.

In August 2011, Gross filed an order to show cause requesting modification of child support, and to enforce the college expense provision of the MSA, as incorporated into the judgment. Specifically, Gross sought an order requiring Drescher to pay [her half of the college expenses of Lila].

In November 2011, the trial court entered an order modifying the child support Gross paid for Lila's and Noah's maintenance. The court also granted Gross's request to enforce the college expense provision of the judgment.

In June 2012, Drescher filed an order to show cause requesting modification of the college expense provision of the judgment. Drescher asserted her disability and the resulting change in the parties' relative incomes since the judgment was entered constituted a material change in circumstances. Her order to show cause asked the court to reallocate the shared support obligation based on the disparity in their current incomes.

Gross opposed the request, arguing the court had no authority to modify the provision because college expenses are not child support, and the parties' stipulation to pay their children's college expenses was entirely contractual. He also argued Drescher had failed to establish a change in circumstances since the court had last modified child support in November 2011. While Drescher's request for modification was pending, Gross brought a competing order to show cause seeking payment from Drescher of her share of tuition and living expenses.

On November 12, 2013, the trial court denied Drescher's request to modify the judgment and granted Gross's request for reimbursement of college expenses incurred on Lila's behalf. With respect to modification, the court concluded, as a matter of contract interpretation, that it lacked jurisdiction to modify because the parties had not intended the college expense provision to be treated as child support. The court reasoned that nothing in the language of the MSA indicated the parties intended "shared expenses for adult children to be treated as equivalent to statutorily mandated child support," citing the fact that "[t]he MSA specifically identified certain items as child support, but [the college expense provision] is not among them." Drescher appealed.

DISCUSSION
We begin with Drescher's contention that an agreement to pay an adult child's college expenses is modifiable as a matter of law, regardless of whether the parents contract to restrict the court's jurisdiction.

FC § 3587 authorizes the court to order adult child support, as follows: "Notwithstanding any other provision of law, the court has the authority to approve a stipulated agreement by the parents to pay for the support of an adult child or for the continuation of child support after a child attains the age of 18 years and to make a support order to effectuate the agreement."

FC § 3651 states the general rule for modification or termination of support orders, "whether or not the support order is based upon an agreement between the parties." (FC § 3651(e).) Subject to other provisions of the Family Code—including FC § 3587, as we will discuss—FC § 3651 authorizes prospective modification of all child support orders, even those based upon the parents' agreement. In turn, FC § 3585 states that "provisions of an agreement between the parents for child support shall be deemed to be separate and severable from all other provisions ... ," and "[a]n order for child support based on the agreement shall be law-imposed and shall be made under the power of the court to order child support." Thus, with respect to support for a minor child, our Supreme Court has held, "[w]hen a child support agreement is incorporated in a child support order, the obligation created is deemed court-imposed rather than contractual, and the order is subsequently modifiable despite the agreement's language to the contrary." (Citations omitted.)

[The] court's authority to order adult child support under FC § 3587 derives entirely from the parents' agreement to pay such support. Because the court's authority is rooted in the parents' contractual agreement, it follows that the parents' agreement also may restrict the court's authority to modify an order for adult child support made under FC § 3587. Construing the "subject to" clause in FC § 3651 to limit the court's authority to modify an adult child support order where the parents have expressly contracted for such a restriction is consistent with the limited grant of jurisdiction under FC § 3587, which authorizes the court to order adult child support to "effectuate the [parents'] agreement."

Accordingly, we conclude that while FC § 3651 generally authorizes the court to modify a child support order, including adult child support ordered pursuant to the parents' agreement, this authority is "subject to," and may be limited by, the parents' express agreement to restrict modification of adult child support ordered pursuant to FC § 3587. We turn now to the trial court's construction of the MSA.
In concluding it lacked jurisdiction to modify the college expense provision, the trial court framed the issue as "fundamentally a question of contract interpretation." Because the "... MSA specifically identified certain items as child support ... ," but the provision concerning college expenses was "not among them," the court reasoned that "[n]othing in the language of the MSA indicates that the parties intended that voluntarily undertaken shared expenses for adult children be treated as equivalent to statutorily mandated child support, or that the equal obligation could later be altered other than by mutual consent."

Though we agree this is a question of contract interpretation, we disagree with the trial court's construction of the MSA. As noted, because no extrinsic evidence was considered, we are not bound by the trial court's construction and interpret the terms of the MSA de novo.

[We have concluded parties' stipulations can be made nonmodifiable to effectuate their agreement and parties may also] contractually restrict the court's jurisdiction to modify spousal support. However, to do so, FC § 3651(d) requires a written or oral agreement made in open court that "specifically provides that the spousal support is not subject to modification or termination." We conclude the same rule should apply in the context of

> adult child support orders. Parties may restrict the court's jurisdiction to modify, but to do so, they must expressly and specifically state in their agreement that any resulting adult child support order made under FC § 3587 will not be subject to modification or termination by the court. In this case, the absence of an express and specific statement in the MSA is alone sufficient to conclude the trial court had jurisdiction to modify the adult child support order pertaining to college expenses.
>
> We conclude the parties' stipulation to pay each minor child's college expenses resulted in a child support order when incorporated into the court's judgment. Though based on an agreement to pay adult child support, the resulting order was subject to the court's jurisdiction to modify, absent an express and specific agreement by the parties to the contrary. Because the MSA does not expressly restrict the court's authority to modify the college expense support order, the trial court erred in concluding it lacked jurisdiction. The court's failure to consider whether the support order should be modified was an abuse of discretion.
>
> Though we hold parents may contract to restrict the court's jurisdiction to modify an adult child support order in this limited circumstance, we conclude the parties' marital settlement agreement in this case did not limit the court's jurisdiction.
>
> **DISPOSITION**
> Accordingly, we reverse the order and remand the matter. The trial court is directed to consider whether the allocation of the college expense support obligation should be modified in light of the parties' respective incomes, other assets they may have to satisfy the support obligation, and any other relevant evidence the court may consider in exercise of its discretion.

A Deferred Sale of the Home Order or *Duke Order*

A deferred sale of the home order is an order that delays the sale of the community residence until the youngest child reaches the eighteen (18) years old. These orders are commonly called **Duke Orders** after the 1980 case entitled *In re Marriage of DUKE* (1980) 101 Cal.App.3d 152, which is the case that follows.

> *In re Marriage of KATHLEEN and JOE WILBUR DUKE. KATHLEEN DUKE, Appellant, v. JOE WILBUR DUKE, Respondent*
> Court of Appeal of California, Fourth Appellate District, Division One
> 101 Cal.App.3d 152
> January 17, 1980
> (*Marriage of Duke*)
>
> Kathleen and Joe were married twenty-three years, had three children and lived in the present family residence more than five years. As of the date of judgment, two children (13 and 16) lived in the home. One child was an adult. Joe was a tenured college instructor, 45 years of age, with a net income of more than $1,900 monthly. Kathleen was 42 years of age and primarily had involved herself in homemaking. She sold Mary Kay cosmetics out of her home and, at trial, netted approximately $50 monthly. She was then enrolled as a second semester junior college student.
>
> Kathleen was awarded custody of the minor children with whom she has resided since their birth. The admittedly large family residence (five bedrooms) had monthly

payments of approximately $ 200, with an existing balance of $ 28,071, and a fair market value of $ 90,000. Property taxes were $ 1,380 per year. The equity in the residence constitutes approximately 60 percent of the total community value. Neither party requested award of the residence as a share of the community property.

DISCUSSION
The value of a family home to its occupants cannot be measured solely by its value in the marketplace. The longer the occupancy, the more important these noneconomic factors become and the more traumatic and disruptive a move to a new environment is to children whose roots have become firmly entwined in the school and social milieu of their neighborhood.

The children's desires to remain in the home were made known to the court.

The trial court's [rejection of Kathleen's request to defer the sale of the family residence] would expose the wife to serious economic factors created by present inflationary impacts on the real estate market with resultant high interest rates, tightening of credit, increased market prices, and shortage of housing at a time when she is still responsible for the shelter of her children. None of these factors are directly addressed by the trial court in its findings.

The impact of inflation on petitioner's ability to effectively utilize her share of the equity to provide adequate housing is compounded by her present limited earning capacity and her need to complete educational requirements abandoned during the 23-year marriage during which she fulfilled the primary role of homemaker and mother. While the inflationary trend may continue until the youngest child reaches majority (April 9, 1983), it is expected Kathleen will at that time have an enhanced earning capacity and be better able to afford to invest in a home if that is her desire.

On the other hand, it appears from the findings Joe's net monthly income adequately provides for his needs and to pay the spousal and child support ordered. While Joe expresses a desire to get his equity out of the residence as soon as possible, he shows no adverse consequence to him by a deferral which outweighs the alleged detrimental impacts on the children reasonably expected to follow an immediate sale of this home. It is clear such a "conditional" award of the family residence may be made in appropriate circumstances.
Civil Code § 4800 (a), allows the court to divide the property at the time of judgment ". . . or at a later time if it expressly reserves jurisdiction to make such property division . . . ." Further, the court may divide the property on "such conditions as it deems proper to effect a substantially equal division" so long as economic circumstances warrant. (Civ. Code, § 4800(b)(1).)
The economics of obtaining equivalent housing for a minor child's welfare is certainly well within the legislative intent expressed by the statute.

[W]e feel the subjective noneconomic impact on the family unit from being deprived of a home environment to which the children have become accustomed is sufficiently significant to allow the court to enter a conditional order such as requested so long as undue hardship is not imposed on the noncustodial parent.

While the parties squarely presented the trial court with the issue of a conditional disposition of the home, no findings relate directly to it. In the record we find no facts which would compel an immediate cash division of the house equity as a matter of

> preference. Facially it appears to be justified only because it is a simple, final disposition of the matter and divides the community dollars equally.
>
> A trial court has a great deal of flexibility in dividing community property to achieve the greatest equity and, indeed, is encouraged to be innovative. A wife's emotional attachment to a family residence of long-time residence is a cognizable factor in determining disposition of property on dissolution
>
> We feel similar recognition should be given to the emotional attachments of a custodial parent and children in weighing respective interests to determine the benefits to be attained in delaying the sale of the family home.
>
> Where there are minor children whose custody is to be awarded to a party, the custodial party is not financially able to acquire the family home as his or her property share, and that person desires a conditional order be made allowing him or her exclusive use of the home, the unique relationship of that asset to the family requires an analysis of all relevant factors including those suggested above in light of the length of delay requested.
>
> Anticipated economic detriments indigenous to the delayed sale should be addressed in terms specific to the individual case so as to counterbalance any adverse impact to the party out of possession resulting from loss of present income. If after applying this process the court finds no adverse impact to the noncustodial parent outweighing the economic and/or subjective impact on the children and custodial parent, it shall grant such relief on terms as may be appropriate to the specific case.
>
> We hold the trial court failed to exercise proper discretion when it rejected Kathleen's request to defer the sale of the family residence in not balancing the significant emotional, economic and social impacts to the family unit of an immediate sale against foreseeable detriment to the noncustodial spouse.
>
> **DISPOSITION**
> The judgment is [reversed] insofar as it orders [the] immediate sale of the residence [and is remanded] for such further proceedings the court deems necessary to enable it to determine whether a conditional award of the family residence is proper after a consideration of relevant factors as suggested in our opinion.

In 1988, the legislature enacted **deferred sale of the home** code sections **FC §§ 3800, 3801, 3802, 3803, 3806, 3807, 3808** and **3809**.

FC § 3800 provides that a **custodial parent** is a party awarded physical custody of a child and a **deferred sale of home order** is an order that temporarily delays the sale of the family home, awarding the temporary exclusive use and possession to the custodial parent of minor children in order to minimize the adverse impact of dissolution of marriage or legal separation of the parties on the welfare of the children.

FC §§ 3801-3809 provide that the court must first determine if it is economically feasible to defer the sale of the family home. **FC § 3801** sets forth conditions that the court must consider in finding feasibility.

Chapter 16: Child Support

FC § 3801(c) provides:

> It is the intent of the Legislature, by requiring the determination under this section, to do all of the following:
> **(1)** Avoid the likelihood of possible defaults on the payments of notes and resulting foreclosures.
> **(2)** Avoid inadequate insurance coverage.
> **(3)** Prevent deterioration of the condition of the family home.
> **(4)** Prevent any other circumstance which would jeopardize both parents' equity in the home.

FC § 3802 provides an additional ten (10) item list of matters that the court must consider before making this order, if the court order has found that the deferred sale of the home is feasible pursuant to **FC § 3801**.[20] In enacting these code sections the legislature makes it clear that a deferred sale of the home order should only be granted in rare cases. And if the parent that is awarded the exclusive use of the home remarries or changes his or her economic status in any way, there is a rebuttable presumption that "further deferral of the sale is no longer an equitable method of minimizing the adverse impact of the dissolution of marriage or legal separation of the parties on the children." **FC § 3808**.

A deferred sale of home order must provide the duration of the order and may include the legal description and assessor's parcel number of the real property that is subject to the order. **FC § 3803**. The order must be in writing and specify the parties' respective responsibilities for the payment of the costs of routine maintenance and capital improvements. **FC § 3806** and **FC § 3807**.

Finally, the court has the discretion to modify or terminate a deferred sale of home order. The court must reserve jurisdiction to determine any issues that arise with respect to the deferred sale of home order including, but not limited to, the maintenance of the home and the tax consequences to each party. **FC § 3807** and **FC § 3809**.

---

[20] The 10 matters set forth in FC § 3802 are:
"(1) The length of time the child has resided in the home;
(2) The child's placement or grade in school;
(3) The accessibility and convenience of the home to the child's school and other services or facilities used by and available to the child, including child care;
(4) Whether the home has been adapted or modified to accommodate any physical disabilities of a child or a resident parent in a manner that a change in residence may adversely affect the ability of the resident parent to meet the needs of the child;
(5) The emotional detriment to the child associated with a change in residence;
(6) The extent to which the location of the home permits the resident parent to continue employment;
(7) The financial ability of each parent to obtain suitable housing;
(8) The tax consequences to the parents;
(9) The economic detriment to the nonresident parent in the event of a deferred sale of home order; and
(10) Any other factors the court deems just and equitable."

Expedited Child Support

In an action for child support that has been filed and served, the court may, without a hearing, make an order requiring a parent or parents to pay for the support of their minor children during the pendency of that action, the amount required by **FC § 4055** or, if the income of the obligated parent or parents is unknown to the applicant, then the minimum amount of support as provided in **Welfare and Institutions Code § 11452**. **FC § 3621**.

The court must make an expedited support order if all of the following are filed:

> **(a)** An application for an expedited child support order, setting forth the minimum amount the obligated parent or parents are required to pay pursuant to Section 4055 of this code or the minimum basic standards of adequate care for Region 1 as specified in Sections 11452 and 11452.018 of the Welfare and Institutions Code.
> **(b)** An income and expense declaration for both parents, completed by the applicant.
> **(c)** A worksheet setting forth the basis of the amount of support requested.
> **(d)** A proposed expedited child support order. FC § 3622.

An application for the expedited support order confers jurisdiction on the court to hear only the issue of support of the children for whom support may be ordered. **FC § 3623**.

An expedited support order becomes effective thirty (30) days after service on the obligated parent of all of the following:

> **(1)** The application for an expedited child support order.
> **(2)** The proposed expedited child support order, which shall include a notice of consequences of failure to file a response.
> **(3)** The completed income and expense declaration for both parents.
> **(4)** A worksheet setting forth the basis of the amount of support requested.
> **(5)** Three blank copies of the income and expense declaration form.
> **(6)** Three blank copies of the response to an application for expedited child support order and notice of hearing form. FC § 3624(a).

Service of an expedited support order may be by personal service or by any method available under **CCP §§ 415.10 to 415.40**, inclusive. **FC § 3624(b)**.

The obligated parent must cause the court clerk to set a hearing on the application for the expedited support order not less than twenty (20) nor more than thirty (30) days after the filing of the response to the application for the expedited support order and *Income and Expense Declaration*. **FC § 3626**.

The obligated parent must give notice of the hearing to the other parties or their counsel by first-class mail not less than fifteen (15) days before the hearing. **FC § 3627**.

At the hearing on the application for the expedited support order, all parties who are parents of the child(ren) who are the subject of the action must produce copies of their most recently filed federal and state income tax returns. **FC § 3629(a)**.

Unless there is a response to the application for an expedited support order as provided in **FC § 3625**, the expedited support order is effective on the obligated parent without further action by the court. **FC § 3624(c)**.

If a tax return is submitted, it may be reviewed and examined by the other parties as to the contents of the return. **FC § 3629(b)**.

The amount of the expedited support order must be the minimum amount the obligated parent is required to pay as set forth in the application. **FC § 3630(a)**.

When there is a hearing, the resulting order is called an order after hearing. **FC § 3631**.

An order after hearing becomes effective not more than thirty (30) days after the filing of the response to the application for the expedited support order and may be given retroactive effect to the date of the filing of the application. **FC § 3632**.

And finally, an expedited child support order may be modified or terminated at any time on the same basis as any other order for child support. **FC § 3633**.

Chapter 16: Child Support

EDUCATIONAL EXERCISES

I. Fill in the blanks

1. In almost all cases, _____ will pay the child support for the minor children to the CP.
2. The NCP is then the _____; the CP, or the person that receives the support for the minor child is called the payee or obligee. FC § 3550.
3. Parents are legally obligated to _____ and care of their child until that child reaches his or her majority.
4. The parents' duty of support imposed by _____ continues for an unmarried child who has reached the age of 18, is a full-time high school student, and not self-supporting until the time the child completes the 12th grade or reaches the age of 19, whichever occurs first.
5. In any case in which an amount is set for current child support, the court must require that _____ for a supported child be maintained by either or both parents if that insurance is available at no cost or at a reasonable cost to the parent. FC § 3751(b).
6. All child support orders must include a provision requiring the child support obligor to keep the obligee informed of _____ made available through his or her employer or has other group health insurance and, if so, the health insurance policy information.
7. Whenever a parent accrues or pays costs on behalf of the minor child, if that parent wants to be reimbursed for his or share, that parent MUST provide the other parent with an _____.
8. A parent MUST utilize the _____ including, but not limited to, coverage for emergency treatment for the children, provided by a parent pursuant to a court order at all times, unless the other parent can show that it is inadequate to meet the child's needs. FC § 4063(e)(1).
9. If either parent uses a health care provider other than the preferred provider, the parent obtaining that care must bear _____ for any non-reimbursable health care costs in excess of the costs that would have been incurred under the court-ordered health care insurance coverage had the preferred provider been used. FC § 4063(f)(2).
10. An employer or insurer cannot deny enrollment of a child under the health insurance coverage of a child's parent because the child was _____.
11. The income of a parent's subsequent spouse may only be considered in the _____ where excluding that income would lead to extreme and severe hardship to any child subject to the child support award. FC § 4057.5.
12. _____ is the time that is spent with the minor children and is usually calculated by determining the number of days in a year that the parent spends with the minor children. The number of days is then divided by the number of days in the year, 365, in order to get a percentage of time. Parents can, and often do, dispute this figure. Sometimes the _____ can be determined by the number of hours that a parent spends with the children with that number divided by the number of hours in a year, which is 8,760.

Chapter 16: Child Support

13. "In adopting the _____ provided in this article, it is the intention of the Legislature to ensure that this state remains in compliance with federal regulations for child support guidelines." FC § 4050.
14. _____ sets forth the formula to determine the amount of child support that the noncustodial parent (NCP) must pay to the custodial parent (CP) for the support of their children.
15. Only _____ are used to calculate the amount of child support to be paid except in an extraordinary case where excluding that income would lead to extreme and severe hardship to any child that is the subject of a child support award. In the extraordinary case, the court must also consider whether including that income would lead to an extreme and severe hardship to any child supported by the obligor or by the obligor's subsequent spouse or nonmarital partner. FC § 4057.5.
16. If a parent is unemployed or underemployed, the court can consider the _____ of a parent in lieu of the parent's income, consistent with the best interests of the children. FC § 4058(c).
17. The amount of child support established by the formula provided in FC § 4055(a) is _____ of child support to be ordered. FC § 4057(a).
18. _____ are: (1) extraordinary health expenses for which the parent is financially responsible, (2) uninsured catastrophic losses and (3) the minimum basic living expenses of natural or adopted children for whom the parent has the obligation to support from other relationships who reside with the parent. FC § 4071(a).
19. If a _____ is awarded to a parent, basic expenses for each child who resides with the parent will be deducted from that parent's income up to the amount of support allocated for each child subject to the order. FC § 4071(c). _____ are completely within the _____. In almost all cases, _____ is used to calculate child support.
20. The child support guideline formula is to be used except where the application of the formula would be _____. A court MUST adhere to the statewide uniform guideline and can deviate from the guideline only in the special circumstances where the court finds a good cause to deviate. FC § 4052. CRC Rule 5.260(b).
21. In a proceeding for child support the court must consider the _____, if any, of the parties to the proceeding. FC § 4006.
22. The court may adjust the child support order to accommodate _____ of either parent, as it deems appropriate. FC § 4064.
23. The _____ ordered by the court must be made before the payment of any debts the paying parent owes to creditors. FC § 4011.
24. It is important to note that even if the CP refuses to allow the court ordered visitation, the NCP still _____. FC § 3556.
25. If the parents have _____, the support order is not enforceable during the time that they are living together, unless the order specifies otherwise. FC § 3602.
26. When the court orders a party to pay child support, the court MUST include in its order an earnings assignment order, known as an _____.

Chapter 16: Child Support

27. An _____ for the payment of child support that orders the employer of the obligor to pay to the obligee (the person to whom the support was ordered to be paid) that portion of the obligor's earnings due or to become due in the future, as will be sufficient to pay an amount to cover the monthly amount ordered by the court for support or arrearages. FC § 5230.
28. If the request for child support is not the initial request, any order modifying or terminating a support order may be made retroactive to the date of the filing of the _____ to modify or terminate, or to any subsequent date. FC § 3653(a).
29. When a person who has been court-ordered to pay child support gets behind in his or her payments, the amount of money owed but not paid on time is called _____.
30. _____ of limitations on child support arrearages.
31. A support order may be _____ as the court determines to be necessary. FC § 3651(a). A support order may not be modified or terminated as to an amount that accrued before the date of the filing of the RFO to modify or terminate.
32. At the request of either party, an order _____ a support order must include a _____. FC § 3654.
33. An order for child support _____ pursuant to FC §§ 3900, 3901, 4007 and 4013. FC § 3601(a).
34. Parties may stipulate to an amount of child support, but this stipulation is _____.
35. The Family Code section that sets forth all of the provisions that MUST be in a child support stipulation is _____.
36. Pursuant to FC § 3901(a)(1) the _____ continues until the time the child completes the 12th grade or attains 19 years of age, whichever occurs first.
37. FC § 3901(b) provides that the parents are free to agree to provide _____ after their obligation ceases.
38. If parties agree to pay _____, the court has jurisdiction to modify the amount of the payment as additional child support, if there is no provision providing otherwise, as the case below demonstrates.
39. A _____ order is an order that delays the sale of the community residence until the youngest child reaches the eighteen (18) years old.
40. In 1988, the legislature enacted _____ code sections FC §§ 3800, 3801, 3802, 3803, 3806, 3807, 3808 and 3809.
41. FC § 3800 provides that a _____ is a party awarded physical custody of a child and a _____ is an order that temporarily delays the sale of the family home, awarding the temporary exclusive use and possession to the custodial parent of minor children in order to minimize the adverse impact of dissolution of marriage or legal separation of the parties on the welfare of the children.
42. In FC §§ 3800-3809, the legislature makes it clear that a _____ should only be granted in _____. And if the parent that is awarded the exclusive use of the home remarries or changes his or her economic status in any way, there is a rebuttable presumption that "_____ is no longer an equitable method of

minimizing the adverse impact of the dissolution of marriage or legal separation of the parties on the children." FC § 3808.

43. A _____ must provide the duration of the order and may include the legal description and assessor's parcel number of the real property that is subject to the _____. FC § 3803. The _____ must be in writing and specify the parties' respective responsibilities for the payment of the costs of routine maintenance and capital improvements. FC § 3806 and FC § 3807.

44. The court must reserve jurisdiction to determine any issues that arise with respect to the _____ including, but not limited to, the maintenance of the home and the tax consequences to each party. FC § 3807 and FC § 3809.

CHAPTER 17: Spousal & Family Support

In Brief...

SPOUSAL SUPPORT:
- Is **court-ordered support that one spouse pays to the other spouse**; and
- It is tax deductible for the supporting spouse, includible in the supported spouse's income.
- **It is a discretionary decision made by a trial court judge who decides after considering all of the factors enumerated in FC § 4320:**
    - If spousal support should be ordered, modified or terminated;
    - The duration and amount of spousal support to be ordered; and
    - Retroactivity to the date of filing the request or any subsequent date, **FC § 4333**.

THE MARITAL STANDARD OF LIVING:
- Is the general station in life enjoyed by the parties;
- Should be weighed under the circumstances of the case along with all other applicable factors;
- May decrease in relative importance over time; *Marriage of Shaughnessy*;
- Examines the supported spouse's needs, not the supporting spouse's standard of living due to post-separation separate property earnings; *Marriage of Ackerman*;
- Entitles the supported party to support commensurate with his or her lifestyle before separation;

SPOUSAL SUPPORT IN MARRIAGES LASTING: FC § 4336:
- **Less than 10 years,** the court has discretion to decide if spousal support is ordered, how much, for how long;
- **More than 10 years,** the court decides if spousal support will be ordered, how much and for how long; and Jurisdiction cannot be terminated as to a spouse's right to receive spousal support.

RETIREMENT AND SPOUSAL SUPPORT:
- Must take into consideration that the retirement age is 65; and
- No one should be compelled to work after the age of 65. ***MARRIAGE of RENOLDS***

A TEMPORARY SPOUSAL SUPPORT ORDER:
- Is made to maintain the status quo pending trial;
- Requires a judge to consider all factors enumerated in **FC § 4320** before making the order;
- Requires a material change of circumstances to modify; and
- Is usually a higher amount than permanent support orders.

PERMANENT SPOUSAL SUPPORT:
- Is ordered to provide financial assistance after dissolution;

Chapter 17: Spousal Support

> - Requires a judge to consider all factors enumerated in **FC § 4320** before making the order;
> - Requires a material change of circumstances to modify;
> - May be ordered in a short marriage or a marriage of long duration; and
> - Is usually a lower amount of money than temporary support.
>
> ***SPECIFIC SPOUSAL SUPPORT ORDERS:***
> - A **Richmond Order** terminates spousal support on a specific date unless the supported spouse files a motion to modify. *Marriage of Richmond*.
> - A **Substantive Stepdown** order decreases the amount of spousal support in designated steps until it becomes a minimal amount or is reduced to $0.
> - A **Jurisdictional Stepdown** orders spousal support to be paid until a certain date.
>
> ***WHEN A SUPPORTED SPOUSE COHABITATES WITH A ROMANTIC PARTNER:***
> - There is a rebuttable presumption of a **decreased need** for spousal support; and
> - The supported party has burden to prove no decreased need by a preponderance.
>
> ***FAMILY SUPPORT, FC § 92:***
> - Is an agreement order or judgment that combines child support and spousal support; and
> - The entire amount is tax deductible to obligor and includible in obligee's income, **FC § 4066**.

Introduction

Spousal support[1] is court-ordered support that one spouse pays to the other spouse during the divorce or legal separation proceedings, and it may continue until sometime after the judgment is rendered, depending upon the length of the marriage and a judge's discretion. If the marriage was ten (10) years or longer, one spouse can be court-ordered to pay support until his or her ex-spouse dies or remarries. Spousal support orders are completely within the discretion of the court, including the amount of the support, the duration and the retention of jurisdiction.

There are no code sections setting a guideline amount to be ordered. There are no code sections that provide how long one spouse must support the other spouse.

There is, however, a code section that provides that a judge may not terminate a spouse's right to receive support if the marriage lasted ten (10) years or longer. For

---

[1] Spousal support may also be called "maintenance" or "alimony". The Family Law Act did not use the word "alimony" because it "evoked an almost automatic glandular reaction and the resulting accumulations of bile did nothing to ease the unhappy lot of counsel and court." *In re Marriage of Morrison* (1978) 20 Cal.3d 437, footnote 7, quoting Attorney's Guide to Family Law Act Practice (Continuing Education Bar 1970) § 3.1, p. 138. Current California codes use "spousal support."

marriages lasting less than ten (10) years, a court may decide when jurisdiction will be terminated.

Although a judge does not have a statutory guideline to determine if and how much spousal support must be ordered, there are circumstances that a judge MUST consider before making a spousal support order. These circumstances are found in **FC § 4320**, which is set forth below.

The obligation of spouses to support each other dates back to 1872 when the legislature enacted Civil Code § 155, which provided that husband and wife have mutual obligations of support. Presently, California codes have essentially the same provision without reference to gender. **FC § 4300** provides that a person must support the person's spouse.

Court-ordered spousal support is a legal obligation, and as such it may not be withheld by the party paying (supporting spouse) as a punishment to the party receiving the support (supported) for any reason at all. Further, a court cannot make an order for spousal support to reward or punish either party.

The purpose for spousal support varies from case to case, depending upon the parties, the facts and their specific circumstances. The facts and the equities in one case may call for no spousal support, or for very short-term support for the purpose of financially assisting one spouse in the transition to single status; or the facts and equities of a case may provide that a spouse needs financial assistance because the supported spouse is not able to generate enough income from whatever source to sufficiently provide for his or her own reasonable living expenses.

> The purpose of spousal support cannot be defined by the Legislature; it is a determination to be made by the trial court based upon the facts and equities of that case, weighing each of the circumstances or guidelines specified by the Legislature in FC § 4320, which are applicable to that case, as well as those specified by appropriate appellate case law. In making its order on the issue of spousal support, it is essential that the trial court possess broad discretion in order to fairly exercise the weighing process contemplated by FC § 4320 with the goal of accomplishing substantial justice for the parties in the case before the court. The issue of spousal support, including its purpose, is one which is truly personal to the parties. *In re MARRIAGE of SMITH* (1990) 225 Cal.App.3d 469 at p. 480-481.

Spousal support is a common request in family law. In many cases, one spouse earns the majority of the money to support the family and the other spouse earns less money or does not work at all outside the home. So, when the spouses divorce, the higher-earning spouse is usually able to support himself or herself, but the lower earning spouse or home-working spouse requires support.

Chapter 17: Spousal Support

Awarding Spousal Support is a Discretionary Decision

There are no codes that set an amount or duration of spousal support. A judge decides if spousal support will be ordered and, if ordered, the amount and the duration. As the case that follows demonstrates, a judge's latitude is not limitless in making these decisions; the law must be followed.

> *In re Marriage of JULIE A. and GREG A. FICKE. JULIE A. FICKE, Appellant, v. GREG A. FICKE, Respondent.*
> COURT OF APPEAL OF CALIFORNIA, FOURTH APPELLATE DISTRICT, DIVISION THREE
> 217 Cal.App.4th 10; 157 Cal.Rptr.3d 870
> June 12, 2013, Opinion Filed
> (*Marriage of Ficke*)
>
> Julie A. and Greg A. Ficke were married in spring 1993, and they separated in midsummer 2008, so the marriage lasted just a little more than 15 years. During that time they had two children, a boy and a girl, who, by the time of the judgment in November 2011, were 17 and 16 years old, respectively.
>
> At the time of the marriage, Julie worked for Beckman Instruments, Inc., as a product planning manager for capillary electrophoresis and liquid chromatography equipment (to 1994), later as a marketing director for a manufacturer of sterilizers for surgical equipment (1994 to 2004). She then took a job as vice-president of marketing for a manufacturer of dental implants and other dental products in Yorba Linda. Julie's 2007 W-2 from the dental implant manufacturer showed total compensation of just over $729,000. Even so, Julie was terminated in spring 2008. Her explanation to a vocational examiner was that a new CEO "came on board and wanted a male in the job."
>
> In the three months after her layoff, Julie conducted a job search which eventually yielded one offer: a marketing management job for a biotech company at $125,000. She declined that job because, when the offer arrived, she had already started a pet health care membership insurance program modeled after a similar business run by her mother in Arizona, and because the job would require considerable travel and not allow her to be home evenings with the two children. At least the startup pet insurance business would allow her to do that.
>
> The evidence is uncontroverted that Julie has worked full time at her pet insurance business since its inception, "probably working very hard" as the trial judge put it. The business, however, has not yet made any money; Julie has been living off loans from her mother and past savings. Thus, at the time of trial, Julie's hard money income was only $251 a month. However, Greg presented evidence in the form of a vocational examination report that Julie was highly marketable and employable in the marketing end of various biotech industries, and could have (at least as of Nov. 2010) found employment in marketing management in such industries at low, mid and high ranges of $120,000, $155,000, and $185,000 a year, respectively.
>
> Meanwhile, Greg worked as a real estate broker for a large realty company and successfully ran for the City Council of Aliso Viejo. He also received income from two rental properties. Greg's total monthly income at the time of trial was found to be $8,088, [$483 from Greg's pay as a city council member, a monthly net average of $3,493 from his position as a real estate broker and net rental income of $4112]. The $8,088 figure is

not challenged by either party in this appeal.

While the initial custody arrangement had been 50/50, sometime afterwards the children made it clear they wanted to be with their mother. Greg does not challenge the fact the court awarded Julie physical custody of the children 95 percent of the time, a fact which certainly undermines any idea he should be getting support from the mother.

[In the judge's statement of decision] the court imputed a whopping $13,333-a-month income to Julie. The figure was based on the "income she would have earned had she taken the position that was offered to her."

Based on the imputation of monthly income of $13,584 to the custodial parent in light of the noncustodial parent's monthly income of $8,088 and a 95 percent time-share factor, child support was figured at $1,368 a month. However, in light of the trial court's imputation of—to use its own word—"phantom" income to the custodial parent of $13,333, the trial court imposed a spousal support award of $700 a month in favor of the noncustodial parent. The difference between the two meant that Greg would owe Julie, net, $668 a month. The mother has appealed from these orders.

DISCUSSION
There are very few—"a handful" overstates it—published appellate decisions which have upheld the imputation of income to custodial parents. The reason is pretty obvious. Since the child support statutes expressly state the purpose of California's guideline child support system is to "place the interests of children as the state's top priority" (FC § 4053(e)), it is counterintuitive—often counterproductive —to impute income to a custodial parent, because the objective effect of such an imputation will be to reduce the money otherwise available for the support of any minor children.

In the case before us now there was no finding imputation would be in the children's best interests. Nor was there any finding Greg needs any monetary break to increase his visitation time. And in fact, what evidence there is all points to an affirmative detriment to the children resulting from imputation. First, obviously, imputation has the objective effect of making less money available for the children. Second, imputation under the circumstances of this case means giving the custodial parent an incentive to leave two teenagers alone on evenings and weekends. Here, Julie turned down the job with the biotech firm because she knew it would involve travel and lost evenings, which would be costs in time that she would not have to incur running a nascent pet insurance firm.

While there might have been abstract justice in penalizing Julie for not putting her own time to its most monetarily efficient Gradgrindian[2] use, there was—to use a monetary metaphor—no "percentage" in it for the children. It did not prioritize the needs of the children, and therefore, with regard to child support, does not pass muster under FC § 4058(b).

Child support is one thing, spousal support quite another. "Child support and spousal support serve different purposes, implicate different policies, and are governed by different rules." In re Marriage of Padilla (1995) 38 Cal.App.4th 1212, 1218, fn. 2.

---

[2] The word comes from Charles Dickens's novel *Hard Times*, in which headmaster Mr. Gradgrind was so materialistic that he only considered the profits in his business. The word "gradgrind" is now used to describe someone who really is only concerned with the bottom line.

Chapter 17: Spousal Support

> For one thing, the statutory basis for imputation of income to the payor litigant is different. For child support, the basis for imputation is FC § 4058(b), which hastens to the best interests of the children in the next breath. By contrast, for spousal support, the basis for imputation is but one factor among many, embedded in a reference to "earning capacity" in FC § 4320(a), and that factor itself is quickly put into the context of possibly impaired earning capacity due to periods of unemployment during the marriage to devote time to "domestic duties." (FC § 4320(a)(2).)
>
> For another, while the child support guideline statutes reflect the explicitly high priority the Legislature has placed on the support of children (FC § 4053(e)), there is, as commentators have noted, no one single legislative purpose behind spousal support. But a spousal support award cannot undercut the child support statutes. Implicit in the high priority given the best interests of the children in the child support statutes is the Legislature's intent there be no legerdemain[3] on the spousal support side to take with one hand what the child support statutes give with the other.
>
> Moreover, an examination of the spousal support statute, FC § 4320, shows it to be not just a mélange of factors, but an expression of several affirmative policy preferences. FC § 4320 (l) expresses the goal each party will be "self-supporting within a reasonable period of time." One can also detect policy preferences that seek to equitably account for the value of "domestic" work, even if it means the impairment of formal job market skills, in subdivision (a)(1) (requirement to consider need for retraining)and (2) [impairment by "periods of unemployment … . incurred during the marriage … to devote time to domestic duties"]. The same policy preference also crops up in subdivision (b), recognizing the contribution of a homemaker spouse to the job skills of the supporting spouse.
>
> Applying these considerations to the instant matter, we first note Greg has excellent skills, political connections, two houses free and clear, no periods of unemployment, good assets, good health, a great career, and is self-sufficient. By the trial court's own reckoning, Greg is pretty much the last divorcing spouse who should receive spousal support. Not only does the spousal support order cut against the express grain of section 4320, subdivision (l) (Greg is already self-supporting), it is also impliedly inconsistent with section 4320, subdivisions (d) (Greg has no need); (e) (Greg has plenty of assets for his own support); (g) (Greg has plenty of ability to engage in his own employment); and (h) (Greg is in good health and is in the prime of life).) It is pretty clear from an examination of the totality of factors enumerated by the Legislature in section 4320 that spousal support was meant for ex-spouses [that are not self-sufficient].
>
> We do recognize, of course, that Julie's preference for a full-time job that actually allows her to be with the children on weeknights and weekends does [provide], to some degree, a unilateral shift of monetary child support costs from her to Greg. But the unilateral shift theory is an equitable factor that might arguably, under the child support statutes allow Greg to get a break on his child support order. [However, in light of the legislative priority given children, the shift theory cannot be the reason for a spousal support order that undercuts] a child support order. In sum, even tested on a traditional abuse-of-discretion review of a spousal support award, this support award is untenable.
>
> (1) As to child support, the trial court abused its discretion in imputing income to the mother without an express finding supported by substantial evidence that the imputation

---

[3] A legerdemain is skillful with the hands, such as in a magic act; now you see it, now you don't.

> would benefit the children. We do not say, of course, that a court may never impute income to a "custodial" parent, but we do say, as does the Family Code itself, if it does so, any imputation must be supported by substantial evidence that the imputation is in the children's interest. (Fam. Code, § 4058(b).)
>
> (2) As to spousal support, the trial court abused its discretion in making a spousal support award running from the mother under the particular circumstances of this case. The economic circumstances of the parties after the divorce did not support making the mother support the father. Independent of any imputation based on the mother's "earning capacity" is the simple fact that the father is self-supporting and does not need any additional help from the mother.
>
> **DISPOSITION**
> Accordingly, we reverse both the child and spousal support orders and remand both the child and spousal support issues for further proceedings consistent with this opinion.

The Legislature and the appellate courts specify guidelines that a trial court must consider when deciding spousal support issues, but in the final analysis trial courts possess broad discretion to decide the applicability and weight of these guidelines as they apply to the facts and equities of each case. "The trial court, in exercising its discretion on the issue of spousal support, must endeavor to make an order which will achieve a 'just and reasonable' result in each case." *In re MARRIAGE of SMITH* (1990) 225 Cal.App.3d 469 at p. 480-481.

The Spousal Support Order

During a dissolution or legal separation preceding a court may order one party to pay support to the other party. The amount of the support must be just and reasonable, based upon the standard of living established during the marriage and taking into consideration the circumstances in **FC § 4320**. **FC § 4330(a)**.

1. FC § 4320

If a court is entertaining the idea of making a spousal support order, the court MUST take all of the factors set forth in **FC § 4320** into consideration. The court must consider these circumstances whether it is an initial spousal support order, a modification or a request to terminate.

FC § 4320 provides:

> In ordering spousal support under this part, the court shall consider all of the following circumstances:
> **(a)** The extent to which the earning capacity of each party is sufficient to maintain the standard of living established during the marriage, taking into account all of the following:
>   **(1)** The marketable skills of the supported party; the job market for those skills; the time and expenses required for the supported party to acquire the appropriate education or training to develop those skills; and the possible need for retraining or education to acquire other, more marketable skills or employment.

> (2) The extent to which the supported party's present or future earning capacity is impaired by periods of unemployment that were incurred during the marriage to permit the supported party to devote time to domestic duties.
> **(b)** The extent to which the supported party contributed to the attainment of an education, training, a career position, or a license by the supporting party.
> **(c)** The ability of the supporting party to pay spousal support, taking into account the supporting party's earning capacity, earned and unearned income, assets, and standard of living.
> **(d)** The needs of each party based on the standard of living established during the marriage.
> **(e)** The obligations and assets, including the separate property, of each party.
> **(f)** The duration of the marriage.
> **(g)** The ability of the supported party to engage in gainful employment without unduly interfering with the interests of dependent children in the custody of the party.
> **(h)** The age and health of the parties.
> **(i)** All documented evidence of any history of domestic violence, as defined in Section 6211, between the parties or perpetrated by either party against either party's child, including, but not limited to, consideration of:
> (1) A plea of nolo contendere.
> (2) Emotional distress resulting from domestic violence perpetrated against the supported party by the supporting party,
> (3) Any history of violence against the supporting party by the supported party.
> (4) Issuance of a protective order after a hearing pursuant to Section 6340.
> (5) A finding by the court during the pendency of the divorce, separation, or child custody proceeding, or other proceeding under Division 10 (commencing with Section 6200), that the spouse has committed domestic violence,
> **(j)** The immediate and specific tax consequences to each party.
> **(k)** The balance of the hardships to each party.
> **(l)** The goal that the supported party shall be self-supporting within a reasonable period of time. Except in the case of a marriage of long duration as described in Section 4336, a "reasonable period of time" for purposes of this section generally shall be one-half the length of the marriage. However, nothing in this section is intended to limit the court's discretion to order support for a greater or lesser length of time, based on any of the other factors listed in this section, Section 4336, and the circumstances of the parties.
> **(m)** The criminal conviction of an abusive spouse shall be considered in making a reduction or elimination of a spousal support award in accordance with Section 4324.5 or 4325.
> **(n)** Any other factors the court determines are just and equitable.

2. The Marital Standard of Living

In a dissolution or legal separation procedure, the court must make specific findings with respect to the standard of living during the marriage. Additionally, at the request of either party, the court must make appropriate factual determinations with respect to other circumstances presented in **FC § 4320**. **FC § 4332**.

> The marital standard of living is intended by the Legislature to mean the general station in life enjoyed by the parties during their marriage. The Legislature did not intend it to be a precise mathematical calculation, but rather a general reference point for the trial court in deciding this issue. *In re Marriage of SMITH* (1990) 225 Cal.App.3d 469 at p. 475-476.

Chapter 17: Spousal Support

When both parties have retired and are past the common age of retirement, then the marital standard of living is the standard that the couple enjoyed in retirement. *In re Marriage of MCLAIN* (2017) 7 Cal.App.5th 262.

"The marital standard of living ... is set at the date of separation." *In re Marriage of ACKERMAN* (2006) 146 Cal.App.4th 191 at p. 209.

The marital standard of living should be weighed under the circumstances of the case along with all other applicable factors contained in **FC § 4320**.

Courts have held that the goal of achieving the marital standard of living may decrease in relative importance over time. *In re Marriage of SHAUGHNESSY* (2006) 139 Cal.App.4th 1225 at p. 1247.

"It is the supported spouse's needs which must be examined, not the supporting spouse's standard of living due to post-separation separate property earnings." *In re Marriage of ACKERMAN, supra.*

The marital standard of living entitles the supported party to financial support commensurate with his or her lifestyle before separation. However, the law does not guarantee the supported spouse a dollar-for-dollar equality between his or her post-separation income and the supporting party's income. *In re MARRIAGE of HOFFMEISTER* (1987) 191 Cal.App.3d 351 at p. 363.

It would be an abuse of discretion to order support that leaves the supported spouse at a standard of living significantly lower than that enjoyed during marriage, while allowing the supporting spouse a significantly higher one. *In re MARRIAGE of ANDREEN* (1978) 76 Cal.App.3d 667 at p. 671.

When post-separation earnings allow the supporting spouse a higher standard of living that does not invalidate the award. *In re Marriage of WEINSTEIN* (1991) 4 Cal.App.4th 555 at p. 565.

In assessing the parties' marital standard of living, the trial court may consider their income, expenses, and lifestyle during their marriage. *In re Marriage of CHERITON* (2001) 92 Cal.App.4th 269 at p. 307.

The court may consider the family's average income, rather than expenses. *In re MARRIAGE of WEINSTEIN* (1991) 4 Cal.App.4th 555 at p. 566.

And finally, in *In re Marriage of KACIK* (2009) 179 Cal.App.4th 410; 101 Cal.Rptr.3d 745, the court used the average of the incomes of the parties to calculate the marital standard of living:

> [The judge] took the $ 11,336 gross per month that Richard was making at the time of the 2001 judgment and halved it, arriving at the figure of $ 5,668. The trial judge then declared the $5,668 figure to be the "marital standard of living." *Id.* at p. 416.

The trial court in *Kacik* calculated the marital standard of living for a divorced spouse to be one-half of the total amount of money earned in a month by both spouses.

3. Self-Supporting Goal FC § 4320(l)

> The goal that the supported party shall be self-supporting within a reasonable period of time. Except in the case of a marriage of long duration as described in FC § 4336[4], a "reasonable period of time" for purposes of this section generally shall be one-half the length of the marriage. However, nothing in this section is intended to limit the court's discretion to order support for a greater or lesser length of time, based on any of the other factors listed in this section, FC § 4336, and the circumstances of the parties.

Employability and the efforts one makes to become self-supporting are not always just a matter of one or two years; sometimes longer periods are required for patterns to emerge. *In re MARRIAGE of SCHAFFER* (1999) 69 Cal.App.4th 801 at p. 811.

Trial courts have broad discretion in determining the meaning of **self-supporting** in any particular case. In general, the meaning of the term **self-supporting** is "achieving the marital standard of living".

When a court is making an order for spousal support, the court may advise the party that will be receiving the spousal support that he or she should make reasonable efforts to assist in providing for his or her support needs. **FC § 4330(b)**.

A court may order that a party submit to an examination by a vocational training counselor during the proceeding for dissolution or legal separation. The examination must include an assessment of the party's ability to obtain employment based upon the party's age, health, education, marketable skills, employment history and the current availability of employment opportunities. The focus of the examination is on the party's ability to obtain employment toward supporting himself or herself, taking into consideration the marital standard of living. **FC § 4331(a)**.[5]

---

[4] FC § 4336 provides:
"(a) Except on written agreement of the parties to the contrary or a court order terminating spousal support, the court retains jurisdiction indefinitely in a proceeding for dissolution of marriage or for legal separation of the parties where the marriage is of long duration.
(b) For the purpose of retaining jurisdiction, there is a presumption affecting the burden of producing evidence that a marriage of 10 years or more, from the date of marriage to the date of separation, is a marriage of long duration. However, the court may consider periods of separation during the marriage in determining whether the marriage is in fact of long duration. Nothing in this subdivision precludes a court from determining that a marriage of less than 10 years is a marriage of long duration.
(c) Nothing in this section limits the court's discretion to terminate spousal support in later proceedings on a showing of changed circumstances.
(d) This section applies to the following: (1) a proceeding filed on or after January 1, 1988.; and (2) a proceeding pending on January 1, 1988, in which the court has not entered a permanent spousal support order or in which the court order is subject to modification."
[5] This code was amended effective January 1, 2019. The quoted language above did not change.

Chapter 17: Spousal Support

FC § 4320(*l*) provides that the supported spouse should become self-supporting within a reasonable period of time. A reasonable period of time is generally considered to be one-half the length of the marriage. However, for a marriage of long duration, as described in **FC § 4336**, a marriage of ten (10) years or more, **FC § 4320**, subdivision (*l*) is inapplicable. *In re Marriage of WEST* (2007) 152 Cal.App.4th 240 at p. 251-252.

A supported party in a marriage of medium or short duration must become self-supporting within a reasonable period of time. **FC § 4320(l)**; *In re Marriage of GAVRON* (1988) 203 Cal.App.3d 705.

In re Marriage of GAVRON (1988) 203 Cal.App.3d 705

In *Gavron*, husband and wife were married for 25 years before they divorced. In the final judgment the wife was granted $1,100 per month in spousal support until further order of the court. Two years after the judgment was rendered, the husband unsuccessfully tried to reduce the spousal support for a year.

Four years after the husband's unsuccessful attempt to reduce and terminate spousal support, the husband filed a motion, once again, seeking modification and termination of spousal support. At that hearing, the court ordered that spousal support would continue for four more months, at which time it would cease and the court would retain jurisdiction over the issue of spousal support until the death or remarriage of the wife. The trial court held that wife's "failure to become employable or to seek training after so many years shifts the burden to her to demonstrate her continued need for support in light of her continued inaction in this regard." *Id.* at p. 711. The wife appealed.

The court of appeal held that "to the contrary, absent stated or reasonably undisputed prior expectations as to the supported spouse's future self-sufficiency at the time of the previous support order, after a lengthy marriage and an appropriate retention of jurisdiction to modify spousal support, 'the burden of justification is on the party seeking termination.'" In reversing the trial court's order, the appellate court stated that "the record does not indicate that this unemployed, 57-year-old wife had any prior awareness that the court would require her to become self-sufficient." *Id.* at p. 712. In other words, she was given no warning that she was expected to become self-sufficient. This warning that the trial court failed to make became known as the **Gavron warning**.

Since that time, a Gavron warning is commonly given to supported spouses whose marriages lasted less than ten (10) ten years. The warning provides that a supported spouse is expected to become self-sufficient within a reasonable period of time with, "reasonable period of time" being defined as generally half the length of the marriage.

However, a judge is not obligated to find that a "reasonable period of time" is half the length of the marriage. In *In re Marriage of HUNTINGTON* (1992) 10

Cal.App.4th 1513, the parties were married three years and seven months. The court held, and the appellate court affirmed, the trial court's order that spousal support of $ 5,000 per month would continue for a period of six months, and then spousal support and the jurisdiction to award spousal support would permanently terminate. *Id.* at p. 1516.

4. Duration of the Marriage

a. Marriages Lasting Less than Ten (10) Years

A marriage lasting less than ten (10) years is either a marriage of medium or short duration. In these marriages, the court has the discretion to decide if spousal support will be ordered, how much will be ordered and for what length of time it will be paid, considering the factors set forth in **FC § 4320** and **FC § 4336**[6], and the circumstances of the parties. **FC § 4320(l)**. Additionally, the court decides how long jurisdiction will be retained.

Finally, in a short time marriage a court is under no obligation to make a spousal support order or even reserve jurisdiction.

b. Marriages of Long Duration

A marriage of long duration is one that lasted ten (10) years or longer.

"There is a presumption affecting the burden of producing evidence that a marriage of ten (10) years or more, from the date of marriage to the date of separation, is a marriage of long duration." **FC § 4336(b)**.

In making the decision as to whether or not the marriage lasted ten (10) years or longer, the court may consider periods of separation during the marriage. A court may determine that a marriage of less than ten (10) years is a marriage of long duration. **FC § 4336(b)**.

While the court still has the discretion to decide how much and how long spousal support will be paid, the court MAY NOT terminate jurisdiction in a long-term marriage at the dissolution trial.

---

[6] FC § 4336 provides:
"(a) Except on written agreement of the parties to the contrary or a court order terminating spousal support, the court retains jurisdiction indefinitely in a proceeding for dissolution of marriage or for legal separation of the parties when the marriage is of long duration.
(b) For the purpose of retaining jurisdiction, there is a presumption affecting the burden of producing evidence that a marriage of 10 years or more, from the date of marriage to the date of separation, is a marriage of long duration. However, the court may consider periods of separation during the marriage in determining whether the marriage is in fact of long duration. Nothing in this subdivision precludes a court from determining that a marriage of less than 10 years is a marriage of long duration.
(c) Nothing in this section limits the court's discretion to terminate spousal support in later proceedings on a showing of changed circumstances."

> Except on written agreement of the parties to the contrary or a court order terminating spousal support, the court retains jurisdiction indefinitely in a proceeding for dissolution of marriage or for legal separation of the parties where the marriage is of long duration. FC § 4336(a); *In re Marriage of HIBBARD* (2013) 212 Cal.App.4th 1007 at p. 1014.

5. Disparity of Income, Retraining or Education & Reconciliation

A disparity in income alone does not justify an award of spousal support. *In re MARRIAGE of ZYWICIEL* (2000) 83 Cal.App.4th 1078 at p. 1081.

The court can order the supporting spouse to pay, in addition to spousal support, the necessary expenses and costs of the counseling, retraining or education. **FC § 4331(f)**.

On the issue of spousal support, retention over jurisdiction is one of the main components, and each spousal support order usually provides the duration of jurisdiction.

Unless the order specifies otherwise, during any period in which the parties have reconciled and are living together support is not enforceable. **FC § 3602**.

Spousal support is tax deductible by the supporting spouse and must be included in the supported spouse's income.

And finally, pursuant to **FC § 2313**:

> No dissolution of marriage granted on the ground of permanent legal incapacity to make decisions relieves a spouse from any obligation imposed by law as a result of the marriage for the support of the spouse who lacks legal capacity to make decisions, and the court may make an order for support, or require a bond therefor, as the circumstances require.

6. Retroactivity

A request for an order for spousal support in a proceeding for dissolution of marriage, legal separation or a request made postjudgment may be made retroactive to the date of filing the request for spousal support, or to any subsequent date. **FC § 4333**. The retroactivity of an order is within a judge's discretion to decide.

In *In re Marriage of LEFT* (2012) 208 Cal.App.4th 1137, the court made the modification of spousal support order retroactive to three months before the hearing instead of the date that the issue was filed, which was eleven months prior to the hearing. The judge stated that he was choosing this later date because the moving party did not file his *Income and Expense Declaration* (form FL-*150*) until three months before the hearing. *Id.* at p. 1151.

7. Security for Spousal Support Orders

A court may order the supporting party to give reasonable security for the payment of spousal support. **FC § 4339.**

Further:

> where it is just and reasonable in view of the circumstances of the parties, the court, in determining the needs of a supported spouse, may include an amount sufficient to purchase an annuity for the supported spouse or to maintain insurance for the benefit of the supported spouse on the life of the spouse required to make the payment of support, or may require the spouse required to make the payment of support to establish a trust to provide for the support of the supported spouse, so that the supported spouse will not be left without means of support in the event that the spousal support is terminated by the death of the party required to make the payment of support. FC § 4360(a).

If a trust is ordered, it may be modified or terminated at any time before the death of the party required to make the payment of support at the court's discretion, provided the parties have not agreed otherwise in writing. **FC § 4360.**

8. Spousal Support Enforceability

Pursuant to **FC § 4350**, when a court makes or has made an order requiring the payment of spousal support, the court may direct that payment to be made to the county officer designated by the court for that purpose. The court may include in its order any service charge imposed under the authority of **Welfare and Institutions Code § 279**.

Additionally, a court may also refer the matter of enforcement of the spousal support order to the local child support agency. The local child support agency may bring those enforcement proceedings it determines to be appropriate. **FC § 4351**.

The obligee spouse, or the county on behalf of the obligee spouse, may bring a civil action against the obligor spouse to enforce the duty of support, and if the county furnishes support to a spouse, the county has the same right as the spouse to whom the support was furnished to secure reimbursement and obtain continuing support. **FC § 4303**.

Finally, a contempt action can be brought if spousal support has not been paid. However, a contempt action is a punitive action, not an enforcement measure. (See Chapter 32 RE: Enforcement, *infra*.)

9. Documented Evidence of Domestic Violence

In 2001, the legislature passed Senate Bill No. 1221 (2001–2002 Reg. Sess.), which removed the domestic violence language from former subdivision (h) of section 4320 and placed it in a separate subdivision for consideration by the trial court.

Chapter 17: Spousal Support

(Senate Bill No. 1221 also added **FC § 4325**, which created a rebuttable presumption against awarding temporary or permanent spousal support to an abusive spouse and added subdivision (m) to section 4320.)

The criminal conviction of an abusive spouse MUST be considered in making a reduction or elimination of a spousal support award in accordance with **FC § 4325**. *In re Marriage of MACMANUS* (2010) 182 Cal.App.4th 330 at p. 336.

One of the circumstances set forth in **FC § 4320(i)** provides:

> (i) All documented evidence of any history of domestic violence, as defined in Section 6211, between the parties or perpetrated by either party against either party's child, including, but not limited to, consideration of:
> (1) A plea of nolo contendere.
> (2) Emotional distress resulting from domestic violence perpetrated against the supported party by the supporting party.
> (3) Any history of violence against the supporting party by the supported party.
> (4) Issuance of a protective order after a hearing pursuant to Section 6340.
> (5) A finding by a court during the pendency of a divorce, separation, or child custody proceeding, or other proceeding under Division 10 (commencing with Section 6200), that the spouse has committed domestic violence.[7]

> In any proceeding for dissolution of marriage where there is a criminal conviction for an act of domestic violence perpetrated by one spouse against the other spouse entered by the court within five years prior to the filing of the dissolution proceeding, or at any time thereafter, there shall be a rebuttable presumption affecting the burden of proof that any award of temporary or permanent spousal support to the abusive spouse otherwise awardable pursuant to the standards of this part should not be made. FC § 4325(a).

The presumption with regard to **FC § 4325(a)** above can be rebutted by a preponderance of the evidence. **FC § 4325(c)**.

The court can consider documented evidence of a convicted spouse's history as a victim of domestic violence, as defined in **FC § 6211**, perpetrated by the other spouse, or any other factors the court deems just and equitable as conditions for rebutting this presumption.

A conviction of domestic violence that occurred before or after the last court order could be a material change in circumstances. If the conviction occurred before the last order, it must be shown that the right to assert this argument was not waved. (See *In re Marriage of KELKAR* (2014) 229 Cal.App.4th 833 at p. 846, where the court allowed a conviction occurring ten (10) years in the past to be used as a change in circumstances to terminate the paying of spousal support to the abuser.) (Also, see Chapter 36 RE: Domestic Violence, *infra*.)

---

[7] FC § 4320(i) was amended effective January 1, 2019. The quoted code reflects the amended language.

Chapter 17: Spousal Support

10. A Criminal Conviction Bars Spousal Support

If a spouse has a criminal conviction for a violent sexual felony perpetrated on the other spouse and the petition for dissolution is filed before five (5) years following the conviction or any time served in custody, on probation or on parole, an award of spousal support to the convicted spouse from the injured spouse is prohibited.

Violent sexual felonies are the offenses described in paragraphs (3), (4), (5), (11) and (18) of **Penal Code § 667.5(c)**[8]. An injured spouse is a spouse who has been the subject of the violent sexual felony for which the other spouse was convicted. **FC § 4324.5**.

> FC § 4320(m): The criminal conviction of an abusive spouse shall be considered in making a reduction or elimination of a spousal support award in accordance with FC § 4324.5[9] or 4325[10].

---

[8] Some of the violent felonies set forth in Penal Code § 667.5(c) are: Murder or voluntary manslaughter, Mayhem, Rape, Sodomy, Oral copulation, Any felony punishable by death or imprisonment in the state prison for life, Any robbery, Arson, Attempted murder, Kidnapping, Carjacking, Spousal rape, Extortion.

[9] FC § 4324.5 was amended effective January 1, 2019. The added language is bolded.
"(a) In any proceeding for dissolution of marriage where there is a criminal conviction for a violent sexual felony or **a domestic violence felony** perpetrated by one spouse against the other spouse and the petition for dissolution is filed before five years following the conviction and any time served in custody, on probation, or on parole, the following shall apply:
(1) An award of spousal support to the convicted spouse from the injured spouse is prohibited.
(2) If economic circumstances warrant, the court shall order the attorney's fees and costs incurred by the parties to be paid from the community assets. The injured spouse shall not be required to pay any attorney's fees of the convicted spouse out of the injured spouse's separate property.
(3) At the request of the injured spouse, the date of separation, as defined in Section 70, shall be the date of the incident giving rise to the conviction, or earlier, if the court finds circumstances that justify an earlier date.
(4) The injured spouse shall be entitled to 100 percent of the community property interest in the retirement and pension benefits of the injured spouse.
(b) As used in this section, the following definitions apply:
(1) "Domestic violence felony" means a felony offense for an act of abuse, as described in Section 6203, perpetrated by one spouse against the other spouse.
(2) "Injured spouse" means the spouse who has been the subject of the violent sexual felony or domestic violence felony for which the other spouse was convicted.
(3) "Violent sexual felony" means those offenses described in paragraphs (3), (4), (5), (11), and (18) of subdivision (c) of Section 667.5 of the Penal Code.
(c) If a convicted spouse presents documented evidence of the convicted spouse's history as a victim of a violent sexual offense, as described in paragraphs (3), (4), (5), (11), and (18) of subdivision (c) of Section 667.5 of the Penal Code, or domestic violence, as defined in Section 6211, perpetrated by the other spouse, the court may determine, based on the facts of the particular case, that one or more of paragraphs (1) to (4), inclusive, of subdivision (a) do not apply .
(d) The changes made to this section by the bill that added this subdivision shall only apply to convictions that occur on or after January 1, 2019."

[10] FC § 4325 was amended effective January 1, 2019. The added language is bolded.
§ 4325. Rebuttable presumption for conviction of domestic violence
(a) In any proceeding for dissolution of marriage where there is a criminal conviction for **a domestic violence misdemeanor or a criminal conviction for a misdemeanor that results in a term of probation pursuant to Section 1203.097 of the Penal Code** perpetrated by one spouse against the

Chapter 17: Spousal Support

11. Retirement

Retirement is another factor to be considered when determining if spousal support will be ordered, how much will be ordered and for how long.

---

other spouse entered by the court within five years prior to the filing of the dissolution proceeding, **or during the course of the dissolution proceeding,** there shall be a rebuttable presumption **that the following shall apply:**
(1) An award of spousal support to the convicted spouse from the injured spouse is prohibited.
(2) If economic circumstances warrant, the court shall order the attorney's fees and costs incurred by the parties to be paid from the community assets. The injured spouse shall not be required to pay any attorney's fees of the convicted spouse out of the injured spouse's separate property.
(3) At the request of the injured spouse, the date of separation, as defined in Section 70, shall be the date of the incident giving rise to the conviction, or earlier, if the court finds circumstances that justify an earlier date.
(b) The court may consider documented evidence of a convicted spouse's history as a victim of domestic violence, as defined in Section 6211, perpetrated by the other spouse, or any other factors the court deems just and equitable, as conditions for rebutting this presumption.
(c) The rebuttable presumption created in this section may be rebutted by a preponderance of the evidence.
(d) The court may determine, based on the facts of a particular case, that the injured spouse is entitled to up to 100 percent of the community property interest in his or her retirement and pension benefits. In determining whether and how to apportion the community property interest in the retirement and pension benefits of the injured spouse, the court shall consider all of the following factors:
(1) The misdemeanor domestic violence conviction, as well as documented evidence of other instances of domestic violence, as defined in Section 6211, between the parties or perpetrated by either party against either party's child, including, but not limited to, consideration of emotional distress resulting from domestic violence. The court shall also consider documented evidence of a convicted spouse's history as a victim of domestic violence, as defined in Section 6211, perpetrated by the other spouse.
(2) The duration of the marriage and when, based on documented evidence, incidents of domestic violence, as defined in Section 6211, occurred.
(3) The extent to which the convicted spouse's present or future earning capacity is impaired by periods of unemployment that were incurred during the marriage to permit the convicted spouse to devote time to domestic duties.
(4) The extent to which the convicted spouse contributed to the attainment of an education, training, a career position, or a license by the injured spouse.
(5) The balance of the hardships to each party.
(6) Any other factors the court determines are just and equitable.
(e) As used in this section, the following definitions apply:
(1) "Domestic violence misdemeanor" means a misdemeanor offense for an act of abuse, as described in paragraphs (1) to (3), inclusive, of subdivision (a) of Section 6203, perpetrated by one spouse against the other spouse.
(2) "Injured spouse" means the spouse who has been the subject of the domestic violence misdemeanor for which the other spouse was convicted.
(f) The changes made to this section by the bill that added this subdivision shall only apply to convictions that occur on or after January 1, 2019.

Chapter 17: Spousal Support

The family court should not enter an order that effectively requires a spouse to forgo retirement. *In re Marriage of KOCHAN* (2011) 193 Cal.App.4th 420 at pp. 429–430.

While a support spouse may not retire prematurely, the supporting spouse has a right to retire at age 65 even when the retirement could lead to a lower income.

The Court held that: "no one may be compelled to work after the usual retirement age of 65 in order to pay the same level of spousal support as when he was employed." *In re Marriage of REYNOLDS* (1998) 63 Cal.App.4th 1373 at p. 1378.)

So how does "self-supporting" fit into retirement? The following case discusses the issue of self-supporting and retirement.

In re Marriage of COLLEEN and BRUCE Y. McLAIN. COLLEEN McLAIN, Respondent, v. BRUCE Y. McLAIN, Appellant.
COURT OF APPEAL OF CALIFORNIA, FOURTH APPELLATE DISTRICT, DIVISION TWO
7 Cal.App.5th 262
January 6, 2017, Opinion Filed
(*Marriage of McLain*)

Husband and Wife married on October 13, 2001. They separated on March 14, 2013. They did not share any children. In May 2014, Husband was 68 years old and Wife was 66 years old. Husband had worked as a firefighter. Wife had worked as a personal assistant and transaction coordinator for a real estate agent and broker. Wife was a licensed real estate agent, but never used her license.

Both Husband and Wife retired in 2005. At that time, Husband was ready to retire and urged Wife to retire as well so they could travel and she could spend time with her grandchildren. In 2005, Wife began training her daughter to take over Wife's job in the real estate office. Through 2011 or 2012, as payment for a loan, Wife continued working as a personal assistant two to five hours per week for the real estate agent/broker. However, Wife's primary focus since 2005 had been cooking, cleaning, laundry, and household chores. Wife was in good health. Wife had a monthly Social Security income of $746 less $198 for Medicare payments. Husband's retirement income was approximately $10,000 per month.

After retiring in 2005, Husband was busy working with a contractor on building a house for Husband and Wife in Big Bear City (the Big Bear house). There was not a mortgage on the house; it was built as cash was available from 2006 through 2011. The Big Bear house was approximately 3,900 square feet and had a stipulated value of $775,000. The lot on which the Big Bear house was built was purchased in 2003.

Wife owned a residence in Fawnskin, which she had owned since 1987. During Husband and Wife's marriage, the loan on the Fawnskin property was refinanced three times. The first refinance allowed approximately $95,000 to be taken out. The second refinance left approximately $100,000 in cash. The third refinance generated an extra $130,000 in cash. The cash from the refinancing, at least from the second and third refinancing, went into a joint account and was used for construction of the Big Bear house. During the construction period Husband and Wife always had joint accounts. The Fawnskin house was ultimately sold in a short sale.

Husband owned a residence in San Dimas, which he acquired in 1974 (the San Dimas house). In 2004, the San Dimas house was sold. Wife's name was added to the title of the San Dimas house at the time of the sale for title insurance purposes. Money from the sale of the San Dimas house went into a joint account and a portion of it was used to construct the Big Bear house. Husband had a "401-A" account and an IRA that he also used to pay for the construction. The cost of the Big Bear house was approximately $507,700.

The family court issued a ruling on submitted matter. In the written ruling, the family court wrote, in relevant part, "In this matter, the Court finds that [Wife] needs spousal support to help her meet her financial needs as well as to put her as close as possible to the marital standard of living. This Court does not believe that it is appropriate to impute income to [Wife]. No evidence was presented which would support an income to her, or that there were jobs available for which she qualified and could earn an income. Furthermore, she is retired, just as [Husband] is retired, with both of them beyond retirement age. The parties have a right to retire, and they did that. [Husband] knew [Wife] substantially retired in 2006, a year after he did, and that she fully retired in 2011. Their retirement has been part of the marital standard of living since well before the dissolution of marriage was filed, and [Wife] is not now going to be thrown out of retirement. For these same reasons, this Court will also not be issuing a *Gavron* warning to [Wife]." The court awarded Wife $4,000 per month in spousal support and $5,500 in attorney's fees.

DISCUSSION
Husband contends the family court erred by concluding Wife has the same right to retire as Husband. Husband asserts Wife, as the supported spouse, has an obligation to become self-supporting and therefore does not have a right to retire.

FC § 4320 lists a variety of factors the family court should consider when ordering spousal support. Two of the factors are "[t]he age and health of the parties." (FC § 4320(h).) The statute also provides the family court should consider "[t]he goal that the supported party shall be self-supporting within a reasonable period of time… However, nothing in this section is intended to limit the court's discretion to order support for a greater or lesser length of time, based on any of the other factors listed in this section, FC § 4336, and the circumstances of the parties." (FC § 4320(*l*).) The family court may also take into account "[a]ny other factors the court determines are just and equitable." (FC § 4320(n).)

The conflict in this case arises between the portion of the statute that authorizes the family court to consider "age," which could be interpreted as retirement age, and the portion of the statute that sets forth the goal of the supported party becoming self-supporting. In other words, can the family court determine that a supported spouse being of retirement age outweighs the "self-supporting" factor? In order to determine this, we need to understand what is meant by the "age" factor in the statute.

The plain language of the statute reflects the family court is to consider "[t]he age and health of the parties" when ordering spousal support. (FC § 4320(h).) For the age factor to have meaning, the family court would need to consider whether the parties are young and

Chapter 17: Spousal Support

therefore presumably more likely to work and earn a living wage, or whether the parties are older and perhaps no longer working. In other words, the plain language of the statute reflects age is a factor in determining spousal support. The point of considering age when determining spousal support, in part, is that there comes an age when people commonly stop working.

The age of 65 is the customary retirement age. Thus, given the plain language of the statute, a relevant consideration for a court when ordering spousal support is the age of the parties, and the point of that factor is to determine if the parties are younger or older, and if the parties are older, whether they have reached the customary retirement age of 65.

"An award of spousal support is a determination to be made by the trial court in each case before it, based upon the facts and equities of that case, after weighing each of the circumstances and applicable statutory guidelines. In making its spousal support order, the trial court possesses broad discretion so as to fairly exercise the weighing process contemplated by FC § 4320, with the goal of accomplishing substantial justice for the parties in the case before it. 'The issue of spousal support, including its purpose, is one which is truly personal to the parties.' In awarding spousal support, the court must consider the mandatory guidelines of FC § 4320. Once the court does so, the ultimate decision as to amount and duration of spousal support rests within its broad discretion and will not be reversed on appeal absent an abuse of that discretion. 'Because trial courts have such broad discretion, appellate courts must act with cautious judicial restraint in reviewing these orders.'" (*In re Marriage of Kerr* (1999) 77 Cal.App.4th 87, 93 [91 Cal. Rptr. 2d 374], fn. omitted.)

Under section 4320, the family court is to consider (1) "[t]he extent to which the earning capacity of each party is sufficient to maintain the standard of living established during the marriage" (FC § 4320(a)) and (2) "[t]he needs of each party based on the standard of living established during the marriage" (FC § 4320(d)). The marital standard of living is "a general description of the station in life the parties had achieved by the date of separation," rather than a "mathematical standard." (*In re Marriage of Smith* (1990) 225 Cal.App.3d 469, 491 [274 Cal. Rptr. 911].)

In the family court's ruling on submitted matter, it concluded that Wife needed spousal support to put her near the marital standard of living. Thus, the court was properly considering the marital standard of living as well as Wife's needs. (FC § 4320(a) & (d).)

Next, the court determined that it would not impute income to Wife because (1) there was no evidence she had an income; (2) there was no evidence of jobs available to Wife; (3) Wife was retired; and (4) Wife had a right to remain retired. The court's consideration of Wife being retired reflects the court taking into account "the station in life the parties had achieved," i.e., that they were both retired. (*In re Marriage of Smith, supra*, 225 Cal.App.3d at p. 491; see FC § 4320(a) & (d)). The court's comment that Wife had a right to remain retired reflects consideration of both the parties' "station in life" as well as Wife's age because Wife was beyond the customary retirement age of 65. The family court's reasoning reflects it was following the requirements of section 4320, taking into account the marital "standard of living" as well as the ages of the parties. (FC § 4320(a), (d) & (h).) The family court's comments concerning Wife's lack of income and the lack of available jobs are related to Wife being retired and thus is a proper consideration. (FC § 4320(a), (d) & (h).)

The court also took into account "[t]he goal that the supported party shall be self-supporting within a reasonable period of time." (§ 4320, subd. (*l*).) The court explained, "Their retirement has been part of the marital standard of living since well before the dissolution of marriage was filed, and [Wife] is not now going to be thrown out of retirement. For these same reasons, this Court will also not be issuing a *Gavron* warning to [Wife]." "[A] '*Gavron* warning' is a fair warning to the supported spouse [that] he or she is expected to become self-supporting." (*In re Marriage of Schmir* (2005) 134 Cal.App.4th 43, 55 [35 Cal. Rptr. 3d 716].)

The court's reasoning reflects it weighed the goal of the supported party becoming self-supporting against the marital standard of living, and reconciled that the goal of self-support would conflict with maintaining the marital standard of living because the marital standard of living included being retired. The court's reasoning shows it considered the relevant factors. Further, the court's reasoning is tied to the evidence, which reflects the parties retired in 2005, and in 2014 Wife was 66 years old. Accordingly, the family court did not abuse its discretion because its reasoning directly relates to the evidence and the factors it is legally required to consider. The family court's decision is within the law and within the bounds of reason. Accordingly, we conclude the family court did not err.

Husband contends the family court erred by not requiring Wife to make an effort to become self-supporting because the court has effectively ordered Husband to pay Wife spousal support for the rest of her life. Husband's argument focuses on the evidence that Wife has the ability to work. Husband is asking this court to reweigh the factors and afford greater weight to Wife's ability to work than to Wife's age. As explained *ante*, the family court's weighing of the factors was reasonable and within the bounds of the law. We cannot reweigh the factors to accord greater weight to the supported spouse's ability to work.

Husband contends the family court erred by failing to consider the factor set forth in FC § 4320(a) —"[t]he extent to which the earning capacity of each party is sufficient to maintain the standard of living established during the marriage." Husband asserts the family court failed to include in its weighing process the length of time it would take for Wife to become self-supporting. Contrary to Husband's position, the family court did consider this factor. The family court explained that Wife did not have an income, that retirement was part of the marital standard of living, that Wife was beyond retirement age, that Wife could not be expected to start working again, and that the Court did not expect Wife to become self-supporting. The family court considered Wife's ability to work as shown by the court's discussion of Wife's retirement status. The family court's reasoning shows it accorded greater weight to the supported spouse's age than to the supported spouse's ability to work. Thus, we are not persuaded that the family court missed a factor in the weighing process.

Next, Husband contends the family court erred because it did not consider "[t]he goal that the supported party shall be self-supporting." (FC § 4320(*l*)) The family court did consider this goal as shown by the court's decision that it would not issue a *Gavron* warning. "[A] '*Gavron* warning' is a fair warning to the supported spouse [that] he or she is expected to become self-supporting." (*In re Marriage of Schmir, supra*, 134 Cal.App.4th at p. 55.) The family court explained it was not issuing a *Gavron* warning because Wife was retired and past the age of retirement. The court's decision shows it considered the goal of the supported party becoming self-supporting, but accorded greater weight to Wife's age. Thus, the court did not miss a required factor;

> rather, it afforded greater weight to the age factor.
>
> **DISPOSITION**
>
> The judgment is affirmed. Respondent is awarded her costs on appeal.

12. A Professional License That is Obtained During the Marriage

As shown in the following case, when one of the parties obtains a professional license during the marriage, that license should be considered in deciding spousal support.

> *In re Marriage of JANET LINNEA and MARK JAYE SULLIVAN. MARK JAYE SULLIVAN, Appellant, v. JANET LINNEA SULLIVAN, Appellant*
> Supreme Court of California
> 37 Cal.3d 762; 691 P.2d 1020; 209 Cal.Rptr. 354
> December 31, 1984
>
> Is a spouse, who has made economic sacrifices to enable the other spouse to obtain a professional education, entitled to any compensation for his or her contribution upon dissolution of the marriage?
>
> Janet and Mark Sullivan were married in September of 1967. The following year, Mark (respondent) entered medical school at Irvine and Janet (appellant) began her final year of undergraduate college at UCLA.[11]
>
> Appellant gives the following abbreviated account of the ensuing years.[12] From 1968 through 1971, respondent attended medical school. Until 1969, appellant worked part time while completing her undergraduate education. After graduation, she obtained a full-time position which she held through 1971.
>
> In 1972, respondent began his internship at Portland, Oregon. Appellant gave up her full-time job to accompany him there. Shortly after the move, she obtained part-time employment. The couple's daughter, Treisa, was born in May of 1974. Appellant ceased work until 1975 when she resumed part-time employment. From 1976 through 1977, she worked full-time. During this period, respondent completed his residency. Both parties then moved back to California. Shortly afterward, they separated. In August 1978, respondent petitioned for dissolution of the marriage.
>
> During the marriage, the couple had accumulated some used furniture and two automobiles, both with payments outstanding. This property was disposed of by agreement. Appellant received $ 500, some used furniture and her automobile, including

---

[11] Both parties appealed from the judgment. However, Janet appealed on the issue that prompted this court to grant a hearing. Therefore, Janet will be referred to as appellant and Mark as respondent.
[12] This account is contained in appellant's trial brief, which was added to the record on appeal by stipulation, and which was before the trial court at the time of its rulings on the motions at issue here. Respondent has stated that he does not object to the use of these facts as general background.
It is not disputed that respondent obtained his professional education during the marriage or that appellant worked to support the couple. Also undisputed are the facts relating to the couple's property settlement and to the dissolution proceedings. (See post, at p. 766.)

the obligation to complete the payments.

At the dissolution proceeding, appellant sought to introduce evidence of the value of respondent's medical education. She argued that the education was obtained by the joint efforts and sacrifices of the couple, that it constituted the greatest asset of the marriage, and that -- accordingly -- both parties should share in its benefits.

The superior court rejected these arguments and granted respondent's motion *in limine* to exclude all evidence pertaining to the value of the education. At the same time, the court granted partial summary judgment to the effect that respondent's education did not constitute community property. The court indicated that it was barred from awarding appellant any compensation for her contribution to respondent's education by the rule of *In re Marriage of Aufmuth* (1979) 89 Cal.App.3d 446, 461 (professional education does not constitute community property).

In May of 1980, the court issued its interlocutory judgment of dissolution. Appellant was awarded no spousal support, but the court reserved jurisdiction for five years to modify that determination. The parties were awarded joint custody of their daughter. Respondent was ordered to pay appellant $ 250 per month for child support and to reimburse her for half the cost of the child's medical insurance. Finally, the court directed respondent to pay appellant $ 1,250 in attorney fees and $ 1,000 in costs. Both parties appealed.

DISCUSSION
This court originally granted a hearing in this case primarily to determine whether a spouse, who has made economic sacrifices to enable the other spouse to obtain an education, is entitled to compensation upon dissolution of the marriage. While the case was pending before this court, the Legislature amended the Family Law Act to provide compensation in all cases not yet final on January 1, 1985. (Stats. 1984, ch. 1661, §§ 2-4.)[13]

The amendments provide for the community to be reimbursed, absent an express written agreement to the contrary, for "community contributions to education or training of a party that substantially enhances the earning capacity of the party." (Civ. Code, § 4800.3, added by Stats. 1984, ch. 1661, § 2.) The compensable community contributions are defined as "payments made with community property for education or training or for the repayment of a loan incurred for education or training." (*Ibid.*) The reimbursement award may be reduced or modified where an injustice would otherwise result. (*Ibid.*)[14]

---

[13] Chapter 1661 amended sections 4800 and 4801 of the Civil Code and added section 4800.3. At the time of filing of this opinion, the changes had not been published in code form. Accordingly, the citations in this opinion are to session and chapter number.

[14] The reimbursement provision states in full: "Section 4800.3 is added to the Civil Code, to read: "4800.3. (a) As used in this section, 'community contributions to education or training' means payments made with community property for education or training or for the repayment of a loan incurred for education or training.

"(b) Subject to the limitations provided in this section, upon dissolution of marriage or legal separation:

"(1) The community shall be reimbursed for community contributions to education or training of a party that substantially enhances the earning capacity of the party. The amount reimbursed shall be with interest at the legal rate, accruing from the end of the calendar year in which the contributions were made.

"(2) A loan incurred during marriage for the education or training of a party shall not be included

Chapter 17: Spousal Support

> In addition to providing for reimbursement, the amendments require the court to consider, in awarding spousal support, "the extent to which the supported spouse contributed to the attainment of an education, training, or a license by the other spouse." (Civ. Code, § 4801, as amended by Stats. 1984, ch. 1661, § 3.)
>
> Since the property settlement in the present proceeding will not be final on January 1, 1985 (see Cal. Rules of Court, rule 24(a)), appellant is entitled to the benefit of the new amendments. (Stats. 1984, ch. 1661, § 4.) The trial court did not, of course, make the findings necessary to determine whether and in what amount reimbursement and/or support should be awarded under these provisions since they were not in existence at that time. Accordingly, the judgment denying any compensation for contributions to education must be reversed.
>
> Respondent has cross-appealed from that portion of the trial court's judgment ordering him to pay $ 1,250 for appellant's attorney fees and $ 1,000 for her costs. He contends that the decision was an abuse of the trial court's discretion.
>
> Civil Code section 4370 provides that "[in] respect to services rendered or costs incurred after the entry of judgment, the court may award such costs and attorneys' fees as may be reasonably necessary to maintain or defend any subsequent proceeding . . . ." The purpose of the award is to provide one of the parties, if necessary, with an amount adequate to properly litigate the controversy.
>
> In making its determination as to whether or not attorney fees and costs should be awarded, the trial court considers the respective needs and incomes of the parties. Further, the trial court is not restricted in its assessment of ability to pay to a consideration of salary alone, but may consider all the evidence concerning the parties' income, assets and abilities.

---

among the liabilities of the community for the purpose of division pursuant to Section 4800 but shall be assigned for payment by the party.

"(c) The reimbursement and assignment required by this section shall be reduced or modified to the extent circumstances render such a disposition unjust, including but not limited to any of the following:

"(1) The community has substantially benefited from the education, training, or loan incurred for the education or training of the party. There is a rebuttable presumption, affecting the burden of proof, that the community has not substantially benefited from community contributions to the education or training made less than 10 years before the commencement of the proceeding, and that the community has substantially benefited from community contributions to the education or training made more than 10 years before the commencement of the proceeding.

"(2) The education or training received by the party is offset by the education or training received by the other party for which community contributions have been made.

"(3) The education or training enables the party receiving the education or training to engage in gainful employment that substantially reduces the need of the party for support that would otherwise be required.

"(d) Reimbursement for community contributions and assignment of loans pursuant to this section is the exclusive remedy of the community or a party for the education or training and any resulting enhancement of the earning capacity of a party. However, nothing in this subdivision shall limit consideration of the effect of the education, training, or enhancement, or the amount reimbursed pursuant to this section, on the circumstances of the parties for the purpose of an order for support pursuant to Section 4801.

"(e) This section is subject to an express written agreement of the parties to the contrary."

> Respondent's financial statement, prepared in the spring of 1980, also reflected monthly expenses which exceeded his net monthly income by over $ 800. Similarly, respondent's assets, although greater than appellant's, would also have been depleted within a few months if his income and expenses remained the same.
>
> However, the court also had before it a comparative statement of respondent's business revenue and expenditures for the years 1978 and 1979, respondent's first two years of medical practice. Significantly, this comparative statement demonstrated that the fees which respondent collected during his second year of practice were more than double the fees he collected during the first. His annual net income increased by over $ 40,000 in one year. On the other hand, there was no corresponding statement or testimony to indicate any likelihood of an increase in appellant's income.
>
> Given this evidence, this court can only conclude that the trial court made the reasonable inference that respondent's burgeoning medical practice would continue to flourish and that his income would increase dramatically. The facts of this case fall woefully short of establishing any abuse of discretion by the trial court. "[The] cases have frequently and uniformly held that the court may base its decision on the [paying spouse's] ability to earn, rather than his [or her] current earnings . . ." for the simple reason that in cases such as this, current earnings give a grossly distorted view of the paying spouse's financial ability. (*Meagher v. Meagher (1961) 190 Cal.App.2d 62* at p. 64.)
>
> **DISPOSITION**
> That portion of the judgment ordering respondent to pay appellant's costs and attorney fees is affirmed. The judgment denying compensation for contributions to spousal education is reversed and the cause remanded for further proceedings consistent with the views expressed in this opinion. Appellant to recover costs on both appeals.

Temporary and Permanent Spousal Support

1. Temporary Support

Temporary spousal support is support that is ordered during the period of time between the initial filing of the petition and the final judgment. Additionally, support can be temporary if the judge so declares.

Temporary and permanent spousal support are two diverse kinds of support, and the purposes of temporary and permanent support are vastly different. "The purpose of temporary spousal support is to maintain the status quo as much as possible pending trial." *In re Marriage of SCHULZE* (1997) 60 Cal.App.4th 519 at p. 525. It is to maintain the status quo until the issue is tried or settled. *In re Marriage of SMITH* (1990) 225 Cal.App.3d 469 Footnote 16 at p. 495.

"Temporary spousal support is utilized to maintain the living conditions and standards of the parties in as close as possible to the status quo position realized during the marriage pending trial and the division of their assets and obligations." *In re Marriage of WINTER* (1992) 7 Cal.App.4th 1926 at p. 1932 quoting: *In re MARRIAGE of BURLINI* (1983) 143 Cal.App.3d 65 at p. 68.

Temporary spousal support may be ordered in "any amount that is necessary for … support and maintenance." **FC §§ 3600-3604**. **FC § 3600** provides in pertinent part: "in any proceeding for dissolution of marriage or for legal separation the court may order (a) either spouse to pay any amount that is necessary for the support of the other spouse, consistent with the requirements of subdivisions (i) and (m) of **FC §§ 4320** and **4325**." "[T]emporary support is intended 'to assure a spouse substantially the same living conditions to which he or she has been accustomed pending final judgment.'" Hogoboom & King, Cal. Practice Guide: Family Law 1 (The Rutter Group 1992) § 5:7.4, p. 5-6.

A temporary support order is operative from the time of pronouncement, and it is directly appealable. *In re MARRIAGE of SKELLEY* (1976) 18 Cal.3d 365, 368.

A change of circumstances is required for the modification of support orders, including temporary ones. (See *In re MARRIAGE of BIDERMAN* (1992) 5 Cal.App.4th 409, where the court stated that a "motion for modification of spousal support may only be granted if there has been a material change of circumstances since the last order. Otherwise, dissolution cases would have no finality and unhappy former spouses could bring repeated actions for modification with no burden of showing a justification to change the order. *Id.* at p. 412-413.)

Temporary support is usually a higher amount than permanent support orders. (See *In re Marriage of SCHULZE* (1997) 60 Cal.App.4th 519, where the court stated that "the purpose of temporary spousal support is to maintain the status quo as much as possible pending trial.

Temporary spousal support is utilized to maintain the living conditions and standards of the parties in as close to the status quo position as possible pending trial and the division of their assets and obligations." *Id.* at p. 525.)

2. Permanent Spousal Support

As provided above, temporary and permanent spousal support are two different kinds of support.

The purpose of permanent spousal support is "to provide financial assistance, if appropriate, as determined by the financial circumstances of the parties after their dissolution and the division of their community property." *In re Marriage of SCHULZE* (1997) 60 Cal.App.4th 519 at p. 522; *In re Marriage of BURLINI* (1983) 43 Cal.App.3d 65 at p. 69.[15]

In determining spousal support at trial, the court must base the amount and duration of spousal support upon the statutory factors enumerated in **FC § 4320**.

---

[15] Actually, *In re Marriage of Burlini* stated the factors that were set forth Civil Code § 4801. CC § 4801 was repealed in 1994 and continued without substantive change in FC §4320.

Permanent spousal support may be ordered in a short marriage or a marriage of long duration.

> Permanent spousal support is supposed to reflect a complex variety of factors established by statute and legislatively committed to the trial judge's discretion, including several factors which tend to favor reduced support, such as the 'goal' that the supported spouse should become self-supporting within a reasonable period of time. *In re Marriage of SCHULZE* (1997) 60 Cal.App.4th 519 at p. 525.

Permanent support is usually a lower amount of money than in temporary orders, and a modification of permanent spousal support requires a change in circumstances. *In re Marriage of HEISTERMAN* (1991) 234 Cal.App.3d 1195 at p. 1201.

If an order for spousal support has a termination date set forth in the order, the court may not extend the time unless the court retained jurisdiction in that order. **FC § 4336**.

Modifiable and Nonmodifiable Spousal Support

1. Modification/Change of Circumstances

FC § 3591 provides that the provisions of an agreement with regard to spousal support are subject to modification or termination by the court. However, an agreement cannot be modified or terminated as to an amount accrued before the filing of a motion to modify or terminate.

"A motion for modification of spousal support may only be granted if there has been a material change of circumstances since the last order." *In re MARRIAGE of SMITH* (1990) 225 Cal.App.3d 469 at p. 480.

The material change in circumstances must be proven to the satisfaction of the court. *In re Marriage of ROSENFELD & GROSS* (2014) 225 Cal.App.4th 478 at p. 479. Otherwise, dissolution cases would have no finality, and unhappy former spouses could bring repeated actions for modification with no burden of showing a justification to change the order. Parties are entitled to attempt, with some degree of certainty, to reorder their finances and lifestyles in reliance upon the finality of the decree.

"Absent a change of circumstances, a motion for modification is nothing more than an impermissible collateral attack on a prior final order." *In re MARRIAGE of SMITH* (1990) 225 Cal.App.3d 469 at p. 480.

Modification of spousal support based on consideration of the **FC § 4320** factors constitutes error when the evidence does not show a material change of circumstances. *In re MARRIAGE of DIETZ* (2009) 176 Cal.App.4th 387, 401–403. The court must first find that there is a material change in circumstances and then consider the circumstances set forth in **FC § 4320**.

Chapter 17: Spousal Support

The moving party bears the burden of establishing that a material change of circumstances has occurred since the last order was made in order to obtain modification of the spousal support order.

In re MARRIAGE of TYDLASKA (2003) 114 Cal.App.4th 572 at p. 575; *In re MARRIAGE of NORVALL* (1987) 192 Cal.App.3d 1047 at p. 1060. After showing to the satisfaction of the court that a change of circumstance occurred, "it does not ensure that a modification will be granted." *In re MARRIAGE of STEPHENSON* (1995) 39 Cal.App.4th 71 at p. 78 quoting Samuels & Mandabach, Practice Under the Cal. Family Code (Cont.Ed.Bar 1995) § 6.24, p. 168.

A change of circumstances sufficient for either party to request a modification of spousal support may exist where there is a spousal support order and a companion child support order and the child support is terminating pursuant to **FC § 3901(a)(1)**.[16] The court must have retained jurisdiction over the spousal support in order for there to be a modification. **FC § 4326(a)**. The motion to modify or terminate spousal support must be filed no later than six months after the child support has terminated. **FC § 4326(b)**.

Changed expectations regarding the ability of a supported spouse to become self-supporting may constitute a change of circumstances warranting a modification of spousal support. If the court's last order provided that the supported spouse decrease his or her needs and did not, a court could modify the award on the ground of changed circumstances. *In re Marriage of SHAUGHNESSY* (2006) 139 Cal.App.4th 1225 at p. 1239.

If either the supported or supporting spouse develops a serious health condition or a serious health condition has worsened after the last order, that may constitute a change in circumstances sufficient for a modification. *Id.* at p. 1245.

If a supporting spouse reaches the appropriate age for retirement and his or her retirement income is less, this could be a material change in circumstances for purposes of modifying a support order. *In re Marriage of DIETZ* (2009) 176 Cal.App.4th 387 at p. 405.

> The propriety of an order modifying spousal support rests within the trial court's sound discretion. So long as the court exercised its discretion along legal lines, its decision will not be reversed on appeal if there is substantial evidence to support it. Reversal requires a clear showing of abuse of discretion. *In re Marriage of SMITH* (1990) 225 Cal.App.3d 469 at p. 480.

---

[16] FC § 3901(a)(1) provides that the duty of support continues until the child attains the 19 years of age or completes the 12th grade, whichever occurs first.

Chapter 17: Spousal Support

A voluntary decision to pursue a doctoral degree rather than entering the working world full time does not constitute a material change of circumstances in most cases. *KHERA and SAMEER v. MADHU* (2012) Cal.App.4th 1467 at p. 1482.

What if the parties define "changed circumstances"? Must the court use that definition? As the following case demonstrates, FC § 4320 allows a court to decide if there are "changed circumstances" even if that term is defined in the parties' agreement.

> ***In re the Marriage of T.C. and D.C.T.C., Respondent, v. D.C., Appellant.***
> Court of Appeal of California, Fourth Appellate District, Division One
> 30 Cal. App. 5th 419
> December 18, 2018, Opinion Filed
>
> Husband and Wife were married for 18 and a half years and have two children together. Both worked outside the home during their marriage. They separated in 2012 and in 2014 dissolved their marriage according to the terms of two agreements, a marriage settlement agreement (MSA) incorporated into the court's judgment in March 2014, and an August 2014 postjudgment stipulation (PJS) (collectively, the Agreements) that reflected newly available details regarding Husband's benefits and compensation.
>
> In the MSA, the parties agreed Wife would pay Husband $850 per month as base spousal support from July 2013 through the end of 2020. According to the MSA, "[t]his spousal support award meets Husband's reasonable needs. These needs are consistent with the standard of living established during the marriage." On top of the $850, Wife would also pay as additional spousal support 10 percent of any earnings in a calendar year in excess of $180,000. The parties further agreed the parties could petition the court to modify the spousal support: "Upon application of either party to modify or terminate support, the court may consider the annual incomes of each party during marriage and at date of separation. At date of separation, Husband had gross monthly income of $12,932.81 (primarily non-taxable income per his income and expense declaration filed on October 30, 2012), and Wife had gross monthly income of $10,300 plus bonus potential (per her income and expense declaration filed on November 29, 2012). After separation and after the filing of the dissolution, Husband changed employers wherein his monthly income decreased to $7,500, and Wife changed employers wherein her monthly income increased to $15,000, plus bonus potential." Wife also agreed to provide Husband with written notice each time she changed employment.
>
> The PJS maintained the general structure and termination terms of spousal support obligations but modified the specific payment amounts. For July to November 2013, Wife's support was reduced to $760 per month; for December 2013, $754; for January to March 2014, $755 per month; and from April 2014 through the end of 2020, $551 per month.
>
> In December 2016, Wife filed a request for order (RFO) to modify her spousal support obligations. She had found a new job with a higher salary and contended that in light of these changed circumstances, her obligations under the Agreements exceeded the marital standard of living and would result in a windfall to Husband. Whereas in 2012 Wife's earnings included a $180,000 base salary and a potential bonus capped at 20 percent of her salary, in 2016 Wife earned $265,000 with a possible bonus of up to 40 percent of her

salary. At the initial hearing the court issued an oral decision denying Wife's petition. But on the following day, it filed a minute order indicating it would reconsider its prior decision on its own motion. Several months later the court issued its findings and order after hearing.

The court found that while Husband's expectation at the time of the Agreements was to receive 10 percent of Wife's bonus of $9,900, i.e. $990, if Wife received all of her potential new bonus, Wife's additional payment would climb to $19,100. Primarily because of the significant disparity between $990 and $19,100, the court found sufficient evidence for changed circumstances. After analyzing the spousal support factors outlined in section 4320, the court maintained the base spousal support as dictated by the Agreements, and it maintained additional spousal support at 10 percent of Wife's earnings above $180,000. But the court added a new restriction, capping additional spousal support at $990 per year irrespective of Wife's actual earnings.

Husband filed objections and requests for findings and rulings relating to the court's findings and order after hearing. The court declined to address the objections, and to the extent Husband sought a statement of decision consistent with Code of Civil Procedure section 632 or rule 3.1590 of the California Rules of Court, the court denied the request as untimely.

DISCUSSION
To modify spousal support, a trial court must first find "'"a material change of circumstances since the last order."'" (*Minkin, supra*, 11 Cal.App.5th at p. 956.) In its changed-circumstances analysis, the court considers all factors affecting the supported spouse's needs and the supporting spouse's ability to pay. An "increase in the supporting spouse's ability to pay" may constitute a change in circumstances. (*In re Marriage of McCann* (1996) 41 Cal.App.4th 978, 982 [48 Cal. Rptr. 2d 864], citing *In re Marriage of Hoffmeister* (1984) 161 Cal.App.3d 1163, 1173 [208 Cal. Rptr. 345].) When support is governed by a marital settlement agreement or stipulated judgment, the trial court's changed-circumstances determination must "'"give effect to the intent and reasonable expectations of the parties as expressed in the agreement."'" (*Minkin, supra*, 11 Cal.App.5th at p. 957.)

Likewise, the "'trial court's discretion to modify the spousal support order is constrained by the terms of the marital settlement agreement.'" (*In re Marriage of Dietz* (2009) 176 Cal.App.4th 347 at p. 398.) Marital settlement agreements incorporated into a dissolution judgment are interpreted under the same rules governing contract interpretation generally. "'"The fundamental goal of contractual interpretation is to give effect to the mutual intention of the parties.If contractual language is clear and explicit, it governs."'" ((*In re Marriage of Hibbard* (2013) 212 Cal.App.4th 1007, 1013.)

Husband argues the Agreements themselves reflect the parties' reasonable expectations upon entering the agreements that an increase in Wife's salary would not constitute changed circumstances. Specifically, he points to the fact the parties did not cap the spousal support but did include a termination date in 2020, years before spousal support obligations would ordinarily terminate after dissolution of a lengthy marriage. Alternatively, Husband argues there is insufficient evidence of changed circumstances. He contends the 2012 marital standard of living "was roughly $475,000," based on Wife's 2012 taxable income of $189,000 and Husband's income of $156,516, $151,899 of which was nontaxable. Husband further points out that at the time of Wife's petition, he was earning $125,000, while Wife's base salary was $265,000, which is short of the marital standard of living even without accounting for inflation.

Chapter 17: Spousal Support

The court found changed circumstances as a result of Wife's "dramatic[]" increase in earnings. The court noted several relevant facts regarding the relative earnings increase. When she entered into the Agreements, Wife had "earned more than $180,000.00 only twice: $189,900 in 2012, and $189,717 in 2013." Under the terms of Wife's employment at that time, "[t]he maximum additional spousal support, had such bonuses been earned, could not have exceeded $3,600.00 per year." Wife's "new remuneration ($265,000.00) is $85,000.00 greater than her salary at the date of separation; additional bonuses of up to 40 percent of her new base salary could add another $106,000.00." As additional spousal support, Wife would thus be required to pay "between $8,500.00 (10% of $85,000.00) and $19,100.00 (10% of $191,000.00)."

We disagree with Husband that the Agreements demonstrate a reasonable expectation that an increase in Wife's earnings could never amount to a change in circumstances. Certainly, the trial court is required to take the Agreements into account in determining whether there are changed circumstances. And the Agreements do reflect the parties' reasonable expectation that Wife's earnings would continue to increase, which we discuss below. But nothing in the Agreements compels a leap from that expectation to an understanding that an earnings increase could *never* constitute changed circumstances.

The real question is what *magnitude* of earnings increase would be necessary to create changed circumstances. On this point we are forced to conclude substantial evidence supports the trial court's finding that Wife's dramatic one-year leap in earnings constitutes a material change in circumstances such that it could consider modification of spousal support. Not only did Wife's bonus potential go from $36,000 to $106,000 in one year, but also by November 2016 records indicate she had already earned $96,152 in bonus income above her $265,000 annual base salary. Thus, we can set aside the speculation regarding potential bonuses and distill the key facts for an appropriate apples-to-apples analysis as follows. In the year prior to filing her RFO, Wife's total earnings climbed from $242,252 in 2015 to $361,403.84 in 2016, a 49 percent increase. Wife's earnings in the five years prior to the Agreements increased at an average rate of 12 percent with a standard deviation of 8.7 percent. Through a broader lens, Wife's earnings in the 10 years prior to the Agreements increased at an average rate of 11 percent with a standard deviation of 9.4 percent. In that context, an increase of 49 percent in one-year amounts to substantial evidence of changed circumstances.

Although its ability to modify a spousal support order is constrained by the terms of the marital settlement agreement, the trial court has significant discretion when weighing the various section 4320 factors. For the same reasons substantial evidence supported the court's changed-circumstances finding, particularly Wife's dramatic earnings increase, substantial evidence likewise supports the court's conclusion that some reduction of Wife's spousal support obligations was appropriate. However, by revising the parties' agreement to cap additional spousal support payment at "10% of Wife's income above $180,000.00 per year, up to $189,900" (i.e., the amount of Wife's earnings in 2012), the order fails to account for the parties' reasonable expectation that Wife's earnings would continue to increase. The order thus exceeds the constraints imposed by the terms of the MSA.

The Agreements reflect the parties' reasonable expectation that Wife's earnings would continue to increase, primarily through the way the parties agreed to calculate spousal support. The MSA divides spousal support into two tiers, base "spousal support" and "additional spousal support." The tiers are distinguished in two ways. First, whereas the base spousal support is set at a specific monthly figure, the additional spousal support is determined as a percentage of the amount by which Wife's annual earnings exceed $180,000. Second, before discussing additional spousal support, the MSA asserts the base "spousal support award meets Husband's reasonable needs. These needs are consistent with the standard of living established during the marriage." These distinctions thus evidence the expectation that while base support would be linked to Husband's reasonable needs and the marital standard of living, the additional spousal support provision—one bargained-for term among many in the expansive dissolution Agreements—would allow Husband to receive a percentage of Wife's likely earnings increase, irrespective of the marital standard of living or Husband's reasonable needs. The PJS maintains the MSA's distinction between the tiers of support.

Furthermore, the parties' earnings history is expressly contemplated in the Agreements' modification provision: "the court may consider the annual incomes of each party *during marriage and* at date of separation." Later in the same paragraph, the Agreements recite, "[a]fter separation and after the filing of the dissolution … Wife changed employers wherein her monthly income *increased* to $15,000, plus bonus potential." (Italics added.) And the Agreements' provision that Wife provide notice regarding any change in employment anticipates the possibility, or perhaps likelihood, that she would again change jobs. The inclusion of these details relating to Wife's new job and her increased earnings reinforces the parties' understanding implicit in the Agreements that her earnings would continue to increase. As discussed above, Wife's annual earnings unmistakably show a pattern of significant increases throughout the marriage, including the five- and 10-year periods before execution of the reements.

In summary, the parties' Agreements reflected their understanding that Wife's relatively recent earnings history included a pattern of increases, averaging 11–12 percent per year. Thus, future increases consistent with this pattern would not amount to changed circumstances sufficient to justify a modification of spousal support. Here, however, the trial court properly found that the unusual—what it termed "dramatic[]"—increase received by Wife in 2016 *was* a changed circumstance because it fell outside the normal pattern of increases reasonably contemplated by the parties at the time of their Agreements. As a result, modification of the "additional spousal support" component of the Agreements was appropriate. In fashioning the modification, however, what the trial court failed to do was incorporate the parties' demonstrated understanding that Wife would likely receive not insignificant increases in her earnings. It thus erred in simply capping additional spousal support at pre-2016 levels.

Because of its history with the parties and firsthand experience, it is for the trial court to craft a specific modification to spousal support in light of its finding of changed circumstances. But any restriction on additional spousal support should not deny Husband what the parties reasonably contemplated at the time they entered into the Agreements. For our part, we only direct that on remand the court (1) take account of the parties' reasonable expectation that Wife's earnings would continue to increase, and (2) modify the spousal support obligations accordingly.

DISPOSITION

The order is reversed and the matter is remanded to the superior court to modify the spousal support obligations in accordance with this opinion. Appellant is entitled to costs on appeal. McConnell, P. J., and Benke, J., concurred.

Finally, even when there is a showing of changed circumstances a "court may not retroactively modify a prior order for temporary spousal support." *In re MARRIAGE of MURRAY* (2002) 101 Cal.App.4th 581 at p. 525. **FC § 3603** "makes no provision for 'suspending' a spousal support order, or for modifying it retroactively beyond the date the underlying request for modification was filed." "The filing date…establishes the outermost limit of retroactivity." *Ibid.*

2. Nonmodifiable Spousal Support

FC § 3591 provides that the provisions of an agreement with regard to spousal support are subject to modification or termination by the court. However, an agreement cannot be modified or terminated as to an amount accrued before the filing of a motion to modify or terminate.

An agreement for spousal support may not be modified or revoked to the extent that a written agreement or, if there is no written agreement, an oral agreement entered into in open court between the parties, specifically provides that the spousal support is not subject to modification or termination. **FC § 3591(c)**.

A court will not modify an order for spousal support if the parties have specifically agreed in writing that the spousal support order is not subject to modification. In *In re Marriage of HIBBARD* (2013) 212 Cal.App.4th 1007, the husband filed a motion to modify the spousal support that he paid to his ex-spouse, claiming that he had become disabled. The parties had agreed to and signed a marital settlement agreement (*MSA*). The *MSA* provided that spousal support was nonmodifiable.

The husband argued that his disability was not foreseeable and, thus, because of either changed circumstances or impossibility, the agreement should be subject to modification. The court denied the husband's request stating that the parties did not intend that a reduction in the husband's income, either through disability or retirement, or some combination thereof, would create changed circumstances warranting modification of the support agreement. *Id.* at p. 1018. The court concluded that the language in the parties' *MSA* and stipulated judgment was very specific providing that spousal support will only terminate upon wife's death, wife's remarriage or the death of the husband. *Ibid.*

FC § 4337 provides:

> Except as otherwise agreed by the parties in writing, the obligation of a party under an order for the support of the other party terminates upon the death of either party or the remarriage of the other party.

However, there may be situations where remarriage does not terminate spousal support, as shown by the following case.

Chapter 17: Spousal Support

> *In re Marriage of GLENDA HILL and EDWARD JOHN CESNALIS. GLENDA HILL CESNALIS, Respondent, v. EDWARD JOHN CESNALIS, Appellant.*
> COURT OF APPEAL OF CALIFORNIA, THIRD APPELLATE DISTRICT
> 106 Cal.App.4th 1267
> March 12, 2003, Decided March 12, 2003, Filed
> (*Marriage of Cesnalis*)
>
> Edward and Glenda were married on November 30, 1992. A little over seven years later, they separated and Glenda filed for divorce. Edward's counsel drafted a stipulated judgment for dissolution of marriage (Stipulated Judgment). Shortly thereafter, the two parties and their attorneys met to discuss the draft.
>
> At this meeting, Glenda demanded that paragraph 4 of the Stipulated Judgment, pertaining to spousal support (Paragraph 4), be modified. As originally drafted, Paragraph 4 stated in relevant part: "4. SPOUSAL SUPPORT. Husband shall pay spousal support in the amount of $ 4,000.00 per month, … beginning October 1, 2000, and continuing until either party's death, the remarriage of Wife, or September 30, 2003, whichever occurs first, at which point spousal support will terminate absolutely. The duration of spousal support will not be modifiable under any circumstances, and the termination date stated herein is absolute, and no court shall have jurisdiction over the issue of spousal support, regardless of whether any motion is made on, before or after September 30, 2003. The parties stipulate that the marriage was one of short duration, and otherwise have bargained carefully for the termination of support contained herein."
>
> Glenda insisted that the words "the remarriage of Wife" be removed from the list of terminating events in Paragraph 4.
>
> Edward removed the remarriage language. Edward also added other language reiterating the three-year duration of support and moved the starting and ending dates of support back a month. Paragraph 4 now stated in relevant part: "4. SPOUSAL SUPPORT. Husband shall pay spousal support in the amount of $ 4,000.00 per month for a period of three years, … beginning November 1, 2000, and continuing until either party's death, or October 30, 2003, whichever occurs first, at which point spousal support will terminate absolutely. The duration of spousal support will not be modifiable under any circumstances, and the termination date stated herein is absolute, and no court shall have jurisdiction over the issue of spousal support, regardless of whether any motion is made on, before or after October 30, 2003. The parties stipulate that the marriage was one of short duration, and otherwise have bargained carefully for the termination of support contained herein."
>
> The parties then agreed to the Stipulated Judgment with this redrafted Paragraph 4, and the court entered the judgment on October 25, 2000. Glenda remarried on August 6, 2001. Upon learning of Glenda's remarriage, Edward moved unsuccessfully to terminate spousal support. This appeal ensued.
>
> **DISCUSSION**
> FC § 4337 states: "Except as otherwise agreed by the parties in writing, the obligation of a party under an order for the support of the other party terminates upon the death of either party or the remarriage of the other party." The issue here is whether Paragraph 4 evidences an agreement between the parties to waive FC § 4337.
>
> Paragraph 4 of the Stipulated Judgment is the relevant written agreement here. The

> specificity is centered on the duration of support and the limited circumstances that can end it. Under the wording of Paragraph 4, Edward "shall pay spousal support ... for a period of three years ... beginning November 1, 2000, and continuing until either party's death, or October 30, 2003, whichever occurs first, at which point spousal support will terminate absolutely." For good measure, Paragraph 4 adds that "[t]he duration of spousal support will not be modifiable under any circumstances, and the termination date stated herein is absolute[.]"
>
> Paragraph 4 reiterates that the three-year duration cannot be changed under any other circumstances; it is no stretch to say that a supported spouse's remarriage would generally be considered one of the most prominent of such circumstances. Viewed in this light, Paragraph 4 cannot be said to be altogether silent on remarriage as a terminating event.
>
> The extrinsic evidence admitted here showed the following. As originally drafted by Edward's counsel, Paragraph 4 specified that Glenda's remarriage ("the remarriage of Wife") would terminate spousal support. Glenda refused to agree to the Stipulated Judgment unless this language was removed from Paragraph 4. Edward removed the language and Glenda signed the Stipulated Judgment. Another significant distinction between the two drafts of Paragraph 4 is that the redrafted Paragraph 4 reiterated, in clear terms, that Edward would pay spousal support "for a period of three years."
>
> The trial court reasonably determined that Glenda would not agree to the Stipulated Judgment if the remarriage termination language was not removed, and that the removal of that language from Paragraph 4, in light of the language that remained, was clear and convincing evidence that the parties had agreed in writing that Glenda's remarriage would not terminate spousal support. Consequently, substantial evidence supports the trial court's determination that Edward waived FC § 4337's remarriage termination provision.
>
> We conclude the record supports the trial court's finding that the parties had agreed in writing that Glenda's remarriage would not terminate spousal support, and therefore Edward had waived FC § 4337. The order is affirmed.

Specific Reduction Spousal Support Orders

1. The Richmond Order

A Richmond order, so named after *In re MARRIAGE of RICHMOND* (1980) 105 Cal.App.3d 352 (*Richmond*), is a spousal support order made in which spousal support payments will terminate on a specific date unless the supported spouse files a motion to modify the support order.

A Richmond order, in effect, lets each spouse know that:

> the supported spouse has a specific period of time to become self-supporting, after which the obligation of the supporting spouse will cease. A **Richmond** order psychologically prepares the supported spouse for the time when he or she must be self-supporting. It also places the burden of showing good cause for a change in the order upon the one who is most able to exercise the control necessary to meet the expectations the trial judge had in making the order. *In re Marriage of Prietsch & Calhoun*, 190 Cal.App.3d 645 at p. 666.

Chapter 17: Spousal Support

Although it is expected, and probably greatly hoped for by the supporting spouse, that a supported spouse will be able to support him or herself by the set date, the court retains jurisdiction in case the supported spouse cannot sufficiently support him or herself by the specified date.

The Richmond court was sensitive to the fact that the desired objective will not be obtained in all cases, and, by retaining jurisdiction, the court has the power to adjust the order as needed. This is said to avoid the situation in *In re Marriage of MORRISON* (1978) 20 Cal.3d 437, where jurisdiction was terminated on the date specific with no allowance to modify in the event that spousal support was still needed after the date. *Morrison*, in effect, "burned its bridges" with regard to spousal support.

2. Substantive Stepdown

A substantive stepdown order of spousal support is an order where the amount of spousal support decreases in designated steps until the spousal support becomes a minimal amount such as $1 or reduced to $0. The court retains jurisdiction until death of either party or remarriage of the supported party if the marriage lasted ten (10) years or more. **FC § 4336**. If the marriage lasted less than ten (10) years, jurisdiction may be terminated at a date set by the court.

Spousal support orders must be based on reasonable inferences to be drawn from the evidence, not mere hopes or speculative expectations. *In re MARRIAGE of PRIETSCH & CALHOUN* (1987) 190 Cal.App.3d 645. The court in *Prietsch* held that it was reversible error to order a substantive stepdown lessening the amount of spousal support in steps over a nine-year period and, thereafter, terminating jurisdiction without any foundation in the evidence that the relevant factors would significantly improve during that nine-year period. *Id.* at p. 659.)

In *In re Marriage of WEST* (2007) 152 Cal.App.4th 240 a stepdown order was made, assuming that the supported spouse's income would increase over the next two years. The order did not prevent the supported spouse from requesting a modification above the amount ordered, but it did shift the burden of showing changed circumstances from the supporting spouse to the supported spouse. Both spouses could then seek a modification. The supported spouse would be entitled to seek a modification because of an unrealized expectation of her future earnings.

While the appellate court found no fault with the stepdown order to the extent that it stepped down support on the assumption that the supported spouse's income would rise over the next couple of years, it reversed the trial court's stepdown order, finding that it was not supported by the **FC § 4320** factors articulated by the court. *Id.* at p. 252.

If a marriage is not of long duration, the judge decides when jurisdiction over spousal support is terminated.

Chapter 17: Spousal Support

3. Jurisdictional Stepdown

A jurisdictional stepdown order is where spousal support is ordered to be paid until a certain date. After that date the amount of spousal support drops to $1 or $0. The court continues to reserve jurisdiction over this matter until the death of either party or the remarriage of the supported spouse, if the marriage was of long duration (10 years or more). If the marriage lasted less than ten (10) years, the judge can set the date that jurisdiction will be terminated.

A jurisdictional stepdown is only appropriate when there is certainty that the supported spouse will be able to support him or herself when jurisdiction is terminated.

Cohabitation

Contrary to what many people believe, when an ex-spouse cohabits with a romantic partner, the law does not provide that spousal support paid by the ex-spouse will be terminated. Instead, there is a rebuttable presumption, affecting the burden of proof, that the supported ex-spouse has a **decreased need** for spousal support. This means that the supported spouse has the burden to **prove by a preponderance of the evidence that his or her need for spousal support has not decreased**. The supported ex-spouse does not have to be holding himself or herself out as a spouse of the person that he or she is living with in order for the court to find a decreased need. If the court determines that the circumstances of the supported ex-spouse have changed, the court may modify or terminate the spousal support paid to the supported ex-spouse. When the court is determining if there is a decreased need, the income of a supporting spouse's subsequent spouse or nonmarital partner will not be considered. **FC § 4323.**

In *In re Marriage of BOWER* (2002) 96 Cal.App.4th 893; 117 Cal.Rptr.2d 520, the case that follows presents an interesting cohabitation issue.

In re Marriage of LYNN and JACK ALAN BOWER. LYNN BOWER, Appellant, v. JACK ALAN BOWER, Respondent.
COURT OF APPEAL OF CALIFORNIA, SECOND APPELLATE DISTRICT, DIVISION SIX
96 Cal.App.4th 893
March 4, 2002, Decided
(*Marriage of Bower*)

Wife unsuccessfully appeals from orders reducing and then terminating spousal support. She contends that the trial court (1) erroneously applied Family Code section 4323 (presumption of decreased need for spousal support if the supported party is cohabiting with a person of the opposite sex), and (2) failed to give adequate reasons for its order reducing and terminating spousal support.

Chapter 17: Spousal Support

1995 ORDER
The parties' 15-year marriage was dissolved in October 1995. Husband was ordered to pay $ 1,700 per month spousal support. At that time, wife's monthly gross income was $ 2,586.

1997 ORDER
In February 1997 husband sought modification or termination of spousal support. He alleged that wife was cohabiting with Mr. S. and that her earnings had increased.[17] Wife admitted only that she had "moved in" with Mr. S. and was splitting "living expenses" with him. She referred to Mr. S. as "a roommate." Wife attached checks payable to S. "evidencing [her] one half [payment] of the rent, utilities, and food." By this arrangement, wife was saving "a little bit of money on rent." Her income and expense declaration showed a current monthly gross income of $ 2,690.

The trial court denied husband's request to modify or terminate spousal support. It found that wife and Mr. S. were only "roommates" and ". . . that she pays her fair share of living expenses in regards to rent, utilities, and food." Had husband appealed from this order, he would not have prevailed. He wisely recognized the trial court's ruling as an adverse factual finding on the issue of cohabitation.

2000 ORDER
In October 2000 husband again sought termination of spousal support. Husband alleged that wife's income had increased to a level approaching her standard of living when the marriage was dissolved. He again claimed that wife was cohabiting with Mr. S. This time, he had proof. Husband submitted a bank statement showing that wife and Mr. S. maintained a joint savings account. The parties stipulated that wife was cohabiting with Mr. S.

Notwithstanding the stipulation, wife insisted that her circumstances had not changed since the 1997 proceeding. She alleged that she had received "only a modest increase in earnings" and that she "live[d] in an apartment with a roommate [*sic*]." Wife's income and expense declaration showed a current monthly gross income of $ 3,598. She had $ 500 in cash, $ 3,000 in savings, and $ 13,347 in other liquid assets.

The trial court found that wife "is now cohabiting with Mr.[S.] and [is] not merely a roommate . . . ." Noting section 4323, the trial court applied the presumption that wife had a reduced need for spousal support. It ruled that wife had "failed to meet her burden to refute the presumption . . . ." It did not immediately terminate spousal support because wife's "standard of living during the marriage was higher than what she has now, and [husband] continues to have the financial ability to provide support." The court reduced monthly spousal support to $ 500 and ordered that it be terminated after one year. The court believed that the "additional year period will allow [wife] the time and income to be able to obtain her own residence . . . without having to invade the savings and other assets that she has been able to accumulate . . . ." The court denied wife's request for attorney's fees and costs.

DISCUSSION
In exercising discretion whether to modify a spousal support order, "the court considers the same criteria set forth in section 4320 as it considered when making the initial order . .

---

[17] Although not required to do so, we refer to the wife's cohabitant by his last initial only.

. . These factors include the ability of the supporting party to pay; the needs of each party based on the standard of living established during the marriage; the obligations and assets of each party; and the balance of hardships to each party. (§ 4320, subds. (c)-(e), (j).)" (*In re Marriage of Terry* (2000) 80 Cal.App.4th 921, 928 [95 Cal.Rptr.2d 760].) " 'Modification of spousal support . . . requires a material change of circumstances since the last order. Change of circumstances means a reduction or increase in the supporting spouse's ability to pay and/or an increase or decrease in the supported spouse's needs. It includes all factors affecting need and the ability to pay. . . . [A]n abuse [of discretion] occurs when a court modifies a support order without substantial evidence of a material change of circumstances."(*Id.* at pp. 936-937.)

A material change of circumstances may occur if the supported spouse alters his or her lifestyle and cohabits with a person of the opposite sex. Cohabitation may reduce the need for spousal support because "sharing a household gives rise to economies of scale. Also, more importantly, the cohabitant's income may be available to the obligee spouse." (*In re Marriage of Schroeder* (1987) 192 Cal.App.3d 1154, 1159 [238 Cal.Rptr. 12].) Section 4323, subdivision (a)(1), provides, "[T]here is a rebuttable presumption, affecting the burden of proof, of decreased need for spousal support if the supported party is cohabiting with a person of the opposite sex." "[T]he Legislature created the presumption . . . based on thinking that cohabitation . . . creates a change of circumstances so tied in with the payment of spousal support as to be significant enough by itself to require a re-examination of whether such need for support continues in such a way that it still should be charged to the prior spouse." (*In re Marriage of Lieb* (1978) 80 Cal.App.3d 629, 643 [145 Cal.Rptr. 763].)

In its statement of decision, the trial court observed that in the 1997 proceeding it had "found that the person with whom [wife] was residing . . . in effect, was a roommate." It concluded that the evidence in the present proceeding clearly established "that [wife] is now cohabiting with Mr. [S.] and [is] not merely a roommate . . . ." It therefore applied the presumption of section 4323 that wife had a decreased need for support.

Wife alleges that the trial court abused its discretion because her cohabitation with Mr. S. "was clear in 1997" and the trial court "in effect found" cohabitation in the 1997 proceeding. She submits that the 1997 order's reference to *In re Marriage of Lieb, supra*, 80 Cal.App.3d 629, 643, shows that the trial court found that she was cohabiting with Mr. S. in 1997. The 1997 order cites *In re Marriage of Lieb* and says that she is "not 'giving away household services at the expense of obligor former spouse.' " Thus, wife argues, cohabitation was not a change of circumstances and could not have triggered the presumption of section 4323.

Wife's interpretation of the 1997 order flies in the face of the rules on appeal (*ante*, pp. 898-899) and violates the "obligation of the reader," articulated by Justice Gilbert in *Harris v. Superior Court* (1992) 3 Cal.App.4th 661, 665-667 [4 Cal.Rptr.2d 564].) [3] In 1997 the trial court neither expressly nor impliedly found cohabitation. The fair and only import of that order is that the trial court factually found that there was no cohabitation at that time. That the order says she was not making a gift of the value of household services does not show that she was cohabiting with Mr. S. The 1997 ruling does not mention any presumption of decreased need that a cohabitation finding would entail. In 1997 the trial court credited wife's representation that Mr. S. was merely a roommate: "[Wife] indicates that Mr. [S.] is, in effect, a roommate. She attaches persuasive evidence that she pays her fair share of living expenses in regards to rent, utilities, and food." Thus, the reader has let

> "the wish for a particular result color the meaning" of the order. (*Id.*, at p. 666.)
>
> The 1997 evidence that wife and Mr. S. were roommates sharing expenses was insufficient by itself to establish cohabitation: "When the Legislature chose to use 'cohabiting' it was selecting a word of particular legal significance that carries more meaning than two persons of the opposite sex living under the same roof." (*In re Marriage of Thweatt* (1979) 96 Cal.App.3d 530, 534 [157 Cal.Rptr. 826].) In *Thweatt* the appellate court found no cohabitation where the wife shared expenses with two male boarders and there was "no evidence of a sexual relationship, a romantic involvement, or even a homemaker-companion relationship between either of the men and wife." (*Id.* at p. 535.) The 1997 proceeding was similarly devoid of such evidence.
>
> In the 2000 proceeding there was substantial evidence showing that wife's relationship with Mr. S. had ripened into more than just an arrangement for sharing expenses. The stipulation to cohabitation is tantamount to a concession that, at least on a practical level, wife was living with Mr. S. as though he were her husband. In addition, they maintained a joint savings account to "which they equally contribute[d] to save up for vacations and trips taken together." This was a material change of circumstances triggering the presumption of section 4323.
>
> Wife contends that the trial court failed to give adequate reasons for its order reducing spousal support and terminating it after one year. Wife alleges: "[T]here is no explanation for the step down order in support other than [that] the . . . Trial Court found that [wife] is **now** cohabiting." But the statement of decision shows that the court also considered the increase in wife's earnings and assets. The court observed that, since the 1997 proceeding, wife's monthly earnings had increased from $ 2,700 to $ 3,600. It also noted that in 1997 wife had "listed savings of $ 400, and no stock, bonds or other liquid assets." In the present proceeding wife listed "savings of $ 3,000 and stocks, bonds and other liquid assets of approximately $ 13,000." The trial court explained that it was continuing reduced spousal support for one year to enable wife to purchase a residence "without having to invade [her] savings and other assets . . . ." The record permits intelligent appellate review. The trial court's articulated rationale cannot be equated with an abuse of discretion. In fact, the record would justify an outright termination of spousal support. It need not explain in detail why it extended largesse to wife.
>
> **DISPOSITION**
> The 2000 order is affirmed.

Family Support

Pursuant to **FC § 92**, family support means "an agreement between the parents, or an order or judgment, that combines child support and spousal support without designating the amount to be paid for child support and the amount to be paid for spousal support." It is similar to spousal support in that it is tax deductible to the obligor and includible in the obligee's taxable income.

Because child support is not deductible to the obligor and not includible to the obligee, there are no tax benefits for either spouse. However, since the entire family support amount is tax deductible from the obligor's taxable income and is includible in the obligee's income, the amount of family support can be adjusted so that the obligor has basically the same net income, when the tax benefits are taken into consideration. This additional deductibility maximizes the tax benefits and provides additional money to the receiving or obligee spouse. **FC § 4066**.

Thus, a family support order made during a dissolution can help the spouses maintain a standard of living that is closer to that which the couple enjoyed during the marriage. For this reason, family support is most commonly used prior to the final judgment.

If the parties enter into an agreement where family support is paid but no allocation is made between child and spousal support, "the court is not required to make a separate order for child support." **FC § 3586**.

Finally, a family support order is enforceable in the same manner and to the same extent as a child support order. **FC § 4501**.

EDUCATIONAL EXERCISES

I. Answer the following questions

1. Who decides how much spousal is awarded to the requesting party?

2. Is there a spousal support amount guideline in the Family Code?

3. Who pays the taxes on spousal support?

4. What is Family Support?

5. If family support is taxable, who pays the tax?

6. What is a "Richmond Order" and when is it used?

7. In what Family Code section are the circumstances that a judge must consider when making a spousal support order set forth?

8. With regard to a spousal support order, what is the difference between a "temporary order" and a "permanent order"? Give one example of each.

9. What does "marital standard of living" mean?

10. Discuss *In re Marriage of Gavron* and the meaning of a Gavron warning.

11. Can a party be awarded or continue to receive spousal support even though he or she is cohabitating with a romantic partner? Explain.

12. Is spousal support always ordered when there is a long-term marriage? Why or why not?

13. What is the one difference between a short-term marriage and a long-term marriage?

14. What do the Courts consider to be a long-term marriage?

15. Can a spouse who has been convicted of sexually abusing the other spouse still be awarded spousal support? Why or why not?

16. List ten factors set forth in FC §4320 that a court must consider when awarding or declining toward spousal support.

17. List the three kinds of orders that reduce spousal support. Give an example of each one.

18. What do the words "decreased need" mean? When is this phrase used?

II.   Fill in the Blanks using the Word List that follows

1. _____A court order that spousal support be paid until a certain date. After that date the amount of spousal support drops to $1 or $0.

2. _____A marriage lasting ten (10) years or longer.

3. _____A request for an order for spousal support in a proceeding for dissolution, legal separation postjudgment that a judge may be made back to the date of the filing of the issue.

4. _____A spousal support order made in which spousal support payments will terminate on a specific date unless the supported spouse files a motion to modify the support order.

5. _____A supported party in a marriage of medium or short duration must become self-supporting within a reasonable period of time.

6. _____An order of spousal support where the amount of spousal support decreases in designated steps until the spousal support becomes a minimal amount such as $1 or reduced to $0.

7. _____Court-ordered support that one spouse pays to the other spouse during the divorce or legal separation proceedings, and it may continue until sometime after the judgment is rendered, depending upon the length of the marriage and a judge's discretion.

8. _____Except as otherwise agreed by the parties in writing, the obligation of a party under an order for the support of the other party terminates when?

9. _____In determining spousal support amount at trial, the court must base the amount and duration of spousal support upon the statutory factors enumerated in this code section.

10. _____In order to request and to be granted a change in the amount of spousal support previously order there must be this.

Chapter 17: Spousal Support

11. _____ Support that is ordered during the period of time between the initial filing of the petition and the final judgment.

12. _____ The Legislature intended this to mean the general station in life enjoyed by the parties during their marriage.

13. _____ The party that bears the burden of establishing that a material change of circumstances has occurred since the last order was made in order to obtain modification of the spousal support order.

14. _____ The purpose of this kind of support "to provide financial assistance, if appropriate, as determined by the financial circumstances of the parties after their dissolution and the division of their community property."

15. _____ This code section provides that the provisions of an agreement with regard to spousal support are subject to modification or termination by the court.

16. _____ This motion may only be granted if there has been a material change of circumstances since the last order.

17. _____ When setting an amount of spousal support to be paid, the court can consider this kind of documented evidence.

18. _____ When a support ex-spouse cohabits with a romantic partner, the rebuttable presumption, affecting the burden of proof is this.

19. _____ This kind of support means an agreement between the parents, or an order or judgment, that combines child support and spousal support without designating the amount to be paid for child support and the amount to be paid for spousal support.

Word List

A. Fc § 3591
B. Fc § 4320
C. A Jurisdictional Stepdown Order
D. A Richmond Order
E. A Substantial Change of Circumstances
F. A Substantive Stepdown Order
G. Family Support.
H. Gavron Warning
I. History of Domestic Violence
J. Marriage of Long Duration
K. Modification of Spousal Support
L. Moving Party
M. Permanent Spousal Support
N. Retroactivity
O. Spousal Support
P. Temporary Spousal Support
Q. The Ex-Spouse Has A Decreased Need
R. The Marital Standard of Living
S. Upon the Death or Marriage of the Supported Party

CHAPTER 18: Disclosure & Fiduciary Duty

In Brief...

***FAMILY CODE DISCLOSURE PROVISIONS*, FC § 2100** et seq.:
- **FC § 2100**: CA public policy is full disclosure and cooperative discovery.
- **FC § 2101**: Definitions:
- **Asset** includes any real or personal property of any nature, whether tangible or intangible, and whether currently existing or contingent.
- **Default judgment** does not include a stipulated judgment or any judgment pursuant to a marital settlement agreement.
- **Earnings and accumulations** include income from whatever source derived, as provided in **FC § 4058**.
- **Expenses** include, but are not limited to, all personal living expenses, but do not include business-related expenses.
- **FC § 2101** sets forth applicable definitions.
- **FC § 2102**: Both parties are subject to the standards provided in **FC § 721,** as to all activities that affect the assets and liabilities of the other party. The fiduciary duty ends when the final dissolution judgment is rendered.
- **FC § 2103**: Each party must serve a preliminary and final declaration of disclosure.
- **FC § 2104**: When preliminary declaration of disclosure FL-140 must be served.
- **FC § 2105**: Final declaration of disclosure FL-140 and current FL-150.
- **FC § 2106**: No judgment until final disclosure declaration; current FL-150 served.
- **FC § 2107**: Failure to serve declaration of disclosure can result in motion to compel.
- **FC § 2108**: Court can order liquidation of community assets.
- **FC § 2109**: Final disclosure declaration does not apply to a summary dissolution.
- **FC § 2110**: Final declaration of disclosure requirements can be waived in a default.
- **FC § 2111**: Work product privilege applies; protective orders can be issued.
- **FC § 2112**: Adaptation of Judicial Council Forms.
- **FC § 2113**: Applies to any proceeding on or after January 1, 1993.

RELATION OF SPOUSES AND FIDUCIARY DUTY:
- Spouses have mutual obligations of respect, fidelity and support, **FC § 720**.
- Spouses have a confidential relationship that imposes a fiduciary duty.

BREACH OF FIDUCIARY DUTY:
- Fiduciary comes from the Latin word *fiducia*, which means **trust**.

Chapter 18: Disclosure & Fiduciary Duty

> - Spouses have a fiduciary duty to always act in good faith and honesty toward one another.
> - When spouses have control of the community property they must act in the best interests of the community or they are breaching their fiduciary duty.
> - A spouse has a claim against the other spouse for any breach of the fiduciary duty that results in impairment to the claimant spouse's present undivided one-half interest in the community estate, **FC § 1101(a)**.
>
> ***REMEDIES*** for the breach of a spouse's fiduciary duty:
> - May be in an award of up to 100% of any asset undisclosed or transferred for a deliberate breach of the fiduciary duty, **FC § 1101(h)**.
> - A 100% award can be made "for the sake of example and by way of punishing the defendant." CC § 3294.

Introduction

California legislature enacted very specific rules regarding spouses disclosing all of their information in a marital dissolution or legal separation action. Spouses MUST, by law, disclose all of their assets and debts in a dissolution or legal separation action, and the judge has discretion to decide the penalty when one spouse fails to disclose information.

Fiduciary comes from the Latin word *fiducia*, which means **trust**. Spouses have a fiduciary duty to always act in good faith and honesty toward one another. When spouses have control of the community property they must act in the best interests of the community or they are breaching their fiduciary duty.

Family Code Disclosure Provisions FC § 2100 et seq.

The disclosure laws set forth at **FC § 2100** et seq. are included in family law discovery rules. **CRC Rule 5.12**. Some of the following rules are verbatim and some of the rules are summarized:

1. FC § 2100

> The Legislature finds and declares the following:
> **(a)** It is the policy of the State of California (1) to marshal, preserve, and protect community and quasi-community assets and liabilities that exist at the date of separation so as to avoid dissipation of the community estate before distribution, (2) to ensure fair and sufficient child and spousal support awards, and (3) to achieve a division of community and quasi-community assets and liabilities on the dissolution or nullity of marriage or legal separation of the parties as provided under California law.
> **(b)** Sound public policy further favors the reduction of the adversarial nature of marital dissolution and the attendant costs by fostering full disclosure and cooperative discovery.
> **(c)** In order to promote this public policy, a full and accurate disclosure of all assets and liabilities in which one or both parties have or may have an interest must be made in the early stages of a proceeding for dissolution of marriage or legal separation of the parties,

Chapter 18: Disclosure & Fiduciary Duty

> regardless of the characterization as community or separate, together with a disclosure of all income and expenses of the parties. Moreover, each party has a continuing duty to immediately, fully, and accurately update and augment that disclosure to the extent there have been any material changes so that at the time the parties enter into an agreement for the resolution of any of these issues, or at the time of trial on these issues, each party will have a full and complete knowledge of the relevant underlying facts. FC § 2100.

2. FC § 2101

The definitions that apply to this chapter are:

(a) Asset includes, but is not limited to, any real or personal property of any nature, whether tangible or intangible, and whether currently existing or contingent.

(b) Default judgment does not include a stipulated judgment or any judgment pursuant to a marital settlement agreement.

(c) Earnings and accumulations include income from whatever source derived, as provided in **FC § 4058**.

(d) Expenses include, but are not limited to, all personal living expenses, but do not include business-related expenses.

(e) *Income and Expense Declaration* includes the *Income and Expense Declaration* form approved for use by the Judicial Council and any other financial statement that is approved for use by the Judicial Council in lieu of the *Income and Expense Declaration*, if the financial statement form satisfies all other applicable criteria. Both parties are subject to the standards provided in **FC § 721**[1], as to all activities that affect the assets and liabilities of the other party. From the date of separation to the date of the distribution of the community or quasi-community asset or liability in question, each party is subject to the standards provided in **FC § 721**, as to all activities that affect the assets and liabilities of the other party.

3. FC § 2102

FC § 2102 sets forth the duties of a fiduciary. It provides:

> **(a)** From the date of separation to the date of the distribution of the community or quasi-community asset or liability in question, each party is subject to the standards provided in Section 721, as to all activities that affect the assets and liabilities of the other party, including, but not limited to, the following activities:
> **(1)** The accurate and complete disclosure of all assets and liabilities in which the party has or may have an interest or obligation and all current earnings, accumulations, and expenses, including an immediate, full, and accurate update or augmentation to the extent

---

[1] FC § 721 in pertinent part provides that "either spouse may enter into any transaction with the other, or with any other person, respecting property, which either might if unmarried." In transactions between spouses the general rules governing fiduciary relationships control. "This confidential relationship imposes a duty of the highest good faith and fair dealing on each spouse, and neither shall take any unfair advantage of the other. This confidential relationship is a fiduciary relationship."

Chapter 18: Disclosure & Fiduciary Duty

> there have been any material changes.
> (2) The accurate and complete written disclosure of any investment opportunity, business opportunity, or other income-producing opportunity that presents itself after the date of separation, but that results from any investment, significant business activity outside the ordinary course of business, or other income-producing opportunity of either spouse from the date of marriage to the date of separation, inclusive. The written disclosure shall be made in sufficient time for the other spouse to make an informed decision as to whether he or she desires to participate in the investment opportunity, business, or other potential income-producing opportunity, and for the court to resolve any dispute regarding the right of the other spouse to participate in the opportunity. In the event of nondisclosure of an investment opportunity, the division of any gain resulting from that opportunity is governed by the standard provided in Section 2556.
> (3) The operation or management of a business or an interest in a business in which the community may have an interest.
> **(b)** From the date that a valid, enforceable, and binding resolution of the disposition of the asset or liability in question is reached, until the asset or liability has actually been distributed, each party is subject to the standards provided in Section 721 as to all activities that affect the assets or liabilities of the other party. Once a particular asset or liability has been distributed, the duties and standards set forth in Section 721 shall end as to that asset or liability.
> **(c)** From the date of separation to the date of a valid, enforceable, and binding resolution of all issues relating to child or spousal support and professional fees, each party is subject to the standards provided in Section 721 as to all issues relating to the support and fees, including immediate, full, and accurate disclosure of all material facts and information regarding the income or expenses of the party.

The fiduciary duty between divorcing spouses ends when the final judgment is rendered and the paying of child support and/or spousal support does not lengthen the duty past the rendering of the judgment in the dissolution matter. There is no "continuing fiduciary duty to disclose all material facts regarding a party's income after a final custody and support order has been entered." *In re Marriage of Sorge* (2012) 202 Cal.App.4th 626 at p. 655.

4. FC § 2103

In order to provide complete and accurate disclosure of all assets and liabilities in which one or both of the parties may have an interest, each party to a dissolution or legal separation proceeding must serve:

(a) A *Preliminary Declaration of Disclosure* on the other party under **FC § 2104;** and
(b) A *Final Declaration of Disclosure* under **FC § 2105**, unless service of the final declaration of disclosure is waived pursuant to **FC § 2105** or **FC § 2110**.

Further, a proof of service must be filed for each declaration. The *FL-140* is a mandatory form used for both the preliminary and final declaration of disclosure.

Chapter 18: Disclosure & Fiduciary Duty

The proof of service form is called a *Declaration Regarding Service of Declaration of Disclosure* and *Income and Expense Declaration* (form *FL-141*); it is a mandatory use form.

5. FC § 2104

Each party must serve on the other a preliminary declaration of disclosure, executed under penalty of perjury on a form prescribed by the Judicial Council, *FL-140*. The commission of perjury on the preliminary declaration of disclosure may be grounds for setting aside the judgment, or any part or parts thereof. The preliminary declaration of disclosure must include all tax returns filed by the declarant within the two years prior to the date that the party served the declaration. The preliminary declaration of disclosure is not filed with the court, except pursuant to a court order.

Additionally, the parties must file a proof of service of the *Preliminary Declaration of Disclosure* with the court, *FL-141*. The petitioner must serve the other party with the *Preliminary Declaration of Disclosure* either concurrently with the *Petition* for dissolution or within sixty (60) days of filing the *Petition*.

The respondent must serve the other party with the preliminary declaration of disclosure either concurrently with the *Response* to the *Petition* or within sixty (60) days of filing the *Response*. The time periods specified in this subdivision may be extended by written agreement of the parties or by court order.

6. FC § 2105

Before or at the time the parties enter into an agreement for the resolution of property or support issues other than pendente lite support[2], or, if the case goes to trial, no later than forty-five (45) days before the first assigned trial date, each party, or the attorney for the party in this matter, must serve on the other party a *Final Declaration of Disclosure* and a current *Income and Expense Declaration*.

The parties may stipulate to a mutual waiver of the requirements of the *Final Declaration of Disclosure* by execution of a waiver under penalty of perjury entered into in open court, by separate stipulation or by using the *Stipulation and Waiver of Final Declaration of Disclosure* (form *FL-144*). The *FL-144* has been approved for optional use and is, thus, not mandatory.

7. FC § 2106

No judgment may be entered with respect to the parties' property rights without each party, or the attorney for that party in this matter, executing and serving a copy of the *Final Declaration of Disclosure* and current *Income and Expense*

---

[2] *Pendente lite* means "pending the trial". Pendente lite support is interim, temporary support before the trial or final proceedings.

Chapter 18: Disclosure & Fiduciary Duty

Declaration. Each party, or his or her attorney, must execute and file with the court a declaration signed under penalty of perjury stating that service of the *Final Declaration of Disclosure* and current *Income and Expense Declaration* was made on the other party or that service of the *Final Declaration of Disclosure* has been waived.

8. FC § 2107

If one party fails to serve on the other party a preliminary declaration of disclosure under **FC § 2104** and a final declaration of disclosure under **FC § 2105**, or fails to provide the information required in the respective declarations with sufficient particularity, and if the other party has served the respective declaration of disclosure on the noncomplying party, the complying party may, within a reasonable time, request preparation of the appropriate declaration of disclosure or further particularity. If the noncomplying party fails to comply with the request, the complying party may file a motion to compel a further response and/or file a motion for an order preventing the noncomplying party from presenting evidence on issues that are covered in the declaration of disclosure.

If a party fails to comply with any provision of this chapter, the court must impose money sanctions against the noncomplying party. Sanctions are ordered in an amount sufficient to deter repetition of the conduct or comparable conduct, and will include reasonable attorney fees, costs incurred or both, unless the court finds that the noncomplying party acted with substantial justification or that other circumstances make the imposition of the sanction unjust.

9. FC § 2108

The court has the authority, at any time during the proceeding, on application of a party and for good cause, to order the liquidation of community or quasi-community assets so as to avoid unreasonable market or investment risks, given the relative nature, scope and extent of the community estate. However, the court must not grant such an application unless the appropriate declaration of disclosure has been served by the moving party.

10. FC § 2109

A final declaration of disclosure is not required for a summary dissolution, but a preliminary declaration of disclosure is required.

11. FC § 2110

In the case of a default judgment, the petitioner may waive the *Final Declaration of Disclosure* requirements and is not required to serve a *Final Declaration of Disclosure* on the respondent, nor receive a final declaration of disclosure from the respondent. However, a *Preliminary Declaration of Disclosure* by the petitioner is required.

12. FC § 2111

A disclosure required by this chapter does not nullify the attorney work product privilege or impede the power of the court to issue protective orders.

13. FC § 2112

"The Judicial Council shall adopt appropriate forms and modify existing forms to effectuate the purposes of this chapter."

14. FC § 2113

"This chapter applies to any proceeding commenced on or after January 1, 1993."

As the following case demonstrates, failing to disclose assets during a divorce can have severe consequences.

> **In re Marriage of DENISE and THOMAS ROSSI. DENISE ROSSI, Appellant, v. THOMAS ROSSI, Respondent.**
> COURT OF APPEAL OF CALIFORNIA, SECOND APPELLATE DISTRICT, DIVISION FOUR
> 90 Cal.App.4th 34; 108 Cal.Rptr.2d 270
> June 22, 2001, Decided
> (*Marriage of Rossi*)
>
> Denise and Thomas were married in 1971. In early November 1996, Bernadette Quercio formed a lottery pool with a group of her coworkers, including Denise. Each member of the pool contributed $5 per week. Denise contributed her $5 for a short time--three weeks--but, according to her papers, on December 1, 1996, or about that date, she withdrew from the pool.
>
> In late December 1996, Ms. Quercio called Denise to say that their group had won the lottery jackpot. The jackpot prize was $6,680,000 and Denise's share was $1,336,000, to be paid in 20 equal annual installments of $66,800 less taxes, from 1996 through 2015. According to declarations by Denise and by Ms. Quercio, Ms. Quercio told her that she wanted to give Denise a share in the jackpot as a gift. Denise explained: "I went to the Lottery Commission office and told them I was married but contemplating divorce.
>
> They told me to file before I got my first check, which I did. I believed that the lottery winnings were my separate property because they were a gift." In early January 1997, Denise filed a petition for dissolution of marriage in the Los Angeles Superior Court. She never told Thomas about the lottery jackpot. She used her mother's address to receive checks and other information from the California Lottery because it would be safer since Thomas would not see the lottery checks.
>
> Thomas was served with the dissolution petition in January 1997. He and Denise talked

about a settlement the same day. Thomas was not represented by counsel in the dissolution proceedings. He and Denise met with Denise's attorney. According to Thomas, he was given several papers to sign to finalize the dissolution. These included a marital settlement agreement and a judgment of dissolution.

Denise filled out a schedule of assets and debts dated January 27, 1997; a final declaration of disclosure; and an income and expense declaration dated January 30, 1997. She did not reveal the lottery winnings in any of these documents, either as community or separate property. Because Thomas did not have an attorney, Denise also filled out Thomas's schedule of assets and debts. The marital settlement agreement was approved as part of the judgment of dissolution.[3]

The lottery winnings are not listed on the schedules attached to the marital settlement agreement. Denise testified that the lottery winnings were not listed on the schedules.

The marital settlement agreement also provided that concealment of assets was a basis to seek to set aside the agreement and that the party who was wronged by the concealment could seek payment of one-half of the concealed property or its value plus one-half of any income derived from the property.

Judgment of dissolution was entered April 7, 1997. In 1998, Thomas filed for bankruptcy. In May 1999, a letter was sent to Thomas's home address, asking if Denise was interested in a lump-sum buyout of her lottery winnings. This was the first Thomas knew about the lottery prize. He confirmed that Denise was a winner with the California Lottery. Thomas retained counsel, who contacted Denise's attorney. According to a declaration filed by Thomas's counsel, Denise's attorney confirmed that she had won a share of a lottery prize, "however, his client was unwilling to share any 'meaningful' amount of the Lottery proceeds . . . ." In July 1999, Denise withdrew $ 33,000 in lottery winnings to repay a loan made by her mother in 1980.

In July 1999, Thomas filed a motion to set aside the dissolution of marriage based on fraud, breach of fiduciary duty and failure to disclose; for adjudication of the lottery winnings as an omitted asset; and sought the award of 100 percent of the lottery winnings pursuant to FC § 1101(h). Thomas also sought an award of his attorney's fees under FC § 1101(g).[4]

---

[33] The parties' Marital Settlement Agreement provided:
Paragraph 9.1: "Each party warrants to the other that prior to the effective date of this Agreement neither was possessed of any property of any kind or description whatsoever other than the property specifically mentioned in this Agreement, and that such party has not made, without the knowledge and consent of the other, any gift or transfer of any property within the past three years. If it shall hereafter be determined by a Court of competent jurisdiction that one party is now possessed of any property not set forth herein . . . such party hereby covenants and agrees to pay to the other on demand an amount equal to the full market value of such property on the date hereof or on the date of judgment in any action to enforce the provisions of this paragraph."
Paragraph 9.4: "Each party has fairly and with candor disclosed all of the property in which either has a claim or interest, whether or not the claim or interest is separate or joint property. Each party has fully disclosed to the other the nature and extent of any interest in all property and warrants that its valuation is, to the best knowledge of that party, a fair and candid valuation and that there have been no events which would materially affect the value of any property."
[4] FC § 1101(g) provides: "Remedies for breach of the fiduciary duty by one spouse, including those set out in Sections 721 and 1100, shall include, but not be limited to, an award to the other spouse of 50

In his points and authorities, Thomas asked the court to enforce the disclosure penalty provision of the judgment of dissolution, provision E.[5] Based on this provision, Thomas claimed at least half of the lottery winnings. In the alternative, Thomas asked the court to set aside the dissolution based on concealment and breach of fiduciary duty. Alternatively, Thomas sought an award of 100 percent of the lottery winnings pursuant to FC § 1101(h), which penalizes a breach of fiduciary duty by a spouse in dissolution proceedings. As a final alternative ground, Thomas argued the lottery proceedings should be adjudicated an omitted asset pursuant to FC § 2556[6].

Denise asserted [in her supporting declaration that] the lottery winnings are her separate property because the share she received was a gift, and because the parties were already separated when the group hit the jackpot.

The trial court found that Denise intentionally failed to disclose her lottery winnings in the marital settlement agreement, the judgment, and her declaration of disclosure. It found that Denise breached her fiduciary duties under FC §§ 721, 1100, 2100 and 2101 by fraudulently failing to disclose the lottery winnings and that she intentionally breached her warranties and representations set forth in paragraphs 9.1, 9.4 and 9.7 of the marital settlement agreement. The court specifically found that Denise's failure to disclose the lottery winnings constituted fraud, oppression and malice within the meaning of CC § 3294 and FC § 1101(h).

The trial court awarded Thomas 100 percent of the lottery winnings pursuant to provision E of the judgment of dissolution, paragraph 9.1 of the marital settlement agreement, and FC § 1101(g) and (h). The trial court found that Denise's evidence that her share of the lottery winnings was a gift was not credible, and concluded that the lottery winnings were community property. Denise filed a timely notice of appeal.

DISCUSSION
FC § 721(b) imposes a fiduciary duty on spouses in transactions between themselves.[7]

---

percent, or an amount equal to 50 percent, of any asset undisclosed or transferred in breach of the fiduciary duty plus attorney's fees and court costs. The value of the asset shall be determined to be its highest value at the date of the breach of the fiduciary duty, the date of the sale or disposition of the asset, or the date of the award by the court."

FC § 1101(h) provides: " Remedies for the breach of the fiduciary duty by one spouse, as set forth in FC §§ 721 and 1100, when the breach falls within the ambit of CC § 3294 shall include, but not be limited to, an award to the other spouse of 100 percent, or an amount equal to 100 percent, of any asset undisclosed or transferred in breach of the fiduciary duty."

[5] Provision E provided that if the court determined that one party failed to disclose property in the dissolution proceedings, that party would pay "at least one-half of the full market value of such property" to the other party.

[6] In a proceeding for dissolution of marriage, for nullity of marriage, or for legal separation of the parties, the court has continuing jurisdiction to award community estate assets or community estate liabilities to the parties that have not been previously adjudicated by a judgment in the proceeding. A party may file a postjudgment motion or order to show cause in the proceeding in order to obtain adjudication of any community estate asset or liability omitted or not adjudicated by the judgment. In these cases, the court shall equally divide the omitted or unadjudicated community estate asset or liability, unless the court finds upon good cause shown that the interests of justice require an unequal division of the asset or liability.

[7] FC § 721(b) provides in pertinent part: "…spouses are subject to the general rules governing fiduciary relationships that control the actions of persons occupying confidential relations with each other. This confidential relationship imposes a duty of the highest good faith and fair dealing on each spouse, and neither shall take any unfair advantage of the other. This confidential relationship is a

Chapter 18: Disclosure & Fiduciary Duty

> Thomas argues that imposition of the 100 percent penalty under FC § 1101(h) was mandatory, once the family court found that Denise acted with fraud, oppression or malice in concealing the lottery winnings during the dissolution proceedings.
>
> The correctness of the family court's order awarding Thomas all of the lottery winnings is based on the finding that Denise's conduct constituted fraud within the meaning of CC § 3294.[8]
>
> The evidence established that Denise filed for dissolution after learning that she had won a share of a substantial lottery jackpot; that she consulted the Lottery Commission personnel about ways in which she could avoid sharing the jackpot with her husband; that she used her mother's address for all communications with the Lottery Commission to avoid notifying Thomas of her winnings; and that she failed to disclose the winnings at any time during the dissolution proceedings, despite her warranties in the marital settlement agreement and the judgment that all assets had been disclosed. The family court expressly rejected her evidence that the winnings constituted a gift and, as such, were her separate property.
>
> The court expressly found that Denise intentionally failed to disclose her lottery winnings in the marital settlement agreement, the judgment and her declaration of disclosure. This case presents precisely the circumstance that FC § 1101(h) is intended to address. Here, one spouse intentionally concealed a significant community property asset. She intentionally consulted with the Lottery Commission as to how to deprive Thomas of a share of the prize; used her mother's address for all communications with the lottery; and did not disclose the winnings in the dissolution proceedings. This supports a finding of fraud within the meaning of CC § 3294. The family court properly concluded that under these circumstances, Thomas was entitled to 100 percent of the lottery winnings under FC § 1101(h).
>
> The strong language of FC § 1101(h) serves an important purpose: full disclosure of marital assets is absolutely essential to the trial court in determining the proper dissolution of property and resolving support issues. The statutory scheme for dissolution depends on the parties' full disclosure of all assets so they may be taken into account by the trial court. A failure to make such disclosure is properly subject to the severe sanction of FC § 1101(h).

---

fiduciary relationship subject to the same rights and duties of nonmarital business partners, as provided in Corporations Code §§ 16403, 16404 and 16503..."

[8] CC § 3294 provides in pertinent part:
"(a) In an action for the breach of an obligation not arising from contract, where it is proven by clear and convincing evidence that the defendant has been guilty of oppression, fraud, or malice, the plaintiff, in addition to the actual damages, may recover damages for the sake of example and by way of punishing the defendant...
(c) As used in this section, the following definitions shall apply:
(1) 'Malice' means conduct which is intended by the defendant to cause injury to the plaintiff or despicable conduct which is carried on by the defendant with a willful and conscious disregard of the rights or safety of others.
(2) 'Oppression' means despicable conduct that subjects a person to cruel and unjust hardship in conscious disregard of that person's rights.
(3) 'Fraud' means an intentional misrepresentation, deceit, or concealment of a material fact known to the defendant with the intention on the part of the defendant of thereby depriving a person of property or legal rights or otherwise causing injury..."

> We find nothing in the language of the statute to justify an exception to the penalty provision of FC § 1101(h) because of the supposed unclean hands of the spouse from whom the asset was concealed. The statute provides that, where a spouse conceals assets under circumstances satisfying the criteria for punitive damages under CC § 3294, a penalty representing 100 percent of the concealed asset is warranted. The statute is unambiguous, and no exception is provided.
>
> The family court could have imposed attorney's fees on Denise as an additional penalty under FC § 1101(h). It chose not to do so. It was within its discretion in making this order.
>
> The evidence which we have summarized supports the family court's order on the alternative ground that Denise violated the terms of the judgment of dissolution and the marital settlement agreement by concealing the lottery winnings. This violation triggered paragraph 9.1 of the marital settlement agreement.
>
> **DISPOSITION**
> The order of the family court is affirmed.

As shown by the case above, a deliberate misappropriation can result in an award of up to 100% of any asset undisclosed or transferred in breach of the fiduciary duty, as the case above demonstrates. **FC § 1101(h)**. The 100% award can be made "for the sake of example and by way of punishing the defendant." **CC § 3294**.

Fiduciary Duty

Spouses have mutual obligations of respect, fidelity and support. **FC § 720**. (See *In re Marriage of RAMIREZ* (2008) 165 Cal.App.4th 751 at p. 759, where the court found that Jorge Ramirez "manifestly intended not to perform his marriage obligation of fidelity" and this breach invalidated the marriage.) Additionally, spouses have a confidential relationship that imposes a fiduciary duty of the highest good faith and fair dealing on each spouse, and neither must take any unfair advantage of the other.

Spouses, in transaction between themselves, are subject to the general rules governing fiduciary relationships that control the actions of persons occupying confidential relations with each other. This confidential relationship imposes a duty of the highest good faith and fair dealing on each spouse, and one spouse must NEVER take any unfair advantage of the other spouse. **FC § 721**.

Either spouse may manage and control the community property. **FC § 1100(a)**. However, with that right comes the obligation of acting in the best interests of the community.

A spouse may not make a gift of community property. However, this does not apply to gifts mutually given by both spouses to third parties and to gifts given by one spouse to the other spouse. **FC § 1100(b)**.

Chapter 18: Disclosure & Fiduciary Duty

Spouses may not dispose of community for less that the reasonable value without the written permission of the other spouse. **FC § 1100(b)**.

A spouse may not sell, convey or encumber community personal property used as the family dwelling; the furniture, furnishings or fittings of the home; or the clothing or wearing apparel of the other spouse or minor children that is community personal property without the written consent of the other spouse. **FC § 1100(c)**.

Remedies for the failure by a managing spouse to give prior written notice as required by this subdivision are only as specified in **FC § 1101**. Failure to give prior written notice does not adversely affect the validity of a transaction, nor of any interest transferred. **FC § 1100(d)**.

Spouses must act with respect to each other in the management and control of the community assets and liabilities, in accordance with the general rules governing fiduciary relationships that control the actions of persons having relationships of personal confidence, as specified in **FC § 721**, until such time as the assets and liabilities have been divided by the parties or by a court. This duty includes the obligation to make full disclosure to the other spouse of all material facts and information regarding the existence, characterization and valuation of all assets in which the community has or may have an interest and debts for which the community is or may be liable, and to provide equal access to all information, records and books that pertain to the value and character of those assets and debts, upon request. **FC § 1100(e)**.

From the date of separation to the date of the distribution of the community or quasi-community asset or liability in question, each party is subject to the standards provided in **FC § 721**, as to all activities that affect the assets and liabilities of the other party, including, but not limited to, the following activities:

> **(1)** The accurate and complete disclosure of all assets and liabilities in which the party has or may have an interest or obligation and all current earnings, accumulations, and expenses, including an immediate, full, and accurate update or augmentation to the extent there have been any material changes.
> **(2)** The accurate and complete written disclosure of any investment opportunity, business opportunity, or other income-producing opportunity that presents itself after the date of separation, but that results from any investment, significant business activity outside the ordinary course of business, or other income-producing opportunity of either spouse from the date of marriage to the date of separation, inclusive. The written disclosure shall be made in sufficient time for the other spouse to make an informed decision as to whether he or she desires to participate in the investment opportunity, business, or other potential income-producing opportunity, and for the court to resolve any dispute regarding the right of the other spouse to participate in the opportunity. In the event of nondisclosure of an investment opportunity, the division of any gain resulting from that opportunity is governed by the standard provided in FC § 2556.
> **(3)** The operation or management of a business or an interest in a business in which the community may have an interest. FC § 2102(a).

Chapter 18: Disclosure & Fiduciary Duty

From the date that a valid, enforceable and binding resolution of the disposition of the asset or liability in question is reached until the asset or liability has actually been distributed, each party is subject to the standards provided in **FC § 721** as to all activities that affect the assets or liabilities of the other party. Once a particular asset or liability has been distributed, the duties and standards set forth in **FC § 721** end as to that asset or liability. **FC § 2102(b)**.

From the date of separation to the date of a valid, enforceable and binding resolution of all issues relating to child or spousal support and professional fees, each party is subject to the standards provided in **FC § 721** as to all issues relating to the support and fees, including immediate, full and accurate disclosure of all material facts and information regarding the income or expenses of the party. **FC § 2102(c)**.

After division of community and quasi-community property, the separate property owned by a married person at the time of the division and the property received by the person in the division is liable for a debt incurred by the person before or during marriage, and the person is personally liable for the debt, whether or not the debt was assigned for payment by the person's spouse in the division. Further, the separate property owned by a married person at the time of the division and the property received by the person in the division is not liable for a debt incurred by the person's spouse before or during marriage, and the person is not personally liable for the debt, unless the debt was assigned for payment by the person in the division of the property. **FC § 916**.

The separate property owned by a married person at the time of the division and the property received by the person in the division is liable for a debt incurred by the person's spouse before or during marriage, and the person is personally liable for the debt if the debt was assigned for payment by the person in the division of the property. If a money judgment for the debt is entered after the division, the property is not subject to enforcement of the judgment, and the judgment may not be enforced against the married person unless the person is made a party to the judgment for the purpose of this paragraph.

If property of a married person is applied to the satisfaction of a money judgment pursuant to subdivision (a) for a debt incurred by the person that is assigned for payment by the person's spouse, the person has a right of reimbursement from the person's spouse to the extent of the property applied, with interest at the legal rate, and may recover reasonable attorney fees incurred in enforcing the right of reimbursement.

"[T]he fiduciary duty statutes that can trigger application of the value-of-the-asset remedy, FC § 1101(h) refers to two Family Code sections: FC §§ 721 and 1100. FC § 1100 is, by its terms, exclusively applicable to the fiduciary duty concerning community property. In contrast, the spousal fiduciary duty specified in FC § 721 is broad enough to encompass the duty to disclose separate property assets during

Chapter 18: Disclosure & Fiduciary Duty

dissolution proceedings." *In re Marriage of SIMMONS* (2013) 215 Cal. App. 4th 584 at p. 594.

As set forth above, the fiduciary duty between spouse ends when the final judgment of dissolution is entered. FC § 2102; *In re Marriage of SORGE* (2012) 202 Cal. App. 4th 626 at p. 655.

Breach of Fiduciary Duty FC § 1101

A spouse has a claim against the other spouse for any breach of the fiduciary duty that results in impairment to the claimant spouse's present undivided one-half interest in the community estate, including, but not limited to, a single transaction or a pattern or series of transactions that have caused or will cause a detrimental impact to the claimant spouse's undivided one-half interest in the community estate. **FC § 1101(a)**.

A court may order an accounting of the property and obligations of the spouses and may determine the rights of ownership in the beneficial enjoyment of, or access to, community property, and the classification of all property of the parties to a marriage. **FC § 1101(b)**.

In any transaction affecting community property in which the consent of both spouses is required, the court may, upon the motion of a spouse, dispense with the requirement of the other spouse's consent if the proposed transaction is in the best interests of the community and the consent has been arbitrarily refused or cannot be obtained due to the physical incapacity, mental incapacity or prolonged absence of the nonconsenting spouse. **FC § 1101(e)**.

Any action may be brought under this section without filing an action for dissolution of marriage, legal separation or nullity; or an action under this section may be brought in conjunction with the action or upon the death of a spouse. **FC § 1101(f)**.

Remedies for breach of the fiduciary duty by one spouse must include an award to the other spouse of fifty (50) percent, or an amount equal to fifty (50) percent, of any asset undisclosed or transferred in breach of the fiduciary duty, plus attorney fees and court costs. The value of the asset will be determined to be its highest value at the date of the breach of the fiduciary duty, the date of the sale or disposition of the asset or the date of the award by the court. **FC § 1101(g)**.

Remedies for the breach of the fiduciary duty by one spouse, as set forth in **FC §§ 721** and **1100**, when the breach falls within the ambit of **Civil Code § 3294**[9] include, but are not limited to, an award to the other spouse of 100 percent, or an

---

[9] Civil Code § 3294(a) provides: "In an action for the breach of an obligation not arising from contract, where it is proven by clear and convincing evidence that the defendant has been guilty of oppression, fraud or malice, the plaintiff, in addition to the actual damages, may recover damages for the sake of example and by way of punishing the defendant."

amount equal to 100 percent, of any asset undisclosed or transferred in breach of the fiduciary duty. **FC § 1101(h)**.

EDUCATIONAL EXERCISES

I. Answer the following Questions.

1. If a party truly believes that a specific asset is his separate property, does he have to disclose it on the Judicial Council form *FL-142, Schedule of Assets and Debts*? Why or why not?
2. If a party knowingly fails to disclose an asset that could be community property, what percent of the asset can be given to the other party pursuant to the Family Code?
3. If a party knowingly fails to disclose an asset that could be community property, what percent of the asset can be given to the other party pursuant to the Civil Code?
4. What does "fiduciary" mean?
5. What are the family code section(s) that discuss the meaning of a fiduciary in a marriage?
6. If one party that has control over community money investments then later loses all of the money that she invested in the stock market, does she have to repay the community for the money lost? Why or why not?
7. Does one spouse have the right to take the management of community property from the other spouse even if one spouse has always taken control and has made a 30% profit on all of the community investments? Discuss.

I. Match the letter to the number

A. FC § 2100
B. FC § 2101
C. FC § 2103
D. FC § 2106

E. FC § 2108
F. FC § 2109
G. FC § 2110
H. FC § 2111

1. ____ In order to provide full and accurate disclosure of all assets and liabilities in which one or both parties may have an interest, each party to a proceeding for dissolution of the marriage or legal separation of the parties shall serve on the other party a preliminary declaration of disclosure under Section 2104, unless service of the preliminary declaration of disclosure is waived as provided in Section 2107 or is not required pursuant to Section 2110, and a final declaration of disclosure under Section 2105, unless service of the final declaration of disclosure is waived pursuant to Section 2105, 2107, or 2110, and shall file proof of service of each with the court.

2. ____ The provisions of this chapter requiring a final declaration of disclosure do not apply to a summary dissolution of marriage, but a preliminary declaration of disclosure is required.

Chapter 18: Disclosure & Fiduciary Duty

3. _____ Unless the provision or context otherwise requires, the following definitions apply to this chapter:
   (a) "Asset" includes, but is not limited to, any real or personal property of any nature, whether tangible or intangible, and whether currently existing or contingent.
   (b) "Default judgment" does not include a stipulated judgment or any judgment pursuant to a marital settlement agreement.
   (c) "Earnings and accumulations" includes income from whatever source derived, as provided in Section 4058.
   (d) "Expenses" includes, but is not limited to, all personal living expenses, but does not include business related expenses.
   (e) "Income and expense declaration" includes the Income and Expense Declaration forms approved for use by the Judicial Council, and any other financial statement that is approved for use by the Judicial Council in lieu of the Income and Expense Declaration, if the financial statement form satisfies all other applicable criteria.
   (f) "Liability" includes, but is not limited to, any debt or obligation, whether currently existing or contingent.

4. _____ The Legislature finds and declares the following:
   (a) It is the policy of the State of California (1) to marshal, preserve, and protect community and quasi-community assets and liabilities that exist at the date of separation so as to avoid dissipation of the community estate before distribution, (2) to ensure fair and sufficient child and spousal support awards, and (3) to achieve a division of community and quasi-community assets and liabilities on the dissolution or nullity of marriage or legal separation of the parties as provided under California law.

5. _____ disclosure required by this chapter does not abrogate the attorney work product privilege or impede the power of the court to issue protective orders.

6. _____ Except as provided in subdivision (d) of Section 2105, Section 2110, or absent good cause as provided in Section 2107, no judgment shall be entered with respect to the parties' property rights without each party, or the attorney for that party in this matter, having executed and served a copy of the final declaration of disclosure and current income and expense declaration.

7. _____ At any time during the proceeding, the court has the authority, on application of a party and for good cause, to order the liquidation of community or quasi- community assets so as to avoid unreasonable market or investment risks, given the relative nature, scope, and extent of the community estate. However, in no event shall the court grant the application unless, as provided in this chapter, the appropriate declaration of disclosure has been served by the moving party.

8. _____ In the case of a default judgment, the petitioner may waive the final declaration of disclosure requirements provided in this chapter and shall not be required to serve a final declaration of disclosure on the respondent nor receive a final declaration of disclosure from the respondent.

CHAPTER 19: Bifurcation

In Brief...

A BIFURCATION:
- Is the common name for separating one or more issues from the other issues of the dissolution;
- Is commonly used to terminate the marital status of one of the parties;
- Requires the filing of a noticed motion or a court order;
- Is requested on a *FL-315* (mandatory) attached to a *FL-300 (Request for Order)*, **CRC Rule 5.390(a)**;
- Requires that a *Preliminary Declaration of Disclosure* (form *FL-140*) be served, **FC § 2337(b)**;
- Requires that a completed *Schedule of Assets and Debts* (form *FL-142*) be served, **FC § 2337(b)**; and
- Is a request for a special trial on the separated (bifurcated) issue(s), which requires:
    - A completed *Request for Separate Trial* (form *FL-315*) (with the Request for Order box checked) attached to the *Request for Order* (form *FL-300*);
    - The completion of an *Application or Response to Application for Separate Trial* (form *FL-315*). **CRC Rule 5.390(a)**; and
    - A declaration that must accompany the request if the request is regarding the alternate date of valuation under **FC § 2552(b)**.

THERE ARE MANY ISSUES THAT CAN BE BIFURCATED SUCH AS:
- Validity of a postnuptial or premarital agreement;
- Date of separation;
- Date to use for valuation of assets;
- Whether property is separate or community;
- How to apportion increase in value of a business;
- Existence or value of business or professional goodwill;
- Termination of marital status;
- Child custody and visitation (parenting time);
- Child, spousal or domestic partner support;
- Attorney fees and costs;
- Division of property and debts;
- Reimbursement claims; or
- Other issues specific to a family law case. **CRC Rule 5.390(b)**.

WHEN A BIFURCATION IS GRANTED:
- The court MUST order that the party's retirement or pension plan be joined as a party;
- The moving party must serve the other party with a copy of any order including attachments and judgments that grant dissolution of the retirement or pension plan administration. **FC § 2337(e)**;
- The court MUST reserve jurisdiction for later determination of all remaining issues, **FC § 2337(f)**; and

Chapter 19: Bifurcation

> - The court MAY impose additional conditions upon the moving party under **FC § 2337(c)**; and
> - If the moving party dies after the entry of judgment granting a dissolution of marriage, all obligations set forth in this code section are enforceable against any asset, **FC § 2337(g)**.
>
> *THE FORMAL BIFURCATION ORDER:*
> - Provides that within 10 days after the order deciding the bifurcated issue and any statement of decision under **CRC Rule 3.1591** has been filed, the clerk must mail copies to the parties and file a certificate of mailing, **CRC Rule 5.390(e)**;
> - Requires the use of a *FL-347* (*Bifurcation of Status of Marriage or Domestic Partnership*); and
> - An attachment of either a *FL-340* (*Findings and Order After Hearing*) or a *FL-180* (*Judgment*) is required.

Introduction

In a dissolution proceeding the court, upon noticed motion, may sever and grant an early and separate trial on any issue of the dissolution. This action is commonly called a **bifurcation**. A party may request this action to terminate his or her marital status in order to remarry before all of the issues in the divorce have been resolved.

Codes, Rules and Forms RE: Requesting a Bifurcation

To make a request to separate a trial issue, a completed *Request for Separate Trial* (form *FL-315*) (with the Request for Order box checked) attached to the *Request for Order* (form *FL-300*) must be used. As part of the noticed *Request for Order* (form *FL-300*) of a party, the stipulation of the parties, case management or the court's own motion, the court may bifurcate one or more issues to be tried separately before other issues are tried.

A party requesting a separate trial or responding to a request for a separate trial must complete an *Application or Response to Application for Separate Trial* (form *FL-315*). **CRC Rule 5.390(a)**.

Additionally, a preliminary *Declaration of Disclosure* (form *FL-140*) and a completed *Schedule of Assets and Debts* (form *FL-142*) must accompany the *FL-300* and the *FL-315*, unless previously served or unless the parties stipulate in writing to defer service of the preliminary declaration of disclosure until a later time. **FC § 2337(b)**.

The court can separately try one or more issues before the trial on the other issues if the resolution of the bifurcated issue is likely to simplify the determination of the other issues. Issues that may be appropriate to try separately in advance include:
  (1) Validity of a postnuptial or premarital agreement;
  (2) Date of separation;

(3) Date to use for valuation of assets;
(4) Whether property is separate or community;
(5) How to apportion increase in value of a business;
(6) Existence or value of business or professional goodwill;
(7) Termination of marital status;
(8) Child custody and visitation (parenting time);
(9) Child, spousal or domestic partner support;
(10) Attorney fees and costs;
(11) Division of property and debts;
(12) Reimbursement claims; or
(13) Other issues specific to a family law case. **CRC Rule 5.390(b).**

When making a request for a separate trial regarding the alternate date of valuation under **FC § 2552(b)**, the declaration must accompany the request stating the following:

---

(1) The proposed alternate valuation date;
(2) Whether the proposed alternate valuation date applies to all or only a portion of the assets and, if the *Request for Order* (FL-300) is directed to only a portion of the assets, the declaration must separately identify each such asset; and
(3) The reasons supporting the alternate valuation date. CRC Rule 5.390(c).

Any and all pension plans that require joinder and have not been divided by court order must be joined as a party to the case before a petitioner or respondent may file a request for a separate trial to terminate marital status. Parties may refer to the *Retirement Plan Joinder-Information Sheet* (form *FL-318-INFO*) to help determine whether their retirement benefit plans must be joined.

The party not requesting termination of status may ask the court:
(1) To order that the judgment granting a dissolution include conditions that preserve his or her claims in retirement benefit plans, health insurance and other assets; and
(2) For other orders made as conditions to terminating the parties' marital status or domestic partnership.

The court must use the *Bifurcation of Status of Marriage or Domestic Partnership-Attachment* (form *FL-347*) as an attachment to the order after a hearing.

In cases involving a division of pension benefits acquired by the parties during the marriage or domestic partnership, the court must use *Pension Benefits-Attachment to Judgment* (form *FL-348*) to set out the orders upon severance of the status of marriage or domestic partnership. The form serves as a temporary qualified domestic relations order and must be attached to the status-only judgment and then served on the plan administrator. It can also be attached to a judgment to allow the parties time to prepare a qualified domestic relations order.

Chapter 19: Bifurcation

Pursuant to **FC § 2337(c)**, before granting a bifurcation, the court may impose upon a party any of the following conditions and, in case of that party's death, an order of any of the following conditions continues to be binding upon that party's estate:

(1) The moving party must indemnify and hold the other party harmless from any taxes, reassessments, interest and penalties payable by the other party in connection with the division of the community estate that would not have been payable if the parties were still married at the time the division was made.

(2) Until judgment has been entered on all remaining issues and has become final:

a. All existing health and medical insurance coverage for the other party and any minor children named as dependents must be maintained, so long as the party is eligible to do so. If at any time during this period the party is not eligible to maintain that coverage, the party must, at the party's sole expense, provide and maintain health and medical insurance coverage that is comparable to the existing health and medical insurance coverage to the extent available.

b. The moving party must indemnify and hold the other party harmless from any adverse consequences if the bifurcation results in a termination of the other party's right to a probate homestead in the residence in which the other party resides at the time the severance is granted.

c. The moving party must indemnify and hold the other party harmless from any adverse consequences if the bifurcation results in the loss of the rights of the other party to a probate family allowance as the surviving spouse of the party.

d. The party must indemnify and hold the other party harmless from any adverse consequences if the bifurcation results in the loss of the other party's rights with respect to any retirement, survivor or deferred compensation benefits under any plan, fund or arrangement, or to any elections or options associated therewith, to the extent that the other party would have been entitled to those benefits or elections as the spouse or surviving spouse of the party.

(3) The moving party must indemnify and hold the other party harmless from any adverse consequences if the bifurcation results in the loss of rights to social security benefits or elections to the extent the other party would have been entitled to those benefits or elections as the surviving spouse of the party.

(4) The moving party must maintain a beneficiary designation for a nonprobate transfer, as described in **Probate Code § 5000**, for a spouse or domestic partner for up to one-half of or, upon a showing of good cause, all of a nonprobate transfer asset until judgment has been entered with respect to the community ownership of that asset, and until the other party's interest therein has been distributed to him or her.

Chapter 19: Bifurcation

(5) The court may require that one-half or all, upon a showing of good cause, of the community interest in any independent retirement account by or for the benefit of the party be assigned and transferred to the other party.

(6) Upon a showing that circumstances exist that would place a substantial burden of enforcement upon either party's community property rights or would eliminate the ability of the surviving party to enforce his or her community property rights if the other party died before the division and distribution or compliance with any court-ordered payment of any community property interest therein, including, but not limited to, a situation in which preemption under federal law applies to an asset of a party, or purchase by a bona fide purchaser has occurred, the court may order a specific security interest designed to reduce or eliminate the likelihood that a postmortem enforcement proceeding would be ineffective or unduly burdensome to the surviving party.

(7) Any other condition the court determines is just and equitable.

Additionally, prior to, or simultaneously with, the entry of a judgment granting bifurcation, all of the following must occur:

(1) Any and all pension plans that have not been divided by court order that require joinder must be joined as a party to the case before a petitioner or respondent may file a request for a separate trial to terminate marital status or the domestic partnership, unless joinder is precluded or made unnecessary by Title 1 of the federal Employee Retirement Income Security Act of 1974 (29 U.S.C. Sec. 1001 et seq.), as amended (ERISA), or any other applicable law. Parties may refer to the *Retirement Plan Joinder-Information Sheet* (form *FL-318-INFO*) to help determine whether their retirement benefit plans must be joined.

(2) The party's retirement or pension plan must be joined as a party to the proceeding for dissolution, unless joinder is precluded or made unnecessary by Title 1 of the federal Employee Retirement Income Security Act of 1974 **(29 U.S.C. Sec. 1001** et seq.), as amended (ERISA), or any other applicable law.

The court must enter one of the following in connection with the judgment for each retirement plan in which either party is a participant:

> **(1)** An order pursuant to FC § 2610 disposing of each party's interest in retirement plan benefits, including survivor and death benefits.
> **(2)** An interim order preserving the nonemployee party's right to retirement plan benefits, including survivor and death benefits, pending entry of judgment on all remaining issues.
> **(3)** An attachment to the judgment granting a dissolution of the status of the marriage, as follows:
> EACH PARTY (insert names and addresses) IS PROVISIONALLY AWARDED WITHOUT PREJUDICE AND SUBJECT TO ADJUSTMENT BY A SUBSEQUENT DOMESTIC RELATIONS ORDER, A SEPARATE INTEREST EQUAL TO ONE-HALF OF ALL BENEFITS ACCRUED OR TO BE ACCRUED UNDER THE PLAN (name each plan individually) AS A RESULT OF EMPLOYMENT OF THE OTHER

Chapter 19: Bifurcation

> PARTY DURING THE MARRIAGE OR DOMESTIC PARTNERSHIP AND PRIOR TO THE DATE OF SEPARATION. IN ADDITION, PENDING FURTHER NOTICE, THE PLAN SHALL, AS ALLOWED BY LAW, OR IN THE CASE OF A GOVERNMENTAL PLAN, AS ALLOWED BY THE TERMS OF THE PLAN, CONTINUE TO TREAT THE PARTIES AS MARRIED OR DOMESTIC PARTNERS FOR PURPOSES OF ANY SURVIVOR RIGHTS OR BENEFITS AVAILABLE UNDER THE PLAN TO THE EXTENT NECESSARY TO PROVIDE FOR PAYMENT OF AN AMOUNT EQUAL TO THAT SEPARATE INTEREST OR FOR ALL OF THE SURVIVOR BENEFIT IF AT THE TIME OF THE DEATH OF THE PARTICIPANT, THERE IS NO OTHER ELIGIBLE RECIPIENT OF THE SURVIVOR BENEFIT. FC § 2337(d)(2).

The moving party must promptly serve a copy of any order, interim order or attachment entered pursuant to paragraph (2) of subdivision (d)[1], as well a copy of the judgment granting a dissolution of the status of the marriage, on the retirement or pension plan administrator. **FC § 2337(e)**.

The court must reserve jurisdiction for later determination of all pending issues. **FC § 2337(f)**.

Within ten (10) days after the order deciding the bifurcated issue and any statement of decision pursuant to **CRC Rule 3.1591** has been filed, the clerk must mail copies to the parties and file a certificate of mailing. **CRC Rule 5.390(e)**.

Pursuant to **FC § 2337(g)**, if the moving party dies after the entry of judgment granting a dissolution of marriage, all obligations set forth in this code section are enforceable against any asset, including the proceeds thereof, against which these obligations would have been enforceable prior to the person's death.

In the case that follows, the trial court refused to grant a bifurcation of the marital status of the petitioner, harboring under the mistaken belief that the petitioner was required to justify his request with a compelling showing of need. The appellate court stated that "only slight evidence is necessary to obtain bifurcation and resolution of marital status." On the other hand, a spouse opposing a bifurcation must present compelling reasons for denial.

---

[1] Paragraph 2 of division (d) provides: "To preserve the claims of each spouse in all retirement plan benefits upon entry of judgment granting a dissolution of the status of the marriage, the court shall enter one of the following in connection with the judgment for each retirement plan in which either party is a participant:
  (A) An order pursuant to Section 2610 disposing of each party's interest in retirement plan benefits, including survivor and death benefits.
  (B) An interim order preserving the nonemployee party's right to retirement plan benefits, including survivor and death benefits, pending entry of judgment on all remaining issues."

Chapter 19: Bifurcation

> **THOMAS A. GIONIS, Petitioner, v. THE SUPERIOR COURT OF ORANGE COUNTY, Respondent; AISSA WAYNE GIONIS, Real Party in Interest**
> Court of Appeal of California, Fourth Appellate District, Division Three
> 202 Cal.App.3d 786; 248 Cal.Rptr. 741
> June 30, 1988
> *(Gionis v. Superior Court)*

Thomas A. Gionis seeks a writ of mandate compelling the superior court to vacate its order denying his motion to bifurcate the issue of his marital status from all other issues. He claims the trial court abused its discretion by denying his motion as untimely. We agree with petitioner and issue the writ.

Aissa and Thomas Gionis were married on February 14, 1986. In June 1987 Aissa filed a petition for legal separation and a separate petition for dissolution of marriage. Both petitions requested sole custody of the parties' infant daughter as well as child and spousal support.

Thomas responded and filed a motion to change venue. The declarations supporting and opposing the motion revealed deep bitterness between the parties over the issue of child custody. The parties then stipulated to proceed with the petition for dissolution of marriage, and agreed that the court acquired jurisdiction over both parties for that purpose in June 1987.

On January 29, 1988, Thomas moved to bifurcate the issue of marital status from the issues of custody, support and property division. His declaration stated the marriage had irrevocably failed, reconciliation was not possible and although the trial of the dissolution would be brief, the remaining issues would require discovery and a more lengthy trial. He further stated he wanted his marital status resolved so he could make investments and obtain credit without having to seek quitclaim deeds from Aissa or worry that a lender might rely on community rather than separate credit. Aissa's opposition to the motion raised procedural objections; she set forth no substantive reasons why bifurcation would be against her interests.

The court denied the motion, stating there was no compelling reason to bifurcate since the petition had been on file less than a year.

In his declaration Thomas maintained reconciliation was impossible and the issues other than status would require a lengthy trial. He continued with extensive personal reasons why he wanted his brief marriage to Aissa dissolved quickly. Absent a showing by Aissa why bifurcation should not be granted, Thomas's declaration provided a proper basis for the motion.

We need not decide whether the court could have denied the motion because of these procedural defects; the record reveals it did not. The court gave no indication it found the declaration unacceptable or refused to consider any of its contents. Rather, it clearly stated the showing made was insufficient. "This is a hotly contested matter, obviously. Obviously, there is [sic] a lot of emotions involved here. But there's no reason stated in the affidavit why I should grant the motion."

Thomas's declaration contained sufficient reasons supporting his motion to bifurcate, and

Chapter 19: Bifurcation

> the trial court abused its discretion by refusing to grant it. Consistent with the legislative policy favoring no fault dissolution of marriage, only slight evidence is necessary to obtain bifurcation and resolution of marital status. On the other hand, a spouse opposing bifurcation must present compelling reasons for denial.
>
> Since the issue presented is one of law and the opposing parties have received due notice, the issuance of a peremptory writ in the first instance is appropriate. Therefore, let a peremptory writ of mandate issue directing the Orange County Superior Court to vacate its order denying the motion to bifurcate the issue of marital status from all other issues and to enter a new order granting bifurcation and dissolving the parties' marital status.

Drafting the formal order for a bifurcation requires completing the mandatory use *FL-347 Bifurcation of Status of Marriage or Domestic Partnership-Attachment* (Family Law) and attaching it either to a *Judgment* (form *FL-180*) or a *Findings and Order After Hearing* (form *FL-340*).

Finally, **CRC Rule 5.392** pertains to appeals and bifurcations and this rule provides:

> **(a)** Applicability - This rule does not apply to appeals from the court's termination of marital status as a separate issue, or to appeals from other orders that are separately appealable.
> **(b)** Certificate of probable cause for appeal
>   **(1)** The order deciding the bifurcated issue may include an order certifying that there is probable cause for immediate appellate review of the issue.
>   **(2)** If it was not in the order, within 10 days after the clerk mails the order deciding the bifurcated issue, a party may notice a motion asking the court to certify that there is probable cause for immediate appellate review of the order. The motion must be heard within 30 days after the order deciding the bifurcated issue is mailed.
>   **(3)** The clerk must promptly mail notice of the decision on the motion to the parties. If the motion is not determined within 40 days after mailing of the order on the bifurcated issue, it is deemed granted on the grounds stated in the motion.
> **(c)** Content and effect of certificate
>   **(1)** A certificate of probable cause must state, in general terms, the reason immediate appellate review is desirable, such as a statement that final resolution of the issue:
>   **(A)** Is likely to lead to settlement of the entire case;
>   **(B)** Will simplify remaining issues;
>   **(C)** Will conserve the courts' resources; or
>   **(D)** Will benefit the well-being of a child of the marriage or the parties.
>   **(2)** If a certificate is granted, trial of the remaining issues may be stayed. If trial of the remaining issues is stayed, unless otherwise ordered by the trial court on noticed motion, further discovery must be stayed while the certification is pending. These stays terminate upon the expiration of time for filing a motion to appeal if none is filed, or upon the Court of Appeal denying all motions to appeal, or upon the Court of Appeal decision becoming final.
> **(d)** Motion to appeal
>   **(1)** If the certificate is granted, a party may, within 15 days after the mailing of the notice of the order granting it, serve and file in the Court of Appeal a motion to appeal the decision on the bifurcated issue. On ex parte application served and filed within 15 days, the Court of Appeal or the trial court may extend the time for filing the motion to appeal by not more than an additional 20 days.
>   **(2)** The motion must contain:

Chapter 19: Bifurcation

　　(A) A brief statement of the facts necessary to an understanding of the issue;
　　(B) A statement of the issue; and
　　(C) A statement of why, in the context of the case, an immediate appeal is desirable.
　(3) The motion must include or have attached:
　　(A) A copy of the decision of the trial court on the bifurcated issue;
　　(B) Any statement of decision;
　　(C) The certification of the appeal; and
　　(D) A sufficient partial record to enable the Court of Appeal to determine whether to grant the motion.
　(4) A summary of evidence and oral proceedings, if relevant, supported by a declaration of counsel may be used when a transcript is not available.
　(5) The motion must be accompanied by the filing fee for an appeal under rule 8.100(c) and Government Code sections 68926 and 68926.1.
　(6) A copy of the motion must be served on the trial court.
(e) Proceedings to determine motion
　(1) Within 10 days after service of the motion, an adverse party may serve and file an opposition to it.
　(2) The motion to appeal and any opposition will be submitted without oral argument, unless otherwise ordered.
　(3) The motion to appeal is deemed granted unless it is denied within 30 days from the date of filing the opposition or the last document requested by the court, whichever is later.
　(4) Denial of a motion to appeal is final forthwith and is not subject to rehearing. A party aggrieved by the denial of the motion may petition for review by the Supreme Court.
(f) Proceedings if motion to appeal is granted
　(1) If the motion to appeal is granted, the moving party is deemed an appellant, and the rules governing other civil appeals apply except as provided in this rule.
　(2) The partial record filed with the motion will be considered the record for the appeal unless, within 10 days from the date notice of the grant of the motion is mailed, a party notifies the Court of Appeal of additional portions of the record that are needed for a full consideration of the appeal.
　(3) If a party notifies the court of the need for an additional record, the additional material must be secured from the trial court by augmentation under rule 8.155, unless it appears to the Court of Appeal that some of the material is not needed.
　(4) Briefs must be filed under a schedule set for the matter by the Court of Appeal.
(g) Review by writ or appeal The trial court's denial of a certification motion under (b) does not preclude review of the decision on the bifurcated issue by extraordinary writ.
(h) Review by appeal None of the following precludes review of the decision on the bifurcated issue upon appeal of the final judgment:
　(1) A party's failure to move for certification under (b) for immediate appeal;
　(2) The trial court's denial of a certification motion under (b) for immediate appeal;
　(3) A party's failure to move to appeal under (d); and
　(4) The Court of Appeals denial of a motion to appeal under (d).

EDUCATIONAL EXERCISES

Answer the following questions

1. What is a Bifurcated Judgment?
2. Under what circumstances is a bifurcation commonly used?
3. Are there judicial Council forms specifically designed for bifurcations? If so, list them.
4. What forms are used in requesting a bifurcation?
5. Using the information in Appendix One draft a Bifurcation Motion on the appropriate Judicial Council forms for Marilyn's attorney because Marilyn wants to get married as soon as possible.

CHAPTER 20: Title, Kinds of Property & Valuation

In Brief...

SPOUSES CAN HOLD TITLE TO PROPERTY AS:
- **Joint tenants:**
  - The title must so state with both names on the deed;
  - Each spouse has an equal, undivided equal right to possess the property; and
  - When a spouse dies, title is automatically conveyed to the surviving spouse. **FC § 251**.
- **Tenants in common:**
  - Spouses do not have to own equal shares;
  - Each spouse has a deed stating the fractional percentage owned; and
  - There is no right to survivorship.
- Community property:
  - The interests of each spouse are present, existing and equal, **FC §§ 760, 751**;
  - Each spouse has the right to include one-half of the property in his or her will; and
  - When one spouse dies without disposing of his or her share, title is automatically conveyed to the surviving spouse.
- **Community property with right of survivorship:**
  - Each spouse owns an equal undivided one-half interest in the property;
  - There is no right to will or dispose his or her share of the property; and
  - When a spouse dies, title is automatically conveyed to the surviving spouse.

THE SIX KINDS OF PROPERTY ARE:
1. Personal Property which is every kind of property that is not real, **CC § 663**.
2. Real or immovable property is land and any and all property that is affixed to, incidental or appurtenant to it, including condominiums, **CC § 658**.
3. Separate property is real or personal property owned by a person before marriage, after separation or acquired at any time by gift, bequest, devise, or descent, **FC § 770(a)**.
4. Quasi-marital property is property that would have been community property or quasi-community property if the marriage had not been void or voidable.
5. Quasi-community property is real or personal property, acquired while not domiciled in CA that would have been community property if acquired while domiciled in CA, **FC § 125(a)**.

Chapter 20: Title, Kinds of Property & Valuation

> 6. Community property is all property, real or personal, wherever situated, acquired by a married person or a married couple during the marriage while domiciled in CA, **FC § 760**.
>
> ***PROPERTY TERMS/PHRASES/RULES:***
> - The community property presumption provides that property acquired during marriage is community, unless the presumption is rebutted, **FC § 2581**.
> - Commingled property is separate property that was mixed with community property or vice versa; and if funds have been so commingled that it is virtually impossible to trace them back to their source, the funds are entirely community property.
> - Transmutations are written waivers that change the character of property from separate to community or vice versa, **FC § 852(a)**.
>
> ***VALUATION OF COMMUNITY ASSETS:***
> - Upon dissolution or legal separation of the parties, the court must value the assets and liabilities as near as practicable to the time of trial, **FC § 2552(a)**.
> - Upon 30 days' notice by the moving party to the other party, the court may value all or any portion of the assets and liabilities at a date after separation and before trial, **FC § 2552(b)**.

Introduction

There are several different ways that spouses can hold title to real property. The most common is – as community property.

"Property includes real and personal property and any interest therein." **FC § 113**. There are six (6) kinds of property and each is discussed in this chapter.

Finally, the date that community property is valued is the time nearest to the trial. However, for a good cause, a different date may be chosen that is after the separation of the parties and before the trial.

Kinds of Property

There are six (6) kinds of property:

(1) Personal property,
(2) Real property,
(3) Separate property,
(4) Quasi-marital property
(5) Community property, and
(6) Quasi-community property.

1. Personal Property

Personal property is movable property owned by an individual; it is not land or attached to land. "Every kind of property that is not real is personal." **CC § 663**.

Chapter 20: Title, Kinds of Property & Valuation

A joint tenancy in personal property may be created by a written transfer, instrument or agreement. **CC § 683(a)**.

If a married woman acquired real or personal property before January 1, 1975, pursuant to an instrument in writing, the following conclusive presumptions apply:

> **(a)** If acquired by the married woman, the presumption is that the property is the married woman's separate property.
> **(b)** If acquired by the married woman and any other person, the presumption is that the married woman takes the part acquired by her as tenant in common, unless a different intention is expressed in the instrument.
> **(c)** If acquired by husband and wife by an instrument in which they are described as husband and wife, the presumption is that the property is the community property of the husband and wife, unless a different intention is expressed in the instrument. FC § 803.

2. Real Property

Real or immovable property is land and any and all property that is affixed to, incidental or appurtenant to it. **CC § 658**. Real Property includes land and buildings, and anything attached to the land and condominiums. **CC § 783**.

Spouses may hold title to real property as **joint tenants**, **tenants in common**, **community property**, **community property with a right of survivorship** or **in trust**. **FC § 750**.

Holding title to property as **joint tenants** gives each spouse an undivided equal right to possess the property. Each spouse has an equal ownership interest in the property and the names of both spouses are on one deed. Title must have been acquired at the same time, by the same conveyance, and the title must expressly state that the spouses hold the title to the property as joint tenants.

When a joint tenant dies, title to the property is automatically conveyed by operation of law to the surviving joint tenant. However, if a joint tenant feloniously and intentionally kills the other joint tenant, the property passes as the decedent's property and the killer has no rights by survivorship. **FC § 251**.

If spouses hold title to real property as **tenants in common**, they do not have to own equal shares and the property can be owned by multiple people with each person owning an undivided fractional interest. Each tenant in common has a deed that sets forth his or her name and the fractional percentage of interest in the property owned. There is no right to survivorship in property owned as tenants in common.

If spouses hold the title to real property as **community property**, then the respective interests of each spouse in community property during the marriage are present, existing and equal. **FC §§ 760** and **751**. When the title to property is held as community property, each spouse has equal rights of management and control of the property and the right to include one-half of the community property in his or her will. If one of the spouses dies without disposing of his or his share of community property, the property automatically passes to the surviving spouse without the need of a probate procedure.

When spouses hold property as **community property with the right of survivorship**, each spouse owns an equal undivided one-half interest in the property, but there is no right to will or dispose his or her share of the property. And just as the property held in joint tenancy passes to the surviving spouse upon the death of one of the spouses, title held as community property with the right of survivorship is automatically conveyed by operation of law to the surviving spouse.

Spouses can also hold property in a **trust**. If a spouse transfers community property into a trust, unless the trust provides otherwise, the transferred property remains community property. The trust must be revocable as to that property transferred. A modification of property in the trust during the marriage requires the consent of both spouses. **FC § 761(a)**. Either spouse can revoke a trust instrument unless the trust instrument expressly provides otherwise.

Community property that is distributed or withdrawn from a trust by revocation, power of withdrawal or otherwise remains community property unless there is a valid transmutation of the property at the time of distribution or withdrawal. This includes any appreciation of the property. **FC § 761(b)**.
Spouses can alter their property rights with a premarital agreement or other marital property agreement. **FC § 1500**. (See Chapter 30 RE: Marital Agreements, *infra*.)

3. Separate Property

Separate property is any property (real or personal) acquired by a spouse before the marriage, after the parties separate or at any time by gift, devise or bequest, unless the spouses agree in writing otherwise.

The case that follows demonstrates that property acquired after separation is separate property, including spousal support.

In re Marriage of BOBBIE VERNON and VIOLET L. WALL. BOBBIE VERNON WALL, Appellant, v. VIOLET L. WALL, Respondent
Court of Appeal of California, Second Appellate District, Division One
29 Cal.App.3d 76; 105 Cal.Rptr. 201
November 30, 1972
(*Marriage of Wall*)

Appellant (husband) and respondent (wife) were married in 1965. They originally separated in 1968. In December of that year, husband filed a complaint for divorce and wife filed a cross-complaint for the same relief. They reconciled but the action was not dismissed. In March 1971, husband and wife again separated. Wife moved from the family home. She lived for a brief period with her daughter by a prior marriage, and then in the home occupied by her first husband and their son.

Chapter 20: Title, Kinds of Property & Valuation

Wife pursued the pending marital dissolution proceeding, prosecuting an order to show cause for temporary support. On April 29, the court awarded her support in the sum of $ 150 per month, payable on the first and fifteenth of each succeeding month. Husband made the May payments required by the order. Although his checks were dated May 1 and May 15, each was delivered several days after its date. Wife paid one-half of the rent on the home occupied by her son and first husband, and a portion of the grocery and utility bills. Her expenses exceeded $ 150 per month, and she supplemented her income by baby-sitting fees of $ 40 to $ 45 in May. Her total expenses exceeded the support payments and her baby-sitting income. Wife had no funds on the date of separation. In the latter part of May 1971, wife purchased a ticket on the Irish Sweepstakes for $ 2.50, taking the ticket in the name of Violet Foster, her name when married to her first husband. On July 1, 1971, wife was notified that she had won $ 120,000 on her ticket.

The matter at bench reached trial on the issues of dissolution of marriage and disposition of community property on February 17, 1972. The proceeds of the sweepstakes ticket had not yet been paid. Husband claimed that the ticket was community property of the marriage in which he had a one-half interest. The trial court found to the contrary, and awarded the ticket to wife as her separate property. Husband perfected his appeal to this court, contending that the record establishes a community interest in the ticket as a matter of law because the ticket was acquired by wife with commingled separate and community funds. Analysis of applicable law dictates rejection of appellant's contention.

"The earnings and accumulations of a spouse . . . while [living] separate and apart from the other spouse, are the separate property of the spouse." (Civ. Code, § 5118.) Here the source of the funds with which the sweepstakes ticket was purchased was either earnings of the wife (baby-sitting fees) or her accumulations (support payments received by her), acquired while she was living separate and apart from appellant husband.

The characterization as separate property of wife's baby-sitting fees is clear. Husband admits that those fees are earnings after separation and hence wife's separate property.

The status of the temporary support payments received by wife from husband presents a more difficult problem. "Accumulations," as used in the statute as a definition of separate property, is by no means as precise a term as "earnings." The few California cases that have dealt with the concept of "accumulations" after separation have applied a very broad definition to the term. Our Supreme Court in 1910 stated that the term applies "to any property which a person acquires and retains" except for property obtained in exchange for community property or community funds.

Here the temporary support payments received by respondent wife are property acquired or retained by her after separation from her husband. They are not property acquired by the wife in exchange for community property or funds. Temporary support payments are of a nature incompatible with their treatment as the community property of the separated marital partners. The purpose of the award is to enable the separated wife to live in her accustomed manner pending the dissolution action. The payments are ordered to prevent diminution of the wife's separate estate as nearly as practicable until the chancellor shall finally determine whether either party is entitled to relief in equity.

The purpose of those payments would be totally frustrated if they were to be treated as community property and thus subject to the management and control of the separated husband. The policy underlying payment of temporary support thus requires that the

> payments when made are the separate property of the recipient.
>
> We conclude that whether the source of payment for the sweepstakes ticket is treated as the baby-sitting earnings of wife or as in the accumulations from temporary support received by her, the source is wife's separate property.
>
> The judgment is affirmed.

Except as otherwise provided by statute, or the spouses agree otherwise, neither spouse has any interest in the separate property of the other. **FC § 752**.

Separate property of a married person includes all of the following:

> **(1)** All property owned by the person before marriage.
> **(2)** All property acquired by the person after marriage by gift, bequest, devise, or descent.
> **(3)** The rents, issues, and profits of the property described in this section. FC § 770(a).

During a dissolution, nullity or legal separation proceeding, if a notice of the pendency of the proceeding is recorded in any county in which either spouse resides on real property that is the separate property of the other, the real property may not be transferred, encumbered or otherwise disposed of voluntarily or involuntarily without the joinder of both spouses for a period of three months thereafter, unless the court otherwise orders. **FC § 754.**

A married person may convey his or her separate property without the consent of his or her spouse. **FC § 770(b).**

"The earnings and accumulations of a spouse and the minor children living with, or in the custody of, the spouse, after the date of separation, are the separate property of the spouse." **FC § 771(a)**.[1]

After entry of a judgment of the legal separation of the parties, the earnings or accumulations of each party are the separate property of the party acquiring the earnings or accumulations. **FC § 772**.

Separate property does not include quasi-community property. **FC § 2502.**

During a dissolution or legal separation, the court has jurisdiction to determine and thereafter divide community and separate property interests, if so requested by either party. The property can be real or personal and must be held by the parties as joint tenants or tenants in common. The property will be divided under the same rules as other community property is divided. **FC § 2650**.

---

[1] Fc § 771(a) provides
The earnings and accumulations of a spouse and the minor children living with, or in the custody of, the spouse, after the date of separation of the spouses, are the separate property of the spouse. This law was amended from "while living separate and apart from the other spouse" to "after the date of separation of the spouses" effective **January 1, 2017.**

Chapter 20: Title, Kinds of Property & Valuation

4. Quasi-Marital Property

If a court makes the determination that a marriage is void or voidable and finds that either party or both parties had a reasonable, good-faith belief that the marriage was valid, the court must declare the marriage to be putative and divide any property equally that was acquired during the union. The property so acquired, which would have been community property or quasi-community property if the union had not been void or voidable, is called **quasi-marital property**.

In the case that follows, the trial court found that the parties were both putative spouses. As such, the property acquired during the invalid marriage was found to be quasi-marital property.

> *In re Marriage of PABLO and PETRA TEJEDA. PABLO TEJEDA, Respondent, v. PETRA TEJEDA, Appellant.*
> COURT OF APPEAL OF CALIFORNIA, SIXTH APPELLATE DISTRICT
> 179 Cal.App.4th 973; 102 Cal.Rptr.3d 361
> November 25, 2009, Filed
> (*Marriage of Tejeda*)
>
> In 1973, appellant Petra Tejeda (Petra) and respondent Pablo Tejeda (Pablo) were married in Las Vegas. At the time of the marriage ceremony, and unbeknownst to Petra, Pablo was married to Margarita Rivera Tejeda (Margarita). In 1975, Pablo petitioned to dissolve his marriage to Margarita, and a judgment of dissolution was entered the following year. In 1988, Pablo and Petra participated in a marriage ceremony in a Mexican church, unaccompanied by any civil formalities.
>
> The parties' union lasted more than 30 years. During this time, Petra and Pablo had five children together. Petra began acquiring real property in 1994, taking title in her name, together with other relatives, but not with Pablo.
>
> In March 2006, Pablo filed an action to end his union with Petra, petitioning for dissolution in San Benito County. In a response filed in May 2006, Petra likewise requested dissolution of marriage. Thereafter, she amended her response to seek a judgment of nullity of marriage.
>
> In January 2008, the trial court made an oral finding that the marriage is either void or voidable because Mr. Tejeda was already married. The court also found that at all times, Mrs. Tejeda believed that she was married to someone who at the time of their marriage ceremony was single. That belief, the court said, was reaffirmed "by her actions over some period of time" such as filing joint tax returns, confirming her marital status for immigration purposes, taking Pablo's name, and using "medical benefits under his insurance, social security benefits under his name."
>
> Given these factual findings, the court concluded, the matter was governed by FC § 2251, which required the court to "declare the party or parties to have the status of a putative spouse." The property thus was quasi-marital property.
> In June 2008, the court entered a judgment of nullity, which incorporated its earlier determinations. The court found that since "either party or both parties believed in good faith that the marriage was valid," the court was statutorily required to "declare the party

or parties to have a status of putative spouse." Under "the mandatory language" of FC § 2251, the court stated, it was "obligated to find that the property of the parties is quasi-marital … property." This appeal ensued.

DISCUSSION
Where a marriage is invalid due to some legal infirmity, an innocent party may be entitled to relief under the putative spouse doctrine. (Citations omitted.) Invalid marriages include those that are void or voidable. Bigamy renders the later marriage either void or voidable, depending on the circumstances. (FC § 2201(a).)

Under the equitable putative spouse doctrine, a person's reasonable, good faith belief that his or her marriage is valid entitles that person to the benefits of marriage, even if the marriage is not, in fact, valid.

The putative spouse doctrine is "an equitable doctrine first recognized by the judiciary, and later codified by the Legislature. The current version of the putative spouse doctrine is contained in FC § 2251(a), which provides in relevant part: 'If a determination is made that a marriage is void or voidable and the court finds that either party or both parties believed in good faith that the marriage was valid, the court shall: (1) Declare the party or parties to have the status of a putative spouse.'"

Quasi-marital property is "property acquired during the union which would have been community property or quasi-community property if the union had not been void or voidable." (FC § 2251(a)(2). The theory of "quasi-marital property" equates property rights acquired during a putative marriage with community property rights acquired during a legal marriage. (Citations omitted.)

Upon declaration of putative spouse status, the court is required to divide the quasi-marital property as if it were community property. (FC § 2251(a)(2). Thus, the share to which the putative spouse is entitled is the same share of the quasi-marital property as the spouse would receive as an actual and legal spouse if there had been a valid marriage, i.e., it shall be divided equally between the parties.

The statute commands the court to divide the quasi-marital property as if it were community property, using these words: If the division of property is in issue, the court shall "divide, in accordance with Division 7 (commencing with FC § 2500), that property acquired during the union which would have been community property or quasi-community property if the union had not been void or voidable. (FC § 2251(a)(2).) Division 7 governs the division of property; FC § 2550 generally requires the court to "divide the community estate of the parties equally."

DISPOSITION
The June 2008 judgment of nullity is affirmed.

5. Quasi-Community Property

Quasi-community property is real or personal property, wherever situated, acquired by either spouse while domiciled elsewhere that would have been community property if the spouse(s) who acquired the property had been domiciled in this state at the time of its acquisition. **FC § 125(a), Probate Code § 66.**

6. Community Property

Community property is all property, real or personal, wherever situated, acquired by a married person or a married couple during the marriage while domiciled in this state; the respective interests of each spouse in community property during the marriage are present, existing and equal. **FC §§ 760** and **751.**

When community property is used to buy a Ferrari, the Ferrari is community property, as the case that follows demonstrates.

> *In re Marriage of FRANCES MAE and JOHN ASHLEY SHELTON. FRANCES MAE SHELTON, Respondent, v. JOHN ASHLEY SHELTON, Appellant*
> Court of Appeal of California, Third Appellate District
> 118 Cal.App.3d 811; 173 Cal.Rptr. 629
> May 5, 1981
> (*Marriage of Shelton*)
>
> On July 13, 1979, approximately one year after the parties' separation but prior to the interlocutory judgment of dissolution of marriage, husband took $ 500 in cash (withdrawn from a community property bank account) and $ 9,500 in cashier's checks (purchased with the proceeds from the sale of community personal property) to a casino at Lake Tahoe, Nevada, where he won $ 21,000 or $ 22,000. The following day he used the winnings and the original $ 10,000 "stake" to purchase a Ferrari car. During the trial, wife argued that the entire value of the car was community, whereas husband argued that that portion of the car purchased with his gambling winnings was his separate property. In its rulings of November 21, 1979, the trial court held "the $ 32,000.00[2] used to purchase the Ferrari was a community asset and the wife is entitled to $ 16,000.00 of that asset."
>
> Husband contends his postseparation gambling proceeds constituted his separate property because he acquired them after separation from wife. He argues the income arose from his separate "skill, efforts and industry," thus commingling community property and separate property, and he should receive a fair share of the profits as his separate property.
>
> Here we have a conflict between two general rules: Proceeds follow the character of their source and property acquired after separation is separate property. The source here was community property; the proceeds were acquired by husband after his separation from wife.
>
> Husband's "skill, efforts, and industry" were minimal. Although perhaps involving some slight element of skill, successful gambling of the type afforded at the Lake Tahoe casinos depends mainly upon good luck.[3] Husband's separate property contribution was the minimal skill and effort required at games of chance, an inconsiderable factor

---

[2] Husband testified he won "approximately $ 21,000" but he also testified he paid $ 31,000 or $ 32,000 cash for the car, plus some additional money not pertinent here, which he borrowed. It would appear the court impliedly found the winnings to be $ 22,000, since it expressly found he "won $ 32,000 gambling with the $ 10,000" and neither party challenges this figure.

[3] We take judicial notice that the gambling offered at the casinos at Lake Tahoe consists primarily of "games of chance" insofar as the law is concerned, i.e., games which by definition are contests in which chance predominates over skill. There is no claim made nor a showing in the record that husband made his winnings at true games of skill.

Chapter 20: Title, Kinds of Property & Valuation

> compared to the community property contribution of $ 10,000. The entire winnings are therefore community property and the trial court's judgment was correct.
>
> The judgment is affirmed.

Also, a married couple may agree in writing to divide their community property on the basis of a non pro rata division of the aggregate value of the community property or on the basis of a division of each individual item or asset of community property or in any manner, provided that both spouses have agreed in writing to so divide. **Probate Code § 100(b)**.

Spouses cannot give away or dispose of community property for less than the fair and reasonable value without the written consent of the other spouse. However, this rule does not apply to gifts that are mutually given by both spouses to third parties and gifts given by one spouse to the other. **FC § 1100(b)**.

A spouse may not sell, convey or encumber community personal property used as the family dwelling, or the furniture, furnishings or fittings of the home. Additionally, a spouse may not sell the clothing or wearing apparel of the other spouse or minor children that is community personal property without the written consent of the other spouse. **FC § 1100(c)**.

Either spouse has the right to management and control of the community personal property, but both spouses must join in executing any instrument by which that community real property or any interest therein is leased for a longer period than one year, or is sold, conveyed, or encumbered. **FC §§ 1100(a)** and **1102(a)**.

Community property that is distributed or withdrawn from a trust by revocation, power of withdrawal or otherwise remains community property unless there is a valid transmutation of the property at the time of distribution or withdrawal. This includes any appreciation of the property. **FC § 761(b)**.

The **community estate** includes both community property and quasi-community property. **FC § 63**.

Spouses have mutual obligations of respect, fidelity and support. **FC § 720**. They have a confidential relationship that imposes a fiduciary duty of the highest good faith and fair dealing on each spouse, and neither must take any unfair advantage of the other. In transactions between themselves, spouses are subject to the general rules governing fiduciary relationships that control the actions of persons occupying confidential relations with each other. **FC § 721**. (See Chapter 18 RE: Disclosure & Fiduciary Duty, *supra.*)

Commingling is mixing separate property assets with community property assets or vice versa.

Chapter 20: Title, Kinds of Property & Valuation

Property that is **commingled** is presumed to be community property. The presumption can be rebutted by tracing or following the money trail and providing proof of the separate claim. Proof of a separate claim could be demonstrated by bank account statements, real estate purchase agreements and deeds. If the tracing successfully proves that the source of the funds was only from a separate property source, the property that was commingled becomes **uncommingled**. If funds have been so commingled that it is virtually impossible to trace them back to their source, the funds are entirely community property.

Pursuant to **FC § 2581**, **property** that is **acquired during marriage in joint form is presumed to be community property**. The presumption affects the burden of proof and can be rebutted by
a clear statement in the deed or other documentary evidence of title by which the property is acquired or proof that the parties made a written agreement providing that the property is separate property.

If parties to a bank account are married to each other, whether or not they are so described in the deposit agreement, their net contribution to the account is presumed to be and remains their community property. **Probate Code § 5305**. This presumption affects the burden of proof and can be rebutted by:

> (1) The sums on deposit that are claimed to be separate property can be traced from separate property unless it is proved that the married persons made a written agreement that expressed their clear intent that the sums be their community property.
> (2) The married persons made a written agreement, separate from the deposit agreement, that expressly provided that the sums on deposit, claimed not to be community property, were not to be community property.

The standard of proof for **FC § 2581** is a preponderance of the evidence.

Finally, it should be noted that the community property presumption is not the same as the presumption that the owner of the legal title to property is presumed to be the owner of the full beneficial title. **Evid. Code § 662**.[4] In order to be rebutted, this presumption requires clear and convincing evidence.

Transmuting or Changing the Character of Property

When one kind of property is changed to another kind of property for any reason the character of the property has been changed. The character of property can be personal, real, separate, quasi-marital, community or quasi-community property. *In re Marriage of HAINES* (1995) 33 Cal.App.4th 277 at p. 291.

The word **transmutation** means change or changing. It is a written waiver of property that changes the character of the property such as changing separate

---

[4] Evid. Code § 662 provides: "The owner of the legal title to property is presumed to be the owner of the full beneficial title. This presumption may be rebutted only by clear and convincing proof."

property into community property. The rules set forth in **FC § 852** must be followed in order to have a valid transmutation. (See *In re Marriage of BONVINO* (2015) 241 Cal.App.4th 1411 where the stated that to "show an agreement changing the character of property from separate to community, or community to separate, the requirements of the transmutation statutes must be met.

If the form of title to property changes the character of the property without meeting the requirements of **FC § 852**, then the title presumption of **Evid. Code § 662**[5] does not apply." *Id.* at p. 1429.)

Married persons may agree with or without consideration to transmute community property to the separate property of either spouse, to transmute the separate property of either spouse to community property and/or transmute the separate property of one spouse to separate property of the other spouse. **FC § 850**.

However, a transmutation of real or personal property is not valid unless it is made in writing and is joined in, consented to or accepted by the spouse whose interest in the property is adversely affected. **FC § 852(a)**. A transmutation is subject to the laws governing fraudulent transfers. **FC § 851**.

How clear must the language be in a transmutation of real property? The following case answers this question.

> In re Marriage of RICHARD BEGIAN and IDA SARAJIAN.RICHARD BEGIAN, Appellant, v. IDA SARAJIAN, Respondent.
> Court of Appeal of California, Second Appellate District, Division Three
> December 20, 2018, Opinion Filed
>
> Richard and Ida married in August 1993 and lived together until their separation in September 2015. They have two children. This appeal concerns a residential property located on Avonoak Terrace in Glendale, California (Avonoak).
>
> On April 29, 1996, Ida's mother, Rose, executed a "QUITCLAIM DEED" transferring a 48 percent undivided interest in Avonoak to Ida. Rose retained a 52 percent interest in the property. On the same day, Richard executed a "QUITCLAIM DEED" transferring his ownership interest in Avonoak to Ida, as her sole and separate property. The deed stated: "IT IS THE EXPRESS INTENT OF THE GRANTOR, BEING THE SPOUSE OF THE GRANTEE, TO CONVEY ALL RIGHT, TITLE AND INTEREST OF THE GRANTOR COMMUNITY OR OTHERWISE, IN AND TO THE HEREIN DESCRIBED PROPERTY, TO THE GRANTEE AS HIS/HER SOLE AND SEPARATE PROPERTY."
>
> On June 21, 2001, Rose and Ida executed an "INDIVIDUAL GRANT DEED" granting their respective 52 percent and 48 percent interests in Avonoak to "ROSE SARAJIAN, a Widow[,] and IDA SARAJIAN and RICHARD BEGIAN, Wife and Husband, All as

---

[5] Evid. Code § 662 provides: "The owner of the legal title to property is presumed to be the owner of the full beneficial title. This presumption may be rebutted only by clear and convincing proof."

Chapter 20: Title, Kinds of Property & Valuation

Joint Tenants." Ida does not dispute that the deed effectively granted Richard a community property interest in Avonoak.

On May 1, 2006, Rose, Ida, and Richard executed a "Trust Transfer Deed." The deed stated: "FOR NO CONSIDERATION, GRANTORS ROSE SARAJIAN, a Widow, and IDA SARAJIAN and RICHARD BEGIAN, Wife and Husband, all as joint tenants, hereby GRANT to IDA SARAJIAN, the following real property [legal description of Avonoak]." The deed stated the conveyance was not subject to a documentary transfer tax because "'this is a bonafide gift and the grantor received nothing in return, R & T 11911.'"

On December 19, 2014, Ida created the "Ida Sarajian Separate Property Trust," naming herself as trustee and her children as beneficiaries. The same day, Ida executed another "Trust Transfer Deed" stating "FOR NO CONSIDERATION, GRANTOR Ida Sarajian, a married woman as her separate property, hereby GRANTS to Ida Sarajian, Trustee of The Ida Sarajian Separate Property Trust dated December 19, 2014, the following described real property [legal description of Avonoak]."

On October 9, 2015, Richard commenced the underlying dissolution action, and requested the court confirm Avonoak as community property. Ida asserted the residence was her separate property.

On June 29, 2016, the trial court bifurcated the question of Avonoak's characterization from the remaining issues in the case. Richard argued the 2006 Trust Transfer Deed lacked an unambiguous declaration of his intention, as the adversely affected spouse, to transmute his community property interest into Ida's separate property. He maintained the document "was prepared and signed in connection with estate planning," as demonstrated by the document's title, and the document made "absolutely no mention of the property rights being changed or the fact that [Richard's] interest [was] being adversely affected." Because "[n]othing on the face of the document explicitly state[d] that [he] was waiving away all of his community property ownership interest," Richard maintained the Trust Transfer Deed failed to meet section 852(a)'s express declaration requirement.

Ida argued the use of the word "grant" in the 2006 Trust Transfer Deed unambiguously demonstrated the parties' intention to change the characterization and ownership of Avonoak from a joint tenancy into Ida's separate property. Anticipating Richard's argument, Ida maintained the document's title was irrelevant to the express declaration analysis, because the Trust Transfer Deed named the grantee only as "'Ida Sarajian,'" and it made no reference to "her capacity as trustee of any trust," let alone the Ida Sarajian Separate Property Trust, which did not exist in 2006.

On August 29, 2016, the trial court issued a statement of decision finding the 2006 Trust Transfer Deed validly transmuted Richard's community interest in Avonoak into Ida's separate property. The court observed that "'"grant" is the historically operative word for transferring interests in real property,'" and reasoned the parties' use of the word in the Trust Transfer Deed thus satisfied section 852(a)'s express declaration requirement. The court added that its conclusion was reinforced by the phrase "bonafide gift," explaining "this provision gave [Richard] clear notice that he was making a gift to [Ida] through the deed and, thus, making a change in the characterization or ownership of the property." Finally, the court determined the deed's title did "not undermine the clear expression" of intent, because "the deed transfers Avonoak to [Ida], not to any trust, and there is no trust identified on the face of the document."

On September 14, 2016, the trial court filed an order deeming Avonoak to be Ida's separate property for the reasons stated in its statement of decision.

On October 3, 2016, the trial court filed a certificate of probable cause for immediate appeal of its order on the bifurcated issue. On October 10, 2016, Richard filed a motion with this court for leave to appeal the bifurcated issue. We granted the motion and now consider the matter.

DISCUSSION

The question presented in this case is whether the trial court correctly determined Richard's execution of the 2006 Trust Transfer Deed effectively transmuted his community interest in Avonoak into Ida's separate property. Section 850, subdivision (a) provides that married persons may transmute the community property of either spouse into separate property "by agreement or transfer," subject to the provisions of sections 851 to 853. Section 852(a) provides: "A transmutation of real or personal property is not valid unless made in writing by an *express declaration* that is made, joined in, consented to, or accepted by the spouse whose interest in the property is adversely affected."

An "express declaration" does not require use of the terms "transmutation," "community property," "separate property," or any other particular locution. However, while "no particular terminology is required the writing must reflect a transmutation on its face, and must eliminate the need to consider other evidence in divining this intent." (*Benson, supra*, 36 Cal.4th at p. 1106.) In other words, "[t]he express declaration must *unambiguously* indicate a change in character or ownership of property." (*In re Marriage of Starkman* (2005) 129 Cal.App.4th 659, 664.) An instrument is ambiguous if "'the written language is fairly susceptible of two or more constructions.'" (*Estate of Russell* (1968) 69 Cal.2d 200, 211.)

Richard argues the Trust Transfer Deed contains two critical ambiguities that together preclude a finding that it meets section 852(a)'s express declaration requirement. First, Richard emphasizes the instrument's title—"Trust Transfer Deed," which he says necessarily "suggests the transfer is associated with a trust." Second, he points to the conveyance language itself, stressing "the deed does not say what interest is being granted." Taken together with the reference to a "Trust Transfer," Richard maintains the conveyance language is reasonably susceptible of the interpretation that he granted his community interest in Avonoak to Ida to be held in trust, and not to effect a change in the marital character or ownership of the property. Because his intention as gleaned solely from the face of the Trust Transfer Deed is ambiguous, Richard argues the writing does not satisfy the express declaration requirement. We agree.

Ida argues the Trust Transfer Deed did not use only the word "transfer," but also stated "that the transfer was 'a bonafide gift' and that Richard was 'granting' the property to Ida."

Richard's use of the word likewise must be viewed as an unambiguous expression of his intent to transfer an interest in Avonoak to Ida. Richard's mere use of the word "grant" does not dictate a definite conclusion about what interest in Avonoak he meant to convey to Ida. In other words, as was true of the phrase "'sell, assign, and transfer'" Richard's use of the word "grant" is ambiguous, because the word only establishes his intention to transfer an interest in real property, "without specifying *what interest* was to be transferred." (*Barneson, supra*, 69 Cal.App.4th at p. 590)

The reference to a "Trust Transfer" in the deed's title compounds this ambiguity, because it suggests, as Richard maintains, that the conveyance to Ida may have been made for the purpose of placing the property into a trust, and not with the intention to change its marital character or ownership. Ida argues the reference to a trust transfer should raise no concern, because under established principles of contract and statutory construction a "title" or "label in a legal document" is "not controlling" of its effect, and because the body of the deed "does not mention any trust." We are not persuaded.

While it may be that a title or label is not "controlling" where specific provisions of the writing dictate a definite interpretation, it is not true that the characterization of a transfer in a deed's title is irrelevant to the express declaration inquiry. Absent an unambiguous statement that the transfer would change the character or ownership of Avonoak, the document's title makes it reasonable to entertain the possibility that Richard executed the deed for the purpose of making only a "Trust Transfer."

The absence of a named trust or trustee in the Trust Transfer Deed does not clarify the ambiguity. Thus, regardless of what extrinsic evidence would show about the existence of a trust, Richard's intention remains ambiguous in that "[n]othing on the face of the document[ ] upon which the transmutation claim is based precludes the possibility the transfer was made in trust." (*Barneson, supra*, 69 Cal.App.4th at p. 591.) Indeed, here we have more than just a lack of language precluding the possibility. In this case we actually have language in the proffered transmutation instrument that expressly refers to a "Trust Transfer." Basing our judgment solely on the face of the document, we are forced to acknowledge it is reasonably susceptible of the interpretation that Richard transferred his interest in Avonoak to Ida only for the purpose of depositing it into a trust, without changing the character or ownership of the property.

The same analysis applies to the language characterizing the transfer as a "bonafide gift" for which the grantors "received nothing in return." As Richard points out, if he had transferred Avonoak to Ida in connection with a trust, he also would have received no consideration, and the transfer would have been a "gift" exempt from the tax.

None of this is to say that Ida's proffered interpretation of the Trust Transfer Deed is unreasonable. All we hold is that the deed is fairly susceptible of at least two interpretations—the one Ida proffers, whereby Richard granted *all of his interest* in Avonoak to her, thereby transmuting the residence into her separate property, and the one Richard proffers, whereby he granted *only an interest in trust* to Ida for the couple's estate planning purposes. As numerous other courts have observed, this ambiguity would have been eliminated by including language in the Trust Transfer Deed specifying that Richard granted all or any interest he had in Avonoak to Ida, or, as he had in the 1996 quitclaim deed, by stating he granted Avonoak to Ida "as her sole and separate property." However, because no definitive judgment about the adversely affected spouse's intention can be made from the face of the Trust Transfer Deed alone, and because the court is barred from considering extrinsic evidence that might allow it to resolve the conflicting interpretations in favor of finding a transmutation, we are left with the default presumption that this interspousal transaction was not a transmutation of Richard's community interest in the property.

DISPOSITION

The trial court's decision on the bifurcated issue is reversed. Each party to bear his and her own costs.

A transmutation of real property is not effective as to third parties without notice, unless the transmutation has been recorded. **FC § 852(b)**.

However, a transmutation is not required for gifts between spouses of clothing, wearing apparel, jewelry or other tangible articles of a personal nature that are used solely or principally by the spouse to whom the gift is made and that is not substantial in value, taking into account the circumstances of the marriage. **FC § 852(c)**.[6]

A statement in a will pertaining to the character of property is not admissible as evidence of a transmutation of the property in a proceeding commenced before the death of the person who made the will. **FC § 853**.

Finally, it is the public policy of California to provide uniformly and consistently for the standard of proof in establishing the character of property acquired by spouses during marriage in joint title form and for the allocation of community and separate interests in that property between the spouses. **FC § 2580(a)**.

Valuation of Community Assets

For the purpose of division of the community estate upon dissolution or legal separation of the parties, when the court reserves jurisdiction, the court must value the assets and liabilities as near as practicable to the time of trial. **FC § 2552(a)**.

However, upon thirty (30) days' notice by the moving party to the other party, the court may value all or any portion of the assets and liabilities at a date after separation and before trial to accomplish an equal division of the community estate of the parties in an equitable manner, provided good cause is shown. **FC § 2552(b)**.

The good cause exception to trial date valuation typically applies to professional practices, as well as small personal service businesses, which rely on the skill and reputation of the spouse who operates them. (See *In re MARRIAGE of KILBOURNE* (1991) 232 Cal.App.3d 1518 where the court stated that the exception to trial date valuation applies because the value of such businesses, "including goodwill, is primarily a reflection of the practitioner's services (accounts receivable and work in progress) and not capital assets such as desks, chairs, law books and computers.

Because earnings and accumulations following separation are the spouse's separate property, it follows the community interest should be valued as of the date of separation; the cutoff date for the acquisition of community assets." *Id.* at p. 253–254.)

---

[6] This section does not apply to or affect a transmutation of property made before January 1, 1985.

EDUCATIONAL EXERCISES

FILL IN THE BLANKS

1. Holding property in _____ gives each spouse an undivided equal right to possess the property. Each spouse has an equal ownership interest in the property and the names of both spouses are on one deed. Title must have been acquired at the same time, by the same conveyance. When a spouse dies, title to the property is automatically conveyed by operation of law to the surviving spouse.
2. A _____ that feloniously and intentionally kills the other owner no rights by survivorship. FC § 251.
3. _____ provides that if spouses hold title to real property, they do not have to own equal shares and the property can be owned by multiple people with each person owning an undivided fractional interest. Each owner has a deed that sets forth his or her name and the fractional percentage of interest in the property owned. There is no right to survivorship.
4. When the title to property is held as _____ each spouse has equal rights of management and control of the property. If one of the spouses dies without disposing of his or his share of the property, automatically passes to the surviving spouse without the need of a probate procedure.
5. When spouses hold property as _____ each spouse owns an equal undivided one-half interest in the property, but there is no right to will or dispose his or her share of the property and upon the death of one of the spouses, title is automatically conveyed by operation of law to the surviving spouse.
6. Spouses can also hold property in a _____. If a spouse transfers community property by this instrument, the transferred property remains community property and must be revocable as to that property transferred. A modification of this transferred property during the marriage requires the consent of both spouses. FC § 761(a). Either spouse can revoke unless this instrument expressly provides otherwise.
7. _____ is movable property owned by an individual; it is not land or attached to land.
8. _____ is land and any and all property that is affixed to, incidental or appurtenant to it. CC § 658. It not only includes land but also buildings and anything attached to the land. Condominiums are also included. CC § 783.
9. _____ is any property (real or personal) acquired by a spouse before the marriage, after the parties separate or at any time by gift, devise or bequest, unless the spouses agree in writing otherwise.
10. The earnings and accumulations of a spouse and the minor children living with, or in the custody of, the spouse, after the date of separation of the spouses, are the _____ of the spouse. FC § 771(a).

Chapter 20: Title, Kinds of Property & Valuation

11. _____ is property that is divided equally when a court makes the determination that a marriage is void or voidable and finds that either party or both parties had a reasonable, good-faith belief that the marriage was valid.
12. _____ is real or personal property, wherever situated, acquired by either spouse while domiciled elsewhere that would have been community property if the spouse(s) who acquired the property had been domiciled in this state at the time of its acquisition. FC § 125(a), Probate Code § 66.
13. _____ is all property, real or personal, wherever situated, acquired by a married person or a married couple during the marriage while domiciled in this state; the respective interests of each spouse during the marriage are present, existing and equal. FC §§ 760 and 751. This property cannot be given away or disposed of for less than the fair and reasonable value without the written consent of the other spouse.
14. The rule that all property acquired during the marriage is presumed to be community property does not apply to _____ by both spouses to third parties and gifts given by one spouse to the other. FC § 1100(b). And pursuant to the law, this property must be divided equally between the spouses, but not necessarily in kind. FC § 2550.
15. Either spouse has the right to management and control of the _____, but both spouses must join in executing any interest that is leased for a longer period than one year, or is sold, conveyed, or encumbered. FC §§ 1100(a) and 1102(a).
16. The _____ includes both community property and quasi-community property.
17. Spouses have mutual obligations of _____. FC § 720. They have a confidential relationship that imposes a _____ of the highest good faith and fair dealing on each spouse, and neither must take any unfair advantage of the other.
18. _____ is mixing separate property assets with community property assets or vice versa. This property is presumed to be community property.
19. If the tracing successfully proves that the source of the funds was only from a separate property source, the property that was commingled becomes_____.
20. There is a presumption that property acquired during marriage in joint form is _____. This presumption affects the burden of proof and can be rebutted by a clear statement in the deed or other documentary evidence of title by which the property is acquired or proof that the parties made a written agreement providing that the property is separate property.
21. If parties to a bank account are married to each other, whether or not they are so described in the deposit agreement, their net contribution to the account is presumed to be and remains their _____. Probate Code § 5305. When one kind of property is changed to another kind of property for any reason the character of the property has been changed. The character of property can be personal, real, separate, quasi-marital, community or quasi-community property.

22. The word _____ means change or changing. It is a written waiver of property that changes the character of the property such as changing separate property into community property. The rules set forth in FC § 852 must be followed in order for this change to be valid.
23. Married persons may agree with or without consideration to _____ to the separate property of either spouse, to community property and/or to the separate property of one spouse to separate property of the other spouse. FC § 850.
24. A _____ of real or personal property is not valid unless it is made in writing and is joined in, consented to or accepted by the spouse whose interest in the property is adversely affected. FC § 852(a). Notice to the other party is required when property is transferred to third parties.
25. Gifts between spouses of clothing, wearing apparel, jewelry or other tangible articles of a personal nature that are used solely or principally by the spouse to whom the gift is made and that is not substantial in value do not require a _____.
26. A _____ of assets and liabilities must be made as near as practicable to the time of trial unless the court makes a determination that an equal division of the community estate requires otherwise.

CHAPTER 21: Community & Separate Debts/Liabilities

In Brief...

A DEBT:
- Is an obligation, whether based on contract, tort or otherwise, **FC § 902**;
- Becomes viable at the time a contract is made, **FC § 903**;
- Is typically money that is owed;
- Can also be called a liability.

THE COMMUNITY ESTATE DEBTS/LIABILITIES:
- Are debts incurred after the date of marriage but before the date of separation, **FC § 2622**;
- Can be paid with community or quasi-community property, **FC § 912**;
- Do include debts incurred after the date of marriage but before separation that have benefited the community estate, **FC § 2622**; and
- Do include contracts entered into while the parties are married, **FC § 903**.

SEPARATE DEBTS/LIABILITIES:
- Are debts that were incurred by a spouse before the marriage or after separation, **FC § 2621**;
- Are debts that were not incurred for the benefit of the community, **FC § 2625**;
- **Include child support or spousal support obligations not from the marriage, FC § 915;**
- Are debts incurred after entry of a judgment but before termination of the parties' marital status, **FC § 2624**;
- Are educational loans and liabilities of the spouse whose act or omission provided the basis for the liability, **FC § 2627**; and
- Incurred by either spouse for nonnecessaries of that spouse or children of the marriage for whom support may be ordered, **FC § 2623**.

COURT HAS DISCRETION TO ASSIGN ASSETS/DEBTS TO EITHER OR BOTH PARTIES:
- After characterizing the debts as separate or community, **FC § 2551**;
- If community debts exceed community and quasi-community assets, **FC § 2622**;
- Including joint California income tax liabilities, **FC § 2623**;
- If incurred after separation but before entry of a judgment, **FC § 2623**;
- Include debts incurred by a person's spouse during marriage if the debt was incurred for the necessaries of life of the person's spouse while the spouses were living together, **FC 2623**;
- Include debts incurred after the date of separation but before the entry of a judgment for the common necessaries of life of either spouse or the children of the marriage for whom support may be ordered, **FC § 2623**; and

415

Chapter 21: Community & Separate Debts/Liabilities

> - And the court has continuing jurisdiction to award community estate assets or community estate liabilities to the parties that have not been previously adjudicated by a judgment, **FC § 2556**.

Introduction

This chapter discusses community debts/liabilities and separate debts. Debts are community if they were incurred after the date of marriage but before separation. The community is liable only for debts that were incurred for the benefit of the community.
Separate debts are debts that were not incurred for the benefit of the community. Separate debts are usually those debts that were incurred prior to marriage or after the date of separation.

Debts/Liabilities

1. Community Estate Debts/Liabilities

A **debt** is an obligation incurred by a married person before or during marriage, whether based on contract, tort or otherwise. **FC § 902**.

Community debts are debts incurred after the date of marriage but before the date of separation. **FC § 2622**.

Pursuant to **FC § 912**, quasi-community property is liable to the same extent and is treated the same as community property with regard to debts.

The community estate is liable for a debt incurred by either spouse before or during marriage, regardless of which spouse has the management and control of the property and regardless of whether one or both spouses are parties to the debt or to a judgment for the debt, except where the spouses are living separate and apart before a judgment of dissolution or legal separation. **FC § 910**.[1]

If there was a death or injury based upon an act or omission that occurred while a married person was performing an activity for the benefit of the community, the liability will first be satisfied from the community estate and second from the separate property of the married person. **FC § 1000(b)(1)**.

---

[1] 2017 version of FC § 910 provides:
(a) Except as otherwise expressly provided by statute, the community estate is liable for a debt incurred by either spouse before or during marriage, regardless of which spouse has the management and control of the property and regardless of whether one or both spouses are parties to the debt or to a judgment for the debt.
(b) "During marriage" for purposes of this section does not include the period after the date of separation, as defined in Section 70, and before a judgment of dissolution of marriage or legal separation of the parties.
The language "after the date of separation, as defined in Section 70, and" was amended to "during which the spouses are living separate and apart" in subdivision (b).

416

Chapter 21: Community & Separate Debts/Liabilities

Liabilities that were incurred after the date of marriage but before separation that have benefited the community estate are a community liability, as the case that follows demonstrates.

> *In re Marriage of JOHN L. and BETH E. BELL. JOHN L. BELL, Respondent, v. BETH E. BELL, Appellant.*
> COURT OF APPEAL OF CALIFORNIA, FOURTH APPELLATE DISTRICT, DIVISION TWO
> 49 Cal.App.4th 300; 56 Cal.Rptr.2d 623
> September 12, 1996, Decided
> (*Marriage of Bell*)
>
> The facts underlying this case are largely undisputed. Husband and Wife were married in 1971 and separated in May 1991. During the early part of the marriage both parties worked, but in 1979 Husband became ill and retired from active employment. They sold their home in Pasadena on a contract of sale and moved to Palm Desert where they purchased their present mobile home and lot. Following the move the parties started a sandwich-making business. They sold the sandwich shop in 1982 or 1983 and Wife started work as a ticket taker for the Palm Springs Aerial Tramway, (Wife's employer), earning an hourly salary.
>
> Starting in 1985 and continuing until her arrest on September 20, 1990, Wife embezzled funds from her employer. A civil action was filed against both parties by Wife's employer in 1990 seeking to recover the embezzled funds. The parties settled that suit for $150,000, and the suit was dismissed.
>
> The parties separated in May 1991 and Husband filed a petition for dissolution in August 1991. In December 1992 the parties entered a stipulation to bifurcate the status of the marriage from the property issues, and the marriage was dissolved at that time.
>
> On the second day of trial, in January 1993, it was stipulated that Wife had not told Husband that she had embezzled funds, and that Husband's first actual knowledge of the embezzlement was when Wife was arrested. Wife testified that she had subsequently been convicted of the crime of embezzlement. Also on the second day of trial the court reiterated that "I indicated that . . . Mrs. Bell is going to bear the burden of the wrongdoing between these two people. [P] When it comes to allocating assets, every question I have is going to be resolved against her about [who is] going to bear this burden . . . ." The court then stated that evidence of whether the community benefited from the embezzled funds was irrelevant.
>
> During trial the court heard testimony from Husband, from Wife, and from Karl Anderson, an accountant hired by the attorney who had represented Husband and Wife in the civil action brought by Wife's employer. Mr. Anderson testified that he had been retained "in order to compute a calculation as to the embezzlement by Mrs. Bell."
>
> Wife testified that she had deposited the embezzled funds in bank accounts and had used the funds to buy certificates of deposit. She also testified that she had used the money to buy groceries, go to the hairdresser and go out to dinner, and that she had given Husband a $100 per month allowance. She stated that she had bought presents for Husband with the money, including a $2,500 watch and an identification bracelet. Wife testified that she had never opened an account in her name alone and that all the money had been deposited in joint accounts.

417

Wife testified that the mortgage on the residence of the parties had been prepaid for about 19 months at the time of her arrest. She also testified that the parties had purchased a Cadillac in 1989 and had accelerated the payments so that the car was completely paid for by 1990.

Counsel for Wife offered to the court a chart prepared by him, on the basis of information given to him by Wife that purported to demonstrate that during the period 1985 to 1990 the community spent $129,000 more than it earned through legitimate sources.

In an effort to establish that the community was not harmed and was in fact benefited by the embezzlement, counsel for Wife elicited testimony to show that cash assets remained after the civil settlement. The parties stipulated that there was about $20,000, plus savings bonds, left after payment of the $150,000 settlement and $55,000 in attorney fees.

Mr. Anderson stated that according to amended tax returns prepared by him, the federal tax due as of December 1992 was $60,874.07, and the state tax due was $18,974. Of those amounts, a total of $28,290 was attributable to penalties and interest.

At the end of trial Husband argued that [Wife should be accessed with the] interest and penalties due on the income tax. Wife agreed that she should be held liable for the interest and penalties due on the income tax. She contended, however, that the tax itself should be paid by the community since the community had had the benefit of the income.

On July 1, 1993, the court ordered that Wife was to hold Husband harmless from the debts,[2] and ordered Wife to pay the debts. Wife filed a motion for a new trial, which was denied, and she then filed this appeal. Wife objects to the trial court decision to attribute to Wife all the costs, but not the benefits, resulting from her embezzlement from her employer over a period of five years.

DISCUSSION
Wife was still engaged in [the intentional tort of embezzlement] and Husband knew nothing about it. There was uncontradicted testimony that the community received the benefit of the embezzlement. Even if the numbers were somewhat uncertain, it was apparent that the community had received a major infusion of funds over the years, and it was clear that all the embezzled funds had been put to community, and not separate, use. Mr. Anderson testified that the amount of the settlement was based on estimates of the amount that had been taken, so the settlement was no more than an attempt at restitution.

We hold that the trial court erred by allocating the entire $150,000 settlement, which had previously been paid out of community property, to Wife as part of her share of the community property distribution. The community had shared in the benefit and could properly be asked to share in the cost.

Here we find that the trial court's resolution of this issue was not supported by the evidence presented and does not reflect a correct analysis and application of the law and we therefore reverse on this issue.

The judgment on the bifurcated property issues is reversed.

---

[2] Federal tax liability $61,000.00 approx. State tax liability $23,000.00 approx. Total tax liability $84,000.00 approx.
Karl Anderson, C.P.A. $1,240.40. Total debts related to embezzlement $85,240.40.

Finally, **FC § 903** provides that a debt becomes viable at the time a contract is made. If the contract was entered into while the parties were married, it is a community liability, even if the parties separated before the completion of the contract. *In re Marriage of FELDNER* (1995) 40 Cal.App.4th 312 at p. 629.

2. Separate Debts/Liabilities

Debts incurred by either spouse before the date of marriage will be confirmed without offset to the spouse who incurred the debt. **FC § 2621**.

FC § 913(a) provides that the separate property of a married person is liable for a debt incurred by the person before or during marriage.

The separate property of a married person is not liable for a debt incurred by the person's spouse before or during marriage. **FC § 911**.

Separate debts are debts, including those incurred by a spouse during marriage and before the date of separation, that were not incurred for the benefit of the community; they will be confirmed without offset to the spouse who incurred the debt. **FC § 2625**.

A married person is personally liable for a debt incurred for necessaries of life of the person's spouse while the spouses are living together and a debt incurred for common necessaries of life of the person's spouse while the spouses are living separately, provided there is no written agreement to the contrary[3]. **FC § 914(a)(1)**.

Debts incurred by either spouse after entry of a judgment of dissolution of marriage but before termination of the parties' marital status or after entry of a judgment of legal separation of the parties will be confirmed without offset to the spouse who incurred the debt. **FC § 2624**.

Pursuant to **FC § 914**[4], a married person is personally liable for the debts incurred by the person's spouse during marriage if the debt was incurred for the necessaries of life of the person's spouse while the spouses were living together.

---

[3] Pursuant to FC § 4302: a person is not liable for support of the person's spouse when the person is living separate from the spouse by agreement unless support is stipulated in the agreement.

[4] Effective 2017 FC § 914 was amended to the following:
(a) Notwithstanding Section 913, a married person is personally liable for the following debts incurred by the person's spouse during marriage:
 (1) A debt incurred for necessaries of life of the person's spouse before the date of separation of the spouses.
 (2) Except as provided in Section 4302, a debt incurred for common necessaries of life of the person's spouse after the date of separation of the spouses.
(b) The separate property of a married person may be applied to the satisfaction of a debt for which the person is personally liable pursuant to this section. If separate property is so applied at a time when nonexempt property in the community estate or separate property of the person's spouse is available but is not applied to the satisfaction of the debt, the married person is entitled to reimbursement to the extent such property was available.
(c)

Chapter 21: Community & Separate Debts/Liabilities

However, if the parties separated before the debt was incurred, only the spouse that incurred the debt is responsible for the debt, as the case that follows demonstrates.

> ***CMRE FINANCIAL SERVICES, INC., Plaintiff, Cross-defendant and Respondent, v. PAMELA D. PARTON, Defendant, Cross-complainant and Appellant.***
> COURT OF APPEAL OF CALIFORNIA, FOURTH APPELLATE DISTRICT, DIVISION ONE
> 184 Cal.App.4th 263; 109 Cal.Rptr.3d 139
> April 29, 2010, Filed
> (*CMRE Financial Services v. Parton*)

On February 16, 2006, Pamela D. Parton (Pamela) called police to the home she shared with her then husband, Daniel W. Parton (Daniel). Pamela told the police her husband had engaged in domestic violence against her. Very shortly thereafter Pamela obtained a restraining order and the couple separated.

On February 23, 2006, after the Partons had separated, Daniel was admitted to Tri-City Medical Center. The record suggests he was suffering from severe emotional illness. Daniel was released from the hospital on February 27, 2006.

On May 17, 2006, Pamela filed a petition for dissolution of her marriage. In her schedule of assets and debts, Pamela stated the Tri-City hospital debt belonged to Daniel. A judgment of dissolution was entered on September 26, 2006. The judgment did not assign the hospital obligation to Pamela.

On January 24, 2008, CMRE Financial Services, Inc. (CMRE), as assignee of Tri-City hospital, filed a complaint against both Partons. The complaint alleged the Partons owed CMRE $26,083, plus interest and attorney fees. Pamela filed an answer denying the material allegations of the complaint.

CMRE alleged Pamela was liable for Daniel's necessaries under FC § 914 and that, notwithstanding FC § 916, Pamela was not relieved of that liability by virtue of her dissolution judgment. Thereafter the trial court tried CMRE's claims and entered judgment against Pamela for $26,083, plus interest, attorney fees and costs. Pamela timely appealed.

DISCUSSION
On appeal, Pamela argues her dissolution judgment relieved her of any liability to CMRE that may have arisen under FC § 914. We agree.

FC § 914(a), states: "Notwithstanding FC § 913, a married person is personally liable for

---

(1) Except as provided in paragraph (2), the statute of limitations set forth in Section 366.2 of the Code of Civil Procedure shall apply if the spouse for whom the married person is personally liable dies.
(2) If the surviving spouse had actual knowledge of the debt prior to expiration of the period set forth in Section 366.2 of the Code of Civil Procedure and the personal representative of the deceased spouse's estate failed to provide the creditor asserting the claim under this section with a timely written notice of the probate administration of the estate in the manner provided for pursuant to Section 9050 of the Probate Code, the statute of limitations set forth in Section 337 or 339 of the Code of Civil Procedure, as applicable, shall apply.
(d) For purposes of this section, "date of separation" has the same meaning as set forth in Section 70.

Chapter 21: Community & Separate Debts/Liabilities

the following debts incurred by the person's spouse during marriage:
"(1) A debt incurred for necessaries of life of the person's spouse while the spouses are living together.

"(2) Except as provided in FC § 4302, a debt incurred for common necessaries of life of the person's spouse while the spouses are living separately."

As Pamela argues, one spouse's liability for the other spouse's necessaries while the spouses are living separately is subject not only to the terms of any separation agreement between them, it is also subject to any assignment of debts made at the time their marriage is dissolved. FC § 916(a), states in pertinent part: "(a) *Notwithstanding any other provision of this chapter*, after division of community and quasi-community property pursuant to Division 7 (commencing with FC § 2500):

"(1) The separate property owned by a married person at the time of the division and the property received by the person in the division is liable for a debt incurred by the person before or during marriage and the person is personally liable for the debt, whether or not the debt was assigned for payment by the person's spouse in the division.

"(2) The separate property owned by a married person at the time of the division and the property received by the person in the division is not liable for a debt incurred by the person's spouse before or during marriage, and *the person is not personally liable for the debt*, unless the debt was assigned for payment by the person in the division of the property. Nothing in this paragraph affects the liability of property for the satisfaction of a lien on the property." (Italics added.)

Prior to enactment of the statutory predecessor to FC § 916, spouses were liable for community debts following dissolution of a marriage. "In 1984, however, the Legislature substantially changed the postmarital liability of spouses. 'The Legislature determined that, under most circumstances, after a marriage has ended, it is unwise to continue the liability of spouses for community debts incurred by former spouses.' It enacted former CC § 5120.160, which provided in pertinent part that, upon the dissolution of the marriage, 'the property received by [a married] person in the division is not liable for a debt incurred by the person's spouse before or during marriage, and the person is not personally liable for the debt, unless the debt was assigned for payment by the person in the division of the property.' When the Family Code was enacted in 1992, CC § 5120.160 became FC § 916." (*Mejia v. Reed* (2003) 31 Cal.4th 657, 665.)

Contrary to CMRE's contention, FC § 914 is not a species of a joint and several liability which is personally incurred by both spouses and for that reason outside the scope of FC § 916. Such an interpretation is inconsistent with the express terms of FC § 914 itself. By its terms FC § 914 governs "debts incurred by the person's spouse." This language confirms that the Legislature views one spouse's liability for the other spouse's post-separation necessaries as entirely derivative and not personally incurred by the supporting spouse.

Our conclusion [that] a dissolution judgment relieves a spouse of liability imposed by FC § 914 is of course supported by the express terms of FC § 916, which make all other provisions of that chapter of the Family Code, including FC § 914, subject to the protection FC § 916 provides to former spouses following dissolution of a marriage. It is also consistent with the manner in which our courts have applied FC § 916.

> The only exception to application of FC § 916 our courts have recognized is where a creditor alleges a marital settlement agreement violates the separate provisions of the Uniform Fraudulent Transfer Act, CC §§ 3439 through 3439.12 (UFTA). Significantly, in reaching that conclusion the court noted that the legislative history of both FC § 916 and the UFTA shed no light on what the Legislature intended when a conflict between the two statutes arose. The court upheld application of the UFTA solely because it found the antifraud policies of the UFTA took precedence over the finality policies embodied in FC § 916. Here of course no such countervailing fundamental policy is implicated.
>
> In sum, as we interpret FC §§ 914 and 916, although spouses have an obligation to support each other while separated, they can avoid that obligation by way of agreement between themselves. Moreover, any liability for support which arose during the parties' separation ceases following dissolution of the marriage, unless the court orders it extended.
>
> In light of our interpretation of FC §§ 914 and 916, Pamela is not liable for the cost of Daniel's hospitalization. The dissolution judgment did not assign that debt to her and FC § 916(a)(2) relieved her of any liability for it.
>
> **DISPOSTION**
> Thus, the judgment entered against Pamela must be reversed with instructions that CMRE's complaint be dismissed.

The earnings of a married person during marriage are not liable for a debt incurred by the person's spouse before marriage. **FC § 911(a)**.

Debts that are incurred by either spouse after the entry of a judgment of dissolution but before termination of the parties' marital status or after entry of a judgment of legal separation of the parties will be confirmed without offset to the spouse who incurred the debt. **FC § 2624**.

The separate property of a married person is liable for a debt incurred by the person before or during marriage but is not liable for a debt incurred by the person's spouse before or during marriage. **FC § 913(a), (b)**.

The separate property owned by a married person at the time of the division and the property received by the person in the division is liable for a debt incurred by the person before or during marriage and the person is personally liable for the debt, whether or not the debt was assigned for payment by the person's spouse in the division. **FC § 916(a)(1)**.

However, the separate property owned by a married person at the time of the division and the property received by the person in the division is not liable for a debt incurred by the person's spouse before or during marriage, and the person is not personally liable for the debt, unless the debt was assigned for payment by the person in the division of the property. **FC § 916(a)(2)**.

Educational loans and liabilities will be assigned to the spouse whose act or omission provided the basis for the liability, without offset. **FC § 2627**.

Chapter 21: Community & Separate Debts/Liabilities

Debts incurred by either spouse after the date of separation but before the entry of a judgment of dissolution or legal separation for the common necessaries of life of either spouse or the children of the marriage for whom support may be ordered, in the absence of a court order or written agreement for support or for the payment of these debts, can be confirmed to either spouse according to the parties' respective needs and abilities to pay at the time the debt was incurred. If the debts are for nonnecessaries, they will be confirmed without offset to the spouse who incurred the debt. **FC § 2623(a),(b)**.

3. The Court has the Discretion to Assign Assets and Debts Party

To the extent that community debts exceed total community and quasi-community assets, the excess of debt will be assigned as the court deems just and equitable, taking into account factors such as the parties' relative ability to pay. **FC § 2622(b)**.

The court must characterize liabilities as separate or community and confirm or assign them to the parties for the purposes of division and in confirming or assigning the liabilities of the parties for which the community estate is liable. **FC § 2551**.

Joint California income tax liabilities may be revised by a court in a proceeding for dissolution of marriage, provided the requirements of **Revenue and Taxation Code § 19006** are satisfied. **FC § 2628**.

Debts incurred by either spouse after the date of separation but before entry of a judgment of dissolution or legal separation may be assigned by the court to either party. The court will make this determination based upon the parties' respective needs and abilities to pay at the time the debt was incurred. **FC § 2623(a)**.

Finally, in a proceeding for dissolution, nullity or legal separation, the court has continuing jurisdiction to award community estate assets or community estate liabilities to the parties that have not been previously adjudicated by a judgment in the proceeding. A party may file a postjudgment motion or order to show cause in the proceeding in order to obtain adjudication of any community estate asset or liability omitted or not adjudicated by the judgment. In these cases, the court must equally divide the omitted or unadjudicated community estate asset or liability, unless the court finds upon good cause shown that the interests of justice require an unequal division of the asset or liability. **FC § 2556**.

Chapter 21: Community & Separate Debts/Liabilities

EDUCATIONAL EXERCISES

FILL IN THE BLANKS

1. A _____ is an obligation incurred by a married person before or during marriage, whether based on contract, tort or otherwise. FC § 902.
2. _____ are those that are incurred after the date of marriage but before the date of separation. FC § 2622.
3. Pursuant to FC § 912, _____ is liable to the same extent, and is treated the same as community property with regard to debts.
4. Liabilities that were incurred after the date of marriage but before separation that have benefited the community estate are a_____.
5. FC § 903 provides that a debt becomes viable at the time a contract is made. If the contract was entered into while the parties were married, it is a _____, even if the parties separated before the completion of the contract.
6. FC § 913(a) provides that the _____ is liable for a debt incurred by the person before or during marriage. It is not liable for a debt incurred by the person's spouse before or during marriage. FC § 911.
7. _____ include those incurred by a spouse during marriage and before the date of separation, that were not incurred for the benefit of the community; they will be confirmed without offset to the spouse who incurred the debt. FC § 2625.
8. A married person is personally liable for a _____ of the person's spouse while the spouses are living together.
9. A debt incurred for the _____ of life of the person's spouse before the date of separation of the spouses. FC § 914(a)(1).
10. The earnings of a married person during marriage are not liable for _____ _____ before marriage. FC § 911(a).
11. Debts that are incurred by either spouse after the entry of a judgment of dissolution but before termination of the parties' marital status or after entry of a judgment of legal separation of the parties will be confirmed _____. FC § 2624.
12. The _____ of a married person is liable for a debt incurred by the person before or during marriage but is not liable for a debt incurred by the person's spouse before or during marriage. FC § 913(a), (b).
13. _____ and liabilities will be assigned to the spouse whose act or omission provided the basis for the liability, without offset. FC § 2627.
14. The court must characterize liabilities as _____ and confirm or assign them to the parties for the purposes of division and in confirming or assigning the liabilities of the parties for which the community estate is liable. FC § 2551.
15. In a dissolution, nullity or legal separation, the court has continuing jurisdiction to award _____ to the parties that have not been previously adjudicated by a judgment in the proceeding.

CHAPTER 22: Division, Tracing & Reimbursement

In Brief...

IN DIVIDING THE COMMUNITY PROPERTY ESTATE:
- The law provides that it must be divided equally between the spouses, **FC § 2550**;
- The community assets do not have to be divided in kind;
- The court may award a community asset to one party if to effect an equal division of the community estate, **FC § 2601**;
- Any real community or real quasi-community property that is in another state must be divided by the court so that it is not necessary to change the nature of the interest, **FC § 2660**;
- The court may award from a party's share of the community property any amount determined to have been deliberately misappropriated by one spouse to the exclusion of the other spouse, **FC § 2602**; and
- The disposition of the community estate is subject to revision on appeal, **FC § 2555**.

TRACING is a process used to prove a separate property claim; there are 2 methods:
- **Direct tracing:**
    - is following the money trail of a commingled asset and tracing it to the source of the asset.
    - To a separate source has traditionally been subject to a requirement that it be done by specific records. Mere oral testimony of **intent** has been held to be inadequate, in light of the general presumption that property acquired during a marriage is community.
    - The direct tracing method follows the money trail to a separate property source. It is commonly called the *Pereira* [*Pereira v. Pereira* (1909) 156 Cal. 1] fair rate of return method or recapitalization.
- **Family Expense Method:**
    - Is commonly called the *Van Camp* [*Van Camp v. Van Camp* (1921) 53 Cal.App. 17] method.
    - Is used if all of the community income was exhausted when the asset was purchased.

REIMBURSEMENT: THE COMMUNITY ESTATE MAY BE REIMBURSED FOR:
- Debts paid by a spouse after separation but before trial. This reimbursement is called Epstein credits from *In re Marriage of EPSTEIN* [(1979) 24 Cal.3d 76] now codified at **FC § 2626**;
- Exclusive use of a community asset by one spouse. This charge to a spouse is called Watts charges from *In re Marriage of WATTS* [(1985) 171 Cal.App.3d 366]; and

Chapter 22: Division, racing & Reimbursement

> - For contributions made to one spouse's education because in most cases, educational loans belong to student, **FC § 2641**.
> - For community debts paid after separation but before trial, **FC § 2626**; and
> - For child/spousal support paid during the marriage when the obligation did not arise from the marriage, **FC § 915**.
> - Separate property contributions made to community property may be reimbursed if there is no written waiver and the contribution can be traced to a separate property source, **FC § 2640**.
>
> *PERSONAL INJURY:*
> - Damages are money paid in satisfaction of a judgment for personal injuries, **FC § 781**;
> - Damages are community property if the cause of action arose during the marriage, **FC § 780**; and
> - Damages must be assigned to the party who suffered the injuries unless the court determines that the interests of justice require another disposition, **FC § 781**.

Introduction

The law provides that community property must be divided equally between the spouses. However, the community property does not have to be divided in kind.

Tracing is the procedure that is followed to prove a claim that an asset is separate property. It is following the paper/money trail back to a separate source and producing documents to demonstrate that the property came from a separate source.

Tracing is necessary in the scenario where a wealthy person marries a person with little or no means and the wealthy person pays for everything during the marriage from his or her separate property. In this case, the community property interest is difficult to discern. The court has developed two different tracing approaches to make this determination. These tracing methods are named after two cases, *PEREIRA v. PEREIRA* (1909) 156 Cal. 1 and *VAN CAMP v. VAN CAMP* (1921) 53 Cal.App. 17.

In certain circumstances, the community or one of the spouses is entitled to a reimbursement. The reimbursement can be demanded when one spouse pays any community property debt after the date of separation but before the final judgment or when one of the spouses has complete and exclusive use of one of the community property assets.

Division of Community Property

In a proceeding for dissolution of marriage or legal separation of the parties, the court MUST, either in its judgment of dissolution of the marriage, in its judgment of

Chapter 22: Division, racing & Reimbursement

legal separation of the parties, or at a later time if it expressly reserves jurisdiction to make such a property division, divide the entire community estate of the parties equally. **FC § 2550**.

However, this does not mean that each community asset must be split equally. There is no requirement that property be divided in kind.

When parties cannot agree in writing to a voluntary division of the community estate, the character, the value and the division of the community estate, a court may submit the matter to arbitration for resolution, if the total value of the community and quasi-community property in controversy in the opinion of the court does not exceed fifty thousand dollars ($50,000). This decision regarding the value of the community and quasi-community property is not appealable. **FC § 2554(a)**.

> In a proceeding for dissolution of marriage, for nullity of marriage, or for legal separation of the parties, the court has continuing jurisdiction to award community estate assets or community estate liabilities to the parties that have not been previously adjudicated by a judgment in the proceeding. A party may file a postjudgment motion or order to show cause in the proceeding in order to obtain adjudication of any community estate asset or liability omitted or not adjudicated by the judgment. In these cases, the court shall equally divide the omitted or unadjudicated community estate asset or liability, unless the court finds upon good cause shown that the interests of justice require an unequal division of the asset or liability. FC § 2556.

"Where economic circumstances warrant, the court may award an asset of the community estate to one party on such conditions as the court deems proper to effect a substantially equal division of the community estate." **FC § 2601**.

If the property subject to division includes real property situated in another state, the court must, if possible, divide the community property and quasi-community property in such a manner that it is not necessary to change the nature of the interests held in the real property situated in the other state. **FC § 2660(a)**.

If it is not possible to divide the property in another state and not change the nature of the assets, then the court may: **(1)** require the parties to execute conveyances or take other actions with respect to the real property situated in the other state as are necessary, or **(2)** award to the party who would have been benefited by the conveyances the money value of the interest in the property that the party would have received if the conveyances had been executed or other actions taken. **FC § 2660(b).**

The court may award from a party's share any amount that is determined to have been deliberately misappropriated by one spouse to the exclusion of the interest of the other spouse in the community estate. **FC § 2602**.

Further, a deliberate misappropriation can result in an award of up to 100% of any asset undisclosed or transferred in breach of the fiduciary duty. **FC § 1101(h)**. The

Chapter 22: Division, racing & Reimbursement

100% award can be made "for the sake of example and by way of punishing the defendant." **CC § 3294**.

The disposition of the community estate is subject to revision on appeal in all particulars, including those which are stated to be in the discretion of the court. **FC § 2555**.

FC § 2552 was designed to remedy certain inequities such as "when the hard work and actions of one spouse **alone** and after separation ... greatly increases the 'community' estate which must then be divided with the other spouse." *In re MARRIAGE of BARNERT* (1978) 85 Cal.App.3d 413 at p. 423. In this regard, **FC § 2552(b)** gives the trial court considerable discretion to divide community property in order to ensure an equitable settlement is reached. *In re Marriage of GERACI* (2006) 144 Cal.App.4th 1278 at p. 1290-1291.

Finally, "if the net value of the community estate is less than five thousand dollars ($5,000) and one party cannot be located through the exercise of reasonable diligence, the court may award all the community estate to the other party on conditions the court deems proper in its judgment of dissolution of marriage or legal separation of the parties." **FC § 2604**.

Tracing Claims

Tracing is the procedure that is followed to prove a claim that an asset is separate property. Since there is a rebuttable presumption that property acquired during marriage is community property, successful tracing—or following the money trail back to a separate source and producing documents to demonstrate that the property came from a separate source—can rebut the community property presumption.

As provided in the last chapter, **commingling** is mixing separate property assets with community property assets or vice versa. Property that is **commingled** is presumed to be community property. The presumption can be rebutted by tracing or following the paper/money trail and providing proof of the separate claim.

If the tracing successfully proves that the source of the funds was only from a separate property source, the property that was commingled becomes **uncommingled**. If funds have been so commingled that it is virtually impossible to trace them back to their source, the funds are entirely community property.

There are **two basic systems of tracing** that can be used to uncommingle assets: direct tracing and the **family expense method**.

(1) Direct tracing is following the money trail of a commingled asset and tracing it to the source of the asset.

Direct tracing to a separate source has traditionally been subject to a requirement that it be done by specific records. Mere oral testimony of **intent** has been held to be inadequate, in light of the general presumption that property acquired during a marriage is community.

> The granddaddy of the specific-record requirement was our Supreme Court's decision in *See v. See* (1966) 64 Cal.2d 778 [51 Cal.Rptr. 888, 415 P.2d 776]. The relevant text concerning recordkeeping and tracing appears at pages 783 and 784 of the opinion. The context of the discussion is the *commingling of funds in a bank account* and a rich husband's attempt to trace his separate property in that account. (See 64 Cal.2d at p. 783.) The court explained, in light of the general community property presumption, that a spouse cannot "invoke the burden of record keeping as a justification for a recapitulation of income and expenses at the termination of the marriage that disregards any acquisitions that *may* have been made during the marriage with *community funds*." (*Id.* at p. 784, italics added.) Hence the court concluded that, once the husband "commingles, he assumes the burden of keeping records adequate to establish the balance of community income and expenditures at the time an asset is acquired with commingled property." *In re Marriage of STOLL* (1998) 63 Cal.App.4th 837 at p. 841.

(2) The **Family expense or recapitulation** method:

> involves a consideration of family expenses. It is based upon the presumption that family expenses are paid from community funds. If at the time of the acquisition of the property in dispute, it can be shown that all community income in the commingled account had been exhausted by family expenses, then all funds remaining in the account at the time the property was purchased were separate funds. *In re Marriage of MIX* (1975) 14 Cal.3d. 604 at p. 612.

> [T]he recapitulation method may be employed only when, through no fault of the spouse asserting a separate property interest, it is impossible to ascertain the balance of income and expenditures at the time the property was acquired. (*SEE v. SEE* (1966) 64 Cal.2d 778 at p. 783.)

1. The *Pereira* Method

The case that follows uses one of the methods to determine the community property interest. This method is called the *Pereira* method, or the **fair rate of return** approach.

> *ANNA AGNES PEREIRA, Respondent, v. FRANK PEREIRA, Appellant.*
> SUPREME COURT OF CALIFORNIA
> 156 Cal. 1; 103 P. 488
> June 30, 1909, Decided
> (*Pereira v. Pereira*)
>
> The plaintiff obtained an interlocutory judgment of divorce on the ground of extreme cruelty. This judgment also declared that the plaintiff should have three fifths of the community property when the divorce became final. The defendant appealed.
>
> The findings state that this property consisted of the real estate on which the defendant carried on business, which was of the value of forty-five thousand dollars and certain

> money on hand, making up the remainder. The evidence shows that the plaintiff and defendant intermarried on April 19, 1900. At that time the defendant was, and he ever since has been, carrying on a saloon and cigar business, then producing a net income of about five thousand dollars annually. He owned the cigar and saloon stock and fixtures, worth in all about fifteen thousand five hundred dollars, and had, besides, some six thousand dollars in cash. Soon after the marriage he bought the home wherein the parties afterwards lived, paying twenty-seven hundred dollars therefor, and he afterwards expended thereon twenty-three hundred dollars in improving it. This home is adjudged to be his separate property and plaintiff is given no interest in it. A year and a half after his marriage he bought the property in which he was carrying on business at the price of forty thousand dollars. He paid in cash therefor five thousand dollars and afterwards, out of his income, he paid the balance of the price and accumulated the cash on hand at the time of trial, in addition, amounting to over twelve thousand dollars. His net income at the time of trial was about eleven thousand dollars a year.
>
> There is an unexplained discrepancy between the total amount of his income less the household expenses, and his total gains. He must have received more than he was willing to disclose, if his net income over household expenses amounted to as much as the money which he admits he has received, not allowing anything for his personal expenses.
> It appears, however, that the decision of the court was made upon the theory that all of his gains received after marriage, from whatever sources, were to be classed as community property, and that no allowance was made in favor of his separate estate. The separate property should have been credited with some amount as profit on this capital. It was not a losing business but a very profitable one. It is true that is very clearly shown that the principal part of the large income was due to the personal character, energy, ability, and capacity of the husband. This share of the earnings was, of course, community property. But without capital he could not have carried on the business. In the absence of circumstances showing a different result, it is to be presumed that some of the profits were justly due to the capital invested. The probable contribution of the capital to the income should have been determined from all the circumstances of the case, and as the business was profitable it would amount at least to the usual interest on a long investment well secured.
>
> We think the court erred in refusing to increase the proportion of separate property and decrease the community property to the extent of the reasonable gain to the separate estate from the earnings properly allowable on account of the capital invested.
>
> The judgment as to the amount and value of the community property and as to the disposition thereof between the parties is reversed.

The *Pereira* method of determining the amount of community property allocates a fair rate of return on the separate property investment. By the process of elimination, any excess in value over the amount allocated as separate property is community property arising from the spouse's labor and efforts.

2. The *Van Camp* Method

The *Van Camp* case below demonstrates the other approach utilized by the court to determine the community property with this same scenario. This method is called the **Van Camp approach**.

Chapter 22: Division, racing & Reimbursement

> ***EUPHRASIA VAN CAMP, Respondent, v. FRANK VAN CAMP, Appellant.***
> ***EUPHRASIA VAN CAMP, Appellant, v. FRANK VAN CAMP, Respondent***
> COURT OF APPEAL OF CALIFORNIA, SECOND APPELLATE DISTRICT,
> DIVISION ONE
> 53 Cal.App. 17; 199 P. 885
> May 26, 1921, Decided
> (*Van Camp v. Van Camp*)
>
> In the year 1914 defendant Van Camp came from Indianapolis to Los Angeles. His family then consisted of a grown son. He was a man of large affairs and had been the directing head of an extensive packing establishment in Indianapolis bearing his name. He brought to California property of great value, consisting largely of cash and stock securities. After his arrival in Los Angeles he organized the Van Camp Sea Food Company. The company was capitalized with 2,000 shares of stock at a par value of $ 100 each. He became the president and general manager of the corporation and received up to January, 1918, a salary of $ 1,000 per month. This salary was increased on January 1, 1918, to $ 1,500 per month and so remained at all times subsequent thereto. The packing plant was located at the seaport town of San Pedro.
>
> In March of 1916 defendant Van Camp married the plaintiff, who was or had been an employee in the post office at San Pedro. Plaintiff was then twenty-one years of age; the defendant was about fifty-four years old. Immediately upon the marriage, defendant purchased a home in the city of Los Angeles, expending therefor about the sum of $ 15,000, and the deed to the place was made to the wife. Not long thereafter defendant delivered to the wife a certificate of deposit representing a cash credit of $ 10,000 and a deed to a lot at San Pedro. Defendant further provided each month for the plaintiff a cash allowance for household expenses which, at the time of the commencement of this proceeding, was $ 450; he also provided plaintiff with an automobile.
>
> From the evidence it appears without dispute that at the time of his marriage to plaintiff, defendant was a man of large means, which included cash, notes, real estate, and corporate stock; that at the time he was president and manager of a corporation known as the Van Camp Sea Food Company, to the management of the affairs of which he devoted his exclusive attention, and for the services so rendered to said corporation received therefrom, up to January, 1918, the sum of $ 1,000 per month, which, commencing with January, 1918, was increased to $ 1,500 per month; that in addition to such salary he received from said company during the period of the marital relation an additional sum of $ 12,203 for the purpose of meeting expenses incurred by him in connection with the business; that during the period in question he was engaged in no other business whatsoever, and, excepting the money so received from said corporation, he had no income other than that derived as rents, issues, and profits from the property owned by him at the time of his marriage. The total amount received by him from said corporation on account of salary and expense money during the existence of the marital relation was the sum of $ 69,203. It therefore follows that all other income, large or small and regardless of the amount thereof, must necessarily have been derived from the property which he owned at the time of his marriage.
> [T]he rule is that the community earnings of husband and wife are chargeable with the family support. Hence any amounts of money expended for such purpose by either spouse during the existence of the marital relation are presumed to have been paid out of the community estate. It appears that during such period defendant expended for the support of his family, and for income tax and premiums on policies of life insurance wherein his estate was made the beneficiary, the sum of $ 84,576. The premiums on his life insurance

> so paid were not a charge upon the community estate. Neither was the entire sum of $ 18,380 paid by defendant on account of income tax, a charge thereon. Just what proportion of said income tax should be charged to defendant's personal earnings is not made to appear; but conceding for the purpose of the argument that the community estate be deemed free from such burden and the entire sum so paid be imposed upon defendant's other income, and deducting both the life insurance premiums and income tax, the aggregate of which is $ 23,946, from the total of $ 84,576 so expended, leaves a balance of $ 60,630 as the amount actually expended for the community benefit and chargeable to his community earnings of $ 69,203. This leaves to the credit of the community estate the amount of $ 8,573, which sum, however, should be further reduced to the extent of the amount chargeable against it on account of its proportion of the income tax so paid by defendant.
>
> It thus appears that the evidence is insufficient to show the existence of a community estate of plaintiff and defendant of the value of $ 90,000, and since his earnings from personal service rendered did not exceed the sum of $ 69,203, the balance of his income, whatever it may have been, was necessarily derived from the rents, issues, and profits of the property which he owned at the time of his marriage.
>
> The judgment as to the amount and value of the community property and as to the disposition thereof between the parties is reversed and the cause is remanded for a new trial upon that issue alone.

The *Van Camp* approach determines how much the owner spouse's effort and labor is worth, and that figure is the community property, with the balance of the increase in value being characterized as separate property by process of elimination.

Reimbursement

1. The Right to Claim Reimbursement

The right to reimbursement arises regardless of which spouse applies the property to the satisfaction of the debt, regardless of whether the property is applied to the satisfaction of the debt voluntarily or involuntarily, and regardless of whether the debt to which the property is applied is satisfied in whole or in part. This right is subject to an express written waiver of the right by the spouse in whose favor the right arises. **FC § 920(a)**.

A right of reimbursement must be exercised within three years after the spouse in whose favor the right arises has actual knowledge of the application of the property to the satisfaction of the debt. **FC § 920(c)**.
The measure of reimbursement is the value of the property or interest in property at the time the right arises. **FC § 920(b)**.

2. *Epstein* Credits

The court has jurisdiction to order reimbursement in cases in which it deems appropriate for debts paid after separation but before trial. **FC § 2626**. The

Chapter 22: Division, racing & Reimbursement

reimbursement of credit for these payments is called *Epstein* **credits** after *In re Marriage OF EPSTEIN* (1979) 24 Cal.3d 76, which is the case that follows.

> *In re Marriage of ELAYNE C. and LEON J. EPSTEIN. LEON J. EPSTEIN, Respondent, v. ELAYNE C. EPSTEIN, Appellant*
> Supreme Court of California
> 24 Cal.3d 76; 592 P.2d 1165; 154 Cal.Rptr. 413
> April 12, 1979
> (*Marriage of Epstein*)
>
> The parties were married on August 8, 1954, and separated on April 15, 1972. At the time of trial wife was 48 years old and husband was 57. There were 2 children of the marriage, a daughter, over 18 years old at the time of trial and in college, and a son, age 16, residing with wife.
>
> Wife has had no employment or job training since 1954. Before marriage she had held a temporary job as a doctor's receptionist for six months, had worked for her father for a brief period in his business, and for a wholesale firm in Los Angeles for slightly less than a year. She had a B.A. degree from the University of California, where she had majored in social work.
>
> The husband, a professor of psychiatry at University of California Medical School, also engages in part-time private practice of psychiatry. His gross income from all sources in 1973 totaled $67,000; his net income from all sources after taxes, retirement and deduction for certain health and life insurance premiums amounted to about $ 31,200.
>
> After the parties separated, husband continued to provide to his wife approximately $ 650 every month and in addition paid utilities, telephone, department store bills, gardener, gasoline card, house insurance, house taxes, and mortgage payment. In February 1974, he modified his monthly payments to $ 950, from which wife was expected to pay utilities, food, car expenses, gardening, and other incidental expenses. Throughout the pendente lite[1] period wife and the son, David, remained in the family residence while husband made all the mortgage, insurance, and tax payments on the home. Wife maintains that because of this arrangement she never sought an order for support pendente lite.
>
> The trial court allowed the husband reimbursement for the money spent to maintain the family residence during the separation period.
>
> Upon consideration of that matter, we agree with the conclusion of In re Marriage of Smith, and adopt as the view of this court the following portion of the Court of Appeal opinion of Justice Kaufman:
>
> "The rule denying reimbursement in the absence of an agreement therefor is based largely on the presumption the paying spouse intended a gift. When the parties have separated in anticipation of dissolution of the marriage, the rational basis for presuming an intention on the part of the paying spouse to make a gift is gone.
>
> "So, we are persuaded the rule disallowing reimbursement in the absence of an agreement for reimbursement should not apply and that, as a general rule, a spouse who, after

---

[1] *Pendente lite* is Latin for "pending the trial".

Chapter 22: Division, racing & Reimbursement

> separation of the parties, uses earnings or other separate funds to pay preexisting community obligations should be reimbursed therefor out of the community property upon dissolution.
>
> In the instant case the trial court did not determine whether husband's payments constituted in reality a discharge in part of his obligation of support.
>
> The portion of the trial court order granting husband reimbursement for traceable funds he has expended during the period of the parties' separation to preserve and maintain the family home is reversed, and the cause is remanded to the trial court for further proceedings consistent with this opinion.

The *Epstein* case was codified by the legislature in 1992 and became operative in 1994 as **FC § 2626**, which provides that "the court has jurisdiction to order reimbursement in cases it deems appropriate for debts paid after separation but before trial."

3. *Watts* Charges

If a spouse, who has the exclusive use a community asset, is paying a lesser amount than the fair market value of that asset, then he or she may be charged the difference between the amount paid and the fair market value. This charge is called a **watts charge**, after the case that follows.

> *In re Marriage of CAROL D. and JOHN D. WATTS. CAROL D. WATTS, Appellant, v. JOHN D. WATTS, Appellant*
> Court of Appeal of California, Fifth Appellate District
> 171 Cal.App.3d 366; 217 Cal.Rptr. 301
> August 21, 1985
> (*Marriage of Watts*)
>
> The parties in this dissolution of marriage proceeding were married on September 30, 1975, and separated on April 29, 1979. Carol D. Watts (hereinafter referred to as Carol) filed her petition for dissolution of marriage on May 15, 1979. John D. Watts (hereinafter referred to as John) filed his response on June 14, 1979. Trial was held on September 14, 1981, and the interlocutory judgment was filed on April 12, 1982.
>
> At the time of marriage, John was a board-certified surgeon who left the employment of the Kern Medical Center as the chief of the department of surgery approximately four months prior to marriage. During the said four-month period which commenced on June 1, 1975, he was associated in a medical partnership with Dr. Charles Ashmore. The practice continued until sometime in 1976 when a medical corporation was formed. The practice was then transferred to the corporation in exchange for stock. The partnership was not dissolved at that time.
>
> The trial court found that John had the "use of" both the family residence and the medical practice between the date of separation and the date of trial. The court then found that 10 percent was a fair rate of return to the community for the use of the residence and the medical practice by John. However, the trial court concluded that it did not have the authority to require John to reimburse the community for his exclusive use of the

Chapter 22: Division, racing & Reimbursement

> community property after separation. Carol contends this conclusion by the trial court is erroneous and contrary to existing case law.
>
> We hold that the trial court erred in concluding that it had no authority to reimburse the community for the value of John's exclusive use of the family residence and the medical practice between the date of separation and the date of trial.
>
> Upon remand, the trial court will determine whether John should be required to reimburse the community for the value of his use of community assets after the date of separation in accordance with its findings. That determination should be made after taking into account all the circumstances under which exclusive possession was ordered.

4. Community Contributions to Education

Community contributions to education or training are payments made with community or quasi-community property for education or training or for the repayment of a loan incurred for education or training, whether the payments were made while the parties were residents in this state or residents outside this state. **FC § 2641(a)**. These reimbursement rights are not absolute.

Upon a dissolution or legal separation, the community is reimbursed for community contributions to education or training of a party that substantially enhances the earning capacity of one of the spouses. The amount reimbursed will include interest at the legal rate, accruing from the end of the calendar year in which the contributions were made. **FC § 2641(b)(1)**.

A loan incurred during marriage for the education or training of one of the spouses is not included among the liabilities of the community. It is assigned to the borrowing spouse for payment. **FC § 2641(b)(2)**.

When the community has substantially benefited from the education, training or loan incurred for the education or training of the party, reimbursement and assignment to the community is reduced or modified to the extent that circumstances render such a disposition unjust. **FC § 2641(c)(1)**.

There is a rebuttable presumption affecting the burden of proof that the community has substantially benefited from community contributions to the education or training made more than ten (10) years before the commencement of the dissolution or legal separation.

However, there is a rebuttable presumption that the community did not substantially benefit from community contributions to the education or training made less than ten (10) years before the commencement of the dissolution or legal separation. **FC § 2641(c)(1)**.

Reimbursement to the community is reduced or modified when the education or training received by the party is offset by the education or training received by the other party for which community contributions have been made. **FC § 2641(c)(2)**.

Chapter 22: Division, racing & Reimbursement

The question of whether the education or training has **substantially enhanced** the student spouse's earning capacity is one of fact for the judge to decide.

Reimbursement for community contributions and assignment of loans pursuant to this section is the exclusive remedy of the community or a party for the education or training and any resulting enhancement of the earning capacity of a spouse. However, nothing limits consideration of the effect of the education, training or enhancement, or the amount reimbursed, on the circumstances of the parties for the purpose of an order for support, pursuant to **FC § 4320. FC § 2641(d)**.

5. Other Reimbursements

The court has jurisdiction to order reimbursement in cases it deems appropriate for debts paid after separation but before trial. **FC § 2626**.

Unless a party has made a written waiver of his or her right to receive reimbursement when contributing to the acquisition of community property, the contributor is entitled to reimbursement if he or she can trace the contributions to a separate property source. Any reimbursement is made without interest or adjustment for any change in the monetary value and may not exceed the net value of the property at the time of division. **FC § 2640**.

Contributions include down payments, payments for improvements and payments that reduce the principal of a loan used to finance the purchase or improvement of the property. Contributions do not include payments of interest on the loan or payments made for maintenance, insurance or taxation of the property.

If the property of a married person is applied to the satisfaction of a money judgment pursuant to **FC § 916(a)** for a debt incurred by the person that is assigned for payment by the person's spouse, the person has a right of reimbursement from the person's spouse to the extent of the property applied, with interest at the legal rate, and may recover reasonable attorney fees incurred in enforcing the right of reimbursement. **FC § 916(b)**.

The child or spousal support obligation of a married person that does not arise out of the marriage will be treated as a debt incurred before marriage, regardless of whether a court order for support is made or modified before or during marriage and regardless of whether any installment payment on the obligation accrues before or during marriage. If community property is used to pay a child or spousal support order that is not related to the marriage, the community estate is entitled to reimbursement from the person in the amount of the separate income, not exceeding the property in the community estate so applied. **FC § 915.**

> A right of reimbursement provided by this part is subject to the following provisions:
> **(a)** The right arises regardless of which spouse applies the property to the satisfaction of the debt, regardless of whether the property is applied to the satisfaction of the debt voluntarily or involuntarily, and regardless of whether the debt to which the property is

Chapter 22: Division, racing & Reimbursement

> applied is satisfied in whole or in part. The right is subject to an express written waiver of the right by the spouse in whose favor the right arises.
> **(b)** The measure of reimbursement is the value of the property or interest in property at the time the right arises. FC § 920.

However, the right of reimbursement set forth above in **FC § 920** must be exercised within three years after the spouse in whose favor the right arises has actual knowledge of the application of the property to the satisfaction of the debt. **FC § 920(c)**.

Personal Injury

Pursuant to **FC § 2603,** community estate personal injury damages are money or other property received or to be received by a person in satisfaction of a judgment for damages for the person's personal injuries or pursuant to an agreement for the settlement or compromise of a claim for the damages, if the cause of action for the damages arose during the marriage, except as provided in **FC § 780**.[2]

However, it is the separate property of the injured spouse if the cause of action arose after the entry of the judgment or while the spouses were living separate and apart. **FC § 781**.

The community may be entitled to part of a personal injury award when one of the spouses has a claim for his or her injuries that occurred during the marriage. However, it should be noted that the parties may agree that no reimbursement to the community is necessary. **FC § 2641(e)**.

If the spouse of the injured person has paid expenses by reason of the personal injuries from separate property or from the community property, that spouse is entitled to reimbursement of the separate or community property for those expenses from the separate property received by the injured person under **FC § 781(a)**. **FC § 781(b)**.

If one spouse has a cause of action against the other spouse that arose during the marriage of the parties, money or property paid or to be paid by or on behalf of a party to the party's spouse of that marriage in satisfaction of a judgment for damages for personal injuries to that spouse, or pursuant to an agreement for the settlement or compromise of a claim for the damages, it is the separate property of the injured spouse. **FC § 781(c)**.

Finally, community estate personal injury damages must be assigned to the party who suffered the injuries unless the court, after taking into account the economic condition and needs of each party, the time that has elapsed since the recovery of

---

[2] FC § 780 provides that "money and other property received or to be received by a married person in satisfaction of a judgment for damages for personal injuries, or pursuant to an agreement for the settlement or compromise of a claim for such damages, is community property if the cause of action for the damages arose during the marriage."

Chapter 22: Division, racing & Reimbursement

the damages or the accrual of the cause of action and all other facts of the case, determines that the interests of justice require another disposition. In such a case, the community estate personal injury damages will be assigned to the respective parties in such proportions as the court determines to be just, except that at least one-half of the damages must be assigned to the party who suffered the injuries. **FC § 781(b)**.

Community Estate Debts/Liabilities

A **debt** is an obligation incurred by a married person before or during marriage, whether based on contract, tort or otherwise. **FC § 902**.

Community debts are debts incurred after the date of marriage but before the date of separation. **FC § 2622**.

Pursuant to **FC § 912**, quasi-community property is liable to the same extent, and is treated the same as community property with regard to debts.

The community estate is liable for a debt incurred by either spouse before or during marriage, regardless of which spouse has the management and control of the property and regardless of whether one or both spouses are parties to the debt or to a judgment for the debt, except where the spouses are living separate and apart before a judgment of dissolution or legal separation. **FC § 910**.[3]

If there was a death or injury based upon an act or omission that occurred while a married person was performing an activity for the benefit of the community, the liability will first be satisfied from the community estate and second from the separate property of the married person. **FC § 1000(b)(1)**.
Liabilities that were incurred after the date of marriage but before separation that have benefited the community estate are a community liability, as the case that follows demonstrates.

---

[3] 2017 version of FC § 910 provides:
(a) Except as otherwise expressly provided by statute, the community estate is liable for a debt incurred by either spouse before or during marriage, regardless of which spouse has the management and control of the property and regardless of whether one or both spouses are parties to the debt or to a judgment for the debt.
(b) "During marriage" for purposes of this section does not include the period after the date of separation, as defined in Section 70, and before a judgment of dissolution of marriage or legal separation of the parties.
The language "after the date of separation, as defined in Section 70, and" was amended to "during which the spouses are living separate and apart" in subdivision (b).

Chapter 22: Division, racing & Reimbursement

> *In re Marriage of JOHN L. and BETH E. BELL. JOHN L. BELL, Respondent, v. BETH E. BELL, Appellant.*
> COURT OF APPEAL OF CALIFORNIA, FOURTH APPELLATE DISTRICT, DIVISION TWO
> 49 Cal.App.4th 300; 56 Cal.Rptr.2d 623
> September 12, 1996, Decided
> (*Marriage of Bell*)

The facts underlying this case are largely undisputed. Husband and Wife were married in 1971 and separated in May 1991. During the early part of the marriage both parties worked, but in 1979 Husband became ill and retired from active employment. They sold their home in Pasadena on a contract of sale and moved to Palm Desert where they purchased their present mobile home and lot. Following the move the parties started a sandwich-making business. They sold the sandwich shop in 1982 or 1983 and Wife started work as a ticket taker for the Palm Springs Aerial Tramway, (Wife's employer), earning an hourly salary.

Starting in 1985 and continuing until her arrest on September 20, 1990, Wife embezzled funds from her employer. A civil action was filed against both parties by Wife's employer in 1990 seeking to recover the embezzled funds. The parties settled that suit for $ 150,000, and the suit was dismissed.

The parties separated in May 1991 and Husband filed a petition for dissolution in August 1991. In December 1992 the parties entered a stipulation to bifurcate the status of the marriage from the property issues, and the marriage was dissolved at that time.

On the second day of trial, in January 1993, it was stipulated that Wife had not told Husband that she had embezzled funds, and that Husband's first actual knowledge of the embezzlement was when Wife was arrested. Wife testified that she had subsequently been convicted of the crime of embezzlement. Also on the second day of trial the court reiterated that "I indicated that . . . Mrs. Bell is going to bear the burden of the wrongdoing between these two people. [P] When it comes to allocating assets, every question I have is going to be resolved against her about [who is] going to bear this burden . . . ." The court then stated that evidence of whether the community benefited from the embezzled funds was irrelevant.

During trial the court heard testimony from Husband, from Wife, and from Karl Anderson, an accountant hired by the attorney who had represented Husband and Wife in the civil action brought by Wife's employer. Mr. Anderson testified that he had been retained "in order to compute a calculation as to the embezzlement by Mrs. Bell."

Wife testified that she had deposited the embezzled funds in bank accounts and had used the funds to buy certificates of deposit. She also testified that she had used the money to buy groceries, go to the hairdresser and go out to dinner, and that she had given Husband a $100 per month allowance. She stated that she had bought presents for Husband with the money, including a $2,500 watch and an identification bracelet. Wife testified that she had never opened an account in her name alone and that all the money had been deposited in joint accounts.

Wife testified that the mortgage on the residence of the parties had been prepaid for about 19 months at the time of her arrest. She also testified that the parties had purchased a Cadillac in 1989 and had accelerated the payments so that the car was completely paid for by 1990.

Counsel for Wife offered to the court a chart prepared by him, on the basis of information given to him by Wife that purported to demonstrate that during the period 1985 to 1990 the community spent $129,000 more than it earned through legitimate sources.

In an effort to establish that the community was not harmed and was in fact benefited by the embezzlement, counsel for Wife elicited testimony to show that cash assets remained after the civil settlement. The parties stipulated that there was about $20,000, plus savings bonds, left after payment of the $150,000 settlement and $55,000 in attorney fees.

Mr. Anderson stated that according to amended tax returns prepared by him, the federal tax due as of December 1992 was $60,874.07, and the state tax due was $18,974. Of those amounts, a total of $28,290 was attributable to penalties and interest.

At the end of trial Husband argued that [Wife should be accessed with the] interest and penalties due on the income tax. Wife agreed that she should be held liable for the interest and penalties due on the income tax. She contended, however, that the tax itself should be paid by the community since the community had had the benefit of the income.

On July 1, 1993, the court ordered that Wife was to hold Husband harmless from the debts,[4] and ordered Wife to pay the debts. Wife filed a motion for a new trial, which was denied, and she then filed this appeal. Wife objects to the trial court decision to attribute to Wife all the costs, but not the benefits, resulting from her embezzlement from her employer over a period of five years.

DISCUSSION
Wife was still engaged in [the intentional tort of embezzlement] and Husband knew nothing about it. There was uncontradicted testimony that the community received the benefit of the embezzlement. Even if the numbers were somewhat uncertain, it was apparent that the community had received a major infusion of funds over the years, and it was clear that all the embezzled funds had been put to community, and not separate, use. Mr. Anderson testified that the amount of the settlement was based on estimates of the amount that had been taken, so the settlement was no more than an attempt at restitution.

We hold that the trial court erred by allocating the entire $150,000 settlement, which had previously been paid out of community property, to Wife as part of her share of the community property distribution. The community had shared in the benefit and could properly be asked to share in the cost.

Here we find that the trial court's resolution of this issue was not supported by the evidence presented and does not reflect a correct analysis and application of the law and we therefore reverse on this issue.

The judgment on the bifurcated property issues is reversed.

---

[4] Federal tax liability $61,000.00 approx. State tax liability $23,000.00 approx. Total tax liability $84,000.00 approx.
Karl Anderson, C.P.A. $1,240.40. Total debts related to embezzlement $85,240.40.

Finally, **FC § 903** provides that a debt becomes viable at the time a contract is made. If the contract was entered into while the parties were married, it is a community liability, even if the parties separated before the completion of the contract. *In re Marriage of FELDNER* (1995) 40 Cal.App.4th 312 at p. 629.

1. Separate Debts/Liabilities

Debts incurred by either spouse before the date of marriage will be confirmed without offset to the spouse who incurred the debt. **FC § 2621**.

FC § 913(a) provides that the separate property of a married person is liable for a debt incurred by the person before or during marriage.

The separate property of a married person is not liable for a debt incurred by the person's spouse before or during marriage. **FC § 911**.

Separate debts are debts, including those incurred by a spouse during marriage and before the date of separation, that were not incurred for the benefit of the community; they will be confirmed without offset to the spouse who incurred the debt. **FC § 2625**.

A married person is personally liable for a debt incurred for necessaries of life of the person's spouse while the spouses are living together and a debt incurred for common necessaries of life of the person's spouse while the spouses are living separately, provided there is no written agreement to the contrary[5]. **FC § 914(a)(1)**.

Debts incurred by either spouse after entry of a judgment of dissolution of marriage but before termination of the parties' marital status or after entry of a judgment of legal separation of the parties will be confirmed without offset to the spouse who incurred the debt. **FC § 2624**.

Pursuant to **FC § 914**[6], a married person is personally liable for the debts incurred by the person's spouse during marriage if the debt was incurred for the necessaries of life of the person's spouse while the spouses were living together.

---

[5] Pursuant to FC § 4302: a person is not liable for support of the person's spouse when the person is living separate from the spouse by agreement unless support is stipulated in the agreement.

[6] Effective 2017 FC § 914 was amended to the following:
(a) Notwithstanding Section 913, a married person is personally liable for the following debts incurred by the person's spouse during marriage:
 (1) A debt incurred for necessaries of life of the person's spouse before the date of separation of the spouses.
 (2) Except as provided in Section 4302, a debt incurred for common necessaries of life of the person's spouse after the date of separation of the spouses.
(b) The separate property of a married person may be applied to the satisfaction of a debt for which the person is personally liable pursuant to this section. If separate property is so applied at a time when nonexempt property in the community estate or separate property of the person's spouse is available but is not applied to the satisfaction of the debt, the married person is entitled to reimbursement to the extent such property was available.
(c)

Chapter 22: Division, racing & Reimbursement

However, if the parties separated before the debt was incurred, only the spouse that incurred the debt is responsible for the debt, as the case that follows demonstrates.

> ***CMRE FINANCIAL SERVICES, INC., Plaintiff, Cross-defendant and Respondent, v. PAMELA D. PARTON, Defendant, Cross-complainant and Appellant.***
> COURT OF APPEAL OF CALIFORNIA, FOURTH APPELLATE DISTRICT, DIVISION ONE
> 184 Cal.App.4th 263; 109 Cal.Rptr.3d 139
> April 29, 2010, Filed
> (*CMRE Financial Services v. Parton*)
>
> On February 16, 2006, Pamela D. Parton (Pamela) called police to the home she shared with her then husband, Daniel W. Parton (Daniel). Pamela told the police her husband had engaged in domestic violence against her. Very shortly thereafter Pamela obtained a restraining order and the couple separated.
>
> On February 23, 2006, after the Partons had separated, Daniel was admitted to Tri-City Medical Center. The record suggests he was suffering from severe emotional illness. Daniel was released from the hospital on February 27, 2006.
>
> On May 17, 2006, Pamela filed a petition for dissolution of her marriage. In her schedule of assets and debts, Pamela stated the Tri-City hospital debt belonged to Daniel. A judgment of dissolution was entered on September 26, 2006. The judgment did not assign the hospital obligation to Pamela.
>
> On January 24, 2008, CMRE Financial Services, Inc. (CMRE), as assignee of Tri-City hospital, filed a complaint against both Partons. The complaint alleged the Partons owed CMRE $26,083, plus interest and attorney fees. Pamela filed an answer denying the material allegations of the complaint.
>
> CMRE alleged Pamela was liable for Daniel's necessaries under FC § 914 and that, notwithstanding FC § 916, Pamela was not relieved of that liability by virtue of her dissolution judgment. Thereafter the trial court tried CMRE's claims and entered judgment against Pamela for $26,083, plus interest, attorney fees and costs. Pamela timely appealed.
>
> **DISCUSSION**
> On appeal, Pamela argues her dissolution judgment relieved her of any liability to CMRE that may have arisen under FC § 914. We agree.

---

(1) Except as provided in paragraph (2), the statute of limitations set forth in Section 366.2 of the Code of Civil Procedure shall apply if the spouse for whom the married person is personally liable dies.
(2) If the surviving spouse had actual knowledge of the debt prior to expiration of the period set forth in Section 366.2 of the Code of Civil Procedure and the personal representative of the deceased spouse's estate failed to provide the creditor asserting the claim under this section with a timely written notice of the probate administration of the estate in the manner provided for pursuant to Section 9050 of the Probate Code, the statute of limitations set forth in Section 337 or 339 of the Code of Civil Procedure, as applicable, shall apply.
(d) For purposes of this section, "date of separation" has the same meaning as set forth in Section 70.

FC § 914(a), states: "Notwithstanding FC § 913, a married person is personally liable for the following debts incurred by the person's spouse during marriage:
"(1) A debt incurred for necessaries of life of the person's spouse while the spouses are living together.

"(2) Except as provided in FC § 4302, a debt incurred for common necessaries of life of the person's spouse while the spouses are living separately."

As Pamela argues, one spouse's liability for the other spouse's necessaries while the spouses are living separately is subject not only to the terms of any separation agreement between them, it is also subject to any assignment of debts made at the time their marriage is dissolved. FC § 916(a), states in pertinent part: "(a) *Notwithstanding any other provision of this chapter*, after division of community and quasi-community property pursuant to Division 7 (commencing with FC § 2500):

"(1) The separate property owned by a married person at the time of the division and the property received by the person in the division is liable for a debt incurred by the person before or during marriage and the person is personally liable for the debt, whether or not the debt was assigned for payment by the person's spouse in the division.

"(2) The separate property owned by a married person at the time of the division and the property received by the person in the division is not liable for a debt incurred by the person's spouse before or during marriage, and *the person is not personally liable for the debt*, unless the debt was assigned for payment by the person in the division of the property. Nothing in this paragraph affects the liability of property for the satisfaction of a lien on the property." (Italics added.)

Prior to enactment of the statutory predecessor to FC § 916, spouses were liable for community debts following dissolution of a marriage. "In 1984, however, the Legislature substantially changed the postmarital liability of spouses. 'The Legislature determined that, under most circumstances, after a marriage has ended, it is unwise to continue the liability of spouses for community debts incurred by former spouses.' It enacted former CC § 5120.160, which provided in pertinent part that, upon the dissolution of the marriage, 'the property received by [a married] person in the division is not liable for a debt incurred by the person's spouse before or during marriage, and the person is not personally liable for the debt, unless the debt was assigned for payment by the person in the division of the property.' When the Family Code was enacted in 1992, CC § 5120.160 became FC § 916." (*Mejia v. Reed* (2003) 31 Cal.4th 657, 665.)

Contrary to CMRE's contention, FC § 914 is not a species of a joint and several liability which is personally incurred by both spouses and for that reason outside the scope of FC § 916. Such an interpretation is inconsistent with the express terms of FC § 914 itself. By its terms FC § 914 governs "debts incurred by the person's spouse." This language confirms that the Legislature views one spouse's liability for the other spouse's post-separation necessaries as entirely derivative and not personally incurred by the supporting spouse.

Our conclusion [that] a dissolution judgment relieves a spouse of liability imposed by FC § 914 is of course supported by the express terms of FC § 916, which make all other provisions of that chapter of the Family Code, including FC § 914, subject to the protection FC § 916 provides to former spouses following dissolution of a marriage. It is also consistent with the manner in which our courts have applied FC § 916.

Chapter 22: Division, racing & Reimbursement

> The only exception to application of FC § 916 our courts have recognized is where a creditor alleges a marital settlement agreement violates the separate provisions of the Uniform Fraudulent Transfer Act, CC §§ 3439 through 3439.12 (UFTA). Significantly, in reaching that conclusion the court noted that the legislative history of both FC § 916 and the UFTA shed no light on what the Legislature intended when a conflict between the two statutes arose. The court upheld application of the UFTA solely because it found the antifraud policies of the UFTA took precedence over the finality policies embodied in FC § 916. Here of course no such countervailing fundamental policy is implicated.
>
> In sum, as we interpret FC §§ 914 and 916, although spouses have an obligation to support each other while separated, they can avoid that obligation by way of agreement between themselves. Moreover, any liability for support which arose during the parties' separation ceases following dissolution of the marriage, unless the court orders it extended.
>
> In light of our interpretation of FC §§ 914 and 916, Pamela is not liable for the cost of Daniel's hospitalization. The dissolution judgment did not assign that debt to her and FC § 916(a)(2) relieved her of any liability for it.
>
> Thus, the judgment entered against Pamela must be reversed with instructions that CMRE's complaint be dismissed.

The earnings of a married person during marriage are not liable for a debt incurred by the person's spouse before marriage. **FC § 911(a)**.

Debts that are incurred by either spouse after the entry of a judgment of dissolution but before termination of the parties' marital status or after entry of a judgment of legal separation of the parties will be confirmed without offset to the spouse who incurred the debt. **FC § 2624**.

The separate property of a married person is liable for a debt incurred by the person before or during marriage but is not liable for a debt incurred by the person's spouse before or during marriage. **FC § 913(a), (b)**.

The separate property owned by a married person at the time of the division and the property received by the person in the division is liable for a debt incurred by the person before or during marriage and the person is personally liable for the debt, whether or not the debt was assigned for payment by the person's spouse in the division. **FC § 916(a)(1)**.

However, the separate property owned by a married person at the time of the division and the property received by the person in the division is not liable for a debt incurred by the person's spouse before or during marriage, and the person is not personally liable for the debt, unless the debt was assigned for payment by the person in the division of the property. **FC § 916(a)(2)**.

Educational loans and liabilities will be assigned to the spouse whose act or omission provided the basis for the liability, without offset. **FC § 2627**.

Debts incurred by either spouse after the date of separation but before the entry of a judgment of dissolution or legal separation for the common necessaries of life of either spouse or the children of the marriage for whom support may be ordered, in the absence of a court order or written agreement for support or for the payment of these debts, can be confirmed to either spouse according to the parties' respective needs and abilities to pay at the time the debt was incurred. If the debts are for nonnecessaries, they will be confirmed without offset to the spouse who incurred the debt. **FC § 2623(a),(b)**.

2. The Court has the Discretion to Assign Assets and Debts Party

To the extent that community debts exceed total community and quasi-community assets, the excess of debt will be assigned as the court deems just and equitable, taking into account factors such as the parties' relative ability to pay. **FC § 2622(b)**.

The court must characterize liabilities as separate or community and confirm or assign them to the parties for the purposes of division and in confirming or assigning the liabilities of the parties for which the community estate is liable. **FC § 2551**.

Joint California income tax liabilities may be revised by a court in a proceeding for dissolution of marriage, provided the requirements of **Revenue and Taxation Code § 19006** are satisfied. **FC § 2628**.

Debts incurred by either spouse after the date of separation but before entry of a judgment of dissolution or legal separation may be assigned by the court to either party. The court will make this determination based upon the parties' respective needs and abilities to pay at the time the debt was incurred. **FC § 2623(a)**.

Finally, in a proceeding for dissolution, nullity or legal separation, the court has continuing jurisdiction to award community estate assets or community estate liabilities to the parties that have not been previously adjudicated by a judgment in the proceeding. A party may file a postjudgment motion or order to show cause in the proceeding in order to obtain adjudication of any community estate asset or liability omitted or not adjudicated by the judgment. In these cases, the court must equally divide the omitted or unadjudicated community estate asset or liability, unless the court finds upon good cause shown that the interests of justice require an unequal division of the asset or liability. **FC § 2556**.

Chapter 22: Division, racing & Reimbursement

EDUCATIONAL EXERCISES

FILL IN THE BLANKS

1. A _____ is an obligation incurred by a married person before or during marriage, whether based on contract, tort or otherwise. FC § 902.
2. _____ are those that are incurred after the date of marriage but before the date of separation. FC § 2622.
3. Pursuant to FC § 912, _____ is liable to the same extent, and is treated the same as community property with regard to debts.
4. Liabilities that were incurred after the date of marriage but before separation that have benefited the community estate are a _____.
5. FC § 903 provides that a debt becomes viable at the time a contract is made. If the contract was entered into while the parties were married, it is a _____, even if the parties separated before the completion of the contract.
6. FC § 913(a) provides that the _____ is liable for a debt incurred by the person before or during marriage. It is not liable for a debt incurred by the person's spouse before or during marriage. FC § 911.
7. _____ include those incurred by a spouse during marriage and before the date of separation, that were not incurred for the benefit of the community; they will be confirmed without offset to the spouse who incurred the debt. FC § 2625.
8. A married person is personally liable for a _____ of the person's spouse while the spouses are living together.
9. A debt incurred for the _____ of life of the person's spouse before the date of separation of the spouses. FC § 914(a)(1).
10. The earnings of a married person during marriage are not liable for _____ _____ before marriage. FC § 911(a).
11. Debts that are incurred by either spouse after the entry of a judgment of dissolution but before termination of the parties' marital status or after entry of a judgment of legal separation of the parties will be confirmed _____. FC § 2624.
12. The _____ of a married person is liable for a debt incurred by the person before or during marriage but is not liable for a debt incurred by the person's spouse before or during marriage. FC § 913(a), (b).
13. _____ and liabilities will be assigned to the spouse whose act or omission provided the basis for the liability, without offset. FC § 2627.
14. The court must characterize liabilities as _____ and confirm or assign them to the parties for the purposes of division and in confirming or assigning the liabilities of the parties for which the community estate is liable. FC § 2551.
15. In a dissolution, nullity or legal separation, the court has continuing jurisdiction to award _____ to the parties that have not been previously adjudicated by a judgment in the proceeding.

CHAPTER 23: Retirement & Disability

In Brief...

DEFINITIONS OF PENSION/RETIREMENT WORDS/TERMS ARE:
- **A pension plan** is exclusively funded by an employer and is received by the employee at retirement;
- **A retirement plan** is primarily funded by an employee but may include contributions from an employer. If the employer contributes to the plan, the employee must continue to be employed by the company for a set number of years to be able to collect the employer-contributed amount.
- **A 401(k) retirement plan** allows an employee to elect to have a percentage of his or her salary contributed to a defined contribution plan. to have a percentage of his or her salary contributed to a defined contribution plan;
- **A Keogh plan** is for self-employed persons, whereby they can contribute pre-taxed money for their retirement.
- **A defined benefit pension plan** is based upon a formula that can include compensation and years of service as factors;
- With a **defined contribution plan**, the ultimate amount of the benefits to be provided at retirement will not be known until the date of retirement because they depend upon the future investment performance of the fund.
- **Deferred compensation** is compensation earned by an employee and taxed when paid;
- **An employee benefit plan** is a plan for employees that can include stock, profit sharing, bonuses or other incentives;
- **The term time rule** is a formula based upon the ratio of the length of employment between the date of marriage and the date of separation to the total length of employment; and
- **The Employee Retirement Income Security Act** is a federal statute passed to protect employees and their pensions in case an employer declares bankruptcy or goes out of business.

PENSIONS, RETIREMENT AND THE LIKE ARE COMMUNITY PROPERTY:
- If acquired during the marriage; and
- The court can make any orders to divide retirement plans, including survivor and death benefits. **FC § 2610(a)**. *MARRIAGE of HUG* (1984) 154 Cal.App.3d 780.

A Qualified Domestic Relations Order (QDRO) divides retirement between spouses.

A joinder action joins the pension plan into the dissolution action as a party litigant, **FC § 2660, CRC Rule 5.24**.

DISABILITY:
- Pay is compensation paid for income that will be lost or has lost due a diminished ability to earn a living;

Chapter 23: Retirement & Disability

> - Is usually designated as separate property and confirmed to the disabled spouse, **FC § 781**;
> - Is not retirement; and
> - If chosen instead of retirement is part separate property because only the net amount over what would have been received as retirement is disability, *MARRIAGE of MUELLER* (1977) 70 Cal.App.3d 66.

Introduction

Pensions, retirement and the like are community property is acquired during the marriage. Retirement and pension plans must be joined into the dissolution action in order for the court to have jurisdiction to make court orders regarding these plans. Further, dividing these plans may require a specific court order.

Pensions, Retirement and the Like

1. Definitions

A **pension plan** is a plan that is exclusively funded by an employer and is received by the employee upon retirement after working at a company for a specified number of years.

A **retirement plan** is one that is primarily funded by the employee but may include contributions from an employer. If the employer contributes to the plan, the employee must continue to be employed by the company for a set number of years to be able to collect the employer-contributed amount.

A **401(k) retirement plan** allows an employee to elect to have a percentage of his or her salary contributed to a defined contribution plan. The employee's contribution portion is contributed before taxes are paid (pretax).

A **Keogh plan** is for self-employed persons, whereby they can contribute pre-taxed money for their retirement.

A defined benefit pension plan is a pension plan in which the employer agrees to pay an employee a specific benefit for life, which commences at retirement.

A defined benefit retirement plan is based upon a formula that can include compensation and years of service as factors. The plan specifies payments in advance in accordance with a formula that comprises factors such as final compensation, age, length of service and a per-service-year multiplier. *In re Marriage of LEHMAN* (1998) 18 Cal.4th 169; 955 P.2d 451; 74 Cal.Rptr. 2d 825.

With a **defined benefit plan**, a separate account is kept for each participant that shows sums contributed by him or her and on the employee's behalf by the employer. The plan manager invests the funds and keeps a record of how much

Chapter 23: Retirement & Disability

profit or loss the investments produce for each participant. With such records a court can, at the end of a marriage, make a "money" apportionment of the pension into community and separate components.

With a **defined contribution plan**, the ultimate amount of the benefits to be provided at retirement will not be known until the date of retirement because they depend upon the future investment performance of the fund. The benefits are defined by a formula for contribution.

Deferred compensation is compensation earned by an employee and taxed when paid, which is a future date. Deferred compensation can be tied to a specific event and payable when that event occurs.

An employee benefit plan is a plan for employees that can include stock, profit sharing, bonuses or other incentives.

Deferred compensation, retirement benefits, pensions, 401(k) accounts and Keogh plans constitute community property if accrued during marriage.

And finally, the Employee Retirement Income Security Act (ERISA) is a federal statute passed in 1974 to protect employees and their pensions in case an employer declares bankruptcy or goes out of business.

2. Matured, Unmatured Vested and Nonvested Retirement Plans

Retirement plans may be called deferred compensation, profit sharing, pension plans or 401k plans. These plans are provided by an employer as incentive for an employee to work for the company or remain working for the company. Since all of these plans provide for an employee to receive these benefits at a later date—retirement age—there is the additional benefit of deferring the tax paid on the money earned to a time when the employee will be in a lower tax bracket.

However, no matter what plan is used, an employee has the right to receive the contributions that he or she made in either periodic payments or lump sum payments upon retirement. It is the contributions of the employer that can be matured, unmatured vested or nonvested.

Retirement plans can be funded by the employee's earnings, contributions from an employer or both. A matured right is unconditional, and the employee can receive payment immediately. "Unmatured vested retirement rights are frequently subject to the condition, among others, that the employee survive until retirement." *In re Marriage of BROWN* (1976) 15 Cal.3d 838, at p. 842 (*Brown*). An unmatured vested retirement right is essentially a right that survives discharge or voluntary termination of an employee, and it is paid on a date certain.

Prior to *Brown*, a nonvested retirement plan was not a property right that was subject to division upon divorce. However, in *Brown* the Supreme Court of

Chapter 23: Retirement & Disability

California disapproved and overruled prior decisions that so held, holding that nonvested retirement rights were a property right and were subject to division upon divorce. *Id.* at p. 841.

In *Brown*, the trial court held that since the husband had not yet acquired a vested right to the retirement pension, the value of his pension rights did not become community property subject to division by the court. *Id.* at p. 843. The wife challenged this decision because if the husband continued to work at that company for just three more years, he could retire and receive a pension amount of $310.94 per month. The wife argued that the husband was entitled to retire after only three years because of the many years that he worked for this company when he was married to her. The Supreme Court agreed with the wife. *Id.* at p. 851.

Thus, retirement rights are community property if accrued during the marriage, whether the rights are matured, unmatured vested or nonvested.

3. The Time Rule

The term **time rule** has been used to describe a formula for determining the community interest in retirement benefits according to the ratio of the length of employment between the date of marriage (or date of commencement of employment, if later) and the date of separation to the total length of employment. *In re Marriage of HUG* (1984) 154 Cal.App.3d 780 at p. 784.

Under the **time rule**:

> the community property interest in retirement benefits is the percentage representing the fraction whose numerator is the employee spouse's length of service during marriage before separation … and whose denominator is the employee spouse's length of service in total … ; the separate property interest is the percentage representing the remainder of 100 percent minus the community property interest percentage. *In re MARRIAGE of LEHMAN* (1998) 18 Cal.4th 169, 176.

4. Court Orders

A court may make an order reserving jurisdiction until the employed spouse's retirement, at which time the other spouse will receive a specified percentage of each pension check. The percentage is calculated by determining the years of marriage that the employee spouse was participating in the pension plan, from the date of marriage or date of employment commencement during the marriage and ending at the date of separation, divided by the total number of years that the employed spouse has been participating in the plan. This calculation is commonly called the **time rule**.

The court has the authority to make whatever orders are necessary or appropriate to ensure that both parties receive their full community share of any retirement plan,

Chapter 23: Retirement & Disability

including survivor and death benefits, regardless of whether the plan is public or private. **FC § 2610(a)**.

A court may order the disposition of any retirement benefits payable upon or after the death of either party in a manner consistent with **FC § 2550**. **FC § 2610(a)(1)**.

A court may order a party to elect a survivor benefit annuity or other similar election for the benefit of the other party, as specified by the court, in any case in which a retirement plan provides for such an election, provided that no court orders a retirement plan to provide increased benefits determined on the basis of its actuarial value. **FC § 2610(a)(2)**.

Additionally, a court may order a retirement plan to make payments directly to a nonmember party of his or her community property interest in retirement benefits. **FC § 2610(a)(4)**.

The court cannot make any order that requires a retirement plan to make payments in any manner that will result in an increase in the amount of benefits provided by the plan or make the payment of benefits to any party at any time before the member retires, unless the plan so provides. **FC § 2610(b)**.

Pursuant to **FC § 2610**, a court can:

---

(1) Order the disposition of any retirement benefits payable upon or after the death of either party in a manner consistent with FC § 2550.
(2) Order a party to elect a survivor benefit annuity or other similar election for the benefit of the other party, as specified by the court, in any case in which a retirement plan provides for such an election, provided that no court shall order a retirement plan to provide increased benefits determined on the basis of actuarial value.
(3) Upon the agreement of the nonemployee spouse, order the division of accumulated community property contributions and service credit; and as provided in the following or similar enactments:
    (A) Article 2 (commencing with Section 21290) of Chapter 9 of Part 3 of Division 5 of Title 2 of the Government Code.
    (B) Chapter 12 (commencing with Section 22650) of Part 13 of the Education Code.
    (C) Article 8.4 (commencing with Section 31685) of Chapter 3 of Part 3 of Division 4 of Title 3 of the Government Code.
    (D) Article 2.5 (commencing with Section 75050) of Chapter 11 of Title 8 of the Government Code.
    (E) Chapter 15 (commencing with Section 27400) of Part 14 of the Education Code.
(4) Order a retirement plan to make payments directly to a nonmember party of his or her community property interest in retirement benefits.

A **Qualified Domestic Relations Order** (**QDRO**) is a court order that requires approval from the pension plan administrator and the court in order to divide community property retirement monies between divorcing spouses. It was created by the Federal Retirement Equity Act of 1984. When the Court makes an order

Chapter 23: Retirement & Disability

concerning a spouse's retirement plan and the order is prepared in the correct form, federal law requires the employer to comply with the terms of the order. There is no set form for a QDRO and, accordingly, drafting a QDRO requires obtaining the specific form used by that plan administrator. Because drafting QDRO requires knowledge of the rules and laws and obtainment of plan information, most law firms do not prepare their own QDROs. Some law firms have limited their practice to just drafting QDROs. It is advisable to retain the services of a law firm or lawyer that is knowledgeable and experienced in drafting QDROs.

Finally, when a spouse is convicted of attempting to murder the other spouse or of soliciting the murder of the other spouse, the injured spouse is entitled to an award of 100 percent of the community property interest in the retirement and pension benefits. **FC § 782.5**.

5. Joinder and Joinder Forms

A joinder action joins the pension plan into the dissolution action as a party litigant. The joinder is necessary in order for the pension plan to be subject to the orders of the court.

Pursuant to **CRC Rule 5.24,** a person who claims or controls an interest in any matter subject to disposition in the proceeding may be joined as a party to the family law case.

CRC Rule 5.24(b) provides that the "claimant is an individual or an entity joined or sought or seeking to be joined as a party to the family law proceeding."

CRC Rule 5.29(a) provides that requests for the joinder of an employee pension benefit plan and order and every pleading on joinder must be submitted on a *Request for Joinder of Employee Benefit Plan and Order* (form *FL-372*) and *Pleading on Joinder-Employee Benefit Plan* (form *FL-370*).

Every summons issued for the joinder of an employee pension benefit plan must be on a *Summons (Joinder)* (form *FL-375*). **CRC Rule 5.29(b)**.

Every notice of appearance of an employee pension benefit plan and responsive pleading filed under **FC § 2063(b)** must be made on a *Notice of Appearance and Response of Employee Benefit Plan* (form *FL-374*). **CRC Rule 5.29(c)**.

6. Early Retirement

When a supporting ex-spouse elects to retire early and not seek reasonably remunerative available employment under the circumstances, the court can properly impute income to that supporting spouse, given that spouse's obligation to provide support and the general notion that a supporting spouse must make reasonable efforts to obtain employment that would generate a reasonable income under the circumstances to meet a continuing support obligation. *In re Marriage of*

STEPHENSON (1992) 39 Cal.App.4th 71 at p. 80. (*See* Chapter 17 RE: Spousal Support & Family Support, *supra*.)

Disability Benefits

Disability is usually designated as separate property and is confirmed to the disabled spouse. It is compensation paid for income that the spouse lost or will lose due to the spouse's diminished ability to earn a living. In determining compensation, it is necessary to discern when the disability occurred and what injury a spouse has sustained.

Disability is not retirement, and if a spouse elects to receive disability benefits instead of a matured right to retirement benefits, only the net amount over and above what would have been received as retirement benefits is disability and separate property.

In the case that follows, the husband could have collected retirement or disability. Husband chose disability, believing that the entire amount would be his separate property.

> *In re Marriage of CHARLOTTE and FREDERICK W. MUELLER. CHARLOTTE MUELLER, Appellant, v. FREDERICK W. MUELLER, Respondent*
> Court of Appeal of California, Fourth Appellate District, Division Two
> 70 Cal.App.3d 66; 137 Cal.Rptr. 129
> May 24, 1977
> (*Marriage of Mueller*)
>
> Husband and wife were married in 1949. After a marriage of nearly 26 years, they separated on January 28, 1975. On January 31, 1975, wife filed a petition for dissolution of the marriage. The interlocutory judgment of dissolution was entered June 23, 1976.
>
> In 1942 husband entered military service as a pilot with the United States Army Air Corps. He served until 1946 when he became a pilot for Pan American Airlines. In 1950 husband rejoined the military as a pilot. He developed arteriosclerotic heart disease in 1967 and several months later sought retirement. Early in 1968 a physical evaluation board found that due to his disability he was "not qualified for military service." It ordered him retired effective July 1, 1968, with a 30 percent permanent disability rating due to his heart condition. Although the trial court found husband's retirement to be involuntary, it also found that on the effective date of his retirement, July 1, 1968, husband was eligible for voluntary longevity retirement.
>
> The parties agreed upon a division of husband's longevity retirement benefits prior to trial. Following trial, the court determined the right to disability pay to be husband's sole and separate property. Husband maintains the right to disability pay was properly classified as his separate property. Wife contends that it is community property subject to division upon dissolution of the marriage. We do not wholly agree with either party.
>
> However, disability benefits received prior to vesting of a right to retirement benefits are held to constitute separate property of the employee spouse upon dissolution of marriage.

Chapter 23: Retirement & Disability

The rationale underlying the distinction between retirement benefits and disability benefits is that whereas retirement pay is deferred compensation for past services rendered and therefore community property, disability pay is compensation for personal anguish and diminished earning capacity, which, being comparable to damages for personal injuries received after separation or dissolution is the recipient spouse's separate property.

However, in In re Marriage of Cavnar (1976) 62 Cal.App.3d 660, we held that where the right to retirement pay had already matured and the employee spouse elected to receive disability benefits in lieu of retirement benefits, only the amount received in excess of the amount of the retirement benefits that would have been received could truly be said to compensate the employee spouse for personal anguish and loss of earning capacity and, thus, be properly classified as separate property, the balance being received only in lieu of retirement pay and, thus, properly classified as community property.

Husband attempts to distinguish Cavnar on the basis that we there dealt with matured retirement benefits whereas here his right to retirement pay was merely vested. [H]usband is incorrect in characterizing his right to retirement pay in the case at bench as merely vested. The trial court found husband was eligible to receive retirement benefits as of July 1, 1968, the effective date of his disability retirement, and, in fact, he is receiving some longevity retirement pay as a result of his retirement on that date. A vested retirement right refers to one which is not subject to forfeiture if the employment relationship terminates before retirement; a matured right to retirement pay refers to a right to immediate payment. On July 1, 1968, husband had the right to immediate payment of retirement benefits. Thus, his right to retirement payments matured on that date. Cavnar is not distinguishable on any significant legal basis and is controlling. We thus conclude that where the employee spouse elects to receive disability benefits in lieu of a matured right to retirement benefits, only the net amount thus received over and above what would have been received as retirement benefits constitutes compensation for personal anguish and loss of earning capacity and is, thus, the employee spouse's separate property. The amount received in lieu of matured retirement benefits remains community property subject to division on dissolution.

The interlocutory judgment of dissolution is reversed insofar as it adjudicates the right to disability payments is husband's separate property. The trial court is directed to redetermine the division of the community property and in so doing to determine the net amount after taxes by which the disability payments exceed the net amount after taxes that would have been received by virtue of retirement payments. That amount together with that portion of the disability payments attributable to husband's employment prior to marriage shall be adjudged to be husband's separate property. The remainder of the disability payments shall be adjudged to be community property.

Chapter 23: Retirement & Disability

EDUCATIONAL EXERCISES

Matching words/Terms/Forms with appropriate definitions

Words/Terms/Forms

A. 401(K) Retirement Plan
B. Deferred Compensation
C. Defined Benefit Pension Plan
D. Defined Benefit Plan
E. FL-374
F. Defined Benefit Retirement Plan
G. Defined Contribution Plan
H. Employee Benefit Plan
I. FL-371
J. Joinder
K. Keogh Plan
L. Pension Plan
M. FL-375
N. QDRO
O. Retirement Plan
P. Time Rule
Q. FL-374

Match the sentence with the term

1. _____ An action that joins the pension plan into the dissolution action as a party litigant. It is necessary in order for the pension plan to be subject to the orders of the court.
2. _____ A plan that is exclusively funded by an employer and is received by the employee upon retirement after working at a company for a specified number of years.
3. _____ A plan that is primarily funded by the employee but may include contributions from an employer. If the employer contributes to the plan, the employee must continue to be employed by the company for a set number of years to be able to collect the employer-contributed amount.
4. _____ A plan for employees in which the employer agrees to pay an employee a specific benefit for life, which commences at retirement.
5. _____ A plan that is based upon a formula that can include compensation and years of service as factors. The plan specifies payments in advance in accordance with a formula that comprises factors such as final compensation, age, length of service and a per-service-year multiplier.
6. _____ The Judicial Council form number for the summons used with joinder actions.
7. _____ A plan whereby the ultimate amount of the benefits to be provided at retirement will not be known until the date of retirement because they depend upon the future investment performance of the fund. The benefits are defined by a formula for contribution.
8. _____ Money that is earned by an employee and taxed when paid, which is a future date. It can be tied to a specific event and payable when that event occurs.
9. _____ A plan for employees that can include stock, profit sharing, bonuses or other incentives.

455

Chapter 23: Retirement & Disability

10. _____ A court order that requires approval from the pension plan administrator and the court in order to divide community property retirement monies between divorcing spouses. It was created by the Federal Retirement Equity Act of 1984. When the Court makes an order concerning a spouse's retirement plan and the order is prepared in the correct form, federal law requires the employer to comply with the terms of the order.
11. _____ A term used to describe a formula for determining the community interest in retirement benefits according to the ratio of the length of employment between the date of marriage (or date of commencement of employment, if later) and the date of separation to the total length of employment.
12. _____ It designated as separate property and is confirmed to the one of the spouses. It is compensation paid for income that the spouse lost or will lose due to the spouse's diminished ability to earn a living.
13. _____ The one of the two Judicial Council forms that must be used for the joinder of an employee pension benefit plan and order.
14. _____ The Judicial Council form that every notice of appearance of an employee pension benefit plan and responsive pleading must be made.
15. _____ The Judicial Council form number for the summons used with joinder actions.
16. _____ A plan that is for self-employed persons, whereby they can contribute pre-taxed money for their retirement.

CHAPTER 24: Apportionment

In Brief...

PURCHASING A HOME by borrowing the money:
- Requires a down payment on the purchase price;
- Requires that the remaining balance be secured by a mortgage loan.
- Interest is the amount that it costs to borrow the money.
- The principal is the amount of money paid toward the money borrowed or owed.
- Most loans use a simple interest method, meaning that the interest is calculated after each payment on the remaining loan balance.
- Most loans are amortization which means that each payment made over the life of the loan is an equal amount.

APPORTIONMENT is determining the community and separate interests in an asset.

FAMILY RESIDENCE:
- Is usually one of the married couple's most substantial assets; &
- Community interest & separate interests must be determined at divorce.
- **When purchased before marriage and title was changed** to joint owners after marriage:
  - The separate property interest is reimbursed to the original purchaser spouse, **FC § 2640**; and
  - No appreciation is added to the separate property reimbursement.
- **When purchased before marriage and title was not changed after marriage:**
  - There is a community property interest in the family residence if mortgage payments were paid with community property earnings;
  - A formula is used to calculate the community interest in a family residence; and
  - This formula is called the Moore/Marsden formula, after the two cases *In re Marriage of MOORE* (1980) 28 Cal.3d 366 and *In re Marriage of MARSDEN* (1982) 130 Cal.App.3d 426.

MOORE/MARSDEN FORMULA:
- Is used to calculate the community and separate property interests;
- Uses the formula determined by the court in *Moore* which uses the FMV at date of trial minus the purchase price of the home to determine the appreciation of the home;
- Was then fine-tuned by the court in *Marsden* by using only the amount that the property actually appreciated during the marriage; and
- It requires the following information to calculate:
  1. The purchase price of the home;
  2. The amount the loan principal was paid down during marriage;
  3. The fair market value of the home at date of marriage;
  4. The fair market value at the date of trial; &
  5. The down payment + principal paid before marriage + principal paid after separation.

Chapter 24: Apportionment

Introduction

The word **apportionment** refers to apportioning separate and community property, or determining what part of the property is separate property and what part is community. In some situations, it is difficult to determine the community property amount. In making this determination, tracing may be used. **Tracing** is a process used to prove a separate property claim.

The concept of apportionment is used when a home is purchased by one of the spouses prior to marriage and the couple resides in the home after marriage. After marriage, the title to the property: **(1)** is changed to joint, or **(2)** is not changed and remains in the name of the purchasing spouse. In either case, the community has an interest in the property.

Principal and Interest in a Mortgage Loan

A basic understanding of the terms **principal** and **interest** is necessary in order to understand the concepts in this section. An explanation and example follow.

When a residence or home is purchased, the purchaser makes a down payment on the purchase price and the remaining balance is secured by a mortgage loan. As with any loan, there is interest and principal. Interest is the amount that it costs to borrow the money. The principal is the actual amount of money paid toward the money borrowed or owed. Most loans use a simple interest method, meaning that the interest is calculated after each payment on the remaining loan balance. In order to understand how the community interest is determined in a residence that was purchased before marriage, a basic understanding of the home loan process is necessary. The following example should provide a basic understanding of principal and interest.

If a buyer purchased a condo for $200,000 and made a down payment of $40,000, the buyer would have to secure a loan in the amount of $160,000. If the interest rate on the simple interest loan was 4% and the loan was for 30 years, or 360 months, the buyer would make loan payments in the amount of $763.87 each month for 360 months, or 30 years. When the loan payments are all an equal amount, that is called amortizing the loan.

Chapter 24: Apportionment

Payment Number 1-360	Date Payment is Due	Amount of Payment	Amount of Payment Paid on Principal	Amount of Payment Paid for Interest	Remaining Balance after Payment
1	Jan 1, 2016	$763.86	$230.53	$533.33	$159,769.47
2	Feb 1, 2016	$763.86	$231.30	$532.56	$159,538.17
3	Mar 1, 2016	$763.86	$232.07	$531.79	$159,306.10
4	April 1, 2016	$763.86	$232.84	$531.02	$159,073.25
5	May 1, 2016	$763.86	$233.62	$530.24	$158,839.63
⋮	⋮	⋮	⋮	⋮	⋮
356	Oct 1, 2045	$763.86	$751.26	$12.60	$3,030.16
357	Nov 1, 2045	$763.86	$753.76	$10.10	$2,276.40
358	Dec 1, 2045	$763.86	$756.28	$7.59	$1,520.12
359	Jan 1, 2046	$763.86	$758.80	$5.07	$761.33
360	Feb 1, 2046	$763.86	$761.33	$2.54	$0.00

Amount paid for condo: $200,000
Amount of down payment: $40,000
Amount borrowed or amount of loan: $160,000
Interest rate: 4%
Type of interest loan: simple interest loan (the interest is calculated after each payment)
Term of loan: 30 years or 360 payments

Pursuant to the above example, the amount of interest that will be paid over the life of the loan (30 years) is $114,991.21. In other words, to borrow $160,000 for 30 years it will cost $114,991.21.

Chapter 24: Apportionment

Home Purchased Before Marriage, Title Changed During Marriage

The family residence is usually one of the married couple's most substantial assets; the other major asset is retirement. Upon divorce the community interest in the family residence must be determined. **FC § 2640** governs reimbursement for separate property contributions made to community property. "**FC § 2640** was enacted to avoid the inequity that may result in a case where property taken in joint tenancy form is divided equally between the spouses despite a showing that one spouse contributed a substantial portion of separate funds to the acquisition." *In re MARRIAGE of WALRATH* (1998) 17 Cal.4th 907 at p. 915.

FC § 2640 provides:

> **(a)** "Contributions to the acquisition of property," as used in this section, include downpayments, payments for improvements, and payments that reduce the principal of a loan used to finance the purchase or improvement of the property but do not include payments of interest on the loan or payments made for maintenance, insurance, or taxation of the property.
> **(b)** In the division of the community estate under this division, unless a party has made a written waiver of the right to reimbursement or has signed a writing that has the effect of a waiver, the party shall be reimbursed for the party's contributions to the acquisition of property of the community property estate to the extent the party traces the contributions to a separate property source. The amount reimbursed shall be without interest or adjustment for change in monetary values and may not exceed the net value of the property at the time of the division.
> **(c)** A party shall be reimbursed for the party's separate property contributions to the acquisition of property of the other spouse's separate property estate during the marriage, unless there has been a transmutation in writing pursuant to Chapter 5 (commencing with Section 850) of Part 2 of Division 4, or a written waiver of the right to reimbursement. The amount reimbursed shall be without interest or adjustment for change in monetary values and may not exceed the net value of the property at the time of the division.

The word **property** in **FC § 2640** encompasses not only the specific community property to which the separate property was originally contributed, but also any other community property that is subsequently acquired from the proceeds of the initial property, and to which the separate property contribution can be traced. **FC § 2640** envisions some tracing, and the "only exceptions to the statutory reimbursement right are a signed written waiver or a signed writing that has the effect of a waiver." *In re MARRIAGE of WALRATH, supra* at p. 918.

The court in *Walrath* stated:

> interpreting FC § 2640 to allow tracing to subsequently acquired assets is supported by important policy considerations. It encourages married persons to freely and without reservation contribute their separate property assets to benefit the community, and alleviates the need for spouses to negotiate with each other during marriage regarding continuing reimbursement rights. Under this interpretation, FC § 2640 protects the

Chapter 24: Apportionment

> general expectations of most people in marriage, i.e., that spouses will be reimbursed for significant monetary contributions to the community should the community dissolve…if both parties are entitled to reimbursement and the property has insufficient value to permit full reimbursement of both, reimbursement should be on a proportionate basis. *Id.* at p. 919, 922.

The examples given in *Walrath* clarify how the proportionate basis works.

> We emphasize that a contributing spouse cannot randomly seek reimbursement from any asset through which his or her separate property contribution has at some time passed. For example, assume prior to marriage, a husband buys a San Francisco property. After marriage, the property is placed in joint tenancy; at that time there is $ 100,000 of equity in the property. The couple immediately borrows $ 90,000, and buys a Los Angeles property. Ten years later they divorce. The San Francisco property is worth $ 500,000, and the Los Angeles property is worth nothing. Under section 2640, the husband may only be reimbursed $ 10,000 of his $ 100,000 contribution from the San Francisco property. Conversely, if the San Francisco property is worth nothing, and the Los Angeles property is worth $ 500,000, he may only be reimbursed $ 90,000 of his contribution from the Los Angeles property.
>
> [To use another example]: suppose a wife contributes $ 300,000 of her separate property so that the couple can purchase a home for the same amount. They immediately refinance, taking out a $ 200,000 30-year loan, and use this money to purchase a vacation home. After 15 years, they divorce. At this time, the original house has only $ 100,000 of equity, and most of what has been paid on the loan is interest, not principal. The vacation home still has $ 200,000 of equity. Under section 2640, the wife is reimbursed for her $ 300,000 contribution by receiving $ 100,000 from the original home, and $ 200,000 from the vacation home. The community receives nothing, and is responsible for the remaining loan obligation. The $ 300,000 contributed by the wife made the acquisition of both homes possible. She conceivably may have spent years sacrificing for and saving these funds, just as the community spent 15 years making payments on the $ 200,000 loan. There is always a risk to both the contributing party and the community that the value of the property purchased will decrease. *Id.* at p. 924.

Thus, a straight tracing is done to determine the separate property interest in a family residence purchased before marriage but transmuted into a community asset. However, it should be noted that in tracing a separate property interest, an owner may testify as to the estimated value of the property.

This estimate "may be the best that can be achieved because homeowners often do not receive copies of written appraisals at the time real property is refinanced." *In re Marriage of STOLL, supra* at p. 842. So, an owner is competent to testify as to the value of his or her own property.

Home Purchased Before Marriage, Title Not Changed

In a dissolution or legal separation, there is a community property interest in the family residence if any amount of the mortgage payment was paid with community property earnings.

Chapter 24: Apportionment

Currently, there is a formula that is used to calculate the community interest in a family residence when one party purchased a home prior to marriage in his or her own name, the couple lived in the home during the marriage and made payments on the loan with community property. This formula is called **the Moore/Marsden formula,** after the two cases *In re Marriage of MOORE* (1980) 28 Cal.3d 366 and *In re Marriage of MARSDEN* (1982) 130 Cal.App.3d 426. A shortened version of both cases follow and an explanation of the formulas used in both cases is provided after each case. Note that in both cases the court was asked to add the interest paid and the property tax on the home to the formula, and the court declined in both cases.

1. The *Moore* Case

> *In re Marriage of LYDIE D. and DAVID E. MOORE. DAVID E. MOORE, Appellant,*
> *v. LYDIE D. MOORE, Respondent*
> Supreme Court of California
> 28 Cal.3d 366; 618 P.2d 208; 168 Cal.Rptr. 662
> October 30, 1980
> (*Marriage of Moore*)
>
> David E. Moore appeals [contesting] the trial court's determination of the community property interest in the residence located at 121 Mira Way, Menlo Park.
> The principal issue to be decided in this case is the proper method of calculating the interest obtained by the community as a result of payments made during marriage on the indebtedness secured by a deed of trust on a residence which had been purchased by one of the parties before marriage.
>
> Lydie purchased the house at 121 Mira Way in Menlo Park in April 1966, about eight months before the parties' marriage. The purchase price was $ 56,640.57. Lydie made a down payment of $ 16,640.57 and secured a loan for the balance of the purchase price. She took title in her name alone as "Lydie S. Doak, a single woman." Prior to the marriage she made seven monthly payments and reduced the principal loan balance by $ 245.18.
>
> The parties lived in the house during their marriage and until their separation in June 1977. They made payments during this time with community funds and reduced the loan principal by $ 5,986.20.
>
> Lydie remained in the house and continued to make payments, reducing the principal by an additional $ 581.07 up to the time of trial. At that time the total principal paid on the purchase price was $ 23,453.02, the balance owing was $ 33,187.55, the market value of the house was $ 160,000, and the equity therein $ 126,812.45.
>
> The trial court concluded that the residence was Lydie's separate property but that the community had an interest in it by virtue of the community property payments made during the course of the parties' marriage.
>
> The community interest was calculated by multiplying the equity value of the house by the ratio of the community's reduction of principal to the total amount of principal reduction by both community and separate property ($ 5,986.20 divided by $ 23,453.02

equals 25.5242 percent). The amount of the community interest was thus determined to be $ 32,367.86.

Lydie's separate property interest was calculated by multiplying the equity value of the house by the ratio of the separate property reduction of principal to the total amount of principal reduction ($ 17,466.82 divided by $ 23,453.02 equals 74.4758 percent). Lydie's separate property interest was thus determined to be $ 94,444.59.

The parties agree that the community has acquired an interest in the house by virtue of the community funds used to make the payments. They disagree, however, as to how the interest is to be determined. Appellant contends that the community property interest should be based upon the full amount of the payments made, which includes interest, taxes and insurance, rather than only on the amount by which the payments reduce the principal.

Where community funds are used to make payments on property purchased by one of the spouses before marriage the rule developed through decisions in California gives to the community a pro tanto[1] community property interest in such property in the ratio that the payments on the purchase price with community funds bear to the payments made with separate funds. (Citations omitted.) This rule has been commonly understood as excluding payments for interest and taxes.

Appellant argues, however, that interest and taxes should be included in the computation because they often represent a substantial part of current home purchase payments. We do not agree. Since such expenditures do not increase the equity value of the property, they should not be considered in its division upon dissolution of marriage. The value of real property is generally represented by the owners' equity in it, and the equity value does not include finance charges or other expenses incurred to maintain the investment. Amounts paid for interest, taxes and insurance do not contribute to the capital investment and are not considered part of it. Upon dissolution, it is the court's duty to account for and divide the assets and the debts of the community. Payments previously made for interest, taxes and insurance are neither.

In summary, we find no basis for departing from the present rule which excludes amounts paid for interest, taxes, and insurance from the calculation of the respective separate and community interests. We turn to that calculation in this case.

In the present situation, the loan was based on separate assets and was thus a separate property contribution; the down payment was also a separate property contribution. Therefore the proceeds of the loan must be treated as a separate property contribution. Accordingly, the formula would be applied as follows:

The separate property percentage interest is determined by crediting the separate property with the down payment and the full amount of the loan less the amount by which the community property payments reduced the principal balance of the loan ($ 16,640.57 plus ($ 40,000 minus $ 5,986.20) equals $ 50,654.37).

This sum is divided by the purchase price for the separate property percentage share ($ 50,654.37 divided by $ 56,640.57 equals 89.43 percent).

---

[1] A Latin phrase meaning "for so much" or "to that extent" or "as far as it goes." Commonly associated with a partial payment on a legal claim.

Chapter 24: Apportionment

> The separate property interest would be $ 109,901.16, which represents the amount of capital appreciation attributable to the separate funds (89.43 percent of $ 103,359.43) added to the amount of equity paid by separate funds ($ 17,466.82).
>
> The community property percentage interest is found by dividing the amount by which community property payments reduced the principal by the purchase price ($ 5,986.20 divided by $ 56,640.57 equals 10.57 percent).
>
> The community property share would be $ 16,911.29, which represents the amount of capital appreciation attributable to community funds (10.57 percent of $ 103,359.43) added to the amount of equity paid by community funds ($ 5,986.20).
>
> The portion of the judgment determining the rights of the parties in and awarding the community property is reversed with directions to redetermine the amount. The judgment is affirmed in all other respects.

2. The *Moore* formula:

(1) The purchase price of the home: $56,640.57
(2) The amount the loan principal was paid down during the marriage with community property: $5,986.20
(3) The fair market value of the home at date of marriage: (price paid was used) $56,640.57
(4) The fair market value at the date of trial: $160,000
(5) The down payment amount, the principal paid down before marriage and principal paid after separation: $16,640.57 + $245.18 + $581.07 = $17,466.25.

Community interest

Principal paid by community property $5986.20 = .1057 (fraction) or 10.57% of community in home.
Purchase price was $56640.37.

Fraction (.1057) is multiplied by the total appreciation of the home: $103,359.43; .1057 X $103,359.43 = $10,925.09

Community interest is $10,925.09 plus amount paid on the principal with community property:
$10,925.09 + $5,986.20 = $16,911.29

Separate interest

Down-payment plus+ loan amount minus– Principal paid by community:
$16,640.57   + $40,000   - $5,986.20 = $50,654.37

$50,654.37 = .8943 (fraction).
$56,640.57

Total appreciation is FMV -minus purchase price:
$160,000   − 56640.57 = $103,359.43

Fraction of interest multiplied by appreciation during marriage:
.8943   X $103,359.43 = $92,434.34..

Percent share +plus total amount of separate property paid equals the separate property interest:
$92,434.34   + $17,466.25   = $ 109,901.16.

Wife's total interest including ½ of community property interest: $109,901.16 + $8,455.65 = $118,356.81.

3. The *Marsden* Case

> *In re Marriage of NANCY E. and SULLIVAN S. MARSDEN. NANCY E. MARSDEN, Respondent, v. SULLIVAN S. MARSDEN, Appellant*
> Court of Appeal of California, First Appellate District, Division Three
> 130 Cal.App.3d 426; 181 Cal.Rptr. 910
> April 1, 1982
> (*Marriage of Marsden*)
>
> In 1962, husband paid to Stanford University $ 6,300 for an 80-year lease of a parcel of property owned by Stanford. That same year, he had a house constructed on the property which he financed by a $ 2,000 cash payment and the proceeds from a $ 30,000 loan from Stanford. Thus, the cost of the property in 1962 was $ 38,300.
> By the time the parties were married in February 1971, husband had reduced the loan by $ 7,000, so the outstanding balance was $ 23,000. During the marriage, payments from community funds further reduced the principal due on the loan by $ 9,200. Between the time of separation in July 1978 and trial in February 1979, husband paid $ 655 on the principal.
>
> The trial court found the fair market value (FMV) of the house and leasehold interest was $ 65,000 at the time of the marriage in February 1971 and $ 182,500 at the time of trial. It computed the appreciation as "$ 136,700 [sic; $ 126,700]", the difference between the equity at the time of trial ($ 182,500 less a loan balance of $ 13,800 equals $ 168,700) and the equity in 1971 ($ 65,000 less the $ 23,000 loan balance equals "$ 32,000 [sic; $ 42,000]"). It then allocated "$ 77,632 [sic; $ 71,953]" as the community interest based on the ratio of separate property loan payments ($ 7,000 or 43.21 percent) to the community property loan payments ($ 9,200 or 56.79 percent). This was clearly in error.
>
> Where community funds are used to make payments on property purchased by one of the spouses before marriage 'the rule developed through decisions in California gives to the community a pro tanto community property interest in such property in the ratio that the payments on the purchase price with community funds bear to the payments made with separate funds. (Citations omitted.) In clarifying the application of the rule, the Supreme Court has recently reaffirmed a formula to determine the respective community and separate interests in the property. The formula gives recognition to the economic value of any loan proceeds contributed toward the purchase of the property. Where, as in Moore and in the case before us, the loan was extended before marriage and was based on

Chapter 24: Apportionment

separate assets, it is a separate property contribution. The Moore court also negated the inclusion of such expenses as loan interest and taxes in the computation.

Under the formula, husband's separate property percentage interest is determined by crediting the separate property with the down payments and the full amount of the loan, less the amount by which the community property payments reduced the principal balance of the loan ($ 8,300) plus ($ 30,000 less $ 9,200) equals $ 29,100). This sum is divided by the purchase price for the separate property percentage share ($ 29,100 divided by $ 38,300 equals 75.98 percent). The community property percentage interest is found by dividing the community property payments on the loan principal by the purchase price ($ 9,200 divided by $ 38,300 equals 24.02 percent).

Husband contends, and we agree, that he should have the benefit of approximately nine years of appreciation in the value of the property before the marriage in 1971. Husband argues that his separate property percentage interest should be 85.85 percent, based on the FMV[2] of the property at the time of marriage ($ 65,000), rather than the purchase price in 1962 ($ 38,300).

The fair market value at or near the time of purchase is usually equivalent to the purchase price. In short, the appraised value equals the cost value. Such was the case in Moore, where the respondent wife had purchased the property eight months before the marriage, and thus no question of the fair market value of the home at the time of marriage was posed.

Where the separate property is owned for a considerable period before marriage, the increase in value in an inflationary market, such as we have had for the past several decades, is substantial. The fair market value at the time of marriage would usually be significantly greater than the purchase price, and this is true in the case before us. We think it is equitable to credit the separate property interest with this prenuptial appreciation. As previously stated, the Moore court in explaining the pro tanto allocation rule noted the direction in Bare to the trial court to determine the increase in equity in the house during marriage and the fair market value of it before and after the marriage . . . . (Citations omitted.)

We therefore compute the pro tanto community and separate property interests in the house and leasehold interest as follows:

Purchase price in 1962		$ 38,300.00	
Less community payments		9,200.00	(24.02%)
Separate property interest		$ 29,100.00	(75.98%)
FMV at time of trial		$ 182,500.00	
Less purchase price	$ 38,300.00		
Appreciation before marriage	26,700.00	65,000.00	
Appreciation during marriage		$ 117,500.00	
Separate property interest:			
Down payments	$ 8,300.00		

---

[2] "FMV" means fair market value.

Chapter 24: Apportionment

Loan payments			
Before marriage	7,000.00		
After separation	655.00		
		$ 15,955.00	
Appreciation before marriage		26,700.00	
75.98% of appreciation after marriage		89,276.50	
			$ 131,931.50
Community property interest:			
Loan payments		$ 9,200.00	
24.02% of appreciation after marriage		28,223.50	
			37,423.50
Balance on loan at time of trial			13,145.00
			$ 182,500.00

Based upon the above computations, the trial court should have awarded husband a separate property interest of $ 131,931.50, plus one-half of the community interest, or $ 18,711.75, for a total of $ 150,643.25. The wife's one-half share of the community interest is $ 18,711.75, and husband, of course, is responsible for the balance due on the loan.

The judgment is reversed insofar as it determines the respective interest of the parties in the house.

4. The *Marsden* formula:

(1) The purchase price of the home: $38,300
(2) The amount the loan principal was paid down during marriage with community property: $9,200
(3) The fair market value (FMV) of the home at date of marriage=(price +appreciation before marriage): $38,300+$26,700= $65,000
(4) The FMV at the date of trial: $182,500
(5) The down payment amount, the principal paid down before marriage and principal paid after separation: $8300+$7000+$655=$15955.

Community interest

Principal paid during marriage $9,200 = .2402 or 24.02%
Purchase price $38,300.

The percent .2402 is multiplied by the appreciation of the home: $182,500:
.2402 X $182500 = $117,500; $117,500 is the appreciation during marriage

.2404 X $117,500 = $28,223.50:
Add the principal paid down during marriage $9200+ appreciation during marriage $28223.50:

Chapter 24: Apportionment

$9200+$28223.50= $37,423.50.

$37,423.50 is the amount of the community interest;
½ of community to each spouse or $18,711.75 to each spouse

Separate interest

Purchase price subtract principal paid by the community $38,300 minus $9200 = $29,100 and the
Purchase price is $38,300:
$\frac{$29,100}{$38,300}$ = .7598 is the fraction or percent of interest.

FMV at date of trial -minus FMV at date of marriage = appreciation during the marriage: $182,500 - $65,000   = $117,500.

Percent of interest multiplied by the appreciation during marriage = Separate property share of appreciation: .7598   X $117,500   = $89,276.50.

Separate property share of the appreciation before the marriage + the appreciation before the marriage + all separate property paid:
$89,276.50 + $26,700 + $15955 = $131,931.50.
Husband's total interest including ½ of community is $131,931.50 + $18,711.75 =$150,643.25.

5. The Moore/Marsden Formula

The court in *Moore* used the FMV at date of trial minus the purchase price of the home to determine the appreciation of the home. The court in *Marsden* refined the formula by using only the amount that the property actually appreciated during the marriage. Thus, the Moore formula, fine-tuned by the *Marsden* case became the Moore/Marsden formula. This formula is currently used to determine separate and community interest when the home was purchased before marriage by one of the spouses and the title was never changed to add the other spouse. It is especially important for the paralegal to understand this formula and be able to discern what information is needed for the formula because the paralegal is the person who gathers the client's information. In order use the Moore/Marsden formula, the following information must be obtained:

(1) The purchase price of the home;
(2) The amount the loan principal was paid down during marriage with community property;
(3) The fair market value of the home at date of marriage;
(4) The fair market value at the date of trial; and
(5) The down payment amount, the principal paid down before marriage and principal paid after separation.

Chapter 24: Apportionment

EDUCATIONAL EXERCISES

I. Answer the following:

Explain what the Marsden court changed with regard to a formula to determine community interest in a home purchased before marriage.

II. Name that Case - Chapters 20-24

Use the brief description of the important cases in Chapters 20-24 below to name the case. The list of cases follows the descriptions.

1. When community property is used to buy a Ferrari, the Ferrari is community property. **Name that case:**

2. When both parties are putative spouses, the property acquired during the invalid marriage is quasi-marital property. **Name that case:**

3. Liabilities that were incurred after the date of marriage but before separation that have benefited the community estate are a community liability. **Name that case:**

4. Property acquired after separation is separate property, including spousal support. **Name that case:**

5. One method of determining the amount of community property allocates a fair rate of return on the separate property investment. By the process of elimination, any excess in value over the amount allocated as separate property is community property arising from the spouse's labor and efforts. **Name that case:**

6. Where the separate property is owned for a considerable period before marriage, the increase in value in an inflationary market is credited to the separate property interest. **Name that case:**

7. The court has jurisdiction to order reimbursement in cases in which it deems appropriate for debts paid after separation but before trial. FC § 2626. **Name that case:**

8. If a party chooses to collect disability instead of retirement, the entire amount is not separate property. **Name that case:**

9. Where community funds are used to make payments on property purchased by one of the spouses before marriage the rule developed through decisions in California gives to the community a pro tanto community property interest in such property in the ratio that the

Chapter 24: Apportionment

payments on the purchase price with community funds bear to the payments made with separate funds. This rule has been commonly understood as excluding payments for interest and taxes.
Name that case:

10. One approach that determines the amount of community property is how much the owner spouse's effort and labor is worth, and that figure is the community property, with the balance of the increase in value being characterized as separate property by process of elimination.
Name that case:

11. If a spouse, who has the exclusive use a community asset, is paying a lesser amount than the fair market value of that asset, then he or she may be charged the difference between the amount paid and the fair market value. **Name that case:**

List of possible cases for the descriptions above.

1. *In re Marriage of BELL* (1996) 49 Cal.App.4th 300; 56 Cal.Rptr.2d 623
2. *In re Marriage of EPSTEIN* (1979) 24 Cal.3d 76; 592 P.2d 1165; 154 Cal.Rptr. 413
3. *In re Marriage of MARSDEN* (1982) 130 Cal.App.3d 426; 181 Cal.Rptr. 910
4. *In re Marriage of MOORE* (1980) 28 Cal.3d 366; 618 P.2d 208; 168 Cal.Rptr. 662
5. *In re Marriage of MUELLER* (1977) 70 Cal.App.3d 66; 137 Cal.Rptr. 129
6. *In re Marriage of SHELTON* (1981) 118 Cal.App.3d 811; 173 Cal.Rptr. 629
7. *VAN CAMP v. VAN CAMP* (1921) 53 Cal.App. 17; 199 P. 885
8. *In re Marriage of TEJEDA* (2009) 179 Cal.App.4th 973; 102 Cal.Rptr.3d 361
9. *In re Marriage of WALL* (1972) 29 Cal.App.3d 76; 105 Cal.Rptr. 201
10. *In re Marriage of WATTS* (1985) 171 Cal.App.3d 366; 217 Cal.Rptr. 301
11. *PEREIRA v. PEREIRA* (1909) 156 Cal. 1; 103 P. 488

CHAPTER 25: Degrees of Proof & Presumptions

In Brief...

THERE ARE 3 LEVELS OF PROOF, Evid. Code § 502:
1. **Preponderance of the evidence:**
   - Means evidence that has more convincing force than that opposed to it;
   - Refers to lowest degree of proof necessary to prove a proposition in a civil or family law matter; and
   - Provides that a party must demonstrate that his or her version of the facts, causes, damages or fault is more likely true than not true.
2. **Clear and convincing proof:**
   - Is a medium-level of proof;
   - Is evidence of such convincing force that it demonstrates high probability of the truth of the facts for which it is offered as proof;
   - Is the level of proof used in cases regarding deeds;
   - Is evidence that is substantially, more likely to be true; and
   - Is employed in both civil and criminal trials.
3. **Beyond a reasonable doubt:**
   - Is the greatest degree of proof; and
   - Is only used in criminal matters.

AN INFERENCE:
- Is a deduction of fact;
- May logically and reasonably be drawn from another fact or group of facts found or otherwise established in the action. **Evid. Code § 600(a).**

PRESUMPTIONS, **there are 2 types:**
1. **REBUTTABLE PRESUMPTIONS:**
   - Are rules of law that permit a court to assume that facts are true until such time as there is a level of proof that rebuts or disproves the presumption, **Evid. Code § 600**;
   - Are based upon a particular set of apparent facts paired with established laws, logic, reasoning or individual rights;
   - Are NOT evidence; and
   - **There are two kinds:**
     1. **Presumptions that affect the burden of producing evidence** means that there is an obligation of a party to introduce evidence sufficient to avoid a ruling against him or her on the issue, **Evid. Code § 110**; and
     2. **Presumptions that affect the burden of proof** are presumptions established to implement some public policy other than to facilitate the determination of the particular action in which the presumption is applied, such as the policy in favor of establishment of a parent and child relationship, the validity of marriage, the stability of titles to property, or the security of

> those who entrust themselves or their property to the administration of others. **Evid. Code § 605**.
> 2. **CONCLUSIVE PRESUMPTIONS:**
>   - Cannot be rebutted or disproved, regardless of the evidence presented, **Evid. Code § 620**.
>   - It is a conclusive presumption that decedent would have outlived the killer when decedent and the killer co-own property. **Probate Code § 251**; *ABBEY v. LORD* (1959) 168 Cal.App.2d 499; 336 P.2d 226.
>   - **FC § 7540** provides that the child of spouses who cohabited at the time of conception and birth is conclusively presumed to be a child of the marriage.

Introduction

There are three degrees of proof that may be required to prove a claim legally: **(1)** preponderance, **(2)** clear and convincing and **(3)** beyond a reasonable doubt. However, only the first two are used in family law matters.

A presumption is a rule of law that allows a court to assume facts are true until such time as there is a preponderance (greater weight) of evidence that rebuts or disproves the presumption. Each presumption is based upon a particular set of apparent facts paired with established laws, logic, reasoning or individual rights. If a presumption is rebuttable, it can be refuted by evidence that is more likely than not (preponderance) or very likely to be true (clear and convincing). If a presumption is conclusive there is no amount of evidence that can be presented that will rebut the presumption.

Degrees of Proof

Pursuant to **Evid. Code § 502**, there are three (3) levels of proof:

1. Preponderance of the Evidence

A preponderance of the evidence refers to lowest degree of proof necessary to prove a proposition in a civil or family law matter. Demonstrating that a party's version of the facts, causes, damages or fault by a preponderance of the evidence requires demonstrating that the evidence presented is more likely true than not true.

To prove a fact by a preponderance of the evidence, a party must demonstrate that his or her version of the facts, causes, damages or fault is more likely true than not true.

> Preponderance of the evidence means evidence that has more convincing force than that opposed to it. If the evidence is so evenly balanced that you are unable to say that the evidence on either side of an issue preponderates, your finding on that issue must be

> against the party who had the burden of proving it. *GLAGE v. HAWES FIREARMS COMPANY* (1990) 226 Cal.App.3d 314, footnote 7 p. 324.

2. Clear and Convincing Proof

A clear and convincing level of proof is a medium-level of proof. In order to meet the standard and prove a proposition by clear and convincing evidence, a party must prove that it is substantially, more likely to be true.

> "Clear and convincing" evidence means evidence of such convincing force that it demonstrates, in contrast to the opposing evidence, a high probability of the truth of the facts for which it is offered as proof. Such evidence requires a higher standard of proof than proof by a preponderance of the evidence. *MATTCO FORGE, INC. v. ARTHUR YOUNG & CO.* (1997) 52 Cal.App.4th 820 at p. 848.

It is employed in both civil and criminal trials.

3. Beyond a Reasonable Doubt

This is the greatest degree of proof. It is only used in criminal matters.

Presumptions

> **(a)** A presumption is an assumption of fact that the law requires to be made from another fact or group of facts found or otherwise established in the action. A presumption is not evidence.
> **(b)** An inference is a deduction of fact that may logically and reasonably be drawn from another fact or group of facts found or otherwise established in the action. Evidence Code § 600(a).

A presumption is either conclusive or rebuttable. **Evid. Code § 601**.

1. Rebuttable Presumptions

"A statute providing that a fact or group of facts is prima facie evidence of another fact establishes a rebuttable presumption." **Evid. Code § 602**.

"Every rebuttable presumption is either (a) a presumption affecting the burden of producing evidence or (b) a presumption affecting the burden of proof." **Evid. Code § 601**.

a. A Presumption Affecting the Burden of Producing Evidence

"A presumption affecting the burden of producing evidence is a presumption established to implement no public policy other than to facilitate the determination of the particular action in which the presumption is applied." **Evid. Code § 603**.

Chapter 25: Degrees of Proof & Presumptions

The burden of producing evidence as to a particular fact is: **(1)** on the party against whom a finding on the fact would be required in the absence of further evidence; or **(2)** The burden of producing evidence as to a particular fact is initially on the party with the burden of proof as to that fact. **Evid. Code § 550**.

> The effect of a **presumption affecting the burden of producing evidence** is to require the trier of fact to assume the existence of the presumed fact unless and until evidence is introduced which would support a finding of its nonexistence, in which case the trier of fact shall determine the existence or nonexistence of the presumed fact from the evidence and without regard to the presumption. Nothing in this section shall be construed to prevent the drawing of any inference that may be appropriate. (Emphasis added.) Evid. Code § 604.

b. A Presumption Affecting the Burden of Proof

> A **presumption affecting the burden of proof** is a presumption established to implement some public policy other than to facilitate the determination of the particular action in which the presumption is applied, such as the policy in favor of establishment of a parent and child relationship, the validity of marriage, the stability of titles to property, or the security of those who entrust themselves or their property to the administration of others. Evid. Code § 605. (Emphasis added.)

The effect of a presumption affecting the burden of proof is to impose upon the party against whom it operates the burden of proof as to the nonexistence of the presumed fact. **Evid. Code § 606**.

c. Presumptions in the Law

FC § 2581 provides in pertinent part:

> For the purpose of division of property on dissolution of marriage or legal separation of the parties, property acquired by the parties during marriage in joint form, including property held in tenancy in common, joint tenancy, or tenancy by the entirety, or as community property, is **presumed to be community property**. (Emphasis added.)

In *In re Marriage of FOSSUM* (2011) 192 Cal.App.4th 336 the husband and the wife purchased a house. To obtain the best interest rate, the property was purchased in the husband's name alone, but later title was placed in both spouses' names. Thereafter the parties decided to refinance the home and once again the wife quitclaimed the home to the husband. The husband never restored the wife's name to the title. Because there is a presumption that property purchased while married is community property and the husband failed to rebut the presumption, the trial court determined the house was community property. *Id.* at 339.

FC § 2641 provides in pertinent part:

> **(c)** The reimbursement and assignment required by this section shall be reduced or modified to the extent circumstances render such a disposition unjust, including, but not

Chapter 25: Degrees of Proof & Presumptions

> limited to, any of the following:
> **(1)** The community has substantially benefited from the education, training, or loan incurred for the education or training of the party. There is a **rebuttable presumption, affecting the burden of proof**, that the community has not substantially benefited from community contributions to the education or training made less than 10 years before the commencement of the proceeding, and that the community has substantially benefited from community contributions to the education or training made more than 10 years before the commencement of the proceeding. (Emphasis added.)

In *In re Marriage of WEINER* (2003) 105 Cal.App.4th 235 the husband graduated from medical school in 1991. Two years later, in 1993, Husband and the wife were married. Eight years later the couple separated. They had no children. During the marriage the couple paid a total of $12,217.14 on loans the husband had incurred while in medical school. The husband presented evidence his medical education provided him with monthly allotments which increased to $1,000 a month and annual bonuses of $15,000, neither of which would have been paid to him by the Navy if he had not been a doctor. The Appellate court stated that given that evidence, the husband was entitled to a determination by the trial court as to whether he had overcome the presumption set forth in **FC § 2641(c)(1)**, that the community had not substantially benefited from his medical school education. If on remand such a benefit is found, the trial court must then determine under **FC § 2641(c)**, whether it is just to require that he reimburse the community for all of its educational loan payments. *Id.* at p. 241.

FC § 3103 in pertinent part provides:

> (d) There is a **rebuttable presumption** affecting the burden of proof that the visitation of a grandparent is not in the best interest of a minor child if the child's parents agree that the grandparent should not be granted visitation rights. (Emphasis added.)

In the case that follows the court discusses presumptions and the degree of proof that is required to rebut a presumption.

> ***CAROL RICH, Plaintiff and Appellant, v. ROCHELLE THATCHER, Defendant and Respondent.***
> COURT OF APPEAL OF CALIFORNIA, SECOND APPELLATE DISTRICT, DIVISION SIX
> 200 Cal.App.4th 1176; 132 Cal.Rptr.3d 897
> November 14, 2011, Filed
> (*Rich v. Thatcher*)
>
> In December 2006 Rochelle Thatcher (mother) gave birth to grandchild. The father was grandmother's son. Mother and father were not married. Mother has physical custody of grandchild. Grandmother and mother "do not get along." Among other disputes, they have differences of opinion concerning father's long-term use of drugs. Father died in 2010 of a drug overdose and left two suicide notes. Grandmother disputed the coroner's determination of death by suicide and told the coroner that mother may have been responsible for his death. Their hostility is open and clear.

Father had previously filed a "Petition to Establish Parental Relationship" and grandmother petitioned for joinder. Grandmother claimed that she should be joined in the action "to assert her visitation rights" pursuant to section 3102. Mother opposed joinder and grandparent visitation. The trial court granted the petition for joinder.

In June 2010 the trial court conducted a lengthy evidentiary hearing on visitation. The trial court denied grandmother's request for visitation. The court stated that its decision was based on "[d]eclarations of the parties and witnesses" and on testimony at the hearing. It expressed "great concern over [grandmother's] veracity." It also noted that, although grandmother had shown that she had a relationship with grandchild, she had failed to show "a deep and abiding relationship." The trial court found that "Grandmother's relationship with [grandchild] was rather limited to interaction with [grandchild] during [grandchild's] supervised visits with Father, largely due to the fact that Grandmother was the court-appointed supervisor for Father's visits with [grandchild]."

The trial court summarized the relevant law as follows: "The case law applicable to FC § 3102 requires the Court to apply a rebuttable presumption that a fit parent will act in the best interest of her child. This presumption can only be overcome by clear and convincing evidence that denial of the grandparent visitation would be detrimental to the child."

The court concluded: "[N]o evidence was presented to the Court to suggest that Mother is an unfit parent. As such, the Court ... finds that Grandmother has not provided clear and convincing evidence to rebut the presumption that Mother is acting in the best interest of [grandchild] in denying visitation to Grandmother at this time or that denial of visitation with Grandmother would be detrimental to [grandchild]." The court went on to find that, regardless of whether the "detrimental" requirement was satisfied, the granting of visitation to grandmother would not be in grandchild's best interest: "Even if the Court were to find that Grandmother had overcome the presumption by clear and convincing evidence that denial of the visitation by Grandmother was detrimental to [grandchild], the Court hereby finds that it would not be in [grandchild's] best interest to interject court-ordered visitation with Grandmother, particularly in light of the longstanding animosity between Mother and Grandmother."

"Grandparents' rights to court-ordered visitation with their grandchildren are purely statutory. " (*In re Marriage of Harris* (2004) 34 Cal.4th 210, 219 [17 Cal.Rptr.3d 842, 96 P.3d 141].) The applicable statute here, FC § 3102, provides in relevant part: "(a) If either parent of an unemancipated minor child is deceased, the ... parents ... of the deceased parent may be granted reasonable visitation with the child during the child's minority upon a finding that the visitation would be in the best interest of the minor child."

Courts have construed FC § 3102 as requiring a rebuttable presumption in favor of a fit surviving parent's decision that grandparent visitation would not be in the best interest of the child.

Grandmother contends that the trial court erred in applying the clear and convincing burden. We disagree with her and agree with the trial court's legal conclusion. We hold as follows: To overcome the presumption that a fit parent will act in the best interest of the grandchild, a grandparent has the burden of proof and must show, by clear and convincing evidence that denial of visitation is not in the best interest of the grandchild, i.e., denial of visitation would be detrimental to the grandchild. The fair import of the word "detriment" is damage, harm, or loss. If grandparent visitation is in the grandchild's "best interest," it is not "detrimental." If grandparent visitation is not in the grandchild's

Chapter 25: Degrees of Proof & Presumptions

> "best interest," it is "detrimental." (*In re Randalynne G.* (2002) 97 Cal.App.4th 1156, 1169 [118 Cal.Rptr.2d 880].)
>
> "The degree of burden of proof applied in a particular situation is an expression of the degree of confidence society wishes to require of the resolution of a question of fact. (*In re Marriage of Peters* (1997) 52 Cal.App.4th 1487, 1490 [61 Cal.Rptr.2d 493].) There is no question that a grandparent has an important interest in visiting with a grandchild. But the higher degree of the burden of proof that we adopt simply demonstrates that there is a preference in favor of the presumably correct choice of a fit sole surviving parent. Such a choice is "first."
>
> Grandmother has not fully developed an argument that the trial court reasonably concluded that visitation would not be in grandchild's best interest. Nine witnesses testified at the hearing on the visitation issue, but grandmother does not specifically discuss their testimony, which the trial court considered. Instead she refers only to her own testimony, which the trial court impliedly, if not expressly, disbelieved.
>
> The judgment (order denying grandparent visitation) is affirmed.

FC § 4325 provides in pertinent part:

> In any proceeding for dissolution of marriage where there is a criminal conviction for an act of domestic violence perpetrated by one spouse against the other spouse entered by the court within five years prior to the filing of the dissolution proceeding, or at any time thereafter, there shall be a **rebuttable presumption affecting the burden of proof** that any award of temporary or permanent spousal support to the abusive spouse otherwise awardable pursuant to the standards of this part should not be made. (Emphasis added.)

In *In re Marriage of KELKAR* (2014) 229 Cal.App.4th 833 the wife pleaded no contest and was convicted of an act of domestic violence before the enactment of **FC § 4325**. The appellate court in affirming the trial court's decision terminating the wife's support stated that **FC § 4325** must be given retroactive application, the stipulated judgment was modifiable, and the doctrines of res judicata, waiver, and equitable estoppel did not bar the application of the presumption of **FC § 4325**.

FC § 4057 provides that the amount of child support established by the formula set forth at **FC § 4055(a)** is **presumed** to be the correct amount of child support to be court ordered.

In re Marriage of GIGLIOTTI (1995) 33 Cal.App.4th 518; 39 Cal.Rptr. 2d 367 the court reduced the statewide uniform guideline child support amount of $717 by $266.67 without complying with the provisions of **FC § 4056(a)**. The appellate court reversed the decision of the trial court upholding the presumption that the guideline amount was the correct amount.

Chapter 25: Degrees of Proof & Presumptions

2. Conclusive Presumptions

A conclusive presumption cannot be rebutted or disproved, regardless of the evidence presented.

Probate Code § 251 provides:

> A joint tenant who feloniously and intentionally kills another joint tenant thereby effects a severance of the interest of the decedent so that the share of the decedent passes as the decedent's property and the killer has no rights by survivorship.

It is a conclusive presumption that decedent would have outlived the killer. *ABBEY v. LORD* (1959) 168 Cal.App.2d 499; 336 P.2d 226.

In *Estate of CASTIGLIONI* (1995) 40 Cal.App.4th 367 after the wife and the husband married, the husband put all of his separate property in joint tenancy with the wife. After 5 years of marriage, the wife murdered the husband. The wife was convicted of first-degree murder. Because there is a conclusive presumption that the deceased joint tenant would have survived the killer, the killer had no rights of survivorship. The property passed as though the wife predeceased her husband. *Id.* at 369.

FC § 7540 provides that "the child of spouses who cohabited at the time of conception and birth is conclusively presumed to be a child of the marriage." In the case that follows, the court upheld this conclusive presumption set forth in **FC § 7540**.

> ***MICHELLE W., a Minor, etc., et al., Plaintiffs and Appellants, v. RONALD W. et al., Defendants and Respondents***
> Supreme Court of California
> 39 Cal.3d 354; 703 P.2d 88; 216 Cal.Rptr. 748
> August 5, 1985
> (*Michelle W. v. Ronald W.*)
>
> Defendants Ronald and Judith W. were married on May 7, 1965, and lived together as husband and wife until their separation approximately 12 years later. Judith gave birth to two daughters, Tamara and Michelle, who were raised as the children of that marriage. During the marriage to Judith, Ronald W. provided the necessary support for the children.
>
> As the father of Tamara and Michelle, he tended, nurtured and loved them and received affection from them. Through their daily interchanges with Ronald and Judith, Tamara and Michelle were provided with the security, as well as the restraints, they needed for their growth and development.
>
> Donald R., the second claimant to the paternity of Michelle, met Judith in 1973. Donald R. and Judith began having sexual relations in that year, although Judith and Ronald W. were married and living together. On October 24, 1974, Judith gave birth to Michelle. Donald R. did not claim paternity at the time of birth nor thereafter for four years while Judith and Ronald W. remained married and continued to live together. Donald R.

asserted no claim nor accepted any responsibility. Throughout that time, without objection from Donald R., the obligation of parenting was fulfilled by Ronald W.

When Ronald and Judith W. separated they executed a marriage settlement agreement; Ronald was granted custody of Tamara, Michelle's sister, and Judith custody of Michelle, by then nearly five years of age. The issue of paternity was not raised. Ronald's obligation to provide child support for Michelle was also not at issue; it was agreed upon.

Following the dissolution of their marriage, Ronald W. regularly and continually exercised his visitation rights with Michelle. In November 1980, when Donald R. married Judith, Ronald W. was refused further visitation. That right was restored when he threatened court action to enforce the settlement agreement. Since Judith's marriage to Donald R., Michelle has lived in Donald R.'s home and he has held her out to be his natural child.

In March 1981, this action to establish paternity was brought by Donald R. and Michelle, age six, through her guardian ad litem. Upon the uncontradicted facts that Ronald W. and Judith were living together as a married couple for nine years before Michelle's birth and that Ronald W. was neither impotent nor sterile, the trial court applied the presumption of Evid. Code § 621[1] and established that Ronald W. is the father of Michelle. Plaintiffs appeal.

The presumption of paternity established by Evid. Code § 621 is limited. The following prerequisites must be satisfied: first, the child's mother must be married; second, the mother must be cohabiting with her husband; third, the husband must be neither impotent nor sterile; fourth, two years must have passed since the birth of the child and during those two years the husband -- or the mother in conjunction with the putative father -- must have failed to rebut the presumption in court.

Plaintiffs assert alternative grounds for holding Evid. Code § 621 unconstitutional. First, Evid. Code § 621 prevents them from establishing the biological parent-child relationship in a court of law, thus depriving them of a liberty interest protected by the due process clause. Second, the gender-based classification of the statute which accords the natural father fewer procedural protections than the married natural mother violates the equal protection guarantee of the California and United States Constitutions. In addition, they argue that the classifications in the statute deny them a fundamental right and thus the law should be strictly scrutinized.

This is not a case where the state has attempted to intervene or to prevent the establishment of a relationship between putative father and child. Rather, Donald R. seeks a determination that he is Michelle's "legal" father, notwithstanding the established and continuing emotional and financial father-daughter relationship between Michelle and Ronald.

We turn to the interests of the state. Numerous policy considerations have been cited in favor of a conclusive presumption of paternity, including certain social policies upholding the integrity of the family and protecting the child's welfare.

---

[1] Evid. Code § 621 was repealed in 1993 and enacted as FC § 7540 in 1994 without substantial change. FC § 7540 was repealed effective January 1, 2019 and a new FC § 7540 became effective January 1, 2019.

Here, Donald R.'s private interest in establishing a biological relationship in a court of law is overridden by the substantial state interests in familial stability and the welfare of the child.

Accordingly, the application of Evid. Code § 621 to the instant case comported with the requirement of due process of law.

Given the facts that Michelle has a legal father and that he opposes this attempt to have Donald R. declared the biological father, we are unpersuaded that a judicial juggling of Michelle's family relationships is warranted by her abstract interest in establishing paternity.

Evid. Code § 621 allows the natural mother of the child to bring a suit to rebut the presumption that her husband is the child's father. Plaintiffs claim that this constitutes an impermissible gender-based distinction because the putative father is not allowed to rebut the presumption. We disagree.

Evid. Code § 621(d) states: "The notice of motion for blood tests under subdivision (b) may be raised by the mother of the child not later than two years from the date of birth if the child's biological father has filed an affidavit with the court acknowledging paternity of the child." We note that the plain word of the statute indicates that the rights of the natural married mother and the natural unwed father are conditioned upon each other.

Thus, we fail to find that the statutory scheme, as interpreted by the courts and as applied to plaintiffs' case, violates the guarantee of equal protection of the laws.

The judgment is affirmed.

Chapter 25: Degrees of Proof & Presumptions

EDUCATIONAL EXERCISES

I. Answer the following questions

1. What is the difference between a rebuttable and a conclusive presumption?
2. What is the presumption if separate and community funds have been comingled after marriage but before separation? Is the presumption rebuttable or conclusive?
3. What are the degrees of proof?
4. What degrees of proof are used in family law?

Fill in the blanks using the Word List that follows

1. _____ includes all types of proof that are presented at a hearing or trial; it is intended to sway a judge toward a specific conclusion.
2. A _____ of the evidence refers to lowest degree of proof necessary to prove a proposition in a civil or family law matter.
3. "A presumption affecting the ___ ___ ___ (3 words together) evidence is a presumption established to implement no public policy other than to facilitate the determination of the particular action in which the presumption is applied." Evid. Code § 603.
4. The ___ ___ ___ (3 words together) evidence as to a particular fact is initially on the party with the burden of proof as to that fact.
5. A presumption is either _____ or rebuttable. Evid. Code § 601.
6. "A statute providing that a fact or group of facts is prima facie evidence of another fact establishes a _____ presumption." Evid. Code § 602.
7. ___ ___ ___ (3 words together counting the "A") doubt is the ___ ___ (2 words together) of proof. It is only used in ___ ___ ___ (2 words together).
8. There are two types of _____.
9. There are three ___ ___ ___ (3 words together).
10. FC § 7540 provides that "the child of a wife cohabiting with her husband, who is not impotent or sterile, is _____ presumed to be a child of the marriage."
11. ___ ___ ___ (3 words together) proof is a medium level of proof.
12. An _____ is a deduction of fact; that may logically and reasonably be drawn from another fact or group of facts found or otherwise established in the action. Evid. Code § 600(a).
13. If a presumption is rebuttable, it can be refuted by evidence that is ___ ___ ___ ___ ___ (4 words together).
14. If a presumption is conclusive there is ___ ___ ___ ___ (4 words together) that can be presented that will rebut the presumption.

Word List

Beyond a reasonable
Burden of producing
Burden of proof
Clear and convincing
Conclusive
Conclusively
Criminal matters
Evidence
Greatest degree
Inference
Medium level
More likely than not
No amount of evidence
Preponderance
Presumptions
Rebuttable

CHAPTER 26: The Hearing

In Brief...

THE REQUEST FOR ORDER, (RFO):
- Is made on a *FL-300*;
- Requires all parties and attorneys to meet and confer prior to the filing, **CRC Rule 5.98(a)**;
- Requires that the *RFO* and the supporting papers state facts sufficient enough to give notice what is being requested;
- Requires a completed *FL-150* to be filed if there are financial issues;
- Requires all moving/supporting papers be filed and served in accordance with **CCP § 1005**;
- Requires the moving party to file, obtain a court date, and serve all of the documents filed with the court to the responding party;
- Requires all documents served must include blank copies for responding, **CRC Rule 5.92**;
- May be served postjudgment by First Class Mail, **FC § 215**; and
- A memorandum of points and authorities is only required if it is requested by the court.

THE RFO RESPONSE:
- Is made on a *Responsive Declaration to Request for Order*, *FL-320*;
- Requires that the Responsive Declaration and the supporting papers that are sufficient to notify the other party of the declarant's contentions in response to the *RFO*;
- Must include a completed *FL-150* if there are financial issues; and
- A memorandum of points and authorities is only required if requested by the court.

DECLARATIONS: SUPPORTING AND RESPONDING TO THE RFO:
- Must accompany the *FL-300* or *FL-320*;
- The form and format of each declaration submitted in a case filed under the Family Code must comply with the requirements set out in **CRC Rule 2.100** et seq.;
- Must not exceed 10 pages if responding and 5 pages if replying, (the form is not counted);
- Must be from personal knowledge and must state how the knowledge was obtained, **CRC Rule 5.111**; and
- Must contain admissible evidence.

AT THE HEARING:
- If both parties have filed initial pleadings (*Petition* and *Response*), there may be no default entered on an amended pleading of either party, **CRC Rule 5.76**;
- The court must receive live, competent, admissible testimony that is relevant, **FC § 217**;
- The court must consider the factors in making a good cause finding to refuse to live testimony, **CRC Rule 5.113(c)**;

Chapter 26: The Hearing

> - A party requesting judicial notice of a document or documents under **Evid. Code § 452** or **453** must provide the court and each party with a copy, **CRC Rule 5.115**; and
> - When a brief continuance is granted to allow time to prepare for questioning witnesses, the court should make appropriate temporary orders, **CRC Rule 5.113(f)**.
>
> **Prior to January 2013**, a Request for Order (RFO) was called an **Order to Show Cause** (OSC).
>
> **Demurrers, motions for summary adjudication and motions for summary judgment** must not be used in family law actions, **CRC 5.76**.

Introduction

Sometimes in family law, partners, spouses or ex-spouses require the assistance of the court system to resolve issues. A hearing must be requested in order for the court to provide this assistance. The request is made on a *FL-300* or *Request for Order* form. A supporting declaration must accompany the *FL-300*. The responding party files an answer on a *FL-320*, *Response to a Request for Order*. If financial issues are requested, the parties must also include a *FL-150* included with the *RFO* or included with the *Responsive Declaration to RFO*.

Prior to Filing a Request for a Hearing

Prior to the filing of a *Request for Order* (*RFO*) (form *FL-300*), all parties and all attorneys are required to meet and confer in person, by telephone or as ordered by the court. During this meeting, the parties must discuss and make a good faith attempt to settle all issues, even if a complete settlement is not possible and only conditional agreements are made. The requirement to meet and confer does not apply to cases involving domestic violence. **CRC Rule 5.98(a)**.

Before or while conferring, the parties must exchange all documentary evidence that is to be relied on for proof of any material fact. At the hearing, the court may decline to consider documents that were not served to the other party before the hearing, as required by the rules. The requirement to exchange documents does not relate to documents that are submitted primarily for rebuttal or impeachment purposes. **CRC Rule 5.98(b)**

1. *Request for Order* and Responding to a *Request for Order*

    a. *Request for Order* (*FL-300* and *FL-300-INFO*)

In a family law proceeding other than an action under the Domestic Violence Prevention Act or a local child support agency action under the Family Code, a request for a hearing must be filed on a *RFO* (form *FL-300*). The *RFO* must set forth facts sufficient to notify the other party of the declarant's contentions in support of the relief requested. A completed *Income and Expense Declaration* (form

FL-150) or *Financial Statement* (form *FL-155*) must be filed with the *RFO when there are any financial issues, including a request for attorney fees and/or court costs*. The moving party must file the documents with the court to obtain a court date and then serve a copy of all of the paperwork filed with the court on the responding party. **CRC Rule 5.92.**

If the *RFO* seeks court orders pending a hearing, or seeks an order that the other party attend the hearing, the *RFO* (form *FL-300*) and appropriate attachments must be served in the manner specified for the service of a *Summons* in **CCP § 413.10** et seq.

If the *RFO* is filed after the entry of a judgment of dissolution of marriage, nullity of marriage, legal separation of the parties, paternity or after a permanent order in any other proceeding in which the visitation, custody or support of a child was at issue, it may be served by first-class mail or airmail, postage prepaid, to the persons to be served. For any party served by mail, the proof of service must include an address verification. **FC § 215**.

When a *RFO* is served, a blank copy of a *Responsive Declaration to Request for Order* (form *FL-320*) must be included. Additionally, if there financial issues involved, a blank *Income and Expense Declaration* (form *FL-150*) or *Financial Statement (Simplified)* (form *FL-155*) must be included. **CRC Rule 5.92.** No memorandum of points and authorities needs to be filed with a *RFO* (form *FL-300*) unless required by the court.

The moving and responding parties may be required to complete, file and serve additional papers to request or respond to a *RFO* (form *FL-300*) about child custody and visitation (parenting time), attorney fees and costs, support and other financial matters. When a party is served with a *RFO*, the party can agree to the relief sought or oppose the request.

The following documents may accompany a *RFO*:

(1) An *Income and Expense Declaration* (form *FL-150*) and its required attachments;
(2) A *Financial Statement* (form *FL-155*) and its required attachments;
(3) A *Property Declaration* (form *FL-160*) and its required attachments;
(4) Exhibits attached to declarations; and
(5) A memorandum of points and authorities.

Prior to January 2013, a *Request for Order* was called an **Order to Show Cause** (*OSC*).

b. Responding to the *Request for Order* (form *FL-320*)

To respond to the issues raised in the *RFO* and any attached papers, the responding party must complete, file and serve a *Responsive Declaration to Request for Order* (form *FL-320*). The *FL-320* and supporting papers must set forth facts sufficient to notify the other party of the declarant's contentions in response to the *RFO* and in support of any relief requested.

The responding papers may request relief related to the orders requested in the moving papers. If the responding party wishes to have orders made on issues not included on the moving party's papers, he or she must file his or her own *RFO*.

A completed *Income and Expense Declaration* (form *FL-150*) or *Financial Statement (Simplified)* (form *FL-155*) must be attached to the *Responsive Declaration to Request for Order* (form *FL-320*) when financial relief is requested.

The moving and responding parties may be required to complete, file and serve additional papers to request or respond to a *RFO* (form *FL-300*) about child custody and visitation (parenting time), attorney fees and costs, support and other financial matters.

The responding party must file and serve his or her opposition papers at least ten (10) calendar days prior to the hearing.

A memorandum of points and authorities is not necessary when filing a *FL-320* unless required by the court.

2. Declarations: Supporting and Responding to the *Request for Order*

A supporting declaration must accompany a *Request for Order (FL-300)* or a *Responsive Declaration to Request for Order (FL-320)*. A declaration included with a *RFO* or a *Responsive Declaration to RFO* must not exceed ten (10) pages in length. A reply declaration must not exceed 5 pages in length, unless the declaration is of an expert witness or the court grants permission to extend the length of a declaration.

The form and format of each declaration submitted in a case filed under the Family Code must comply with the requirements set out in **CRC Rule 2.100** et seq.

A declaration must be based on personal knowledge and explain how the person acquired that knowledge. Also, the statements in the declaration must be admissible in evidence. **CRC Rule 5.111**.

If a party believes that an opposition declaration is not from a party's personal knowledge, the party must file and serve his or her objections in writing at least 2 court days before the time of the hearing, or any objection will be considered waived, and the declaration may be considered as evidence. Upon a finding of good cause, objections may be made in writing or orally at the time of the hearing.

Chapter 26: The Hearing

The following documents may accompany a *Request for Order* or a *Responsive Declaration* without being counted toward the page limitation for declarations:
(1) An *Income and Expense Declaration* (form *FL-150*) and its required attachments;
(2) A *Financial Statement* (form *FL-155*) and its required attachments;
(3) A *Property Declaration* (form *FL-160*) and its required attachments;
(4) Exhibits attached to declarations; and
(5) A memorandum of points and authorities.

CRC Rule 3.1300 provides that all moving and supporting papers must be filed and served in accordance with **CCP § 1005**, and the proof of service of the moving papers must be filed no later than five (5) court days before the time appointed for the hearing.

3. Other Rules

Demurrers, motions for summary adjudication and motions for summary judgment must not be used in family law actions. **CRC 5.76**.

Amendments to pleadings, amended pleadings and supplemental pleadings are served and filed according to the provisions of law civil actions generally, but the petitioner is not required to file a reply if the respondent has filed a *Response*.

If both parties have filed initial pleadings (*Petition* and *Response*), there may be no default entered on an amended pleading of either party. **CRC Rule 5.76**.

And finally, pursuant to **CRC 2.100** no trial court, or any division or branch of a trial court, may enact or enforce any local rule concerning the form or format of papers.

The Hearing

At a hearing on any request for an order brought under the Family Code, absent a stipulation of the parties or a finding of good cause, the court must receive any live, competent and admissible testimony that is relevant and within the scope of the hearing. *ELKINS v. SUPERIOR COURT* (2007) 41 Cal.4th 1337.

ELKINS v. SUPERIOR COURT (2007) 41 Cal.4th 1337(*Elkins*)

In *Elkins*, Petitioner/Husband represented himself during a marital dissolution. A local superior court rule and a trial scheduling order in the family law court provided that in dissolution trials, parties must present their cases by means of written declarations. The testimony of witnesses under direct examination was not allowed except in "unusual circumstances", although upon request parties were permitted to cross-examine declarants. In addition, parties were required to establish in their pretrial declarations the admissibility of all exhibits they sought to introduce at trial.

Chapter 26: The Hearing

Petitioner's pretrial declaration failed to establish the evidentiary foundation for all but two of his exhibits. Accordingly, the court excluded the 34 remaining exhibits. Without the exhibits, and without the ability through oral testimony to present his case or establish a foundation for his exhibits, Petitioner was prevented from presenting his case; he was prevented from having his day in court.

Petitioner, thereafter, filed a petition for writ of mandate or prohibition in the Court of Appeal of California, First Appellate District and Division One, which was denied. Petitioner sought review from the California Supreme Court.

The Supreme Court reversed the judgment rendered by the Court of Appeal summarily denying the Petition for Writ of Mandate or prohibition and remanded the matter to that court with directions to issue the writ. The court found that the rule and order that prevented Petitioner from presenting his case was inconsistent with various statutory provisions. The court concluded that the trial court abused its discretion in sanctioning

Petitioner, by excluding the bulk of his evidence simply because he failed to file a declaration establishing the admissibility of his trial evidence prior to trial. The sanction was disproportionate and inconsistent with the policy favoring determination of cases on their merits.

After and because of the *Elkins* case, California legislature enacted **FC § 217,**[1] which became operative January 1, 2011 and provides that, in addition to the rules of evidence, a court must consider the following factors in making a finding of good cause to refuse to receive live testimony under **FC § 217**:

> **(1)** Whether a substantive matter is at issue--such as child custody, visitation (parenting time), parentage, child support, spousal support, requests for restraining orders, or the characterization, division, or temporary use and control of the property or debt of the parties;
> **(2)** Whether material facts are in controversy;
> **(3)** Whether live testimony is necessary for the court to assess the credibility of the parties or other witnesses;
> **(4)** The right of the parties to question anyone submitting reports or other information to the court;

---

[1] FC § 217 provides:
"(a) At a hearing on any order to show cause or notice of motion brought pursuant to this code, absent a stipulation of the parties or a finding of good cause pursuant to subdivision (b), the court shall receive any live, competent testimony that is relevant and within the scope of the hearing, and the court may ask questions of the parties.
(b) In appropriate cases, a court may make a finding of good cause to refuse to receive live testimony and shall state its reasons for the finding on the record or in writing. The Judicial Council shall, by January 1, 2012, adopt a statewide rule of court regarding the factors a court shall consider in making a finding of good cause.
(c) A party seeking to present live testimony from witnesses other than the parties shall, prior to the hearing, file and serve a witness list with a brief description of the anticipated testimony. If the witness list is not served prior to the hearing, the court may, on request, grant a brief continuance and may make appropriate temporary orders pending the continued hearing."

> **(5)** Whether a party offering testimony from a non-party has complied with Family Code section 217(c); and
> **(6)** Any other factor that is just and equitable. CRC Rule 5.113(b).

If the court makes a finding of good cause to exclude live testimony, it must state its reasons on the record or in writing. The court is required to state only those factors on which the finding of good cause is based. **CRC Rule 5.113(c)**.

Whenever the court receives live testimony from a party or any witness, the court may ask questions of the parties and other witnesses. **CRC Rule 5.113(g)**.

The court must consider whether or not a brief continuance is necessary to allow a litigant adequate opportunity to prepare for the questioning of any witness. When a brief continuance is granted to allow time to prepare for questioning witnesses, the court should make appropriate temporary orders. **CRC Rule 5.113(f)**.

A party requesting judicial notice of a document or documents under **Evid. Code § 452**[2] or **453** must provide the court and each party with a copy of the material of the documents. If the material is part of a file in the court in which the matter is being heard, the party must specify in writing the part of the court file sought to be judicially noticed and make arrangements with the clerk to have the file in the courtroom at the time of the hearing. **CRC Rule 5.115**.

A court that does not regularly provide for reporting of hearings on a *RFO* or motion must so state in its local rules. The county's local rules should provide a procedure by which a party may obtain a court reporter in order to provide the party with an official verbatim transcript. **CRC Rule 5.123**.

Procedure and Forms

1. **Prior to the filing of a *RFO*,** all parties and all attorneys are required to **meet and confer** in person, by telephone or as ordered by the court.

---

[2] Evidence Code § 452 provides judicial notice may be taken of the following matters:
"(a) The decisional, constitutional and statutory law of any state of the US and the resolutions and private acts of the Congress of the US and of the legislature of this state.
(b) Regulations and legislative enactments issued by or under the authority of the US or any public entity in the US.
(c) Official acts of the legislative, executive and judicial departments of the US and of any state of the US.
(d) Records of (1) any court of this state, or (2) any court of record of the US or of any state of the US.
(e) Rules of court of (1) any court of this state or (2) any court of record of the US or of any state of the US.
(f) The law of an organization of nations and of foreign nations and public entities in foreign nations.
(g) Facts and propositions that are of such common knowledge within the territorial jurisdiction of the court that they cannot reasonably be the subject of dispute.
(h) Facts and propositions that are not reasonably subject to dispute and are capable of immediate and accurate determination by resort to sources of reasonably indisputable accuracy."

2. Before or while conferring, the **parties must exchange all documentary evidence** that is to be relied on for proof of any material fact.
3. The following documents **may accompany a *RFO***:
   - An *Income and Expense Declaration* (form *FL-150*) and its required attachments;
   - A *Financial Statement* (form *FL-155*) and its required attachments;
   - A *Property Declaration* (form *FL-160*) and its required attachments;
   - Exhibits attached to declarations; and
   - A memorandum of points and authorities.
4. **When responding to a *RFO*, a *Responsive Declaration to Request for Order*** (form *FL-320*) is used.
5. **The *FL-320*** and supporting papers **must set forth facts sufficient to notify** the other party of the declarant's contentions in response to the *RFO* and in support of any relief requested.
6. A **completed *Income and Expense Declaration*** (form ***FL-150***) or *Financial Statement (Simplified)* (form *FL-155*) **must be attached to the *Responsive Declaration*** to Request for Order (form *FL-320*) when financial relief is requested.
7. A **supporting declaration** must accompany a *Request for Order* (*FL-300*) or a *Responsive Declaration to Request for Order* (*FL-320*).
8. The following documents may accompany a *Request for Order* or a *Responsive Declaration* without being counted toward the page limitation for declarations:
   - An *Income and Expense Declaration* (form *FL-150*) and its required attachments;
   - A *Financial Statement* (form *FL-155*) and its required attachments;
   - A *Property Declaration* (form *FL-160*) and its required attachments;
   - Exhibits attached to declarations; and
   - A memorandum of points and authorities.

EDUCATIONAL EXERCISES

I.   Use the information set forth in Appendix One to complete the following forms:

Filed by Marilyn John's attorney:

    a.   RFO (FL-300) with a declaration
    b.   Income & Expense Declaration (FL-150)

II.   List all of the forms that will be filed with this RFO motion.

CHAPTER 27: *Ex Parte*

In Brief...

EX PARTE:
- Procedure rules are set forth in **CRC Rule 5.151**;
- May be used to set a hearing date or an order shortening time for a hearing;
- Orders shortening time for filing and service of papers can be made for other times than the times specified in **CCP § 1005**, **CRC Rule 5.94(a)**; and
- Hearings require that service has been effected unless there are exceptional circumstances, **CRC Rule 5.167**.

EX PARTE EMERGENCY ORDERS:
- Procedure rules set forth at CRC Rule 5.151 are referred to as emergency orders rules;
- Applications are also known as *ex parte* applications;
- Are for matters that cannot wait for the court's regular calendar;
- Are to help prevent an immediate danger or irreparable harm to a party or the children; and
- Are to help prevent immediate loss or damage to property.

A REQUEST FOR EMERGENCY ORDERS MUST BE IN WRITING AND:
- Must include a *Request for Order* (form *FL-300*) that identifies the relief requested;
- Must include a current *Income and Expense Declaration* (form *FL-150*) (if financial issues);
- Must include *Temporary Orders* (form *FL-305*) to serve as the proposed temporary order;
- Must include a written declaration based on personal knowledge;
- Must include a copy of the current custody orders, if there is one;
- Must include a completed *Declaration Under Uniform Child Custody Jurisdiction and Enforcement Act* (*UCCJEA*) (form *FL-105*) if the emergency request involves children of the marriage/relationship; and
- Must include a full, detailed description of the most recent incidents showing "immediate harm to the child or immediate risk that the child will be removed from the State of California", **FC § 3064**.

EX PARTE NOTICE:
- To request emergency orders may be given by telephone, in writing or by voicemail message; and
- For emergency orders may be waived under exceptional circumstances.
- After providing notice, each party must be served with the documents requesting emergency orders as described in **CRC Rule 5.167** or as required by local rule.

WHEN EX PARTE ORDERS HAVE BEEN GRANTED:
- The applicant must obtain conformed copies of the orders and personally serve then on all parties, **CRC Rule 5.167**.

Chapter 27: *Ex Parte*

> - They may include emergency orders that grant or modify child custody or visitation (parenting time) under **FC § 3064**.
>
> **The court must not make an order granting or modifying a custody order on an *ex parte* basis unless there has been a showing of immediate harm to the child or immediate risk that the child will be removed from the State of California.**

Introduction

Applications for emergency orders are also known as *ex parte* applications. The rules regarding *ex parte* procedures are set forth in **CRC Rule 5.151.** These rules are referred to as **the emergency orders rules**. Unless specifically stated, these rules do not apply to *ex parte* applications for domestic violence restraining orders under the Domestic Violence Prevention Act. (See Chapter 36 RE: Domestic Violence, *infra*.)

The purpose of a request for emergency orders is to address matters that cannot wait to be heard on the court's regular hearing calendar. In this type of proceeding, notice to the other party is shorter than in other proceedings. Notice to the other party can also be waived under exceptional circumstances, as provided in **CRC Rule 5.151**.

A party seeking emergency orders and a party providing written opposition must serve the papers on the other party or on the other party's attorney at the first reasonable opportunity before the hearing. Absent exceptional circumstances, no hearing may be conducted unless such service has been made. The court may waive this requirement in extraordinary circumstances if good cause is shown and imminent harm is likely. This rule does not apply in cases filed under the Domestic Violence Prevention Act. **CRC Rule 5.167.**

If the judicial officer signs the applicant's proposed emergency orders, the applicant must obtain and have the conformed copy of the orders personally served on all parties.

Pursuant to **CRC Rule 5.169**, courts may require all parties to appear at a hearing before ruling on a request for emergency orders. Courts may also make emergency orders based on the documents submitted without requiring the parties to appear at a hearing.

And finally, the court, on its own motion or on application for an order shortening time supported by a declaration showing good cause, may prescribe shorter times for the filing and service of papers other than the times specified in **CCP § 1005**. **CRC Rule 5.94(a).**

Chapter 27: *Ex Parte*

The Process

The *ex parte* process is used to request that the court:
(1) Make orders to help prevent an immediate danger or irreparable harm to a party or to the children involved in the matter;
(2) Make orders to help prevent immediate loss or damage to property subject to disposition in the case; or

(3) Make orders about procedural matters, such as setting a date for a hearing on the matter that is sooner than that of a regular hearing (granting an order shortening time for hearing) or shortening or extending the time required for the moving party to serve the other party with the notice of the hearing and supporting papers (grant an order shortening time for service), or continuing a hearing or trial. **CRC Rule 5.151.**

A request for emergency orders must be in writing and must include all of the following completed documents when relevant to the relief requested:

(1) *Request for Order* (form *FL-300*) that identifies the relief requested;
(2) A current *Income and Expense Declaration* (form *FL-150*) or *Financial Statement (Simplified)* (form *FL-155*) and *Property Declaration* (form *FL-160*) (if there are financial issues);
(3) *Temporary Orders* (form *FL-305*) to serve as the proposed temporary order;
(4) A written declaration regarding notice of application for emergency orders based on personal knowledge; and
(5) And only if required, a memorandum of points and authorities.

The application and declaration for emergency orders must state the name, address and telephone number of any attorney known to the applicant to be an attorney for any party or, if no such attorney is known, the name, address and telephone number of the party, if known to the applicant. **CRC Rule 5.151.**

The declarations must contain facts within the personal knowledge of the declarant that demonstrate why the matter should be handled as an emergency hearing, as opposed to being on the court's regular hearing calendar.

An applicant must make an affirmative factual showing of irreparable harm, immediate danger or any other statutory basis for granting relief without notice or with shortened notice to the other party. The applicant has a duty to disclose that an emergency order will result in a change in the current situation or status quo. Absent such disclosure, attorney fees and costs incurred to reinstate the status quo may be awarded.

Applications for emergency orders granting or modifying child custody or visitation (parenting time) under **FC § 3064** must provide a full, detailed description of the most recent incidents showing "immediate harm to the child or immediate risk that the child will be removed from the State of California." **FC § 3064**.

Chapter 27: *Ex Parte*

If immediate harm to the child or immediate risk that the child will be removed from the State of California is not set forth in an *ex parte* declaration, the trial court should deny the request to shorten the time. If, however, the trial court grants such a request, the appellate court will most assuredly reverse, as was the case in *In re Marriage of SEAGONDOLLAR* (2006) 139 Cal.App.4th 1116, (*Seagondollar*). In *Seagondollar*, the Appellate Court reversed the trial court's decision granting an *ex parte* request to shorten the time for the hearing on a custody/moveaway issue where there was no immediate harm or immediate risk that the children would be removed from California. *Id.* at p. 1129.

Additionally, the description in the *ex parte* request must specify the date of each incident and advise the court of the existing custody and visitation (parenting time) arrangements and how they would be changed by the request for emergency orders.

A copy of the current custody orders, if they are available, must be included in the application. If no orders exist, the accompanying declaration must explain where and with whom the child is currently living.

A completed *Declaration Under Uniform Child Custody Jurisdiction and Enforcement Act* (*UCCJEA*) (form *FL-105*) must accompany an *ex parte* application if the emergency request involves children of the marriage/relationship, if the form was not already filed by a party or if the information has changed since it was filed.

Notice of an *ex parte* appearance at a hearing to request emergency orders may be given by telephone, in writing or by voicemail message.

A party seeking emergency orders must give notice to all parties or their attorneys so that it is received no later than 10:00 a.m. on the court day before the matter is to be considered by the court.

After providing notice, each party must be served with the documents requesting emergency orders as described in **CRC Rule 5.167** or as required by local rule. This rule does not apply to a party seeking emergency orders under the Domestic Violence Prevention Act. **CRC Rule 5.165.**

A party seeking emergency orders and a party providing written opposition must serve the papers on the other party or on the other party's attorney at the first reasonable opportunity before the hearing. Absent exceptional circumstances, no hearing may be conducted unless such service has been made. The court may waive this requirement in extraordinary circumstances if good cause is shown that imminent harm is likely if documents are provided to the other party before the hearing. This rule does not apply in cases filed under the Domestic Violence Prevention Act.

If the judicial officer signs the applicant's proposed emergency orders, the applicant must obtain and have the conformed copy of the orders personally served on all parties. **CRC Rule 5.167**.

Often the county's local family law rules will set forth the procedures to be followed in making *ex parte* requests.

Temporary Ex Parte Orders

Temporary child support orders are usually orders made after a dissolution or paternity petition is filed and before the final judgment is rendered. Temporary child support orders must comply with **FC § 4065**.

If the parties have agreed to or reached an understanding on the custody or temporary custody of their children, a copy of the agreement or an affidavit as to their understanding must be attached to the petition or action that is to be filed with the court. As promptly as possible after this filing, the court must, except in exceptional circumstances, enter an order granting temporary custody in accordance with the agreement or understanding or in accordance with any stipulation of the parties. **FC § 3061**.

Temporary orders are often made on an *ex parte* basis when there are orders made in emergency situations. In the absence of an agreement, understanding, or stipulation, the court may, if jurisdiction is appropriate, enter an *ex parte* temporary custody order, set a hearing date within 20 days, and issue a *Request for Order* (*RFO*) on the responding party. If the responding party does not appear or respond within the time set, the temporary custody order may be extended as necessary, pending the termination of the proceedings. **FC § 3062(a)**.

If, despite good faith efforts, service of the *ex parte* order and the *RFO* has not been effected in a timely fashion and there is reason to believe, based on an affidavit or other manner of proof made under penalty of perjury by the petitioner, that the responding party has possession of the minor child and seeks to avoid the jurisdiction of the court or is concealing the whereabouts of the child, then the hearing date may be reset and the *ex parte* order extended up to an additional 90 days. After service has been affected, either party may request *ex parte* that the hearing date be advanced or the *ex parte* order be dissolved or modified. **FC § 3062(b)**.

When making an *ex parte* order seeking or modifying an order of custody, the court must order that the person receiving custody is restrained from removing the child from the state pending notice and a hearing on the order seeking or modifying custody. **FC § 3063.**

Finally, the court must not make an order granting or modifying a custody order on an *ex parte* basis unless there has been a showing of immediate harm to the child or immediate risk that the child will be removed from the State of California. **FC § 3064. Immediate harm to the child includes**, but is not limited to, the following:

(1) Having a parent who has committed acts of domestic violence, where the court determines that the acts of domestic violence are of recent origin or are a part of a demonstrated and continuing pattern of acts of domestic violence; or

(2) Sexual abuse of the child, where the court determines that the acts of sexual abuse are of recent origin or are a part of a demonstrated and continuing pattern of acts of sexual abuse. **FC § 3064(b)**.

EDUCATIONAL EXERCISES

1. Explain the term "*Ex Parte*" and describe under what conditions it is usually requested.
2. List the 4 Judicial Council forms that must be completed and filed when requesting an *ex parte* appearance.

CHAPTER 28: Defaults

In Brief...

DEFAULTS:
- **The 2 Ways That a Default Can occur are:**
  - When a responding party fails to appear at a court hearing after being appropriately and timely noticed; or
  - When a responding party fails to respond to the paperwork after being appropriately and timely served.
- **There Are 2 Kinds of Judgment Defaults:**
  - A complete, or true, default when the responding party does not respond to the *Petition*; and
  - A default with an agreement in which the parties make an agreement (*MSA*) but the respondent still does not file a *Response* (form *FL-120*), **FC § 2338.5**.

DEFAULT RULES AND PROCEDURES:
- If both parties have filed initial pleadings (*Petition* and *Response*), no default may be entered, **CRC Rule 5.76**.
- Pursuant to the *Summons*, the respondent has thirty (30) days to respond to the *Petition*.
- If no *Response* is filed within 30 days after service was effected, the petitioner can file the default paperwork.
- Local rules determine whether a default has to be "proven up".
- No default may be entered in any proceeding unless a request has been completed on a *Request to Enter Default* (form *FL-165*) and filed with the court by the petitioner, **CRC RULE 5.401**.

THE JUDGMENT DEFAULT PROCESS:
- The Petitioner must wait 30 days after service of the Summons and Petition;
- After the 30 days, the Petitioner must file:
  - *FL-165 Request to Enter Default*
  - *FL-170 Declaration for Default* **or** *Uncontested Dissolution*
  - *FL-180 Judgment* and **Proposed Judgment**
  - *FL-190 Notice of Entry of Judgment*
- In some counties, the petitioner or the petitioner's attorney must appear in court to **prove up** the default. The local rules of the county will provide whether or not **a prove up** is necessary.
- **CRC RULE 5.401** sets forth the rules and procedures for defaults.

SETTING ASIDE THE DEFAULT:
- Pursuant to **FC § 2122**, a default may be set aside within one year after the judgment has rendered for actual fraud, perjury, duress and mental incapacity.
- Pursuant to **CCP § 473(b)**, a request to set aside a default must be filed within six months after the judgment was entered; and

Chapter 28: Defaults

> - May not be set aside because it was inequitable when made or because the division of assets or liabilities was divided inequitably.

Introduction

A default occurs when the responding party fails to respond to the *Petition* or appear at a hearing when the notice to the responding party has been timely and appropriate. When a party fails to respond to a *Petition* or responds after the time allowed to timely respond (30 days), a default judgment can be filed by the petitioner against that party.

Many family law matters are resolved by default proceedings. Some couples make their marital settlement agreements prior to the filing of the dissolution *Petition* so that both parties do not each need to pay the expensive first paper filing fees.

There are two ways that a default can occur:
(1) When a responding party fails to appear at a court hearing after being duly and timely noticed; or
(2) When a responding party fails to respond to paperwork after being duly and timely served that paperwork.

If both parties have filed initial pleadings (*Petition* and *Response*), there may be no default entered on an amended pleading of either party. **CRC Rule 5.76**.

Pursuant to **FC § 4253,** when hearing child support matters, a commissioner or referee may enter default orders if the defendant does not respond to notice or other process within the time prescribed to respond to that notice.

When an action is filed by the local child support agency pursuant to **FC § 17400, 17402** or **17404**, a judgment will be entered without a hearing, without the presentation of any other evidence or further notice to the defendant, upon the filing of proof of service by the local child support agency evidencing that more than thirty (30) days have passed since the simplified summons and complaint, proposed judgment, blank answer, blank income and expense declaration and all notices required by this division were served on the defendant.

The moving party can still present his or her case, even when the responding party fails to appear. However, all of the requests made by the moving party are not necessarily granted. A court will most likely grant the moving party's reasonable requests.

When a *Request for Order*, (*RFO* prepared on a *FL-300* form), has been filed and calendared by the moving party, the responding party's failure to appear at the hearing could be by agreement of the parties. If the responding party agrees to the moving party's requests in the *RFO*, the responding party does not necessarily have to appear at the hearing. He or she can choose not to appear, and if the court finds that all of the moving party's requests are reasonable, the responding party will be defaulted.

Also, pursuant to the *Summons*, the respondent has thirty (30) days to respond to the *Petition* after service has been affected. If he or she does not respond within that period of time, the respondent can be **defaulted,** or the petitioner can file the default paperwork. When no responsive paperwork is filed by a party, that party has no voice or input in the proceedings. In *BROOKS v. NELSON* (1928) 95 Cal.App. 144 at pp. 147-148, the court stated that:

> A defendant against whom a default has been entered is out of court and is not entitled to take any further steps in the cause affecting plaintiff's right of action; he cannot thereafter, until such default is set aside in a proper proceeding, file pleadings or move for a new trial, or demand notice of subsequent proceedings.

Finally, besides the two ways to default, there are two kinds of judgment defaults. One default is a complete, or true default that occurs when the responding party just does not respond to the *Petition*. The other kind of default occurs when the parties have made an agreement (a marital settlement agreement, *MSA*) before the filing of the *Judgment*. The *MSA* is attached to the Judgment when it is filed. Again no *Response* is filed. The parties can share the cost of filing of the *Petition* or not, but only one filing fee will need to be paid.

The Two Kinds of Judgment Defaults

1. Default without an Agreement

Sometimes in a divorce situation there is a party who does not want to participate in any of the court procedures. This party can be defaulted and will thereafter have no say in any of the court actions or paperwork unless the default is set aside.

In order to file a default against the respondent, the petitioner must so request and complete and file the following paperwork:

FL-165 Request to Enter Default
FL-170 Declaration for Default **or** *Uncontested Dissolution*
FL-180 Judgment and **Proposed Judgment**
FL-190 Notice of Entry of Judgment

The petitioner can start the default process after thirty (30) days have passed since service was affected on the respondent and the respondent has not filed a *Response* (form *FL-120*).

Chapter 28: Defaults

2. Default with an Agreement

The second kind of default judgment occurs when the parties have agreed to all issues of the divorce and have made a written agreement containing a resolution of all issues of the divorce. This agreement is called a *Marital Settlement Agreement* (*MSA*), and this subject is covered more fully in Chapter 30, *infra*. This default is a common use of the default procedure, because some parties can resolve their divorce issues without court intervention.

As stated above, if the parties agree to this default, only one party pays the filing fee. However, the agreement or *MSA* must be written, contain the signature of the spouse who has defaulted and be notarized. **FC § 2338.5**.

Along with the *MSA*, the petitioner must complete and file the following paperwork:

In a default with a *Marital Settlement Agreement* (*MSA*), the final paperwork consists of:

FL-141 Declaration Regarding Service of Declaration of Disclosure and Income and Expense Declaration **or**
FL-144 Stipulation and Waiver of Final Declaration of Disclosure
FL-170 Declaration for Default or Uncontested Dissolution
FL-180 Judgment **with a signed and notarized *MSA* attached**
FL-190 Notice of Entry of Judgment

Default Procedures, Rules and Forms

Even though a parent defaults in the divorce case, he or she still has standing to request a modification of a child custody agreement, as shown by the case that follows.

> *In re Marriage of CHRISTOPHER DALE OLSON and HEATHER RAE OLSON.*
> *CHRISTOPHER DALE OLSON, Petitioner, v. THE SUPERIOR COURT OF LOS ANGELES COUNTY, Respondent; HEATHER RAE OLSON, Real Party in Interest.*
> COURT OF APPEAL OF CALIFORNIA, SECOND APPELLATE DISTRICT, DIVISION ONE
> 238 Cal.App.4th 1458
> July 30, 2015, Opinion Filed
> (*Marriage of Olson*)
>
> On October 12, 2011, Christopher filed a petition for dissolution of marriage to obtain a divorce from Heather, his wife of nine years. Heather did not file a response, and on February 19, 2013, the court granted the divorce in a default judgment. Heather was present in court as a witness. The court granted a judgment of dissolution of the marriage and granted the parties joint legal custody of their twin seven-year-old daughters. Each parent was entitled to physical custody of the children approximately half the time. The judgment reserved spousal and child support to be determined at a later date.

The relationship between Christopher and Heather subsequently deteriorated, and in June 2014, Heather filed a petition to modify joint custody. Heather proposed that Christopher have custody of the twins only on Thursday nights and alternate weekends. The remainder of the week, they would stay with Heather. Christopher opposed Heather's request, arguing for the existing joint custody schedule to remain in effect.
Christopher also filed a separate petition in which he contended that because the divorce judgment was granted by default judgment against Heather, Heather lacked the standing to request a change in the judgment, and that the court lacked jurisdiction to consider her petition.

On August 20, 2014, the court denied Christopher's petition, ruling that Heather did have standing, and the court did have jurisdiction to decide her petition.

On September 9, 2014, Heather filed a motion requesting child support from Christopher. The next day, September 10, Heather filed a petition requesting that the court order Christopher to produce documents in response to a discovery request. On the same day, Christopher filed a notice of appeal from the court's order accepting jurisdiction and proceeding on the merits of Heather's child custody request.

After participating in the parenting plan assessment, the parties agreed to a stipulated order, filed October 16, 2014, which confirmed the existing joint custody schedule as had been provided in the default judgment. The court entered this stipulated order.

DISCUSSION
Christopher claims that the trial court's entry of a default judgment against Heather bars Heather from seeking a modification of the joint custody arrangement unless she first obtains relief from the default judgment. We disagree.

Christopher argues that this case should be viewed as if it were any other civil dispute. He relies on FC § 210, which provides that unless another law or rule specifies otherwise, family court cases are governed by the same procedural rules as civil cases generally. Because a defendant in a civil case who has had a default judgment against her may not file pleadings or take further steps in the case while the default judgment remains in effect, Christopher contends that Heather has no standing to seek a modification of the joint custody arrangement ordered in the default judgment.

We disagree. The supervision of the custody of children is fundamentally different from other court functions. The court's primary concern must be the well-being of the children, not the preferences of the parties themselves. For this reason, the court retains jurisdiction of a divorce case in order to supervise issues such as custody: "The court may, during the pendency of a proceeding or at any time thereafter, make an order for the custody of a child during minority that seems necessary or proper." (FC § 3022.) The court's power to order modifications of custody for the benefit of children when circumstances change must take precedence over the wishes of the parents. (In re Marriage of Brown & Yana (2006) 37 Cal.4th 947, 957 [38 Cal.Rptr.3d 610, 127 P.3d 28].)

Indeed, the Family Code expressly authorizes parents to seek modifications: "An order for joint custody may be modified or terminated upon the petition of one or both parents or on the court's own motion if it is shown that the best interest of the child requires modification or termination of the order." (FC § 3087.) Nothing in this section or any provision of the Family Code suggests that it does not apply in cases where a divorce was granted via default judgment. To the extent that this provision conflicts with the general

Chapter 28: Defaults

> rules applicable to default judgments, the "general ... provision must yield to one that is special." (Kroupa v. Kroupa (1949) 91 Cal.App.2d 647, 651 [205 P.2d 683] [court's statutory authority to modify alimony decisions takes precedence over the general rules regarding default judgments]; see FC § 210 ["Except to the extent that any other statute or rules adopted by the Judicial Council provide applicable rules, the rules of practice and procedure applicable to civil actions generally ... apply to, and constitute the rules of practice and procedure in, proceedings ..." in family court.
>
> As Christopher notes, the case law regarding custody disputes after default judgments is sparse. The relevant cases that exist suggest that a default divorce judgment does not bar the defaulted parent from petitioning the court regarding custody. In Osgood v. Landon (2005) 127 Cal.App.4th 425 [25 Cal.Rptr.3d 379], the court decided on the merits an ex-husband's petition to prevent his ex-wife from moving with their child out of state. The court was aware that the man had been defaulted in his divorce proceeding, but it did not question his right to petition the court regarding the custody arrangement. As early as 1947, Justice Traynor recognized in an analogous case that the existence of a default divorce judgment did not prevent the court from using its jurisdiction to modify a spousal support award. (See Bowman v. Bowman (1947) 29 Cal.2d 808, 814 [178 P.2d 751] (Bowman), abrogated on other grounds in In re Marriage of Lippel (1990) 51 Cal.3d 1160, 1168–1170 [276 Cal.Rptr. 290, 801 P.2d 1041].) In Bowman, the defendant husband sought to have a default judgment of divorce set aside in order to challenge an award that the court characterized as support and maintenance. (Bowman, at pp. 811–812.) The court ruled that he had waited too long after the entry of default to attack the default judgment. (Id. at p. 813.) The court recognized, however, that in spite of the default, it had continuing jurisdiction to modify spousal and child support decrees in cases where a party could demonstrate changed circumstances. (Bowman, at p. 814.)
>
> Christopher suggests that if his position were adopted, Heather would not necessarily be barred from obtaining a modification of the joint custody order because Heather could petition the court for relief from the default judgment. But relief from the default is not what Heather sought. She did not ask that the dissolution of the marriage be set aside.
>
> We hold that a parent has standing under FC § 3087 to request a modification of a child custody judgment notwithstanding that the judgment sought to be modified was a default judgment taken against the parent who is petitioning for the change.

1. To Prove Up or Not

In some counties, the petitioner or the petitioner's attorney must appear in court to **prove up** the default. The local rules of the county will provide whether or not a **prove up** is necessary. If it is, the prove-up appearance requires the petitioner or the petitioner's attorney and the petitioner to tell the court that there are irreconcilable differences in the marriage that have caused an irrevocable break down in the marriage such that the marriage cannot be saved. If the court agrees with the petitioner or petitioner's council, then the judge will declare the marriage dissolved.

No judgment of dissolution or of legal separation of the parties may be granted upon the default of one of the parties or upon a statement or finding of fact made by a referee; but the court must, in addition to the statement or finding of the referee, require proof of the grounds alleged, and the proof, if not taken before the court, must be by affidavit. In all cases in which there are minor children of the parties, each affidavit or offer of proof must include an estimate by the declarant or affiant of the monthly gross income of each party. If the declarant or affiant has no knowledge of the estimated monthly income of a party, the declarant or affiant must state why he or she has no knowledge. In all cases in which there is a community estate, each affidavit or offer of proof must include an estimate of the value of the assets and the debts the declarant or affiant proposes to be distributed to each party, unless the declarant or affiant has filed, or concurrently files, a complete and accurate property declaration with the court. **FC § 2336(a)**.

In some counties no prove up will be necessary. Again, the local rules of that county should be consulted to make this determination. If a prove-up is not necessary, then all of the final paperwork, including the declaration of the petitioner (form *FL-170*) and a proposed judgment (form *FL-180*), must be delivered to the court clerk. The paperwork will then be reviewed by the clerk and processed, thus completing and finalizing the divorce.

If the proof is by affidavit, the personal appearance of the affiant is required only when it appears to the court that any of the following circumstances exist:

(1) Reconciliation of the parties is reasonably possible.
(2) A proposed child custody order is not in the best interests of the child.
(3) A proposed child support order is less than a noncustodial parent is capable of paying.
(4) A personal appearance of a party or interested person would be in the best interests of justice.

An affidavit submitted pursuant to this section must contain a stipulation by the affiant that the affiant understands that proof will be by affidavit and that the affiant will not appear before the court unless so ordered by the court. **FC § 2336(b), (c)**.

2. Default Rules and Codes

CRC RULE 5.401 sets forth the rules and procedures for defaults. **CRC RULE 5.401** provides:

> **(a)** Upon proper application of the petitioner, the clerk must enter a default if the respondent or defendant fails within the time permitted to:
> **(1)** Make an appearance as stated in CRC Rule 5.62;
> **(2)** File a notice of motion to quash service of summons under section 418.10 of the Code of Civil Procedure; or
> **(3)** File a petition for writ of mandate under section 418.10 of the Code of Civil Procedure.
> **(b)** Proof of facts
> **(1)** The petitioner may apply to the court for the relief sought in the petition at the time default is entered. The court must require proof to be made of the facts stated in the petition and may enter its judgment based on that proof.
> **(2)** The court may permit the use of a completed *Income and Expense Declaration* (form FL-150) or *Financial Statement (Simplified)* (form FL-155) and *Property Declaration*

Chapter 28: Defaults

> (form FL-160) for all or any part of the proof required or permitted to be offered on any issue to which they are relevant.
> **(c)** Disposition of all matters required A judgment based on a default must include disposition of all matters subject to the court's jurisdiction for which a party seeks adjudication or an explicit reservation of jurisdiction over any matter not proposed for disposition at that time.

CRC RULE 5.402 provides:

> **(a)** No default may be entered in any proceeding unless a request has been completed on a *Request to Enter Default* (form FL-165) and filed by the petitioner. However, an Income and *Expense Declaration* (form FL-150) or *Financial Statement (Simplified)* (form FL-155) are not required if the petition contains no request for support, costs, or attorney's fees. A *Property Declaration* (form FL-160) is not required if the petition contains no request for property.
> **(b)** For the purpose of completing the declaration of mailing, unless service was by publication and the address of respondent is unknown, it is not sufficient to state that the address of the party to whom notice is given is unknown or unavailable.

When requesting a default, the court clerk must give the *Notice of the Entry of Judgment of Dissolution of Marriage, Nullity of Marriage, or Legal Separation* (form *FL-190*) to the attorney for each party or to the party, if unrepresented. **FC § 2338.5(b)**.

When the default paperwork is completely and appropriately filled out, it must be submitted to the court clerk, the original and two (2) copies. The court clerk then enters the default of the respondent. Once the default is filed, the respondent will no longer have any voice in the action, unless the default is set aside, which will only be allowed if there is a mistake of fact or law.

When filing, it is necessary to include an original and two copies of each of the documents to be filed. If the default was with a marital settlement agreement, the signed original marital settlement agreement must be included with two copies.

If there has been no appearance by the other party, the address stated in the affidavit of mailing in part 3 of the *Request to Enter Default* (form *FL-165*) must be the party's last known address and must be used for mailing form *FL-190* to that party. If service was by publication and the address of respondent or defendant is unknown, those facts must be stated in place of the required address. **CRC Rule 5.415(c)**.

Setting Aside a Default

The grounds to set aside a default judgment are: actual fraud, perjury, duress and mental incapacity. Usually the time limit for requesting a default is one year from the date of the discovery of the fraud. **FC §2122.**

However, it must be noted that a judgment may not be set aside simply because the court finds that it was inequitable when made, nor simply because subsequent circumstances caused the division of assets or liabilities to become inequitable, or the support to become inadequate. **FC § 2123**.

Further, relief can be sought to set aside a default pursuant to **CCP § 473 (b),** which provides that relief may be granted from a judgment for the following reasons: mistake, inadvertence, surprise or excusable neglect. This request to set aside a default judgment must be filed within six (6) months after the judgment was entered. **CCP § 473 (b)**.

Additional Forms

The following additional forms for child custody, child support, spousal or partner support, division of community property and pensions may need to be completed and filed with the court.

If the client seeks custody orders, some of the following forms may need to be completed and filed:

FL-341 Child Custody and Visitation Order Attachment
FL-341A Supervised Visitation Order
FL-341B Child Abduction Prevention Order Attachment
FL-341C Children's Holiday Schedule Attachment
FL-341D Additional Provisions – Physical Custody Attachment
FL-341E Joint Legal Custody Attachment

If the client is seeks child support orders, some of the following forms may need to be completed and filed:

FL-150 Income and Expense Declaration or
FL-155 Financial Statement (Simplified)
FL-191 Child Support Case Registry Form
FL-195 Income Withholding for Support
FL-342 Child Support Information and Order Attachment

If the client seeks spousal or partner support, some of the following forms may need to be completed and filed with the court:

FL-150 Income and Expense Declaration
FL-157 Spousal or Partner Support Declaration Attachment
FL-343 Spousal, Partner or Family Support Attachment
FL-435 Earnings Assignment Order for Spousal or Partner Support

If the client is requesting spousal support and/or child support, a wage assignment or order for support, *FL-195*, must be filed. The *FL-195* is used for both spousal and child support.

If the client seeks an order dividing his or her community property and debt, some of the following forms may need to be completed and filed with the court:

Chapter 28: Defaults

FL-160 Property Declaration
FL-345 Property Order Attachment to Judgment
FL-348 Pension Benefits - Attachment to Judgment **if the couple has a pension plan**.

Chapter 28

EDUCATIONAL EXERCISES

MATCH THE TERMS/WORDS/PHRASES TO THEIR CORRESPONDING DESCRIPTION.

A. Actual fraud, perjury, duress and mental incapacity
B. An estimate of the value of the assets and the debts
C. An original and two copies
D. Default
E. Inequitable
F. Local rules of the county
G. Made an agreement
H. Monthly gross income of each party
I. No default entered
J. Prove up
K. Request a modification
L. The marriage cannot be saved
M. The party's last known address
N. Thirty (30) days
O. Thirty (30) days
P. True default
Q. Two kinds

1. A _____ occurs when the responding party fails to respond to the *Petition* or appear at a hearing when the notice to the responding party has been timely and appropriate. When a party fails to respond to a *Petition* or responds after the time allowed to timely respond (30 days), a default judgment can be filed by the petitioner against that party.
2. If both parties have filed initial pleadings (*Petition* and *Response*), there may be - _____ on an amended pleading of either party.
3. Pursuant to the *Summons*, the respondent has _____ to respond to the *Petition* after service has been affected.
4. There are _____ of judgment defaults.
5. A _____ occurs when the responding party just does not respond the *Petition*.
6. The other kind of default occurs when the parties have _____.
7. The petitioner can start the default process after _____ have passed since service was affected on the respondent and the respondent has not filed a *Response* (form *FL-120*).
8. Even though a parent defaults in the divorce case, he or she still has standing to _____ of a child custody agreement.
9. In some counties, the petitioner or the petitioner's attorney must appear in court to _____ the default.
10. The _____ will provide whether or not a prove up is necessary.
11. The prove-up appearance requires the petitioner or the petitioner's attorney and the petitioner to tell the court that there are irreconcilable differences in the marriage that have caused an irrevocable break down in the marriage such that _____.
12. In all cases in which there are minor children of the parties, each affidavit or offer of proof must include an estimate by the declarant or affiant of the _____ unless the declarant or affiant has no knowledge of the estimated monthly income of a party.
13. In all cases in which there is a community estate, each affidavit or offer of proof must include _____ the declarant or affiant proposes to be distributed to each party, unless the declarant or affiant has filed, or concurrently files, a complete and accurate property declaration with the court.
14. When filing, it is necessary to include _____ of each of the documents to be filed. If the default was with a marital settlement agreement, the signed original marital settlement agreement must be included with two copies.

Chapter 28: Defaults

15. If there has been no appearance by the other party, the address stated in the affidavit of mailing in part 3 of the *Request to Enter Default* (form *FL-165*) must be _____ and must be used for mailing form *FL-190* to that party.
16. The grounds to set aside a default judgment are: _____. Usually the time limit for requesting a default is one year from the date of the discovery of the fraud.
17. A judgment may not be set aside because the court finds that it was ___ when made.

CHAPTER 29: Drafting Court Orders

In Brief...

STIPULATIONS:
- Are agreements made between opposing parties settling one or more disputed issues;
- Can be made regarding any family law matter;
- RE: child support must contain the requirements in **FC § 4065**;
- Can be court orders if the agreements are signed by a judge;
- Can be drafted on Judicial Council forms, if there is a form for the stipulation;
- When there is no specific form for a stipulation, the stipulation is usually drafted on pleader or numbered paper; and
- If the parties agree to stipulate to a child support amount that is below the amount established by the statewide uniform guideline for child support, a change of circumstances is not required to modify the child support amount to guideline or above. **FC § 4065(d)**.

PENDENTE LITE HEARINGS, CRC Rule 5.125:
- Are hearings that occur before or while a final judgment is pending; and
- Court orders are drafted on the *FL-340, Findings and Order After Hearing.*

A MODIFICATION HEARING:
- May be requested to change or terminate a court order; and
- Request can be made during the proceeding or after the judgment.

COURT ORDERS RE: MODIFICATIONS, CRC Rule 5.570:
- Rules RE: filing a request are set forth in **CRC Rule 5.570**;
- Child support order may be modified to consolidate orders for support;
- Support order may not be modified or terminated as to an amount that accrued before the date of the filing of the notice of motion or order to show cause (*RFO*) to modify or terminate. **FC § 3651(c)(1)**.
- When there is an agreement, written or oral, providing that spousal support is nonmodifiable, then the court may not modify it;
- The court may make order for adult child support pursuant to **FC § 3587**; and
- If the child is receiving public assistance pursuant to **FC § 4004**, a court may not make a court order without the appearance or agreement of the county that is providing the assistance.

DRAFTING THE FINDINGS AND ORDER AFTER HEARING, (FOAH):
- A court order after a hearing is most commonly drafted on *Findings and Order After Hearing FL-340*, plus any attachment forms;
- The form can be found at: ***www.courts.ca.gov/documents/fl340.pdf***;
- **CRC Rule 5.125** sets forth the procedure for preparation, service and submission of the *Findings and Order After Hearing*; and
- Postjudgment orders are drafted pursuant to **CRC Rule 5.125**.

Chapter 29: Drafting Court Orders

> **FORMAL FORM FOR TRIALS vs. FINAL FORM FOR HEARINGS:**
> - A *Findings and Order After Hearing* is used to draft the formal order for hearings; and
> - The form used to draft the formal order for a trial is a *Judgment*.

Introduction

There are many Judicial Council forms that were promulgated for stipulations, court orders and judgments in family law matters. The forms for a stipulation include *Stipulation to Establish or Modify Child Support* and *Order and Stipulation and Order for Custody and/or Visitation of Children*. (There is a list of the forms, both optional and mandatory, that may be used for stipulations at the end of this chapter.)

The forms that may be used for drafting a court order include *Findings and Order After Hearing*, *Earnings Assignment Order for Spousal or Partner Support (Family Law)* (also called a wage assignment), *Temporary Emergency Court Order*, *Supervised Visitation Order* and *Expedited Child Support Order*. (There is a more complete list of Judicial Council forms for court orders at the end of this chapter.)

The forms that are used to attach to stipulations and court orders include *Child Custody and Visitation (Parenting Time) Order Attachment*, *Child Support Information and Order Attachment*, *Non-Guideline Child Support Findings Attachment* and *Spousal, Partner or Family Support Order Attachment*.

The forms for hearings and trial are different because hearings and trials are different. The evidence presented at hearings is usually by declaration[1] and the evidence at trials is usually presented by testimony.

Court Orders

1. Stipulations

A *stipulation* is an agreement made between opposing parties in a legal action that settles one or more disputed issues. If the stipulation is in regard to issues that are currently before a court and a hearing is pending, then the stipulation can be signed by the court to make the stipulation a court order. If, however, the stipulation does

---

[1] After and because of the *Elkins* case, California legislature enacted FC § 217, which provides that a court must consider the following factors in making a finding of good cause to refuse to receive live testimony under FC § 217:
"(1) Whether a substantive matter is at issue--such as child custody, visitation (parenting time), parentage, child support, spousal support, requests for restraining orders, or the characterization, division, or temporary use and control of the property or debt of the parties;
(2) Whether material facts are in controversy;
(3) Whether live testimony is necessary for the court to assess the credibility of the parties or other witnesses;
(4) The right of the parties to question anyone submitting reports or other information to the court;
(5) Whether a party offering testimony from a non-party has complied with FC § 217(c); and
(6) Any other factor that is just and equitable."

Chapter 29: Drafting Court Orders

not settle disputed issues currently before the court, then when the parties sign the agreement, it is a stipulation, not a court order.

Stipulations can be made regarding any disputed issue or issues in a family law matter. They are often made with regard to child support, spousal support, custody and visitation of the children. If the stipulation is regarding child support, **FC § 4065** sets forth the following requirements:

> Unless prohibited by applicable federal law, the parties may stipulate to a child support amount subject to approval of the court. However, the court shall not approve a stipulated agreement for child support below the guideline formula amount unless the parties declare all of the following:
> (1) They are fully informed of their rights concerning child support.
> (2) The order is being agreed to without coercion or duress.
> (3) The agreement is in the best interests of the children involved.
> (4) The needs of the children will be adequately met by the stipulated amount.
> (5) The right to support has not been assigned to the county pursuant to Welfare and Institutions Code § 11477 and no public assistance application is pending.

There are stipulation forms whose use is mandatory and forms for optional use. However, if there is no specific form for a stipulation, the stipulation is usually drafted on pleader or numbered paper.

If the local child support agency is involved in the case, no stipulation may be made unless the child support agency has joined in the stipulation. **FC § 4065(b)**.

If the parties agree to stipulate to a child support amount that is below the amount established by the statewide uniform guideline for child support, a change of circumstances is not required to modify the child support amount to guideline or above. **FC § 4065(d)**.

Finally, a party or a party's attorney can request that a stipulation be signed by a judge. The normal procedure for this request is the filing of a *Request for Order* (form *FL-300*).

2. *Pendente Lite* Hearings and Court Orders

Pendente lite means "while the trial is pending". A *pendente lite* hearing is a hearing that occurs after the *Petition* is filed and before the final judgment is rendered. The request is normally made pursuant to a *Request for Order* (*RFO*) (form *FL-300*).

A court order for a *pendente lite* hearing is most commonly drafted on a *Findings and Order After Hearing* form, a *FL-340*

3. Postjudgment Modifications or Terminations

a. In General

A modification is a change or termination of an existing court order. A request for a

Chapter 29: Drafting Court Orders

modification hearing can be made during the divorce or after the paternity or divorce judgment.

A support order may not be modified or terminated as to an amount that accrued before the date of the filing of the notice of motion or order to show cause (*RFO*) to modify or terminate. **FC § 3651(c)(1)**.

A found error in the amount of the current support or arrearage in an order, or if the amount exceeds federal or state limits, is not grounds to vacate the assignment order. However, the court must modify the order to reflect the correct or allowable amount of support or arrearages. **FC § 5272**.

After the hearing and decision of the trial court, the formal order is drafted on an *Order and Findings After Hearing* (form *FL-340*) that can be found at: ***www.courts.ca.gov/documents/fl340.pdf***.

The rules with regard to filing a request are set forth **CRC Rule 5.570**, which provides that the following must be included:

A petition for modification must be liberally construed in favor of its sufficiency. The petition must be verified and, to the extent known to the petitioner, must contain the following:
(1) The name of the court to which the petition is addressed;
(2) The title and action number of the original proceeding;
(3) The name and age of the child, nonminor, or nonminor dependent;
(4) The address of the child, nonminor, or nonminor dependent unless confidential under (c);
(5) The name and address of the parent or guardian of the child or nonminor;
(6) The date and general nature of the order sought to be modified;
(7) A concise statement of any change of circumstance or new evidence that requires changing the order or, for requests under section 388(c)(1)(B), a concise statement of the relevant action or inaction of the parent or guardian;
(8) A concise statement of the proposed change of the order;
(9) A statement of the petitioner's relationship or interest in the child, nonminor, or nonminor dependent, if the petition is made by a person other than the child, nonminor, or nonminor dependent; and
(10) A statement whether or not all parties agree to the proposed change.

---

b. Child Support Orders

Pursuant to **FC § 3651,** a child support order may be modified or terminated at any time as the court determines to be necessary, with the following exceptions:

(1) An amount that accrued before the date of the filing of the notice of motion or order to show cause to modify or terminate;
(2) If there is a written agreement or oral agreement made in open court between the parties, providing that the spousal support is nonmodifiable;

(3) An order for adult child support pursuant to **FC § 3587**[2]; and
(4) An order where a child is receiving public assistance pursuant to **FC § 4004**[3].

A child support order may be modified, in conformity with the statewide uniform guideline, to consolidate arrearages and wage assignments for children of the parties and to consolidate orders for support. **FC § 3651(b)**.

To request a modification of a child support order, *Request for Order* (form *FL-300*) is used. This form can be found on the official California court website at: ***www.courts.ca.gov/documents/fl300.pdf***.

Other than forms providing custody and visitation (parenting time) orders to be filed in the family court, the clerk must file information where the identification of a related case includes a disclosure of information relating to a juvenile dependency or delinquency matter involving the children of the parties in the pending family law case in the confidential portion of the court file. **CRC Rule 5.440**.

c. Spousal Support Orders

An order for spousal support may not be modified or terminated to the extent that a written agreement or, if there is no written agreement, an oral agreement entered into in open court between the parties, specifically provides that the spousal support is not subject to modification or termination. **FC § 3651(d)**.

4. The *Findings and Order After Hearing* form

To draft a formal court order after a pendente lite or postjudgment modification hearing, the form commonly used is the *Findings and Order After Hearing* (form *FL-340*) (*FOAH*).

CRC Rule 5.125 sets forth the procedure for preparation, objections, service and submission of the *Order After Hearing*. **CRC Rule 5.125** provides:

> The court may prepare the order after hearing and serve copies on the parties or their attorneys. Alternatively, the court may order one of the parties or attorneys to prepare the proposed order as provided in these rules. The court may also modify the timelines and procedures in this rule when appropriate to the case.
> **(a)** The term "party" or "parties" includes both self-represented persons and persons represented by an attorney of record. The procedures in this rule requiring a party to perform action related to the preparation, service, and submission of an order after

---

[2] FC § 3587 provides: "Notwithstanding any other provision of law, the court has the authority to approve a stipulated agreement by the parents to pay for the support of an adult child or for the continuation of child support after a child attains the age of 18 years and to make a support order to effectuate the agreement."

[3] FC § 4004 provides: "In a proceeding where there is at issue the support of a child, the court shall require the parties to reveal whether a party is currently receiving, or intends to apply for, public assistance under the Family Economic Security Act of 1982 (Chapter 2 [commencing with Section 11200] of Part 3 of Division 9 of the Welfare and Institutions Code) for the maintenance of the child."

hearing include the party's attorney of record.

(b) Within 10 calendar days of the court hearing, the party ordered to prepare the proposed order must:

  (1) Serve the proposed order to the other party for approval; or

  (2) If the other party did not appear at the hearing or the matter was uncontested, submit the proposed order directly to the court without the other party's approval. A copy must also be served to the other party or attorney.

(c) Other party approves or rejects proposed order after hearing

  (1) Within 20 calendar days from the court hearing, the other party must review the proposed order to determine if it accurately reflects the orders made by the court and take one of the following actions:

    (A) Approve the proposed order by signing and serving it on the party or attorney who drafted the proposed order; or

    (B) State any objections to the proposed order and prepare an alternate proposed order. Any alternate proposed order prepared by the objecting party must list the findings and orders in the same sequence as the proposed order. After serving any objections and the alternate proposed order to the party or attorney, both parties must follow the procedure in (e).

  (2) If the other party does not respond to the proposed order within 20 calendar days of the court hearing, the party ordered to prepare the proposed order must submit the proposed order to the court without approval within 25 calendar days of the hearing date. The correspondence to the court and to the other party must include:

    (A) The date the proposed order was served on the other party;

    (B) The other party's reasons for not approving the proposed order, if known;

    (C) The date and results of any attempts to meet and confer, if relevant; and

    (D) A request that the court sign the proposed order.

(d) Failure to prepare proposed order after hearing

  (1) If the party ordered by the court to prepare the proposed order fails to serve the proposed order to the other party within 10 calendar days from the court hearing, the other party may prepare the proposed order and serve it to the party or attorney whom the court ordered to prepare the proposed order.

  (2) Within 5 calendar days from service of the proposed order, the party who had been ordered to prepare the order must review the proposed order to determine if it accurately reflects the orders made by the court and take one of the following actions:

    (A) Approve the proposed order by signing and serving it to the party or attorney who drafted the proposed order; or

    (B) State any objections to the proposed order and prepare an alternate proposed order. Any alternate proposed order by the objecting party must list the findings and orders in the same sequence as the proposed order. After serving any objections and the alternate proposed order to the other party or attorney, both parties must follow the procedure in (e).

  (3) If the party does not respond as described in (2), the party who prepared the proposed order must submit the proposed order to the court without approval within 5 calendar days. The cover letter to the court and to the other party or attorney must include:

    (A) The facts relating to the preparation of the order, including the date the proposed order was due and the date the proposed order was served to the party whom the court ordered to draft the proposed order;

    (B) The party's reasons for not preparing or approving the proposed order, if known;

    (C) The date and results of any attempts to meet and confer, if relevant; and

    (D) A request that the court sign the proposed order.

(e) Objections to proposed order after hearing

Chapter 29: Drafting Court Orders

> (1) If a party objects to the proposed order after hearing, both parties have 10 calendar days following service of the objections and the alternate proposed order after hearing to meet and confer by telephone or in person to attempt to resolve the disputed language.
>
> (2) If the parties reach an agreement, the proposed findings and order after hearing must be submitted to the court within 10 calendar days following the meeting.
>
> (3) If the parties fail to resolve their disagreement after meeting and conferring, each party will have 10 calendar days following the date of the meeting to submit to the court and serve on each other the following documents:
>
>   (A) A proposed *Findings and Order After Hearing* (FL-340) (and any form attachments);
>
>   (B) A copy of the minute order or official transcript of the court hearing; and
>
>   (C) A cover letter that explains the objections, describes the differences in the two proposed orders, references the relevant sections of the transcript or minute order, and includes the date and results of the meet-and-confer conferences.
>
> (f) Before signing a proposed order submitted to the court without the other party's approval, the court must first compare the proposed order after hearing to the minute order; official transcript, if available; or other court record.
>
> (g) After the proposed order is signed by the court, the court clerk must file the order. The party who prepared the order must serve an endorsed-filed copy to the other party.

Forms for Stipulations, Court Orders and Attachments

The following is a list of many of the Judicial Council forms to be used for family law stipulations, court orders, judgments and attachments. The asterisk indicates that the form is a mandatory use form.

1. Stipulations

FL-240* Stipulation for Entry of Judgment RE: Establishment of Parental Relationship
FL-350* Stipulation to Establish or Modify Child Support and Order
FL-355 Stipulation and Order for Custody and/or Visitation of Children
FL-615* Stipulation for Judgment or Supplemental Judgment Regarding Parental Obligations and Judgment (Governmental)
FL-625* Stipulation and Order (Governmental)
FL-626 Stipulation and Order Waiving Unassigned Arrears (Governmental)
FL-663* Stipulation and Order for Joinder of Other Parent (Governmental)

2. Court Orders

FL-192* Minutes and Order or Judgment
FL-195 Income Withholding for Support
FL-278* Order After Hearing on Motion to Set Aside Judgment of Paternity (Family Law – Governmental)
FL-279 Order After Hearing on Motion to Set Aside Judgment of Paternity (Family Law—Governmental)
FL-290* Order After Hearing on Motion to Set Aside Voluntary Declaration of Paternity (Family Law – Governmental)

Chapter 29: Drafting Court Orders

FL-305* Temporary Emergency Court Orders
FL-306 Application and Order for Reissuance of Request for Order and Temporary Emergency Orders
FL-323 Order Appointing Counsel for a Child
FL-327* Order Appointing Child Custody Evaluator
FL-336* Order to Pay Waived Court Fees and Costs (Superior Court)
FL-338* Order After Hearing on Motion to Set Aside Order to Pay Waived Court Fees (Superior Court)
FL-340* Findings and Order After Hearing (Family Law – Custody and Support – Uniform Parentage)
FL-341(A)* Supervised Visitation Order
FL-367* Order After Hearing on Motion to Set Aside Support Order
FL-382* Expedited Child Support Order
FL-395* Ex Parte Application for Restoration of Former Name After Entry of Judgment and Order (Family Law)
FL-400* Order for Child Support Security Deposit and Evidence Deposit
FL-401* Application for Disbursement and Order for Disbursement From Child Support Security Deposit
FL-410* Order to Show Cause and Affidavit for Contempt
FL-415 Findings and Order Regarding Contempt (Family Law – Domestic Violence Prevention – Uniform Parentage – Governmental)
FL-435* Earnings Assignment Order for Spousal or Partner Support (Family Law)
FL-455* Stay of Service of Earnings Assignment and Order
FL-460 Qualified Domestic Relations Order for Support (Earning Assignment Order for Support)
FL-470* Application and Order for Health Coverage
FL-511* Ex Parte Application for Order for Nondisclosure of Address and Order (UIFSA)
FL-560 Ex Parte Application for Transfer and Order (UIFSA)
FL-627* Order for Genetic (Parentage) Testing
FL-665* Findings and Recommendation of Commissioner (Governmental)
FL-675* Order After Judicial Review of License Denial (Governmental)
FL-678* Order Determining Claim of Exemption or Third-Party Claim (Governmental)
FL-683* Order to Show Cause (Governmental)
FL-687* Order After Hearing (Governmental)
FL-688* Short Form Order After Hearing (Governmental)
FL-192* Minutes and Order or Judgment
FL-915 Order on Request of Minor to Marry or Establish a Domestic Partnership
FL-958 Order on Application to Be Relieved As Counsel Upon Completion of Limited Scope Representation
FL-982 Order for Publication or Posting

3. **Attachments to Stipulations and Orders**

FL-341 Child Custody and Visitation (Parenting Time) Order Attachment
FL-341(B)* Child Abduction Prevention Order Attachment

FL-341(C) Children's Holiday Schedule Attachment
FL-341(D) Additional Provisions-Physical Custody Attachment
FL-341(E) Joint Legal Custody Attachment
FL-342* Child Support Information and Order Attachment
FL-342(A)* Non-Guideline Child Support Findings Attachment
FL-343 Spousal, Partner or Family Support Order Attachment
FL-344 * Property Order Attachment to Findings and Order After Hearing
FL-346 Attorney's Fees and Costs Order Attachment
FL-347* Bifurcation of Status of Marriage or Domestic Partnership – Attachment (Family Law)
FL-461 Attachment to Qualified Domestic Relations Order for Support (Earning Assignment Order for Support)
FL-693 Guideline Findings Attachment (Governmental)

EDUCATIONAL EXERCISES

1. What judicial council form is used to draft the formal court order after a "pendente lite" hearing?
2. If a stipulation made by the parties is not made pursuant to an issue that is currently before the court, can it still become a court order? Explain.

CHAPTER 30: Marital Agreements

In Brief...

PREMARITAL AGREEMENTS FC § 1610:
- Are agreements that prospective spouses make in contemplation of marriage that are effective upon marriage;
- Require no consideration; and
- There is no fiduciary relationship between the parties because they are not yet married.

Premarital agreements executed prior to 1986:
- Could not alter a spouse's obligation to support the other spouse or would most likely be held void and unenforceable as promoting or encouraging divorce; and
- An unenforceable or illegal provision does not invalidate an entire agreement.

Premarital agreements executed from 1986 to 2001:
- Were not *per se* invalid if the agreement contained a spousal support waiver; and
- The validity of the agreement is a discretionary decision made by a trial court.

Premarital agreements executed from 2002 to the present, FC § 1612(c), FC § 1615(c):
- Provide that there is a rebuttable presumption that the agreements were not entered into voluntarily unless the party against whom enforcement was sought:
- Was represented by independent legal counsel or expressly waived in writing;
- Had not less than 7 calendar days to seek independent legal counsel;
- If unrepresented, was fully informed of the terms and basic effect of the agreement;
- Was not executed under duress, fraud or undue influence; and
- Was not entered into **voluntarily by factors the court deems rlevant.**

Drafting a premarital agreement

CHART 9: Checklist for a Premarital Agreement

POSTMARITAL AGREEMENTS, (transmutations FC § 850):
- Are contracts made by and between the spouses during the marriage are called postmarital agreements;
- Are not construed and enforced under the same standards as premarital agreements;
- Have a fiduciary relationship between the spouses in postmarital agreements; and
- Are often executed to change separate property into community property or vice versa.

CHART 10: Checklist for a Post Marital Agreement

Chapter 30: Marital Agreements

> ***MARITAL SETTLEMENT AGREEMENTS:***
> - Are the most common type of marital agreement;
> - Memorialize the facts and issues that are undisputed or have been agreed upon;
> - Are contracts and the laws regarding contracts apply; and
> - There is no judicial council form so most family law firms have their own version (template).
>
> **CHART 11: Marital Settlement Agreement - Check List with Codes**

Introduction

From the time that laws were first enacted in California to the present day, parties have entered into marital agreements prior to marrying, during the marriage and when separating and/or divorcing.[1]

These three common types of marital agreements are currently called premarital, postmarital and marital settlement agreements, respectively. The main difference between the three is the time of the signing of the agreement.

1. Premarital Agreements

Agreements made prior to marriage are called premarital, prenuptial or antenuptial agreements.

The Family Code uses the term **premarital** to describe "an agreement between prospective spouses made in contemplation of marriage and to be effective upon marriage." **FC § 1610**. **Premarital agreement** is the preferred term and the California legislature changed the word **prenuptial** to **premarital** in all of the California laws.

Premarital agreements do not require consideration, and there is no fiduciary duty between the parties because they are not yet married.

When the California Civil Code was established in 1872, California legislature enacted a law that provided that a husband and wife could enter into a marital agreement if:

(1) it was in writing;
(2) it did not alter their legal rights; and

---

[1] See *Graham v. Bennet* (1852) 2 Cal. 503, where a premarital agreement was found to be void because Defendant was married to another when it was executed; *Gough v. Ferguson et al.* (1864) 26 Cal. 546 at pp. 572-573, where the court held an agreement executed during marriage giving the real property to wife was valid; and *In re Estate of Noah* (1887) 73 Cal. 583, where a separation agreement was held to be valid.

Chapter 30: Marital Agreements

(3) it concerned only property and support during separation.[2]

Although the law specifically provided that a marital agreement had to be in writing to be valid, the court held in *KENNEY v. KENNEY* (1934) 220 Cal. 134 that a fully executed, oral marital agreement could also be upheld, if it was a legal contract in all other respects. *Id.* at p. 137. In *Kenney*, the court concluded that an oral contract that the parties confirmed by their acts and their conduct during their marriage was a valid, enforceable contract. *Id.* (See also *WOODS v. SECURITY-FIRST NATIONAL BANK* (1956) 46 Cal.2d 697 at 700, where the court upheld an oral agreement between spouses that changed the character of the separate property owned by one spouse prior to the marriage into community property after the marriage.)

Premarital agreements commonly have provisions regarding: **(1)** real and personal property owned prior to the marriage and that will be acquired during the marriage; **(2)** income earned prior to the marriage and will be earned during the marriage; and **(3)** support upon separation or dissolution.
Laws regarding property and income have changed very little over the years, but the laws concerning support have changed substantially.

Written separation agreements between a husband and wife that provide for support during that separation date back to the first laws enacted in California and are usually held to be valid. Child-support provisions that adversely affect children or provide that a parent does not have to support his or her children have always been void and against public policy. However, the laws regarding the validity of a premarital agreement have changed over the years from: **(1)** disfavoring provisions in marital agreements that alter a spouse's duty to support the other spouse, **(2)** allowing the court complete discretion to decide the validity of a premarital agreement and **(3)** to providing that there is rebuttable presumption that the agreement was entered into involuntarily if the five conditions set forth in **FC § 1615** were not met.

1. Premarital Agreements Executed Prior to 1986

In 1850, the California legislature enacted laws regarding community property and the rights of parties to enter into contracts that contain stipulations that are contrary to these laws.[3] The legislature also enacted laws that provide that the property rights of spouses may be altered by a premarital agreement or other marital property agreement.[4]

---

[2] Former Civil Code § 159 provides that: "[a] husband and wife cannot, by any contract with each other, alter their legal relations, except as to property, and except that they may agree, in writing…and may make provision for the support of either of them and of their children during such separation." Former Civil Code § 1624 enacted in 1872 provides "[t]he following contracts are invalid, unless the same or some note of memorandum thereof be in writing and subscribed by the party to be charged, or by his agent." Former Civil Code § 178, also enacted in 1872 provides: "[a]ll contracts for marriage settlements must be in writing and executed and acknowledged or proved in like manner as a grant of land is required to be executed and acknowledged or proved."
[3] Statutes of California passed at the First Session of the Legislature, 1850, chapter 103, § 14, p. 255.
[4] FC § 1500; former Civil Code: § 5200 (1985) § 5133 (1969).

Chapter 30: Marital Agreements

Parties contemplating marriage and parties already married could enter into a contract with each other concerning the property of either party. Former Civil Code § 159. Additionally, parties could make a contract waiving rights to receive a family allowance[5] when one of the parties died. Parties could make an agreement for the support of either of them and of their children during a separation period. These contracts, if legal in all other respects, would be upheld providing a court did not find that the agreement fostered or promoted divorce.

However, if an agreement had a provision that altered support obligations other than support during separation, courts held that this provision was void as against public policy. A husband and wife had a reciprocal statutory obligation to support the other and "agreements that [were] designed to waive, diminish or alter the statutory obligation of spouses to mutually support each other were contrary to public policy and therefore void and unenforceable…" The rationale for this rule was that marriage was considered more than a mere contract. It was "regarded as a social institution vital to society's stability." *In re Marriage of MELISSA* (2012) 212 Cal.App.4th 598 at p. 604. This public policy was still in effect more than one hundred years later when the Supreme Court of California decided *In re Marriage of HIGGASON* (1973) 10 Cal.3d 476 (*Higgason*).

In *Higgason*, a 73-year-old woman with substantial assets married a 48-year-old man with little to no means. They executed a marital agreement prior to marriage that waived the statutory obligations that spouses have to support each other. The husband became ill during the marriage and required extensive hospitalization, surgery and medical attention. When the parties separated he had no separate property, and there was no community or quasi-community property; so, he was unable to care for himself or seek employment. Even though the wife had the ability to provide support to the husband, the trial court refused to award the husband any support at all "acting under the erroneous conviction that the [premarital agreement that the parties signed] precluded an award of post-dissolution support to the husband." *Id.* at p. 488. The Supreme Court reversed the trial court's decision and held that: **(1)** contracts entered into prior to marriage could not waive the statutory obligations that spouses have to support each other, and **(2)** that contracts that facilitate divorce or separation by providing for a settlement only in the event of such an occurrence are void as against public policy. *Id.*

---

[5] A family allowance is payments made from a deceased person's estate to surviving family members who were dependent on the decedent for support prior to the decedent's death. A family allowance is payments made from a deceased person's estate to surviving family members who were dependent on the decedent for support prior to the decedent's death. (See *Estate of Schwartz* (1947) 79 Cal.App.2d 308, where the court denied the wife a family allowance because the parties executed a premarital agreement that she had clearly waived her right to receive a family allowance. *Id.* at p. 311. Also see *Estate of Wallace* (1977) 74 Cal.App.3d 196 where the court granted a family allowance stating that "the purpose of the family allowance is to continue, during settlement of the estate, the support of the surviving spouse (or eligible child) that he or she was receiving or was entitled to receive during the decedent's life." *Id.* at 202.)

Chapter 30: Marital Agreements

Three years after *Higgason, supra*, the Supreme Court in *In re Marriage of DAWLEY* (1976) 17 Cal.3d 342 held that when a spousal support provision in a premarital agreement:

> violates the state policy favoring divorce only insofar as its terms encourage or promote dissolution... [this] does not require the invalidation of the entire agreement... it requires only that the courts refuse to enforce [the] specific contractual provisions which by their terms seek to promote the dissolution of a marriage. *Id.* at pp. 352, 350, respectively.

Thus, from 1850 until the law changed in 1986, provisions in premarital agreements that altered a spouse's obligation to support the other spouse would mostly likely be held as void and unenforceable as promoting or encouraging divorce. But if an agreement had such a provision and the provision was held to be void, the entire contract was not necessarily void and unenforceable because the remainder of the provisions could still be held as a valid agreement providing all of the other provisions were not illegal or unenforceable and did not foster divorce

2. Agreements Executed from 1986 to 2001

The Uniform Premarital Agreement Act (UPAA)[6] was promulgated in 1983. Senate Bill 1143, which contained the entire UPAA, was introduced in the California legislature as a proposed law in March of 1985. However, as the following case explains, before the UPAA was signed into law, the legislature deleted Section 3(a)(4) and Section 6(b). Senate Bill No. 1143 with these deletions became Civil Code § 5300 et seq. operative on January 1, 1986.[7]

a. *The Pendleton Case*

> **In re MARRIAGE of CANDACE PENDLETON and BARRY I. FIREMAN.**
> **CANDACE PENDLETON, Respondent, v. BARRY I. FIREMAN, Appellant.**
> **SUPREME COURT OF CALIFORNIA**
> **24 Cal.4th 39; 5 P.3d 839; 99 Cal.Rptr.2d 278**
> **August 21, 2000, Decided**
> **(Marriage of Pendleton)**
>
> Candace Pendleton and Barry I. Fireman married on July 13, 1991. On July 1, 1991, they had executed a premarital agreement which provided, inter alia: "[B]oth parties now and forever waive, in the event of a dissolution of the marriage, all rights to any type of spousal support or child support from the other; . . ." The agreement acknowledged that each party had been represented by independent counsel in the negotiation and preparation of the agreement, that counsel had advised each of the meaning and legal consequences of the agreement, and that each party had read and understood the

---

[6] "Uniform Premarital Agreement Act Drafted by the National Conference of Commissioners on Uniform State Laws" and by it approved and recommended for enactment in all the states at its Annual Conference Meeting in its Ninety-Second Year in Boca Raton, Florida July 22-29, 1983. Referred to as "UPAA."

[7] It was repealed December 31, 1993 and reenacted as FC § 1600 et seq. on January 1, 1994 with no substantial change.

527

Chapter 30: Marital Agreements

agreement and its legal consequences. Their respective counsel certified that this had been done and that their clients understood the meaning and legal consequences of the agreement and executed it freely and voluntarily.

The couple separated in 1995, and on April 3, 1996, Candace filed a petition for dissolution of the marriage and subsequently sought spousal support. Candace acknowledged the existence of a premarital agreement in a declaration that accompanied her request for spousal support, stating that she was then investigating its validity. At the time the dissolution petition was filed, each party had a net worth of approximately $ 2.5 million. Candace, who had two children from a prior marriage, held a master's degree and was an aspiring writer. Barry, who held a doctorate in pharmacology and a law degree, was a businessman with ownership interests in numerous companies and business ventures.

Candace declared that her monthly gross income was $ 5,772, consisting of $ 1,352 in Social Security benefits for two children from a prior marriage, $ 2,000 from a brokerage account, and $ 2,420 in rental income. Her net monthly income was $ 4,233. Barry sought to strike the pleading seeking support or to have a separate trial on the validity of the prenuptial agreement. The court denied the motion for separate trial, concluding that discovery on the issue of validity would overlap that on other issues and would not result in saving time or litigation costs. The court ruled that the waiver of spousal support was against public policy and thus was unenforceable, noted that the couple had maintained a lifestyle in the high $ 20,000 to $ 32,000 per month range, and ordered Barry to pay temporary spousal support of $ 8,500 per month.

On Barry's appeal, the Court of Appeal reversed the order for temporary spousal support. The Court of Appeal acknowledged that the Legislature had deleted subdivision (a)(4) from section 3 of the Uniform Premarital Agreement Act (Uniform Act) prior to adopting the act in 1985.[8] The omitted subdivision would have expressly permitted the parties to a premarital agreement to contract with respect to modification or elimination of spousal support. The Court of Appeal concluded, however, that the Legislature intended to leave the question of whether spousal support waivers in premarital agreements violate public policy to the courts and that there was presently no authority governing the public policy question. In reaching the latter conclusion, the court reasoned that the question had not been reconsidered after the adoption of the Family Law Act of 1969, which repealed the law permitting divorce only on a showing of fault, or in light of current law that gives both spouses equal control over management and control of community property (FC §§ 1100- 1103) and mandates equal division on dissolution (FC § 2550). In the view of the Court of Appeal, the current state of family law is one that "should not per se prohibit premarital spousal support waivers or limitations. All the protection the parties need is expressly provided by the California [version of the Uniform] Act." The Court of Appeal therefore remanded the matter to the trial court which, in the belief that such waivers were per se unenforceable, had not determined whether this agreement was enforceable under the rules set forth in section 1615 and the policies underlying the Uniform Act and the California version thereof.[9]

---

[8] The California version of the Uniform Act was enacted in 1985 as Civil Code § 5300 et seq., which was repealed in 1992, and effective January 1, 1994 it was reenacted as part of the new FC § 1600 et seq. (FC § 1601.) The California version of section 3 of the Uniform Act is now FC § 1612. (Stats. 1992, ch. 162, § 3, p. 464; *id.*, § 10, p. 500.)

[9] FC § 1615 provides: "(a) A premarital agreement is not enforceable if the party against whom enforcement is sought proves either of the following:

Chapter 30: Marital Agreements

DISCUSSION

The California version of the Uniform Act omits subdivision (a)(4) of section 3 of the Uniform Act (subdivision (a)(4)). When first introduced on March 7, 1985, Senate Bill No. 1143 (1985-1986 Reg. Sess.) (Senate Bill 1143), the California version of the Uniform Act, included subdivision (a)(4), and thus listed among the permissible subjects of a premarital agreement "the modification or elimination of spousal support." The spousal support waiver provision was deleted by amendment. (Assem. Amend. to Sen. Bill No. 1143 (1985-1986 Reg. Sess.) Aug. 28, 1985.) The amendment of Senate Bill 1143 that deleted subdivision (a)(4) simultaneously deleted a provision, subdivision (b) of section 6 of the Uniform Act, which provided: "If a provision of a premarital agreement modifies or eliminates spousal support and that modification or elimination causes one party to the agreement to be eligible for support under a program of public assistance at the time of separation or marital dissolution, a court, notwithstanding the terms of the agreement, may require the other party to provide support to the extent necessary to avoid that eligibility." (Sen. Bill No. 1143 (1985-1986 Reg. Sess.) Mar. 7, 1985; Assem. Amend. to Sen. Bill No. 1143 (1985-1986 Reg. Sess.) Aug. 28, 1985.) As enacted, Senate Bill 1143 became Civil Code former section 5315, now FC § 1612.

The Court of Appeal held that neither the Legislature's deletion from the legislation of express authorization for premarital waivers of spousal support, nor past cases refusing to enforce waivers of spousal support, preclude such waivers today. **The court reasoned that the legislative history of section 1612 suggested that, in omitting subdivision (a)(4) of the Uniform Act, the Legislature intended to leave the enforceability of spousal support waivers to the courts.** It found support for that conclusion in two reports by the Assembly Subcommittee on Administration of Justice. The first was prepared for an August 19, 1985, hearing on Senate Bill 1143. Senate Bill 1143 repealed prior statutory law governing premarital agreements and enacted the Uniform Act. In the first report staff advised that California courts did not permit enforcement of premarital agreements on spousal support and recommended deletion "to allow California case law to continue to prevail on the issue of spousal support in premarital agreements." (Assem. Subcom. on Admin. of Justice, Rep. on Sen. Bill No. 1143 (1985-1986 Reg. Sess.) for Aug. 19, 1985, hearing, p. 3.)

It is clear that the Legislature understood that the omission of authorization for premarital waivers of spousal support in section 1612 would leave the law as it was in 1985. The subcommittee reports reflect that understanding. We do not agree with respondent and the dissent, however, that in so doing the Legislature thereby abrogated the role of the courts in developing the law governing premarital waivers of spousal support. We will not presume that the Legislature intended that the law remain static. It would be unreasonable to assume that the Legislature intended the common law of the 19th century to govern the

---

(1) That party did not execute the agreement voluntarily.
(2) The agreement was unconscionable when it was executed and, before execution of the agreement, all of the following applied to that party:
(A) That party was not provided a fair and reasonable disclosure of the property or financial obligations of the other party.
(B) That party did not voluntarily and expressly waive, in writing, any right to disclosure of the property or financial obligations of the other party beyond the disclosure provided.
(C) That party did not have, or reasonably could not have had, an adequate knowledge of the property or financial obligations of the other party.
(b) An issue of unconscionability of a premarital agreement shall be decided by the court as a matter of law."

marital relationship in the 21st century. The most reasonable understanding of the Legislature's purpose when it omitted subdivision (a)(4) is that it was satisfied with the evolution of the common law governing premarital waivers of spousal support and intended to permit that evolution to continue. Had the Legislature intended to forbid spousal support waivers, it is logical to assume that it would have done so by expressly including spousal support in FC § 1621(b), which reads: "The right of a child to support may not be adversely affected by a premarital agreement." We agree with the Court of Appeal, therefore, that the court is free to reexamine the assumptions that underlie the common law rule that premarital spousal support waivers promote dissolution and for that reason contravene public policy. Having done so, we also agree with the Court of Appeal that the common law policy, based on assumptions that dissolution of marriage is contrary to public policy and that premarital waivers of spousal support may promote dissolution, is anachronistic.

Section 1612 expressly permits the parties to contract with regard to numerous property rights, including "[t]he dispositions of property upon separation, marital dissolution, death, or the occurrence or nonoccurrence of any other event." (FC § 1612(a)(3).) No basis appears on which to distinguish premarital waivers of spousal support from agreements governing property rights insofar as either has a potential for promoting dissolution. As the Court of Appeal recognized, today the availability of an enforceable premarital agreement "may in fact encourage rather than discourage marriage." We agree with the Court of Appeal, therefore, that, when entered into voluntarily by parties who are aware of the effect of the agreement, a premarital waiver of spousal support does not offend contemporary public policy. Such agreements are, therefore, permitted under FC § 1612(a)(7), which authorizes the parties to contract in a premarital agreement regarding "[a]ny other matter, including their personal rights and obligations, not in violation of public policy or a statute imposing a criminal penalty."

It is enough to conclude here that no public policy is violated by permitting enforcement of a waiver of spousal support executed by intelligent, well-educated persons, each of whom appears to be self-sufficient in property and earning ability, and both of whom have the advice of counsel regarding their rights and obligations as marital partners at the time they execute the waiver. Such a waiver does not violate public policy and is not per se unenforceable as the trial court believed.

We conclude that no policy of this state makes an agreement like that entered into by the parties to this action per se unenforceable, and affirm the judgment of the Court of Appeal.

b. *The Bonds' Cases*

Barry Bonds, a famous baseball player, and his wife Susann entered into a premarital agreement during this time period. During their divorce, Barry sought to enforce the premarital agreement. The trial court case was first heard before Commissioner George Taylor, who later recused himself sua sponte after the media reported that he had requested an autograph from Barry.

The case was then transferred to the Honorable Judith W. Kozloski. The issue of the validity of the premarital agreement had been previously bifurcated to be

Chapter 30: Marital Agreements

determined before the other divorce issues. And now, Judge Kozloski had to decide whether or not the premarital agreement was valid.

The Appellate case that follows contains the findings of the trial court.

> *In re Marriage of SUSANN MARGRETH and BARRY LAMAR BONDS. SUSANN MARGRETH BONDS, Appellant, v. BARRY LAMAR BONDS, Respondent.*
> **COURT OF APPEAL OF CALIFORNIA, FIRST APPELLATE DISTRICT, DIVISION TWO**
> 71 Cal.App.4th 290; 83 Cal.Rptr.2d 783
> April 12, 1999, Filed
>
> Both Barry and Sun were 23 years old when they met in Montreal in August 1987. At that time, Barry earned $106,000 a year as a major league baseball player for the Pittsburgh Pirates.
>
> Sun had been in Montreal since the spring of 1985, when, at the age of 21, she left her native home in Sweden to live with her father in Canada and work in his small restaurant. She attended classes to become a cosmetologist or an aesthetician, and hoped someday to have her own business serving celebrity clients.
>
> After they met for the first time in August, Sun and Barry spent two days together in Montreal. Subsequently, Sun visited Barry in Arizona for 10 days and returned to Montreal to attend beautician school. On November 7, 1987, Sun moved to Phoenix to live with Barry. Seven days later Barry proposed to Sun. The parties set their wedding date for February 7, 1988.
>
> The wedding was to occur in Las Vegas, and Barry's godfather, Willie Mays, secured hotel rooms there for the wedding party. Sun invited her Swedish friend Margareta Forsberg (Forsberg), who currently lived in Montreal, to attend the wedding, and she arrived in Phoenix on January 29, 1988. She stayed with Sun and Barry until after the wedding.
>
> Barry's banker and financial advisor, Mel Wilcox (Wilcox), referred him to Arizona attorneys Sabinus Megwa (Megwa) and Leonard Brown (Brown) to prepare a prenuptial agreement for him. Brown, who had been practicing law for about seven years, assigned to Megwa the task of preparing the premarital agreement. Megwa had been admitted to the Arizona Bar 10 months earlier and had no experience in drafting premarital agreements.
>
> Barry, Sun, and Forsberg had reservations to fly from Phoenix to Las Vegas in the early afternoon of February 5, 1987. Barry and Sun planned to get married on February 6 but needed to obtain their marriage license and select a wedding chapel once they arrived in Las Vegas.
>
> On the morning of February 5, just prior to their scheduled flight departure, Barry and Sun, as well as Sun's friend Forsberg, met with Megwa and Brown in their law office for two to three hours. Wilcox met them as they entered the building and told Sun that there would not be a wedding if she did not sign the premarital agreement.
>
> At the meeting, Megwa and Brown provided Barry and Sun with copies of the premarital

agreement. Neither Sun nor Barry had an opportunity to review the agreement before the February 5 meeting. Brown and Megwa informed Sun that she "may" want to seek counsel.

The agreement presented at trial contained numerous typographical errors, and a portion of one provision was typed twice. Moreover, the pages were not numbered and none of the pages contained the parties' initials. The agreement also appeared to be incomplete. It ended abruptly with the statement "OTHER PROVISIONS AS FOLLOWS:"; and the immediately following page contained only the signature block and signature lines for the parties and their attorneys and a notarization block. Barry and Sun had signed above their names, but Brown had signed only the notary subscription. Brown did not sign the signature line indicating he was Barry's attorney.

Although the agreement referred to schedules of the parties' separate property, no schedules were attached. This was despite a provision which provided: "Both parties have initialed each page of the attached lists as evidence that they have read and concur with the classification of each item on each list." Inexplicably, a handwritten list of such properties, used at the meeting for discussion purposes, was not attached. Brown testified that he "believed" both parties were aware of the other's assets.

A heading in the agreement stated "SPOUSAL MAINTENANCE AND CHILD SUPPORT." Following that heading, the agreement contained an illegal provision regarding the parties' contributions for child support but stated nothing regarding spousal support.

Brown specifically remembered explaining the provision regarding earnings during marriage entitled, "CONTROL AND EARNINGS OF BOTH HUSBAND AND WIFE DURING MARRIAGE." This provision provided the following: "We agree that all the earnings and accumulations resulting from the other's personal services, skill, efforts and work, together with all property acquired with funds and income derived therefrom, shall be the separate property of that spouse. [P] The earnings from husband and wife during marriage shall be: [P] separate property of that spouse. . . ." After the parties signed the agreement they left the originals with the attorneys.

The case was first heard before Commissioner George Taylor, who later recused himself sua sponte after the media reported that he had requested an autograph from Barry. The case was transferred to the Honorable Judith W. Kozloski. The legal separation action was later converted to one for divorce, and a status-only dissolution judgment was entered on December 8, 1994.

Prior to trial, the court considered whether Arizona or California law should be applied to the agreement. The agreement contained an obscure provision entitled "Situs," which stated the following: "This Agreement shall be subject to and governed by the laws of the state set forth as the effective place of this Agreement." Although it is undisputed that the agreement took place in Arizona, the agreement itself never defined "effective place" within the meaning of its own language.

In her appeal, Sun challenges the trial court's determination that the prenuptial agreement was valid.

By its failure to define "effective place," the choice of law provision--like so many of the provisions in this contract--is both incomplete and ambiguous.

Sun maintains, the existence of two different "copies" of the agreement, which could not have both been made from the same original, raised questions of authenticity. A photocopy which had been received from an attorney in Pennsylvania was introduced as exhibit 1, while another copy, exhibit A, was also presented at trial, but it incorrectly spelled Barry's last name as "Bond" on its first page. This difference was particularly consequential, Sun asserts, because neither document had page numbers or initials on the pages. Furthermore, since an identical copy of the same original signature page had been attached to both exhibits, there was an inference of obvious tampering. Because Sun and Barry testified that they had only signed one draft, someone must have improperly attached a copy of the signature page to at least one of the alleged duplicates of the original.

The agreement ended with the statement "OTHER PROVISIONS AS FOLLOWS:"; but the following page only contained the signature block and the signature lines for the parties and their attorneys, followed by a notarization block. Brown did not sign the line provided for Barry's attorney.

Inexplicably, the agreement referred to schedules of the parties' separate property, but no such schedules were attached. The agreement also referred to a listing of the community property, but no such listing was attached. The absence of these schedules contradicted another provision in the agreement which stated: "Both parties have initialed each page of the attached lists as evidence that they have read and concur with the classification of each item on each list."

Barry's own testimony indicated that Sun did not understand *why* she needed an attorney. Barry testified: ". . . Sun said she didn't want a lawyer. Sun didn't have anything. I paid for everything. Sun said, what do I need a lawyer for? I don't have anything. I mean, I know exactly what she said in that conversation." This is precisely the problem: Sun thought she did not have anything and did not need a lawyer, and no one disabused her of that incorrect perception. The fact was that she did have something: she had the potential legal right to community property. The whole purpose of the agreement was to divest her of rights which would accrue to her as a matter of law unless she waived them before the wedding.

In this context, the comment that Sun "may want" to obtain an attorney was worse than worthless; it was misleading. There was not even a superficial attempt to explain to Sun the reasons for needing an attorney, and attorneys cannot avoid their ethical obligation to avoid conflicts of interest by merely telling the unrepresented party that he or she may obtain an attorney. Not only did Brown fail to identify any conflict of interest, but, he frequently acted in a manner that made him appear to be an independent legal advisor rather than Barry's advocate.

Further, the agreement's signature line for Barry's attorney remained blank, and Brown only signed the signature line provided for the notary.
Specifically, Barry contends that Sun understood that she was waiving her statutory rights to community property.[10] The critical provision regarding the community property waiver

---

[10] Primarily at issue is paragraph 10 of the agreement, which provided, in pertinent part, as follows: "Control and Earnings of Both Husband and Wife During Marriage. We agree that all the earnings and accumulations resulting from the other's personal services, skill, efforts and work, together with all property acquired with funds and income derived therefrom, shall be the separate property of that spouse. [P] The earnings from husband and wife during marriage shall be: [P] separate property of that

was paragraph 10 in the agreement, which provided, in pertinent part, as follows: "CONTROL AND EARNINGS OF BOTH HUSBAND AND WIFE DURING MARRIAGE. We agree that all the earnings and accumulations resulting from the other's personal services, skill, efforts and work, together with all property acquired with funds and income derived therefrom, shall be the separate property of that spouse. [P] The earnings from husband and wife during marriage shall be: [P] separate property of that spouse."

Nothing in this paragraph explained that such earnings would ordinarily be community property. No waiver of right can be inferred from a written stipulation except where an intentional relinquishment of the known right is explicit, the terms and scope of the waiver are spelled out and the express reason for the waiver set forth . . . .

Barry, who had negotiated legal contracts before, had his attorneys Brown and Megwa and his financial agent Wilcox at the meeting as his advocates. Sun only had her Swedish friend, Forsberg, and herself. Neither Sun nor Forsberg had any special legal knowledge or business experience in negotiating contracts.

The court therefore should have scrutinized the other factors related to duress, coercion, and fraud. As we have already stressed, not only did Sun lack any legal counsel, but Barry's attorneys actually gave her legal advice and acted in a manner that contaminated the entire process. Moreover, Sun was neither given a copy of the agreement to review prior to the meeting nor given a copy of the agreement even after she signed it. Any delay would have resulted in a postponement of the wedding. The wedding may have been planned as a "small affair," but guests such as Willie Mays, Bond's relatives, and Sun's friend who had traveled from Canada had made special arrangements to be there. Finally, as already noted, as she arrived at the attorneys' office, Wilcox aggressively threatened Sun with "no wedding" if she did not sign the agreement.

Although the trial court stated it was considering the question of voluntariness, we conclude that the trial court, as a matter of law, did not properly give the absence of legal representation the proper weight when determining this issue. We hold that when a party challenging a premarital agreement establishes that he or she did not have legal counsel while the other party had such assistance, and the unrepresented party did not have the opportunity to obtain legal counsel or did not knowingly refuse legal counsel, the court must strictly scrutinize the totality of the circumstances involved in the execution of the contract. [T]he trial court erred in failing to give the proper weight to the factor of Sun's not having any legal counsel while Barry had two attorneys and his agent advising him. As with settlement agreements in divorce actions, the court should "carefully scrutinize the agreements" when the party challenging the agreement did not have the advice of counsel.

We reverse that part of the judgment which upheld the validity of the prenuptial agreement, and remand the matter of the validity of the prenuptial agreement.

---

spouse." The agreement also contained provisions concerning support obligations and the disposition of property upon dissolution of the marriage, including a proviso that "Each of us shall receive free and clear of all claim of the other spouse that property which was the separate property of each spouse prior to marriage . . . and as may be later acquired as separate property."

Chapter 30: Marital Agreements

Regardless of all of the problems with the premarital agreement that the trial court found, Judge Kozloski decided that the premarital agreement was valid. Sun appealed.

The appellate court reversed the trial court decision and Barry appealed to the California Supreme Court. The Supreme Court opinion follows.

> *In re Marriage of SUSANN MARGRETH BONDS and BARRY LAMAR BONDS.*
> *SUSANN MARGRETH BONDS, Appellant, v. BARRY LAMAR BONDS, Respondent.*
> **SUPREME COURT OF CALIFORNIA**
> 24 Cal.4th 1; 5 P.3d 815; 99 Cal.Rptr.2d 252
> August 21, 2000, Decided
>
> [The facts are set forth in the Appellate decision above.]
>
> The trial court observed that the case turned upon the credibility of the witnesses. In support of its determination that Sun entered into the agreement voluntarily, "free from the taint of fraud, coercion and undue influence . . . with full knowledge of the property involved and her rights therein," the trial court made the following findings of fact:
>
> (1) "Respondent [Sun] knew Petitioner [Barry] wished to protect his present property and future earnings.
> (2) Respondent knew . . . that the Agreement provided that . . . Petitioner's present and future earnings would remain his separate property. . . .
> (3) Respondent is an intelligent woman and though English is not her native language, she was capable of understanding the discussion by Attorney Brown and Attorney Megwa regarding the terms of the agreement and the effect of the Agreement on each [party's] rights. [P] . . . [P] . . .
> (4) Respondent was not forced to execute the document, nor did anyone threaten Respondent in any way.
> (5) Respondent never questioned signing the Agreement or requested that she not sign the Agreement.
> (6) Respondent's refusal to sign the Agreement would have caused little embarrassment to her. The wedding was a small impromptu affair that could have been easily postponed. [P]
> (7) Respondent had sufficient knowledge of the nature, value and extent of the property affected by the Agreement.
> (8) Petitioner fully disclosed the nature, approximate value and extent of all of his assets to Petitioner, both prior to and on the day of the execution of the agreement. [P]
> (9) Respondent had sufficient knowledge and understanding of her rights regarding the property affected by the Agreement, and how the Agreement adversely affected those rights.
> (10) Respondent had the opportunity to read the Agreement prior to executing it.
> (11) Attorneys Brown and Megwa explained to both parties their rights regarding the property affected by the Agreement, and how the Agreement adversely affected those rights.
> (12) Respondent never stated prior to execution that she did not understand the meaning of the Agreement or the explanations provided by Petitioner's attorneys. [P]
> (13) Respondent had sufficient awareness and understanding of her right to, and need for, independent counsel.

(14) Respondent also had an adequate and reasonable opportunity to obtain independent counsel prior to execution of the Agreement.
(15) Respondent was advised at a meeting with Attorney Brown at least one week prior to execution of the Agreement that she had the right to have an attorney represent her and that Attorneys Brown and Megwa represented Petitioner, not Respondent.
(16) On at least two occasions during the February 5, 1988, meeting, Respondent was told that she could have separate counsel if she chose. Respondent declined. Respondent was capable of understanding this admonition. The wedding was a small impromptu affair that could have been easily postponed."

The Court of Appeal in a split decision reversed the judgment rendered by the trial court and directed a retrial on the issue of voluntariness. We granted Barry's petition for review.

We first consider whether the Court of Appeal majority applied the appropriate legal standard in resolving the question whether the premarital agreement was entered into voluntarily. We conclude it erred in holding that a premarital agreement in which one party is not represented by independent counsel should be subjected to strict scrutiny for voluntariness. Such a holding is inconsistent with FC § 1615, which governs the enforceability of premarital agreements.

The California enactment, like the Uniform Act, sets out the law of premarital agreements, including such matters as the nature of property subject to such agreements, the requirement of a writing, and provision for amendments. FC § 1615, like section 6 of the Uniform Act, regulates the enforceability of such agreements. It provides in pertinent part: "(a) A premarital agreement is not enforceable if the party against whom enforcement is sought proves either of the following: [P] (1) That party did not execute the agreement voluntarily. [P] (2) The agreement was unconscionable when it was executed and, before execution of the agreement, all of the following applied to that party: [P] (A) That party was not provided a fair and reasonable disclosure of the property or financial obligations of the other party. [P] (B) That party did not voluntarily and expressly waive, in writing, any right to disclosure of the property or financial obligations of the other party beyond the disclosure provided. [P] (C) That party did not have, or reasonably could not have had, an adequate knowledge of the property or financial obligations of the other party."

Pursuant to FC § 1615, a premarital agreement will be enforced unless the party resisting enforcement of the agreement can demonstrate either (1) that he or she did not enter into the contract voluntarily, or (2) that the contract was unconscionable when entered into *and* that he or she did not have actual or constructive knowledge of the assets and obligations of the other party and did not voluntarily waive knowledge of such assets and obligations.

Neither the article of the Family Code in which section 1615 is located, nor the Uniform Act, defines the term "voluntarily."

We have considered the range of factors that may be relevant to establish the involuntariness of a premarital agreement in order to consider whether the Court of Appeal erred in according such great weight to one factor--the presence or absence of independent counsel for each party. As we shall explain, we do not believe that the terms or history of FC § 1615 support the conclusion of the Court of Appeal majority that a premarital agreement should be subjected to strict scrutiny for voluntariness in the absence of independent counsel for the less sophisticated party or of an assuredly

Chapter 30: Marital Agreements

effective and knowing waiver of counsel comparable to that occurring in the criminal law setting (and potentially also requiring an offer by the represented party to pay for independent counsel for the other party).

It seems evident that the commissioners who enacted the Uniform Act intended that the presence of independent counsel (or a reasonable opportunity to consult counsel) should be merely one factor among several that a court should consider in examining a challenge to the voluntariness of a premarital agreement. Moreover, the overall purpose of the Uniform Act was to *enhance* the enforceability of premarital agreements, a goal that would not be furthered if agreements were presumed to be of doubtful voluntariness unless both parties were represented by independent counsel.

Finally, and perhaps most significantly, the rule created by the Court of Appeal would have the effect of shifting the burden of proof on the question of voluntariness to the party seeking enforcement of the premarital agreement, even though the statute expressly places the burden upon the party challenging the voluntariness of the agreement. Because the commissioners and our Legislature placed the burden of proof of involuntariness upon the party *challenging* a premarital agreement, it seems obvious that the party seeking enforcement should not be required to prove that the *absence* of any factor tending to establish voluntariness did *not* render the agreement involuntary--the inevitable result were we to adopt the strict scrutiny standard suggested by the Court of Appeal.

We conclude that although the ability of the party challenging the agreement to obtain independent counsel is an important factor in determining whether that party entered into the agreement voluntarily, the Court of Appeal majority erred in directing trial courts to subject premarital agreements to strict scrutiny where the less sophisticated party does not have independent counsel and has not waived counsel according to exacting waiver requirements.

Because the Uniform Act was intended to enhance the enforceability of premarital agreements, because it expressly places the burden of proof upon the person challenging the agreement, and finally because the California statute imposing fiduciary duties in the family law setting applies only to spouses, we do not believe that the commissioners or our Legislature contemplated that the voluntariness of a premarital agreement would be examined in light of the strict fiduciary duties imposed on persons such as lawyers, or imposed expressly by statute upon persons who are married.

Finally, we conclude that the trial court's determination that Sun voluntarily entered into the premarital agreement in the present case is supported by substantial evidence.

The Court of Appeal held the trial court erred in finding the parties' agreement to be voluntary. The appellate court stressed the absence of counsel for Sun, and, strictly examining the totality of the circumstances to determine voluntariness, pointed to Sun's limited English language skills and lack of "legal or business sophistication," and stated that she "received no explanation of the legal consequences to her ensuing from signing the contract" and "was told there would be 'no marriage' if she did not immediately sign the agreement." It also referred to typographical errors and omissions in the agreement, the imminence of the wedding and the inconvenience and embarrassment of cancelling it, and Sun's asserted lack of understanding that she was waiving her statutory right to a community property interest in Barry's earnings.

The trial court determined that there had been no coercion. It declared that Sun had not

Chapter 30: Marital Agreements

been subjected to any threats, that she had not been forced to sign the agreement, and that she never expressed any reluctance to sign the agreement.

With respect to the presence of independent counsel, although Sun lacked legal counsel, the trial court determined that she had a reasonable opportunity to obtain counsel. The trial court stated: "Respondent had sufficient awareness and understanding of her right to, and need for, independent counsel. Respondent also had an adequate and reasonable opportunity to obtain independent counsel prior to execution of the Agreement. Respondent was advised at a meeting with Attorney Brown at least one week prior to execution of the Agreement that she had the right to have an attorney represent her and that Attorneys Brown and Megwa represented Petitioner, not Respondent. On at least two occasions during the February 5, 1988, meeting, Respondent was told that she could have separate counsel if she chose. Respondent declined. Respondent was capable of understanding this admonition."

With respect to the question of inequality of bargaining power, the trial court determined that Sun was intelligent and, evidently not crediting her claim that limited English made her unable to understand the import of the agreement or the explanations offered by Barry's counsel, found that she was capable of understanding the agreement and the explanations proffered by Barry's attorneys. There is ample evidence to support the trial court's determination regarding Sun's English-language skills, in view of the circumstances that for two years prior to marriage she had undertaken employment and education in a trade that required such skills and before meeting Barry had maintained close personal relationships with persons speaking only English. In addition, Barry and his witnesses all testified that Sun appeared to have no language problems at the time she signed the agreement.

[T]here is substantial evidence that they did not pressure Sun or even urge her to sign the agreement. Further, although Barry had three years of college studies as well as some experience in negotiating contracts, while Sun had only recently passed her high school equivalency exam (in English) and had little commercial experience, there is evidence that Barry did not understand the legal fine points of the agreement any more than Sun did. In addition, the basic purport of the agreement--that the parties would hold their earnings and accumulations during marriage as separate property, thereby giving up the protection of marital property law--was a relatively simple concept that did not require great legal sophistication to comprehend and that was, as the trial court found, understood by Sun.

Finally, we observe that the evidence supports the inference that Sun was intrepid rather than a person whose will is easily overborne. She emigrated from her homeland at a young age, found employment and friends in a new country using two languages other than her native tongue, and in two years moved to yet another country, expressing the desire to take up a career and declaring to Barry that she "didn't want his money." These circumstances support the inference that any inequality in bargaining power--arising primarily from the absence of independent counsel who could have advised Sun not to sign the agreement or urged Barry to abandon the idea of keeping his earnings separate--was not coercive.

With respect to full disclosure of the property involved, the trial court found that Sun was aware of what separate property was held by Barry prior to the marriage, and as the Court of Appeal noted, she failed to identify any property of which she later became aware that was not on the list of property referred to by the parties when they executed the contract.

Chapter 30: Marital Agreements

> The trial court also determined that Sun was aware of what was at stake--of what normally would be community property, namely the earnings and acquisitions of the parties during marriage. Substantial evidence supports this conclusion, including Sun's statements to Barry before marriage, the terms used in the contract, and Brown's and Megwa's testimony that they painstakingly explained this matter to Sun.
>
> The factors we have identified in assessing the voluntariness of the agreement entered into between Barry and Sun are not rigidly separate considerations; rather the presence of one factor may influence the weight to be given evidence considered primarily under another factor. In this respect, the trial court's finding that Sun had advance knowledge of the meaning and intent of the agreement and what was at stake for her is influential, as we have seen, in considering some of the other factors.
>
> In considering evidence that Sun responded to Barry's suggestion that she secure independent counsel with the observation that she did not need counsel because she had nothing, the Court of Appeal majority drew the inference *least* in support of the judgment--namely, that this statement indicated Sun did not understand that she did have property interests at stake in the form of the community property rights that would accrue to her under applicable statutes, in the absence of a premarital agreement. We believe that this was error on the part of the appellate court, because substantial evidence supported the trial court's determination to the contrary.
>
> FC § 1615 places on the party seeking to avoid a premarital agreement the burden of demonstrating that the agreement was involuntary. The trial court determined that Sun did not carry her burden, and we believe that its factual findings in support of this conclusion are supported by substantial evidence.
>
> The judgment of the Court of Appeal is reversed to the extent that it reversed the judgment of the trial court on the issue of the voluntariness of the premarital agreement. The matter is remanded to the Court of Appeal to determine [among other things] whether the trial court erred in various respects in interpreting and enforcing the agreement.

The Supreme Court of California determined that the findings of the trial court were supported by substantial evidence and, accordingly held that Sun had entered into the premarital agreement voluntarily. Supreme Court at p. 37-38. Some of the substantial evidence that the Supreme Court referred to was the following 10 findings of fact. The Appellate Court's findings on the same subject follow in the indented boxes.

Supreme Court Fact ONE:

> Respondent [Sun] knew Petitioner [Barry] wished to protect his present property and future earnings."[11]

Supreme Court Fact TWO:

> There is evidence that Barry did not understand the legal fine points of the agreement any more than Sun did.

---

[11] The fact is set forth in bold.

Chapter 30: Marital Agreements

> Barry, who had negotiated legal contracts before, had his attorneys Brown and Megwa and his financial agent Wilcox at the meeting as his advocates. Sun only had her Swedish friend, Forsberg, and herself. Neither Sun nor Forsberg had any special legal knowledge or business experience in negotiating contracts. **Appellate Court at p. 331.**

Supreme Court Fact THREE:

> Respondent is an intelligent woman and though English is not her native language, she was capable of understanding the discussion by Attorney Brown and Attorney Megwa regarding the terms of the agreement and the effect of the Agreement on each [party's] rights.

> Brown testified that he believed Sun understood his explanations and that, although Swedish is her first language, she never indicated that she was having any difficulty understanding English." **Appellate Court at p. 298**.

> Barry's own testimony indicated that Sun did not understand *why* she needed an attorney. **Appellate Court at p. 325.**

Supreme Court Fact FOUR:

> Respondent was not forced to execute the document, nor did anyone threaten Respondent in any way.

> Sun arrived at the law office, on her way to the wedding, [where] she was greeted by Barry's agent, who threatened that there would be 'no wedding' if she did not sign the agreement. **Appellate Court at p. 295.**

Supreme Court Fact FIVE:

> Respondent had sufficient knowledge of the nature, value and extent of the property affected by the Agreement. Respondent knew . . . that the Agreement provided that . . . Petitioner's present and future earnings would remain his separate property…

(Information about Barry Bonds baseball earnings by year:

In 1986 Barry earned $60,000,
In 1987 Barry earned $100,000,
In 1988 Barry earned $220,000,
In 1989 Barry earned $360,000,
In 1990 Barry earned $850,000, won MVP award for Pittsburg Pirates
In 1991 Barry earned $2,300,000,
In 1992 Barry earned $4,800,000, won MVP award playing for Pittsburgh Pirates
In 1993 Barry earned $4,516,666, won MVP award playing for San Francisco Giants
In 1994 Barry earned $5,166,666,
In 1995 Barry earned $8,166,666,

Chapter 30: Marital Agreements

In 1996 Barry earned $8,416,667,
In 1997 Barry earned $8,666,667,
In 1998 Barry earned $8,916,667,
In 1999 Barry earned $9,381,057,
In 2000 Barry earned $10,658,826,
In 2001 Barry earned $10,300,000, won MVP award with San Francisco Giants
In 2002 Barry earned $15,000,000, won MVP award with San Francisco Giants
In 2003 Barry earned $15,500,000, won MVP award with San Francisco Giants
In 2004 Barry earned $18,000,000, won MVP award with San Francisco Giants
In 2005 Barry earned $22,000,000,
In 2006 Barry earned $19,331,470,
In 2007 Barry earned $15,533,970.

Barry was to receive bonuses pursuant to his contract with the San Francisco Giants whenever he received a Most Valuable Player award. He won that award s follows:
1 MVP award.. .. .. $100,000
2 MVP awards.. .. ..$250,000
3 MVP awards.. .. ..$500,000
4 MVP awards.. .. ..$1 million)

Supreme Court Fact SIX:

> Petitioner fully disclosed the nature, approximate value and extent of all of his assets to Petitioner, both prior to and on the day of the execution of the agreement.

There was a provision which provided:

> Both parties have initialed each page of the attached lists as evidence that they have read and concur with the classification of each item on each [separate property] list. **Appellate Court at p. 297.**

[There were no lists attached to the agreement and there were no initials on any of the pages of the agreement.]

Supreme Court Fact SEVEN:

> Respondent had the opportunity to read the Agreement prior to executing it.

> Neither Sun nor Barry had an opportunity to review the agreement before the February 5 meeting. **Appellate Court at p. 297.**

> Barry's attorneys answered her questions about the agreement and also attempted to explain to her each provision in the contract. Sun signed the document a short time later, after seeing it for the first time at the meeting in the law office. After the meeting with Barry's attorneys, Barry and Sun went directly to the airport to catch a plane for Las Vegas to attend the wedding scheduled for the following day. **Appellate Court at p. 295.**

Chapter 30: Marital Agreements

Supreme Court Fact EIGHT:

Respondent had sufficient awareness and understanding of her right to, and need for, independent counsel.

> [At trial, Brown stated he did not believe that he] ever made an affirmative declaration to Sun that she should seek counsel. Rather, he told her that "she may want to do that." **Appellate Court at p. 297.**

> Merely being told one may seek counsel does not establish any understanding of the need for counsel. **Appellate Court at p. 322-323.**

> In this context, the comment that Sun 'may want' to obtain an attorney was worse than worthless; it was misleading. There was not even a superficial attempt to explain to Sun the reasons for needing an attorney, and attorneys cannot avoid their ethical obligation to avoid conflicts of interest by merely telling the unrepresented party that he or she may obtain an attorney. Not only did Brown fail to identify any conflict of interest, but he frequently acted in a manner that made him appear to be an independent legal advisor rather than Barry's advocate. **Appellate Court at p. 326.**

Supreme Court Fact NINE:

Respondent also had an adequate and reasonable opportunity to obtain independent counsel prior to execution of the Agreement. Respondent was advised at a meeting with Attorney Brown at least one week prior to execution of the Agreement that she had the right to have an attorney represent her and that Attorneys Brown and Megwa represented Petitioner, not Respondent."

> At the meeting, Megwa and Brown provided Barry and Sun with copies of the premarital agreement [to read]. Neither Sun nor Barry had an opportunity to review the agreement before the February 5 meeting. **Appellate Court at p. 297.**

Supreme Court Fact TEN:

On at least two occasions during the February 5, 1988, meeting, Respondent was told that she could have separate counsel if she chose. Respondent declined. Respondent was capable of understanding this admonition.

> [When asked why she did not believe she needed another attorney, Sun responded:] Because Barry--Barry and I were there together, and they were attorneys. And they didn't come out and, you know, in the sense that they were not here for you. I don't recall them ever coming out to me that way. I didn't know anything about attorneys. I didn't know how it worked with attorneys, that you have one and I have one. **Appellate Court at p. 297.**

The Supreme Court of California reversed the decision of the Appellate Court and affirmed the trial Court's decision.

Chapter 30: Marital Agreements

c. *Senate Bill No. 78*

In footnote 12 of the *PENDLETON* case, the Supreme Court issued the following invitation to the legislature:

> The Legislature may, of course, limit the right to enter into premarital waivers of spousal support and/or specify the circumstances in which enforcement should be denied. Supreme Court at p. 54.

Less than five months after the decision in *BONDS* and *PENDLETON*, Senator Sheila Kuehl introduced Senate Bill No. 78, taking up the Supreme Court's challenge.

The crux of Senate Bill No. 78 was that two existing laws, **FC § 1612** and **FC § 1615,** be amended so that premarital agreements were presumed to be entered into involuntarily unless certain conditions were met. One those conditions was that a party had the time to retain independent counsel.[12]

The "legislature responded swiftly with amendments to section 1615." *In re Marriage of CADWELL-FASO & FASO* (2011) 191 Cal.App.4th 945 at p. 956.

Bill No. 78 was enacted by the legislature as **FC §§ 1612** and **1615**. They were signed into law by the governor on September 11, 2001 and became effective January 1, 2002. Thus, as of January 1, 2002 the validity of a premarital agreement would be determined by law, not judicial discretion.

3. Agreements Executed from 2002 to Present

As provided above, the legislature added **FC § 1612(c)** and **FC § 1615(c),** to become effective January 1, 2002. **FC § 1612(c)** provides:

> Any provision in a premarital agreement regarding spousal support, including, but not limited to, a waiver of it, is not enforceable if the party against whom enforcement of the spousal support provision is sought was not represented by independent counsel at the time the agreement containing the provision was signed, or if the provision regarding spousal support is unconscionable at the time of enforcement. An otherwise unenforceable provision in a premarital agreement regarding spousal support may not become enforceable solely because the party against whom enforcement is sought was represented by independent counsel.

FC § 1615(c) provides:

> For the purposes of subdivision (a), it shall be deemed that a premarital agreement was not executed voluntarily unless the court finds in writing or on the record all of the following:
> **(1)** The party against whom enforcement is sought was represented by independent legal counsel at the time of signing the agreement or, after being advised to seek independent

---

[12] The actual laws are set forth in the next section.

Chapter 30: Marital Agreements

> legal counsel, expressly waived, in a separate writing, representation by independent legal counsel.
> (2) The party against whom enforcement is sought had not less than seven calendar days between the time that party was first presented with the agreement and advised to seek independent legal counsel and the time the agreement was signed.
> (3) The party against whom enforcement is sought, if unrepresented by legal counsel, was fully informed of the terms and basic effect of the agreement as well as the rights and obligations he or she was giving up by signing the agreement, and was proficient in the language in which the explanation of the party's rights was conducted and in which the agreement was written. The explanation of the rights and obligations relinquished shall be memorialized in writing and delivered to the party prior to signing the agreement. The unrepresented party shall, on or before the signing of the premarital agreement, execute a document declaring that he or she received the information required by this paragraph and indicating who provided that information.
> (4) The agreement and the writings executed pursuant to paragraphs (1) and (3) were not executed under duress, fraud, or undue influence and the parties did not lack capacity to enter into the agreement.
> (5) Any other factors the court deems relevant.

With this enactment, the law changed from courts having absolute discretion to decide the validity of premarital agreements to a rebuttable presumption that the agreement was not entered into voluntarily, unless the five conditions set forth in **FC § 1615(c)** were met.

After new law is enacted, the question of retroactivity is usually litigated unless the legislature addresses this issue within the newly enacted law. Retroactivity of **FC § 1615(c)** was the issue presented in *In re Marriage of HOWELL* (2011) 195 Cal.App.4th 1062. In *Howell*, the parties signed a premarital agreement in 1999 that waived "any right to receive future spousal support, maintenance or alimony from the other in the event of a Dissolution of Marriage or Legal Separation."

Husband's attorney, at Husband's request, prepared a premarital agreement in late 1998. The agreement was given to the Wife-to-be, in December 1998. The parties signed their premarital agreement on January 30, 1999 and were married in May of 1999.

The trial court held that **FC § 1615(c)** applies retroactively to the parties' 1999 premarital agreement. The appellate court reversed the trial court's decision, stating that:

> [o]ur review of the legislative history shows the Legislature did not intend FC § 1615(c) to apply retroactively. *Id.* at pp. 1074, 1078. [This amendment was not merely] the result of a legislative attempt to clarify the true meaning of a statute, [it is a substantive change in the law. To apply a retroactive application to an agreement that was signed before these amendments became law] creates new obligations by raising a standard of care and imposing, for the first time, a specific penalty for breach of the new standard. [This would impair the vested rights of one or both the parties without due process of law. *Id.* at p. 1074.]

Chapter 30: Marital Agreements

In *In re Marriage of CADWELL-FASO* (2011) 191 Cal.App.4th 945; 119 Cal.Rptr.3d 818, the issue also concerned whether the premarital agreement was signed voluntarily. However, since their premarital agreement was signed in May of 2006, the amendments to **FC §§ 1612(c)** and **1615(c)** were the laws to apply to decide validity.

In *CADWELL-FASO*, Faso (husband) moved to set aside an Addendum to the premarital agreement, arguing that the document was invalid because he did not have seven days between the time of presentation and execution, as required by section 1615(c)(2). *Id.* at p. 952.

The trial court held because the Addenda had [not] been presented within seven days of the day that they were signing, the Addenda was unenforceable because:

> the seven-day rule applied. The court held that the seven-day rule was mandatory, and the statute as drafted did not limit the rule to the unrepresented. Because presentation of the Addendum ran afoul of the seven-day rule in this case, Faso's execution of the document was deemed involuntary and the Addendum was unenforceable. *Id.* at p.954.

The appellate court reversed the trial court decision, stating that:

> section 1615(c)(2) does not pertain to Faso, a party who was represented in the transaction from the outset. Hence the trial court erred in deeming that his execution of the Addendum was involuntary and therefore unenforceable. The Addendum is enforceable. *Id.* at p. 962. [T]he sole purpose [of FC § 1615(c)(2)] is not simply to allow the unrepresented party seven days to obtain counsel; the purpose is to allow seven days to seek and obtain legal advice *prior to* execution. *Id.*

The two sections of the Family Code that were amended, adding a part (c) to both, substantially changed the law regarding the validity of premarital agreements. The law moved from giving a trial court judge complete discretion to decide the validity of premarital agreements to a rebuttable presumption that an agreement was signed involuntarily if the five conditions in **FC § 1615(c)(2)** were not met. The new law cannot be applied to agreements signed prior to its enactment. *HOWELL, supra*. And finally, that the seven-days clause in **FC § 1615(c)(2)** does not apply to parties who were represented from the onset.

In re Marriage of Clarke (2018) 19 Cal.App.5th 914, one of the parties was not given 7 days pursuant to FC § 1615 and the court held that the agreement was not valid, even though the party (Matthew) who was not represented by an attorney made the first draft of the agreement. After making the first draft, Matthew retained an attorney for his soon-to-be wife (Claudia) did not retain an attorney for himself. The attorney representing Claudia, redrafted the agreement adding additional provisions before sending it to Matthew to sign. Matthew was not given 7 days between the time that the agreement was sent and the time that Matthew signed the agreement. The trial court found that the agreement was invalid because of lack of compliance with FC § 1615(c)(2) and (3). The appellate court affirmed this decision. *In re Marriage Clarke* (2018) 19 Cal.App.5th 914 at p. 922.

Chapter 30: Marital Agreements

4. Drafting Premarital Agreements

The Family Code uses the term **premarital** to describe "an agreement between prospective spouses made in contemplation of marriage and to be effective upon marriage." FC § 1610. Pursuant to FC § 1500 property rights of spouses may be altered by a premarital agreement. It should be noted that the California legislature changed the word **prenuptial** to **premarital** in all of the California laws. Perhaps, it would be advisable to use premarital instead of prenuptial in all agreements that are signed prior to marriage.

> (a) A premarital agreement or other marital property agreement that is executed and acknowledged or proved in the manner that a grant of real property is required to be executed and acknowledged or proved may be recorded in the office of the recorder of each county in which real property affected by the agreement is situated.
> (b) Recording or nonrecording of a premarital agreement or other marital property agreement has the same effect as recording or nonrecording of a grant of real property. Premarital agreements do not require consideration, and there is no fiduciary duty between the parties because they are not yet married. FC § 1502.

The Uniform Premarital Agreement Act is set forth in the Family Code §1600-1617. It applies to any premarital agreement drafted on or after January 1, 1986. **FC § 1601**.

Pursuant to **FC § 1610(a)** a premarital agreement is an "agreement between prospective spouses made in contemplation of marriage and to be effective upon marriage."

Also defined in **FC § 1610** is the word property. **Property** "means an interest, present or future, legal or equitable, vested or contingent, in real or personal property, including income and earnings." **FC § 1610**.

FC § 1611 provides that a premarital agreement must be in writing and signed by both parties. **It is enforceable without consideration.**

A premarital agreement becomes effective upon marriage. **FC § 1613**.

FC § 1612 sets forth what terms may be present in a premarital agreement:

> (1) The rights and obligations of each of the parties in any of the property of either or both of them whenever and wherever acquired or located.
> (2) The right to buy, sell, use, transfer, exchange, abandon, lease, consume, expend, assign, create a security interest in, mortgage, encumber, dispose of, or otherwise manage and control property.
> (3) The disposition of property upon separation, marital dissolution, death, or the occurrence or nonoccurrence of any other event.
> (4) The making of a will, trust, or other arrangement to carry out the provisions of the agreement.
> (5) The ownership rights in and disposition of the death benefit from a life insurance

Chapter 30: Marital Agreements

> policy.
> **(6)** The choice of law governing the construction of the agreement.
> **(7)** Any other matter, including their personal rights and obligations, not in violation of public policy or a statute imposing a criminal penalty.

After marriage, a premarital agreement may be amended or revoked only by a written agreement signed by the parties. The amended agreement or the revocation is enforceable without consideration. **FC § 1614.**

FC § 1615 is the law that discusses enforceability/involuntariness. It provides:

> **(a)** A premarital agreement is not enforceable if the party against whom enforcement is sought proves either of the following:
> **(1)** That party did not execute the agreement voluntarily.
> **(2)** The agreement was unconscionable when it was executed and, before execution of the agreement, all of the following applied to that party:
>   **(A)** That party was not provided a fair, reasonable, and full disclosure of the property or financial obligations of the other party.
>   **(B)** That party did not voluntarily and expressly waive, in writing, any right to disclosure of the property or financial obligations of the other party beyond the disclosure provided.
>   **(C)** That party did not have, or reasonably could not have had, an adequate knowledge of the property or financial obligations of the other party.
> **(b)** An issue of unconscionability of a premarital agreement shall be decided by the court as a matter of law.
> **(c)** For the purposes of subdivision (a), it shall be deemed that a premarital agreement was not executed voluntarily unless the court finds in writing or on the record all of the following:
> **(1)** The party against whom enforcement is sought was represented by independent legal counsel at the time of signing the agreement or, after being advised to seek independent legal counsel, expressly waived, in a separate writing, representation by independent legal counsel.
> **(2)** The party against whom enforcement is sought had not less than seven calendar days between the time that party was first presented with the agreement and advised to seek independent legal counsel and the time the agreement was signed.
> **(3)** The party against whom enforcement is sought, if unrepresented by legal counsel, was fully informed of the terms and basic effect of the agreement as well as the rights and obligations he or she was giving up by signing the agreement, and was proficient in the language in which the explanation of the party's rights was conducted and in which the agreement was written. The explanation of the rights and obligations relinquished shall be memorialized in writing and delivered to the party prior to signing the agreement. The unrepresented party shall, on or before the signing of the premarital agreement, execute a document declaring that he or she received the information required by this paragraph and indicating who provided that information.
> **(4)** The agreement and the writings executed pursuant to paragraphs (1) and (3) were not executed under duress, fraud, or undue influence, and the parties did not lack capacity to enter into the agreement.
> **(5)** Any other factors the court deems relevant.

Chapter 30: Marital Agreements

In light of the above laws, it must be stressed that the opposing party MUST have at a minimum SEVEN days prior to signing the Agreement to allow opposing party the time to meet with his or her independent counsel. It would be wise to extend this time period to more than seven days because many attorneys require more notice for an appointment to review a premarital agreement.

If the opposing party decides against retaining independent counsel and so provides in writing, the seven days should still be given before opposing party is required to sign the agreement.

Finally, a minor can make a valid premarital agreement: (1) if the minor is emancipated; (2) is capable of contracting pursuant to FC §§ 302,303; or (3) has entered into a marriage that is valid in jurisdiction where the marriage will soon be solemnized or has been solemnized. **FC § 1501**.

CHART 9: Check List for a Premarital Agreement

1.   **Introductory Provisions**
1.1   ☐ Identification of Parties
1.2   ☐ Names, addresses and dates of birth

2.0   **Purpose of Agreement**
2.2   ☐ Ownership and division of property owned before, during and after separation;
2.3   ☐ The parties desire to set forth their respective rights and liabilities from this relationship
2.4   ☐ The parties recognize that differences may arise between them that may become irreconcilable

3.0   **Status of Property Premarriage/Disclosure**
3.1   **Real property**
3.1.1   ☐ Husband-to-be's separate real property (Exhibit A1)
3.1.2   ☐ Wife-to-be's separate real property (Exhibit A2)
3.2   **Personal property**
3.2.1   ☐ Husband-to-be's separate real property (Exhibit A1)
3.2.2   ☐ Wife-to-be's separate real property (Exhibit A2)

4.0   **Disclosure of Income/Liabilities**
4.1   ☐ Income & Expense Declarations/Disclosure of income for husband-to-be (Exhibit B1)
4.2   ☐ Income & Expense Declarations/Disclosure of income for wife-to-be (Exhibit B2)
4.2   ☐ Schedule of Assets and Debts/Disclosure statement for husband-to-be (Exhibit C1)
4.2   ☐ Schedule of Assets and Debts/Disclosure statement for wife-to-be (Exhibit C2)

5.0   **Status of Property acquired after marriage**
5.1   ☐ Community real property
5.2   ☐ Community separate property
5.5   ☐ Transmutations FC §§ 850-852
5.5   ☐ Reimbursements FC §§ 2640-2641

6.0   **Distribution of property**
6.1   ☐ Property will be distributed as set forth in this Agreement and property acquired before marriage will remain the sole and separate property
6.2   ☐ Property acquired during marriage will be as set forth in Exhibit D
6.3   ☐ Gifts from one party to the other
6.4   ☐ Commingled property is presumed to be community property
6.5   ☐ Distribution of property after death of either or simultaneous death of both parties
7.0   **Children**

Chapter 30: Marital Agreements

7.1 □ Children born prior to marriage from a different relationship
7.1.1 □ Names, Dates of birth
7.1.2 □ In the event of separation of the parties any rights and obligations any rights and/or obligation relating to children born prior to this marriage from another relationship
7.2 □ Children of the marriage
7.2.1 □ Arrangement for custody and/or support shall be in bests interests of the children as determined by the court

8.0 **Spousal Support at and after date of separation**
8.1 □ Duty of support
8.2 □ Waiver of spousal support
8.3 □ Facts/circumstances/ conditions regarding spousal support
8.4 □ Temporary spousal support
8.4.1 □ Amount of temporary support
8.4.2 □ Duration of Temporary spousal support
8.5 □ Permanent spousal support
8.5.1 □ Amount of permanent spousal support
8.5.2 □ Duration of permanent spousal support
8.6 □ Modifications of amount of spousal support
8.8 □ Modifiable or remarriage/death termination
8.9 □ Reservation of jurisdiction
8.10 □ Termination of jurisdiction

9.0 **The Family Residence**
9.1 □ Disposition
9.2 □ Occupancy
9.3 □ Deferred Sale of the Home (*Duke*)
9.4 □ Terms and conditions for the selling of residence
9.5 □ Maintenance, repairs and improvements
9.6 □ Reservation of jurisdiction
9.7 □ Modifiability

10.0 **Retirement/Pension/Ira/Sep/Deferred Compensation**
10.1 □ Retirement accrued before date of marriage
10.2 □ Retirement accrued after date of marriage
10.3 □ Joinder
10.4 □ Division/Court Order
10.5 □ Waiver of Benefits

11.0 **Debts**
11.1 □ All debts accrued before marriage
11.2 □ Community property debts acquired during marriage
11.3 □ Separate property debts acquired during marriage
11.4 □ Debts accrued after date of marriage
12.0 **Attorney Fees**
12.1 □ Equal access to representation

Chapter 30: Marital Agreements

12.2 ☐ Prevailing party
12.3 ☐ Enforcement

13.0 ☐ **Representation by separate counsel.** (Pursuant to **FC § 1615** an opposing party must be given at least SEVEN days to retain independent counsel to review the agreement. **FC § 1615.**
14.0 ☐ **Taxes**
14.1 ☐ Filing State and Federal income taxes
14.2 ☐ Income tax liabilities before marriage
14.3 ☐ Income tax liabilities after date of marriage
14.4 ☐ Income tax refunds

15.0 **Amendments/Termination**
15.1 ☐ All amendments to this Agreement require the signature of both parties
15.2 ☐ Termination of this Agreement requires the signature of both parties

16.0 **Warranties and Remedies**
16.1 ☐ Hidden/omitted assets unintentional
16.2 ☐ Hidden/omitted assets intentional
16.3 ☐ Penalty for hidden/omitted assets unintentional
17.0 ☐ **Execution of Wills**
18.0 **General contract provisions**
18.1 ☐ Release of Liabilities and Claims CC §§ 1541-1549
18.2 ☐ Waiver of Rights on Death of Other Party
18.3 ☐ Entire Agreement CC § 1695.3
18.4 ☐ Modification by Subsequent Agreement
18.5 ☐ Invalid Provision Remaining Provisions Valid and Enforceable (severability clause)
18.6 ☐ Choice of Law
18.7 ☐ Notice of Bankruptcy Filing
18.8 ☐ Inurement
18.9 ☐ Cooperation in Implementation of Agreement
18.10 ☐ Further documentation
18.11 ☐ Effective Date of Agreement
18.12 ☐ Execution of Instruments to achieve intent of Agreement

19.0 **Affirmations**
19.1 ☐ That both parties desire that distribution of all property be governed by this Agreement
19.2 ☐ That both parties had the opportunity to receive independent legal advice
19.3 ☐ That both parties have exchanged financial statements providing complete disclosure of assets/liabilities before marriage
19.4 ☐ That both parties voluntarily and expressly waive any other rights to disclosure property/assets/liabilities
19.5 ☐ That both parties were given at least 7 days to review this Agreement and retain legal advice before signing

Chapter 30: Marital Agreements

19.6 ☐ That both parties entered into this Agreement voluntarily
19.7 ☐ That this Agreement was not unconscionable when executed
19.8 ☐ That both parties have fully and completely disclosed all information without any omissions

20.0 ☐ **Dates and Signatures of Parties and Attorneys**
21.0 ☐ **Approved as to Form and Content**
22.0 ☐ **Date and Signature of Attorney/Party Approving as to Form and Content**
23.0 ☐ **Notarization**

2. Postmarital Agreements

Pursuant to **FC § 1620**, spouses cannot, by a contract with each other, alter their legal relations, but the "property rights of spouses prescribed by statute may be altered by a premarital agreement or other marital property agreement." **FC § 1500**.

Postmarital agreements are marital agreements that parties enter into while they are married. Often, postmarital agreements are made to change the character of property from community to separate or separate to community. Sometimes the parties desire to change the character of property purchased during the marriage to separate property or property received as a gift or bequest or property that was purchased with separate property to community property. Agreeing to change the character of property from separate to community or vice versa requires a **transmutation**.[13]

When a transmutation is made regarding real or personal property, it is not valid unless it is in writing and signed by the spouse whose interest in the property is adversely affected. However, if the item or items are a gift between spouses of clothing, wearing apparel, jewelry or other tangible articles of a personal nature that are used solely or principally by the spouse to whom the gift is made and that is not substantial in value, a written agreement is not necessary. **FC § 852**.

Premarital agreements and postmarital agreements are not construed and enforced under the same standards. *In re Marriage of BENSON* (2005) 36 Cal.4th 1096 at p. 1111. There is a fiduciary relationship between the parties in a postmarital agreement that is not present in a premarital agreement. *Id.* at p. 1110.

In *In re Marriage of BURKLE* (1997) 139 Cal.App.4th 712 at p. 733-734 the court stated that:

> Interspousal transactions are expressly governed by FC § 721(b)[14], which prohibits a spouse from taking "any unfair advantage of the other," and treats the fiduciary duties of

---

[13] FC § 850 provides that, subject to FC §§ 851 to 853, "inclusive, married persons may by agreement or transfer, with or without consideration, do any of the following:
(a) Transmute community property to separate property of either spouse.
(b) Transmute separate property of either spouse to community property.
(c) Transmute separate property of one spouse to separate property of the other spouse."

[14] FC § 721(b) provides: "(b) Except as provided in Sections 143, 144, 146, 16040 and 16047 of the Probate Code, in transactions between themselves, spouses are subject to the general rules governing fiduciary relationships that control the actions of persons occupying confidential relations with each other. This confidential relationship imposes a duty of the highest good faith and fair dealing on each spouse, and neither shall take any unfair advantage of the other. This confidential relationship is a fiduciary relationship subject to the same rights and duties of nonmarital business partners, as provided in Sections 16403, 16404 and 16503 of the Corporations Code, including, but not limited to, the following:
(1) Providing each spouse access at all times to any books kept regarding a transaction for the purposes of inspection and copying.
(2) Rendering upon request, true and full information of all things affecting any transaction that concerns the community property. Nothing in this section is intended to impose a duty for either spouse to keep detailed books and records of community property transactions.

> spouses like those of business partners. The distinction between the two types of fiduciary relationship—trustee-beneficiary on the one hand, and spouses or business partners on the other—is entirely reasonable, because in the latter fiduciary duties run in both directions. Indeed, just as it would be patently irrational to presume undue influence in a contract between business partners, it would likewise be unreasonable to presume undue influence in a contract between spouses, unless one of the spouses has obtained an unfair advantage. For these reasons, we conclude that a contract between spouses that "advantages one spouse" and therefore raises a presumption the transaction was induced by undue influence, is a transaction in which one spouse obtains an unfair advantage over the other.

In *BURKLE* the issue was the enforceability of a postmarital agreement. Ms. Burkle contended the postmarital agreement was void and unenforceable because: **(1)** she was so depressed and emotionally dependent upon Mr. Burkle that she did not sign the agreement of her own free will, and **(2)** that Mr. Burkle concealed assets or significant financial information from Ms. Burkle. After a 10-day trial, the trial court's ultimate findings were that Ms. Burkle signed the agreement "freely and voluntarily, and free from any emotional influence that interfered with an exercise of her own free will," and that Mr. Burkle did not conceal assets or significant financial information from Ms. Burkle. The agreement was valid and enforceable. *Id.* at p. 717.

Thus, unlike a premarital agreement, a postmarital agreement carries with it the duty of the highest good faith and fair dealing. Accordingly, when drafting a postmarital agreement, the greatest care should be taken to ensure that:

(1) The agreement was entered into freely, willingly and voluntarily;
(2) There was no fraud, duress, medical condition or undue influence; and
(3) Neither party gains an advantage over the other.

Further, it would be wise to give both parties at least seven days to take the agreement to independent counsel of his or her choice. Although this is the rule for premarital agreements, extending the rule postmarital agreements is a very good idea.

---

(3) Accounting to the spouse and holding as a trustee, any benefit or profit derived from any transaction by one spouse without the consent of the other spouse that concerns the community property."

CHART 10: Check List for a Post Marital Agreement

1.0		**Introductory Provisions**
1.1	□	Identification of Parties
1.2	□	Names, addresses and dates of birth

2.0   **Purpose of Agreement**
2.2   □   Ownership and division of property owned before, during and after separation;
2.3   □   The parties desire to set forth their respective rights and liabilities from this relationship
2.4   □   The parties recognize that differences may arise between them that may become irreconcilable

3.0   **Status of property prior to this Agreement.**
3.1   **Real property**
3.1.1   □   Husband's separate real property (Exhibit A1)
3.1.2   □   Wife's separate real property (Exhibit A2)
3.2   **Personal property**
3.2.1   □   Husband's separate real property (Exhibit A1)
3.2.2   □   Wife's separate real property (Exhibit A2)
3.3   □   Community property

4.0   **Transmutation of property**
4.1   □   Real property described in Exhibit A from separate property to community property.
4.2   □   Personal property described in Exhibit A from separate property to community property.
4.3   □   Real property described in Exhibit A from community property to separate property.
4.4   □   Personal property described in Exhibit A from community property to separate property.
4.5   □   Declaration from spouse or spouse that are transmuting the property.

IF SPOUSAL SUPPORT AFTER SEPARATION IS ONE OF THE REASONS FOR THIS AGREEMENT:

5.0   **Spousal Support at and after date of separation**
5.1   □ Duty of support
5.2   □ Waiver of spousal support
5.3   □ Facts/circumstances/ conditions regarding spousal support
5.4   □   Temporary spousal support
5.4.1   □   Amount of temporary support
5.4.2   □   Duration of Temporary spousal support
5.5   □   Permanent spousal support
5.5.1   □   Amount of permanent spousal support
5.5.2   □   Duration of permanent spousal support

Chapter 30: Marital Agreements

5.6 ☐ Modifications of amount of spousal support
5.8 ☐ Modifiable or remarriage/death termination
5.9 ☐ Reservation of jurisdiction
5.10 ☐ Termination of jurisdiction

IF DETERMINATION OF THE FAMILY RESIDENCE AT SEPARATION IS ONE OF THE REASONS FOR THIS AGREEMENT

6.0   **The Family Residence**
6.1 ☐ Disposition
6.2 ☐ Occupancy
6.3 ☐ Deferred Sale of the Home (*Duke*)
6.4 ☐ Terms and conditions for the selling of residence
6.5 ☐ Maintenance, repairs and improvements
6.6 ☐ Reservation of jurisdiction
6.7 ☐ Modifiability

IF RETIREMENT OR THE LIKE IS ONE OF THE REASONS FOR THIS AGREEMENT.

7.0   **Retirement/Pension/Ira/Sep/Deferred Compensation**
7.1 ☐ Retirement accrued before date of marriage
7.2 ☐ Retirement accrued after date of marriage
7.3 ☐ Joinder
7.4 ☐ Division/Court Order
7.5 ☐ Waiver of Benefits

8.0 ☐ **Representation by separate counsel** (There should be a time period allowing both spouses the time to take this Agreement to independent counsel of his or her choice.)

9.0   **Amendments/Termination**
9.1 ☐ All amendments to this Agreement require the signature of both parties
9.2 ☐ Termination of this Agreement requires the signature of both parties

10.0   **General contract provisions**
10.1 ☐ Release of Liabilities and Claims
10.3 ☐ Entire Agreement CC § 1695.3
10.4 ☐ Modification by Subsequent Agreement
10.5 ☐ Invalid Provision Remaining Provisions Valid and Enforceable (severability clause)
10.6 ☐ Choice of Law
10.8 ☐ Inurement
10.9 ☐ Cooperation in Implementation of Agreement
10.10 ☐ Further documentation
10.11 ☐ Effective Date of Agreement

10.12 ☐ Execution of Instruments to achieve the parties' intent of this Agreement

11.0 Affirmations
11.1 ☐ That both parties understand that this Agreement is governed by **FC § 721** which provides that "spouses are subject to the general rules governing **fiduciary relationships** that control the actions of persons occupying **confidential** relations with each other. This **confidential** relationship imposes a duty of the highest good faith and fair dealing on each spouse, and neither shall take any unfair advantage of the other."
11.5 ☐ That both parties were given at least 7 days to review this Agreement and retain legal advice of his or her own choosing before signing
11.6 ☐ That both parties entered into this Agreement voluntarily
11.7 ☐ That this Agreement was not unconscionable when executed
11.8 ☐ That both parties have fully and completely disclosed all information without any omissions.

12.0 ☐ **Dates and Signatures of Parties and Attorneys**
13.0 ☐ **Approved as to Form and Content**
14.0 ☐ **Date and Signature of Attorney/Party Approving as to Form and Content**
15.0 ☐ **Notarization**

Chapter 30: Marital Agreements

3. Marital Settlement Agreements

The third category of marital agreements, and by far the most common, is the marital settlement agreement.[15] A marital settlement agreement is an agreement that memorializes the settled issues in a legal separation or dissolution. Marital settlement agreements are contracts and, as such, are governed by many of the same rules and regulations as **normal** contracts. In family law cases, a marital settlement agreement is prepared when an agreement is reached on one or more settled issues. Undisputed facts and issues are also made part of the agreement, such as the date that the parties were married and the names and dates of birth of the children of the marriage.

Marital settlement agreements begin with the basic facts, such as when the parties were married, their date of separation and if there are children of the marriage. The provisions containing the basic facts are usually followed by the agreements regarding the custody and visitation of the children.

Then, most marital settlement agreements discuss the child and spousal support issues. After the support issues, the provisions vary greatly. Most family law firms have their own version of a marital settlement agreement and that is the template that the paralegal will use. However, because every family law case is different, the family law paralegal should remember that every marital settlement agreement will also be different.

Oral agreements made prior to separation regarding property may be enforced. However, once the dissolution is filed, oral agreements regarding the division of property will not be upheld, pursuant to **FC § 2550**. *In re Marriage of DELLARIA* (2009) 172 Cal.App.4th 196.

One final note: as with the other marital agreements, it would be wise to give both parties at least seven days to obtain independent counsel to review the agreement prior to signing.

---

[15] A marital settlement agreement is often referred to as an "*MSA*."

CHART 12: Marital Settlement Agreement - Check List

1.0   **Introductory Provisions**
1.1   ☐   Identification of Parties
1.2   ☐   Date of Marriage
1.3   ☐   Date of Separation
1.4   ☐   Number and Dates of Birth of Minor Child or Children of the Marriage
1.5   ☐   Purpose of Agreement
1.6   ☐   Disclosure of Assets FC §§ 2100-2113
1.6.1 ☐ Preliminary Declaration of Disclosure FC § 2104 (*FL-140*)
1.6.2 ☐ Waiver of Final Declarations of Disclosure FC § 2105 (*FL-144*)
1.6.3 ☐ Income and Expense Declarations FC § 2101 (*FL-150*)
1.6.4 ☐ Schedule of Assets and Debts CCP § 2030 (*FL-142*)
1.7   ☐   Restoration of Wife's Former Name FC § 2080 (*FL-395*)

2.0   **Custody and Visitation FC §§ 3000-3465**
2.1   ☐ Custody FC §§ 3000-3007
2.2   ☐ Parenting Time/Visitation FC § 3100
2.3   ☐ Notice of Change of Residence FC§ 3024

3.0   **Child Support**
3.1.1 ☐ Dependency Exception
3.1.2 ☐ Child Support – Pursuant to FC § 4055
3.1.3 ☐ Annual Gross Income of Parents FC § 4058 (*FL-150*)
3.1.4 ☐ Timeshare Percent FC § 4055
3.2   ☐ Additional Child Support FC §§ 4061-4062
3.3.1 ☐ Health Insurance for Child or Children FC §§ 3751-3753
3.3.2 ☐ Uninsured Health care for children
3.4. ☐ Child Support Stipulation Acknowledgments. FC § 4065
3.5   ☐ Hardships FC §§ 4070-4073
3.6   ☐ Stipulated Agreement for Adult Child Support/College Expenses FC § 3587
3.7   ☐ Modifications FC § 4076, FC § 3651
3.8   ☐ Uninsured Costs FC § 4063
3.9   ☐ Private school tuition
3.10 ☐ College expenses for the children
3.11 ☐ Extracurricular activity costs for the children

4.0   **Spousal Support FC §§ 4300- 4360**
4.0   ☐ Duty of Support FC § 4300
4.1.1 ☐ Amount
4.1.2 ☐ Temporary Support
4.1.3 ☐ Amount and Duration of Temporary Support
4.1.4 ☐ Permanent Support
4.1.5 ☐ Amount
4.1.6 ☐ Duration
4.1.7 ☐ 10-year Marriage FC § 4336

Chapter 30: Marital Agreements

4.2	☐	Modification of Amount FC § 3591
4.3	☐	Conditions
4.3.1	☐	Spousal Support amount to vary with supported spouse's income
4.3.2	☐	Period fixed sum of support payments
4.3.3	☐	Payment of medical/housing/education
4.4	☐	Cohabitation Presumption of "Decreased Need" FC § 4323
4.5	☐	Waiver of Spousal Support FC § 4320
4.6	☐	Reservation of Jurisdiction FC § 4336
4.7	☐	Modifiable or Remarriage/Death Termination FC §§ 360[16], 3590, 4326, 4360
4.8	☐	Facts and Circumstances Regarding Spousal Support FC § 4320
4.9	☐	Marital Standard of Living FC § 4337
4.10	☐	Reservation/Termination of Jurisdiction FC § 4335
4.11	☐	Cobra Cal Ins. Code § 10116.5
4.12	☐	Notification of Happening of Contingency
4.13	☐	Survival of support obligation after remarriage
4.14	☐	Security for spousal support
4.15	☐	Family support

5.0   **Property**
5.1	☐	Separate Property FC § 770
5.2	☐	Division of Community Property Assets FC §§ 2550-2581
5.3	☐	Division of Community Property Debts FC §§ 2620-2628
5.4	☐	Equalizing Payment FC § 2550
5.5	☐	Transmutations FC §§ 850-852
5.5	☐	Reimbursements FC §§ 2640-2641
5.6	☐	Liability after Property Division FC § 916
5.7	☐	Other Real Property (Timeshare, vacation home)

6.0   **The Family Residence**
6.1	☐	Disposition FC §§ 2554-2555
6.2	☐	Occupancy
6.3	☐	Deferred Sale of the Home (*Duke*) FC §§ 3800-3810
6.4	☐	Selling of Residence Terms
6.5	☐	Maintenance, Repairs and Improvements
6.6	☐	Reservation of Jurisdiction
6.7	☐	Modifiability

7.0   **Retirement/Pension/Ira/Sep/Deferred Compensation FC § 2610**
7.1	☐	Joinder FC § 2021
7.2	☐	Division/Court Order
7.3	☐	Waiver of Benefits

---

[16] Effective January 1, 2017 FC § 360 Amended subd (b) by substituting (1) "shall not be" for "may not be"; (2) "the date of marriage" for "issuance of the original license"; and (3) "date of marriage" for "issuance date shown on the original marriage license" at the end.

8.0		**Attorney Fees**
8.1	☐	"Equal Access to Representation" FC § 2030
8.2	☐	Prevailing Party FC § 3652
8.3	☐	Enforcement FC § 3557

9.0   **Representation Clause** (Both spouses should have t least 7 days to obtain independent counsel prior to signing.)

10.0		**Other Property Provisions**
10.1	☐	Hidden/Omitted Assets FC § 721
10.2	☐	Income Tax Liability/Refunds FC § 2628, Cal Rev & Tax Code § 19006
10.3	☐	Other

11.0	**Property Warranties and Remedies**
12.0	**Wills Revoked Probate Code §122**
13.0	**Grounds for Relief/Set Aside FC §§ 2122-2123, CCP § 473**

14.0		**General Provisions**
14.1	☐	Release of Liabilities and Claims CC §§ 1541-1549
14.2	☐	Status of Temporary Orders
14.3	☐	Waiver of Rights on Death of Other Party
14.4	☐	Entire Agreement CC § 1695.3
14.5	☐	Reconciliation
14.6	☐	Modification by Subsequent Agreement
14.7	☐	Invalid Provision Remaining Provisions Valid and Enforceable
14.8	☐	Choice of Law
14.9	☐	Notice of Bankruptcy Filing
14.10	☐	Cooperation in Implementation of Agreement
14.11	☐	Effective Date of Agreement
14.12	☐	Further documentation
14.13	☐	Inurement

15.0	**Dates and Signatures of Parties and Attorneys**
16.0	**Approved as to Form and Content**
17.0	**Date and Signature of Attorney/Party Approving as to Form and Content**

© 2019 LW Greenberg

EDUCATIONAL EXERCISES

Use the information is Appendix One to draft the following. You may make up any facts that do not conflict with the information presented.

1. Draft two provisions that could be in a premarital agreement between Marilyn and Trevor.
2. Draft two provisions that could be in a postmarital agreement between Marilyn and Trevor.
3. **Draft two provisions that could be in a Marital Settlement Agreement for the Johns' divorce.

CHAPTER 31: Settlements, Trial & the Final Paperwork

In Brief...

IN AN UNCONTESTED DISSOLUTION:
- The respondent files a *Response*, the parties resolve all issues and there is no trial, **CRC Rule 5.404**; &
- All issues of the divorce are reduced to a written agreement called a *MSA*.

IN A CONTESTED DISSOLUTION:

Before the trial
- A *MSA* is prepared for undisputed and resolved issues;
- A settlement conference may be required (check local rules of the county); and
- A trial notebook is prepared for the trial (if required), **CRC Rule 5.393** and **5.394**.

At the trial:
- Only disputed issues are presented for a decision; and
- The judge decides all of the disputed issues.

THE FINAL PAPERWORK:
1. ***The Declaration of Disclosure:***
   - Both a preliminary and a final declaration of disclosure must be prepared and served, **FC § 2105**;
   - Is not filed with the court;
   - May be waived if it is a final declaration and the parties so agree in writing; and
   - In the case of a default, only the petitioner files the *Declaration of Disclosure*, **FC § 2110**.
2. **The *Notice of Entry of Judgment:***
   - Is the mandatory form *FL-190*; and
   - Must include 2 stamped envelopes addressed to the parties or their attorneys that have the address of the court clerk as the return address, **FC § 2338** and **CRC Rule 5.415**.
3. The judgment:
   - Includes any judgment, decree or signed order from which an appeal lies;
   - Contains the final resolution of all issues, **FC § 664.5**;
   - Contains decision(s) made by the judge that resolve contested issues, **FC § 2403**;
   - For dissolutions, legal separations and annulments form *FL-180* is used; for paternities, it is form *FL-250* that is used; and for summary dissolutions form *FL-825* is used.
   - Can be a stipulated judgment which is a written agreement similar to a *MSA*, **CRC Rule 5.411**;

Chapter 31: Settlements, Trial, & the Final Paperwork

> - That was mistakenly, negligently or inadvertently not signed or not filed or entered when submitted is called a nunc pro tunc judgment, **FC § 2346**.
>
> **WHEN FILING THE FINAL PAPERWORK:**
> - A signed, original *MSA*, if the parties have executed one;
> - An original +2 copies of all paperwork submitted must be submitted to the clerk for filing;
> - **There is a 6 month cooling off period, FC § 2339:**
>   - That begins when the Summons is served or the respondent makes an appearance;
>   - Before the judgment becomes final.

Introduction

Sometime parties agree to all issues regarding the divorce and a default can be entered to finalize the divorce. If the respondent has filed a *Response* or appeared in the action, then the default process is no longer available. If however, the parties thereafter agree to resolve all of their disputed issues without court intervention, the dissolution can become an uncontested dissolution. In either case, a marital settlement agreement (*MSA*) should be drafted that sets forth all of the parties' resolutions/agreements. Then the final paperwork can be prepared, signed, copied and filed.

If, however, after all of the agreements have been made and reduced to a writing and there are still disputed issues, a settlement conference and trial date will be set. At the settlement conference, disputed issues will be discussed toward reaching a full settlement. If disputed issues of the divorce still remain after the settlement conference, then the parties or their respective attorneys must give the court a time estimate as to how much time will be needed to try the case.

Additionally, a trial brief will need to be drafted and most family law firms prepare a trial notebook whenever a trial is set.

At the trial, the judge will decide all disputed issues because there is no jury in a family law trial. After the trial has finished, the final paperwork must be prepared, signed, copied and filed.

Dissolutions

1. Uncontested Dissolutions

When a respondent files a *Response* to the *Petition* and, thereafter, the parties resolve all issues of the divorce, the divorce becomes **uncontested**. In an uncontested dissolution, all resolved issues are reduced to a written agreement called a **Marital Settlement Agreement (*MSA*)**. The original *MSA* is signed by

both parties and all attorneys, attached to the *Judgment*, copied and filed, along with all of the other final paperwork.
Courts must allow judgments in uncontested cases to be submitted by declaration pursuant to **FC § 2336** and must not require that a hearing be conducted in all such cases.

Once the *Proof of Service of Summons (Family Law)* (form *FL-115*) has been filed with the court or the respondent has made a general appearance in the case, the court must conduct a procedural review of all the documents submitted for judgment based on default or uncontested judgments submitted under **FC § 2336** and notify the attorneys or self-represented litigants who submitted them of all identified defects. Basic information for correction of the defects are included in any notification to attorneys or self-represented litigants. **CRC Rule 5.407**.

In an uncontested dissolution, the final paperwork may need to be prepared for filing:

FL-130 - Appearance, Stipulations and Waivers;
FL-141 - Declaration Regarding Service of Declaration of Disclosure and Income and Expense Declaration **OR**
FL-144 - Stipulation and Waiver of Final Declaration of Disclosure (if the parties have so agreed);
FL-170 - Declaration for Default or Uncontested Dissolution;
FL-190 - Notice of Entry of Judgment; and
FL-180 - Judgment with the *MSA* attached.

2. Contested Dissolutions

a. The Settlement Conference

A settlement conference with the parties and their attorneys, if the parties have retained counsel, may be requested or required before a long cause hearing or trial date will be set. During the conference, disputed issues will be discussed toward resolving them. If there are still disputed issues, a trial date will be set and each party must provide an estimate of the amount of time that will be needed to complete the trial or long-cause hearing. The estimate must take into account the time needed to examine witnesses and introduce evidence at the trial. **CRC Rule 5.393(b)**.

Additionally, at the settlement conference, the settlement judge must determine if a trial brief will be required. If trial briefs will be required, they must comply with the requirements of **CRC Rule 5.394**. The local rules of the county should be consulted with regard to the form of a trial brief. Any additional requirements to the brief must be provided to the parties in writing before the end of the conference.

Chapter 31: Settlements, Trial, & the Final Paperwork

b. The Trial

CRC Rule 5.393 provides the following definitions with regard to trials:
A **trial day** is defined as a period no less than two and a half hours of a single court day.

A **long-cause hearing** is defined as a hearing on a request for an order that extends more than a single court day.

A **trial brief** or **hearing brief** is a written summary or statement submitted by a party that explains to a judge the party's position on particular issues that will be part of the trial or hearing.

In many jurisdictions each party will have to prepare a trial brief, a hearing brief or other pleading; the contents of the brief must minimally include:

1. The statistical facts and any disputes about the statistical facts. Statistical facts that may apply to the case could include:
    a. Date of the marriage or domestic partnership;
    b. Date of separation;
    c. Length of marriage or domestic partnership in years and months; and
    d. Names and ages of the parties' minor children;
2. A brief summary of the case;
3. A list of all issues that need to be resolved at trial;
4. A brief statement summarizing the contents of any appraisal or expert report to be offered at trial;
5. A list of the witnesses to be called at trial and a brief description of the anticipated testimony of each witness, as well as name, business address and statement of qualifications of any expert witness;
6. Any legal arguments on that are going to be presented; and
7. Any other matters determined by the judge to be necessary.

The parties must serve the trial brief on all parties and file the brief with the court a minimum of five (5) court days before the trial or long-cause hearing. **CRC Rule 5.393(b)**.

After the judge makes a decision regarding the disputed issues, the judgment and all necessary paperwork must be prepared to finalize the divorce.

The Final Paperwork

1. The Declaration of Disclosure

In a dissolution, legal separation or nullity action, both a preliminary and a final declaration of disclosure (both are on a *FL-140* form, *Declaration of Disclosure - Family Law*) must be prepared and served on the other party with certain

exceptions. Neither disclosure is filed with the court, but a declaration stating that service of the disclosure documents (*FL-141, Declaration of Service of Declaration of Disclosure and Income and Expense Declaration*) was completed or waived must be filed with the court. The use of a *FL-140* is mandatory.
A *FL-140* can be found at the following website:
www.courts.ca.gov/documents/fl140.pdf. A *FL-141* can be found at:
www.courts.ca.gov/documents/fl141.pdf.

A preliminary declaration of disclosure must be served at the same time as or within sixty (60) days of service of the *Petition*. The respondent must serve a preliminary declaration of disclosure at the same time as or within sixty (60) days of serving of the *Response*. The parties can execute a written agreement and the court can order an extension of these time periods pursuant to **FC § 2104(f)**.

In summary dissolution cases, each spouse or domestic partner must exchange preliminary disclosures on a *FL-810*. However, pursuant to **FC § 2109,** final disclosures are not required.

In a default judgment case that is not a stipulated judgment or a default with a marital settlement agreement, only the petitioner is required to complete and serve a preliminary declaration of disclosure. Pursuant to **FC § 2110**, a final disclosure is not required of either party.

The following forms may need to be attached to a *Declaration of Disclosure* (form *FL-141*):

(1) A completed *Schedule of Assets and Debts* (form *FL-142*) or a *Property Declaration* (form *FL-160*) for community and quasi-community property and/or separate property;
(2) A completed *Income and Expense Declaration* (form *FL-150*);
(3) All income tax returns filed by the parties in the two years before the date that the disclosure documents were served;[1]
(4) A statement of all material facts and information regarding valuation of all assets that are community property or in which the community has an interest; [2]
(5) A statement of all material facts and information regarding obligations for which the community is liable;[3] and
(6) An accurate and complete written disclosure of any investment opportunity, business opportunity or other income-producing opportunity presented since the date of separation that results from any investment, significant business or other income-producing opportunity from the date of marriage to the date of separation.[4]

---

[1] Income tax returns are usually lodged with the court and not filed. If an income tax return is filed, it must be sufficiently redacted.
[2] There is no Judicial Council form for this statement.
[3] There is no Judicial Council form for this statement.
[4] There is no Judicial Council form for this disclosure.

Chapter 31: Settlements, Trial, & the Final Paperwork

Service of preliminary declarations of disclosure may not be waived by an agreement between the parties. The parties, however, can agree in writing to waive the filing of the final declarations of disclosure. **FC § 2103**. Although the use of a *FL-144* to waive this filing is not mandatory, it is recommended. A *FL-144* can be found at: ***www.courts.ca.gov/documents/fl144.pdf***.

In the case that follows, one of the parties was trying to have the *Declarations of Disclosure* be declared inadmissible because the parties attended a mediation.

> ***GILDA LAPPE, Petitioner, v. THE SUPERIOR COURT OF LOS ANGELES COUNTY, Respondent; MURRAY LAPPE, Real Party in Interest.***
> COURT OF APPEAL OF CALIFORNIA, SECOND APPELLATE DISTRICT, DIVISION THREE
> 232 Cal.App.4th 774; 181 Cal.Rptr.3d 510
> December 19, 2014, Opinion Filed
> (*Lappe v. Superior Court*)
>
> Gilda and Murray were married for 16 years and have two children together. Gilda was a stay-at-home mother during their marriage. Murray is trained as a medical doctor and is a successful businessman.
>
> On February 10, 2011, Gilda filed a petition for dissolution of the marriage. The parties agreed to settle their property and support issues through mediation without representation by counsel. During the mediation, Gilda and Murray signed declarations stating that service of the preliminary and final declarations of disclosure had been made on the other party as required by the Family Code. Notwithstanding these declarations, Gilda maintains that she did not serve Murray with a preliminary or final declaration of disclosure, nor did she receive a preliminary or final declaration from Murray. She avers the declaration regarding service was one of several documents that Murray "coerced" her to sign while they were alone in the mediator's office. Murray denies the allegation.
>
> During the mediation, the parties also executed a marital settlement agreement. As pertinent to the instant proceeding, the agreement provides that Murray shall pay Gilda a total of $10 million in full satisfaction of her entire community interest in shares of eScreen, Inc. With respect to the declarations of disclosure, the agreement also states: "The parties' Preliminary/Final Declarations of Disclosure shall be inadmissible in a court of law, and otherwise protected from disclosure, pursuant to the provisions of Evidence Code § 1119(b)." Evidence Code § 1119(b) bars discovery or admissibility of writings "prepared for the purpose of, in the course of, or pursuant to, a mediation." On August 2, 2011, the trial court entered a stipulated judgment, which incorporated the marital settlement agreement.
>
> On April 24, 2012, Gilda filed an application to set aside the judgment on grounds of fraud, perjury, duress, and mistake. In her supporting declaration, Gilda asserted that in January 2012, less than five months after the judgment was entered, she learned Murray was in the process of selling eScreen and all equity shares he acquired in the company through the marital settlement agreement. As a result of the sale, Murray received approximately $75 million pretax for the eScreen shares. Gilda averred that Murray never disclosed he was shopping eScreen for sale, and had she known as much, she would not have agreed to surrender her community interest in the company for only $10 million.

Chapter 31: Settlements, Trial, & the Final Paperwork

In connection with her application to set aside the judgment, Gilda served a request for production of documents on Murray, which included a request for the declaration of disclosure that Murray served upon Gilda prior to entry of judgment. Murray objected to the request and refused to produce the declaration on the ground that it was protected from disclosure by the mediation confidentiality statutes. Gilda brought a motion to compel production.

The trial court appointed a referee to make recommendations regarding the discovery dispute. The referee concluded the declaration of disclosure was not subject to mediation confidentiality because the document had "independent legal significance" and the "public policy" declared by the Family Code favoring disclosure to ensure fair and equal property divisions "overrides" mediation confidentiality. Gilda applied for an order confirming the referee's recommendation and findings. Murray objected to the recommendation [arguing that the] recommendation ignored the parties' express agreement that the declarations of disclosure were to be deemed inadmissible and shielded from discovery under the mediation confidentiality provisions of the Evidence Code.

The trial court agreed with Murray [ruling that Evidence Code § 1119 applied and the declarations of disclosure were inadmissible.]

DISCUSSION
Gilda contends the Evidence Code's mediation confidentiality provisions cannot be applied in a marital dissolution proceeding to bar the discovery and admissibility of financial disclosures mandated by the Family Code.

As codified in FC § 2100 et seq., California law recognizes the vital importance of "full and accurate disclosure of all assets and liabilities" at the "early stages" of a marital dissolution proceeding to ensure fair and sufficient child and spousal support awards and to achieve a proper division of community and quasi-community assets and liabilities. (FC § 2100(c).) This includes a "continuing duty" on the part of each spouse to "immediately, fully, and accurately update and augment that disclosure" so both will have "full and complete knowledge of the relevant underlying facts." (FC § 2100(c).)

To implement this policy, the Family Code mandates that each spouse "shall serve on the other party" a "preliminary" and a "final" declaration of disclosure. (FC § 2103.) The preliminary declaration of disclosure provides a general inventory of the parties' respective assets at the outset of dissolution proceedings. The final declaration requires far more extensive disclosures.

The Family Code mandates that the final declaration of disclosure "shall include" "[a]ll material facts and information" regarding (1) the characterization of all assets and liabilities, (2) the valuation of all assets that are contended to be community property, (3) the amounts of all obligations that are contended to be community obligations, and (4) the earnings, accumulations, and expenses of each party. (FC § 2105(b).) The final declaration must also contain "accurate and complete written disclosure of any investment opportunity, business opportunity, or other income-producing opportunity that presents itself after the date of separation, but that results from any investment, significant business activity outside the ordinary course of business, or other income-producing opportunity of either spouse from the date of marriage to the date of separation, inclusive." (FC § 2102(a)(2).) This written disclosure "shall be made in sufficient time for the other spouse to make an informed decision as to whether he or she desires to

> participate in the investment opportunity, business, or other potential income-producing opportunity, and for the court to resolve any dispute regarding the right of the other spouse to participate in the opportunity." (FC § 2102(a)(2).)
> Because the Family Code's extensive disclosure requirements could reveal sensitive financial information, the final declarations of disclosure, like the preliminary declarations, must be served on the other spouse, but are not to be filed with the court. Mediation confidentiality is codified in Evidence Code § 1115 et seq. As delineated in Evidence Code § 1119, mediation confidentiality applies to any oral or written communication made or "prepared for the purpose of, in the course of, or pursuant to, a mediation or a mediation consultation … ." (Evid. Code, § 1119(b).) Section 1119 specifies that such evidence is neither subject to discovery nor admissible in any civil action or other noncriminal proceeding. Even after mediation ends, communications and writings protected by the statutes are to remain confidential. (Evid. Code, § 1126.)
>
> The declarations of disclosure at issue in this case—in particular the final declarations that must be exchanged before judgment can be entered (FC § 2106)—do not come within the categories delineated by Evidence Code § 1119. These declarations were not prepared "for the purpose of" a mediation; rather, they were prepared for the purpose of complying with FC § 2100 et seq. Nor were the declarations prepared "pursuant to" a mediation; again, they were prepared pursuant to a statutory duty imposed by the Family Code, and a mandate requiring exchange of the final declarations before judgment will be entered. As Gilda aptly puts it in her writ petition, "the disclosure documents are not created and exchanged because a mediation is contemplated and they will form a part of the party's negotiation strategy. Rather, they are created and exchanged because the [L]egislature demands it, so that divorcing spouses will have full and accurate information upon which to base fair and equitable divisions of assets." We agree.
>
> Accordingly, the declarations were not prepared "for the purpose of, in the course of, or pursuant to, a mediation." (Evid. Code, § 1119(b).) In so holding, we are not crafting an exception to the mediation confidentiality statutes. On the contrary, we simply recognize that the confidentiality statutes do not apply in the first instance, because these statutorily mandated declarations do not fall within any category delineated by Evid. Code §1119.
>
> Because Evidence Code § 1119 does not apply to the subject declarations of disclosure, [they are admissible.] The trial court should have ordered production of the declarations of disclosure and the failure to do so was an abuse of discretion.
>
> Let a writ of mandate issue directing the trial court to vacate its order denying Gilda Lappe's motion to compel and to enter a new and different order granting the motion with respect to the declarations of disclosure.

Finally, final declarations do not have to be served prior to agreements made in contemplation of a dissolution. *In re Marriage of EVANS* (2014) 229 Cal.App.4th 374 at p. 384.

2. The Notice of Entry of Judgment FL-190

A *Notice of Entry of Judgment* is a mandatory use form. It must be completed and filed with the judgment or proposed judgment whether the dissolution was contested or uncontested.

Further, for the purpose of mailing the *Notice of Entry of Judgment*, the party submitting the judgment must provide the court clerk with a stamped envelope bearing sufficient postage addressed to the attorney for the other party or to the party, if unrepresented, with the address of the court clerk as the return address. The court clerk must maintain any such document returned by the post office as part of the court file in the case. **FC § 2338.5(c)**.

The *FL-190* must be fully completed except for the designation of the date entered, the date of mailing and the signatures. The certificate of mailing must specify the place where the notices have been given to the other party. **CRC Rule 5.415(b)**.

Failure to complete the *FL-190* or to submit the envelopes is cause for refusal to sign the judgment until compliance with the requirements of this rule. **CRC Rule 5.415(d)**.

Every person who submits a judgment for a signature by the court must submit an original and at least two additional copies of the *Notice of Entry of Judgment* (form *FL-190*). **CRC Rule 5.415(a)**.

Upon order of the court entry of a judgment in a contested action or any action or special proceeding, the clerk must mail a notice of entry of any judgment or ruling, whether or not it is appealable. **FC § 664.5(d)**.

3. Judgments

a. The Judgment for Dissolutions, Legal separations and Annulments

In a proceeding for a dissolution of the marriage, legal separation of the parties or nullity, the court determines whether or not a judgment should be granted. A judgment is any judgment, decree or signed order from which an appeal lies and it is the final part of the action. **FC § 664.5(c)**.

If the judge determines that no dissolution should be granted, a judgment so providing will be entered. If the judge determines that a dissolution should be granted, a judgment of dissolution of marriage, legal separation or nullity will be entered.

After a the parties have resolved all disputed issues and/or the court has made a decision that resolves the contested issues, the formal order for all three actions are drafted on a *Judgment* (form *FL-180*).

A judgment in a paternity action is drafted on a *FL-250* form; a judgment in a summary dissolution is drafted on a *FL-825* form.

After the entry of the judgment and before it becomes final, neither party has the right to dismiss the proceeding without the consent of the other. **FC § 2338**.

Chapter 31: Settlements, Trial, & the Final Paperwork

A judgment of dissolution of marriage must specify the date on which the judgment becomes finally effective for the purpose of terminating the marriage relationship of the parties. **FC § 2340**.

Pursuant to **FC § 7637**, a judgment[5] may contain any other provision directed against the appropriate party to the proceeding, concerning:

(1) The duty of support, the custody and guardianship of the child,
(2) Visitation privileges with the child,
(3) The furnishing of a bond or other security for the payment of the judgment, or
(4) Any other matter that is in the best interests of the child.

Additionally, the judgment may direct the parent to pay the reasonable expenses of the mother's pregnancy and confinement in parentage matters.

CRC Rule 5.405 provides a judgment checklist, *Dissolution/Legal Separation* (form *FL-182*), which lists the forms that courts may require to complete a judgment based on a default or uncontested judgment in dissolution or legal separation cases based on a declaration under **FC § 2336**.

Entry of the judgment pursuant to **FC § 2403**[6] constitutes a final adjudication of the rights and obligations of the parties with respect to the status of the marriage and property rights and a waiver of their respective rights to spousal support, rights to appeal, and rights to move for a new trial. **FC § 2404**.

Notwithstanding any other provision of law, in any action filed by the local child support agency pursuant to **FC § 17400, 17402** or **17404**, a judgment must be entered without a hearing; without the presentation of any other evidence or further notice to the defendant; upon the filing of proof of service by the local child support agency evidencing that more than thirty (30) days have passed since the simplified summons and complaint, proposed judgment, blank answer, blank income and expense declaration; and all notices required by this division were served on the defendant. **FC § 17430**.

Finally, the death of either party after the entry of the judgment does not prevent the judgment from becoming a final judgment under **FC §§ 2339** to **2343**, inclusive. **FC § 2344**.

---

[5] In a dissolution matter, the *Judgment* form is the *FL-180*. In a paternity action, the Judicial Council form is the *FL-250*. In a summary dissolution mater, the judgment form is the *FL-825*.

[6] FC § 2403 provides that when six months have expired from the date of the filing of the joint petition for summary dissolution, the court must, unless a revocation has been filed pursuant to FC § 2402, enter the judgment dissolving the marriage. The judgment restores to the parties the status of single persons, and either party may marry after the entry of the judgment. The clerk must send a notice of entry of judgment to each of the parties at the party's last known address.

Chapter 31: Settlements, Trial, & the Final Paperwork

b. Stipulated Judgments

A stipulated judgment (which must be attached to a *Judgment* [form *FL-180*] or a *Judgment [Uniform Parentage]* [form *FL-250*]) may be submitted to the court for signature as an uncontested matter or at the time of the trial on the merits and must contain the exact terms of any judgment proposed to be entered in the case. At the bottom of the form, immediately above the space reserved for the judge's signature, the stipulated judgment must contain the signatures of both the petitioner and the respondent and the signatures of their respective attorneys. **CRC Rule 5.411(a)**.

A stipulated judgment must include the disposition of all matters subject to the court's jurisdiction for which a party seeks adjudication or an explicit reservation of jurisdiction over any matter not proposed for disposition at that time. A stipulated judgment constitutes a written agreement between the parties as to all matters covered by the stipulation. **CRC Rule 5.411(b)**.

Finally, a stipulated judgment is very similar to a *MSA*. It may, however, be shorter than a *MSA* and more abbreviated. In any case, it has the same effect as a *MSA* once it is attached to a judgment and filed.

c. The *Nunc Pro Tunc* Judgment

A ***nunc pro tunc*** judgment is a judgment that mistakenly, negligently or inadvertently was not signed, filed or entered. The court can cause the judgment to be signed, dated, filed and entered in the proceeding as of the date when the judgment could have been signed, dated, filed and entered originally. However, it must appear to the satisfaction of the court that no appeal is going to be taken in the proceeding or no motion will be made for a new trial to annul or to set aside the judgment. **FC § 2346(a)**.

The court may cause a *nunc pro tunc* judgment to be entered on its own motion or upon the motion of either party to the proceeding. However, in contested cases notice of the *nunc pro tunc* judgment request must be given to the opposing party. **FC § 2346(b)**.

The court may cause the judgment to be entered *nunc pro tunc* even though the judgment may have been previously entered, where through mistake, negligence or inadvertence the judgment was not entered as soon as it could have been entered under the law. **FC § 2346(c)**.

A court, however, may not cause a judgment to be entered *nunc pro tunc* as of a date before trial in the matter, before the date of an uncontested judgment hearing in the matter or before the date of submission to the court of an application for judgment on affidavit, pursuant to **FC § 2336**.

After a *nunc pro tunc* judgment is entered, the parties have the same rights with regard to the dissolution of marriage becoming final on the date that it would have become final had the judgment been entered upon the date when it could have been originally entered. **FC § 2346(d)**.

Filing the Final Paperwork

When filing the final paperwork, it is necessary to include an original and two copies of every document to be filed. If there is a marital settlement agreement, the signed original marital settlement agreement must be included with two copies.

The final paperwork can either be mailed to the court or taken to the courthouse by the attorney, the paralegal, an attorney service or any other person. If the paperwork is mailed and the attorney desires that the court return the processed paperwork by mail, a pre-postaged or stamped envelope must be included that will hold all of the papers that will be file-stamped by the clerk to be returned.

If the paperwork is taken to the courthouse, it will be placed in a bin or box for pickup after the clerk has completely processed the final paperwork.

If the *Petition* and proposed *Judgment* do not contain a demand for money, property costs or attorney fees, the default will be entered (filed with the court) and an *Income and Expense Declaration* (form *FL-150*) and *Property Declaration* (form *FL-160*) will not be required. **FC § 2330.5**.

Once a valid proof of service of the *Summons* has been filed with the court or the respondent has made a general appearance in the case, the court must conduct a procedural review of all the documents submitted for judgment based on default or uncontested judgments submitted under **FC § 2336** and notify the attorneys or self-represented litigants who submitted them of all identified defects in their paperwork. Basic information for correction of the defects will be included. **CRC Rule 5.407**.

If child custody orders, child support orders, spousal or partner support, division of community property and pensions are sought, additional forms will need to be added to the final paperwork.

The Six-Month Waiting Period

No judgment of dissolution is final such that either or both of the parties may remarry until six (6) months after: **(1)** the date of service of the *Summons* and *Petition* or **(2)** the date of the appearance of the respondent, whichever occurs first. **FC § 2339(a)**. (See Chapter 5, *supra*, for more information re: "Cooling Off Period".)

It is within the judge's discretion to retain jurisdiction over the date of termination of the marital status or order that the marital status be terminated at a future specified date. This reservation requires notice and good cause or a stipulation of the parties.

On the date of termination of the parties' marital status, the parties are restored to the status of unmarried persons. **FC § 2343**. **FC § 2339(b)**. (See Chapter 5 RE: Annulment, Dissolution & Legal Separation, *supra*.)

EDUCATIONAL EXERCISES

1. What is the length of time that parties to a dissolution have to set aside their Marital Settlement Agreement when they reach a complete agreement on all issues and sign an agreement?
2. What are the codes section(s) that can give a party the right to set aside a Judgment?
3. List the forms that must be filed with a Marital Settlement Agreement and a Judgment before the judgment can be processed.
4. If the parties are really fighting about everything, can all issues of the marriage be litigated?
5. Can there be 3 judgments issued in one dissolution? Explain.
6. How long does one party have to set aside a court order pursuant to CCP § 473?
7. When filing the final paperwork in a dissolution, how many copies should be made of each original document?
8. What must be included with A Notice of Entry of Judgment?
9. If the final paperwork is "dropped" at the court for processing, what does that mean?

CHAPTER 32: Enforcement

In Brief...

A WRIT OF EXECUTION is a court order that gives the sheriff the power to seize the debtor's property in order to pay a judgment debt, **CCP § 699.520**.

AN ABSTRACT OF JUDGMENT is a document filed with the county recorder that makes the debt a public record and creates a lien on any real property owned by a debtor in that county, **FC § 4506**.

AN ELISOR can be appointed to sign necessary documents if a party cannot or will not sign them, **CCP § 262.10** and the county's local rules.

CONTEMPT OF COURT, **CCP § 1209**:
- The contempt process is not enforcement; it is a punishment for violating a court order.
- The civil law that applies to contempts also applies to family law, **FC §292, CCP §§ 1211, 1211.5, 1212**.
- There are contempt forms that MUST be used when requesting a contempt.
- In order to sustain a cause of action for contempt, it must be proven that:
    1. Citee has willfully disobeyed certain orders of the court:
    2. Citee had knowledge of the court order in that:
        - Citee was present in court at the time the order was made;
        - Citee was served with a copy of the order;
        - Citee signed a stipulation upon which the order was based; or
        - Other (must specify how citee knew about the order).
    3. Citee was able to comply with each order when it was disobeyed.
- Orders for contempt of court are final and conclusive, **CCP § 1222**.
- Statute of limitations for a contempt is 3 years for failure to pay support, **CCP § 1218.5**.

CONTEMPT OF COURT JUDGMENTS:
- May be enforced by any method determined by the court;
- Are enforceable for child, spousal and family support owed and arrearages, **FC §§ 4500, 4501**; and
- Are enforceable in any manner provided by law for the enforcement of judgments.

INCOME WITHHOLDING ORDERS FOR SUPPORT/WAGE ASSIGNMENTS:
- Must be issued when child, spousal or family support is ordered, **FC § 5208**;
- May be stayed if the court finds a good cause to stay the assignment, **FC § 5260**;
- May be served on an employer by first-class mail, **CCP § 1013**;
- Are effective and binding on any existing or future employer, unless stayed, **FC §§ 5232-5233**; and
- The *Income Withholding for Support FL-195* may be used for both child support and spousal support.

SANCTIONS:

Chapter 32: Enforcement

> - Are monetary fines or penalties ordered by the court against a person; and
> - May be used to enforce a family law court order, **FC § 4500**.

Introduction

This chapter discusses methods that can be used to enforce court orders. While there is some general information in this chapter regarding enforcement, the focus is primarily on orders made pursuant to the Family Code.

The Writ of Execution

The writ of execution is the most common method for collecting on a money judgment. If a judgment debtor has not paid the judgment debt when it is due or made arrangements to pay it over time, California law allows the judgment creditor to collect property or levy on property pursuant to a writ of execution. A writ of execution is a court order giving the sheriff (or other levying officer) the power to seize the judgment debtor's property in order to pay a judgment debt.

When a court issues a *Writ of Execution* (form *EJ-130*), the court directs the sheriff or marshal to enforce the judgment in the county where the assets are located. Writs of execution are only good for 180 days.

A writ of execution must be issued by the clerk of the court, upon application of the judgment creditor, and must be directed to the levying officer in the county in which the levy is to be made and to any registered process server. The clerk of the court must give priority to the application for, and issuance of, writs of execution on orders or judgments for child support and spousal support. A separate writ shall be issued for each county in which a levy is to be made. Writs may be issued successively until the money judgment is satisfied, but a new writ may not be issued for a county until the expiration of 180 days after the issuance of a prior writ for that county unless the prior writ is first returned.

The writ of execution is issued in the name of the judgment debtor as listed on the judgment. The writ of execution must include the additional name or names, and the type of legal entity by which the judgment debtor is known, as set forth in the affidavit of identity, as defined in **CCP § 680.135**. It is filed by the judgment creditor with the application for issuance of the writ of execution.

The property that is to be collected must be described and the place where the property is to be collected must be set forth. The clerk may only issue a writ if thirty (30) days have passed since the court mailed the *Notice of Entry of Judgment* (Form *SC-130*) to the judgment creditor and the judgment debtor.

The writ of execution requires the levying officer to whom it is directed to enforce the money judgment, and it must include the following information:

> (a) The date of issuance of the writ.
> (b) The title of the court where the judgment is entered and the cause and number of the action.
> (c) The name and address of the judgment creditor and the name and last known address of the judgment debtor. If the judgment debtor is other than a natural person, the type of legal entity shall be stated.
> (d) The date of the entry of the judgment and of any subsequent renewals and where entered in the records of the court.
> (e) The total amount of the money judgment as entered or renewed, together with costs thereafter added to the judgment pursuant to CCP § 685.090 and the accrued interest on the judgment from the date of entry or renewal of the judgment to the date of issuance of the writ, reduced by any partial satisfactions and by any amounts no longer enforceable.
> (f) The amount required to satisfy the money judgment on the date the writ is issued.
> (g) The amount of interest accruing daily on the principal amount of the judgment from the date the writ is issued.
> (h) Whether any person has requested notice of sale under the judgment and, if so, the name and mailing address of that person.
> (i) The sum of the fees and costs added to the judgment pursuant to Government Code § 6103.5 or 68511.3, and which is in addition to the amount owing to the judgment creditor on the judgment.
> (j) Whether the writ of execution includes any additional names of the judgment debtor pursuant to an affidavit of identity, as defined in Section 680.135.
> (k) A statement indicating whether the case is limited or unlimited. CCP § 699.520.

Writs of execution on judgments or orders in a fixed amount, or based on judgments or orders providing for installment payments, do not require a judicial officer's signature or notice to the opposing party before presentation to the records division of the clerk's office for approval and issuance.

With a writ of execution, a judgment creditor can:

1. Collect from the debtor's wages;
2. Collect from the debtor's bank account or safe deposit box;
3. Put a lien on the debtor's real property;
4. Have the debtor's house or other real property sold at public auction;
5. Put a lien on the debtor's personal property;
6. Take and sell the debtor's car (the sheriff must take and sell the car); and
7. Put a lien on a lawsuit that the debtor has against someone else.

The application for a writ of execution is required if the writ was issued for child or spousal support.

The Abstract of Judgment

An abstract of judgment is a document issued by the clerk of the court that certifies the general contents of a judgment entered in a court proceeding. The document

Chapter 32: Enforcement

provides how much money the debtor owes to the judgment creditor, the rate of interest to be paid on the judgment amount, court costs and any specific orders that the debtor must obey. The abstract of judgment is acknowledged and stamped; it is then recorded in the county where the debtor, hopefully, owns real property. The purpose of an abstract of judgment is so that the debt owed is made a public record and a lien is created on any property owned by the debtor in that county. Once issued, the abstract of judgment can be recorded with the county recorder in every county in which the debtor may own property.

Pursuant to **FC § 4506**, an abstract of judgment ordering a party to pay spousal, child or family support to the other party must be certified by the clerk of the court where the judgment was entered and must contain all of the following:

---

(1) The title of the court where the judgment is entered and the cause and number of the proceeding.
(2) The date of entry of the judgment and of any renewal of the judgment.
(3) Where the judgment and any renewals are entered in the records of the court.
(4) The name and last known address of the party ordered to pay support.
(5) The name and address of the party to whom support payments are ordered to be paid.
(6) Only the last four digits of the social security number, birth date, and driver's license number of the party who is ordered to pay support. If any of those numbers are not known to the party to whom support payments are to be paid, that fact shall be indicated on the abstract of the court judgment. This paragraph shall not apply to documents created prior to January 1, 2010.
(7) Whether a stay of enforcement has been ordered by the court and, if so, the date the stay ends.
(8) The date of issuance of the abstract.
(9) Any other information deemed reasonable and appropriate by the Judicial Council.

A judgment includes an order for child, family or spousal support. **FC § 4506(d)**. As a judgment, it may be punished by a contempt of court.

An *Abstract of Support Judgment FL-480* form must be used for support judgments. This form can be found at ***www.courts.ca.gov/documents/fl480.pdf***. An *Abstract of Judgment EJ-001* form must be used for any other judgments. This form can be found at: ***www.courts.ca.gov/documents/ej001.pdf***.

The Elisor[1]

When a party will not or cannot execute a document necessary to carry out a court order, the clerk of the court, or his or her authorized representative or designee, may be appointed as an elisor to sign the document.

The specific rules regarding an elisor are usually set forth in the local rules of each county.

---

[1] Elisor is pronounced with a long E Liz with a long I, or o is a short o.

An application for the appointment of an elisor requires a supporting declaration that must provide specific facts that establish the necessity of an elisor. If the documents being signed by the elisor require notarization, it is the responsibility of the applicant to arrange for a notary public to be present when the elisor signs the documents.

Whenever an act is performed by an elisor, he or she must receive a reasonable compensation, to be fixed by the court, to be paid by the person or party requiring the service in all other cases in private action. **CCP § 262.10**.

Contempt of Court

1. The Contempt Process

The contempt process is not really enforcement; it is a punishment for violating a court order. Because the punishments for violations of family law court orders can include actual jail time, the contempt process is considered quasi-criminal. In quasi-criminal proceedings, a defendant or offender is entitled to all of the due process protections that are afforded a criminal defendant.[2]

CCP § 1209 provides that disobedience of lawful judgments, orders or processes of the court are within the authority of the court to cite for contempt. Pursuant to **FC § 292**, there are forms promulgated by the Judicial Council that MUST be used when requesting a contempt. These forms are: *Order to Show Cause and Affidavit for Contempt* (Family Law) *FL-410* and the *Affidavit of Facts Constituting Contempt*, to be used for *Financial and Injunctive Orders FL-411*, and a *FL-412*, to be used for *Domestic Violence/ Custody and Visitation*. The *FL-411* and the *FL-412* forms need to be attached to the *FL-410*.

The *FL-410* contains (on pages 3 and 4) instructions on how to prepare and submit the *Order to Show Cause and Affidavit for Contempt (Family Law)*.

FC § 292(c) provides that **CCP § 1211.5** applies to the *Order to Show Cause and Affidavit for Contempt* (*Family Law*) and the *Affidavit of Facts Constituting Contempt*.

2. Proving a Contempt

A **citee** or **contemner** is the person who allegedly violated the court order.

In order to prove the basic information needed to sustain a cause of action for contempt, it must be proven that the citee has willfully disobeyed certain orders of the court:

---

[2] In family law the parties are referred to as the petitioner and the respondent. In civil or criminal law the parties are referred to as the plaintiff and the defendant. Since the contempt process is quasi-criminal, the party or offender is referred to as a defendant.

Chapter 32: Enforcement

      a. Citee had knowledge of the court order in that:

          i. Citee was present in court at the time the order was made;
          ii. Citee was served with a copy of the order;
          iii. Citee signed a stipulation upon which the order was based; or
          iv. Other (must specify how citee knew about the order).

      b. Citee was able to comply with each order when it was disobeyed.[3]

For an alleged contemner to be found guilty of contempt of court, the court must find that:

1. There are valid court orders;
2. Citee had knowledge of the orders; and
3. Citee violated the orders.

The civil law that applies to contempts (**CCP §§ 1211, 1211.5** and **1212**) also applies to contempts in family law. **FC § 292(c), CCP § 1211(b)**.

CCP § 1211(a) provides that when the contempt is not committed in the immediate view and presence of the court or judge, an affidavit must be presented to the court or judge of the facts constituting the contempt, or a statement of the facts by the referees, arbitrators or other judicial officers. A warrant of attachment may be issued to bring the person charged to answer, or, without a previous arrest, a warrant of commitment may, upon notice or an order to show cause, be granted.

No warrant of commitment can be issued without such previous attachment to answer or such notice or order to show cause. **CCP § 1212**.

If there is no objection as to the sufficiency of the affidavit or statement during the hearing on the contempt charges, jurisdiction of the subject matter does not depend on the averments of such affidavit or statement, but may be established by the facts found by the trial court to have been proved at such hearing, and the court must amend the affidavit or statement to be amended to conform to proof. **CCP § 1211.5(a)**.

An affidavit may be amended by court order if there is a defect or insufficiency at any stage of the proceedings. The person accused of contempt must continue as if the affidavit or statement had been originally filed as amended, unless his or her substantial rights are prejudiced, in which event a reasonable postponement not longer than the ends of justice requires may be granted. **CCP § 1211.5(b)**.

---

[3] Inability to pay may be used as an affirmative defense only in child support cases. *KOEHLER v. THE SUPERIOR COURT OF SAN MATEO COUNTY* (2010) 181 Cal.App.4th 1153; 104 Cal.Rptr.3d 877. The *FL-410* form (*Affidavit Supporting Order to Show Cause for Contempt*) sets forth these rules.

3. Court Orders

A person who is subject to a court order as a party to the action, or any agent of this person who is adjudged guilty of contempt for violating that court order, may be ordered to pay to the party initiating the contempt proceeding the reasonable attorney fees and costs incurred by this party in connection with the contempt proceeding. **CCP § 1218**.

Any party who is in contempt of a court order or judgment in a dissolution of marriage, dissolution of domestic partnership or legal separation action is not permitted to enforce such an order or judgment, by way of execution or otherwise, either in the same action or by way of a separate action, against the other party. This restriction does not affect nor apply to the enforcement of child or spousal support orders. **CCP § 1218(b)**.

Pursuant to **CCP § 1218(c)**, if a party is found in contempt of court for failure to comply with a court order pursuant to the Family Code, the court MUST order the following:

> **(1)** Upon a first finding of contempt, the court shall order the contemner to perform community service of up to 120 hours, or to be imprisoned up to 120 hours, for each count of contempt.
> **(2)** Upon the second finding of contempt, the court shall order the contemner to perform community service of up to 120 hours, in addition to ordering imprisonment of the contemner up to 120 hours, for each count of contempt.
> **(3)** Upon the third or any subsequent finding of contempt, the court shall order both of the following:
>   **(A)** The court shall order the contemner to serve a term of imprisonment of up to 240 hours, and to perform community service of up to 240 hours, for each count of contempt.
>   **(B)** The court shall order the contemner to pay an administrative fee, not to exceed the actual cost of the contemner's administration and supervision, while assigned to a community service program pursuant to this paragraph.

When a court orders either community service, imprisonment or both, the court must take the parties' employment schedules into consideration. **CCP § 1218(c)**.

Each month where child, spousal or family support is not paid in full constitutes a separate count of contempt. **CCP § 1218.5(a)**.

The judgment and orders of the court or judge made in cases of contempt are final and conclusive. **CCP § 1222**.

The contempt action is a powerful weapon. It must be pled with specificity, and a court must find that all of the elements of the contempt have been met before finding a person guilty of contempt.

As the case below demonstrates, it is essential that the judge know the contempt laws and act within them.

Chapter 32: Enforcement

> **HENRY JAMES KOEHLER, Petitioner, v. THE SUPERIOR COURT OF SAN MATEO COUNTY, Respondent; GILBERT PAPAZIAN et al., Real Parties in Interest.**
> COURT OF APPEAL OF CALIFORNIA, FIRST APPELLATE DISTRICT, DIVISION TWO
> 181 Cal.App.4th 1153; 104 Cal.Rptr.3d 877
> February 5, 2010, Filed
> (*Koehler v. Superior Court*)
>
> **Petitioner became wife's attorney** [in a bitter divorce matter] in July 2005. During the course of discovery, documents containing certain confidential information belonging to Lucky Strike Farms, Inc., Papazian Properties Company, and Gilbert and Margaret Papazian (collectively, third parties) had been provided to wife. On April 25, 2006, third parties filed for a protective order requiring, inter alia, the return of these documents, and on August 8, 2006, they obtained an order to that effect, ordering return of the documents by no later than August 18. The documents were not returned.
>
> On October 17, 2006, third parties moved for an award of discovery sanctions under CCP §§ 2017.020(b), and 2023.030(a), and for mandatory injunctive relief. A hearing on this motion was held on November 27, 2006, before the Honorable Clifford Cretan. After considering the arguments presented by both sides, Judge Cretan ordered both petitioner and wife to pay third parties sanctions in the amount of $ 10,000.
>
> [This case involves an indirect contempt.] In indirect contempt proceedings based on disobedience of a prior court order, a valid judgment must meet strict requirements. Each of the following must be established. (Citations omitted.)
>
> "• Facts establishing court's jurisdiction (e.g., personal service or subpoena, validity of court order allegedly violated, etc.);
>
> "• Defendant's knowledge of the order disobeyed;
>
> "• Defendant's ability to comply; and
> "• Defendant's willful disobedience of the order."
>
> Petitioner never paid the $ 10,000 sanctions, and on May 30, 2007, third parties initiated contempt proceedings against him by submitting an affidavit of facts allegedly constituting contempt. Represented by a major law firm, third parties filed an "Order to Show Cause and Affidavit for Contempt." The factual showing in the affidavit included a lengthy attachment and five exhibits, providing evidence of third parties' unsuccessful attempts to negotiate a settlement of the issue, and to recover the sanctions award.
>
> On July 16, 2007, the matter came before Judge Cretan, the judge who had issued the sanction order. Petitioner appeared on his own behalf and requested the services of a public defender. Judge Cretan paused the proceeding to have petitioner fill out a financial statement, and then questioned petitioner concerning it. Apparently satisfied with petitioner's inability to pay for counsel, Judge Cretan ruled that it would appoint a private defender to represent petitioner, which he later did.
>
> Third parties resumed the contempt proceedings on July 3, 2008, proceeding under CCP §§ 1209(a)(5) and 1218(a), and the matter came on for hearing on July 10, 2008. Third parties were represented by counsel, as was petitioner, by his court-appointed counsel. Third parties presented documents and testimony demonstrating that Judge Cretan had

issued a valid order in November 2006, requiring petitioner to pay $ 10,000 as a discovery sanction; that petitioner was aware of this order; and that he had made no payments in compliance with it.

At the conclusion of the hearing, the trial court found petitioner in contempt for failing to comply with the November 2006 order and sentenced him to five days in jail. Petitioner served the five-day jail sentence.

On February 24, 2009, a second contempt proceeding was initiated via an "Order to Show Cause Re: Contempt." The order to show cause has no counsel of record, and is signed by the trial court; it is not under oath. The record does not indicate what caused this second contempt proceeding to be generated, and we assume the court generated it on its own accord.

The contempt hearing was held on March 25, 2009, as ordered. There was no appearance on behalf of third parties. [Petitioner's] counsel challenged the court's jurisdiction on the basis that the reference to FC § 271 and the statement that sanctions were payable to the court were inaccuracies in the order to show cause, and that petitioner was never properly joined as a party. The trial court responded as follows:

"THE COURT: Mr. Koehler knows we had a huge hearing on this where he was found in contempt. So if the court misstated that it was payable to this court or to Lucky Strikes Farm in any event, that's—that may just be—that doesn't affect these proceedings, counsel. He knows what the issue is before the court. He was ordered to pay a $ 10,000 discovery sanction by the trial court. We had a hearing on it. He was found in contempt of court. And he hasn't as yet paid that $ 10,000. So that's why we are here today." Petitioner's counsel responded that he believed "the need for accuracy in the order to show cause re contempt is jurisdictional," and then complained that petitioner was improperly joined in the case.

"THE COURT: Counselor, I was taking a look at the file [at the brief recess], and unfortunately I think you are incorrect on both issues. According to the minutes of the court on November 27, 2006, the minutes of the court clearly say sanctions in the sum of $ 10,000 dollars are imposed against Henry James Koehler per FC § 271 to be paid to the court on or before January 30, 2007.

"PETITIONER'S ATTORNEY: I'm sorry, 271 is only against parties as a matter of law.

"THE COURT: I am just reading to you the exact language in the minutes which the court adopted in the re contempt."

Petitioner's counsel pressed on, concluding that there was a "defective order" to show cause regarding contempt, and objected to "any order for contempt based on payment of 271 sanctions … as such 271 sanctions are not enforceable against him as a matter of law." It was all to no avail.

The trial court found that the elements of contempt were previously established at the July 10, 2008 hearing, and that petitioner had still refused to pay the sanctions award. The trial court again sentenced petitioner to another five days of confinement. Petitioner served that second five-day sentence in early April 2009.
On May 14, 2009, another "Order to Show Cause Re: Contempt" was filed, once again signed by the trial court. As before, the order to show cause appears to be generated by

Chapter 32: Enforcement

the court itself. As before, it is not under oath. And as before, it concludes with this: "Note that all of the elements of contempt were found true at the contempt proceedings against Henry James Koehler on July 10, 2008. Therefore, there is no need for an initiating affidavit in this new contempt proceeding. The factual findings made at the conclusion of the July 10, 2008 hearing have been substituted for an initiating affidavit for this new Order to Show Cause Re: Contempt."

Petitioner filed opposition and on May 27, 2009, made a "special appearance" before the trial court, this time in propria persona. The trial court inquired as to whether petitioner had paid the $10,000. Petitioner refused to answer, asserting his constitutional rights. Petitioner objected to the form of service of the notice of hearing, specifically noting that he had not been personally served. He argued that the matter should be continued to permit him to obtain legal representation and witnesses.

The trial court rejected all [of petitioner's arguments] and again sentenced petitioner to five days in jail.

On May 29, 2009, petitioner filed in this court a petition for a writ of habeas corpus. That same day we issued a stay of the trial court's contempt order and a request for informal opposition.

DISCUSSION
We begin with discussion of what occurred at the third hearing, on May 27, 2009, which began at 10:44 a.m. and was over by 10:55 a.m. Again, there was no appearance by third parties [and petitioner appeared in propria persona. The] trial court started with this:

"THE COURT: Mr. Koehler, you are before the court on an in re contempt for the third time for failure to pay a $10,000 discovery sanction that was payable to Lucky Strike Farms, Inc. that was the order of the trial court on November 27, 2006; was to be paid by January 30, 2007. We had a hearing in this matter in July of 2008 and I brought you before the court twice before and sentenced you to county jail on two prior occasions. This is the third time I've brought you back before the court. Have you paid that $10,000 discovery sanction, sir?

"THE DEFENDANT: Without counsel here obviously that would be a Fifth Amendment testimony matter. I am making a special appearance. I take it the court has gotten and read the motion to quash today, but my offer is and the court read it is that I'm willing to accept service because it wasn't personally served. I would accept it today with the condition that I get the required 16-day court time under CCP §1005. Did the court get a chance to read that?
"THE COURT: Yes. We mailed you the notice of the hearing to appear before the court. [T]his time you're objecting that the court has to personally serve you is your position; is that correct, Mr. Koehler?

"THE DEFENDANT: I believe that's the law. That's CCP § 1016 is the Cedars-Sinai [Imaging Medical Group v. Superior Court (2000) 83 Cal.App.4th 1281 [100 Cal.Rptr.2d 320]] case, but you notice that on the last page of that, I've said that as an officer of the court, I'm not trying to hide and I'm more than willing to accept service of it today, personal service if I get in exchange for the required 16 court days that I would get anyway under a motion.

> "THE COURT: The court is going to respectfully deny your request. …In any event, the court has already conducted a hearing in this matter and found you in contempt of court for failure to abide by a ruling of the trial court back in 2006. Again, this is the third time you've been before the court. Very well, sir, is there anything else you'd like to say?
>
> "THE DEFENDANT: Yes. … Clearly this is a third trial. It's a separate trial. It is not a continuing trial; it is a third one. The notice at any rate even if it had been served correctly on May 14, only gave me eight court days, this is the 8th court day; and therefore, I make my motion to have my 16 court days, which would continue this matter, I believe until June 15 so that I have the necessary notice and opportunity for obtaining counsel and obtaining witnesses and evidence and so on.
>
> "THE COURT: Sir, I think you misunderstand the procedure before the court. We've already had a hearing on this matter and all of the elements of contempt were found true on July 10 of 2008. You had a hearing, you were represented by counsel, and the court found you in contempt; therefore, there is no need for an initial hearing or affidavit in these new contempt proceedings. We don't have hearing after hearing on the same facts, sir. You were found guilty of contempt for failure to pay a $10,000 discovery sanction as an attorney of law, so you misunderstand the law, sir. It would make no sense to have a hearing each and every time on the very same issue. [T]he court is going to sentence you to five days in the county jail. …
>
> The third contempt proceeding was improper in at least four particulars.
>
> First, it was not properly begun. It has long been the rule that the filing of a sufficient affidavit is a jurisdictional prerequisite to a contempt proceeding. CCP § 1211 requires that an affidavit be presented to the judge reciting the facts constituting contempt. No such affidavit was presented. … [An] indirect contempt requires there be an initiating affidavit, and without one any contempt order is void.
>
> Second, a contempt citation must be served personally. Service of an order to show cause to bring a party into contempt is insufficient if made by mail on the party's attorney of record.
>
> Third, because the contemptuous act occurred outside the judge's presence, a valid order and judgment of indirect contempt must cover the following elements: the issuance of an order, the contemner's knowledge of the order, the contemner's ability to obey it, and the contemner's willful disobedience. The order and judgment must state evidentiary facts supporting a finding of each of these elements, except that it need not state such facts in support of the finding of willfulness, which may be inferred from the circumstances. (Citations omitted.) The minute order here falls short in all respects.
>
> Fourth, the trial court responded to petitioner's argument of "triple jeopardy" by asserting that each day that petitioner had not paid the $ 10,000 was "technically … a new contempt." This was wrong. The preclusion of multiple punishment in Penal Code § 654 applies in civil contempt, to the extent the punishment is punitive in nature. In sum and in short, the third contempt was improper, both procedurally and substantively.
>
> As noted, from the outset petitioner's counsel took the position that third parties had the burden to prove that petitioner had the ability to pay. Third parties' position was that inability to pay was an "affirmative defense." The trial court expressly agreed. The law is

Chapter 32: Enforcement

> contrary. Thus, there was no substantial evidence that petitioner had the ability to comply with the order, so the contempt must be reversed and annulled. (Citations omitted.)
>
> Not only did the trial court hold petitioner in contempt, but on May 27, 2009, it also caused a discipline referral form to be submitted to the State Bar. Despite all that had occurred, the form inexplicably stated that the referral was "for a $ 10,000 discovery sanction imposed against Mr. Koehler on November 27, 2006, pursuant to FC § 271." And, the form said, the "nature of the criminal offense" was petitioner's "contempt of court failed to comply with November 27, 2006 court order." This referral apparently had a drastic effect, as at oral argument his counsel represented that petitioner has been "disbarred."
>
> One of the many inexplicable aspects of this case is how a person deemed sufficiently impecunious[4] to be entitled to appointed counsel can be held in contempt and incarcerated for failure to pay a $ 10,000 fine—indeed, on the trial court's theory, repeatedly so held and repeatedly incarcerated, apparently ad infinitum.
>
> **A judge is obliged to know proper contempt procedures.** The contempt power, which permits a single official to deprive a citizen of his [or her] fundamental liberty interest without all of the procedural safeguards normally accompanying such a deprivation, must be used with great prudence and caution. It is essential that judges know and follow proper procedures in exercising this power, which has been called a court's "ultimate weapon." [A]ny trial court exercising the "ultimate weapon" must be absolutely certain that it not only knows the law, but that it has also dotted all the i's and crossed all the t's. What happened here was a far cry.
>
> [Petitioner] like all others, is entitled to the due process the law requires. This, he did not get.
>
> Petitioner's petition is treated as one for prohibition, and is granted, and the order of contempt is reversed and annulled. (Emphasis added.)

4. The Statute of Limitations

The Statute of Limitations for a contempt is three (3) years from the date that the payment was due if the contempt alleged is the failure to pay child, spousal or family support.

If the action before the court is enforcement of another order under the Family Code, the period of limitations for commencing a contempt action is two years from the time that the alleged contempt occurred. **CCP § 1218.5(b)**.

Judgments

A judgment or order made or entered pursuant to the Family Code may be enforced by the court by execution, the appointment of a receiver, contempt, or by any other

---

[4] Impecunious means penniless, having very little money.

Chapter 32: Enforcement

order as the court in its discretion determines from time to time to be necessary. **FC § 290**.

If child support is owed, or any arrearages, interest or penalty remains unpaid more than thirty (30) days after serving the notice of delinquency, the support obligee may file a motion to obtain a judgment for the amount owed, which is enforceable in any manner provided by law for the enforcement of judgments. **FC § 4725**.

If a parent has been ordered to make payments for the support of a minor child, an action to recover any arrearages may be maintained at any time within the period otherwise specified for the enforcement of such a judgment, notwithstanding the fact that the child has attained the age of 18 years. **FC § 4503**.

In an action to enforce a judgment for child, family or spousal support, the defendant may raise, and the court may consider, the defense of laches only with respect to any portion of the judgment that is owed to the state. **FC § 291(d).**

A money judgment or judgment for possession or sale of property that is made or entered under the Family Code, including a judgment for child, family or spousal support, is enforceable until paid in full or otherwise satisfied. **FC § 291(a)**.

Unless the judgment otherwise provides, interest commences to accrue as to each installment if a money judgment is payable in installments; interest commences to accrue on a money judgment on the date of entry of that judgment. **CCP § 685.020**. (See *In re Marriage of HOFFEE* (1976) 60 Cal.App.3d 337 at p. 340, where the court held that a "review of the cases concerned with interest on money judgments discloses a consistent series of holdings that all money judgments draw interest" and money judgments with regard to marital agreements are not excluded from this rule.)

An order for child, family or spousal support that is made, entered or enforceable in this state is enforceable under this code, whether or not the order was made or entered pursuant to this code. **FC § 4500**.

A family support order is enforceable in the same manner and to the same extent as a child support order. **FC § 4501**.

The enforcement procedure when a parent who alleges that his or her default in a child or family support order is due to unemployment is to submit a list of at least five (5) different places the parent has applied for employment. The list must be submitted to the appropriate child support enforcement agency or any other entity designated by the court, including, but not limited to, the court itself, every two weeks, or at a frequency deemed appropriate by the court. **FC § 4505(a)**.

Finally, disobedience of any lawful judgment, order, or process of the court is a contempt of the authority of the court **CCP § 1209(a)(5)**.

Chapter 32: Enforcement

Income Withholding Orders for Support /Wage Assignment

1. Definitions

A **withholding order for support** is an earnings withholding order issued on a writ of execution to collect delinquent amounts payable under a judgment for the support of a child or a spouse or former spouse of the judgment debtor. A withholding order for support must be indicated as such on its face. **CCP § 706.030.**

Assignment order has the same meaning as **earnings assignment order for support**. **FC § 5202**.

Earnings assignment order for support means an order that assigns to an obligee a portion of the earnings of a support obligor due or to become due in the future. **FC § 5208(a)**. This form is also referred to as a Wage Assignment which was the name of the first form of this type.

In family law the Judicial Council form that is used is called an *Income Withholding Order for Support*, **FL-195**. Instructions on the completion of this form are in the FL-196,

An **obligee** or **assigned obligee** can be: **(1)** the person to whom support has been ordered to be paid, **(2)** the local child support agency, or **(3)** another person designated by the court to receive the payment. **FC § 5214**.

An **obligor** is the person owing a duty of support. **FC § 5216**.

A **timely payment** means receipt of support payments by the obligee or assigned obligee within five days of the due date. **FC § 5220**.

Due date of support payments is the date specifically stated in the order of support or, if no date is stated in the support order, the last day of the month in which the support payment is to be paid. **FC § 5204**.

Earnings that are subject to an earnings assignment order for support under **CCP § 703.010** et seq. include:

> **(a)** Wages, salary, bonus, money, and benefits described in CCP §§ 704.119, 704.113 and 704.115.
> **(b)** Payments due for services of independent contractors, interest, dividends, rents, royalties, residuals, patent rights, or mineral or other natural resource rights.
> **(c)** Payments or credits due or becoming due as a result of written or oral contracts for services or sales whether denominated as wages, salary, commission, bonus, or otherwise.
> **(d)** Payments due for workers' compensation temporary disability benefits.
> **(e)** Payments due as a result of disability from benefits described in CCP § 704.130.
> **(f)** Any other payments or credits due or becoming due, regardless of source. FC § 5206.

Chapter 32: Enforcement

Employer includes: **(1)** a person for whom an individual performs services as an employee, as defined in **CCP § 706.011**, **(2)** the United States government and any public entity as defined in **Government Code § 811.2** and **(3)** any person or entity paying earnings as defined under **FC § 5206**. **FC § 5210**.

2. Arrearages

Arrearages accrue when a support obligor fails to pay the court-ordered support when it was due. Arrearages are the amount necessary to satisfy a support judgment or order pursuant to **CCP § 695.210**. **FC § 5201**.

Arrearages of support payments must be computed on the basis of the payments owed and unpaid on the date that the obligor has been given notice of the assignment order, as required by **FC § 5234**. **FC § 5239**.

Any obligee alleging arrearages in child support must specify the amount thereof under penalty of perjury. **FC § 5230.5**.

Where an assignment order or assignment orders include both current support and payments towards the liquidation of arrearages, priority must be given first to the current child support obligation, followed by the current spousal support obligation, and thereafter to the liquidation of child and then spousal support arrearages. **FC § 5238(a)**.

3. Court Orders

An assignment order for support has priority against any attachment, execution or other assignment as specified in **CCP § 706.031**. **FC § 5243**.

A different procedure is employed for a support order first issued or modified before July 1, 1990, when the court, in ordering support or modification of support, did not issue an assignment order. **FC § 5250**.

The obligee seeking issuance of an assignment order to enforce a support order described in **FC § 5250** may file an application under **FC § 5252**, by notice of motion or order to show cause or pursuant **to FC § 5230(b)**. **FC § 5251**.

An assignment order required or authorized by this chapter must include a requirement that the obligor notify the obligee of any change of employment and of the name and address of the obligor's new employer within ten (10) days of obtaining new employment. **FC § 5281**.

An income-withholding order issued in another state may be sent by or on behalf of the obligee, or by the support enforcement agency, to the person defined as the obligor's employer, pursuant to **FC § 5210,** without first filing a petition or comparable pleading or registering the order with a tribunal of this state. **FC 4940**.

Chapter 32: Enforcement

A finding of error in the amount of the current support or arrearage or a finding that the amount exceeds federal or state limits is not grounds to vacate the assignment order. The court must modify the order to reflect the correct or allowable amount of support or arrearages. The fact that the obligor may have subsequently paid the arrearages does not relieve the court of its duty to enter the assignment order. **FC § 5272**.

CRC Rule 5.335 provides a procedure for a hearing under **FC § 4945** in response to an income- withholding order. **CRC Rule 5.335** provides:

> [1] A support obligor may contest the validity or enforcement of an income withholding order by filing a completed request for hearing. A copy of the income withholding order must be attached.
> [2] The court must not require a filing fee to file the request for hearing under this rule. Upon receipt of the completed request for hearing and a copy of the income withholding order, the clerk must assign a case number and schedule a court date. The court date must be no earlier than 30 days from the date of filing and no later than 45 days from the date of filing.
> [3] The support obligor must provide the clerk with envelopes addressed to the obligor, the support enforcement agency that sent the income withholding order, and the obligor's employer. The support obligor must also provide an envelope addressed to the person or agency designated to receive the support payments if that person or agency is different than the support enforcement agency that sent the income withholding order. The support obligor must provide sufficient postage to mail each envelope provided. Upon scheduling the hearing, the clerk must mail a copy of the request for hearing in each envelope provided by the support obligor.
> [4] Any subsequent proceedings filed in the same court that involve the same parties and are filed under the Uniform Interstate Family Support Act (UIFSA) must use the file number created under this rule.

4. Obligor's Employer

When the court orders a party to pay an amount for support or orders a modification of the amount of support to be paid, the court must include in its order an earnings assignment order for support that orders the employer of the obligor to pay to the obligee that portion of the obligor's earnings due, or to become due in the future, as will be sufficient to pay an amount to cover the amount ordered by the court for support and an amount paid toward the liquidation of any arrearage. **FC § 5230(a)**.

An earnings assignment order for support must be issued and is effective and enforceable pursuant to **FC § 5231**, notwithstanding the absence of the name, address or other identifying information regarding the obligor's employer. **FC § 5230(b)**.

Service on an employer of an assignment order may be made by first-class mail in the manner prescribed in **CCP § 1013**. The obligee shall serve the documents specified in **FC § 5234**. **FC § 5232**.

Chapter 32: Enforcement

Service of the assignment order creates a lien on the earnings of the employee and the property of the employer to the same extent as the service of an earnings withholding order as provided in **CCP § 706.029**. **FC § 5242.**

Unless the order states a later date, the employer must commence withholding pursuant to the assignment order from all earnings payable to the employee as soon as possible after service of the order on the employer but not later than ten (10) days after service of the order on the employer. **FC § 5233.**

Within ten (10) days of service of an assignment order or an order/notice to withhold income for child support on an employer, the employer must deliver both of the following to the obligor/employee:

> **(a)** A copy of the assignment order or the order/notice to withhold income for child support.
> **(b)** A written statement of the obligor's rights under the law to seek to quash, modify, or stay service of the earnings assignment order, together with a blank form that the obligor can file with the court to request a hearing to quash, modify, or stay service of the earnings assignment order with instructions on how to file the form and obtain a hearing date. FC § 5234.

An employer must continue to withhold, and forward support as required by the assignment order until served with notice terminating the assignment order. **FC § 5235(a)**. Some counties allow the *ex parte* procedure to be used for this purpose.

Within ten (10) days of service of a substitution of payee on the employer, the employer must forward all subsequent support to the governmental entity or other payee that sent the substitution. **FC § 5235(b).**

The employer must send the amounts withheld to the obligee within the timeframe specified in federal law and report to the obligee the date on which the amount was withheld from the obligor's wages. **FC § 5235(c)**.

The employer may deduct from the earnings of the employee the sum of one dollar and fifty cents ($1.50) for each payment made pursuant to the order. **FC § 5235(d)**.

Unless stayed, an assignment order is effective and binding upon any existing or future employer of the obligor upon whom a copy of the order is served in compliance with **FC §§ 5232** and **5233**, notwithstanding the absence of the name, address or other identifying information regarding the obligor's employer, or the inclusion of incorrect information regarding the support obligor's employer. **FC § 5231**.

After the obligor has left employment with the employer, the employer, at the time the next payment is due on the assignment order, must notify the obligee designated in the assignment order by first-class mail, postage prepaid, to the last known address of the obligee that the obligor has left employment. **FC § 6282**.

Chapter 32: Enforcement

When an employer receives an earnings assignment order or an income withholding order for support from a court or administrative agency in another state, all of the provisions of this chapter apply. **FC § 5230.1(b)**.

5. Failure of an Employer to Withhold Employee Wages

An employer who willfully fails to withhold and forward support pursuant to a currently valid assignment order entered and served upon the employer is liable to the obligee for the amount of support not withheld, forwarded or otherwise paid to the obligee, including any interest thereon. **FC § 5241(a)**.

In addition to any other penalty or liability provided by law, willful failure by an employer to comply with an assignment order is punishable as a contempt, pursuant to **CCP § 1218**. **FC § 5252**.

6. Staying and Terminating Assignment Orders

The court may order that service of the assignment order be stayed only if the court makes a finding of good cause or if an alternative arrangement exists for payment in accordance with **FC § 5260(b)**, set forth below.

Pursuant to **FC § 5260(b)**, there is good cause to stay a wage assignment when all of the following conditions exist:

> **(A)** The court provides a written explanation of why the stay of the wage assignment would be in the best interests of the child.
> **(B)** The obligor has a history of uninterrupted, full, and timely payment, other than through a wage assignment or other mandatory process of previously ordered support, during the previous 12 months.
> **(C)** The obligor does not owe an arrearage for prior support.
> **(D)** The obligor proves, and the court finds, by clear and convincing evidence that service of the wage assignment would cause extraordinary hardship upon the obligor. Whenever possible, the court shall specify a date that any stay ordered under this section will automatically terminate.

An alternative arrangement for staying an earnings assignment order (wage assignment) requires a written agreement between the parties that provides for payment of the support obligation as ordered, other than through the immediate service of a wage assignment. Any agreement between the parties that includes the staying of a service of a wage assignment must include the concurrence of the local child support agency in any case in which support is ordered to be paid through a county officer designated for that purpose. The execution of an agreement pursuant to this paragraph does not preclude a party from thereafter seeking a wage assignment in accordance with the procedures specified in **FC § 5261** upon violation of the agreement. **FC § 5260(b)**.

Service of wage assignments issued for foreign orders for support and service of foreign orders for the assignment of wages registered pursuant to **FC § 4950**[5] will not be stayed pursuant to this subdivision. **FC § 5260(a)**.

If service of the assignment order has been ordered stayed, the order will terminate upon the obligor's failure to make timely support payments or earlier, by court order, if requested by the local child support agency or by the obligor. The stay may terminate earlier by court order if requested by any other obligee who can establish that good cause, as defined in **FC § 5260**, no longer exists. **FC § 5261(a)**.

To terminate a stay of the service of the assignment order, the obligee must file a declaration signed under penalty of perjury by the obligee that the obligor is in arrears in payment of any portion of the support. At the time of filing the declaration, the stay terminates by operation of law without notice to the obligor. **FC § 5261(b)**.

With regard to termination of an order to stay an assignment order, the filing of a declaration with knowledge of the falsity of its contents is punishable as a contempt and any other penalty provided by law, pursuant to **CCP § 1209**. **FC § 5261(c)**.

When an obligor files and serves a motion and a notice of motion to terminate the service of an assignment order, the court must so terminate if past due support has been paid in full, including any interest due, and if any of the following conditions exist:

(1) With regard to orders for spousal support, the death or remarriage of the spouse to whom support is owed.
(2) With regard to orders for child support, the death or emancipation of the child for whom support is owed.
(3) The court determines that there is good cause, as defined in **FC § 5260**, to terminate the assignment order. This subdivision does not apply if there has been more than one application for an assignment order.
(4) The obligor meets the conditions of an alternative arrangement and a wage assignment has not been previously terminated and subsequently initiated.
(5) There is no longer a current order for support.
(6) The termination of the stay of an assignment order under **FC § 5261** was improper, but only if that termination was based upon the obligor's failure to make timely support payments as described in **FC § 5261(b)**. **FC § 5240**.

Finally, in lieu of filing and serving a motion and a notice of motion pursuant to **FC § 5261**, an earnings and assignment order may be terminated by an *EX PARTE*

---

[5] Pursuant to FC § 4950, a support order or an income-withholding order issued by a tribunal of another state may be registered in this state for enforcement.

appearance if the obligation to pay support has ended and/or if past due support has been paid in full, including any interest due. **FC § 5240**.

7. Judicial Council Forms for Wage Assignment Orders

Commencing January 1, 2000, all earnings- assignment orders for support in any action in which child support or family support is ordered MUST be issued on an "order/notice to withhold income for child support" mandated by Section 666 of Title 42 of the United States Code. **FC § 5208(b)**.

The *Income Withholding for Support FL-195*, may be used for both child support and spousal support. However, the *Earnings Assignment Order FL-435* may only be used for spousal support.

Sanctions for Violations under the Family Code

Another means that the court has to enforce a family law court order is by sanctions. **CRC Rule 5.14.** Sanctions are monetary fines or penalties ordered by the court against a person. A person is defined as a party, a party's attorney, a law firm, a witness or any other individual or entity whose consent is necessary for the disposition of the case. **CRC Rule 5.14 provides:**

> In addition to any other sanctions permitted by law, the court may order a person, after written notice and an opportunity to be heard, to pay reasonable monetary sanctions to the court or to an aggrieved person, or both, for failure without good cause to comply with the applicable rules. The sanction must not put an unreasonable financial burden on the person ordered to pay.

If a party seeks sanctions against another party, the party's request must:

    1. State the applicable rule of court that has been violated;
    2. Describe the specific conduct that is alleged to have violated the rule; and
    3. Identify the party, attorney, law firm, witness or other person against whom sanctions are sought.

Additionally, the court, on its own motion, may issue an order to show cause that:

    1. States the applicable rule of court that has been violated;
    2. Describes the specific conduct that appears to have violated the rule; and
    3. Directs the attorney, law firm, party, witness or other person to show cause why sanctions should not be imposed for violation of the rule.

A court may also order a person who has violated an applicable rule of court to pay to the party aggrieved by the violation that party's reasonable expenses, including reasonable attorney fees and costs incurred in connection with the motion or request for an order for sanctions.

When the court makes an order awarding sanctions, the order must be in writing and must recite in detail the conduct or circumstances justifying the order.

An order for child, family or spousal support that is made, entered or enforceable in this state is enforceable under this code, whether or not the order was made or entered pursuant to this code. **FC § 4500**.

A family support order is enforceable in the same manner and to the same extent as a child support order. **FC § 4501**.

Finally, the enforcement procedure when a parent who alleges that his or her default in a child or family support order is due to unemployment is to submit a list of at least five (5) different places the parent has applied for employment. The list must be submitted to the appropriate child support enforcement agency or any other entity designated by the court, including, but not limited to, the court itself, every two weeks, or at a frequency deemed appropriate by the court. **FC § 4505(a)**.

EDUCATIONAL EXERCISES

Match the Letter to the appropriate number

A. Abstract of Judgment
B. An Obligee or Assigned Obligee
C. Arrearages
D. Assignment Order
E. Citee
F. Earnings Assignment Order for Support
G. Elisor
H. Obligor
I. Timely Payment
J. Writ of Execution

1. _____ California law allows the judgment creditor to collect property or levy on property pursuant to a writ of execution. It is a court order giving the sheriff (or other levying officer) the power to seize the judgment debtor's property in order to pay a judgment debt.
2. _____ A document issued by the clerk of the court that certifies the general contents of a judgment entered in a court proceeding. The document provides how much money the debtor owes to the judgment creditor, the rate of interest to be paid on the judgment amount, court costs and any specific orders that the debtor must obey. It is acknowledged and stamped; it is then recorded in the county where the debtor, hopefully, owns real property. It purpose is to make a public record and a lien is created on any property owned by the debtor in that county. Once issued, it can be recorded with the county recorder in every county in which the debtor may own property.
3. _____ When a party will not or cannot execute a document necessary to carry out a court order, the clerk of the court, or his or her authorized representative or designee, may be appointed to sign the document. The specific rules regarding this appointee are usually set forth in the local rules of each county. An application for the appointment requires a supporting declaration that must provide specific facts that establish the necessity of an appointee.
4. _____ It has the same meaning as earnings assignment order for support. FC § 5202.
5. _____ An order that assigns to an obligee a portion of the earnings of a support obligor due or to become due in the future. FC § 5208(a).
6. _____ The person to whom support has been ordered to be paid, (2) the local child support agency, or (3) another person designated by the court to receive the payment. FC § 5214.
7. _____ The person owing a duty of support. FC § 5216.
8. _____ This is a receipt of support payments by the obligee or assigned obligee within five days of the due date. FC § 5220.
9. _____ This is the amount necessary to satisfy a support judgment or order pursuant to CCP § 695.210.
10. _____ They accrue when a support obligor fails to pay the court-ordered support when it was due. They must be computed on the basis of the payments owed and unpaid on the date that the obligor has been given notice of the assignment order, as required by FC § 5234. FC § 5239.
11. _____ The person who allegedly violated the court order.

CHAPTER 33: Postjudgment

In Brief...

FOR POSTJUDGMENT MOTIONS, FC § 3651:
- A decree of divorce for custody, care and maintenance of minor children is not finality; the trial court retains continuing jurisdiction. *Marriage of Kreiss* (2004) 122 Cal.App.4th 1082.
- Motions to modify a court order postjudgment follow the same procedure as modifying motions prior to the final judgment.
- Modification or termination of a support order can occur at any time the court deems necessary, **FC § 3651**.
- Motion to modify support or child visitation may be served by first class mail, postage prepaid, **FC § 215**.
- A court has jurisdiction to modify a *MSA* to pay college expenses. *Marriage of Rosenfeld and Gross* (2014) 225 Cal.App.4th 478.
- Unpaid child support can be upheld, even if the child is 18. *Marriage of Hubner* (1999) 94 Cal.App.4th 175.
- Procedures for enforcement by execution do not violate due process. *Wyshak v. Wyshak* (1977) 70 Cal.App.3d 384.
- An order for spousal support may not be modified or terminated to the extent that a written agreement or, if there is no written agreement, an oral agreement entered into in open court between the parties that specifically provides that the spousal support is not subject to modification or termination. **FC § 3651**.
- A party can file a postjudgment action to enforce a provision of the parties' stipulated judgment, *In re Marriage of KREMPIN* (1999) 70 Cal.App.4th 1008.

A JUDGMENT MAY BE SET ASIDE:
- If there was actual fraud committed;
- If there was perjury;
- If there was duress in the procuring,
- If one or both of the parties had a mental incapacity,
- If a stipulated or uncontested judgment was based with a mistake;
- If there was a failure to comply with the disclosure requirements, **FC § 2107(b)(3)**;
- When there is a mistake, inadvertence, surprise or excusable neglect, and action is brought within 6 months, **CCP § 473(b)**.

THE APPEAL PROCESS:
- The dissolution does not become final until all issues are decided and finalized, **FC § 2341**;
- The disposition of the community estate is subject to revision, **FC § 2555**;
- The notice of appeal includes a cross-appeal, **CRC Rule 8.100**;
- A notice of appeal must be filed and served, **CRC Rule 8.100**; and
- The notice of appeal must be accompanied by the filing fee, **CRC Rule 8.26**.

> - An order from the trial court finding a stipulated custody order that was meant to be a final determination of custody can be appealed. *MONTENEGRO v. DIAZ* (2001) 26 Cal.4th 249.
> - An appellate court will not interpose its judgment on factual issues over the opinion of the trial judge.

Introduction

Following the entry of the court's decision and judgment with respect to the issues presented at trial, if one or both of the parties are unhappy with the outcome and there appears to be an abuse of discretion, a mistake in applying the law or a mistake in the choice of the law, either or both parties may have the right to appeal the decision.

However, an appellate court will not interpose its judgment on factual issues over the opinion of the trial judge. The basic function of the appellate court is to determine if the law chosen was the right law, if the judge applied the right law properly and if the facts presented at trial support the judgment of the trial court.

The Appeal Process

The disposition of the community estate is subject to revision on appeal in all, including those which are stated to be in the discretion of the court. **FC § 2555**.

If an appeal is taken from the judgment or a motion for a new trial is made, the dissolution of marriage does not become final until the motion or appeal has been finally disposed of, nor if the motion has been granted or judgment reversed. **FC § 2341(a)**.

An appeal may be taken from a final order in accordance with expedited appellate procedures in other civil cases and unless the court enters a temporary emergency order under **FC § 3424**, the enforcing court may not stay an order enforcing a child custody determination pending appeal.

To appeal from a superior court judgment or an appealable order of a superior court, other than in a limited civil case, an appellant must serve and file a notice of appeal in that superior court. The appellant or the appellant's attorney must sign the notice. The notice of appeal is sufficient if it identifies the particular judgment or order being appealed. The notice need not specify the court to which the appeal is taken; the appeal will be treated as taken to the Court of Appeal for the district in which the superior court is located. Note that the failure to serve the notice of appeal neither prevents its filing nor affects its validity, but the appellant may be required to remedy the failure. **CRC Rule 8.100(a)**.

Chapter 33: Postjudgment

A **notice of appeal** includes a notice of cross-appeal, and **appellant** includes a respondent filing a notice of cross-appeal. **CRC Rule 8.100(f)**.

The notice of appeal must be accompanied by the $775 filing fee under **Government Code §§ 68926** and **68926.1(b)**, an application for a waiver of court fees and costs on appeal under **CRC Rule 8.26** or an order granting such an application. The fee should be paid by check or money order, payable to **Clerk, Court of Appeal**; if the fee is paid in cash, the clerk must give a receipt.

Further, the appellant must also deposit $100 with the superior court clerk as required under **Government Code $ 68926.1**, unless otherwise provided by law or the superior court waives the deposit. The clerk must file the notice of appeal, even if the appellant does not present the filing fee, the deposit or an application for or order granting a waiver of fees and costs. **CRC Rule 8.100(b)**.

Finally, the filing of an appeal or of a motion for a new trial does not stay the effect of a judgment insofar as it relates to the dissolution of the marriage status and restoring the parties to the status of unmarried persons, unless the appealing or moving party specifies in the notice of appeal or motion for new trial an objection to the termination of the marriage status. No party may make such an objection to the termination of the marriage status unless such an objection was also made at the time of trial. **FC § 2341(b)**.

Postjudgment Motions[1]

Motions to modify orders for visitation, custody and support of children and spousal support may be common, allowable postjudgment modifications.

> [T]he entry of a decree of divorce ..., in so far as it relates to the custody, care, and maintenance of the minor children ... is not a finality, but the trial court retains a continuing jurisdiction which is as complete as that possessed by it prior to the entry of said final decree. ... *In re MARRIAGE of KREISS* (2004) 122 Cal.App.4th 1082; 19 Cal.Rptr.3d 260.

A **support order** may be modified or terminated at any time the court determines to be necessary; however, a support order may not be modified or terminated as to an amount that accrued before the date of the filing of the notice of motion or order to show cause to modify or terminate.

Further, an order for spousal support may not be modified or terminated to the extent that a written agreement or, if there is no written agreement, an oral agreement entered into in open court between the parties that specifically provides that the spousal support is not subject to modification or termination. **FC § 3651**.

---

[1] Postjudgment is one word and there is no e after the g.

Chapter 33: Postjudgment

A court has jurisdiction to modify the amount and allocation of college expenses in a marital settlement agreement when the agreement provides that the parties agreed to equally share their children's college expenses. *In re Marriage of ROSENFELD and GROSS* (2014) 225 Cal.App.4th 478 at pp. 488-489.

> The parties' stipulation to pay each minor child's college expenses resulted in a child support order when incorporated into the court's judgment. Though based on an agreement to pay adult child support, the resulting order was subject to the court's jurisdiction to modify, absent an express and specific agreement by the parties to the contrary. *In re Marriage of ROSENFELD and GROSS* (2014) 225 Cal.App.4th 478 at p. 490.)

While the trial court has the authority, in most cases, to modify a college-expense support order in a marital settlement agreement postjudgment, there must still be a substantial change in circumstances to so modify. *Ibid.*

In most cases, a court will not revise a child support order unless there has been a **material change of circumstances**. This rule applies to any form of child support order—i.e., whether pendente lite or 'permanent. *In re Marriage of STANTON* (2010) 190 Cal.App.4th 547 at pp. 543-554.

Additionally, an order from the trial court finding a stipulated custody order that was meant to be a final determination of custody can be appealed. *MONTENEGRO v. DIAZ* (2001) 26 Cal.4th 249. In *Montenegro*, Deborah Diaz and Alex Montenegro could not agree on custody and visitation over their son, Gregory. During the child custody proceedings, Diaz and Montenegro entered into various stipulations, confirmed by the trial court, **resolving** their disputes over Gregory. In the last such stipulation, Diaz and Montenegro agreed to joint legal custody of Gregory, with Diaz having primary physical custody. When Gregory was to start kindergarten, however, they were unable to resolve their differences and asked the trial court to modify its last stipulated custody order. After an adversarial hearing, the trial court awarded primary physical custody to Montenegro, based on the **best interests** of the child. The Court of Appeal reversed, concluding that the trial court applied the wrong standard. Finding that two of the stipulated orders were final judicial custody determinations, the Court of Appeal held that the custody arrangement was subject to modification only if Montenegro established a significant change in circumstances.

The Supreme Court of California reversed the Appellate Court's decision, finding that the trial court properly applied the best interests standard, rather than the changed circumstance rule and a stipulated custody order is a final custody determination for purposes of the changed circumstance rule only if there is a clear, affirmative indication the parties intended such a result. *Id.* at p. 258-260.

Motions to modify a court order postjudgment follow the same procedure as modifying motions prior to the final judgment.

Chapter 33: Postjudgment

A party can file a postjudgment action to enforce a provision of the parties' stipulated judgment, which gave Wife a share of Husband's military pension. *In re Marriage of KREMPIN* (1999) 70 Cal.App.4th 1008.

A postjudgment motion for unpaid child support was upheld, even though the child had reached the age of 18 and had finished high school. *In re Marriage of HUBNER* (2004) 94 Cal.App.4th 175.

California postjudgment procedures for enforcement, by execution, of judgments providing for installment support payments are reasonable and are not violative of due process. *WYSHAK v. WYSHAK* (1977) 70 Cal.App.3d 384; 138 Cal.Rptr. 811.

Finally, a postjudgment motion to modify a custody, visitation, or child support order may be served on the other party or parties by first-class mail, postage prepaid. FC § 215.

Setting Aside the Judgment

Pursuant to FC § 2122, a motion to set aside a judgment, or any part or parts thereof, may be set aside only if it is one of the following:

1. Actual fraud where the defrauded party was kept in ignorance or in some other manner was fraudulently prevented from fully participating in the proceeding. An action or motion based on fraud shall be brought **within one year** after the date on which the complaining party either did discover or should have discovered the fraud.
2. Perjury when an action or motion based on perjury in the preliminary or final declaration of disclosure and the waiver of the final declaration of disclosure, or in the current income and expense statement, was brought **within one year** after the date on which the complaining party either did discover or should have discovered the perjury.
3. Duress when an action or motion based upon duress was brought **within two years** after the date of entry of judgment.
4. Mental incapacity when an action or motion based on mental incapacity was brought **within two years** after the date of entry of judgment.
5. A stipulated or uncontested judgment or that part of a judgment stipulated to by the parties when an action to set aside was based on mistake and brought **within one year** after the date of entry of judgment.
6. Failure to comply with the disclosure requirements and the action to set aside was brought **within one year** after the date on which the complaining party either did discover or should have discovered the failure to comply.

The court may, upon any terms as may be just, relieve a party or his or her legal representative from a judgment, dismissal, order or other proceeding taken against him or her through his or her mistake, inadvertence, surprise or excusable neglect. The motion must be made within a reasonable time, in no case exceeding six

Chapter 33: Postjudgment

months, after the judgment, dismissal, order or proceeding was taken. **CCP § 473(b)**.

If a court enters a judgment when the parties have failed to comply with all disclosure requirements of this chapter, the court must set aside the judgment. Failure to comply with the disclosure requirements does not constitute harmless error. If the court granted the complying party's voluntary waiver of receipt of the noncomplying party's preliminary declaration of disclosure pursuant to **FC § 2107(b)(3)**[2], the court must set aside the judgment only at the request of the complying party, unless the motion to set aside the judgment is based on: **(1)** actual fraud if the defrauded party was kept in ignorance, or in some other manner was fraudulently prevented from fully participating in the proceeding; or **(2)** perjury, as defined in **Penal Code § 118**[3], in the preliminary or final declaration of disclosure, in the waiver of the final declaration of disclosure, or in the current income and expense statement. **FC § 2107(d)**.

Pursuant to **FC § 7648.3**, a court may not issue an order setting aside or vacating a judgment establishing parentage if the judgment was made or entered by a tribunal of another state, even if the enforcement of that judgment is sought in this state, or the judgment was made or entered in this state and genetic tests that did not exclude the previously established father as the biological father of the child were conducted prior to the entry of the judgment.

In any action filed by the local child support agency pursuant to **FC § 17400, 17402** or **17404**, the court may, on any terms that may be just, set aside that part of the judgment or order concerning the amount of child support to be paid. This relief may be granted after the six-month time limit of **CCP § 473** has elapsed, based on the grounds, and within one year of the first collection of money by the local child support agency or obligee that begins to run from the date that the local child support agency receives the first collection. **FC § 17432**.

Finally, for good cause, the presiding judge of the appellate division may relieve a party from a default for any failure to comply with these rules, except the failure to file a timely notice of appeal. **CRC Rule 8.812**.

---

[2] FC § 2107(b)(3) provides "that if the noncomplying party fails to comply with a request the preparation of the appropriate declaration of disclosure or further particularity, the complying party may file a motion showing good cause for the court to grant the complying party's voluntary waiver of receipt of the noncomplying party's preliminary declaration of disclosure, pursuant to FC § 2104 or final declaration of disclosure pursuant to FC § 2105." FC § 2107(b).

[3] Penal Code § 118(a) provides: "Every person who, having taken an oath that he or she will testify, declare, depose or certify truly before any competent tribunal, officer or person, in any of the cases in which the oath may by law of the State of California be administered, willfully and contrary to the oath, states as true any material matter which he or she knows to be false, and every person who testifies, declares, deposes or certifies under penalty of perjury in any of the cases in which the testimony, declarations, depositions or certification is permitted by law of the State of California under penalty of perjury and willfully states as true any material matter which he or she knows to be false, is guilty of perjury."

EDUCATIONAL EXERCISES

Draft a Postjudgment Motion (RFO) for Marilyn; she wants more time with the children. Add the facts below to the facts set forth in Appendix One.

1. Marilyn won $10 million in the California lottery.
2. She opted for 26 equal payments.
3. She gets $384,982 each year for 26 years.
4. She quit working as a teacher.
5. Her boyfriend moved in with her.

CHAPTER 34: Parentage

In Brief...

> ***PARENTAGE:***
> - Parentage is the act of becoming a parent;
> - Paternity means fatherhood or the act of becoming a father;
> - Parentage actions/lawsuits are filed to determine or declare parentage; and
> - Parentage files are sealed.
>
> **The establishment of parentage by voluntary declaration FC § 7570 et seq.:**
> - Has the same force and effect as a parentage judgment, **FC § 7573**;
> - That has been signed by a minor is not effective until 60 days after emancipation;
> - Grants a court authority to order support; and
> - Can be rescinded under certain conditions.
>
> ***THE UNIFORM PARENTAGE ACT,*** **FC § 7600** et seq.:
> **The parent-child relationship:**
> - Extends equally to every child/parent, regardless of the parent's marital status, **FC § 7602**;
> - Can include more than two parents, **FC § 7601**.
>
> **The parentage presumption FC § 7540:**
> - A child is conclusively presumed to be a child of the marriage if:
>   - The spouses cohabited at the time of conception and birth;
>   - The husband is not sterile; &
>   - The child was not conceived through assisted reproduction.
>
> **There are two ways for the father to rebut the conclusive presumption:**
> - By proving sterility or impotency at the time of conception; or
> - By requesting blood tests within two years of the child's birth.
>
> **A parentage action:**
> - May be brought to determine a father-child/mother-child relationship, **FC § 7611**;
> - Allows a child under 12 years may be made a party to the action & a child 12 years or older must be made a party to the action, **FC § 7635**.
> - A minor who is a party, must be represented by a Guardian ad Litem, **FC § 6735**.
>
> **Setting aside or vacating a judgment of parentage:**
> - Requires that the request be made by a Noticed Motion, **FC § 7666**; and
> - Requires that the request be filed within a two-year time limit.
>
> **Assisted reproduction is conception by means other than sexual intercourse, FC § 7606.**
>
> **Adoption and termination of parental rights in parentage cases:**
> - Require no filing fee for a petition to terminate parental rights of alleged father, **FC § 7670**;
> - Can include the signing of a voluntary waiver of father's right to notice of adoption; and

Chapter 34: Parentage

> - Can include a mother or other parent relinquishing/consenting to termination, **FC § 7611**.
>
> ***ATTORNEY FEES:***
> - Can be awarded to ensure that both parties have equal access to legal representation; and
> - Can be ordered for one party pay the fees of the other party, **FC § 7605**.
>
> **CHART 13: Parentage Codes and Titles (Code Number Order)**
> **CHART 14: Parentage Family Codes (Alphabetical by Subject)**

Introduction

Assembly Bill Number 2684 was signed into law in 2018. This bill deleted, amended, added to and rewrote many of the "paternity" codes. And, it should be noted that the word **paternity** was replaced with the word **parentage**. And although the word **paternity** will be replaced with the word **parentage** in many codes effective January 1, 2019 and many code sections effective January 1, 2020, this chapter with be replacing **parentage** for **paternity** every place where appropriate. The word **paternity** is NOT changed in cases or current codes.

Parentage is the act of becoming a parent and paternity is fatherhood or the act of becoming a father. The father does not have to be married to the mother in order to request that he be declared the father of their child. The parent-child relationship extends equally to every child and to every parent, regardless of the marital status of the parents. **FC § 7602**.

Parentage actions/lawsuits and parentage issues are a large part of family law. Parentage actions can be filed to determine or declare parentage, to request support or to request custody and/or visitation of a child.

Finally, all codes from Assembly Bill No. 2684 that are effective or operative commencing January 1, 2020 are set forth in Appendix Three.

Establishment of Parentage by Voluntary Declaration FC § 7570[1]

Pursuant to **FC § 7570**, the legislature hereby finds and declares as follows:

> **(1)** There is a compelling state interest in establishing paternity for all children. Establishing paternity is the first step toward a child support award, which, in turn, provides children with equal rights and access to benefits, including, but not limited to, social security, health insurance, survivors' benefits, military benefits, and inheritance rights. Knowledge of family medical history is often necessary for correct medical diagnosis and treatment. Additionally, knowing one's father is important to a child's

---

[1] FC § 7570 provided here will be repealed effective January 1, 2020. The new FC § 7570 effective January 1, 2020 is set forth in Appendix Three, *infra*.

Chapter 34: Parentage

> development.
> **(2)** A simple system allowing for establishment of voluntary paternity will result in a significant increase in the ease of establishing paternity, a significant increase in paternity establishment, an increase in the number of children who have greater access to child support and other benefits, and a significant decrease in the time and money required to establish paternity due to the removal of the need for a lengthy and expensive court process to determine and establish paternity and is in the public interest.

1. The Declaration of Parentage FC § 7571[2]

On or after January 1, 1995, when an unmarried mother gives birth to a live child, prior to leaving any hospital, the person responsible for registering live births under **Health and Safety Code § 102405** must provide to the mother and the man identified by the mother as the father, a voluntary declaration of parentage together with the written materials described in **FC § 7572**.[3] The hospital staff in the hospital should witness the signatures of the parents signing a voluntary declaration of parentage; within 20 days of the signing of declaration, the staff must forward the signed declaration to the Department of Child Support Services. A copy of the declaration must be made available to both parents. **FC § 7571(a)**.

If the declaration is not registered by the person responsible for registering live births at the hospital, it may be completed by the parents, notarized and then mailed to the Department of Child Support Services at any time after the child's birth. **FC § 7571(d)**.

Copies of the declaration and any rescissions filed with the Department of Child Support Services must be made available only to the parents, the child, the local child support agency, the county welfare department, the county counsel, the State Department of Health Services and the courts. **FC § 7571(i)**.

A completed voluntary declaration of parentage, as described in **FC § 7574**[4], that has been filed with the Department of Child Support Services establishes the parentage of a child and has the same force and effect as a judgment for parentage issued by a court of competent jurisdiction. **FC § 7573**. The voluntary declaration of parentage is recognized as a basis for the establishment of an order for child custody, visitation or child support. **FC § 7573**. (See *KEVIN Q. v. LAUREN W.* (2009) 175 Cal.App.4th 1119 at p. 1132 where the Court of Appeal stated that a voluntary declaration of paternity that was signed by adult parents on or after January 1, 1997 is treated as a judgment.)

---

[2] FC § 7571 will be repealed effective January 1, 2020 and a new FC § 7571 will be effective January 1, 2020. The new code section is set forth in Appendix C.

[3] FC § 7572 sets forth the written materials that must be attached to the *Declaration of Paternity* form and provided to unmarried parents. This code section will be repealed effective January 1, 2020 and a new code section will replace it with the only changes being replacing the word paternity" with the word "parentage" and "assisted reproduction" added.

[4] This code will be repealed effective January 1, 2019 and the new code is set forth in Appendix C, *infra*.

Chapter 34: Parentage

The court must make appropriate orders as specified in **FC § 7637**[5], based upon the voluntary declaration of parentage, unless evidence is presented that the voluntary declaration of parentage has been rescinded by the parties or set aside, as provided in **FC § 7575** of the Family Code. **FC § 7644(b)**.

A voluntary declaration of parentage is invalid if, at the time the declaration was signed, any of the following conditions existed:

> **(1)** The child already had a presumed parent under FC § 7540.
> **(2)** The child already had a presumed parent under FC § 7611(a), (b), or (c).
> **(3)** The man signing the declaration is a sperm donor, consistent with FC § 7613(b). FC § 7612(f).

"If the court finds that the person who executed the voluntary declaration is not identified as a genetic parent of the child, the question of parentage will be resolved accordingly." **FC § 7575(c)(5)**.

If a person who executed a parentage declaration as the father of the child is not excluded as a possible father, the question of parentage must be resolved as otherwise provided by law. **FC § 7575(c)(5)**.

If there is a voluntary declaration of paternity in place, the court may order support payments to be made to: **(1)** the other parent; **(2)** the clerk of the court; and/or **(3)** a person, corporation or agency designated to administer the payments for the benefit of the child under the supervision of the court. **FC § 7641(b)**.

2. The Form for the Declaration of Parentage FC § 7574

A Declaration of Parentage form is used to legally establish the parentage of a child when the mother and father are not married to each other.

In California, the voluntary declaration of parentage is executed on form CS 909. It is set forth, along with additional information and instructions for completion, at *www.childsup.ca.gov/portals/0/cp/docs/cs909_english.pdf*.
(Note there is an "underscore" between the 909 and the word "English".)

The form includes the following information:

> **(1)** The name and the signature of the mother.
> **(2)** The name and the signature of the father.
> **(3)** The name of the child.
> **(4)** The date of birth of the child.
> **(5)** A statement by the mother that she has read and understands the written materials described in Section 7572, that the man who has signed the voluntary declaration of paternity is the only possible father, and that she consents to the establishment of

---

[5] FC § 7637 provides that a judgment or order may contain support, custody, guardianship, visitation bond or security for support or any other matter that is in the best interests of the child.

> paternity by signing the voluntary declaration of paternity.
> **(6)** A statement by the father that he has read and understands the written materials described in Section 7572, that he understands that by signing the voluntary declaration of paternity he is waiving his rights as described in the written materials, that he is the biological father of the child, and that he consents to the establishment of paternity by signing the voluntary declaration of paternity.
> **(7)** The name and the signature of the person who witnesses the signing of the declaration by the mother and the father. FC § 7574(b).

3. Declarations Signed on or Before December 31, 1996

Except as provided in **FC § 7576(d)** below, the child of a woman and a man executing a declaration of paternity under this chapter is conclusively presumed to be the man's child.

A voluntary declaration of paternity is recognized as the basis for the establishment of an order for child custody or support. **FC § 7576(b)**.

In any action to rebut the presumption created by this section, a voluntary declaration of paternity is admissible as evidence to determine paternity of the child named in the voluntary declaration of paternity. **FC § 7576(c)**.

Any interested person can rebut the paternity presumption established by this chapter by requesting blood or genetic tests. The notice of motion for blood or genetic tests pursuant to this section must be supported by a declaration under oath submitted by the moving party, stating the factual basis for placing the issue of paternity before the court. **FC § 7576(d)**.

A notice of motion requesting blood tests must be made within three years from the date of execution of the declaration by the attesting father or attesting mother, whichever signature is later. The two-year statute of limitations specified in **FC § 7541(b)**[6] is inapplicable for purposes of this section. **FC § 7576(d)**.

---

[6] FC § 7541 was amended effective January 1, 2019. The bolded text that follows represents the amended language. "(a) If the court finds that **the spouse who is a presumed parent under Section 7540 is not a genetic parent of the child** pursuant to Chapter 2 (commencing with Section 7550), **the question of parentage** shall be resolved **in accordance with all other applicable provisions of this division, including, but not limited to, Section 7612.**
(b) An action to challenge the parentage of the spouse who is a presumed parent under Section 7540 shall be filed not later than two years from the child's date of birth **and may only be filed by any of the following:**
(1) By either spouse.
(2) By a person who is a presumed parent under Section 7611 or by the child, through or by the child's guardian ad litem, to establish the parentage of the person who is a presumed parent under Section 7611.
(c) The petition or motion to challenge a presumption under Section 7540 pursuant to this section shall be supported by a declaration under oath submitted by the moving party stating the factual basis for placing the issue of **parentage** before the court.
(d) Genetic testing may not be used to challenge **parentage,** in either of the following cases:
(1) A case that reached final judgment of **parentage** on or before September 30, 1980.

Chapter 34: Parentage

A presumption under **FC § 7612** is a rebuttable presumption affecting the burden of proof and may be rebutted in an appropriate action only by clear and convincing evidence. **FC § 7612**.

4. A Declaration Signed by a Parent Who is a Minor

A voluntary declaration of parentage or a rescission of the voluntary declaration of parentage that is signed by a minor parent or minor parents does not establish parentage until sixty (60) days after both parents have reached the age of 18 years or are emancipated, whichever first occurs.

Accordingly, if minor parents marry after the birth of their child, they become emancipated and the declaration of parentage or the rescission becomes effective sixty (60) days after the date of the marriage. **FC § 7577**.

A voluntary declaration of parentage signed by a minor creates a rebuttable presumption of parentage until the date that it establishes parentage, as specified in **FC § 7577(a)** above. **FC § 7577(c)**.

A voluntary declaration of parentage signed by a minor is admissible as evidence in any civil action to establish parentage of the minor named in the voluntary declaration. **FC § 7577(d)**.

A voluntary declaration of parentage that is signed by a minor is not be admissible as evidence in a criminal prosecution for violation of **Penal Code § 261.5**. [7]

5. Custody, Visitation and Child Support

It is necessary to establish parentage before custody, visitation, or child support before it will be ordered by a court. A voluntary declaration of parentage is recognized as the basis for the establishment of an order for child custody and/or support.

An order for custody, visitation or child support remains in effect until the court determines that the voluntary declaration of parentage should be set aside, subject to the court's power to modify the orders as otherwise provided by law. **FC § 7575(c)(3)**.

If the person who executed the declaration of parentage is ultimately determined to be the father of the child, any child support that accrued under an order based upon the voluntary declaration of parentage remains due and owing. **FC § 7575(c)(5)**.

---

(2) A case **challenging the parentage of a spouse who is a parent pursuant to Section 7962 or subdivision (a) of Section 7613, except to resolve a dispute regarding whether the child was conceived through assisted reproduction.**

[7] Penal Code § 261.5 pertains to unlawful sexual intercourse with a minor, misdemeanor or felony violation upon conviction and the civil penalties."

If there is a parentage order in place and the couple thereafter marries, the parentage order is nullified.

However, whatever support was owed and not paid prior to the marriage remains due. In *In re Marriage of Wilson* (2012) 207 Cal.App.4th 768, a child was born to an unwed couple. M filed a paternity action and child support was set at $1,600 per month. Thereafter, the parties moved in together, had another child and then married. Approximately three years later, the parties began divorce proceedings. At the first hearing M contended that F owed the $1,600 per month from the time that they separated after the marriage ended until the present time. F contended that the marriage terminated the paternity support order. The trial court sided with M, and F appealed. The Court of Appeals reversed the trial court's decision and held that the marriage did not terminate the support order but nullified it. Accordingly, F did not owe the support from the date that they separated to the present. Further, F did not owe support for the time that the couple resided together.

And, any support that was not paid prior to the couple moving in together was due and owed. *Id.* at p. 810.

If there is a voluntary declaration of parentage in place, the court may order support payments to be made to: **(1)** the other parent; **(2)** the clerk of the court; **(3)** a person, corporation or agency designated to administer the payments for the benefit of the child under the supervision of the court. **FC § 7641(b)**.

A court may order pendente lite relief for custody or visitation[8], if the court finds that a parent and child relationship exists based upon tests authorized pursuant to **FC § 7540** or **FC § 7541** AND the custody or visitation order would be in the best interests of the child. **FC § 7604**.

An action for custody and child support may be based upon a voluntary declaration of parentage. **FC § 7644(a)**.

FC § 7614 provides:

> **(a)** A promise in writing to furnish support for a child, growing out of a presumed parent or alleged father and child relationship, does not require consideration and, subject to Section 7632, is enforceable according to its terms.
> **(b)** In the best interest of the child or the other parent, the court may, and upon the promisor's request shall, order the promise to be kept in confidence and designate a person or agency to receive and disburse on behalf of the child all amounts paid in performance of the promise.

---

[8] Relief that is pending a hearing or a trial may be called "pendente lite relief."

Chapter 34: Parentage

6. Rescission of a Declaration of Parentage FC § 7575

Either parent may rescind the voluntary declaration of parentage by filing a rescission form with the Department of Child Support Services within sixty (60) days of the date of execution of the declaration of the attesting father or attesting mother, whichever signature is later, unless a court order for custody, visitation or child support has been entered in an action in which the signatory seeking to rescind was a party. **FC § 7575(a)**.

If a court finds from the conclusions of all of the experts, based upon the results of the genetic tests performed, that the man who signed the voluntary declaration is not the father of the child, the court may set aside the voluntary declaration of parentage unless the court determines that denial of the request to set aside the voluntary declaration of parentage is in the best interests of the child. In making this decision, the court must consider all of the following factors:

> (A) The age of the child.
> (B) The length of time since the execution of the voluntary declaration of paternity by the man who signed the voluntary declaration.
> (C) The nature, duration, and quality of any relationship between the man who signed the voluntary declaration and the child, including the duration and frequency of any time periods during which the child and the man who signed the voluntary declaration resided in the same household or enjoyed a parent-child relationship.
> (D) The request of the man who signed the voluntary declaration that the parent-child relationship continue.
> (E) Notice by the biological father of the child that he does not oppose preservation of the relationship between the man who signed the voluntary declaration and the child.
> (F) The benefit or detriment to the child in establishing the biological parentage of the child.
> (G) Whether the conduct of the man who signed the voluntary declaration has impaired the ability to ascertain the identity of, or get support from, the biological father.
> (H) Additional factors deemed by the court to be relevant to its determination of the best interest of the child. FC § 7575(b).

In the event of any conflict between the presumption under **FC § 7611** and the voluntary declaration of parentage, the weightier considerations of policy and logic will control. **FC § 7612(e)**.

If the court denies the action requesting a rescission, the court must state on the record the basis for the denial of the action and any supporting facts. **FC § 7575(b)(2)**.

If the voluntary declaration of parentage is set aside, the court must order that the mother, child and alleged father submit to genetic tests. **FC § 7575(c)(5)**.

A court's ruling on the petition to set aside the voluntary declaration of parentage must be made taking into account: **(1)** the validity of the voluntary declaration of parentage, **(2)** the best interests of the child, based upon the court's consideration of the factors set forth in **FC § 7575(b)**, **(3)** the best interests of the child based upon the nature, duration and quality of the petitioning party's relationship with the child and **(4)** the benefit or detriment to the child of continuing that relationship.

A Declaration to Rescind a Declaration of Parentage form, along with instructions on completion, is set forth at:
www.childsup.ca.gov/portals/0/cp/docs/cs915_english.pdf. It is form *CS 915*.

The Uniform Parentage Act (UPA) FC § 7600 et seq.

1. The Parent-Child Relationship

A **natural parent** is a nonadoptive parent, whether biologically related to the child or not. **FC § 7601(a)**. "The parent and child relationship extends equally to every child and to every parent, regardless of the marital status of the parents." **FC § 7602**.

A **parent-child relationship** is a legal relationship existing between a child and the child's natural or adoptive parents, incident to which the law confers or imposes rights, privileges, duties and obligations. The term includes the mother-child relationship and the father-child relationship. A parent-child relationship can include more than two parents. **FC § 7601**.

The parent and child relationship may be established between a child and the natural parent by proof of having given birth to the child or between a child and an adoptive parent by proof of adoption. **FC § 7610**.

2. The Presumption of Parentage FC § 7611

A person is presumed to be the natural parent of a child if the person meets the conditions set forth in **FC § 7540** et seq. (presumption arising from birth of child during marriage), or in any of the following:

> **(a)** The presumed parent and the child's natural mother are or have been married to each other and the child is born during the marriage, or within 300 days after the marriage is terminated by death, annulment, declaration of invalidity, or divorce, or after a judgment of separation is entered by a court.
> **(b)** Before the child's birth, the presumed parent and the child's natural mother have attempted to marry each other by a marriage solemnized in apparent compliance with law, although the attempted marriage is or could be declared invalid, and either of the following is true:
>   **(1)** If the attempted marriage could be declared invalid only by a court, the child is born during the attempted marriage, or within 300 days after its termination by death, annulment, declaration of invalidity, or divorce.
>   **(2)** If the attempted marriage is invalid without a court order, the child is born within 300 days after the termination of cohabitation.
> **(c)** After the child's birth, the presumed parent and the child's natural mother have married, or attempted to marry, each other by a marriage solemnized in apparent

Chapter 34: Parentage

> compliance with law, although the attempted marriage is or could be declared invalid, and either of the following is true:
>
> **(1)** With his or her consent, the presumed parent is named as the child's parent on the child's birth certificate.
>
> **(2)** The presumed parent is obligated to support the child under a written voluntary promise or by court order.
>
> **(d)** The presumed parent receives the child into his or her home and openly holds out the child as his or her natural child. **FC § 7611.**

If two or more presumptions conflict, either conflicting with each other or a conflict by a person identified as a genetic parent, the presumption on which the facts are founded on the weightier considerations of policy and logic controls. **FC § 7612(b).**

If one of the parents is also a presumed parent under **FC § 7540**, the **FC § 7540** presumption can only be rebutted pursuant to **FC § 7541. FC § 7612(b).**

In an appropriate action, a court may find that more than two persons with a claim to parentage under this division are parents. If, in determining, the court finds that recognizing only two parents would be detrimental to the child, the court must consider all relevant factors, including, but not limited to, the harm of removing the child from a stable placement with a parent who has fulfilled the child's physical needs and psychological needs for care and affection, and who has assumed that role for a substantial period of time. A finding of detriment to the child does not require a finding of unfitness of any of the parents or persons with a claim to parentage. **FC § 7612(c).**

A presumption under **FC § 7611** is a rebuttable presumption affecting the burden of proof and may be rebutted in an appropriate action only by clear and convincing evidence. **FC § 7612.**

In the case that follows, Husband and Wife may have been cohabiting when the child was conceived; this fact is unclear. However, because Wife's former lover (S.G.) signed a Declaration of Paternity and Wife was married at the time, Wife had the option to rescind her former lover's declaration, which would make her husband the presumed father pursuant to **FC § 7611.**

> ***H.S. et al., Petitioners, v. The Superior Court of Riverside County, Respondent; S.G., Real Party in Interest.***
> COURT OF APPEAL OF CALIFORNIA, FOURTH APPELLATE DISTRICT, DIVISION TWO
> 183 Cal.App.4th 1502
> April 22, 2010, Filed
> (*H.S. v. Superior Court*)
>
> This is a paternity action involving a married couple, who will be referred to as petitioners or husband and wife, and wife's former lover, [will be referred to as] S.G. Husband and wife are from China where they first married. They divorced in Riverside in September 2001, but reconciled and remarried in 2002.

Chapter 34: Parentage

Wife became pregnant in 2005 and gave birth to a daughter, A. At the time wife became pregnant, she and husband were living apart during the workweek but claim that they spent the weekends together. Wife had an affair with S.G [during this time]. Wife separated from husband prior to the child's birth.

Wife admits that she told S.G. about her pregnancy, and [w]hen she did give birth, she called S.G., who came with his mother to the hospital.

Wife and S.G. executed a voluntary declaration of paternity or POP[9] declaration about 90 minutes after the birth. [Wife] does not have a good command of English and uses an electronic translator, but she did not have this device with her in the hospital and did not understand the explanation about the form given by the hospital personnel.

Within 60 days, wife executed a rescission of the declaration after using her translator to figure out what it meant. S.G. admits receiving this rescission, although the proof of service is defective.

Two weeks after A. was born, husband learned of her birth. He went to see her and husband and wife reconciled. Husband has accepted A. as his daughter. Husband and wife have lived together since then, along with the child, and a father-daughter relationship has developed between husband and A. Initially, the couple allowed S.G. to visit A. twice a month for two hours in their home. Husband became dissatisfied with this situation; they consulted a lawyer who advised them that they did not have to allow this. Husband and wife refused S.G. further visits in June 2008.

In May 2008, S.G. filed a petition to establish paternity and requested genetic testing. If it is determined he is the biological father, then he seeks visitation as well as support.

Wife responded to S.G.'s action with a motion to quash the proceedings and a motion to set aside the POP. The trial court denied the former, but granted the latter under FC § 7575(c)(1). In September 2008, the trial court ordered genetic testing under FC § 7575(c)(5).[However, the]testing did not take place because wife asked for reconsideration. Meanwhile, husband moved to join in the proceedings.

At the November 2009 hearing, the trial court found that wife and husband had not been cohabiting at the time of conception and, thus, the conclusive presumption of paternity under FC § 7540 did not apply. It did find husband was a presumed father under FC § 7611(a) and (d).

The trial court reaffirmed its order for genetic testing under FC § 7575(c)(5) and husband and wife petitioned this court for a writ of supersedeas, mandate, or prohibition. [We granted their Petition.]

DISCUSSION
The POP procedure establishes a simple procedure so that children can be assured of having child support and other benefits. The statute is primarily for the protection of children of unwed mothers to make sure that they have financial support. The Department of Child Support Services maintains that the POP should not be given to married mothers, and FC § 7571 provides only that the POP forms shall be offered to unmarried mothers in

---

[9] Paternity Opportunity Program, referred to hereinafter as "POP."

Chapter 34: Parentage

> the event of a live birth. The trial court indicated that the department's literature was not binding on it and noted that the statute does not specifically prohibit a POP from being executed by a married mother and another person. It concluded, therefore, that such a POP was not void on its face. It then considered whether allowing a voluntary POP would somehow "frustrate the purpose of the legislative intent and frustrate the purpose or policy of the statute." The trial court found it did not because the child would be provided for financially either by husband or the POP father.
>
> [T]he trial court focused only on the policies behind the POP statutes and ignored the policies underlying the marital presumption and standing statutes to maintain the stability of the family. We find that recognizing a POP declaration executed by a married woman does undermine these latter purposes, at least under certain circumstances. This appears to be just such a case, where the wife tried to rescind the POP and she and her husband have raised the child as his child in a stable family relationship.
>
> Moreover, the trial court set aside the POP, but ordered genetic testing pursuant to FC § 7575. S.G. has no standing as a presumed father other than the POP declaration and would have no standing to challenge husband's presumption of paternity under FC § 7630.
>
> Even in a contest between presumed fathers, the biological father does not automatically prevail against the mother's husband under FC § 7611(a) and (d). Rather, the court must weigh all relevant factors, including biology, in determining which presumption is founded on weightier considerations of policy and logic.
>
> In conclusion, we hold that requiring the parties to undergo genetic testing would be burdensome and serve no useful purpose when there is no basis to recognize S.G. as a presumed father other than the POP declaration. As previously discussed, that declaration is voidable when executed by a married woman. Under the circumstances of this case, the trial court should have found it was void and of no effect, when it granted wife's motion to set it aside.
>
> Let a peremptory writ of mandate issue directing the Superior Court of Riverside County to vacate its order for genetic testing and to issue a new and different order in accordance with the views expressed herein.

Unless a court orders otherwise after making the determination that there are more than two parents, a presumption under **FC § 7611** is rebutted by a judgment establishing parentage of the child by another person. **FC § 7612(d)**.

Within two years of the execution of a voluntary declaration of parentage[10], a person who is presumed to be a parent under **FC § 7611** may file a petition pursuant to **FC § 7630**[11] to set aside a voluntary declaration of parentage.

In the case that follows, there are two possible presumed fathers, the plaintiff and mother's new husband, whom she married after the child was born. When the trial

---

[10] Note that because the codes commencing January 1, 2020 will replace the word "paternity" with the word "parentage", that correction has already been made wherever it was appropriate to do so in this book.

[11] FC § 7630 sets forth who can file a paternity action.

court decided that the biological father prevailed as the presumed father, the mother and her new husband appealed.

> ### *J.R., Plaintiff and Respondent, v. D.P. et al., Defendants and Appellants.*
> COURT OF APPEAL OF CALIFORNIA, SECOND APPELLATE DISTRICT, DIVISION EIGHT
> 212 Cal.App.4th 374
> December 21, 2012, Opinion Filed
> (*J.R. v. D.P.*)
>
> Plaintiff and the mother of the child had an intimate sexual relationship which, according to plaintiff, began in December 2003. [They] were intimate in July 2009, when the child was conceived. At that time, plaintiff was married to another woman with whom he had two children, and the mother was living with and having sexual relations with R.M., who was named as father on the child's birth certificate. The child's mother (mother) had been living with R.M. since 2005.
>
> Mother discovered she was pregnant in August 2009. She thought R.M. was the father. She told plaintiff she was pregnant three months later. In late November 2009, she and plaintiff had testing done at the University of California at Los Angeles (UCLA) to determine if plaintiff was the father of the child. The results, received in December 2009, showed plaintiff was the father. Mother discussed the results with plaintiff in early January 2010, but she continued to believe R.M. was the father, because plaintiff told her [that he had a vasectomy.] Mother said that plaintiff tried to speak with her during the two months after they learned of the test results, but she told him not to call her anymore and did not respond to his phone calls. Mother changed her telephone number and did not give her new number to plaintiff.
>
> Plaintiff did not go to mother's house because she was living with R.M. and he did not want to provoke a violent reaction. He tried to reach R.M., but R.M. did not return his calls. In May 2010, he sent a letter to mother, but it was returned as undeliverable. He filed his lawsuit four months after the child was born, though he began preparing to file the lawsuit in June 2010. Mother and R.M. married on October 22, 2010.
>
> In August 2011, the court found that both plaintiff and R.M. qualified as presumed fathers under FC § 7611(d). Under that subdivision, a man is presumed to be the natural father if he "receives the child into his home and openly holds out the child as his natural child." FC § 7611(d). Plainly, R.M. qualified as a presumed father under FC § 7611(d). The court reasoned that plaintiff also qualified as a presumed father because he persisted throughout the pregnancy and after the child's birth to secure a relationship with the child but met extensive resistance from mother, who was determined to exclude plaintiff from the child's life. The court addressed the conflicting presumptions and the FC § 7611 requirement that "the presumption which on the facts is founded on the weightier considerations of policy and logic controls." FC § 7611(b).
>
> The court found it would offend basic human rights to deny plaintiff's claim of paternity since plaintiff had taken all reasonable steps to establish his paternity, yet mother thwarted his efforts by doing everything within her power to prevent him from establishing a parent-child relationship. The court reasoned it would be illogical to, in effect, permit mother to pick and choose who would be the child's father. The court concluded the law should not extinguish a biological relationship with a father who

sought to be responsible for the child's needs, solely because R.M. also loved the child, particularly since the vicissitudes[12] of life do not guarantee a lifelong relationship between mother and R.M., in which event the child could be left fatherless. The court acknowledged that recognizing plaintiff's parentage would interfere with the stability of the child's life, but found mother had created a false sense of stability by deceiving R.M. into believing he was the father.

The parents were given joint legal custody starting February 8, 2012. Mother and R.M. filed this appeal on September 13, 2011.

DISCUSSION
Mother and R.M. contend plaintiff had no standing to bring a paternity action and the trial court abused its discretion when it weighed competing presumptions and "allow[ed] biology to trump family stability." We find no merit in any of these contentions.

We begin with a brief description of the interrelated statutes that govern paternity decisions. The Uniform Parentage Act FC § 7600 et seq. enumerates the circumstances under which a man is presumed to be the natural father of a child. As relevant to this case, a man is presumed to be the natural father if he meets the conditions specified by statute for a voluntary declaration of paternity FC § 7570 et seq., or if he "receives the child into his home and openly holds out the child as his natural child." FC § 7611(d) A presumption under FC § 7611 (here, receiving the child into one's home) "is rebutted by a judgment establishing paternity of the child by another man." FC § 7611(c).

FC § 7630 as it reads today, would give plaintiff standing: "[A]n action to determine the existence of the father and child relationship may be brought by … a man alleged or alleging himself to be the father … ." FC § 7630(c). This provision was not in effect in August 2010 when plaintiff sued. At that time, FC § 7630(c) provided only for an action to determine the existence of a father and child relationship "with respect to a child who has no presumed father under FC § 7611… ." Defendants argue the FC § 7630 standing provision should not be applied retroactively, but, in practical effect, there is no retroactive application in this case. While the court found standing on September 30, 2010, before the provision was amended, its substantive rulings in the case all occurred after January 1, 2011. And, if the court had ruled on September 30 that plaintiff had no standing, plaintiff had only to refile his case 90 days later, after January 1, 2011, when the amended provision became effective, as there are no time constraints on when such an action may be brought.

The trial court found both plaintiff and R.M. to be presumed fathers under FC § 7611(d), and resolved the conflicting presumptions in plaintiff's favor. The issue is which father's presumption of paternity "on the facts is founded on the weightier considerations of policy and logic." FC § 7611(b). In weighing the conflicting interests, "the trial court must in the end make a determination which gives the greatest weight to [the child's] well-being." (Craig L. v. Sandy S. (2004) 125 Cal.App.4th 36, 53). Here, the trial court clearly believed that both men loved the child and would be good fathers, and that it was "illogical" to allow mother, in effect, to "pick and choose who the father's going to be." The court thought it was in the child's best interest to know his biological father, in circumstances where that father "did everything within his power to

---

[12] Vicissitudes means fluctuations and deviations.

> establish parentage."
>
> [W]e see no error in the court's use of the biology factor in this case. In the end, the court's determination must "give the greatest weight to [the child's] well-being" (Craig L., supra, 125 Cal.App.4th at p. 53), and that is what the court did. With plaintiff as the presumed father, the child will continue to have two loving families, both of which are currently a part of his life. If R.M. were found to be the presumed father, mother has left no doubt that plaintiff would have no part in the child's life.
>
> The judgment is affirmed.

3. The Parentage Action

a. Who Can Bring a Parentage Action FC § 7630

Any interested party may bring an action at any time for the purpose of determining the existence or nonexistence of the father-child relationship presumed under **FC § 7611(d)** or **(f)**. **FC § 7630(b)**.

Any interested person may bring an action to determine the existence or nonexistence of a mother-child relationship. **FC § 7650**.

A child, the child's natural mother, a person presumed to be the child's parent under **FC § 7611(a), (b)** or **(c)**, a person seeking to be adjudicated as a parent under **FC § 7613**, an adoption agency to whom the child has been relinquished or a prospective adoptive parent of the child may bring an action to determine paternity:

(1) at any time for the purpose of declaring the existence of the parent-child relationship presumed under **FC § 7611(a), (b)** or **(c)**; or
(2) for the purpose of declaring the nonexistence of the parent-child relationship presumed under **FC § 7611(a), (b)** or **(c)** only if the action is brought within a reasonable time after obtaining knowledge of relevant facts; or
(3) at any time for the purpose of declaring the nonexistence of the parent and child relationship of a donor under **FC § 7613**.

After the presumption has been rebutted, parentage of the child by another person may be determined in the same action, if that person has been made a party. **FC § 7630(a)(2)**.

Pursuant to **FC § 7630(c)**, an action to determine the existence of the parent-child relationship may be brought by:

1. The child,
2. A personal representative of the child,
3. The Department of Child Support Services,
4. A presumed parent,
5. The personal representative

6. A parent of that presumed parent if that parent has died or is a minor, or, in cases in which the natural mother is the only presumed parent or an action under Welfare and Institutions Code § 300 or adoption is pending, or
7. A man alleged or alleging himself to be the father or the personal representative or a parent of the alleged father if the alleged father has died or is a minor.

A child may be made a party to the action if the child is under 12 years old. If the child is 12 years or older, the child must be joined as a party to the action. If the child is a minor and a party to the action, the child must be represented by guardian ad litem[13] appointed by the court. If the guardian ad litem is related to the child, attorney representation is not mandatory. **FC § 7635(a)**.

> The natural parent, each person presumed to be a parent under Section 7611 or 7540, each person who is a parent of the child under Section 7613 or 7962, and each person, and each person alleged to be the genetic parent unless precluded under this division from establishing parentage based on genetic testing shall be given notice of the action in the manner prescribed in Section 7666 and an opportunity to be heard, and shall be made a party if they request to be joined. Appointment of a guardian ad litem shall not be required for a minor who is a parent of the child who is the subject of the petition to establish parental relationship, unless the minor parent is unable to understand the nature of the proceedings or to assist counsel in preparing the case. FC § 7635(b).

Regardless of its terms, an agreement between an alleged father or a presumed parent and the other parent or child does not bar an action under this chapter. **FC § 7632**.

Finally, a parent or guardian pursuant to **FC § 7638** may bring an action to change the name of a minor or adult child for whom a parent-child relationship is established pursuant to **FC § 7676**.

b. Genetic Tests to Determine Parentage

Genetic testing means any genetic testing that complies with **FC § 7552**. **FC § 7552** provides:

> (a) Genetic testing shall be of a type reasonably relied on by experts in the field of genetic testing and performed in a testing laboratory accredited by either of the following:
> (1) The AABB, formerly known as the American Association of Blood Banks, or a successor organization.
> (2) An accrediting body designated by the Secretary of the United States Department of Health and Human Services.
> (b) A specimen used in genetic testing may consist of a sample or a combination of samples of blood, buccal cells, bone, hair, or other body tissue or fluid. The specimen used in the testing need not be of the same kind for each person undergoing genetic testing.

---

[13] Guardian ad litem is a court appointed representative appointed to represent the best interests of the child. **FC § 7647.5**.

> **(c)** Based on the ethnic or racial group of a person undergoing genetic testing, a testing laboratory shall determine the databases from which to select frequencies for use in calculating a relationship index. If a person or a local child support agency objects to the laboratory's choice, the following rules shall apply:
> **(1)** Not later than 30 days after receipt of the report of the test, the objecting person or local child support agency may request the court to require the laboratory to recalculate the relationship index using an ethnic or racial group different from that used by the laboratory.
> **(2)** The person or local child support agency objecting to the choice of laboratories under this subdivision shall do either of the following:
> **(A)** If the requested frequencies are not available to the laboratory for the ethnic or racial group requested, provide the requested frequencies compiled in a manner recognized by accrediting bodies.
> **(B)** Engage another laboratory to perform the calculations.
> **(3)** The laboratory may use its own statistical estimate if there is a question of which ethnic or racial group is appropriate. The laboratory shall calculate the frequencies using statistics, if available, for any other ethnic or racial group requested.
> **(d)** If, after recalculation of the relationship index pursuant to subdivision (c) using a different ethnic or racial group, genetic testing does not identify a person as a genetic parent of the child, the court may require a person who has been tested to submit to additional genetic testing to identify a genetic parent.

A child of spouses who cohabited at the time of conception and birth is conclusively[14] presumed to be a child of the marriage. This is called the **conclusive marital presumption**. The conclusive marital presumption does not apply if the court determines the husband of the woman who gave birth was impotent or sterile at time of conception or assisted reproduction was not used. **FC § 7540**.

As set forth above, FC § 7540 provides two means for the father to rebut the presumption: **(1)** by proving sterility or impotency at the time of conception, or **(2)** by proving that assisted reproduction was used.

A notice of motion for challenging blood tests may be filed no later than two years from the child's date of birth by:
"**(1)** By either spouse.
(2) By a person who is a presumed parent[15] under Section 7611 or by the child, through or by the child's guardian ad litem, to establish the parentage of the person who is a presumed parent under Section 7611." **FC § 7541**.

However, blood tests may not be used to challenge paternity in: **(1)** a case that reached final judgment of parentage on or before September 30, 1980, **(2)** a case challenging the parentage of a spouse who is a parent pursuant to FC § 7962 or FC

---

[14] Pursuant to Evid. Code § 600(a), a "'presumption' is an assumption of fact that the law requires to be made from another fact or group of facts found or otherwise established in the action." "A presumption is either conclusive or rebuttable. Every rebuttable presumption is either (a) a presumption affecting the burden of producing evidence or (b) a presumption affecting the burden of proof." Evid. Code § 601. A conclusive presumption cannot be rebutted or disproved regardless of the evidence presented.
[15] The definition of a "presumed parent" is set forth in FC §§ 7611 and 7612, *infra*.

Chapter 34: Parentage

§ 7613(a), except to resolve a dispute regarding whether the child was conceived through assisted reproduction. **FC § 7541(d)**.

Pursuant to **FC § 7551**, when parentage is a relevant fact, a court, upon its own motion, initiative or upon suggestion made by or on behalf any person who is involved, must order the woman who gave birth, the child and the alleged genetic parent to submit to genetic testing. If, however, a party refuses to submit to genetic testing, is admissible as evidence in any proceeding to determine parentage. **FC § 7551(d)(2)**. An order to submit to genetic testing is enforceable by a contempt. **FC § (d)(5)**.

A person is identified as a genetic parent of a child if the genetic testing results disclose:

> **(1)** The person has at least a 99 percent probability of parentage, using a prior probability of 0.50, as calculated by using the combined relationship index obtained in the testing.
> **(2)** A combined relationship index of at least 100 to 1.
> **(b)** A person identified pursuant to subdivision (a) as a genetic parent of the child may challenge the genetic testing results only by other genetic testing satisfying the requirements of this chapter that either excludes the person as a genetic parent of the child or identifies another person as a possible genetic parent of the child other than the woman who gave birth to the child or the person challenging parentage.
> **(c)** If more than one person, other than the woman who gave birth to the child, is identified by genetic testing as a possible genetic parent of the child, the court shall order each person to submit to further genetic testing to identify a genetic parent. FC § 7555(a).

A party to an action may produce expert evidence on the issue of genetic testing. However, when expert witnesses are called by a party to the action or proceeding, their fees will be paid by the party calling them and only ordinary witness fees shall be taxed as costs. **FC § 7557**.

c. The Court Hearing or Trial

A parentage hearing or trial held under this part may be held in closed court without admittance of any person other than those necessary to the action or proceeding.

In an action where the alleged father in present in court, the court must inform him of his right to have genetic testing performed to determine if he is the biological father of the child. **FC § 7635.5**.

Except as provided in **FC § 7643(b)**, all papers and records, other than the final judgment, pertaining to the action or proceeding are subject to inspection and copying only in exceptional cases upon an order of the court for good cause shown. **FC § 7643(a)**.

4. The Parentage Judgment

Although an action under this chapter may be brought and an order/judgment made and entered before the birth of the child, enforcement of that order or judgment must be stayed until the birth of the child. **FC § 7633**.

A parentage judgment or order may contain any other provision directed against the appropriate party to the proceeding, concerning the duty of support, the custody and guardianship of the child, visitation privileges with the child, the furnishing of bond or other security for the payment of the judgment or any other matter in the best interests of the child. The judgment or order may direct the parent to pay the reasonable expenses of the mother's pregnancy and confinement. **FC § 7637**.

If the judgment or order of the court varies from the child's birth certificate, the court must order that a new birth certificate be issued. **FC § 7639**.

Pursuant to **FC § 7642**, the court has continuing jurisdiction to modify or set aside a judgment or order made under this part. A judgment or order relating to an adoption may only be modified or set aside in the same manner and under the same conditions as an order of adoption may be modified or set aside under **FC § 9100** or **9102**.

FC § 7643(b) provides that papers, documents and records pertaining to the action or proceeding that are part of the permanent record of the court are subject to inspection and copying only by the parties to the action, their attorneys and by agents acting pursuant to written authorization from the parties to the action or their attorneys. An attorney must obtain the consent of the party to the action prior to authorizing an agent to inspect and copy the permanent record. An attorney must state on the written authorization that he or she has obtained the consent of the party to authorize an agent to inspect and copy the permanent record.

The judgment or order of the court determining the existence or nonexistence of the parent-child relationship is determinative for all purposes, except for actions brought pursuant to **Penal Code § 270**.[16] **FC § 7636**.

Willful failure to obey the judgment or order of the court is a civil contempt of the court, and all remedies for the enforcement of judgments, including imprisonment for contempt, apply. **FC § 7641(c)**.

---

[16] Penal Code § 270 is pertains to the failure to support a child.

Chapter 34: Parentage

5. Setting Aside or Vacating the Judgment of Paternity

FC § 7645 provides the following definitions:

Child means the child of a previously established father or mother, as determined by the superior court in a judgment that is the subject of a motion brought pursuant to this article, or as a matter of law. **FC § 7545(a)**.

Judgment means a judgment, order or decree entered in a court of this state that establishes parentage, including a determination of parentage made pursuant to a petition filed under **Welfare and Institutions Code §§ 300, 601** or **602.** For the purposes of this article, **judgment** does not include a judgment in any action for marital dissolution, legal separation or nullity. **FC § 7645(b)**.

Previously established father means a person identified as the father of a child in a judgment that is the subject of a motion brought pursuant to this article. **FC § 7645(c)**.
Previously established mother means a person identified as the mother of a child in a judgment that is the subject of a motion brought pursuant to this article. **FC § 7645(d)**.

A court must inform an alleged father who is in court of his right to set aside or vacate a judgment of paternity pursuant to **FC § 7646** within two years of the date he received notice of the action to establish paternity. After that time has passed, he may not move to set aside or vacate the judgment of paternity, regardless of whether genetic testing shows him not to be the biological father of the child. **FC § 7635.5**.

A judgment establishing parentage may be set aside or vacated upon a motion by: A previously established parent; (2) the child; (3) or the legal representative of any of these persons if the genetic testing shows that the previously established father is not the genetic father. The motion must be brought: within two years commencing with the previously established father knew or should have known that a judgment had been made adjudicating parentage; (2) If there is a legal father as the result of a default judgment as of the effective date of this section, within a two-year period from January 1, 2005 to December 31, 2006, inclusive. **FC § 7646(a)**.

FC § 7646(a) does not apply if the child is presumed to be a child of the marriage (**FC § 7540**), the previously established parent is a parent under **FC § 7613** or **FC § 7962**, or the action is barred by **FC § 7630(a)(2)**.[17]

If the court grants a motion to set aside or vacate a parentage judgment pursuant to this article, the court must also vacate any order for child support and arrearages

---

[17] FC § 7630(a)(2) provides: "For the purpose of declaring the nonexistence of the parent and child relationship presumed under subdivision (a), (b), or (c) of Section 7611 only if the action is brought within a reasonable time after obtaining knowledge of relevant facts. After the presumption has been rebutted, parentage of the child by another person may be determined in the same action, if that person has been made a party."

Chapter 34: Parentage

issued on the basis of that previous judgment of parentage. The previously established father has no right of reimbursement for any amount of support paid prior to the granting of the motion. **FC § 7648.4.**

A motion for reconsideration requesting reconsideration of a paternity decision may be requested and granted if: **(1)** the motion was filed with the court between September 24, 2006, and December 31, 2006, inclusive, **(2)** the motion was denied solely on the basis that it was untimely AND **(3)** the request for reconsideration of the motion is filed on or before December 31, 2009. **FC § 7646(c).**

Any genetic testing used to support the motion to set aside or vacate must be conducted in accordance with **FC § 7552**[18]. A court may set aside or vacate a judgment establishing parentage only if:

> **(1)** The motion is filed in a court of proper venue.
> **(2)** The motion contains, at a minimum, all of the following information, if known:
> **(A)** The legal name, age, county of residence, and residence address of the child.
> **(B)** The names, mailing addresses, and counties of residence, or, if deceased, the date and place of death, of the following persons:
> **(i)** The previously established parents and the alleged father of the child.
> **(ii)** The guardian of the child, if any.
> **(iii)** Any person who has physical custody of the child.
> **(iv)** The guardian ad litem of the child, if any, as appointed pursuant to Section 7647.5.
> **(C)** A declaration that the person filing the motion believes that the previously established father is not the genetic father of the child, the specific reasons for this belief, and a

---

[18] FC § 7552 was repealed and the new FC § 7552 became effective January 1, 2019. The new FC § 7552 provides: "**(a)** Genetic testing shall be of a type reasonably relied on by experts in the field of genetic testing and performed in a testing laboratory accredited by either of the following:
(1) The AABB, formerly known as the American Association of Blood Banks, or a successor organization.
(2) An accrediting body designated by the Secretary of the United States Department of Health and Human Services.
(b) A specimen used in genetic testing may consist of a sample or a combination of samples of blood, buccal cells, bone, hair, or other body tissue or fluid. The specimen used in the testing need not be of the same kind for each person undergoing genetic testing. laboratory shall determine the databases from which to select frequencies for use in calculating a relationship index. If
(c) Based on the ethnic or racial group of a person undergoing genetic testing, a testing a person or a local child support agency objects to the laboratory's choice, the following rules shall apply:
(1) Not later than 30 days after receipt of the report of the test, the objecting person or local child support agency may request the court to require the laboratory to recalculate the relationship index using an ethnic or racial group different from that used by the laboratory.
(2) The person or local child support agency objecting to the choice of laboratories under this subdivision shall do either of the following:
(A) If the requested frequencies are not available to the laboratory for the ethnic or racial group requested, provide the requested frequencies compiled in a manner recognized by accrediting bodies.
(B) Engage another laboratory to perform the calculations.
(3) The laboratory may use its own statistical estimate if there is a question of which ethnic or racial group is appropriate. The laboratory shall calculate the frequencies using statistics, if available, for any other ethnic or racial group requested.
(d) If, after recalculation of the relationship index pursuant to subdivision (c) using a different ethnic or racial group, genetic testing does not identify a person as a genetic parent of the child, the court may require a person who has been tested to submit to additional genetic testing to identify a genetic parent.

Chapter 34: Parentage

> declaration that the person desires that the motion be granted. The moving party is not required to present evidence of genetic testing indicating that the previously established father is not the genetic father of the child in order to bring this motion pursuant to Section 7646.
> **(D)** A declaration that the marital presumption set forth in Section 7540 does not apply and that an action is not barred under paragraph (2) of subdivision (a) of Section 7630.
> **(3)** The court finds that the previously established father is not a genetic parent pursuant to Section 7555. FC § 7647.

A court may deny a motion to set aside the paternity judgment if it determines that denial of the motion is in the best interests of the child, after consideration of:

- **(a)** The age of the child;
- **(b)** The length of time since the entry of the judgment establishing parentage;
- **(c)** The nature, duration, and quality of any relationship between the previously established father and the child, including the duration and frequency of any time periods during which the child and the previously established father resided in the same household or enjoyed a parent and child relationship;
- **(d)** The request of the previously established father that the parent and child relationship continue;
- **(e)** Notice by the biological father of the child that he does not oppose preservation of the relationship between the previously established father and the child;
- **(f)** The benefit or detriment to the child in establishing the genetic father as the parent of the child.
- **(g)** Whether the conduct of the previously established father has impaired the ability to ascertain the identity of, or get support from, the biological father; and
- **(h)** Additional factors deemed by the court to be relevant to its determination of the best interests of the child. **FC § 7648**.

Pursuant to **FC § 7648.3**, a court may not issue an order setting aside or vacating a judgment establishing paternity where the judgment was made or entered:

(1) By a tribunal of another state or
(2) The judgment was made or entered in this state and the genetic testing were conducted prior to the entry of the judgment which did not exclude the previously established father as the biological father of the child.

Nothing in this article limits the rights and remedies available under any other law with regard to setting aside or vacating a parentage. **FC § 7649**.

6. Assisted Reproduction

Assisted reproduction means conception by any means other than sexual intercourse. And an **assisted reproduction agreement** means a written contract that includes a person who intends to be the legal parent of a children born through

Chapter 34: Parentage

assisted reproduction and that defines the terms of the relationship between the parties to the contract. **FC § 7606**.

A person who has sexual intercourse or causes conception with the intent to become a legal parent by assisted reproduction in this state thereby submits to the jurisdiction of the courts of this state with respect to a child who may have been conceived by that act of intercourse or assisted reproduction. **FC § 7620(a)**.

An action under this part must be brought in one of the following:

> **(b)** If a child is conceived pursuant to an assisted reproduction agreement for gestational carriers, as defined in Section 7960 and as described in Section 7962, the courts of this state shall have jurisdiction over a proceeding to determine parentage of the child if any of the following conditions is satisfied:
> **(1)** One or more of the parties to the assisted reproduction agreement for gestational carriers resides in this state, or resided in this state at the time the assisted reproduction agreement for gestational carriers was executed.
> **(2)** The medical procedures leading to conception, including in vitro fertilization or embryo transfer, or both, were carried out in this state.
> **(3)** The child is born in this state. FC § 7620(b).

FC § 7613 provides:

> **(a)**
> **(1)** If a woman conceives through assisted reproduction with semen or ova or both donated by a donor not her spouse, with the consent of another intended parent, that intended parent is treated in law as if he or she were the natural parent of a child thereby conceived. The other intended parent's consent shall be in writing and signed by the other intended parent and the woman conceiving through assisted reproduction.
> **(2)** Failure to consent in writing, as required by paragraph (1), does not preclude the court from finding that the intended parent consented if the court finds by clear and convincing evidence that, prior to the conception of the child, the woman and the intended parent had an oral agreement that the woman and the intended parent would both be parents of the child.
> **(b)**
> **(1)** The donor of semen provided to a licensed physician and surgeon or to a licensed sperm bank for use in assisted reproduction by a woman other than the donor's spouse is treated in law as if he were not the natural parent of a child thereby conceived, unless otherwise agreed to in a writing signed by the donor and the woman prior to the conception of the child.
> **(2)** If the semen is not provided to a licensed physician and surgeon or a licensed sperm bank as specified in paragraph (1), the donor of semen for use in assisted reproduction by a woman other than the donor's spouse is treated in law as if he were not the natural parent of a child thereby conceived if either of the following are met:
> **(A)** The donor and the woman agreed in a writing signed prior to conception that the donor would not be a parent.
> **(B)** A court finds by clear and convincing evidence that the child was conceived through assisted reproduction and that, prior to the conception of the child, the woman and the donor had an oral agreement that the donor would not be a parent.

Chapter 34: Parentage

> **(3)** Paragraphs (1) and (2) do not apply to a man who provided semen for use in assisted reproduction by a woman other than the man's spouse pursuant to a written agreement signed by the man and the woman prior to conception of the child stating that they intended for the man to be a parent.
>
> **(c)** The donor of ova for use in assisted reproduction by a person other than the donor's spouse or nonmarital partner is treated in law as if the donor were not the natural parent of a child thereby conceived unless the court finds satisfactory evidence that the person providing ova and the person intended for the person providing ova to be a parent. FC § 7613.

In the case that follows, Jason and Danielle cohabitated for many years, but they never married. Their child, Gus, was conceived through in vitro fertilization (IVF), with Jason providing the sperm used in the procedure. Because Jason provided his sperm, he contended that he was Gus' natural father and, accordingly, filed a paternity action. Danielle opposed the petition, arguing that Jason was not the natural father, but a sperm donor, pursuant to **FC § 7613(b)**.

> ***JASON P., Plaintiff and Appellant, v. DANIELLE S., Defendant and Respondent.***
> COURT OF APPEAL OF CALIFORNIA, SECOND APPELLATE DISTRICT, DIVISION FOUR
> 226 Cal.App.4th 167
> May 14, 2014, Opinion Filed
> (*Jason P. v. Danielle S.*)
>
> In June 2012, appellant Jason P. filed a petition to establish a parental relationship with Gus S., a child born to respondent Danielle S. in December 2009. Danielle opposed the petition, arguing that Jason was a sperm donor under FC § 7613(b) and therefore was not Gus's natural father as a matter of law.
>
> Jason is not listed on Gus's birth certificate, and there is no voluntary declaration of paternity. Gus has no other natural, presumed, or potential biological father.
>
> Jason presented evidence that he and Danielle tried to have a baby naturally beginning in 2006. In 2007, Danielle had two intrauterine insemination (IUI) procedures using Jason's sperm, but neither resulted in a pregnancy. In October 2007, after being advised that their inability to conceive might be due to issues regarding Jason's sperm count, Jason had a surgical procedure to address that problem. She and Jason also began to look into having an IVF procedure.
>
> After having an unsuccessful IUI procedure in January 2009 using Jason's sperm, Danielle decided to try an IVF procedure. On March 9, 2009, Jason took Danielle to California Fertility Partners for the IVF procedure. The procedure was successful, and Gus was born in December 2009.
>
> At trial, Jason presented evidence regarding his relationship with Gus and Danielle over the next two and a half years. For example, he presented evidence that Danielle referred to Jason as "Dada" when speaking to Gus, and Gus called Jason "Dada." When Jason was working in New York for six months, Danielle and Gus flew there several times and stayed with Jason at his apartment. When Danielle and Gus were not in New York with Jason, Jason communicated with Gus over the Internet by Skype. Jason continued to maintain contact with Gus until the middle of 2012, when Danielle terminated her

relationship with Jason.

At the close of evidence in the first phase of the trial, Danielle moved for nonsuit under CCP § 631.8. The court granted the motion. In announcing its ruling, the court stated, "I don't think anyone is going to prevail as a result of this. I think at the end of the day that everyone turns out to be worse off, and certainly I think Gus turns out to be worse off as a result of where we're going to end up. But it just is what it is, because I think that's the legislative policy that's been articulated." The court provided its oral statement of decision, and subsequently issued a written statement of decision.

The court found that the undisputed evidence that Jason's semen was provided to a licensed physician and surgeon, that Gus was conceived through IVF using Jason's sperm, and that he and Danielle were never married conclusively established that FC § 7613(b) applies.

Next, the trial court found that Jason could not establish paternity under FC § 7611(d) because FC § 7613(b) is the exclusive means of determining paternity in cases involving sperm donors and unmarried women.
Having found that Jason did not have a parent and child relationship with Gus, the trial court found Jason was not entitled to custody of, or visitation with, Gus, and vacated the pendente lite visitation order. Judgment was entered in favor of Danielle, from which Jason appeals.

DISCUSSION
[It is our opinion that] the trial court's ruling was incorrect. [W]e hold that FC § 7613(b should be interpreted only to preclude a sperm donor from establishing paternity based upon his biological connection to the child, and does not preclude him from establishing that he is a presumed parent under FC § 7611(d) based upon postbirth conduct.

We reach this conclusion because we must construe FC § 7611(d) with reference to the entire scheme of law of which it is part so that the whole may be harmonized and retain effectiveness. We choose the construction that comports most closely with the Legislature's apparent intent, endeavoring to promote rather than defeat the statute's general purpose, and avoiding a construction that would lead to absurd consequences. "The paternity presumptions are driven by state interest in preserving the integrity of the family and legitimate concern for the welfare of the child. The state has an interest in preserving and protecting the developed parent-child … relationships which give young children social and emotional strength and stability." (In re Nicholas H. (2002) 28 Cal.4th 56, 65.) "This interest is served notwithstanding termination of the mother's marital relationship with the presumed father." (Susan H. v. Jack S. (1994) 30 Cal.App.4th 1435, 1443.)

By interpreting FC § 7613(b) only to preclude a sperm donor from establishing paternity based upon his biological connection to the child, while allowing him to establish that he is a presumed parent under FC § 7611 based upon a demonstrated familial relationship, we allow both statutes to retain effectiveness and promote the purpose of each.
Our holding that a sperm donor is not precluded from establishing presumed parentage does not mean that a mother who conceives through assisted reproduction and allows the sperm donor to have some kind of relationship with the child necessarily loses her right to be the sole parent.

Chapter 34: Parentage

> First, FC § 7611 requires a familial relationship. To qualify as a presumed parent under subdivision (d), the presumed parent must show that he or she "receives the child into his or her home and openly holds out the child as his or her natural child." FC § 7611(d). A mother wishing to retain her sole right to parent her child conceived through assisted reproduction can limit the kind of contact she allows the sperm donor to have with her child to ensure that the relationship does not rise to the level of presumed parent and child.[10]
>
> Second, the presumption of parentage under FC § 7611 is, with certain exceptions, a rebuttable presumption. FC § 7612(a). Thus, even if a sperm donor can establish that he received the child into his home and openly held out the child as his natural child, the trial court nevertheless may conclude based on other evidence that the presumption has been rebutted and the sperm donor is not the child's natural father.
>
> In this case, Jason was denied the opportunity to present evidence to show that he is Gus's presumed father under [FC § 7611(d)]. Therefore, the judgment must be reversed and the matter remanded for further proceedings.
> The judgment is reversed. The matter is remanded with directions to the trial court to conduct further proceedings to determine whether Jason qualifies as a presumed parent under FC § 7611.

"A party to an assisted reproduction agreement may bring an action at any time to establish a parent and child relationship consistent with the intent expressed in that assisted reproduction agreement." **FC § 7630(f)**.

An intended parent may, but is not required to, use the optional forms to demonstrate his or her intent to be a legal parent of a child conceived through assisted reproduction. These forms satisfy the writing requirements specified in **FC § 7613** and are designed to provide clarity regarding the intentions, at the time of conception, of intended parents using assisted reproduction. **FC § 7613.5(a)**.

7. Adoption and Termination of Parental Rights in Paternity Cases

There is no filing fee charged for a petition filed to terminate parental rights of an alleged father. **FC § 7670**.

In an effort to identify all alleged fathers and presumed parents, an inquiry must be made by the court. The inquiry must include all of the following:

> **(1)** Whether the mother was married at the time of conception of the child or at any time thereafter.
> **(2)** Whether the mother was cohabiting with a man at the time of conception or birth of the child.
> **(3)** Whether the mother has received support payments or promises of support with respect to the child or in connection with her pregnancy.
> **(4)** Whether any person has formally or informally acknowledged or declared his or her possible parentage of the child.
> **(5)** The names and whereabouts, if known, of every person presumed or man alleged to be the parent of the child, and the efforts made to give notice of the proposed adoption to each person identified. FC § 7663(b).

Chapter 34: Parentage

If, after the inquiry, the biological father is identified to the satisfaction of the court, or if more than one man is identified as a possible biological father, notice of the proceeding must be given in accordance with **FC § 7666**. If any alleged biological father fails to appear or, if appearing, fails to claim parental rights, his parental rights with reference to the child will be terminated. **FC § 7664(a)**.

If, after the inquiry, the court is unable to identify the biological father or any possible biological father and no person has appeared claiming to be the biological father and claiming custodial rights, the court must enter an order terminating the unknown biological father's parental rights with reference to the child. **FC § 7665**.

If the biological father or a man representing himself to be the biological father claims parental rights, the court must determine if he is the biological father. The court must next determine if it is in the best interests of the child that the biological father retains his parental rights, or if an adoption of the child should be allowed to proceed. The court, in making that determination, may consider all relevant evidence, including the efforts made by the biological father to obtain custody, the age and prior placement of the child and the effects of a change of placement on the child. **FC § 7664(b).**

If the court finds that it is in the best interests of the child that the biological father should be allowed to retain his parental rights, the court must order that his consent is necessary for an adoption. If the court finds that the man claiming parental rights is not the biological father, or that, if he is the biological father, it is in the child's best interests that an adoption be allowed to proceed, the court must order that the consent of that man is not required for an adoption. This finding terminates all parental rights and responsibilities with respect to the child. **FC § 7664(c)**.

In the case that follows, Mother (M) gave birth to Kelsey on May 18, 1988. Father (F) and M were not married to one another. At that time, F was aware that M planned to place their child for adoption, and he objected to her decision because he wanted to rear the child; it was undisputed that F was the child's natural (biological) father.

> *Adoption of KELSEY S., a Minor. STEVEN A. et al., Plaintiffs and Respondents, v. RICKIE M., Defendant and Appellant. RICKIE M., Plaintiff and Appellant, v. M S., Defendant and Respondent.*
> SUPREME COURT OF CALIFORNIA
> 1 Cal.4th 816
> February 20, 1992, Decided and Filed
> *(Kelsey S. v. Rickie M.)*
>
> Two days after the child's birth, F filed an action in superior court under Civil Code § 7006[19] to establish his parental relationship with the child and to obtain custody of the child.

---

[19] Civil Code § 7004 was repealed and recodified as FC § 7611 without substantial change.

Chapter 34: Parentage

On May 24, 1988, the prospective adoptive parents, filed an adoption petition under Civil Code § 226 [alleging that only the mother's consent to the adoption was required because there was no presumed father under Civil Code § 7004(a). Seven days later, filed a petition under Civil Code § 7017[20] to terminate F's parental rights.]

The parties subsequently stipulated that F was the child's natural father. The superior court, however, ruled that he was not a "presumed father" within the meaning of Civil Code § 7004(a)(4). The court held four days of hearings to determine whether it was in the child's best interest for F to retain his parental rights and whether the adoption should be allowed to proceed. On August 26, 1988, the court found "by a bare preponderance" of the evidence that the child's best interest required termination of F's parental rights.

F appealed. He contended the superior court erred by: (1) concluding that he was not the child's presumed father; (2) not granting him a parental placement preference; and (3) applying a preponderance-of-the-evidence standard of proof. The Court of Appeal rejected each of his contentions and affirmed the judgment.

DISCUSSION
Civil Code § 7004 states, "A man is presumed to be the natural father of a child . . ." if the man meets any of several conditions set forth in the statute. Whether a biological father is a "presumed father" under Civil Code 7004 is critical to his parental rights. If the mother of a child who does not have a presumed father consents to the child's adoption, a petition must, except in certain narrow circumstances, be filed in the superior court to terminate the natural father's parental rights. If the natural father or a man representing himself to be the natural father claims parental rights, the court first must determine whether he is the natural father. If so, [the court must then determine if it is in the best interest of the child that the father retain his parental rights, or that an adoption of the child be allowed to proceed. If the court finds that it is in the best interest of the child that the father should be allowed to retain his parental rights, it must order that his consent is necessary for an adoption.] The child's best interest is the sole criterion where there is no presumed father.

Mothers and presumed fathers have far greater rights. Under Civil Code § 221.20, either a mother or presumed father can withhold consent to the adoption except in certain specified and narrow circumstances. Moreover, Civil Code § 7017(d)(2) states that its provision for allowing termination of a natural father's parental rights based on the child's best interest does not apply to presumed fathers. In short, a mother or a presumed father must consent to an adoption absent a showing by clear and convincing evidence of that parent's unfitness.

This statutory scheme creates three classifications of parents: mothers, biological fathers who are presumed fathers, and biological fathers who are not presumed fathers (i.e., natural fathers). A natural father's consent to an adoption of his child by third parties is not required unless the father makes the required showing that retention of his parental rights is in the child's best interest. Consent, however, is required of a mother and a presumed father regardless of the child's best interest. The natural father is therefore treated differently from both mothers and presumed fathers.

A man becomes a "presumed father" under Civil Code § 7004(a)(4) if "[h]e receives the child into his home and openly holds out the child as his natural child." (Italics added.) It

---

[20] Civil Code § 7017 was repealed and recodified as FC § 7660-7666.

is undisputed in this case that F openly held out the child as being his own. F, however, did not physically receive the child into his home. He was prevented from doing so.

F asked the mother for custody of their child and, when rebuffed, immediately (as soon as the child was born) went to court seeking legal custody. He continues to seek legal recognition of his parental rights. The record is clear that F did attempt through legal channels to shoulder full responsibility for his child.

We agree that the courts have the authority under this state's Uniform Parentage Act to grant custody to the natural father despite the mother's objection. In the present case, the superior court had the authority to grant F custody of his child so that he could qualify as a presumed father under Civil Code § 7004(a).

We [also] agree that a biological father has a constitutionally cognizable opportunity interest in developing a relationship with his child. However, it is clear that the Legislature meant to provide natural fathers with far less rights than both mothers and presumed fathers have under California's statutory system. The question is whether that distinction is constitutionally tenable.

F asserts a violation of equal protection and due process under the federal Constitution; more specifically, that he should not be treated differently from his child's mother. In constitutional terms, the question is whether California's sex-based statutory distinction between biological mothers and fathers serves "'. . . important governmental objectives and [is] substantially related to achievement of those objectives.'" Does the mother's ability to determine the father's rights substantially serve an important governmental interest?

The issue is whether the statutory treatment of natural fathers (i.e., biological fathers without presumed status under Civil Code § 7004) is substantially related to the achievement of that objective. On the facts of this case, the question must be framed as follows: Is the state's important interest in the well-being of a child born out of wedlock substantially furthered by allowing the mother to deny the child's biological father an opportunity to form a relationship with the child that would give the father the same statutory rights as the mother (or a presumed father) in deciding whether the child will be adopted by third parties?

We do not in our society take children away from their mothers--married or otherwise--because a "better" adoptive parent can be found. We see no valid reason why we should be less solicitous of a father's efforts to establish a parental relationship with his child. [In this case] the mother seeks to sever all ties with her child. The natural father, by contrast, has come forward to assume the legal and practical burdens of being a parent. Even if it could be said, either in general or in a particular case, that the mother somehow has a greater connection than the father with their child, and thus should have greater rights in the child, the same result need not obtain when she seeks to relinquish custody and to sever her legal ties with the child and the father seeks to assume his legal burdens.

In summary, we hold that Civil Code § 7004(a) and the related statutory scheme violates the federal constitutional guarantees of equal protection and due process for unwed fathers to the extent that the statutes allow a mother unilaterally to preclude her child's biological father from becoming a presumed father and thereby allowing the state to terminate his parental rights on nothing more than a showing of the child's best interest. If an unwed father promptly comes forward and demonstrates a full commitment to his

Chapter 34: Parentage

> parental responsibilities--emotional, financial, and otherwise--his federal constitutional right to due process prohibits the termination of his parental relationship absent a showing of his unfitness as a parent. Absent such a showing, the child's well-being is presumptively best served by continuation of the father's parental relationship. Similarly, when the father has come forward to grasp his parental responsibilities, his parental rights are entitled to equal protection as those of the mother.
>
> A court should consider all factors relevant to that determination. The father's conduct both before and after the child's birth must be considered. Once the father knows or reasonably should know of the pregnancy, he must promptly attempt to assume his parental responsibilities as fully as the mother will allow and his circumstances permit. In particular, the father must demonstrate "a willingness himself to assume full custody of the child--not merely to block adoption by others." A court should also consider the father's public acknowledgement of paternity, payment of pregnancy and birth expenses commensurate with his ability to do so, and prompt legal action to seek custody of the child.
>
> If the trial court finds on remand that F failed to demonstrate the required commitment to his parental responsibilities that will be the end of the matter. He will hot have suffered any deprivation of a constitutional right. If, however, the required commitment is found, the result under our constitutional analysis will necessarily be a decision that F's rights to equal protection and due process under the federal Constitution were violated to the extent that he was deprived of the same statutory protections granted the mother. Therefore, if (but only if) the trial court finds F demonstrated the necessary commitment to his parental responsibilities, there will arise the further question of whether he can be deprived of the right to withhold his consent to the adoption.
>
> In deciding this question, the trial court shall take into account (as it must also do on the threshold question of whether F assumed his parental responsibilities) F's conduct and circumstances up to and including the time of the decision on remand. The proper standard is whether he is now fit or unfit. For purposes of remand, we also note Civil Code § 232 (c), which states: "A finding pursuant to this section shall be supported by clear and convincing evidence." (Italics added.) Thus, any finding of F's unfitness must be supported by clear and convincing evidence. Absent such evidence, he shall be permitted to withhold his consent to the adoption.
>
> We reverse the judgment of the Court of Appeal with directions to remand to the superior court for further proceedings consistent with our decision.

The *Kelsey S.* case above set a precedent in the termination of parental rights by holding that if an unwed biological father promptly comes forward and demonstrates a full commitment to his parental responsibilities, including the child's well-being, the emotional and financial commitment and demonstrates that he has a willingness to assume full custody of the child, his federal constitutional right to due process prohibits the termination of his parental relationship, absent a showing of his unfitness as a parent. (See *In re JASON J.* (2009) 175 Cal.App.4th 922 at p. 931 where the court held that the father did not rise to the level of the father in *Kelsey S.*)

Notice in most cases must be given to the father before his parental rights are terminated. **FC § 7666(a)** provides that notice of the proceeding must be given to every person identified as the biological father or a possible biological father in accordance with the Code of Civil Procedure for the service of process in a civil action in this state at least ten (10) days before the date of the proceeding, except that publication or posting of the notice of the proceeding is not required, and service on the parent or guardian of a biological father or possible biological father who is a minor is not required unless the minor has previously provided written authorization to serve his or her parent or guardian. Proof of giving the notice must be filed with the court before the proceeding goes forward.

Notice is not required to be given to a man identified as, or alleged to be, the biological father, and the court must issue an order dispensing with notice to him under any of the following circumstances:

> **(1)** The relationship to the child has been previously terminated or determined not to exist by a court.
> **(2)** The alleged father has executed a written form to waive notice, deny his paternity, relinquish the child for adoption, or consent to the adoption of the child.
> **(3)** The whereabouts or identity of the alleged father are unknown or cannot be ascertained.
> **(4)** The alleged father has been served with written notice of his alleged paternity and the proposed adoption, and he has failed to bring an action pursuant to subdivision (c) of Section 7630 within 30 days of service of the notice or the birth of the child, whichever is later. FC § 7666(b).

If a mother relinquishes, or consents to, or proposes to relinquish or consent to, the adoption of a child who has a presumed parent under **FC § 7611**, the presumed parent must be given notice of the adoption proceeding unless that parent's relationship to the child has been previously terminated or determined by a court not to exist, or the presumed parent has voluntarily relinquished for or consented to the adoption of the child. **FC § 7660**. lg

If the other parent relinquishes or consents to, or proposes to relinquish or consent to, the adoption of a child, the mother must be given notice of the adoption proceeding unless the mother's relationship to the child has been previously terminated by a court or the mother has voluntarily relinquished for or consented to the adoption of the child. **FC § 7661**.

If a mother relinquishes or consents to, or proposes to relinquish or consent to, the adoption of a child, or if a child otherwise becomes the subject of an adoption proceeding, the agency or person to whom the child has been or is to be relinquished to, or the mother or person having physical or legal custody of the child, or the prospective adoptive parent, must file a petition to terminate the parental rights of the alleged father, unless one of the following occurs:

> **(1)** The alleged father's relationship to the child has been previously terminated or determined not to exist by a court.

Chapter 34: Parentage

> **(2)** The alleged father has been served as prescribed in Section 7666 with a written notice alleging that he is or could be the biological father of the child to be adopted or placed for adoption and has failed to bring an action for the purpose of declaring the existence of the father and child relationship pursuant to subdivision (c) of Section 7630 within 30 days of service of the notice or the birth of the child, whichever is later.
> **(3)** The alleged father has executed a written form developed by the department to waive notice, to deny his paternity, relinquish the child for adoption, or consent to the adoption of the child. FC § 7662(a).

An alleged father may validly execute a waiver or denial of paternity before or after the birth of the child, and, once signed, no notice of, relinquishment or consent to the adoption of the child is required from the alleged father for the adoption to proceed. **FC § 7662(b)**.

Any motion or petition for custody or visitation filed in a proceeding under this part must be stayed. The petition to terminate parental rights under this section is the only matter that may be heard during the stay until the court issues a final ruling on the petition. **FC § 7662(c).**

An action to terminate the parental rights of an alleged father of a child as specified in this part must be set for hearing not more than forty-five (45) days after filing of the petition, except as provided in **FC § 7667(c)** below. **FC § 7667(a)**.

Pursuant to **FC § 7667(c)**, a court may dispense with a hearing and issue an *ex parte* order terminating parental rights if any of the following applies:

> **(1)** The identity or whereabouts of the alleged father are unknown.
> **(2)** The alleged father has validly executed a waiver of the right to notice or a denial of paternity.
> **(3)** The alleged father has been served with written notice of his alleged paternity and the proposed adoption, and he has failed to bring an action pursuant to subdivision (c) of Section 7630 within 30 days of service of the notice or the birth of the child, whichever is later.

The court may continue the paternity proceedings for not more than thirty (30) days, as necessary to appoint counsel and to enable counsel to prepare for the case adequately or for other good cause. **FC § 7668(a)**.

In order to obtain an order for a continuance of the hearing, written notice must be filed within two court days of the date set for the hearing, together with affidavits or declarations detailing specific facts showing that a continuance is necessary, unless the court for good cause entertains an oral motion for continuance. **FC § 7668(b)**.

Continuances will be granted only upon a showing of good cause. Neither a stipulation between counsel, nor the convenience of the parties is in and of itself a good cause. **FC § 7668(c)**.

Chapter 34: Parentage

An order requiring or dispensing with an alleged father's consent for the adoption of a child may be appealed from in the same manner as an order of the juvenile court declaring a person to be a ward of the juvenile court and is conclusive and binding upon the alleged father. **FC § 7669(a).**

A court has no power to set aside, change or modify an order requiring or dispensing with the alleged father's consent. However, the order and/or judgment may be appealed. **FC § 7669.**

Attorney Fees

In any action brought to establish physical or legal custody of a child or a visitation order and/or any subsequent action, the court must ensure that each party has access to legal representation to preserve each party's rights by ordering one party to pay to the other party, or to the other party's attorney, whatever amount is reasonably necessary for attorney fees and for the cost of maintaining or defending the proceeding. **FC § 7605(a).**

In any initial or subsequent proceeding where custody of, or visitation with, a minor child is an issue, the court may, if it determines it would be in the best interests of the minor child, appoint private counsel to represent the interests of the minor. **FC § 7635(d).**

When a request for attorney fees and costs is made, the court must make findings on whether: **(1)** an award of attorney fees and costs is appropriate, **(2)** whether there is a disparity in access to funds to retain counsel, and **(3)** whether one party is able to pay for legal representation of both parties. If the findings demonstrate disparity in access and ability to pay, the court must make an order awarding attorney fees and costs. **FC § 7605(b).**

The party requesting that the other party pay his or her attorney fees must make a noticed motion so requesting. **FC § 7605(d).**

Finally, the court may order reasonable fees if a party lacks the financial ability to hire an attorney when there is a pro per litigant and the court finds that the other party has the financial ability to pay a reasonable amount to allow the unrepresented party to retain an attorney, the court may grant the unrepresented litigant's request in a timely manner before proceedings in the matter go forward. **FC § 7605 (b).** Further, a request can be made to augment a fee order.

Attorney fees and costs may also be awarded for legal services rendered or costs incurred before or after the commencement of counsel, experts, the child's guardian ad litem and other costs of the action and pretrial proceedings, including genetic

Chapter 34: Parentage

testing to be paid by the parties, excluding any governmental entity. The court may apply the standards set forth in **FC § 2032**[21] and **FC § 7605**[22]. **FC § 7640**.

---

[21] FC § 2030 provides:
(a)
(1) In a proceeding for dissolution of marriage, nullity of marriage, or legal separation of the parties, and in any proceeding subsequent to entry of a related judgment, the court shall ensure that each party has access to legal representation, including access early in the proceedings, to preserve each party's rights by ordering, if necessary based on the income and needs assessments, one party, except a governmental entity, to pay to the other party, or to the other party's attorney, whatever amount is reasonably necessary for attorney's fees and for the cost of maintaining or defending the proceeding during the pendency of the proceeding.
(2) When a request for attorney's fees and costs is made, the court shall make findings on whether an award of attorney's fees and costs under this section is appropriate, whether there is a disparity in access to funds to retain counsel, and whether one party is able to pay for legal representation of both parties. If the findings demonstrate disparity in access and ability to pay, the court shall make an order awarding attorney's fees and costs. A party who lacks the financial ability to hire an attorney may request, as an in pro per litigant, that the court order the other party, if that other party has the financial ability, to pay a reasonable amount to allow the unrepresented party to retain an attorney in a timely manner before proceedings in the matter go forward.
(b) Attorney's fees and costs within this section may be awarded for legal services rendered or costs incurred before or after the commencement of the proceeding.
(c) The court shall augment or modify the original award for attorney's fees and costs as may be reasonably necessary for the prosecution or defense of the proceeding, or any proceeding related thereto, including after any appeal has been concluded.
(d) Any order requiring a party who is not the spouse of another party to the proceeding to pay attorney's fees or costs shall be limited to an amount reasonably necessary to maintain or defend the action on the issues relating to that party.
(e) The Judicial Council shall, by January 1, 2012, adopt a statewide rule of court to implement this section and develop a form for the information that shall be submitted to the court to obtain an award of attorney's fees under this section.
[22] (a) In any proceeding to establish physical or legal custody of a child or a visitation order under this part, and in any proceeding subsequent to entry of a related judgment, the court shall ensure that each party has access to legal representation to preserve each party's rights by ordering, if necessary based on the income and needs assessments, one party, except a government entity, to pay to the other party, or to the other party's attorney, whatever amount is reasonably necessary for attorney's fees and for the cost of maintaining or defending the proceeding during the pendency of the proceeding.
(b) When a request for attorney's fees and costs is made under this section, the court shall make findings on whether an award of attorney's fees and costs is appropriate, whether there is a disparity in access to funds to retain counsel, and whether one party is able to pay for legal representation of both parties. If the findings demonstrate disparity in access and ability to pay, the court shall make an order awarding attorney's fees and costs. A party who lacks the financial ability to hire an attorney may request, as an in pro per litigant, that the court order the other party, if that other party has the financial ability, to pay a reasonable amount to allow the unrepresented party to retain an attorney in a timely manner before proceedings in the matter go forward.
(c) Attorney's fees and costs within this section may be awarded for legal services rendered or costs incurred before or after the commencement of the proceeding.
(d) The court shall augment or modify the original award for attorney's fees and costs as may be reasonably necessary for the prosecution or defense of a proceeding described in subdivision (a), or any proceeding related thereto, including after any appeal has been concluded.
(e) Except as provided in subdivision (f), an application for a temporary order making, augmenting, or modifying an award of attorney's fees, including a reasonable retainer to hire an attorney, or costs, or both, shall be made by motion on notice or by an order to show cause during the pendency of any proceeding described in subdivision (a).
(f) The court shall rule on an application for fees under this section within 15 days of the hearing on the motion or order to show cause. An order described in subdivision (a) may be made without notice by an oral motion in open court at either of the following times:

Chapter 34: Parentage

---
(1) At the time of the hearing of the cause on the merits.
(2) At any time before entry of judgment against a party whose default has been entered pursuant to Section 585 or 586 of the Code of Civil Procedure. The court shall rule on any motion made pursuant to this subdivision within 15 days and prior to the entry of any judgment.

CHART 13: Parentage Codes & Titles (Code No. Order)

Code §	Code Title
FC § 7540	Presumption arising from birth of child during marriage
FC § 7541	Use of blood (genetic) tests to determine parentage
FC § 7550	Uniform Act on Blood Tests to Determine Parentage
FC § 7551	Order for genetic testing in action involving parentage
FC § 7551.5	Facilitation of genetic tests
FC § 7552	Requirements for genetic testing
FC § 7553	Compensation of experts
FC § 7554	Finding of parentage
FC § 7555	ID as genetic parent; challenge to tests
FC § 7556	Limitation on application in criminal matters
FC § 7557	Right to produce other expert evidence
FC § 7558	Administrative order requiring genetic testing; Costs; Motion for relief
FC § 7570	Legislative findings and declaration
FC § 7571	Declaration of parentage
FC § 7572	Informational and training materials; Regulations
FC § 7573	Effect of declaration of parentage
FC § 7573.5	Voiding voluntary declaration of parentage
FC § 7574	Form for declaration of parentage
FC § 7575	Rescission of voluntary declaration of parentage; Setting aside declaration
FC § 7576	Presumption of parentage applicable to declarations signed on specified date
FC § 7577	Effect of declaration executed by minor parent
FC § 7600	Uniform Parentage Act
FC § 7601	"Natural parent" and "parent and child relationship"
FC § 7602	Relationship not dependent on marriage
FC § 7604	Pendente lite relief of custody or grant of visitation rights
FC § 7604.5	Bills for pregnancy, childbirth, and genetic testing as evidence
FC § 7605	Equal access to representation in custody and visitation proceedings; Attorney fees and costs; Disparity of income.
FC § 7606	Definitions: Assisted reproduction and Assisted reproduction agreement
FC § 7611	Presumption of parentage
FC § 7611.5	Prohibition on presumption of parentage

Chapter 34: Parentage

FC § 7612	Rebuttal of parentage presumption; Controlling presumption; Conflicts; Validity of voluntary declaration of parentage; refusal to sign or not sign is only a factor.
FC § 7613	Assisted reproduction procedure
FC § 7613.5	Optional statutory forms for assisted reproduction
FC § 7614	Promise to furnish support enforceable
FC § 7620	Sexual intercourse or conception in this state provides Jurisdiction; Venue
FC § 7630	Who may bring action and when; Consolidation of proceedings; Joinder of parties; Service; Notice of proceedings
FC § 7632	Agreement between alleged father or presumed parent and other parent or child does not bar action
FC § 7633	Action, order or judgment before birth of child
FC § 7634	Action by local child support agency; lg
FC § 7635	Parties
FC § 7635.5	Right to genetic testing; Right to move to set aside or vacate judgment
FC § 7636	Effect of judgment determining existence or nonexistence of parent and child relationship
FC § 7637	Judgment may contain provision for payment and parent to pay reasonable expenses of pregnancy
FC § 7638	Change of name of child
FC § 7639	Issuance of new birth certificate
FC § 7640	Award of attorney fees and other costs
FC § 7641	Enforcement of judgment
FC § 7642	Modification of judgment
FC § 7643	Confidentiality of hearings and records
FC § 7644	Action based on declaration; Effect of declaration
FC § 7645	Definitions: Child, Judgment, Previously established father and mother
FC § 7646	Motion challenging parentage judgment upon genetic testing showing non-parentage; Time limitations; Request for reconsideration
FC § 7647	Conditions for granting motion; Proof of service on specified persons required
FC § 7647.5	Guardian ad litem
FC § 7647.7	Genetic testing
FC § 7648	Denial of motion in best interests of child; Factors of consideration
FC § 7648.1	Statement on record after denial of motion
FC § 7648.3	Circumstances where setting aside or vacating judgment not allowed

Chapter 34: Parentage

FC § 7648.4	Vacating order of child support and arrearages
FC § 7648.8	Effect on adoption
FC § 7648.9	Child conceived by assisted reproduction or pursuant to surrogacy agreement
FC § 7649	No limitation on rights and remedies provided by other law
FC § 7649.5	Effect on distribution or payment made in good faith reliance on parentage judgment; Immunity from liability for such distribution or payment
FC § 7650	Action to determine mother and child relationship; Presumption
FC § 7660	Relinquishment or consent by mother; Notice to and rights of presumed parent
FC § 7660.5	Voluntary waiver of father's right to notice of adoption proceedings; Indian tribe Rights
FC § 7661	Relinquishment or consent by other parent; Notice to and rights of mother
FC § 7662	Proceeding to terminate parental rights of alleged father; Stay pending final determination; Domestic violence orders
FC § 7663	Effort to identify alleged father and presumed parent
FC § 7664	Notice to man identified as possible biological father; Determination and order concerning parental rights
FC § 7665	Order terminating parental rights of unknown biological father
FC § 7666	Manner of giving notice; Order dispensing with notice
FC § 7667	Setting hearing; Preference for trial; Issuance of *ex parte* order terminating parental rights
FC § 7668	Continuance only for good cause; stipulation or convenience not good cause
FC § 7669	Order requiring or dispensing with alleged father's consent; Appeal; Binding effect
FC § 7670	No filing fee for a FC § 7662 petition
FC § 7671	Petition to terminate parental rights of alleged father

© 2019 LW Greenberg

Chapter 34: Parentage

CHART 14: Parentage Family Codes (Alphabetical by Subject)

SUBJECT	CODE	Code *In Brief*
Adoption	7648.8	This article does not establish a basis for termination of any adoption.
Agreement	7632	Agreement between alleged father, presumed parent, other parent, child action not barred
Assisted Reproduction	7606	**Assisted reproduction:** conception by any means other than sexual intercourse. **Assisted reproduction agreement:** a written contract through assisted reproduction.
	7613	Assisted reproduction procedure
	7613.5	Optional statutory forms for assisted reproduction
	7648.9	Child conceived by assisted reproduction or pursuant to surrogacy agreement
Attorney Fees	7605	Equal access to representation in custody and visitation proceedings; Attorney fees
	7640	Award of attorney fees and other costs
Blood and Genetic Testing	7541	The notice of motion for blood tests may be filed not later than 2 years from child's DOB.
	7550	Uniform Act on Blood Tests to Determine Parentage
	7551	Upon motion of any party, the mother, child, and alleged father to submit to genetic tests.
	7551.5	All hospitals, local child support agencies, welfare offices, and family courts shall facilitate genetic tests for purposes of enforcement of this chapter.
	7552	A copy of all genetic tests shall be served upon all parties, no later than 20 days prior to any hearing in which the genetic test results may be admitted into evidence.
	7554	If the experts disagree in their findings the question shall be submitted upon the evidence.
	7558	Administrative order requiring genetic testing; Costs; Motion for relief; Additional test
	7604.5	Bills for pregnancy, childbirth, and genetic testing are admissible as evidence without third-party foundation testimony and constitute prima facie evidence of costs incurred.
	7635.5	If the alleged father is present in court, the court shall inform him of his right to have genetic testing and set aside a judgment of parentage within 2 years of the date of the notice of the action.
	7647.7	Genetic testing used to support a set aside or vacate must in accordance with FC § 7552.
Change Name	7638	The procedure to change the name of a minor or adult child for whom a parent and child relationship is established pursuant to FC § 7636.
Consent	7660	Relinquishment or consent by mother; Notice to and rights of presumed parent

645

Chapter 34: Parentage

	7660.5	Voluntary waiver of father's right to notice of adoption proceedings; Indian tribe Rights
	7661	Relinquishment or consent by other parent; Notice to and rights of mother
	7669	Order requiring or dispensing with alleged father's consent; Appeal; Binding effect
Custody and Visitation	7604	A court may order pendente lite relief consisting of a custody or visitation order, if tests have determined a parent & child relationship exists or in the best interests of child.
Declarations of Paternity/ Parentage	7571	On and after 1/1/1995, upon the event of a live birth the institution must provide to the natural mother and at the place of birth, to the man identified by the natural mother as the natural father, a voluntary declaration of parentage.
	7573	A completed voluntary declaration of parentage has the same force and effect as a judgment for parentage issued by a court of competent jurisdiction.
	7574	The voluntary declaration of parentage shall contain the following: (1) The name and the signature of the mother. (2) The name and the signature of the father. (3) The name of the child. (4) The date of birth of the child. (5) A statement by mother that she has read and understands the written materials. (6) A statement by the father that he has read and understands the written materials (7) Name and the signature of witnesses to the he signing of the declaration.
	7575	Rescission of voluntary declaration of parentage; Setting aside declaration. lg
	7577	(1) A voluntary declaration of parentage signed by a minor parent or minor parents does not establish parentage until 60 days after both parents are 18 or are emancipated. (2) The minor may rescind the voluntary declaration at any time up to 60 days after reaching the age of 18. (3) A voluntary declaration of parentage signed by a minor creates a rebuttable presumption of parentage until the date that it establishes parentage. (4) A voluntary declaration of parentage signed by a minor shall be admissible as evidence in any civil action to establish parentage of the minor named in the voluntary declaration.
	7644	The voluntary declaration of parentage shall be given the same force and effect as a judgment of parentage entered by a court of competent jurisdiction.
Definitions	7645	**Child**: child of a previously established father. **Judgment**: a judgment, order, or decree entered in a court of this state that establishes parentage, including a determination of parentage or a voluntary declaration of parentage.

Chapter 34: Parentage

		Previously established father means a person identified as the father of a child in a judgment that is the subject of a motion brought pursuant to this article. **Previously established mother** means a person identified as the mother of a child in a judgment that is the subject of a motion brought pursuant to this article.
Experts	7553	Experts appointed by the court shall be paid as the court determines and fixed at a reasonable amount.
	7557	Right to produce other expert evidence
Guardian ad Litem	7647.5	A guardian ad litem may be appointed for the child to represent the best interests of the child in an action brought pursuant to this article.
Identification	7663	Effort to identify alleged father and presumed parent
Judgments	7636	Effect of judgment determining existence or nonexistence of parent and child relationship
	7637	Judgment may contain provision for payment and parent to pay reasonable expenses of pregnancy
	7641	If there is a voluntary declaration of parentage in place the obligation of the parent may be enforced.
	7642	The court has continuing jurisdiction to modify or set aside a judgment or order made under this part.
	7648.3	Circumstances where setting aside or vacating judgment not allowed
Jurisdiction	7620	Sexual intercourse or conception in this state provides Jurisdiction; Venue
Legislature	7570	The Legislature finds and declares that there is a compelling state interest in establishing parentage for all children.
Limitation	7556	Limitation on application in criminal matters
Motions, Proceedings, Hearings and Orders	7643	A hearing or trial held under this part may be closed without admittance of any person other than those necessary to the action or proceeding
	7646	Motion challenging parentage judgment upon genetic testing showing non-parentage; Time limitations; Request for reconsideration
	7647	Conditions for granting motion; Proof of service on specified persons required
	7648	Denial of motion in best interests of child; Factors of consideration
	7648.1	Statement on record after denial of motion
	7662	Proceeding to terminate parental rights of alleged father; Stay pending final determination; Domestic violence orders
	7665	If, after the inquiry, the court is unable to identify the biological father the court shall enter an order terminating the unknown biological father's parental rights.
	7667	Setting hearing; Preference for trial; Issuance of order terminating parental rights
	7668	No continuances for more than 30 days to appoint counsel or for other good cause. Neither a stipulation between counsel nor convenience of the parties is a good cause.

Chapter 34: Parentage

New Birth Certificate	7639	If the judgment or order of the court is at variance with the child's birth certificate, the court shall order that a new birth certificate be issued.
Notice	7664	Notice to man identified as possible biological father; Determination and order concerning parental rights
	7666	Manner of giving notice; Order dispensing with notice
Parties	7635	The child may, if under the age of 12 years, and if 12 years of age or older, shall be made a party to the action. The natural parent, each person presumed to be a parent under FC § 7611, and each man alleged to be the natural father, may be made parties. The court may, if it determines it would be in the best interests of the minor child, appoint private counsel to represent the minor child.
Petitions and Actions	7630	Who may bring action and when; Consolidation of proceedings; Joinder of parties; Notice
	7633	An action may be brought, an order or judgment may be entered before the birth of the child, and enforcement of that order or judgment shall be stayed until the birth of the child.
	7634	Action by local child support agency; lg.
	7670	**No filing fee for a FC § 7662 petition**
	7671	Petition to terminate parental rights of alleged father
Presumptions	7540	Except as provided in FC § 7541, the child of a wife cohabiting with her husband, who is not impotent or sterile, is conclusively presumed to be a child of the marriage.
	7555	There is a rebuttable presumption if the court finds that the parentage index, as calculated by the experts qualified as examiners of genetic markers, is 100 or greater.
	7576	(1) The child of a woman and a man executing a declaration of parentage under this chapter is conclusively presumed to be the man's child. (2) A voluntary declaration of parentage shall be recognized as the basis for the establishment of an order for child custody or support. (3) In any action to rebut the presumption created, a voluntary declaration of parentage is admissible as evidence to determine parentage. (4) The presumption may be rebutted by requesting blood or genetic tests. (5) A presumption shall override all statutory presumptions of parentage.
	7611	A person is presumed to be the natural parent of a child if the person meets the conditions provided in FC § 7541 or in any of the following subdivisions: (1) The presumed parent and the child's natural mother are or have been married to each other and child was born during the marriage, or within 300 days before ended.

Chapter 34: Parentage

		(2) Before the child's birth, the presumed parent and natural mother attempted to marry. **(3)** After the child's birth, the presumed parent and natural mother have married, or attempted to marry, although the attempted marriage is or could be declared invalid. **(4)** The presumed parent receives the child into his or her home and openly holds out the child as his or her natural child. **(5)** The child is in utero after the death of the decedent.
	7611.5	A man shall not be presumed to be the natural father of a child if the child was conceived as a result of an act in violation of Penal Code § 261 and father was convicted of that violation; or the child was conceived as a result of an act in violation of PC § 261.5, the father was convicted of that violation, and mother was under the age of 15 years.
	7612	Rebuttal of parentage presumption; Controlling presumption; Conflicts; Validity of voluntary declaration of parentage; signing or not signing is only a factor to consider.
	7650	Any interested person may bring an action to determine the existence or nonexistence of a mother and child relationship.
Relationship	7601	**Natural parent**: a nonadoptive parent, whether biologically related to the child or not. **Parent and child relationship:** the legal relationship existing between a child and the child's natural or adoptive parent. This part does not preclude a finding that a child has **a parent and child relationship with more than two parents.**
Rights	7649	No limitation on rights and remedies provided by other law
Support	7614	Promise to furnish support enforceable
	7648.4	If the court grants a motion to set aside or vacate a parentage judgment, the court shall vacate any order for child support and arrearages issued on the basis of that previous judgment of parentage. The father has no right of reimbursement.
	7649.5	Effect on distribution or payment made in good faith reliance on parentage judgment; Immunity from liability for such distribution or payment
UPA	7600	Uniform Parentage Act

© 2019 LW Greenberg

EDUCATIONAL EXERCISES

Name the case that each paragraph briefly describes

This is a paternity action involving a married couple. Wife became pregnant in 2005 and gave birth to a daughter, A. At the time wife became pregnant, she and husband were living apart during the workweek but claim that they spent the weekends together. Wife had an affair with S.G. [during this time]. Wife separated from husband prior to the child's birth. Wife and S.G. executed a voluntary declaration of paternity or POP declaration about 90 minutes after the birth. Within 60 days, wife executed a rescission of the declaration after using her translator to figure out what it meant. S.G. admits receiving this rescission, although the proof of service is defective. Two weeks after A. was born, husband learned of her birth. He went to see her and husband and wife reconciled. Husband has accepted A. as his daughter. S.G. filed a petition to establish paternity and requested genetic testing. If it is determined he is the biological father, then he seeks visitation as well as support. Wife responded to S.G.'s action with a motion to quash the proceedings and a motion to set aside the POP. The trial court denied the former, but granted the latter under FC § 7575(c)(1). At the hearing, the trial court found that wife and husband had not been cohabiting at the time of conception and, thus, the conclusive presumption of paternity under FC § 7540 did not apply. It did find husband was a presumed father under FC § 7611(a) and (d).

The trial court reaffirmed its order for genetic testing under FC § 7575(c)(5) and husband and wife petitioned this court for a writ of supersedeas, mandate, or prohibition. Appellate court held that requiring the parties to undergo genetic testing would be burdensome and serve no useful purpose when there is no basis to recognize S.G. as a presumed father other than the POP declaration. As previously discussed, that declaration is voidable when executed by a married woman. Under the circumstances of this case, the trial court should have found it was void and of no effect, when it granted wife's motion to set it aside. **Name that Case**

Plaintiff and the mother of the child had an intimate sexual relationship which, according to plaintiff, began in December 2003. [They] were intimate in July 2009, when the child was conceived. At that time, plaintiff was married to another woman with whom he had two children, and the mother was living with and having sexual relations with R.M., who was named as father on the child's birth certificate. The child's mother (mother) had been living with R.M. since 2005. Mother discovered she was pregnant in August 2009. She thought R.M. was the father. She told plaintiff she was pregnant three months later. In late November 2009, she and plaintiff had testing done at the University of California at Los Angeles (UCLA) to determine if plaintiff was the father of the child. The results, received in December 2009, showed plaintiff was the father. In August 2011, the court found that both plaintiff and R.M. qualified as presumed fathers under FC § 7611(d). The court addressed the conflicting presumptions and the FC § 7611 requirement that "the presumption which on the facts is founded on the weightier considerations of policy

Chapter 34: Parentage

and logic controls." FC § 7611(b). The trial court found both plaintiff and R.M. to be presumed fathers under FC § 7611(d) and resolved the conflicting presumptions in plaintiff's favor. The issue is which father's presumption of paternity "on the facts is founded on the weightier considerations of policy and logic." FC § 7611(b). The court thought it was in the child's best interest to know his biological father, in circumstances where that father "did everything within his power to establish parentage. In the end, the court's determination must "give the greatest weight to [the child's] well-being" and that is what the court did. With plaintiff as the presumed father, the child will continue to have two loving families, both of which are currently a part of his life. If R.M. were found to be the presumed father, mother has left no doubt that plaintiff would have no part in the child's life. **Name that Case.**

In June 2012, appellant J filed a petition to establish a parental relationship with G, a child born to respondent D. in December 2009. D opposed the petition, arguing that Jason was a sperm donor under FC § 7613(b) and therefore was not G's natural father as a matter of law. J is not listed on G's birth certificate, and there is no voluntary declaration of paternity. Gus has no other natural, presumed, or potential biological father. J presented evidence that he and D tried to have a baby naturally beginning in 2006. In 2007, D had two intrauterine insemination (IUI) procedures using J's sperm, but neither resulted in a pregnancy. In October 2007, after being advised that their inability to conceive might be due to issues regarding J's sperm count, J had a surgical procedure to address that problem. She and J also began to look into having an IVF procedure. After having an unsuccessful IUI procedure in January 2009 using J's sperm, D decided to try an IVF procedure. On March 9, 2009, J took D to California Fertility Partners for the IVF procedure. The procedure was successful, and G was born in December 2009.Having found that J did not have a parent and child relationship with G, the trial court found J was not entitled to custody of, or visitation with, G, and vacated the pendente lite visitation order. Judgment was entered in favor of D, from which J appeals. We hold that FC § 7613(b should be interpreted only to preclude a sperm donor from establishing paternity based upon his biological connection to the child, and does not preclude him from establishing that he is a presumed parent under FC § 7611(d) based upon postbirth conduct. Our holding that a sperm donor is not precluded from establishing presumed parentage does not mean that a mother who conceives through assisted reproduction and allows the sperm donor to have some kind of relationship with the child necessarily loses her right to be the sole parent. **Name that Case**

Two days after the child's birth, F filed an action in superior court under Civil Code § 7006 to establish his parental relationship with the child and to obtain custody of the child. On May 24, 1988, the prospective adoptive parents, filed an adoption petition under Civil Code § 226 [alleging that only the mother's consent to the adoption was required because there was no presumed father under Civil Code § 7004(a). Seven days later, filed a petition under Civil Code § 7017 to terminate F's

Chapter 34: Parentage

parental rights.]

The parties subsequently stipulated that F was the child's natural father. The superior court, however, ruled that he was not a "presumed father" within the meaning of Civil Code § 7004(a)(4). The court held four days of hearings to determine whether it was in the child's best interest for F to retain his parental rights and whether the adoption should be allowed to proceed. On August 26, 1988, the court found "by a bare preponderance" of the evidence that the child's best interest required termination of F's parental rights. F appealed. He contended the superior court erred by: (1) concluding that he was not the child's presumed father; (2) not granting him a parental placement preference; and (3) applying a preponderance-of-the-evidence standard of proof. The Court of Appeal rejected each of his contentions and affirmed the judgment. In summary, we hold that Civil Code § 7004(a) and the related statutory scheme violates the federal constitutional guarantees of equal protection and due process for unwed fathers to the extent that the statutes allow a mother unilaterally to preclude her child's biological father from becoming a presumed father and thereby allowing the state to terminate his parental rights on nothing more than a showing of the child's best interest. If an unwed father promptly comes forward and demonstrates a full commitment to his parental responsibilities--emotional, financial, and otherwise--his federal constitutional right to due process prohibits the termination of his parental relationship absent a showing of his unfitness as a parent. Absent such a showing, the child's well-being is presumptively best served by continuation of the father's parental relationship. Similarly, when the father has come forward to grasp his parental responsibilities, his parental rights are entitled to equal protection as those of the mother. **Name that Case.**

Match the sentence with the word/phrase/code/term

1. Child
2. Previously established father
3. Conclusive marital presumption
4. Judgment
5. FC § 7552

_____A decree entered in a court that establishes parentage
_____A person identified as the father of a child in a judgment
_____Genetic testing
_____A child of a previous established father
_____A child of spouses who cohabited at time of conception and birth

CHAPTER 35: Minors

In Brief...

A MINOR:
- Is an individual under the age of 18, **FC § 6500**;
- Becomes an adult the first minute of his or her 18th birthday; this is called the **birthday rule**, **FC § 6501**.

COOGAN'S LAW, FC § 6752:
- Is a trust account;
- That was named after the childhood actor Jackie Coogan;
- It provides that 15% of a minor's earnings must be placed into a Coogan Trust Account, **FC § 6753**; and
- Provides that at least one of the parents must be the trustee of the account, **FC § 6752**.

MINORS MAY ENTER INTO CONTRACTS:
- For employment to render artistic or creative services;
- For employment to render services as a player in a sport; and/or
- To purchase, sell, lease or license for use in motion pictures, television or production of sound recordings. **FC § 6750**.

MEDICAL TREATMENT:
- A minor can consent to medical treatment under certain conditions, **FC § 6922**.
- Sterilization and abortion require the consent of the minor's parent, guardian or the court, **FC § 6925**.

PARENT'S RIGHTS:
- Both parents are equally entitled to the services and earnings of their child, **FC § 7500**.
- An employer must pay a minor's earnings to a parent if so noticed by the parent, **FC § 7503**.
- Parental authority ends when a guardian is appointed, the minor marries or the minor turns 18 years old, **FC § 7505**.

A MINOR MAY PETITION FOR DECLARATION OF EMANCIPATION IF:
- The minor is at least 14 years of age;
- The minor willingly lives separate and apart from his or her parents with their consent;
- The minor is managing his or her own financial affairs; and
- The Minor's income is not from an illegal source, **FC § 7120**.

A MINOR CAN BE DECLARED FREE FROM PARENTAL CUSTODY/CONTROL:
- If the child is abandoned, **FC § 7822**;
- If the child is neglected or cruelly treated, **FC § 7823**;
- If the parent or parents suffer a disability because of the habitual use of alcohol or any controlled substances, **FC § 7824**;
- If the parent or parents are convicted of a felony, **FC § 7825**;

Chapter 35: Minors

> - If the parent or parents have been declared to be developmentally disabled or mentally ill, **FC § 7826**; and
> - If so declared, all parental rights are permanently severed/terminated, FC § 7893.

Introduction

"A minor is an individual who is under 18 years of age. The period of minority is calculated from the first minute of the day on which the individual is born to the same minute of the corresponding day completing the period of minority." **FC § 6500**. This is called the **birthday rule**. When the minor reaches his or her majority, he or she becomes an **adult**. **FC § 6501**.

Before March 4, 1972, a minor was an individual who was under 21 years of age. **FC § 6502**.

Minors and Contracts

A minor may enter into a valid contract in the manner as an adult, subject to the power of disaffirmance. However, a minor cannot: **(1)** give a delegation of power; **(2)** make a contract relating to real property or any interest therein; or **(3)** make a contract relating to any personal property not in the immediate possession or control of the minor. **FC § 6701**.

A minor can enter into a contract:

1. For employment to render artistic or creative services;[1]
2. For employment to render services as a player in a sport; and/or
3. To purchase, sell, lease or license for use in motion pictures, television or production of sound recordings. **FC § 6750**.

A contract entered into by a minor may be disaffirmed by the minor before his or her majority or within a reasonable time afterwards or, in case of the minor's death, within that period by the minor's heirs or personal representative. **FC § 6710**.

In *RIMES v. CURB RECORDS, INC.* (2001) 129 F.Supp.2d 984, Singer LeAnn Rimes filed an action in Texas requesting that the court declare the contract void that she entered into with Curb Records, Inc., when she was 12 years old. This contract contained a forum clause in Section 7(e), which provided:

> This agreement shall be construed in accordance with the laws of the State of Tennessee applicable to agreements entered into and to be wholly performed therein. Any and all actions, proceedings or claims relative to this agreement shall be brought before a court of

---

[1] Artistic or creative services includes services as an actor, actress, dancer, musician, comedian, singer, stunt-person, voice-over artist or other performer or entertainer, or as a songwriter, musical producer or arranger, writer, director, producer, production executive, choreographer, composer, conductor, or designer.

Chapter 35: Minors

> competent jurisdiction in Davidson County and the courts sitting in the State of Tennessee shall have exclusive jurisdiction over all disputes hereunder.

Ms. Rimes' argument was that because she was eighteen (18) years old, she has right to disaffirm her contract with Curb. Since she was disaffirming her contract, it became void so that the forum selection clause was without effect. Curb Records replied, requesting that either the case be dismissed or transferred to Tennessee because of the forum selection clause. The court denied Ms. Rimes' request to disaffirm, denied Curb Records' request to dismiss the case and granted Curb Records' request to transfer the case. The opinion by Judge Jerry Buchmeyer, in the case that follows was written in rhyme.

> ***MARGARET LEANN RIMES, Plaintiff, vs. CURB RECORDS, INC. and LEANN RIMES ENTERTAINMENT, INC., Defendant.***
> UNITED STATES DISTRICT COURT FOR THE NORTHERN DISTRICT OF TEXAS, DALLAS DIVISION
> 129 F.Supp.2d 984
> January 10, 2001, Decided
> (*Rimes v. Curb Records*)
>
> **MEMORANDUM OPINION AND ORDER**
>
> Plaintiff Margaret LeAnn Rimes ("LeAnn Rimes" or "Ms. Rimes") seeks a declaratory judgment against Defendant Curb Records Inc. ("Curb") to disaffirm a recording contract she entered into as a minor on April 27, 1995. This Court has diversity jurisdiction pursuant to 28 U.S.C.A. § 1332. Now before this Court is Defendant's Motion to Dismiss, or in the alternative. Motion to Transfer Venue, pursuant to Rule 12(b) of the Federal Rules of Civil Procedure and 28 U.S.C. § 1404(a) and § 1406. For the reasons stated below, Defendant's Motion to Dismiss is **DENIED** and its Motion to Transfer Venue is **GRANTED**.
>
> **STATEMENT OF FACTS**
> **(To be sung to the tune of LeAnn Rimes, "How Do I Live." & (r) 1997 Curb Records, Inc.)**
>
> LeAnn Rimes
> A very rich and famous star
> Wasn't so rich in times afar
> But what a talent she had!
> Enter Curb[2]
> To sign a contract, they hoped
> After her talent they scoped
> They saw the cash in her eyes
> But LeAnn
> Who at twelve was hardly dumb herself
> Wanted to retain her future wealth
> Oh
> If you could have seen
> Baby those attorneys changed everything

---

[2] Repeat Verse One Instrumental for this section.

Chapter 35: Minors

But so many lines!
They missed one thing.

CHORUS # 1:
Why did you sign, LeAnn Rimes?[3]
So long ago
Off on that choice of forum?[4]
Your attorneys didn't know?
They made lots of changes, but one thing survived....
Forum clause, to that clause, what weight do we give?

INSTRUMENTAL INTERLUDE

VERSE # 3:
Many times
Back and forth from judge to attorney
Both in Texas and in Tennessee
There was so much to review.
And LeAnn
With a guardian to oversee
She disavowed her own minority
Oh
Now she believes
Her age will invalidate everything[5]
She ever signed
We must decide

CHORUS # 2:
How do we read the forum clause?
Binding or no?
How could she see, at age twelve
Or truly know
That the Curb-Rimes relations, would never survive?
Forum clause, to that clause, how much weight do we give?

LEGAL ANALYSIS
(To be sung to the tune of LeAnn Rimes, "I Need You" (r) 2000, Curb Records, Inc.)
The law ain't clear on lots of things
Sometimes it tells you nothing
To their arguments the parties cling
You never know what motions bring
But we've got all we need to decide on this venue

Forum selection clauses, they point us towards the truth

---

[3] On April 27, 1995, Ms. Rimes entered into a recording contract with Defendant Curb Records, Inc.
[4] As neither party disputes, the recording contract contains a forum selection clause.
[5] In response to Curb's Motion to Dismiss or Transfer, Ms. Rimes' foremost argument is that the contract is void because she signed it as a minor, and that she has the absolute right to disaffirm the contract, and all the provisions within, if she does not ratify it after reaching majority. This Court acknowledges that under Texas law, this presumption is generally true.

Chapter 35: Minors

CHORUS # 1:
That Venue! A clause, clear to all to see
That Venue! It says "go to Tennessee."
There's a freedom of contract, that carries on to
The Venue

VERSE # 2:
State courts never liked these things
They never found them valid
But revolution the High Court can bring
Changed that policy -- the High Court did
They first upheld a forum clause, in admiralty
Then they pushed the holding, to cases in diversity

CHORUS # 2:
Then came Shute! Slip- and-fall, while on a cruise
That darn Shute! Filed in Washington, they lose
The ticket said "you come to Florida, if you want a suit"
That darn Shute

VERSE # 3:
Now LeAnn has arguments
That there's a balancing of interests
That her case has a twisted bent
That her minor status ends this mess
But minority can't void this clause before the case is tried[6]
And the Fifth Circuit has spoken, balancing tests won't fly

CHORUS # 3:
Through and through! Mitsui[7] Amplicon[8], Kessmann[9]
Require proof! She's not met the burden.

While there's freedom as a judge, re-inventing the rule
I won't do.

---

[6] Ms. Rimes' main argument in response to Curb's transfer motion is that the entire contract, including the forum clause, is void because she entered into it as a minor. However, until and unless she successfully voids the declaratory order of the Tennessee Chancery Court disaffirming her minor status on July 5, 1995, this Court must afford full faith and credit to the judgment of that court. For the purposes of determining venue at this early stage in the litigation, this Court will not adjudicate this case on the merits before the order removing the disability of Rimes' minority is properly challenged in the Tennessee state court system. As this Court does not yet view Rimes as a minor at the time the contract was signed, her defense of minority fails, and the proper weight to afford this particular forum selection clause under § 1404(a) is the only remaining legal issue.

[7] In *Mitsui & Co. Inc. v. Mira M/V*, 111 F.3d 33, 35 (5th Cir. 1997) the Supreme Court held that forum selection clauses are presumptively valid…the burden of proving unreasonableness [in a forum selection clause] is a heavy one.

[8] Federal courts are required to give full effect to the final judgment of state courts, subject only to narrowly circumscribed areas of collateral attack. *Midessa Television Co. v. Motion Pictures for Television* (1961) 290 F.2d 203 (5th Cir. 1961).

[9] *Kessmann and Associates Inc. v. Barton-Aschman Associates, Inc*, 10 F. Supp.2d 682, 688, (S.D. Tex. 1997), "Valid forum selection clauses must receive controlling consideration 'in all but the most exceptional cases."

Chapter 35: Minors

> **CONCLUSION**
> (Also to be sung to the tune of LeAnn Rimes, "How Do I Live." & (r) 1997, Curb Records, Inc.
>
> How Do I
> Deem this forum the right place
> If I were to sit and hear this case
> What kind of judge would I be?
> Although I
> Would love to meet LeAnn Rimes
> It's gonna have to be another time.
> Oh
> This case must now leave
> Baby you must take away everything
> Away from my court
> I order now
>
> **CHORUS:**
> This case now lives in Tennessee
> Following Ricoh
> The Middle District of Tennessee
> Not because I say so.
> 'Cause forum clauses forever, ever survive!
> 'Cause that's the way, that's the way, that's the way the law is.
>
> **IT IS SO ORDERED**[10]

The case was then transferred to Tennessee.[11] A contract, otherwise valid, entered into by a minor may not be disaffirmed during his or her minority, or at any time thereafter, if all of the following requirements are satisfied:

> [1] The contract is to pay the reasonable value of things necessary for the support of the minor or the minor's family.
> [2] These things have been actually furnished to the minor or to the minor's family.
> [3] The contract is entered into by the minor when not under the care of a parent or guardian able to provide for the minor or the minor's family. FC § 6712.

The Coogan Trust Account/Coogan's Law

The case that follows explains Coogan's Law, why it is so named, why it was enacted and how it is to be applied.

> *JASMINE PHILLIPS, as Trustee, etc., et al., Plaintiffs and Appellants, v. BANK OF AMERICA, N.A., Defendant and Respondent.*

---

[10] Credit for both the words and the lyrics in this opinion go entirely to Judge Buchmeyer's law clerk, Elizabeth Falk, a devoted LeAnn Rimes fan.
[11] After the case was transferred to Tennessee, the judge that heard the matter denied Ms. Rimes' request to set aside the contract. She appealed. Thereafter, Ms. Rimes and Curb Records reached an agreement whereby she signed another recording contract with Curb Records and dismissed her appeal.

COURT OF APPEAL OF CALIFORNIA, SECOND APPELLATE DISTRICT, DIVISION FIVE
236 Cal.App.4th 217
April 27, 2015, Opinion Filed
(*Phillips v. Bank of America*)

We hold that a bank may not for account service fees debit a so-called "Coogan Trust Account"—a statutorily required account to preserve 15 percent of a minor's gross earnings for artistic or creative services for the benefit of the minor until the minor turns 18 or is emancipated) (Coogan Law)—because of the statutory ban on withdrawals from a Coogan Trust Account without court approval. [FC § 6753(b)] Such a debit, without court approval, is a prohibited withdrawal under the applicable state statute, and that state law prohibition on a debit by a national bank is not preempted by federal law. We therefore reverse the judgment entered on a demurrer sustained without leave to amend.

FACTUAL AND PROCEDURAL BACKGROUND

Plaintiffs and appellants Jasmine Phillips, also known as Jasmine Gonzales (Phillips), as trustee for Alex Gonzales, and Anesha L. Colemen, as trustee for Jadon I. Monroe, filed a class action lawsuit on behalf of themselves and all others similarly situated against defendant and respondent Bank of America, N.A., a national bank association.

Plaintiffs breach of written contract, breach of the implied covenant of good faith and fair dealing, conversion, and unlawful and unfair business practices. Plaintiffs alleged that they were "the parents or guardians of unemancipated minors who have been paid for performing artistic or creative services."

Plaintiffs alleged that, as trustees for their minor children, they "opened accounts entitled 'Coogan Trust' Accounts for the minors at [defendant] in full compliance with ... [FC § 6750 et seq.] [(the Coogan Law)]. From time to time, wages or other monies earned by the minors for performing artistic services were deposited into Plaintiffs' Coogan Trust Accounts for the benefit of the minors. ... During the four years preceding the filing of the initial Complaint in this action, defendant[] ha[s] made withdrawals from Plaintiffs' Coogan Trust Accounts, including but not limited to withdrawals for monthly service fees, without court approval."

[Plaintiffs allege] that they entered into written agreements with defendant [pursuant to which defendant agreed to open and maintain ... Coogan Trust Accounts ... . Notwithstanding these written agreements ... defendant regularly and systematically breached these agreements by making withdrawals from the Coogan Trust Accounts, including but not limited to monthly service charges, without court approval.]

[Additionally plaintiffs allege that despite defendant's representations that defendant would open and maintain the subject accounts as Coogan Trust Accounts, defendant unlawfully took and converted monies from the Coogan Trust Accounts for monthly service charges. Defendant, thus, failed to maintain the accounts as Coogan Trust Accounts.]

Plaintiffs sought as relief compensatory damages, issuance of a temporary restraining order and a preliminary and permanent injunction, disgorgement of all profits resulting, punitive damages, costs of suit, attorney fees, and such other and further relief as the trial court might deem just and proper.

Chapter 35: Minors

The trial court sustained defendant's demurrer to plaintiffs' complaint without leave to amend, finding that the term "withdrawal" as used in the Coogan Law did not include the debiting of an account by a financial institution for service charges. The trial court thereafter entered a final judgment of dismissal, and plaintiffs filed a timely notice of appeal.

The parties have confirmed that the issue on appeal is whether the Coogan Law precludes defendant from debiting the Coogan Trust Accounts for account service fees, including whether the debits by defendant are withdrawals under the Coogan Law and if so whether the state law that has the effect of banning such debits by a national bank is preempted by federal law.

DISCUSSION
The history of the Coogan Law has been summarized in legislative documents. "The Coogan Law was enacted in 1938 in response to childhood star Jackie Coogan's plight. Even though he earned millions as a child, Coogan was surprised to find out when he reached adulthood that he was flat broke, because his mother and stepfather spent all his money—legally. ...

Thus, the Coogan Law was passed in order to preserve a portion of the minor's earnings for the minor's use when he or she reaches the age of majority." Inadequacies in the statutory scheme, however, resulted in additional abuses of the finances of such child-actors as Shirley Temple, Macauly Culkin, Lee Aaker, and Gary Coleman—whose parents left the minors with at best only a small percentage of what they earned during their careers [and the] Legislature amended the Coogan Law in 1999, 2003, and 2013 [accordingly].

As relevant to this case, the Coogan Law provides that for a contract pursuant to which a minor is employed or agrees to render artistic or creative services, the minor's employer must set aside 15 percent "of the minor's gross earnings pursuant to the contract" in trust "in an account or other savings plan, and preserved for the benefit of the minor." [FC § 6752(b)(1)] At least one of the minor's parents or legal guardians must "be appointed as trustee of the funds," unless the superior court determines that the appointment "of a different individual, individuals, entity, or entities" is required in the best interests of the minor. [FC § 6752(b)(2),(c)(1)]

The Coogan Law provides that within seven business days after execution of the contract, the trustee must establish a trust account, "known as a Coogan Trust Account," at a "bank, savings and loan institution, credit union, brokerage firm, or company registered under the Investment Company Act of 1940, that is located in the State of California." [FC § 6753(a)] Within 15 business days after receiving [the necessary documents, the minor's employer must deposit into the Coogan Trust Account "15 percent of the minor's gross earnings pursuant to the contract." [FC § 6752(b)(4),(c)(3)] The parent or guardian "acting in his or her fiduciary relationship, shall, with the earnings and accumulations of the minor under the contract, pay all liabilities incurred by the minor under the contract, including, but not limited to, payments for taxes on all earnings, including taxes on the amounts set aside under [FC §6752(b) and (c) ... ." [FC §6752(d)] As 15 percent of the gross earnings is deposited in the Coogan Trust Account, it follows that these liabilities would be payable out of the remaining 85 percent of the earnings.

Chapter 35: Minors

Plaintiffs assert that defendant, without written orders of the superior court, debited Coogan Trust Accounts for account service fees, thereby violating the prohibition against withdrawals from Coogan Trust Accounts. Defendant contends that such debits are not withdrawals and that even if they were, any state law that prohibits such debits is preempted by federal law, which permits the imposition of account service fees and precludes the application of state law that prevents or significantly interferes with a national bank's exercise of its powers.

[FC § 6753(b)] prohibits the "withdrawal" of funds on deposit in a Coogan Trust Account by the beneficiary "or any other individual, individuals, entity, or entities," without court approval. Defendant contends that its "debit" of a Coogan Trust Account for account service fees is not a "withdrawal" of funds, and the use of the phrase "any other individual, individuals, entity, or entities" shows that the ban on withdrawals is meant only "to reach trustees—a parent or guardian or other individual or entity—who are responsible for managing and controlling a child-actors' earnings." [However, when] a bank debits an account, it necessarily withdraws money from that account.

Moreover, courts have used the word "withdrawal" to include a bank's debiting an account for, or charging, a service fee or charge. The purpose of the Coogan Trust Account is for the "preserving for the benefit of the minor [15 percent] of the minor's gross earnings" until the minor reaches majority. [FC § 6753(a)] Preserving the gross amount of earnings contemplates no deductions for taxes or fees of any kind without court approval.

Defendant reads the statute to mean that its prohibition on withdrawals applies only to the minor and his or her parents, guardians, and trustees and not to others, such as banks. Under this reading, as defendant concedes, others could execute on the amounts in the Coogan Trust Account or otherwise lawfully obtain portions of what is supposed to be protected monies, which actions are inconsistent with the purpose of a Coogan Trust Account.

[FC § 6753(b)] specifies that prior to the time the minor becomes 18 years old or is emancipated, "no withdrawal by the beneficiary or any other individual, individuals, entity, or entities may be made of funds on deposit in trust without written order of the superior court ... ." (Italics added.) Thus, the statute explicitly provides that the withdrawal prohibition is not limited to the beneficiary, parent, or trustee.

Defendant argues that as only beneficiaries (minors through their guardians), trustees, parents, and guardians can petition for an order amending or terminating the trust [FC § 6752(b)(7), (c)(5)]; they are the only ones who can seek an order permitting a withdrawal from the Coogan Trust Account and thus the restriction on withdrawals only applies to them—not to third parties. That those with a fiduciary duty can seek to amend or terminate the trust does not mean that a third party without such a fiduciary duty cannot seek court approval to withdraw funds from the trust or that the restriction on withdrawals does not apply to such third parties.

If a parent, guardian, or trustee does not timely supply the employers with [the appropriate documents] establishing the Coogan Trust Account, the minor's employer must forward to The Actors' Fund of America the 15 percent of the minor's gross earnings. [FC § 6752(b)(9)(A), (c)(7)(A).] The Actors' Fund of America then becomes the trustee of such funds. The Legislature specifically provided that the Actors' Fund of

America "may assess and deduct from the balance in the beneficiary's account reasonable management, administrative, and investment expenses." [FC § 6752(f)(2)]

Thus, when a withdrawal for charges from a minor's trust account is permissible, the Legislature specifically provided for it. No such authorization is given to a depository bank. For all of these reasons, by debiting the Coogan Trust Accounts, defendants have made impermissible withdrawals from those accounts.

Plaintiffs alleged that although defendant entered into contracts and otherwise represented "that the subject accounts would be opened and maintained as 'Coogan Trust Accounts,'" it "failed to maintain the accounts as Coogan Trust Accounts and instead ... made withdrawals from these accounts, including but not limited to 'monthly service charges,' without court approval." Defendant asserts that the application of the Coogan Law (specifically, [FC § 6753(b)] to prevent its debits is preempted by federal law. We disagree.

The Coogan Law is a "State consumer financial law." It does not discriminate against national banks; it provides that a withdrawal from a Coogan Trust Account may not be made by anyone. [FC § 6753(b)].

There has been no determination of preemption by the OCC[12] of the state law involved here. Moreover, the regulation authorizing account service charges does not purport to preempt any state restriction on the method of obtaining bank fees for accounts such as Coogan Trust Accounts. National banks are authorized to "charge" their customers noninterest fees, including deposit account service charges. (12 C.F.R. § 7.4002(a) (2015).)

The OCC regulation (12 C.F.R. § 7.4002(a) (2015)) does not provide that the account service fees must be taken from a trust account or any specific account. The regulation merely provides that a bank is authorized to "charge" for the fees.

Plaintiffs' claims are premised on the theory that withdrawing account service fees from the Coogan Trust Accounts without court approval is inconsistent with the accounts being Coogan Trust Accounts. Plaintiffs do not challenge defendant's right to "charge" the fee. The account service fees may be charged to the parent or guardian, at least one of whom must be the trustee [FC § 6752(b)(1),(2)], and may be paid from the nontrust fund assets that are the source from which all other liabilities incurred by the minors under the employment contracts, including taxes, are paid. [FC § 6752(d)] If a trustee prefers that the fee be taken out of the Coogan Trust Account, or defendant federal bank desires to debit the Coogan Trust Account, either may seek court approval for such a withdrawal. [FC § 6753(b)].

As noted, by contrast, in the case of The Actors' Fund of America acting as trustee for the funds because the trustee failed to provide timely the minor's employer with a copy of the trustee's statement pursuant to [FC § 6753] the State Legislature specifically stated that The Actors' Fund of America "may assess and deduct from the balance in the beneficiary's account reasonable management, administrative, and investment expenses ..." [FC § 6752(f)(2)] Here, the Coogan Law's restriction on withdrawals does not

---

[12] Office of the Comptroller of the Currency, which is charged with assuring the safety and soundness of and compliance with laws and regulations, fair access to financial services and fair treatment of customers by the institutions and other persons subject to its jurisdiction.

> "prevent or significantly interfere with" the exercise by a national bank of its power. Accordingly, [FC § 6753(b)] is not preempted by federal law.
>
> **DISPOSITION**
> The judgment is reversed.

Coogan's Law requires that fifteen (15) percent of a minor's gross earnings pursuant to his or employment contract be set aside by the minor's employer. The amounts set aside must be in trust, in an account or other savings plan and preserved for the benefit of the minor in accordance with **FC § 6753**. **FC § 6752(b)**.

The court requires that at least one parent or legal guardian entitled to the physical custody, care and control of the minor be appointed as trustee of the funds ordered to be set aside in trust for the benefit of the minor, "unless the court shall determine that appointment of a different individual, individuals, entity or entities as trustee or trustees is required in the best interests of the minor." **FC § 6752(b)(2).** The trust account is entitled and known as a **Coogan Trust Account**.

Prior to the date on which the beneficiary of the trust attains the age of eighteen (18) years or the issuance of a declaration of emancipation of the minor under **FC § 7122**, no withdrawal by the beneficiary or any other individual, individuals, entity or entities may be made of funds on deposit in trust without written order of the superior court. Upon reaching the age of 18 years, the beneficiary may withdraw the funds on deposit in trust only after providing a certified copy of the beneficiary's birth certificate to the financial institution where the trust is located. **FC § 6753(b)**.

The trust must be established in California, either with a financial institution that is and remains insured at all times by the Federal Deposit Insurance Corporation (FDIC), the Securities Investor Protection Corporation (SIPC) or the National Credit Union Share Insurance Fund (NCUSIF) or their respective successors, or with a company that is and remains registered under the Investment Company Act of 1940.

The trustee or trustees of the trust must be the only individual, individuals, entity or entities with the obligation or duty to ensure that the funds remain in trust, in an account or other savings plan insured in accordance with this section or with a company that is and remains registered under the Investment Company Act of 1940, as authorized by this section. **FC § 6753**.

The court has continuing jurisdiction over the trust account established pursuant to the order and may, at any time, order that the trust be amended or terminated. **FC § 6752(b)(7)**.

Medical Treatment

The **FC §§ 6901-6903** set forth the following definitions:

Chapter 35: Minors

Dental care means X-ray examination, anesthetic, dental or surgical diagnosis or treatment, and hospital care by a dentist licensed under the Dental Practice Act.

Medical care means X-ray examination, anesthetic, medical or surgical diagnosis or treatment, and hospital care under the general or special supervision and upon the advice of or to be rendered by a physician and surgeon licensed under the Medical Practice Act.

Parent or guardian means either parent if both parents have legal custody, or the parent or person having legal custody, or the guardian, of a minor.

A parent or guardian of a minor who is a relative of the minor and who may authorize medical care and dental care under **FC § 6550** may authorize in writing an adult into whose care a minor has been entrusted to consent to medical care or dental care, or both, for the minor. **FC § 6910**.

A minor may consent to medical or dental care if he or she is 15 years of age or older, living separate and apart from his or her parents or guardian, whether with or without the consent of a parent or guardian and regardless of the duration of the separate residence and is managing his or her own financial affairs, regardless of the source of the minor's income. **FC § 6922(a)**.

> A physician and surgeon or dentist may, with or without the consent of the minor patient, advise the minor's parent or guardian of the treatment given or needed if the physician and surgeon or dentist has reason to know, on the basis of the information given by the minor, the whereabouts of the parent or guardian. FC § 6922.

> **(1) Mental health treatment or counseling** services means the provision of mental health treatment or counseling on an outpatient basis by any of the following:
> (A) A governmental agency.
> (B) A person or agency having a contract with a governmental agency to provide the services.
> (C) An agency that receives funding from community united funds.
> (D) A runaway house or crisis resolution center.
> (E) A professional person, as defined in paragraph (2). FC § 6924(1).

Pursuant to **FC § 6924(a)(2)**, a **professional person** is any of the following:

> (A) A person designated as a mental health professional in Sections 622 to 626, inclusive, of Article 8 of Subchapter 3 of Chapter 1 of Title 9 of the California Code of Regulations.
> (B) A marriage and family therapist as defined in Chapter 13 (commencing with B & P Code § 4980.
> (C) A licensed educational psychologist as defined in Article 5 (commencing with B & P Code § 4986.
> (D) A credentialed school psychologist as described in Education Code § 49424.
> (E) A clinical psychologist as defined in Health and Safety Code § 1316.5.
> (F) The chief administrator of an agency referred to in paragraph (1) or (3).
> (G) A person registered as an associate marriage and family therapist intern, as defined in Chapter 13 (commencing with B & P Code § 4980. while working under the

Chapter 35: Minors

> supervision of a licensed professional specified in B & P Code § 4980.03(g).
> (H) A licensed professional clinical counselor, as defined in Chapter 16 (commencing with B & P Code § 4999.10.
> (I) A person registered as an associate professional clinical counselor, as defined in Chapter 16 (commencing with B & P Code § 4999.10, while working under the supervision of a licensed professional specified in B & P Code § 4999.12(h).

> The mental health treatment or counseling of a minor authorized by this section shall include involvement of the minor's parent or guardian unless, in the opinion of the professional person who is treating or counseling the minor, the involvement would be inappropriate. The professional person who is treating or counseling the minor shall state in the client record whether and when the person attempted to contact the minor's parent or guardian, and whether the attempt to contact was successful or unsuccessful, or the reason why, in the professional person's opinion, it would be inappropriate to contact the minor's parent or guardian. FC § 6924(d).

"A minor may consent to medical care related to the prevention or treatment of pregnancy." **FC § 6925**. However, **FC § 6925** does not authorize a minor **(1)** to be sterilized without the consent of the minor's parent or guardian or **(2)** to receive an abortion without the consent of a parent or guardian other than as provided in **Health and Safety Code § 123450**.

Health and Safety Code § 123450 provides in pertinent part:

> **(a)** Except in a medical emergency requiring immediate medical action, no abortion shall be performed upon an unemancipated minor unless she first has given her written consent to the abortion and also has obtained the written consent of one of her parents or legal guardian.
> **(b)** If one or both of an unemancipated, pregnant minor's parents or her guardian refuse to consent to the performance of an abortion, or if the minor elects not to seek the consent of one or both of her parents or her guardian, an unemancipated pregnant minor may file a petition with the juvenile court. If, pursuant to this subdivision, a minor seeks a petition, the court shall assist the minor or person designated by the minor in preparing the petition and notices required pursuant to this section. The petition shall set forth with specificity the minor's reasons for the request. The court shall ensure that the minor's identity is confidential. The minor may file the petition using only her initials or a pseudonym. An unemancipated pregnant minor may participate in the proceedings in juvenile court on her own behalf, and the court may appoint a guardian ad litem for her. The court shall, however, advise her that she has a right to court-appointed counsel upon request. The hearing shall be set within three days of the filing of the petition. A notice shall be given to the minor of the date, time, and place of the hearing on the petition.
> **(c)** At the hearing on a minor's petition brought pursuant to subdivision (b) for the authorization of an abortion, the court shall consider all evidence duly presented, and order either of the following:
> **(1)** If the court finds that the minor is sufficiently mature and sufficiently informed to make the decision on her own regarding an abortion, and that the minor has, on that basis, consented thereto, the court shall grant the petition.
> **(2)** If the court finds that the minor is not sufficiently mature and sufficiently informed to make the decision on her own regarding an abortion, the court shall then consider whether performance of the abortion would be in the best interest of the minor. In the event that

Chapter 35: Minors

> the court finds that the performance of the abortion would be in the minor's best interest, the court shall grant the petition ordering the performance of the abortion without consent of, or notice to, the parents or guardian. In the event that the court finds that the performance of the abortion is not in the best interest of the minor, the court shall deny the petition.

If a minor who is twelve (12) years of age or older comes into contact with an infectious, contagious or communicable disease, that minor may consent to medical care related to the diagnosis or treatment of the disease, if the disease or condition is one that is required by law or regulation adopted pursuant to law to be reported to the local health officer, or is a related sexually transmitted disease, as may be determined by the State Public Health Officer. **FC § 6926(a)**.

Additionally, a minor who is twelve (12) years of age or older may consent to medical care related to the prevention of a sexually transmitted disease, and the minor's parent or guardian is not liable for payment for medical care. **FC § 6926**.

A minor who is twelve (12) years of age or older and who is alleged to have been raped may consent to medical care related to the diagnosis or treatment of the condition and the collection of medical evidence with regard to the alleged rape. **FC § 6927**.

A minor who is alleged to have been sexually assaulted may consent to medical care related to the diagnosis and treatment of the condition and the collection of medical evidence with regard to the alleged sexual assault. However, the person providing medical treatment must attempt to contact the minor's parent or guardian. Further, such attempts to contact the parent must be recorded and noted, whether or not the contact was successful. **FC § 6928**.

A minor who is twelve (12) years of age or older may consent to medical care and counseling relating to the diagnosis and treatment of a drug- or alcohol-related problem. **FC § 6929(b)**.

Parents' Rights

The mother of an unemancipated minor child and the father, if presumed to be the father under **FC § 7611**, are equally entitled to the services and earnings of the child. **FC § 7500(a)**. If one parent is dead, is unable or refuses to take custody, or has abandoned the child, the other parent is entitled to the services and earnings of the child. **FC § 7500**.

A parent entitled to the custody of a child has a right to change the residence of the child, subject to the power of the court to restrain a removal that would prejudice the rights or the welfare of the child. **FC § 7501(a)**,

The parent has no control over the property of the parent's child. **FC § 7502**.

Chapter 35: Minors

The employer of a minor must pay the earnings of the minor to the minor until the parent or guardian of that minor gives the employer notice that the parent or guardian is claiming the minor's earnings. **FC § 7503**.
The authority of a parent ceases when a guardian is appointed, when the minor marries or when the minor reaches his or her majority. **FC § 7505**.

If a child, after attaining the age of majority, continues to be supported by his or her parent, neither party is entitled to compensation, in the absence of an agreement for the compensation. **FC § 7506**.
Except as provided in **FC § 7541**, the child of a wife cohabiting with her husband, who is not impotent or sterile, is conclusively presumed to be a child of the marriage. **FC § 7540**.

Emancipation of Minors

A person under the age of 18 years is an emancipated minor without filing a *Petition* for Emancipation if: **(1)** he or she has entered into a valid marriage, whether or not the marriage has been dissolved; or **(2)** he or she is on active duty with the armed forces of the United States or if an individual has received a Declaration of Emancipation pursuant to **FC § 7122**. **FC § 7002**.

A minor may petition the superior court of the county in which the minor resides or is temporarily domiciled for a Declaration of Emancipation. The *Petition* must provide that:

> **(1)** The minor is at least 14 years of age.
> **(2)** The minor willingly lives separate and apart from the minor's parents or guardian with the consent or acquiescence of the minor's parents or guardian.
> **(3)** The minor is managing his or her own financial affairs. As evidence of this, the minor shall complete and attach a declaration of income and expenses as provided in Judicial Council form FL-150.
> **(4)** The source of the minor's income is not derived from any activity declared to be a crime by the laws of this state or the laws of the United States. FC § 7120.

Before a *Petition for Declaration of Emancipation* is heard, reasonable notice must be given to the minor's parents, guardian or other person entitled to the custody of the minor. **FC § 7121**.

The court must order that the *Petition* for Emancipation be granted if it finds that the minor is a person described by **FC § 7120** and that emancipation would not be contrary to the minor's best interests.

If the *Petition* is granted, the court must forthwith issue a Declaration of Emancipation, which will be filed by the clerk of the court. A Declaration of Emancipation is conclusive evidence that the minor is emancipated. **FC § 7122**.
In the following case, the court found that two of the requirements necessary to be granted a Declaration of Emancipation (the minor willingly lives separate and apart

Chapter 35: Minors

from his or her parents with their consent and the minor must be managing her own his or her own financial affairs) were not met and accordingly reversed the trial court's decision.

> **BONNIE P. et al., Petitioners, v. THE SUPERIOR COURT OF SAN DIEGO COUNTY, Respondent. JACQUELINE P., Real Party in Interest.**
> **COURT OF APPEAL OF CALIFORNIA, FOURTH APPELLATE DISTRICT, DIVISION ONE**
> 134 Cal.App.4th 1249
> December 15, 2005, Filed
> (*Bonnie P. v. Superior Court*)

On April 30, 2005, Jacqueline, at age 16, gave birth to a daughter. Jacqueline then left [her mother's house (M) M's] home and began living with her boyfriend and the baby's father, Rafael P., and his parents, Josephine P. and Rafael P. (Rafael Sr.).

On May 19, 2005, Jacqueline filed a petition for a declaration of emancipation under FC § 7129. The petition stated she was managing her own financial affairs and began living apart from her parents on May 2, 2005, but not with their consent. An accompanying income and expense declaration stated she worked at a grocery store for about three weeks in the summer of 2004. It specified no current employment or salary or wages received the preceding month, and it reported for the preceding 12 months an average gross monthly income of $ 600 from salary or wages. It estimated total average monthly expenses of $ 2,070 and noted they were paid entirely by others.

A hearing on Jacqueline's petition was held June 16, 2005. [Jacqueline's father (F)] had notified the court he contested the petition, and the court allowed him to appear by telephone because he lives in Van Nuys and is disabled. Jacqueline appeared with Josephine and Rafael Sr. The bailiff informed the court that Rafael was arrested outside the courtroom before the hearing on outstanding felony warrants.

The court did not swear in any of the witnesses. Jacqueline said she was working full time during the summer and would work part time when she returned to school. She liked school, her grade point average was 3.5 and she would be a senior in high school and 17 years of age during the 2005–2006 school year. Rafael's family helped her by paying utilities and providing food and childcare when she went to school and work.

Jacqueline said she was not living with [M] because she receives welfare and provides nothing for Jacqueline. Jacqueline was not living with [F] because her parents had been separated for about two years and were going through a divorce, and her mother had primary custody of her.

Jacqueline [stated that F] could not afford to support her and her baby because he was unemployed and received approximately $ 800 a month from disability. She stopped living with him because he had an anger management problem and refused to take anger management classes, and she lacks a working relationship with him.

Josephine and Rafael Sr. addressed the court through an interpreter, but the court did not swear the interpreter in as a witness or identify him or her on the record. Rafael Sr. addressed questions about the legality of his presence in the United States. He said he was "waiting for his adjustment of status through INS for 14 years" and was due to get an appointment to "go get their green card." The interpreter spoke to the court off the record to "shed some light" on Rafael Sr.'s statements, after which the court expressed concern that if Rafael Sr. did not "have a legal basis to stay here, some or all family members could be deported which will impact Jacqueline's plans."

The court nonetheless granted Jacqueline's petition and issued a declaration of emancipation under FC § 7122, as she had a child and was doing well in school. The court also found that [M] has not "been there" for Jacqueline and [F] is not financially or otherwise able to provide a stable home, and Rafael's family provides Jacqueline with support. [F and M] separately appeal the order, and we treat their notices of appeal as petitions for writ of mandate under FC § 7123(b).

DISCUSSION
[F] contends the informal nature of Jacqueline's emancipation hearing violated statutory procedural requirements and his right to due process of law in the following respects: the court did not swear the witnesses and interpreter at the hearing to tell the truth; the interpreter's off-the-record discussion with the court to "shed some light" on Rafael Sr.'s statements about his immigration status deprived [F] of the opportunity to challenge her statements; and [F] did not get a meaningful opportunity to be heard because the court cut him off at the end of the hearing when he indicated he had further comments.

We agree that emancipation proceedings are subject to certain procedural requirements the court did not meet here.

The due process clause of the Fourteenth Amendment protects against governmental interference with the fundamental liberty interest of parents in making decisions concerning the care, custody, control, and education of their children. "[T]he due process clause does not permit a State to infringe on the fundamental right of parents to make childrearing decisions simply because a state judge believes a 'better' decision could be made." (Troxel v. Granville (2000) 530 U.S. 57 at p. 72-73.)

FC § 7110 conveys "the intent of the Legislature that [emancipation] proceedings … be as simple and inexpensive as possible." However, considering fundamental parental rights and interests at stake when a parent opposes an emancipation petition, we do not view FC § 7110's directive for simplicity as statutory authorization for courts to dispense with the basic requirements of the Evidence Code for evidentiary hearings. Evidence Code § 300 states that "[e]xcept as otherwise provided by statute, this code applies in every action before … a … superior court …." "If this command were not clear enough, the Law Revision Commission Comment to Evidence Code § 300 resolves any conceivable ambiguity in the statutory language; the Commission states that [Evidence Code] § 300 'makes the Evidence Code applicable to all proceedings conducted by California courts except those court proceedings to which it is made inapplicable by statute. …'The case law is equally explicit: 'Evidence Code § 300 makes it clear that, except as otherwise provided by statute, the Evidence Code applies to every evidentiary hearing in the state courts. …' " (Citation omitted.)

Moreover, the necessity of an evidentiary hearing in emancipation proceedings under FC § 7120 et seq. is implicit in the statutory requirements of a formal petition (id., § 7120), notice of the proceedings before the petition is heard (id., § 7121), and formal findings on the petition by the court (id., § 7122). Accordingly, the court should have placed all witnesses who testified at Jacqueline's emancipation hearing under oath. (Evid. Code, § 710.) Further, it should have sworn the interpreter who translated for Rafael Sr. and Josephine as a witness (id., §§ 750, 751, 752, subd. (a)) and identified him or her on the record (id., § 752, subd. (b)).

A petition for a declaration of emancipation must set forth with specificity certain facts, including that the "minor is at least 14 years of age," the minor "willingly lives separate and apart from the minor's parents or guardian with the consent or acquiescence of the minor's parents or guardian," and the "minor is managing his or her own financial affairs." (§ 7120, subd. (b)(1)–(3).) "The emancipation of a minor child must be proved; it is never presumed, and the burden of proof is on the one asserting it... In determining whether a child has been emancipated, the intention of the parent governs."

[F] challenges the sufficiency of the evidence to support the court's implied findings that Jacqueline was living apart from her parents with their consent or acquiescence and that she was managing her own financial affairs. When a judgment is attacked as being unsupported by the evidence, 'the power of the appellate court begins and ends with a determination as to whether there is any substantial evidence, contradicted or uncontradicted, which will support the conclusion reached by the [trier of fact]." (Citation omitted.) " '[I]f the word "substantial" means anything at all, it clearly implies that such evidence must be of ponderable legal significance. Obviously the word cannot be deemed synonymous with "any" evidence. It must be reasonable in nature, credible, and of solid value; it must actually be "substantial" proof of the essentials which the law requires in a particular case.' " (Citations omitted.)

Here, there was no evidence to support a finding that [F or M] consented to or acquiesced in Jacqueline's living apart from them. Indeed, Jacqueline declared under penalty of perjury on her emancipation petition that she did not have her parents' consent. At the hearing, [F]opposed Jacqueline's emancipation [and] the court officer noted Jacqueline's parents oppose her emancipation.

Jacqueline asserts "[t]he information gathered by the ... court during its questioning of all present indicated Jacqueline's parents had indeed acquiesced to Jacqueline's willing absence from her mother's home in that neither parent had made an effort to provide adequately for her." However, any arguable parental failure to adequately provide for a minor does not constitute parental consent or acquiescence to the minor's living apart from the parents. Parental neglect may be a basis for invoking the jurisdiction of the juvenile court under California's juvenile dependency scheme (Welf. & Inst. Code, § 300 et seq.), but it is not a statutory basis for emancipation under FC § 7120.

Although the lack of parental consent is dispositive, we also find the evidence does not support a finding Jacqueline was managing her own financial affairs. Her petition asserted she was doing so, but her accompanying income and expense declaration (declaration) and the information presented at the emancipation hearing do not support the assertion. The declaration noted Jacqueline's employment for three weeks in August 2004, several months before the hearing. The declaration stated she received $ 600 average monthly gross income from salary or wages during the preceding 12 months, but it reported no current employment and no income from salary or wages the preceding month. The declaration listed varying amounts of gross monthly income earned by Rafael and his family members, and stated they each contributed to household expenses. It estimated Jacqueline's monthly expenses to be $ 2,070 and specified that others, presumably Rafael and his family, paid that entire amount.

Additionally, the petition showed Jacqueline had been living apart from her parents for only six weeks at the time of the hearing, and the court understandably expressed

Chapter 35: Minors

> concern about the ability of Rafael and his family to continue supporting Jacqueline in the future, as Rafael had just been incarcerated on outstanding warrants and it was questionable whether his parents were living in the United States legally.
>
> We conclude substantial evidence does not support the court's implied factual findings that [F and M] consented to or acquiesced in Jacqueline's living arrangement or that Jacqueline was adequately managing her own financial affairs within the meaning of FC § 7120(b)(2) and (3). Thus, its order of emancipation was improper.
>
> Let a writ of mandate issue directing the superior court to vacate its order of June 16, 2005, granting Jacqueline P.'s petition for declaration of emancipation, and to enter an order denying the petition.

The court noted in its footnote 6 that there had been no reported opinions that interpret the requirement that to be emancipated a minor must be "managing his or her own financial affairs." *Id.* at p. 1258. An emancipated minor is considered an adult for the following purposes:

> (a) The minor's right to support by the minor's parents.
> (b) The right of the minor's parents to the minor's earnings and to control the minor.
> (c) The application of Welfare and Institutions Code §§ 300 and 601.
> (d) Ending all vicarious or imputed liability of the minor's parents or guardian for the minor's torts. Nothing in this section affects any liability of a parent, guardian, spouse, or employer imposed by the Vehicle Code, or any vicarious liability that arises from an agency relationship.
> (e) The minor's capacity to do any of the following:
>   (1) Consent to medical, dental, or psychiatric care, without parental consent, knowledge, or liability.
>   (2) Enter into a binding contract or give a delegation of power.
>   (3) Buy, sell, lease, encumber, exchange, or transfer an interest in real or personal property, including, but not limited to, shares of stock in a domestic or foreign corporation or a membership in a nonprofit corporation.
>   (4) Sue or be sued in the minor's own name.
>   (5) Compromise, settle, arbitrate, or otherwise adjust a claim, action, or proceeding by or against the minor.
>   (6) Make or revoke a will.
>   (7) Make a gift, outright or in trust.
>   (8) Convey or release contingent or expectant interests in property, including marital property rights and any right of survivorship incident to joint tenancy, and consent to a transfer, encumbrance, or gift of marital property.
>   (9) Exercise or release the minor's powers as donee of a power of appointment unless the creating instrument otherwise provides.
>   (10) Create for the minor's own benefit or for the benefit of others a revocable or irrevocable trust.
>   (11) Revoke a revocable trust.
>   (12) Elect to take under or against a will.
>   (13) Renounce or disclaim any interest acquired by testate or intestate succession or by inter vivos transfer, including exercise of the right to surrender the right to revoke a revocable trust.
>   (14) Make an election referred to in Section 13502 of, or an election and agreement referred to in Probate Code § 13503.

Chapter 35: Minors

> (15) Establish the minor's own residence.
> (16) Apply for a work permit pursuant to Education Code § 49110 without the request of the minor's parents.
> (17) Enroll in a school or college. FC § 7050(e).

An insurance contract entered into by an emancipated minor has the same effect as if it were entered into by an adult and, with respect to that contract, the minor has the same rights, duties and liabilities as an adult. **FC § 7051**.

If an emancipation petition is denied, the minor has a right to file a petition for a writ of mandate. If the petition is sustained, the parents or guardian have a right to file a petition for a writ of mandate if they have appeared in the proceeding and opposed the granting of the petition. **FC § 7123**.

A Declaration of Emancipation obtained by fraud or by the withholding of material information is voidable and a Declaration of Emancipation of a minor who is indigent and has no means of support is subject to rescission. **FC § 7130**.

A petition to void a Declaration of Emancipation on the ground that the declaration was obtained by fraud or by the withholding of material information may be filed by any person or by any public or private agency. The petition must be filed in the court that granted the declaration. **FC § 7131**.

Pursuant to **FC § 7132**, a petition to rescind a Declaration of Emancipation on the ground that the minor is indigent and has no means of support may be filed by the minor declared emancipated, by the minor's conservator or by the district attorney of the county in which the minor resides. The petition must be filed in the county in which the minor or the conservator resides. A minor may be considered indigent if the minor's only source of income is from public assistance benefits.

The court must consider the impact of the rescission of the Declaration of Emancipation on the minor and must find the rescission of the Declaration of Emancipation will not be contrary to the best interests of the minor before granting the order to rescind.

Before a petition to rescind a Declaration of Emancipation, reasonable notice must be given to the minor's parents or guardians. **FC § 7133**.

When a minor is declared emancipated, the minor may apply to the Department of Motor Vehicles for an identification card. **FC § 7140**.

Termination of Parental Rights

The purpose of the laws providing for termination of parental rights is to serve the welfare and best interests of a child by providing the stability and security of an adoptive home when those conditions are otherwise missing from the child's life. **FC § 7800**.

Chapter 35: Minors

A proceeding may be brought under this part for the purpose of having a minor child declared free from the custody and control of either or both parents. **FC § 7802**. The evidence presented must be liberally construed to serve and protect the interests and welfare of the child. **FC § 7801**. There is no filing fee charged for a proceeding brought under this part. **FC § 7806**.

A declaration of freedom from parental custody and control pursuant to this part terminates all parental rights and responsibilities with regard to the child. **FC § 7803**.

When a child is declared free from parental custody and control, the court may appoint a suitable party to act on behalf of the child and may order such further notice of the proceedings to be given as the court deems proper. **FC § 7804**.

A petition or a report or records of a probation officer may only be inspected by:

> **(1)** Court personnel.
> **(2)** The child who is the subject of the proceeding.
> **(3)** The parents or guardian of the child.
> **(4)** The attorneys for the parties.
> **(5)** Any other person designated by the judge. FC § 7805(a).

In a proceeding before the court of appeal or Supreme Court to review a judgment or order entered in a proceeding under this part, the court record and briefs filed by the parties may be inspected only by the following persons:

> **(1)** Court personnel.
> **(2)** The child who is the subject of the proceeding.
> **(3)** The parents or guardian of the child.
> **(4)** The attorneys for the parties.
> **(5)** Any other person designated by the judge. FC § 7805(b).

A proceeding to declare a minor child free may be brought under this part for the purpose of having a child under the age of 18 years declared free from the custody and control of either or both parents if the child comes within any of the descriptions set out in this chapter. **FC § 7820**. The finding by the court must be supported by clear and convincing evidence. **FC § 7821**.

A proceeding may be brought pursuant to this section if:

- A child is abandoned (**FC § 7822**);
- A child neglected or cruelly treated (**FC § 7823**);
- If the **parent** or parents suffer a disability because of the habitual use of alcohol or any controlled substances (**FC § 7824**);
- If the parent or parents are convicted of a felony (**FC § 7825**); or
- If the parent or parents have been declared to be developmentally disabled or mentally ill (**FC § 7826**).

EDUCATIONAL EXERCISES

Fill in the blanks using the Word List that follows

1. Someone who is under the age of 18 years is called a _____.
2. A person becomes an adult the first minute of his or her birthday and this is called the _____ _____ (2 words together).
3. The name of the account that provides that 15% of a minor's earnings must be placed into a bank account is called _____ _____ _____ (3 words together).
4. Both parents are equally entitled to the _____ and _____ of their child (2 words not together).
5. An employer must pay a minor's earnings to a _____ if so noticed.
6. _____ _____ ends when a guardian is appointed, the minor marries or the minor turns 18 years old (2 words together).
7. A minor can request adult status by filing a Petition for _____ of _____ (2 words not together).
8. The requirements for filing the Petition mentioned above are:
   a. The minor must be at least 14 years of age;
   b. The minor must be living separate and apart from his or her parents with _____ _____ (two words together);
   c. The minor is managing his or her own _____ _____ (2 words together); and
   d. The Minor's income may not be from an _____ _____ (two words together).
9. The main person in the rhyming opinion case was _____ _____ (first and last name that are together).
10. In the case mentioned above, the issue was a minor requesting to _____ _____ her recording contract (two words together).
11. If a Petition discussed above is denied, the minor has a right to file a petition for a _____ _____ _____ (three words together).
12. The Petition mentioned above must be filed in the _____ in which the minor or the conservator resides.
13. A contract provision that must be litigated in the same venue as where the contract was made is called a _____ _____ (two words together).
14. A minor may consent to _____ (single word) or _____ _____ (two words together) if he or she is 15 years of age or older, living separate and apart from his or her parents or guardian, whether with or without the consent of a parent or guardian and regardless of the duration of the separate residence and is managing his or her own financial affairs, regardless of the source of the minor's income.

Word List

1. Minor
2. Birthday Rule
3. Coogan Trust Account
4. Service and Earnings (2 words no together)
5. Parent
6. Parental Authority
7. Declaration Emancipation (2 words not together).
8. The requirements for filing the Petition mentioned above are:
9. The minor must be at least 14 years of age ental ca
10. Their consent
11. Financial affairs
12. Illegal Source
13. LeAnn Rimes
14. Set Aside (two words together).
15. Writ of mandate
16. County
17. Forum clause (two words together).
18. Medical
19.

CHAPTER 36: Domestic Violence

In Brief...

DOMESTIC VIOLENCE, (DV):
- Is violence committed by one member of the household against another member, most commonly a spouse, former spouse, cohabitant or former cohabitant, **FC § 6211**;
- Can happen to anyone regardless of race, age, sexual orientation, religion, gender, socioeconomic background and education; and
- Crimes include assault, assault with a deadly weapon, battery, sexual battery, traumatic injury, murder and attempted murder, **FC § 6203**; and
- Includes true information disseminated by email that causes extreme emotional distress.

THERE ARE 3 KINDS OF PROTECTIVE ORDERS:

1. Emergency protective orders (EPOs), CRC Rule 5.420, FC §§ 6215, 6218:
- Are restraining order requests made to a judge by law enforcement officers responding to a DV call who believe that a victim is in immediate and present danger;
- Are valid for either five business days or seven calendar days (whichever is shorter);
- Are issued to give the victim time to go to court to ask for a DV restraining order; and
- Include a FIREARMS EMERGENCY PROTECTIVE ORDER.

2. DV restraining orders (ROs), Welfare and Inst. Code § 213.5, CRC Rule 5.151:
- Are court orders that are issued to prevent further violence by ordering that abusers stop abusing and stay away from their victims;
- May be granted to a spouse, former spouse, current/past cohabitant, a person with whom a dating or engagement relationship is shared or the unmarried biological coparent, **FC § 6211**;
- May grant to a victim exclusive possession of the communal residence, **FC § 6321**;
- May grant to a victim temporary custody or visitation of the minor children, **FC § 6323**; and
- There are no filing fees to make the request.
- When **denied**, the court must include the reason(s) for the denial on the record; and
- **Mutual ROs** require detailed on the record findings that both parties were aggressors.
- **Temporary DVROs:**
  - Can be obtained *ex parte* if there is danger/need for immediate protection, **FC § 6320**;
  - Can be issued with or without notice, **FC § 6220**; and

Chapter 36: Domestic Violence

> - Can be issued solely upon testimony or affidavit of the person so requesting, **FC § 6300**.
> - **Can order that the restrained person comply with court orders AND:**
>   - Move out of and stay away from the family house with very little notice;
>   - Relinquish any and all firearms and ammunition in his or her possession;
>   - Stay away from his/her children and/or have little/no visitation with his or her children;
>   - Stay away from the family pets;
>   - Stay away from the children's school;
>   - Pay child support, spousal support, specified bills, attorney fees and court costs;
>   - Not do anything that significantly affects the victim's property;
>   - Return or release certain property;
>   - Attend parenting, domestic violence or anger management classes.
> - **Permanent DVRO, FC § 6345:**
>   - May be renewed 5 years or permanently, without showing of further abuse, **FC § 6345**.
>   - Permanent DVROs are effective when made.
> 3. **Emergency orders, CRC 5.151:**
>   - Are requests that require the immediate attention of the court;
>   - Can request to modify child custody or visitation if there is a possibility of immediate harm to the child or an immediate risk that the child will be removed from CA, **FC § 3064**.

Introduction

The words "domestic violence have said and heard in may situations. However, there are many who really do not understand what the words actually mean. So what is domestic violence?

Black's Law Dictionary defines **domestic violence** as "violence between members of a household, usually spouses; an assault or other violent act committed by one member of a household against another; domestic abuse, family violence."[1] **FC § 6211** defines **domestic violence** as abuse by a spouse or former spouse, a cohabitant or former cohabitant, a person with whom the respondent is having or has had a dating or engagement relationship or a person with whom the respondent has had a child.[2] Additionally, domestic violence can include third-party injuries that occurred

---

[1] *Black's Law Dictionary, Ninth Edition*, 2009, p. 1705.
[2] "Cohabitant means a person who regularly resides in the household. 'Former cohabitant' means a person who formerly regularly resided in the household." FC § 6209.

Chapter 36: Domestic Violence

under circumstances involving domestic violence. (See *PEOPLE v. TRUONG* (2001) 90 Cal.App.4th 887 where the court stated that:

> by its plain language, Penal Code § 12022.7(d), establishes an enhancement for any person who inflicts great bodily injury upon a person in the course of an incident of domestic violence. No person of ordinary intelligence would be left guessing as to the meaning of this language. Rather, the statute clearly informs a defendant who commits domestic violence that infliction of great bodily injury on any person involved in the incident, whether or not a victim of domestic violence under the definition of Penal Code § 13700, will result in an enhanced sentence. It is easy to conjure the circumstances in which the statute might come into play, such as when the defendant inflicts great bodily injury upon a friend or relative who has attempted to come to the aid of the domestic violence victim, or upon a peace officer responding to an incident of domestic violence. The reach of the statute certainly includes the circumstances presented here, in which an angry husband physically abuses his wife and, as part of the same incident, inflicts great bodily injury upon the man with whom she is having an affair." *Id.* at pp. 899-900.)

Abuse includes: **(1)** intentionally or recklessly causing or attempting to cause bodily injury; **(2)** sexual assault; and **(3)** placing a family member in reasonable apprehension of imminent serious bodily injury to that person or to another.

But that is not all, because abuse is not limited to the actual infliction of physical injury or assault. It additionally includes terrorizing, shoving, pushing, kicking, pulling hair, throwing objects, scaring or following a person and keeping someone from freely coming and going. Abuse can be verbal, emotional or psychological. Behaviors that intimidate, manipulate, humiliate, isolate, frighten, terrorize, coerce, threaten, blame, hurt, injure or wound a family member are also considered domestic violence. **FC § 6203. PC § 13700.** Additionally, domestic abuse includes the physical abuse of the family pets.

The abuse can be the distribution of information that causes "grave emotional distress" as the following case demonstrates; it does not matter whether or not the statements made are true or not true.

> ***CAROLINA ALTAFULLA, Plaintiff and Respondent, v. JOHN ERVIN, Defendant and Appellant.***
> COURT OF APPEAL OF CALIFORNIA, FOURTH APPELLATE DISTRICT, DIVISION ONE
> 238 Cal.App.4th 571; 189 Cal.Rptr.3d 316
> June 9, 2015, Opinion Filed
> (*Altafulla v. Ervin*)
>
> In 2011, Ervin was married to Michal Ben-Nun. According to Ben-Nun, in August 2011, Ervin threatened her and their three children by stating: "One day I will take a gun and shoot all four of you." Ben-Nun called the police, Ervin was removed from the family home and Ben-Nun obtained two temporary DVPA orders preventing Ervin from coming

---

"Dating relationship means frequent, intimate associations primarily characterized by the expectation of affection or sexual involvement independent of financial considerations." FC § 6210.

near her or their home. Ervin and Ben-Nun's marriage was eventually dissolved.

Ervin has consistently denied threatening Ben-Nun or his children. However, in civil litigation he pursued against Ben-Nun based on her repetition of the alleged threat to others, Ervin conceded he made an "unfortunate and irresponsible statement" to Ben-Nun.

Shortly after his separation from Ben-Nun, Ervin began a romantic relationship with Altafulla. Eventually, Ervin and Altafulla purchased a home together, where they lived with two of Altafulla's daughters, ages nine and 17.

In February 2014, Ervin received a surveillance report, of unknown origin, which provided photographic and narrative evidence that Altafulla had been engaged in a romantic affair with what the record suggests was someone associated with a client of her employer. In the trial court, Altafulla tacitly acknowledged that the affair took place.

Ervin created a digital image of the report, including photographs of Altafulla and the man she was having an affair with, and e-mailed the report to a number of Ervin and Altafulla's mutual friends, relatives, and coworkers. Ervin's e-mail stated: "I am deeply hurt, so take this with a grain of salt. But I invested my life savings, and countless hours with this women's [sic] children to try to make it work. Imagine you are taking care of another person's children—not your own children, but another person's children—only to find out the parent is not travelling for work, as they say, but cheating on you—during the very time you are investing your life savings in a common house. [¶] I'm not asking for sympathy, but here I am stuck, with this woman who cheated on me. I invite you to have read [sic] of this report. [¶] Please let me know if you have any ideas how to overcome this."

Although immediately following disclosure of the affair both Altafulla and Ervin remained in the home, Altafulla attempted to avoid contact with Ervin. However, on the evening of February 25, 2014, Ervin would not let Altafulla into the master bedroom to retrieve her pajamas and she called the police; the police arrived, and, after speaking with Ervin, Altafulla was able to retrieve belongings from her bedroom. After the police left, Ervin began angrily disassembling the two children's bedroom furniture and insisting that different sleeping arrangements in the home were necessary.

According to Altafulla, while Ervin was disassembling the children's furniture, Ervin disclosed to the children that their mother had been having an affair with another man, explained "blow jobs" to the girls, and warned them that their mother might have a sexually transmitted disease that they could contract if they shared towels with her.

Altafulla's 17-year-old daughter was severely traumatized by Ervin's behavior and fled the home in her car. Altafulla learned that her daughter had gone to a psychiatric facility and had been admitted. The following day, a psychologist at the facility contacted Altafulla and told her that her daughter was afraid of Ervin and that the facility would not release her daughter to Altafulla until Ervin left their home.

On February 27, 2014, Altafulla obtained a temporary restraining order requiring that Ervin leave the home and preventing him from having any contact with Altafulla or her children. On March 17, 2014, the trial court conducted a hearing on Altafulla's application for a permanent DVPA order against Ervin and Ervin's application for a restraining order against Altafulla.

The trial court granted Altafulla's application and denied Ervin's application. In granting Altafulla's application, the trial court stated: "The court has had the opportunity to review the pleadings in the file and observe the witnesses on the witness stand. The court is satisfied that Ms. Altafulla is legitimately in fear of ongoing harassing behavior from Mr. Ervin. Based upon the testimony that I have heard today and observing the demeanor and content of that testimony, as well as the pleadings, she is afraid for herself and on behalf of her children. An order will be issued for a period of five years protecting her."

In particular, the trial court ordered that Ervin leave the home he shared with Altafulla and stay away from it.

With respect to Ervin's application and the trial court's decision to deny it, the trial court stated: "Mr. Ervin testified he did not believe that Ms. Altafulla was violent. The activity that Mr. Ervin is complaining of—while it is personally upsetting to him and I can understand why it is personally upsetting, it is not harassing, it does not come within the purview of the granting of a restraining order. His request is denied."

Ervin filed a second request for a DVPA restraining order, which the trial court also denied. Ervin filed a timely notice of appeal from the trial court's orders.

DISCUSSION
Ervin asserts that because Altafulla has never disputed the affair occurred and admitted to him that, following one of her trips with her lover, she experienced a yeast infection, his e-mails and statements to her children were literally true. Given the factual accuracy of his statements, Ervin contends they were not abusive and could not be the basis for a restraining order. He also argues that the trial court could not rely on the statements he made to Ben-Nun, which he contends were not death threats. We reject Ervin's arguments.

The factual accuracy of information used to otherwise harass the victims of domestic violence does not take abusive conduct outside the scope of the DVPA. Moreover, Ervin's earlier statements to Ben-Nun and their children, even if they were not meant by him as actual death threats, demonstrate an appalling lack of judgment on his part, as even he acknowledged. Thus, they were relevant in determining whether Altafulla needed protection from Ervin.

The DVPA was enacted to protect domestic partners from abusive conduct, which, as the record here amply demonstrates, may involve the use of arguably accurate information in a manner that causes severe emotional distress.

Here, Ervin's distribution of information about Altafulla's affair, which she plainly did not want to share with her coworkers, relatives, and friends, did cause and no doubt was calculated to cause, Altafulla grave emotional distress. The statements Ervin made to Altafulla's children were similarly calculated to and did in fact cause significant emotional distress to both Altafulla, as well as her children. The outrageous statement Ervin had previously made to Ben-Nun, even if the trial court accepted his interpretation of it as not intended to be a serious death threat, displayed a serious lack of judgment and self-control.

Chapter 36: Domestic Violence

> Taken together, this history of abusive and outrageous conduct was more than sufficient to support intervention by the trial court by way of an order keeping Ervin away from Altafulla and her children.
>
> Next, Ervin contends the trial court erred in making its order effective for a term of five years. He contends Altafulla only requested a three-year order. The record in fact shows that although in her application for a permanent order Altafulla asked for a three-year order, at the hearing Altafulla asked for a five-year order. Given the impact of Ervin's conduct on Altafulla's daughter, the trial court did not abuse its discretion in restraining Ervin for the full five years permitted under the DVPA. (See § 6345, subd. (a).) Altafulla's earlier request for a three-year order did not prejudice her later request for a five-year order, especially in light of Ervin's ability to seek relief from the order if he can show that it is no longer necessary. (*Ibid.*)
>
> Ervin's conduct here gave rise to far more than an incipient or inchoate fear of him. Because the e-mails Ervin sent in no way portray him in a positive light but nonetheless were plainly designed to embarrass Altafulla, they were an unmistakable manifestation of his extreme anger towards her; Ervin's emotional abuse of Altafulla's two daughters was even more worrisome. In light of these circumstances, Altafulla's fears were well developed and reasonable, and, in addressing the very real fears of such victims of harassment, the Legislature acted rationally.
>
> Ervin also argues that the trial court abused its discretion in failing to grant his application for a restraining order against Altafulla. We find no abuse of discretion. There is no evidence in the record that suggests Altafulla engaged in any abusive or harassing conduct directed toward Ervin or was likely to do so. Her affair, the fact she developed a yeast infection and her own application for a restraining order are not abusive or harassing conduct circumstances within the meaning of the DVPA. Thus, there is nothing in the record that would support such an order.
>
> Finally, we reject Altafulla's request that we impose sanctions on Ervin. Although we have rejected Ervin's arguments on appeal, they are not so lacking merit that no reasonable attorney would assert them.
>
> **DISPOSITION**
> The trial court's orders are affirmed.

Domestic violence can happen to anyone, regardless of race, age, sexual orientation, religion or gender. Domestic violence affects people of all socioeconomic backgrounds and educational levels.

Domestic violence is perpetrated by both men and women. It occurs in both opposite-sex and same-sex relationships and between intimate partners who are married, living together or dating.

Domestic violence not only affects those persons who are abused, but it also has a substantial effect on other family members, friends, co-workers, other witnesses and the community at large. Children who grow up witnessing domestic violence often become abusers themselves, making children some of those most seriously affected by this crime. Frequent exposure to violence in the home not only predisposes

Chapter 36: Domestic Violence

children to numerous social and physical problems, but it also teaches them that violence is okay on many levels and is a normal way of life.[3]

> ...on-going violence and abuse is the norm in domestic violence cases... there [is] a great likelihood that any one battering episode is part of a larger scheme of dominance and control... If we fail to address the very essence of domestic violence, we will continue to see cases where perpetrators of this violence will beat their intimate partners, even kill them, and go on to beat or kill the next intimate partner. [C]riminal prosecution is one of the few factors which may interrupt the escalating pattern of domestic violence...
> *PEOPLE v. HOOVER* (2000) 77 Cal.App.4th 1020 at p. 1028 quoting Assem. Com. on Public Safety, Rep. on Sen. Bill No. 1876 (1995-1996 Reg. Sess.) June 25, 1996, pp. 3-4.

The Crimes

Domestic violence crimes are penal code crimes perpetrated against:

(1) A spouse or former spouse;
(2) A cohabitant or former cohabitant;
(3) A person with whom the respondent is having or has had a dating or engagement relationship;
(4) A person with whom the respondent has had a child, where the presumption applies that the male parent is the father of the child of the female parent;
(5) A child of a party or a child who is the subject of an action under the Uniform Parentage Act, where the presumption applies that the male parent is the father of the child to be protected; and
(6) Any other person **related by consanguinity or affinity within the second degree. FC § 6211.**[4]

Not only are heinous domestic violence crimes perpetrated against the people that were once loved and trusted most, domestic violence crimes include the added element of anger. Anger that belittles, demoralizes, intimidates and permanently scars both physically and emotionally.

The list of crimes that follow is not exhaustive because domestic violence crimes include any and all violence perpetrated against other family members.

---

[3] From the California Courts website at *www.courts.ca.gov/selfhelp-domesticviolence.htm*.
[4] The Family Code includes the following definitions:
FC § 6205. "Affinity, when applied to the marriage relation, signifies the connection existing in consequence of marriage between each of the married persons and the blood relatives of the other."
FC § 6209. "Cohabitant means a person who regularly resides in the household. 'Former cohabitant' means a person who formerly regularly resided in the household."
FC § 6210. "Dating relationship means frequent, intimate associations primarily characterized by the expectation of affection or sexual involvement independent of financial considerations."

Chapter 36: Domestic Violence

1. Assault

Assault "is an unlawful attempt, coupled with a present ability, to commit a violent injury on the person of another." **PC § 240**. A **domestic violence assault** is the unlawful attempt to angrily commit a violent injury on a family member.

2. Assault with deadly weapon or by force likely to produce great bodily injury

This is an assault "upon the person of another with a deadly weapon or instrument other than a firearm." **PC § 245(a)(1)**. A domestic violence assault with a deadly weapon is angrily terrorizing a family member with a gun or knife.

3. Battery

Battery "is any willful and unlawful use of force or violence upon the person of another." **PC § 242**. A domestic violence battery is violently and angrily attacking, hitting, punching and/or hurting a family member.

4. Sexual Battery

Sexual battery is touching an intimate part of another person:

(1)	While that person is unlawfully restrained by the accused or an accomplice, and if the touching is against the will of the person touched and is for the purpose of sexual arousal, sexual gratification or sexual abuse, is guilty of sexual battery.
(2)	Who is institutionalized for medical treatment and who is seriously disabled or medically incapacitated, if the touching is against the will of the person touched, and if the touching is for the purpose of sexual arousal, sexual gratification, or sexual abuse, is guilty of sexual battery.
(3)	For the purpose of sexual arousal, sexual gratification, or sexual abuse, and the victim is at the time unconscious of the nature of the act because the perpetrator fraudulently represented that the touching served a professional purpose, is guilty of sexual battery.
(4)	Who, for the purpose of sexual arousal, sexual gratification, or sexual abuse, causes another, against that person's will while that person is unlawfully restrained either by the accused or an accomplice, or is institutionalized for medical treatment and is seriously disabled or medically incapacitated, to masturbate or touch an intimate part of either of those persons or a third person, is guilty of sexual battery.

PC § 243.4. A **domestic violence sexual battery** is using sex to hurt a family member—using what should be a loving act to belittle and terrorize.

5. Traumatic Injury

A willful infliction of corporal injury resulting in a traumatic condition upon a victim who is or was the offender's spouse or former spouse, cohabitant or former cohabitant, fiancée, someone with whom the offender has, or previously had, an

Chapter 36: Domestic Violence

engagement or dating relationship or the mother or father of the offender's child is the crime of traumatic injury. **PC § 273.5(a), (b)**. **Traumatic condition** means a condition of the body, such as a wound, or external or internal injury, including, but not limited to, injury as a result of strangulation or suffocation, whether of a minor or serious nature, caused by a physical force. **Strangulation** and **suffocation** include impeding the normal breathing or circulation of the blood of a person by applying pressure on the throat or neck.

A **domestic violence traumatic injury** occurs when an abuser beats a family member senseless such that the victim sustains a permanent, disabling injury.

6. Murder in the First Degree

First degree murder "is the unlawful killing of a human being, or a fetus, with malice aforethought." **PC § 187(a)**. **Malice** is described as a deliberate intention. **PC § 188**.

First degree murder is:

> murder which is perpetrated by means of a destructive device or explosive, a weapon of mass destruction, knowing use of ammunition designed primarily to penetrate metal or armor, poison, lying in wait, torture, or by any other kind of willful, deliberate, and premeditated killing, or which is committed in the perpetration of, or attempt to perpetrate, arson, rape, carjacking, robbery, burglary, mayhem, kidnapping, train wrecking, or any act punishable under Section 206, 286, 288, 288a or 289, or any murder which is perpetrated by means of discharging a firearm from a motor vehicle, intentionally at another person outside of the vehicle with the intent to inflict death, is murder of the first degree. PC § 189.

7. Murder in the Second Degree

Murder in the second degree is all other murder not set forth above. **PC § 189**.

8. Attempted Murder

Attempted murder is an attempt to commit a murder with specific intent to commit the crime, and a direct but ineffectual act done toward its commission. **PC § 21a**.

Access is greatly enhanced when a family member is the victim making murder the most heinous of all crimes.

Additionally, domestic violence includes violence against family pets. Angry violence, maliciously and intentionally killing an animal, is a CRIME! **PC § 597**.

> Defendant's abusive behavior extended to the family dog. In August 1982, about a month before Janet disappeared, Fuzz [the family dog] was taken to the veterinary clinic in critical condition. The dog died on the examination table, reflexively gasping [for air] because its brain [was] deprived of oxygen and blood. ...Defendant admitted that he

> kicked the dog several times in order to discipline the animal [for getting into the] garage, but denied causing the dog's death. At a Placer County Deputy Sheriffs' Association barbeque, Janet cried as she told Gail Easter that defendant had kicked the dog to death... *PEOPLE v. KOVACICH, JR.* (2011) 201 Cal.App.4th 863 at pp. 870-871.

Domestic violence crimes **ARE REAL CRIMES.** (See *In re Marriage of FAJOTA* (2014) 230 Cal.App.4th 1487 at pp. 1490-1491, where the judge denied issuing a permanent restraining order even though the victim met the legal requirements for a restraining order.)

Protective Orders

First of all, there are three kinds of protective orders that may be available to a victim: **(1)** emergency protective orders (EPOs[5]), **(2)** restraining orders (both temporary and permanent) and **(3)** emergency orders.

CRC Rule 5.420(b) provides that a **protective order** is synonymous with a **domestic violence restraining order,** as well as the following:

(1) Emergency protective order under **FC § 6215**;
(2) Protective order under **FC § 6218**;
(3) Restraining order under **Welfare and Institutions Code § 213.5**; and
(4) Orders by court under **PC § 136.2**.

FC § 6218 provides that a **protective order** includes any of the following restraining orders, whether issued *ex parte*, after notice and hearing or in a judgment:

(a) An order described in **FC § 6320,** enjoining specific acts of abuse;
(b) An order described in **FC § 6321,** excluding a person from a dwelling; and
(c) An order described in **FC § 6322,** enjoining other specified behavior.

1. The Emergency Protective Order (EPO)

When a family member is abused by another family member, law enforcement officers are often summoned for help. It is no secret that law enforcement officers do not want to take these kinds of domestic violence calls. What may be a secret is that when a person is abused, the responding law enforcement officers have the discretion to decide if an abuser will be arrested for his or her crime.[6]

---

[5] FC § 6215.
[6] PC § 836(d) provides: "if a suspect commits an assault or battery upon a current or former spouse, fiance, fiancée, a current or former cohabitant as defined in FC § 6209, a person with whom the suspect currently is having or has previously had an engagement or dating relationship [and] has parented a child... a peace officer may arrest the suspect without a warrant where both of the following circumstances apply:

Chapter 36: Domestic Violence

A law enforcement officer who responds to a DV situation can also request that an emergency protective order (EPO) be issued. An officer must request an EPO if the officer believes that the victim is in immediate and present danger. **FC § 6275**.

The request for an EPO is made to a judge. It must be made in writing and signed by the officer making the request. **FC § 6270**. There are judges that are available to issue EPOs 24 hours each day.

A law enforcement officer answering a domestic violence call has the discretion to request that a judge issue an EPO at any time of the day or night.

A judicial officer may issue an *ex parte* EPO when a law enforcement officer asserts reasonable grounds to believe any of the following:

> **(a)** That a person is in immediate and present danger of domestic violence, based on the person's allegation of a recent incident of abuse or threat of abuse by the person against whom the order is sought.
> **(b)** That a child is in immediate and present danger of abuse by a family or household member, based on an allegation of a recent incident of abuse or threat of abuse by the family or household member.
> **(c)** That a child is in immediate and present danger of being abducted by a parent or relative, based on a reasonable belief that a person has an intent to abduct the child or flee with the child from the jurisdiction or based on an allegation of a recent threat to abduct the child or flee with the child from the jurisdiction.
> **(d)** That an elder or dependent adult is in immediate and present danger of abuse as defined in Welfare and Institutions Code § 15610.07, based on an allegation of a recent incident of abuse or threat of abuse by the person against whom the order is sought, except that no emergency protective order shall be issued based solely on an allegation of financial abuse. FC § 6250.

Pursuant to **FC § 6251**, an EPO may be issued only if the judicial officer finds both of the following:

> **(a)** That reasonable grounds have been asserted to believe that an immediate and present danger of domestic violence exists, that a child is in immediate and present danger of abuse or abduction, or that an elder or dependent adult is in immediate and present danger of abuse as defined in Welfare and Institutions Code § 15610.07.
> **(b)** That an emergency protective order is necessary to prevent the occurrence or recurrence of domestic violence, child abuse, child abduction, or abuse of an elder or dependent adult.

An EPO is only valid if it is issued by a judicial officer after making the findings required by **FC § 6251,** and pursuant to a specific request by a law enforcement officer. **FC § 6250.3**.

---

(1) The peace officer has probable cause to believe that the person to be arrested has committed the assault or battery, whether or not it has in fact been committed."

Chapter 36: Domestic Violence

An EPO lasts either five business days or seven calendar days (whichever is shorter). An EPO is issued to give the victim time to go to court to request a domestic violence restraining order (DVRO). An EPO can provide most of the protections available in a regular DVRO (Domestic Violence Restraining Order), such as removing the abuser from the home, ordering that the abuser have no contact with the victim and temporary custody of children.

An EPO may include any of the following specific orders:
(1) A protective order, as defined in **FC § 6218**;
(2) An order determining the temporary care and control of any minor child of the endangered person and the person against whom the order is sought;
(3) An order placing the temporary care and control of the endangered child and any other minor children in the family or household with the parent or guardian of the endangered child who is not a restrained party; and
(4) An order determining the temporary care and control of any minor child who is in danger of being abducted.

2. Restraining Orders (ROs)

a. Requesting a Temporary Restraining Order (TRO)

If there is immediate danger and a need for protection right away, a temporary (*ex parte*) restraining order (TRO) can be requested. A TRO is an immediate court order that orders that the abuser have no contact with the victim. Additionally, a TRO can order the abuser to leave the home, as well as many other forms of protection.

A TRO may be granted to:

1. A spouse or former spouse;
2. A cohabitant or former cohabitant, as defined in **FC § 6209**;
3. A person with whom the respondent is having or has had a dating or engagement relationship;
4. A person with whom the respondent has had a child, where the presumption applies that the male parent is the father of the child of the female parent under the Uniform Parentage Act;
5. A child of a party or a child who is the subject of an action under the Uniform Parentage Act, where the presumption applies that the male parent is the father of the child to be protected; and
6. Any other person related by consanguinity or affinity within the second degree. **FC § 6211**.

Additionally, if a TRO concerns an endangered child, the child's parent or guardian who is not a restrained person, or a person having temporary custody of the endangered child, may apply to the court for a TRO under **Welfare and Institutions Code § 213.5**. **FC § 6257**.

Chapter 36: Domestic Violence

When a **TRO** is requested, the court clerk sets a date for the hearing that is usually within the next three weeks. After a hearing date is scheduled, there will be a hearing in which the judge will decide whether or not a RO will be issued. A judge can grant a RO that can last up to five years. If the judge does issue a RO, a request can be made to extend that RO if the request is made within the last three months of the previous order. The judge can make this extension without proof of any further abuse.

Once the paperwork has been filed with the court, it will be taken to a judge for review. An *ex parte* order must be issued or denied on the same day that the application is submitted to the court, unless the application is filed too late in the day to permit effective review. In the case where the application is filed too late, the order must be reviewed and issued or denied on the next day of judicial business in sufficient time for the order to be filed that day with the clerk of the court. **FC § 6326**.

The judge has the discretion to decide whether or not to grant the TRO. Additionally, the judge must decide whether the TRO should be effective immediately or can wait until the court date. If the judge decides that the TRO should take effect immediately, the TRO is effective until the court date. This court date and hearing time will be set forth on the paperwork. TROs usually last between 20 and 25 days until the court hearing date on the matter.

Temporary Restraining Orders (TROs) Pending the Hearing

The court may issue an *ex parte* order enjoining a party from molesting, attacking, striking, stalking, threatening, sexually assaulting, battering, harassing, telephoning (including, but not limited to, making annoying telephone calls), destroying personal property, contacting (either directly or indirectly, by mail or otherwise), coming within a specified distance of or disturbing the peace of the other party and, in the discretion of the court, on a showing of good cause, of other named family or household members. **FC § 6320(a)**.

The court may include in a protective order a grant to the petitioner of the exclusive care, possession or control of any animal owned, possessed, leased, kept or held by either the petitioner or the respondent or a minor child residing in the residence or household of either the petitioner or the respondent. **FC § 6320(b)**.

The court may issue an *ex parte* order excluding a party from the family dwelling, the dwelling of the other party, the common dwelling of both parties or the dwelling of the person who has care, custody and control of a child to be protected from domestic violence for the period of time and on the conditions the court determines, regardless of which party holds legal or equitable title or is the lessee of the dwelling. **FC § 6321(a)**.

Chapter 36: Domestic Violence

The court may issue an *ex parte* order determining the temporary use, possession and control of real or personal property of the parties and the payment of any liens or encumbrances coming due during the period the order is in effect. **FC § 6324.**

The court may issue an *ex parte* order determining the temporary custody and visitation of a minor child(ren). **FC 6323** and **CRC Rule 5.381**.

A TRO can order that the restrained person:

1. Move out of the family house with very little notice[7];
2. Stay away from the family house;
3. Relinquish any and all firearms and ammunition in his or her possession;
4. Stay away from the children, as requested by the victim;
5. Have little or no visitation with his or her children;
6. Stay away from the family pets[8];
7. Stay away from the children's school;
8. Pay certain bills, as requested by the victim;
9. Pay child support;
10. Pay spousal support to the other spouse;
11. Pay the other's spouse's attorney fees and court costs,
12. Not make any changes to insurance policies;
13. Not incur large expenses or do anything significant to affect the victim's property;
14. Return or release certain property;
15. Attend parenting, domestic violence or anger management classes[9]; and/or
16. Comply with the orders of the court.[10]

---

[7] FC § 6321 provides: "(a) The court may issue an ex parte order excluding a party from the family dwelling, the dwelling of the other party, the common dwelling of both parties, or the dwelling of the person who has care, custody, and control of a child to be protected from domestic violence for the period of time and on the conditions the court determines, regardless of which party holds legal or equitable title or is the lessee of the dwelling.
(b) The court may issue an order under subdivision (a) only on a showing of all of the following:
(1) Facts sufficient for the court to ascertain that the party who will stay in the dwelling has a right under color of law to possession of the premises.
(2) That the party to be excluded has assaulted or threatens to assault the other party or any other person under the care, custody, and control of the other party, or any minor child of the parties or of the other party.
(3) That physical or emotional harm would otherwise result to the other party, to any person under the care, custody, and control of the other party, or to any minor child of the parties or of the other party."
[8] FC § 6320(b) provides: "On a showing of good cause, the court may include in a protective order a grant to the petitioner of the exclusive care, possession, or control of any animal owned, possessed, leased, kept, or held by either the petitioner or the respondent or a minor child residing in the residence or household of either the petitioner or the respondent. The court may order the respondent to stay away from the animal and forbid the respondent from taking, transferring, encumbering, concealing, molesting, attacking, striking, threatening, harming, or otherwise disposing of the animal."
[9] Judicial Council form DV-110 so provides.
[10] FC § 6322 provides that "The court may issue an ex parte order enjoining a party from specified behavior that the court determines is necessary to effectuate orders under FC § 6320 or 6321."

Chapter 36: Domestic Violence

While this TRO provides that the abuser is court-ordered to refrain from certain behavior, this does not mean that the victim will be safe from the abuser. A RO only protects the victim on paper.

The RO orders that the abuser stay away from the victim for a specified period of time. It does not prevent the domestic violence from continuing.

Once the soon-to-be restrained person has been served, he or she has a right to file an answer to the RO request. The answer will contain the restrained person's side of the story.
It should be noted that a RO is NOT a dissolution/divorce such that it ends a marriage or domestic partnership, nor does it establish parentage of the children with the restrained person.

b. Notice of the Temporary Restraining Order (TRO)

A TRO may be issued with or without notice to restrain any person for the purpose specified in **FC § 6220**[11], if an affidavit or testimony and any additional information provided to the court pursuant to **FC § 6306**[12] shows, to the satisfaction of the court, reasonable proof of a past act or acts of abuse. The court may issue an order under this part based solely on the affidavit or testimony of the person requesting the RO. **FC § 6300**.[13]

After the TRO has been granted, the abuser or soon-to-be-restrained person has to be personally served with all of the paperwork filed with the court. Any person who is at least 18 years old and not a party to the case can serve this paperwork.

In making a protective order, as defined in **FC § 6218**[14], when both parties are present in court, the court must inform both the petitioner and the respondent of the terms of the order, including notice that the respondent is prohibited from owning, possessing, purchasing or receiving or attempting to own, possess, purchase or

---

[11] FC § 6220 provides: "The purpose of this division is to prevent acts of domestic violence, abuse, and sexual abuse and to provide for a separation of the persons involved in the domestic violence for a period sufficient to enable these persons to seek a resolution of the causes of the violence."
[12] FC § 6306 discusses searching of specific records and databases prior to issuance or denial of order; information to be obtained; release of information to parties; and confidentiality.
[13] This code was amended effective January 1, 2019. The amended code provides: "(a) An order may be issued under this part to restrain any person for the purpose specified in Section 6220, if an affidavit or testimony and any additional information provided to the court pursuant to Section 6306, shows, to the satisfaction of the court, reasonable proof of a past act or acts of abuse. The court may issue an order under this part based solely on the affidavit or testimony of the person requesting the restraining order.
(b) An ex parte restraining order issued pursuant to Article 1 (commencing with Section 6320) shall not be denied solely because the other party was not provided with notice."
[14] FC § 6218 provides: "Protective order means an order that includes any of the following restraining orders, whether issued ex parte, after notice and hearing, or in a judgment:
(a) An order described in Section 6320 enjoining specific acts of abuse.
(b) An order described in Section 6321 excluding a person from a dwelling.
(c) An order described in Section 6322 enjoining other specified behavior."

receive a firearm or ammunition, and including notice of the penalty for violation. **FC § 6304**.

c. The Restraining Order (RO) Hearing

Pursuant to **CRC Rule 5.151** the court may be requested to:

(1) Make orders to help prevent an immediate danger or irreparable harm to a party or to the children involved in the matter;
(2) Make orders to help prevent immediate loss or damage to property subject to disposition in the case; or
(3) Make orders about procedural matters, including the following:

> **(a)** Setting a date for a hearing on the matter that is sooner than that of a regular hearing (granting an order shortening time for hearing);
> **(b)** Shortening or extending the time required for the moving party to serve the other party with the notice of the hearing and supporting papers (grant an order shortening time for service); and
> **(c)** Continuing a hearing or trial.

At the hearing on the date set forth on the TRO, it is within the judge's discretion to decide whether or not to continue the RO. If the judge decides to extend the RO, it becomes a **permanent** order that may last for up to five years. **FC § 6345**.

The permanent order is effective when made. The law enforcement agency must enforce it immediately on receipt. "It is enforceable anywhere in California by any law enforcement agency that has received the order or is shown a copy of the order." If proof of service on the restrained person has not been received, the law enforcement agency will advise the restrained person of the terms of the order and then enforce it. **FC § 6224.**

The personal conduct, stay-away and residence exclusion orders contained in a court order issued after notice and a hearing may have a duration of not more than five years, subject to termination or modification by further order of the court either on written stipulation filed with the court or on the motion of a party depending upon the discretion of the court. These orders may be renewed, upon the request of a party, either for five years or permanently, without a showing of any further abuse since the issuance of the original order, subject to termination or modification by further order of the court either on written stipulation filed with the court or on the motion of a party. The request for renewal may be brought at any time within the three months before the expiration of the orders. **FC § 6345**.

The court can grant or deny the TRO request at the hearing. When determining whether to make any orders under this subdivision, the court must consider whether failure to make any of these orders may jeopardize the safety of the petitioner and the children for whom the custody or visitation orders are sought. If the court makes any order for custody, visitation or support, that order continues or survives the termination of any protective order. If a court denies a request for a RO, a brief written statement of the reasons must be included in the record. **FC § 6340(1a), (b)**.[15]

An order denying a petition for an *ex parte* order pursuant to **FC § 6320** must include the reasons for denying the petition.

An order denying a jurisdictionally adequate petition for an *ex parte* order, pursuant to **FC § 6320**, must provide the petitioner the right to a noticed hearing on the earliest date that the business of the court will permit, but not later than 21 days or, if good cause appears to the court, twenty-five (25) days from the date of the order. The petitioner must serve on the respondent, at least five (5) days before the hearing, copies of all supporting papers filed with the court, including the application and affidavits.

If there is no expiration date on the face of the form, then the order has a duration of three years from the date of issuance. **FC § 6345(c)**.

Finally, pursuant to **FC § 3044,** there is a rebuttable presumption that it would be detrimental to a child's best interests to grant custody to a parent who has been convicted of perpetrating a domestic violence crime against the other party seeking custody of the child, against the child or the child's siblings "or against any person in subparagraph (C) of paragraph (1) of subdivision (b) of Section 3011 with whom the party has a relationship, there is a rebuttable presumption that an award of sole

---

[15] FC § 6340 was amended effective January 1, 2019. The added language is bolded. (1) The court may issue any of the orders described in Article 1 (commencing with Section 6320) after notice and a hearing. When determining whether to make any orders under this subdivision, the court shall consider whether failure to make any of these orders may jeopardize the safety of the petitioner and the children for whom the custody or visitation orders are sought. If the court makes any order for custody, visitation, or support, that order shall survive the termination of any protective order. The Judicial Council shall provide notice of this provision on any Judicial Council forms related to this subdivision. **(2)**
(A) If at the time of a hearing with respect to an order issued pursuant to this part based on an ex parte temporary restraining order, the court determines that, after diligent effort, the petitioner has been unable to accomplish personal service, and that there is reason to believe that the restrained party is evading service, the court may permit an alternative method of service designed to give reasonable notice of the action to the respondent. Alternative methods of service include, but are not limited to, the following:
(i) Service by publication pursuant to the standards set forth in Section 415.50 of the Code of Civil Procedure.
(ii) Service by first-class mail sent to the respondent at the most current address for the respondent that is available to the court or delivering a copy of the pleadings and orders at the respondent's home or place of employment, pursuant to the standards set forth in Sections 415.20 to 415.40, inclusive, of the Code of Civil Procedure.
(B) If the court permits an alternative method of service under this paragraph, the court shall grant a continuance to allow for the alternative service pursuant to Section 245.
(b) The court shall, upon denying a petition under this part, provide a brief statement of the reasons for the decision in writing or on the record. A decision statin g "denied" is insufficient.
(c) The court may issue an order described in Section 6321 excluding a person from a dwelling if the court finds that physical or emotional harm would otherwise result to the other party, to a person under the care, custody, and control of the other party, or to a minor child of the parties or of the other party. FC § 6340 was amended effective January 1, 2019.

or joint physical or legal custody of a child to a person who has perpetrated domestic violence is detrimental to the best interests of the child, pursuant to Sections 3011 and 3020. This presumption may only be rebutted by a preponderance of the evidence.[16]

d. Mutual Restraining Orders (ROs)

As the following case demonstrates, **FC § 6305** requires that the court make detailed findings of fact "indicating that both parties acted as a primary aggressor and that neither party acted primarily in self-defense" before the issuance of mutual ROs.

> ***MAURA MONTERROSO, Plaintiff and Appellant, v. MARIO LOPEZ MORAN, Defendant and Respondent.***
> COURT OF APPEAL OF CALIFORNIA, SECOND APPELLATE DISTRICT, DIVISION TWO
> 135 Cal.App.4th 732; 37 Cal.Rptr.3d 694
> January 11, 2006, Filed
> (*Monterroso v. Moran*)

Maura Monterroso (Monterroso) and Mario Lopez Moran (Moran) are married, they used to live together, and they have minor children together. In the proceeding below, Monterroso sought temporary restraining orders against Moran under the Domestic Violence Prevention Act.[17] She requested that the trial court order Moran not to harass or contact her or her children, and to stay at least 100 yards away. She also requested that the trial court order Moran to attend a batterer intervention program, and that he not borrow against, sell or destroy any possessions or property.

Her application detailed the following facts: She and Moran separated in August 2004. Once he found out where she was living, he came into her home without permission and threatened their children, telling them that they needed to come see him. In October of that year, because he was angry at their 16-year-old daughter for having a boyfriend, he told Monterroso and their 13-year-old daughter that ?you are going to die." He was driving Monterroso's car at the time. When she tried to get the keys, he grabbed her arm and left bruises. A few days later, when she went to pick up her son from a babysitter across the street from Moran's house, Moran showed her a knife, pointed it at several areas of his body and said that he would hurt himself to show his love for her. Moran accused Monterroso of having an affair with a friend that was giving Monterroso a place to stay. Subsequently, she found videotapes that Moran took of her without her knowledge.

On January 1, 2005, Moran came to her house and began verbally abusing her. He was upset that she would not move back in with him and told her that she was trash. He took her keys, car, wallet and house-cleaning materials that she uses for her job. A few days later she went to Moran's house to retrieve her house-cleaning materials from her car. He grabbed her by the hair, dragged her into his house and told her that he was going to kill

---

[16] This code was amended effective January 1, 2019.

[17] This code was amended effective January 1, 2019.

her. Then he covered her face with a pillow. After she struggled to get free, he put his hand on her throat and choked her. He picked her up by her hair and hit her head on a heater. He slapped her. She ended up with a cut lip and a chipped tooth. When she screamed, he stuck his hand in her mouth and scratched the roof of her mouth. He went to the kitchen and she ran outside to where her daughter was waiting and called the police.

After the police arrived, she was told that Moran had already called and accused her of trying to kill him. Moran had apparently cut his chest with a knife. Both Monterroso and Moran were arrested. Eventually, Moran admitted that Monterroso had not tried to kill him. She was released.

Attached to Monterroso's application was a copy of an emergency protective order issued the date Moran was arrested. The emergency protective order lasted four days and instructed Moran not to contact or harass Monterroso. It instructed him to stay at least 100 yards away from her.

Moran filed an answer.

The matter came on for hearing. Moran was represented by counsel, but Monterroso was not. Both parties were assisted by a Spanish-language interpreter.
According to the trial court, it read Monterroso's papers, but it did not read Moran's answer. The reason given for not reading Moran's answer was that he had been arrested and the trial court wanted to respect his constitutional right to remain silent in case he was charged with a crime.

When the trial court asked if the matter could be resolved, Moran's counsel indicated that the parties went to conciliation court that very morning and had agreed to make the restraining orders mutual, but they could not agree on child custody and visitation. The trial court asked Monterroso if she would be agreeable to mutual restraining orders. She said "yes."

The trial court altered the proposed restraining order submitted by Monterroso to make it mutual. Each party signed it. The altered order prohibited each party from, inter alia, harassing, attacking, striking, threatening, assaulting, or stalking the other, or from destroying the personal property of the other, for a period of six months. Thereafter, the order was entered. The trial court made no findings of fact.

[Monterroso timely appealed the] order entering a mutual restraining order enjoining her and her husband, Mario Lopez Moran (Moran), from specific acts of abuse. She argues that the trial court failed to make detailed findings, as required by FC § 6305.

DISCUSSION
This case presents the following question: Is reversal required if the trial court did not make the detailed findings of fact required by FC § 6305. This is a question of law. We review questions of law de novo.

The language of FC § 6305 is clear and its plain meaning must be respected. A trial court has no statutory power to issue a mutual order enjoining parties from specific acts of abuse described in FC § 6320 without the required findings of fact. When a trial court issues such an order in contravention of its statutory obligation to make the required findings of fact, it acts in excess of its jurisdiction.

Chapter 36: Domestic Violence

> Having agreed to the mutual restraining order, the question arises whether Monterroso can challenge it on appeal.
>
> Our Supreme Court recently summarized the pertinent body of law this way: "[W]hen a statute authorizes [a] prescribed procedure, and the court acts contrary to the authority thus conferred, it has exceeded its jurisdiction. When a court has fundamental jurisdiction, but acts in excess of its jurisdiction, its act or judgment is merely voidable. That is, its act or judgment is valid until it is set aside, and a party may be precluded from setting it aside by 'principles of estoppel, disfavor of collateral attack or res judicata." (People v. American Contractors Indemnity Co. (2004) 33 Cal.4th 653, 661 [16 Cal.Rptr.3d 76, 93 P.3d 1020].)
>
> There is nothing in the record suggesting that the principles of estoppel bar this direct appeal. We note that Monterroso cleans houses for a living. She appeared at the hearing without representation and needed a Spanish-language interpreter. She did not display any legal sophistication. Though the trial court asked if she was amenable to a mutual restraining order, the trial court did not ask her if she understood that a mutual restraining order required a detailed finding that both parties acted primarily as aggressors and not primarily in self-defense during a prior incident. Nor did the trial court ask her to stipulate to such facts. Because the trial court did not fully explain the import of a mutual restraining order, there is no indication that Monterroso could appreciate all of its ramifications. Under these circumstances, it cannot be said that Monterroso consented to the mutual restraining order such that she is estopped from seeking redress on appeal.
>
> Monterroso was never informed that she had every right to insist that the trial court rule on the merits of her application for restraining orders against Moran. At the hearing, it was Moran's counsel who brought up the idea of a mutual restraining order. The trial court did not inquire about the allegations of terrible domestic violence in Monterroso's application. Instead, it expressed concern over protecting Moran's constitutional right against self-incrimination and declined to review his answer. Then the trial court asked if Monterroso was amenable to a mutual restraining order. The inference is that the trial court decided that a mutual restraining order was an expedient way to protect or mollify Moran and resolve the matter without reaching the merits.
>
> **We write with an eye toward the role of the courts in our community. Though we do not know what actually transpired between Monterroso and Moran, we do know this: Domestic violence is a grievous problem in today's world, and its victims often have few places to turn. The courts must be sensitive to allegations of domestic violence, root out the truth in each case, and protect victims when possible. Victims should be guided through our judicial system, not herded.**
>
> We hold that unless a trial court makes the detailed findings required by FC § 6305, it acts in excess of its jurisdiction by entering a mutual restraining order. The order is reversed. Upon remand, the trial court is directed to rule upon the merits of Monterroso's application for restraining orders against Moran.

In *Melissa G. v. Raymond M.* (2018) 27 Cal.App.5th 360 the trial court issued mutual restraining orders against mother and father. Father appealed, and even though it appeared in the record that father was the aggressor, the Appellate Court stated that:

Chapter 36: Domestic Violence

> our inquiry is limited to whether there is substantial evidence to support such a finding (a restraining order against father only) and we find sufficient evidence in the record to warrant a remand for the court to make its own factual determination. *Id.* at 374.

3. Emergency Orders

Emergency orders are requests for court orders that cannot wait until a judge can hear the matter on the court's regular business calendar. These orders are not made pursuant to the Domestic Violence Prevention Act.

CRC Rule 5.151 provides that emergency orders, also known as *ex parte* applications in family law cases, are governed by this rule and may be referred to as the **emergency orders rules**.

Applications for emergency orders can request to modify child custody or visitation (**FC § 3064**) because there is a possibility of immediate harm to the child or an immediate risk that the child will be removed from the State of California.

CRC Rule 5.165 provides that a party requesting an emergency order must give notice by telephone, in writing or by voicemail message. All parties and their attorneys must be given notice no later than 10:00 a.m. on the court day before the matter is heard. After giving notice, each party must be served a copy of all documents that are being used to request an emergency order. There are some exceptions to giving the notice.[18] This rule does not apply to a party seeking emergency orders under the Domestic Violence Prevention Act.

4. The Restraining Order (RO) Paperwork

If the law enforcement officers do request that an EPO be issued, that order lasts for only five to seven days, just long enough for the victim to seek a temporary RO. In order to make this request, the victim must complete the following mandatory judicial council forms:

(1) *Confidential CLETS Information* (form *CLETS-001*);
(2) *Request for Domestic Violence Restraining Order* (form *DV-100*);
(3) *Description of Abuse* (*Domestic Violence Prevention*) (form *DV-101*);
(4) *Notice of Court Hearing* (*Domestic Violence*) (form *DV-109*); and
(5) *Temporary Restraining Order* (CLETS–TRO) (form *DV-110*).

---

[18] The exceptions for notice are:
"(1) Giving notice would frustrate the purpose of the order;
(2) Giving notice would result in immediate and irreparable harm to the applicant or the children who may be affected by the order sought;
(3) Giving notice would result in immediate and irreparable damage to or loss of property subject to disposition in the case;
(4) The parties agreed in advance that notice will not be necessary with respect to the matter that is the subject of the request for emergency orders; and
(5) The party made reasonable and good faith efforts to give notice to the other party, and further efforts to give notice would probably be futile or unduly burdensome."

Chapter 36: Domestic Violence

If there are children and custody and/or visitation orders for the children are requested, then *Request for Child Custody and Visitation Orders* (form *DV-105*) may be added.

The documents that are required for emergency orders must be in writing and must include all of the following completed documents when relevant to the relief requested:

(1) *Request for Order* (form *FL-300*) that identifies the relief requested;
(2) A current *Income and Expense Declaration* (form *FL-150*) or *Financial Statement (Simplified)* (form *FL-155*) and *Property Declaration* (form *FL-160*);
(3) *Temporary Orders* (form *FL-305*) to serve as the proposed temporary order;
(4) A written declaration regarding notice of application for emergency orders based on personal knowledge; and
(5) A memorandum of points and authorities only if required by the court. **CRC Rule 5.151**.

After all of the necessary forms are completed, the forms must be filed with the court at the venue set forth by the local rules of that county. There is no filing fee for an application, a responsive pleading or an order to show cause that seeks to obtain, modify or enforce a protective order or other order authorized by this division when the request for the other order is necessary to obtain or give effect to a protective order. **FC § 6222.**

The Tort Action

As the following case demonstrates, a victim in a domestic violence case has a right to sue the abuser. The statute of limitations is three years from the last time the abuse occurred to file a civil case for damages against the abuser.

> ***MICHELE NOEL PUGLIESE, Petitioner, v. THE SUPERIOR COURT OF LOS ANGELES COUNTY, Respondent; DANTE J. PUGLIESE, Real Party in Interest.***
> COURT OF APPEAL OF CALIFORNIA, SECOND APPELLATE DISTRICT, DIVISION TWO
> 146 Cal.App.4th 1444; 53 Cal.Rptr.3d 681
> January 23, 2007, Filed
> (*Pugliese v. Superior Court*)
>
> Michele and Dante were married in January 1989. Michele filed a petition for dissolution of that marriage on April 22, 2002. On April 2, 2004, Michele sued Dante for assault, battery, intentional infliction of emotional distress and violation of civil rights. Michele alleged Dante had engaged in a pattern of domestic abuse, both physical and mental, which began within a few months of the marriage. Although the physical acts allegedly ceased in April 2001, Michele claims the emotional abuse continued until April 2004. In September 2005, Dante filed a motion in limine to exclude evidence of any assaults and batteries alleged to have occurred more than three years prior to the filing of the complaint, claiming that Michele could not recover damages for acts occurring prior to that time because the statute of limitations set forth in CCP § 340.15 barred such

recovery. The trial court granted Dante's in limine motion, and this petition followed.

The issue presented is whether Michele is barred, pursuant to the three-year limitations period set forth in CCP § 340.15(a), from recovering damages for acts of domestic violence occurring prior to April 2001.

DISCUSSION

Spouses are permitted to pursue appropriate civil remedies against each other, including lawsuits asserting the tort of domestic violence. (CC § 1708.6.)

CC § 1708.6(a) provides: "A person is liable for the tort of domestic violence if the plaintiff proves both of the following elements: (1) The infliction of injury upon the plaintiff resulting from abuse, as defined in PC § 13700(a). (2) The abuse was committed by the defendant, a person having a relationship with the plaintiff as defined in PC § 13700(b)."

The time for commencement of an action under CC § 1708.6 is governed by CCP § 340.15, which provides: "(a) In any civil action for recovery of damages suffered as a result of domestic violence, the time for commencement of the action shall be the later of the following:

"(1) Within three years from the date of the last act of domestic violence by the defendant against the plaintiff.

"(2) Within three years from the date the plaintiff discovers or reasonably should have discovered that an injury or illness resulted from an act of domestic violence by the defendant against the plaintiff.

"(B) As used in this section, 'domestic violence' has the same meaning as defined in FC § 6211."

FC § 6211 defines "domestic violence" as "abuse perpetrated against ... [a] spouse or former spouse." (FC § 6211(a).)

"Abuse" is defined as any of the following: "(a) Intentionally or recklessly to cause or attempt to cause bodily injury. (b) Sexual assault. (c) To place a person in reasonable apprehension of imminent serious bodily injury to that person or to another. (d) To engage in any behavior that has been or could be enjoined pursuant to Section 6320."[19] (FC § 6203.)

The rights and remedies provided in CC § 1708.6 are in addition to any other rights and remedies provided by law. (CC § 1708.6(d).) Thus, spouses and ex-spouses are entitled to allege, as did Michele, causes of action for assault, battery and intentional infliction of emotional distress. When such counts are alleged, we look to the limitations period applicable to each of these causes of action to determine if they are barred by the statute of limitations. Causes of action for assault, battery and intentional infliction of emotional distress are governed by the two-year statute of limitations set forth in CCP § 335.1.

---

[19] FC § 6320 permits a court to enjoin a party from "molesting, attacking, striking, stalking, threatening, sexually assaulting, battering, harassing, telephoning, including, but not limited to, annoying telephone calls as described in PC § 653m, destroying personal property, contacting, either directly or indirectly, by mail or otherwise, coming within a specified distance of, or disturbing the peace of the other party ... ." (FC § 6320.)

Chapter 36: Domestic Violence

(CCP § 335.1.) Michele alleges the last physical act of abuse occurred in April 2001. Thus, her assault and battery causes of action are barred by CCP § 335.1. As for Michele's intentional infliction of emotional distress claim, she alleges the last act of emotional abuse occurred in April 2004, less than two years prior to the filing of the complaint. Thus, her intentional infliction of emotional distress claim was timely filed pursuant to CCP § 335.1.

Although the assault and battery causes of action are barred by the applicable statute of limitations, the complaint, taken as a whole, alleges a violation of CC § 1708.6. Michele claims that during the period June 1989 to April 2004, Dante shoved, pushed, kicked, hit, slapped, shook, choked and sexually abused her. She also alleges he pulled her hair, pinched and twisted her flesh, threatened to kill her, threatened her with bodily harm, confined her in the family car while driving erratically and drunkenly and infected her with sexually transmitted diseases. Clearly, Michele has alleged that Dante intentionally or recklessly caused or attempted to cause her bodily injury, sexually assaulted her, placed her in reasonable apprehension of imminent serious bodily injury and engaged in behavior that could have been enjoined pursuant to FC § 6320. We therefore conclude Michele has set forth a cognizable claim for domestic violence. Accordingly, the three-year limitations period set forth in CCP § 340.15 applies. (CCP § 340.15.)

Because Michele alleges the last physical act of abuse occurred in April 2001 and the last act of emotional abuse occurred in April 2004, and because the complaint was filed within three years of these dates, Michele's CC § 1708.6 domestic violence claim was timely filed. Michele contends she is entitled to seek damages for acts of domestic abuse occurring beyond the three-year limitations period set forth in CCP § 340.15(a). We agree.

CCP § 335.1, the statute setting forth the limitations period for assault and battery between nondomestic partners, views each incident of abuse separately and the limitations period commences at the time the incident occurs. By contrast, CCP § 340.15 provides that domestic violence lawsuits must be commenced within three years "from the date of the *last act* of domestic violence … ." (CCP § 340.15(a)(1), italics added.) The words "last act" are superfluous if they have no meaning. By adding these words, we believe the Legislature adopted by statute the continuing tort theory, thus allowing domestic violence victims to recover damages for all acts of domestic violence occurring during the marriage, provided the victim proves a continuing course of abusive conduct and files suit within three years of the "last act of domestic violence."

Dante makes little attempt to explain the Legislature's use of the words "last act," focusing instead on the purpose of statutes of limitations, which is to "prevent the resurgence of stale claims after the lapse of long periods of time as a result of which loss of papers, disappearance of witnesses, [and] feeble recollections … make ineffectual or extremely difficult a fair presentation of the case." (*County of L. A. v. Security First Nat. Bank* (1948) 84 Cal.App.2d 575, 580 [191 P.2d 78].) Dante concludes the situation at hand is precisely the sort in which statutes of limitations must be strictly enforced; otherwise he will be forced to combat evidence that has long since faded in amount, potency, reliability, and relevance.

While we recognize the difficulty a spouse or ex-spouse may have in defending against domestic violence cases, the continuing tort doctrine seems especially applicable in such cases. Generally, a limitations period begins to run upon the occurrence of the last fact essential to the cause of action. However, where a tort involves a continuing wrong, the statute of limitations does not begin to run until the date of the last injury or when the tortious acts cease.

Dante contends that the continuing tort doctrine should not be applied to violations of CC § 1708.6. He claims, in essence, that the tort of domestic violence is made up of essentially three separate torts, i.e., assault, battery and the infliction of emotional distress. According to Dante, because a victim knows she or he has been injured at the time the assault, battery or infliction of emotional distress occurs, the victim must file suit against the abuser within two years of the act or forever lose the right to do so. However, the tort of domestic violence is more complex than Dante concedes. Domestic violence is the physical, sexual, psychological, and/or emotional abuse of a victim by his or her intimate partner, with the goal of asserting and maintaining power and control over the victim. Most domestic violence victims are subjected to "an ongoing strategy of intimidation, isolation, and control that extends to all areas of a woman's life, including sexuality; material necessities; relations with family, children, and friends; and work." (Stark, Re-Presenting Woman Battering: From Battered Woman Syndrome to Coercive Control (1995) 58 Alb. L.Rev. 973, 986, fn. omitted.) Pursuing a remedy, criminal or civil, while in such an environment defies the abuser's control, thus exposing the victim to considerable risk of violence.

The conduct set forth in Michele's complaint could be considered separate offenses of assault, battery and intentional infliction of emotional distress. However, Michele has alleged continual domestic abuse over a 15-year period, and that Dante's tortious conduct did not completely cease until April 2004. Accordingly, Michele's CC § 1708.6 cause of action did not accrue until April 2004 and she is entitled to seek recovery of damages for acts occurring prior to that time.

A considerable portion of Dante's brief is devoted to a discussion of the legislative history of CCP § 340.15. While it is clear the Legislature, in adopting the three-year limitations period, understood that victims of domestic violence need additional time within which to file suit, nothing contained in the legislative history conclusively establishes whether the Legislature intended courts to treat a CC § 1708.6 tort as a continuing wrong. The legislative history of CC §1708.6 is more enlightening.

In adopting CC § 1708.6, our Legislature declared: "(a) Acts of violence occurring in a domestic context are increasingly widespread. (b) These acts merit special consideration as torts, because the elements of trust, physical proximity, and emotional intimacy necessary to domestic relationships in a healthy society makes participants in those relationships particularly vulnerable to physical attack by their partners. (c) It is the purpose of this act to enhance the civil remedies available to victims of domestic violence in order to underscore society's condemnation of these acts, to ensure complete recovery to victims, and to impose significant financial consequences upon perpetrators."

Clearly our Legislature understood that domestic violence encompasses a series of acts, including assault, battery and intentional infliction of emotional distress, and that when these acts are coupled with an oppressive atmosphere of control, the continuing tort of domestic violence results.

The legislative history of CC § 1708.6 and the plain language of CCP § 340.15 convince us that damages are available to victims of domestic violence, not just for the "last act" of abuse, but for acts occurring prior to the date of the "last act." Accordingly, we conclude

Chapter 36: Domestic Violence

> the trial court erred in granting Dante's in limine motion to exclude all references to acts of domestic violence alleged to have occurred three years prior to the date Michele filed her domestic violence complaint.
>
> We conclude that domestic violence litigants are entitled to seek recovery for all acts of domestic abuse occurring during the domestic relationship, so long as the litigant proves a continuing course of abusive conduct.

Real-time GPS Monitoring

Currently, California uses a system of passive monitoring, whereby an abuser wears a GPS bracelet that checks the abuser's whereabouts once a day or even less frequently. With an active or real-time GPS tracking system, the abuser (restrained person) wears a GPS leg bracelet that transmits in real-time. The victim is given a transmitter so that he or she can be reached at any time, night or day. Both the victim and the restrained person's movements are monitored 24/7.

A real person monitors the screen showing the movements of the restrained person and the victim. If the restrained person comes within a certain distance of the victim, the victim is alerted, which gives the victim the time to leave the area. Then the police are called to let them know that the abuser has violated his or her restraining order. Because the victim is notified PRIOR TO THE ARRIVAL OF HIS OR HER ABUSER, the victim has the time to leave and is, thus, less likely to become a murder statistic.[20]

While it may seem that this GPS monitoring system would cost more than the current system, it actually can cost less. The current passive check-maybe-once-a-day system costs about $18-$20 each day for each abuser; the real-time or active GPS system costs about $12 per day.[21]

FC § 6326 the bolded text shows the addition.

> An ex parte order under this article shall be issued or denied on the same day that the application is submitted to the court, unless the application is filed too late in the day to permit effective review, in which case the order shall be issued or denied on the next day of judicial business in sufficient time for the order to be filed that day with the clerk of the court. **A petition for an ex parte order pursuant to this article shall not be denied solely because the other side was not provided with notice.**

---

[20] The *San Diego Union Tribune* reported that "murders attributed to domestic and family violence increased by 43% from 2013 to 2014."
[20] These figures are based upon Jeff Zevely's report on channel 8 that aired in 2010. In his report Mr. Zevely showed how the system worked and how much it would cost to use using a tracking device call a "tracker pal".
[21] These figures are based upon Jeff Zevely's report on channel 8 that aired in 2010. In his report Mr. Zevely showed how the system worked and how much it would cost to use using a tracking device call a "tracker pal".

Chapter 36: Domestic Violence

EDUCATIONAL EXERCISES

1. What is Domestic Violence?

2. Are domestic violence acts real crimes? Explain.

3. Who most often commits domestic violence?

4. List the 3 kinds of protective orders:

5. List 5 restraining orders that a court can make re: the restrained person
6. Explain the procedure that a victim must follow to get a temporary restraining order from the court.

CHAPTER 37: Living Together/*Marvin* Actions

In Brief...

MARVIN CASES:
- Were named after the case **Marvin v. Marvin**;
- Are cases with issues involving unmarried couples who have separated after cohabitation;
- Are decided by case law because there is no codified law;
- Have contract issues that follow the same rules and rights as other contract cases (*Schafer v. Superior Court*); and
- Can be tried in family or civil court, depending upon the local rules where the action lies.

MARVIN PROPERTY CLAIMS:
- Courts usually sever illicit parts of *Marvin* agreements, if possible, so that if a contract can be proven, it may be upheld (*Bergen*);
- Parties can agree to pool their assets that are acquired during their cohabitation (*Trutalli*);
- If both parties contribute to the purchase of the property, then it will be divided equally;
- When title to property is taken in joint names, the property is jointly owned and will be partitioned if necessary to divide (*Milian*); and
- If title to property is in only one cohabiting party's name, the nonowner party must prove that the owner is not as set forth on the title by clear and convincing evidence (*Toney*).

MARVIN SUPPORT CLAIMS, (Palimony):
- Are support that one unmarried, no-longer cohabiting partner pays to the other after separation pursuant to their agreement; and
- Support will only be court-ordered if it can be shown that the parties agreed to support the other after separation (*Friedman v. Friedman*).

REMEDIES IN MARVIN ACTIONS:
- That might be appropriate are: constructive trust, resulting trust, quantum meruit (*Marvin*);
- May be a variety of remedies to protect the parties' expectations (*Marvin*);
- May evolve to protect expectations where existing remedies prove inadequate (*Marvin*);
- Cannot be fashioned by a court because existing remedies are inadequate to effect justice *Friedman v. Friedman*); and
- Will not be ordered where no implied *Marvin* contract is found (*Taylor v. Polackwich*).

MARVIN CONTRACTS ARE BREACHED:
- When one partner terminates the relationship (*Whorton v. Dillingham*); and/or
- When the party charged with a duty to perform refuses to do so (*Cochran*

Chapter 37: Living together/*Marvin* Actions

> *v. Cochran*).
> **Statute of Limitations:**
> - The statute of limitations for a cause of action based on equitable grounds is 4 years (*Whorton*); and
> - *Marvin* actions based on an express oral agreement are governed by the 2 year statute of limitations applicable to unwritten contracts (*Cochran*).
>
> **CHART 15: (*Marvin*)/Living Together Rules from Case Law**

Introduction

According to the United States Census Bureau, more and more couples are choosing to remain unmarried. In 2009, there were 6.7 million unmarried couples, and in 2010 that number had risen to 7.5 million. In 2015 there were more cohabiting unmarried couples than married couples.[1]

For unmarried couples, problems often occur when one of the parties wants out of the relationship or one party dies without making the arrangements promised. Unfortunately, even though unmarried couples living together are now the majority, there is no codified law that directly addresses the issues presented by unmarried, cohabiting parties, who are no longer living together. Accordingly, it is the precedents that are set by case law that are used to decide these cases.

Cases with issues involving unmarried couples who have separated after cohabitation are commonly called ***Marvin*** cases after the 1976 case ***Marvin v. Marvin*** (1976) 18 Cal.3d 660, even though the *Marvin* case was not the first of such cases. Claims between these unmarried persons are commonly called ***Marvin* claims**, which regard "an express or implied enforceable contract between two nonmarital partners, usually arising out of some sort of domestic arrangements between those partners." *ALLEN v. STODDARD* (2013) 212 Cal.App.4th 807 at p. 812.

A *Marvin* relationship usually consists of: **(1)** the partner who cares for the home and the children (the homemaker), and **(2)** the partner who is earning the money to support the couple (the supporter). It is by an express or implied agreement between the parties that the homemaker is not employed outside of the home, allowing the supporter to continue to work fulltime advancing and enhancing his or her career with employment opportunities and promotions.

Marvin claims can involve a request to divide all money, assets and property acquired during the cohabitation upon separation. However, this division will only be considered if the parties made such an agreement. While that agreement can be an express written contract, which likely is not the case for most couples, it can also be an implied agreement, providing:

---
[1] All figures were obtained from the United States Census Bureau.

(1) The conduct of the parties so demonstrates the agreement;
(2) The meretricious relationship, if there is one, is not part of that contract; **and**
(3) The evidence demonstrating the contract is proven by a preponderance of the evidence.

Marvin claims can also involve requests for support to be paid by the supporter to the homemaker; this is called **palimony**.[2] Pursuing a palimony claim is often the only avenue for the homemaker to obtain a support order and support will only be court-ordered if it is proven that the parties had a contract with a palimony or support provision. If the supporter disputes that such an agreement was made, this can be a difficult feat to overcome. Accordingly, palimony is rarely ordered.

When a party in a nonmarital relationship dies, a ***Marvin* claim** can be made pursuant to **CC § 366.3**. "*Marvin* claims sometime manifest themselves as breaches of contract to make a will or other disposition from an estate when one of the nonmarital partners dies." *ALLEN v. STODDARD, supra* at p. 812. This matter will be heard in Probate Court. When the nonmarried parties separate after cohabitation and both partners are still living, the matter can be tried in family court or civil court, depending on the superior court rules of the county where the action lies.

Finally, while many people who enter into these relationships think that their relationship will last forever and that the supporter will continue to forever-support the homemaker after the parties separate that is almost never the case.

The Marvin Cases

The case that follows is an abridged version of the California Supreme Court decision in the action between Michelle Triola Marvin[3] and Lee Marvin.[4]

> ***MICHELLE MARVIN, Plaintiff and Appellant, v. LEE MARVIN, Defendant and Respondent***
> Supreme Court of California
> 18 Cal.3d 660; 557 P.2d 106; 134 Cal.Rptr. 815
> December 27, 1976
> (*Marvin I*)
>
> Plaintiff, Michelle Triola Marvin, hereinafter "Michelle", and defendant, Actor Lee Marvin, hereinafter "Marvin" lived together for seven years without marrying; all property acquired during this period was taken in Marvin's name.

---

[2] Besides the term "*Marvin* claim", the *Marvin* case is also known for the word "palimony." Actually, it was the attorney that represented Michelle Triola Marvin in the *Marvin* case, Marvin Mitchelson, who is credited with coining the term "palimony." Marvin Mitchelson was a famous Hollywood divorce lawyer who represented many famous celebrities. He died September 18, 2004.
[3] Michelle Triola Marvin died October 30, 2009. At her death she was two weeks shy of her 76th birthday. She and Dick Van Dyke began living together in 1976 and remained partners until her death.
[4] Actor Lee Marvin was born February 19, 1924, in New York City. He appeared in about 70 films between 1951 and 1986. He was still married to and living with his third wife when he died at the age of 63 in 1987.

When Michelle sued to enforce a contract under which she was entitled to half the property and to support payments, the trial court granted judgment on the pleadings for Marvin, thus leaving him with all property accumulated by the couple during their relationship.

Since the trial court rendered judgment for Marvin on the pleadings, we must accept the allegations of Michelle's complaint as true, determining whether such allegations state, or can be amended to state, a cause of action. We turn therefore to the specific allegations of the complaint.

Michelle avers that in October of 1964 she and Marvin "entered into an oral agreement" that while "the parties lived together they would combine their efforts and earnings and would share equally any and all property accumulated as a result of their efforts whether individual or combined." Furthermore, they agreed to "hold themselves out to the general public as husband and wife" and that Michelle "would further render her services as a companion, homemaker, housekeeper and cook to Marvin.

Shortly thereafter Michelle agreed to "give up her lucrative career as an entertainer [and] singer" in order to "devote her full time to Marvin . . . as a companion, homemaker, housekeeper and cook;" in return Marvin agreed to "provide for all of Michelle's financial support and needs for the rest of her life."

Michelle alleges that she lived with Marvin from October of 1964 through May of 1970 and fulfilled her obligations under the agreement. During this period the parties as a result of their efforts and earnings acquired in Marvin's name substantial real and personal property, including motion picture rights worth over $ 1 million. In May of 1970, however, Marvin compelled Michelle to leave his household. He continued to support Michelle until November of 1971, but thereafter refused to provide further support.

On the basis of these allegations Michelle [asserts a cause of action for declaratory relief, asking the court to determine her contract and property rights.]

After hearing argument the court granted Marvin's motion and entered judgment for Marvin. Michelle moved to set aside the judgment and asked leave to amend her complaint. The trial court denied Michelle's motion, and she appealed from the judgment.

In the case before us Michelle maintains that the trial court erred in denying her a trial on the merits of her contention. Although that court did not specify the ground for its conclusion that Michelle's contractual allegations stated no cause of action, Marvin offers some four theories to sustain the ruling; we proceed to examine them.

[1] Marvin first and principally relies on the contention that the alleged contract is so closely related to the supposed "immoral" character of the relationship between Michelle and himself that the enforcement of the contract would violate public policy. He points to cases asserting that a contract between nonmarital partners is unenforceable if it is "involved in" an illicit relationship or made in "contemplation" of such a relationship.[5] A review of the numerous California decisions concerning contracts between nonmarital partners, however, reveals that the courts have not employed such broad and uncertain standards to strike down contracts.

---

[5] Penal Code section 269a provided that living "in a state of cohabitation and adultery" was prohibited.

[2] Marvin secondly relies upon the ground suggested by the trial court: that the 1964 contract violated public policy because it impaired the community property rights of Betty Marvin, Marvin's lawful wife. Marvin points out that his earnings while living apart from his wife before rendition of the interlocutory decree were community property under 1964 statutory law[6] and that Marvin's agreement with Michelle purported to transfer to her a half interest in that community property. But whether or not Marvin's contract with Michelle exceeded his authority as manager of the community property, Marvin's argument fails for the reason that an improper transfer of community property is not void ab initio, but merely voidable at the instance of the aggrieved spouse.

[3] Marvin's third contention is noteworthy for the lack of authority advanced in its support. He contends that enforcement of the oral agreement between Michelle and himself is barred by Civil Code § 5134, which provides that "All contracts for marriage settlements must be in writing. . . ." A marriage settlement, however, is an agreement in contemplation of marriage in which each party agrees to release or modify the property rights which would otherwise arise from the marriage. The contract at issue here does not conceivably fall within that definition, and thus is beyond the compass of CC § 5134.

[4] Marvin finally argues that enforcement of the contract is barred by Civil Code § 43.5(d), which provides that "No cause of action arises for . . . breach of promise of marriage." This rather strained contention proceeds from the premise that a promise of marriage impliedly includes a promise to support and to pool property acquired after marriage to the conclusion that pooling and support agreements not part of or accompanied by promise of marriage are barred by the section. We conclude that CC § 43.5 is not reasonably susceptible to the interpretation advanced by Marvin, a conclusion demonstrated by the fact that since CC § 43.5 was enacted in 1939, numerous cases have enforced pooling agreements between nonmarital partners, and in none did court or counsel refer to CC § 43.5.

In summary, we base our opinion on the principle that adults who voluntarily live together and engage in sexual relations are nonetheless as competent as any other persons to contract respecting their earnings and property rights.

Of course, they cannot lawfully contract to pay for the performance of sexual services, for such a contract is, in essence, an agreement for prostitution and unlawful for that reason. But they may agree to pool their earnings and to hold all property acquired during the relationship in accord with the law governing community property; conversely they may agree that each partner's earnings and the property acquired from those earnings remains the separate property of the earning partner. So long as the agreement does not rest upon illicit meretricious consideration, the parties may order their economic affairs as they choose, and no policy precludes the courts from enforcing such agreements.

In the present instance, Michelle alleges that the parties agreed to pool their earnings, that they contracted to share equally in all property acquired, and that Marvin agreed to support Michelle. The terms of the contract as alleged do not rest upon any unlawful consideration. We therefore conclude that the complaint furnishes a suitable basis upon which the trial court can render declaratory relief. The trial court consequently erred in

---

[6] Civil Code §§ 169 and 169.2 were replaced in 1970 by CC § 5118. In 1972, CC § 5118 was amended to provide that the earnings and accumulations of both spouses "while living separate and apart from the other spouse, are the separate property of the spouse."

Chapter 37: Living together/*Marvin* Actions

> granting Marvin's motion for judgment on the pleadings.
>
> We conclude that the judicial barriers that may stand in the way of a policy based upon the fulfillment of the reasonable expectations of the parties to a nonmarital relationship should be removed. As we have explained, the courts now hold that express agreements will be enforced unless they rest on an unlawful meretricious consideration.
>
> We add that in the absence of an express agreement, the courts may look to a variety of other remedies in order to protect the parties' lawful expectations.
>
> The courts may inquire into the conduct of the parties to determine whether that conduct demonstrates an implied contract or implied agreement of partnership or joint venture or some other tacit understanding between the parties.
> The courts may, when appropriate, employ principles of constructive trust or resulting trust. Finally, a nonmarital partner may recover in quantum meruit for the reasonable value of household services rendered less the reasonable value of support received if he can show that he rendered services with the expectation of monetary reward.
>
> Since we have determined that Michelle's complaint states a cause of action for breach of an express contract, and, as we have explained, can be amended to state a cause of action independent of allegations of express contract, we must conclude that the trial court erred in granting Marvin a judgment on the pleadings.
>
> The judgment is reversed and the cause is remanded for further proceedings consistent with the views expressed herein.

In remanding the case, the Supreme Court of California stated:

(1) That the trial court should have determined whether or not there was an agreement instead of rendering a judgment on the pleadings;
(2) That parties may agree to pool their earnings and to hold all property acquired during the relationship in accord with the law governing community property… So long as the agreement does not rest upon illicit meretricious consideration, the parties may order their economic affairs as they choose, and no policy precludes the courts from enforcing such agreements;
(3) That courts can look to the conduct of the parties to determine whether the conduct demonstrates an implied contract;
(4) That a nonmarital partner may recover in *quantum meruit* for the reasonable value of household services rendered less the reasonable value of support received if he can show that he rendered services with the expectation of monetary reward; and
(5) If a contract is shown, courts may, when appropriate, employ principles of constructive trust or resulting trust.

After the case was remanded, the trial court found that Michelle was in need of rehabilitation to learn new employable skills and that she should be able to accomplish such rehabilitation in two years. The trial court awarded her the sum of $104,000 for the rehabilitation and for her living expenses (including her debts) during this period of rehabilitation. The trial court explained that it fixed the award at the highest salary that the Michelle had ever earned, namely, $1,000 a week for two years, although Michelle's salary had been at that level for only two weeks and she ordinarily earned less than one-half that amount weekly. Lee Marvin appealed, and that opinion follows.

> **MICHELLE MARVIN, Plaintiff and Respondent, v. LEE MARVIN, Defendant and Appellant**
> Court of Appeal of California, Second Appellate District, Division Three
> 122 Cal.App.3d 871; 176 Cal.Rptr. 555
> August 11, 1981
> (*Marvin II*)
>
> Michelle's amended complaint, upon which this action went to trial, asks, with respect to the support of Michelle by defendant, only that defendant be ordered to pay to Michelle a reasonable sum per month as and for her support and maintenance. Michelle did not ask in this basic pleading for any limited rehabilitative support of the type the trial court apparently on its own initiative subsequently awarded her. Consequently, the special findings of fact and conclusions of law in support of this award must be disregarded as not being within the issues framed by the pleadings. When this is done, the challenged portion of the judgment becomes devoid of any support whatsoever and therefore must be deleted.
>
> [T]he trial court expressly found that Michelle benefited economically and socially from her relationship with defendant and suffered no damage therefrom, even with respect to its termination. Furthermore, the trial court also expressly found that defendant never had any obligation to pay Michelle a reasonable sum as and for her maintenance and that defendant had not been unjustly enriched by reason of the relationship or its termination and that defendant had never acquired anything of value from Michelle by any wrongful act.
>
> Furthermore, the special findings in support of the challenged rehabilitative award merely established Michelle's need therefor and defendant's ability to respond to that need. This is not enough. The award, being nonconsensual in nature, must be supported by some recognized underlying obligation in law or in equity. A court of equity admittedly has broad powers, but it may not create totally new substantive rights under the guise of doing equity.
>
> The trial court in its special conclusions of law addressed to this point attempted to state an underlying obligation by saying that Michelle had a right to assistance from defendant until she became self-supporting. But this special conclusion obviously conflicts with the earlier, more general, finding of the court that defendant has never had and did not then have any obligation to provide Michelle with a reasonable sum for her support and maintenance and, in view of the already-mentioned findings of no damage (but benefit instead), no unjust enrichment and no wrongful act on the part of defendant with respect to either the relationship or its termination, it is clear that no basis whatsoever, either in equity or in law, exists for the challenged rehabilitative award. It therefore must be deleted from the judgment.
>
> The judgment under appeal is modified by deleting therefrom the portion thereof under

Chapter 37: Living together/*Marvin* Actions

> appeal, namely, the rehabilitative award of $ 104,000 to Michelle Marvin. As modified it is affirmed.

The net result from both of these *Marvin* decisions was that Michelle had "benefited economically and socially from her relationship with Lee Marvin and suffered no damage therefrom, even with respect to its termination" and was, thus, not entitled to anything from the major motion picture star, Lee Marvin.

Marvin Property Claims

A *Marvin* property claim is a claim that one of the unmarried, newly separated, cohabiting parties is entitled to one-half of all of the property that was acquired during the cohabitation. However, in order to prevail, it must be proven that the parties so agreed and their agreement was not simply meretricious[7].

1. The Meretricious Agreement

In ***BERGEN v. WOOD*** (1993) 14 Cal.App.4th 854, Wood, a Bel-Air resident, was a former president of Lockheed and a widower. He met Bergen, a German actress, in Monte Carlo in the summer of 1981. At that time, Wood was 65 and Bergen was 45. They quickly developed an intimate relationship.

The parties never cohabited. Bergen maintained her apartment in Munich, Germany. While Bergen was in California she kept a room at the Beverly Pavilion Hotel in Beverly Hills. Bergen was Wood's travelling companion and accompanied him to social events. Wood provided Bergen with money, and paid for travel expenses and hotel accommodations.

The relationship ended after seven years and Bergen retained Attorney Marvin M. Mitchelson to file a complaint against Wood for breach of express contract, breach of implied contract and fraud and deceit.

Bergen alleged: In July 1982, the parties entered into an oral agreement whereby she agreed to be Wood's "companion, his confidante, homemaker, and assist [Wood] with his business affairs by acting as a social hostess." In return, Wood would provide for her financial support in accordance with her needs and his ability to pay.

The trial court found that there was no implied-in-fact contract and no conduct by Wood to support the claim of fraud and deceit. However, there was an oral contract between the parties that Wood would provide for Bergen's support. While Wood repeatedly promised Bergen he would always provide for her, there were no discussions or promises between the parties regarding the *specific* duration or amount of support, or whether support would continue after the relationship ended. Despite the lack of express terms, the duration and amount of support could be

---
[7] The word used in this context means having to do with prostitution.

ascertained from the circumstances, including the prior level of support. Based thereon, Bergen was entitled to $ 3,500 per month for 48 months.

Wood appealed from the judgment. The Appellate court in reversing the trial court's decision stated that services as a social companion and hostess are not normally compensated; they are inextricably intertwined with the sexual relationship. Since Bergen failed to show any consideration independent of the sexual aspect of the relationship, the agreement was unenforceable for lack of consideration.

In ***CROSLIN v. SCOTT*** (1957) 154 Cal.App.2d 767, the parties lived together as man and wife, though not married, agreeing that he would furnish the home and that she would furnish the food and do the cooking and housekeeping. This relationship was terminated when the plaintiff left and married another. The defendant thereafter wrote to the plaintiff telling him that she missed him, and she asked him to return to her. She said that she would give him the extra lot for the work he had done and the money that he put into other property belonging to her.

The plaintiff accepted. His marriage was thereafter annulled, and the plaintiff moved back. The plaintiff purchased lumber and started building a house. When the house was completed, the parties moved in. When the parties separated, sometime later, the defendant refused to give the plaintiff a share of the property. The plaintiff sued. The trial court granted the defendant's motion for a nonsuit, based upon the ground of illegality of the alleged agreement. The appellate court reversed and remanded stating that the contract did not have to be based upon a meretricious relationship and that it could be a valid contract.

Finally, the principal argument advanced by Lee Marvin in the first *Marvin* case was that the contract alleged by Michelle was so closely related to the immoral character of the relationship between Michelle and him that the enforcement of the contract would violate public policy. *Id.* at p. 671.

The court stated that:

> a standard which inquires whether an agreement is "involved" in or "contemplates" a nonmarital relationship is vague and unworkable. Virtually all agreements between nonmarital partners can be said to be "involved" in some sense in the fact of their mutual sexual relationship, or to "contemplate" the existence of that relationship. Thus defendant's proposed standards, if taken literally, might invalidate all agreements between nonmarital partners, a result no one favors. Moreover, those standards offer no basis to distinguish between valid and invalid agreements. By looking not to such uncertain tests, but only to the consideration underlying the agreement, we provide the parties and the courts with a practical guide to determine when an agreement between nonmarital partners should be enforced. *Id.* at p. 672.

2. Parties Can Agree to Pool Assets Acquired During their Cohabitation

In the cases that are summarized below, the court found that there were two contracts; one was the meretricious one and the other was the agreement to pool the assets during the cohabitation. In this way, if an agreement to pool their assets was proven, the court could uphold it.

In **TRUTALLI v. MERAVIGLIA** (1932) 215 Cal. 698, the parties, Charles and Rita, agreed to live together without being married and to hold themselves out as husband and wife to the world. Thereafter, they cohabited "publicly and notoriously." They had two children during the cohabitation. Charles and Rita also agreed that Rita would perform all the necessary household services and that all monies derived by either or both parties would be paid to Charles to be invested by him for the benefit of both parties from time to time; the parties additionally agreed that all property, real and personal, acquired by Charles would be held by him for the joint benefit of both parties, each having an undivided one-half (1/2) interest.

When the parties separated, Charles filed an action to quiet title the real property that was acquired during the cohabitation. Rita cross-complained alleging that she owned an undivided one-half of the real property. The judgment was entered in favor of the Rita.

The trial court found that the parties had an agreement to live together as husband and wife without the formality of a marriage ceremony and to invest their separate earnings for their joint benefit and that all property so acquired should be owned by them jointly. In affirming the judgment, the Supreme Court of California stated that there were two contracts: **(1)** to live unlawfully together and **(2)** to invest their separate earning for the benefit of both of them. The two agreements, although made at the same time, were separate and distinct contracts, and neither was made dependent upon the other. The court held that there was a valid agreement and Rita was the owner of an undivided half.

In **GARCIA v. VENEGAS** (1951) 106 Cal.App.2d 364 appellant/defendant Jose Venegas (Jose) appealed from a judgment against him and in favor of the respondent, Julia Maria Garcia (Julia), in the sum of $1,860, representing the amount by which the value of her services exceeded the value of the maintenance and support which he furnished to her during the period of time these parties, unmarried, lived together as man and wife.

The trial court found that Jose and Julia lived together as man and wife for a period 62 months; that during this period Julia contributed money, work and services equally with Jose; that Jose agreed with Julia during this relationship that everything they acquired would belong to both of them; that as a result of joint contributions of money, work and services they jointly accumulated real and personal property; that the reasonable value of Julia's services during this period of 62 months exceeded in value the maintenance and support furnished by Jose to Julia by the sum of $30 per month, or a total sum of $1,860.

The trial court stated that: **(1)** there was no express agreement, oral or written, by Jose to compensate Julia for her services that was within the issues presented by the pleadings; **(2)** there was no evidence of any such an agreement; and **(3)** there was no basis for an implied or quasi-contractual obligation upon the part of Jose to compensate Julia for her services.

The appellate court held that when two people enter into a contract to pool their work and earnings and share equally in the property accumulated and the illicit relationship was not so involved in the contract as to render it illegal, the law recognizes the contract and enforces the rights arising out of it. Such a joint business enterprise, somewhat akin to a partnership, is one which any two persons might undertake." *Id.* at p. 368. The judgment was reversed with directions to the trial court, to amend its findings of fact and conclusions of law appropriately to declare that Julia owned an undivided one-half interest in the real property mentioned.

In ***BRIDGES v. BRIDGES*** (1954)125 Cal.App.2d 359 the parties cohabited for about four years. They had one child together. During the entire period the parties worked together with the common purpose and design of accumulating property, money and other assets. They agreed verbally that they would pool their joint assets, work, labor and services. The man worked as a salesman and used his savings to purchase properties. The woman kept house, cared for seven children, three from each former marriage and one from the nonmarital relationship, and helped construct improvements on the properties. By virtue of their common efforts they acquired real property in Chico and in Redding. The court found that the parties had made an agreement to pool their assets and divided the property equally. Defendant appealed and the appellate court affirmed. *Id.* at p. 363.

3. Contributions and Sharing Can be Proportional

In ***VALLERA v. VALLERA*** (1943) 21 Cal.2d 681, the plaintiff (Marian) brought an action for separate maintenance and for a division of community property, which she alleged was worth at least $60,000. The trial court concluded that: **(1)** Marian and the defendant (Concezio) had never been husband and wife; **(2)** that Marian was not entitled to maintenance; and **(3)** that there was no community property. It found that all property acquired by the parties between December 16, 1938, and July 6, 1940, except such property as either might have acquired by gift, devise, bequest or descent, was held by them as tenants in common, each owning an undivided one-half thereof, and Concezio appealed.

Concezio contended that since there was no marriage, no attempt to contract marriage, no belief in the existence of a valid marriage, no evidence of any agreement between the parties as to their property rights and no evidence concerning the accumulation of property or contributions by the parties thereto, Marian could not acquire the rights of a cotenant in property acquired by him during the period of illicit cohabitation.
In reversing the trial court's decision, the Supreme Court of California stated that there was no evidence that the parties made any agreement concerning their property or property rights, that Marian was, thus, not entitled to one-half of the

property. However, "even in the absence of an express agreement to that effect, [Marian was] entitled to share in the property jointly accumulated, in the proportion that her funds contributed toward its acquisition." *Id.* at p. 685.

4. When the Property is Held in Joint Title

In **MILIAN v. DE LEON** (1986) 181 Cal.App.3d 1185, the plaintiff challenged a decision of the trial court that ordered a partitioning and selling of the home and dividing the proceeds equally between plaintiff and defendant based on an implied contract between the parties to own and to divide their property equally. The parties held title to the property as joint tenants. The trial court found that substantial evidence supported a finding that the parties intended that each was to contribute what he or she could and that both intended the property to be owned equally irrespective of inequality in the amounts contributed by each. The appellate court affirmed.

5. When the Real Property is only in the Name of One of the Parties

In **TONEY v. NOLDER** (1985) 173 Cal.App.3d 791, the sole question presented was whether the statutory presumption that the owner of the legal title to property is the owner of the full beneficial title, **Evid. Code § 662**[8], may be overcome by less than clear and convincing evidence when the parties to the dispute were in a confidential relationship at the time of the transaction. The trial court found for the nonowner, but the appellate court reversed stating that irrespective of whether a confidential relationship is shown, to overcome the presumption of title the evidence presented must be clear and convincing.

In **TANNEHILL v. FINCH** (1986) 188 Cal.App.3d 224, the property in question was in the sole name of only one of the cohabiting parties, Finch. Tannehill argued that there was a pooling agreement. Finch disagreed. The jury found for Tannehill by a preponderance of the evidence pursuant to a jury instruction. The appellate court reversed the trial court's decision ruling that the statutory presumption that the owner of the legal title to property is the owner of the full beneficial title may only be overcome by clear and convincing evidence. The appellate court declared that there is no "confidential relationship" exception to the clear and convincing evidence requirement.

Finally, it would "certainly be an honorable thing for a man to divide with a woman for whom he held a strong affection the accumulations [during the time when the parties cohabitate], especially where it appears that the woman involved was, during the whole period, working with constant industry on behalf of both of them." **FERGUSON v. SCHUENEMANN** (1959) 167 Cal.App.2d 413 at p. 418.

---

[8] Evid. Code § 662 provides that "The owner of the legal title to property is presumed to be the owner of the full beneficial title. This presumption may be rebutted only by clear and convincing proof."

Chapter 37: Living together/*Marvin* Actions

Marvin Support Claims (Palimony)

Marvin support claims are called palimony. It is support that one unmarried, no-longer cohabiting partner pays to the other party after separation pursuant to an agreement. Palimony in *Marvin* cases will only be ordered where the court finds that the unmarried parties clearly made a contract so agreeing.

In the case that follows, the appellate court majority opinion by P. J. Anderson did not approve of the trial court fashioning its own equitable remedy when the trial court judge found that the existing remedies had proven inadequate to effect justice. J. Poch disagreed with the majority and his opinion on this matter follows the majority opinion.

> ***TERRI FRIEDMAN, Plaintiff and Respondent, v. ELLIOTT FRIEDMAN, Defendant and Appellant.***
> COURT OF APPEAL OF CALIFORNIA, FIRST APPELLATE DISTRICT, DIVISION FOUR
> 20 Cal.App.4th 876; 24 Cal.Rptr.2d 892
> November 30, 1993, Decided
> (*Friedman v. Friedman*)
>
> Respondent and appellant began living together in 1967, when respondent was 25 years old. Respondent had a child from a previous marriage when she and appellant began their cohabitation. Respondent and appellant did not believe that a license for marriage was necessary to bond together in a lifetime commitment. Thus, they vowed to be husband and wife and to strive to be partners in all respects "without any sanction by the State."
>
> In 1971 respondent and appellant purchased land in Alaska in partnership with several other individuals; title to their portion referred to them as "Husband and Wife." Over a period of two years, they built a home on their property. Appellant worked as an investigator the entire time they were in Alaska. Respondent initially worked as a waitress; however, her principal work was in contributing to appellant's career, building up and maintaining the property, and caring for their first child, who was born in 1974. Along the way they also acquired an interest in some commercial property, the deed to which listed respondent as "Terri Friedman." When they decided to leave Alaska that property was sold.
>
> In 1978 or 1979 respondent and appellant moved back to the Bay Area; appellant began attending law school in 1979. Their plans for respondent to complete her college education fell through in part due to illness of their second child, who was born in 1981. Also in 1981 they purchased and fixed up a home in Berkeley; they apparently sold that home and purchased a new home in Kensington in 1986.
>
> After law school appellant became a practicing attorney and entered into a small partnership; respondent assisted in designing and decorating his office. When that partnership dissolved appellant continued in practice and did well economically. Respondent involved herself in upgrading and maintaining their homes, cooking, cleaning, entertaining and caring for their children.
>
> In the mid-1980's respondent was experiencing back trouble; ultimately, she was

Chapter 37: Living together/*Marvin* Actions

diagnosed as having a herniated disc which required surgery. Respondent is currently disabled; her ability to walk is extremely limited, and she must wear a back brace at all times, except when she is asleep.

On January 13, 1992, respondent filed a complaint, seeking damages and various forms of equitable relief from appellant, following termination of a relationship in which the two had cohabited for twenty-one years. On April 21, 1992, respondent filed a motion, requesting "temporary support" pending trial. The motion was supported by a lengthy declaration by respondent, chronicling the history of her relationship with appellant. Appellant filed opposition to the motion, including a declaration which contradicted a number of facts set forth in respondent's declaration. The trial court conducted a two-day evidentiary hearing, rendering its decision shortly thereafter.

In its Statement of Decision the court found insufficient evidence to support a finding of an express agreement to provide support but that it was adequate to support a finding of an "implied" agreement. Specifically, the court found that there was an implied contract between the parties "that if they separated, [respondent] would be supported by [appellant] in the same manner as if they had been legally married."

The court: (1) found that a trial could be years in the future, leaving respondent "in poor health living off her dwindling personal assets"; (2) found that such an award was proper because there were no other adequate remedies, respondent would suffer irreparable injury (if the award were not made) and respondent had a "reasonable probability of success at trial on the merits"; and (3) the court awarded $1,426 per month in temporary support, based on Alameda County spousal support guidelines.

Shortly thereafter appellant filed a motion to dissolve the injunction and, in the alternative, to fix the amount of security for undertaking. During the course of that hearing, the court noted that its original order, indeed, had been framed as an injunctive order. However, the court ultimately "changed [its] mind" and denied "appellant's motion to dissolve injunction and to require security" because the earlier order was not an injunctive order but rather, an "order to pay money . . .." Appellant appealed.

THE MAJORITY OPINION

Appellant argued that: (1) the trial court erred in issuing a pretrial "order to pay money"; (2) if the order to pay money is considered to be, in reality, a preliminary injunction, it was granted in error because (a) respondent has an adequate remedy at law; (b) insufficient evidence was presented that respondent would suffer irreparable harm; and (c) respondent failed to demonstrate that she has a reasonable probability of success on the merits; and (3) the trial court erred in making its support award retroactive to the date on which respondent's motion for temporary support was filed.

The trial court's statement of decision makes it clear that the court found that there was an "implied" agreement between appellant and respondent. However, the statement of decision does not reflect what specific conduct of the parties led to its conclusion that such an implied agreement existed. Moreover, the statement of decision fails to set forth the terms of the implied agreement with regard to support. Specifically, the statement of decision does not make findings on such questions as (a) the amount of support one party impliedly agreed to provide to the other, following termination of the relationship; (b) how long such support would last; and (c) most significantly, whether or not such support should be paid from the moment the relationship terminated and before any other rights of the parties were determined by a court of law.

[W]e conclude that an amorphous "order to pay money" is not a cognizable provisional remedy under California law and that appellant is not estopped from asserting that the trial court exceeded its authority in making such an order. The effect of the trial court's order was to give respondent relief to which other, noncohabiting contracting parties would not have been entitled. An award of such relief constitutes an abuse of discretion. [The trial court's findings would resurrect common law marriages in California.]

We share the trial court's concern with the economic situation confronted by respondent, and we regret that there is no basis upon which her short-term needs can be met under existing law. Justice Mosk's lament (concerning another law) also applies to the situation we face here: "As a judge, I am bound by the law as I find it to be and not as I might fervently wish it to be." (*In re Anderson* (1968) 69 Cal.2d 613, 635 [73 Cal.Rptr. 21, 447 P.2d 117].)

[W]e reverse and remand to the trial court to vacate its order granting temporary support to respondent.

THE DISSENT by J. Poch

I dissent. From our lofty perch my colleagues perceive a very different reality than I do. They fault the trial judge for awarding to a now disabled woman interim support from her partner in a 21-year relationship during which the couple lived as a family and raised 3 children. The majority instead tell her she has no more recourse than a buyer of widgets faced with breach of a sale contract by its supplier. Their advice to her: Stand in line; we'll offer you a trial someday.

Judge Duncan was candid and direct: "If ever there is to be an award of support based on an implied contract in a Marvin case, it is difficult to imagine a scenario more compelling than [the one] presented herein."

The evidence fully supports the trial court's finding that the parties did have an implied contract whereby defendant agreed to support plaintiff in the event they separated. Uncontradicted evidence shows that defendant voluntarily paid approximately $190,000 in monthly support payments to plaintiff following their separation, and that these payments were still being made at the time the order for support was made. As an implied contract is one identified by conduct, this alone constitutes substantial evidence in support of the trial court's finding. There is also the matter of the "situation or mutual relation of the parties" from which an implied contract may be inferred. The evidence on this score goes beyond abundant to become overwhelming.

In light of these circumstances, the trial court was fully justified in concluding that the parties were "maintaining a marriage relationship" in all respects except that of legal sanction. As this court has recently noted, the duty of support is inherent to the marital relationship. It is therefore no great jurisprudential leap to conclude that parties who treat themselves as married may have made provision for this duty of support should they separate.

The majority speak of the trial court exceeding its jurisdiction by "creat[ing a] totally new substantive right under the guise of doing equity." The only "right" involved here is the right to support based directly and solely on the parties' agreement. The trial court was

> thus not creating a right, but only an equitable remedy to preserve that right. Granted, the remedy it did award is probably unprecedented, but that is not to say, as do the majority, that it is illegitimate. In my view Judge Duncan was following the explicit guidelines set forth by the Supreme Court in Marvin v. Marvin: fashioning an additional equitable remedy to protect the expectations of the parties to a nonmarital relationship in a situation where existing remedies were inadequate. Far from being illegitimate, the remedy was suggested by the California Supreme Court.
>
> If 21 years of living together in a mutually supportive family relationship, of taking title to property and otherwise conducting one's financial affairs as if one were married is insufficient evidence of an implied contract to conduct oneself as married with all the moral and legal obligations to the other spouse that such a relationship entails, then I simply cannot imagine any relationship which the majority would find sufficient. **The result reached by the majority may be, in the eyes of some, good law; it is lousy justice.**

Proving that an agreement existed whereby one party agreed that he/she would forever-more support the other party is almost non-existent. In fact, the only published California court opinion where palimony was proven to be the agreement of the parties was ***COCHRAN V. COCHRAN*** (*Cochran I*) (1997) 56 Cal.App.4th 378. However, in that case the court was not deciding the issue of palimony entitlement, but rather when a support agreement is breached such that the statute of limitations has begun to run.[9]

Remedies in Marvin Actions

Remedies in *Marvin* matters can be equitable or in law. However, most of the *Marvin* cases do refer to the remedy as an equitable one.

An equitable remedy is a court order that a person do something or refrain from doing something. Equitable remedies can include specific performance, restitution, declaratory relief, accountings and constructive and resulting trusts.

A constructive trust is an equitable remedy that is imposed upon a person who wrongfully acquires title to property that belongs to another. The wrongful owner has a duty to transfer the property to the party who rightfully owns it. This legal concept is used to prevent the party having the property from obtaining an unjust enrichment at the true owner's expense.

A resulting trust arises by operation of law. It is a legal presumption that the person who holds title to specific property actually holds that property as a trustee for the true owner.

Quantum meruit is a Latin term that means "as much as is deserved". A party who performs a service for another without an agreement or formal contract can recover

---

[9] In the entire United States, there are only 2 published opinions where palimony was ordered and the decision was upheld - *Connell v. Diehl* (2008) 397 N.J. Super. 477 and *Crowe v. De Gioia* (1985) 203 N.J. Super. 22.

the reasonable amount for the labor and materials expended. If no recovery was allowed, the person who received the service and did not pay for it would be unjustly and unfairly enriched.

The Supreme Court in *Marvin* case above, made the following statements with regard to remedies in a *Marvin* matter:
1. In the absence of an express agreement, the courts may look to a variety of remedies to protect the parties' expectations.
2. Remedies that might be appropriate in a *Marvin* action are: constructive trust, resulting trust or *quantum meruit*.
3. Additional equitable remedies [may evolve] to protect the expectations of the parties to a nonmarital relationship in cases in which existing remedies prove inadequate. MARVIN v. MARVIN (1976) 18 Cal.3d 660.

In **PADILLA v. PADILLA** (1940) 38 Cal.App.2d 319, the court held that when an unmarried couple who have separated after cohabitation, agreed to purchase and own real property jointly, with each paying one-half of the purchase price, and the property is in only one party's name, a resulting trust will be established.

In **CLINE v. FESTERSEN** (1954) 128 Cal.App.2d 380 the court reached the same decision as the *Padilla* case. In *Cline*, the plaintiff and the defendant cohabited without marriage for about thirteen years. They had one child. One day during the parties' cohabitation, they entered into an agreement to purchase property. They agreed that they would make the purchase jointly, that each would pay one-half of the purchase price, and that they would own the property jointly.

However, the property was conveyed to defendant as her separate property without the knowledge or consent of the plaintiff. After the parties separated, the plaintiff found out that the property had been deeded solely to the defendant. He filed an action requesting his one-half share. The jury decided in favor of the plaintiff and the defendant appealed. The appellate court affirmed the trial court's decision holding that where an unmarried couple who separated after the cohabitation, agreed to purchase and own real property jointly, with each paying one-half of the purchase price, and the property is in only one party's name, a resulting trust will be established.

Finally, the court in **TAYLOR v. POLACKWICH** (1983) 145 Cal.App.3d 1014 stated that when no implied *Marvin* contract is found, there is no basis for any equitable remedy.

Marvin Contract Breaches & the Statute of Limitations

The *Cochran* case mentioned above, **COCHRAN V. COCHRAN** (*Cochran I*) (1997) 56 Cal.App.4th 1115, discusses when a palimony agreement is breached. In that case, Patricia Cochran alleged that she and Johnnie began a romantic relationship in the mid-1960's, during which time they had a child together and, though unmarried, lived together as husband and wife for many years. She legally changed her surname to match Johnnie's. During this time, Johnnie allegedly promised that property acquired during the relationship belonged to him and appellant equally and promised Patricia lifetime support. In October 1983, Patricia and Johnnie entered into an agreement that settled their rights as to property acquired up to that point. At the same time, Johnnie again promised to support Patricia for the rest of her life. In 1984, Johnnie ratified his agreement to equally share all property acquired during the relationship.

Patricia and Johnnie lived together until 1986, when Johnnie told Patricia that he had married another woman. Even though Johnnie moved out of the house that he shared with Patricia to live with his wife, he continued to support Patricia financially until February 1995. Johnnie continued his relationship with Patricia during those years and through both words and conduct, ratified or renewed his promises regarding support and property acquisition. Patricia quit her job in 1991 at Johnnie's request, based on his promise of continued support.

Johnnie contended, and the trial court agreed that their *Marvin* agreement was breached in 1986, when he moved out and married another woman and the statute of limitations had already run. However, the appellate court held that "a *Marvin* agreement is breached when the party charged with a duty to perform refuses to do so. If the parties have separated, but the obligor performs as required by the *Marvin* agreement, there has been no breach, no cause of action has accrued, and the statute of limitations has not begun to run." *Id.* at p. 1124.

In **WHORTON v. DILLINGHAM** (1988) 202 Cal.App.3d 447, Donnis and Ben began dating and entered into a relationship. When the parties began living together in 1977, they orally agreed that Donnis's exclusive, fulltime occupation was to be Ben's chauffeur, bodyguard, social and business secretary, partner and counselor in real estate investments, and to appear on his behalf when requested. Donnis was to render labor, skills and personal services for the benefit of Ben's business and investment endeavors. Additionally, Donnis was to be Ben's constant companion, confidant, traveling and social companion and lover, to terminate his schooling upon obtaining his Associate of Arts degree, and to make no investment without first consulting Ben.

In consideration of Donnis's promises, Ben was to give him a one-half equity interest in all real estate acquired in their joint names, and in all property thereafter acquired by Ben. Ben agreed to financially support Donnis for life and to open bank accounts, maintain a positive balance in those accounts, grant Donnis invasionary powers to savings accounts held in Ben's name and permit Donnis to charge on Ben's personal accounts. Ben was also to engage in a homosexual relationship with Donnis. Importantly, for the purpose of our analysis, the parties specifically agreed that any portion of the agreement found to be legally unenforceable was severable and the balance of the provisions would remain in full force and effect.

Thereafter, Ben barred him from his premises and refused to perform his part of the contract by giving Donnis the promised consideration for the business services rendered.

Donnis sued claiming that Ben breached their agreement. Ben demurred to the complaint and the trial court sustained the demur. Donnis appealed. The appellate court reversed the trial court's decision. The appellate court stated that Donnis's claim was not barred by the statute of limitations.

> The general rule is that a cause of action for breach of contract accrues at the time of breach. A *Marvin*-type contract is breached when one partner terminates the relationship. The statute of limitations for an action upon a contract not founded on a writing is two years. The complaint states the breach occurred "on or about the latter part of 1984." The complaint was filed in June 1986. The complaint on its face does not show the contract cause of action is barred by the statute of limitations. Id. at pp. 456-457.

CHART 15: (*Marvin*)/Living Together Rules from Case Law
© 2017 LW Greenberg

RULE	CASE NAME & CITE
1. Courts should enforce contracts between nonmarital partners.	***MARVIN* v. *MARVIN*** (1976) 18 Cal.3d 660; 557 P.2d 106
2. In the absence of an express contract, the courts should look to the conduct of the parties to determine whether or not that conduct demonstrates an implied contract, agreement of partnership or joint venture or some other tacit understanding between the parties.	
3. In the absence of an express agreement, the courts may look to a variety of remedies to protect the parties' expectations.	
4. Remedies that might be appropriate in a *Marvin* action are: constructive trust, resulting trust or quantum meruit.	
5. Additional equitable remedies [may evolve] to protect the expectations of the parties to a nonmarital relationship in cases in which existing remedies prove inadequate.	
6. Services as a social companion and hostess are inextricably intertwined with the sexual relationship between the parties and do not form lawful consideration supporting a *Marvin* agreement.	***BERGEN* v. *WOOD*** (1993) 14 Cal.App.4th 854
7. Cohabitation is required for recovery under *Marvin* because from cohabitation flows the rendition of domestic services which amount to lawful consideration for a contract.	
8. When parties previously lived in a meretricious relationship and agreed to a contract based upon past services and later, while the parties were living together, made a new agreement, the court could find that the continuance of such relationship was not a part of either agreement, and the new agreement was enforceable.	***CROSLIN* v. *SCOTT*** (1957) 154 Cal.App.2d 767
9. The fact that parties agreed to invest their earnings in property to be held jointly between them while they were living together in an unlawful relations does not disqualify them from entering into a lawful agreement with each other, so long as such immoral relation was not made a consideration of the agreement.	***TRUTALLI* v. *MERAVIGLIA*** (1932) 215 Cal. 698
10. When two people enter into a contract to pool their work and earnings and share equally in the property accumulated therewith, and the illicit relationship was not so involved in the contract as to render it illegal, the law recognizes the contract and enforces the rights arising out of it.	***GARCIA* v. *VENEGAS*** (1951) 106 Cal.App.2d 364
11. The court will divide the property acquired between parties when a contract is proven that the parties agreed to pool their earnings and services for their mutual benefit.	***BRIDGES* v. *BRIDGES*** (1954) 125 Cal.App.2d 359
12. Not having a good faith belief that the marriage is valid does not preclude a woman from recovering property to which she would otherwise be entitled.	***VALLERA* v. *VALLERA*** (1943) 21 Cal.2d

13. If a man and woman live together as husband and wife under an agreement to pool their earnings and share equally in their joint accumulations, equity will protect the interests of each in such property.	681
14. Even in the absence of an express agreement to that effect, the woman would be entitled to share in the property jointly accumulated in the proportion that her funds contributed toward its acquisition.	
15. Cohabitation is not a prerequisite to the finding of an implied agreement between unmarried persons concerning their property.	*MILIAN v. DE LEON* (1986) 181 Cal.App.3d 1185
16. The only limitation upon the right of unmarried persons to contract with respect to their property and financial arrangements is that the contract must not be illegal or against public policy. Such an agreement is unenforceable only to the extent that it explicitly rests upon the immoral and illicit consideration of meretricious sexual services.	*MILIAN v. DE LEON* (1986) 181 Cal.App.3d 1185
17. The statutory presumption that the owner of the legal title to property is the owner of the full beneficial title may only be overcome by clear and convincing evidence. There is no "confidential relationship" exception to the clear and convincing evidence requirement.	*TONEY v. NOLDER* (1985) 173 Cal.App.3d 791
18. Property claims made pursuant to a *Marvin* claim must be proven by clear and convincing evidence.	*TANNEHILL v. FINCH* (1986) 188 Cal.App.3d 224
19. When there is a viable remedy at law, a trial court cannot fashion its own equitable remedy just because the existing remedies had proven inadequate to effect justice.	*FRIEDMAN v. FRIEDMAN* (1993) 20 Cal.App.4th 876
20. When an unmarried couple who separated after cohabitation and agreed to purchase and own real property jointly, with each paying one-half of the purchase price, a resulting trust will be established.	*PADILLA v. PADILLA* (1940) 38 Cal.App.2d 319
21. An administrator of the man's estate is estopped to assert the statute of frauds when the woman trusted and believed the deceased man's statements to her that everything would be owned in common and he never repudiated this agreement.	*CLINE v. FESTERSEN* (1954) 128 Cal.App.2d 380
22. An administrator of the man's estate is estopped to assert the statute of frauds when the woman trusted and believed the deceased man's statements to her that everything would be owned in common and he never repudiated this agreement.	
23. When parties have cohabited without marriage and agreed to pool their interests in income and property acquired during their cohabitation, each party will acquire an equitable interest in that real and personal property.	*FERGUSON v. SCHUENEMANN* (1959) 167 Cal.App.2d 413
24. When two people enter into a contract to pool their work and earnings and share equally in the property accumulated therewith, and the illicit relationship was not so involved in the contract as to render it illegal, the law recognizes the contract	*GARCIA v. VENEGAS* (1951) 106 Cal.App.2d 364

Chapter 37: Living Together/*Marvin* Actions

and enforces the rights arising out of it.	
25. Where no implied *Marvin* contract is found, there is no basis for an equitable remedy.	***TAYLOR v. POLACKWICH*** (1983) 145 Cal.App.3d 1014
26. A claim to real property when the legal title is in the name of another must be established by clear, satisfactory and convincing evidence.	
27. So long as the agreement does not rest upon illicit meretricious consideration, the parties may order their economic affairs as they choose.	***COCHRAN v. COCHRAN*** (*Cochran II*) (2001) 89 Cal.App.4th 283
29. Full-time cohabitation is not necessary in proving a *Marvin* relationship.	
30. A *Marvin* agreement is breached when the party charged with a duty to perform refuses to do so.	***COCHRAN V. COCHRAN*** (*Cochran I*) (1997) 56 Cal.App.4th 378
31. A cause of action for breach of contract accrues at the time of breach.	***WHORTON v. DILLINGHAM*** (1988) 202 Cal.App.3d 447
32. A *Marvin*-type contract is breached when one partner terminates the relationship.	
33. The statute of limitations for an action upon a contract not founded on a writing is two years.	
34. The statute of limitations for a cause of action based on equitable grounds is four years.	

© 2019 LW Greenberg

EDUCATIONAL EXERCISES

1. What was the main issue in the *Marvin v. Marvin* case?
2. What was Michelle Triola Marvin seeking when she filed her initial lawsuit against Lee Marvin?
3. Are living together cases filed in family or civil court? Where does one find the answer to this question?

Appendix One: Johns' Intake Sheets & Timeline

Marilyn Johns Intake Sheet
Date of Attorney visit: 1/5/2018
Attorney for Marilyn Johns: Gary Hanson, Esq. State Bar No. 179998
Hanson, Williams & Howard, 196 First Street, Suite 1400 San Diego, CA 92101
619 402-9602

PARTIES, RESIDENCY AND CHILDREN
Petitioner: Name: Marilyn Johns Maiden Name: Williams Would you like your maiden name restored? Yes
Address: 5111 Applewood Street, El Cajon, CA 92019 Telephone: Home 619 203-8801, Cell 619 668-8801
Date of Birth: 6/1/80 Place of Birth San Diego, CA Social Security No.:555-11-9021
California Driver's License Number Z09087620
State Residency: CA Length of time in county: Entire life

Married in Las Vegas, Nevada - 01/01/2006

TWO Children of the marriage
Trevor, Jr Date of birth: 7/1/2009 Born: San Diego, CA
Christina Date of birth: 12/31/2010 Born: San Diego, CA

PROPERTY
Family Residence: Address: 5111 Applewood Street, El Cajon, CA 92019
Title held as community property with right of survivorship, Date of Purchase: 6/1/2006 Purchase Price: $350,000
Amount borrowed at time of purchase: $300,000 Current loan Balance: $157,650
Current fair market value: $700,000

Other Real Property: Hilton Timeshare purchased for $64,000 in 2010; paid off.

Personal Property

Automobiles:
Marilyn: 2012 Lexus RX 300 paid off; Trevor: leased 2016 Lexus GS 450h monthly payment of $550.

Bank Accounts:

Chase Bank	La Mesa	Checking	Balance: $3,267.77;
Union Bank	El Cajon	Savings	Balance: $88,688.50

Stocks and Bonds: 100 shares of Apple stock (Current worth $500,000)

Pension Plans/401ks/IRAs/Retirement/Deferred Compensation:
Marilyn: Retirement thru employer approx. current amount $45,700;
Trevor: Retirement thru Quality Plus $18,800 will not be vested until 2020

Furniture and furnishings approximate value $25,000.

THE FOLLOWING INFORMATION HAS THE SAME NUMBERING AS A *FL-150*.

1. **Employment:**
   a. Employer: Spring Valley School District
   b. Employer's address: 997 Madison Ave. Spring Valley, CA 92045
   c. Occupation: 5th grade teacher

Employer's phone number: (619) 454-6621
Date job started: If unemployed, date job ended: 9/2006

Appendix One: Johns' Intake Sheets & Timeline

I get paid $6,000 gross each month (before taxes)
I work about hours per week: 40

2. **Age and Education:**
   1) My age is:
   2) I have completed high school or the equivalent: Y
   3) Number of years of college school completed: 5
   4) Number of years of graduate school completed: 1
   5) Degree(s) obtained: BA Elementary Education
   6) I have Profession/occupational license: Teaching credential

3. **Tax information:**
   a. I last filed taxes for tax year: 2016
   b. My tax filing status is: Head of Household
   c. I file state tax returns in: CA
   d. I claim the following number of exemptions (including myself) on my taxes: 3

   4. **Other party's income:** $12,500. We have a joint bank account where our paychecks are auto deposited
   5. **Income:** (annual): $72,000

10. **Deductions:**
    1. Required union dues: $25/mo
    2. Required retirement payments (not social security, FICA, 401(k), or IRA): 0
    3. Medical, hospital, dental, and other health insurance premiums (total monthly amount: 0

11. **Assets**
    a. Cash and checking accounts, savings, credit union, money market, and other deposit accounts: $3,500
    b. Stocks, bonds, and other assets I could easily sell: $500,000
    c. All other property real and personal: $300,000

13. **Average monthly expenses**
    a. Home:
        I. Mortgage: $3,300, average principal: $2,945, $ average interest: $355
        II. Real property taxes: $1,500
        III. Homeowner's or renter's insurance (if not included above): $110
        IV. Maintenance and repair: $250
    b. Health care costs not paid by insurance: $200
    c. Child care: $800
    d. Groceries and household supplies: $1,200
    e. Eating out: $1,000
    f. Utilities (gas, electric, water, trash): $340
    g. Telephone, cell phone, and e-mail (internet): $210
    h. Laundry and cleaning: $125
    i. Clothes: $450
    j. Education: $225
    k. Entertainment, gifts, and vacation: $300
    l. Auto expenses and transportation (insurance, gas, repairs, bus, etc.): $300
    m. Insurance (life, accident, etc. Not auto, home, health insurance): $27

Appendix One: Johns' Intake Sheets & Timeline

    n.   Savings and investments: 0
    o.   Charitable contributions: 0
    p.   Monthly payments listed in #14 (itemize below #14, insert total here): $125
    q.   Other
    r.   TOTAL EXPENSES (a–q) (do not add in the amounts in (a) and (b) $5,302
    s.   Amount of expenses paid by others: $0

14. Installment payments and debts not listed above:

Paid to	For	Mo/Amount	Balance	Date of last payment
VISA	Misc.	$125	$3,368	12/2017
MasterCard	Misc.	$225	$7,218	12/2017
Lexus International	auto	$450	N/A	12/2017

Marilyn's name is on the VISA; she uses it & pays the bill. Trevor's name is on the MasterCard; he uses it & pays the bill.

15. Attorney fees:
    a.   To date I have paid my attorney this amount is fees and costs: $25,000
    b.   The source of this money was: Loan from parents
    c.   I still owe the following fees and costs to my attorney: $0
    d.   My attorney's hourly rate is: $450

17. Children's health-care expenses
    a.   I do XXXX have health insurance available to me for the children through my job:
    b.   Name of insurance company: Aetna
    c.   Address of insurance company: 2400 West Parkway, Philadelphia, PA 19133
    d.   The monthly cost for the children's health insurance is or would be: $50

18. Additional expenses for the children in this case:
    a.   Child care so that I can work or get job training: $50
    b.   Children's health care not covered by insurance: $200
    c.   Travel expenses for visitation: $0

Appendix One: Johns' Intake Sheets & Timeline

Trevor Johns Intake Sheet

Date of Attorney Visit 2/16/2018
Attorney: Maria Garcia, Esq. State Bar No. 134090
Garcia & Jones 500 Fifth Ave. Street, Suite 901 San Diego, CA 92101 619 405-8831

PARTIES, RESIDENCY AND CHILDREN
Respondent
Name: Trevor Johns
Address: 2140 Highland Ave. Lakeside, CA 92040, Condo
Telephone: Home 619 891-7768, Cell 619 699-8451
Date of Birth: 1/4/80 Place of Birth Orange, CA Social Security No.:557-88-0201
California Driver's License Number N661098
State Residency: CA Length of time in county: 10+ years
Married in Las Vegas, Nevada - 01/01/2006– TWO Children of the marriage
Trevor, Jr. Date of Birth: 7/1/2009   Born: San Diego, CA
Christina   Date of Birth: 12/31/2010   Born: San Diego, CA
Family Residence: Address: 5111 Applewood Street, El Cajon, CA 92019
How title is held: Husband and wife, as community property with right of survivorship
Date of Purchase: 6/1/2006 and the Purchase Price: $350,000 Amount borrowed at time of purchase: $300,000 and the current loan Balance: $157,650 Current fair market value: $700,000.
Other Real Property: Hilton Timeshare purchased for $64,000 in 2010 paid off.
Personal Property
Automobiles:
Marilyn: 2013 Lexus RX 300-paid off; Trevor: leased 2016 Lexus GS 450h monthly payment of $550.
Bank Accounts:
Chase Bank   La Mesa   Checking   Balance: $3,267.77
Union Bank   El Cajon   Savings   Balance: $86,572.50
Stocks and Bonds: 100 shares of Apple stock (Current worth $500,000).
Pension Plans/401ks/IRAs/Retirement/Deferred Compensation:
Marilyn: Retirement thru her employer approx. current amount $45,700.
Trevor: Retirement thru Quality Plus $9,800 will not be vested until 2019.
Furniture and furnishings approximate value $25,000
Trevor's Expenses
Name: Trevor Johns Address: 2140 Highland Ave. Lakeside, CA 92040, Cell: 619 201-5977
THE FOLLOWING INFORMATION HAS THE SAME NUMBERING AS A FL-150.
1. **Employment:**
   a. Employer: Quality Plus, Inc.
   b. Employer's address: 5800 Fifth Ave. San Diego, CA 92705

Appendix One: Johns' Intake Sheets & Timeline

   c. Occupation: Director of Engineering
   d. Employer's phone number: (619) 626-5189
   e. Date job started: 1/2006 If unemployed, date job ended
   f. I get paid $12,500 gross (before taxes) per month
   g. I work about hours per week: 40
2. **Age and Education:**
   a. My age is:
   b. I have completed high school or the equivalent: Y
   c. Number of years of college school completed: 7
   d. Number of years of graduate school completed: 3
   e. Degree(s) obtained: MS EE (electrical engineering)
   f. I have Profession/occupational license: N/A
3. **Tax information:**
   a. I last filed taxes for tax year: 2016
   b. My tax filing status is: Single
   c. I file state tax returns in: CA
   d. I claim the following number of exemptions (including myself) on my taxes: 1
4. **Other party's income: $6,000 We still have a joint bank account where our paychecks are auto deposited**
5. **Income:** (annual): $150,000
10. **Deductions: a-g zero or N/A**
11. **Assets**
    a. Cash and checking accounts, savings, credit union, money market, and other deposit accounts: $3,500
    b. Stocks, bonds, and other assets I could easily sell: $500,000
    c. All other property real and personal: $300,000
13. **Average monthly expenses**
    a. Home:
    b. Rent $1500
    c. Renter's insurance (if not included above): $45
    d. Health care costs not paid by insurance: $50
    e. Child care: $1,500 Trevor is paying for Trevor, Jr.'s school $1,500.
    f. Groceries and household supplies: $700
    g. Eating out: $2,000
    h. Utilities (gas, electric, water, trash): only electricity $55
    i. Telephone, cell phone, and e-mail (internet): $405
    j. Laundry and cleaning: $150
    k. Clothes: $200
    l. Education: $0
    m. Entertainment, gifts, and vacation: $1,000
    n. Auto expenses and transportation (insurance, gas, repairs, bus, etc.): $500
    o. Insurance (life, accident, etc. do not include auto, home or health insurance): $82
    p. Savings and investments: 0
    q. Charitable contributions: 0

r. Monthly payments listed in item 14 (itemize below in 14 and insert total here): $875
s. Other
t. TOTAL EXPENSES (a–q) (do not add in the amounts in a(1)(a) and (b): $7,517
u. Amount of expenses paid by others: $0

14. Installment payments and debts not listed above:

Paid to	For	Amount	Balance	Date of last payment
VISA	Misc.	$125	$3,368	12/2017
MasterCard	Misc.	$225	$7,218	12/2017
Lexus International	auto	$650	N/A	12/2017

Marilyn's name is on the VISA; she uses it and pays the bill; Trevor's name is on the MasterCard; he uses it and pay the bill.

15. Attorney fees:
 a. To date I have paid my attorney this amount is fees and costs: $25,000
 b. The source of this money was: Loan from father
 c. I still owe the following fees and costs to my attorney: $0
 d. My attorneys hourly rate is: $550

17. Children's health-care expenses
 1. I do not have health insurance available to me for the children through my job:
 2. Name of insurance company: Aetna
 3. Address of insurance company: 2400 West Parkway, Philadelphia, PA 19133
 4. The monthly cost for the children's health insurance is or would be: $50

18. Additional expenses for the children in this case:
 a. Child care so that I can work or get job training: $50
 b. Children's health care not covered by insurance: $200
 c. Travel expenses for visitation: $0

Appendix One: Johns' Intake Sheets & Timeline

Appendix One: Johns' Intake Sheets & Timeline

TIME LINE: the Johns Dissolution
January 2018
1/1/2006 Date of marriage (DOM)
6/1/2006 Purchase of home located at 5111 Applewood Street, El Cajon, CA 92019.
1/1/2018 Marilyn's date of separation (DOS) (married 10 years)
1/5/2018 Date of Marilyn's 1st interview with Gary Hanson, Esq. (Hanson) and paralegal Mel Ho
1/5/2018 Signs retainer agreement, engaging Hanson
1/26/2018 Date of filing of Summons, Petition, UCCJEA (FL-100, FL-110, FL-105)
February 2018
2/16/2018 **Trevor retains attorney, Maria Garcia, Esq. (Garcia)**
2/23/2018 Response, UCCJEA (FL-120, FL-105) filed by Garcia
March 2018
3/2/2018 Discovery was mailed to Garcia:
  1. Demand for Documents requesting: recent payroll and Retirement info
  2. Five special interrogatories.
3/28/2018 Discovery responses sent to Hanson with a verification signed by Trevor.
3/28/2018 Discovery was mailed to Hanson:
  1. Demand for Documents requesting: recent payroll and Retirement info
  2. Five special interrogatories.
April 2018
4/6/2018 Request For Order (RFO) (FL-300) filed by Hanson in El Cajon, CA Case No. ED 123456
Paperwork filed by sent to Garcia:
  1. RFO (FL-300)
  2. Spousal support ($1,000/mo)
  3. Custody and Visitation Marilyn wants:
  4. Joint legal, sole physical custody
  5. Attorney fees ($25,000) and Court costs (($435)
  6. Child support (Guideline)
  7. **FCS date set at filing for 5/22/2018 10:00 a.m.**
  8. **Hearing set for 6/14/2018 at 1:30 p.m.**
4/18/2018 Discovery responses sent to Garcia with a verification signed by Marilyn.
May 2018
5/15/2018 Response to RFO (FL-320) filed by Hanson and sent to Garcia
5/22/2018 Parties reach agreement at FCS regarding custody and visitation
June 2018
6/14/2018 Court made the following order at RFO hearing:
  1. Custody and visitation agreement made by the parties at FCS becomes Order of the Court
  2. Court ordered $1000/mo spousal support payable by Trevor to Marilyn (temporary order)
  3. Court set child support at $1240/mo total payable by Trevor to Marilyn
  4. Court awarded attorney fees of $7,500 payable by Trevor to Hanson
6/21/2018 FOAH prepared by Marilyn's attorney; sent to Garcia the same day
6/22/2018 FOAH sent back to Hanson with 1 objection
6/27/2018 redrafted FOAH sent to Garcia

6/29/2018 sent back to Hanson signed by Garcia

July 2018
7/9/2018 FOAH dropped at Court for court's signing and filing
7/13/2018 FOAH filed stamped by Court
7/17/2018 Conformed copy of FOAH received at Marilyn's Attorney office from court
7/20/2018 Conformed copy of FOAH sent to Garcia
7/25/2018 Demand for Documents sent to Hanson requesting payroll and retirement information.

August 2018
8/15/2018 Response to discovery sent to Garcia with a verification signed by Marilyn
8/24/2018 Received dates for
1. **Settlement Conference date set for 9/21/2018 at 9:00 a.m.**
2. **Trial date set for December 28, 2018**

September 2018
9/24/2018 Settlement Conference. Parties are negotiating so a continuing private settlement date was then set for 9/26/2018.
9/26/2018 4-way with Marilyn and Hanson and Trevor and Garcia; the parties reach an agreement as to all disputed issues except spousal support; the parties agree to have a mutually agreed upon mediator decide the issue.

October 2018
10/11/2018 Mutual mediator agreed upon to decide spousal support. **Mediation date: 10/30/2018**
10/30/2018 Mediation: Mediator sets spousal support at $800 per month (permanent order until December 31, 2020 at which time jurisdiction on this issue for both parties is terminated.

November 2018
11/7/2018 MSA prepared by Hanson and sent to Garcia along with all final paperwork for signatures.
11/21/2018 MSA and all final paperwork signed by Trevor and Garcia and sent back to Hanson
11/29/2018 MSA & final paperwork dropped at Court for Court's signature and filing

December 2018 12/3/2018 Effective date of MSA
12/4/2018 MSA & accompanying paperwork processed and filed stamp dated
12/14/2018 Copy of MSA & paperwork mailed to Garcia.

Appendix Two: 2019 Family Code Changes & Bill Nos.

	FC §	Bill #	RE:
1	297.1	273	Domestic partnership, child under 18 yrs
2	298.8	273	Domestic partnership document
3	302	273	Issuance of marriage license
4	303	273	Consent of court, minor has no parent
5	304	273	Interview of parties; counseling
6	423	273	Return of license to local registrar
7	1501	273	Premarital agreements
8	2210	273	Grounds for nullity
9	2605	2214	Division of ownership of pets
10	3011	2044	Factors considered in determining best interests of child
11	3020	2044	Legislative findings and declarations
12	3044	2044	Rebuttable presumption that DV was perpetrated
13	3100	2044	Visitation rights
14	3110.5	2296	Qualifications for child custody evaluator
15	3901	3248	Duration of duty (child support)
16	4007.5		Suspension of spousal support due to incarceration
17	4014	695	Updating current forms, employer
18	4058	2780	Annual gross income of parent
19	4320	929	Circumstances court must consider when awarding spousal support
20	4324.5	1129	Proceeding for dissolution when criminal conviction
21	4325	1129	Rebuttable presumption conviction
22	4331	2789	Exam by vocational counselor
23	5614	3248	Duties & prohibitions
24	6228	1494	Provision to make reports available to victims
25	6300	2684	Affidavit proof of past acts
26	6326	2684	Time for issuance or denial of ex parte motion R.O.
27	6380	2780	Electronic transfer of info to Justice Dept.
28	6340	2694	Ex parte orders
29	6924	2780	Consent by minor for mental health treatment
30	6928	1494	Consent by assault victim for treatment
31	6930	3189	Consent to treatment by DV victim
32	7002	273	Emancipation of minors
33	7540	2684	Presumption arising from birth of child during marriage
34	7541	2684	Use of blood tests to determine paternity
35	7550	2684	Scope of chapter
36	7550.5	2684	Definitions: combined relationship index, ethnic or racial group…
37	7551	2684	Order for genetic testing in action involving parentage
38	7551.5	2684	Facilitation of genetic tests
39	7552	2684	Requirements for genetic testing
40	7552.5	2684	Service of copies of results of genetic testing
41	7553	2684	Compensation of experts
42	7554	2684	Finding of parentage

Appendix Two: 2019 Family Code Changes & Bill Nos.

	FC §	Bill#	RE:
43	7555	2684	ID as genetic parent; challenge to results
44	7556	2684	Limitation on application in criminal matters
45	7557	2684	Right to produce other experts
46	7558	2684	Administrative order requiring genetic testing
47	7559	2684	Advance payment of initial genetic testing cost
48	7560	2684	Order for additional genetic testing upon request
49	7562	2684	Order for genetic testing of deceased person
50	7570	2684	Legislative findings and declarations
51	7571	2684	Declaration of paternity
52	7572	2684	Informational and training materials
53	7573	2684	Effect of declaration of paternity
54	7573.5	2684	Voiding voluntary declaration of paternity
55	7574	2684	Form of declaration of paternity
56	7575	2684	Rescission of voluntary declaration of paternity
57	7576	2684	Presumption of paternity applicable to declarations
58	7577	2684	Effect of declaration executed by minor parent
59	7578	2684	Will become effective 1/1/2020
60	7580	2684	Will become effective 1/1/2020
61	7581	2684	Will become effective 1/1/2020
62	7604	2684	Pendente lite relief of custody
63	7612	2684	Rebuttal of paternity presumption
64	7613	2684	Assisted reproduction
65	7630	2684	Who may bring action
66	7635	2684	Parties
67	7640	2684	Award of attorney fees and other costs
68	7643	2684	Confidentiality of hearings/records
69	7644	2684	Action based on declaration
70	7645	2684	Definitions: child, judgment, previously established father/mother
71	7646	2684	Motion challenging paternity judgment
72	7647	2684	Conditions for granting motion
73	7647.5	2684	Genetic testing
74	7648	2684	Denial of motion in best interests of child
75	7649	2684	No limitation on rights and remedies provided by other law
76	7650	2684	Action to determine mother and child relationship
77	7663	2684	Effort to ID father and presumed parent
78	7823	2684	Neglected or cruelly treated child
79	7827	2684	Parent mentally disabled
80	7850	2684	Investigation of circumstances of child
81	7851	2684	Report and recommendations to court
82	7911.1	2684	Investigations of threats to children
83	8502	2296	Adoption service provider
84	9001	2296	Investigation – written report
85	17311.7	3248	Payments state disbursement unit
86	17412	2684	Effect of voluntary declaration of paternity
87	17506	695	Parent locator service
88	17520	695	Consolidated lists

Appendix Two: 2019 Family Code Changes & Bill Nos.

Brief summary of Senate/Assembly Bills[1] Effective 2019

Bill No. 273: "Existing law establishes eligibility requirements and requires families to meet at least one requirement in each of 2 specified areas, including the area relating to why the family has a need for the child care service.
This bill would include in the area relating to need, as a requirement that may be satisfied for purposes of eligibility, that the family needs the child care services because the parents are engaged in an educational program for English language learners or to attain a high school diploma or general educational development certificate."

Bill No. 695: "(1) Existing law requires the driver of a vehicle or pedestrian to cross a railroad, a rail transit grade crossing, or a railroad grade crossing in a specified manner to safely avoid a train or car. A violation of these requirements is a crime.
This bill would make this requirement applicable to avoid on-track equipment, as defined. By expanding the scope of a crime, this bill would impose a state-mandated local program.
(2) The California Constitution requires the state to reimburse local agencies and school districts for certain costs mandated by the state. Statutory provisions establish procedures for making that reimbursement.
This bill would provide that no reimbursement is required by this act for a specified reason."

Bill No. 929: "Existing law authorizes a court to order spousal support in an amount, and for a period of time, that the court determines is just and reasonable based on the standard of living established during the marriage. In making spousal support awards, the court is required to consider, among other factors, documented evidence of any history of domestic violence between the parties or against the child of either party.
This bill would specify that all documented evidence of any history of domestic violence be considered by the court in ordering spousal support, including, but not limited to, issuance of a protective order or a finding by a court during the pendency of a divorce, separation, or child custody proceeding, or other specified proceeding, that the spouse has committed domestic violence."

Bill No. 1129: "Existing law requires a local EMS agency to plan, implement, and evaluate an emergency medical services system, as specified, and authorizes the local EMS agency to develop and submit a plan to the authority for an emergency medical services system according to prescribed guidelines that address data collection and evaluation, among other things.
This bill would require an emergency medical care provider to, when collecting and submitting data to a local EMS agency, use an electronic health record system that exports data in a format that is compliant with the current versions of the California Emergency Medical Services Information System (CEMSIS) and the National Emergency Medical Services Information System (NEMSIS) standards, includes those data elements required by the local EMS agency, and uses an electronic health record system that can be integrated with the local EMS agency's data system, as specified. The bill would prohibit a local EMS agency from mandating that a provider use a specific electronic health record system to collect and share data with the agency. The bill would not modify or affect a written contract or agreement executed before January 1, 2016, between a local EMS agency and an emergency medical care provider."

Bill No. 1494: "Existing law prohibits a voter from showing his or her ballot to any person after it is marked in such a way as to reveal its contents. Existing law provides that a person who interferes or attempts to interfere with the secrecy of voting is guilty of a felony, and authorizes the Secretary of State, the Attorney General, or a local election official to bring an action to impose additional civil penalties for committing those acts.
This bill would create an exception to that prohibition that would permit a voter to voluntarily disclose how he or she voted if that voluntary act does not violate any other law." Existing law requires a family court to determine the best interests of the child for purposes of deciding child custody in proceedings for dissolution of marriage, nullity of marriage, legal separation of the parties, petitions

---

[1] Unless provided otherwise, each bill contains shortened text with the exact language that is in that bill. Bill numbers are in chronological order.

Appendix Two: 2019 Family Code Changes & Bill Nos.

for exclusive custody of a child, and proceedings under the Domestic Violence Prevention Act. In making that determination, existing law requires the court to consider specified factors, including whether either of the child's parents habitually or continually uses alcohol or illegal drugs.

This bill would require the court to make the determination consistent with specified findings. The bill would include in those findings that children have the right to be safe and free from abuse and that domestic violence in a household where a child resides is detrimental to the health, safety, and welfare of the child.

Existing law establishes a rebuttable presumption that an award of sole or joint physical or legal custody of a child to a person who has perpetrated domestic violence against the other party seeking custody of the child or against the child or the child's siblings within the previous five years is detrimental to the best interests of the child. In overcoming that presumption, existing law requires the court to consider specified factors, including whether the perpetrator of domestic violence has committed any further acts of domestic violence.

This bill would extend this presumption to a person who has committed domestic violence against another person with whom that party has a specified relationship. The bill would require the court, in determining whether the presumption is overcome, to find that the perpetrator of domestic violence has demonstrated that giving sole or joint physical or legal custody of a child to the perpetrator is in the best interests of the child and would specify additional factors that, on balance, are required to support the grant of custody. The bill would require the court to state its reasons for finding that the presumption has been overcome in writing or on the record.

Existing law requires a court to grant reasonable visitation rights to a parent unless it is shown that the visitation would be detrimental to the best interest of the child.

This bill, instead, would require the court to grant reasonable visitation rights when it is shown that the visitation would be in the best interest of the child, as defined, and consistent with the above provisions for ordering custody.

Existing law requires the Judicial Council to establish judicial training programs for individuals who perform duties in domestic violence matters, including judges, referees, and mediators, among others, and requires that the training programs include instruction in all aspects of domestic violence.

This bill would require the training to include the detriment to children of residing in a home with a person who perpetrates domestic violence and that domestic violence can occur without a party seeking or obtaining a restraining order, without a substantiated child protective services finding, and without other documented evidence of abuse."

Bill No. 2214: "Existing law provides for the licensure and regulation of community care facilities by the State Department of Social Services. Existing law also provides for the licensure and regulation by the State Department of Health Care Services of adult alcoholism and drug abuse recovery and treatment facilities for adults.

This bill would, among other things, define a "recovery residence" as a residential property that is operated as a cooperative living arrangement to provide an alcohol and drug free environment for persons recovering from alcoholism or drug abuse, or both, who seek a living environment that supports personal recovery. The bill would authorize a recovery residence to demonstrate its commitment to providing a supportive recovery environment by applying and becoming certified by a certifying organization that is approved by the State Department of Health Care Services. The bill would require an approved certifying organization to, among other things, maintain an affiliation with a national organization recognized by the department, establish and use procedures to administer the application, certification, renewal, and disciplinary processes for a recovery residence, and investigate and enforce violations by a residence of the organization's code of conduct, as provided. The bill would specify the information and documentation that an operator who seeks to have a residence certified is required to submit to an approved certifying organization.

This bill would require an approved certifying organization to maintain and post on its Internet Web site a registry containing specified information of a residence that has been certified pursuant to these provisions and would require the department to maintain and post on its Internet Web site a registry that contains specified information regarding each residence and operator that has had its certification revoked.

This bill would require, on and after January 1, 2020, specified entities, including a state agency, state-contracted vendor, county agency, or county-contracted vendor, certified alcohol drug counselor, and person or entity licensed in the healing arts that directs substance use treatment, or a judge or parole

Appendix Two: 2019 Family Code Changes & Bill Nos.

board that sets terms and conditions for the release, parole, or discharge of a person from custody, if it requires that person to reside in a sober living environment, to first refer that person to a residence listed as a certified recovery residence on a registry posted by an approved certifying organization, if available. The bill would authorize those entities to refer persons to noncertified recovery residences, if they determine it is in the best interests of those persons, and, in that case, and would authorize those entities to notify the State Department of Health Care Services department of their decision. The bill would require the department to report to the Legislature on or before January 1, 2021, regarding the efficacy of its regulation of certifying organizations' impact on complaint resolution, as specified. By imposing additional duties on local governments, this bill would create a state-mandated local program.

The bill would provide for the repeal of all of these provisions on January 1, 2026.

The California Constitution requires the state to reimburse local agencies and school districts for certain costs mandated by the state. Statutory provisions establish procedures for making that reimbursement.

This bill would provide that, if the Commission on State Mandates determines that the bill contains costs mandated by the state, reimbursement for those costs shall be made pursuant to the statutory provisions noted above."

Bill No. 2296: "Existing law, the Uniform Electronic Transactions Act, provides that a record or signature may not be denied legal effect or enforceability solely because it is in electronic form and defines an electronic signature for purposes of the act. Existing provisions of the Government Code authorize the use of a digital signature in any written communication with a public entity, and specifies that in those communications, the use of a digital signature has the same force and effect as the use of a manual signature if it complies with specified requirements.

This bill would express the intent of the Legislature to clarify that a digital signature may be used to satisfy the requirements of an electronic signature under the Uniform Electronic Transactions Act. The bill would, for purposes of the Uniform Electronic Transactions Act, provide that an electronic signature includes a digital signature under the above described provisions of the Government Code and that a digital signature under those provisions is a type of an electronic signature as set forth in the Uniform Electronic Transaction Act. The bill would also revise the above-described provisions of the Government Code by specifying that if a public entity elects to use a digital signature, that meets specified requirements, the digital signature has the same force and effect of a manual signature in any communication with the public entity."

Bill No. 2684: "(1) The Uniform Parentage Act defines the parent and child relationship as the legal relationship existing between a child and the child's parents, and provides rebuttable presumptions as to the parentage of a child born under certain circumstances. The Uniform Act on Blood Tests to Determine Paternity provides the procedures for the use of genetic testing, as defined, to determine paternity.

This bill would delete the name of the Uniform Act on Blood Tests to Determine Paternity and would revise and recast provisions relating to establishing a parent and child relationship to, among other things, refer instead to genetic testing and parentage. The bill would revise the presumptions and procedures for establishing and challenging parentage based on a genetic or nongenetic relationship with a child, including to modify the procedures for genetic testing for parentage. The bill would authorize the court to apply existing standards for awarding attorney's fees and costs in actions related to marriage and child custody and visitation to awarding fees and costs in actions related to determining a parent and child relationship.

This bill would, beginning on January 1, 2020, modify the procedures and requirements under which a voluntary declaration of parentage may be established and challenged.

(2) Existing law requires the State Department of Public Health to license and regulate tissue banks, which process, store, or distribute human tissue for transplantation into human beings.

This bill would define gamete bank as a tissue bank that collects, processes, stores, or distributes gametes, including a facility that provides reproductive services. The bill would require a gamete bank licensed in this state, for gametes collected on or after January 1, 2020, to collect specified identifying information and medical information, as defined, from a gamete donor, to provide the gamete donor with specified information, and to obtain a declaration from the gamete donor regarding the disclosure or nondisclosure of his or her identity to a child that results from the donation, upon the child turning 18 years of age and requesting the information."

Appendix Two: 2019 Family Code Changes & Bill Nos.

Bill No. 2694: "Existing law authorizes a court to issue various ex parte orders, including, among other orders, orders enjoining a party from assaulting, contacting, coming within a specified distance of, or disturbing the peace of the other party, or excluding a party from a dwelling or enjoining a party from specified behavior that the court determines is necessary to effectuate these orders.
This bill would prohibit a petition for an ex parte order for the purposes described above from being denied solely because the other party was not provided with notice. The bill would also authorize, if at the time of a hearing with respect to an order based on an ex parte temporary restraining order the court determines that, after diligent effort, the petitioner has been unable to accomplish personal service, and that there is reason to believe that the restrained party is evading service, the court to permit an alternative method of service designed to give reasonable notice of the action to the respondent, as specified."

Bill No. 2780: "(1) Existing law authorizes the court, in a proceeding for dissolution of marriage or for legal separation of the parties, to order a party to submit to an examination by a vocational training counselor to assess the party's ability to obtain certain employment, as specified. Existing law requires a vocational training counselor performing these examinations to possess specific educational and professional experiences, including, among other qualifications, a master's degree in the behavioral sciences.

This bill would modify the required qualification to serve as a vocational training counselor by allowing, in the alternative to the master's degree, a vocational training counselor to possess another postgraduate degree that the court finds provides sufficient training to perform a vocational evaluation.
(2) Existing law requires a court, in a proceeding for court-ordered child support, to follow the statewide uniform guideline to determine the amount of child support to order, unless special circumstances exist. Existing law also requires a court to adhere to certain principles in these proceedings, including, among others, that each parent should pay for the support of the children according to his or her ability. Existing law defines the annual gross income of the parent for purposes of the statewide uniform guideline, and authorizes the court, in its discretion, to consider the earning capacity of a parent in lieu of the parent's income, consistent with the best interests of the children.
This bill would specify that a court may, in exercising its discretion to consider the earning capacity of the parent as described above, take into consideration the overall welfare and developmental needs of the children, and the time that parent spends with the children."

Bill No. 3189: "(1) Existing law authorizes a minor who is 12 years of age or older and is alleged to have been raped, or a minor who is alleged to have been sexually assaulted, to consent to medical care related to the diagnosis and treatment of the condition and the collection of medical evidence with regard to the alleged rape or sexual assault.
This bill would authorize a minor who is 12 years of age or older and who states he or she is injured as a result of intimate partner violence, as defined, to consent to medical care related to the diagnosis or treatment of the injury and the collection of medical evidence with regard to the alleged intimate partner violence. The bill would specify that this provision would not apply to a case in which a minor is an alleged victim of rape or is alleged to have been sexually assaulted, in which case the above-described provisions would apply.
(2) Existing law requires a health practitioner who works in a certain type of health facility and provides medical services for a patient he or she knows or reasonably suspects is suffering from an injury caused by a firearm or assaultive or abusive conduct to make a report to a local law enforcement agency about the patient and the extent of the injuries.
This bill would require a health practitioner that believes a report is required pursuant to these provisions, when providing treatment to an above-described minor injured as a result of alleged intimate partner violence, to inform the minor that the report will be made and attempt to contact the minor's parent or guardian and inform him or her of the report, except as specified."

Bill No. 3248: "(1) Existing law continues the parental duty to support an unmarried child who has attained 18 years of age, is a full-time high school student, and who is not self-supporting, until the time the child completes the 12th grade or attains 19 years of age, whichever occurs first.

Appendix Two: 2019 Family Code Changes & Bill Nos.

This bill would excuse a child from the requirement to be a full-time high school student for purposes of these provisions if the child has a medical condition documented by a physician that prevents full-time school attendance.

(2) Existing law provides various procedures for the collection of child support and establishes, within the Department of Child Support Services, the State Disbursement Unit for the collection and disbursement of payments pursuant to support orders. Existing law also provides for the collection of child support by private child support collectors and requires those entities to take specified actions, including establishing a direct deposit account with the State Disbursement Unit and, within 2 business days from the date the funds are disbursed from the State Disbursement Unit to the private child support collector, if a portion of the funds constitute an obligor's fee, to notify the department of the portion of each collection that constitutes a fee.

This bill would remove the requirement that a private child support collector establish a direct deposit account with the State Disbursement Unit and would remove the notification requirement. The bill would require any payment required to be made to a family through the State Disbursement Unit to be made directly to the obligee parent in the child support order requiring the payment, a special needs trust for the benefit of the obligee parent, or other specified individuals.

The bill would also remove requirements relating to the transfer of child support collection and distribution functions to the state, including a requirement that all child support collections remaining undisbursed, with interest earned on these funds, be transferred to the department for deposit in the Child Support Payment Trust Fund.

(3) The Uniform Parentage Act authorizes a hearing or trial held under its provisions to be held in closed court without admittance of any person other than those necessary to the action or proceeding. Under the act, all papers and records, other than the final judgment, pertaining to an action or proceeding are subject to inspection and copying only in exceptional cases upon an order of the court for good cause shown, except as specified.

This bill would authorize the papers and records relating to establishing paternity and establishing and enforcing child support orders in a proceeding under the act to be subject to inspection and copying by any local child support agency.

(4) Existing law authorizes a trial court to, by local rule, require the electronic filing and service of documents in civil actions, subject to certain conditions. Existing law exempts, until January 1, 2019, a local child support agency from a trial court's mandatory electronic filing and service requirements, unless the Department of Child Support Services and the local child support agency determine it has the capacity and functionality to comply with those requirements."

Appendix Three: Family Codes Effective 1/1/2020

FC § 7550 This chapter shall govern both of the following:
(a) The genetic testing of a person who either voluntarily submits to genetic testing or is ordered to submit to genetic testing pursuant to an order of a court or local child support agency.
(b) The use of genetic testing in a proceeding to determine parentage.

FC § 7551

(a) Except as provided in subdivisions (b) and (c), in a civil action or proceeding in which parentage is a relevant fact, the court may, upon its own initiative or upon suggestion made by or on behalf of any person who is involved, and shall upon motion of any party to the action or proceeding made at a time so as not to delay the proceedings unduly, order the woman who gave birth, the child, and the alleged genetic parent to submit to genetic testing.
(b)
(1) Genetic testing shall not be used for any of the following purposes:
(A) To challenge the parentage of a person who is a parent pursuant to subdivision (a) of Section 7613, except to resolve a dispute whether the child was conceived through assisted reproduction.
(B) To challenge the parentage of a person who is a parent pursuant to Section 7962, except to resolve a dispute whether the gestational carrier surrogate is a genetic parent.
(C) To establish the parentage of a person who is a donor pursuant to subdivision (b) or (c) of Section 7613, except to resolve a dispute whether the child was conceived through assisted reproduction.
(2) If the child has a presumed parent pursuant to Section 7540, a motion for genetic testing is governed by Section 7541.
(3) If the child has a parent whose parentage has been previously established in a judgment, a request for genetic testing shall be governed by Section 7647.7.
(4) A court shall not order genetic testing if the genetic testing would be used to establish the parentage of a person who is prohibited under this division from establishing parentage based on evidence of genetic testing.
(c) A court shall not order in utero genetic testing.
(d) In any case under this division in which genetic testing is ordered, the following shall apply:
(1) If a party refuses to submit to genetic testing, the court may resolve the question of parentage against that party or enforce its order if the rights of others and the interests of justice so require.
(2) The refusal of a party to submit to genetic testing is admissible in evidence in any proceeding to determine parentage.
(3) If two or more persons are subject to court-ordered genetic testing, the court may order that the testing be completed concurrently or sequentially.
(4) Genetic testing of a woman who gave birth to a child is not a condition precedent to the testing of the child and a person whose genetic parentage of the child is being determined. If the woman is unavailable for genetic testing, the court may order genetic testing of the child and each person whose genetic parentage of the child is at issue.
(5) An order under this division for genetic testing is enforceable by contempt.

FC § 7552

(a) Genetic testing shall be of a type reasonably relied on by experts in the field of genetic testing and performed in a testing laboratory accredited by either of the following:
(1) The AABB, formerly known as the American Association of Blood Banks, or a successor organization.
(2) An accrediting body designated by the Secretary of the United States Department of Health and Human Services.
(b) A specimen used in genetic testing may consist of a sample or a combination of samples of blood, buccal cells, bone, hair, or other body tissue or fluid. The specimen used in the testing need not be of the same kind for each person undergoing genetic testing.
(c) Based on the ethnic or racial group of a person undergoing genetic testing, a testing laboratory shall determine the databases from which to select frequencies for use in calculating a relationship index. If a person or a local child support agency objects to the laboratory's choice, the following rules shall apply:
(1) Not later than 30 days after receipt of the report of the test, the objecting person or local child support agency may request the court to require the laboratory to recalculate the relationship index using an ethnic or racial group different from that used by the laboratory.
(2) The person or local child support agency objecting to the choice of laboratories under this subdivision shall do either of the following:
(A) If the requested frequencies are not available to the laboratory for the ethnic or racial group requested, provide the requested frequencies compiled in a manner recognized by accrediting bodies.
(B) Engage another laboratory to perform the calculations.
(3) The laboratory may use its own statistical estimate if there is a question of which ethnic or racial group is appropriate. The laboratory shall calculate the frequencies using statistics, if available, for any other ethnic or racial group requested.
(d) If, after recalculation of the relationship index pursuant to subdivision (c) using a different ethnic or racial group, genetic testing does not identify a person as a genetic parent of the child, the court may require a person who has been tested to submit to additional genetic testing to identify a genetic parent.

FC § 7554

(a) If the woman who gave birth to the child is the only other person who is a parent or has a claim to parentage of the child under this division, the court shall find the alleged father or genetic parent who is not a donor under Section 7613 to be a parent of the child if he or she meets any of the following:
(1) Is identified pursuant to Section 7555 as a genetic parent of the child and the identification is not successfully challenged.
(2) Admits parentage in a pleading, when making an appearance, or during a hearing, the court accepts the admission, and the court determines that he or she is a genetic parent of the child.
(3) Declines to submit to genetic testing ordered by the court or a local child support agency, in which case, the court may find that the person is a parent of the child even if he or she denies a genetic relationship with the child.
(4) Is in default after service of process and the court determines the person to be a genetic parent of the child.
(5) Is neither identified nor excluded as a genetic parent by genetic testing and, based on other evidence, the court determines the person to be a genetic parent of the child.
(b) If more than one person other than the woman who gave birth asserts a claim under this division to be the child's parent, parentage shall be determined under provisions of this division.

FC § 7555

(a) Subject to a challenge under subdivision (b), a person is identified under this part as a genetic parent of a child if genetic testing complies with this part and the results of the testing disclose both of the following:
(1) The person has at least a 99 percent probability of parentage, using a prior probability of 0.50, as calculated by using the combined relationship index obtained in the testing.
(2) A combined relationship index of at least 100 to 1.
(b) A person identified pursuant to subdivision (a) as a genetic parent of the child may challenge the genetic testing results only by other genetic testing satisfying the requirements of this chapter that either excludes the person as a genetic parent of the child or identifies another person as a possible genetic parent of the child other than the woman who gave birth to the child or the person challenging parentage.
(c) If more than one person, other than the woman who gave birth to the child, is identified by genetic testing as a possible genetic parent of the child, the court shall order each person to submit to further genetic testing to identify a genetic parent.

FC § 7570.

(a) The Legislature hereby finds and declares as follows:
(1) There is a compelling state interest in establishing parentage for all children. Establishing parentage is the first step toward a child support award, which, in turn, provides children with equal rights and access to benefits, including, but not limited to, social security, health insurance, survivors' benefits, military benefits, and inheritance rights.
(2) A simple administrative system allowing for establishment of voluntary parentage will result in a significant increase in the ease of establishing parentage, a significant increase in parentage establishment, an increase in the number of children who have greater access to child support and other benefits, and a significant decrease in the time and money required to establish parentage due to the removal of the need for a lengthy and expensive court process to determine and establish parentage and is in the public interest.
(b) This section shall become **operative on January 1, 2020.**

FC § 7571

(a) On and after January 1, 1995, upon the event of a live birth, prior to an unmarried mother or a mother who gave birth to a child conceived through assisted reproduction leaving a hospital, the person responsible for registering live births under Section 102405 of the Health and Safety Code shall provide to the woman giving birth and shall attempt to provide, at the place of birth, to the person identified by the woman giving birth as either the only possible genetic parent other than the woman who gave birth or the intended parent of a child conceived through assisted reproduction, a voluntary declaration of parentage together with the written materials described in Section 7572. Staff in the hospital shall witness the signatures of parents signing a voluntary declaration of parentage and shall forward the signed declaration to the Department of Child Support Services within 20 days of the date the declaration was signed. A copy of the declaration shall be made available to each of the attesting parents.
(b) A health care provider shall not be subject to civil, criminal, or administrative liability for a negligent act or omission relative to the accuracy of the information provided, or for filing the declaration with the appropriate state or local agencies.
(c) The local child support agency shall pay the sum of ten dollars ($10) to birthing hospitals and other entities that provide prenatal services for each completed declaration of parentage that is filed with the Department of Child Support Services, provided that the local child support agency and the hospital or other entity providing prenatal services has entered into a written agreement that specifies the terms and conditions for the payment as required by federal law.

(d) If the declaration is not registered by the person responsible for registering live births at the hospital, it may be completed by the attesting parents, notarized, and mailed to the Department of Child Support Services at any time after the child's birth.
(e) Prenatal clinics shall offer prospective parents the opportunity to sign a voluntary declaration of parentage. In order to be paid for their services as provided in subdivision (c), prenatal clinics must ensure that the form is witnessed and forwarded to the Department of Child Support Services within 20 days of the date the declaration was signed.
(f) Declarations shall be made available without charge at all local child support agency offices, offices of local registrars of births and deaths, courts, and county welfare departments within this state. Staff in these offices shall witness the signatures of parents wishing to sign a voluntary declaration of parentage and shall be responsible for forwarding the signed declaration to the Department of Child Support Services within 20 days of the date the declaration was signed.
(g) The Department of Child Support Services, at its option, may pay the sum of ten dollars ($10) to local registrars of births and deaths, county welfare departments, or courts for each completed declaration of parentage that is witnessed by staff in these offices and filed with the Department of Child Support Services. In order to receive payment, the Department of Child Support Services and the entity shall enter into a written agreement that specifies the terms and conditions for payment as required by federal law. The Department of Child Support Services shall study the effect of the ten dollar ($10) payment on obtaining completed voluntary declaration of parentage forms.
(h) The Department of Child Support Services and local child support agencies shall publicize the availability of the declarations. The local child support agency shall make the declaration, together with the written materials described in subdivision (a) of Section 7572, available upon request to any parent and any agency or organization that is required to offer parents the opportunity to sign a voluntary declaration of parentage. The local child support agency shall also provide qualified staff to answer parents' questions regarding the declaration and the process of establishing parentage.
(i) Copies of the declaration and any rescissions filed with the Department of Child Support Services shall be made available only to the parents, the child, the local child support agency, the county welfare department, the county counsel, the State Department of Public Health, and the courts.
(j) Publicly funded or licensed health clinics, pediatric offices, Head Start programs, child care centers, social services providers, prisons, and schools may offer parents the opportunity to sign a voluntary declaration of parentage. In order to be paid for their services as provided in subdivision (c), publicly funded or licensed health clinics, pediatric offices, Head Start programs, child care centers, social services providers, prisons, and schools shall ensure that the form is witnessed and forwarded to the Department of Child Support Services.
(k) An agency or organization required to offer parents the opportunity to sign a voluntary declaration of parentage shall also identify parents who are willing to sign, but were unavailable when the child was born. The organization shall then contact these parents within 10 days and again offer the parent the opportunity to sign a voluntary declaration of parentage.
(*l*) This section shall become **operative on January 1, 2020.**

FC § 7572

(a) The Department of Child Support Services, in consultation with the State Department of Health Care Services, the California Association of Hospitals and Health Systems, and other affected health provider organizations, shall work cooperatively to develop written materials to assist providers and parents in complying with this chapter. This written material shall be updated periodically by the Department of Child Support Services to reflect changes in law, procedures, or public need.

(b) The written materials for unmarried parents or parents of a child conceived through assisted reproduction that shall be attached to the form specified in Section 7574 and shall contain the following information:

(1) A signed voluntary declaration of parentage that is filed with the Department of Child Support Services legally establishes parentage.

(2) The legal rights and obligations of both parents and the child that result from the establishment of parentage.

(3) An alleged father's constitutional rights to have the issue of parentage decided by a court; to notice of any hearing on the issue of parentage; to have an opportunity to present his case to the court, including his right to present and cross-examine witnesses; to have an attorney represent him; and to have an attorney appointed to represent him if he cannot afford one in a parentage action filed by a local child support agency.

(4) That by signing the voluntary declaration of parentage, the father is voluntarily waiving his constitutional rights.

(c) Parents shall also be given oral notice of the rights and responsibilities specified in subdivision (b). Oral notice may be accomplished through the use of audio or video recorded programs developed by the Department of Child Support Services to the extent permitted by federal law.

(d) The Department of Child Support Services shall, free of charge, make available to hospitals, clinics, and other places of birth any and all informational and training materials for the program under this chapter, as well as the declaration of parentage form. The Department of Child Support Services shall make training available to every participating hospital, clinic, local registrar of births and deaths, and other place of birth no later than June 30, 1999.

(e) The Department of Child Support Services may adopt regulations, including emergency regulations, necessary to implement this chapter.

(f) This section shall become **operative on January 1, 2020.**

FC § 7573

(a) The following persons may sign a voluntary declaration of parentage to establish the parentage of the child:

(1) An unmarried woman who gave birth to the child and another person who is a genetic parent.

(2) A married or unmarried woman who gave birth to the child and another person who is a parent under Section 7613 of a child conceived through assisted reproduction.

(b) A voluntary declaration of parentage shall be in a record signed by the woman who gave birth to the child and by either the only possible genetic parent other than the woman who gave birth or the intended parent of a child conceived through assisted reproduction, and the signatures shall be attested by a notary or witnessed.

(c) Except as provided by Section 7580, a voluntary declaration of parentage takes effect on the filing of the document with the Department of Child Support Services.

(d) Except as provided in Sections 7573.5, 7575, 7576, 7577, and 7580, a completed voluntary declaration of parentage that complies with this chapter and that has been filed with the Department of Child Support Services is equivalent to a judgment of parentage of the child and confers on the declarant all rights and duties of a parent.

(e) The court shall give full faith and credit to a voluntary declaration of parentage effective in another state if the declaration was in a signed record and otherwise complies with the law of the other state.

(f) This section shall become **operative on January 1, 2020.**

FC § 7573.5.

(a) A voluntary declaration of parentage is void if, at the time of signing, any of the following are true:

(1) A person other than the woman who gave birth to the child or a person seeking to establish parentage through a voluntary declaration of parentage is a presumed parent under Section 7540 or subdivision (a), (b), or (c) of Section 7611.

(2) A court has entered a judgment of parentage of the child.

(3) Another person has signed a valid voluntary declaration of parentage.

(4) The child has a parent under Section 7613 or 7962 other than the signatories.

(5) The person seeking to establish parentage is a sperm or ova donor under subdivision (b) or (c) of Section 7613.

(6) The person seeking to establish parentage asserts that he or she is a parent under Section 7613 and the child was not conceived through assisted reproduction.

(b) In an action in which a party is seeking a determination that a voluntary declaration of parentage is void under this section, notice shall be provided pursuant to Section 7635.

(c) This section shall become **operative on January 1, 2020.**

FC § 7574

(a) The voluntary declaration of parentage shall be executed on a form developed by the Department of Child Support Services in consultation with the State Department of Public Health and groups addressing child support, child custody, assisted reproduction issues, and lesbian, gay, bisexual, and transgender rights.

(b) The form described in subdivision (a) shall contain, at a minimum, all of the following:

(1) The name and the signature of the woman who gave birth to the child.

(2) The name and the signature of the person seeking to establish parentage.

(3) The name of the child.

(4) The date of birth of the child.

(5) For a voluntary declaration of parentage signed pursuant to paragraph (1) of subdivision (a) of Section 7573, all of the following:

(A) A statement by the woman who gave birth that she is unmarried and understands the written materials described in Section 7572, that the person who is signing the voluntary declaration of parentage is the only possible genetic parent other than the woman who gave birth, that the woman who gave birth consents to the establishment of parentage by the genetic parent signing the voluntary declaration of parentage, and that the woman who gave birth understands that a challenge by a signatory to a valid declaration of parentage is permitted only under limited circumstances and is barred two years after the effective date of the declaration.

(B) A statement by the genetic parent signing the voluntary declaration of parentage that he or she has read and understands the written materials described in Section 7572, understands that by signing the voluntary declaration of parentage he or she is waiving his or her rights as described in the written materials, that he or she is the genetic parent of the child, that he or she consents to the establishment of parentage by signing the voluntary declaration of parentage, that he or she is assuming all the rights and responsibilities of a parent and wishes to be named on the child's birth certificate, and that he or she understands that a challenge by a signatory to a valid declaration of parentage is permitted only under limited circumstances and is barred two years after the effective date of the declaration.

(6) For a voluntary declaration of parentage signed pursuant to paragraph (2) of subdivision (a) of Section 7573, all of the following:

(A) A statement by the woman who gave birth that she has read and understands the written materials described in Section 7572, that the person who is signing the voluntary declaration of parentage is the intended parent of a child conceived through assisted reproduction, that the woman who gave birth consents to the establishment of parentage by the other person signing the voluntary declaration of parentage, and that the woman who gave birth understands that a challenge by a signatory to a valid declaration of parentage is permitted only under limited circumstances and is barred two years after the effective date of the declaration.

(B) A statement that the person seeking to establish parentage has read and understands the written materials described in Section 7572, understands that by signing the voluntary declaration of parentage he or she is waiving his or her rights as described in the written materials, that he or she is the intended parent of the child conceived through assisted reproduction, that he or she consents to the establishment of parentage by signing the voluntary declaration of parentage, that he or she is assuming all the rights and responsibilities of a parent and wishes to be named on the child's birth certificate, and that he or she understands that a challenge by a signatory to a valid declaration of parentage is permitted only under limited circumstances and is barred two years after the effective date of the declaration.

(7) The name and the signature of the person who witnesses the signing of the declaration.

(c) This section shall become **operative on January 1, 2020.**

FC § 7575

(a) Either parent may rescind the voluntary declaration of parentage by filing a rescission form with the Department of Child Support Services within 60 days of the date of execution of the declaration by the attesting parents, whichever signature is later, unless a court order for custody, visitation, or child support has been entered in an action in which the signatory seeking to rescind was a party. The Department of Child Support Services shall develop a form to be used by parents to rescind the declaration of parentage and instructions on how to complete and file the rescission with the Department of Child Support Services. The form shall include a declaration under penalty of perjury completed by the person filing the rescission form that certifies that a copy of the rescission form was sent by any form of mail requiring a return receipt to the other person who signed the voluntary declaration of parentage. A copy of the return receipt shall be attached to the rescission form when filed with the Department of Child Support Services. The form and instructions shall be written in simple, easy to understand language and shall be made available at the local family support office and the office of local registrar of births and deaths. The department shall, upon written request, provide to a court or commissioner a copy of any rescission form filed with the department that is relevant to proceedings before the court or commissioner.

(b) This section shall become **operative on January 1, 2020.**

FC § 7576

(a) After the period for rescission provided in Section 7575 expires, but not later than two years after the effective date provided in subdivision (c) of Section 7573 of a voluntary declaration of parentage, a signatory of the voluntary declaration of parentage may commence a proceeding to challenge the declaration on the basis of fraud, duress, or material mistake of fact.

(b) The limitations period provided in subdivision (a) shall not apply if the voluntary declaration of parentage is void under Section 7573.5.

(c) This section shall become **operative on January 1, 2020.**

FC § 7577

The following rules apply in an action to challenge a valid voluntary declaration of parentage brought by a person who is not a signatory to the declaration. This section does not apply to a voluntary declaration of parentage that is void under Section **7573.5.**

(a) A person has standing under this section if he or she is an alleged genetic parent who is not a donor under Section 7613, is a presumed parent under Section 7611, or any person who has standing under Section 7630.
(b) The petition challenging a voluntary declaration of parentage pursuant to this section shall be supported by a declaration under oath alleging specific facts to support standing under this section.
(c) If the court holds a hearing to determine standing, the hearing shall be held on an expedited basis. If the person challenging the voluntary declaration of parentage is an alleged genetic parent, genetic testing shall be ordered on an expedited basis.
(d) The action shall be filed not later than two years after the effective date of the declaration. This limitations period shall not apply if the voluntary declaration of parentage is void under Section 7573.5.
(e) Notice shall be provided to the signatories of the declaration and to any person entitled to notice under Section 7635. Any person who asserts a claim to parentage under this division shall be joined in the action.
(f) With respect to whether the voluntary declaration of parentage should be set aside, the person petitioning to set aside the voluntary declaration of parentage shall have the burden of proof by a preponderance of the evidence.
(g) The court may grant the petition to set aside the voluntary declaration of parentage only if the court finds that setting aside the voluntary declaration of parentage is in the best interests of the child, based on consideration of all of the following factors:
(1) The age of the child.
(2) The length of time since the effective date of the voluntary declaration of parentage.
(3) The nature, duration, and quality of any relationship between the person who signed the voluntary declaration of parentage and the child, including the duration and frequency of any time periods during which the child and the person resided in the same household or enjoyed a parent and child relationship.
(4) The request of the person who signed the voluntary declaration of parentage that the parent and child relationship continue.
(5) If the person challenges a voluntary declaration of parentage signed pursuant to paragraph (1) of subdivision (a) of Section 7573, the court shall additionally consider all of the following:
(A) Notice by the genetic parent of the child that the genetic parent does not oppose preservation of the relationship between the person who signed the declaration of parentage and the child.
(B) Whether any conduct of the person who signed the voluntary declaration has impaired the ability to ascertain the identity of, or obtain support from, the genetic parent.
(6) Additional factors deemed by the court to be relevant to its determination of the best interests of the child.
(h) If the voluntary declaration of parentage is challenged by a person who is presumed to be a parent under subdivision (d) of Section 7611, the court's ruling on the petition to set aside the voluntary declaration of parentage shall, in addition to the factors under subdivision (g), also take into account the nature, duration, and quality of the relationship between the petitioning party and the child and the benefit or detriment to the child of continuing that relationship.
(i) If the court denies the petition to set aside the voluntary declaration of parentage, the court shall state on the record the basis for the denial of the action and any supporting facts.
(j)
(1) If the court grants the petition to set aside the voluntary declaration of parentage, the court shall adjudicate parentage pursuant to Section 7612.

(2) Any order for custody, visitation, or child support shall remain in effect until the court determines that the voluntary declaration of parentage should be set aside, subject to the court's power to modify the orders as otherwise provided by law.

(k) Nothing in this section shall be construed to prejudice or bar the rights of a person who is not a signatory and has standing under subdivision (a) to file an action or motion to set aside the voluntary declaration of parentage on any of the grounds described in, and within the time limits specified in, Section 473 of the Code of Civil Procedure. If the action or motion to set aside a judgment is required to be filed within a specified time period under Section 473 of the Code of Civil Procedure, the period within which the action or motion to set aside the voluntary declaration of parentage must be filed shall commence on the date that the court makes an initial order for custody, visitation, or child support based upon a voluntary declaration of parentage.

(*l*) Nothing in this section is intended to restrict a court from acting as a court of equity.

(m) The Judicial Council shall develop the forms and procedures necessary to effectuate this section.

(n) This section shall become **operative on January 1, 2020.**

FC § 7578

(a) Every signatory to a voluntary declaration of parentage shall be made a party to a proceeding to challenge the declaration.

(b) By signing a voluntary declaration, a signatory submits to personal jurisdiction in this state in a proceeding to challenge the declaration, effective on the filing of the declaration with the Department of Child Support Services.

(c) The court shall not suspend the legal responsibilities arising from a voluntary declaration of parentage, including the duty to pay child support, during the pendency of a proceeding to challenge the voluntary declaration of parentage, unless the party challenging the declaration shows good cause.

(d) A party challenging a voluntary declaration of parentage has the burden of proof by a preponderance of the evidence.

(e) If the judgment or order of the court is at variance with the child's birth certificate, the court shall order that a new birth certificate be issued as prescribed in Article 2 (commencing with Section 102725) of Chapter 5 of Part 1 of Division 102 of the Health and Safety Code.

(f) This section shall become **operative on January 1, 2020.**

FC § 7580

(a) Notwithstanding subdivision (c) of Section 7573, a voluntary declaration of parentage that is signed by a minor parent or minor parents shall not establish parentage until 60 days after both signatories have reached 18 years of age or are emancipated, whichever first occurs.

(b) A person who signs a voluntary declaration of parentage when he or she is a minor may rescind the voluntary declaration of parentage at any time up to 60 days after the signatory reaches 18 years of age or becomes emancipated, whichever first occurs.

(c) A voluntary declaration of parentage signed by a minor creates a rebuttable presumption for or against parentage until the date that it establishes parentage as specified in subdivision (a).

(d) A voluntary declaration of parentage signed by a minor shall be admissible as evidence in any civil action to establish parentage of the minor named in the voluntary declaration.

(e) A voluntary declaration of parentage that is signed by a minor shall not be admissible as evidence in a criminal prosecution for violation of Section 261.5 of the Penal Code.

(f) This section shall become **operative on January 1, 2020.**

Appendix Three: Family Codes Effective 1/1/2020

FC § 7581 The following provisions shall apply for voluntary declarations signed on or before December 31, 1996.
(a) Except as provided in subdivision (d), the child of a woman and a man executing a declaration of paternity under this chapter is conclusively presumed to be the man's child. The presumption under this section has the same force and effect as the presumption under Section 7540.
(b) A voluntary declaration of paternity shall be recognized as the basis for the establishment of an order for child custody or support.
(c) In an action to rebut the presumption created by this section, a voluntary declaration of paternity shall be admissible as evidence to determine paternity of the child named in the voluntary declaration of paternity.
(d) The presumption established by this section may be rebutted by any person by requesting genetic testing pursuant to Chapter 2 (commencing with Section 7550). The notice of motion for genetic testing pursuant to this section shall be supported by a declaration under oath submitted by the moving party stating the factual basis for placing the issue of paternity before the court. The notice of motion for genetic testing shall be made within three years from the date of execution of the declaration by the attesting father, or by the attesting mother, whichever signature is later. The two-year statute of limitations specified in subdivision (b) of Section 7541 is inapplicable for purposes of this section.
(e) A presumption under this section shall override all statutory presumptions of paternity, except a presumption arising under Section 7540, a claim made pursuant to Section 7555, or as provided in Section 7612.
(f) This section shall become **operative on January 1, 2020.**

FC § 7612

(a) Except as provided in Chapter 1 (commencing with Section 7540) and Chapter 3 (commencing with Section 7570) of Part 2, a presumption under Section 7611 is a rebuttable presumption affecting the burden of proof and may be rebutted in an appropriate action only by clear and convincing evidence.
(b) If two or more presumptions arise under Section 7611 that conflict with each other, or if one or more presumptions under Section 7611 conflict with a claim by a person identified as a genetic parent pursuant to Section 7555, the presumption that on the facts is founded on the weightier considerations of policy and logic controls. If one of the presumed parents is also a presumed parent under Section 7540, the presumption arising under Section 7540 may only be rebutted pursuant to Section 7541.
(c) In an appropriate action, a court may find that more than two persons with a claim to parentage under this division are parents if the court finds that recognizing only two parents would be detrimental to the child. In determining detriment to the child, the court shall consider all relevant factors, including, but not limited to, the harm of removing the child from a stable placement with a parent who has fulfilled the child's physical needs and the child's psychological needs for care and affection, and who has assumed that role for a substantial period of time. A finding of detriment to the child does not require a finding of unfitness of any of the parents or persons with a claim to parentage.
(d) Unless a court orders otherwise after making the determination specified in subdivision (c), a presumption under Section 7611 is rebutted by a judgment establishing parentage of the child by another person.
(e) A person's offer or refusal to sign a voluntary declaration of parentage may be considered as a factor, but shall not be determinative, as to the issue of legal parentage in a proceeding regarding the establishment or termination of parental rights.
(f) This section shall become **operative on January 1, 2020.**

FC § 7644.

(a) Notwithstanding any other law, an action for child custody and support and for other relief as provided in Section 7637 may be filed based upon a voluntary declaration of parentage as provided in Chapter 3 (commencing with Section 7570) of Part 2.

(b) Except as provided in Section 7581, the voluntary declaration of parentage shall be given the same force and effect as a judgment of parentage entered by a court of competent jurisdiction. The court shall make appropriate orders as specified in Section 7637 based upon the voluntary declaration of parentage unless evidence is presented that the voluntary declaration of parentage has been rescinded by the parties, set aside as provided in Section 7575, 7576, or 7577, or is void under Section 7573.5.

(c) The Judicial Council shall develop the forms and procedures necessary to implement this section.

(d) This section shall become **operative on January 1, 2020.**

FC § 17412

(a) Notwithstanding any other law, an action for child support may be brought by the local child support agency on behalf of a minor child or caretaker parent based upon a voluntary declaration of parentage as provided in Chapter 3 (commencing with Section 7570) of Part 2 of Division 12.

(b) Except as provided in Sections 7580 and 7581, the voluntary declaration of parentage shall be given the same force and effect as a judgment for parentage entered by a court of competent jurisdiction. The court shall make appropriate orders for support of the minor child based upon the voluntary declaration of parentage unless evidence is presented that the voluntary declaration of parentage has been rescinded by the parties or set aside by a court as provided in Section 7575, 7576, or 7577.

(c) The Judicial Council shall develop the forms and procedures necessary to implement this section.

(d) This section shall become **operative on January 1, 2020.**

GLOSSARY

Ability to pay: FC § 270 provides that if a court orders a party to pay attorney's fees or costs pursuant to this code, the court must first determine that the party so ordered has or is reasonably likely to have the ability to pay. FC § 7605(b) provides when a request for attorney's fees and costs is made and the court finds that there is disparity in access and ability to pay, the court must make an order awarding attorney's fees and costs. See Chapter 7: Attorney Fees & Limited Scope Representation.

Abstract of judgment: A summary of the court's final decision with regard to money owed on a judgment. The form is filed with the county recorder. It becomes a lien on any real property the judgment debtor owns in that county. See Chapter 32: Enforcement.

Acknowledgment: Accepting the existence or truth of something; or a form used in notarization.

Action: A lawsuit; actions can be criminal, civil or family law.

Adjudication: The act of a court in making an order, judgment, or decree.

Admission: Making a statement agreeing that certain facts are true.

Adoption: The process whereby a person assumes the parenting of another, usually a child. It is a way to legalize a relationship between a parent and child when they are not related by blood. See Chapter 14: Child Visitation and Chapter 34: Paternity.

Adversary system: Two opposing advocates, who each represent their parties' positions, present their theory or facts before an impartial person (judge) and/or jury, in an effort to determine the truth.

Affidavit: A sworn statement confirmed by an oath or affirmation taken by someone who is legally authorized to take the statement such as a judge or notary public.

Affirm: To state as a fact or a statement made that is strongly and publically asserted.

Affirmed: When a higher court agrees that the lower court has applied the right law correctly, the higher court will agree or affirm the lower court's decision

Affirmative defense: A defense in which one of the parties in a lawsuit introduces evidence, which, if found to be credible, will negate criminal or civil liability, even if it is proven that the party committed the alleged act.

Agent: Someone who has authority to act for another.

Alimony: See **spousal support**, *infra*.

Allegation: A statement or claim that is made and that has not been proven to be true or false.

Alternative dispute resolution (ADR): A methods of resolving disputes without official court proceedings. These methods include mediation and arbitration.

Alternate valuation date: For the purpose of division of the community estate upon dissolution or legal separation of the parties, the court must value the assets and liabilities as near as practicable to the time of trial. However, upon 30 days' notice by the moving party to the other party, the court may value all or any portion of the assets and liabilities at a date after separation and before trial (alternate valuation date) to accomplish an equal division of the community estate of the parties in an equitable manner, provided a good cause is shown. FC § 2552. See Chapter 20: Title, Kinds of Property & Valuation.

Amend: to alter, rephrase, modify, delete or add to.

***Amicus curiae*:** Advice formally offered to the court in a brief filed by a person or an entity interested in, but not a party to, the case.

Annulment or nullity of marriage: An action filed by a married person to change his or her marital status from married person to unmarried person. If an annulment is granted, the marriage never existed. FC § 2212 provides that "the effect of a judgment of nullity of marriage is to restore the parties to the status of unmarried persons." See Chapter 5: Annulment, Dissolution & Legal Separation.

Appeal: Asking a higher court to review a decision for mistakes of law or applying the law. The person who appeals a court's decision is called an **appellant** and the appeal is made to the Appellate Court.

Appearance: Going to court or filing responsive paperwork.

Apportionment: The concept of apportionment refers to determining the community and separate property interests in an asset. In making this determination, tracing may be used. See Chapter 24: Apportionment.

Arbitration: Having a neutral person not involved in the case consider all of the evidence, and then make a decision.

Arrearage: Child support that is overdue or unpaid. A parent that has arrearages is **in arrears**. See Chapter 32: Enforcement.

Assets: Property of all kinds, including real and personal, tangible and intangible.

At-issue memorandum: A legal document filed in a civil case to tell the court that the case is ready for trial.

Attorney of record: The lawyer whose name is listed in a case record as representing a party in the case.

Audit: When records or accounts are looked at to check that they are accurate and complete.

Bankruptcy: The procedure that can be used by a debtor (person or organization) to eliminate all current debts and get a fresh start with regard to his or her monetary obligations. (See **Chapters in bankruptcy** in this **Glossary**, *infra*.)

Bankruptcy code: The informal name for title 11 of the United States Code (11 U.S.C. §§ 101-1330), the federal bankruptcy law. (See **Chapters in bankruptcy** in this **Glossary**, *infra*.)

Bankruptcy court: A specific court that decides whether a bankruptcy will be granted and which assets are excluded and included, a unit of the district court.

Battery: Any willful and unlawful use of force or violence upon the person of another." PC § 242. A domestic violence battery is violently and angrily attacking, hitting, punching and/or hurting a family member. See Chapter 36: Domestic Violence.

Best interest of the child: The standard that courts use to decide custody and visitation issues. Some of the factors courts look at are: the age of the child, the health of the child, the emotional ties between the parents and the child, the ability of the parents to care for the child, and the child's ties to school, home, and the community.

Glossary

Bifurcation: Separating one or more legal issues in a case. Commonly used to separate marital status from the rest of the divorce issues so that one the parties is free to remarry before all of the issues of the divorce are decided. See Chapter 19: Bifurcation.

Blocked account: An account with a financial institution in which money or securities are placed and that cannot be withdrawn without the court's permission.

***Bona fide*:** Sincere, real, without fraud or deceit. Comes from the Latin for **in good faith**.

Brief: A written statement submitted in a trial or appellate preceding that explains one side's legal and factual arguments.

Burden of proof: The duty to go forward and present evidence in a lawsuit. There are three levels of Proof; preponderance, clear and convincing and beyond a reasonable doubt. See Chapter 25: Degrees of Proof & Presumptions.

California Rules of Court: The rules for practices and procedures in the court of California. See Chapter 1: Laws, Rules & Forms.

California Rules of Professional Conduct: Rules enacted to regulate the professional conduct of attorneys in the State of California.

Caption: Part of a pleading that contains the case name, court, and case number.

Case law: The law as established from previous court decisions.

Case number: The identification number that the clerk of the court gives to a case.

Cause of action: The charges (or **counts**) that allege behavior for a legal claim.

***Caveat emptor*:** A theory that you buy things at your own risk. Comes from the Latin for **let the buyer beware**.

Certified copy: An official copy of a paper that is marked as being true, complete, and a real copy of the original paper filed.

***Certiorari*:** Latin for **to be informed of or to be made certain in regard to**. A procedure whereby a higher court reviews a lower court's decision when the circumstances described in a petition are sufficient enough to merit a review. Certiorari is requested via a Petition.

Chambers: A judge's office where the judge and his or her staff (clerks) usually work.

Change of venue: When a case is moved from one court jurisdiction to another.

Chapters in bankruptcy: Chapter 11: A reorganization bankruptcy, usually involving a corporation or partnership. Chapter 12: The chapter of the Bankruptcy Code providing for adjustment of debts of a **family farmer**. Chapter 13: The chapter of the Bankruptcy Code providing for the adjustment of debts of an individual with regular income, often referred to as a **wage-earner plan**. Chapter 13 allows a debtor to keep property and use his or her disposable income to pay debts over time, usually three to five years. Chapter 7: The chapter of the Bankruptcy Code providing for **liquidation**.

Chattel: A piece of personal property

Child abuse: Injuring or harming a child physically, sexually or emotionally. See Chapter 14: Child Visitation and Chapter 37: Domestic Violence.

Child advocate: Someone with special training appointed by the court to help a child in a case.

Child custody:

Glossary

- **Legal custody** - the right to make decisions regarding the health, education and welfare of the children.
- **Sole legal custody** - one parent has the right to make the decisions relating to the health, education, and welfare of the children.
- **Joint legal custody** - both parents share the right and responsibility to make the decisions relating to the health, education, and welfare of the children.
- **Sole physical custody** – the children reside with and are under the supervision of one parent, subject to the power of the court to order visitation.
- **Joint physical custody** - parents have significant periods of physical custody such that there is frequent and continuing contact with both parents.

Child custody evaluation: An investigation and analysis by a mental health expert ordered by a court to resolve custody and visitation issues.

Child Protective Services (CPS): A state agency that responds to reports of child abuse and neglect. A case is opened if the case worker determines that there is possible abuse or neglect. See Chapter 36: Domestic Violence.

Child support: Money paid by the one parent to the other parent to help support a child or children. FC § 4055 sets forth the State guideline amount of child support that should be ordered by the court. Child support payments are made to the custodial parent for the support of the children of divorced or separated parents while the children are minors or until they emancipate. FC § 3901(a) sets forth the terminate date for child support. See Chapter 16: Child Support.

Child support guidelines: Guidelines established by FC § 4055 that sets forth the formula to determine the amount of child support to be paid to one parent by the other parent. Only the income of the parents and the timeshare with the children are considered in the formula. The amount determined by the formula is presumed to be the correct amount of support to be paid. See Chapter 16: Child Support.

Citation of contempt: A document that sets forth the violation of a court order in a contempt proceeding. See Chapter 32: Enforcement.

Citee: the person who violated the court order in a contempt proceeding. See Chapter 32: Enforcement.

Class action: A lawsuit in which members of a large group, or class, of individuals or other entities sue on behalf of the entire class. The district court must find that the claims of the class members contain questions of law or fact that are in common before the lawsuit can proceed as a class action.

Clerk of court: An assistant chosen by a judge to manage cases, keep court records, deal with financial matters, and give other administrative support.

Codicil: An addition to a will that modifies the will.

Cohabitation: Unmarried parties that are living together and are usually in a romantic relationship together. See Chapter 17: Spousal & Family Support.

Collaborative Law: A way to solve conflicts without going to court. Both sides have a lawyer, but they agree not to go to court unless it is impossible to settle the case. See Chapter 38: Collaborative Divorce.

Commingling: Mixing separate property assets with community property assets or vice versa.

Property that is **commingled** is presumed to be community property. The presumption can be rebutted by tracing or following the money trail and providing proof of the separate claim. See Chapter 20: Title, Kinds of Property & Valuation.

Commissioner: A person chosen by the court and given the power to hear and make decisions in certain kinds of legal matters. Commissioners are commonly appointed to family courts.

Common law: Rules from court decisions and not from statutes or constitutions. Uncodified law. See Chapter 5: Annulment, Dissolution & Legal Separation.

Community: Property acquired during marriage or owned jointly by both spouses. It is presumed that all property acquired during the marriage is community property. The marriage estate. See Chapter 20: Title, Kinds of Property & Valuation.

Community property: All property, real or personal, wherever situated, acquired by a married person or a married couple during the marriage while domiciled in this state; the respective interests of each spouse in community property during the marriage are present, existing and equal. FC §§ 760 and 751. Property so acquired is presumed to be community property. See Chapter 20: Title, Kinds of Property & Valuation.

Complaint: In civil cases, a request filed by the plaintiff that begins a case and sets forth allegations of the plaintiff, the actionable acts of the defendant and the remedies requested for those actionable acts.

Conciliation Court: A mediation service provided by the Superior Court where court-appointed, experienced mediators try to assist couples to reconcile by resolving their differences in an effort to save their marriage. A *Petition* is required to invoke conciliation court services. Only some counties have conciliation courts because it is not a requirement that all Superior Courts provide this service. FC § 3160. See Chapter 12: Mediation.

Conclusive presumption: A matter that is presumed and cannot be rebutted or disproved regardless of the evidence presented. See Chapter 25: Degrees of Proof & Presumptions.

Confidential marriage: A marriage whereby the record of the marriage is not open to public inspection. The county clerk may conduct a search for a confidential marriage certificate for the purpose of confirming the existence of a marriage, but the date of the marriage and any other information contained in the certificate may not be disclosed. FC § 511(c). See Chapter 4: Validity of Marriage.

Conformed copies: Copies of original documents that are file-stamped by the clerk of the court and returned to the person who filed them.

Conservatorship: A legal concept whereby a guardian is appointed by a judge to and mange a person and/or his or her affairs. There are two parts to a conservatorship (conservator of the person and conservator of the state).

Conservator of the person: A person or business chosen by a judge to care for and protect a person when the judge orders a conservatorship because a person (called the "conservatee") cannot care for himself or herself.

Conservator of the estate is the person or business chosen by a judge to handle the financial matters of a person when the judge orders a conservatorship because the person (called the **conservatee**) cannot handle his or her own financial affairs.

Consolidation of actions: When at least 2 court files that involve the same people are combined into one file.

Constructive trust: A constructive trust is an equitable remedy that is imposed upon a person who wrongfully acquires title to property that belongs to another. The wrongful owner has a duty to transfer the property to the party who rightfully owns it. This legal concept is used to prevent the party having the property from obtaining an unjust enrichment at the true owner's expense.

Contempt of court: When a person violates a court order that person is in contempt of court and maybe subject to fines and/or imprisonment.

Contested: Disputed.

Continuance: Postponing a hearing or trial to a later date.

Continuing exclusive jurisdiction: A court's authority to hear and keep jurisdiction of a case. See Chapter 3: Jurisdiction & Venue.

Convey: To transfer the title to property.

Court order: A legal decision issued by a court that commands or directs that something be done or not done. It can be made by a judge, commissioner, court referee, or magistrate.

Court reporter: A person who uses a special machine to record all that is said in courtroom. The account made by the court reporter can then be transcribed. It is customarily used as proof or for an appeal. See Chapter 11: Family Law Discovery.

Court stamp: A stamp that contains a seal that is imprinted on court papers. The copies that are stamped are called conformed copies.

Creditor: A person or business to whom money is owed.

Custodial parent: (CP) The parent who has primary care, custody, and control of the child or children. See Chapter 14: Child Visitation.

Custody order: A court order that provides who a child will live with and who will make the decisions about their health, education and welfare.

Damages: Money for losses or injuries.

Debtor: A person or business that owes a debt.

Debtor's examination: An examination of a debtor whereby the judgment creditor asks questions of the debtor to ascertain any assets that the debtor may have or when the asset was purchased. The debtor must answer the questions under penalty of perjury.

Decedent: A person who has died.

Declaration: A written statement that is made under penalty of perjury under the laws of the State of California that is used as evidence in court proceedings.

Declaratory judgment: A statement by a court that decides the rights of a person.

De facto: Latin, meaning **in fact** or **actually**. Something that exists in fact but not as a matter of law.

Default: A default occurs when a party in a lawsuit does not file a response after being appropriately and timely served or when a person does not appear in a court action after being appropriately and timely served to appear. See Chapter 28: Defaults.

Default judgment: A court decision that is made when only one party to a lawsuit or action appears at a hearing. A court will not grant all requests made by the appearing party unless the requests are fair and reasonable. See Chapter 28: Defaults.

Deferred compensation: money paid by an employer to an employee that is payable at some time in the future. See Chapter 23: Retirement & Disability.

Deferred sale of the home order: The act of deferring the sale of the community residence until the youngest child reaches the age of emancipation. Commonly called a **Duke Order**. Codified at FC §3801 et seq. See Chapter 16: Child Support.

Defined benefit plan: A pension plan where the employer agrees to pay an employee a specific benefit for life that commences at retirement. With a defined benefit plan, a separate account is kept for each participant that shows sums contributed by him or her and on the employee's behalf by the employer. See Chapter 23: Retirement & Disability.

Defined benefit retirement plan: A plan that is based upon a formula that can include compensation and years of service as factors. The plan specifies payments in advance in accordance with a formula that comprises factors such as final compensation, age, length of service, and a per-service-year multiplier. See Chapter 23: Retirement & Disability.

Defined contribution plan: The ultimate amount of the benefits to be provided at retirement will not be known until the date of retirement because they depend upon the future investment performance of the fund. The benefits are defined by a formula for contribution. See Chapter 23: Retirement & Disability.

De novo: Latin for **anew**. Hearing the case as if it were the first time.

Dependency court: Another name for juvenile court. Dependency matters typically originate when Child Protective Services (CPS) or the County Department of Public Social Services (DPSS) remove a child from his or her home. This removal can be prompted by a report from the child's teacher, a doctor or any child abuse mandated person that there is a situation where a minor may be in danger. In these matters, the dependency court has jurisdiction to decide the course of action that will be followed.

Dependent: A minor who is financially supported by another person.

Deposition: Written or oral testimony given under oath in front of an authorized third person such as a court reporter. The court reporter records all of the testimony and makes a book of that testimony. Depositions take place outside of court. See Chapter 11: Family Law Discovery.

Dictum: A part of a written court case opinion that is related to the case, but is not the holding in the case. See Chapter 1: Introduction, Laws, Rules & Forms.

Disaffirm: Common term used in contract law whereby a party to the contract repudiates, denies or sets aside the contract. See Chapter 35: Minors: Codes & Cases.

Discovery: The name given to gathering of information, facts, documents, or testimony to amass the evidence needed to pursue a case. See Chapter 11: Family Law Discovery.

Dismiss with prejudice: When a court dismisses a case with prejudice, the same claim cannot be refiled.

Dismiss without prejudice: When a court dismisses a case without prejudice, the same claim or action may be refiled.

Disposable income: the money from earnings that is left after taxes and necessary bills are paid. See Chapter 16: Child Support.
Disposition: The final decision by the court in a case.
Dissolution: A divorce or termination of a marriage. See Chapter 5: Annulment, Dissolution & Legal Separation.
Divorce: A generic term for dissolution. See Chapter 5: Annulment, Dissolution & Legal Separation.
Doctrine of recrimination: The Doctrine of Recrimination is a countercharge in a divorce action in which the filing party is shown to be guilty of an offense constituting a ground for divorce.. When both parties to the marriage have committed marital misconduct that would be grounds for divorce, neither may obtain a complete divorce, a divorce from the bonds of matrimony under the laws of the late 1800s. See Chapter 5: Annulment, Dissolution & Legal Separation.
Document production demand: One of the six methods of discovery whereby one party requests that another party in the lawsuit produce specific documents. See Chapter 11: Family Law Discovery.
Domestic Violence Prevention Act: An Act intended to prevent acts of domestic violence, abuse, and sexual abuse and to provide for a separation of the persons involved in the domestic violence for a period sufficient to enable these persons to seek a resolution of the causes of the violence. FC § 6220. See Chapter 36: Domestic Violence.
Domicile: A person's legal address. A person may have only one domicile. See Chapter 4: Validity of Marriage.
Due process: The fundamental, constitutional guarantee that all persons will be given notice of any legal proceedings and have an opportunity to be heard. It is a constitutional guarantee that a law will not be unreasonable, capricious or arbitrary. The constitutional guarantee of due process of law is set forth in the Fifth and Fourteenth Amendments to the U.S. Constitution.
Duke Order: An order to defer the sale of the community residence. See deferred sale of the home *supra*. Codified at FC § 3801 et seq. See Chapter 16: Child Support.
Earning capacity: Earning capacity is composed of: (1) the ability to work, including such factors as age, occupation, skills, education, health, background, work experience and qualifications; (2) the willingness to work exemplified through good faith efforts, due diligence and meaningful attempts to secure employment; and (3) an opportunity to work, which means an employer who is willing to hire. *In re MARRIAGE of REGNERY* (1989) 214 Cal.App.3d 1367 at p. 1372. The opportunity to work exists when there is substantial evidence of a reasonable likelihood that a party could, with reasonable effort, apply his or her education, skills and training to produce income. The statewide uniform guideline for determining child support permits the court, in lieu of using actual income, to impute income to a parent based on his or her earning capacity. *In re Marriage of SMITH* (2001) 90 Cal.App.4th 74 at p. 77. See Chapter 16: Child Support.

Earnings withholding order: A court order that directs an obligor's employer to withhold the earnings of the obligor to pay a debt such as child or spousal support to an obligee. See Chapter 32: Enforcement.

Elisor: When a party will not or cannot execute a document necessary to carry out a court order, the clerk of the court, or his or her authorized representative or designee may be appointed by the court as an elisor to sign the document. See Chapter 32: Enforcement.

Emancipation: a legal mechanism by which a minor (any person under the age of 18 years in the State of California) is freed from control by his or her parents or guardians, and the parents or guardians are freed from any and all responsibility toward the child. Emancipation requires meeting certain requirements and filing a *Petition* to make the request. See Chapter 35: Minors: Codes & Cases.

En banc: Court sessions where all of the judges of a court are present.

Enforce: To take legal steps to make sure of compliance to a court order or judgment. (See Chapter 32: Enforcement.

Epstein **credits**: When a person pays community property debts after separation but before the judgment has been rendered he or she may receive reimbursement for the debts paid. This reimbursement is called **Epstein credits** after *In re Marriage of EPSTEIN* (1979) 24 Cal.3d 76. Epstein credits have been codified at FC § 2626. See Chapter 22: Division, Tracing & Reimbursement.

Enjoin: To require, command or positively direct by an injunction from a court of equity, to perform, or to abstain or desist from some act.

Equitable distribution: The distribution of marital assets and debt obligations by a court in a divorce action pursuant to statute; such distribution does not have to be kind. Chapter 22: Division, Tracing & Reimbursement.

Equity: (1) English common law system where cases are tried seeking non-monetary remedies. **Court of Equity**. **(2)** When one purchases an asset with a down payment and the remainder of the purchase price is borrowed, the down payment represents the equity in that asset. As payments toward the loan are made, the equity of the asset is increased.

Estoppel: An act or statement that prevents a person from later making claims to the contrary. An To stop an action.

Et al.: In Latin, this means **and others**. Refers to parties not included in the formal name of a court case.

Evidence: Any proof legally presented at trial through witnesses, records, and/or exhibits.

Executor: A person named in a will to carry out the deceased party's instructions and requests.

Executory contracts: Contracts or leases under which both parties to the agreement have duties remaining to be performed.

Ex parte: These Latin words mean from **one side only**. Where one party appears in court to make a request without the other party. Commonly, ex parte requests are made because there is an emergency situation that cannot wait to be litigated in the normal course of the court's business.

Family Court Services (FCS): A part of the family court that assists parents to make parenting plans for their children.

Glossary

Family Law Facilitator: A lawyer with experience in family law who works for the superior court to help parents and children involved in family law cases with family law issues such as child, spousal, and partner support. It is a free service.

Family support: Pursuant to FC § 92, family support means "an agreement between the parents, or an order or judgment, that combines child support and spousal support without designating the amount to be paid for child support and the amount to be paid for spousal support." It is similar to spousal support in that it is tax deductible to the obligor and includible in the obligee's taxable income. See Chapter 17: Spousal & Family Support.

Federal Parental Kidnapping Prevention Act 28 U.S.C. § 1738A: An act that became law in 1980 to address parental kidnapping and interstate/international child custody and visitation disputes. Its intent was to prevent forum shopping by preventing other states that were not the home state of the child from taking jurisdiction to decide the custody disputes. See Chapter 13: Child Custody.

Fee waiver: Official permission not to pay the filing or other fees of the court. A court can order that one party or both parties reimbursement the court the filing in some family law matters. Chapter 7: Filing, Service & Family Centered Case Resolution.

Fiduciary: A trustee or trusted person such as spouses in a marital relationship; spouses have a confidential relationship that imposes a fiduciary duty of the highest good faith and fair dealing on each spouse, and neither must take any unfair advantage of the other. In transactions between themselves, spouses are subject to the general rules governing fiduciary relationships that control the actions of persons occupying confidential relations with each other. FC § 721. See Chapter 18: Disclosure & Fiduciary Duty.

***Forum non conveniens*:** A forum that is not convenient. A litigant can file an action to change a venue because the current venue is inconvenient.

Fraud: A false representation of a fact by words or conduct that is or has misleading allegations; concealment of a fact that should have been disclosed. Fraud is intentionally deceiving another so that a person will act upon it to her or his legal injury. See Chapter 5: Annulment, Dissolution & Legal Separation.

Freeman order: A visitation order whereby the noncustodial parent has custody of the child for approximately 20% of the time. Customarily, the 20% time with the child or children is every other weekend and some time on every Wednesday. See Chapter 14: Child Visitation.

Full faith and credit: Article IV, Section 1, of the U.S. Constitution provides that states must recognize legislative acts, public records, and judicial decisions of the other states within the U.S. "Full Faith and Credit shall be given in each State to the public Acts, Records, and judicial Proceedings of every other State." It also prevents parties from forum shopping or seeking litigation of an issue already litigated in another state.

Garnishment: A legal process that allows part of a person's wages and/or assets to be withheld for payment of a debt. Wage or income garnishment is usually involuntary.

Genetic testing: A medical test to determine legal paternity or fatherhood of a child. See Chapter 34: Paternity.

Glossary

Gift: An item that is given to another gratuitously. In family law, gifts are most often separate property regardless if the gift was given before, during or after the marriage. See Chapter 20: Title, Kinds of Property & Valuation.

Goodwill: In business, an intangible asset that represents the portion of the business value that cannot be attributed to other business assets.

Gross income: Income that is earned and calculated before taxes. See Chapter 16: Child Support.

Guardian: A person who has the legal rights and responsibilities to care for a child whose parents are unavailable to care for him or her. A guardian can be a guardian of the person, taking care of the personal needs of a child like care, custody, schooling and medical decisions and/or a guardian of the estate, managing the child's finances.

Guardian ad litem: A court-appointed adult that represents a minor child or legally incompetent person.

Guardianship: The court process for a person to obtain legal custody to care for a child.

Hearing: A formal court proceeding with the judge and opposing sides present, but there is no jury in family law hearings. Evidence is customarily presented by declaration in a hearing.

Hearsay: An out-of-court statement made to prove the truth of the matter asserted. Hearsay is inadmissible in court unless a there is a specific exception to the rule.

Imputed income: It is the income that can be attributed to a person when he or she is seeking to avoid paying for debts or services. See Chapter 16: Child Support.

In camera: Latin for in chamber. A hearing held in the judge's chambers.

Income: Money that is earned, received through investments or from any source. Income includes wages, salaries, commissions, bonuses, workers' compensation, disability, pension or retirement program payments, and interest. See Chapter 16: Child Support, Chapter 17: Spousal & Family Support.

Income withholding: When the court orders a party to pay child support, the court MUST include in its order an earnings assignment order, known as an *Income Withholding for Support* (IWO) or wage assignment. Pursuant to this court order, the money is deducted from the obligor's earnings to pay court ordered support. It is also called wage assignment. See Chapter 16: Child Support, Chapter 17: Spousal & Family Support.

Indemnity: An obligation to another to provide compensation for a loss, injury, or damage.

Inheritance: A gift that is given at the death of the donor.

Injunction: A court order that requires a person to do or to refrain from doing a specific act.

In propria persona **or** *in pro per*: Latin for **in one's own proper person**. When a person represents him or herself and has not retained the services of a lawyer.

Interrogatories: Written questions sent by one side in a lawsuit to an opposing side as part of pretrial discovery. The side that receives the interrogatories must answer them in writing under oath within 30 days. See Chapter 11: Family Law Discovery.

Intestate: To die without making a will or leaving instructions for disposal of one's property after death.

Glossary

Irreconcilable differences: Differences in a marriage that cannot be reconciled. A total breakdown of a marriage such that the marriage can never be repaired. See Chapter 5: Annulment, Dissolution & Legal Separation.

Issue: The disputed claim or point between parties in a lawsuit.

Joinder: Bringing or joining another or others into a lawsuit.

Judgment: The official decision of a court that resolves the dispute(s) between the parties to the lawsuit.

Judicial Council: In 1926 an amendment to the California Constitution created the Judicial Council to make policy decisions for the California Courts. The main focus of the Judicial Council was and is to enact uniform rules of court practice and procedure. The Judicial Council is chaired by the Chief Justice. Most of its members are appointed by the Chief Justice or by the State Bar Board of Trustees. All council members are volunteers and receive no compensation. Most Judicial Council members serve three-year terms. Each year, about one-third of the membership rotates out, and a new group is sworn in. The Judicial Council is responsible for adopting legal forms for use in the California Courts. The forms and rules have been enacted, adapted or adopted by the Judicial Council under the authority of **FC§ 211, article VI, section 6** of the **California Constitution** and other applicable law. See Chapter 1: Introduction, Laws, Rules & Forms.

Judicial Council forms: Forms that have been promulgated by the Judicial Council. Some of these forms are prescribed by the council and are mandatory; others are approved for optional use. The printed language in the lower left corner of the first page of each form specifies: **(1)** whether the form is adapted (mandatory) or approved (optional) and **(2)** the date of revision or implementation. Only the latest version of the form may be filed with the court. See Chapter 1: Introduction, Laws, Rules & Forms.

Jurisdiction: It is the right to exercise authority over persons and their property and apply the law of the land. There are 4 types: Subject matter jurisdiction, Personal jurisdiction, *In personam* jurisdiction and *In rem* jurisdiction. See Chapter 3: Jurisdiction & Venue.

Jurisdictional stepdown: A jurisdictional stepdown order is where spousal support is ordered to be paid until a certain date. After that date the amount of spousal support drops to $1 or $0. The court continues to reserve jurisdiction over this matter until the death of either party or the remarriage of the supported spouse, if the marriage was of long duration (10 years or more). If the marriage lasted less than 10 years, the judge can set the date that jurisdiction is terminated. A jurisdictional stepdown is only appropriate when there is certainty that the supported spouse will be able to support him or herself when jurisdiction is terminated. See Chapter 17: Spousal & Family Support.

Jurisprudence: The study of law and the structure of the legal system.

Juvenile: A person younger than the legal age of adulthood or a minor; a person who is under the age of 18 years old in this state. See Chapter 35: Minors.

Juvenile court or juvenile dependency court: The Juvenile Dependency Court has jurisdiction to hear many kinds of cases involving minors, including criminal acts that have been committed by minors. Even though the superior court and the juvenile court are equal branches of the court system, juvenile court decisions take precedence over matters heard in the family court. The Juvenile Court maintains jurisdiction over these matters until it decides that it no longer needs to intervene. See Chapter 13: Child Custody.

Laches: Laches provides that the claimant cannot pursue the claim because of his or her failure to act within a reasonable amount of time.

Legal separation: A procedure that is virtually identical to a dissolution, except that the parties in the legal separation retain their marital status; they remain married and are not free to remarry. Just as in a dissolution, issues regarding child custody and child support, spousal support and the division of property are all resolved in a legal separation. See Chapter 5: Annulment, Dissolution & Legal Separation.

Lesterizing: A term (derived from the *Lester* case) used to describe the creation of "family support," which seeks to capitalize on the fact that spousal support is deductible from one's income while child support is not. Family support is spousal support and child support together. Family support is taxable. Lesterizing is calculating the family support so that the parties can maximize the support by figuring out the amount of family support taking into consideration the tax ramifications to both parties. See Chapter 17: Spousal & Family Support.

Lien: A claim on property to prevent the sale or transfer of that property until a debt is paid. The lien may be enforced or collected by levying on the property.

Limited-scope representation: An arrangement with a lawyer to receive help on some parts of a case for a set fee or limited fees. Also called unbundled legal services or unbundling. See Chapter 7: Attorney Fess & Limited Scope Representation.

***Lis pendens*:** Latin for **a pending suit**. A written notice that a lawsuit involving title or ownership of a certain parcel of property has been filed. The *lis pendens* is filed with the county recorder in the county where the land is located. The property cannot be conveyed to another when there is a *lis pendens* on the property.

Litigation: The process of taking legal action; a case, a controversy, or a lawsuit. The people involved in lawsuits (petitioners/plaintiffs and respondents/defendants) are called **litigants**.

Magistrate: A judicial officer with the power to issue arrest warrants and find probable cause at preliminary hearings.

Marital settlement agreement: A marital settlement agreement is an agreement that memorializes the settled issues in a legal separation or dissolution. Marital settlement agreements are contracts and they are governed by many of the same rules and regulations as **normal** contracts. In family law cases, a marital settlement agreement is prepared when an agreement is reached on one or more settled issues. Undisputed facts and issues are also made part of the agreement, such as the date that the parties were married and the names and dates of birth of the children of the marriage. See Chapter 17: Spousal & Family Support.

Marriage of long duration: A marriage lasting ten years or more. In a marriage of long duration, a judge may not terminate a spouse's right to receive support. There is a presumption affecting the burden of producing evidence that a marriage of 10 years or more, from the date of marriage to the date of separation, is a marriage of long duration. However, the court may consider periods of separation during the marriage in determining whether the marriage is in fact of long duration. Nothing in this subdivision precludes a court from determining that a marriage of less than 10 years is a marriage of long duration. See Chapter 17: Spousal & Family Support.

Mediation: Mediation is a required service provided by the Superior Court for divorcing or separating parents. Only custody and visitation issues will be discussed in the mediation. The mediators at Family Court Services (FCS) try to help parents reach a parenting plan with regard to custody and visitation of their children. Every divorcing or separating couple MUST attend FCS prior to setting any hearing if custody and visitation issues are disputed. See Chapter 12: Mediation.

Minimum contacts: A term used in civil procedure to determine when it is appropriate for a court in one state to assert personal jurisdiction over a defendant from another state. Specifically, before someone can be forced to adjudicate a matter in a state other than one's home state, the person must have at least minimum contacts with that state.

Minor: A person under the age of 18 years or an unemancipated person. See Chapter 35: Minors.

Minute order: The courtroom clerk's written notes or minutes of the court's order.

Modification: A change, alteration or termination of a court order.

Moore/Marsden Formula: The court in *Moore* used the FMV at date of trial minus the purchase price of the home to determine the appreciation of the home. The court in *Marsden* refined the formula by using only the amount that the property actually appreciated during the marriage. Thus, the Moore formula fine-tuned by the *Marsden* case became the Moore/Marsden formula. This formula is currently used to determine separate and community interest when the home was purchased before marriage by one of the spouses and the title was never changed to add the other spouse. See Chapter 24: Apportionment.

Motion: An oral or written request that a party makes to the court for a ruling or an order on a particular issue.

Motion in *Limine*: A pretrial motion requesting that the court prohibit the other side from presenting or even referring to, evidence on matters that can be highly prejudicial.

Moveaway case: A moveaway or relocation case is where one party moves away or relocates with the child or children. Pursuant to *In re Marriage of Burgess* (1996) 13 Cal.4th 25, the custodial parent has a fundamental right to relocate with the minor child or children subject to the court's power ensuring that the move is in the best interests of the child or children. See Chapter 15: Moveaways or Relocations.

Negligence: The failure to use reasonable care that results in damage or injury to another.

Net income: The amount of income left after deducting the appropriate amount of taxes.

Nolo contendere: No contest; from the Latin for "I do not wish to contend".

Noncustodial parent (NCP): The parent that does not have primary care, custody, or control of a child. See Chapter 14: Child Visitation.

Glossary

Non-marital property: Property that is not community. Usually called separate property which is property owned by either spouse prior to marriage, after date of separation or acquired by gift or inheritance at any time. See Chapter 20: Title, Kinds of Property & Valuation.

Notary public: A person authorized by law to administer oaths, to affirm and certify that certain documents are genuine and authentic.

Notice and opportunity to be heard: The Fifth and Fourteenth Amendments to the Constitution provide that no person can be deprived of life, liberty or property with being given the right to notice and opportunity to defend and present evidence.

Nunc pro tunc: Latin for **now for then**. When a court order is issued on a later date than the date that it was originally filed or meant to be filed but was not because of a mistake. The court order is effective as of the date that it would have been effective if there was no error.

Obligation: Law or duty that requires parties to adhere to the agreement that they made. An obligation can be a debt created by a judgment, contract or court order such as child support.

Obligee: The person, state agency, or institution who is owed a debt.

Obligor: The person who must pay the debt to the obligee or some other financial obligation.

Opinion: A judge's written explanation of the decision of the court in appellate cases. If all the judges completely agree on the result, one judge will write the opinion for all. If all of the judges do not agree, the formal decision will be based on the majority view, and one member of the majority will usually write the opinion. The judges that do not agree with the majority may write their own dissenting or concurring opinions to state their views. A dissenting opinion disagrees with the majority opinion because of the reasoning and/or the principles of law the majority used to decide the case. A concurring opinion agrees with the decision of the majority opinion, but offers comment or clarification or a completely different reason for reaching the same result.

Order to show cause: A request for a hearing. Renamed in 2013 to *Request for Order* (*RFO*).

Parentage: A legal determination of a child's parents.

Parenting plan: A detailed custody and visitation agreement that states when the child will be with each parent and how decisions will be made regarding the children. The parenting plan may be developed by the parents, through mediation, with the help of lawyers, or by a judge at a trial or hearing. See Chapter 14: Child Visitation.

Party: One of the litigants in a court case.

Passive income: Not earned income; income from investments.

Paternity: Legal determination of fatherhood. Paternity must be determined before a court can order child support or medical support. See Chapter 34: Paternity.

Pendente lite: Latin for **while the action is pending**. Court orders that are made before the final judgment in the case is rendered.

Pereira/Van Camp methods of calculating community property: The ***Pereira*** method of determining the amount of community property is allocating a **fair rate of return** on the separate property investment. By the process of elimination, any excess in value over the amount allocated as separate property is community property arising from the spouse's labor and efforts. Under the *Van Camp* approach it is determined how much the owner **spouse's effort and labor** is worth and that figure is the community property, with the balance of the increase in value being characterized as separate property by process of elimination. See Chapter 22: Division, Tracing & Reimbursement.

Perjury: A knowingly false statement made under oath.

Permanent spousal support: Spousal support intended "to provide financial assistance, if appropriate, as determined by the financial circumstances of the parties after their dissolution and the division of their community property." *In re Marriage of SCHULZE* (1997) 60 Cal.App.4th 519 at p. 522. In determining spousal support at trial, the court must base the amount and duration of spousal support upon the statutory factors enumerated in FC § 4320. See Chapter 17: Spousal & Family Support.

Personal jurisdiction: Personal jurisdiction gives a party notice of the lawsuit and an opportunity to be heard. It gives the court the authority over a person to make a decision regarding a person's personal rights. Personal jurisdiction is necessary for both *in personam* jurisdiction and *in rem* jurisdiction. See Chapter 3: Jurisdiction & Venue.

Personal property: Personal property is movable property owned by an individual; it is not land or attached to land. "Every kind of property that is not real is personal." Civil Code § 663. See Chapter 20: Title, Kinds of Property & Valuation.

Personal service: Personally delivering court documents. See Chapter 9: Filing & Service.

Petition: A formal written request given to the court asking for a specific judicial remedy. A person that presents a *Petition* to the court is called the petitioner. See Chapter 8: Initial Forms & Checkboxes.

Pleading: A formal written document that sets forth the filing party's allegations, claims or defenses in a lawsuit. Pleadings define the issues to be adjudicated.

Points and authorities: Also called **P's and A's**. **Points and authorities** refer to the written legal argument given to support or oppose a motion. It includes references to filed cases, statutes and other statements of law that emphasize either the legality of the motion requested or the legal basis for the court to grant or deny a motion.

Precedent: A court decision in an earlier case with facts and legal issues similar to a dispute currently before a court. Judges will generally follow precedent, meaning that they use the principles established in earlier cases to decide new cases dealing with similar facts and legal issues. A judge will overlook precedent if a party can show that the earlier case was decided incorrectly or that it differed in some significant way from the current case.

Premarital agreement: Agreements made prior to marriage are called premarital, prenuptial or antenuptial agreements. The Family Code uses the term premarital to describe "an agreement between prospective spouses made in contemplation of marriage and to be effective upon marriage." FC § 1610. Premarital agreement is the preferred term and the California legislature changed the word prenuptial to premarital in all of the California laws. Premarital agreements do not require consideration, and there is no fiduciary duty between the parties because they are not yet married. See Chapter 30: Marital Agreements.

Preponderance of the evidence: Evidence that has more convincing force than that opposed to it. See Chapter 25: Degrees of Proof & Presumptions.

Presiding judge/justice: In a court with more than one judicial officer, the judge that acts as the administrator of the court's business.

Presumption: A "**presumption** is an assumption of fact that the law requires to be made from another fact or group of facts found or otherwise established in the action." Evid, Code § 600(a). A presumption can be either conclusive or rebuttable. See Chapter 25: Degrees of Proof & Presumptions.

Prima facie: Latin for **at first face or from first view**. Not requiring further support to establish existence, credibility, or validity. A prima facie case is sufficient on its face because it is supported by the necessary minimum evidence and free from obvious defects. Prima facie evidence is sufficient to support a certain conclusion unless contradictory evidence is presented.

Probable cause: A reasonable basis for assuming that a charge or fact is well founded or true.

Probate: The judicial process to determine if a will of a deceased person is genuine or not; lawful distribution of a decedent's estate.

Pro bono: Latin for **for the good**. Legal work done for free.

Process server: A person that serves court papers to a party to a lawsuit.

Pro hac vice: The status of a lawyer that gets special permission to try a case in California because he or she is licensed to practice law in another state.

Promissory note: A written document that states that a person promises to pay money to another.

Proof of service: The form filed with the court that proves that court papers were formally delivered to a party in a court action on a certain date. See Chapter 9: Filing & Service.

Pro per: A short form of **in propria persona**. Refers to persons that present their own cases in court without lawyers; from the Latin for **in one's own proper person**. Also called **pro se**: Latin for **on one's own behalf**.

Property: Tangible items that are capable of being and that have a value.

Pro tem **judge:** A lawyer that volunteers his or her time to hear and decide cases. Also called a **temporary judge**.

Public record: A court record available for inspection by the general public.

Putative spouse: A spouse who reasonably and in good faith believes that his or her marriage is legally valid when it is not. This marriage can be void (a marriage that was never valid) or voidable (a marriage that had a defect at the beginning of the marriage but remains in effect until challenged) depending on the circumstances. The court makes the putative spouse determination. When the court finds that the party, who in good faith believed that the marriage was legal when it was not, is a putative spouse, this innocent party is entitled to all of the benefits of a valid marriage. One such benefit is that all of the property acquired during the marriage by the spouse who knew or should have known that the marriage was not valid is divided equally as though it was community property. See Chapter 5: Annulment, Dissolution & Legal Separation.

Glossary

Qualified domestic relations order (QDRO): An order or judgment issued by a court and approved by a pension plan that divides a pension plan in order to make a fair division of property in a divorce. See Chapter 23: Retirement & Disability.

Quantum meruit: A Latin term that means "as much as is deserved". A party who performs a service for another without an agreement or formal contract can recover the reasonable amount for the labor and materials expended. If no recovery was allowed, the person who received the service and did not pay for it would be unjustly and unfairly enriched. See Chapter 37: Living Together/*Marvin* Actions.

Quash: To make void, to vacate, to annul and to set aside. For example, to quash a subpoena means that the court will not enforce the subpoena because it has been voided or set aside.

Quasi-community property: Quasi-community property is any type of property that was acquired by either one or both spouses when living in another state that, had it been acquired while living in California, it would have been considered community property. See Chapter 20: Title, Kinds of Property & Valuation.

Real property: Land and any and all property that is affixed to, incidental or appurtenant to it. Civil Code § 658. Real property includes land and buildings, and anything attached to the land. See Chapter 20: Title, Kinds of Property & Valuation.

Rebuttable presumption: A rebuttable presumption may be rebutted by credible evidence. It affects the burden of producing evidence. "A statute providing that a fact or group of facts is prima facie evidence of another fact establishes a rebuttable presumption." Evid. Code § 602. "Every rebuttable presumption is either (a) a presumption affecting the burden of producing evidence or (b) a presumption affecting the burden of proof." Evid. Code § 601. See Chapter 25: Degrees of Proof & Presumptions.

Recuse: To excuse oneself or be excused from a criminal or civil proceeding because of conflict of interest.

Request for admission: Requests for Admissions are requests to an opposing party to admit the genuineness of specific documents and/or the truth of specific statements that are relevant to the action. See Chapter 11: Family Law Discovery.

Request for Order: *RFO* A request for a hearing made on Judicial Council form *FL-300*.

Reservation of jurisdiction: A court reserving or keeping the right to continue to hear natters regarding the case.

Residence: The place where a person lives; can be the same the domicile. A person can have many residences but can have only one domicile.

Residency requirement: In order to dissolve a marriage in the state of California, a person filing the *Petition* must have resided in the state for six months and the county for three month prior to the filing of the *Petition*. See Chapter 5: Annulment, Dissolution & Legal Separation.

Respondent superior: A legal theory where a person's employer may be held liable for the wrong or tort done by the employee.

Response: In family law, the form used to respond to a *Petition* for dissolution, legal separation or annulment. It is judicial council form *FL-120*. The responding party in a dissolution, nullity, adoption, or probate case is called the respondent. See Chapter 8: Initial Forms & Checkboxes.

Restitution: The act of restoring or giving the equivalent value to compensate for an injury, damage, or loss.

Restraining order: A court order that orders that a person refrain from a certain action such as ordering that an abuser stay away from his/her victim. See Chapter 36: Domestic Violence.

Resulting trust: A trust that arises by operation of law. It is a legal presumption that the person who holds title to specific property actually holds that property as a trustee for the true owner. See Chapter 37: Living Together/Marvin Actions.

Retirement benefits: Benefits earned by an employee to be paid at a later date. See Chapter 23: Retirement & Disability.

Reverse: When an appellate court sets aside the decision of a trial court. A reversal is often accompanied by a remand to the lower court for further proceedings.

Richmond order: So named after *In re Marriage of Richmond* (1980)105 Cal.App.3d 352. It is a spousal support order made where spousal support payments will terminate on a specific date unless the supported spouse files a motion to modify the support order. See Chapter 17: Spousal & Family Support.

Sanction: A penalty or punishment intended to make someone obey the law.

Satisfaction: Payment of a judgment.

Sealed record: A record closed by a court to further inspection; requires a court order to permit viewing. Paternity actions are sealed.

Separation date: In deciding a date of separation for a divorce, there are several case rules that must be considered. Also, the court will consider the following conduct of the parties: **(1)** Clearly communicate the intention to separate; **(2)** Move out of or physically partition the house; **(3)** Divide all formerly joint bank and credit accounts; **(4)** Decline counseling; **(5)** Cancel any prepaid vacation plans; **(6)** Refrain from socializing or in having the estranged spouse perform **spouse-like** duties; **(7)** Stop being intimate with each other; **(8)** Stop receiving mail at the home of the estranged spouse; and **(9)** file for Dissolution. See Chapter 6: Date of Separation.

Separate property: Property owned before marriage, after separation or received anytime by gift or bequest. See Chapter 20: Title, Kinds of Property & Valuation.

Service by publication: When service of process is done by publishing a notice in a newspaper or by posting on a bulletin board of a courthouse or other public facility after a court determines that other means of service are impractical or have been unsuccessful. See Chapter 9: Filing & Service.

Service of process: The delivery of all legal papers filed with the court in a lawsuit to the opposing party. The papers must be delivered by an adult aged 18 or older that is not involved in the case. See Chapter 9: Filing & Service.

Settlement conference: A meeting where parties and their lawyers attempt to settle the case before trial. Sometimes called a **four-way**. See Chapter 31: Settlements, Trial & the Final Paperwork.

Glossary

Sole proprietorship: An unincorporated business that is owned by one individual.

Spousal support: Court-ordered support that one spouse must pay a sum of money to the other spouse; also called **maintenance** or **alimony**. See Chapter 17: Spousal & Family Support.

Standard of proof: Degree of proof required. In criminal cases, prosecutors must prove a defendant's guilt **beyond a reasonable doubt**. The majority of civil lawsuits require proof **by a preponderance of the evidence**, but in some cases the standard may be higher and requiring **clear and convincing proof**. See Chapter 25: Degrees of Proof & Presumptions.

Statute: A law passed by Congress or a state legislature.

Statute of limitations: A law that sets forth the deadline for a party to pursue a specific claim.

Stay order: An order issued by a court stopping court proceedings until the disputed event takes place.

Stipulated judgment: An agreement between the parties to a case that settles a case.

Stipulation: An agreement between the parties and their attorneys, if represented, relating to disputed issues. See Chapter 16: Child Support and Chapter 29: Drafting Court Orders.

Sua sponte: Commonly used to describe when a judge does something without being asked to by either party in a case; from the Latin for **of one's own will**.

Subject matter jurisdiction: "the power to hear and determine the cause" and to "describe the range of power to apply remedies in various fields of substantive law." *HAHN v. DIAZ-BARBA* (2011) 194 Cal.App.4th 1177 at 1188. See Chapter 3: Jurisdiction & Venue.

Subpoena: A court order to appear at court or a deposition and/or to produce documents. See Chapter 11: Family Law Discovery.

Subpoena duces tecum: An official court order to bring documents/ records to a stated place at a stated time. See Chapter 11: Family Law Discovery.

Substantive stepdown: A court order where the amount of spousal support decreases in designated steps until the spousal support becomes a minimal amount such as $1 or the support amount is reduced to $0. The court retains jurisdiction until death of either party or remarriage of the supported party if the marriage lasted 10 years or more (FC § 4336). If the marriage lasted less than 10 years, jurisdiction would be terminated at a date set by the court. See Chapter 17: Spousal & Family Support.

Summary dissolution: A less expensive process for parties to dissolve their marriage and is usually done without the participation of attorneys. It is less expensive because only one filing fee is paid to the court, as opposed to each party paying a filing fee in a dissolution. A summary dissolution requires that both parties consent to the procedure. Either party can revoke the *Joint Petition* and terminate the summary dissolution proceeding at any time prior to the filing of the judgment of summary dissolution if they so desire. FC § 2402. See Chapter 5: Annulment, Dissolution & Legal Separation.

Summons: A notice to a defendant or respondent that an action against him or her was filed in the court that provides the time that a responding party has to answer the lawsuit. See Chapter 8: Initial Forms & Checkboxes.

Superior court: The trial court in each county of the State of California.

Supervised visitation: Visitation between a parent and a child that requires a supervisor to monitor the visitation. See Chapter 14: Child Visitation.

Surrogate parent: A person that substitutes for the legal parent to advocate for a child's special educational rights and needs; can be selected by the child's parent or appointed by the local educational agency (LEA). See Chapter 34: Paternity.

Temporary restraining order: A court order, sometimes called a **TRO** that prevents an action. In domestic violence actions a TRO is an immediate court order that orders that the abuser have no contact with the victim. See Chapter 36: Domestic Violence.

Temporary spousal support: Temporary spousal support is the support that is ordered during the period of time between the initial filing of the *Petition* and the final judgment. "The purpose of temporary spousal support is to maintain the status quo as much as possible pending trial." *In re Marriage of Schulze* (1997) 60 Cal.App.4th 519 at p. 525. Temporary spousal support "is utilized to maintain the living conditions and standards of the parties in as close as possible to the status quo position realized during the marriage pending trial and the division of their assets and obligations." *In re Marriage of Winter* (1992) 7 Cal.App.4th 1926 at p. 1932 quoting: *In re Marriage of Burlini* (1983) 143 Cal.App.3d 65 at p. 68. See Chapter 17: Spousal & Family Support.

Testator: A person who made a will prior to his/her death.

Testify: To give evidence under oath as a witness in a court proceeding.

Testimony: Evidence presented orally by witnesses during trials or depositions, before grand juries, or during administrative proceedings.

Timeshare: The percent of time that a parent has custody of his/her children. See Chapter 14: Child Visitation.

Title: The ownership or evidence of ownership of land or other property. **Title documents** include a Certificate of Title for cars and Grant Deed or Quitclaim Deed for real estate. See Chapter 20: Title, Kinds of Property & Valuation.

Toll: Stopping the statute of limitations.

Tort: A private or civil wrong and a person who is found guilty of a tort is called a tortfeasor.

Tracing: A process that is used to prove a separate property claim when there is a dispute as to ownership, either separate or community. There are two methods of tracing, direct and family expense. See Chapter 22: Division, Tracing & Reimbursement.

Transcript: A written, word-for-word record of what was said at a trial or some other formal conversation like a hearing or deposition. See Chapter 11: Family Law Discovery.

Transmutation: A change in the character of property. The character of real property can be separate, community or quasi-community property. Married persons may agree with or without consideration to transmute community property to the separate property of either spouse, to transmute the separate property of either spouse to community property and/or transmute the separate property of one spouse to separate property of the other spouse. FC § 850. However, a transmutation of real or personal property is not valid unless it is made in writing and is joined in, consented to, or accepted by the spouse whose interest in the property is adversely affected. FC § 852(a). A transmutation is subject to the laws governing fraudulent transfers. FC § 851. See Chapter 20: Title, Kinds of Property & Valuations.

Trustee: The person that has custody of or control over funds or items for the benefit of another.

Unbundled legal services (or unbundling): An arrangement with a lawyer to receive help on some parts of a case for a set fee or limited fees. Also called **limited-scope representation**. See Chapter 7: Attorney Fees & Limited Scope Representation.

Uniform Child Custody Jurisdiction and Enforcement Act (UCCJEA): An Act that provides the bases for custody jurisdiction. The purpose of the UCCJEA is to promote uniformity among the states, minimize competition among the jurisdictions, and encourage the states to cooperate with one another with regard to child custody matters. FC § 3461. See Chapter 13: Child Custody.

Unliquidated claim: A claim for which a specific value has not been determined.

Venue: The particular court in which an action may be brought.

Verification: An oral or written statement, usually made under oath, saying that something is true.

Vesting: The account owned by employee who is receiving retirement benefits from his/her employer is completely vested in his or her account when he/she owns 100% of it and the employer cannot reclaim or take it back for any reason. See Chapter 23: Retirement & Disability.

Visitation: The time that a parent may visit with his/her children. All parents must be granted a reasonable amount of time to visit with their children unless it is shown that the visitation would be detrimental to the best interest of the child. See Chapter 14: Child Visitation.

Vocational training counselor - an individual with sufficient knowledge, skill, experience, training, or education in interviewing, administering, and interpreting tests for analysis of marketable skills, formulating career goals, planning courses of training and study, and assessing the job market, to qualify as an expert in vocational training under Evidence Code § 720. See Chapter 17: Spousal & Family Support.

Void marriage: Marriages that were never valid under any circumstances at any time. There are only two grounds for a void marriage, incest and bigamy/polygamy. See Chapter 5: Annulment, Dissolution & Legal Separation.

Voidable marriage: A marriage that may be declared invalid by an annulment judgment at some time after the marriage takes place because a defect existed at the time of the marriage. See Chapter 5: Annulment, Dissolution & Legal Separation.

Wage assignment: A court order to an employer to withhold a portion of the employee's wages and pay the withheld money to the other parent or person who has custody of the children. See Chapter 32: Enforcement.

Waiver: To give up a legal right voluntarily, intentionally, and with full knowledge of the consequences.

Will: A legal document that lists a person's wishes about his or her personal property upon his or her death.

***Watts* charges:** If a spouse, who has the exclusive use a community asset, is paying a lesser amount than the fair market value of that asset, then he or she may be charged the difference between the amount paid and the fair market value. This charge is called a **watts charge**, after *In re Marriage of WATTS* (1985) 171 Cal.App.3d 366. See Chapter 22: Division, Tracing & Reimbursement.

Writ: A written court order stating that certain action must be taken.

Writ of Execution: A court order giving the sheriff (or other levying officer) the power to seize the judgment debtor's property in order to pay a judgment debt. When a court issues a *Writ of Execution* (Form *EJ-130*), the court directs the sheriff or marshal to enforce the judgment in the county where the assets are located. Writs of execution are only good for 180 days. See Chapter 32: Enforcement.

Writ of Mandate: A court order to another court, to follow the law by correcting its prior actions or ceasing illegal acts.

INDEX (Terms & Cases)

Ability to pay, 757
Abstract of judgment, 757
Abuse, 118, 677, 695, 697
acknowledgement, 634
adoption, 211, 230, 231, 232, 247, 248, 250, 251, 252, 526, 605, 613, 619, 620, 623, 631, 632, 634, 635, 636, 637, 642, 643, 644, 649, 775
adoptive parent, 184, 251, 613, 619, 632, 633, 636, 647, 649
adultery, 71, 706
agreement, 734, 735
Alicia R. v. Timothy M., 93
Alimony, 757
Altafulla v. Ervin, 677
Amicus curiae, 758
Anderson, 13, 14, 415, 416, 437, 438, 715, 717
annulment, 49, 50, 57, 58, 59, 60, 61, 62, 63, 64, 65, 67, 78, 79, 91, 103, 121, 124, 125, 137, 613, 758, 775, 778
antenuptial, 99, 120, 522, 772
appeal, 7, 17, 20, 33, 35, 60, 63, 76, 93, 98, 101, 105, 106, 109, 110, 122, 129, 149, 171, 174, 188, 217, 219, 222, 241, 250, 251, 258, 263, 275, 296, 306, 307, 308, 327, 333, 350, 356, 361, 390, 391, 397, 400, 416, 418, 423, 426, 438, 440, 477, 526, 561, 569, 570, 571, 597, 598, 599, 618, 656, 658, 667, 671, 680, 693, 709, 758, 762
appealable, 348, 390, 425, 569, 598
appearance, 16, 31, 52, 85, 113, 114, 137, 141, 144, 154, 155, 214, 450, 454, 494, 504, 505, 506, 509, 510, 562, 563, 572, 583, 584, 594
apportionment, 447, 456, 758
arrearage, 25, 306, 307, 308, 514, 590, 592
assignment, 17

assignment order, 295, 514, 588, 589, 590, 591, 592, 593, 594, 596
assistant, 9, 12
assisted reproduction, 8, 627, 630, 641, 642, 643, 649
attorney, 90, 392, 729, 732, 734
authorization, 52, 527, 623, 635, 660, 663, 667
bankruptcy, 13, 14, 15, 92, 111, 112, 309, 374, 445, 447, 758, 759
battery, 675, 682, 684, 696, 697, 758
best interests, 76, 104, 105, 162, 177, 178, 182, 185, 189, 196, 201, 203, 204, 206, 207, 208, 209, 210, 213, 218, 229, 234, 237, 238, 239, 240, 241, 242, 244, 247, 248, 249, 251, 252, 256, 259, 260, 261, 262, 263, 264, 265, 266, 267, 268, 271, 273, 274, 276, 277, 278, 280, 281, 282, 283, 284, 285, 287, 288, 292, 299, 303, 309, 320, 327, 328, 368, 377, 380, 505, 513, 570, 592, 600, 608, 611, 612, 620, 623, 626, 631, 637, 641, 644, 645, 646, 658, 661, 665, 670, 671, 691, 770
bifurcate, 384, 389, 390, 415, 437
bifurcation, 33, 384, 386, 387, 388, 389, 390
Bifurcation of Status of Marriage, 384, 385, 390, 519
bigamy, 57, 59, 60, 778
biological father, 94, 119, 208, 478, 602, 609, 612, 615, 617, 618, 626, 628, 631, 632, 633, 634, 635, 636, 642, 645, 646, 648, 649, 650
blood test, 94, 111, 119, 274, 289, 478, 605, 609, 621, 640, 643
Bonnie P. v. Superior Court, 666
breach, 16, 542
breach of fiduciary duty, 91, 133, 374
brief, 150
Burchard, 209, 274, 284

Index

Burchard v. Garay, 284
burden of proof, 203, 234, 240, 246, 300, 337, 359, 361, 365, 403, 410, 433, 469, 471, 472, 473, 474, 475, 479, 535, 614, 621, 668, 774
Calendar days, 141
California Rules of Court, 5, 116, 123, 124, 142, 143, 759
Cassady v. Signorelli, 283
certiorari, 241
change of circumstances, 209, 228, 241, 255, 264, 265, 267, 278, 279, 281, 283, 286, 288, 323, 324, 348, 349, 350, 361, 362, 365, 366, 511, 513, 600
changed-circumstance, 209, 259, 260, 267, 268, 283
checkbox, 122, 131, 133, 134
checklist, 570
child custody, 2, 73, 96, 104, 127, 129, 132, 133, 138, 178, 179, 180, 183, 189, 190, 191, 192, 193, 195, 196, 197, 202, 209, 211, 212, 213, 216, 220, 221, 222, 223, 224, 225, 227, 229, 231, 234, 235, 249, 257, 268, 273, 289, 311, 389, 483, 484, 486, 492, 493, 502, 503, 504, 505, 507, 509, 512, 572, 598, 600, 607, 609, 610, 646, 676, 693, 695, 766, 769, 778
child custody evaluators, 193, 196, 197
Child Protective Services (CPS), 232, 760, 763
Child support, 298, 302, 327, 734, 758, 760
Child support guidelines, 760
Citation of contempt, 760
Citee, 575, 580, 760
Cochran I, 718, 719, 724
Cochran II, 724
Cochran v. Cochran, 704
cohabit, 64
cohabitation, 359, 360, 361, 362, 613, 703, 704, 705, 706, 710, 712, 713, 715, 719, 722, 723, 724
Collaborative Law, 760

commingling, 401, 426, 427
common law, 3, 39, 47, 48, 58, 527, 717, 765
community property, 32, 35, 52, 66, 75, 77, 78, 84, 85, 95, 97, 99, 100, 112, 134, 187, 314, 315, 348, 365, 368, 375, 377, 380, 387, 393, 394, 395, 396, 397, 398, 399, 400, 401, 402, 403, 404, 409, 410, 411, 414, 416, 422, 423, 424, 425, 426, 427, 428, 430, 432, 433, 434, 435, 436, 438, 444, 446, 447, 448, 449, 450, 451, 454, 455, 456, 458, 459, 460, 461, 462, 463, 465, 466, 467, 468, 472, 507, 521, 523, 524, 526, 531, 535, 537, 547, 551, 553, 565, 567, 572, 707, 708, 713, 727, 730, 760, 761, 765, 771, 772, 773, 774, 777
community property debts, 765
community property with right of survivorship, 727, 730
Complex Asbestos Litigation v. Owens-Corning, 20
conceive, 628, 649
conception, 605, 615, 621, 627, 630, 641, 643, 645, 648
Conciliation Court, 178, 761
conclusive presumption, 94, 119, 395, 470, 476, 477, 605, 615, 621, 648
conduct of the parties, 8, 705, 708, 716, 722, 775
confidential marriage, 51, 52, 53, 55, 66, 761
Conflict of Interest, 9, 23
conservator, 72, 670, 761
constitutional, 163, 241, 242, 245, 246, 247, 487, 584, 633, 634, 635, 650, 693, 694
constitutionality, 240, 242
contempt, 95, 96, 100, 119, 123, 222, 295, 336, 575, 578, 579, 580, 581, 582, 583, 584, 585, 586, 587, 592, 593, 623, 760, 762
contempt of court, 222, 295, 575, 578, 580, 581, 583, 585, 586, 762
contempt process, 575, 579
Coogan, 651, 656, 657, 658, 660, 661

court days, 130, 136, 141, 142, 143, 144, 146, 148, 149, 151, 152, 153, 156, 484, 485, 564, 584, 585, 637
custodial parent, 107, 237, 238, 249, 255, 256, 258, 260, 270, 272, 274, 283, 292, 295, 296, 297, 315, 320, 327, 760, 770
custody, 734
custody evaluation, 192, 193, 196, 197, 261, 284, 760
date of separation, 75, 77, 83, 84, 87, 88, 276, 331, 332, 334, 368, 369, 378, 379, 397, 408, 413, 414, 417, 421, 422, 424, 432, 436, 439, 443, 444, 445, 448, 454, 548, 553, 556, 565, 567, 734, 770, 771, 775
daycare, 269, 274, 288
debtor, 14, 92, 111, 575, 576, 577, 578, 588, 596, 757, 758, 759, 762, 779
debts, 99, 100, 102, 120, 291, 304, 320, 368, 374, 378, 383, 385, 413, 414, 416, 417, 418, 419, 421, 422, 424, 430, 432, 434, 436, 438, 439, 440, 441, 443, 444, 461, 467, 505, 509, 708, 729, 732, 758, 759, 765
decedent, 251, 395, 470, 476, 524, 647, 773
Declaration of Disclosure, 77, 135, 157, 370, 371, 372, 383, 384, 502, 557, 561, 563, 564, 565
Declaration of Emancipation, 651, 665, 666, 670
Declaration of Paternity, 517, 607, 608, 612, 613, 614
decreased need, 324, 359, 361
default, 16, 73, 79, 98, 105, 111, 121, 125, 132, 133, 134, 136, 137, 215, 262, 295, 297, 301, 367, 372, 481, 485, 499, 500, 501, 502, 503, 504, 505, 506, 507, 509, 510, 561, 562, 563, 565, 570, 572, 587, 595, 602, 762
default judgment, 16, 133, 134, 215, 262, 372, 500, 502, 503, 504, 506, 507, 509, 510, 565

defect, 57, 59, 61, 66, 78, 116, 580, 773, 778
deferred compensation, 75, 165, 386, 447, 452
deferred sale of the home, 291, 313, 315, 316, 764
defined benefit plan, 446, 453, 763
defined contribution plan, 445, 446, 447, 453
degrees of proof, 470
Department of Child Support Services, 607, 612, 615, 619
dependency court, 233, 763
deposition, 131, 142, 144, 149, 162, 166, 167, 168, 173, 776, 777
dicta, 6
direct tracing, 423, 426
disability, 206, 234, 237, 276, 298, 311, 355, 446, 451, 467, 588, 651, 655, 666, 672, 767
disclose, 13, 64, 100, 102, 113, 114, 120, 183, 185, 192, 214, 249, 296, 368, 373, 374, 375, 376, 428, 493
disclosure, 21, 25, 102, 103, 160, 163, 170, 183, 188, 197, 367, 368, 370, 371, 372, 373, 374, 375, 376, 378, 379, 384, 493, 515, 527, 561, 564, 565, 566, 568, 597, 601, 602, 678
disclosure forms, 25
discoverable, 128, 131, 138
discovery, 20, 25, 64, 99, 100, 102, 116, 120, 131, 133, 142, 144, 159, 160, 161, 162, 163, 164, 165, 166, 168, 169, 171, 172, 173, 174, 175, 188, 261, 367, 368, 389, 390, 503, 506, 510, 526, 566, 582, 583, 584, 585, 586, 735, 764, 767
disparity of income, 99, 100, 101, 102, 120
divorce, 90
domestic violence, 108, 109, 179, 180, 181, 182, 186, 195, 198, 212, 219, 249, 268, 330, 336, 337, 418, 440, 475, 482, 492, 495, 676, 677, 679, 680, 681, 682, 683, 684, 685,

687, 688, 689, 691, 694, 696, 697, 698, 700, 758, 764, 777
Domestic Violence Prevention Act, 123, 205, 482, 492, 494, 692, 695, 764
domicile, 31, 68, 78, 764, 774
down payment, 434, 455, 456, 457, 460, 461, 462, 464, 465, 466, 765
Duke, 313, 548, 554, 558, 763, 764
Duke Order, 313, 763, 764
earning capacity, 299, 314, 328, 329, 433, 434, 452, 764
earnings assignment, 134, 136, 305, 320, 588, 590, 591, 592, 596, 767
earnings withholding order, 588, 591
electronic service, 142, 145, 146, 155
elisor, 578, 579, 765
Elkins, 485, 486, 512
Emancipation, 651, 665, 670, 765
Emergency Order, 518, 695
Employee Benefit Plan, 450
Employee Retirement Income Security Act, 387, 445, 447
employment, 149
encumbrance, 669
Epstein Credits, 430
equity, 1, 3, 306, 307, 314, 316, 397, 459, 460, 461, 462, 463, 566, 709, 717, 720, 723, 765
ERISA, 387, 447
Estoppel, 765
Evilsizor v. Sweeney, 169
ex parte, 33, 177, 183, 191, 193, 194, 214, 390, 491, 492, 493, 494, 495, 591, 636, 642, 675, 684, 685, 686, 687, 688, 689, 691, 695, 765
expedited child support, 317, 318
ex-spouse, 324, 328, 355, 359, 450, 482, 697
extramarital, 67
ex-wife, 504
F.T. v. L.J., 262, 282
facsimile, 148
fair market value, 75, 314, 432, 455, 462, 463, 464, 465, 466, 468, 727, 730, 779

fair rate of return, 423, 427, 428, 432, 467, 771
Family Code, 1, 3, 4, 5, 35, 59, 66, 92, 93, 97, 111, 118, 122, 123, 124, 133, 136, 142, 154, 174, 187, 193, 202, 227, 230, 247, 251, 299, 309, 312, 329, 350, 359, 368, 419, 441, 481, 482, 484, 485, 487, 503, 522, 534, 543, 544, 566, 576, 581, 586, 587, 594, 606, 608, 643, 681, 772
Family Court Services, 25, 178, 181, 261, 268, 765, 770
Family expense, 427
family law facilitator, 308
family support, 99, 120, 308, 362, 363, 429, 575, 578, 581, 586, 587, 594, 595, 766, 769
father, 732
FCS, 178, 181, 261, 268, 765, 770
Federal Parental Kidnapping Prevention Act, 202, 220, 766
fee waiver, 122, 129, 130, 136, 154
fertilization, 628
fidelity, 67, 367, 377, 402
fiduciary, 7, 44, 102, 103, 120, 133, 367, 368, 369, 374, 375, 377, 378, 380, 402, 425, 521, 522, 535, 544, 551, 555, 658, 766, 773
fiduciary duty, 102, 103, 120, 133, 367, 368, 374, 375, 377, 380, 402, 425, 522, 544, 659, 766, 773
file-stamped, 572, 761
filing, 149, 150, 728, 731, 734, 735
filing fee, 129, 130, 134, 136, 138, 308, 391, 500, 501, 502, 590, 597, 599, 605, 630, 642, 646, 671, 675, 696, 776
final disclosure, 367, 565
final paperwork, 25, 502, 505, 562, 563, 572
FMV, 455, 463, 464, 465, 466, 770
forfeiture, 452
fraud, 61, 62, 63, 64, 65, 67, 76, 103, 217, 295, 374, 375, 376, 380, 499, 506, 509, 521, 542, 552, 566, 597, 601, 602, 670, 710, 759

Frederick v. Superior Court of Los Angeles, 33
frequent and continuing, 182, 201, 203, 204, 206, 234, 760
Friedman v. Friedman, 703, 715
frustrate, 267, 283, 616, 695
frustration, 283
Garnishment, 305, 766
Gavron, 333
Gavron warning, 333
genetic testing, 615, 616, 622, 625, 640, 641, 643, 645, 648
goodwill, 383, 385, 408
grandparent, 182, 184, 237, 240, 242, 244, 245, 246, 250, 251, 473, 474, 475
gross income, 94, 298, 301, 303, 360, 431, 505, 509, 526, 668
guardianship, 212, 230, 570, 608, 623
guideline, 291, 292, 296, 299, 301, 302, 303, 305, 309, 310, 320, 324, 325, 327, 328, 475, 511, 513, 515, 760, 764
guideline formula, 291, 301, 302, 303, 320, 513
H.S. v. Superior Court, 614
Hague Convention, 156, 202, 225, 226, 227, 235
handicap, 239, 256, 276, 285
hardship, 219, 270, 291, 296, 298, 301, 302, 314, 319, 320, 376, 592
hearing, 148, 149, 734
Henderson v. Pacific Gas and Electric, 16
Huffman v. Grob, 250
illegitimate, 59, 718
impute, 299, 327, 328, 450, 764
imputed income, 296
in camera, 162
in personam, 29, 30, 31, 32, 37, 222, 772
in pro per, 110, 637, 767
in propria persona, 584, 773
In re J.T v. JASMINE, 247
in rem, 29, 30, 31, 32, 772
incest, 57, 59, 778
incestuous, 59

income, 90, 728, 731
Income and Expense Declaration, 77, 115, 121, 127, 128, 135, 157, 171, 172, 292, 301, 317, 335, 369, 371, 482, 483, 484, 485, 488, 491, 493, 502, 505, 506, 507, 547, 557, 563, 565, 572, 696
income withholding, 590, 592
income withholding order, 590, 592
inheritance, 7, 44, 606, 771
injunction, 14, 657, 716
installment, 434, 577, 587, 601
intake, 21, 26, 27, 182
interest, 728
interlocutory, 34, 73, 132, 247, 401, 427, 432, 451, 707
internet, 728, 731
interrogatories, 99, 100, 102, 131, 159, 161, 164, 165, 176, 734, 767
interstate, 202, 211, 220, 221, 224, 234, 235, 766
interview, 13, 26, 177, 185, 191, 195, 199, 734
intestate, 670
investigated, 162
investigating, 226, 526
investigation, 104, 177, 183, 195, 196, 198, 203, 268, 273, 289, 760
irreconcilable differences, 57, 71, 72, 73, 78, 79, 504, 509
irremediable, 71, 72, 73, 75, 78, 79
irreparable, 491, 493, 689, 695, 716
irrevocable, 504, 509, 669
IWO, 305, 767
J.M. v. G.H., 256, 277, 285
J.R. v. D.P., 617, 648
jackpot, 373, 375, 376
Jason P. v. Danielle S., 628
Joinder, 385, 387, 450, 517, 548, 554, 558, 641, 646, 768
Joint legal custody, 201, 203, 234, 760
Joint Petition, 58, 75, 80, 776
Joint physical custody, 201, 203, 234, 760
Joint tenants, 393

Judgment, 19, 208, 356, 357, 374, 384, 385, 390, 481, 499, 501, 502, 506, 508, 517, 518, 561, 563, 568, 569, 570, 571, 572, 576, 577, 578, 596, 601, 623, 624, 629, 641, 644, 645, 649, 768
Judgment of Paternity, 517, 624
judicial council, 4, 522, 695, 768, 775
judicial council form, 522, 695, 775
jurisdictional stepdown, 359, 366, 768
jury, 3
juvenile, 5
juvenile court, 195, 231, 232, 637, 663, 668, 763, 768
Kelsey S. v. Rickie M., 632
Keogh plan, 445, 446, 447, 453
kidnapping, 202, 203, 211, 215, 217, 219, 220, 234, 235, 683, 766
Koehler v. Superior Court, 582
laches, 308, 587
Lappe v. Superior Court, 566
leasehold, 463
legal custody, 110, 184, 192, 194, 201, 202, 203, 204, 205, 206, 208, 212, 234, 257, 259, 260, 263, 268, 269, 275, 277, 287, 288, 502, 600, 618, 633, 636, 637, 662, 760, 767
legal separation, 29, 30, 35, 57, 60, 69, 71, 72, 73, 78, 79, 91, 97, 98, 104, 121, 123, 124, 125, 126, 137, 172, 179, 180, 186, 212, 291, 303, 315, 316, 321, 322, 324, 329, 330, 332, 334, 335, 348, 364, 365, 368, 370, 375, 380, 389, 394, 398, 408, 414, 417, 420, 421, 422, 424, 425, 426, 433, 436, 439, 442, 443, 444, 459, 472, 483, 504, 530, 556, 561, 564, 569, 570, 581, 624, 757, 769, 775
Lesterizing, 769
liability, 96, 103, 134, 301, 369, 375, 378, 413, 414, 415, 416, 417, 418, 419, 420, 421, 422, 425, 436, 438, 439, 440, 441, 442, 443, 444, 592, 642, 647, 669, 757
license, 728, 731

limited scope representation, 113, 114
liquidation, 367, 372, 589, 590, 759
living separate and apart, 82, 84, 85, 397, 414, 435, 436, 662, 673, 707
Loeffler v. Medina, 108
lottery, 373, 374, 375
lower-earning spouse, 92, 102
magistrate, 762
mailbox, 149, 152
maintenance, 31, 49, 92, 111, 112, 179, 311, 316, 322, 324, 347, 434, 458, 504, 515, 542, 597, 599, 709, 712, 713, 776
Marckwardt, 247, 248
marital settlement agreement, 187, 188, 259, 310, 313, 355, 367, 369, 374, 375, 420, 442, 500, 501, 506, 509, 522, 556, 562, 565, 566, 572, 600
marital standard of living, 330, 331, 332
Mark T. v. Jamie Z., 282
Marriage of Adams, 189
Marriage of Boblitt, 173
Marriage of Boswell, 306
Marriage of Bower, 359
Marriage of Brown, 503
Marriage of Burgess, 255, 265, 271, 770
Marriage of Burlini, 348, 777
Marriage of Candiotti, 159, 162
Marriage of Cantarella, 43
Marriage of Carney, 271
Marriage of Cesnalis, 356
Marriage of Duke, 313
Marriage of Epstein, 431, 765
Marriage of Ficke, 326
Marriage of Harris, 243, 474
Marriage of Hubner, 597
Marriage of Johnston, 62, 65
Marriage of Kahn, 133
Marriage of Lippel, 131, 504
Marriage of Lisi, 105
Marriage of long duration, 769
Marriage of Marsden, 463
Marriage of Michalik, 221
Marriage of Moore, 460

Marriage of Morrison, 324
Marriage of Mueller, 451
Marriage of Nurie, 213
Marriage of Olson, 502
Marriage of Pendleton, 525
Marriage of Prietsch & Calhoun, 357
Marriage of Ramirez, 64, 66
Marriage of Richmond, 324, 775
Marriage of Rosenfeld & Gross, 292, 310
Marriage of Rossi, 373
Marriage of Seagondollar, 256
Marriage of Seaton, 59
Marriage of Sharples, 115
Marriage of Shelton, 401
Marriage of Smith, 299, 431, 764
Marriage of Tejeda, 399
Marriage of Tharp, 92, 99
Marriage of Thornton, 31
Marriage of Wall, 396
Marriage of Watts, 432
Marriage of Winter, 777
Marriage of Witherspoon, 226
Marriage of Woolsey, 186
Marsden, 85, 455, 463, 465, 466, 770
Marsden formula, 465, 466, 770
Marvin, 8, 703, 704, 705, 706, 707, 708, 709, 710, 711, 715, 717, 718, 719, 720, 721, 722, 723, 724
Marvin II, 709
Marvin v. Marvin, 703, 704, 718
Marvin-type, 721, 724
matrimony, 40, 69, 71, 177, 178, 181, 198, 764
McDonald v. McDonald, 49
mediation, 129, 138, 177, 178, 179, 181, 182, 183, 184, 185, 186, 187, 188, 196, 198, 199, 207, 243, 268, 269, 277, 288, 566, 568, 757, 761, 770, 771
mediator, 177, 181, 182, 183, 184, 185, 186, 188, 189, 192, 195, 198, 261, 278, 566, 735
meet-and-confer, 517
meretricious, 8, 705, 707, 708, 710, 711, 712, 722, 723, 724
meruit, 718, 774

minimum contacts, 31, 32, 770
minority, 248, 307, 309, 474, 503, 652, 654, 655, 656
minute order, 7, 15, 35, 116, 208, 210, 265, 517, 585
modifiable, 261, 287, 311, 312, 356, 357, 475
modification, 43, 115, 127, 160, 171, 172, 174, 175, 192, 194, 209, 218, 219, 222, 223, 238, 248, 255, 263, 265, 267, 269, 273, 275, 278, 279, 281, 283, 284, 286, 305, 307, 308, 310, 311, 312, 329, 332, 333, 335, 348, 349, 350, 355, 358, 360, 365, 366, 396, 409, 502, 503, 504, 509, 513, 515, 526, 527, 589, 590, 597, 599, 600, 690
Montenegro v. Diaz, 207, 281, 283
Monterroso v. Moran, 692
Moore, 455, 460, 462, 463, 466, 770
Moore formula, 462, 466, 770
Moore/Marsden, 455, 460, 466, 770
mortgage, 300, 416, 431, 437, 455, 456, 459, 544
motion in limine, 696
moveaway, 256, 257, 259, 260, 261, 265, 266, 268, 270, 272, 273, 277, 280, 283, 284, 285, 287, 288, 289, 494, 770
murder, 97, 249, 338, 450, 476, 675, 683, 700
necessaries, 413, 417, 418, 419, 421, 439, 440, 441, 443
negligence, 13, 17, 34, 571
negotiate, 458, 582
negotiation, 525, 568
net income, 298, 313, 428, 431
nolo contendere, 330
noncustodial parent, 206, 237, 238, 239, 255, 260, 267, 269, 270, 272, 293, 296, 297, 314, 320, 327, 505, 766
non-custodial parent, 211
non-custodial parent, 234
nonmodifiable, 312, 355, 511, 514
notice of appeal, 101, 146, 263, 375, 503, 597, 598, 599, 602, 658, 679

Index

nullity, 29, 30, 35, 58, 59, 60, 61, 63, 68, 78, 79, 80, 94, 97, 98, 103, 121, 123, 126, 179, 180, 188, 368, 375, 380, 398, 399, 400, 421, 422, 425, 443, 444, 483, 564, 569, 624, 758, 775
nunc pro tunc, 33, 34, 35, 221, 562, 571
obligee, 293, 294, 305, 319, 321, 324, 336, 361, 362, 587, 588, 589, 590, 591, 592, 593, 596, 602, 765, 766, 771
obligor, 293, 294, 298, 305, 319, 320, 321, 324, 336, 361, 362, 588, 589, 590, 591, 592, 593, 596, 720, 765, 766
Order to Show Cause, 15, 189, 208, 264, 482, 483, 518, 579, 580, 582, 583
OSC, 15, 16, 115, 116, 117, 189, 191, 192, 227, 264, 265, 288, 482, 483
palimony, 705, 715, 718, 719
paralegal, 9, 10, 11, 12, 13, 16, 17, 19, 20, 24, 25, 26, 466, 556, 572, 734
parentage, 8, 94, 119, 125, 127, 486, 512, 610, 612, 614, 616, 618, 619, 626, 630, 631, 640, 644, 649, 689
Parental Kidnapping Prevention Act, 211, 220, 224, 235
parent-child relationship, 251, 477, 605, 606, 612, 613, 614, 617, 619, 620, 623, 626
parenting plan, 25, 177, 178, 181, 183, 185, 196, 206, 209, 260, 264, 265, 503, 765, 770, 771
Parker v. Harbert, 93, 95
partnership, 12
paternity, 172, 177, 184, 202, 207, 212, 262, 264, 265, 266, 274, 277, 279, 288, 289, 476, 483, 495, 514, 569, 570, 602, 605, 606, 607, 608, 609, 610, 611, 612, 614, 616, 617, 618, 619, 621, 622, 623, 624, 625, 626, 628, 629, 634, 635, 636, 640, 641, 642, 643, 644, 645, 646, 647, 648, 649, 766

paternity judgment, 266, 605, 623, 624, 626, 641, 642, 645, 647
pendente lite, 112, 371, 431, 513, 515, 600, 611, 629, 644, 649
pension, 165, 383, 385, 387, 388, 445, 446, 447, 448, 449, 450, 453, 454, 508, 597, 601, 763, 767, 774
Pereira Method, 427, 467
Pereira v. Pereira, 427
permanent spousal support, 43, 332, 337, 347, 348, 349, 366, 475, 548, 553
personal jurisdiction, 30, 31, 32, 37, 212, 234, 770
personal property, 29, 126, 367, 369, 378, 393, 394, 395, 400, 401, 402, 404, 410, 411, 523, 544, 551, 577, 652, 669, 687, 693, 697, 706, 712, 723, 759, 777, 778
personal service, 31, 137, 138, 153, 154, 157, 182, 317, 408, 430, 530, 531, 532, 582, 584, 720
petition, 150
Petition, 58, 60, 68, 69, 72, 74, 75, 76, 78, 79, 81, 84, 86, 90, 107, 121, 124, 125, 126, 127, 131, 133, 134, 135, 136, 137, 138, 144, 151, 153, 154, 155, 156, 178, 181, 198, 279, 291, 371, 474, 481, 485, 486, 499, 500, 501, 509, 513, 562, 565, 572, 615, 642, 646, 665, 761, 765, 772, 774, 775, 777
Phillips v. Bank of America, 657
PKPA, 211, 220, 221, 222, 223, 224, 235
polygamous, 85
polygamy, 59, 778
posting, 134, 136, 137, 138, 151, 154, 156, 635, 775
postjudgment, 160, 173, 174, 175, 265, 291, 335, 364, 375, 421, 425, 443, 481, 515, 597, 599, 600, 601
postmarital, 419, 441, 521, 522, 551, 552
postnuptial, 383, 384
precedent, 6
preliminary disclosure, 77, 565

premarital agreement, 100, 102, 383, 384, 396, 521, 522, 523, 524, 525, 526, 527, 528, 529, 532, 534, 537, 541, 542, 543, 544, 545, 546, 551, 552
prenuptial, 464, 468, 522, 526, 529, 530, 544, 772
preponderance, 88, 228, 300, 324, 337, 359, 403, 470, 471, 479, 632, 650, 705, 714, 776
preponderance of the evidence, 88, 228, 300, 337, 359, 403, 470, 471, 479, 705, 714, 776
presumed father, 614, 615, 616, 617, 618, 619, 621, 629, 630, 632, 633, 634, 648, 649, 650
presumption, 521, 523, 542, 543, 552
presumption of parentage, 630
prima facie, 112, 228, 239, 276, 285, 471, 479, 643, 773, 774
primary custody, 257, 261, 263, 273, 277, 287, 666
principal, 728
pro tanto, 461, 463, 467
probate, 2, 5, 33, 128, 386, 396, 409, 775
probation, 107, 185, 230, 231, 338, 671
process server, 576
professional, 19, 20, 24
proof of service, 114, 136, 138, 146, 151, 155, 156, 157, 159, 161, 167, 370, 371, 483, 485, 500, 570, 572, 615, 648, 690
property, 728, 731
Property Declaration, 77, 135, 483, 485, 488, 493, 505, 506, 508, 565, 572, 696
prove-up, 133, 504, 505, 509
Pugliese v. Superior Court, 696
putative spouse, 57, 66, 67, 68, 103, 399, 400, 467, 773
QDRO, 445, 449, 774
qualified domestic relations order, 385
quantum meruit, 8, 703, 708, 719, 722

quash, 31, 169, 170, 171, 214, 505, 584, 591, 615, 648, 774
quasi-community, 32, 83, 368, 369, 372, 378, 379, 393, 398, 399, 400, 402, 403, 410, 413, 414, 419, 421, 423, 425, 433, 436, 441, 443, 524, 565, 567, 777
quasi-criminal, 579
quasi-marital, 66, 103, 399, 400, 403, 410, 467
quitclaim, 389
Ragghanti v. Reyes, 282
rebuttable presumption, 237, 240, 245, 246, 295, 298, 300, 316, 321, 324, 337, 359, 361, 365, 426, 433, 471, 473, 474, 475, 479, 521, 523, 542, 543, 610, 614, 621, 630, 644, 646, 691, 774
recapitulation, 427
recuse, 191, 194
reimbursement, 132, 174, 294, 311, 336, 379, 423, 424, 430, 431, 432, 433, 434, 435, 455, 458, 459, 467, 472, 625, 647, 765
religion, 178, 189, 675, 680
relocate, 30, 35, 256, 257, 260, 261, 263, 265, 266, 268, 270, 272, 273, 275, 281, 282, 283, 287, 288, 289, 770
relocation, 255, 256, 257, 260, 261, 262, 263, 269, 270, 272, 279, 282, 283, 287, 770
remarriage, 257, 333, 355, 356, 357, 358, 359, 548, 554, 558, 593, 768, 776
remunerative, 450
representation, 25, 57, 65, 91, 92, 97, 104, 105, 107, 110, 111, 112, 113, 361, 542, 566, 584, 606, 637, 640, 643, 694, 769, 778
Request for Order, 15, 98, 105, 115, 143, 153, 169, 181, 182, 189, 198, 264, 306, 383, 384, 385, 481, 482, 483, 484, 485, 488, 491, 493, 495, 500, 513, 515, 518, 696, 771, 774
rescind, 65, 612, 614, 616, 644, 670
rescission, 610, 612, 615, 648, 670

Index

reservation of jurisdiction, 506, 571
residence, 30, 31, 36, 57, 68, 72, 75, 78, 83, 84, 87, 88, 93, 105, 137, 149, 151, 153, 167, 176, 207, 217, 218, 221, 223, 225, 227, 237, 238, 240, 249, 255, 257, 258, 260, 263, 268, 271, 272, 275, 277, 278, 279, 283, 286, 289, 300, 313, 314, 315, 316, 321, 360, 362, 386, 416, 431, 432, 437, 455, 456, 458, 459, 460, 548, 554, 662, 665, 670, 673, 675, 687, 688, 690, 763, 764
respondent, 176
response, 149
Response, 121, 124, 125, 127, 128, 132, 135, 136, 137, 154, 155, 156, 160, 170, 181, 198, 273, 289, 371, 383, 384, 450, 481, 482, 485, 499, 500, 501, 509, 561, 562, 565, 775
restitution, 296, 416, 438, 718
retirement, 75, 165, 350, 355, 383, 385, 386, 387, 388, 431, 445, 446, 447, 448, 449, 450, 451, 453, 454, 458, 467, 728, 735, 763, 767, 778
retirement benefits, 447, 448, 449, 451, 454, 778
retirement plan, 75, 165, 387, 388, 445, 446, 447, 448, 449, 450, 453, 454, 763
retroactive, 291, 305, 306, 307, 318, 321, 335, 475, 542, 618, 716
retroactivity, 335, 355, 366, 542
RFO, 15, 98, 105, 130, 143, 144, 153, 169, 182, 189, 259, 264, 287, 306, 308, 321, 481, 482, 483, 484, 487, 488, 495, 500, 511, 513, 514, 734, 771
Rich v. Thatcher, 473
Richmond Order, 324, 357
Rimes, 652, 653, 654, 655, 656
Rimes v. Curb Records, 653
Rules of Court, 5, 116, 122, 136, 160, 192
sanction, 91, 93, 95, 96, 97, 100, 103, 109, 120, 159, 161, 169, 172, 197, 271, 308, 372, 376, 486, 582, 583, 584, 585, 586, 594, 715, 717

Schafer v. Superior Court, 703
Schaub v. Schaub, 62, 64
See v. See, 427
self-employed, 292, 296, 445, 446, 454
self-represented, 123, 155, 156, 515, 563, 572
self-supporting, 293, 309, 319, 328, 330, 332, 333, 349, 350, 357, 364, 709
separate property, 35, 75, 99, 102, 108, 120, 323, 330, 331, 373, 375, 376, 379, 394, 395, 396, 397, 398, 401, 402, 403, 404, 408, 410, 411, 414, 417, 419, 420, 422, 423, 424, 426, 427, 428, 430, 434, 435, 436, 439, 441, 442, 444, 446, 448, 451, 454, 455, 456, 458, 459, 460, 461, 462, 463, 465, 466, 467, 468, 476, 521, 523, 524, 530, 531, 533, 536, 547, 551, 553, 565, 707, 719, 758, 760, 767, 771, 777
separation date, 83, 523
service by mail, 137, 149, 152, 153
service by posting, 137, 153
service by publication, 137, 151, 153, 154
service of process, 25, 31, 32, 153, 635, 775
service of Summons, 57, 144
set aside, 16, 17, 34, 76, 217, 247, 307, 374, 499, 500, 501, 504, 506, 507, 510, 543, 566, 571, 601, 602, 608, 610, 612, 615, 616, 623, 624, 625, 626, 637, 641, 643, 645, 647, 648, 658, 661, 693, 706, 774
settlement conference, 173, 561, 562, 563
Sharon v. Sharon, 40
sole legal custody, 189, 192, 194, 272, 277, 289
sole physical custody, 203, 207, 257, 264, 269, 270, 272, 288, 289
solemnization, 39, 40, 41, 42, 46, 47, 48, 51, 52, 53, 54, 55
sperm, 8, 608, 628, 629, 630, 649

spousal support, 43, 58, 66, 73, 76, 92, 107, 108, 115, 127, 128, 132, 133, 137, 171, 174, 298, 301, 302, 311, 312, 323, 324, 325, 326, 327, 328, 329, 332, 333, 334, 335, 336, 337, 338, 347, 348, 349, 350, 354, 355, 356, 357, 358, 359, 360, 362, 364, 365, 366, 368, 379, 389, 396, 413, 424, 434, 467, 486, 504, 507, 511, 512, 513, 514, 515, 521, 525, 526, 527, 528, 530, 541, 542, 548, 553, 554, 556, 558, 567, 570, 575, 576, 577, 578, 581, 587, 589, 593, 594, 595, 597, 599, 688, 716, 734, 735, 757, 766, 768, 769, 772, 775, 776, 777
spousal support order, 43, 128, 302, 325, 328, 329, 334, 335, 336, 350, 354, 355, 357, 360, 364, 365, 434, 581, 775
standard of proof, 403, 408, 471, 632, 650
Statute of Limitations, 586, 704, 719
stay order, 592
stepdown, 358, 768, 776
stepparent, 2, 182, 184, 238, 247, 248, 250, 251
sterile, 477, 479, 605, 621, 646, 665
sterility, 64, 605, 621
stipulated judgment, 189, 277, 279, 355, 356, 367, 369, 475, 561, 565, 566, 571, 597, 601
stipulation, 105, 131, 162, 183, 187, 197, 208, 216, 222, 243, 264, 269, 288, 309, 311, 313, 321, 360, 362, 371, 384, 415, 437, 485, 486, 495, 505, 512, 513, 571, 572, 575, 580, 600, 637, 642, 645, 690
Stipulation and Order, 208, 269, 288, 512, 517
Stipulation and Waiver, 371, 502, 563
sua sponte, 530
subject matter jurisdiction, 30, 37, 214, 216, 218, 222, 248
subpoena, 116, 142, 144, 149, 167, 169, 170, 171, 582, 774
substantive stepdown, 358, 366

suicide, 191, 240, 245, 473
Summary dissolution, 776
Summons, 72, 121, 125, 126, 127, 132, 135, 136, 137, 138, 141, 144, 151, 152, 153, 154, 155, 156, 157, 450, 483, 499, 501, 509, 562, 563, 572, 734, 776
supersedeas, 101, 275, 290, 615, 648
supervised visitation, 238, 249
supervision, 11, 12, 186, 201, 203, 234, 503, 581, 608, 611, 662, 663, 760
supervisor, 186, 474, 777
supporting declaration, 227, 375, 482, 484, 488, 566, 579, 596
Sylvia Wei-Ting Hu, Plaintiff and Respondent, v. Amy Fang, 15
Taylor v. Polackwich, 703
Temporary Restraining Order (TRO), 686, 689
temporary spousal support, 35, 100, 347, 348, 354, 526, 777
temporary support, 100, 324, 348, 371, 397, 548, 553, 716, 717
tenancy, 395, 396, 458, 459, 472, 476, 669
tenant, 395, 409, 476
tenants in common, 173, 395, 398, 713
termination of parental rights, 212, 230, 232, 605, 635, 671
time for filing, 149
time rule, 445, 448
timely filing, 142
timeshare, 237, 239, 291, 292, 293, 296, 298, 760
title, 32, 66, 75, 82, 86, 90, 165, 231, 393, 394, 395, 396, 399, 403, 404, 408, 409, 410, 455, 456, 460, 466, 472, 577, 578, 687, 688, 703, 712, 714, 715, 718, 723, 724, 730, 758, 762, 769, 770, 775
tort, 413, 414, 416, 422, 436, 438, 444, 697, 698, 774, 777
tortfeasor, 777
Totten, 126

Index

tracing, 403, 423, 424, 426, 427, 456, 458, 459, 758, 760, 777
transmutation, 396, 402, 403, 404, 408, 411, 458, 551, 777
transmute, 404, 777
tribunal, 589, 593, 602, 626
Troxel, 240, 242, 245, 246, 667
Troxel v. Granville, 240, 245, 667
trust account, 651, 658, 660, 661
trustee, 552, 651, 657, 658, 660, 661, 718, 775
UCCJA, 211, 217, 220
UCCJEA, 92, 106, 118, 127, 135, 201, 211, 212, 213, 214, 216, 218, 219, 220, 226, 491, 494, 734, 778
unbundled legal services, 769
uncodified, 39, 47, 54
uncommingled, 403, 410, 426
unconstitutional, 244, 477
undisputed, 522, 530
Uniform Child Custody Jurisdiction Act, 4, 211, 217, 220, 222
Uniform Child Custody Jurisdiction and Enforcement Act, 106, 121, 123, 127, 135, 201, 211, 227, 491, 494, 778
valuation, 374, 378, 383, 385, 408, 565, 567, 757
valuation date, 385, 757
Van Camp, 423, 428, 429, 430, 771
vasectomy, 617
venue, 30, 35, 36, 37, 389, 654, 655, 696, 759, 766
verification, 483, 734, 735
vesting, 451
videoconference, 131
visitation, 98, 105, 110, 123, 129, 132, 138, 162, 177, 178, 179, 181, 182, 183, 184, 185, 186, 187, 188, 191, 196, 198, 199, 201, 202, 203, 204, 205, 206, 207, 208, 209, 211, 212, 215, 217, 218, 220, 221, 222, 223, 227, 234, 235, 237, 238, 239, 240, 241, 242, 243, 244, 245, 246, 247, 248, 249, 250, 251, 252, 256, 257, 259, 261, 262, 263, 264, 265, 266, 267, 268, 269, 270, 271, 273, 274, 275, 277, 281, 283, 285, 286, 287, 288, 290, 300, 305, 320, 327, 383, 385, 473, 474, 475, 477, 483, 484, 486, 492, 493, 494, 512, 513, 515, 556, 597, 599, 600, 601, 606, 607, 608, 610, 611, 612, 615, 623, 629, 636, 637, 640, 643, 644, 648, 649, 675, 676, 687, 688, 690, 693, 695, 696, 758, 760, 766, 770, 771, 777, 778
vocational training counselor, 332
void marriage, 57, 58, 59, 80, 778
voidable marriage, 57, 59, 60, 61, 80, 103
voluntary declaration, 277, 605, 607, 608, 609, 610, 611, 612, 615, 616, 618, 626, 628, 640, 641, 644, 645, 646, 647, 648, 649
wage assignment, 291, 305, 309, 320, 507, 512, 515, 592, 593, 767
Watts charge, 423, 779
Whorton v. Dillingham, 703
will, 90, 727, 730
witness, 149
writ, 7, 33, 35, 101, 248, 260, 268, 273, 275, 289, 290, 389, 390, 391, 486, 505, 568, 576, 577, 584, 588, 615, 616, 648, 667, 669, 670
Writ of Execution, 576, 779
Writ of Mandate, 486, 779

Made in the USA
San Bernardino, CA
30 January 2020